THE SAGE HANDBOOK
of
SOCIOLOGY

THE SAGE HANDBOOK
of
SOCIOLOGY

Edited by
CRAIG CALHOUN, CHRIS ROJEK
and BRYAN TURNER

SAGE Publications
London ● Thousand Oaks ● New Delhi

Chapter 1 has been edited by the author, with the permission of
the ASA, from the original publication, Adrian E. Raftery, 2001,
'Statistics in Sociology, 1950–2000: A Selective Review', *Sociological
Methodology*, 31: 1–45 © American Sociological Association, 1307
New York Avenue, NW, Suite 700, Washington DC 20005–4701

Chapter 19 © Dalton Conley 2005

First published 2005

SAGE Publications Ltd
1 Oliver's Yard
55 City Road
London EC1Y 1SP

SAGE Publications Inc.
2455 Teller Road
Thousand Oaks, California 91320

SAGE Publications India Pvt Ltd
B-42, Panchsheel Enclave
Post Box 4109
New Delhi 110 017

British Library Cataloguing in Publication data

A catalogue record for this book is available from
the British Library

ISBN 0 7619 6821 0

Library of Congress Control Number: 2004099525

Typeset by C&M Digitals (P) Ltd., Chennai, India
Printed in Great Britain by Cromwell Press, Trowbridge, Wiltshire

Contents

Contributors

Gary L. Albrecht is Professor of Public Health and of Disability and Human Development at the University of Illinois at Chicago. His current work focuses on the quality of life of disabled persons and the political economy of disability. His most recent books are the *Handbook of Social Studies in Health and Medicine* (with Ray Fitzpatrick and Susan Scrimshaw, Sage, 2000) and the *Handbook of Disability Studies* (with Katherine Seelman and Michael Bury, Sage, 2001), both of which have been released in softback in 2003. He is a Fellow of the American Association for the Advancement of Science (AAAS), in 2003 a Visiting Fellow at Nuffield College, University of Oxford, and scholar in residence at Maison des Sciences de l'Homme (MSH) and Centre de Recherche Médecine Maladie et Sciences Sociales (CERMES), Paris.

David E. Apter is Henry J. Heinz Professor Emeritus of Comparative Political and Social Development and Senior Research Scientist, Yale University. Before coming to Yale he taught at Northwestern University, the University of Chicago and the University of California at Berkeley where he was Director of the Institute of International Studies. Professor Apter is currently a fellow of the Center for Comparative Culture at Yale. He has done research on politics and development in many parts of the world and written case studies on Ghana, Uganda, Japan and China. He has also written extensively on comparative politics. His book, *Choice and the Politics of Allocation*, was the recipient of the Woodrow Wilson Award of the American Political Science Association.

Paul Atkinson is Distinguished Research Professor in Sociology at Cardiff University, UK. He is Associate Director of the ESRC Research Centre on Social and Economic Aspects of Genomics. His main research interests are the sociology of medical knowledge and the development of qualitative research methods. His publications include: *Ethnography: Principles in Practice* (with Martyn Hammersley, Routledge,1983 and 1995), *The Clinical Experience* (Ashgate, 1981 and 1997), *The Ethnographic Imagination* (Routledge, 1990), *Understanding Ethnographic Texts* (Sage, 1992), *Medical Talk and Medical Work* (Sage, 1995), *Fighting Familiarity* (with Sara Delamont, Hampton, 1995), *Making Sense of Qualitative Data* (with Amanda Coffey, Sage, 1996), *Sociological Readings and Re-Readings* (Ashgate, 1996) and *Interactionism* (with William Housley, Sage 2003). Together with Sara Delamont he edits the journal *Qualitative Research*. He was co-editor of *The Handbook of Ethnography* (Sage, 2002). His ethnographic study of an international opera company is published as *Everyday Arias: Making Opera Work* (Alta Mira, 2005). He is an Academician of the Academy for the Learned Societies in the Social Sciences.

Craig Calhoun is President of the Social Science Research Council and University Professor of Social Sciences at New York University, where he was previously Chair of the Sociology Department. He received his doctorate from Oxford University and taught at the University of North Carolina, Chapel Hill from 1977 to 1996, where he was also Dean of the Graduate School and founding Director of the University Center for International Studies. His publications include *Nationalism* (University of Minnesota Press, 1997), *Critical Social Theory: Culture, History and the Challenge of Difference* (Blackwell, 1995), *The Roots of Radicalism* (University of Chicago Press, forthcoming) and the co-edited anthologies *Understanding September 11th* (New Press, 2002) and *Lessons of Empire?* (New Press, 2004). He was the editor of *Sociological Theory* from 1994 to 1999 and is currently editing a history of sociology in America for the American Sociological Association's Centennial.

Stewart R. Clegg is a Professor at the University of Technology, Sydney, and Director of ICAN Research (Innovative Collaborations, Alliances and Networks Research), a Key University Research Centre of the University. He also holds Visiting Professorships at the University of Aston Business School, Maastricht University, and the Vrije Universiteit of Amsterdam.

Born in Bradford, England, he migrated to Australia in 1976, after completing a first degree at the University of Aston (1971) and a Doctorate at Bradford University (1974). Previously he held positions at the University of St Andrews, Scotland; University of New England; University of Western Sydney, in all of which he was Professor and Head of Department, and Griffith University, Brisbane, where he was Reader.

He has written extensively on power and organizations. His most recent books are *Debating Organization: Point–Counterpoint in Organization Studies* (with Robert Westwood, Blackwell, 2003) and *Managing and Organizations: An Introduction to Theory and Practice* (with Martin Kornberger and Tyrone Pitsis, Sage, 2005). He publishes regularly in leading journals such as the *Academy of Management Education and Learning, Organization Science, Organization Studies, Organization, Human Relations* and *Administrative Science Quarterly.*

Randall Collins is Professor of Sociology at the University of Pennsylvania. Recent publications include *Interaction Ritual Chains* (Princeton University Press, 2004) and *Macro-History: Essays in Sociology of the Long Run* (Stanford University Press, 1999).

Dalton Conley is Professor of Sociology and Public Policy at New York University and Director of NYU's Center for Advanced Social Science Research (CASSR). He is also Adjunct Professor of Community Medicine at Mount Sinai School of Medicine and a Research Associate at the National Bureau of Economic Research (NBER).

His scholarly research focuses on how socio-economic status is transmitted across generations and the public policies that affect that process. In this vein, he studies siblings' differences in socio-economic success, racial inequalities, the measurement of class and social status, and how health and biology affect (and are affected by) social position. Conley is author of *Being Black, Living in the Red: Race, Wealth and Social Policy in America* (winner of the American Sociological Association 1997 Dissertation Award), *Honky*, a sociological memoir, and *The Starting Gate: Birth Weight and Life Chances* (with Kate Strully and Neil G. Bennett). His most recent book is *The Pecking Order: Which Siblings Succeed and Why* (Pantheon Books, 2004).

Nick Crossley is a Reader in Sociology at the University of Manchester, UK. He works in the areas of embodiment, social movements and social theory. He has published a number of books and articles on these areas, including *The Social Body*

(Sage, 2001) and *Making Sense of Social Movements* (Open University Press, 2002). He is currently working on a book about reflexive embodiment in late modernity.

Charles Crothers is Professor of Sociology at Auckland University of Technology, having previously been Chair of Sociology at the University of Natal, Durban. Earlier postings included periods in the Departments of Sociology at the University of Auckland, Victoria University of Wellington and the Ministry of Works and Development. His interests lie particularly in the theory of social structure, its history and the sociology of its production, and its applicability in the analysis of settler societies, such as New Zealand and South Africa. Related writing is on Robert K. Merton and recent trends in sociology, including its traditions.

Sara Delamont is Reader in Sociology at Cardiff University, UK, and an Academician of the Academy for the Learned Societies in the Social Sciences. She was the first woman to be President of the British Education Research Association, and the first woman to be Dean of Social Sciences at Cardiff. Her research interests are educational ethnography, the anthropology of the Mediterranean and Brazil, and gender. Of her twelve published books the best known is *Interaction in the Classroom* (Methuen, 1976 and 1983), her favourites are *Knowledgeable Women* (Routledge, 1989) and *Appetites and Identities* (Routledge, 1995). Her most recent books are *Fieldwork in Educational Settings* (Routledge, 2002), *Feminist Sociology* (Sage, 2003) and *Key Themes in Qualitative Research* (with Paul Atkinson and Amanda Coffey, Alta Mira, 2003). She is co-editor of the journal *Qualitative Research* with Paul Atkinson. She is currently doing an ethnography of *capoeira* teaching in the UK.

Gerard Delanty is Professor of Sociology in the University of Liverpool, UK. His books include *Inventing Europe: Idea, Identity, Reality* (Macmillan, 1995), *Rethinking Irish History: Nationalism, Identity, Ideology* (with P. O'Mahony, Macmillan, 1998), *Social Science: Beyond Constructivism and Realism* (Open University Press, 1997), *Social Theory in a Changing World* (Polity Press, 1999), *Modernity and Postmodernity: Knowledge, Power and the Self* (Sage, 2000), *Citizenship in a Global Age* (Open University Press, 2000), *Challenging Knowledge: The University in the Knowledge Society* (Open University Press, 2001), *Nationalism and Social Theory* (Sage, 2002), *Community* (Routledge, 2003) and *Rethinking Europe* (with C. Rumford, Routledge, 2005).

Wendy Griswold is Professor of Sociology and Comparative Literary Studies at Northwestern University. Recent books include *Bearing Witness: Readers, Writers, and The Novel in Nigeria* (Princeton University Press, 2000) and *Cultures and Societies in a Changing World*, 2nd edition (Pine Forge, 2004), which has been translated into Japanese and Italian.

John A. Hall is Professor of Sociology, James McGill Chair and Dean of Arts at McGill University. He is the author of several books, including *Powers and Liberties: Liberalism, Coercion and Consent*, and of forthcoming edited collections on the work of Michael Mann, the state of Denmark and civil society.

Patricia Hill Collins is Charles Phelps Taft Professor of Sociology at the Department of African American Studies, University of Cincinnati. Professor Collins received her BA and PhD degrees in sociology from Brandeis University, and an MAT degree from Harvard University. A social theorist, her research and scholarship have dealt primarily with issues of race, gender, social class, sexuality and/or nation specifically relating to African American women. Her first book, *Black Feminist Thought: Knowledge, Consciousness, and the Politics of Empowerment*, won the Jessie Bernard Award of the American Sociological Association for significant scholarship in gender, and the C. Wright Mills Award of the Society for the Study of Social Problems. She is also the author of *Race, Class, and Gender: An Anthology* (edited with Margaret Andersen, currently in its fifth edition) and *Fighting Words: Black Women and the Search for Justice.* Her fourth book, *Black Sexual Politics: African Americans, Gender, and the New Racism*, was published by Routledge in 2004. She is currently completing a book of essays titled *From Black Power to Hip Hop: Essays on Racism, Nationalism, and Feminism*, to be published by Temple University Press in 2005.

Charles Hirschman is Boeing International Professor in the Department of Sociology and the Daniel J. Evans School of Public Affairs at the University of Washington. He received his PhD from the University of Wisconsin in 1972 and then taught at Duke University (1972 to 1981) and Cornell University (1981 to 1987) before joining the faculty at the University of Washington in 1987. He is the author of *Ethnic and Social Stratification in Peninsular Malaysia* (American Sociological Association, 1975), the co-editor of *Southeast Asian Studies in the Balance: Reflections from America* (Association for Asian Studies, 1992), and *The Handbook of International Migration: The American Experience* (Russell Sage Foundation, 1999), and has written more than one hundred articles and book chapters on demography, race and ethnicity, social stratification, and Southeast Asia. He is the current (2005) president of the Population Association of America.

Geoffrey Ingham is Fellow and Director of Studies in Social and Political Sciences, Christ's College, Cambridge and teaches in the Faculty of Social and Political Sciences, University of Cambridge. Over the recent past he has published numerous articles on the sociology of money in *Economy and Society*, *British Journal of Sociology*, *Acta Sociologica* and *Journal of Classical Sociology*; his book *The Nature of Money* (Polity) was published in 2004.

Karin Knorr Cetina is Professor of Sociology at the University of Konstanz (DE), Visiting Professor at the University of Chicago, and a member of the Institute for World-Society Studies, University of Bielefeld, Germany. In addition to her three degrees, she has received several honours, including Vienna University's Fellowship for the Gifted and she was a Ford Foundation Post-Doctoral Fellow, a member of the Institute for Advanced Study, Princeton, president of the International Society for Social Studies of Science, and she is a future member of the Center for Advanced Study in the Behavioral Sciences in Palo Alto, CA. She has published numerous papers and books, including *Epistemic Cultures: How the Sciences Make Knowledge* (1999, Harvard University Press), which received the Ludwik Fleck Prize of the Society for Social Studies of Science and the Robert K. Merton Prize of the American Sociological Association. Among other things, she is currently working on global financial markets and preparing a book that analyses postsocial developments and the impact of the life sciences on social and cultural change in Western societies.

David Lyon is Director of the Surveillance Project and Professor of Sociology at Queen's University, Kingston, Ontario, Canada. His main research and writing are in the area of the social aspects of communication and information technologies with particular reference to surveillance, religion and culture, and social theory. His most recent work in each area is *Surveillance after September 11* (Polity Press, 2003); *Jesus in Disneyland* (Polity Press, 2000) and *Postmodernity* (Open University Press, 1999). See http://www.queensu.ca/sociology/Faculty/Lyon.htm/

Siniša Malešević is a Lecturer in the Department of Political Science and Sociology, National University of Ireland, Galway. His recent publications include *The Sociology of Ethnicity* (Sage, 2004), *Ideology, Legitimacy and the New State* (Frank Cass, 2002), and the co-edited volumes *Making Sense of Collectivity* (Pluto, 2002) and *Ideology after Poststructuralism* (Pluto, 2002).

Jan Nederveen Pieterse, Professor of Sociology at University of Illinois Urbana-Champaign, specializes in transnational sociology with research interests in globalization, development studies and intercultural studies. He taught in the Netherlands and Ghana, and as visiting professor in Japan, Indonesia, Pakistan, Sri Lanka and Thailand. He is associate editor of several journals and Fellow of the World Academy of Art and Science. Recent books are *Globalization or Empire?* (Routledge, 2004), *Globalization and Culture: Global Mélange* (Rowman and Littlefield, 2003) and *Development Theory: Deconstructions/Reconstructions* (Sage, 2001). Website http://netfiles.uiue.edu/jnp/www/

Elspeth Probyn has taught media studies, sociology and literature in Canada and the United States, and is now the Professor of Gender Studies at the University of Sydney, Australia. Her work focuses on questions of identity, sexuality and bodies. She has been constantly interested in what people think and do with their bodies, from eating and sex, to emotions and writing. Her books include *Sexing the Self* (Routledge, 1993), *Outside Belongings* (Routledge, 1996), *Carnal Appetites* (Routledge, 2000) and *Sexy Bodies* (co-edited with Elizabeth Grosz, Routledge, 1995). Her latest book, *Blush: Faces of Shame* (University of Minnesota Press, and UNSW Press, 2005) focuses on shame as a positive force in society. She is also interested in ethics, the media and popular culture, and recently co-edited *Remote Control* (with Catharine Lumby, Cambridge University Press, 2003), a book on media ethics, and new forms of television such as reality TV and food shows.

Adrian E. Raftery is Professor of Statistics and Sociology, and founding Director of the Center for Statistics and Social Sciences at the University of Washington in Seattle. He was born in Ireland and obtained his BA in Mathematics (1976) and his MSc in Statistics and Operations Research (1977) both at Trinity College, Dublin. He obtained a doctorate in mathematical statistics in 1980 from the Université Pierre et Marie Curie in Paris, France. He was a Lecturer in Statistics at Trinity College, Dublin from 1980 to 1986, and since then has been on the faculty at the University of Washington. Raftery has published over 100 articles in peer-reviewed statistical, sociological and other journals. His research focuses on Bayesian model selection and Bayesian model averaging, model-based clustering, inference for deterministic simulation models, and statistical methodology for sociology, demography and the environmental and health sciences. He is a Fellow of the American Academy of Arts and Sciences, a Fellow of the American Statistical Association, an elected Member of the Sociological Research Association, a winner of the Population Association of America's Clifford C. Clogg Award, and a winner of the American Sociological Association's Paul F. Lazarsfeld Award for Distinguished Contribution to Knowledge.

He is also a former coordinating and applications editor of the *Journal of the American Statistical Association* and a former editor of *Sociological Methodology*.

Roland Robertson is Distinguished Service Professor of Sociology at the University of Pittsburgh and Professor of Sociology and Global Society at the University of Aberdeen, UK. One of the world's pioneers in the study of globalization, he has also published extensively in the sociology of religion and culture, as well as social theory. He has served on the editorial boards of the *Journal of Mathematical Sociology*, the *Review of Religious Research, Sociological Analysis* (recently renamed *The Sociology of Religion*), *Theory, Culture and Society*, the *Journal of International Communication, Globalizations* and *Citizenship Studies*. Recent publications include *Globalization: Social Theory and Global Culture* (Sage, 1992), *Global Modernities* (with Mike Featherstone and Scott Lash, Sage 1995) and *Globalization: Critical Concepts in Sociology* (with Kathleen E. White, six volumes, Routledge, 2003). His work has been translated into numerous languages.

Chris Rojek is Professor of Sociology and Culture at Nottingham Trent University. His most recent books are *Celebrity* (2001), *Stuart Hall* (2003), *Frank Sinatra* (2004) and *Leisure Theory: Principles and Practice* (2005).

Saskia Sassen is the Ralph Lewis Professor of Sociology at the University of Chicago, and Centennial Visiting Professor at the London School of Economics. Her latest book is *Territory, Authority and Rights: From Medieval to Global Assemblages* (Princeton University Press, 2005). She has just completed for UNESCO a five-year project on sustainable human settlement for which she set up a network of researchers and activists in over 30 countries. Her most recent books are the edited *Global Networks, Linked Cities* (Routledge, 2002) and the co-edited *Socio-Digital Formations: New Architectures for Global Order.* (Princeton University Press, 2005). *The Global City* came out in a new fully updated edition in 2001. Her books are translated into sixteen languages. She serves on several editorial boards and is an advisor to several international bodies. She is a Member of the Council on Foreign Relations, a member of the National Academy of Sciences Panel on Cities, and Chair of the Information Technology and International Cooperation Committee of the Social Science Research Council (USA). Her comments have appeared in *The Guardian, The New York Times, Le Monde Diplomatique, The International Herald Tribune* and *The Financial Times,* among others.

Mike Savage is Professor of Sociology and Director of the ESRC Centre for Socio-Cultural Change at the University of Manchester. He has research interests in the areas of social stratification, urban sociology and historical sociology. Recent publications include *Class Analysis and Social Transformation* (Open University Press, 2000), and *Globalization and Belonging* (with Gaynor Bagnall and Brian Longhurst, Sage, 2004). He is currently working on a project, *Cultural Capital and Social Exclusion,* with Tony Bennett, Elizabeth Silva and Alan Warde, conducting a survey on cultural taste, knowledge and participation in the UK which will lead to a major book on social inequality and culture.

Richard Sennett trained with David Riesman, Erik Erikson and Oscar Handlin at Harvard. His intellectual life as an urbanist came into focus through the time he spent at the Joint Center for Urban Studies of Harvard and MIT. The two unifying themes of this work and writing are how people interpret the social structures in which they dwell and the relation of social structure to visual design.

His earliest book, *Families Against the City*, was a study of the relation between family structure and social mobility in nineteenth-century Chicago. Subsequent books explored urban culture more largely: *The Uses of Disorder, The Fall of Public Man, The Conscience of the Eye* and *Flesh and Stone*. Further books address work, welfare and class in the city: *The Hidden Injuries of Class, The Corrosion of Character* and *Respect*. *Authority* is an essay in political theory which does not have a specifically urban focus; this book addresses the tools of interpretation by which people recast raw power into either legitimate or illegitimate authority.

He is currently working on two large projects, the first about cultural materialism, the second a large-scale history of urban design. In the public realm, he founded and directed for a decade, the New York Institute of the Humanities which has served as a working space for artists and intellectuals. He chaired a United Nations commission on urban development and design and as president of the American Council on Work, he led a forum, sponsored by the Rockefeller Foundation, for researchers trying to understand the changing pattern of American labour. Most recently he helped create the Cities Programme at the London School of Economics, which aims to bridge the divide between training, research and consultancy in urban design.

Roger Silverstone is Professor of Media and Communications at the London School of Economics. His recent publications include: *Television and Everyday Life* (Routledge, 1994), *Why Study the Media?* (Sage, 1999), *Media, Technology and Everyday Life in Europe* (Ashgate, 2005) and *Morality and Media* (Polity, in press).

Don Slater is Reader in Sociology at the London School of Economics. His recent books include *Consumer Culture and Modernity* (Polity, 1997) *Market Society* (with Fran Tonkiss, Polity, 2000), *The Internet: An Ethnographic Approach* (with Daniel Miller, Berg, 2000) and *The Technological Economy* (with Andrew Barry, Routledge, in press 2005). His research interests include consumption and economic sociology, ethnographic studies of new technologies in non-Western regions and visual sociology.

Heinz Steinert is Professor of Sociology at the J.W. Goethe-University Frankfurt-am-Main. He received his doctorate (in psychology) from Vienna University, had psychoanalytic training in Vienna and was founding Director of the Vienna Institut für Rechts- und Kriminalsoziologie and visiting professor at the University of Melbourne and New York University. His research interests are criminology, deviance and social exclusion; culture industry, sociology of art (mainly twentieth century) and music (mainly jazz); Symbolic Interactionism and Critical Theory (several books on Adorno). His most recent publications are *Welfare Policy from Below: Struggles Against Social Exclusion in Europe* (co-editor, Ashgate, 2003) and *Culture Industry* (Cambridge, 2003).

Bryan Turner is a Professor in the Asian Research Institute and the Department of Sociology at the National University of Singapore. He was Professor of Sociology at the University of Cambridge (1998–2005). He has held professorial and research positions in Australia, the Netherlands and Germany. He is the founding editor of the journal *Citizenship Studies*, founding co-editor (with Mike Featherstone) of *Body & Society* and founding co-editor (with John O'Neill) of the *Journal of Classical Sociology*. His research interests range over the sociology of the body, rights and citizenship, civil society and voluntary associations, and the sociology of religion. His early publications on Islam include *Weber and Islam* (Routledge, 1974), *Marx and the End of Orientalism* (Allen & Unwin, 1978) and *Religion and Social Theory* (HEB, 1983). His recent publications include *Society and Culture* (with Chris Rojek, Sage, 2001), *Profiles in Contemporary Social Theory* (with Anthony Elliott, Sage, 2001), and *Classical Sociology* (Sage, 1999). He published *Generations, Culture and Society* (with June Edmunds, OUP, 2002) and edited *Generational Consciousness: Narrative and Politics* (with June Edmunds, Rowman & Littlefield, 2002). He edited *Islam. Critical Concepts in Sociology* (Routledge, 2003). His most recent publication is *The New Medical Sociology* (W.W. Norton, 2004). He is currently editing the *Cambridge Dictionary of Sociology*.

Jonathan H. Turner is Distinguished Professor of Sociology at the University of California at Riverside. He is primarily a general sociological theorist, with substantive interests in stratification, ethnic relations, social institutions, emotions and biosociology. He is the author of some 29 books and many articles and chapters. His works have been translated into most major languages. He is currently writing in the area of emotions, neurology of the brain and evolutionary sociology.

Sylvia Walby is a Professor in the Institute for Women's Studies at Lancaster University. She has been Professor of Sociology in the University of Leeds and the University of Bristol, UK and was the founding Director of the Gender Institute at the LSE. Her recent research has been funded by the Luxembourg Presidency of the EU, the Economic and Social Research Council, the Department for Trade and Industry Women and Equality Unit, the Equal Opportunities Commission and the Home Office. Her books include: *Gender Transformations* (Routledge, 1997), *Theorizing Patriarchy* (Blackwell, 1990) and *Patriarchy at Work* (Polity Press, 1986). Papers from her ESRC-funded seminar series on 'Gender Mainstreaming' are being published in special issues of *Social Politics* and the *International Feminist Journal of Politics* in December 2005. Her next book, *Complex Social Systems: Theorizations and Comparisons in a Postcolonial Global Era* (Sage, forthcoming 2006), integrates gender relations into the heart of social theory using complexity theory.

Kathleen E. White is an independent consultant specializing in research and writing on topics relating to globalization, education and international academic exchanges. Currently based in Aberdeen, Scotland, she has had a long career in teaching, curriculum development and higher education administration. She was a founder and long-serving Director of the Pennsylvania Governor's School for International Studies at the University of Pittsburgh as well as the first Director of the Maryland Summer Center for International Studies. In recent years she has held visiting appointments at the UNESCO Institute on Cultural Pluralism, Candido Mendes University, Rio de Janiero, Brazil; at Koc University, Istanbul, Turkey; and at the University of Nuoro, Sardinia, Italy. She is the co-editor (with Roland Robertson) of the six-volume compendium, *Globalization: Critical Concepts in Sociology* (Routledge, 2003) and co-author of a number of articles and chapters on globalization, glocalization, and global education.

Steve Yearley is Professor and Chair of Sociology at the University of York, UK and Senior Research Fellow of the Stockholm Environment Institute. He works on environmental sociology and the sociology of science and focuses in particular on areas where these topics overlap. He is the author of many books, including: *Making Sense of Science* (Sage, 2004) and *Cultures of Environmentalism* (Palgrave, 2004).

Acknowledgement

This was a complex book to assemble and the editors would like to thank Kay Bridger for her help in easing the task. Kay played an indispensable role in processing the various chapters, in their diverse states of readiness from contributors who live and work in many different countries around the world. That the Handbook was ever finished at all, is a tribute to her resourcefulness and grace.

Introduction

CRAIG CALHOUN, CHRIS ROJEK AND
BRYAN TURNER

Sociology, like human society, is varied, contested and constantly changing. It is hard to capture from a single perspective, and hard to describe with finality. This does not mean there are no regular patterns, no enduring features, or no basis for science. But it does mean that as a science sociology faces a distinctive challenge. Its object of study – society or social relations – is more subject to historical change and human choice than the objects of the physical and biological sciences. It is also broader and more complex than the specific dimensions of social life singled out by the narrower, more specialized social sciences like politics, economics, and geography. And precisely because human society is open to choice and historical change, and social life is so internally complex, it is always possible to see things a little differently by looking again or looking from a different perspective. Not least of all, sociological findings – even when very clearly confirmed – are liable to be contested not only by other scientists with different theories but by people with political or personal commitments to certain views of the social world.

All of this makes sociology hard, but also exciting. Likewise, it makes editing a Handbook that attempts to give an overview of the field a daunting but stimulating task. When Sage last published a major Handbook of Sociology, in 1988, the social world itself was different. That earlier Handbook came at the tail end of a period of consolidation after the upheavals of the 1960s and in the midst of a high moment for global conservatism signalled by the overlapping tenures of Margaret Thatcher and Ronald Reagan. Although Reagan had actually been an undergraduate sociology major, as a president his views, like Thatcher's, tilted away from social concerns towards an idealization of individualism. Thatcher famously asserted, in fact, that there was no such thing as society. By this she meant, it seems, that there is nothing distinct about society as a whole that is not contained in the wills of individual members. Reagan, similarly, focused on the freedom of choice that citizens of Western capitalist democracies enjoyed and that was denied to citizens of Soviet communist societies. But he was not much interested in the economic or social conditions on which active citizenship rested.

Reagan and Thatcher both contributed to changes in global society, not least to the rise of neoliberalism, an ideology of free markets and economic individualism. But they also missed important things that were happening. The crisis of the Soviet Union and East European communism did not simply bring peace or freedom, it brought nationalist wars and ethnic cleansing. The intensification of global capitalism did not simply bring new prosperity – though for a time it did, at least in the world's rich countries. It also brought a sharp backlash. So too did the position of the United States as the world's unrivalled superpower. The two converged in the attacks of 11 September 2001. Islamic radicals flew hijacked airplanes into symbols of global capitalism – the twin towers of the World Trade Center in New York – and of American power – the Pentagon in Washington, DC. At about the same time the high-tech bubble collapsed, bringing global stock markets down from their unrealistic highs. Suddenly, anxieties about globalization were as much in fashion as enthusiasms. And of course there were also a host of other social issues that demanded attention, including many that had been obscured while neoliberalism, high-tech and American power seemed clearly ascendant.

One of the basic goals of this new Handbook has been to reflect the new reality of social life and the processes of change that have produced it and are still at work – from globalization to shifting gender relations. Another goal is to reveal the continuities that persist in the face of change – from the long-term trend towards urbanization to the deep patterns of inequality. A third goal is to indicate the methodological and substantive improvements in sociological knowledge, the new knowledge that has been created. And finally, a fourth central goal has been to do justice to the internal diversity of the field. Some of that diversity involves differences of theory and intellectual perspective, some is the product of different research methods and some grows out of emphasis on different topics – science studies, for example, compared to family or popular culture. And of course, different perspectives also reflect the identities and social locations of authors.

The 1988 Handbook was written entirely by Americans and reflected mainly American research on American society. Smelser (1988: 15) himself recognized that '[t]his volume is … predominantly a book on sociology as it stands in the United States'. We have tried to reduce this bias. Although globalization has become a major aspect of contemporary sociology, national differences in research topics and forms of sociological theory clearly persist. In editing this Handbook we have been conscious of the growth of globalization, but we have also been concerned to reflect national differences. Smelser's Handbook was assembled in the context of a long-standing debate about the professionalization and institutionalization of sociology in American higher education. It is clear that Smelser was in part responding to Talcott Parsons's essay of 1959 on 'Some remarks of confronting sociology as a profession' and

also thinking about Robert E. Lee Faris's (1964) *Handbook of Modern Sociology*. Parsons's article had been relatively optimistic about the consolidation of sociology and Faris's Handbook had contained outstanding contributions from leading sociologists. By contrast, the tone of Smelser's introduction was more defensive. He (1988: 12) noted that sociology had experienced 'increased specialization of inquiry, diversification of both perspectives and subject matter studied, and considerable fragmentation and conflict'. In addition, he pointed to a range of new areas of specialization and growth such as the sociologies of medicine, gender and age stratification. Our Handbook recognizes that these trends identified by Smelser in the 1980s have, if anything, intensified. Sociology lacks an integrative theoretical paradigm and the topics it addresses continue to multiply. We can mention such topics as the globalization of society, the sociology of the body, queer theory, risk sociology, environmental sociology, the sociology of animals and many more. Once more there is a clear difference between American sociology, which has a strong and active professional association, and the sociology elsewhere in which professional development is generally much weaker. Opinion is divided about both the benefits and drawbacks of academic professionalization. Some would argue that diversity, fragmentation and conflict are healthy consequences of a discipline engaged with controversial issues in contemporary society. Professionalization is clearly a process of social closure. By contrast, it can be argued that sociology in Western Europe, Australia, New Zealand and particularly the UK, where professionalization is relatively underdeveloped, has suffered from encroachment and dilution from interdisciplinarity as represented by cultural studies, gender studies, film studies and so on.

Trying to reduce the American bias that was evident in Smelser's Handbook does not mean eliminating the United States from the picture – American society is important and American sociology perhaps the largest and most influential national branch of the discipline. But it does mean complementing American perspectives with many more international ones. We are not perfect in that regard; our contents are still biased towards English-language sociology. And sociology itself is not perfect, for it is still disproportionately produced in the global north. But we hope this volume does bring out the increasingly global character of twenty-first-century sociology.

GLOBAL SOCIAL TRANSFORMATIONS

There is always both continuity and change in social life. Even the most stable and most traditional social orders reveal patterns of change. There is change within a more or less consistent overall structure as new individuals are born or as some families prosper and others suffer. There are external shocks like plagues and crop failures that may decimate the population of a society near the subsistence level. Wars can do the same – and also lead to more centralized power and the dominion of some groups over others. But in none of these cases is change built in to a social order.

These cyclical and episodic changes contrast with long-term trends of more cumulative change. Population growth, technological innovation, early urbanization and long-distance trade all show a pattern of gradual increase over millennia. They have been central concerns for evolutionary approaches to social change, from nineteenth-century founders like Spencer (1885) to contemporary leaders like Lenski (Lenski and Nolan, 2004). Two major generalizations come from such studies. First, the overall pattern is one of increasing scale and differentiation. Through this long pattern of historical change societies grew larger as their economies, communications infrastructures and political systems gained in capacity. And as they grew larger they were also subdivided into more complex arrangements of subunits. At first these were relatively similar to each other, as families, or farming villages may be similar within a society. But eventually there were also differentiations of occupations, of farming from craft production and different crafts from each other, of military and religious

specialists from primarily economic producers, of rulers from subjects, and so forth. These changes were crucial to the several dichotomous contrasts that great nineteenth-century sociologists elaborated. Spencer wrote of the more differentiated industrial society by comparison to 'militant' societies in which armed power was basic. Durkheim (1893) wrote of the more complex patterns of organic solidarity that united people across lines of difference, by contrast to the mechanical solidarity that united people in relatively similar groups. Toennies (1886) contrasted community to association, emphasizing the more abstract structures and formal organizations necessary to organize large-scale, internally differentiated societies by contrast to the sentiments of commonality and face-to-face relations adequate to smaller, less complex societies.

Second, there are some 'tipping points' where quantitative change produces qualitative transformation. The rise of agriculture with its capacity to support cities and literate civilizations is one example. The industrial revolution another. In each case, a long pattern of changes eventually cumulated in far reaching transformations. We are arguably living through another of these qualitative changes as capitalism becomes more truly global and economic activity increasingly a matter of control over 'information' rather than only material production (Bell, 1973; Castells, 1996; and David Lyon's chapter in this Handbook). Although there are debates about just how to analyse contemporary global transformations of society, there is little doubt that they are dramatic.

Many sociologists would reject evolutionary theories, suggesting that they exaggerate the extent to which the patterns of change are the same all over the world and tend in the same directions. Rather than an explanation in terms of a single evolutionary mechanism like survival of the fittest, they would suggest that a variety of historical processes overlap. Michael Mann (1986) argues that the central pattern is one of cross-cutting circles of power, state formation, and growing capacity both to keep domestic peace and to manage inter-state relations. Tilly (1990) links the growth of coercive power to capital as well as state capacity, at least taking a long view of European history. Other historical sociologists place greater emphasis on cultural or on economic factors (drawing on thinkers from Foucault to Marx). But they concur that evolutionary theories build too much presumption of 'progress' and necessity into patterns of historical change that bring evil as well as good and reveal the results of purposive human action even if the results are not always what actors intend. Indeed, one of the major transformations in global sociology during the last third of the twentieth-century was the rise of historical sociology, in part as a renewal of classical sociology, asking questions with roots in Marx, Weber, Tocqueville and Durkheim but answering them on empirical as well as theoretical grounds and for the most part rejecting those evolutionary theories that assumed monocausal, unidirectional courses of change.

It was not evolutionary theory in general that was typically monocausal and unidirectional – there is nothing in Darwin to suggest this and many evolutionary sociologists like Lenski were careful to avoid such assumptions. This was more specifically true of modernization theory, developed as an offshoot of the dominant functionalist sociology of the 1950s. The ideas that there was one way to be modern, and that developing societies could and should follow the examples of Western Europe and the United States to achieve this were enormously influential, not only in sociology but throughout the social sciences (e.g., Inkeles and Smith, 1974; Parsons, 1977). But by the late 1960s this approach was being challenged both by sociological research and by the manifest problems of the approaches to development it encouraged. Dependency theory revealed the extent to which early leaders in economic development retained power over other countries (including their former colonies) (Cardoso and Faletto, 1978; Frank, 1980). World systems theory demonstrated the importance of position within a global structure to shaping the options open and chances for economic growth in any country (Wallerstein, 1974, 1988).

As problematic as a unidirectional, Western-biased modernization theory was revealed to

be, there remained a widespread consensus that one of the most important of the large-scale, qualitative transformations in world history was the transition to modernity. This involved multiple different factors – capitalism and/or markets, state formation and science to name just three. Different theories emphasized different combinations of these and other factors – secularization, nation-building, proactive social movements and individualism. This suggested different patterns within the modern era, as for example communist countries formed strong states but without market economies, while others attempted to modernize government and economics without limiting religion by secularization. More recently, many sociologists have argued that instead of speaking of a single modernization we should recognize 'multiple' or 'alternative' modernities (Eisenstadt and Schlucter, 1998; Gaonkar, 2001).

None of this reduces the importance of the transition to modernity, it only complicates the picture of what modernity means. Rather than one ideal model to which different societies approximate more or less, contemporary theorists see a range of different forms of modern societies co-existing with each other. And modernity is not only a characteristic of each society (or of the culture or character of its members). It is a characteristic of the whole era. What is common to this era, even as different societies produce different forms of modernity? Four transformations are crucial:

1   An increasing scale and intensity of interconnection, for which globalization is the most common shorthand. Events in one place can have unprecedentedly rapid repercussions around the world – as was revealed on 11 September 2001, or earlier in the Asian monetary crisis of 1997.
2   A 'disembedding' of individuals from close local communities and traditional, face-to-face cultures – accomplished by media, education, migration, economic choices and citizenship in large-scale societies.
3   A concentration of effective power, not necessarily in the hands of individuals as in the kings and emperors of the past, but in

powerful bureaucracies and social elites. A medieval king could order a subordinate killed, but if the unfortunate vassal was not close at hand it could take weeks to reach remote corners of even a small kingdom. Today few rulers can yell 'off with her head', but state capacities for surveillance and effective action reach effectively throughout whole countries and into individual lives and households – for good or ill, and ranging from tax collection to mandating school attendance to requiring vaccinations or persecuting religious minorities.

4 A process of self-sustaining change. Perhaps the single most distinctive feature of modernity has been its embrace of both the idea of progress and a set of institutional and organizational features that encourage continual and often dramatic social change. Capitalist competition, for example, means that businesses must constantly innovate or lose their market edge to other firms. Science continues not only to add to knowledge but to technology, which not only solves the problems inventors had in mind but enables a range of new activities (and often creates new problems). The idea of free and equal citizenship encourages claims for equal recognition on the part of a variety of lifestyles, sexual orientations, ethnic groups and social movements that might have been repressed in earlier eras. If modernity is about one thing, it is about the latest thing, the new, the idea of change as a virtue, as progress, growth and the struggle to get ahead.

A strange feature of modernization theory had been its tendency to treat the former colonies of European powers as though they were simply separate societies competing on a level playing field rather than societies constructed in part through and on the basis of colonial domination – and societies dealing not only with the domestic implications of colonization but the continuing international power of former colonial rulers. To give blunt examples, Jamaicans and Indians do not migrate to the UK just because they happen to like the former colonial power, but because the UK remains relatively rich and offers a range of economic opportunities.

Understanding the nature of modernity took on new prominence in the sociological agenda because of the critique of modernization theory, and also because of the growing interconnection of different kinds of societies in a common global order. But instead of being seen as simply a goal for all societies, modernity was subjected to critical examination. Zygmunt Bauman (1991), for example, prominently showed that the Holocaust was possible only in and because of modernity. While rulers exercised ruthless power in all historical periods, the idea of totalitarianism, with its ambition not just to dominate but to control and even change the conditions of individual existence, was shown to be distinctively modern. And a range of dark sides to modernity and globalization continue to worry us: AIDS and other infectious diseases, the development of ever-deadlier weapons based on science and their global trade in illegal but still active capitalist markets, threats to privacy from the surveillance capacity of new electronic technologies.

Surprisingly few of these issues were prominent when the previous Handbook was published (Smelser, 1988). A few might have been emerging, and one could wish they had been included. But though the Handbook produced its own, highly contestable, account of where the centre of the discipline lay, the issue was not just the selectivity of the editor but the dramatic social changes that were launched – many in the symbolically famous year, 1989.[1]

Before asking how sociology itself has changed, it may be worthwhile – however schematically – to indicate the recent global social transformations to which it has responded and which shape its current context. Some of the most important changes (at least centred if not contained in the past 15 years) include the following.

1 The collapse of the Soviet Union and the end of the Cold War. This set in train a range of other transitions, including a range of civil wars and nationalist upheavals from the former Yugoslavia through Central Asia to parts of Africa and the enlargement of

the European Union as formerly communist societies were invited to join. Inside the former Soviet Union there were new freedoms – in personal life, in religion, and in business. But there were also crises. Division of the USSR into newly independent national states created unstable borders and unhappy minority populations. There was a troubling brain drain as skilled workers from the former state sector sought better-paying jobs in the West. The health care systems of Russia and many other states largely collapsed. State industries were privatized in corrupt deals that created a new class of extremely wealthy individuals but did little to help ordinary workers. Some turned to right-wing nationalism, some became nostalgic for communism. But while crisis remained deep in Russia and Central Asia, more successful transitions to market economies and democracy were accomplished in parts of Eastern Europe.

2   The ascendancy of the United States as an unrivalled but not unchallenged global power. Some called it empire, some a new global hegemony, some simply a unipolar world but there was widespread agreement that the US wielded an unprecedented level of power both economically and militarily. And at least under President George W. Bush it was prepared to exert this power unilaterally, bypassing the United Nations and other multilateral organizations and partnerships. The US invaded Iraq twice, and on the second occasion, in 2003–4, did so in defiance of its long-standing allies. American dominance made the US the target of terrorist attacks, most famously on 11 September 2001 ('9/11'). But terrorists also attacked Spain and other countries that supported the US.

3   The intensification of globalization. In a host of ways the interconnection of the entire world became more visible and the flows of money, people, information and even disease more powerful. This was simultaneously as a matter of international markets, the organization of production and business corporations on a global scale, the availability of new communications technologies, the development of international organizations, and the spread of English as a global language. Markets for financial instruments – including the huge global market for 'derivatives' (including 'hedge funds') – both fuelled speculation and reduced the fiscal autonomy of individual countries. Risk management became big business as international financial markets tried to anticipate shifts in currency valuations and other events. But a sense of shared risk affected many without much money as they worried about the possibilities of environmental or other catastrophes on a global scale. The 1990s and early twenty-first century saw a wave of emergencies and humanitarian crises and a dramatic expansion of global NGOs and philanthropy as ways of dealing with these. Nationalist struggles, ethnic cleansing, civil wars and genocides each produced flows of refugees. Humanitarian organizations like Médecins sans Frontières became increasingly prominent.

4   The dramatic expansion of mass communication which made the events of 1989 and thereafter simultaneously visible throughout the word. If this was true of the Tiananmen Square massacre and the fall of the Berlin Wall, it was almost as true of the horrors of ethnic cleansing in Yugoslavia and Rwanda and two successive American invasions of Iraq. CNN became a global media source, alongside the BBC, and was joined by SkyNews and other Western-dominated networks. But the hegemony of these was eventually challenged by Al-Jazeera among others. While access to information was unequal, it was increasingly global. Films from 'Bollywood' in India circulated at least as widely as those from Hollywood. Latin American telenovelas were eagerly watched in China. Egyptian soap operas were popular throughout the Middle East and in Africa. World music became a popular taste category in the West, but in fact a range of musical styles enjoyed global support. The Internet fuelled globalization of cultural consumption. Its chat rooms joined virtual

communities based on shared interests from sports to illnesses to politics. That pornography was among its most popular offerings worried many traditionalists; that it helped political dissenters organize worried many governments. And communications technologies continued to proliferate as cell phones not only spread but merged with computing for text messages.

5 A demographic division characterized more than anything else by the ageing of the advanced industrial societies (especially with immigration not taken into account) and the relative youth of less developed societies. The 'greying' of the world's richer countries is becoming a major issue as life expectancy grows – and with it demand for care. This contributed to migration – as for example an ageing Europe imported workers for its service industries – and to economic divisions. Those with the money to purchase care were often racially, ethnically, and nationally distinct from those providing care. The demographic division also helped sustain international economic inequalities, impeding economic development. And it was complicated as AIDS became a global pandemic. As AIDS has struck increasingly hard at women, this further changes gender structures – and in many countries selection of male over female babies (before or after birth) has substantially altered sex ratios.

6 The crisis of the Western welfare state and the ascendancy of neoliberalism. The latter refers both to a domestic ideology focused on reduction in entitlements and dependency within relatively rich societies and an international ideology promoting 'free markets' and a reduced role for governments as a path towards development for less rich societies. To many, neoliberalism seemed to be the imposition of an American (or Anglo-American) model by means of global market pressure. Workers were often told there was no choice but to accept lower wages or reduced benefits or an elimination of job security because that was the only way to keep jobs from moving to less developed countries. Both private pension funds and government social security systems have been financially challenged and many have collapsed. Health care systems have become increasingly expensive and in many countries both the services provided and the structure of who pays for them have changed. A growing privatization of education has reversed a long-term trend of growing state support for equal access.

7 Upheavals in the global and domestic labour markets. Old patterns of secure, sometimes lifelong employment began to erode – even in Japan, where this had been so developed many regarded lifetime jobs as a right. Productivity-enhancing technologies reduced demand for some kinds of labour, international economic competition forced firms to look for ways to cut costs, and a wave of mergers and acquisitions led to consolidations and loss of jobs in many industries. 'Outsourcing' moved some jobs from wealthy countries to mid-level ones, as for example corporate 'call centres' in Ireland and India answered queries from customers around the world for firms based in the United States. A growing 'casualization' of labour meant that workers often had to move from job to job, and frequently lost benefits in each transition.

8 Dramatic new technologies fuelled economic growth but also speculative boom and bust cycles. They also changed everyday life. Information technology and biotechnology are the most visible. Not only did computers spread to nearly every desktop, they became wearable, played music and videos, facilitated a growing proportion of purchases, and recorded a wealth of personal data on nearly everyone in the world's richer societies, raising concerns about privacy and surveillance. At the same time, biotechnology yielded genetically modified crops – to the enthusiasm of some and the fear of others (both over the effects on humans and the potential for environmental damage). New drugs prolonged life, enhanced sexual performance, controlled moods, and led to deep ethical concerns.

9 Social movement activity grew stronger than it had been since the 1960s and 1970s, challenging corporations and governments and focusing attention on a variety of issues. In some cases, like controversies over abortion rights, there were active mobilizations on both sides. In other cases, like the widespread opposition to global neoliberalism, activism was the tactic of those not represented on corporate boards of directors and in elite government circles. The movement against corporate-dominated globalization brought together environmentalists, advocates for indigenous peoples, anarchists worried about the centralization of power, citizens worried about the loss of sovereignty for their countries, and labour unions facing the loss of hard won rights for workers. Social movements also demanded better responses to AIDS, equal recognition for gay men and lesbians, rights for ethnic minorities and provisions for the disabled.

10 A resurgence of religion in the public sphere. While an older sociology had often suggested that secularization, was a normal part of modernization, it became increasingly apparent that religion did not always fade. The United States has long retained high rates of religious participation and in recent years has seen a boom in fundamentalist churches and engagement of both evangelical Protestants and conservative Catholics in politics. Church attendance is lower in much of Western Europe, but religious commitments became an important tension between new and old members of the European Union. But Christianity has seen its most rapid growth in Africa, Asia, and Latin America – and the new Christian communities are often more conservative than the old, both on theological matters and on lifestyle questions like gay rights. At the same time, immigration has changed the character of religion around the developed world. Buddhism, Islam and Hinduism are all now American religions alongside Christianity and Judaism. Large Islamic minorities are a major issue in many European countries that have thought of themselves as Christian even if largely secular, and where secular traditions are challenged by a desire for public religious recognition (as for example the French government banned Muslim girls from wearing headscarves to school). And Islam has itself become a global religion, with increasing flows of communication joining Muslims from the Middle East to those in South and South-East Asia, the former Soviet Union, Europe, America and Africa. Often stigmatized as anti-modern, Islam is better seen as resurgent among those seeking ways of dealing with modernity. And the same goes for Hinduism, increasingly organized as both a religious and a political force among Indians.

TRANSFORMATIONS OF GLOBAL SOCIOLOGY

Sociology has not been standing still as the world changed. On the contrary, the past 15 years have seen exciting new perspectives on earlier social changes and also important advances in methods and theory. Equally, however, sociology continues to engage the social world around it. In a sense, the late 1980s were a low time for sociology, well after the enthusiasms of the 1960s – and indeed, reeling from some backlash – and not yet focused on the post-Cold War world. During the past few years sociology has enjoyed a remarkable renewal. This is reflected both in the intellectual excitement of the discipline and in the numbers of new students. One simple indicator was the American Sociological Association annual meeting for 2004 – which drew the biggest crowd of any such meeting ever. The International Sociological Association has been undergoing a similar renewal as well. The reason is straightforward: the sense of how crucial sociology is to understanding what is going on in the world today.

So what are the big changes in sociology since the previous Handbook? Obviously there are scientific advances in every sub-field. Our list focuses, however, on those that have influenced the discipline as a whole. These are themes brought out by the chapters in this new Handbook, even while they also update readers on developments in specific sub-fields.

1 *Globalization as topic and engagement.* Trying to understand globalization in general has become an increasingly central concern for sociologists. One of the pioneers in this pursuit, Roland Robertson, writes with Kathleen White on both the patterns of globalization and the ways in which they change sociology's relationship to other disciplines. But globalization figures in other ways. It is a major reason for the resurgence of comparative sociology, discussed by David Apter. It is a crucial reason why sociological analyses of money and finance have grown in importance, as Geoffrey Ingham shows. Stewart Clegg analyzes the globalization of business, Jan Pieterse the structures of global inequality, and Siniša Malešević and John Hall the ways in which citizenship and the nation-state fare in a global era. Globalization is also an important dimension of issues in communication (discussed by Roger Silverstone), information (discussed by David Lyon), health and illness (discussed by Gary Albrecht), demography (discussed by Charles Hirschman), and higher education (discussed by Gerard Delanty).

2 *The 'cultural turn'.* One of the most dramatic changes in sociology in recent years was the resurgence of culture as a topic for sociological attention. This included both 'cultural sociology' (signalling a cultural approach to all sociological issues) and 'sociology of culture' (signalling a specialization of inquiry focused on cultural production, including especially art, music, literature and film). Wendy Griswold addresses culture in both senses. But like globalization, this is a theme that has shaped work across the discipline. This is apparent in Richard Sennett's account of 'the culture of work', Bryan Turner's analysis of the sociology of religion, Karin Knorr Cetina's examination of science

and technology, Don Slater's chapter on consumption and lifestyle and Chris Rojek's on leisure and recreation.

3 *Economic sociology.* If there is another sub-field of sociology which has grown as dramatically as the sociology of culture, and with comparable implications for the discipline as a whole, it is economic sociology. From roots mainly in the sociology of organizations, this has become one of the most influential parts of the discipline and an important field in business schools as well as sociology departments. Geoffrey Ingham, Stewart Clegg, Don Slater and Richard Sennett all address aspects of economic sociology. But it is a notable perspective in other fields as well, visible for example in Saskia Sassen's chapter on cities, Mike Savage's on stratification and power, and Dalton Conley's on poverty.

4 *Identity.* One of the features of the recent unsettled era in global society has been the destabilization of identities that were in the past often treated as relatively fixed – like race, gender, sexuality, ethnicity and nationality. These have been the focus of social movements and campaigns for both change and recognition. This has changed the nature of sociological research. Work on inequality between men and women and on sex roles, thus, has been complemented by examination of gender identities – and indeed the recognition that gender is a central category for sociology in general (not simply a special topic). This is a focus of Sylvia Walby's chapter, most centrally, but also an important theme for Patricia Hill Collins, who shows the way in which gender and race interrelate, for Bryan Turner, who considers changes in the sociology of the family, and for Nick Crossley who examines the development of the new field of the sociology of the body. Obviously gender issues also overlap with sexuality as well, examined in Elspeth Probyn's chapter. Gender, race, ethnicity, and sexuality all inform patterns of consumption and lifestyle (analysed by Don Slater), shape issues of health and illness

(addressed by Gary Albrecht), inform the way deviance and social exclusion operate (as Heinz Steinert shows) and indeed figure in a range of fields.

5   *Renewal of public sociology.* Sociology has always had a voice in public affairs, and sociological research has informed both government policy-making and debates among citizens. During much of the postwar era, however, there was also a notion of 'pure science' that suggested sociology was most appropriately produced for other sociologists, and minimized or treated as mere popularization efforts to introduce sociology into broader public debates. This was challenged in the 1960s and early 1970s with calls for research and teaching focused on issues of greater 'relevance' and in the past few years it has been challenged again. In the United States, where the ideology of 'pure science' was perhaps stronger than in most other countries, Michael Burawoy used his 2004 term as president of the American Sociological Association to promote 'public sociology'. In Europe similar trends were evident, as Pierre Bourdieu in the last years of his life focused on the struggle against neoliberal globalization, as Alain Touraine pursued action research in relation to social movements and citizenship, and as Boris Kagarlitsky struggled to revitalize public discourse in post-Soviet Russia. Anthony Giddens not only wrote about the Third Way and helped to inform New Labour policies in the UK but also helped to remake the London School of Economics as a publicly engaged scientific institution. Jürgen Habermas, the most prominent theorist of the public sphere, has been a publicly prominent sociologist throughout his career and most recently a key voice on European unification. Around the world, indeed, the growth of attention to 'civil society' has made sociological research more prominent. And throughout almost every chapter in the present book readers will find not only sociological knowledge relevant to public debates, but evidence of the ways in which sociology is shaped by its engagements with public issues.

These transformations of sociology are of basic importance. But each builds on long-standing strengths of the discipline, renews parts of its tradition, and represents an ongoing scientific effort to improve knowledge of society and social change. It is appropriate, thus, that in the first section of the Handbook we consider some of the new directions in basic development of theory and method. We make no effort to survey all that is available – this would produce a completely different (and much larger) book. Rather, we have asked authors to focus on major changes and issues that have informed recent work and are the basis for new research now. Adrian Raftery analyses the growth and transformation of quantitative methods in sociological research. Paul Atkinson and Sara Delamont focus on the qualitative research traditions. In each case, the authors reveal that more is at stake than mere technique; method is a matter of structuring intellectual inquiry. Randall Collins examines the relationship between sociology and philosophy which is basic to sociological theory and also to sociology's reflexive self-understanding of what it means to be a science. Charles Crothers demonstrates both the diversity of sociological traditions and the need for more effort to overcome the insularity of many in order to take advantage of what the field as a whole offers. David Apter reviews the revitalization of comparative sociology that has been especially important in an era of globalization.

Sometimes, the desire to succeed in various practical projects encourages the illusion that it is easier to change the social world than it really is. Revolutionaries, for example, may find more followers if they can persuade people that the risks of revolution are low. Those who promote the restoration of traditional values, by contrast, may find more supporters if they can convince people that traditions are undermined just by individual choices to deviate and not by the capitalist economy with its search for new products, new markets, and advertising techniques to make people feel new needs. Most generally, the truth that human beings have some choice over the social conditions under which they live – and indeed more choice in modern societies than in most of history – and the fact that people would like even more often leads to individualistic ideologies that underestimate the power of social structure. At the very least, sociology continually reminds us, abstract freedom of individual choice is different from concrete capacity to make one's choices effective. It is easier for an individual to choose what candidate to vote for in an election than to choose what kind of political system to live under. The latter is subject to laws, immigration controls, economic resources, the cooperation of others and power relations. Changes can be made to political systems, but they are made only through social processes and they usually work well only when other aspects of social life change in reinforcing ways.

At other times, the speed of social change encourages the sense that social life is so unstable as to be completely unpredictable. This too is an illusion. Even while many features of social life undergo dramatic changes, others may be highly stable. The past 20 years, for example, have seen the breakup of the Soviet Union and the end of the Cold War, dramatic changes in information technology, and a major wave of international migration that has made many societies more multicultural. Part of the job of sociology is to make sense of these historically specific transformations (and indeed, chapters in this Handbook help to do so). But just as we need to be clear what has changed, we also need to recognize that many things did not. Conflict and competition between political powers are still basic to world affairs, even if reorganized. Capitalist corporations are still more powerful than some countries, and the collapse of communism only made this more true in some cases. The control of information is still a fundamental source of power. And immigration is still a source of both tension and creativity, the growing prominence of minorities still challenged by prejudice and helped by understanding.

In sum, sociology is needed as much today as ever to make sense of the possibility for choice and change and the pressures that reproduce existing structures. Sociology is enjoying a renewal, revitalized as it rises to the challenges of a rapidly changing world. This Handbook offers an introduction to a wide range of themes, theories, research methods and empirical topics. They do not exhaust the subject, but they should whet the appetite for more.

NOTE

1 The editor claimed that establishing a sociological 'canon' was not his intention, but the Handbook was widely perceived as offering an 'orthodox' account of the discipline. For a symposium of review essays discussing it, see Calhoun and Land (1989).

REFERENCES

Bell, Daniel (1973) *The Coming of Post-Industrial Society*. New York: Basic Books.

Bauman, Zygmunt (1991) *The Holocaust and Modernity*. Cambridge: Polity Press.

Calhoun, Craig and Land, Kenneth (eds) (1989) 'Smelser's *Handbook*: an assessment', *Contemporary Sociology*, 8 (4): 475–501.

Cardoso, Fernando H. and Faletto, Enzo (1978) *Dependency and Development in Latin America*. Berkeley, CA: University of California Press.

Castells, Manuel (1996) *The Rise of the Network Society*. Cambridge, MA: Blackwell.

Durkheim, Emile (1893) *The Division of Labor in Society*. New York: The Free Press.

Eisenstadt, Shmuel and Schlucter, Wolfgang (1998) 'Introduction: Paths to early modernities – a comparative view', *Daedalus*, 127 (3: 'Early Modernities'): 1–18.

Faris, Robert E. Lee (ed.) (1964) *Handbook of Modern Sociology*. Chicago: Rand McNally.

Frank, Andre Gunder (1980) *Dependent Accumulation and Underdevelopment*. New York: New York University Press.

Gaonkar, Dilip (2001) *Alternative Modernities*. Durham, NC: Duke University Press.

Inkeles, Alex and Smith, David (1974) *Becoming Modern*. Cambridge, MA: Harvard University Press.

Lenski, Gerhard and Nolan, Patrick (2004) *Human Societies*. Herndon, VA: Paradigm Publishers.

Mann, Michael (1986) *The Sources of Social Power*. Cambridge: Cambridge University Press.

Parsons, Talcott (1959) 'Some remarks confronting sociology as a profession', *American Sociological Review*, 29: 547–559.

Parsons, Talcott (1977) *The Evolution of Societies*. Englewood Cliffs, NJ: Prentice–Hall.

Smelser, Neil (ed.) (1988) *Handbook of Sociology*. Newbury Park, CA: Sage.

Spencer, Herbert (1885) *The Principles of Sociology*. New York: Greenwood.

Tilly, Charles (1990) *Coercion, Capital, and European States AD 990–1990*. Cambridge, MA: Blackwell.

Toennies, Ferdinand (1886) *Community and Society*. New York: Harper.

Wallerstein, Immanuel (1974, 1988) *The Modern World System*, vols 1 and 2. La Jolla, CA: Academic Books.

Part 1

Theory and Method

1

Quantitative Research Methods

ADRIAN E. RAFTERY

INTRODUCTION

The roots of sociology go back to the mid-nineteenth century and to seminal work by Auguste Comte (who invented the word 'sociology'), Karl Marx, Max Weber and Emile Durkheim on the kind of society then newly emerging from the Industrial Revolution. Sociology has used quantitative methods and data from the beginning. Comte, who launched the discipline, was quite explicit about its grounding in statistical data. Durkheim's (1897) *Le Suicide*, for example, made extensive use of statistical data.

However, prior to the Second World War, the data tended to be fragmentary, often bordering on the anecdotal, and the statistical methods simple and descriptive. Camic and Yu (1994) identified Franklin H. Giddings as the father of quantitative sociology in the United States. Giddings, who was appointed Professor of Sociology at Columbia in 1894 and died in 1931, defined sociology as a field that studies social phenomena at the aggregate level. He held that statistical analysis in sociology consists largely of counting the individuals in each of several categories and finding average characteristics of each category. From a modern statistical perspective, a striking feature of his work was his relative lack of concern with variation.

Since then, the data available have grown in complexity, and statistical methods have been developed to deal with them. Much of this statistical development has been due to sociologists rather than statisticians; Clogg (1992) and the discussants of his article made this point emphatically, and documented it well. This partly reflects the fact that the number of statisticians working on sociological problems has always been relatively small. Statisticians have tended to work in greater numbers on problems emerging from medicine, engineering and the biological sciences; this probably reflects the balance of available funding in the latter half of the twentieth century. There are some signs recently that this situation is changing, as I mention at the end of the chapter.

The overall trend in sociology in the past 50 years has been towards more rigorous formulation of hypotheses, larger and more detailed data sets, statistical models growing in complexity to match the data, and a higher level of statistical analysis in the major sociological journals. Statistical methods have had a successful half-century in sociology, contributing to a greatly improved standard of scientific rigor in the discipline.

Sociology has made extensive use of a wide variety of statistical methods and models. I will focus here on the ones developed by sociologists, those whose development was directly motivated by sociological problems, and those that were first published in sociological journals. Many other methods, such as those for limited dependent variables (logistic regression springs to mind), have been used extensively in sociology, but were primarily developed in other disciplines in response to other problems. Important though they are for sociology, I will mention these areas more briefly.

A major omission from this chapter is any in-depth discussion of statistical methods that have come to sociology from econometrics rather than from statistics; this would merit a separate chapter in its own right. Econometrics has been influential in sociological methodology, but here I do not review this important influence except incidentally.

At the risk of controversy, I will classify statistical methods in sociology by the kind of data that they address, rather than by the method itself. I will distinguish three postwar generations of statistical methods in sociology, each defined by the kind of data to which they are most often applied: cross-tabulations, unit-level survey data, and newer data forms. Like real generations, these intellectual generations overlap and the boundaries between them are not clearcut; they all remain active today, albeit at different levels of maturity, and even their starting points are not uniquely defined.

In the period starting after the Second World War, much of the data that sociologists had to work with came in the form of cross-tabulations of counts from surveys and censuses. The first generation of methods I will discuss deals with data of this kind. Typically these cross-classifications involved only a small number of variables such as sex, age group and occupational category; social mobility tables provided the canonical example for much of the methodological work. This is perhaps the area of statistics to which sociologists have contributed the most; indeed, it could be argued that sociologists have dominated this sub-field and that the methods they have developed have been diffusing out from sociology into other disciplines. Schuessler's survey in 1980 largely reflects this first-generation work.

By the early 1960s, sociologists no longer had to rely on cross-tabulations of counts, and unit-level data from surveys that measured many variables were becoming available. Computing power was also developing to the point where it could handle such data fairly easily. The second generation of methods was developed to deal with data of this kind. This generation of methods was galvanized by Blau and Duncan's (1967) highly influential book *The American Occupational Structure*, and also by the establishment of *Sociological Methodology* in 1969 and *Sociological Methods and Research* in 1972 as publication outlets. Edgar Borgatta established both of these publications, the second when it became rapidly apparent that there was both the supply and demand for more articles than could be published by *Sociological Methodology* alone. These developments marked the coming of age of research of quantitative methodology in sociology.

By the late 1980s, sociologists had conceived the ambition of analyzing data that do not fit easily into the standard straightjackets of cross-tabulations or data matrices (although they can sometimes be forced into them). These include texts or narratives, and data in which dependence is a crucial aspect, such as social network data and data in which spatial referencing is important. They also include datasets that combine multiple types of data, such as satellite images, enthnographic accounts and quantitative measurements. The third generation of methods is being developed to address data such as these. As befits its youth, so far it is a lively and exciting grab-bag of ideas and developments, not having yet achieved the well-organized maturity of the first two generations.

My classification of statistical methods in sociology into generations defined by the kind of data addressed, rather than the kind of method used, does not reflect the usual organization of graduate training, and is bound to be somewhat controversial. Perhaps for reasons of convenience and efficiency in training, the major methods of sociology have tended to be grouped together under categories such as regression models, limited dependent variable models, loglinear models, structural equation models, event history analysis, and so on. However, I have found it easier to attempt to discern past trends and to think about future developments by focusing on the types of data that motivate the development of the methods in the first place.

We have come a long way in the past 50 years. Today, much sociological research is based on the re-analysis of large high-quality survey sample datasets, often collected with public funds and publicly available to researchers, with typical sample sizes in the range 5000–20,000, or greater. This has opened the way to easy replication of results and has helped to produce standards of scientific rigor in sociology comparable to and greater than those in many of the natural and medical sciences. Perhaps in part because of this, social statistics has recently started a rapid expansion as a research area, and several major institutions have launched initiatives in this area in the past few years.

THE FIRST GENERATION: CROSS-TABULATIONS

Categorical data analysis

Initially, much of the data that quantitative sociologists had to work with came in the form of cross-classified tables, and so it is not surprising that this is perhaps the area of statistics to which sociology has contributed the most. A canonical example has been the analysis of social mobility tables, usually in the form of two-way tables of father's against respondent's occupational category; typically the number of categories used is between 5 and 17.

At first the focus was on measures of association, or mobility indices as they were called in the social mobility context (Glass, 1954; Rogoff, 1953), but these indices failed to do the job of separating structural mobility from exchange (or circulation) mobility. The solution to this key problem in the analysis of mobility tables turned out to require explicit probability models for the tables. Birch (1963) proposed the loglinear model for the observed counts $\{x_{ij}\}$, given by

$$\log(E[x_{ij}]) = u + u_{1(i)} + u_{2(j)} + u_{12(ij)}, \qquad (1)$$

where i indexes rows and j columns, $u_{1(i)}$ and $u_{2(j)}$ are the main effects for the rows and columns, and $u_{12(ij)}$ is the interaction term, measuring departures from independence. This provided the overall framework needed for the rigorous analysis of mobility and similar tables. However, the difficulty with model (1) in its original form for social mobility and similar tables is that the number of parameters is too large for inference and interpretation. For example in the US datasets 17 categories were used, so the interaction term involves $16^2 = 256$ parameters.

To make progress, it was necessary to model the interaction term parsimoniously (that is, with few parameters), but in a way that fits the data. A successful general approach to doing this is the association model of Duncan (1979) and Goodman (1979):

$$u_{12(ij)} = \sum_{m=1}^{M} \gamma_m \alpha_i^{(m)} \beta_j^{(m)} + \phi_i \delta(i,j), \qquad (2)$$

where $\delta(i, j) = 1$ if $i = j$ and 0 otherwise. In (2), $\alpha_i^{(m)}$ is the score for the ith row on the kth scoring dimension, and $\beta_j^{(m)}$ is the corresponding score for the jth column; these can be either specified in advance or estimated from the data. The last term allows a different strength of association on the diagonal. (The model (2) is unidentified as written; various identifying constraints are possible.) This is often called the RC(M) model. In most applications to date, $M = 1$; the first genuine substantive application of the model in sociology with $M > 1$ was to labor market experiences and outcomes by Clogg, Eliason and Wahl (1990).

Goodman (1979) initially derived this model as a way of describing association in terms of local odds ratios. Goodman (1985) has shown that this model is closely related to canonical correlations and to correspondence analysis (Benzécri, 1976), and provides an inferential framework for these methodologies. When the categories are ordered, the uniform association model with $\alpha_i = \beta_i = i$ is a useful starting point (Haberman, 1979). In this model, the odds ratios in all 2×2 sub-tables are equal, so this can be viewed as a discrete analogue to the bivariate normal distribution, with $\gamma \equiv \gamma_k$ specifying the correlation.

Table 1.1   *Observed counts from the largest US social mobility study and expected values from a Goodman association model with 4 degrees of freedom. Sample size is 19,912*

	Son's occupation									
	Upper non-manual		Lower non-manual		Upper manual		Lower manual		Farm	
Father's occupation	Obs.	Exp.	Obs.	Exp.	Obs.	Exp.	Obs.	Exp.	Obs.	Exp.
Upper non-manual	1414	1414	521	534	302	278	643	652	40	42
Lower non-manual	724	716	524	524	254	272	703	698	48	43
Upper manual	798	790	648	662	856	856	1676	1666	108	112
Lower manual	756	794	914	835	771	813	3325	3325	237	236
Farm	409	386	357	409	441	405	1611	1617	1832	1832

Source: Hout (1983)

Table 1.1 shows the actual counts for a reduced version of the most extensive US social mobility study, and the fitted values from an association model; the model accounts for 99.6% of the association in the table and its success is evident. Hout (1984) extended the range of application of these models by modeling the scores and diagonal terms in (2) as sums or products of covariates, such as characteristics of the occupational categories in question; this is an extension of Birch's (1965) linear-by-linear interaction model.

This methodology has also made it feasible to model relatively high-dimensional tables with large numbers of categories in a parsimonious and interpretable way. This has led to important discoveries, including Hout's (1988) finding that social mobility has been increasing in the United States. This is a subtle result because of the complex nature of the data underlying it, and it would have been hard to discover it without using the association model methodology. This substantive result was confirmed and refined in Ganzeboom, Luijkx and Treiman's (1989) discovery, based on several hundred social mobility tables from different countries at different time points, that social mobility increased by about 1% a year in industrialized countries throughout the second half of the twentieth century.

Biblarz and Raftery (1993) and Biblarz, Raftery and Bucur (1997) adapted the models to higher dimensional tables to study social mobility in non-intact families. The tables they used had up to five dimensions: father's occupation, offspring's occupation, gender, race, and period, and up to about 7000 cells. Thus

standard loglinear models would not have revealed anything, but association modeling, extending the models mentioned earlier, did provide interpretable results, parameter estimates and conclusions. They showed that occupational resemblance is weaker in non-intact families than in intact ones, that offspring raised by working single mothers succeed much better on average than those from other non-intact families, and that these patterns have remained essentially constant from the 1960s through the 1990s, in spite of the many changes in family structure, occupational distribution and the relationship between gender, race and occupational and labor force status. Other important applications of loglinear and related models include the analysis of sex segregation (Charles and Grusky, 1995), and assortative mating (Kalmijn, 1991). From sociology, the use of association models has diffused to other disciplines, such as epidemiology (Becker, 1989).

One common reason for analyzing tables with more than two dimensions is to assess how two-way associations vary across a third (or several other) dimension(s). Yamaguchi (1987) and Xie (1992) have proposed specific forms of the higher-dimensional association model that are adapted for this purpose, and these were unified and extended by Goodman and Hout (1998). A particularly appealing aspect of the latter approach is the availability of a range of graphical displays that facilitate the interpretation of the rather complex data and model parameters that arise in this setting.

These models are for situations with discrete independent variables. Perhaps the most successful models for the dependence of cross-classifications on *continuous* independent variables are Sobel's (1981, 1985) diagonal mobility models. These have been applied in a variety of settings, for example to marital fertility (Sorensen, 1989), cultural consumption (De Graaf, 1991) and voting behavior (Weakliem, 1992).

An intuitive alternative formulation of the basic ideas underlying (1) and (2) is in terms of marginal *distributions* rather than the main effects in (1). The resulting marginal models specify a model for the marginal distributions and a model for the odds ratios, and this implies a model for the joint distribution that is not loglinear (Lang and Agresti, 1994; Becker, 1994; Becker and Yang, 1998). The first substantive application of these models in sociology was to modeling social mobility (Sobel et al., 1998).

Latent class models

An alternative approach that answers different questions is the latent class model (Lazarsfeld, 1950; Lazarsfeld and Henry, 1968; Goodman, 1974a,b). In its basic form, this represents the distribution of counts as a finite mixture of distributions within each of which the different variables are independent. The model was introduced to account for observed associations in multivariate discrete data, the original motivation being somewhat akin to that for factor analysis for multivariate continuous data.

Hagenaars (1988, 1990) has extended the latent class model to the situation where each component in the mixture can exhibit dependence. Clogg (1995) gives a survey of this area. There have been many applications of this model. One interesting recent application to criminology is by Roeder, Lynch and Nagin (1999).

This basic model has been formulated and used in other contexts. Chickering and Heckerman (1997) formulated it as a Bayesian graphical model with one hidden node. This formulation facilitates estimation of latent class models with many variables, and also makes it easier to estimate the model when there is missing data for some individuals, and to make inference about the missing data. Celeux and Govaert (1991) used the same basic model for clustering multivariate discrete observations, again potentially with a large number of variables.

Hypothesis testing and model selection

Sociologists often have sample sizes in the thousands, and so they came up early and hard against the problem that standard *P*-values can indicate rejection of null hypotheses in large samples, even when the null model seems reasonable theoretically and inspection of the data fails to reveal any striking discrepancies with it. The problem is compounded by the fact that there are often many models rather than just the two envisaged by significance tests, and by the need to use stepwise or other multiple comparison methods for model selection (e.g. Goodman, 1971). By the early 1980s, some sociologists were dealing with this problem by ignoring the results of *P*-value-based tests when they seemed counterintuitive and by basing model selection instead on theoretical considerations and informal assessment of discrepancies between model and data.

Then it was pointed out that this problem could be alleviated by basing model selection instead on Bayes factors (Raftery, 1986a), and that this can be simply approximated for loglinear models by preferring a model if BIC (Bayesian Information Criterion), defined by BIC = Deviance − (Degrees of freedom) $\log(n)$, is smaller (Schwarz, 1978; Raftery, 1986b). For nested hypotheses, this can be viewed as defining a significance level for a test that decreases automatically with sample size. Since then, this approach has been used in many sociological applications of loglinear models. Kass and Wasserman (1995) showed that the approximation is quite accurate if the Bayesian prior used for the model parameters is a unit information prior, that is, a prior distribution that contains about the same amount of information as a single 'typical' observation. Raftery (1995) indicated how the methodology can be extended to a range of other models.

Weakliem (1999) criticized the use of BIC on the grounds that the unit information prior to which it corresponds may be too diffuse in practice, leading BIC to tend to favor the null hypothesis too often. However, Raftery (1999) pointed out that the unit information prior does provide a reasonable representation of the prior knowledge of an investigator who has some advance information, but not a great deal, about the parameter values for the model being estimated. It can thus be viewed as approximating the situation where there is little prior information. A more knowledgeable investigator would have a tighter prior distribution, and thus might have a basis for rejecting a null hypothesis when BIC does not, but this would be based on prior information rather than on data, and this should be made explicit in any report that does so. BIC provides a conservative assessment of evidence: one can be quite confident of the reality of any 'effect', evidence of whose existence is favored strongly by BIC. Weakliem's arguments can be viewed as implying that if real prior information is indeed available it should be used, and I would agree with this. This points towards using Bayes factors based on priors that reflect the actual information available; this is easy to do for loglinear and other generalized linear models (Raftery, 1996).

THE SECOND GENERATION: UNIT-LEVEL SURVEY DATA

The second generation of statistical models responded to the availability of unit-level survey data in the form of large data matrices of independent cases. The methods that have proved successful for answering questions about such data have mostly been based on the linear regression model and its extensions to path models, structural equation models, generalized linear models and event history models. For questions about the *distribution* of variables rather than about their predicted value, however, nonparametric methods have proven useful (Morris et al., 1994; Bernhardt et al., 1995; Handcock and Morris, 1998, 1999). We start by reviewing the development of the measurement of occupational status, which provided a major impetus for the growth of the second generation of methods.

Measuring occupational status

Occupational status is an important concept in sociology and developing a useful continuous measure of it was a signal achievement of the field. It was important for the development of statistical methods in sociology because, starting in the early 1960s, it encouraged greater use of regression analysis and related methods among scholars with an interest in the sources and consequences of job-holding. These methodological approaches diffused rapidly into other areas of the discipline.

Initially, the status of an occupation was equated with its perceived prestige, as measured in national surveys beginning in the 1940s. However, surveys could measure the prestige of only a small number of the several hundred occupations identified in each decennial Census classification. To fill in missing prestige scores for the 1960 Census classification, Duncan (1961) regressed the prestige scores for the 45 occupations for which they were available on measures of the proportion of occupational incumbents who had completed high school and the proportion of incumbents who earned more than $10,000. He found that the predictions were very good ($R^2 = 0.91$) and that the two predictors were about equally weighted. Based on this, he created a predicted prestige score for all occupations in the 1960 classification, which became known as the Duncan Socioeconomic Index (SEI); the SEI later turned out to be a better predictor of various social outcomes than the prestige scores themselves. Duncan's initial work has been updated several times for subsequent Census classifications, but has recently been critiqued on conceptual and empirical grounds (Hauser and Warren, 1997; Warren et al., 1998).

In much social research, particularly in economics, current income is used as a predictor of social outcomes, but there are good reasons to prefer occupational status. It has proven to be a good predictor of many social outcomes. Jobs and occupations can be measured accurately, in contrast to income or wealth, whose measurement is plagued by problems of refusal, recall and reliability. Also, occupational status is more stable over time than income, both within careers and between generations. This suggests that occupational status may actually be a better indicator of long-term or permanent income than (current) income itself. The status of occupations tends to be fairly constant both in time and across countries (Treiman, 1977).

The many uses of structural equation models

Figure 1.1 shows the basic path model of occupational attainment at the heart of Blau and Duncan (1967) (see Duncan, 1966). Wright (1921) introduced path analysis, and Blalock (1961) gave it a causal interpretation in a social science context. One of the important uses and motivations of structural equation models was to decompose a total effect into direct and indirect effects. Alwin and Hauser (1975) played an important role in showing how to do this for sociological data. See Freedman (1987) and Sobel (1998) for critiques, and later in this chapter for more discussion of causality in the social sciences.

Often, variables of interest in a causal model are not observed directly, but other variables are observed that can be viewed as measurements of the variables, or 'constructs' of interest, such as prejudice, alienation, conservatism, self-esteem, discrimination, motivation or ability. Jöreskog (1973) dealt with this by maximum likelihood estimation of a structural equation model with latent variables; this is sometimes called a LISREL model, from the name of Jöreskog's software. Duncan (1975) played a big role in introducing these ideas into sociology, and Long (1984a,b) and Bollen (1989) provide well-written and accessible accounts geared to sociologists. A typical model of this kind is shown in Figure 1.2: the goal of the analysis is testing and estimating the strength of the relationship between the

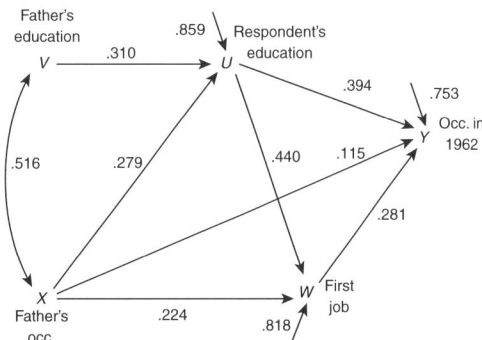

Figure 1.1   A famous path model: the process of stratification, US 1962. The numbers on the arrows from one variable to another are regression coefficients, 0.516 is the correlation between V and X, and the numbers on the arrows with no sources are residual standard deviations. All the variables have been centered and scaled. (Blau and Duncan, 1967)

unobserved latent variables represented by the thick arrow. Diagrams such as Figures 1.1 and 1.2 have proven useful to sociologists for specifying theories and hypotheses and for building causal models.

The LISREL framework has been extended and used ingeniously for purposes beyond those for which it was originally intended. Muthén (1983) extended it to categorical variables, and Muthén (1997) showed how it can be used to represent longitudinal data, growth curve models and multi-level data. Kuo and Hauser (1996) used data on siblings to control for unobserved family effects on socioeconomic outcomes, and cast the resulting random effects model in a LISREL framework.

The advent of graphical Markov models (Spiegelhalter et al., 1993), specified by conditional independencies rather than by regression-like relationships, is important for the analysis of multivariate dependencies, although they can seem less interpretable to sociologists. They have been particularly useful for propagating information about some variables through a system of dependent variables, to yield information about other, unobserved variables, as is needed, for example, in the construction of expert systems for medical diagnosis and other

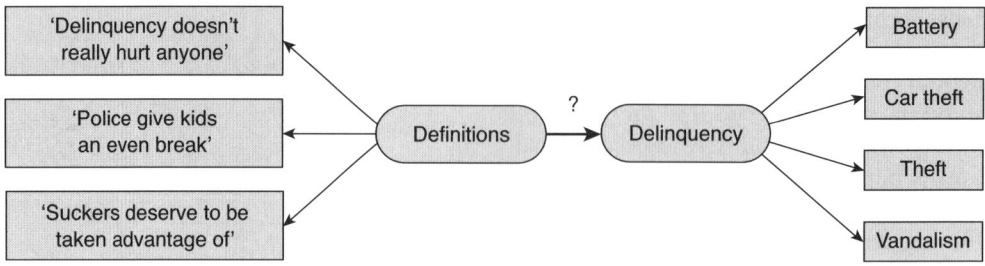

Figure 1.2   *Part of a structural equation model to assess the hypothesis that learned definitions of delinquency cause delinquent behavior. The key goal is testing and estimating the relationship represented by the thick arrow. The constructs of interest, 'Definitions' and 'Delinquency', are not measured directly. The variables inside the rectangles are measured. (Matsueda and Heimer, 1987)*

applications. They have been less used so far for inference and modeling in social research, perhaps because sociological hypotheses tend to be formulated more often in terms of regression or causal relationships than in terms of conditional independencies between variables.

The relationship between graphical Markov models and structural equation models has begun to be understood (Koster, 1996; Spirtes et al., 1998). Also, the LISREL model seems ideally suited to Gibbs sampling and Markov chain Monte Carlo (MCMC) methods (Gilks et al., 1996), and this is likely to permit useful extensions of the framework.

Event history analysis

Unit-level survey data often include or allow the reconstruction of life histories. These include the times of crucial events such as marriages, divorces, births, commitals to and releases from prison, job changes, or going on or off welfare.

Prior to 1972, two approaches were available for the analysis of the distribution of the time to a single event such as death, and of the factors influencing it. One was life table analysis from demography, but this did not allow easy analysis of the factors influencing time to an event. The other was regression analysis of the observed times to the event, but this was plagued by censoring, and by the often extreme non-normality of the response.

This field was revolutionized by the introduction of the Cox (1972) proportional hazards model, which brought together these two approaches. Tuma (1976) and Tuma and Hannan (1984) generalized this approach to allow for repeated events, for multiple types of events, such as marriages and divorces, and for events consisting of movement between different types of states, such as different job categories. Yamaguchi (1991) and Petersen (1991) have provided accessible accounts of the methodology, emphasizing sociological applications, and Mayer and Tuma (1990) described a collection of case studies from social science. One important area of application of hazard rate models has been organizational birth and death processes; this is unique to sociology. Petersen (1995) extended the basic model further to multiple types of events where the events are interdependent, that is, where the occurrence or non-occurrence of one type of event affects the probability that the other type of event happens. An example is the relationship between becoming unemployed and getting divorced. Xie (2000) has discussed the roots of event history analysis in demography and life table analysis.

Users of the Cox model in medicine have tended to treat the baseline hazard non-parametrically, but in social science it has sometimes been found useful to model it parametrically. For example, Yamaguchi (1992) analyzed permanent employment in Japan where the surviving fraction (those who never change jobs) and its determinants are of key interest; he found that covariates were associated both with the timing of job change and with the surviving fraction. Yamaguchi and Ferguson (1995) provide another application of this idea, to the stopping and spacing of childbirths.

Social science event history data are often recorded in discrete time, for example, by year, either because events tend to happen at particular times of year (e.g. graduating), or because of measurement constraints. As a result, discrete-time event history models have been popular (Allison, 1984), and in some ways are easier to handle than their continuous-time analogues. Ways of dealing with multi-level event history data, smoothly time-varying covariates and other complications have been introduced in this context (e.g. Raftery et al., 1995b; Fahrmeir and Knorr-Held, 1997).

This basic framework has also been found useful to model a different kind of phenomenon: that of diffusion of innovations and social influence. Burt (1987) provided a theoretical framework for this work, and the extended event-history framework proposed for modeling it was developed by Marsden and Podolny (1990), Strang (1991) and Strang and Tuma (1993). A different approach, using accelerated failure-time models rather than proportional hazards models, was developed by Diekmann (1989) and Yamaguchi (1994).

One problem with social science event history data is that dropping out can be related to the event of interest. For example, people may tend to leave a study shortly before a divorce, which will play havoc with estimation of divorce rates. The problem seems almost insoluble at first sight, but Hill (1997) produced an elegant solution using the Shared Unmeasured Risk Factor (SURF) model of Hill, Axinn and Thornton (1993). The basic trick is to observe that, although one does not know which of the people who dropped out actually got divorced soon afterwards, one can estimate which ones were most at risk of divorcing. One can then use this information to adjust the empirical divorce rates in the study by modeling divorce and dropout simultaneously.

Binary dependent variables

The term 'limited dependent variable' is usually used to refer to a scalar dependent variable in a regression model, the set of whose possible values is restricted in a way that violates the assumptions of normal linear regression too severely for it to be used. The canonical example is binary dependent variables; others include nominal, ordinal and compositional variables, and, in some contexts, variables that are constrained to be positive.

Limited dependent variables, especially binary variables, arise frequently in social research, and many articles in leading sociological journals use models and methods specifically developed for this situation. Nevertheless, much of the methodological development in this area has come from disciplines other than sociology. However, sociologists have played a major role in expositing, adapting and synthesizing these methods; see, for example, the books by Long (1997) and Xie and Powers (2000).

For binary responses, the method of choice in sociology in the past 20 years has been logistic regression. Much of the early development was for medical applications, and the monograph by Cox (1970) helped to introduce the methods to a wide audience. The advent of generalized linear models (Nelder and Wedderburn, 1972), and the recognition that logistic regression is a special case, as well as the development of the associated GLIM software (Baker and Nelder, 1977), helped to make logistic regression a standard tool in many disciplines, particularly in the social and health sciences. Some version or descendant of the GLIM software is now included in most major commercial statistical packages.

Logistic regression is not the only possible model for regression with binary responses. Ordinary linear regression gives similar results if most of the probabilities are far enough from 0 and 1 (say between 0.1 and 0.9). Logistic regression is more 'correct' than linear regression, since, for example, it constrains fitted probabilities to lie between 0 and 1. Nevertheless, in the 1970s and 1980s there was a debate about whether logistic regression is really needed, given that it is more complex to estimate and needs more computer time than linear regression. The subsequent increase in computer speed made the additional computer time negligible, and the debate was settled in favor of logistic regression.

Another alternative is probit regression, in which the dependent variable is assumed to arise by truncating an unobserved normal random variable whose expectation depends linearly on the independent variables. This is soundly based and easy to estimate, because it is also a generalized linear model and so can be estimated using GLIM; it tends to give results that are very similar to those from logistic regression. However, in sociology, as in many other disciplines, it has lost out to logistic regression, perhaps because of the appealing interpretation of the logistic regression coefficients as odds ratios. There has been a revival of interest in probit regression recently among statisticians. This is because it is defined in terms of latent variables, and so can be included relatively easily as a component in more complex Bayesian models that are estimated using MCMC (e.g. Albert and Chib, 1993).

A further alternative is complementary log–log regression, in which $\log(-\log(p))$ is assumed to be a linear combination of independent variables, where p is the conditional probability of the event of interest, given the independent variables. This is also a generalized linear model and so is easy to estimate. It can fit much better than logistic regression, and often gives quite different predicted probabilities, particularly for more extreme values of the independent variables. One example of this is the Irish educational transition data discussed by Raftery and Hout (1985); see Kass and Raftery (1995).

The introduction of two-sided logit models by Logan (1996, 1997) was an important development. This recognizes that in many situations in social life where individuals choose between different outcomes, there are two types of force in play: the preferences and attributes of the individual, and those of the possible choices. For example, in the labor market, which job an individual ends up in depends not only on his or her own attributes and preferences or utilities, but also on those of the other candidates in the job market, and those of the available employers and jobs. Logan's approach is to model both of these processes explicitly and simultaneously, and to explain the final labor market outcomes in terms of the interaction between them. The model can be estimated using either individual-level data or data aggregated into a cross-classification.

Other limited dependent variables

Logistic regression has been extended to nominal dependent variables with more than two categories (see, for example, Hosmer and Lemeshow, 1989). Maximum likelihood estimation of the resulting multinomial logistic regression model is relatively straightforward, and software to do it is available. Begg and Gray (1984) have shown that this can be very well approximated by an appropriately set up (binary) logistic regression (see also Hosmer and Lemeshow, 1989). Logistic regression has also been extended to ordinal dependent variables; see, for example, McCullagh and Nelder, 1989 and Agresti, 1990).

Another important kind of limited dependent variable arises when the variable is positive, but has a non-negligible probability of being exactly equal to zero. One example is income from work: some people are out of the labor force or unemployed, and have zero income from work, while all others have positive income. Data of this kind have often been analyzed using the Tobit model of Tobin (1958). In this model, it is assumed that those with zero income actually have an unobserved negative income, and the true income (now assumed to be capable of taking all positive and negative values) is modeled using ordinary linear regression.

The Tobit model in its original form seems rather unsatisfactory. For one thing, the postulated unobserved value does not exist: those who have zero income actually do have zero income (ignoring measurement error), not some unobserved negative income. Also, and perhaps more seriously, the model assumes that the mechanism determining whether or not someone has income from work, is essentially the same as the one that determines how much they earn. It could easily be the case, however, that the mechanism that determines whether or not someone is in the labor force is quite different from the mechanism that determines how much they earn if they are in the labor force, and with the Tobit model it is hard to make this distinction.

The Tobit model was developed before the widespread availability of specific methods for binary dependent variables. Now, however, there is a simple alternative approach that avoids the problems with the Tobit model. One simply models the data in two steps. In the first step, the dependent variable is whether or not the dependent variable is zero, and this is modeled using probit regression. Then, in the second step, the dependent variable is the amount earned and only individuals with positive earnings are included. This is the standard sample selection model, which led to the development of the Heckman (1979) two-stage estimator. Amemiya (1985) calls this the Type II Tobit model. Winship and Mare (1992) review subsequent developments in this area.

A further kind of limited dependent variable arises in the analysis of compositional data. Here the dependent variable is a vector of positive values that sum up to one, and consist of proportions. An example is the analysis of household budgets: the response is a vector, each element of which is the proportion of total household expenditure spent on some category, such as rent, food, utilities, education and so on. One's first idea might be to model each proportion separately using regression, or perhaps to use a multivariate regression method that takes account of the correlation between the different responses. These methods do not work, however, because of the constraint that the responses add up to one, and so standard distributional assumptions do not apply. The observations lie on a *simplex*, the high-dimensional analogue of the triangle, not on the full Euclidean space. Literature studying this situation has been summarized in part by Aitchison (1986); his main recommendation is to first transform the p-dimensional vector of proportions to a $(p-1)$-dimensional vector on the full Euclidean space using the multivariate logistic transform, and then to proceed using standard methods.

Multi-level models

Multi-level models extend the regression models and their generalizations to situations where individual-level outcomes depend not just on individual-level covariates, but also on social context. Much of the development in the social sciences has been in the context of education. A canonical example is where the individual-level outcomes are grades or test scores, and the contexts are the class, the school, the school district, the state, or some subset of these.

Often there is interest in the situation where the effect of an individual-level attribute, such as household income, depends on the context. For example, it might be hypothesized that in some schools the effects on test scores of inequalities due to differences in household income would be less than in other schools. The simplest approach to modeling such situations, with a view to estimating and testing the hypothesized effects, is via a fixed effects multi-level model. Suppose that y_i is the outcome for student i who attends school $s(i)$, where there are S schools represented in the data, and that x_i is his or her family income. Then a simple fixed effects model is

$$y_i = \alpha + \beta_{s(i)} x_i + \varepsilon_i, \qquad (3)$$

where $\beta_{s(i)}$ is the effect of household income on test score in student i's school, and $\varepsilon_i \overset{iid}{\sim} N(0, \sigma_\varepsilon^2)$. There is a different regression coefficient β_j for each school j. This model can be estimated by ordinary least squares regression (see, for example, Boyd and Iversen, 1979 and Blalock, 1984).

There are several difficulties with this model. One is that the number of parameters to be estimated, equal to $(S+2)$, is large if there are many contexts (schools) involved, and so the model is hard both to estimate accurately and to interpret. Another is that, if the number of students from a particular school is small, and the estimated regression coefficient for that school is extreme relative to the estimates for the other schools, the resulting estimate is likely to be poor. This can be a problem, as it is often precisely these more extreme estimates that are of most interest.

There has been a great deal of work on overcoming these difficulties, and analogous ones in more complex and realistic multi-level situations, using random effects models. In a simple formulation, (3) is supplemented by:

$$\beta_j = \psi + \delta_j, \qquad (4)$$

where $\delta_j \overset{iid}{\sim} N(0, \sigma_\delta^2)$. Combining (3) and (4) we get

$$y_i = \alpha + \psi x_i + u_i, \qquad (5)$$

where

$$u_i \overset{indep}{\sim} N(0, \sigma_\varepsilon^2 + \sigma_\delta^2 x_i^2).$$

Equation (5) differs from (3) in having only four parameters to be estimated, instead of $(S + 2)$, and also in that the error variances differ, and depend on the value of the independent variable. One consequence is that the estimated 'school effects' tend to be less extreme. It has been shown in several contexts that less extreme 'shrunken' estimates such as those tend to be better on average (e.g. Morris, 1983).

The basic idea of random effect multi-level models goes back at least to Lindley and Smith (1972), who introduced the idea in a Bayesian context. Many different names have been used for the general class of models, including multi-level models, hierarchical models, random effect models, variance component models, contextual models, random coefficient models, and parametric empirical Bayes models: for expositions, see Bryk and Raudenbush (1992), Goldstein (1995), and Snijders and Bosker (1999). Easy to use software is available, notably HLM, MLn and VARCL.

Many of the applications have been in education, but there have been important applications in other areas of sociology. One successful application that helped to spread the methodology arose in demography, to modeling fertility decline (Wong and Mason, 1985).

Another fruitful area of application is meta-analysis, that is, the pooling of results from different studies (Hedges and Olkin, 1985; Goldstein et al., 2000).

The model can be estimated by maximum likelihood using the EM algorithm, viewing the random effects as 'missing data' (Dempster et al., 1977). The Bayesian formulation has proved useful in recent years, particularly for going beyond the hierarchical linear model, of which (5) is an example, to other more complex situations, such as multi-level models with limited dependent variables, event history outcomes, multivariate outcomes and so on. This has proved quite amenable to estimation using MCMC (e.g. Gelman et al., 1995; Daniels and Gatsonis, 1999).

Missing data

Missing data is pervasive in social science. By far the most common approach to dealing with it has been listwise deletion, in which cases with missing data on any of the relevant variables are removed from the analysis. Sometimes variables with a great deal of missing data are removed from the analysis as well. This works well as long as it does not lead to too many cases being removed: unbiased parameter estimators remain unbiased given that the missing data are missing at random, and the main problem is the loss of precision due to the reduction in the amount of data.

However, this approach starts to break down if the number of variables is considerable and the amount of missing data significant, as then much of the data can end up being removed. Various ways around this problem have been tried. One of these, mean imputation, in which the missing value is replaced by the mean of the variable over the cases for which it is observed, can lead to biased estimates and is not to be recommended; unfortunately, it is frequently used, and it is even available in some widely distributed commercial software. Single imputation, also called regression imputation, consists of replacing the missing value by its conditional expectation given the values of the other variables for the case, estimated by regression. This gives unbiased estimates, but tends to underestimate standard errors and other measures of uncertainty, to an extent that increases with the amount of missing information.

A consensus seems to be building that the method of choice for missing data is multiple imputation (Rubin, 1977). This consists of simulating several replicates of the missing data from an approximate conditional or posterior distribution of the missing data given the observed data. These can then be combined to provide a composite inference that takes account of uncertainty about the missing data, does not discard any data, and is relatively easy to use (Little and Rubin, 1987; Rubin, 1987, 1996). This consensus is not a total one, and multiple imputation has been criticized and alternative suggestions made (e.g. Fay, 1996; Rao, 1996). It is possible, but more complicated, to specify a model for the missing data, and to compute maximum likelihood estimates for the model (regression) parameters using the EM algorithm, taking account of the missing data and of uncertainty about them (Little and Rubin, 1989; Little, 1992).

The motivation for multiple imputation was Bayesian, and the resulting inferences are approximately Bayesian. Recently, a more exact Bayesian approach to this problem has been developed using MCMC (e.g. Schafer, 1997). This extends multiple imputation by allowing one to simulate values of the missing data and of the parameters at the same time, to yield a sample from a posterior distribution of the parameters that takes full account of the missingness. This yields more accurate estimates and statements of uncertainty than Rubin's original version of multiple imputation, but it is also more cumbersome to implement.

Multiple imputation relies for its validity on the assumption that whether or not a particular value is missing is in some sense random and independent of the other data. The technical term 'missing completely at random' (MCAR) was coined to denote the situation in which missingness is statistically independent of all the data, observed and unobserved. It turns out, fortunately, that this rather demanding assumption does not have to be met for multiple imputation to be valid. Instead, the missingness needs only to be conditionally independent of the unobserved data given the observed data, a condition technically referred to as 'missing at random' (MAR). This latter condition holds, at least approximately, in many situations. It does not hold, however, if the missingness is related to the missing data themselves (for example, if people with higher incomes are more likely to refuse to say what their income is). We have previously discussed one approach to this more difficult problem of 'non-ignorable missingness' in the specific case of event history data, using the SURF model.

Causality

The goal of much of the regression and other statistical modeling that we have been discussing is, at least implicitly, to make statements about the mechanisms that underlie social life, social behavior and social structure. In other words, to make causal statements. Statisticians, on the other hand, have tended to avoid the language of causality, cautioning that statistical models can show association between variables, but cannot prove that the association is causal in origin.

The regression approach to causality has loomed large in social science because it seems to fit well with how empirical social researchers proceed. Much of (social) science proceeds by a researcher positing a causal theory of how and why a phenomenon occurs, implying that the presence of some attribute X causes an outcome Y. Data on observed values of X and Y are then collected. If a correlation between X and Y is observed, it provides some support for the causal theory, but does not demonstrate it because there are other possible explanations of the correlation, notably: (a) Y might be causing X instead of the other way round, or (b) some third (set of) attribute(s) Z might be causing both X and Y.

The most common approach in these circumstances is to collect time-ordered or longitudinal data on X and Y to try to exclude (a), and to collect data on as many hypothesized common causes Z as possible to try to render (b) less plausible. This is done by 'controlling' for Z, that is, by assessing whether X and Y remain correlated when cases with each value of Z are considered separately. If Z can take many possible values (for example, because it consists of several variables, or of variables that can take many values), this will not be feasible, and instead a regression model is built that represents the relationships in a more parsimonious way. If the 'effect' of X on Y remains significant after controlling for Z, that is taken as evidence for the posited causal theory. It does not provide a conclusive demonstration of X causing Y, however. For example, there might be other Z variables that we could not measure or did not think of.

When there is some additional causal information, such as the presence of an independent variable that is known to be causally related to one of X and Y but not to the other, causal inferences can sometimes be made. The basic approach is instrumental variable estimation, and this is a major topic in econometrics, but will not be discussed further here.

Several scientists have been trying to make the case that one *can* infer causation from observational data in the absence of additional causal information, describing methods for doing so, and giving examples of its being done. This contention remains controversial. Two main general approaches to this task have been taken: the structural equation or graphical model approach, and the counterfactual approach.

The first of these traditions of causal inference is that of structural equation modeling, or, more recently, graphical models. This tradition is motivated by the effort to infer causal structure from the multivariate (perhaps simply cross-sectional) structure of data. Perhaps the boldest claims about the possibility of doing this were made by Spirtes, Glymour and Scheines (1993), drawing in part on work by Blalock (1961) and Costner (1969). They argued there that while the saying 'correlation does not imply causation' is clearly true for two variables, it is not necessarily true for three or more variables. As the simplest example, they considered the case where the correlation structure of three variables, X, Y and Z, is of the form X–Y–Z, that is, X and Z are both correlated with Y but uncorrelated with each other. They pointed out that, in this case, most people would agree that the causal structure of the data is of the form $X \to Y \leftarrow Z$, and they gave conditions under which this inference would be correct.

Extending this work, Spirtes et al. (1998) considered linear structural equation models, and asked several questions that arise. If there is a causal model that fits the data well, are there other equivalent models that imply the same covariance structure but a different path diagram, and if so, how many are there? Given that there are equivalent models, is it possible to extract the features common to all of them? When does a non-zero partial regression coefficient correspond to a non-zero coefficient in a structural equation? They provided answers to some of these questions using the key property of *d-separation*, defined by Verma and Pearl (1988). This can be viewed as a generalization of the concept of conditional independence. This makes it possible to read causal relations off the graph.

The second major current approach to causal inference is the counterfactual one. This starts from the idea that the randomized experiment with perfect compliance and no missing data is the gold standard for estimating the causal effects of treatment interventions. In social science, randomized experiments are sometimes done to estimate treatment effects, for example, the effects of social programs. However, unlike randomized experiments in some other areas of science, such experiments suffer from the problem of noncompliance – some subjects refuse the treatment to which they are assigned. These experiments also tend to suffer from missing data.

The counterfactual approach to estimating causal effects from such experiments was first proposed by Rubin (1974) in the context of what later became known as the Rubin Causal Model. An accessible description of this framework was provided by Holland (1986). This approach was illustrated by Barnard et al. (1998), who described methods for dealing with both noncompliance and missing data in this framework, illustrating their points with issues from the analysis of the Milwaukee

Parental Choice Program, a natural randomized experiment.

Sobel (1990) has investigated the application of the counterfactual framework to observational data, which is more common in sociology than the (imperfect) randomized experiments that Rubin and his collaborators have considered. Sobel argues that when using data from observational studies, sociologists should attempt to identify causes, and then think about the covariates that would justify invoking the assumption of conditional random assignment, and attempt to measure these in the study. In Sobel (1998) he applied his reasoning to an attainment model of Featherman and Hauser (1976), concluding that the 'effects' of family background on educational attainment and occupational achievement should not be viewed as causal. Sobel's conclusion in what would often be regarded as a rather clear-cut case of a causal effect suggests that few observational studies in sociology would meet his criteria for causal inference to be possible. Simplistically put, this is because one can rarely be sure that there is no unmeasured common cause out there. This is a useful caveat, as is his detailed description of the relatively rare cases when causal inference from observational studies will be possible.

However, much of sociology is about marshaling evidence for *competing* causal explanations, and observational studies *can* allow one to do this, regardless of whether or not they allow us to show any causal explanation to be correct in an absolute sense. Such studies do provide a basis for saying which of the current causal theories is best supported by the data. The most common way of doing this is by testing one or several coefficients in a regression-type model for significance. This has the limitation that it can be used only to compare pairs of theories that correspond to nested statistical models. Often, however, competing theories do not neatly fit inside one another in this way, but instead correspond to quite different ways of explaining a phenomenon, and so do not correspond to nested hypotheses. In this case, standard statistical significance testing becomes difficult. However, Bayes factors can still be used to make these comparisons (Kass and Raftery, 1995; Raftery, 1995).

The search for causal explanation, although widely accepted as the basis for much social research, is not uncontroversial. For example, Abbott (1998) argued that the regression model of causality, although dominant in American sociology, is too narrow and needs to be expanded to include broader concepts of explanation and to reinstate the central role of description. He put forward the historical narrative-based approach as one way of achieving a more compelling and interesting account of social life. He mentioned nonstatistical simulation models and cluster analysis as potentially useful methods in this context, allowing one to describe relational and spatial aspects of social life, as well as temporal ones. This kind of 'noncausal', or 'postcausal' thinking is an important ingredient in the development of the third generation of methods, to which we now turn.

THE THIRD GENERATION: NEW DATA, NEW CHALLENGES, NEW METHODS

Social networks and spatial data

Social networks consist of sets of pairwise connections, such as friendships between adolescents (Udry and Bearman, 1998), sexual relationships between adults (Laumann et al., 1994), or patterns of marriage exchange and political alliance across social groups (White, 1963; Padgett and Ansell, 1993; Bearman, 1997). The analysis of data about such networks has a long history (Wasserman and Faust, 1994). Frank and Strauss (1986) developed formal statistical models for such networks related to the Markov random field models used in Bayesian image analysis, and derived using the Hammersley–Clifford theorem (Besag, 1974). This has led to the 'p^*' class of models for social networks (Wasserman and Pattison, 1996). An alternative approach to formal statistical modeling of social networks based on Goodman-type association models is due to Yamaguchi (1990).

Methods for the analysis of social networks have focused mostly on small data sets with complete data. In practical applications, however, such as the effect of sexual network patterns on the spread of sexually transmitted diseases (Morris, 1997), the data tend to be large and very incomplete, and current methods are somewhat at a loss. This is the stage that pedigree analysis in statistical genetics was at some years ago, but the use of likelihood and MCMC methods have led to major progress since then (Thompson, 1998). Social networks are more complex than pedigrees in one way, because pedigrees tend to have a tree structure, while social networks often have cycles, but progress does seem possible.

Most social data are spatial, but this fact has been largely ignored in sociological research. A major exception is Massey and Denton's (1993) study of residential segregation by race, reviving a much older sociological tradition of spatial analysis in American society (e.g. Duncan and Duncan, 1957). More recently, the field of research on fertility and contraception in Asia (several major projects focused on China, Thailand and Nepal) has been making fruitful use of satellite image and Geographic Information System (GIS) data (e.g. Entwisle et al., 1997).

More extensive use of spatial statistics in sociology seems likely. Spatial statistics has been making great progress in the past two decades. The two most fruitful approaches to modeling spatial dependence have turned out to be those based on geostatistics (Matheron, 1971; Chilès and Delfiner, 1999), and on Markov random fields (Besag, 1974; Besag et al., 1991). Geostatistics models spatial correlation taking account of distance explicitly. Markov random fields, on the other hand, are based on a notion of neighborhood: an observation is taken to depend directly on its neighbors, and to be conditionally independent of all other cases given its neighbors. Markov random fields seem promising for social data if they are fairly regularly spaced, but for unevenly spaced spatial units, geostatistics may find it easier to account for the spatial dependence. For social data, geographic distance may not be the most relevant; distances defined on the basis, for example, of flows of people or of information may be more germane for some applications. I do not know of any work on spatial statistical models based on distances of this type, however.

Textual and qualitative data

In its rawest form, a great deal of sociological data is textual, for example, interviews, answers to open-ended questions in surveys, enthnographic accounts. How to analyze such data formally and draw inference from it remains a largely open question. Efforts at formal analysis have focused on standard content analysis, consisting mainly of counting words in the text in different ways. It seems likely that using the context in which words and clauses appear would yield better results. Promising recent efforts to do just this include Carley's (1993) map analysis, Franzosi's (1994) set theoretic approach and Roberts's (1997) generic semantic grammar, but the surface has only been scratched. The human mind is very good at analyzing individual texts, but computers are not, at least as yet; in this way the analysis of textual data may be like other problems such as image analysis and speech recognition. A similar challenge is faced on a massive scale by information retrieval for the Web (Jones and Willett, 1997), where most search engines are based on simple content analysis methods. The more contextual methods being developed in sociology might be useful in this area also.

Singer et al. (1998) have made an intriguing use of textual data analysis, blending quantitative and qualitative approaches. They took a standard unit-level data set with over 250 variables per person, and converted them into written 'biographies'. They then examined the biographies for common features, and thinned them to more generic descriptions.

Another approach to the systematic analysis of some kinds of qualitative data has recently been pioneered by Raudenbush and Sampson (1999) under the name 'ecometrics'. Their work was motivated by the study of neighborhood characteristics that could be linked to crime, such as physical decay (e.g. abandoned buildings), physical disorder (e.g. graffiti) and social disorder (e.g. drug dealing on the street).

A standard quantitative approach to this kind of problem has been to estimate neighborhood effects using aggregates of respondents from the neighborhood, but Raudenbush and Sampson argue persuasively that this does not provide independent or 'objective' assessments of the environment based on direct observation. Their data consisted of videotapes and observer logs for about 23,000 street block segments (Sampson and Raudenbush, 1999) They coded these data and developed a hierarchical model for assessing reliabilities and calculating physical and social disorder scales.

Raudenbush and Sampson place their work in Reiss's (1971) framework of systematic social observation, defined to include explicit rules that permit replication, and means of observation that are independent of what is being observed. This seems important for formal analysis of and inference from qualitative, textual and ethnographic data; the work of Carley (1993), Franzosi (1994) and Roberts (1997) is in this spirit.

Raudenbush and Sampson point out that the search for individual and ecological effects may overemphasize the individual component simply because the well-studied individual psychometric measures are likely to be better than the much less studied ecological ones. Indeed, I have noticed that in many sociological studies, the reported contextual and neighborhood effects are weak, and the point that this may be due to poor measures rather than to weak effects is interesting. Data of this kind cry out for spatial statistical analysis. Raudenbush and Sampson acknowledge this and list it as a topic for future research; their work to date has not accounted for spatial dependence.

Narrative and sequence analysis

Life histories are typically analyzed by reducing them to variables and doing regression and multivariate analysis, or by event history analysis. Abbott and Hrycak (1990) argued that these standard approaches obscure vital aspects of a life history (such as a professional career) that emerge when it is considered as a whole. They proposed viewing life histories of this kind as analogous to DNA or protein sequences, using optimal alignment methods adapted from molecular biology (Sankoff and Kruskal, 1983), followed up by cluster analysis, to detect patterns common to groups of careers. Stovel, Savage and Bearman (1996) used these methods to describe changes in career systems at Lloyds Bank over the past century.

Subsequently, Dijkstra and Taris (1995) extended the ideas to include independent variables, and Abbott and Barman (1997) applied the Gibbs sampling sequence detection method of Lawrence et al. (1993), originally also developed for microbiology; this seems to work very well.

The approach is interesting, and there are many open statistical questions. These include questions about the alignment methodology: for example, how should the insertion, deletion and replacement costs be determined? They also include questions about the clustering method: how many clusters are there, which clustering method should be used, how should one deal with outliers? Perhaps a more explicitly model-based approach would help to answer these questions. Cluster analysis was for long a somewhat ad hoc collection of methods, and reformulating it so that it is based on formal statistical models has helped provide principled answers to some of these questions in other contexts (e.g. Banfield and Raftery, 1993; Fraley and Raftery, 2002).

Simulation models

Another way to represent a social process in more detail is via a macro- or micro-simulation model. Such models are often deterministic and quite complicated, representing systems by different compartments that interact, and each compartment by a set of differential or difference equations. They have been used, for example, to explore the implications of different theories about how domestic politics and war interact (Hanneman et al., 1995), the social dynamics of collective action (Kim and Bearman, 1997), and the role of sexual networks in the spread of HIV (Morris, 1997 and references therein).

A difficulty with such models is that ways of estimating the many parameters involved, of assessing the fit of the model, and of comparing competing models are not well established; all this tends to be done by informal trial and error. Methods being developed to put inference for such models on a solid statistical footing in other disciplines may prove helpful in sociology as well (Guttorp and Walden, 1987; Raftery et al., 1995a; Poole and Raftery, 2000).

Macrosociology

Macrosociology deals with large entities, such as states and their interactions. As a result, the number of cases tends to be small, and the use of standard statistical methods such as regression is difficult. This was pointed out trenchantly by Ragin (1987) in an influential book. His own proposed alternative, qualitative comparative analysis, seems unsatisfactory because it does not allow for variability of any kind, and so is sensitive to small changes in the data and in the way the method is applied (Lieberson, 1994).

One solution to the problem is to obtain an at least moderately large sample size, as Bollen and Appold (1993) were able to do, for example. Often, however, this is not possible, so this is not a general solution. Another approach is to use standard regression-type models, but to do Bayesian estimation with strong prior information if available, which it often is from the practice, common in this area, of analyzing specific cases in great detail (Western and Jackman, 1994). Bayes factors may also help, as they tend to be less stringent than standard significance tests in small samples and allow a calibrated assessment of evidence rather than forcing the rejection or acceptance of a hypothesis (Kass and Raftery, 1995) They also provide a way of accounting for model uncertainty, which can be quite large in this context (Western, 1996).

DISCUSSION

Statistical methodology has had a successful half-century in sociology, leading the way in providing models for cross-classifications, and developing well-adapted methods for unit-level datasets. This has contributed to the greatly improved level of scientific rigor in sociology today. New kinds of data and new challenges abound, and the area is ripe for statistical research.

What are the future directions? As is implicit in my categorization of generations, I feel that the questions posed by the types of data that have motivated the third generation of methods may well spark some of the most exciting developments in sociological methodology in the medium term. But there are others, particularly related to the kind of data that may emerge from current technological developments, for example, surveys carried out by giving computers to respondents and inviting them to respond online, perhaps sporadically or repeatedly over an extended period, may generate useful data with new methodological issues of repeated measures at unequal time intervals, missing data, or they may not work at all. More generally, the Web is generating vast amounts of social science data of new types, and developing methods for drawing valid conclusions from such data is bound to be a major future source of challenges.

One direction I would both predict and advocate is that future developments will be interdisciplinary, spanning the social sciences and beyond. This has not been the case for most of the twentieth century, during which one social science discipline after another made the leap to greater quantitative sophistication, but often in relative isolation from one another and from statistics as a whole. Psychology may have been the first to make this transition, with the work of Spearman and Thurstone early in the century, followed by economics, with the development of econometrics in the 1930s and 1940s by Haavelmo, Tinbergen, the Cowles Commission and others. Then sociology made its move in the 1960s, with the work of Blalock, Duncan, Goodman and others that we have been discussing here. In the 1990s, it has been the turn of political science, led by Gary King, Larry Bartels and others, who have been adopting and adapting modern statistical methodology to their discipline, and developing new methods in the process.

The pattern in each of these disciplines has been similar. The quantitative transition has tended to focus on, and in some cases create, the most advanced statistical methods available at the time, and to spawn a dynamic cadre of methodologists, which in the case of the disciplines that made the transition the longest time ago, psychology and economics, have coalesced into their own quasi-disciplines of psychometrics and econometrics. Subsequent quantitative methodological development has been slower in each discipline, however, and has tended to remain tied to the methods that were at the cutting edge at the time of the quantitative transition. Sociology has not escaped this pattern: there quantitative work remains dominated by the methods first developed in the 1960s and early 1970s (structural equation models with latent variables, generalized linear models, event history analysis via the Cox model), and has focused on developments and refinements of these methods. As I have discussed, there are good reasons for this, and it has had a very positive effect on the field as a whole. However, the statistical methods of the 1990s, particularly Bayesian analysis via Markov chain Monte Carlo (MCMC), have been eagerly adopted by the cohorts of young political scientists going through the excitement and turmoil of their own quantitative revolution, but have been slower to penetrate sociology.

Now, in a more interdisciplinary academic world than that of previous decades, the opportunity is there for all the social science disciplines to break out of the disciplinary straightjacket, and to move their quantitative methodologies forward together. Several major institutions have recently launched interdisciplinary centers and initiatives focused on quantitative social science methodology in the past few years, providing resources for doing just this. These include the University of Washington's Center for Statistics and the Social Sciences, and Harvard's Center for Basic Research in the Social Sciences, which emphasizes social statistics. Columbia's new Masters program in Quantitative Social Science is another interdisciplinary enterprise spanning the social sciences and statistics. At the University of Michigan, the new Quantitative Methodology Program is creating and reviving joint graduate programs between the Department of Statistics and several social science departments. These all join what is perhaps the most successful effort of this kind to date: the Social Statistics Department at the University of Southampton.

NOTE

The author is grateful to to Mark Becker, Mark Handock, Don Rubin, Michael Sobel, Tom Snijders, Rob Warren, Yu Xie and Kazuo Yamaguchi for helpful comments.

REFERENCES

Abbott, Andrew (1998) 'The causal devolution', *Sociological Methods and Research*, 27: 148–81.

Abbott, Andrew and Barman, Emily (1997) 'Sequence comparison via alignment and Gibbs sampling: a formal analysis of the emergence of the modern sociological article', *Sociological Methodology*, 27: 47–88.

Abbott, Andrew and Hrycak, Alexandra (1990) 'Measuring sequence resemblance', *American Journal of Sociology*, 96: 144–85.

Agresti, Alan (1990) *Categorical Data Analysis*. New York: Wiley.

Aitchison, John (1986) *The Analysis of Compositional Data*. London: Chapman and Hall.

Albert, James and Chib, Siddartha (1993) 'Bayesian analysis of binary and polychotomous response data', *Journal of the American Statistical Association*, 88: 669–79.

Allison, Paul (1984) *Event History Analysis*. Beverly Hills, CA: Sage.

Amemiya, Takashi (1985) *Advanced Econometrics*. Cambridge, MA: Harvard University Press.

Baker, R.J. and Nelder, John A. (1977) *The GLIM System, Release 3, Generalized Linear Interactive Modeling*. Oxford: Numerical Algorithms Group.

Banfield, Jeffrey D. and Raftery, Adrian E. (1993) 'Model-based Gaussian and non-Guassian clustering', *Biometrics*, 49: 803–21.

Bearman, Peter S. (1997) 'Generalized exchange', *American Journal of Sociology*, 102: 1383–1415.

Becker, Mark P. (1989) 'Using association models to analyze agreement data: two examples', *Statistics in Medicine*, 8: 1199–1207.

Becker, Mark P. (1994) 'Analysis of cross-classifications of counts using models for marginal distributions: an application to trends in attitudes on legalized abortion', *Sociological Methodology*, 24: 229–65.

Becker, Mark P. and Yang, I. (1998) 'Latent class marginal models for cross-classifications of counts', *Sociological Methodology*, 28: 293–326.

Begg, Colin B. and Gray, R. (1984) 'Calculation of polytomous logistic regression parameters using individualized regressions', *Biometrika*, 71: 11–18.

Benzécri, J.-P. (1976) *L'Analyse des données*, 2nd edn. Paris: Dunod.

Bernhardt, Annette D., Morris, Martina and Handcock, Mark S. (1995) 'Women's gains or men's losses? A closer look at the shrinking gender gap in earnings', *American Journal of Sociology*, 101: 302–28.

Besag, Julian E. (1974) 'Spatial interaction and the statistical analysis of lattice systems (with discussion)', *Journal of the Royal Statistical Society, Ser. B*, 36: 192–236.

Besag, Julian E., York, Jeremy and Mollié, Annie (1991) 'Bayesian Image restoration, with two applications in spatial statistics (with discussion)', *Annals of the Institute of Statistical Mathematics*, 43: 1–59.

Biblarz, Timothy J. and Raftery, Adrian E. (1993) 'The effects of family disruption on social mobility', *American Sociological Review*, 58: 97–109.

Biblarz, Timothy J., Raftery, Adrian E. and Bucur, Alexander (1997) 'Family structure and social mobility', *Social Forces*, 75: 1319–39.

Birch, M.W. (1963) 'Maximum likelihood in three-way tables', *Journal of the Royal Statistical Society, Ser. B*, 25: 220–33.

Birch, M.W. (1965) 'The detection of partial association, II: The general case', *Journal of the Royal Statistical Society, Ser. B*, 27: 111–24.

Blalock, Hubert M. (1961) *Causal Inferences in Nonexperimental Research*. New York: W.W. Norton.

Blalock, Hubert M. (1984) 'Contextual-effects models: theoretical and methodological issues', *Annual Review of Sociology*, 10: 353–72.

Blau, Peter M. and Duncan, Otis Dudley (1967) *The American Occupational Structure*, New York: The Free Press.

Bollen, Kenneth A. (1989) *Structural Equation Models with Latent Variables*. New York: Wiley.

Bollen, Kenneth A. and Appold, S.J. (1993) 'National industrial-structure and the global system', *American Sociological Review*, 58: 283–301.

Boyd, L.H. and Iversen, G.R. (1979) *Contextual Analysis: Concepts and Statistical Techniques*. Belmont, CA: Wadsworth.

Bryk, Anthony S. and Raudenbush, Stephen W. (1992) *Hierarchical Linear Models: Applications and Data Analysis Methods*. Newbury Park, CA: Sage.

Burt, Ronald S. (1987) 'Social contagion and innovation: cohesion versus structural equivalence', *American Journal of Sociology*, 92: 1287–1335.

Camic, Charles, and Xie, Yu (1994) 'The advent of statistical methodology in American social science – Columbia University, 1880 to 1915', *American Sociological Review*, 59: 773–805.

Carley, Kathleen M. (1993) 'Coding choices for textual analysis: a comparison of content analysis and map analysis', *Sociological Methodology*, 23: 75–126.

Celeux, Gilles and Govaert, Gérard (1991) 'Clustering criteria for discrete data and latent class models', *Journal of Classification*, 8: 157–76.

Charles, Maria and Grusky, David (1995) 'Models for describing the underlying structure of sex segregation', *American Journal of Sociology*, 100: 931–71.

Chickering, D. Maxwell and Heckerman, David (1997) 'Efficient approximations for the marginal likelihood of Bayesian networks with hidden variables', *Machine Learning*, 29: 181–212.

Chilès, Jean-Paul and Delfiner, Pierre (1999) *Geostatistics: Modeling Spatial Uncertainty*. New York: Wiley.

Clogg, Clifford C. (1992) 'The impact of sociological methodology on statistical methodology (with discussion)', *Statistical Science*, 7: 183–207.

Clogg, Clifford C. (1995) 'Latent class models', in G. Arminger, C.C. Clogg and M.E. Soble (eds), *Handbook of Statistical Modeling for the Social and Behavioral Sciences*. New York: Plenum Press. pp. 311–59.

Clogg, Clifford C., Eliason, Scott R. and Wahl, R.J. (1990) 'Labor market experiences and labor force outcomes', *American Journal of Sociology*, 95: 1536–76.

Costner, Herbert L. (1969) 'Theory, deduction and rules of correspondence', *American Journal of Sociology*, 75: 245–63.

Cox, David R. (1970) *The Analysis of Binary Data*. London: Chapman and Hall.

Cox, David R. (1972) 'Regression models and life tables (with discussion)', *Journal of the Royal Statistical Society, Ser. B*, 34: 187–220.

Daniels, Michael J. and Gatsonis, Constantine (1999) 'Hierarchical generalized linear models in the analysis of variations in health care utilization', *Journal of the American Statistical Association*, 94: 29–42.

De Graaf, Nan (1991) 'Distinction by consumption in Czechoslovakia, Hungary and the Netherlands', *European Sociological Review*, 7: 267–90.

Dempster, Arthur P., Laird, Nan M. and Rubin, Donald B. (1977) 'Maximum likelihood from incomplete data via the EM algorithm (with discussion)', *Journal of the Royal Statistical Society, Ser. B*, 39: 1–38.

Diekmann, Andreas (1989) 'Diffusion and survival models for the process of entry into marriage', *American Journal of Mathematical Sociology*, 14: 31–44.

Dijkstra, W. and Taris, T. (1995) 'Measuring the agreement between sequences', *Sociological Methods and Research,* 24: 214–31.

Duncan, Otis Dudley (1961) 'A socioeconomic index for all occupations', in A.J. Reiss (ed.), *Occupations and Social Status*. New York: The Free Press. pp. 109–38.

Duncan, Otis Dudley (1966) 'Path analysis', *American Journal of Sociology*, 72: 1–16.

Duncan, Otis Dudley (1975) *An Introduction to Structural Equation Models*. New York: Academic Press.

Duncan, Otis Dudley (1979) 'How destination depends on origin in the occupational mobility table', *American Journal of Sociology*, 84: 793–803.

Duncan, Otis Dudley and Duncan, Beverly (1957) *The Negro Population of Chicago*. Chicago: University of Chicago Press.

Durkheim, Emile (1897) *Le Suicide*. Paris: Alcan. (Translated by G. Simpson and J.A. Spaulding (1951) as *Suicide*, New York: The Free Press.)

Entwisle, Barbara, Rindfuss, Ronald R., Walsh, S.J., Evans, T.P., and Curran, Sara R. (1997) 'Geographic Information Systems, spatial network analysis, and contraceptive choice', *Demography*, 34: 171–87.

Fahrmeir, Ludwig, and Knorr-Held, Leo (1997) 'Dynamic discrete-time duration models: estimation via Markov chain Monte Carlo', *Sociological Methodology*, 27: 417–52.

Fay, Robert E. (1996) 'Alternative paradigms for the analysis of imputed survey data', *Journal of the American Statistical Association*, 91: 490–8.

Featherman, David L. and Hauser, Robert M. (1976) 'Sexual inequalities and socioeconomic achievement in the U.S., 1962–1973', *American Sociological Review*, 41: 462–83.

Fraley, Christina, and Raftery, Adrian E. (2002) 'Model-based clustering, discriminant analysis, and density estimation. *Journal of the American Statistical Association*, 97: 611–31.

Frank, Ove, and Strauss, David (1986) 'Markov graphs', *Journal of the American Statistical Association*, 81: 832–42.

Franzosi, Roberto (1994) 'From words to numbers: a set theory framework for the collection, organization and analysis of narrative data', *Sociological Methodology*, 24: 105–36.

Freeman, John, Carroll, Glenn and Hannan, Michael T. (1983) 'The liability of newness: age dependence in organizational death rates', *American Sociological Review*, 48: 692–710.

Freedman, David A. (1987) 'As others see us (with discussion)', *Journal of Educational Statistics*, 12: 101–223.

Ganzeboom, Harry B.G., Luijkx, Ruud, and Treiman, Donald J. (1989) 'Intergenerational class mobility in comparative perspective', *Research in Social Stratification and Mobility*, 9: 3–79.

Gelman, Andrew, Carlin, John B., Stern, Hal S. and Rubin, Donald B. (1995) *Bayesian Data Analysis*. New York: Chapman and Hall.

Gilks, Walter R., Richardson, Sylvia and Spiegelhalter, David J. (eds) (1996) *Markov Chain Monte Carlo in Practice*. London: Chapman and Hall.

Glass, David V. (1954) *Social Mobility in Britain*. Glencoe, IL: The Free Press.

Goldstein, Harvey (1995) *Multilevel Models in Educational and Social Research*, 2nd edn. London: Griffin.

Goldstein, Harvey, Yang, M., Omar, R., Turner, R. and Thompson, S. (2000) 'Meta-analysis using multilevel models with an application to the study of class size effects', *Applied Statistics*, 49: 399–412.

Goodman, Leo A. (1971) 'The analysis of multidimensional contingency tables: stepwise procedures and direct estimation methods for building models for multiple classifications', *Technometrics*, 13: 33–61.

Goodman, Leo A. (1974a) 'The analysis of systems of qualitative variables when some of the variables are unobservable', *American Journal of Sociology*, 79: 1179–1259.

Goodman, Leo A. (1974b) 'Exploratory latent structure analysis using both identifiable and unidentifiable models', *Biometrika*, 61: 215–31.

Goodman, Leo A. (1979) 'Simple models for the analysis of association in cross-classifications having ordered categories', *Journal of the American Statistical Association*, 74: 537–52.

Goodman, Leo A. (1985) 'The analysis of cross-classified data having ordered and/or unordered categories', *Annals of Statistics*, 13: 10–69.

Goodman, Leo A. and Hout, Michael (1998) 'Statistical methods and graphical displays for analyzing how the association between two qualitative variables differs among countries, among groups, or over time: a modified regression-type approach (with discussion)', in Adrian E. Raftery (ed.), *Sociological Methodology*. Cambridge, MA: Blackwell. pp. 175–262.

Guttorp, Peter and Walden, Andrew T. (1987) 'On the evaluation of geophysical models', *Geophysical Journal of the Royal Astronomical Society*, 91: 201–210.

Haberman, Shelby J. (1979) *Analysis of Qualitative Data*, vol. 2. New York: Academic Press.

Hagenaars, Jacques A. (1988) 'Latent structure models with direct effects between indicators: local dependence models', *Sociological Methods and Research*, 16: 379–406.

Hagenaars, Jacques A. (1990) *Categorical Longitudinal Data: Log-Linear Panel, Trend and Cohort Analysis*. Newbury Park, CA: Sage.

Handcock, Mark S. and Morris, Martina (1998) 'Relative distribution methods', *Sociological Methodology*, 28: 53–98.

Handcock, Mark S. and Morris, Martina (1999) *Relative Distribution Methods in the Social Sciences*. New York: Springer-Verlag.

Hanneman, R.A., Collins, Randall and Mordt, Gabriele (1995) 'Discovering theory dynamics by computer simulation: experiments on state legitimacy and imperialist capitalism', *Sociological Methodology*, 25: 1–46.

Hauser, Robert M. and Warren, John R. (1997) 'Socioeconomic indexes for occupations: a review, update and critique', *Sociological Methodology*, 27: 177–298.

Heckman, James J. (1979) 'Sample selection bias as a specification error', *Econometrika*, 47: 153–61.

Hedges, Larry J. and Olkin, Ingram (1985) *Statistical Methods for Meta-Analysis*. New York: Academic Press.

Hill, D.H. (1997) 'Adjusting for attrition in event-history analysis', *Sociological Methodology*, 27: 393–416.

Hill, D.H., Axinn, W.G. and Thornton, A. (1993) 'Competing hazards with shared unmeasured risk factors', *Sociological Methodology*, 23: 245–77.

Holland, Paul (1986) 'Statistics and causal inference', *Journal of the American Statistical Association*, 81: 945–70.

Hosmer, David W. and Lemeshow, Stanley (1989) *Applied Logistic Regression*. New York: Wiley.

Hout, Michael (1983) *Mobility Tables*. Beverly Hills, CA: Sage.

Hout, Michael (1984) 'Status, autonomy and training in occupational mobility', *American Journal of Sociology*, 89: 1379–1409.

Hout, Michael (1988) Expanding universalism, less structural mobility: the American occupational structure in the 1980s', *American Journal of Sociology*, 93: 1358–1400.

Jones, K.S. and Willett, P. (1997) *Readings in Information Retrieval*, San Francisco: Morgan Kaufman.

Jöreskog, Karl G. (1973) 'A general method for estimating a linear structural equation system', in A.S. Goldberger and O.D. Duncan (eds), *Structural Equation Models in the Social Sciences*. New York: Seminar. pp. 85–112.

Kalmijn, M. (1991) 'Status homogamy in the United State', *American Journal of Sociology*, 97: 496–523.

Kass, Robert E. and Raftery, Adrian E. (1995) 'Bayes factors', *Journal of the American Statistical Association*, 90: 773–95.

Kass, Robert E. and Wasserman, Larry (1995) 'A reference Bayesian test for nested hypotheses and its relationship to the Schwarz criterion', *Journal of the American Statistical Association*, 90: 928–34.

Kim, Hyojoung and Bearman, Peter S. (1997) 'The structure and dynamics of movement participation', *American Sociological Review*, 62: 70–93.

Koster, Jan (1996) 'Markov properties of non-recursive causal models', *Annals of Statistics*, 24: 2148–77.

Kuo, H.H.D. and Hauser, Robert M. (1996) 'Gender, family configuration, and the effect of family background on educational attainment', *Social Biology*, 43: 98–131.

Lang, Joseph B. and Agresti, Alan (1994) 'Simultaneously modeling joint and marginal distributions of multivariate categorical responses', *Journal of the American Statistical Association*, 89: 625–32.

Laumann, Edward O., Gagnon, J., Michael, R. and Michaels, S. (1994) *The Social Organization of Sexuality*. Chicago: University of Chicago Press.

Lawrence, C.E., Altschul, S.F., Boguski, M.S., Liu, J.S., Neuwald, A.F. and Wooton, J.C. (1993) 'Detecting subtle sequence signals', *Science*, 262: 208–14.

Lazarsfeld, Paul F. (1950) 'The logical and mathematical foundation of latent structure analysis', in E.A. Schulman, P.F. Lazarsfeld, S.A. Starr and J.A. Clausen (eds), *Studies in Social Psychology in World War II. Vol. 4: Measurement and Prediction*. Princeton, NJ: Princeton University Press. pp. 362–412.

Lazarsfeld, Paul F. and Henry, Neil W. (1968) *Latent Structure Analysis*. Boston, MA: Houghton Mifflin.

Lieberson, Stanley L. (1994) 'More on the uneasy case for using mill-type methods in small-N comparative studies', *Social Forces*, 72: 1225–37.

Little, Roderick J.A. (1992) 'Regression with missing X's: a review', *Journal of the American Statistical Association*, 87: 1227–37.

Little, Roderick J.A. and Rubin, Donald B. (1987) *Statistical Analysis with Missing Data*. New York: Wiley.

Little, Roderick J.A. and Rubin, Donald B. (1989) 'The analysis of social science data with missing values', *Sociological Methods and Research*, 18: 292–326.

Logan, John A. (1996) 'Opportunity and choice in socially structured labor markets', *American Journal of Sociology*, 101: 114–60.

Logan, John A. (1997) 'Estimating two-sided Logit models', *Sociological Methodology*, 28: 139–73.

Long, J. Scott (1984a) *Confirmatory Factor Analysis*. Newbury Park, CA: Sage.

Long, J. Scott (1984b) *Covariance Structure Models*. Newbury Park, CA: Sage.

Long, J. Scott (1997) *Regression Models for Categorical and Limited Dependent Variables*. Thousand Oaks, CA: Sage.

Marsden, Peter V. and Podolny, Joel (1990) 'Dynamic analysis of network diffusion processes', in H. Flap and J. Weesie (eds), *Social Networks Through Time*, Utrecht: ISOR. pp. 197–214.

Massey, Douglas S. and Denton, Nancy A. (1993) *American Apartheid: Segregation and the Making of the Underclass*. Cambridge, MA: Harvard University Press.

Matheron, Georges (1971) *The Theory of Regionalized Variables and its Applications*. Paris: Ecole Nationale Supérieure des Mines.

Matsueda, Ross L. and Heimer, Karen (1987) 'Race, family structure, and delinquency: a test of differential association and social control theories', *American Sociological Review*, 52: 826–40.

Mayer, Karl Ulrich and Tuma, Nancy Brandon (1990) *Event History Analysis in Life Course Research*. Madison, WI: University of Wisconsin Press.

McCullagh, Peter and Nelder, John A. (1989) *Generalized Linear Models*. London: Chapman and Hall.

Morris, Carl N. (1983) 'Parametric empirical Bayes inference: theory and applications (with discussion)', *Journal of the American Statistical Association*, 78: 47–65.

Morris, Martina (1997) 'Sexual networks and HIV', *AIDS*, 11: S209–S216.

Morris, Martina, Bernhardt, Annette D. and Handcock, Mark S. (1994) 'Economic inequality: new methods for new trends', *American Sociological Review*, 59: 205–19.

Muthén, Bengt (1983) 'Latent variable structure equation modeling with categorical data', *Journal of Econometrics*, 22: 43–65.

Muthén, Bengt (1997) 'Latent variable modeling of longitudinal and multilevel data', *Sociological Methodology*, 27: 453–80.

Nelder, John A. and Wedderburn, R.W.M. (1972) 'Generalised linear models', *Journal of the Royal Statistical Society, Ser. A*, 135: 370–84.

Padgett, John F. and Ansell, C.K. (1993) 'Robust action and the rise of the Medici', *American Journal of Sociology*, 948: 1259.

Pearl, Judea (1998) 'Graphs, causality, and structural equation models', *Sociological Methods and Research*, 27: 226–84.

Petersen, Trond (1991) 'The statistical analysis of event histories', *Sociological Methods and Research*, 19: 270–323.

Petersen, Trond (1995) 'Models for interdependent event-history data: specification and estimation', in Peter V. Marsden (ed.), *Sociological Methodology 1995*. Cambridge, MA: Blackwell. pp. 317–76.

Poole, David and Raftery, Adrian E. (2000) 'Inference from deterministic simulation models: the Bayesian melding approach', *Journal of the American Statistical Association*, 95: 1244–55.

Raftery, Adrian E. (1986a) 'Choosing models for cross-classifications', *American Sociological Review*, 51: 145–6.

Raftery, Adrian E. (1986b) 'A note on Bayes factors for log-linear contingency table models with vague prior information', *Journal of the Royal Statistical Society, Ser. B*, 48: 249–50.

Raftery, Adrian E. (1995) 'Bayesian model selection in social research (with discussion)', *Sociological Methodology*, 25: 111–93.

Raftery, Adrian E. (1996) 'Approximate Bayes factors and accounting for model uncertainty in generalized linear models', *Biometrika*, 83: 251–66.

Raftery, Adrian E. (1999) 'Bayes factors and BIC: comment on "A critique of the Bayesian Information Criterion for model selection"', *Sociological Methods and Research*, 27: 411–27.

Raftery, Adrian E. and Hout, Michael (1985) 'Does Irish education approach the meritocratic ideal? A logistic analysis', *Economic and Social Review*, 16: 115–40.

Raftery, Adrian E., Givens, Geof H. and Zeh, Judith E. (1995a) 'Inference from a deterministic population dynamics model for Bowhead Whales (with discussion)', *Journal of the American Statistical Association*, 90: 402–30.

Raftery, Adrian E., Lewis, Steven M. and Aghajanian, Akbar (1995b) 'Demand or ideation? Evidence from the Iranian marital fertility decline', *Demography*, 32: 159–82.

Ragin, Charles (1987) *The Comparative Method: Moving Beyond Qualitative and Quantitative Strategies*. Berkeley, CA: University of California Press.

Rao, J.N.K. (1996) 'On variance estimation with imputed survey data', *Journal of the American Statistical Association*, 91: 499–506.

Raudenbush, Stephen W. and Sampson, Robert J. (1999) 'Ecometrics: toward a science of assessing ecological settings, with application to the systematic social observation of neighborhoods', *Sociological Methodology*, 29: 1–41.

Reiss, Albert J., Jr (1971) 'Systematic observations of natural social phenomena', *Sociological Methodology*, 3: 3–33.

Roberts, Carl W. (1997) 'A generic semantic grammar for quantitative text analysis: applications to East and West Berlin news content from 1979', *Sociological Methodology*, 27: 89–130.

Roeder, Kathryn, Lynch, G.S. and Nagin, Daniel S. (1999) 'Modeling uncertainty in latent class membership: a case study in criminology', *Journal of the American Statistical Association*, 94: 766–76.

Rogoff, Nathalie (1953) *Recent Trends in Occupational Mobility*. Glencoe, IL: The Free Press.

Rubin, Donald, B. (1974) 'Estimating causal effects of treatments in randomized and nonrandomized studies', *Journal of Educational Psychology*, 66: 688–701.

Rubin, Donald, B. (1977) 'Formalizing subjective notions about the effect of nonrespondents in sample surveys', *Journal of the American Statistical Association*, 72: 538–43.

Rubin, Donald, B. (1987) *Multiple Imputation for Nonresponse in Surveys*. New York: Wiley.

Rubin, Donald, B. (1996) 'Multiple imputation after 18+ years', *Journal of the American Statistical Association*, 91: 473–89.

Sampson, Robert J. and Raudenbush, Stephen W. (1999) 'Systematic social observations of public spaces: a new look at neighborhood disorder', *American Journal of Sociology*, 105: 603–51.

Sankoff, D. and Kruskal, J.B. (1983) *Time Warps, String Edits, and Macromolecules*. Reading, MA: Addison–Wesley.

Schafer, Joseph L. (1997) *Analysis of Incomplete Multivariate Data*. London: Chapman and Hall.

Schuessler, Karl F. (1980) 'Quantitative methodology in sociology: the last 25 years', *American Behavioral Scientist*, 23: 835–60.

Schwarz, Gideon (1978) 'Estimating the dimension of a model', *Annals of Statistics*, 6: 461–4.

Singer, Burton, Ryff, Carol D., Carr, Deborah and Magee, W.J. (1998) 'Linking life histories and mental health: a person-centered strategy', *Sociological Methodology*, 28: 1–52.

Snijders, Tom A.B. and Bosker, Roel J. (1999) *Multilevel Analysis: An Introduction to Basic and Advanced Multilevel Modeling*. Beverly Hills, CA: Sage.

Sobel, Michael E. (1981) 'Diagonal mobility models: a substantively motivated class of designs for the analysis of mobility effects', *American Sociological Review*, 46: 893–906.

Sobel, Michael E. (1985) 'Social mobility and fertility revisited: some new methods for the analysis of mobility effects hypothesis', *American Sociological Review*, 50: 699–712.

Sobel, Michael E. (1990) 'Effect analysis and causation in linear structural equation models', *Psychometrika*, 55: 495–515.

Sobel, Michael E. (1998) 'Causal inference in statistical models of the process of socioeconomic achievement: a case study', *Sociological Methods and Research*, 27: 318–48.

Sobel, Michael E., Becker, Mark P. and Minick, Susan S. (1998) 'Origin, destination and association in occupational mobility', *American Journal of Sociology*, 104: 687–701.

Sorensen, Ann Marie (1989) 'Husbands' and wives' characteristics and fertility decisions: a diagonal mobility model', *Demography*, 26: 125–35.

Spiegelhalter, David J., Dawid, A. Philip, Lauritzen, Steffan and Cowell, R. (1993) 'Bayesian analysis in expert systems', *Statistical Science*, 8: 219–82.

Spirtes, Peter, Glymour, Clark and Scheines, Richard (1993) *Causation, Prediction and Search*. New York: Springer-Verlag.

Spirtes, Peter, Richardson, Thomas S., Meek, Christopher, Scheines, Richard and Glymour, Clark (1998) 'Using path diagrams as a structural equation modeling tool', *Sociological Methods and Research*, 27: 182–225.

Stern, R.D. and Coe, R. (1984) 'A model fitting analysis of daily rainfall data (with discussion)', *Journal of the Royal Statistical Society, Ser. A*, 147: 1–34.

Stovel, Katherine, Savage, M. and Bearman, Peter S. (1996) 'Ascription into achievement: models of career systems at Lloyds Bank, 1890–1970', *American Journal of Sociology*, 102: 358–99.

Strang, David (1991) 'Adding social structure to diffusion models: an event history framework', *Sociological Methods and Research*, 19: 324–53.

Strang, David and Tuma, Nancy Brandon (1993) 'Spatial and temporal heterogeneity in diffusion', *American Journal of Sociology*, 99: 614–39.

Thompson, Elizabeth A. (1998) 'Inferring gene ancestry: estimating gene descent', *International Statistical Review*, 66: 29–40.

Tobin, James (1958) 'Estimation of relationships for limited dependent variables', *Econometrika*, 26: 24–36.

Treiman, Donald J. (1977) *Occupational Prestige in Comparative Perspective*. New York: Academic Press.

Tuma, Nancy Brandon (1976) 'Rewards, resources, and rates of mobility: a nonstationary multivariate stochastic model', *American Sociological Review*, 41: 338–60.

Tuma, Nancy Brandon, and Hannan, Michael T. (1984) *Social Dynamics: Models and Methods*. Orlando, FL: Academic Press.

Udry, J.R. and Bearman, Peter S. (1998) 'New methods for new research on adolescent sexual behavior', in R. Jessor (ed.), *New Perspectives on Adolescent Risk Behavior*. Cambridge: Cambridge University Press. pp. 241–69.

Verma, T. and Pearl, Judea (1988) 'Causal networks: semantics and expressiveness', in *Proceedings of the 4th Workshop on Uncertainty in Artificial Intelligence*. Mountain View, CA. pp. 352–9.

Warren, John R., Sheridan, Jennifer T. and Hauser, Robert M. (1998) 'Choosing a measure of occupational standing – how useful are composite measures in analyses of gender inequality in occupational attainment?', *Sociological Methods and Research*, 27: 3–76.

Wasserman, Stanley and Faust, K. (1994) *Social Network Analysis: Methods and Applications*. Cambridge: Cambridge University Press.

Wasserman, Stanley and Pattison, Philippa (1996) 'Logit models and logistic regressions for social networks. 1: An introduction to Markov graphs and *p*', *Psychometrika*, 61: 401–25.

Weakliem, David L. (1992) 'Does social mobility affect political behavior?', *European Sociological Review*, 8: 153–65.

Weakliem, David L. (1999) 'A critique of the Bayesian Information Criterion for model selection (with discussion)', *Sociological Methods and Research*, 27: 359–443.

Western, Bruce (1996) 'Vague theory and model uncertainty in macrosociology', *Sociological Methodology*, 26: 165–92.

Western, Bruce and Jackman, Simon (1994) 'Bayesian inference for comparative research', *American Political Science Review*, 88: 412–23.

White, Harrison C. (1963) *An Anatomy of Kinship: Mathematical Models for Structures of Cumulated Roles*. Englewood Cliffs, NJ: Prentice–Hall.

Winship, Chrisopher and Mare, Robert D. (1992) 'Models for sample selection bias', *Annual Review of Sociology*, 18: 327–50.

Wong, G.Y. and Mason, William M. (1985) 'The hierarchical logistic regression model for multi-level analysis', *Journal of the American Statistical Association*, 80: 513–24.

Wright, Sewall (1921) 'Correlation and causation', *Journal of Agricultural Research*, 20: 557–85.

Xie, Yu (1992) 'The log-multiplicative layer effect model for comparing mobility tables', *American Sociological Review*, 57: 380–95.

Xie, Yu and Powers, Daniel (2000) *Statistical Methods for Categorical Data Models*. New York: Academic Press.

Yamaguchi, Kazuo (1987) 'Models for comparing mobility tables: towards parsimony and substance', *American Sociological Review*, 52: 482–94.

Yamaguchi, Kazuo (1990) 'Homophily and social distance in the choice of multiple friends: an analysis based on conditionally symmetric log-bilinear association models', *Journal of the American Statistical Association*, 85: 356–66.

Yamaguchi, Kazuo (1991) *Event History Analysis*. Newbury Park, CA: Sage.

Yamaguchi, Kazuo (1992) 'Accelerated failure-time regression models with a regression model of surviving fraction: an application to the analysis of "Permanent employment" in Japan', *Journal of the American Statistical Association*, 87: 284–92.

Yamaguchi, Kazuo (1994) 'Some accelerated failure-time models derived from diffusion process models: an application to diffusion process analysis', *Sociological Methodology*, 24: 267–301.

Yamaguchi, Kazuo and Ferguson, Linda R. (1995) 'The stopping and spacing of childbirths and their birth-history predictors: rational-choice theory and event-history analysis', *American Sociological Review*, 60: 272–98.

2

Qualitative Research Traditions

PAUL ATKINSON AND SARA DELAMONT

INTRODUCTION

The art historian Hal Foster (1996) has suggested that 'the ethnographic' has become the dominant methodological model of the contemporary academy (cf. Coles, 2000; Kwon, 2000). Foster's discussion focuses on anthropology rather than sociology, but the general point holds good. The visual arts, cultural studies, sociology and anthropology all share an ethnographic focus on local sites of social relations and cultural forms. They include: a close attention to the particularities of social life; an equally close attention to the forms of their representation; the reflexive attention to the productive work of the artist, writer and ethnographer; an awareness of the work of biographical and autobiographical construction. The ethnographic gaze captures and calls into question the tensions between the self and the other, between the near and the distant, between the familiar and the strange.

Ethnographic and other qualitative research has come to occupy a prominent position in recent sociology and related intellectual fields, such as the emergent traditions of cultural studies (Denzin and Lincoln, 2000; Atkinson et al., 2001). Sociology itself has witnessed a number of theoretical developments that have fuelled the volume of qualitative research – including the introduction of phenomenology,

ethnomethodology, cultural sociology, the so-called linguistic turn, the influence of various strands of feminist scholarship, and the rediscovery of rhetoric in the social and cultural disciplines. These have conjoined with long traditions of research under the auspices of symbolic interactionism, urban ethnography, deviancy studies, and community studies to renew traditions of research that have spanned many decades. In a review essay such as this it is impossible to review comprehensively all of the research that has contributed to these movements and their consequences for empirical sociological inquiry. Furthermore, and partially divorced from the various theoretical and epistemological perspectives, qualitative research methods themselves have burgeoned and grown increasingly varied. They now include ethnographic fieldwork, life-history and narrative analyses, conversation and discourse analysis, documentary and semiotic analysis. Again, a review of all these developments would be impossible within the compass of a single chapter, and in any case would inevitably recapitulate many other treatments of these themes.[1] Readers who wish to follow up the argument can find detailed citations to authoritative literature reviews and other relevant publications in the notes.

A historical chronicle of all these topics, and of the theoretical or epistemological issues that underpin them would be intractable. It would, moreover, fail to capture many of the most significant themes that have informed and emerged from these sociological tendencies. Consequently, we have decided to follow a different approach. We have identified a number of major themes that have informed qualitative research (in its widest sense) over the past century. Necessarily selective in coverage, this will enable us to convey many of the most significant continuities and influences in the development of sociological thought. This thematic treatment will give greater opportunity to explore simultaneously the substantive, theoretical and methodological preoccupations that have informed the sociological work. It is important to re-affirm some of the long-term continuities in sociological research. Recent commentaries on the development of qualitative research, especially those that focus primarily on methodological issues, have stressed discontinuities (Denzin and Lincoln, 1994, 2000). Methodological innovation and development invite an emphasis on novelty and change. When linked to contemporary preoccupations with the claims of postmodernism, then it is all too easy to over-emphasize new departures and disjunctures (Denzin, 1997). While it is important to take full account of change and innovation, it is dangerous to over-emphasize them and so lose sight of deeper and longer intellectual commitments. In that sense, therefore, our remarks here are to be read in contrast to other accounts of qualitative research and its traditions that stress discontinuity.[2]

This selective review, therefore, ranges across a wide variety of literature and across apparently different traditions. This is not an arbitrary selection. Rather, it consciously transcends some of the more conventional divisions – theoretical schools, national traditions and empirical specialisms. We pay attention to the following broad thematic topics: the modern metropolis and urban anonymity; the search for community; the production of selves and identities; the recounting of lives and voices; the aesthetics and politics of representation; and the philosophies and justifications of qualitative sociology. Hence we shall draw together recurrent empirical research preoccupations with recurrent motifs in modern sociological thought. Distinctive forms of sociological imagination have developed qualitative research methods and broad analytic categories to address these and similar phenomena. We are more interested in synthesizing than discriminating between different theoretical and epistemological positions. Fine-grained methodological or theoretical disputation too readily obscures significant shared interests. It is easier to try to establish the uniqueness or novelty of one's own cherished position than it is to remember and acknowledge broader intellectual commitments. We are uninterested in accounts that repeatedly affirm the existence of incommensurable 'paradigms' – or their equivalent – within the field.[3]

In affirming this approach to our subject matter we do not deny the importance of clarifying philosophical and methodological standpoints, and there is no lack of debate and commentary in that vein. There are more profound issues that are shared and that endure. We stress the recurrent rather than the transitory and the fashionable, the issues to which successive generations of sociologists and others have returned. Methodological discourse needs to be placed in the wider context of sociological and cultural analysis that informs it and is informed by it. Rather than starting with qualitative 'method', therefore, we treat our themes from a different perspective. We discuss how general strategies of sociological understanding are grounded in recurrent themes. This treatment allows us to describe how methodological commitments have reflected and informed broader issues in the history of sociological thought.

URBAN EXPLORATION

The inspiration of much ethnographic work is to be found – historically and in contemporary sociology – in the moral ambiguities of the modern city. Ethnographers have repeatedly explored and reported the social and cultural domains of the metropolitan life of Europe and America. There they have juxtaposed estrangement with intimacy, the metropolitan with the local, fragmentation with organization. Urban ethnography has itself been placed between strangeness and familiarity, disengagement and intimacy. The impetus to explore the city has had diverse sources – theoretical, methodological, moral and aesthetic.

City of strangers

The exploration of the metropolis gave a major impetus to the development of ethnographic work in the city: it is no accident that the *Journal of Contemporary Ethnography* was founded under the title of *Urban Life and Culture.* The observation of the urban milieu has various origins. It is to be found in nineteenth-century, *fin-de-siècle* and early twentieth-century literary and social works.

Baudelaire's commentary on modernity in *Les Fleurs du mal* provides a classic point of origin for the literary celebration of the *flâneur* (Tester, 1994). The female *flâneuse* has equally been a recurrent motif in women's literary representations of the urban environment (Parsons, 2000; Wilson, 2001). This archetype inhabits a great deal of early writing on the city. The detached urban explorer, the cool gaze and the ironic tone are among the distinctive traits of this urban explorer. It was a theme taken up by Walter Benjamin in his series of metropolitan observations, most notably in the Moscow diaries and the incomplete Arcades project. In the study of the arcades of Paris, Naples and elsewhere, Benjamin developed a distinctive sociological gaze. In the arcades he undertook the archaeology of a modernity that was already being overcome by new forms of metropolitan construction and consumption. Like Baudelaire, Benjamin identified the *flâneur* as both the model of the social observer and an archetype of the urban dweller. The observer, the rag-picker and the prostitute were among the urban types that corresponded to the detached and nomadic intellectual (Benjamin, 1986, 2000; Buck-Morss, 1997; Coles, 1999). The intellectual style of urban observation in turn reflected the more general optic imagination

of nineteenth-century intellectual and aesthetic life (Crary, 1990, 1999).

Such treatments of metropolitan culture were paralleled by the sociological treatment of modernity by Simmel and Kracauer (cf. Frisby, 1985). Cities like Berlin provided the opportunity to observe the characteristic cultural features of modernity. In particular, modern urban life was held to generate distinctive social types. The city was physically and socially fragmented. Urban life was described in terms of over-stimulation. The senses were bombarded by diverse stimuli at a rapid rate. The modern urbanite was therefore vulnerable to over-excitement. There was, in this treatment, an implicit parallel between the sociological view of modern city dwellers and late nineteenth-century medical anxieties. The medical image of modern social actors was one of *neurasthenia* and the neurasthenic was the victim of over-civilization (Rosenberg, 1978; Oppenheim, 1991).

The neurasthenic personality or social type was vividly present in Simmel's treatment of the metropolis and its inhabitants. As Frisby (1992) makes clear, neurasthenic over-stimulation and depletion were explicitly recognized in Simmel's work by his contemporaries. Indeed, the neurasthenic type of metropolitan dweller is to be found in the European images of modernity to be found in Baudelaire, Benjamin and Kracauer, among others. The *modern* metropolis was, therefore, clearly identified with varieties of degeneracy. Equally, it must be remembered, the connotations of neurasthenia were not unrelievedly negative. It reflected a heightened sensibility and sensitivity to external stimuli. Consequently, the urban observer, the aesthete and the social critic could all be thought to exemplify the positive benefits of the neurasthenic state. The European metropolis and the detached observer were described as 'strangers'. The disengaged intellectual mirrored the anonymous and estranged individuals who were observed: the social observer was a stranger among strangers.

The European tradition of urban sensibility was paralleled in American sociology. It is a major strand in the earliest manifestations of

Chicago sociology.[4] Park provided a direct link with the European tradition, having been exposed directly to Simmel's social thought in Germany. Park brought together his own experiences as a journalist and the sociological exploration of the city (Park and Burgess, 1925). Likewise, Louis Wirth and his Chicago-school contemporaries were at pains to describe the city as something more than and different from a merely physical location. They asserted that the modern metropolis created radically new *forms* and new *social types*. Wirth himself suggested that urbanism constituted a new way of life in its own right. The city was characterized not only in terms of its size, but also its complexity and the density of social life within it. Wirth's portrait of modern urban living, therefore, has echoes of neurasthenic civilization. 'Men and women coping with the pace and congestion of the city became irritable, unstable and insecure' (Smith, 1988: 164). Moreover, the metropolis was a city of strangers. Urban dwellers were pictured as rootless and planetary. The metropolis is thus a setting for the anonymous crowd: primary social ties of kinship and mutual obligation were replaced by weaker, secondary links. In the works of early urban ethnography, therefore, the modern metropolis was a site of social dislocation (Riesman, 1950). The social forms and values of traditional societies in the old world (Europe) and the new (including the rural South) were smashed by the demands of the modern urban environment. Collective modes of social solidarity were being replaced by a new individualism and the values of self-interest.

Among the origins of a qualitative tradition in sociology, then, are to be found the observation and exploration of the urban scene, portrayed as a site of modernity, as a physical and social space within which strangers engage in fleeting encounters and transactions (e.g. Cressey, 1932). The city, moreover, is a site of appearances. The stranger-observer marks the appearance of things and of persons. This preoccupation with strangers and appearances is to be found in a later American manifestation of the ethnographic gaze. The work of Erving Goffman incorporates a series of engagements with those European and American preoccupations.[5] His inspirations and sources are, of course, wider than that, but his core work develops the themes of estrangement in the modern world. He documents the fragility of the social actor in the presence of strangers and the protective work of appearances in the metropolitan setting. Goffman's social actors are engaged in a never-ending series of tasks in order to preserve the possibility of selfhood and moral agency in response to the gaze of anonymous others (Goffman, 1959, 1961, 1963a,b, 1967). In a manner that recalls Sartre's bleak anthropology, the self is always under threat: rendered an object of the other's gaze and judgement. The presentation of self embodies the moral obligations imposed by the presence of strangers. Stigma is only the consequence of normal imperfection writ large and amplified through the judgement of uncomprehending others, when the everyday requirements of tact and face-work break down. The social world that Goffman creates, therefore, becomes a kaleidoscope of intensely magnified microcosms of the modern world – just like Benjamin's shopping arcades. Everyday social life can be understood as a series of projects in which identities are produced and appearances are consumed.

Lyn Lofland's urban ethnography has continued the project (Lofland, 1985, 1998). Her observations of urban estrangement and the work of moral agency are in direct line of descent from Simmel and Park, Wirth and Goffman. She deploys the sociological gaze to show how social actors conduct themselves in anonymous settings – in a city like San Francisco – in the interests of preserving the appearance of self-control and composure. An activity as mundane as waiting at the bus station becomes fraught with moral significance. There is no question of transforming anonymity into acquaintance; rather, the anonymity itself must be managed and controlled, its potential threats guarded against. Her focus on the micro-politics of self-management in part reflects the intellectual and aesthetic tradition of the woman *flâneuse* (Parsons, 2000).

The observation of modern society was given a particular flavour in the United Kingdom by the Mass-Observation project, founded by

Hopkinson and Madge (see Stanley, 2001).[6] It built on an image of the anthropological enterprise and a particular sense of documentary reportage. It drew on the observations of members of the general public rather than professional social scientists. From the 1930s onwards, correspondents kept records and diaries and collected ephemera about specified themes, or about particular social events. The results, although patchy and unpredictable, added up to a remarkable experiment in demotic social observation. Many of the materials remained unpublished. Key publications were also produced. They included the ethnographic observations of 'Worktown' (Bolton in Lancashire), and of working-class life in London and the provinces. At times the observers and the authors who collated and interpreted the records displayed an insouciant capacity to 'other' the British working class. They provided vividly detailed accounts of phenomena such as the dance-craze 'the Lambeth walk', commercial ('all-in') wrestling, and day-trips to the seaside. By no means the same in inspiration as the disengaged observations of the European intellectual, Mass-Observation reflected a rather different mode of observation. Its gaze was an engaged one, in a vernacular genre. It had something in common with the various American New Deal projects of documentary reportage. The combination of text and photographic image contributed to a distinctive mode of attention to the everyday realities of working lives and popular leisure. It also owed something to a strand of surrealist aesthetics.

Contemporary preoccupations have given renewed impetus to the observation of urban spaces and the circulation of social actors within them. Indeed, recent work on culture and consumption have given a new urgency to that same optic impetus that informed Benjamin, Park and Simmel (e.g. Lash and Urry, 1994). Much of the scholarship is conducted under the rubric of late modernity or postmodernity, not least the exploration of urban spaces and consumer cultures. Informed by the theorization of Baudrillard and Lyotard, such contemporary scholarship in many ways returns to the early years of urban observation. It derives in part

from the conviction that contemporary social life is increasingly mediated through the symbolic. Information-society and consumer-society are accomplished through the production, circulation and consumption of signs. The social commentator thus becomes a kind of semiotic *flâneur* amidst a proliferation of spectacles, representations and life-style goods. The identification of tourism as a key topic and as a trope for postmodern living is a telling one (MacCannell, 1976; Urry, 2000). The themes are reflected too in the research literature on the intersection of tourism, museum culture and the ethnographic gaze (Kirshenblatt-Gimblett, 1998). The themes recall earlier sociological analyses of modernity once more: Veblen's pioneering discussion of conspicuous consumption, for example, pre-figures some of the themes, if not the theoretical frames of reference (Veblen, 1899/1970; Diggins, 1978).[7]

Within this renewed sociological gaze, the city itself is a semiotically marked space. It is itself a spectacle, and the sociological imagination is again rendered in terms of the optical. Cultural sociology has engaged anew with sociological classics such as Simmel in rediscovering the world of urban culture and consumption. Simmel's sociology has been 'postmodernized' (Weinstein and Weinstein, 1993). He, Benjamin and others have been rehabilitated as postmodernists *avant la lettre*, as contemporary social theorists have invested them with renewed vitality and urgency. Consumption *of* the city and consumption *in* the city together motivate the newer sociologies (Wilson, 1991, 2001; Urry, 1995).

Urban intimacies

While the early European and American observers found an urban environment of strangers and fleeting anonymity, marked by the dislocations of modernization, they and their contemporaries also explored sites of intimacy and cultural coherence. There were domains of organization that resisted the entropy of urban fragmentation and estrangement, providing sites for personal identity and meaning. The slum, the urban 'quarter' and the workplace were thus reconstructed sociologically as *local* manifestations of order and intimacy. The exploration of such settings implied in turn the transformation of the sociologist from the detached observer to the marginal or conditional participant. The 'strangeness' of the social setting is something to be – partially – overcome. The ethnographic enterprise is portrayed as a process that transcends the gulf of anonymous social difference. The ethnographer of urban settings, while remaining a 'professional stranger' (Agar, 1980), also seeks to gain 'access' to the everyday culture and relationships of local social worlds. The methods of participant observation do not depend on participation in the purely behavioural sense of physical presence, but rest on the social engagement of co-presence in the social world. Gaining access to a social world is not, therefore, a mere methodological preliminary to field research. It is a guiding principle of the research process itself. It transforms the objects of the *flâneur's* observations into the subjects of their own lives and circumstances.[8]

Like the urban observations of the detached European intellectuals, the Chicago ethnographers also found an affinity with the marginalized and the demi-monde. Cressey's taxi-dancers, or Anderson's hobos were the equivalent of Benjamin's prostitute or ragpicker. They represented the 'stranger' in the midst of the urban setting. Likewise, the ethnic quarter or the slum represented the sociologists' *terra incognita*. The ethnographic interest in the American slum, the 'little Italy', or the street corner has been an enduring one. This perspective derived from the conviction of Park and his contemporaries that the modern city was an environment in which diverse ways of life could be sustained (cf. Vidich and Lyman, 1994). So-called 'natural areas' provided opportunities for participant observation, and furnished some of the early classics of urban ethnography (e.g. Anderson, 1923; Wirth, 1928; Zorbaugh, 1929). Not only did such urban domains provide the setting for documenting the 'others' within the fabric of the metropolis, they also allowed the sociologists to demonstrate local order. Even superficially pathological phenomena such as the

gang could be shown to display coherence and to provide the social resources for organization and personal identity (Thrasher, 1927).

This spirit of urban ethnography was established by later classic studies of 'urban villages' and localities. Whyte's study of the Italian community of Boston's North End became not only a classic of urban sociology, but also a methodological exemplar. In recent years it has also become a key exemplar in the critique of classic fieldwork and its products (Whyte, 1943).[9] It was paralleled by Gans (1962) and Suttles (1968). Through their ethnographic engagement with the urban neighbourhoods, they showed the local cultures, the forms of social organization and the modes of rationality. The intensive documentation of the local was brought to a high point by Liebow (1967) in his classic ethnography of unemployed street-corner men in Washington, DC, by Hannerz in his monograph on an urban neighbourhood (Hannerz, 1969), by Anderson (1978) and in Duneier's subsequent study of urban African American men (1992).[10] These ethnographies all exemplify the recurrent American themes: the identification of distinctive ethnic areas within the metropolis and the documentation of local subcultures. The urban worlds of the private eye are the fictional counterpart to some of the urban ethnographies. Rich topographical descriptions of gritty reality characterize this genre – from Chandler's LA in the 1930s through Parker's Boston to Burke's New Orleans or Dawson's Oakland (Willett, 1996).

The ethnographic eye in American sociology, therefore, has repeatedly traversed the ambiguous terrain of the city (Hannerz, 1980). It has sustained images of the city that encompass the overall fragmentation of the city to the intensity of the locality. The quarter, the block, the street corner, the diner – these are all transformed from the specific into the generic. They stand for a series of broader preoccupations. They capture the ironic contrast between the anonymity and disorganization of the 'mainstream' and the endurance of order at the social margin. They subvert the conventional moral order by affirming the rationality and morality of the local community.

More importantly, they have explored one of the most pervasive themes of sociological thought since the beginning of the twentieth century and before. That is, the search for collective social life in the face of individualism, the search for community in the face of anonymity, the search for intimacy in a world of strangers.

THE SEARCH FOR COMMUNITY

The search for community has not been confined to American scholars, nor indeed to urban ethnographers. It would appear that social observers generically have been fretfully engaged with the theme of modern fragmentation and the loss of community. In the UK the classic theme was that of the spatial distribution of social classes in the urban scene rather than the ethnic dimensions of American social science. Young and Willmott (1957, 1973) were responsible for some of the most distinctive and influential of such studies. Their studies of neighbourhood and community in London's Bethnal Green contrast it with the new suburban housing estate to which the East Enders were migrating. They echo the tone of nostalgia for community, for the urban village, for local intimacy. They epitomize a distinctive British sense of class and community: a palpable affection for the compact and intimate village, based on local craft industry and trade, embodying the physical and social warmth of the public house, the social intimacies of neighbouring and the dense networks of mutual obligation based on kinship and shared occupational cultures.

Bethnal Green represents the epitome of London's East End in the immediate postwar period, when memories of the blitz were fresh, when modern re-housing projects were new, and when 'tradition' was confronted by the urgency of social and economic regeneration – embodied in the Festival of Britain just across the Thames on London's South Bank. The coal mining community occupied an equivalent symbolic space. The dense physical inhabitation, its distinct position in the division of labour – mining as a particular kind of aristocracy of organized labour – granted the mining community a particular mythologized significance. Dennis, Henriques and Slaughter (1956) made that concrete in their ethnography of a mining town. It captured the relations of intimacy and trust, the intensity of face-to-face social relations, that were among the abiding characteristics long associated with the sociological analysis of 'community'. It satisfied deeply held, and not always explicitly articulated, feelings associated with a romantic celebration of working class heroism. The mining community stood some way between the modern and the premodern, the urban and the rural. It thus provided a historical link between several traditions of ethnographic research, linking the metropolitan with the rural. The mining 'community' has continued to occupy an iconic position in the canon of sociological topics. It has exerted an interest in the UK, for instance, that has clearly outlasted the mining industry itself. From a recurrent, nostalgic commitment to the occupational traditions and the life of the coalfield community studies have followed the miners into everyday life after mine closure (Dicks, 1996) to the re-creation of coal mining as part of the heritage industry (Dicks, 1997, 1999, 2000; Strangleman et al., 1999): arguably, community sociology itself was already a form of 'heritage' industry.[11]

The fullest expression of community ethnography was to be found, in both the United Kingdom and in the United States, in the genre known as community studies, addressing the small-scale and the rural (Brunt, 2001). They described the persistence of the premodern. They also reflected long-term perspectives on the rural, as described for instance by Raymond Williams, inscribed in long traditions of literary and other representations (Williams, 1975). Images of small-town and rural social life pervade social and literary imaginations. There is a history of intellectual engagement with the rural community and its premodern characteristics that is as long as the equivalent fascination with the modern city. It is to be found influentially in the tradition of German-language sociology – most famously in Toennies and his ideal-type of *Gemeinschaft* (Toennies, 1957), and rather less well known in the work of Schmalenbach, who also theorized the nature of communitas in the *Bund* (Schmalenbach, 1977). It represents in part an intellectual reaction to the perceived pathologies of metropolitan life, a nostalgic return to the small-scale and the intimate, a rediscovery of mutual trust and obligation rather than impersonal contract in a cash nexus. Community studies were a hybrid genre between the 'local' studies of sociology and the 'distant' field research of social or cultural anthropologists. (In this context distance is not governed by mere geographical measurement: many of the 'others' studied by American anthropologists were the indigenous peoples of North America.) Community studies could satisfy an implicit desire for ethnographic fieldwork in self-contained settings, and a search for distance away from the urban milieu. In the UK they typically inhabited the geographical and social margins, most notably in the Celtic fringes and the borders. This is indeed a genre of the liminal. The villages in which community was to be found were poised between premodern and modern social life, between past and present, between the familiar and the strange.[12] There the anthropologist-sociologists found the fine grain of mutual support and obligation, the ties of kinship and trust that sociology had typically found missing in the fragmentations of mass society. The multiplex ties of kinship and mutual obligation were encoded in the networks of reciprocity in the face-to-face community. The pre-contractual basis of trust was rediscovered. In the United States the rural community and the small town encapsulated traits of the American ethos, embodying values that contrasted with the metropolitan centres. Small-town America has for a long time enjoyed a particular mythological status, and there was a close parallelism between literary and other artistic representations of the setting, and the sociological-cum-anthropological tradition of 'community' studies. The search for community and the nostalgia for past intimacies continues, in renewed manifestations. The popular reception of *Bowling Alone* (Putnam, 2000) is but one contemporary manifestation of the general spirit.

SELVES AND IDENTITIES

Self and identity are repeatedly treated as problematic in the sociology of modern society, while postmodern perspectives have given renewed urgency to the treatment of identity. We have already suggested some of the ways in which the modern urban setting was regarded as a site of disrupted and fragmented identities. The tradition also asserts the essentially social character of the social self and of self-identities. Self-awareness is at the heart of interpretative social science, including George Herbert Mead's symbolic interactionist legacy, in which the dialectical relations between mind, self and society are established (Baldwin, 1986; Miller, 1973). Charles Horton Cooley also formulated the 'looking-glass self' in an attempt to capture the processes of mutual regard through which the self is constituted. The judgement of others constitutes a social mirror in which the actor sees himself or herself reflected in the perceptions and evaluations of others, and so experiences a sense of selfhood, accompanied by those feelings of pride or mortification that in turn reflect the degree to which that self matches or falls short of a desired ideal (Cooley, 1930).

Cooley's others constitute a kind of audience, and in Goffman (1959) the sense of audience is rendered most vividly. His dramaturgical metaphor of everyday life portrays it as a kind of performance, and the self as a process of enactment. From the outset, the self of interactionist and Goffmanesque sociology is an embodied process (1963a). The body is at once cultural and physical. It provides the functional and expressive means through which everyday life is articulated. The presentation of self is always accomplished through physical work of some sort. The body is not merely a passive field but an active constituent of social enactments. Goffman develops Mead's reflections on gesture to outline a grammar of performatives. Goffman provides a sociological counterpart to the philosophical consideration of speech acts, through a formulation of performances in which the self is achieved in its worldly presence with others (Goffman, 1963b, 1967). In that sense Goffman recapitulates Mauss's pioneering work on the techniques of the body (Mauss, 1934). Mauss had extended Durkheim's insistence on the pervasiveness of the social into the superficially intractable domain of the physical body, showing how the most mundane of activities inscribed culture in the corporeal.

Goffman's self is also a 'ritually delicate object', in that it is created and sustained through the everyday rituals of social interaction. The social encounter is the fundamental unit of analysis, and in the face-to-face encounter social selves are produced and reproduced. The self is rendered delicate in that it is always a precarious achievement, open to threats and changes in definition. The mutable self thus reflects the plastic 'definition of the situation' – an equally core concept in the interpretative tradition.

The long-term sociological project of work on self and identity has been given renewed urgency under the auspices of scholarship that is conducted under the auspices of late-modernity or postmodernity (Denzin, 1991, 1992, 1995). There has been a new emphasis on the nature of the self under contemporary social conditions. It is argued that the social self is subject to unprecedented forces that lead to fragmented identities, in which analytic emphases are placed on instability and flux. Goffman's contributions have been carried on – though the debt is sometimes unacknowledged – in various guises. The mutability of identity has been stressed. The absolute novelty of such insights has been exaggerated. Likewise, there has been a relatively new fashion for interest in the body.[13] Significant while the new sociology of the body has been, it continues a strand in the interpretative tradition rather than initiating a completely new direction of scholarship. The interpretative tradition of qualitative research has for long recognized and explored such phenomena. But the ethnographic understanding of such things has sometimes been pursued in isolation from the main streams of theoretical fashion and orthodoxy. What is new

in recent years is the congruence of 'high' theory with the abiding concerns with qualitative sociological traditions.

LIVES AND VOICES

From the earliest years of the twentieth century the traditions of qualitative research have included the collection and analysis of documents of life. Indeed, 'lives' have been repeatedly documented and reconstructed, from letters, diaries, life-history interviews, oral testimony, biographical narratives and similar sources. In more recent years, lives have been supplemented by the reproduction of 'voices'. Lives and voices inhabit a long development of humanistic, qualitative research (Plummer, 2000, 2001).

Life documents were among the earliest sources of data collected and analysed by the Chicago-school sociologists. Thomas and Znaniecki's (1918–1920) work with documents from Poles in Chicago and in Poland has long been regarded as a classic. It was one of the first major pieces of empirical sociological research to attain such classic status. It captured one of the main substantive themes of the first Chicago school – the transition from the Old World to the New. The work exemplified the social, cultural and personal consequences of the sudden translation into a modern urban environment. Perhaps, though, the methodological stance of *The Polish Peasant* was more significant than its substance. Certainly it is the research approach that has been an enduring inspiration and reference point.

In the mythologizing of past research methods, it is too easy to reconstruct the heroic golden age of the early Chicago School in terms of a fully fledged ethnographic approach. But participant observation – in today's sense – was not regarded as the sole or even the main kind of data collection.[14] The life and the life-history were promoted as the sociological approach *par excellence*, and documentary data were held up as exemplary sources for such sociological work. Thomas, for instance, not only worked on the life-documents of displaced Poles. He also used texts such as letters to problem pages among the sources for *The Unadjusted Girl* – a work famous for the inclusion of his famous dictum concerning 'the definition of the situation' (Thomas, 1923).

The life-history also gained classic status in Shaw's extended biographical work with an adolescent deviant – the eponymous 'jack-roller' character who is the central character of the resulting monograph (Shaw, 1930). This work too has gained classic status in the canon of American empirical sociology. Again, this reflects primarily the fact that it was one of the first extended works of life-history reconstruction, based on repeated interviews with one informant. It retains its significance as a methodological exemplar rather than for the specific insights it might provide into deviant careers and identities.

At one time, then, life-histories, assembled from interviews or documentary sources, could be regarded as sociological materials *par excellence*. The 'life' encapsulated the personal and the public, social structure with personal subjectivity. In the face of survey methods, however, the life-history rather fell into obscurity. From the centre of sociological interest it was relegated to the margins. There continued to be outstanding life-history studies; Most notably they included Heyl's study of a house-prostitution madam (Heyl, 1979) and Klockars's (1974) study of a professional fence. These exemplified the strength of the life-history tradition.

In more recent years, varieties of the 'life' have been granted renewed currency in the social sciences. The biographical has been reintroduced. This has, in part, been promoted under the aegis of various poststructuralist and postmodernist tendencies in theory and method.[15] In our view it is not necessary to invoke those particular meta-theoretical frames in order to justify a fresh interest in the documentation of lives; those tendencies have undoubtedly provided fresh justifications and have helped to encourage a commitment to such work.

The earlier genre of life-history owed something to other social and cultural forms. They had affinities with literary forms such as the *Bildungsroman* – the novel of personal development. The Chicago School style of work related directly to contemporary fiction. Farrell's *Studs Lonigan* trilogy has an especially close affinity with that sociological tradition, not least from the setting of the fiction, and the fact that the author had himself studied sociology in the Chicago department. The fictional tradition and the sociological tradition alike traced the development of character in predominantly urban settings. They described what Goffman would later call the 'moral career' of characters (1961). In a manner reminiscent of the fiction of Zola, they explored the interaction of character and circumstance. Again, this is not entirely adventitious. We are told that the younger sociologists at Chicago were encouraged to read Zola as an exemplar of realist writing about social life.

Late twentieth-century interest in life-history took on a different array of connotations from earlier work and this continues into the new century. There has been a special emphasis on biographical and autobiographical *narratives*. Indeed, one can argue that the personal narrative has become one of the central modes of social and cultural inquiry of recent years. Biographical narrative has taken on a different kind of significance from the earlier representations of life-histories. As Atkinson and Silverman (1997) have suggested, this in part seems to reflect the growing cultural significance of the interview and the biographical confessional mode in contemporary society. The cultural work of the print media and television constantly reproduced the personal interview as the preferred way of capturing and disseminating information. There is a strong cultural preference for self-revelation through the interview. In contemporary society at large, the interview is a site for much more than the rehearsal of events. It is a genre for the expression of feelings. Events without emotional responses seem devoid of significance in this discourse. Rather, feelings have precedence over actions; emotions are granted greater significance than events.

The impetus for recent biographical work shares similar preoccupations. Atkinson and Silverman argue that the sociology reproduces the obsessions of the 'interview society'.

Sociological attention is paid to actors' 'experiences' and 'feelings' with diminished attention to social organization and social action. The interview becomes a technology of self-construction and the reconstruction of lives. Interview sociology and the interview society become complicit in the celebration of lives. The interview has, they argue, become a contemporary technology of the self.[16]

The interview society and interview sociology stress the identity of the social actor, and her or his biographical distinctiveness. It is, moreover, paralleled by a similar attention to the biographical work of the social scientist. The biographical and the autobiographical thus converge. This is a particular application of the principle of *reflexivity*. The autobiographical account of the research process has long been an aspect of field research, and it has been identified with a 'confessional' genre (Van Maanen, 1988). The confessional mode has become increasingly urgent in recent writing, however. Where once the confessional was confined to a methodological appendix or to a separate essay (often in anthologies of retrospective essays by experienced researchers) it has become central to the research itself (Coffey, 1999). In some cases the autobiographical self-absorption of the ethnographer can assume greater importance than the social actors or social setting that provide the ostensible subject matter. The sociological work echoes more vernacular reproductions of lives and voices, such as Terkel's collections of *vox populi* interviews (e.g. Terkel, 1970, 1974).

The transformations in 'lives' and 'voices' mark the culmination in a major series of changes in the applications of qualitative research strategies. The celebration of biography in the so-called postmodern period marks the move from action to experience. The sociological gaze has moved decisively from observable actions to reported emotions and experiences. Everyday life is no longer conceived in terms of shared cultural resources and interaction; it is conceived primarily in terms of the personal and the private. The researcher no longer seeks 'access' to a shared social world, but 'access' to the private realm. It is a move from a distinctively *social* domain to

a *personal* one. It ceases to be the exploration of a 'strange' exterior world and becomes the exploration of the interior world of feeling. This is no longer the detached gaze of the *flâneur*, nor even the conditional engagement of the professional stranger. It is more akin to a therapeutic relationship than a disengaged research-oriented undertaking (Atkinson, 1997). The analytic metaphor of qualitative research seems to have shifted from the *visual* observation of action to one of *listening* to the voices of others and to the interior monologue of personal reflection.

The celebration of voices accompanies ethical as well as methodological transformations. Under the auspices of postcolonial and other critical standpoints, scholars have increasingly sought to reinstate the voice of the 'other'. It has been argued repeatedly that previous, conventional modes of ethnographic research privileged the voice of the ideal-typical observer (prototypically white, Western, male and privileged) while subsuming or muting the voices of the objects of the research gaze. In the process, however, the celebration of voices seems to have become privileged over the analysis of actions.

AESTHETICS AND REPRESENTATIONS

We have alluded to a number of affinities between the social sciences and literary and other cultural forms already. It is important to note that there have been direct or indirect influences between the wider cultural and representational sphere and the conduct of the social sciences. Ethnographic and other qualitative research has not developed in a vacuum. While widespread and explicit literary experimentation may be a recent phenomenon among qualitative researchers, that does not mean that for most of the twentieth century there was no interplay between the literary, the artistic and the ethnographic. On the contrary, the affinities are an integral part of the intellectual history.

There were, for example, significant parallels between the development of the first Chicago

School of urban ethnography and the literary imagination of realist fiction. Cappetti (1993) has documented such literary parallels in some detail. In a similar vein, it has been possible to trace intellectual and aesthetic convergences between Malinowski's ethnography and Conrad's literary preoccupations, and there are significant surrealist influences on anthropology (Clifford, 1981). More generally, of course, the modernist encounter with the 'primitive' plastic art developed over a similar period of time that twentieth-century ethnographic fieldwork practices were established by British, European and North American scholars. It is wrong, therefore, to assume that an awareness of the literary and aesthetic possibilities of ethnography is an exclusively recent topic of interest. As early as 1935 Zora Neale Hurston was experimenting with literary forms for the expression of anthropological texts: hers was one of the first experiments in what has later been called 'blurred genres' forms of representation (Hernandez, 1995). Likewise, Bateson's *Naven* must be recognized as an early essay in 'alternative' textual forms (Bateson, 1936).

Since the early to mid-1980s, however, sociologists and anthropologists have become increasingly aware of the textual conventions through which even the most orthodox of ethnographic texts has been constructed. The conventionality of ethnographic writing extends to the homology between functionalist anthropological work and the arrangement of ethnographic monographs, the use of textual practices like the 'ethnographic present', and the textual inscription of the ethnographer's authority.[17] As well as a heightened awareness of textual forms, an increasing number of ethnographers have experimented with 'alternative' literary forms for the reconstruction of social reality. These have included the construction of 'ethno-drama', of 'ethno-fiction', of poems and other self-consciously aesthetic experimentations (Angrosino, 1998; Banks and Banks, 1998; Handler, 1988; Jones, 1998; Mienczakowski, 2001; Wolf, 1992). These in part reflect the call for 'messy texts' that in turn reflect the complexity and indeterminacy of ethnographic understanding, and stand in opposition to texts that rest on realist conventions, and enshrine a monolithically authorial gaze.

PHILOSOPHIES AND JUSTIFICATIONS

Ethnographic and cognate social research have not developed for over a century completely divorced from broader intellectual currents, as we have seen. Equally, they have not been entirely separated from theoretical and epistemological currents. It is not appropriate here to review all the possible theoretical claims that have been invoked for or against particular research strategies. We do, however, want to sketch out some general themes and in doing so correct some current misrepresentations. In general terms, one cannot point to definitive links between specific theories or philosophies of science and particular research approaches. It is sometimes convenient to do so for pedagogical purposes, but like most such pedagogical devices, at best it incorporates half-truths.

Qualitative research traditions clearly have a long-standing elective affinity with various strands of 'interpretative' social thought. In the United States there are strong family resemblances, personal and institutional links between the tradition of symbolic interactionism and qualitative research. The institutional links include the Chicago School of sociology. George Herbert Mead's social philosophy and social psychology – most notably in his profoundly social characterization of 'mind, self and society' – provide a significant point of reference (Baldwin, 1986; Miller, 1973). In the subsequent work of scholars like Herbert Blumer the strands of symbolic interactionism were to some extent codified into a coherent justification for a distinctive sociology. Blumer's was a particular reading of symbolic interactionism that articulated a distinctive methodological vision (Hammersley, 1989). In the 'Second Chicago School' (Fine, 1995) there is a clear continuity between the interactionist and the ethnographic strands of work in the institutional ethnographies of Becker, Geer, Strauss and their contemporaries (e.g. Becker, Geer, Hughes and Strauss, 1961; Olesen and

Whittaker, 1968). The transformations of the self through occupational and organizational socialization, for instance, provide a major programme of empirical research studies that portray the systemic relationships between institutions and persons (Becker, 1970; Hughes, 1971). The social psychology of interactionism also furnishes a major methodological warrant for ethnographic fieldwork. There is, as we have seen, a homology between the interactionist model of the social actor and that of the reflexive ethnographer (Rock, 1979).

Interactionism is not, however, the sole inspiration or justification for qualitative research. Versions of social phenomenology and existential sociology have also been of some influence. Indeed, it is noticeable that at various times in the development of qualitative or interpretative sociology, distinctions between those perspectives have not been especially clearly demarcated. At crucial periods in the dissemination of the relevant ideas, for instance, 'symbolic interactionism' has included work inspired by social phenomenology, ethnomethodology, existentialism and other philosophical or methodological tendencies.[18]

The phenomenological tradition has been a major influence on the conceptualization of qualitative research. Alfred Schutz's marriage of Weberian sociology and Husserlian phenomenology, together with his own migration to the United States, provides one significant link between European social philosophy and Anglo-American sociology (e.g. Schutz, 1967) Not an empirical social researcher himself, Schutz provides one philosophical justification for a distinctive approach to social research. This was given greater impetus by the work of Berger and Luckmann (1967) in their synthesis and exegesis of phenomenological sociology. The movement legitimated serious attention to social constructivism, including the social construction of expert knowledge, and the mechanisms of everyday practical reasoning. The affinities between social phenomenology and qualitative research lay in the former's close attention to the practicalities of mundane action and common sense reasoning. Those included the use of typifications. Empirical research on the use of typifications – in

professional reasoning, the everyday organization of work and organizations – was directly influenced by the phenomenological turn. The ethnographic study of practical reasoning and processes of categorization *in situ* became a major topic in the development of empirical qualitative research. In recent years, varieties of phenomenology have been given new leases of life in a number of substantive research domains. For instance, a number of practitioners of nursing research have claimed phenomenology as a distinctive foundation for qualitative inquiry into nursing knowledge and practice: the accuracy of those claims is beyond the scope of this chapter.

The phenomenological movement was also paralleled by various programmes of existential sociology and the sociology of the absurd (e.g. Douglas and Johnson, 1977; Lyman and Scott, 1970; Morris, 1977). Drawing inspiration not only from phenomenological philosophy, but also from other continental schools of thought, the existentialist and absurdist standpoints rested on the assertion of the arbitrariness of social life, the absence of intrinsic meaning, and the dissolution of assumptions of stable social order. There are affinities too between these radical sociological perspectives and theories of the spectacle and situationist radical perspectives in politics and aesthetics. The absurdist perspective also self-consciously draws on aesthetic movements: including, of course, the theatre of the absurd. In that sense, it also harks back to earlier affinities with surrealist aesthetics and theories. The emphasis on the essentially arbitrary nature of the social, and the radical view of the 'definition of the situation', were both central to the existential and absurdist positions.

It would be wrong, however, to focus unduly on the purely transitory phenomena of avant-garde epistemologies, or on the novelties of phenomenological or other 'turns' in qualitative sociology. Those movements and moments reflect a longer series of commitments in humanist interpretative sociology. Severyn Bruyn (1966) provides a major statement of humanist sociology that links phenomenological insights and the merits of participant observation. Earlier, Florian Znaniecki (1934, 1940, 1969) articulated a humanistic rationale for a sociology that also reflected his own 'qualitative' research commitments.

We have mentioned from time to time already in this chapter that interests and commitments that have relatively long histories in sociology and other social sciences (notably anthropology) have been granted renewed attention, and endorsed with increasing enthusiasm in recent years. The theoretical enthusiasms that have led to the cultural turn in the social sciences have fuelled interest in qualitative research methods. They have also given renewed urgency to the exploration of representational modes. Likewise, the linguistic turn in the social and cultural sciences has renewed the array of qualitative research strategies. The traditions of conversation and discourse analysis are beyond the confines of this particular chapter. But their distinctive approaches to spoken action have provided an especially powerful way of understanding social interaction, understanding the performance of selves and identities, and the discursive accomplishment of everyday reality. Those interests converge with contemporary work on the biographical, through new programmes of work on narrative, biography and autobiography.

The ethical and epistemological commitments of feminist scholarship have led towards a broadly qualitative agenda. This has drawn on several kinds of justification. Stanley and Wise, for instance, base their methodological commitments to a feminist perspective on everyday life that owes much to the phenomenological spirit and something to the ethnomethodological programme – in treating the everyday world as problematic from a feminist viewpoint (Stanley and Wise, 1983, 1993). Likewise, Smith unites a feminist perspective with that of an interpretative tradition (1987, 1990, 1999) to produce a distinctive synthesis of perspectives. More generally, qualitative research has been claimed as especially congruent. The newer emphasis on intimacy, biography and autobiography owes much to feminist commitments (see Coffey, 1999; Reed-Danahay, 1997; Stanley, 1992). These perspectives transcend vulgar appeals to feminism that uncritically equate quantitative with masculinist and positivist standpoints, while endowing qualitative methods with female and/or feminist qualities. Rather, they suggest that there is a convergence between a feminist commitment to treating everyday categories of thought as problematic, and the fundamental commitments of interpretative social science, including qualitative research methods.

CONCLUSION

A number of characterizations of qualitative research have stressed discontinuities in the development of the tradition(s). Those genealogies are often misleading. They have looked primarily at the explicit statements of methodologists – selectively at that – rather than looking more broadly at the major themes that have characterized the traditions. Other commentators have tried to insist on the existence of mutually exclusive and incommensurable methodological paradigms. Such an approach does violence to the intellectual history of interpretative sociology and qualitative methods. The mutual influences of theories, methods and practical research have been complex. There are no one-to-one relationships between theories and methods. There are no such things as 'paradigms' within these broad traditions. There have been changes of emphasis at various historical junctures, of that there is no doubt. Nevertheless, the identification of more and more historical periods, and more and more distinct paradigms, is equally absurd. Moreover, the authors of those reconstructions of the past frequently ignore significant contributions in order to produce spurious genealogies and developmental sequences.

There have been some remarkably durable and pervasive themes, some of which we have outlined here. Changes in emphasis need to be appreciated against this backcloth of recurrent preoccupations. For that reason, it is important to understand 'qualitative' research traditions in terms of subject-matter, and not just in terms of specific methods of data collection and analysis. We have not made 'methods' the focal topic of this chapter. The development of ethnography in Western urban settings, or in small-scale 'communities', or the use of the life-history interview, need to be understood in the context of generic sociological themes that have informed their use. Qualitative research in sociology has never been defined and practised entirely in terms of method alone. The qualitative research tradition is grounded in a more general set of intellectual commitments. It is not defined solely by the use of participant observation or interviewing. Even the more general commitment to 'ethnographic' perspectives does not equate with those foundational concerns. We have attempted to outline and illustrate just some of those major currents of social thought, of which methodological interests are but a part, however important.

NOTES

1 Major works of reference include anthologies edited by Atkinson, Coffey, Delamont, Lofland and Lofland (2001), Denzin and Lincoln (2000) and Gubrium and Holstein (1997). Recent contributions that cover significant domains of fieldwork research strategy include: Coffey (1999), Davies (1999), Delamont (2002), Denzin (1997), Gubrium and Holstein (1997), Hammersley and Atkinson (1995), Silverman (2000). More detailed treatments of specialist topics include Cortazzi (1993), Holstein and Gubrium (2000) and Plummer (2000) on narrative, biographies and life-histories; ten Have (1999) on spoken discourse; Pink (2001) on visual analysis; Bloor et al. (2001) on focus groups; and Wengraf (2001) on interviewing more generally.

2 Lincoln and Denzin (1994) offered a 'five moments' model of qualitative research that stresses discontinuities, and subsequently expanded to a seven moments model (Denzin, 1997; Denzin and Lincoln, 2000). Our arguments against this position are expanded upon in Atkinson, Delamont and Coffey (1999), Delamont, Coffey and Atkinson (2000), Atkinson, Coffey, Delamont, Lofland and Lofland (2001) and Delamont and Atkinson (2004).

3 Jacob (1987), for instance, offered an elaborate but sterile model of incommensurable paradigms in qualitative research on education, criticized by Atkinson, Delamont and Hammersley (1988). Leininger's (1992) parallel typology in nursing research is criticized by Atkinson (1995) and Delamont and Atkinson (1995). We continue to believe that the tensions within and between traditions of qualitative research are not best approached in terms of separate paradigms. Equally, we are convinced that there are important continuities and commitments that endure, and cross-cut any short-term theoretical or

epistemological fashions: see Atkinson, Coffey and Delamont (2003).

4 There is a large and ever-increasing literature on the history of sociology at Chicago. Deegan (2001) provides a recent review of the topic. Earlier accounts include Rock (1979), Bulmer (1984), Harvey (1987), Smith (1988). Sibley's (1995) account of urban geography also includes a discussion of Chicago urban sociology. The history is contested and mythologized. Abbott (1999) offers an interesting view of the relations between Chicago, American sociology more generally, the ASA and the *American Journal of Sociology*. Fine (1995) encompasses the postwar period (1945–1965). Cappetti (1993) provides a fascinating account of the continuities of literary and sociological representations of Chicago.

5 The work of Goffman has been the subject of an extensive secondary literature: see Burns (1992), Ditton (1980), Drew and Wootton (1988), Manning (1992) Greg Smith (1999).

6 There are many publications from the Mass-Observation archive at Sussex University, as well as reprints of the original publications. See, for instance, Calder and Sheridan (1984), Cross (1990), Jennings and Madge (1937), Mass-Observation (1937, 1939), Sheridan (1990). There is also a modern literature of commentary, including Chaney and Pickering (1985, 1986), Hubble (1998), McClancy (1995) and Stanley (2001).

7 Much of the work in this vein is to be found in the Theory, Culture and Society books series. See, *inter alia*, Falk and Campbell (1997), Featherstone (1990) and Rojek (1995).

8 These issues are explored further in Hammersley and Atkinson (1995) and in Coffey (1999).

9 Whyte's study was originally published in 1943. It has been reissued in several subsequent editions. Controversial re-appraisals of the research and the resulting monograph are to be found in a special issue of *The Journal of Contemporary Ethnography*, 1992, Vol. 21, No. 1.

10 Lyn Lofland's essay (1975) on the 'thereness' of women is a trenchant critique of this genre of work. Burawoy (1991) and Lamphere (1992) show it continues unabated.

11 For general reviews of the community studies tradition, see Bell and Newby (1971), Brunt (2001), Frankenberg (1976), Gusfield (1975) and Stacey (1975).

12 Significant community studies in the UK include: Frankenberg (1957), Rees (1950), Strathern (1981) and Williams (1956, 1963). In addition to indigenous UK studies, there is also a tradition of fieldwork among the Celtic fringes and the Marches by scholars from the United States: see for instance Arensberg (1959) and Scheper-Hughes (1977, 2001). See also Frankenberg (1965).

13 For recent contributions to the sociology of the body see Delamont (1998), Falk (1994), Featherstone, Hepworth and Turner (1991), Monaghan (1999, 2001), Mellor and Shilling (1997), Shilling (1993), Turner (1996), Williams (2000, 2002) and Williams and Bendelow (1998).

14 For discussions of the methodological contributions of the Chicago School, and the relative importance of different methods, see Rock (1979), Bulmer (1984), Harvey (1987) and Platt (1999).

15 The distinctive claims of postmodernism in this context are beyond the scope of this chapter. We make general reference to the claims for postmodernism towards the end of our discussion. For its significance in relation to lives and voices, see Delamont and Atkinson (2004).

16 For samples of the extensive literature on narratives and lives, see Ellis and Flaherty (1992), Josselson (1996), Josselson and Lieblich (1995), Lieblich and Josselson (1994), Mishler (1999), Plummer (2000) and Riessman (1990, 1993).

17 This literature, which has grown enormously in recent years, was most prominent in anthropology: see Boon (1982), Behar and Gordon (1995), Clifford (1988), Clifford and Marcus (1986) and James et al. (1997). In sociology contributions included Atkinson (1981, 1990, 1992), Edmondson (1984), Ellis and Bochner (1996), Goodall (2000), Richardson (1990, 1994) and Van Maanen (1988). See also Spencer (2001).

18 Evidence for this inclusive and eclectic definition can be seen in the early editions of influential anthologies, such as those edited by Manis and Meltzer (1967) and Rose (1962). Authors more readily identified in terms of phenomenology, ethnomethodology and labelling theory are to be found in these collections of 'interactionist' papers. The early contributions by authors such as Cicourel (1968) were also included within a generically interactionist literature at that time.

BIBLIOGRAPHY

Abbott, Andrew (1999) *Department and Discipline: Chicago Sociology at One Hundred*. Chicago: University of Chicago Press.

Agar, Michael (1980) *The Professional Stranger: An Informal Introduction to Ethnography*. New York: Academic Press.

Anderson, Elijah (1978) *A Place on the Corner*. Chicago: University of Chicago Press.

Anderson, Nels (1923) *The Hobo: The Sociology of the Homeless Man*. Chicago: University of Chicago Press.

Angrosino, Michael (1998) *Opportunity House: Ethnographic Stories of Mental Retardation*. Walnut Creek, CA: AltaMira.

Arensberg, Conrad (1959) *The Irish Countryman*. Boston, MA: Smith.

Atkinson, Paul (1981) 'Writing ethnography', in H.J. Helle (cd.), *Kultur und Institution*. Berlin: Duncker and Humblot. pp. 77–105.

Atkinson, Paul (1990) *The Ethnographic Imagination: Textual Constructions of Reality*. London: Routledge.

Atkinson, Paul (1992) *Understanding Ethnographic Texts*. Newbury Park, CA: Sage.

Atkinson, Paul (1995) 'Perils of paradigms', *Qualitative Health Research*, 5 (1): 117–24.

Atkinson, Paul (1997) 'Narrative turn or blind alley?', *Qualitative Health Research*, 7 (3): 325–44.

Atkinson, Paul, Coffey, Amanda and Delamont, Sara (2003) *Key Themes in Qualitative Research*. Walnut Creek, CA: AltaMira.

Atkinson, Paul and Silverman, David (1997) 'Kundera's *Immortality*: the interview society and the invention of the self', *Qualitative Inquiry*, 3: 304–25.

Atkinson, Paul, Coffey, Amanda, Delamont, Sara, Lofland, John and Lofland, Lyn (eds) (2001) *Handbook of Ethnography*. London: Sage.

Atkinson, Paul, Delamont, Sara and Coffey, Amanda (1999) 'Ethnography: post, past and present', *Journal of Contemporary Ethnography*, 28 (5): 460–71.

Atkinson, Paul, Delamont, Sara and Hammersley, Martyn (1988) 'Qualitative research traditions', *Review of Educational Research*, 58 (2): 231–50.

Baldwin, John D. (1986) *George Herbert Mead: A Unifying Theory for Sociology*. Newbury Park, CA: Sage.

Banks, Anna and Banks, Stephen P. (eds) (1998) *Fiction and Social Research: By Ice or Fire*. Walnut Creek, CA: AltaMira.

Bateson, Gregory (1936) *Naven*. Cambridge: Cambridge University Press.

Becker, Howard (1970) *Sociological Work*. Chicago: Aldine.

Becker, Howard, Geer, Blanche, Hughes, Everett and Strauss, Anslem (1961) *Boys in White: Student Culture in Medical School*. Chicago: University of Chicago Press.

Behar, Ruth and Gordon, Deborah A. (eds) (1995) *Women Writing Culture*. Berkeley, CA: University of California Press.

Bell, Colin and Newby, Howard (1971) *Community Studies*. London: Allen and Unwin.

Benjamin, Walter (1986) *Moscow Diary* (ed. Gary Smith, trans. Richard Sieburth). Cambridge, MA: Harvard University Press.

Benjamin, Walter (2000) *The Arcades Project* (ed. Rolf Tiedemann, trans. Howard Eiland and Kevin McLaughlin). Cambridge, MA: Belknap Press/ Harvard University Press.

Berger, Peter and Luckmann, Thomas (1967) *The Social Construction of Reality*. London: Allen Lane.

Bloor, Michael, Frankland, Jane, Thomas, Michelle and Robson, Kate (2001) *Focus Groups in Social Research*. London: Sage.

Boon, J.A. (1982) *Other Tribes, Other Scribes: Symbolic Anthropology in the Comparative Study of Authors, Histories, Religions and Texts*. Cambridge: Cambridge University Press.

Brunt, Lodewijk (2001) 'Into the community', in P. Atkinson, A. Coffey, S. Delamont, J. Lofland and L. Lofland (eds), *Handbook of Ethnography*. London: Sage. pp. 80–91.

Bruyn, Severyn (1966) *The Human Perspective: The Methodology of Participant Observation*. Englewood Cliffs, NJ: Prentice–Hall.

Buck-Morss, Susan (1997) *The Dialectics of Seeing: Walter Benjamin and the Arcades Project*. Cambridge, MA: MIT Press.

Bulmer, Martin (1984) *The Chicago School of Sociology: Institutionalization, Diversity, and the Rise of Sociological Research*. Chicago: University of Chicago Press.

Burawoy, Michael (ed.) (1991) *Ethnography Unbound*. Berkeley, CA: University of California Press.

Burns, Tom (1992) *Erving Goffman*. London: Routledge.

Calder, Angus and Sheridan, Dorothy (eds) (1984) *Speak for Yourself: A Mass-Observation Anthology*. London: Jonathan Cape.

Cappetti, P. (1993) *Writing Chicago*. New York: Columbia University Press.

Chaney, David and Pickering, Michael (1985) 'Democracy and communication: Mass-Observation 1937–1943', *Journal of Communication*, 36: 41–56.

Chaney, David and Pickering, Michael (1986) 'Authorship in documentary: sociology as an art form in Mass-Observation', in John Corner (ed.), *Documentary and the Mass Media*. London: Edward Arnold, pp. 29–44.

Cicourel, Aaron (1968) *The Social Organization of Juvenile Justice*. London: Heinemann.

Clifford, James (1981) 'On ethnographic surrealism', *Comparative Studies in Society and History*, 23 (4): 539–64.

Clifford, James (1988) *The Predicament of Culture*. Cambridge, MA: Harvard University Press.

Clifford, James and Marcus, George (eds) (1986) *Writing Culture: The Poetics and Politics of Ethnography*. Berkeley, CA: University of California Press.

Coffey, Amanda (1999) *The Ethnographic Self*. London: Sage.

Coles, Alex (ed.) (1999) *The Optic of Walter Benjamin*. London: Black Dog Publishing.

Coles, Alex (ed.) (2000) *Site-Specificity: The Ethnographic Turn*. London: Black Dog Publishing.

Cooley, Charles H. (1930) *Sociological Theory and Social Research*. New York: Holt.

Cortazzi, Martin (1993) *Narrative Analysis*. London: Falmer.

Crary, Jonathan (1990) *Techniques of the Observer: On Vision and Modernity in the Nineteenth Century*. Cambridge, MA: MIT Press.

Crary, Jonathan (1999) *Suspensions of Perception: Attention, Spectacle, and Modern Culture*. Cambridge, MA: MIT Press.

Cressey, Paul (1932) *The Taxi-Dance Hall: A Sociological Study on Commercialized Recreation and City Life*. Chicago: University of Chicago Press.

Cross, Gary (ed.) (1990) *Worktowners at Blackpool: Mass-Observation and Popular Leisure in the 1930s*. London: Routledge.

Davies, Charlotte A. (1999) *Reflexive Ethnography: A Guide to Researching Selves and Others*. London: Routledge.

Deegan, Mary-Jo (2001) 'The Chicago School of Ethnography', in P. Atkinson, A. Coffey, S. Delamont, J. Lofland and L. Lofland (eds), *Handbook of Ethnography*. London: Sage. pp. 11–25.

Delamont, Sara (1998) 'You need the leotard', *Sport, Education and Society*, 3 (1): 5–17.

Delamont, Sara (2002) *Fieldwork in Educational Settings: Methods, Pitfalls and Perspectives*, 2nd edn. London: Routledge.

Delamont, Sara and Atkinson, Paul (1995) *Fighting Familiarity: Essays on Education and Ethnography*. Cresskill, NJ: Hampton Press.

Delamont, Sara and Atkinson, Paul (2004) 'Qualitative research and the postmodern turn', in A. Bryman and M. Hardy (eds), *Handbook of Data Analysis*. London: Sage. pp. 667–81.

Delamont, Sara, Coffey, Amanda and Atkinson, Paul (2000) 'The twilight years? Educational ethnography and the five moments model', *International Journal of Qualitative Studies in Education*, 13 (3): 223–38.

Dennis, Norman, Henriques, Fernando and Slaughter, Clifford (1956) *Coal is Our Life*. London: Eyre and Spottiswood (2nd edn, London: Tavistock, 1969).

Denzin, Norman K. (1991) *Images of Postmodern Society: Social Theory and Contemporary Cinema*. Thousand Oaks, CA: Sage.

Denzin, Norman K. (1992) *Symbolic Interactionism and Cultural Studies*. Cambridge, MA: Blackwell.

Denzin, Norman K. (1995) *The Cinematic Society: The Voyeur's Gaze*. Thousand Oaks, CA: Sage.

Denzin, Norman K. (1997) *Interpretive Ethnography*. Thousand Oaks, CA: Sage.

Denzin, Norman and Lincoln, Yvonna (eds) (1994) *Handbook of Qualitative Research*. Thousand Oaks, CA: Sage.

Denzin, Norman and Lincoln, Yvonna (eds) (2000) *Handbook of Qualitative Research*, 2nd edn. Thousand Oaks, CA: Sage.

Dicks, Bella (1996) 'Coping with pit closures in the 1990s', in J. Pilcher and A. Coffey (eds), *Gender and Qualitative Research*. Aldershot: Avebury. pp. 22–43.

Dicks, Bella (1997) 'Regeneration versus representation in the Rhondda', *Contemporary Wales*, 9: 56–73.

Dicks, Bella (1999) 'The view of our town from the hill: communities on display as local heritage', *International Journal of Cultural Studies*, 2 (3): 349–68.

Dicks, Bella (2000) 'Encoding and decoding the people: circuits of communication at a local heritage museum', *European Journal of Communication*, 15 (1): 61–78.

Diggins, John P. (1978) *The Bard of Savagery: Thorstein Veblen and Modern Social Theory*. Hassocks, Sussex: Harvester.

Ditton, Jason (ed.) (1980) *The View from Goffman*. London: Macmillan.

Douglas, Jack D. and Johnson, John M. (eds) (1977) *Existential Sociology*. Cambridge: Cambridge University Press.

Drew, Paul and Wootton, Anthony (eds) (1988) *Erving Goffman: Exploring the Interaction Order*. Cambridge: Polity Press.

Duneier, M. (1992) *Slim's Table: Race, Responsibility and Masculinity*. Chicago: University of Chicago Press.

Edmonson, Ricca (1984) *Rhetoric in Sociology*. London: Macmillan.

Ellis, Carolyn and Bochner, Arthur B. (eds) (1996) *Composing Ethnography*. Walnut Creek, CA: AltaMira.

Ellis, Carolyn and Flaherty, Michael G. (eds) (1992) *Investigating Subjectivity: Research on Lived Experience*. Newbury Park, CA: Sage.

Falk, Pasi (1994) *The Consuming Body*. London: Sage.

Falk, Pasi and Campbell, Colin (eds) (1997) *The Shopping Experience*. London: Sage.

Featherstone, Mike (1990) *Consumer Culture and Postmodernism*. London: Sage.

Featherstone, Mike, Hepworth, Mike and Turner, Bryan S. (eds) (1991) *The Body: Social Process and Cultural Theory*. London: Sage.

Fine, Gary Alan (ed.) (1995) *A Second Chicago School? The Development of a Postwar American Sociology*. Chicago: University of Chicago Press.

Foster, Hal (1996) *The Return of the Real: The Avant-Garde at the End of the Century*. Cambridge, MA: MIT Press.

Frankenberg, Ronald (1957) *Village on the Border*. London: Cohen and West.

Frankenberg, Ronald (1965) *Communities in Britain*. Harmondsworth: Penguin.

Frankenberg, Ronald (1976) 'In the production of their lives', in D.L. Barker and S. Allen (eds), *Sexual Divisions and Society*. London: Tavistock.

Frisby, David (1985) *Fragments of Modernity: Theories of Modernity in the Work of Simmel, Kracauer and Benjamin*. Cambridge: Polity Press.

Frisby, David (1992) *Sociological Impressionism: A Reassessment of Georg Simmel's Social Theory*. London: Routledge.

Gans, Herbert J. (1962) *The Urban Villagers: Group and Class in the Life of Italian-Americans*. New York: The Free Press.

Goffman, Erving (1959) *The Presentation of Self in Everyday Life*. Garden City, NY: Anchor.

Goffman, Erving (1961) *Asylums*. New York: Anchor.

Goffman, Erving (1963a) *Stigma: Notes on the Management of Spoiled Identity*. Englewood Cliffs, NJ: Prentice–Hall.

Goffman, Erving (1963b) *Behavior in Public Places*. Glencoe, IL: The Free Press.

Goffman, Erving (1967) *Interaction Ritual*. New York: Doubleday.

Goodall, H.L. (2000) *Writing the New Ethnography*. Walnut Creek, CA: AltaMira.

Gubrium, Jaber F. and Holstein, James A. (1997) *The New Language of Qualitative Method*. New York: Oxford University Press.

Gusfield, J. (1967) 'Moral passage: the symbolic process in the public designations of deviance', *Social Problems*, 15: 175–88.

Gusfield, Joseph (1975) *Community: A Critical Response*. Oxford: Blackwell.

Hammersley, Martyn (1989) *The Dilemma of Qualitative Method: Herbert Blumer and the Chicago Tradition*. London: Routledge.

Hammersley, Martyn and Atkinson, Paul (1995) *Ethnography: Principles in Practice*, 2nd edn. London: Routledge.

Handler, R. (1988) *Nationalism and the Politics of Culture in Québec*. Madison, WI: University of Wisconsin Press.

Hannerz, Ulf (1969) *Soulside*. New York: Columbia University Press.

Hannerz, Ulf (1980) *Exploring the City*. New York: Columbia University Press.

Harvey, Lee (1987) *Myths of the Chicago School of Sociology*. Aldershot: Avebury.

Hernandez, Graciela (1995) 'Multiple subjectivities and strategic positionality', in R. Behar and D. Gordon (eds) *Women Writing Culture*. Berkeley, CA: University of California Press. pp. 148–66.

Heyl, Barbara (1979) *The Madam as Entrepreneur*. New Brunswick, NJ: Transaction Books.

Holstein, James A. and Gubrium, Jaber F. (2000) *Constructing the Life Course*. Dix Hills, NY: General Hall.

Hubble, Nick (1998) 'Walter Benjamin and the theory of Mass-Observation: surveillance contra surveillance at the first media coronation'. Unpublished paper, Surveillance Conference, Liverpool John Moores University, June 1998.

Hughes, Everett (1971) *The Sociological Eye: Selected Papers*. New York: Aldine–Atherton.

Jacob, Evelyn (1987) 'Qualitative research traditions', *Review of Educational Research*, 57 (1): 1–50.

Jennings, Humphrey and Madge, Charles (1937) *May the Twelfth: Mass-Observation Day Surveys 1937*. London: Faber and Faber.

James, A., Hockey, J. and Dawson, A. (eds) (1997) *After Writing Culture*. London: Routledge.

Jones, Stacy H. (1998) *Kaleidoscope Notes*. Walnut Creek, CA: AltaMira.

Josselson, Ruthellen (1996) *Revising Herself: The Story of Women's Identity from College to Midlife*. New York: Oxford University Press.

Josselson, Ruthellen and Lieblich, Amia (eds) (1995) *Interpreting Experience: The Narrative Study of Lives*. Thousand Oaks, CA: Sage.

Kirshenblatt-Gimblett, Barbara (1998) *Destination Culture: Tourism, Museums, and Heritage*. Berkeley, CA: University of California Press.

Klockars, Carl (1974) *The Professional Fence*. New York: The Free Press.

Kwon, Miwon (2000) 'Experience vs interpretation: traces of ethnography in the works of Lan Tanzon and Nikki S. Lee', in A. Coles (ed.) *Site-Specificity: The Ethnographic Turn*. London: Black Dog Publishing. pp. 74–91.

Lamphere, L. (ed.) (1992) *Structuring Diversity: Ethnographic Perspectives on the New Immigration*. Chicago: University of Chicago Press.

Lash, Scott and Urry, John (1994) *Economies of Signs and Space*. London: Sage.

Leininger, Madeleine (1992) 'Current issues, problems and trends to advance qualitative paradigmatic research for the future', *Qualitative Health Research*, 2 (4): 392–415.

Lieblich, Amia and Josselson, Ruthellen (eds) (1994) *Exploring Identity and Gender: The Narrative Study of Lives*. Thousand Oaks, CA: Sage.

Liebow, Elliott (1967) *Tally's Corner, Washington DC: A Study of Negro Streetcorner Men*. London: Routledge and Kegan Paul.

Lincoln, Yvonna and Denzin, Norman (1994) 'The Fifth Moment', in N. Denzin and Y. Lincoln (eds), *Handbook of Qualitative Research*. Thousand Oaks, CA: Sage.

Lofland, Lyn H. (1975) 'The "Thereness" of Women', in M. Millman and R. Kanter (eds), *Another Voice*. New York: Anchor.

Lofland, Lyn H. (1983) 'Understanding urban life: the Chicago legacy', *Urban Life*, 11 (4): 491–511.

Lofland, Lyn H. (1985 [1973]) *A World of Strangers: Order and Action in Urban Public Space*. Prospect Heights, IL: Waveland Press.

Lofland, Lyn H. (1998) *The Public Realm: Exploring the City's Quintessential Social Territory*. Hawthorne, NY: Aldine de Gruyter.

Lury, Celia (1996) *Consumer Culture*. Cambridge: Polity Press.

Lyman, Stanford and Scott, M. (1970) *A Sociology of the Absurd*. New York: Appleton–Century–Crofts.

MacCannell, Dean (1976) *The Tourist*. New York: Schocken.

Manis, Jerome G. and Meltzer, Bernard N. (eds) (1967) *Symbolic Interaction: A Reader in Social Psychology*. Boston, MA: Allyn and Bacon.

Manning, Philip (1992) *Erving Goffman and Modern Sociology*. Cambridge: Polity Press.

Mass-Observation (1937) *Mass-Observation*. London: Muller.

Mass-Observation (1939) *Britain by Mass-Observation*. Harmondsworth: Penguin.

Mauss, Marcel (1934) 'Techniques of the body', (republished in English translation). *Economy and Society*, 2: 70–88.

McClancy, Jeremy (1995) 'Brief encounter: the meeting, in Mass-Observation, of British surrealism and popular anthropology', *Journal of the Royal Anthropological Institute*, 1: 495–507.

Mellor, Philip A. and Shilling, Chris (1997) *Re-Forming the Body*. London: Sage.

Mienczakowski, Jim (2001) 'Ethnodrama: performed research', in P. Atkinson, A. Coffey, S. Delamont, J. Lofland and L. Lofland (eds), *Handbook of Ethnography*. London: Sage. pp. 468–76.

Miller, David L. (1973) *George Herbert Mead: Self, Language and the World*. Chicago: University of Chicago Press.

Mishler, Elliot G. (1999) *Storylines: Craftartists' Narratives of Identity*. Cambridge, MA: Harvard University Press.

Monaghan, Lee (1999) 'Creating the "perfect body"', *Body and Society*, 5 (2–3): 267–90.

Monaghan, Lee (2001) *Bodybuilding, Drugs and Risk*. London: Routledge.

Morris, Monica B. (1977) *An Excursion into Creative Sociology*. Oxford: Blackwell.

Olesen, Virginia and Whittaker, Elvi (1968) *The Silent Dialogue: A Study in the Social Psychology of Professional Socialization*. San Francisco: Jossey–Bass.

Oppenheim, Janet (1991) *'Shattered Nerves': Doctors, Patients, and Depression in Victorian England*. New York: Oxford University Press.

Park, Robert and Burgess, E. (1925) *The City*. Chicago: University of Chicago Press.

Parsons, Deborah L. (2000) *Streetwalking the Metropolis: Women, the City and Modernity*. Oxford: Oxford University Press.

Pink, Sarah (2001) *Doing Visual Ethnography.* London: Sage.

Platt, Jennifer (1999) *A History of Sociological Research Methods in America.* Cambridge: Cambridge University Press.

Plummer, Ken (2000) *Documents of Life 2: An Invitation to Critical Humanism.* London: Sage.

Plummer, Ken (2001) 'The call of life stories in ethnographic research', in P. Atkinson, A. Coffey, S. Delamont, J. Lofland and S. Lofland (eds) *Handbook of Ethnography.* London: Sage. pp. 395–406.

Putnam, Robert D. (2000) *Bowling Alone: The Collapse and Revival of American Community.* New York: Simon and Schuster.

Rapport, N. (1993) *Diverse World-Views in an English Village.* Edinburgh: Edinburgh University Press.

Reed-Danahay, Deborah (ed.) (1997) *Auto/Biography.* Oxford: Berg.

Rees, Alwyn (1950) *Life in a Welsh Countryside.* Cardiff: University of Wales Press.

Richardson, Laurel (1990) *Writing Strategies: Reaching Diverse Audiences.* Newbury Park, CA: Sage.

Richardson, Laurel (1994) 'Writing: a method of inquiry', in N.K. Denzin and Y. Lincoln (eds), *The Handbook of Qualitative Research.* Thousand Oaks, CA: Sage.

Riesman, David (1950) *The Lonely Crowd: A Study of the Changing American Character.* New Haven, CT: Yale University Press.

Riessman, Catherine K. (1990) *Divorce Talk: Women and Men Make Sense of Personal Relationships.* New Brunswick, NJ: Rutgers University Press.

Riessman, Catherine K. (1993) *Narrative Analysis.* Newbury Park, CA: Sage.

Rock, Paul (1979) *The Making of Symbolic Interactionism.* London: Macmillan.

Rojek, Chris (1995) *Decentring Leisure.* London: Sage.

Rose, Arnold M. (ed.) (1962) *Human Behavior and Social Processes.* London: Routledge and Kegan Paul.

Rosenberg, George (1978) *No Other Gods: On Science and American Social Thought.* Baltimore, MD: Johns Hopkins University Press.

Scheper-Hughes, Nancy (1977) *Saints, Scholars and Schizophrenics: Mental Illness in Rural Ireland.* Berkeley, CA: University of California Press.

Scheper-Hughes, Nancy (2001) *Saints, Scholars and Schizophrenics,* 2nd edn. Berkeley, CA: University of California Press.

Schmalenbach, Herman (1977) *On Society and Experience* (ed. and trans. G. Lüscher and G.P. Stone). Chicago: University of Chicago Press.

Schutz, Alfred (1967) *The Phenomenology of the Social World.* Chicago: Northwestern University Press.

Shaw, R. (1930) *The Jack-Roller: A Delinquent Boy's Own Story.* Chicago: University of Chicago Press.

Sheridan, Dorothy (ed.) (1990) *Wartime Women: A Mass-Observation Anthology.* London: Heinemann.

Shilling, Chris (1993) *The Body and Social Theory.* London: Sage.

Sibley, David (1995) *Geographies of Exclusion: Society and Difference in the West.* London: Routledge.

Silverman, David (2000) *Doing Qualitative Research: A Practical Handbook.* London: Sage.

Smith, Denis (1988) *The Chicago School: A Liberal Critique of Capitalism.* London: Macmillan.

Smith, Dorothy (1987) *The Everyday World as Problematic: A Feminist Sociology.* Toronto: University of Toronto Press.

Smith, Dorothy (1990) *The Conceptual Practices of Power.* Toronto: University of Toronto Press.

Smith, Dorothy (1999) *Writing the Social: Critique, Theory, and Investigations.* Toronto: University of Toronto Press.

Smith, Greg (ed.) (1999) *Goffman and Social Organization: Studies in a Sociological Legacy.* London: Routledge.

Spencer, Jonathan (2001) 'Ethnography after post-modernism', in P. Atkinson, A. Coffey, S. Delamont, J. Lofland and L. Lofland (eds), *Handbook of Ethnography.* London: Sage. pp. 443–52.

Stacey, Margaret (1975) 'The myth of community studies', in C. Lambert and D. Weir (eds), *Cities in Modern Britain.* London: Fontana. pp. 237–47.

Stanley, Liz (ed.) (1992) *The Auto/biographical I.* Manchester: Manchester University Press.

Stanley, Liz (2001) 'Mass-Observation's fieldwork methods', in P. Atkinson, A. Coffey, S. Delamont, J. Lofland and L. Lofland (eds), *Handbook of Ethnography.* London: Sage. pp. 92–108.

Stanley, Liz and Wise, Sue (1983) *Breaking Out.* London: Routledge and Kegan Paul.

Stanley, Liz and Wise, Sue (1993) *Breaking Out Again.* London: Routledge.

Strangleman, Tim, Hollywood, Emma, Beynon, Huw, Bennett, Katy and Hudson, Ray (1999) 'Heritage work: re-representing the work ethic in the coalfields', *Sociological Research Online,* 4: 3. <http://www.socresonline.org.uk/4/3/strangleman.html>.

Strathern, Marilyn (1981) *Kinship at the Core.* Cambridge: Cambridge University Press.

Suttles, Gerald (1968) *The Social Order of the Slum: Ethnicity and Territory in the Inner City.* Chicago: University of Chicago Press.

ten Have, Paul (1999) *Doing Conversation Analysis*. London: Sage.

Terkel, Studs (1970) *Hard Times: An Oral History of the Great Depression*. London: Allen Lane.

Terkel, Studs (1974) *Working*. Harmondsworth: Penguin.

Tester, Keith (ed.) (1994) *The Flâneur*. London: Routledge.

Thomas, W.I. (1923) *The Unadjusted Girl*. Boston, MA: Little, Brown & Co.

Thomas, W.I. and Znaniecki, F. (1918–1920) *The Polish Peasant in Europe and America,* 5 vols. Boston, MA: Richard G. Badger (vols 1 and 2 originally published by University of Chicago Press, 1918).

Thrasher, Frederic (1927) *The Gang: A Study of 1313 Gangs in Chicago*. Chicago: University of Chicago Press.

Toennies, Ferdinand (1957) *Community and Society*. New York: Harper and Row.

Turner, Bryan (1996) *The Body and Society*, 2nd edn. London: Sage.

Urry, John (1995) *Consuming Places*. London: Routledge.

Urry, John (2000) *The Tourist Gaze: Leisure and Travel in Contemporary Societies*, 2nd edn. London: Sage.

Van Maanen, John (1988) *Tales of the Field: On Writing Ethnography*. Chicago: University of Chicago Press.

Veblen, Thorsten (1899/1970) *The Theory of the Leisure Class*. London: Unwin.

Vidich, Arthur J. and Bensman, J. (1968) *Small Town in Mass Society: Class, Power and Religion in a Rural Community*, 2nd edn. Princeton, NJ: Princeton University Press.

Vidich, Arthur J. and Lyman, Stanford. (1994) 'Qualitative methods: their history in sociology and anthropology', in N.K. Denzin and Y. Lincoln (eds), *Handbook of Qualitative Research*. Thousand Oaks, CA: Sage. pp. 23–59.

Weinstein, Dana and Weinstein, Michael A. (1993) 'Georg Simmel: sociological *flâneur bricoleur*', in D. Weinstein and M.A. Weinstein (eds), *Postmodern(ized) Simmel*. London: Routledge.

Wengraf, Tom (2001) *Qualitative Research Interviewing*. London: Sage.

Whyte, William F. (1943) *Street Corner Society*. Chicago: University of Chicago Press.

Willett, Ralph (1996) *The Naked City: Urban Crime Fiction in the USA*. Manchester: Manchester University Press.

Williams, Raymond (1975) *The Country and the City*. London: Paladin.

Williams, Simon (2000) *Emotion and Social Theory*. London: Sage.

Williams, Simon (2002) 'Corporeal reflections on the biological: reductionism, constructionism and beyond?', in G. Bendelow, M. Carpenter, C. Vautier and S. Williams (eds), *Gender, Health and Healing*. London: Warwick. pp. 13–33.

Williams, Simon and Bendelow, Gillian (1998) *The Lived Body: Sociological Themes, Embodied Issues*. London: Routledge.

Williams, William M. (1956) *The Sociology of an English Village: Gosforth*. London: Routledge and Kegan Paul.

Williams, William M. (1963) *A West Country Village: Ashworthy*. London: Routledge and Kegan Paul.

Wilson, Elizabeth (1991) *The Sphinx in the City: Urban Life, the Control of Disorder, and Women*. London: Virago.

Wilson, Elizabeth (2001) *The Contradictions of Culture: Cities, Culture, Women*. London: Sage.

Wirth, Louis (1928) *The Ghetto*. Chicago: University of Chicago Press.

Wirth, Louis (1938) 'Urbanism as a way of life', *American Journal of Sociology*, 44 (1): pp. 1–24.

Wolf, M. (1992) *The Thrice-Told Tale: On Writing Ethnography*. Berkeley, CA: University of California Press.

Young, M. and Willmott, P. (1957) *Family and Kinship in East London*. London: Routledge and Kegan Paul.

Young, M and Willmott, P. (1973) *The Symmetrical Family*. Harmondsworth: Penguin.

Znaniecki, Florian (1934) *The Method of Sociology*. New York: Farrar and Rinehart.

Znaniecki, Florian (1940) *The Social Role of the Man of Knowledge*. New York: Columbia University Press.

Znaniecki, Florian (1969) *Florian Znaniecki on Humanistic Sociology* (ed. R. Bierstedt). Chicago: University of Chicago Press.

Zorbaugh, H. (1929) *The Gold Coast and the Slum*. Chicago: University of Chicago Press.

3

Sociology and Philosophy

RANDALL COLLINS

Sociology and philosophy are connected in at least three ways. First, genealogically, sociology branched off from the lineages of philosophers; and up through the present many of the most influential sociologists have been trained as philosophers. Second, philosophical issues are often raised inside sociology, especially epistemological probings and methodological attempts to legislate the character of sociological knowledge; there is also much exposing of and polemicizing over value questions, making sociology a semi-concretized version of philosophical ethics; and metaphysical questions are raised over the nature of social being, individuals, mind and action; in short, sociology has been a terrain for arguing philosphical questions in both activist and analytical modes. Third, reversing the relationship, philosophy has become a target for sociological research, theorizing the social conditions under which intellectuals have created philosophical topics and which shape what they think about them. The sociology of philosophy is related to earlier and parallel enterprises in the sociology of knowledge, sociology of scientific knowledge, and sociology of culture, as sociologists have aimed to explain all the productions of human consciousness.

And thus we come full circle. Given that sociology branches from philosophy, that philosophy protrudes its questions into sociology, and that sociology has turned back again to analyze philosophy as a social pattern, we can say that the sociology–philosophy relationship is a multiply reflexive one. Providing many layers of reflexive consciousness from one component upon another, the sociology – philosophy nexus exemplifies the hypermodern intellectual situation.

GENEALOGIES AND CROSS-OVERS

Sociology originated historically as a specialized branch breaking off from the older role of the philosopher. Early intellectuals were 'philosophical' in the sense that as unspecialized thinkers they dealt with questions at considerable levels of generality and without regard for boundaries among topics that would later be appropriated as distinctive territories. During times of transition many philosophers jettisoned the old scholarly identity for newer ones such as 'natural philosopher' or 'mechanical philosopher' – terms that in the nineteenth century became transmuted into 'scientist'; the eighteenth-century branching called 'moral philosophy' eventually became such fields as economics, statecraft/political science and psychology. During such times, it was repeatedly claimed that philosophy was disappearing, having been transformed into more advanced content. Descartes and his compatriots in the mid-1600s claimed that what they called the 'scholastic' philosophy of the old church-dominated universities was now superseded by the 'mechanical philosophy' of new mathematical science. Auguste Comte in the 1840s held that cultural history passes through the stages of theology, philosophy and positive science, of which sociology was the latest and crowning achievement. Ordinary language philosophers of the mid-twentieth century spearheaded by Wittgenstein and Austin attacked existing philosophy as a repository of conceptual mistakes to be cleared away; the chief merit of philosophy was that in dying it gave birth to new disciplines such as linguistics and cognitive sciences.

Philosophy has not disappeared through these transformations, but has usually gone on to a new round of creative innovation, digging more deeply into the core territory that becomes revealed as more empirically oriented disciplines have branched off. As philosophy ceased to claim knowledge of the natural world in the same manner as its empirical researchers, it found fruitful dimensions of argument by dealing with conceptual questions at a more abstract level, and with increasingly higher standards of criticism; philosophy has come to take as its turf the most reflexive intellectual enterprises, examining both its own standards of knowledge, and the knowledge claims of all the surrounding disciplines. Its genealogical children, in leaving home, continue to support their philosophical parents, in part because their activities as research scientists, mathematicians, historians, economists and sociologists now provide topics for philosophers who have stayed on the old home base to criticize and examine. Although Cartesians and Baconians held that philosophy had been superseded by mathematical or empirical research, there was room for moves like Berkeley's and Hume's to critique the very basis of belief in scientific findings, and thence for countermoves like Kant, with its chain of consequences for opening up new philosophical terrain. This is a characteristic long-term pattern; the generations following Descartes were highly creative in the abstract core of philosophy, as the new epistemological sharpening opened up innovations

in metaphysics as well. In the same way, later branching between philosophy and the social disciplines did not merely empty out the last contents of philosophical wine cellars, as Comte had proclaimed, but provided a richer field of interaction between new social-scientific disciplines and the increasingly sophisticated reflections of philosophers.

Sociology, as a self-conscious discipline taking as its turf the social, studied by all empirical means in conjunction with theoretical ones, branched off relatively late, even by comparison to other social sciences. Sociology had a complicated genealogy, with its canonical 'founders' coming from a variety of fields. Comte trained as a mathematical scientist at the École Polytechnique; Lester Ward was employed as a geologist; Herbert Spencer was a journalist who found his materials in the evolutionist circle around Darwin; Pareto was an engineer, who shifted to mathematical economics and then devised a sociology to fill in the irrational side left incomplete by the rational-utilitarian side of his work. It is striking that the most influential sociological theorists were those who were trained by philosophers, even as they added other ingredients through their networks of teachers or early career contacts. Consider the 'big five': Marx, Durkheim, Weber, Simmel and Mead.

Marx was intellectually initiated around 1840 in the circle of Young Hegelians. His teacher (Bruno Bauer) and colleagues (Feuerbach, Stirner, Ruge, D.F. Strauss) were Hegel's pupils; his collaborator Friedrich Engels had attended the lectures of Schelling. Marx began in one wing of a movement in the late 1830s/early 1840s, breaking away from the prior generation of Idealists, above all by criticizing the Idealist defense of theology, while transforming the line of argument into a critique of social conditions. Since intellectuals find their distinctive positions – and reputations – by playing off of each other, Marx and Engels went on to critique their fellows (in *The German Ideology*) for remaining too close to a theological world-view, and eventually formulated their own radical slot as dialectical materialism. They were able to do this by combining some aspects of Hegelian (and Fichtean) philosophy – the logical clash of thesis, antithesis and higher synthesis; history as the successive moments of alienation of the spirit from its potentiality for liberation – with quite different intellectual streams in English economics and French radical politics.

Marx and Engels made their move to materialism at just the time that a larger movement sweeping the German academic world did the same; in the late 1840s and 1850s German scientists revolted against *Naturphilosophie*, the Idealist theories of natural phenomena such as electricity, chemical attraction, and living beings; some took an extremely strong stance that only material forces exist and that all spiritual phenomena are to be reduced to them through scientific research. This movement (whose most radical leaders were the scientists Büchner and Moleschott) acquired a material base insofar as German universities now split off a *Naturwissenschaftliches Fakultät* (Faculty of Natural Science) with its own chairs independent of the *Philosophische Fakultät*. Materialist reductionism was a central strand in the writings of Marx and Engels; it was only in the 1930s when their early writings from the Young Hegelian milieu were rediscovered that the Idealist themes began to come to the fore again. And it was in the 1960s and thereafter, with a new generation of intellectual radicals, and in connection with philosophical ingredients from existentialism and phenomenology, that Marx became the canonical referent for a spiritual rather than economic liberation, as his texts became taken as grounds for erotic, gender and ethnic insurgent movements.

Max Weber, educated in the1880s, inhabited a very different milieu. He was a pupil of Wilhelm Dilthey and the colleague of Wilhelm Windelband and Heinrich Rickert; which is to say, he was in the midst of the Neo-Kantians who had revived philosophy in Germany after the materialist onslaught. The Neo-Kantian tactic was to delineate the spheres between academic disciplines according to each's logic of investigation; a typical distinction was between the *Geisteswissenschaften* (the spiritual or humanistic sciences) and the *Naturwissenschaften* (natural sciences), regarded not as a difference in content but in the concepts through which contents are delineated. Weber's methodological

writings for the social sciences (written 1906–1919, translation in Weber, 1949) were straightforwardly Neo-Kantian. Sociology belongs to the *Geisteswissenschaften* and thus its contents are subject to interpretation through categories of meaningful human action, not to causal explanation in the mode of the natural sciences. Weber found his distinctive subject matter in adjudicating the *Methodenstreit* (the struggle of methods), which pitted German-style historical economics against English and Austrian formal economic theory. In good Neo-Kantian style, Weber held that the theoretical concepts of formal economics could be validly used but only as ideal types for the analysis of human action, with the understanding that these are only lenses through which the observer formulates a one-sided picture of the infinite particulars of human history. Weber created his own sociology as a set of these one-sided ideal types (such as bureaucracy *vs.* patrimonial organization; class *vs.* status group) as a means of understanding how the capitalist economy as presented in economic theory could have historically developed.

Weber advocated a value-free stance in scholarship, as opposed to taking a partisan political stand; his point, again in the Neo-Kantian spirit, is that the value-free stance is an orientation on the part of the observer that serves to define a disciplinary subject matter; not that another way of slicing up the world is impossible, such as by political orientation, but conversely one cannot claim that all thought is intrinsically politicized. For Weber these are choices among observational stances. After the 1960s, Weber's choice became an unfashionable one, but other aspects of his interpretative methodology became widely advocated. Other sociologists developed Weber's substantive work on capitalism and other topics, jettisoning the Neo-Kantian methodology; the divergence in interpretations of Weber himself illustrates the point that the same subject matter can be developed in different manners by different observers.

Georg Simmel also was trained in the Neo-Kantian movement; he shared the same teacher – Dilthey – with Weber. Simmel also was a pupil of Franz Brentano, who held that consciousness always intends or posits objects (the 'intentionality of consciousness'), a position developed by other Brentano pupils (including Husserl) who formulated phenomenology. Simmel, who taught for most of his career in low-ranking lectureships in philosophy (in contrast to Weber, who became a professor of historical economics), ranged widely across the fields of culture and aesthetics, demonstrating in Neo-Kantian fashion their formal properties. Simmel was much less of a full-time sociologist than Weber became. Whereas Weber applied Neo-Kantian philosophy mainly in epistemological writings on methodology, Simmel applied it to sociology substantively. For Simmel sociology is the study of the formal properties of sociation; thus he wrote about the forms of conflict, the web of association (what would now be called network analysis), and the formal properties of groups with differing numbers of members. This work later became detached from its philosophical framework when it was developed by empirical researchers.

Durkheim was trained by philosophers but in contrast to his German sociological contemporaries advocated a sharper break between the fields, even reversing their positions so that sociology would pass judgment on philosophy. In his generation, the French academic system was undergoing reform to eliminate religious control; spiritualist philosophers associated with political conservatism were opposed by secularist reformers, among whom Durkheim took a leading position (Collins, 1998: ch. 14; Fabiani, 1988). Nevertheless, he was trained at the elite École Normale Supérieure by the neo-spiritualist philosopher Émile Boutroux, who also taught Durkheim's classmate Henri Bergson; young Durkheim went on to Germany to study with Wundt, who had just founded psychology as a laboratory science and thereby exemplified the pathway for breaking off a social science from philosophy. Durkheim determined to do the same with sociology; his emphasis on the *sui generis* character of sociological explanations and his opposition to explanations in terms of psychological or biological conditions was part of his strategy for creating sociology as an academic discipline independent of these rivals.

Of all the founding sociologists, Durkheim was most concerned to turn the tools of sociology back upon the philosophy from which it had emerged (Durkheim 1898–1911/1953). In *The Elementary Forms of the Religious Life* (1912), he held that sociology can resolve the conflict inside philosophy between empiricism in the style of the British (for example, Hume), who grounded all knowledge of reality in individual sensory experience; and Idealism in the style of Kant, which privileges the screen of mental categories through which all reality is observed. Drawing upon ethnographic comparisons of religion as in the tribal rites of Australian aborigines, Durkheim noted that the Kantian categories of the understanding – time, space, causality – mirror the differences among forms of social organization. The Idealists are right in seeing categories as external and prior to individual experience; but the empiricists are wrong in taking the isolated individual as the starting point of perception and reflection on the world. The categories of perception and the reality of experience are given simultaneously, because those categories arise through social experience. The collective rites that make up the practice of religion exemplify the moments of intense interaction that generate symbols representing membership in the group; these symbols also become the ingredients of world-views, and mental tools which individuals can carry with them as their own minds.

Durkheim's position, establishing the connection between collective symbolism and social structure, was developed by a series of colleagues, pupils and grandpupils, including the linguist Ferdinand de Saussure, Marcel Mauss and Claude Lévi-Strauss, a lineage which eventually became the structuralist movement. French structuralism in the 1950s and 1960s, in conjunction with semiotics and phenomenology, took a quasi-idealist turn rather different from Durkheim's own emphasis on the material reality of human bodies interacting upon an ecological terrain; for the structuralists and especially their post-structuralist successors, the structural code determines social action, even acting as a deeply constraining form of power (a position argued by Foucault 1969/1990). For a lineage of Durkheimian sociologists, on the other hand, it is the social structure of human interaction that determines symbolic codes and their changes (notably, on the macro level, Swanson and Mary Douglas; on the micro level, Goffman and Collins). Durkheim's argument has also been revived as a position solving epistemological problems inside philosophy by Anne Rawls (2005).

George Herbert Mead, the most influential American social theorist, spent his entire career as a philosophy professor. He grew up intellectually in the midst of the pragmatist movement, as a protégé of William James, Royce and Dewey (and thus as grandpupil of Peirce). Mead combined this pragmatist lineage with his own connections with the new experimental psychologists, including Wundt in Germany, and Mead's militant young colleague at Chicago, John B. Watson, the founder of behaviorism. Idealism (exemplified by Royce, and the early work of Peirce and Dewey) had been prominent in America at the time that American universities were breaking free from the old religious colleges, since Idealism was acceptable as a transition from biblical Christianity to a spiritualized quasi-secularism; in the following generation, as secularism came to dominance, pragmatism developed as a further transition from spiritualism to science. Psychology proved attractive to the pragmatists (James and Dewey were both active in the field) because it could be interpreted as a scientific field in which the subject was nevertheless active and dynamic rather than fixed and static, and in which the spiritual qualities of the human mind were vindicated scientifically. Mead developed a theory of the human mind as evolving from the naturalistic interaction of human animals; symbolic language emerges from gestures indicating intentions to act, and thought developed as internalized conversation between the parts of the self and a Generalized Other.

Mead was primarily concerned not with constructing a sociology but with using his social theory of mind to answer long-standing philosophical questions (e.g. Mead, 1932, 1938).

For example, the existence of universals can be explained without either inducing them from particulars or presupposing them as Platonic essences. Universals exist in the natural world because human beings make particular experiences equivalent by marking them out with recurrent symbolic gestures towards them; it is the capacity to think against the frame of a Generalized Other which brings universals into existence. Further levels of human meaning emerge; no longer limited to physical interaction among bodies, humans who have acquired their own internal conversations and Generalized Others now interact by imaginatively taking the role of the other and interpreting one's own actions from the other's viewpoint.

Mead's work was little published during his own lifetime, and was generally ignored by most psychologists and philosophers, who were then taking other directions. It was a sociologist, Herbert Blumer, who assisted in Mead's courses at Chicago, and after Mead's death in 1931 formulated a sociology which he called symbolic interactionism. Blumer developed this as a theory and methodology for empirical research; the movement became prominent in the 1950s and 1960s as an alternative to narrowly positivisitic quantitative research methods promoted by incursions from the Vienna Circle. On the methodological side, ethnographies and sensitivity to meaningful interpretations of human actors should take precedence over quantitative measurement and depersonalized objectivity. On the theoretical side, symbolic interactionists emphasized ongoing process and the potential for emergence as against static structures and restraints, especially as the latter were formulated in functionalist theory. Symbolic interactionism thus appealed to social reformers and to the generation of political activists of the 1960s, although its rather straightforward empiricism and its growing detachment from philosophical roots made it vulnerable to being upstaged by newer intellectual movements in the following decades.

More recent sociologists strongly influenced by philosophy include Harold Garfinkel, a student both of Talcott Parsons (and thus oriented to the theoretical problems of Durkheim and Weber) and of Alfred Schutz (concerned with applying Husserlian phenomenology to the social world). Garfinkel's ethnomethodology (1967), with its sometimes startling methods for piercing the taken-for-granted constructs of everyday life, may be regarded as a hybrid, carrying out philosophical investigations by means of extremely detailed empirical research. Major French sociologists, such as Pierre Bourdieu and Bruno Latour, were also trained in philosophy, giving their works a claim of wide theoretical generality and an ongoing engagement with philosophical issues. This combination is far more characteristic of the Parisian intellectual community than of American sociologists, who tend to be better funded for empirical research and thus to work in narrower disciplinary specializations; British sociology, which was institutionalized in the academic world rather late (mostly after the 1960s), has imported orientations from both French and Americans.

Finally, we should note that a number of individuals who are read as sociological theorists have no training in sociology and little acquaintance with sociological research. For example, Jürgen Habermas is a German philosopher trained by a pupil of Heidegger, but also by members of the Frankfurt School whose Marxist orientation introduced sociological themes. Habermas's work, such as his well-known theory of communicative action (1984), is the attempt to solve the epistemological problem of truth, and the ethical problem of egalitarian democracy, by importing both Anglophone language philosophy and sociological concepts of thinking (and therefore truth-claims) as a process of social interaction. Unsurprisingly, Habermas's theory has been criticized by micro-sociologists for its idealized picture of communication and its crude misunderstandings of the work of Goffman and of the ethnomethodologists. Postmodernists such as Lyotard (1979) built on a series of internal debates within structuralism by importing and widening the sociological notion of a post-industrial society. The border between philosophy and sociology has thus been crossed at many points in the past, and likely will continue to be so in the future.

PHILOSOPHICAL ISSUES IN SOCIOLOGY

In the 1980s and 1990s it became fashionable to say that borders and distinctions do not exist; but this is merely a form of rhetoric, at best a claim made within intellectual politics that hybrids should predominate over local specialists. The fact that borders are social constructs makes them none the less real, as realms of human action; in this case they are separations among regions in intellectual attention space, organized around departments with distinctive sources of funding and independent control over careers. In Bourdieu's terms, we can say they are distinctive regions in the field of intellectual production. From the point of view of the sociology of knowledge, it is hardly surprising that different organizational bases should promote differences in intellectual practice. Let us remind ourselves of what these differences chiefly are.

Sociology has its own substantive theories and research practices. Although philosophy lends a particular emphasis to abstract questions, these are not equivalent to theory *per se*. Sociology is organized around its own topics the study of which constitutes its own social practice: stratification, organizations, social interaction, social movements, population, conflict, and more specialized institutional areas (sociology of the family, education, crime, race and ethnicity, culture, and many others). Some of the theories used in analyzing these topics were originated by sociologists who had training in philosophy, but Weberian, Durkheimian, symbolic interactionist, neo-Marxist and other forms of sociological theory have developed far beyond the philosophical tenets of their founders. And even in Weber and Durkheim, for example, we can distinguish between their philosophical tools, and their substantive theories (such as Weber's theory of the institutional conditions for rationalized capitalism, or Durkheim's theory of the division of labor). Sociological theory-making is an ongoing enterprise that develops according to its own local conditions.

Contrast this distinctively sociological terrain with the topics at the core of philosophical attention space:

1 Epistemology, the theory of knowledge, investigating and questioning truth.
2 Metaphysics, the theory of being and its modes, the general treatment of all that might be claimed to have reality.
3 Value theory, including ethics, aesthetics and other questions about realms of obligation or evaluation.

Philosophy is a meta-discipline, in the sense that it can reflexively examine the contents or methods of all the other disciplines; in so doing they are not necessarily intervening in those disciplines, since philosophers raise their questions on a high level of generality and in relation to their own field of discourse, which implicitly relates any local question in a particular discipline to a larger philosophical tradition.

From time to time philosophers like Kant have made the move of claiming that their philosophical intervention was necessary to shore up the empirical sciences and save them from fatal flaws. But those flaws are ones which philosophers have ferreted out for purposes of arguments in their own attention space. There is no reason to believe that eighteenth-century science would not have carried on with its substantive discoveries whether Kant had given it epistemological 'foundations' or not. In the same way, neither sociologists nor members of any other research field are constrained to listen to what philosophers tell them; pragmatically, members of any intellectual community are capable of generating their own methods and producing interesting findings and theories out of their own invention. Garfinkel's 'breaching experiments' (1967), which launched ethnomethodology; or Goffman's innovative style of using micro-sociological observations (e.g. Goffman, 1961, 1974), were certainly not what was prescribed in methodological textbooks, and indeed violated the philosophical standards prevailing at the time (under the influence of logical positivism); such examples show that philosophical rules are likely to be constraints that must be broken or ignored by sociologists pushing the frontiers of knowledge. As a social enterprise, sociology (or economics, or biology, etc.) has its own resources and would not falter as an organized intellectual activity if philosophers were to disappear (and vice versa).

Border crossings only have meaning insofar as they are few; most practitioners stay within local attention spaces, thus setting up a contrast by which we can pick out the hybrids who do the border crossing. In the previous section I have listed how some of the classic sociologists imported philosophical orientations into the substantive topics that are the empirical focus of sociology. It has not been only thinkers of star reputation who have brought in philosophical issues; this has happened repeatedly, and in recent decades sociologists have frequently argued over issues that are palpably more akin to philosophical issues than to the core topics of sociological research. Now we seem to face a contradiction: can it be the case, as I have argued, both that sociology is well off going its own way without direction from philosophy, and also that philosophical intrusions have shaped some of the most important sociological developments?

Let us separate the question into the influence of epistemological, metaphysical and value theory issues in sociology.

First, epistemological issues in sociology have most typically come in the form of methodological arguments as to how sociologists should do their research. In the 1940s through the 1960s, American methods textbooks were written from the viewpoint of logical positivists, often émigrés from the Vienna Circle; in defense of their own methods, symbolic interactionists struck back by formulating their own philosophical justification; their successors have drawn implicitly on the German Idealist, Neo-Kantian and phenomenological traditions. In *The Sociological Imagination* (1959), C. Wright Mills issued a manifesto for the right of sociologists to invent their own methods according to the problems they face, thereby repudiating the claim of methodologists and meta-commentators of any stripe to legislate what sociologists do.

That is, sociological methods are inherently neither interpretive, subjectivist and focussed on the standpoint of the actor, nor materialist, structural, quantitative or objectivist. The sociologist's one rule is 'get on with it!' following whatever theoretical and empirical pathways seem fruitful; the best justification comes by finding out where they lead.

Mills's advice, essentially a form of pragmatism, still holds in the face of claims at epistemological legislation inside sociology that have been promulgated in recent decades. Poststructuralist and postmodernist philosophers have become influential in many academic disciplines, among other reasons through their adoption by some (but not all) branches of feminist and other insurgent liberationist movements. In this way the stance has become popular that the search for theoretical 'foundations' is an outdated historical relic, and that knowledge is necessarily situated, local, perspectival and (in the eyes of some positions) transitory. It is too little recognized by its partisans that the intellectual sources of this poststructuralist position are a particular blend of philosophical traditions – notably the Hegelian revival which took place in French thinking from the 1930s onwards, along with existentialism, phenomenology, a rather dogmatic Freudianism and the non-materialist aspects of Marxism – and that these are merely one possible choice of philosophical positions. The postmodernist move to exclude systematic theorizing, comparative research, formal modeling and other such options are another case of trying to impose restrictions from 'on high'. Sociologists engaged in their own research and their own theorizing have no obligation to obey restrictions, whether from positivists, interpretivists, phenomenologists, postmodernists, or anyone else except those who are willing to argue it out alongside them on the substantive level of their research.

The epistemological origins of the classic sociologists were not their enduring contributions to sociology. Weber's ideal type method may have helped to orient his own work – and even more likely have given him cover from the prevailing philosophies of the time, under which he could pursue wide-ranging substantive theories based on world comparisons; what Weber turned up in these researches has been transposed into parts of sociology far removed from his Neo-Kantian origins. It is much the same with the research traditions flowing from Marx, Mead and others. The bottom line on epistemological intrusions into sociology is: sometimes they open up new orientations on how to develop sociological work – as in the case of the phenomenology imported by Garfinkel which became an arena of ethnomethodological research with its own emergent theories such as conversation analysis. When epistemological orientations open up new areas, they are creative; when they are restrictive and exclusionary, they are drags upon the possibilities of sociological discovery.

Secondly, metaphysical issues in sociology concern the nature of social being, and thus the kind of concepts implicated in sociological theorizing. Among such issues have been debates over the primacy and reality of micro and macro; and over functionalism versus the motives of individual actors (the latter having evolved from Homans's critique of Parsons into present-day rational choice theory). These have been debates over the ontological reality of individuals versus groups. Further variants have been concerned with long-distance and long-run pressures and structural interconnections vis-à-vis the exigencies of local situations. In these debates, metaphysical errors are often charged against opponents, especially the reciprocal errors of reification (by opponents of high-order structures) and of reductionism (by opponents of low-level independent units). Other issues in social ontology are the existence and explanation of mind, consciousness and culture, vis-à-vis contrary theoretical conceptions which explain such phenomena in terms of ideology, material interests and resources, emotion, evolutionary genetics, or ecology. Given these ingredients, it has been possible to construct a wide mixture of theoretical positions including intermediate ones such as the multi-dimensionality of embodied social action (Rojek and Turner, 2000). The range of positions is too wide to be surveyed here, let alone pull out their philosophical resonances and offer comments on their lines of development and possible future resolution.

In answer to the question raised above, whether philosophical intrusions in sociology are creative or restrictive, the answer is different for metaphysics than for epistemology: whereas epistemological intrusions have often been more restrictive than facilitating, metaphysical issues have broadened the range of sociological theory. A caveat still holds: metaphysical issues in sociology have often been argued out in polemical tones, as if the correct stance on social ontology determines what our truths will be. This overstates the influence of high-level conceptualization in drawing boundaries around the thinkable and the unthinkable. The ongoing process of sociologists engaged in research and in formulating and reformulating theories to encompass their findings has often outstripped whatever metaphysical conceptions may have been popular even a few years earlier.

Finally, issues of value theory. These include issues of *cui bono*, who is and who should be the beneficiary of sociological research; stripping away putative ideological biases in theoretical conceptions; the ethics of the research process itself as it looks into or interferes with the lives of its subjects; and the issue of whether sociological theory should (or indeed must) be politically éngagé or whether it can stand aloof from partisan viewpoints. Sociologists who argue such issues are typically unreflexive about the sources of their own motivations. (On the historical development of moral reflexivity generally, see Collins, 2000b.) Ultimately, moral stances do not rest on reasoned argument; they arise as commitments in particular kinds of social communities (but see also Joas, 2000). The moral claims for activist and engagé sociology appear to arise from participation in social movements (although this has not been adequately studied sociologically), or in social service professions. On the other side, commitments to the value of theorizing and research for their own sake, for the advance of sociological knowledge or for the excitement of discovering new visions of the social world, also arise in social communities: those movements of intellectuals fighting

it out over the center of action inside an intellectual attention space.

The activists are right in saying there is no such thing as an uncommitted, value-free position; but they are blinkered in thinking that the only kinds of commitments and values are those of political activists, and that the political realm, or the practice of social services, are the only social arenas in which values can arise. The concern for finding truth, or more open-endedly, for pressing the frontiers of intellectual discovery, are also value commitments. Competing value commitments, as Weber (following Rickert) noted, struggle over whose project will dominate; this is the case today, and has been the case throughout much of the history of sociology. Once again, it is possible to make a plea for a non-exclusionary stance: rather than decreeing that only political value commitments should exist, or that only the pure scholarly goals are of value, we might find it desirable to have a sociological community which is tolerant of the variety of such value stances among its members.

FROM SOCIOLOGY OF KNOWLEDGE, THROUGH SOCIOLOGY OF SCIENCE, TO SOCIOLOGY OF PHILOSOPHY

Philosophy may be analyzed as a social institution: as a network of persons interacting and reproducing a pattern of discourse across the generations. The sociology of philosophy is an offspring of the older sociology of knowledge, and a cousin of its other contemporary branches. In Durkheim's sociology of knowledge, the structure of society as a whole shapes the ideas and beliefs of its members. We may narrow the analysis to the social community of philosophers, to show how their changing organization produces corresponding changes in philosophical ideas. Another version of the sociology of knowledge stems from Marx and Engels's (1846/1947) thesis that the production of ideas is determined by the material means of intellectual production. Marx and Engels were concerned to show that class ownership of these means of intellectual production ensured that the dominant ideas would be an ideology favoring the dominant class (for the debates over this issue, see Abercrombie et al., 1980); but the question of who owns or controls these means is separable from the more fruitful proposition that the material organization of intellectual and cultural life is what shapes ideas. Mannheim (1929/1936) went on to elaborate a model of the various kinds of ideologies corresponding to the interests of different social groups, while holding out the possibility for a 'free-floating' intelligentsia who acquire their own social bases (as in educational systems) and thus are able to provide objective, ideology-transcending ideas.

One branch of research came to focus on the sociology of science. Initially this was a study of the community of scientists, analyzing their norms, forms of organization, competition over original discoveries, and their outpouring of publications (Hagstrom, 1965; Merton, 1973; Price, 1963/1986). In the 1970s, an ambitious program calling itself 'sociology of scientific knowledge' or 'SSK' argued that sociology should explain not only the social context in which knowledge is discovered but the contents of that knowledge itself. David Bloor (1976, 1983) and Barry Barnes (1975) formulated the 'Strong Programme' which held that the task of the sociologist of science is not merely to show how social factors lead to the production of ideological or false knowledge, but to true knowledge as well (the 'symmetry principle'). That is to say, sociology is not merely a study of how social factors bias the process of scientific discovery, but how the formulation of truths is socially shaped. Sociology thus acquired an ambitious research program, not merely to show the external social conditions which allow the autonomous quest for truth to proceed, but to go inside the laboratory like an anthropologist visiting a strange tribe without assuming any knowledge of the validity of its beliefs, seeking the social conditions by which its truth-beliefs are produced. This was first, and most famously, done by Latour and Woolgar (1983).

SSK raised in an acute form the philosophical or meta-theoretical problem of reflexivity. If sociology can investigate the social conditions for scientific truth, what does this say for the character of its own sociological truths? Is SSK (and indeed all of sociology) self-undermining (Ashmore, 1989)? It is too little appreciated that self-reflexive statements may sometimes be self-exemplifying rather than self-undermining. To say 'I am lying' is a self-undermining paradox (and ancestor to famous paradoxes of early twentieth-century logicist philosophy such as Russell's paradox); but to say 'I am telling the truth' is reflexive but self-reinforcing.

Two notable solutions to the problem of social reflexivity of truth are Latour (1987) and Fuchs (2001). Latour notes on empirical grounds that scientists are oriented in part towards the research frontier, in part towards past bodies of codified knowledge. The first, which Latour calls 'science in the making', is a mode in which scientists are contentious among rival hypotheses, and denigrate their opponents by accusing them of using political tactics to win adherents, funding and research equipment. At the frontier, science is epistemologically open and relativistic. Once a victor has been established in the struggle, however, the black box is closed so that the sordid details of how the discovery had been socially organized are no longer looked into; the idea-contents become items of accepted knowledge, uncontroversial 'facts' which now are propagated in textbooks, taught to students and displayed as achievements to lay people outside the scientific community. This is 'science already made'. (See also Kim (1996) on the role which second-level scientists play in adopting one research program or another and thus determining the victor.) In keeping with the symmetrical principle of the Strong Programme, Latour does not express an epistemological preference between 'science in the making' and 'science already made'; both are observable social patterns, and the most comprehensive and defensible statement one can make about science is that it has two faces, relativistic and socially constructive, but also consensual and objectivistic, and that given items of knowledge pass from one to the other as the research frontier moves onwards.

Stephan Fuchs's (2001) solution may be called a network-location theory of the observer. It is the stance of observers occupying different positions within social networks that determines which distinctions they make. Tightly connected and self-enclosed networks see the world in terms of essences, sharply defined realities; loosely connected, decentralized networks see the world as fluid and relativistic; in between these extremes, category schemes have greater or lesser essentialism or relativism. Over time, networks may transform, so that new, contentious, open networks become solidified into cores which make fixed realities out of their beliefs; conversely, the cores of old networks can break apart and confident realism can shift toward greater relativism. A second key point is the relation between the network in which an observer is located and the network that is being observed; when these locations are close together the interpretations are nuanced and individualized, but when they are distant the interpretations become simplified essences.

A case in point is the 'science wars' of the 1990s between the new constructivist sociology of science allied with radical feminism, standpoint theory, and deconstructionist literary theory on one side, against defenders of the truthfulness, realism and impartiality of the natural sciences on the other (Gross and Levitt, 1994). Fuchs points out how the debate is carried on in terms of dichotomous essences, using popular ideologies on both sides: the defenders of science presenting its idealized Goffmanian frontstage, its attackers tearing away the facade and declaring there is nothing there but another form of privilege and arbitrary power. Both sides are debating over stereotypes; science is not a fixed entity but a variety of fields and subfields with different levels of network tightness or looseness, hence promoting scientific ideas which vary in the realism or relativism with which they are regarded by the scientists themselves. It is the same with technology: here again there is a continuum, historically ever-changing, between the tightly encapsulated techniques in stable networks that work reliably, and technologies in transition where the networks of machines and their users are in flux. For Fuchs, science can neither be replaced with social activism nor reduced to physical objects or brain neurons; these are endpoints of different kinds of network structures, but the world of science is a large number of networks in flux between the extremes.

Sociology of cultural production

Another contemporary offshoot of classical sociology of knowledge is the sociology of cultural production. The most comprehensive theoretical statement, and also the one supported by a program of research, is Bourdieu's *The Field of Cultural Production* (1993). Bourdieu views each branch of culture as the product of a social field, that is, a community of specialists with mutual relations among themselves – whether these be intellectuals, artists, dramatists, couturiers, or other cultural specialists. The internal structure of a field of cultural production is shaped along two main axes. One is the 'horizontal' axis of relative autonomy or heteronomy of orientation; that is, the extent to which practitioners are oriented internally towards each other and their own standards, problems and criteria of prestige, or externally towards their audiences, consumers and patrons (that is, 'lay' people who are not themselves cultural producers). The second axis is the 'vertical' ranking between the prestigious elite whose works have been canonized as classics of art, literature, science, philosophy and the like, as against the avant-garde of the new generation struggling to displace them.

The structure of a field of cultural production is not reducible to the surrounding class structure (which Bourdieu calls the 'field of power'), since it operates by its own specific logic; cultural products are not simply ideologies reflecting class interests. Nevertheless, Bourdieu gives a qualified Marxian conclusion, arguing that there is a 'homology' or correspondence between the structure of relations inside the field of cultural production and the structure of class relations outside; there is an attraction between dominant social classes and canonized cultural works inside the field, and between subordinated classes and the avant-garde struggling to revolutionize culture. As an instance, Bourdieu (1975/1991) attempts to show that Heidegger's philosophy, although formulated in terms of ingredients internal to the generational conflict within the German philosophical field (a phenomenological avant-garde *vs.* the Neo-Kantian establishment), corresponded to the concerns of the lower-middle class disgruntled by modernization who allegedly made up the supporters of the Nazi movement. Bourdieu's principle of the homology among fields is an extension of structuralist theory (promoted by Lévi-Strauss and ultimately deriving from Durkheim) pressed into service of a quasi-Marxian theory of ideological hegemony.

INTELLECTUAL CREATIVITY AS STRUGGLE TO DIVIDE A LIMITED ATTENTION SPACE

Collins's *Sociology of Philosophies* (1998; for a précis, see Collins, 2000a) shares Bourdieu's focus on a self-oriented field of cultural producers, which Collins describes as an 'attention space'. But Collins parts company with Bourdieu in rejecting the adequacy of connecting internal intellectual positions to external class ideologies via a principle of structural homology among fields. The basis of Collins's argument is an historical analysis of the networks of masters and pupils, colleagues and rivals that make up the internal structure of the communities of philosophers across major periods of world history: ancient and medieval China; medieval and early modern Japan; ancient and medieval India; ancient Greece; the medieval Islamic and Jewish world; medieval Christendom; and modern Europe through the early twentieth century. The structure of an attention space is its division into a number of factions according to a 'law of small numbers' which shapes the positions intellectuals occupy as they struggle among themselves for a limited amount of recognition available at any one time. In philosophy, innovators are not generally disprivileged

avant-gardes situated on the margins, but typically come from the heart of the previous elite generation, 'revolts within the citadel'. Classes and political power do not influence ideas so much by correspondence to ideological interests, as by their intermediating effects on changes in the material conditions supporting intellectual life, which force wholesale rearrangements in the factions dividing up intellectual attention space.

The theory of intellectual attention space may be summarized in the following points.

1   Intellectual creativity is concentrated in chains of personal contact. Those who become famous philosophers typically are pupils of those already famous, and/or friends or colleagues early in their careers of those who will also go on to achieve fame. It is typical for a group of young intellectuals to move up together, like the young roommates Hegel, Schelling and Hölderlin who made contact with Fichte at the beginning of his career and went on to become the most famous figures in a closely networked movement of German Idealism and Romanticism; or again, the young Sartre, with his friends de Beauvoir, Merleau-Ponty, Canguilhem, Aron and Lacan, whose lively discussion group became the core of existentialism and its offspring movements in France. From a network viewpoint, prior creativity appears to spark off further creativity, giving a strategic advantage to persons who start off close to the prior centers of intellectual action. This tendency towards network inheritance is mitigated by two further social patterns: creativity is concentrated not only in vertical chains from generation to generation, but horizontally among groups of contemporaries who collectively spawn intellectual movements; and old intergenerational networks are sometimes broken off as changes in material conditions open up opportunities for new networks to form. Sometimes the latter pattern predominates over the former, as we see in point (6) below.

2   Creativity is a collective product of the emotional energy of persons intensely oriented to each other face-to-face. That is to say, what intellectuals on their way to becoming successful

get from each other is not merely cognitive, the passing along of privileged cultural capital, but emotional, an excited buzz of attention upon the forefront of arguments and opportunities for developing new ideas. Success in intellectual creativity cannot be simply a matter of being the recipient of received ideas, no matter their canonical status; to preserve such ideas would make one an epigone, not an independent thinker constructing a reputation in one's own right.

3 Creativity is organized by oppositions; this is why circles of young friends later break up into rivalries as they become successful. The evidence of the historical networks shows this oppositional pattern: comparably important philosophers appear in the same generation, like Parmenides and Heraclitus formulating the first abstract metaphysical positions in Greek philosophy but with opposing notions of being as immutable or inherent flux. This pattern of simultaneous opposing creativity shows the inadequacy of the notion of a *Zeitgeist*, since it is rivalry rather than unity of belief that generates creativity.

Opposition both gives the emotional energy of creative intellectual action, and shapes the contents of philosophies. The intellectual world is a sphere of arguments, not of conclusions; it is where opportunities for rivalries can be exploited within a common focus of attention that creativity occurs. The creative individuals are those who are energized by taking up part of that limited attention space where the buzz of intellectual life is most intense. The network pattern of intellectual life – the vertical connections from one generation to the next between persons successful in dominating the attention space; and the horizontal connections of concentrated friends and rivalries – explains not only who will be successful but also the content of their ideas. It is a theory of who will think what thoughts under what conditions structuring the intellectual community as it moves through historical time. Collins's sociology of philosophies thus makes the same move that the SSK did in moving from the sociology of science in the generation of Merton (showing the institutional supports which allow scientists to operate, but saying

nothing about what ideas are produced, except in the case of distorted, false ideas), to a position in which the content of ideas – scientific *knowledge* – is also to be explained.

In the theory of struggle over attention space, the content of what philosophers produce at a given historical moment is shaped by these two structures of the network: vertically, a thinker is part of a stream of discourse coming down from the past, containing sets of concepts and modes of argument which can be recombined in various ways to yield new ideas. Horizontally, each thinker has to feel his or her way into a distinctive niche in the attention space constituted by arguments among contemporary rivals; this is done by finding a dimension in which one's ideas negate the main ideas of a rival. Rival thinkers implicitly feed off of each other. This tacit dependence reveals yet another reason why successfully creative thinkers appear so close to each other in the networks of personal contact: they need to know, swiftly and intuitively, what tacks each other is taking so that they can shape a position that maximizes attention and emotional energy by sharpening the lines of opposition most fruitful for elaborated argument. Intellectuals operate under the ideology of seeking truth, and this is not an inaccurate way of characterizing the guiding ideal or symbol of their search for arguments which are autonomous from any practical or other external loyalties except those of the argumentative community; but their success at formulating a socially believable truth depends upon picking a highly visible fight, especially in the eyes of their followers and successors.

4 'Golden Ages' of widespread creative outbursts occur in a distinctive network pattern: where several rival circles intersect at a few metropoles. This pattern is found world-wide, in ancient Athens and Alexandria for Greek philosophy, as in medieval Baghdad and Basra at the height of Islamic philosophy, or at the great monastery-university Nalanda in medieval India where the several Buddhist sects debated their Hindu counterparts; similar patterns are found for the multiple schools at Kyoto and Edo in the efflorescence of Tokugawa Japan, and again at the creative moments in the European

West. Conversely, structural extremes are deadly for philosophical creativity: concentration of all resources in a single faction stifles innovation; so does dispersion of intellectual life into a large number of centers, especially when these become closed orthodoxies as in the proliferation of universities in the European late middle ages divided into fortresses of Thomists, Scotists and Nominalists.

5   The 'law of small numbers' holds that the number of positions which can be successful simultaneously, within the same generation, is between three and six. This applies both to the number of distinctive intellectual positions that become stably recognized – the labels by which, as the dust clears from the initial chaos of argument, intellectuals come to define what positions they belong to and what they are reacting against – and also to the network organization of the field, the number of intergenerational chains which successfully keep up their eminence from master to pupil. The law of small numbers is a structural shaper and limit of creativity. The lower limit of three (occasionally as low as two) comes from the oppositional nature of creativity; creating a solitary new position, although logically possible, appears not to be sociologically possible. Historically, we see that when bureaucratic orthodoxy, or some other form of extreme monopoly on intellectual life, limits the number of intellectual factions to one, creativity dries up. But where social conditions allow two new positions to be generated by rivalry, it is always possible to craft a third position ('a plague on both houses'); given the richness of the streams of ideas coming down from previous generations, it is possible to put together many variants, by combining elements and negating some of them. But there is a structural limit to how much elaboration of rival positions can be done; the attention space is limited, so that when there are more than six positions, the surplus positions become lost in attention space – they fail to become recognized. We see this empirically in the history of intellectual networks: in generations where the number of networks splits into more than six schools, the following generation experiences failure of lineages so that the successful ones are brought back down to the limits of the attention space.

As we see in the following point, the upper and lower limits of the law of small numbers generate structural tensions which shape the periods of creative change in intellectual life.

6   There is a two-step causality from the external social surroundings of intellectual life to the changes in contents of philosophies. The first level of causation is what changes the material bases of intellectual life, as when religions are founded or disappear, expanding monasteries provide positions for thinkers, or universities or publishing houses are created. Such changes are caused by larger and more remote shifts in political and economic structures which foster new religious movements, new class audiences for reading books, new government demands for educated officials. These changes do not simply and directly result in ideologies reflecting the dominant social classes or political factions; instead they modify resources for intellectual competition over local attention space, sometimes opening up possibilities for new factions and new lines of opposition, sometimes by closing down existing factions. When the number of factions is changed by these shifts in material bases, the entire attention space is transformed.

Thus the second layer of social causality: strong positions divide, weak positions unite. Schools of thought which are strongly supported by material conditions expand to take up as much of the attention space as is available; thus if a rival position is destroyed, space is opened up for the remaining, victorious position to split into rival factions. We see this, for instance, in medieval India when the Buddhist monasteries lost their economic patronage and eventually were driven out of India; the victorious Hindu thinkers now moved into Buddhist intellectual space, taking over Buddhist philosophical positions, and subdividing among themselves into new rivalries. This pattern has occurred repeatedly in all parts of the world. Structurally, reducing the number of factions below the upper limits of the law of small numbers fosters splits among the remaining factions to fill up the available slots.

Conversely, weak positions, those which are losing their material bases, tend to huddle together into a defensive alliance. When in the later Roman empire Christianity with its coherent networks for training priests began to threaten to gain religious dominance as well as to command the intellectual attention space, the pagan schools ended their rivalries and formed a grand alliance, through the synthesis constructed by Plotinus. Another version of a structural inducement to synthesis occurs when upper limits of the law of small numbers are strained by a proliferation of positions; the impending failure of many positions to find followers motivates synthesizers who reduce the number of factions through combining them on a new level of abstraction; this is what Aristotle did in the generation following the proliferation of schools founded by the many pupils of Socrates. Thus there are two forms of structurally induced creativity: the creativity of factionalizers, splitting off new positions in an expanding intellectual space, and the creativity of synthesizers, reducing the number of positions and shoring up weakening positions by combining them.

This shows another inadequacy of the *Zeitgeist* model of intellectual history as a reflex of changes in the economic or political circumstances of the entire society. There is creativity both on the way up and the way down, in times when material resources are expanding, and when they are contracting; indeed, these often proceed simultaneously and symmetrically, as when one side of the intellectual field (the Christians) are expanding and the other side (the pagans) are contracting. Creativity does not simply consist of the ideas of the social 'progressives' (in contrast to Bourdieu's model, in which innovators are supposed to be a disprivileged avant-garde rebelling against an older Establishment). Because of the oppositional nature of innovation, leading innovators are sometimes conservatives. In their own eyes they oppose the intellectual and social changes of their times; they may even come from a faction inside the intellectual field which holds out for religious tradition or scriptural orthodoxy, or which opposes the self-conscious rationalists and innovators. But because they are situated in networks at the core of the intellectual action, they combat new ideas along lines of sophisticated opposition generated by the entire attention space; conservatives have often been innovators against the letter of their overt ideologies by raising acute epistemological critiques of their rationalist rivals, or by capping those arguments by moving to new levels of abstraction and reflexivity.

Innovation in Asian intellectual history has frequently been carried out in the guise of claiming to restore old orthodoxies; striking examples are the Neo-Confucian metaphysicians in Sung Dynasty China, the Ancient Learning and National Learning schools in Tokugawa Japan, and the Mimamsakas (the most reactionary of the Hindu Vedic factions) who pioneered a new level of epistemological acuteness in medieval Indian philosophy. In the West, we find a pattern of conservative innovators from Rousseau to Heidegger. Given the recombinations of cultural capital from generation to generation, it should not be surprising that the ideas of such thinkers should be picked up by successors (in the case of Heidegger, by the French existentialists and deconstructionists) on a different side of the ideological spectrum. Once again we see the inadequacy of an external-reflection sociology of knowledge, such as explaining Heidegger by his affinities with Nazism.

7 The network theory of attention spaces is integrated with a micro-sociology of thinking. Ideas are symbols of social membership. Durkheim held this is the case for membership in an entire society, but in the case of intellectuals we may say that their specialized ideas and modes of arguing are emblems of membership in particular intellectual factions – just those factions which divide up the attention space. Add Mead's theory, that thinking is internalized conversation; and the empirical observation that intellectuals internalize their ideas from their discourse with their teachers, friends, and rivals. Creative thinking, then, is the rapid formulation of new concepts and strings of argument. The creative individual may be alone at that moment when ideas 'pop into one's head', but his or her ideas are loaded

with membership connotations for factions in the intellectual attention space. Thinking is making coalitions and oppositions in the mind. This shows another reason why face-to-face connections among persons active in the core of attention space are so prominent in the early lives of creative thinkers; it is the emotional resonances of these encounters that give the rapid, intuitive flow of ideas. Creative persons at their peak do not merely labor over putting together their ideas; the new ideas come together as if by magnetism, carried by the emotional energy internalized from experience in excited attention spaces.

OTHER RESEARCH IN SOCIOLOGY OF PHILOSOPHY

A pioneer of the field was C. Wright Mills (1942/1969), who studied the American pragmatists by assembling a portrait of their social origins and sketching the organizational context of the reform of American universities which took place during their lifetime. An impressive recent performance, using the model of the Strong Programme in SSK, is Kusch's (1995) analysis of the movement in German philosophy in the early twentieth century, which formulated the doctrine, subsequently widely accepted, that psychological arguments are an illegitimate way of dealing with philosophical problems, since the latter have their autonomous logic. Kusch shows that this anti-psychologism movement occurred in just those circles in German philosophy faculties which were opposing the development of new laboratories of experimental psychology; in response to the 'role hybridization' of physiological researchers moving into philosophical chairs which created the new specialized discipline of psychology (Ben-David and Collins, 1966), the anti-psychologism movement was a 'role-purification' movement to throw the invaders out.

A number of other recent studies in the sociology of philosophy are collected in Kusch (2000). Chew (2000) broadens beyond the usual Eurocentric focus to show the strategies adopted by philosophers in China and Japan in the late nineteenth and early twentieth centuries as contrasting responses to dominance of the world intellectual scene by the philosophies of the European colonial powers. Henry (2000) analyzed the formation of Afro-Caribbean philosophy in the aftermath of colonialism. Bryant (1996) showed how the changing political conditions, as the ancient Greek city-states lost autonomy to the Hellenistic empires, shut off venues for public debate, and motivated the creation of inwardly oriented moral philosophies withdrawing from public life.

Most reflexively oriented towards analyzing ourselves – the movement in the late twentieth century producing a sociology of scientific knowledge and a sociology of philosophy – is Steve Fuller (2000). Taking the eminence of Thomas Kuhn as the paradigm case of success in the current intellectual world, Fuller shows how Kuhn's theory of scientific revolutions (Kuhn, 1962) was created in the academic circles at the end of the Second World War which were most centrally involved in government-funded 'Big Science' supported by the Cold War military buildup. Kuhn's internalist sociology of science extols an image of autonomously driven paradigm revolutions modeled on historically earlier, individual scientific researchers who had been made anachronistic by Big Science; thus Kuhn's imagery provided ideological legitimation and diversion from the current character of science increasingly driven not by paradigm interests but by external political-military concerns. Fuller calls for an 'external reflexivity', weaving critique of the social grounding of intellectuals (including late twentieth- and early twenty-first-century philosophers and sociologists of science) back into the internally reflexive paradigm struggles within the intellectual world.

In terms of the theory of intellectual attention spaces, Fuller draws attention to the ways in which struggles can cut across the levels of the lay-oriented politics that affects the material bases of intellectual life, as well as the level of struggles over slices of the intellectual attention space. Factions inside the attention space (such as SSK, and now the sociology of philosophy) can be filled not merely along lines of internal opposition, but also along lines which propose to create factions that can contend over state political power. Philosophers can also aspire to export their reflexivity into the larger political arena. Whether they are successful at that, to be sure, will be determined by larger political conditions, not by the local conditions of argument inside intellectual networks. But politically successful or not, Fuller points to a further layer of reflexive self-understanding for the sociology of philosophies and other intellectual positions: sociologically examining the conditions under which politically ambitious factions become prominent within intellectual attention space.

REFERENCES

Abercrombie, Nicholas, Hill, Stephen and Turner, Bryan S. (1980) *The Dominant Ideology Thesis*. London: Allen and Unwin.

Ashmore, Malcolm (1989) *The Reflexive Thesis: Wrighting Sociology of Scientific Knowledge*. Chicago: University of Chicago Press.

Barnes, Barry (1975) *Scientific Knowledge and Sociological Theory*. London: Routledge.

Ben-David, Joseph and Collins, Randall (1966) 'Social factors in the origins of a new science: the case of psychology', *American Sociological Review*, 31: 451–65.

Bloor, David (1976) *Knowledge and Social Imagery*. New York: Columbia University Press.

Bloor, David (1983) *Wittgenstein: A Social Theory of Knowledge*. Chicago: University of Chicago Press.

Bourdieu, Pierre (1975/1991) *The Political Ontology of Martin Heidegger*. Cambridge: Polity Press.

Bourdieu, Pierre (1993) *The Field of Cultural Production*. Chicago: University of Chicago Press.

Bryant, Joseph M. (1996) *Moral Codes and Social Structure in Ancient Greece: A Sociology of Greek Ethics from Homer to the Epicureans and Stoics*. Albany, NY: State University of New York Press.

Chew, Matthew (2000) 'Politics and patterns of developing indigenous knowledge under Western disciplinary compartmentalization: the case of philosophical schools in modern China and Japan', in Martin Kusch (ed.), *The Sociology of Philosophical Knowledge*. Dordrecht: New Synthese Historical Library/Kluwer Publishers. pp. 125–54.

Collins, Randall (1998) *The Sociology of Philosophies: A Global Theory of Intellectual Change*. Cambridge, MA: Harvard University Press.

Collins, Randall (2000a) 'The sociology of philosophies: A précis', *Philosophy of the Social Sciences*, 30: 157–201.

Collins, Randall (2000b) 'Reflexivity and embeddedness in the history of ethical philosophies', in Martin Kusch (ed.), *The Sociology of Philosophical Knowledge*. Dordrecht: New Synthese Historical Library, Kluwer Publishers. pp. 155–78.

Durkheim, Emile (1912/1961) *The Elementary Forms of the Religious Life*. New York: Collier.

Durkheim, Emile (1898–1911/1953) *Sociology and Philosophy*. New York: Free Press.

Fabiani, Jean-Louis (1988) *Les Philosophes de la République*. Paris: Éditions de Minuit.

Foucault, Michel (1969/1990) *The Archeology of Knowledge*. London: Routledge.

Fuchs, Stephan (2001) *Against Essentialism*. Boston, MA: Harvard University Press.

Fuller, Steve (2000) *Thomas Kuhn: A Philosophical History for our Times*. Chicago: University of Chicago Press.

Garfinkel, Harold (1967) *Studies in Ethnomethodology*. Englewood Cliffs, NJ: Prentice–Hall.

Goffman, Erving (1961) *Asylums*. New York: Doubleday.

Goffman, Erving (1974) *Frame Analysis*. New York: Harper and Row.

Gross, Paul and Levitt, Norman (1994) *Higher Superstition: The Academic Left and Its Quarrels with Science*. Baltimore, MD: Johns Hopkins University Press.

Habermas, Jürgen (1984) *Theory of Communicative Action*. Boston: Beacon Press.

Hagstrom, Warren O. (1965) *The Scientific Community*. New York: Basic Books.

Henry, Paget (2000) *Caliban's Reason: Introducing Afro-Caribbean Philosophy*. London: Routledge.

Joas, Hans (2000) *The Genesis of Values*. Chicago: University of Chicago Press.

Kim, Kyung-Man (1996) 'Hierarchy of scientific consensus and the flow of consensus over time', *Philosophy of the Social Sciences*, 26: 3–25.

Kuhn, Thomas S. (1962) *The Structure of Scientific Revolutions*. Chicago: University of Chicago Press.

Kusch, Martin (1995) *Psychologism: A Case Study in the Sociology of Philosophical Knowledge*. London: Routledge.

Kusch, Martin (ed.) (2000) *The Sociology of Philosophical Knowledge*. Dordrecht: New Synthese Historical Library, Kluwer Publishers.

Latour, Bruno (1987) *Science in Action*. Cambridge, MA: Harvard University Press.

Latour, Bruno and Woolgar, Steve (1983) *Laboratory Life: The Social Construction of Scientific Facts*. Beverly Hills, CA: Sage.

Lyotard, Jean-Francois (1979/1983) *The Postmodern Condition*. Minneapolis, MN: University of Minnesota Press.

Mannheim, Karl (1929/1936) *Ideology and Utopia*. New York: Harcourt.

Marx, Karl and Engels, Friedrich (1846/1947) *The German Ideology*. New York: International Publishers.

Mead, George Herbert (1932) *The Philosophy of the Present*. LaSalle, IL: Open Court.

Mead, George Herbert (1938) *The Philosophy of the Act*. Chicago: University of Chicago Press.

Merton, Robert K. (1973) *The Sociology of Science*. Chicago: University of Chicago Press.

Mills, C. Wright (1942/1969) *Sociology and Pragmatism: The Higher Learning in America*. New York: Oxford University Press.

Mills, C. Wright (1959) *The Sociological Imagination*. Oxford: Oxford University Press.

Price, Derek J. de Solla (1963/1986) *Little Science, Big Science, and Beyond*. New York: Columbia University Press.

Rawls, Anne Warfield (2005) *Epistemology and Practice. Durkheim's Elementary Forms of Religious Life*. Cambridge: Cambridge University Press.

Rojek, Chris and Turner, Bryan S. (2000) 'Decorative sociology: toward a critique of the cultural turn', *Sociological Review*, 48: 629–48.

Weber, Max (1949) *Methodology of the Social Sciences*. New York: Free Press.

4

The Diversity and Insularity of Sociological Traditions

CHARLES CROTHERS

THE IMPORTANCE OF TRADITIONS

Sociologists should make the choices at each of the stages of a research or writing project – conceptual approach, methodology, presentational style, etc. – in terms of what is most appropriate for that particular topic. However, almost inevitably, sociologists are strongly, albeit often unconsciously, intellectually influenced at each point in their projects by received or developing traditions, paradigms, lines of thought, and socially influenced by the 'social embedding' of such cognitive structures in 'schools', 'theory-groups', 'research networks' and other forms of intellectual social organization. Such influences and pre-structurings of approaches are, more often than not, complex rather than simple, with different sociological traditions influencing different aspects of the project, and with multiplex strands very often simultaneously in play.

There is room for authorial choice, as well as the play of more determinate shapings imposed by established authorities. Traditions are not necessarily limiting. Very many sociologists would agree that the influence of sociological traditions is in fact *necessary*. After all, as Weber argued, the very choice of research topic cannot be decided on strictly scientific grounds. Where there is more room for disagreement is on whether the press of sociological traditions determines the outcomes of investigations, or whether they merely provide alternative and equivalent paths to much the same final outcome. Will the truth 'out' irrespective of the play of traditions dancing around a bedrock of firm reality, or is 'social reality' varyingly constructed by each tradition?[1] Moreover, there is room for choice along a multiplicity of dimensions, as opposed to the highly simplifying notions often imposed by textbook taxonomists eager to tidy up the messiness in order to inculcate order in the minds of neophyte sociologists.

Indeed, many sociologists would argue for the importance of traditions as providing the continuing backbone of sociological thinking, and are prepared to invest energies in their maintenance and communication. This is so particularly in the teaching activities of sociologists.

What sociologists' understandings of traditions are is an open empirical question. There is likely a considerable range of views about the nature and scope of traditions. A similar empirical question is the extent to which sociologists are conscious and informed in their choices amongst traditions, and the extent to which they are able to follow through the consequences of the assumptions embedded in any particular tradition in ways that are logical and coherent. Some sociologists clearly cleave to a particular approach, but at the other extreme, some deny being influenced by any specific tradition.

DEFINING TRADITIONS

Intellectual traditions can take many forms. It is also difficult to pin down any particular vocabulary in discussing them. The term 'tradition' emphasizes rather too much the connotation of respect for past thinking. But other terms have drawbacks too. 'School' implies rather too much a formal organization, leadership and even intellectual control from that leadership. The ambiguities around Kuhn's (1962) fecund term 'paradigm' have led to a major commentary industry. I would prefer, then, to use the term 'sociological tradition' in a loose sense to refer to any cognitive formation that lends consistency to aspects of thinking amongst sociologists, whether or not the doctrine concerned is unique within sociology or also shared by wider groupings of intellectuals or scientists.

It is important to delimit, within traditions, some of their possible components and dimensions. There is a tendency amongst historians of social theory to restrict their concerns to traditions which are theoretical. But, any sociological work (and thus any fully formed tradition) must inevitably cover, at least, each of meta-methodological, conceptual, methodological and ideological aspects. In terms of their internal state, traditions may vary in terms of their degree of historical development, the tightness of their formal development, the linkages between the theory espoused and the facts considered important in the tradition, the closure of their boundaries, the degree of reflexive consciousness with which they are held by adherents, the moral tone which is pursued etc. In addition, there are more social aspects to traditions which may also affect their trajectory: the degree of social cohesion, organizational contours, shared cultural assumptions of adherents etc., and their fit with the environing culture and society.[2]

Writings on sociological traditions vary in terms of which aspect is emphasized, and over time further salient dimensions have been added for consideration. Important writings in the (historical) sociology of sociology have drawn attention to each of these major dimensions, for example:

- Kuhn: the importance of underlying conceptual assumptions and models, and the intellectual community upholding the 'paradigm'.
- Gouldner: the importance of underlying conceptual assumptions and models, and the grounding of views in personal experiences.
- Friedrichs: the importance of the underlying moral views.
- Platt: the importance of traditions of social research methodology.
- Levine: the importance of the type of 'organizing model' (narrative) about the trajectory of sociological development held by the historian.

Having scouted out some of the complexities of what is involved with traditions, let us return to their central core. Donald Levine (1995) has provided a useful imagery of what is at the heart of any sustained and cumulative sociological discourse. He sees each tradition as a conversation, a dialogue between sociologists. As with other intellectual activities which are largely text-based, time and space are limited in their effect as barriers. Thus, such conversations can take place between generations of sociologists (as well as within generations) and across countries (as well as within them). Levine defines traditions as inter- and intra-generational conversations amongst intellectuals which tend to share particular assumptions about social reality. (A critique of conceptions of Sociological Traditions is provided in Baehr and O'Brien, 1994; Baehr, 2002.)

Any tradition cannot merely be regarded on its own. Rather, it must be placed within the context of the other traditions then pertaining, and on the relations amongst these traditions. Usually, contemporaneous traditions are in competition, and sometimes in conflict, although they may also ignore each other with studied contempt. I shall refer to any prevailing climate of inter-tradition relations as involving 'tradition-sets'.

In this chapter I will: discuss the methodologies of identifying traditions; review conceptualizations of the dynamics of traditions; provide a comparative/historical account of factors shaping traditions; profile views of pre-disciplinary traditions of social theory; typologize contemporary traditions; examine other types of tradition, e.g. methodological; note various mechanisms for linking traditions; and summarize some of the empirical studies of sociological traditions, before concluding.

METHODOLOGY FOR IDENTIFYING TRADITIONS: THE HISTORY OF SOCIOLOGICAL CLASSIFICATIONS

In studying traditions there is a prior methodological question: what is the correct way of proceeding in identifying traditions? As Levine (1995: 13) has remarked, sociology was officially born carrying with it a schema of its own history. Comte coined the term and simultaneously laid out his version of its trajectory. Such histories tend to include a classification of types of sociology, and the various substantive traditions comprising this history. Concern with the classification of types of sociology almost inevitably accompanies any enterprise in theory. The classifying of types of tradition, then, is often a highly contested topic, with rival schema often being pressed into service for purposes other than writing the cool, calm, historical record. It is a process of social production (cf. Connell, 1997; cf. Schumpeter's famous definition of two types of 'schools').

Classifications of theory are not only part and parcel of normal sociological argumentation. A secondary usage then develops by those textbook writers whose contribution it is to provide classifications of theories. Such classifications are sometimes largely historical in orientation and sometimes more contemporary in purpose. Such classifications then tend to become built into classroom teaching, especially in theory and history of sociology courses, and begin to take on a life of their own. However, they risk breaking connections with the linkages between theory developments and on-going sociological debates. Without such organic connections, classifications may ossify.

Much thinking about traditions is concerned with the rather different task of trying to specify the parameters of theoretical possibilities. For example, much recent theorizing consists in cogitations upon dichotomies (or polarities or 'dualities'), between such contrasts as the subjective and the objective, structure and action, macro and micro. These then become cognitive anchors for developing classifications of traditions: for example, those traditions stressing the subjective *vs.* the objective, those emphasizing the micro-level rather than the macro level, etc. But too often the temptation to reify these positions is not resisted. Emphases become essential defining features. Theoretical concern with the alternative possibilities in theorizing is useful in constructing typologies of different traditions, but it has dangers in averting attention from what features are actually expressed in different traditions.

In short, I am wary of commentaries. Traditions must be shown to affect actual sociological writing. For example, in his study of types of sociology, Menzies usefully distinguishes between 'theorist's theory', and 'researcher's theory'. Studies such as that of Mullins (1973) have endeavoured to systematically trace how traditions are passed on through master–apprenticeship pairings, and are sustained by networks of like minds. Accordingly, this account will pay particularly careful attention to such empirical studies of traditions.[3]

THE DYNAMICS OF TRADITIONS: A SOCIOLOGY OF SOCIOLOGY/ICAL CHANGE

Traditions can have an intellectual and a social life of their own, and the qualities of their infrastructure may have an effect on the cognitive characteristics of the tradition. In considering sociological traditions we need to be alert to the social conditions underpinning them and the social processes through which they are formed and change.

A considerable conceptual vocabulary has developed which allows the description of the dynamics of traditions. On to Kuhn's terms such as 'periods of normal science' and 'revolutionary periods' were grafted other terms such as 'progressive and regressive shifts'. More recently, Alexander and Colomy (1992) have added a further slew of terms.[4]

Rather more interestingly, sociologists have also developed 'phase models' of the development of specialities – which might also apply to sociological traditions (cf. Crane, 1972; Mullins, 1973; Rule, 1997). Traditions and specialities are often built on a slowly developed platform, and then break away into a fast-developing growth phase, before hitting a plateau and in some cases then declining. Institutionalization, and obtaining a secure supply of requisite resources and recruits, is necessary for a tradition to be sustained (cf. Turner and Turner, 1990). Traditions often forge strong social ties amongst members, with master–apprenticeship relations being essential for their longer-term growth (cf. Collins, 1994; Mullins, 1973).

Over time, Alexander has argued particular strategic cognitive patterns are likely to emerge, with disciples for example, tending to de-stress the particularities which the tradition's masters tended to emphasize. Mulkay develops a more radical argument whereby 'Theoretical development is regarded as being neither continuous nor, in any direct way, cumulative. Instead, it is seen as arising from a number of discrete and intermittent theoretical reorganizations, which centre upon new strategies devised as replacements for the unsuccessful policies adopted by prior theory' (1971: 3).

THE SHAPING OF TRADITIONS:
A COMPARATIVE/HISTORICAL ACCOUNT
OF FACTORS SHAPING TRADITIONS

The rise and fall of (national and other) traditions are shaped by various cultural, ideological, political, institutional, cognitive and social factors both generally, but also in different ways in different national contexts. Such external influences may override some of the internal dynamics of traditions.

The broadest influence is undoubtedly that of culture. Cultures stressing the importance, in both the natural and social realms, of the acquisition of rational explicit scientific principles and of empirical fact-finding, and even more importantly the importance of developing systematic ways of interfacing the rational and the empirical, are much more likely to foster successful social science. An important influence on the development of social science are the models of natural scientific inquiry admired by social scientists. Each of the main traditions has philosophers, and also scientists of more general importance, whose understandings of science were highly consequential for work in that tradition. For example, Newton's views on science had a particular resonance within subsequent British thinking.

Aspects of religious thinking in a country also affect the development of science and social science. Prior to the reformation and enlightenment, secular social thinking was often discouraged. Moreover, 'In Protestant countries close relations developed between intellectuals and churches. Intellectuals were harnessed in the conflict with Catholic ideas and politics; there was more room for debate since (some) Protestant religions were not anchored by a central dogma; and since Protestant clergymen could raise families, intellectual dynasties could be more readily formed. Thus, in England, and also the Netherlands and Scandinavia, scientific innovation was linked with religious debate. However, in France secularization of intellectual culture took place with support from the state and the court, and did not involve the development of scientific thought, since literary genres were dominant. Therefore scientization without secularization in contrast to secularization without scientization' (Heilbron, 1995: 63–4).

Different cultures house much the same range of ideological perspectives, but some national consistencies can be found. French ideology more often stresses radical change, drawing on its rationalist heritage, whereas in the UK and the United States emphasis is more on reform, flowing from a strain towards empiricism. In Germany ideology is often idealist, humanist and anti-positivist.

Each culture has somewhat different ways of portraying what is covered within the realm of the social sciences. In Germany *sozialwissenschaften* is a broad conceptualization, whereas in the Anglo-US world a sharper distinction is usually drawn between the social sciences and the humanities. France is more complex, with economics located within Faculties of Law whereas the other human sciences are located within the broader humanistic framework of Faculties of Letters. Which particular disciplines are separately identified has also differed: with some continental university systems often presenting more 'policy-oriented' types of knowledge: for example, demography, criminology, sociography in the Netherlands. More recently, the distribution of disciplines which developed in American universities has successfully diffused world-wide, and has become the norm against which the array of disciplines in other countries has come to be measured. The main disciplines of social science, including sociology, tend now to have an American imprimatur. However, even if the general approach of the discipline has been set by its grounding in American institutional structures, the content of sociology has more recently been more often influenced by Continental sources.

Each culture understands the relationships between its component 'social fields' rather differently. Although most modern societies have in common separate economic, political and social realms, together with many minor arenas of social life, how each is constituted and what its relationships are to other spheres may differ considerably, and this has consequences for social science work in that society. The various disciplines tend to have a particular interactive relationship with one or other of the social realms in that society: with the social science discourse being in part constitutive of that realm, and in part being shaped by it. These schema constitute 'deep structures' that may implicitly guide the development of particular national traditions over many generations. For example, in France the state has long been a very central and powerful institution, although there has been a strong discouragement of scholarship in political science. In France, society ('the social') became distinct from church and politics, and then the economy, but in Germany the distinction was resisted. The possibilities of the development of sociology were shaped by these differences.

During the period of German university development from the late 1700s through to the mid-1800s, literary and artistic intellectuals were not accommodated in universities. One result of this appears to have been that 'the independent non-university intellectuals became hostile to the new professorial form of knowledge production' (Heilbron, 1995: 24). This involved a Romanticist rejection of cold hard facts, which developed alongside, and in reaction to, the professionalization of knowledge, and provided an alternative and oppositional stock of intellectual resources, which has most recently been drawn on in the development of postmodernism.

The policy process is different in different states. In the UK, fact-finding was institutionalized in the role of Royal Commissions, inspectorates and social reform research associations, but these were weakly linked (at least as far as formal ties are concerned) with the policy-making. Social network ties amongst various members of the elite could provide channels for information to percolate to policy-makers. However, links between social researchers and policy-makers have remained ever since generally at arm's-length. In Germany, there was also considerable state involvement in statistics collection. On the other hand, in the Netherlands a tradition of longer-term policy-making developed and this was able to articulate with a slew of empirically oriented research approaches such as sociography and social geography, which were particularly well developed there. The interest of states in social research and their capacity to promote it and then to utilize findings vary considerably.

Although the attention of historians of sociology is particularly drawn to examining theoretical traditions, there are also research traditions (or more broadly methodological traditions) which may not be at all strongly linked with the more theoretical traditions. The state, as the key institution in developing statistical information, is particularly important in shaping the types of empirical research and methodological developments which eventuate in a particular country.

Undoubtedly the most important methodological breakthrough in the social sciences was the German historians' concerns with methods for validating the reliability of documents. This led to a more widespread tide of heightened methodological standards. In addition, Levine (1995: 276) suggests that:

> The empirical traditions also bore the mark of national dispositions, if not in such a pronounced form as the philosophical ones. England led the way with social surveys, systematic investigations of living and working conditions, mainly of members of the working class. France and Italy pursued the collection of national social statistics, work that enabled Durkheim to lead off so impressively with his analysis of divorce rates, educational levels, mental illness data, religious affiliation and the like in *Suicide*. Germany pioneered the experimental manipulation of subjects and also the systematic collection of ethnographic data in broadly defined culture areas. The US pioneered in producing census data and later in systematic-gathering of information through personal documents and direct observation as well as interviews.

Later in the United States, content analysis was developed, especially in the context of the Second World War and the Cold War when direct access to totalitarian countries was denied and so more indirect means of study were especially required. The methodological emphasis of US social science led to the very considerable systematization of social research methods there in the mid-nineteenth century.

Besides the state itself, social science's traditions may be shaped through interaction with a range of coalition partners, including scholarly and/or professional organizations of social scientists, the social-science based semi-professions and a wider array of social movement organizations. In many countries there has been a development of semi-professions, at least partly based on sociological knowledge (social workers, planners, nurses, librarians, psychologists, economists, educators and teachers) and their differential association with

sociology has affected the development of national traditions.

A range of coalition partners, which differ in particular circumstances, may shore up the development of social science knowledge, especially where there is a cognitive and moral affinity. Such partners may include political parties, trade unions, pro-business groupings, welfare reform groups or, more generally, social movements. Often some aspects of sociology relate to these in terms of some 'discursive affinity', an overlapping of key concerns and some basic similarity in cognitive assumptions and terms. In such circumstances, the sociological work provides some of the conceptual elaboration and/or the social information required to support the programme of its ally, while the ally may assist in providing treatments of what issues are problematic, empirical material (for example, access to research sites) and assist in mobilizing resource support. Plus providing a more general legitimacy. This relationship is often strengthened when the partner obtains parliamentary power or is in government. More recently, think-tanks have been set up to mobilize social science knowledge for more specifically ideological purposes, especially in support of the doctrines of neoliberalism. Supporting social movements are often especially important in the international linking of national traditions: for example, Marx bequeathed his writings to the German socialist movement (which gained a parliamentary foothold in the 1880s and 1890s), which harboured them to display for widespread trade union and academic utilization at the turn of century.

The effects of different institutional forms and the material basis of the provision of resources has been especially important for fuelling the differential development of sociology. A range of institutional forms have been relevant in different times and places: coffee houses, salons, associations, university teaching departments and research institutes (cf. Coser, 1975). Salons and coffee houses can be significant for the flexible innovation of new ideas. Universities can be important for providing a more secure and longer-staying environment, with systematization required for teaching and some degree of system rationale allowed and pushed for. University settings propel specialization, and divisions of labour, especially in the form of formal development of separate disciplines. However, university teaching departments are not necessarily appropriate institutions to support larger-scale research so that the tackling of larger topics, and also policy research, often requires the development of research centres where a specialized division of labour can be built up and resources for particular products mobilized.

Different national university systems have provided different contexts for the development of sociology. The German universities were reformed from the 1820s on and launched a range of more systematically based scientific work, especially in philology and then extending especially into history, which was placed on a far more scientific footing. The French system, which was not revivified until the 1870s, was (and still is) highly centralized, which can mean the rapid institutionalization of a particular area of knowledge, although the centralization can prove intellectually stultifying. As with natural science, the American university system in which presidents have strong power to develop new areas, where there can be fierce competition for prestige amongst institutions, and where (at least in larger universities) the appointment of several full professors in each department fosters a democratic climate and a diversity of lines of research, seems to have been a particularly successful environment within which social science, including sociology, has flourished.

The timing of reform to university systems seems also to have its own period-effect: witness the intellectual outpourings following eras of educational reform in Germany/Prussia after the 1780s and France during the 1880s and after.

One particular design feature which supports innovation seems to have been the importance of role hybrids; those with one foot in practical concerns and the other in a setting allowing for systematization of ideas are often especially innovative situations. A particular sociological example was the early development of survey research in which academic sociologists played midwives to the more sophisticated methodological development of the research technique.

The institutions within which social science development takes place may also have an effect on the dominant cognitive style through which social knowledge is produced and debated. German scholars often were ensconced in universities whereas French scholars were focused in Paris, housed in academies and grandes écoles and interacted in salons. As a result, 'Whereas the German intellectual was systematic, scholarly, even pedantic, the French intellectual tended to be orientated to science as well as to political controversy and to be brilliant and lucid as well as facile and flowery in exposition' (Collins, 1994: 14).

Cognitive properties may affect the development of national traditions, such as where there is reliance on subject matter that is strongly localized: for example the study of languages seems to have nurtured a considerable degree of longevity of localized scholarship. All cultures are permeated with a reflexive 'folk knowledge', but one of the earliest arenas for the development of social science knowledge were the many prototypical 'folk languages' in which 'native scholars' extracted some of the formal principles of their language in order usually to use these principles in instruction and structuring of the language itself by guiding its development.

Having alerted the reader to the various dimensions of the national matrices within which sociological traditions can develop, we now turn to a more concrete historical exploration of the development of the various traditions within sociology.

PRE-DISCIPLINARY TRADITIONS OF SOCIAL THEORY

Before the mid-twentieth century, classificatory schema purporting to describe types of sociology were about as confusing as the state of sociology itself. Consequently, many of the schemas advanced then have a quaint and distanced feel to them. Moreover, even their authors would abandon them. Over time, there has been a tendency for such schema to be more deductively based, with the different types of sociology identified being grounded in what were theoretically postulated as extreme polarities. Once the possibilities were laid out, it was then possible to 'paint in' various types of sociology or particular sociological writers. One major difficulty with this approach is that it requires the classifier to squeeze the complexities of a writer's sociology into a pre-existing box, and to emphasize the extreme features of an approach, rather than trying to locate where it 'naturally' might fall.

Some broad periodizations of eras in the development of sociological traditions have been developed. Heilbron, for example, argues that understanding the prehistory of sociology is important. In contrast, most sociologists tend to see sociological traditions as only being formed in the immediate wake of the Industrial Revolution. During the Enlightenment, the first major systematic theorizing was carried out. Seidman (1983) argues that both the Anglo-American tradition and the more Continental 'science of man' were developed in this period. Some writers stress the importance of the more conservative impulse of the Counter-Enlightenment. Certainly, the more formal development of sociology was based on these precursor systems of thinking. It was the social sensitivity of much social thought in this period which generated the first concern for such lasting themes as alienation (Seidman, 1983). During this period, too, began the highly exploratory and fragile development of more systematic social research. However, it was not until the *fin-de-siècle* development of major sociological systems that somewhat more substantial links with the entirely fledgling methodological traditions were made, and these were not consolidated until the middle of the nineteenth century.

Levine (1995, 1996, 1997, 2001) argues that more light is thrown on the development of sociological thought by endeavouring to grasp the national channels in which it flowed for some centuries. Levine's schema builds on the (often binary) classifications of traditions set out by other writers, but pursues a more detailed examination. He

define[s] them primarily as national traditions, for two reasons. The originative figures of modern sociology mainly cite fellow nationals, as, for example, Halbwachs is likely to cite Rousseau; von Weise, Simmel; Park, Sumner. More important, over the generations they reproduce what are palpably national characteristics. Moreover, when they engage in dialogue with parties from other national traditions, they do so, openly or by implication, in a more contrastive mode – as when Durkheim explicitly contrasts his French discipline with British and German traditions. (1995: 99, 100)

A national tradition submerges within a more universalistic discourse once these particularities are transcended.

Each national culture tends to make similar ontological assumptions about the nature of social reality, and how it might be known (Levine, 1995). These assumptions underpin social science work in that country, and these views often have been articulated by important philosophers – who then act as something of a 'skirmish-line' for later sociological thought (Crothers, 1997). In particular, cultural choices tend to be made between stressing the individual level as ontologically prior (as in the UK), or the collective level (France), and between an objective approach (as in both the UK and France) compared to a more subjective approach (as in Germany). Although there is a long-term consistency in the development of these approaches, there can be considerable variation within them, and they are often formed in part through a conversation with other theoretical traditions.

Levine identifies the various national traditions in sociology as follows:

- Aristotle, representing the Hellenic tradition, is concerned with the way in which different constitutional arrangements of societies (city-states) shape the conditions for achieving human virtues, and thus human happiness, with the achievement of that potential arising from the deliberative judgements of the participants.
- The British tradition emphasizes the naturally sociable disposition of individual humans, for example, their preoccupation with the properties, rights, liberties and utilities of individual actors, and then the conduct of the actors.

- The French tradition emphasized that 'society formed a supra-personal entity with properties and needs of its own, above all needs for normative regulation and solidaristic integration' and that it was a natural phenomenon.
- The German tradition emphasized human freedom as an essential element of moral decision-making, and also affirmed the creative power of language as a distinctive feature of human action and morality.
- The trans-national Marxian tradition emphasized elements elicited through critique of several of the other traditions in order to combine, in Marx's synthesis 'Kant's notion of self-determination, Hegel's notions of collective historical development, French notions of associated humanity and social classes and the British conception of the competitive pursuit of individual interests in the marketplace' (Levine, 1995: 222).
- The Italian tradition sought laws about societies as natural systems with the prominent features of these systems being the functioning of ruling classes or elites.
- American pragmatism stressed social activism disposed to solve problems on an experimental common-sense basis.

Since this long period of development, indeed throughout the nineteenth century, the national traditions have tended to become overwhelmed by more recent developments in sociology. From mid-century onwards there has been much more a development of a generic sociology. Nevertheless, distinct traces of the older national traditions can be found, and the legacies of particular sociological traditions can often be linked back to these national traditions.

CONTEMPORARY SOCIOLOGICAL TRADITIONS

In the mid-1930s, Talcott Parsons endeavoured to establish a more solid cognitive base on which future social theory might be built. Famously, he attempted this through consideration of a mix of theorists (each perhaps representing different traditions, although it is not a point in Parsons's argumentation) which he argued shared common features critical of utilitarian doctrines and instead positing a more sophisticated 'theory of action': Marshall, Pareto, Durkheim and Weber (with suppressed attention also to Simmel and to Marx). By the immediate post-Second World War period, this synthesis was broadly accepted as a foundation on which specialists in the newly emergent speciality of sociological theory could build.

There is a broadly agreed understanding, at least amongst commentators on this subject, about the range and trajectory of sociological traditions over the past 50 years. Functionalism (or structural-functionalism) is seen as the major approach which dominated sociological discourse in the 1950s and 1960s, beginning earlier than this and certainly carrying on into the 1970s. Alongside this approach was the 'loyal opposition' of symbolic interactionists mainly concerned with micro-sociological processes. Perhaps most poignantly surfacing during the campus violence of the late 1960s and certainly during the 1970s, the hegemony of structuralism was seen as being challenged from below and above. Micro-sociologies became more fashionable, with several new approaches being added to the agenda. On the other hand, macro-sociologies also became more fashionable with (Weberian) comparative/historical and more radical Marxist approaches becoming more prominent. To some extent, a milder version of this period lay in a postulated dichotomy between consensus and conflict sociologies, although it was realized after a while that these were quite complementary and not so penetrating. Also, at the cusp of the late 1960s a series of interesting books carried far-reaching resonance: Glaser and Strauss's *Discovery of Grounded Theory* (1967) and Berger and Luckmann's *Social Construction of Reality* (1967).

Although the above account is plausible and widely accepted, there are several difficulties with it. It is very widely believed, in textbook accounts and also in surveys of sociologists, that functionalism was the dominant perspective of sociology in the 1950s and 1960s. However, closer examination of available content analyses shows that while functionalism was strongly established in the textbook literature, it failed to penetrate far into the research front of sociology. The many meanings of functionalism confuse the picture, and in particular divert attention from the structuralism which underlay so much theoretical analysis and empirical research in this period and subsequently. My argument is that while functionalism was dominant in textbook sociological knowledge, it really had little influence on the research front of sociology, even during its period of supposed dominance. For example, Bryan Turner in his introduction to the *Blackwell Companion to Social Theory*, provides a more distanced account. 'It is often claimed that in the 1950s and 1960s functionalism was the dominant theory paradigm in North America. The dominance of functionalism was closely associated with the career of Talcott Parsons, although the exact relationship between Parsonian sociology and functionalism is open to dispute. ... It is certainly the case that the demise of the influence of Parsons parallels the decline of functionalism as a paradigm' (1996: 9).

The fall of structural-functionalism has itself attracted sociological analysis. This provides a useful case study of the sociology of sociology, which might be extended to the analysis of other traditions. Norbert Wiley (1985) gives an interesting account of the fall of functionalism. He sees this as a combination of: (1) the social protest in the 1960s, (2) the rise of feminism and women's interests and (3) the decline in the capitalist world economy, including the American leadership of that economy' and intellectual attack from macro-level conflict analyses, the qualitative micro-based sociologies and from the quantified positivists, and Homans and exchange theory. To this could be added there was an interactive effect of changes in society which the functionalist approach was unable to understand. In the last quarter-century a much wider range of theoretical material has been 'written into' sociological theory, and the role of Continental and British theorists has become far more prominent. A useful example of the way sociological traditions are re-woven

is the work of Giddens, a recent theorist rather more sensitive to the traditions of sociology than many.[5] At the start of a 15-year theoretical odyssey, Giddens began with a series of essays taking into account each of the received traditions mentioned earlier in this section, largely criticizing their deficiencies but also winnowing out the useful residue that might be reclaimed from their work: he began reviewing the received traditions (functionalism, materialism) but then examined a wide swathe of traditions in order to recruit appropriate ideas for sociology (including ethnomethodology, hermeneutics, poststructuralism). The useful material was then incorporated in his own 'structuration theory'.

Consequently, by the 1980s a considerable agenda of approaches was on the table: one stream emphasized Marxian approaches and more generally political economy, or conflict sociology. There was a rising tide of 'subjectivism' and focus on the individual social actor. In their useful summative presentation, Giddens and Turner suggest (problematically) that the changes were largely driven by a revised underlying philosophy of science inhaled by sociologists. Over the 1970s and 1980s

> ... a dramatic change has occurred. ... developments in the philosophy of natural science have inevitably influenced thinking about the social sciences, while accelerating an increasing disillusionment with the dominant theories of 'mainstream' social science. The result of such changes has been a proliferation of approaches in theoretical thinking. Traditions of thought that previously had been either little known or ignored have become much more prominent: phenomenology, particularly associated with the writings of Alfred Schutz; hermeneutics, as developed in the work of such authors as Gadamer and Ricoeur; and critical theory, as represented by the works of Habermas. Moreover, older traditions of thought, such as symbolic interactionism in the United States and structuralism or post-structuralism in Europe, have more recently developed types of thinking, including ethnomethodology, structuration theory, and the 'theory of practise' associated in particular with Bourdieu. ... There continues to be something of a 'mainstream', even if it is navigated by fewer than before. Parsonian structural-functionalism, for example, still exerts a strong appeal and, in fact, has undergone a considerable revival recently in the writings of Luhmann, Munch, Alexander, Hayes and others. (Giddens and Turner, 1987: 2–3)

Just as this agenda of different traditions had become well established, especially within American sociology, a further wave of social thinkers came to the fore in European sociology. Whereas the earlier wave of groupings operated under doctrinal titles, albeit closely linked with particular key figures, the new round of thinkers were more individualistic. Some of the major figures clearly included Foucault, Derrida, Giddens and Bourdieu. While some attempts have subsequently been made to name and classify the approaches adopted by these latter-day theoretical saints, such classificatory bundlings have, however, been fiercely resisted by their protagonists. Over the past two decades two rather more broad approaches have also gained considerable notoriety and influence, although several announcements of their demise have also been made: poststructuralism and postmodernism.

Perhaps the ultimate depiction of the current situation is that provided by the blurb of a book published in the mid-1980s:

> In this latest volume … a panoramic but acutely critical balance-sheet of the key current of social theory is drawn up, drawing on some of the most profound and trenchant criticism from writers such as Herbert Marcuse, Theodor Adorno, Goran Therborn, Erik Olin Wright, Perry Anderson, Peter Gowan, Peter Des, Norman Geras, Robert Brenner, Sabrina Lovibond, Gregor McLellan, Nicos Poulantzas, Chris Wickham, Kate Soper and others. The volume assesses the historical and sociological theories of both the classical tradition and the more recent schools of thought such as critical theory, world-systems-theory, neo-Weberianism, structuration theory and postmodernism. Combining new studies with classical articles and integrating thorough analyses of individual thinkers – Ulrich Beck, Pierre Bourdieu, Jon Elster, Michel Foucault, Ernest Gellner, Anthony Giddens, Jürgen Habermas, Michael Mann, Carl Schmitt, Theda Skocpol, Richard Rorty, Roberto Unger – with syncretic considerations of themes such as essentialism, structure and agency, individualism and modernism. (Dallmyr, 1987: x, xi)

Alongside the developments of this extended period there may have been changes in the tradition-set. In the 1960s and 1970s there seemed to be a heightened level of rivalry and conflict between traditions. Functionalism as the reigning viewpoint was often attacked with considerable vehemence, and attempts were often made to force a choice between consensus and conflict models. Adherents of Durkheimian, Weberian and Marxist viewpoints would be highly jealous of attempts to confuse their doctrines, or to include them in the sin of eclecticism. Later, some of the lesser theory groupings were often assailed, in an attempt to drive them from the sociological landscape. Such a heightened conflict had an impeccable rationale: a conflict approach to theory flowed quite naturally from conflict modes of social theory. More recently, though, since the mid-1980s vituperation seems to have died down, and eclecticism accepted. This may partly be because of the wider menu of possibilities that are available so that battles might tend to become highly confused. Again, it may also follow from some of the new viewpoints being offered which are more comforting to eclectic and multiple approaches. (It is interesting, though, that postmodernists tend to let a thousand flowers bloom as long as these do not include positivist or scientific approaches!) (The reverberations of such developments for mainstream sociology are addressed in accounts such as Cole, 2001.)

Given the complex layerings of different generations of theories, it may be useful to attend to several detailed classifications of types of tradition. Unfortunately, these are now quite old, but they are important to consider as they illustrate some of the difficulties of classification and also because they 'drive' some of the empirical investigations I report in the next section.

Wallace (1969) provides one of a number of accounts which carefully dissect some of the detailed variation within sociological knowledge. He generates a sophisticated typology of social explanations, derived from a few axioms. Amongst these is social structuralism (SS), which is a broad category within which he distinguishes functional structuralism (FS: e.g. Davis, Robert K. Merton), exchange structuralism (ES: e.g. Thibaut and Kelley, Blau) and conflict structuralism (CS: e.g. Coser, Dahrendorf.) SS endeavours 'to explain the social (defined as objective behaviour relations) mainly through reference to the socially generated, established (i.e. "structured") statuses of participants' (1969: 24).[6]

Table 4.1   *Ritzer's Paradigms*

Name	Exemplar	Constituent theories	Appropriate methods	Definition	% AJS 1940/41	% AJS 1965/66
Social facts	Durkheim	Structural-functional/ conflict/ systems	Questionnaire/ interview	Social phenomena more or less determined by social structures and institutions	36	31
Social definition	Weber on social action	Action theory, symbolic interaction, phenomenology	Observation	The way in which people define social facts	33	32
Social behaviour	Skinner	Behaviouralism, exchange theory	Experimental	Rewards/punishments shaping behaviour	31	37

Another important schema is that developed by Ritzer (1975). As well as describing each of these traditions, Ritzer adds in his views of what their constituent theories are, and what appropriate methods would be for each. Using rather doubtful criteria, he then identifies the proportion of articles taking up each of these traditions in the 1940/41 and 1965/66 issues of the *American Journal of Sociology*. He shows that sociological attention (so measured) was broadly equally divided amongst these three categories and that there was a move from an emphasis on the more macro-level entities associated with the 'social facts' paradigm, to the smaller-scale of the social behavioural paradigm.

Collins (1994, 1985) has identified three broad traditions, before later adding a fourth:

- Conflict sociology (Marx, Weber and class theory more generally).
- The Durkheimian tradition (including functionalism and social anthropology).
- The micro-interactionist traditions (pragmatism, symbolic interactionism, Goffman etc.)
- Rational choice and exchange theories.

A considerable number of other broadly similar classifications could be explored. The ones I have chosen to present are those subsequently used in research to show the prevalence of different traditions over time, which will be covered in a following section. Most of such schemes are essentially deductive, arguing that different approaches are possible, and that

therefore traditions inevitably come to occupy such a slot. But this labelling of 'potential traditions' is to stop once one has identified the bare bones, without exploring the flesh and blood of actual traditions.

Mullins (1973) has developed an interesting inductive classification of theory-groups in American sociology, but beginning with an intuitive leap as to which groupings are worth investigating in more detail. Having identified a grouping of scholars (and usually their students, given that such theory-groups are often based in an institution or set of institutions), his categories include:

- Standard American (this comprises the broad mass of American sociology, indicated by allegiance to structural functional-theory and/or survey methodology)
- Symbolic interaction
- Small group
- New causal (especially causal modelling of occupational mobility)
- Ethnomethodology
- Radical-critical.

For each of these putative theory-groups Mullins identifies its characteristics at each stage of its growth trajectory. The various theory-groups he identifies are of quite different orders of importance, and at quite different growth stages. Standard American and symbolic interaction are both large and well established. The other four are smaller and their continuance is more problematic. Nevertheless, when Mullins returned a decade later (1983) to re-examine the fate of these theory-groups he found them all soldiering on, with little overall change. Mullins's approach is a useful corrective to the more deductive schema.

However, Mullins, too, may have gone too far in one direction: in his case an inductive direction, and has been criticized for turning up some occasionally utterly strange results because he has too readily tried to read off cognitive content from social maps. Clearly, a better methodology for identifying sociological traditions and following their progress is required.

NON-THEORETICAL TRADITIONS

Alongside the theoretical traditions that are most prominent in discussions are arranged a variety of sociological traditions that operate at other levels, for example, substantive, methodological or ideological.

There are several quasi-theoretical traditions which are given space (from time to time) in theory texts but not usually admitted to the core set of recognized theory traditions. Alternatively, some topics are accorded a particular status of more widespread theoretical importance beyond their immediate face value, for example, topics such as 'power' or 'alienation'. Some particular problematics have from time to time been raised to a higher level of visibility, for example, micro–macro linkages. In Germanic fashion, certain 'theoretical struggles' between differing traditions have been sufficiently institutionalized to be named.

One way of identifying some of these 'almost traditions' is to see how various theory collections have included residual topics. For example, Bottomore and Nisbet (1979) include chapter treatments of positivism and of social stratification, but also of power and authority. In Giddens and Turner (1987) these 'additions' include world-systems theory, and class analysis, and also mathematical sociology. Ritzer (1990) includes cultural sociology and micro–macro linkage as a broad problematic issue. Turner (1996) includes systems theory and historical sociology, cultural sociology, the sociology of time/space and feminist social theory.

Besides social science-wide or discipline-wide traditions shared by sociologists, some traditions are specific to particular countries or specific specialities. For example, addressing the speciality area of the sociology of science, Zuckerman (1988: 512) comments: 'Not unlike other specialities … this one is marked also by … different theoretical orientations, no one of which holds sway: constructivism, discourse analysis, relativism, structural analysis, functional analysis, and conflict theory.' She sees (p. 513) differences in views held within the speciality as flowing from national perspectives, especially between US as opposed to UK/European sociologists of science. Again, such national differences apply more broadly but with many exceptions, with the North American approach tending to be more research orientated, functionalist and 'positivist' whereas the European approach is characterized as more comparative/historical and 'critical'. It might be possible to find different patterns of cleavage amongst traditions in different sociology speciality areas – and the resource material is perhaps now available for such assessments (for example, see the chapters in Quah and Sales, 2000) – but no well-established generalizations can be readily offered.

Much more has been written about regional sociologies. Several volumes have been collected which include country-by-country accounts, although not usually country-by-country comparisons. (These include several 'World Handbooks' with country chapters, e.g. Mohan and Wilke, 1994.) There seem to be many claims to regional or country traditions, but not too many of these seem to survive closer examination. As with the overall trajectory of sociology, many countries did include in their prehistories of sociology particular figures who loomed over later sociological developments and who by projecting their particular scholarly idiosyncrasies bequeathed a particular national flavour to the sociology of their country. Such scholars may have been jurists, literary or philosophical theorists or more generic social scientists. However, such national traditions tended to have short lives. In the postwar period, sociology world-wide was invaded by American sociology with its empiricism (symbolized by survey research and a 'scientific' approach) and structural-functional theory. However, by the 1970s other traditions percolated out from the first world core of sociology to challenge the hegemony of the American approach: especially various macro-sociologies and micro-sociologies. This widening of perspectives, too, allowed room for the development of national traditions. But most national sociologies are probably best characterized as particular 'mixes' of the then-current metropolitan (and therefore world) sociological traditions. Nevertheless, since such local versions of the world tradition-set are implemented by discrete sociologists in unique institutions many will pick up a local flavour. Amongst genuine regional sociologies the outstanding example surely is the dependency school of Latin American social scientists, although that is as much claimed by economics as by sociology.

From time to time particular specialities seem of prime importance as pace-setters at the cutting edge in setting traditions. For example, in the 1960s the 'new criminology' emphasized the application of symbolic interactionist and also Marxist approaches to the sociology of deviance, and this had broader implications for sociology as a whole. Another speciality area which has been of importance is that of social stratification, which has been a particularly contested area in which competing sociological traditions have been challenged to exhibit their causal efficacy. For example, in the development period of functional analysis, one of its key contributions was in the area of stratification, with the notion that stratificational orders were of functional consequence for their societies by motivating the filling of key societal roles by people with higher skills and ambitions since incumbents of such positions were rewarded by higher social and economic rewards.

What constitutes methodological traditions, as opposed to more theoretically orientated ones? As with the scientific instrumentation which underpinned a lot of scientific advance, methodological traditions flowed out of concerns to secure social information, which in turn were often an expression of societal

interests. Sometimes, too, there has been opportunity for the sociological exploitation of 'naturally occurring' data sources in particular national sites, such as the population registers developed in many continental countries, or the spread, especially in the suburbanizing and consumer-orientated United States, of market research as the press and then radio became the key link to consumers, and in turn spun off research needs for this industry. (See above for Donald Levine's description of earlier areas of national specialization amongst methodological traditions.) In the post-war era the development of survey methodology was greatly enhanced by the work of sociologists such as Lazarsfeld and Stouffer, whose efforts were assisted by the strong interest of the media industry keen to obtain feedback on their audiences, advertisers needing to know about consumer reactions and the military concerned with questions of morale. Later in the United States, content analysis was developed, especially in the context of the Second World War and then the Cold War, when direct access to totalitarian countries was denied and so more indirect means of study through examining their media outputs were especially required. Although particular methodological traditions grew around each different method (survey, participant observation, content analysis etc.), there was a tendency over time for these separate streams of interest to merge into wider methodological frameworks as the similarities in the issues facing each particular method became more visible. Although particular methodologies tended to have symbolic links to particular disciplines (for example, the link between sociology and surveys), such links have tended to disappear over time, and for methodology to become an interdisciplinary framework shared by all social science disciplines. The broadly methodological emphasis of US social science led to the very considerable systematization of social research methods there from the mid-nineteenth century onwards (Platt, 1996).

The systematization of social research methodology very largely undertaken in the United States in the 1940s and 1950s was in itself anchored in a broader 'philosophical tradition' of positivism, which spanned several more specific traditions. American positivism stressed value-freedom and empiricism (cf. Bryant, 1985) and was strongly advocated in the 1930s by Lundberg and others, and then was taken up by functional theorists and more positivist social researchers.

However, there have been influences other than positivism upon thinking about research methods, especially over more recent decades. The received largely positivist approach to methodological issues has come under attack from viewpoints stemming from a wider array of philosophical and theoretical positions, including postpositivism, feminism, postmodernism, Marxism etc.

There has been relatively little recognition of these broader (philosophical) traditions of thinking which influence how sociological work is carried out. One theme has been that of positivism, which has been deployed by many more specific sociological traditions. Bryant usefully points out that positivism has cycled through several variants, including the French version of Comte and later Durkheim, and the Austrian approach, before being developed with rather different emphases in its more modern form in the United States over the last century. Another theme which has attracted much discussion is the Marxian approach, which seemed to peak in the 1970s. This approach was often quite visible and self-conscious – even sometimes setting itself outside the normal boundaries of bourgeois sociology. Several writers (e.g. Giddens) have struggled to identify a postpositivist philosophical mood that deconstructs each of the various fundamentals of positivism. In the passage I cited above, postpositivist developments in the philosophy of science are even credited with 'driving' other changes in sociology. However, there seems to be rather too much of a spread of thinking to readily encompass some of these themes in any single doctrine, and it is also doubtful if sociologists attend so closely to philosophical writings that these might direct their thinking (cf. Platt, 1996: ch. 4).

There has been a broad differentiation between the (more common) interest in developing sociology as a scientific programme, and those who reiterate its humanist concerns and (often then) interest in fundamental social criticism. Another broad differentiation lies between those impatient to apply their sociology to the real world, as opposed to those wishing to remain firmly ensconced in their ivory towers. On the whole, it seems that either humanistic or applied sociology are too inchoate to be termed traditions as such. Certainly, continuities can often be established, and there may be quite local traditions, but for the most part such tendencies are rather more ephemeral, maintained only through a thinly connected set of texts.

Another line of argument steps right outside the arenas of ideas. Turner and Turner (1990; see also Shils, 1970) argue that the conceptual content in the development of sociology is relatively unimportant compared to the importance of tradition-building amongst cohorts of recruits, institutionalization and generating an adequate flow of resources. (It would be stretching the term 'tradition' rather unduly to see resource regimes as 'traditions', but they are relatively similar in also being institutionalized social patterns.)

Undoubtedly there is a strong tendency amongst sociologists to emphasize social determinations of activities – even when that activity is the process of sociologizing itself. Undoubtedly, the various strands of cognitive thinking other than the formal theoretical apparatus of sociology itself may play important roles in shaping sociological developments. Many ingenious and exciting argumentations in the sociology of sociology have ensued. Nevertheless (as Seidman has alerted, 1983), we must be highly aware of conflation of multi-dimensional complexes into particular forms of single-factor determinism. Each of these various types of tradition may be important at some point, but the central importance of the substantive conceptual content of sociology should never be overlooked. Whatever the collective opportunities and constraints, sociology is constructed by individuals choosing or unconsciously orientated towards particular substantive ideas and 'facts'.

INTEGRATION OF TRADITIONS

There is a tendency, once one has decomposed any phenomenon into its parts, to have some difficulties in reassembling the components back into a working whole. The same is true of traditions. Once isolated, identified, labelled and cleanly packaged we want to see each separate, tradition (of whatever type) as unique and separate, sailing on its own unique course. However, although the linkages often are lost against the bright light of the established positions, the linkages can be discovered, and often revealed to be important.

Some connections are almost purely logical. Some traditions are essentially the flip-sides of others, and developed specifically as a head-on repeal of the other position. However, more complex linkages are more likely. In particular, traditions are often strongly linked through time, since later traditions have the opportunity to forge (or not forge) linkages with their predecessors. Although one tradition often reacts to the temporally adjacent one (as in the Mulkay point cited earlier), there are also instances of temporally non-adjacent, much earlier, traditions being invoked. One example is the postmodern predilection to return to Nietzsche.

Inter-tradition debate can be a major influence on the development of those traditions involved. Despite Levine's strongly nationalistic model of the development of sociological traditions he also stresses the importance of cross-tradition conversations. Intra-tradition conversations differ in their role from inter-tradition conversations: the former usually allow fine-tuning of differences and detailed development where the latter exhibit more the clash of counter-posed postulates. Levine places particular emphasis, for example, on the way 'the divergent postulates that underlie … persisting differences were honed and deepened in the course of centuries of mutual confrontations between British and French social theorists' (1995: 173). He then briefly sketches interactions involving Montesquieu against Hobbes, Rousseau against Hobbes, Smith against Quesnay, Comte against Smith, Mill against Comte, Spencer against Comte,

Durkheim against Mill, and Durkheim against Spencer. More generally, Levine discusses links between American and German and Marxist traditions; British and German and Marxist sociological traditions; French and German traditions; German and American traditions; Anglo-French, Italian and Marxist traditions; Italian and German traditions; and Marxian with British, French and German traditions. The structure of such inter-generation interactions is largely determined by the differential start-times of each of the national traditions which broadly has the pattern of British, French, German, Marxist, Italian and American. Some patterns of 'alliance' can be seen in which some groupings of national traditions band together against others, while sharing internal differences. In particular, Levine sees 'The formidable German defence of subject-orientated assumptions against Anglo-French support for naturalistic assumptions … [as originating] … one of the persistent fault lines in modern social science. Such dialogues can be effective in sharpening differences, as much as they lead to exploration of commonalities.'

In the more recent periods of the development of sociology there has been much discussion of alliances between theoretical traditions and ideologies on the one hand, and methods traditions on the other. One of the more fierce of such battles was the castigation of functional analysis as being inherently conservative, although several defences against this accusation were mounted. Other theoretical traditions seemed to more warmly welcome an ideological commitment. Thus comparative/historical sociologists often openly allied to a radical political position. Many symbolic interactionists felt that their approach fairly decisively led to a sympathy with the 'underdog'.

Links between theoretical and methodological traditions were also sometimes debated. In anthropology there clearly seemed to be a link between functionalist theory and participant observation. A similarly strong link is often postulated between symbolic interactionist and similar theoretical approaches (for example, Weberian 'verstehen sociology') and participant observation. Much of the work of the founding fathers involved consideration of differences amongst societies and therefore implied a link with those methods appropriate for comparative and historical studies (for example, meta-analysis of historical work based on documents or drawing on statistics and on institutional descriptions.) On the other hand, there are major exceptions to such links. Participant observation seems dictated by the circumstances of small-scale societies as much as by theoretical viewpoint, so that ethnographers of different theoretical hues have happily used this field-work approach. There has also been a definite sub-tradition within the broad school of symbolic interactionism which has used survey data or even experimentation as its methodology. The postulated link between functional theory and survey research has been much debated. Platt argues that, surprisingly, although there is an 'ecological correlation' between the two (that is, each is often found in the other's company) there is no intrinsic link. However, that argument is debatable (Crothers, 1990). Some more systematic treatment of the theory-methods link has built up in the textbooks of each speciality: occasionally theory texts allude to the possible methodological consequences, whereas methodology texts now will much more often include advice sensitizing their readers to the theoretical implications of the methods which they might deploy.

It is not sociologically surprising that the sheer spread of sociological ideas over the last couple of decades has given rise to movements of integration. In their introduction to their 1987 collection, Giddens and (Jonathan) Turner suggest that 'the apparent explosion of competing versions of social theory conceals more consistency and integration between rival viewpoints than may appear at first sight' (p. 3). They adduce three grounds in defence of this view:

- '[T]here may be more overlap between different approaches than has generally been perceived' (p. 4). (In earlier phases approaches may seem radically different but over time it becomes recognized that the problems being tackled in a tradition are those common to others, and that there are contributions which each tradition can make to these problems.)
- '[T]here are common lines of development shared by a wide range of the theoretical perspectives which have come into prominence over the past two decades. There has been a concern, for instance, to re-conceptualize the nature of action' (p. 4).
- '[I]t would be difficult to deny that there has been some sort of progress towards resolving issues which previously either appeared intractable or were not analysed in a direct fashion' (p. 4).

However, the story of sociology's successive tradition-sets is not entirely one of movement towards integration. Forces conspire to keep traditions separate from each other. One mechanism is sheer mutual ignorance. The classic example, undoubtedly, is of the mutual unawareness of Durkheim and Weber, two giants of sociology working at exactly the same period and separated by only a few hundred kilometres in physical distance, although perhaps sheltered behind two only partly open national contexts. Another puzzle has been how long it took statistical methods appropriate to social data to emerge and then to link with social investigations and then social theory. Statistical methods were (famously) largely innovated in late Victorian England at a time when there was much social research, but measures such as the correlation coefficient were only pressed into sociological service (at Columbia University by Giddings in particular, see Camic and Xie, 1994) a bit later and on the other side of the Atlantic. In a long and almost despairing essay, Goldthorpe (2000) traces the failure of probabilistic statistical treatments of social phenomena to match with rational choice theory. In each of the main national traditions the possibilities loomed but were never consummated. He suggests that organizational reasons did limit the linkage, but what was more significant were intellectual barriers.

A slightly stronger mechanism of avoidance is merely the expanse of new work awaiting attention by sociologists who are happy enough to continue within their received traditions and are not too concerned to worry about compatibilities or incompatibilities. Indeed, the very notion of cumulation of sociological work, which such bridging of traditions implies, has sometimes been castigated as flowing from a (despised) positivist philosophy.

In some situations rewards flow from establishing difference rather than trying to advance sociology cumulatively by carefully building on the work of others. In Lemert's portrayal of the French intellectual scene for example, he argues that the intense competition for the spotlight encourages the celebration of difference, and underplays the constructive engagement between attentive sociological viewpoints to confront and perhaps reconcile overt differences. Indeed, Lemert argues, appropriate 'rivals' are not even explicitly named as audiences are sure to pick up subtle references.

Rivalry between traditions is often 'social': driven by interests in acquiring resources, recruiting bright students, and catching the attention of policy-makers, funders or the intelligentsia more generally. For example, the 1960s rivalry between Chicago, Columbia and Harvard was not necessarily combative but nevertheless was underlined by snideness and stereotyping. (For an account from the Chicago viewpoint see Fine, 1995.)

But sometimes, too, proponents feel that the whole intellectual and even moral direction of the discipline is at stake, and that this is supremely important. So, sometimes there has been not just competition or even robust competition but outright war between traditions. The 'bad tradition' in some eyes has been Marxism (or its derivatives), which many American sociologists felt to be beyond the pale. But less extreme positions have also yielded occasional vehement fights. Even such a placatory sociologist as Lewis Coser (1975) devoted his ASA Presidential Address to castigating ethnomethodology and also extreme quantitative sociology as inimical to the optimal progress of sociology. Such conflict is of course not the slightest bit unique to sociology, with Kuhn going so far as to suggest that the pre-paradigmatic stage in any science was filled with the clamour of a 'war of the schools'.

Perhaps this has lasted longer in sociology than other disciplines. Perhaps it has become institutionalized.

EMPIRICAL STUDIES OF TRADITIONS

Given my earlier-expressed methodological qualms about the extent to which the theoretical trends commented on actually pertain on the research front or in the textbook and other literature that consolidates research findings, it is important to reach out to empirical studies of sociological traditions, and their interrelationships. Rather than provide an exhaustive review, I will concentrate on two major ones carried out in the early 1980s and a survey conducted in the early 1990s.

In his content analysis of a moderately large sample of articles published in several leading journals over the period of the 1970s Menzies (1982) showed that 'Despite the previous dominance of functionalism, particularly in the United States, functionalist articles constitute only 3.5 per cent of the combined research and theory sample articles'. Even though the sample only covers the 1970s, this is surely a surprising finding, and invites further exploration. It may help such further investigation, though, to look quite carefully at Menzies's 'ethnography' and 'sociography' of the functionalist approach (Table 4.2).

A parallel study (but with a longer coverage) is the content analysis carried out by Wells and Picou (1981) of articles in *American Sociological Review* from its founding until 1978 (see Table 4.3). They examine some 750 articles, and operationalize both Mullins's and Wallace's typologies of theories, as well as other dimensions (especially on type of research, data collection and data analysis designs) relevant to journal articles.[7]

Wells and Picou show that functional imperativism (FI) declined as a theoretical viewpoint over the 1936–78 period, but was not extinguished – averaging 6 per cent. On the other hand, social structuralism (SS) generically all but captured a majority of articles over the whole period, and was the majority viewpoint in the 1965–78 period. Within social

Table 4.2 *Menzies's Empirically Derived Paradigms*

Categories	Overall	Research	Theory
Middle range	15.3	17.7	2.7
Unclassified	10.9	10.5	12.7
Action theory	9.4	10.7	2.7
Description	7.5	8.9	0
Role	7.2	7.4	6.4
Systems theory	6.5	6.3	7.3
Symbolic interaction	6.3	4.6	15.5
Attainment	5.7	6.7	0.9
Interests	5.1	4.9	6.4
Functionalism	3.5	3.2	5.5
Marxism	3.2	2.6	6.4
Greats	2.8	1.8	8.2
Socio-economic determinism	2.5	2.8	0.9
Social issue	2.4	2.3	2.7
Ethnomethodology	1.5	1.4	1.8
Specific thinkers	1.9	0.7	8.2
Exchange	1.0	0.9	1.8
Behaviourism	0.7	0.7	0.9
Phenomenology	0.4	0.4	0.9

Table 4.3 *Wells & Picou's Paradigms*

Mullins's categories	1938–1964	1965–1978
Standard American sociology (SAS)	26.0	61.7
Symbolic interaction	6.3	5.2
Small group theory	–	1.6
New causal theory	5.7	8.3
Ethnomethodology	1.5	–
Radical critical	5.1	1.6
Description	7.5	19.1
Others	47.8	2.6

interpretative method (survey data is a secondary interest), SS articles are heavily involved with survey data (with a tiny commitment to experimental research) and the proportion of 'merely' interpretative articles declines over time. Similarly, FI articles tend to have a low level of sophistication in data analysis compared to SS. (Mind you, since FI articles tend to have been published earlier, there is a need to control for period here.)

Content analyses have some limitations since the theoretical position of the author – let alone other traditions they might adhere to – is not always specifically identified and often has to be inferred by the analyst. Besides content analyses of journals and/or texts, there have been a few (very few) surveys of sociologists' viewpoints. In the Gouldner/Sprehe (1965; Gouldner, 1970) survey of American sociologists' views, evidence for widespread support of functionalism in the mid-1960s is provided: 82.4 per cent favoured functional analysis.[9]

A quarter of a century later, many (a considerable minority) still cling to the functionalist viewpoint. Sanderson and Ellis (1992) found that some 19 per cent of American sociologists they sampled ($n = 162$) identified with functionalism as either a primary (9.9 per cent) or secondary (8.6 per cent) perspective, especially

structuralism, functional structuralism has remained by far the most dominant position, although this importance declined over the period. In terms of Mullins's categories, SAS is characterized as utterly dominant in their earlier period and still a substantial majority in the 1970s.[8]

The cross-tabulations they publish in their book yield further clues into the cognitive character of these perspectives: see Table 4.4 which summarizes several of their tables. First, SS (and also SAS) generates more empirical work than FI. Second, whereas the analysis in FI articles is mainly aimed at the group/family/community/association level – and secondarily at the societal level – SS has a substantial commitment at the individual/role level. Thirdly, whereas FI articles are more likely to involve an

Table 4.4 *Summary of data concerning the research methods linked to the Wallace theory categories*

Theories	Total no.	L L1	L L2	L L3	L L4	Empirical (%)	DC I	DC S	DC E	DA Mv	DA Bi	DA Sq
D	34	5.9	23.5	47.1	23.5	88	6.7	93.3	0	20.7	75.9	3.4
E	30	0	10	90	0	90	14.8	85.2	0	25.9	63	11.1
M	6	0	50	12.5	37.5	100	28.6	71.4	0	57.1	28.6	14.3
P	11	72.7	18.2	9.1	0	73	0	87.6	12.4	0	100	0
T	12	8.3	8.3	25.1	58.3	75	77.8	22.2	0	10	20	70
SS	209	43.3	6.2	34.1	16.4	84	27.3	69.9	2.8	23.2	58.6	18.2
SI	51	74.5	3.9	17.7	3.9	80	34.2	61	4.8	17.1	51.2	31.7
FI	25	0	12.5	50	37.5	64	75	25	0	12.5	25	62.5
SAS	51	51	3.9	19.6	25.5	73	43.2	51.4	5.4	13.6	43.2	43.2
Total	429											

Abbreviations: L, Level; DC, Data collection; DA, Data analysis; L1, Individual/role; L2, Populations/aggregations/classes; L3, Group/family/community/association; L4, Institutions/societies/confederations; N3, Percentage of articles which are empirical; N2, Number of articles; I, Interpretative; S, Survey; E, Experimental; Mv, Multivariate; Bi, Distributional and bivariate; Sq, Sample quotes and typical statements. For abbreviations of theories, see p. 89 above.
Source: Wells and Picou, 1981

Table 4.5 *Paradigms held by United States Sociologists*

Category	%
Conflict theory	28
Eclecticism	26
Symbolic interactionism	25
Functionalism	19
Structuralism	17
Marxism	12
Other	12
Weberianism	11
Phenomenology/ethnomethodology	9
Exchange/rational choice	7
Atheoretical	5
Sociobiology	3
Evolutionism	1

Source: Sanderson and Ellis (1992)

amongst older sociologists, for whom it is the modal category. Nevertheless more expected allegiances include conflict theory (28 per cent), symbolic interactionism (25 per cent), structuralism (17 per cent) and Marxism (12 per cent). On the other hand, they were surprised to find anyone openly identifying themselves as postmodernist.[10]

Sanderson and Ellis's study also points to at least two further complications which empirical research opens up. Almost all respondents were able to identify two responses, and a substantial proportion reported that they were either avowedly atheoretical or eclectic. Both these points clearly indicate that the real world of sociological practice is rather more murky and complex than some schemas might suggest. On the other hand, it must be admitted, the empirical studies do suggest that the views of the textbook classifiers are not too awry. A later extension (Lord and Sanderson, 1999) surveying 375 members of the American Sociological Association's Theory section shows a similar diversification.

It seems rather strange that the very discipline whose business it is to pry into the affairs of other groups knows so little about itself, that there is only very scattered data on its membership, their interests and their theoretical and methodological positions. There is much debate about theory and types of sociology, but little knowledge of what views are held by the vast majority of workaday sociologists who presumably comprise the audience for these debates.

CONCLUSIONS

Sociology is a far-flung science concerned with existing and emerging social phenomena in all their manifestations, at all levels of scale, historical time-period and geographical area.

As undoubtedly the broadest of the social sciences there are few areas where sociological interest fails to penetrate, and sociology can only resist temporarily being brought into any controversies that arise in any corner of the social sciences. The heterodox effects of its massive scanning range are aggravated still further by sociology's theoretical (and more general) highly developed self-consciousness and reflexivity. As a core subject in graduate curricula and as undoubtedly the most prestigious and central speciality area, sociological theorists are under constant pressure to sift through and organize the disparate agenda of sociology.

A broad problem is that there are somewhat inadequate mechanisms for bringing traditions together. Part of this arises because of the essential empiricism of American sociology (albeit laced with middle-range theories), which is globally hegemonic, but which fails to be too concerned with theoretical synthesis. Another general barrier to more active synthesis are the conditions under which Continental social theory is produced which too often stress an emphasis on the idiosyncratic features of theories and theorists, rather than cumulation.

Since its disciplinary origins and through its predisciplinary inheritance, sociology has been host to a bewildering variety of traditions. These have emphasized certain aspects of social phenomena, different scales of analysis, a changing degree of sophistication in engaging with social reality. These traditions have developed under different conditions, exhibited different trajectories etc. Nevertheless, sociology has maintained a reasonably coherent agenda of approaches at each stage, and the individual traditions have fitted, and have been accommodated within the prevailing agenda of the overall tradition-set then pertaining. Since the struggle between traditions takes place in the heart of sociology, at its most prestigious meetings and in its most visible journals, sociologists surely are exposed to the options that are available. Where the direct points at issue are not especially explicit, the stolid patient work of commentators and textbook writers remedies this deficiency. This reflexivity about traditions has allowed sociologists to maintain some degree of control over their own intellectual concerns. But, do traditions rule sociologists, or are they merely epiphenomena resulting from hard and clear choices that sociologists make? It is up to every reader to make up their own mind.

NOTES

1 An interesting example occurred when Hanan Selvin set up an experiment with several data analysts, who were presented with the same dataset to consider, and who in fact came up after several days with similar analyses, despite voyaging on different routes to reach this: see Selvin and Hirshi, 1967.

2 The several aspects of a tradition can more formally be classified into the following:

Levels/Dimensions	Substantive	Methodological	Moral
'Ideas'	Concepts, theories, etc.	Methodology, assumptions etc.	Moral vision
'Facts'	Findings, empirical generalizations etc.	Methods	Practical recommendations.

3 Stephen Cole (1994), in particular, has drawn attention to the difference between the 'core' and the research front. He suggests that the cognitive structure of most sciences consists in a few theories and procedures over which there is complete consensus and which can be readily presented in textbooks, and a 'research front' marked by minimal consensus and much diversity of approaches, methods and models. Another conception is that there is a 'world' of textbook sociology which has a life of its own, with often a minimal connectivity to the research front. Traditions may live rather different lives in each of these two different worlds.

4 Alexander and Colomy's terminology for charting the progress of a tradition includes:

- Elaboration (i.e. refinement), proliferation (extension of scope) and revisions (relating back to the core) as three lines of specification.

- Reconstruction, which involves acknowledging differences with the founder and openings to other traditions.
- Tradition-creation: 'The essence of tradition- creation is the synthesis of elements drawn from several existing and often competing intellectual paradigms, with the aim of generating the theoretical core of a new school', 1992: 37.

5 To say the least, since many other recent theorists seem intent on ignoring major tracts of sociological theorizing: see Mouzelis (1995) for a critique.

6 Wallace attempts to derive his set of 11 (plus one missing!) positions with a logically derived basis. This contrasts determined with socially generated causes of social phenomena (further broken down into characteristics and environments and then into people and non-people sources) and objective versus subjective definitions of social reality.

7 Unfortunately since they do not provide the details of their operationalization in their book it is not possible to check its plausibility. Moreover since (unlike Menzies) they do not provide illustrative case studies the reader cannot readily establish an intuitive feel for what is subsumed under each category.

8 Wells and Picou operationalize Mullins's central category of 'Standard American' as comprising functionalism + role theory + middle range theory (26 per cent theory + research articles). Interestingly, 'Standard American sociology' is higher (61.7 per cent) in the cognate study they carried out of articles published in *Rural Sociology*, which is not surprising given the heavily empiricist reputation of that speciality field within sociology of that era.

9 At that time, other national traditions of sociology may have somewhat similar patterns of allegiance: for example, Lipset (in Blau, 1975: 206) cites a late-1960s survey of Japanese sociologists who endorse Talcott Parsons (24 per cent) and Robert K. Merton (19 per cent) as non-Japanese sociologists worthy of considerable attention.

10 Their methodology was to offer closed-response choices. Up to two were asked for, while allowing an open-ended other category for write-in responses.

BIBLIOGRAPHY

Alexander, Jeffrey (1979) 'Paradigm revision and "Parsonianism"', *Canadian Journal of Sociology*, 4: 343–57.

Alexander, J. (1987) *Sociological Theory since 1945*. London: Hutchinson.

Alexander, J. (1982–83) *Theoretical Logic in Sociology*. Berkeley, CA: University of California Press.

Alexander, Jeffrey and Colomy, Paul (1992) 'Traditions and competition: preface to a post-positivist approach to knowledge cumulation', in George Ritzer (ed.), *Metatheorizing*. Newbury Park, CA: Sage. pp. 27–54.

Baehr, Peter and O'Brien, Mike (1994) 'Founders, classics and the concept of a canon', *Current Sociology*, 42 (1): 1–151.

Baehr, Peter (2002) *Founders, Classics, Canons: modern disputes over the origins and appraisal of Sociology's Heritage*. New Brunswick: Transaction Publishers.

Ben-David, Joseph (1973) 'The state of sociological theory and the sociological community', *Comparative Studies in Society and History*, 15: 448–72.

Berger, P. and Luckmann, T. (1967) *The Social Construction of Reality*. London: Allen Lane.

Blau, Peter (ed.) (1975) *Approaches to the Study of Social Structure*. New York: Free Press.

Bottomore, Tom and Nisbet, Robert (eds) (1979) *A History of Sociological Analysis*. London: Heinemann.

Bryant, C. (1985) *Positivism in Theory and Research*. Basingstoke: Macmillan.

Camic, Charles and Xie, Yu (1994) 'The statistical turn in American social science: Columbia University 1890–1915', *American Sociological Review*, 59: 773–805.

Cole, Stephen (ed.) (2001) *What's Wrong with Sociology?* New Brunswick: Transaction Publishers.

Cole, Stephen (1992) *Making Science*. Cambridge, MA: Harvard University Press.

Collins, Randall (1985) *Three Sociological Traditions*. New York: Oxford University Press.

Collins, Randall (1994) *Four Sociological Traditions*. New York: Oxford University Press.

Connell, R.W. (1997) 'Why is classical theory classical?', *American Journal of Sociology*, 102 (6): 1511–57.

Coser, L. (1965) *Men of Ideas*. New York: The Free Press.

Coser, L. (1975) 'Two methods in search of a substance', *American Sociological Review*, 40 (6): 691–700.

Crane, D. (1972) *Invisible Colleges*. Chicago: University of Chicago Press.

Crothers, Charles (1990) 'The link between "Structural Analysis" and "Systematic Social Research"', unpublished ms. Department of Sociology, University of Auckland.

Crothers, Charles (1997) 'Extending Levine's models of sociological research traditions', *History of the Human Sciences*, 10 (2): 150–64.

Crothers, Charles (1995) *Social Structure*. London: Routledge.

Dallmyr, F. (1987) *Critical Encounters: Between Philosophy and Politics*. Bloomington, IN: University of Notre Dame Press.

Davis, Kingsley (1959) 'The myth of functional analysis as a special method in sociology and anthropology', *American Sociological Review*, 24: 757–72.

Easthope, Gary (1974) *History of Social Research Methods*. London: Longman.

Eisenstadt, S.N. and Curelaru, M. (1976) *Forms of Sociology: Paradigms and Crises*. New York: Wiley.

Fine, Gary (ed.) (1995) *A Second Chicago School?* Chicago: University of Chicago Press.

Friedheim, E. (1979) 'An empirical comparison of Ritzer's paradigms and similar meta-theories: a research note', *Social Forces*, 58: 59–66.

Friedrichs, R.W. (1970) *A Sociology of Sociology*. New York: The Free Press.

Giddens, A. and Turner, J. (eds) (1987) *Social Theory Today*. Cambridge: Polity Press.

Glaser, Barney and Strauss, Anselm (1967) *The Discovery of Grounded Theory*. Chicago: Aldine.

Goldthorpe, John (2000) *On Sociology*. Oxford: Oxford University Press.

Gouldner, A. (1970) *The Coming Crisis of Western Sociology*. New York: Basic Books.

Gouldner, Alvin and Sprehe, Timothy (1965) 'Sociologists look at themselves', *Transaction*, 2 (4): 42–4.

Hays, W. (1977) 'Theorists and theoretical frameworks identified by family sociologists', *Journal of Marriage and the Family*, 39: 59–65.

Heilbron, Johan (1995) *The Rise of Social Theory*. Cambridge: Polity Press.

Kuhn, Thomas (1962/1970) *The Structure of Scientific Revolutions*. Chicago: University of Chicago Press.

Lamont, Michele (1987) 'How to become a dominant French philosopher: the case of Jacques Derrida', *American Journal of Sociology*, 93: 584–622.

Lemert, C. (ed.) (1981) *French Sociology: rupture and renewal since 1968*. New York: Columbia University Press.

Levine, Donald (1995) *Visions of the Sociological Tradition*. Chicago: University of Chicago Press.

Levine, Donald (1996) 'Thoughts on Vision and its Creation', *Sociological Forum*, 11 (4): 675–85.

Levine, Donald (1997) 'On Vision and its Critics', *History of the Human Sciences*, 10 (2): 168–73.

Levine, Donald (2001) 'Dialogues of the Nations: Revisiting Visions and its Critics', *Sociological Quarterly*, 42 (1): 111–20.

Lord, Jane and Sanderson, Stephen (1999) 'Current theoretical and political perspectives of Western sociological theorists', *American Sociologist*, 30 (3): 42–66.

Madge, John (1963) *The Origins of Scientific Sociology*. London: Tavistock.

Martindale, Don (1961) *The Nature and Types of Sociological Theory*. London: Routledge and Kegan Paul.

Menzies, Ken (1982) *Sociological Theory in Use*. London: Routledge and Kegan Paul.

Merton, R.K. (1976) *Sociological Ambivalence*. New York: Free Press.

Merton R.K. and White Riley, Matilda (eds) (1980) *Sociological Traditions from Generation to Generation*. Norwood, NJ: Ablex.

Mohan, Raj and Wilke, Arthur S. (eds) (1994) *International Handbook of Contemporary Developments in Sociology*. Westport, CT: Greenwood Press.

Mouzelis, Nicos (1995) *Sociological Theory: What went Wrong?* London: Routledge.

Mulkay, M. (1971) *Functionalism, Exchange and Theoretical Strategy*. London: Routledge and Kegan Paul.

Mullins, N. (1973) *Theory and Theory Groups in Contemporary American Sociology*. New York: Harper and Row.

Mullins, N. (1983) 'Theory and theory groups revisited', *Sociological Theory*, 1: 319–37.

Munch, Richard (1991) 'American and European social theory: cultural identities and social forms of theory production', *Sociological Perspectives*, 34: 313–35.

Nisbet, Robert (1966) *The Sociological Tradition*. New York: Basic Books.

Oberschall, Anthony (ed.) (1972) *The Establishment of Empirical Sociology*. New York: Harper and Row.

Picou, J., Wells, R. and Nyberg, K. (1978) 'Paradigms, theories and methods in contemporary rural sociology', *Rural Sociology*, 43: 559–83.

Platt, Jennifer (1996) *A History of Sociological Research Methods in America: 1920–1960*. Cambridge: Cambridge University Press.

Quah, Stella R. and Sales, Arnaud (eds) (2000) *The International Handbook of Sociology*. London: Sage.

Ritzer, George (1975) *Sociology: A Multi-paradigm Science*. Boston, MA: Allyn and Bacon.

Ritzer, George (ed.) (1990) *Frontiers of Social Theory: New Syntheses*. New York: Columbia University Press.

Ritzer, George (1996) *Modern Sociological Theory*, 4th edn. New York: McGraw–Hill.

Rule, James (1997) *Theory and Progress in Social Science*. Cambridge, New York: Cambridge University Press.

Sanderson, Stephen and Ellis, Lee (1992) 'Theoretical and political perspectives of American sociologists in the 1990s', *American Sociologist*, 23 (2): 26–43.

Seidman, S. (1983) *Liberalism and the Origins of European Social Theory*. Berkeley, CA: University of California Press.

Selvin, Hanan (1976) 'Durkheim, Booth and Yule: the non-diffusion of an intellectual innovation'. *Archives Européens de Sociologie*, 17: 39–51.

Selvin, H.C. and Hirshi, T. (1967) *Delinquency Research: an appraisal of analytical methods.* New York: Free Press.

Shils, E. (1970) 'Tradition, ecology, and institutions in the history of sociology', *Daedalus*, 99: 760–825.

Snizek, W. (1975) 'The relationship between theory and research: a study in the sociology of sociology', *Sociological Quarterly*, 16: 415–28.

Snizek, W. (1976) 'An empirical assessment of sociology: a multi-paradigmatic science', *American Sociologist*, 11: 217–19.

Sorokin, Pitirim (1966) *Sociological Theories of Today.* New York: Harper and Row.

Stinchcombe, Arthur (1982) 'Should sociologists forget their mothers and fathers?', *American Sociologist*, 17: 2–10.

Turner, Bryan (ed.) (1996) *The Blackwell Companion to Social Theory.* Oxford: Blackwell.

Turner, Jonathan (1986) *The Structure of Sociological Theory.* Chicago: Dorsey Press.

Turner, S. and Turner, J. (1990) *The Impossible Science: An Institutional Analysis of American Sociology.* Newbury Park, CA: Sage.

Wagner, Peter, Weiss, C.H., Wittrock, B. and Wollman, H. (eds), *Social Sciences and Modern States: National Experiences and Theoretical Crossroads.* Cambridge: Cambridge University Press.

Wagner, P., Wittrock, B. and Whitley, R. (eds) (1990) *Discourses on Society XV.* Dordrecht: Kluwer Academic Publishers.

Wallace, Walter (ed.) (1969) *Sociological Theory: An Introduction.* London: Heinemann.

Wells, Richard and Picou, Steven (1981) *American Sociology: Theoretical and Methodological Structures.* Washington, DC: University Press of America.

Wiley, N. (1985) 'The current inter-regnum in American sociology', *Social Research*, 51: 179–207.

Zuckermann, H. (1988) 'Sociology of Science', in N. Smelser (ed.), *Handbook of Sociology.* Thousand Oaks, CA: Sage.

5

Comparative Sociology: Some Paradigms and their Moments

DAVID E. APTER

INTRODUCTION

In the not-so-distant past, comparative sociology was considerably more central in the general field of sociology than it is today. The present discussion will review several periods of its more ample prosperity, suggest reasons for the decline and indicate briefly possible future trends. While it appears unlikely that comparative sociology will be restored to the privileged place it held in the past, it remains important not only because of the pivotal role it played in shaping general sociological inquiry, but because to a considerable extent sociology today continues to rework earlier themes. That said, these remarks are not intended as a catalog or survey of comparative research nor a 'who's who' of contemporary practitioners. Rather, in recuperating several intellectual traditions in the field, I want to strike a balance between their logical and methodological tendencies by approaching comparative sociology in terms of several of its more robust 'paradigms'. Those which were of most concern in the past dealt with such topics as social change, capitalism, socialism, industrialization, modernity and development, that is, the big themes Polyani referred to as the great transformation. Old in terms of comparative theory they remain new in the light of fresh problems (Boudon, 1986b).

Among sociologists who over the years have been both beneficiaries and contributors to these paradigms one might include such figures as Reinhard Bendix, Edward Shils, S.N. Eisenstadt, Seymour Martin Lipset, Neil Smelser, Barrington Moore, Jr, Ralf Dahrendorf, Juan Linz, Theda Skocpol, Craig Calhoun, Anthony Giddens, Rogers Brubaker, David Stark, Karen Barkey, Ivan Szelenyi, Pierre Bourdieu, Raymond Boudon, Norbert Elias, to name only a few. While they vary widely in approach, all owe intellectual debts to one or more of the major antecedent thinkers who constituted comparative sociology as a field. Most have considered comparative sociology as subject as well as object; that is, reviewed and analyzed what it is they do as they do it. Hence there is a large body of literature on comparative research design, frameworks, conceptual schemes and hypothesis-testing not to speak of broader philosophical concerns.[1]

To the extent that this is so, to consider the condition of comparative sociology requires placing it in context. In this regard, perhaps no single earlier figure continues to have the impact of Max Weber, who remains as virtually the ideal type of comparative sociologist. No one dealt as explicitly and effectively with the gap between structural principles and individualistic modes of action, not least of all in terms of rational and non-rational behavior (Shils and Finch, 1949; see also Brubaker, 1984). Perhaps it is for this reason that Weber continues to be a source of research questions today, establishing both the conditions of possibility for comparative theory and substantive ideas (although the Simmel revival in a context of modernity is also extremely interesting). So much so that Weber remains the standard bearer against whom to judge more contemporary approaches, such as rational choice theory, the new institutionalism and discourse theory.[2]

It is also the case that in the past, when the main paradigms to be discussed here were first applied, they seemed ahead of the facts. That is, they illuminated what conventional knowledge obscured. Today, however, one might say that the facts are ahead of theories. Theories are overwhelmed by contingencies, the unanticipated outcomes of anticipated events undermining the implied determinism of structural and logical outcomes. One could argue that the more this is so the greater the need to probe more deeply into cases, to frame, contextualize and, by examining lower levels of generalization, connect subsystem to system. Indeed, each of the paradigms discussed here did so in one way or other, and according to one or other set of rules of scientific logic. Moreover, they concerned themselves as well with the methodological problems of inquiry, and a spectrum of methodologies, conceptual strategies and statistical techniques.[3]

In the absence of these or other paradigms, theory construction falters. It lags behind methodological innovation. And this is one of the present predicaments facing comparative sociology as a field. This at a time when rules of valid evidence have become more stringent to the point where excessive preoccupation with method makes one suspicious of more interpretative approaches. Yet without appropriate knowledge of historical, contextual and multi-layered factors, causal and technically proficient techniques, not least of all cross-sectional matrices, will produce thin results. Hence the considerable intellectual tension between those favoring historical, descriptive and qualitative analysis, and path-dependent theory construction and those relying on survey, questionnaire, multivariate analysis and other quantitative techniques. It would be comforting to conclude that contemporary comparative sociologists need to be equally at home with both insofar as they involve different styles of thinking. In practice it is not as easy as it sounds (Mahoney, 2000).

Doing so was perhaps easier at an earlier period. Lipset,[4] Dogan (Dogan and Pelassy, 1980), Galtung (1967), Linz (Linz and Stepan, 1978) and others made generous use of the survey and other quantitative techniques and data available. They moved easily between analytic and methodological modes. They could combine depth with statistical knowledge. Someone like Charles Tilly played back and forth between historical analysis and quantitative techniques in, for example, his studies of social mobilization and social movements (Tilly, 1978). Today the requirements of both are greater, as are the difficulties of combining them (Hechter and Levi, 1994).

Despite these difficulties, the aims of comparative sociology remain what they have always been, the principled explanation of similarities and differences, resolution or non-resolution of contradictions and inconsistencies. How to find general meaning in the particular event by means of comparative methods is perhaps another way of putting the matter.[5]

As for context and depth, while there are plenty of sociologists who did and continue to use case materials, and with theoretically interesting comparative results, for examples, Ronald Dore (1973) on Japan, or Andrew G. Walder (1995) on China, it is more and more rare to consider such work as in the main stream of sociological thinking. Societal comparisons around problems of power, authority, stratification, mobility etc. continue but a good deal of work is now specialized rather than comparative, and around topical themes like gender, sexuality, race, ethnicity, language etc. Such specialization has shifted the focus away from a comparative perspective as such.

It is with these thoughts in mind that we turn to five paradigms that we consider useful in describing the field of comparative sociology in its early and better days. We use the term paradigm advisedly, not so much as a corpus of knowledge as a framing discourse – less than a school and more than a theory. This is close to Kuhn's original definition of significant paradigms, that is, including an ability to attract an enduring group of adherents away from competing modes of inquiry while remaining sufficiently open-ended as to leave a variety of problems for such adherents to solve (Kuhn, 1962). They are also paradigmatic in the sense that they establish general rules and structural principles from which hypotheses can be derived, examined empirically and applied synchronically, diachronically, or both. The common goal is not only a cumulative body of theory but also an underlying logic of outcomes as the basis of theoretical propositions.

Those discussed here share such purposes but they are neither exhaustive nor mutually exclusive. All have given birth to a very theoretically diverse progeny.[6] Over time these paradigms have replaced each other, although their clienteles often overlap. When shifts occur it is less a result of anomalies, or those kinds of theoretical crises leading to the conviction that an alternative is better. They simply go out of fashion.

If it is the case that each reached a certain intellectual high-water mark of influence, in decline all left important residues. Some, like Marx, or better, Marxism, although very much out of favor at the moment, retain a fluctuating significance, indeed, a gift of eternal return. In this sense a good many of the theorists falling under each paradigm (and not only Max Weber) continue to have theoretical influence. Take for example, the renewed emphasis on modernism, a recurrent central concern in all of the paradigms. As a topic it fell out of favor, not so much replaced as critiqued in terms of dependency theory, conflict theory and other approaches which emphasized the socially and politically negative consequences of modernism, particularly in terms of problems of hegemony, imperialism, colonialism and other forms of domination. Similarly with ideas of jurisdiction and space, territoriality and the proprietary notions that went with it. In the latter instance, for example, social space is back as public space, in ways informed by earlier concerns. Habermas retrieves Weber and Parsons.

Henri Lefebvre retrieves the sociological Marx (e.g. Lefebvre, 1971, 1986; see also Harvey, 1989), David Frisby (2001) retrieves the modernizing Simmel.

The five paradigms owe considerably to their European and British origins. These lent American sociology a cosmopolitan quality it otherwise lacked. The latter was to a significant degree an exploration (if not a celebration) of 'progress', particularly social Darwinian and evolutionary approaches. Applied to problems of societal change the early paradigms represented a major advance over earlier forms of inquiry, including those ranging from an unabashed curiosity about the exotic to a romantic Rousseauean search for an original noble savage, a Lockean original condition, or using simple cultural, racial and other distinctions to distinguish between 'savagery' and 'civilization'. In these terms a 'Science of Man', using an evolutionary metaphor drawn from the natural sciences, was a great advance. Attacking mysticism, idealism and religion, it substituted instead a harmonious teleology – social life as a master plan in keeping with or parallel to evolutionary processes.

For Comte, Spencer, Cooley and others modern society was a social process capable of structural innovation and adaption the consequence of which was societal evolution from inferior to superior forms of social life. In Spencer such evolution took the forms of greater diversification and differentiation, resulting in transitions from simple ('primitive') to complex organizational forms (Radcliffe-Brown, 1952). At once systemic and developmental, it stimulated inquiries into how, where and under what conditions such evolution occurs.

Similarly, Charles Horton Cooley developed the idea of modernity as progress, the unidirectionality of industrialization and the spread of universalized roles and networks.[7] How to sustain social integration given the disturbances and perturbations of modernizing processes became the prism by means of which economic growth and political authority and control tended to be refracted.[8]

One result of this evolutionary emphasis was the introduction of functionalism into the social sciences. Functionalism made comparison more systemically possible. By using it for comparing very different social systems, observers could augment their understanding of their own society. It also enabled the derivation of universals from the diversity of particulars. It took from biology notions of differentiation, complexity, self-maintenance and the like. But it never lost its original connection to social Darwinism. In this sense one could say that comparative sociology remains close to its evolutionary origins.

Such thinking influenced not only sociology but anthropology, not least of all a host of case studies comparing folk- or community-based societies in terms of the impact of modernity (not least of all in the work of Malinowski, Radcliffe-Brown, Evans-Pritchard, S.F. Nadel, Redfield, Egan, Richards, Fallers and many others working in the functionalist tradition of social anthropology). It retains its influence, at least to some extent, in the work of Talcott Parsons.[9]

A second paradigm is represented best by Marx himself as well as in its other *Marxisant* renditions: revisionist, Trotskyist, Gramscian etc. Dialectical as well as evolutionary, it had a preferred historical teleology, with socialism a last instance on a directional, systemic and purposeful scale demarcating irreversible modal stages – a transcendence from lower to higher material modes. Whatever its guises, Marxism was above all concerned to identify the critical and dynamic components of capitalism as a unique engine of productivity while identifying in 'systemic', more general terms the inevitable disarray within it, the cracks occurring willy-nilly as a result of the impact of the productive process itself. By concentrating on the determining, socially necessary and contradictory effects of capitalist productive modes different societies could be characterized in terms of the gaps which grew between the ever-more concentrated wealth and power of property owners on the one hand and the expanding significance of the value-producing labor power of workers (plus their growing and presumably superior insight), resulting in class conflict as the state, embodying the bourgeoisie, became polarized, indeed, against society, as represented by the proletariat

(Therborn, 1980). As a paradigm Marxism sponsored theories about transformation and revolution, work and alienation and, in more Hegelian terms, conditions under which inversionary and revolutionary ruptures would occur, the consequence of which was the periodic transformation of societies from a lower to a higher productive/societal stage.[10]

For Marx the critical cases to examine were Germany, France and England, with some reference to the United States and to colonial countries such as India as well as Turkey, China and elsewhere. His views about the progressive power of capitalism were made almost embarrassingly clear in *The Communist Manifesto*. For example, he described capitalism in terms far more glowing than, for example, the more 'dismal' economists like Adam Smith. Speculating on its rise in the West, Marx compared it to the more hydraulic bureaucracies of the so-called 'Asian mode of production' found in the Turkish or Chinese empires for example. His description of the morally ambiguous transformative effects of colonial capitalism on India are clearly in favor of the first, with only mild regret for the loss of village Indian life and customs.[11]

Of course the so-called historical sociologists were also interested in capitalism and what triggered it. Nevertheless one wonders whether had there not been a Marx there would have been a Weber. In this sense, as a third paradigm, historical sociology takes off from Marx even though its protagonists were hardly enamored of his solutions. It asked all the comparative questions probing deeply into the nature of capitalism itself, the conditions of its emergence: institutions, norms, structural determinants, its relations of power to equity, including core as well as peripheral characteristics of modern corporate society. Within its very generous pantheon are, most significantly, Weber, Durkheim, Toennies, Pareto and Simmel (whom Aron considered the founder of 'formal' sociology – a 'geometry of the social world'). Other, somewhat more peripheral figures included Max Scheler who deplored the elevation in modern society of utility as the last word in rationality, and the equation of market values with ethical truths (Scheler, 1961).

As a group it could be divided into those who like Durkheim reinforced the functional attributes of the organic evolutionists, or Weber, whose emphasis on power and legitimacy was based on a combination of economic organization and existential, indeed phenomenological knowledge. The first influenced the comparative study of religion, its relation to more positivist factors like the division of labor, and in so doing combined structuralism and positivism with the power of belief. The second combined an emphasis on intentionality, economic organization, types of normative legitimacy, bureaucracy, hierarchy and comparative religion.

Just as one might ask about Marx and historical sociology, so too with Weber and Parsons. The Parsonian paradigm, although relatively short-lived, was something of a synthesis of major ingredients from evolutionism in the form of organismic theory, and Weber's and Pareto's emphases on non-economic factors in social systems. The most pretentiously ambitious comparative approach, the Parsonian version of functionalism, 'structural-functionalism', was more of a 'conceptual scheme' than a theory, designed to bring together in one elaborate, all-encompassing framework, three all-encompassing dimensions of social life: culture, social system, behavior (Parsons, 1949).[12] Using these to establish 'systems-problems,' structural-functionalism took over functional theory as hitherto employed in anthropology, added psychological and behavioral components and established binary categories for comparing the varying structural properties on the basis of common functional elements in concrete societies, most particularly between less industrial and industrial societies. These binaries could be regarded as sets (pattern variables), forming components of social systems. They could be applied from one concrete society or sub-system to another, and from the most general to the lower levels of the same system. By so doing Parsons colonized 'organismic' models of society, with survival, integration, adaptation and self-maintenance tests to determine the minimum set of structural requisites necessary for societies to cope with strains, tensions and change (Alexander, 1983b; Mitchell, 1967).

The final paradigm to be mentioned, world system theory, is the most dependent on wide-ranging comparisons over time, and is more a variant of social institutionalism – a kind of structuralism that owes a good deal to Marx, Durkheim and Weber (Alexander, 1982). Concerned with economics-driven change over the *longue durée*, among the key figures in Europe it includes two sociological historians, Fernand Braudel and Marian Malowist, and in the United States, Immanuel Wallerstein. It was the latter who developed further the original particularly Braudelian emphasis on the circulation of trading patterns, inventions and particularly the geography of what is today called globalization, by means of diachronic studies of 'world systems'. An adaptation of dependency theory but with a broader historical sweep, it emphasized the significance of hegemonic relations between centers and peripheries, the origins of the former, their universalizing propensities and totalizing effects, not least of all for the consolidation of a European-centered world economy. Dominant factors are innovation, technology, invention, their impact on trade and markets, their social effects and their impact on the changing relations of power (Wallerstein, 1974, 1980, 1989).[13]

The ideas embodied in these five paradigms have left an indelible mark on comparative sociology today. The evolutionary tradition and Parsonianism emphasized social differentiation, complexity, adaptation and equilibrium, concepts still relevant in systems theory, organization theory, the analysis of institutions, networks, etc. Both Marxism and world system theory emphasized the negative effects of what today is called globalization and growing disparities of wealth and power both between metropoles and peripheries but within countries as well. The historical sociologists pointed out what is just beginning to become respectable among economists, the importance of non-economic factors in limiting the scope of market rationality, the sentiments, residues and ophelmities (rather than optimalities) of Pareto. There is renewed interest in the role of religion in social life (shades of Durkheim), while new concerns with leadership and elites, hierarchy and authority, and differences in legitimization between legal rational and other forms, bring a good many of Weber's concerns back into currency. Similarly with Simmel's interest in the balancing consequences of asymmetrical conflict (Frisby, 1986). In each case comparison was central both as a means to theory construction and as a testing ground for hypotheses.[14]

In contrast to comparative politics, with its emphasis on the state, comparative sociology is on the whole concerned with how power is dispersed, its multiple sources, how it derives from relationships in civil society, and in private life from family to groups, cultural, business, labor, religious, and from voluntary associations as well as formal institutions. Indeed, the closer to formal institutions, and particularly the state, it is, the more indistinguishable is comparative sociology from comparative politics (e.g. Badie and Birnbaum, 1983; Linz, 2000).

One does not want to limit comparative sociology to the five paradigms. There were many others that had considerable significance although were perhaps not quite paradigmatic.[15] One good example is the Frankfurt School, so important in German and European comparative sociology, with its concern with the different faces of rationality, culture and power, according to whether a system was capitalist, socialist, or fascist. Its protagonists, Benjamin, Adorno, Horkheimer and others had a considerable 'aura' effect within sociology even though it can hardly be said to have affected mainstream American sociology.[16]

Whatever else that can be said about it, and regardless of its present condition as a field, as will be shown here, comparative analysis remains relevant as a way of deriving principles of social life from the comparative study of explicit cases, cultures, societies and social systems.[17] In some respects the contrast between the five paradigms is less in terms of theories than the ends that their theories favor. Each has a preferred teleology, a definition of public well-being, and underwrites moral claims to prophylactic or improving ends by references to scientific inquiry. Insofar as such ends remain as relevant so theory in the context of comparative sociology will continue to matter.[18]

Whatever else might be said about them, in their day these paradigms sponsored a wide range of comparative research. While they may have appeared to have outlived their usefulness this is by no means the case. To a considerable extent their once innovative contributions have entered the mainstream of sociology with respect to such diverse matters as class, elites, roles and other social formations, and industrialization, bureaucratization, nationalism, belief systems, etc. even as they have become divorced from their origins and become sociological commonplaces. Some ideas have, at least in their original forms, became obsolete. Few sociologists today take evolutionary notions seriously in the way of a Comte,[19] Spencer and Cooley or regard social life according to evolutionary stages of human knowledge (at its higher end enabling sociology itself as a superior kind of understanding), save perhaps socio-biologists or ethologists.[20] As for the possibilities of finding sociological truths or establishing a science of society, the aim might be accepted while the practice would strike most of today's sociologists as immodest.[21]

Yet if the historical sociologists – and here one might also include Maine, Austen, Sombart, Mosca, Michels and Ostrogorski, in addition to Weber, Durkheim, Toennies, Pareto, Simmel, the basic binaries they all used for comparison (such as 'primitive'/'modern', status/contract, pre-industrial/ industrial, etc.), or Weber's types of authority, Toennies's *Gemeinschaft–Gesellschaft* distinctions, Durkheim's mechanical or organic society, as well as the constructed ideal or modal typologies they favored (and that in their moment seemed so insightful) – lack sufficient nuance from today's perspective, becoming overkill categories for the nature of the phenomena they are supposed to examine, it is also the case that their obsolescence has resulted in contemporary typologies that are more descriptive than theoretically fruitful.[22]

As to Parsonianism, which in its day represented a high-water mark in paradigmatic construction, certainly the most architecturally elaborate and ambitious of comparative schemes, by elevating the more or less heuristic functionalism of such anthropological figures as Malinowski and Radcliffe-Brown into a form of structuralism-functionalism, the effect was to make comparison totally unwieldy. It required one to exhaust each higher level of generalization before moving to lower levels and in terms of multiple combinations of the same 'pattern variables'.[23] These, organized in sets and multiple combinations, were used empirically to compare systems, and also to evaluate them in terms of their propensities towards equilibrium as social steady states (Parsons et al., 1953). The instrumental purpose was to identify and remove sources of strain and facilitate adaption. If in theory it was remedial, the actual research practice became too difficult; the relationships between functional equivalents and requisite variables (functional requisites) necessary for unit maintenance and adaptation becoming simply unmanageable (e.g. Parsons and Shils, 1951). In short, there was no way to refine and operationalize the system.[24] Hence the bias for 'order' over conflict. Not surprisingly efforts to revive it by Jeffrey Alexander and others have not been successful (Alexander, 1983b). But it should be added that Parsons continues to show up in Habermas and other theorists concerned with the role of system in social analysis.

As for world system theory, it never became as central to comparative sociology as the others. But insofar as it emphasized the relations between centers on peripheries, their hegemonic influences, not least of all in terms of imperialism and colonialism, it remains, as with Marxism, a way of interpreting patterns of major social change using economic and technological factors among others. Perhaps its heavy reliance on history, both descriptively and as evidence, went too much against the grain of sociology itself (which on the whole remains largely anti-historical).

MAX WEBER AND THE SPIRIT OF SOCIOLOGICAL COMPARISON

If the paradigms have declined, paradoxically enough Weber retains his stature. One might call him, without too much exaggeration, the godfather of comparative theory (Alexander, 1983a). Insofar as modernism is considered a function of capitalism, Weber's original questions continue to be pertinent. Why did capitalism occur when it did? Why in Europe and not somewhere else?

What are the moral equivalents to the Protestant ethic in other beliefs which might serve to induce the kind of this-worldly asceticism Weber saw as socially essential in order to maintain the disciplined and saving graces of capitalist development, especially in its early stages? If historical processes include more strategic variables than class, what else is relevant in accounting for differences between economic factors, utilitarian individualism and collective behavior? Above all, what are necessary and sufficient conditions for adapting to inputs of modernity, particularly economic but cultural as well in various settings, and in terms of social discipline, civic responsibility, citizenship, work and commitment? Such matters are as important today as when Weber dealt with them.

It was part of Weber's genius to raise such questions in three contexts – historical, economic and legal. Separating acquisitive commercialism elsewhere than Europe in terms of the evolution of legal and financial instruments and activities, Weber showed some of the different ways in which rationality and purposive action were channeled if not defined by value orientations. In Europe the most germane interpretive commitments combined discipline as social strategy with widespread individual sacrifice, not least of all the longer view prevailing over the shorter. Contrasting, for example, the individual harshness of a predestination unknown to the predestined, with the 'meditative piety' of the Buddhism of India and especially the 'genteel intellectualism' of Brahmanism, Weber speculated on the consequence of the latter for a caste which possessed neither the stuff of entrepreneurial commitment nor the competition for virtue as represented in particular by Calvinism (Weber, 1958b: 151). As well, Weber showed how deeply Protestantism contrasted with the Confucian ethic which is not that of a priesthood but rather an ordered convention of laymen, an imperial cosmology originally charismatically endowed and hierarchically enshrined in a bureaucratic Mandarinate order above, while below it was embodied and enshrined in the family unit. Wealth was deified.

> In no other civilized country has material welfare been so exalted as the supreme good … Still economic policy did not create the economic mentality of capitalism. The money profits of the traders in the Period of the Warring States were political profits of commissioners to the state. The great mining *corvées* were used to search for gold. Still no intermediate link led from Confucianism and its ethic – as firmly rooted as Christianity – to a civic and methodical way of life. (Weber, 1951: 237–8)

Indeed, the contrast to Puritanism could not be greater.[25]

So too with the ancient Hebrew prophets, who, showing both ecstatic proclivities and a penchant for chasing visions, delivered their prophecies from on high. Unlike early Christianity, the 'prophets did not think of themselves as members of a supporting spiritual community. On the contrary. Misunderstood and hated by the mass of their listeners they never felt themselves to be supported and protected by them as like-minded sympathizers as did the apostles of the early Christian community. Hence, the prophets spoke at no time of their listeners or addressees as their "brethren", the Christian apostles always did so' (Weber, 1952: 292). Not much opportunity here either for collective order and a truly effective social community, nor the individual tested by a pre-destined fate known less by virtue itself than its fiduciary accomplishment. Rather, the ancient Hebrews suffered from what Weber called the 'pathos of solitude', the 'Deutero-Isaiahic' vision which has at its center the 'positive evaluation of self abasement', and a view of the Messiah not as a redeemer but one who dies in combat (1952: 376–7). Divided between admonishing visions on the one hand and esoteric speculation on the other, there was less space for personal virtue than Jovian suffering. So much for the prefatory tradition among the ancient Hebrews. In none of these societies was a spirit of commercial enterprise lacking, nor entrepreneurial propensities. Nor was there any dearth of highly rationalistic calculating skills. What was missing, for

Weber, was the rationalistic ethic supplied by ascetic Protestantism. Without it magical, religious and ethical ideas of duty became barriers to the evolution of such concomitants of modern capitalism as free labor, the rationalization of technique and, above all, an economic view of the survival of the fittest which, if it is a necessary condition for establishing competitive capitalism, could only be acceptable within the larger context of predestined grace (1958a: 24–7, 55). 'With the consciousness of standing in the fullness of God's grace and being visibly blessed by Him, the bourgeois businessman, as long as he remained within the bounds of formal correctness, as long as his moral conduct was spotless and the use to which he put his wealth was not objectionable, could follow his pecuniary interests as he would and feel that he was fulfilling a duty in doing so. The power of religious asceticism provided him in addition with sober, conscientious and unusually industrious workmen, who clung to their work as to a life purpose willed by God.' Finally, 'it gave him the comforting assurance that the unequal distribution of the goods of this world was a special dispensation of Divine Providence, which in these differences, as in particular grace, pursued secret ends unknown to men' (1958a: 176–7).

As for the second question, whether or not there are or have been genuine functional equivalents which combined both individual commitment and collective belief (which Weber believed necessary), and would be crucial in controlling modernization processes prior to industrialization, while enabling effective authority to be maintained the answer remains open. For modernization theorists generally, the best combination was represented by Japan, its Samurai serving as a mediating *Stand*, negotiating effectively the conditions and limits of acceptable innovation, especially during the Tokugawa period and early Meiji. Here again, scholars have emphasized the critical role of education as the basis of both a mediating instrument and a transcending rationality. For in Japan, unlike in China, and paradoxically enough if one considers Weber, education combined well with Confucianism, serving to reinforce hierarchy with knowledge, and making possible conditions of authority and control which promoted rather than impeded the spread of those qualities necessary for capitalism, moderating the negative effects of modernization (see Dore, 1965; see also Ikegami, 1995).

What Weber shows better than most is the value of cases for comparison, and comparison as an approach to more general theories. And any number of figures followed in his wake – Bendix, Eisenstadt, Lipset, Apter, Moore – and continue to do so – Linz, Evans, Skocpol, Calhoun, Brubaker and many others.

Perhaps more than any other, it was Bendix who was most faithful to Weber's methods in using comparative case materials to examine what were crucial differences in the modernization experience and interpreting what political differences the social differences made. For him, as for Weber, the defining and crucial characteristic of modernization theory was embodied not only in the question of how capitalism and democracy first evolved but how they could best be universalized, their values and their institutions reproduced elsewhere no matter how culturally alien the ground. To deal with this question Bendix focused on troublesome cases specifically where authoritarianism had been a consequence of industrialization rather than democracy – Germany and Japan. He also puzzled over the case of India, which in its democracy seemed to challenge a good many assumptions of both the modernization theorists and its antagonists, not least those of a more sociologically naive variety.[26] Indeed, if anyone tried to 'become' Weber it was Bendix.

Although never a mere clone of Weber, the central theme he picked up from him was democracy in the special institutional sense of necessary and appropriate instruments and procedures, such as bureaucracies and parties, and substantive principles, legislative accountability, legal rational authority etc. For Bendix, the instrumental, procedural and substantive features of democratic society as these evolved in the West, foreshadow an experience which, with varying degrees of appropriateness, might be mirrored elsewhere. It was this which led him to follow in the historical and comparative tradition of Weber by comparing the evolution of Western institutional politics with Russia,

Germany, Japan and India. For Bendix, Weber's types of authority became system types, the 'traditional' and the 'modern' and how in each case they intersected, collided and became mutually accommodated.[27] Crucial for Bendix was the role education might play in fostering an emergent sense of civic obligation.

Even more deeply influenced by the whole of Weber's way of thinking was Talcott Parsons, most of whose earlier ideas were scarcely disguised Weberian concepts redeployed both problematically and as well as in the content rather than the form of 'pattern variables'. Moreover, a line from Weber to Parsons can be drawn that includes a variety of comparative sociologists working in one fashion or other on modernity, as for example in Robert Bellah's work on religion in Japan which suggested that Tokugawa 'values' might be considered as functional equivalents to the Protestant ethic, so central were they in promoting modern developmentalism in that country.[28] Smelser is another example. Where Bellah emphasized the normative, Smelser was more concerned with socio-economic factors associated with the rise of British industrialism, for which analysis he elaborated an explicit comparative framework (Smelser, 1959). Apter, too, especially in his early work combined Parsonian forms of analysis with ideas of legal rational authority, charisma and its routinization, and similar factors to the problem of 'political institutional transfer' in an African setting (Apter, 1972). Both Eisenstadt in his work on tradition and modernity, and also on the rise and fall of bureaucratic empires, and Lipset, not least of all in *Union Democracy*, were inveterate comparativists, moving back and forth between cases as illustrative examples, using general ideas and categories that drew heavily on those of Weber and Parsons in examining the effects of modern bureaucracy on the state and social institutions, but also social variables such as functional specificity and diffuseness, ascription and achievement, universalism and particularism (e.g. Eisenstadt, 1963, 1968). Still others, like David Lockwood and John Goldthorpe, used stratification theory and class analysis comparatively in developing a theory of class 'embourgeoisement'.[29] Other comparativists more indebted to Weber's notions of legitimacy, bureaucracy, charisma, Sultanism, civic consciousness etc. include Juan Linz, Karin Barkey, Rogers Brubaker and others.[30]

RECENT TRENDS IN COMPARATIVE RESEARCH

In these regards Weber has a continuing influence in what has been called the new institutionalism, which is less paradigmatic but no less suggestive of theory than the approaches discussed here. It also has its uneasy counterpart in rational choice theory, which, less derivative from Weber, despite the emphasis on rationality, has become central in comparative studies in recent years, both in sociology and political science (Apter, 1991). Still another, which focuses on the relationship between interpretation and social action, is political discourse theory.

The first is able to combine intentionality with economic and social structural variables, and incorporate elements of rational choice theory. Instead of developmental change, or modernization theory as such, the emphasis is on nationalism, identity formation, cultural norms, citizenship and immigration, and the relationships between jurisdiction, affiliation and social displacement more generally. The second, discourse theory, which occupies one end of the spectrum of which rational choice can be said to be the other, deals with symbolic capital, language as power, and above all the narrative interpretation of reality, especially as these contribute to the creation and maintenance of discourse communities, their role in establishing solidary groups, and the relationship of events, their interpretation, narratives and texts, the constituent elements of symbolic capital. Although the first is more widely accepted than the second, both draw on a large body of earlier thought and research, much of it from fields other than sociology itself.

The new institutionalism fits economic, stratification, culture, normative and organizational variables together with historical, multivariate and case types of analysis (e.g.

Calhoun, 1992). Nee characterizes it as a conjunction of two converging traditions, the Weberian combination of comparative institutionalism, its emphasis and methodological individualism and rationality in the context of cases and comparisons, and Durkheim's methodological holism (Nee, 2003; see also Brinton and Nee, 1998; Powell and DiMaggio, 1991). The debt to Weber is the greater, not least of all in terms of the analysis of rationality (Brubaker, 1987), but also the relevance of law, philosophy and economics. To the extent that rationality is defined by these forces, incentives are structured and the rules of legitimate social action ordained – rules within which individuals and organizations compete for control over resources with institutions, defined as a web of interrelated norms, formal and informal, government social relationships (Nee, 2003). In contrast to the old institutionalism, with its concern with the configuring power of institutions as ordering mechanisms and instrumentalities shaping choice, the new institutionalism emphasizes purposive action, or what Parsons referred to as goal attainment, intentionality.

The new institutionalism emphasizes context as well as form. The old institutionalism used history and so does the new, but within the framework of path dependency as a mode of framing and contextualizing the limits within which choice can take place, and the limits of rationality, whereby choices can be measured. Hence the new institutionalism places greater emphasis on norms. Like the old, it lends itself to case studies but is better able to employ modern multivariate analysis (e.g. Inkeles and Smith, 1974). It is linked to economic sociology, comparative stratification and organizational theory and network analysis. It also uses elements of rational choice theory while rejecting the latter's assumption of unlimited relevant information. In short the new institutionalism as a comparative framework can assimilate a variety of fields and tendencies where and when they seem appropriate.

The problem is that for institutions to work they must configure. That is, they need to frame and delimit the range of options to actors as citizens, subjects, producers, or consumers. Embodied in law, custom, tradition and prevailing or dominant sets of norms, they both establish a framework for order and represent it. Hence institutions are not just any groups. Rather, in both civil and political society they combine strategic networks of roles with systems of norms.

And they do not always work. They may fail to work instrumentally. That is, they may not accomplish what they are supposed to accomplish, or do it so partially that one can speak of institutional failures. When they do configure social action we say that the 'system' works well. But this is misleading. Institutions are not necessarily systems *per se*. A system involves sets of interacting variables so that a change in one results in a change in others. In this sense, for example, checks and balances can be said to be more systemic than institutional while separation of powers is less systemic and more institutional.

Similarly, when institutions fail one might say that the dominant norms embodied in them are no longer authoritative. A certain social discipline is weakened. Another way to describe this would be to say that the discourse associated with them loses force. Or antithetical discourses may arise in opposition. Insofar as this is correct, it might be said that discourse theory picks up where institutionalism leaves off.

Discourse theory is by no means as widely recognized as the new institutionalism. It deals with how people talk themselves into acting, define choices and by interpreting events, circumstances and experiences, collectivize them. In short, it deals with the ways in which people construct their social worlds and communities in terms of signs, symbols, language and meaning, and act on those concentrations. By itself it is not a replacement for other approaches; it adds a dimension of interiority to comparative analysis, a depth of a kind that reveals how interpretation leads to social action. It is particularly appropriate for certain kinds of comparative case materials, particularly the study of power, conflict and the formation of social movements. It goes beyond organizational variables in showing how social bonding occurs through narrative and textual exegesis.

Discourse theory, which attends to the uses of language in public space as well as communication and in ways not entirely dissimilar to, say, Habermas's formulations of discourse in a context of communicative action, is hardly new. Indeed one could trace its pedigree to Plato. Its modern provenance is French structuralism and poststructuralism (Geertz, 1988). It draws heavily on the sociological and linguistic perspectives, to which Claude Lévi-Strauss, Roland Barthes, Paul Ricoeur, Clifford Geertz, Hayden White, W.T. Mitchell, Michel Foucault, Jean Baudrillard, Pierre Clastres, Mary Douglas, Frederic Jameson, Judith Butler, Edward Said and Jerome Bruner might be said to be contributors. There are, of course, many others.

In terms of comparative sociology, in some of these respects discourse theory can be said to represent a next stage in the study of social knowledge. Here the fit is with recent work by Jeffrey Alexander and others working on the role of performance. It also might be said to be one end of a continuum of which rational choice theory is the other. That is, it emphasizes ways in which interpretive narratives both establish and constitute the conditions for, as well as the modes of, rationality, and how meaning becomes symbolically intensified to the point where it constitutes a form of power in its own right. When, as a form of power, it becomes the basis for and embodied in 'discourse communities' the effect on individuals is such that they are persuaded to convey their own discretion over their own lives to the larger community. In turn this enables them to draw down from that community more power, self-esteem etc. than they originally had. If by drawing down more than they put in, actors begin to feel personally enlarged, experiencing both a collective 'overcoming' through collective action and a personal transcendence, instrumental and moral, then the result is what might best be called a kind of collective individualism. Many social movements, religious, radical etc., are examples of how this works. Discourse theory thus constitutes an alternative perspective for comparative analysis but one which is growing in importance, and, one might add, not so different from Weber's 'this worldly asceticism'. Moreover it is also a response to the limitations of rational choice theory which is, in Ferejohns's words, thin. It is not without interest that concern with such thinness in some quarters has led to recent efforts to 'thicken' rational choice theory by the use of narratives (Bates et al., 1998; see also Bruner, 1991).

What discourse theory allows for is in-depth studies that can reveal how language, speech, symbol, metaphors, metonymy, retrievals, projections, myth and logic, as well as other components contribute to building up symbolic density to the point where it constitutes a form of capital. Put in these terms, symbolic capital constitutes a moral fund on which to draw much as money constitutes a fiduciary fund on which to draw. In other words, symbolic capital is analogous economic capital, the two sometimes, as in Weber, mutually reinforcing, and at other times not. Discourse theory then makes choice and rationality far more socially interesting than rational choice notions of 'rationality'.[31]

As indicated, in the context of sociology discourse theory is particularly useful in studying social groups as discourse communities by means of a narrative construction or reconstruction of reality. Insofar as it reconstitutes rationality and provides an alternative logic to action it validates deviance from social norms. In these regards it enables comparative theorists to examine in concrete terms how fictive truths are produced and become performative. It suggests the importance and role of designated interpreters in narrating experience, generating texts and linking events to both, thereby collectivizing personal histories (Butler, 1996). In this manner, specific circumstances are both located in relation to a retrieved past and translated into critical signifiers that provide logical explanations for future choices.[32] The past becomes 'real' in the events of the present. Texts so produced appear to embody truth values; they are widely distributed, or passed around, and begin to take on iconographic properties so as to serve as a source of instruction or a frame of reference for the more general understanding. Symbolic capital, grounded in events, has two components:

myth – which reconstitutes experiences validated as theories – and theories that themselves become mythic, (as for example in Leninism or Maoism, or their religious counterparts). As an approach discourse theory is particularly useful in trying to account for how people try to transcend the limitations of their predicaments by reinterpreting the realities of their experience. If and when, as story and narrative, such reinterpretation becomes intersubjective, capable of forming new codes and tropes, the result is that form of political chemistry which makes for collective individualism. Then, discourse comes to possess performative consequences, changing the world by re-interpreting it.

There are many advantages to discourse theory as an approach to comparison. But it has serious weaknesses as well. It works best in conjunction with intensive case studies in depth. It requires repetitive interviewing. It is not very amenable to operational techniques, survey, path analysis and other statistical methods. It is relativist. It is less concerned with the content of ideologies, the conventional interest of political scientists, than in the structure of beliefs, what forms them and how they become adopted. There is also a bias that over time rationality will triumph over non-rationality; logic over revelation, theory over myth, facts over appearances.

There are other lines of comparative inquiry that have emerged that doubt the validity of large-scale comparative theories and prefer the mobilization of different empirical strategies.

CASES FOR COMPARISON

There are a number of comparative sociological studies falling within the category of new institutionalism. A good transitional example is Barrington Moore's *Social Origins of Dictatorship and Democracy* (1966), which contrasted transitions from peasant and agrarian societies to either democracy or authoritarian outcomes in England, France, America, China, Japan and India. A second is Theda Skocpol, *States and Social Revolutions* (1979), which, following in Moore's footsteps, compared France, Russia and China in terms of state structures and the mobilization of mass politics. There is a cluster of comparative work centering around class, nationalism, identity, jurisdiction, citizenship and ethnic and social conflict both theoretical and empirical. Among them are Craig Calhoun's *The Question of Class Struggle* (1992), as well as his study of nationalism (1995) and Brubaker's two volumes *Citizenship and Nationhood in France and Germany* (1992) and *Nationalism Reframed* (1996), comparative studies which center on nationalism, civic consciousness and citizenship, not least of all in terms of 'communities of descent'.[33] Similarly with other books on nationalism, such as Karen Barkey's *Bandits and Bureaucrats: The Ottoman Route to State Centralization* (1994; see also Barkey and von Hagen, 1997).

Among theoretically informed case/area studies there is indeed a powerful tradition. In terms of an older tradition using organizational variables we have already mentioned Ronald Dore's landmark studies in Japan (1965, 1973). Among newer case studies with comparative theoretical implications are Roger Gould's (1995) analysis of protest in nineteenth century Paris, and Andrew G. Walder's *Communist Neo-traditionalism: Work and Authority in Chinese Industry* (1986; see also Walder, 1995). The latter marks an interesting shift from the kind of concern with capitalism that preoccupied the historical sociologists to the transition from socialism to capitalism, a topic which has stimulated a variety of comparative studies of former communist countries. These include examination of certain central European former socialist states currently wrestling with how to make such a transition, as in the recent work of Ivan Szelenyi and his associates *Making Capitalism Without Capitalists* (Eyal et al., 1998) and David Stark's *Postsocialist Pathways* (Stark and Bruszt, 1998).

As for discourse theory, perhaps because it is the most interdisciplinary of the various paradigms and approaches examined here most of its main practitioners are outside of the field of sociology *per se*. It has aroused considerable interest among historians, especially those working on France, which is not so surprising given the importance of French theoretical contributions. Here one might mention Le Roy Ladurie's (1978) extraordinary reconstruction from the records of the Inquisition, of the 'mentality' and religious commitments of a community of Cathars subjected to persecution in the twelfth century in what might be considered an exemplary example of a discourse community in which word and text appeared to violate Catholic norms totally. Similarly, his analysis of a semiotics of space in *Carnival in Romans* (1979), the latter much influenced by Claude Lévi-Strauss. In a similar vein, examining the influence of texts on revolutionary ideologies Robert Darnton's *The Great Cat Massacre* (1984) was influenced by the ideas of Clifford Geertz. Also using France as the case, examining it in terms of virtually every aspect of its social life in terms of retrievals, is Pierre Nora's monumental *Realms of Memory* (1992). Another study, Mona Ozouf's *La Fête révolutionnaire* (1976), 'decodes' the symbolic, celebratory side of revolutionary events. Still another treats culture and text as originating factors in the French Revolution (Chartier, 1992). The list is virtually endless, but perhaps worth noting is that more and more sociological historians apply aspects of discourse theory to case materials from which they generate more general theory, including François Furet, also dealing with France, Jacques Lafaye on Mexico, Jeffrey Wasserstein on China etc.

It is not surprising that discourse theory remains a diverse and loose combination of ideas drawn from many fields and disciplines. It is above all concerned with how people interpret their lives, an operational project, and as well how to interpret the interpretations, a theoretical one.[34] There have been a number of efforts to formalize it for comparative sociological research ranging from Claude Lévi-Strauss's classic studies of myth and kinship to the specific study of ideology as in the work of Raymond Boudon (1986a). Among the most important influences in comparative sociology was Pierre Bourdieu's *Outline of a Theory of Practice*, which, itself a case study of the Kabyle, generated categories of general application to comparative societies such as *habitus* and symbolic capital (Bourdieu, 1977, 1984).[35]

Other comparative studies loosely following one or other tradition in discourse theory include Prasenjit Duara's *Rescuing History from the Nation* (1995), which uses narrative theory in a context of China, Benedict Anderson's *Imagined Communities* (1983), James C. Scott's, *Seeing Like a State* (1998), which uses multiple cases, as do Jean-François Bayart, *L'Illusion identitaire* (1996a) and *La Greffe de l'état* (1996b). My own more explicit formulations of discourse theory derive from specific field studies, as in *Against the State* (Apter and Sawa, 1984), a study of a protest movement in Japan, and *Revolutionary Discourse in Mao's Republic* (Apter and Saich, 1994), a study of the central and defining 'moment' of the Chinese communist revolution.

MAIN CURRENTS IN COMPARATIVE ANALYSIS TODAY

It is probably fair to say that while comparative analysis has lost its antecedent paradigms it has gained in methodological proficiency and professionalized data analysis. Two studies stand out, if indeed they do not point the way for the succeeding generation of comparativists. The first follows in a tradition emphasizing state instability, revolutionary change and social protest. Most comparative political sociologists who have analyzed, for example, the English, French, Russian, Chinese, Mexican and other revolutions, their putative descendants in nationalist uprisings, anti-colonial struggles etc., try to develop wide-ranging general propositions about disjunctive transformations, as in the works of Wallerstein, Skocpol, Perry Anderson, Hobsbawm and others who rely on a combination of institutional, class and ideological structural variables. Challenging them are scholars like Jack Goldstone and Bruce Western, two of a growing group of comparativists dissatisfied with highly generalized models of 'social change'. In his *Revolution and Rebellion in the Early Modern World*, Goldstone, for example, examines crises as precipitants of revolutionary change in a context of state breakdowns in England, France, the Ottoman Empire (with other comparisons interspersed in the analysis), preferring 'robust processes' over the deployment of omnibus comparative categories (Goldstone, 1991). Favoring multiple models and approaches and coming close to empirical essentialism, he suggests that

> sociology seems to have gotten it backwards. The interminable arguments over whether '*the* social order' is based on conflict or consensus, on whether 'social change' is founded primarily on material or idea factors, and on whether 'micro' or 'macro' behavior is the fundamental object of sociological concern, reflect this notion that there is *a* problem of social order that, once solved, will allow all social behavior to be explained and understood. It should be evident by now that no such single solution is possible. (1991: 45)

Preferring 'case-based method' Goldstone introduces demographic factors as a way of accounting for the social consequences of economic factors germane to state breakdowns and revolutionary uprisings.

Similarly with Bruce Western. Where Goldstone studies comparative revolutions, Western, in *Between Class and Market* (1997), analyzes unionization in 18 advanced capitalist countries. He shares Goldstone's distaste for formalized models and like him favors a problems-oriented approach to comparison. Western, however, relies far more heavily than Goldstone does on statistical analysis and while using institutional materials eschews structural analysis other than in terms of market effects. For Western, whose main hypothesis is that 'labor movements grow where they are institutionally insulated from the market forces that drive up competition among workers', examining the relationship between institutional factors, government support and degrees of insulation of workers from labor market competition using a concept of union density as a standard, illustrates the appropriate way to do comparative analysis. In a very convincing use of multiple measures Western is able to account for variations in unionization (Finland the highest and the United States the lowest), primarily in terms of the relationship between political institutions, parties and labor market vulnerability.

Similarly with the work of Doug McAdam on political movements, as well as many others (McAdam and Diani, 2003).

These more recent tendencies in political and social comparative analysis, while they emphasize quantitative professionalism and in some respects are quite opposite to more historical, institutional, cultural and philosophical approaches, are hardly immune to institutional factors. However, their treatment of these latter is configuring rather than substantive. For example, in this regard Western's treatment of comparative labor movements is utterly different from, say, the work of Ira Katznelson and Aristide R. Zolberg (1986), who employ case materials incorporating ideological, cultural and institutional factors in historical settings in the book they edited on *Working Class Formation*.[36] There unionization is analyzed in terms of radicalization, the nature of the industry, class and political dynamics and what is a more rich and certainly more nuanced way, albeit a less 'scientific' treatment.

Nevertheless, it is clear that in showing how, respectively, multivariate analysis can be applied to a historical phenomenon and, in the latter case, to a kind of time series over a 50 year period and without pretending to formal models, Goldstone and Western arrive at striking conclusions. Both are indubitably comparative and it very much appears as if an important, if not *the*, way of the future points in their direction. Possibly too their successors will be able to incorporate more contextual knowledge, the kind that requires detailed case studies without at the same time diluting the elegance of more precise modes of analysis. Whatever criticism one might have of such elegance, the more it stays away from a specifically Weberian emphasis on case materials, the more its advantage with respect to theoretical closure. The question is what is the cost of such closure.

For some the answer is decidedly that the advantages outweigh the disadvantages. This is certainly the case if one values a more scientific approach to comparative studies for its own sake. For others, while one can learn much about revolutions, or determinants of union density, or political movements, in the absence of greater interior understanding and knowledge of the dynamics involved, closure will be chimerical.

A SYNOPTIC CONCLUSION

These last trends are particularly appropriate to subjects that, in the past, remained mostly outside the concerns of comparative studies, such as problems relating to race, gender, sexuality, immigration etc. Some of these have replaced earlier radical, Marxian and post-Marxian 'projects' whose emphases were mainly of the 'last shall be first' kind, that is, analysis with inversionary intents, and instead deal more realistically with them in terms of pluralistic accommodation. One might well argue that the more of a praxiology methodologically refined comparative research becomes, the more easily it can absorb other related fields such as economic sociology, political sociology, social movements, stratification etc.[37] But there are also attendant dangers. One, a corollary of advancing American professionalism, is a decline in European intellectual influences. In these regards one might argue that as it becomes universalized American-style social analysis also parochializes the scope of what is being studied, and insofar as this occurs, comparative sociology as a distinct sub-field becomes more marginalized (Dogan, 2000).

Another danger is that more recent approaches relegate the contextual knowledge of area and case studies more and more to the fringes of the enterprise just at the moment where new substantive knowledge is required if only to avoid simplistic interpretations and solutions to major problems. Indeed, the need has never been greater for better understanding of complex social processes based on more specialized cultural knowledge.[38]

This is not to say that reliance on quantitative, mainly distributional, criteria for every variety of variable – class, ethnicity, education, religion, income, occupation, residence (urban, rural etc.), patterns of participation, voting, consumption, the influence of the media, and so on, not to speak of organization variables rather than structural ones – can or should be lessened. Quite the contrary, the problem today is how to ensure a better fit between quantitative operationalization and interpretive understanding. In short, what Quentin Skinner once referred to as 'grand theory' should become more important rather than less.[39]

One does not want to overdo this. After all, comparative sociology in the United States was hardly overwhelmed by the intellectual waves that occasionally washed over the field of comparative studies from abroad – interpretive, post-Marxist, semi philosophical. Indeed, the work of European sociologists such as Goldmann, Touraine and others such as Foucault or Baudrillard, all of whom did comparative work themselves and were enormously influential in their intellectual communities, did not make much of a dent in either American or British comparative sociology. There has been far more reservation about using such themes as 'the other' or 'deviant' and redeeming inversionary figures (homosexuality, the 'subaltern', 'blackness', 'orientalism', prisoners etc.) than what has become the catch-all for more radical social analysis, that is, 'cultural studies'. Even where there have been comparative studies centering on emancipatory themes relating to gender, race, marginality, colonialism and, indeed, the hegemonic consequences of language, these were not done in particularly self-reflexive ways. To the point where, comparatively speaking in terms of say, anthropology, American sociology remains quite complacent and approving about the hegemony of its professionality, for the most part ignoring the contributions of such central figures as Pierre Bourdieu and his emphasis on the nature of socially constructed forms of power.

If these are questions for debate, their more immediate purpose is to help draw together the main threads of the analysis and to conclude with a brief assessment of where comparative sociology presently stands. Very briefly, the discussion so far suggests four general characteristics of the field as follows.

First, where earlier analysis was concerned, comparisons between preindustrial and industrial societies, the structural and normative differences between them, and transitions from the one to the other, centering on the nature of capitalism, its components of and types of social integration, modern comparative sociology has moved away from gross categories, breaking them into more complex variables, less deep structures or central norms and values and more differentiated combinations more amenable to statistical and survey data. 'Integration' has become far less central to analysis and systemic theory has declined in favor of inductive modeling.

Secondly, comparative sociology is itself no longer a preoccupation of a relatively small number of scholars working primarily in research centers and universities in the West or mainly in the United States. There has been a remarkable proliferation of centers of comparative sociology in Latin America, Japan, Africa, China etc., much of it involving research teamwork, and supported by philanthropic as well as governmental organizations inside and outside of universities. One result is that comparative sociology is transformed from an analytical framework of its own into a strategic one enabling both shared research and the diversification of projects. The spread of such centers and the wide-ranging character of their investigations has mobilized 'local knowledge' in ways denied to outsiders, while contributing to the kind of deep knowledge (indigenousness as an original ethnography) that relies on statistically grounded sociological methods. This has been particularly the case where comparative analysis focuses on immigration and emigration, ethnicity, religiosity etc., as these intersect with class, gender, race, education, family patterns, urbanism, law, public and private organization, and social pathologies with political violence in the large frame.

Thirdly, the dominance of market economics and the decline of radical and socialist theories of social development has introduced a new emphasis on rational choice, theories of risk, the sociology of the enterprise and connections to social psychology.

Which has, fourthly and finally, in effect universalized comparison in terms of core problems rather than substantive areas, the former including speculation on uneven change, the variable receptivity to modernism (although there continues to be substantial debate over what modernism means in different settings), with emphasis on social instabilities and their political consequences.

Do these four tendencies suggest that comparative sociology in its more original emphasis on institutions, system and process (a tradition that, as we have seen, began with the early evolutionists and extended through both revisionist Marxism and Parsonianism), has more or less disappeared? In some ways yes, it has. Insofar as they were systemic, articulating a logic of modernism, and assuming commonalities of function rather than form, it was possible to deal with comparative societies as such as well as particular components without losing the sense of their wholeness as societies, that is as systems of social structure and cultural entities. Similarly, dialectical modes of analysis, too, despite their alternative emphases, were systemic in their focus on structural contradiction rather than accommodation. But perhaps the very complexity of modern social life has made obsolete the kind of historical/ comparative analysis which sees system in large-scale terms, even when employing more finely tuned distinctions than the old 'traditional – modern' binaries that in their day purported to generalized conclusions. It is also the case that more problems-centered quantitatively nourished modern modes of analysis have given us a more precise knowledge of social life and its political consequences 'round the globe' as it were.

These are real accomplishments. But they open up as many questions as they resolve. Has new knowledge derived from comparative study been widely disseminated and diffused through a more informed and educated citizenry? The answer seems woefully negative. Even more woeful has been the lack of impact on major policy-makers in government. Nor has the expropriation of such approaches by the vastly increased number and spread of think-tanks and policy research centers now found all over the globe led to better advice to

princes. While data has certainly piled up most citizens know less than before, not only because new sociological knowledge of other people and places remains inaccessible in the measure that it becomes available, but also because frameworks of understanding have become objects of suspicion. This both in terms of society at large, which on the whole remains ignorant of them, or among the significant political elites who largely ignore them, the main sources of advice to princes come from think-tanks whose policy recommendations tend to fit preferred ideologies rather than being grounded in basic research. Indeed, policy-makers remain fearful of expert social knowledge because it tends to be politically tone deaf. And, despite the spread of interest in the comparative understanding of other parts of the world, in the United States a general parochialism is built into our firm beliefs in the universality of our own views. Insofar as Americans regard themselves as the measure of all others, the likelihood is that again and again and despite ever-more sophisticated methods of analysis, we will continue to be surprised by unforeseen contingencies.

If it remains among the purposes of social science to be able to reduce the contingent by means of the theoretical, to make better and more testable predictive and projective hypotheses by probing more deeply into the intentions, meanings, actualities and ambiguities of political and social life, this analysis suggests a need to go back to the drawing boards. What is required is greater emphasis on fieldwork and field studies (Bates and other proponents of rational choice theory to the contrary) and less on survey analysis.[40] This even though the implications of the work of Goldstone, Western, McAdam and to some extent Tilly and others are that comparative analysis has outlived its 'paradigmatic phase', especially since, unlike theories, paradigms are not right or wrong and therefore difficult to assess in terms of adequate or inadequate. Moreover, if, as suggested above, paradigm shifts occur in the social sciences according to fashions, rather than fresh insights, then they are fairly dodgy intellectual instruments for all their pretensions.

All of this is true enough. But what it does not take into account is that the kinds of paradigms discussed above contain not so much specific knowledge but knowledge of the nature of relevance for knowledge. This suggests that comparative sociology needs to redefine on its own terms not only the nature of its knowledge but the contexts in which such knowledge is germane. Focusing on problems is not enough. And, more parenthetically, in this regard, neither the new institutionalism nor discourse theory, not to speak of more multivariate forms of analysis, provide structuring paradigms.

It is of course crucial to emphasize problems as the way into comparative research. But it is equally crucial to have a place to stand which effectively grounds whatever the favored theoretical approaches and components. In this sense professional comparative analysis is very much a process of changing the lens on a camera; with each change in the optic, one frames the subject differently. And that holds as true for the old paradigms as well as the newer presumed alternatives.

One can therefore agree on the need for multiple approaches and a problems emphasis. What ought not be excluded is a concern with structural frameworks if not models. It is in providing such materials in the context of interior forms of knowledge that makes Weber still relevant. Yes, evolutionism *per se* is today not very useful, but systemic tendencies and directionality are. Systems theory is now quaint but it focused on the relationship between general systems and sub-systems, the framework for network analysis. Yes, the Parsonian framework fails as such but several of the principles behind it, social equilibria and its time–space components remain relevant for studies of social integration and mal-integration. Yes, Marxist and world system theories have lost the power of their solutions. Nevertheless, in a globalized world as critiques they remain more important than ever, not least of all in questioning the positive accomplishments of capitalism and reflecting on its negative aspects.

The hero of this story about comparative analysis has, of course, been Max Weber. No scholar dealt with so many central issues more fruitfully in his day and perhaps in ours than he. But if he remains the model comparativist (although he could not and did not himself do fieldwork in ancient Israel, China, or India) one might speculate on what direction he would take us today. Perhaps it would be towards a new synthesis in which modern methodological approaches and field techniques would be applied to case materials to generate more depth, while rigorously framing both in the context of new and more abstract ideal types. What he would no doubt disavow is in part what he himself did, derive his material first from plundering the literature without even a brief visit to the site, or relying on a survey or two. Which leads us to the following very modest conclusion. If it is to renew itself, comparative sociology needs more than ever to become a fieldwork discipline in the true sense – with comparative cases more than mere illustrations for what is known, but instead a source of new ideas, new hypotheses and new theories.

NOTES

1 Although somewhat out of date, the best of these remains Adam Przeworski and Henry Teune's *The Logic of Comparative Social Inquiry* (1970).

2 Indeed, the more faithful to the Weberian tradition one is the more likely to be receptive to theoretically informed case and area studies employing the detailed knowledge of social networks, social thought and the social complexities they afford in order to rescue theoretical principles from otherwise contingent events (see Apter, 2001a).

3 One might recall that coterminous with the rise of sociology as a discipline was the effort to examine deviancy empirically. The concept of the normal curve and its associated notion of deviancy as social pathology came out of studies of 'criminal behavior', particularly Bertillion's efforts to distinguish and identify physical traits and characteristics of criminals which distinguished them from 'normal' people (perhaps prefiguring what today is called profiling).

4 In this respect comparative sociology was and continues to be what Merton called middle range, standing somewhere between broad or formalistic theory construction, and validation of empirical information, and either in terms of case materials or distributional variables. In these terms, over half a century ago Lipset employed statistical materials with case studies, both informed by hypotheses drawn from Marx, Weber, Parsons, Michels and a variety of other theorists (see, for example, Lipset,

1950, 1963; Lipset et al., 1956). In other work querying the absence of a European-style proletariat in the United States, the question itself was a refutation of Marxism, while the specific focus came from Louis Hartz's *The Liberal Tradition in America* (1955), itself a comparative study, which makes the argument (presently under attack), that the absence of feudalism in the United States accounts for the lack of a class-based society.

5 For useful appraisals of the comparative theory tradition generally see Giddens (1971a,b).

6 For comparative views of comparative studies see Apter (1996). See also Apter (2001).

7 See for example Cooley's *Social Process* (1918): 'Group struggle has, on the whole, tended to rise to higher levels of intelligence and moral control in accordance with the increasing mental and moral unification of life. History shows a general growth of rational organization; and this means, for one thing, a general situation of which intelligence and the control of the part in the interest of the whole more and more condition every kind of success' (p. 247). Herbert Spencer puts the matter somewhat differently:

> Of course, I do not say that the parallel between an individual organism and a social organism is so close, that the distinction to be clearly drawn in the one case may be drawn with like clearness in the other. The structures and functions of the social organism are obviously far less specific, far more modifiable, far more dependent on conditions that are variable and never twice alike. All I mean is that, as in the one case so in the other, there lie underneath the phenomena of conduct, not forming subject matter for science, certain vital phenomena, which do form subject matter for science. Just as in man there are structures and functions which make possible the doings his biographer tells of, so in the nation there are structures and functions which make possible the doings its historian tells of; and in both cases it is with these structures and functions in their origin, development and decline that science is concerned … And just as Biology discovers certain general traits of development, structure, and function, holding throughout all organisms, others holding throughout certain great groups, others throughout certain sub-groups these contain; so Sociology has to recognize truths of social development, structure, and function, that are some of them universal, some of them general, some of them special. (Spencer, 1961: 52–3)

8 See in particular Talcott Parsons's *The Structure of Social Action* (1949).

9 Precursors of this evolutionary tradition include Montesquieu, who developed a theory of a total social system in which the features of social life are united in a coherent whole, the sociologically inclined historians like Fustel de Coulanges, who, among other things, comparing religious practices and beliefs in the antique world in terms of their difference from modern forms (in part to discount claims to their inheritance) insisted on the role of religion, or beliefs more generally, to shape social structure and give social relationships both purpose and meaning, and Tocqueville, who as Smelser pointed out,

contrasted France and the United States in terms of aristocracy versus equality, revolutionary ideas versus pragmatic goals, centralization and decentralization, and used third party cases to bolster what became causal hypotheses (see Smelser, 1971).

10 For critical commentary see Dahrendorf (1957); see also Aron (1967).

11 As Marx put it, 'England, it is true, in causing a social revolution in Hindostan, was actuated only by the vilest interests, and was stupid in her manner of enforcing them. But that is not the question. The question is, can mankind fulfil its destiny without a fundamental revolution in the social state of Asia? If not, whatever may have been the crimes of England she was the unconscious tool of history in bringing about the revolution' (Marx, 1969: 94).

12 In contrast to evolutionism or linear or unilinear theory, Parsons favored a 'voluntaristic theory of action'.

13 It should be pointed out that Wallerstein eschews the term 'theory' as applied to his work and prefers 'system' instead. See his 'The itinerary of world-systems analysis, or how to resist becoming a theory' in Berger and Zelditch (2000).

14 Above all, however, they defined what might be called the ongoing comparative problematic: the extent to which structure (and structural theories) can serve to narrow the limits of observable discretionary action, reduce the significance of contingency and find explanations for actions which escape structural limitations. In these terms, in one way or another the most general theoretical problem for earlier forms of comparative sociology as well as for current approaches remains how best to narrow the contingency gap and in terms of both rational and non-rational action (see Crozier and Friedberg, 1977). In these terms too it is interesting to speculate on why comparative politics has remained more central to political science than comparative sociology in relation to sociology. Perhaps this is in part because the former has a sharper institutional focus, concerned primarily as it is with how power is concentrated particularly in formal instruments of state power. Indeed, in these terms what might be called heuristic functionalism, loosely a combination of concepts derived from Parsons and both historical sociology and institutionalism, sponsored a main thrust in comparative politics for a considerable period of time in good measure under the influence of Gabriel Almond and including James S. Coleman, Lucian Pye, Leonard Binder and, most particularly, Gabriel Almond and Sidney Verba (see Almond and Coleman, 1960; Almond and Verba, 1963).

15 For example, the so-called 'College of Sociology', which had enormous intellectual significance in France between the two world wars, had virtually no effect on American sociology (Hollier, 1988).

16 Sociologists associated with the Frankfurt School who had considerable influence in the United States included Adorno and Leo Lowenthal, especially the latter's emphasis on the role of culture.

17 In a very different vein, Philip Converse's classic article 'The nature of belief systems in mass publics' (1964) lays out a methodological strategy for examining beliefs and the extent to which information generates social and

political saliency, but applies it, albeit briefly, to Nazi Germany. See in particular Putnam (1973).

18 Whether, for example, Durkheim's emphasis on education, or Weber's on the parliamentary and democratic state. All proposed that their preferred general ideas be applied to specified and critical social problems in ways that would make modern society both more rational and democratic (whether as neo-Kantian forms of *Verstehen*, or liberal 'axiologies' with mildly 'socialist' characteristics).

19 Comte was the first to explicitly claim that sociology was a scientific and nomothetic discipline. He not only invented the term 'sociology' but applied his positivist and empirical approach to variations and differences between cultures, institutions and mentalities. Indeed, embedded in his original emphasis on science is the idea of norm and deviance (whether in statistical terms or others).

20 Cooley's organic society, Znaniecki's concept of roles forming symbiotic relations in a human community considered as interactive, adaptative, capable of learning, Spencer's notion of a division of society that occurred according to its needs, especially those required for self-preservation and also according to that necessary for cultivation of the arts, the graces, civility itself, are all basically metaphors. Which does not mean they were not useful as, for example, in Durkheim's theory of the division of labor, the role of religion in social life and the importance of education for civic responsibility.

21 Similarly, a theory of conflict, class confrontation and revolution linked to a dynamic and transformation class has simply proved wrong, or at least certainly not right enough.

22 Not least of all as a source of interpretative ideas for the comparative study of culture, values, beliefs, religion, gender, ethnicity, institutions, classes, status, hierarchy, organization, roles, attitudes and their consequences for the changing patterns of behavior.

23 It is one of the lesser ironies that Parsons begins *The Structure of Social Action* with Crane Brinton's words, 'Who now reads Spencer?'. Ironic because today one might ask, 'Who reads Parsons?'. As for Spencer, Parsons began taking Spencer seriously enough to write the introduction to an edition of the latter's *The Study of Society*.

24 Despite heroic efforts by Merton and Levy.

25 Weber puts it as follows:

Puritanism represents the polar opposite type of rational dealing with the world, a somewhat ambiguous concept as we have shown elsewhere. The '*ecclesia pura*', in practice and in true meaning, represented the Christian communion at the Lord's Supper in honor of God and purged of all morally rejected participants. This honor might have a Calvinist or Baptist foundation, its church constitution might be more synodical or more congregationalist. Broadly understood, Puritanism may refer to the morally rigoristic and Christian asceticist lay communities in general ... As against the Confucian type, it was peculiar to these types that they should oppose the flight from the world in order to rationalize it, despite or indeed because of their asceticist rejection of the world. Men are equally wicked and fail ethically; the world is a vessel of sin; and there can be no

differences in creatural wickedness in the face of the Lord. Adjustment to vanity fair would be a sign of rejection; self perfection in the sense of Confucianism would be idolatrous blasphemy. Wealth and surrender to its enjoyment would be the specific temptation, reliance on philosophy and literary education would be sinful and creatural pride ... (1951: 238)

26 Especially economists like W.W. Rostow or Clark Kerr (Bendix's colleague at Berkeley), who were persuaded that in the end industrialization was a universalizing process and in capitalist form would sweep all before it so that people would come to resemble each other more and more in their world of belief as well as their worlds of work. The classic in this regard is Rostow's *The Stages of Economic Growth* (1964).

27 As Bendix puts it with respect to tradition and modernity, 'Accordingly, our concept of development must encompass not only the products and by-products of industrialization, but also the various amalgams of tradition modernity which make all developments "partial"' (1964: 11).

28 More dubiously, Bellah speculated that its other functional equivalents might include communism in Russia and China (1957: 193–4). For a far more sophisticated treatment of a similar subject see Ikegami (1995).

29 See John H. Goldthorpe, David Lockwood, Frank Bechhofer and Jennifer Platt's contribution to *Comparative Perspectives on Stratification* (1968), a volume which consists of case studies of Mexico, Britain and Japan, each written by a specialist.

30 In these respects Brubaker's work is directly influenced not only by Weber and the historical sociologists, but social history (Brubaker, 1992, 1996).

31 Good examples by political scientists interested in theoretical questions, what might be called the analytic aspects of case studies, requiring interiority, depth and the detailing of interaction between different networks, jurisdictions and relationships, not to speak of attitudes, beliefs and their complexity rather than over-simplification, are: Kohli (1990) and Mitchell (1988). A good comparative use of case materials is Migdal (1988).

32 For an example of how an interpreter can use this type of translation to shatter the transparency of accepted common sense by means of a logic drawn from mythic narratives see Apter and Sawa (1984) and Apter (1997). See also my contribution 'Political discourse theory' in Smelser and Baltes's *International Encyclopedia of the Social and Behavioral Sciences* (Apter, 2001).

33 In a more historical sociological vein see Greenfeld (1992), which compares England, France, Russia, Germany and America in terms of contrasting routes to modernity.

34 Insofar as sociology was interested in contextuality and intentionality it was influenced by the work of Garfinkle's ethnomethodology and Goffman's phenomenology. See in particular Goffman (1974).

35 Bourdieu has perhaps, more than any other French sociologist, a growing following in American sociology, not least through the work of Paul DiMaggio. See also Calhoun et al. (1993).

36 Much the same comment could be made *vis-à-vis* McAdam's work on social movements and protest and

Mommsen and Hirschfeld's *Social Protest, Violence, and Terror* (1982).

37 Parenthetically it might be noted that in the 1968 edition of the *Encyclopedia of the Social Sciences* there were two long entries on the comparative analysis of social institutions by Eisenstadt. The forthcoming edition has nothing on comparative sociology *per se* but instead has separate entries for comparative case studies, comparative constitutionalism, comparative economic systems, comparative health care systems, comparative history etc., adding up to a total of 12. More parenthetically it might also be pointed out that in the original edition of this Handbook there was no entry on comparative sociology.

38 An exception perhaps is the work of Michael Hechter, most particularly his *Internal Colonialism: The Celtic Fringe in British National Development* (1975).

39 Charles Tilly (1984) to the contrary.

40 For Bates see 'Area studies and political science: rupture and possible synthesis' (1997). See also Przeworski (1991) and, for an early and quite unsuccessful effort at comparative analysis, Rabushka and Shepsle (1972).

BIBLIOGRAPHY

Alexander, Jeffrey (1982) *The Antinomies of Classical Thought: Marx and Durkheim.* Berkeley, CA: University of California Press.

Alexander, Jeffrey (1983a) *The Classical Attempt at Theoretical Synthesis: Max Weber.* Berkeley, CA: University of California Press.

Alexander, Jeffrey (1983b) *The Modern Reconstruction of Classical Thought: Talcott Parsons.* Berkeley, CA: University of California Press.

Almond, Gabriel and Coleman, James S. (eds) (1960) *The Politics of the Developing Areas.* Princeton, NJ: Princeton University Press.

Almond, Gabriel and Verba, Sidney (1963) *The Civic Culture.* Princeton, NJ: Princeton University Press.

Anderson, Benedict (1983) *Imagined Communities.* London: Verso.

Apter, David E. (1972) *Ghana in Transition*, 2nd edn. Princeton, NJ: Princeton University Press.

Apter, David E. (1991) 'Institutionalism reconsidered', *International Social Science Journal*, XLIII (3): 463–81.

Apter, David E. (1996) 'Comparative politics, old and new', in Robert E. Goodin and Hans-Dieter Klingemann (eds), *A New Handbook of Political Science.* Oxford: Oxford University Press.

Apter, David E. (ed.) (1997) *The Legitimization of Violence.* London: Macmillan.

Apter, David E. (2001a) 'Structure, contingency, and choice: a comparison of trends and tendencies in political science', in Debra Keates and Joan W. Scott (eds), *Twenty-Five Years of Interpretive Social Science.* Princeton, NJ: Princeton University Press.

Apter, David E. (2001b) 'Political discourse theory', in Neil Smelser and Paul B. Baltes (eds), *International Encyclopedia of the Social and Behavioral Sciences.* Amsterdam, New York: Elsevier.

Apter, David E. and Sawa, Nagayo (1984) *Against the State.* Cambridge, MA: Harvard University Press.

Apter, David E. and Saich, Tony (1994) *Revolutionary Discourse in Mao's Republic.* Cambridge, MA: Harvard University Press.

Arendt, Hannah (1962) *On Revolution.* New York: Viking Press.

Aron, Raymond (1967) *18 Lectures on Industrial Society.* London: Weidenfeld & Nicolson.

Avineri, Shlomo (1969) *Karl Marx on Colonialism and Modernization.* New York: Doubleday/Anchor Books.

Badie, Bertrand and Birnbaum, Pierre (1983) *The Sociology of the State.* Chicago: University of Chicago Press.

Barkey, Karen (1994) *Bandits and Bureaucrats: The Ottoman Route to State Centralization.* Ithaca, NY: Cornell University Press.

Barkey, Karen and von Hagen, Mark (1997) *After Empire: Multiethnic Societies and Nation-Building: The Soviet Union and Russian, Ottoman, and Habsburg Empires.* Boulder, CO: Westview Press.

Bates, Robert (1997) 'Area studies and political science: rupture and possible synthesis', *Africa Today*, 44 (2): 123–31.

Bates, R. et al. (1998) *Analytical Narratives.* Princeton, NJ: Princeton University Press.

Bayart, Jean-François (1996a) *L'Illusion identitaire.* Paris: Fayard.

Bayart, Jean François (1996b) *La Greffe de l'état.* Paris: Karthala.

Bell, Daniel (1960) *The End of Ideology.* New York: The Free Press.

Bellah, Robert (1957) *Tokugawa Religion.* Glencoe, IL: The Free Press.

Bendix, Reinhard (1964) *Nation-Building and Citizenship.* Berkeley, CA: University of California Press.

Berger, J. and Zelditch, M., Jr (2000) *New Directions in Contemporary Sociological Theory.* Lanham, MD: Rowman and Littlefield. pp. 358–76.

Boudon, Raymond (1986a) *The Analysis of Ideology.* Chicago: University of Chicago Press.

Boudon, Raymond (1986b) *Theories of Social Change.* Cambridge: Polity Press.

Bourdieu, Pierre (1977) *Outline of a Theory of Practice.* Cambridge: Cambridge University Press.

Bourdieu, Pierre (1984) *Distinction.* Cambridge, MA: Harvard University Press.

Braudel, Fernand (1969) *Ecrits sur l'histoire.* Paris: Flammarion.

Braudel, Fernand (1981) *Civilization and Capitalism.* London: Collins.

Brinton, Mary and Nee, Victor (eds) (1998) *The New Institutionalism in Sociology.* New York: Russell Sage.

Brubaker, Rogers (1984) *The Limits of Rationality.* London: George Allen and Unwin.

Brubaker, Rogers (1987) *The Limits of Rationality.* London and New York: Routledge.

Brubaker, Rogers (1992) *Citizenship and Nationhood in France and Germany.* Cambridge, MA: Harvard University Press.

Brubaker, Rogers (1996) *Nationalism Reframed.* Cambridge: Cambridge University Press.

Bruner, Jerome (1991) 'The narrative construction of reality', *Critical Inquiry,* 18 (1): 1–21.

Butler, Judith (1996) *Excitable Speech.* New York: Routledge.

Calhoun, Craig (1992) *The Question of Class Struggle: Social Foundations of Popular Radicalism during the Industrial Revolution.* Chicago: University of Chicago Press.

Calhoun, Craig (1995) *Critical Social Theory: Culture, History and the Challenge of Difference.* Oxford: Blackwell.

Calhoun, Craig, Li Puma, Edward and Postone, Moishe (1993) *Bourdieu: Critical Perspectives.* Cambridge: Polity Press.

Chartier, Roger (1992) *The Cultural Origins of the French Revolution.* Durham, NC: Duke University Press.

Converse, Philip E. (1964) 'The nature of belief systems in mass publics', in D.E. Apter (ed.), *Ideology and Discontent.* New York: The Free Press.

Cooley, Charles Horton (1918) *Social Process.* New York: Charles Scribner's Sons.

Crozier, Michael and Friedberg, Erhard (1977) *L'Acteur et le système.* Paris: Editions du Seuil.

Dahrendorf, Ralf (1957) *Class and Class Conflict in an Industrial Society.* London: Routledge and Kegan Paul.

Darnton, Robert (1984) *The Great Cat Massacre.* New York: Basic Books.

Dogan, Mattei (2000) 'The moving frontier of the social sciences', in Stella R. Quah and Arnaud Sales (eds), *The International Handbook of Sociology.* Beverly Hills, CA: Sage.

Dogan, Mattei and Pelassy, Dominique (1980) *Sociologie politique comparative.* Paris: Economica.

Dore, Ronald (1965) *Education in Tokugawa Japan.* Berkeley, CA: University of California Press.

Dore, Ronald (1973) *British Factory, Japanese Factory: the Origins of National Diversity in Industrial Relations.* London: Allen and Unwin.

Duara, Prasenjit (1995) *Rescuing History from the Nation.* Chicago: University of Chicago Press.

Eisenstadt, S.N. (1963) *The Political Systems of Empires.* New York: The Free Press.

Eisenstadt, S.N. (ed.) (1968) *The Protestant Ethic and Modernization.* New York: Basic Books.

Elias, Norbert (1973) *La Civilisation des moeurs.* Paris: Calmann-Levy.

Eyal, Gil, Szelenyi, Ivan and Townsley, Eleanor (1998) *Making Capitalism Without Capitalists.* London: Verso.

Formisano, Renaldo (2000) 'The concept of political culture', *Journal of Interdisciplinary History,* 31 (3): 393–426.

Frisby, David (1986) *Fragments of Modernity: Theories of Modernity in the work of Simmel, Kracauer and Benjamin.* Cambridge: Polity Press.

Frisby, David (2001) *Cityscapes of Modernity.* Cambridge: Polity Press.

Frognier, Andre-Paul (1999) 'Logique(s) de la politique comparée', *Revue Internationalé de Politique Comparée,* 1 (1): 61–90.

Galtung, Johan (1967) *Theory and Methods of Social Research.* Oslo: Universitetsforlaget.

Geertz, Clifford (1973) *The Interpretation of Cultures.* New York: Basic Books.

Geertz, Clifford (1988) *Works and Lives.* Stanford, CA: Stanford University Press.

Giddens, Anthony (1971a) *Capitalism and Modern Social Theory.* Cambridge: Cambridge University Press.

Giddens, Anthony (1971b) *A Contemporary Critique of Historical Materialism.* Berkeley, CA: University of California Press.

Goffman, Erving (1974) *Frame Analysis.* Cambridge, MA: Harvard University Press.

Goldstone, Jack A. (1991) *Revolution and Rebellion in the Early Modern World.* Berkeley, CA: University of California Press.

Goldthorpe, John H., Lockwood, David, Bechhofer, Frank and Platt, Jennifer (1968) 'The affluent worker and the thesis of embourgeoisement: some preliminary resarch findings', in Joseph A. Kahl (ed.), *Comparative Perspectives on Stratification.* Boston, MA: Little, Brown and Co.

Gould, Roger V. (1995) *Insurgent Identities: Class Community and Protest in Paris from 1848 to the Commune.* Chicago: University of Chicago Press.

Greenfeld, Liah (1992) *Nationalism.* Cambridge, MA: Harvard University Press.

Hartz, Louis (1955) *The Liberal Tradition in America.* New York: Harcourt, Brace.

Harvey, David (1989) *The Condition of Postmodernity.* Oxford: Blackwell.

Hechter, Michael (1975) *Internal Colonialism: The Celtic Fringe in British National Development.* Berkeley, CA: University of California Press.

Hechter, Michael and Levi, Margret (1994) 'Ethno-regional movements in the West', in John Hutchinson and Anthony D. Smith (eds), *Nationalism.* New York: Oxford University Press.

Hollier, Denis (1988) *The College of Sociology.* Minneapolis, MN: University of Minnesota Press.

Ikegami, Eiko (1995) *The Taming of the Samurai.* Cambridge, MA: Harvard University Press.

Inkeles, Alex and Smith, David H. (1974) *Becoming Modern.* Cambridge, MA: Harvard University Press.

Katznelson, Ira and Zolberg, Aristide R. (1986) *Working Class Formation.* Princeton, NJ: Princeton University Press.

Kohli, Atul (1990) *Democracy and Discontent.* Cambridge: Cambridge University Press.

Kuhn, Thomas S. (1962) *The Structure of Scientific Revolutions.* Chicago: University of Chicago Press. p. 10.

Le Roy Ladurie, Emmanuel (1978) *Montaillou.* New York: George Braziller.

Le Roy Ladurie, Emmanuel (1979) *Carnival in Romans.* New York: George Braziller.

Lefebvre, Henri (1971) *The Sociology of Marx.* London: Allen Lane.

Lefebvre, Henri (1986) *La Production de l'espace.* Paris: Editions Anthropos.

Linz, Juan J. (2000) *Totalitarian and Authoritarian Regimes.* Boulder, CO: Lynne Rienner.

Linz, Juan and Stepan, Alfred (1978) *The Breakdown of Democratic Regimes.* Baltimore, MD: Johns Hopkins University Press.

Lipset, S.M. (1950) *Agrarian Socialism.* Berkeley, CA: University of California Press.

Lipset, S.M. (1963) *The First New Nation.* New York: Basic Books.

Lipset, S.M., Trow, M. and Coleman, James (1956) *Union Democracy.* Glencoe, IL: The Free Press.

Mahoney, James (2000) 'Path dependence in historical sociology', *Theory and Society*, 29 (4): 507–48.

Malowist, Marion (1972) *Croissance et regression en Europe.* Paris: Armand Colin.

Marx, Karl (1969) 'The British rule in India', in Shlomo Avineri (ed.), *Karl Marx on Colonialism and Modernization.* New York: Doubleday.

McAdam, Doug and Diani, Mario (2003) *Social Movements and Networks: Relational Approaches to Social Action.* New York: Oxford University Press.

Migdal, Joel S. (1988) *Strong Societies and Weak States.* Princeton, NJ: Princeton University Press.

Mitchell, Timothy (1988) *Colonizing Egypt.* Cambridge: Cambridge University Press.

Mitchell, William C. (1967) *Sociological Analysis and Politics: The Theories of Talcott Parsons.* Englewood Cliffs, NJ: Prentice–Hall.

Mommsen, Wolfgang J. (1999) 'Max Weber's "Grand Sociology": the origins and composition of *Wirtschaft und Gesellschaft Sociologie*', *History and Theory*, 39 (3): 364–83.

Mommsen, Wolfgang J. and Hirschfeld, Gerhard (1982) *Social Protest, Violence, and Terror.* New York: St Martin's Press.

Moore, Barrington, Jr (1966) *Social Origins of Dictatorship and Democracy.* Boston, MA: Beacon Press.

Nee, Victor (2003) *Remaking the American Mainstream.* Cambridge, MA: Harvard University Press.

Nora, Pierre (1992) *Realms of Memory*, 3 vols. New York: Columbia University Press.

Ozouf, Mona (1976) *La Fête révolutionnaire.* Paris: Gallimard.

Parsons, Talcott (1949) *The Structure of Social Action.* Glencoe, IL: The Free Press.

Parsons, Talcott and Shils, Edward (eds) (1951) *Toward a General Theory of Action.* Cambridge, MA: Harvard University Press.

Parsons, T., Bales, R. and Shils, E. (1953) *Working Papers in the Theory of Social Action.* Glencoe, IL: The Free Press.

Powell, Walter and DiMaggio, Paul (1991) *The New Institutionalism in Organizational Analysis.* Chicago: University of Chicago Press.

Przeworski, Adam (1991) *Democracy and the Market.* Cambridge: Cambridge University Press.

Przeworski, Adam and Teune, Henry (1970) *The Logic of Comparative Social Inquiry.* New York: Wiley.

Putnam, Robert P. (1973) *The Belief Systems of Politicans.* New Haven, CT: Yale University Press.

Rabushka, Alvin and Shepsle, Kenneth A. (1972) *Politics in Plural Societies: A Theory of Democratic Instability.* Columbus, OH: Charles E. Merrill.

Radcliffe-Brown, A.R. (1952) *Structure and Function in Primitive Society.* Glencoe, IL: The Free Press.

Rostow, W.W. (1964) *The Stages of Economic Growth.* Cambridge: Cambridge University Press.

Scheler, Max (1961) *Ressentiment.* New York: The Free Press.

Scott, James C. (1998) *Seeing Like a State.* New Haven, CT: Yale University Press.

Shils, Edward A. and Finch, Henry A. (eds) (1949) *Max Weber on the Methodology of the Social Sciences.* Glencoe, IL: The Free Press.

Skocpol, Theda (1979) *States and Social Revolutions.* Cambridge: Cambridge University Press.

Smelser, Neil J. (1959) *Social Change in the Industrial Revolution.* Chicago: University of Chicago Press.

Smelser, Neil J. (1963) *Theory of Collective Behavior.* New York: The Free Press.

Smelser, Neil (1971) 'Alexis de Tocqueville as comparative analyst', in Ivan Vallier (ed.), *Comparative Methods in Sociology.* Berkeley, CA: University of California Press.

Spencer, Herbert (1961) *The Study of Sociology.* Ann Arbor, MI: University of Michigan Press.

Stark, David and Bruszt, Laszlo (1998) *Postsocialist Pathways.* Cambridge: Cambridge University Press.

Therborn, Goran (1980) *The Ideology of Power and the Power of Ideology.* London: Verso.

Tilly, Charles (1978) *From Mobilization to Revolution.* New York: Random House.

Tilly, Charles (1984) *Big Structures, Large Processes, Huge Comparisons.* New York: Russell Sage.

Touraine, Alain (1965) *Sociologie de l'action.* Paris: Editions du Seuil.

Touraine, Alain (1968) *La Parole et le sang: politique et société en Amerique Latine.* Paris: Odile Jacob.

Touraine, Alain (1973) *Production de la société.* Paris: Editions du Seuil.

Walder, Andrew G. (1986) *Communist Neo-traditionalism: Work and Authority in Chinese Industry.* Berkeley, CA: University of California Press.

Walder, Andrew G. (1995) *The Waning of the Communist State: Economic Origins of Political Decline in China and Hungary.* Berkeley, CA: University of California Press.

Wallerstein, Immanuel (1974, 1980, 1989) *The Modern World System,* 3 vols. New York: Academic Press.

Weber, Max (1951) *The Religion of China.* Glencoe, IL: The Free Press.

Weber, Max (1952) *Ancient Judaism.* Glencoe, IL: The Free Press.

Weber, Max (1958a) *The Protestant Ethic and the Spirit of Capitalism.* New York: Charles Scribner's Sons.

Weber, Max (1958b) *The Religion of India.* Glencoe, IL: The Free Press.

Western, Bruce (1997) *Between Class and Market.* Princeton, NJ: Princeton University Press.

Part 2

The Axial Processes of Society

6

The Culture of Work

RICHARD SENNETT

By one of history's ironies, the collapse of the Soviet empire coincided in the West with a renewed scholarly interest in Marxian propositions about labor and the relation of work to class and class consciousness. In part this coincidence occurred because in the last generation capitalism itself has profoundly changed, and the durable legacy of Marx, analytic rather than remedial, seemed to offer sharp tools for an explanation. This renewed radical tradition cannot alone suffice, however, to understand the most radical features of the new capitalism, changes which affect the interpretative activities and subjective experiences of workers.

A simple but profound insight moved Marx: social groups are formed by powers external to themselves. The sociological starting point here is that domination begets differentiation. This insight contests the natural separations of talent or the elective affinities of identity, as a basis for sorting people into different classes; instead it insists that top-down classification is an arbitrary operation conducted for the benefit of those on top, absorbed and naturalized among those below so as to impede their free action and sap their will to resist.

Many recent writings on work take this starting point as their own, even if the writers do not label themselves Marxists. The 'integrative functions' of work, so emphasized in Parsonian sociology in the mid-twentieth century, are played down by these writers, while the dissonances produced by arbitrary differentiation are emphasized. For writers as different as Michele Lamont, Robert Howard and Erik Olin Wright, the labor process itself generates arbitrary differentiation; for others, again as varied as Arlie Hochschild and Judy Wajcman, gender does so; still others, like William Julius Wilson, emphasize race; and finally 'culturalists' like Katherine Newman, Caitlin Zaloom and myself, emphasize communal and urban sources of dissonance at work. (This list is meant to be illustrative rather than inclusive.)

Traditional Marxian writings on labor emphasized oppression, and that emphasis frequently degraded into an ethos of victimology, the oppressed viewed as passive, their powers of resistance viewed as weak so long as resistance did not take the political form of seeking regime-change. All the writers cited above have sought to avoid the error of victimology, focusing instead on arbitrary differentiation as a problem which individuals and groups have to work out in everyday experience.

Alejandro Portes has, in recent writings on class, tried to articulate this anti-victimization emphasis in a systematic way. He focuses on what could be called 'lateral' as well traditional hierarchical forms of class difference. Portes's intensive research on immigration has led him to explore how groups seemingly in roughly the same material condition can use resources like religious ties or shared migratory paths to create quite distinctive associations, with different practical outcomes for themselves or their children. Lateral class conflict – as between Koreans and blacks, Puerto Ricans and Mexicans – may be the result. But the focus is on agency, the focus both of the groups studied and of their student.

One theoretical source for looking at the agency of the working class is the writings of Pierre Bourdieu; as much as he was obsessed by the formation of inequality via social and cultural capital, he equally stressed the agency of all social actors within the social field. Still, mixing in new elements of gender, race, ethnicity, social and cultural capital into the old-fashioned analysis of class poses a large issue: what happens to labor as a measure of class, and of the behavior which follows from class inequality? The sociological break with both Marxism and Parsonian functionalism might occur by arguing that these forces of gender, race, or ethnicity serve as the sources of *arbitrary* differentiation. Another way of relating work to class would look at changes in the organization of work itself; by doing so, the very importance of laboring could be affirmed.

Whereas theorists of 'late' capitalism from Ernest Mandel to Fredric Jameson still return to the images of market exchange which dominated classical Marxism, the labor process has been in fact reorganized by forces that are new rather than late: notably the information revolution, bureaucratic 'flexible' restructuring, the emphasis on shareholder value rather than profitability, and – most controversially – the replacement of national imperialism by firm globalization. The argument here would be that class changes its meaning due to such changes in the organization of work.

Immigration again provides an illustration. Modern patterns of immigration are circulatory rather than linear, immigrants in the global economy establishing multi-country networks based on family, clan, or religion rather than leaving one locality to resettle permanently in another. The immigrants who can participate in these dynamic flows themselves tend to be entrepreneurial and adaptive, able to cope with dislocations built into the modern economy; they form a contrast to poor people rooted to local communities who are likely to suffer from their very immobility. Here, then, is a new divide between classes of people, and it is complex, more than a contrast of the mobile and the rooted. Those who are committed to finding work globally make use of that commitment in small-scale affective networks; in their lives there is the primacy of the experience of flexible labor, but work is not an end in itself.

The point is worth insisting upon because one strand of thinking about modern work wants to argue that labor matters less and less in the subjective and emotional constitution of modern individuals. One thread in this strand is the argument derived from Veblen, then Theodor Adorno, then Guy Debord that leisure, media and consumption activities now dominate mass society; another thread is the argument that work itself consists increasingly of a series of episodes, of a short-term portfolio of tasks, which yield no deeper or coherent sense of self: an argument put forward with sadness by Jeremy Rifkin and in a celebration of its postmodernity by Charles Leadbeater.

These views run counter to simple fact as well as to modern social forces. Juliet Schor has documented the ways in which the sheer time people spend at work has increased dramatically in the last generation, as has the 'contingent time' of commuting to and from jobs. Were work truly to be losing its subjective value, unemployed workers blessed with permanent unemployment support should be happy individuals; as Claus Offe has shown, in Germany those able-bodied workers lacking work suffer greatly from alcoholism, stress, and other psychological disorders, even though the welfare state keeps them in cash; the same data obtain in Scandinavia. We have only to reflect that most adults, now women as well as men, spend most of their conscious hours engaged in work-related activities to doubt that the labor they do is an emotionally neutral subject to them.

One intellectual labor which lies before modern researchers on work concerns consciousness, both the interpretative understanding of work itself and of class consciousness which work inspires. This intellectual inquiry has a political edge.

In my view, the changes in modern work have eroded both the critical grasp of workers on what they do, and a clear view of the place of work in the larger social structure. Rather than 'false consciousness', workers suffer from an occlusion of vision, and this is because modern capitalism is itself an increasingly illegible system. The task incumbent upon us is to try to explain to the people we study why it is so difficult to 'read' the work they do.

Sociologists often treat 'consciousness' as a representational event. Social representations are more than mirrors; as in paintings some elements are highlighted, others obscured but still, these are in intent reflections: something other than consciousness itself is meant to be presented.

Consciousness can, however operate in a way that breaks out of the confines of representational intent. Here there is a dialectic between tacit and explicit knowledge. Tacit knowledge concerns habits, routines and taken-for-granted assumptions which oil the daily social machine. We can be conscious of the behavior and beliefs which have taken form in the tacit realm, and such awareness tends to consist of representing what we are doing. Explicit knowledge can take a further, self-critical step when these behaviors and beliefs go wrong. Then consciousness addresses what is problematic, difficult, resistant, irregular.

The world of Fordist labor elaborated knowledge of the tacit and representative sort. It did so through the articulation of work bureaucracy. When Weber spoke of 'rationalized bureaucracy', he meant to convey its clarity of design, and so of interpretation. In visual terms, we could depict bureaucratic rationality as a pyramid, with clear places at each horizontal slice of the pyramid, and each place allotted a fixed function. Such Fordism dominated white-collar as well as industrial labor for much of the past century, structured public agencies as well as private corporations, dominated the efforts of socialist institution-builders as strongly as those of executives creating multinational businesses.

The 'organization man', or more incisively, David Riesman's 'other-directed individual', is the logical outcome of this bureaucratic rationalization, conscious of who he or she is by virtue of one's place in an organization. The tacit rules of organizational behavior define the working self, as the evolution of bureaucracy in the first two-thirds of the past century tended toward ever-greater elaboration, ever-greater definition of form.

This self-representational, rationalized realm tended to create a categorical class-consciousness which subsumed the self. When strikes and conscious knowledge of a more critical sort appeared, the focus of struggle was 'getting a fair share' within the system, demands for equity and inclusion, worries about belonging and not belonging to the established order. The issue of membership oriented class consciousness: we might think, how could it be otherwise? Precisely the profound changes in work organization in the latter third of the twentieth century, however, have shown it could be otherwise.

It is the institutional hierarchy which has come apart in the past 30 years. In the effort to make private businesses more responsive to changing markets, layers of bureaucrats have been stripped away from organizations, the functions of those who remain have been de-routinized, and the corporations themselves have become more chameleon-like in business focus. The effort to make institutions more flexible is not itself new, but the technologies of the information revolution plus the global sweep of labor and capital flows give this effort a distinctively contemporary edge. Moreover, the effort to dismantle the Weberian pyramid has a public side, as the old bureaucratic apparatus of welfare provision both West and East is challenged as rigid, unresponsive, sclerotic.

Proponents of this institutional revolt claim it will lead to greater democracy, but so far, no greater equality has marked institutions of a more flexible sort. Nor do journalistic images of casino capitalism, or Scott Lash's analysis of 'the end of organized capitalism', really capture how it works. What Portes shows us – and he is not alone; writers like Bennett Harrison, Saskia Sassen and Manuel Castells compose the fuller picture – is instead a new regime of control. In contrast to the Weberian pyramid, we may imagine the flexible institutions shaped like a wheel: from a hub of power, spokes radiate out to the periphery where the mass labors. At the hub, there is a coordination of capital flows and market activities on a global scale, unknown to earlier ages. The new technologies of information make possible control of the periphery from the center on a daily, indeed an hourly basis; the 'spokes' transmitting power are strong. The chaotic aspects of this regime – which are certainly real – emerge on the institutional periphery.

Here illegibility of structure reigns, and for quite concrete reasons: the flux of outsourcing; the frequent recomposition of teams, both in composition and in purpose; the creation of internal markets within organizations in which winners may move rapidly closer to the center but losers are frequently dismissed – there are rewards neither for pure effort nor for dogged service in 'new economy' businesses. One way to understand the structure of instability is Bennett Harrison's; he argues there is a split in the new bureaucracy between command and response, commands from the hub being exigent, while those on the receiving end, on the periphery, are left 'free' to obey – that is, how to respond becomes their own problem. John Gray argues this split evinces an evasion of responsibility and hands-on involvement on the part of the powerful. Whereas the Weberian pyramid resembled a controlled military operation, Harrison and Gray imagine a new kind of regime in which you command, then depart. Those left behind all too often cannot make out what they are supposed to do, in order to obey.

Changes in the new economy and in the public sector embody a different kind of bureaucratic time than that of the Weberian pyramid, an institutional experience of time which profoundly disorients both tacit routines and representational knowledge of institutions themselves. This time is short-term in character: a short-term profit horizon in the private sector, a short-term of care in the public sector. Short-term institutional time creates a particular kind of illegibility. As I have argued (in my book, *The Corrosion of Character*, 1998), short-term social

relations tend toward confusion; they also tend toward superficiality. Institutional loyalties become weak, as are fleeting relationships among peers. Moreover, short-term institutional time weakens risk-taking on the periphery; people without power do not know what will happen if they stick their necks out without support, and so tend to focus on the possible losses rather than the gains entailed by risk. Strategic planning is always difficult under uncertain conditions; however, the institutions of the new economy do not think well, and often not at all, about long-term survival. A focus on short-term results may not be fatal for those at the hub amply provisioned with financial and social capital when failure occurs; the inability to plan defensive action and resistance can be disastrous for those who lack these resources.

For such reasons, consciousness of where one belongs, to what group one belongs, is obscured; this institutional reality is hard to read. The nineteenth-century idea of false consciousness tended to put the blame on the reader of an established social text, whereas flexible institutions prevent clear readings. Over the past decade, I have interviewed people who work in a variety of flexible bureaucracies both public and private; they are hard put to describe the form of the institutions they inhabit, and this is particularly true on the peripheries of institutions, where job definitions, peer groupings and measures of competence shift from year to year, sometimes month to month. Modern bureaucracy is a hermeneutic puzzle, especially hard to solve by those on the receiving end of commands. The realm of tacit knowledge shaped by routine has become fragmented and weak.

What sort of critical self-consciousness might these changes inspire? Portes answers this question by quoting the remark of Maréchal Ney, who, when asked about his family, replied 'Madame, I am my own ancestor.' Maréchal Ney, who was a far more astute military strategist than Napoleon himself, meant in his riposte that by his talents he had created a position for himself in society, indeed, created himself.

In a way the marshal invokes a founding trope of entrepreneurial capitalism, and indeed of modernity itself. The riposte unfolded in novels of the nineteenth century, from Stendhal's *The Red and the Black* to Trollope's *The Way We Live Now*, stories of self-made men and women – but these socially mobile individuals were not our contemporaries. In the world of the nineteenth-century entrepreneur, there was a fixed socio-logical ladder to climb, manners as well as money were defined on each rung; mass consumption and mass media had not yet thrown their veils over inequality. In Stendhal's novel, for example, Julian Sorel quickly learns just how he has to re-adjust his clothing, his speech, his bodily comportment each time he takes a step up. Class consciousness consisted in reading this legible social text; radical consciousness in reading the plain text critically.

Ideologically, 'I am my own ancestor' is the mantra of every new economy business; it is the reform of client consciousness sought by the reformers of the welfare state. But it has lost its nineteenth-century legibility.

To be sure, very few of the new-economy denizens I have interviewed long for the age of rigid bureaucracy, and that lack of longing shows in their behavior. Evincing little loyalty to the corporations in which they work – in businesses that evidence little loyalty to them – these employees in high-tech firms, financial services, or new media are almost impossible to organize through traditional unions. The world in which they struggle for survival seems to have thrived on endless revision and self-willed organization; if they have not thrived – and the majority have not – their resulting problems seem to be their own to solve, if at all; they are certainly insoluble by collective effort.

In the views of Bennett Harrison and John Gray, the operations of the new economy have *abandoned* the mass of individuals on the receiving end of command to self-creation. 'Abandoned' is the key word; hub-power abjures involvement with the periphery. Self-creation is all you have left when you lack institutional power. In particular, the shortening time-framework of institutional life has thrust people back on their own strategic and emotional resources, but this short, amorphous experience of institutional time obscures critical thinking about institutional form and history.

It will not do to label this condition 'individualism'. The strong effort to network, to forge informal alliances in new-economy institutions, signals the recognition of the need for mutually supportive relationships; the difficulty, as Manuel Castells points out, is that the farther from the center you are, the more limited in scope and the more fragile in function become your networks. Moreover, most of the peripheral people I and my colleagues have interviewed are well aware that as individual actors they hardly have the same chances as those in the hub. There is consciousness of differentiation; people are well aware they have been left to their own devices, 'abandoned' in Harrison's sense. The problem is that such consciousness does not prompt the impulse to solidarity with others. Again, this cannot be ascribed to passivity or a failure on the part of peripheral workers: class solidarity is difficult to imagine, and to practice, when there are no solid institutions against which to react. The problem of people on the periphery is that they know they are on their own, but not what to do about it.

In sum, students of the culture of work confront a crisis of representation in the world of work itself. There is class consciousness in the new capitalism in the sense of awareness of domination and subordination, but the new order of work, power and profit takes advantage of its own illegibility of structure. The defeat of Weberian rationality inflicts a wound on the understandings peripheral people have of their own condition.

BIBLIOGRAPHY

Bourdieu, Pierre (1984) *Distinction: A Social Critique of the Judgement of Taste.* London: Routledge and Kegan Paul.

Castells, Manuel (1997) *The Power of Identity.* Cambridge, MA: Blackwell.

Debord, Guy (1995) *The Society of the Spectacle.* New York: Zone Books.

Gray, John (2002) *Straw Dogs: Thoughts on Humans and Other Animals.* London: Granta.

Harrison, Bennett (1994) *Lean and Mean: The Changing Landscape of Corporate Power in the Age of Flexibility.* New York: Basic Books.

Hochschild, Arlie (1989) *The Second Shift: Working Parents and the Revolution at Home*. New York: Viking.

Howard, Robert (1986) *Brave New Workplace*. New York: Penguin Books.

Jameson, Fredric (1991) *Postmodernism, or, the Cultural Logic of Late Capitalism*. London: Verso.

Lamont, Michele (1992) *Money, Morals, and Manners: The Culture of the French and American Middle Class*. Chicago: University of Chicago Press.

Lash, Scott and Urry, John (1987) *The End of Organized Capitalism*. Cambridge: Polity Press.

Leadbeater, Charles (1999) *Living on Thin Air: A Manifesto for the New Economy*. London: Viking.

Mandel, Ernest (1978) *Late Capitalism*. London: Verso.

Newman, Katherine (1999) *No Shame in My Game: The Working Poor in the Inner City*. New York: Knopf and the Russell Sage Foundation.

Offe, Claus and Heinze, Rolfe (1992) *Beyond Employment: Time, Work, and the Informal Economy*. Cambridge: Polity Press.

Portes, Alejandro and Rumbaut, Rubén (2001) *Legacies: The Story of the Immigrant Second Generation*. Berkeley, CA: University of California Press; New York: Russell Sage Foundation.

Riesman, David (1967) *The Lonely Crowd: A Study of the Changing American Character*. New Haven, CT: Yale University Press.

Rifkin, Jeremy (1995) *The End of Work: The Decline of the Global Force and the Dawn of the Post-Market Era*. New York: G.P. Putnam's Sons.

Sassen, Saskia (1998) *Globalization and its Discontents*. New York: New Press.

Schor, Juliet (1991) *The Overworked American: The Unexpected Decline of Leisure*. New York: Basic Books.

Sennett, Richard (1998) *The Corrosion of Character: The Personal Consequences of Work in the New Capitalism*. New York: W.W. Norton.

Sennett, Richard (1972) *The Hidden Injuries of Class*. Cambridge: Cambridge University Press.

Veblen, Thorstein (1902) *The Theory of the Leisure Class: An Economic Study of Institutions*. New York: Macmillan.

Wacjman, Judy (1991) *Feminism Confronts Technology*. University Park, PA: Pennsylvania State University Press.

Wilson, William Julius (1997) *When Work Disappears: The World of the New Urban Poor*. New York: Alfred A. Knopf.

Wright, Erik Olin (1997) *Class Counts: Comparative Studies in Class Analysis*. Cambridge and New York: Cambridge University Press.

Zaloom, Caitlin (2002) 'The Discipline of Spectators: Trading and Technology from Chicago to London'. PhD dissertation, University of California-Berkeley.

7

The Sociology of the Family

B R Y A N   T U R N E R

INTRODUCTION: ISSUES IN THE CONTEMPORARY SOCIOLOGY OF THE FAMILY

The family, which is employed in this chapter as an umbrella term to cover the more general discussion of familial institutions, kinship relations, household structures, intimate couples and friendship networks, is a fundamental institution of all human societies. For reasons that are to be explored, the family is difficult to define. In the twentieth century, there have been profound changes in marriage, family structures, divorce, love and intimacy. It is difficult to use the word 'family' to cover such a diverse collection of social relationships and institutions. There is the further complication that, through much of the previous century, the sociology of the family and marriage was not a dominant or influential topic of sociological inquiry. In American sociology, the family was, of course, a major aspect of the sociological research of Talcott Parsons, W.E. DuBois, Robert F. Bales, Kingsley Davis and William J. Goode (Turner, 1998). In particular, Goode's *World Revolution and Family Patterns* (1970) was an outstanding contribution to sociology as a science of institutions, but few other publications on the family achieved a similar status. In British sociology, there were also a number of classical contributions: Peter

Willmott and Michael Young (1957) *Family and Kinship in East London*, Elizabeth Bott (1957) *Family and Social Network* and Peter Laslett (1972) *Household and Family Life in Past Time*. In his *City Life in Japan*, Ron Dore (1958) made an important contribution to the comparative sociology of the family. Despite this legacy of research and analysis, it is not clear that the sociology of the family can survive as a specific area of inquiry in sociology.

There are four reasons for this analytical crisis in the study of the family. First, sociologists have become interested in romance and intimacy in social life, and have regarded these developments in private life as more significant than traditional marriage patterns as indications of fundamental changes in culture and society (Giddens, 1992; Illouz, 1997). Because sociologists are interested in the transformations of identity in modern societies, they have been more interested in patterns of intimacy than in the family itself. Where there has been considerable interaction between sociology and psychoanalysis in twentieth-century social theory, there has been an important focus on sexuality, sexual identity and the emotions (Elliott, 2001). This scholarly interest in sexuality has not necessarily been connected with the modern family, and, to some extent, research on couples has appeared to be more promising theoretically than research on the family

(Widmer, 2004). Second, sociologists have been concerned to study gay and lesbian patterns of intimacy, and have analysed the challenge of gay and lesbian social movements to the hegemony of traditional heterosexual relationships. The growth of gay and lesbian partnering and the prospects of gay and lesbian marriages have been seen as further developments of intimate relationships. Some sociologists have interpreted these developments as illustrations of the emergence of sexual citizenship (Bell and Binnie, 2002). Third, with high rates of divorce, remarriage and cohabitation, family structures are increasingly complex, giving rise to 'blended families' where new partners bring together children from previous marriages or relationships. There is also a growing proportion of single or lone parent families in modern society. As a result of these changes, many sociologists believe that modern family life is chaotic (Beck and Beck-Gernsheim, 1995). Finally, with globalization, especially the development of global labour markets, families are often dispersed through different societies and, while they retain family ties, their familial structures are stretched in spatial terms. With the global growth of diasporic communities, the territorial and spatial boundaries of the modern family are not necessarily housed or contained within the nation-state; we need new theories of family life that will accommodate these global transformations. For example, *The Globalization Reader* (Lechner and Boli, 2004) has no entry on the family and marriage. Globalization produces multiculturalism, and the development of multicultural societies involves a further differentiation of family forms. There is, however, considerable social endogamy, and in the United States between 80 and 90 per cent marry somebody of their own faith, but interracial marriages are increasing, especially between Hispanic and non-Hispanic communities. While the historical trend is towards increasing interracial marriage (Spickard, 1989), interfaith marriages are not seen to provide a secure basis for a stable marriage. Muslim women, for example, are not, according to custom rather than law, free to marry outside the religious community (Smith, 1999: 112).

The family is currently not a major topic of mainstream sociological inquiry. The sub-field is fragmented and there is no single theoretical paradigm around which the issues of family, marriage, sexuality and intimacy could be effectively integrated. Familial relations are stretched over a variety of issues that in some general sense sociologists are more concerned with intimacy through the life course than with marriage at the beginning of adulthood. The growth of the sociology of emotions is perhaps one indicator of the decline of the family as an area of research (Barbalet, 2002). This stretching of the family across different areas of sociology is well illustrated by the classification in *Contemporary Sociology*, which describes this area as 'Intimate Relationships, Family and Life Course'. The intellectual paradox is that, while reproduction is one of, if not the most important social function of any human society, it is not clear what exactly constitutes the sociology of the family.

DEFINING FAMILIAL INSTITUTIONS

In order to develop an adequate definition of the family, it is instructive to consider a range of accounts in classical sociology. Having examined this legacy of classical sociology, we can begin to evaluate the scale of the transformation of the family in modern society. Basically, the family has evolved from being the cornerstone of property, power and household to being a more or less stable relationship for the enjoyment of sexual satisfaction and emotional companionship. As the institutionalization of intimacy, the family can include both heterosexual and homosexual couples.

The traditional family was obviously concerned with the organization of sexual relations, the satisfaction of sexual needs and the reproduction of society through the biological processes of mating and procreation. In addition to these procreative functions, the family was historically a context for the organization of economic production, the social division of labour, the distribution of property, the transmission of culture and the socialization of children. The economy in traditional societies was not differentiated from the household, and hence the economy was simply the management (*nomos*) of the household (*oikos*). The family unit within the household combined economic production and biological reproduction. Before the development of the modern welfare state, the family was also significant in the provision of welfare services to its members, especially for the care of the elderly. The satisfaction of these social functions positioned the family as the core institution of civil society.

The family may be defined as a group of interacting persons who recognize a social relationship involving common parentage, marriage and/or adoption. While some authors attempt to define the family in terms of function, these functions vary between different societies, and 'there is no central function that all societies grant to the family' (Rose, 1968: 203). This definition draws attention to the fact that, while biological relations are important in defining family membership, the real issue is the recognition of a familial relationship. In the sociology of the family and kinship, it is important to recognize the difference between the significance of 'blood' and 'marriage'. A blood relationship is produced by an act of sexual intercourse, which results in offspring, who may or may not be recognized as legitimate 'produce' of a sexual union. By contrast, marriage is a legal relationship existing between people who are joined by a formal marriage ceremony or religious ritual. In historical terms, marriage was an institution, which ultimately regulated sexual relations. While marriage can be terminated through separation and divorce, 'blood' relations cannot be so easily dissolved. In the majority of modern societies, divorce is relatively easily obtained on a no-fault basis, but biological parenthood is regarded as more or less permanent. This distinction underpins the common sense idea that 'blood is thicker than water', because the social duties of biological relationships cannot be easily ignored or rejected.

While this distinction suggests unambiguously that 'blood' and 'marriage' represent a simple dichotomy between 'nature' and 'culture', the distinction is in fact more complex, because it is the recognition of a blood relationship rather than an actual relationship which is important. Thus, 'kinship is a social interpretation of natural phenomena rather than the natural phenomena themselves' (Allan, 1979: 32). In traditional societies, for example, without the assistance of genetic science and DNA testing, it was almost impossible to prove fatherhood. In feudal societies, where marriage was a treaty between landholding families, the emphasis on primogeniture (that is inheritance by the first-born male child) resulted in endless disputes about paternity. These economic and political arrangements between powerful families partly explain the importance of chastity and virginity in young brides where the legitimacy of the offspring was important to the ownership of land (Duby, 1978).

In classical sociology, the family was seen to be a key institution in the legitimation of property claims by descent, and hence stable familial relationships were recognized as the foundation of social order and political authority. For example, in *Economy and Society*, Max Weber, while relatively uninterested in the family, recognized the importance of the household to stable property relations and inheritance. Weber noted that

> separated from the household as a unit of economic maintenance, the sexually based relationship between husband and wife, and the physiologically determined relationship between father and children are wholly unstable and tenuous. The father relationship cannot exist without a stable economic household unit of father and mother; even where there is such a unit the father relationship may not always be of great import. Of all of the relationships arising from sexual intercourse, only the mother–child relationship is 'natural', because it is a biologically based household unit that lasts until the child is able to search for means of subsistence of his own. (1978: 357)

The important sociological point here is that marriage as a combination of sexual union and socialization exists only with reference to other social groups outside the marriage. Legitimate birth within a stable marriage relationship was important only in relation to property rights within a system of kinship. Sexual exclusivity was required to protect the political stability of the household and the peaceful allocation of goods and labour within the household.

Having recognized the political and economic functions of the traditional household, we can provide a more elaborate account of the characteristics of the family (MacIver, 1937: 197). In conventional terms, a family involves:

1 A mating relationship
2 A form of marriage or other institutional arrangement in accordance with which the mating relationship is established and maintained
3 A system of nomenclature, involving also a mode of reckoning descent
4 Some economic needs associated with childbearing and child-rearing
5 (Generally), a common habitation, home or household, which, however, may not be exclusive to the family group.

A similar list of 'quasi-variables' was provided in Goode's description of the multiple functions of the family. These are fertility, which may be high or low; the placement of members in a stratification system in terms of ascribed and achieved status positions; the biological maintenance of the family; the socialization of children in terms of the degree and effectiveness of obligations of parents; the emotional maintenance and psychological security for the individual; and finally the exercise of social control, especially sexual control over both adults and children (Goode, 1959: 188–9).

DECLINE OR TRANSFORMATION OF THE FAMILY

These conventional definitions of the family have been challenged in contemporary sociology, because it is no longer clear that the family is exclusively important for the economic, reproductive and emotional life of individuals in contemporary society. The modern household is not typically an economic unit of production. In fact, the modern household is characteristically a unit of consumption of services and goods that are produced outside the family. Because reproduction is no longer closely connected with the legitimate ownership

of property, an increasing number of children are born outside of wedlock, and illegitimacy is no longer profoundly stigmatized. Marriage is often justified in terms of companionship rather than reproduction, but for many people emotional and sexual satisfaction is increasingly found outside family life.

The family is changing rapidly. After the Second World War, the general trend in marriage in Western society was towards a younger and more universal marriage pattern that peaked in the 1960s. Marriage rates then declined in the 1970s and the mean age of marriage has increased. In the mid-1970s the mean age of marriage for first-time brides in Western Europe was 22–24, rising to 27 years by 2000 (Kiernan, 2003). The rising age of brides is partly produced by the popularity of cohabitation, which can be either a prelude or an alternative to conventional marriage. In the age group 25–34 years, in Scandinavian societies approximately 50 per cent are cohabiting; in the UK, Germany and the Netherlands, around one-third are cohabiting, and in Catholic Europe the figure is approximately 12 per cent. In Sweden and Denmark, because cohabitation is so extensive, it is almost impossible to distinguish between cohabitation and marriage. Because couples in Europe are delaying marriage and choosing not to reproduce, fertility rates have declined significantly since the 1970s. For example, in 1970 all European societies had fertility rates above two children per woman, but in 2000 no European society had a fertility rate above two. The two extreme cases are Spain and Italy, which declined from 2.88 and 2.42 respectively in 1970 to 1.24 and 1.23 in 2000. While childlessness has increased empirically in Europe, the majority of couples still regard having a child as very important in their lives. However, a significant minority believe that having children is unimportant. The Eurobarometer survey in 1998 found that a quarter of British people thought that having children was unimportant in their lives.

A major change in family life is illustrated by the separation of marriage and reproduction. Although the trend is towards reproduction outside of marriage, there are important European variations. There are significant differences, for example, between Nordic and southern European societies. In the Nordic societies, on average 40 per cent of children in 1999 were born outside of marriage, whereas in Switzerland, Italy and Greece only 10 per cent on average are born outside of marriage. The increase in children born outside of marriage is largely concentrated in couples who are cohabiting. Because cohabitation is more unstable than marriage, these children stand a higher chance of being raised by a lone parent. For example, lone-parent families in the UK increased from 14 per cent in the 1980s to 23 per cent of all families with dependent children, but in the rest of Europe around 10 per cent are lone-parent families. Around 80–90 per cent of lone parents are female. The United States has the highest rate of lone-parent families.

There has been a considerable rise in divorce rates in both the United States and Europe since the 1960s. Changes in the law from fault-based divorce to no-fault divorce have obviously had a significant impact on the rate of divorce in liberal society. If the current rate of divorce in Europe prevails, then over 30 per cent of marriages will end in divorce. The rates for Canada and the United States since the 1970s are 44 and 50 per cent respectively.

In European societies there is considerable internal variation, Sweden being the most liberal society in terms of cohabitation, childlessness, delayed marriage and high divorce rates. The United States has had a similar pattern of social change, with shrinking marriage rates, increasing age at first marriage and growth in cohabitation. However, while comparisons between 1950 and 2000 illustrate this pattern of cohabitation and increasing age at marriage, the comparison between 1900 and 2000 suggests that there have been some important continuities. Rates of marriage were similar, but the most significant change was the rate of divorce. In 1900 less than 1 per cent of the population between 15 and 44 years of age were divorced, as opposed to 9.3 per cent in 1998. In addition, while around 7 per cent of American women are currently cohabiting, they appear to be cohabiting as a prelude not as an alternative to marriage (Newman and Grauerholz,

2002: 249). Despite the prevalence of marriage and cohabitation as preferred arrangements, lone-parenting in America has increased significantly. In 1960, 9 per cent of American children under the age of 18 years lived with a lone parent, but this figure had increased to 32 per cent by 1998. Among African American children, the figure was 64 per cent.

The growth in fatherless homes is perhaps the most dramatic change in family life. It has been found that almost a quarter of children in the United States living with their mothers had not seen their fathers in the past five years. Sociological research on fatherless households has found that children in such households suffer from poor school performance, sexual abuse, drug addiction and depression. In addition, they also marry early, have children and divorce. The National Marriage Project of 2001 came to the conclusion that marriage as an institution for childbearing and child-rearing was in decline and that the consequences for children were 'devastating'.

There are, however, important continuities in attitudes towards marriage. In the United States, around 90 per cent of the population believe that extramarital sex is wrong (Laumann et al., 1994). The same survey found, however, that a quarter of the men claimed to have had sexual relations with a person outside the marriage. Rates of infidelity are slightly higher among cohabitors than among married people. Where emotional compatibility becomes the basis for enduring relationships, couples place significant emphasis on both sexual and emotional fidelity. It is interesting to speculate therefore on the growth of 'cyber affairs' with increasing access to the Internet which permits people to experiment with virtual relationships (Greenfield, 1999). Despite these important changes, voluntary childlessness is both uncommon and stigmatized. While involuntary childlessness is often regarded as a tragedy, couples who are voluntarily without children are often regarded as selfish. However, sociological research suggests that couples who are apparently voluntarily childless may in fact be chronic postponers (Veevers, 1980). The issue of childlessness only serves to underline the fact that the dominant ideology of modern societies is pronatalist. Childlessness and pronatalism raise interesting sociological questions about the impact of new reproductive technologies on family life and the status of gay and lesbian partnering.

There is, therefore, a reproductive pressure for women to enter into parenthood as a normal social role. However, the demands on women in an industrial society are often contradictory, because women may be expected to sustain a position in the labour market while also managing a set of domestic arrangements in the household. In order to fulfil their ambitions in the labour market, women may delay reproduction, opt for voluntary childlessness, or remain single. However, while there is social support for the ideal of a companionate marriage, there is equally, in societies with a strong pronatalist culture, social criticism of voluntary childlessness, which is often regarded as selfish (Marshall, 1993). The result is that women, especially professional women in the middle class, who delay fertility, are nevertheless attentive to their 'biological clocks', and may as a result require medical assistance to ensure safe reproduction. There is therefore a characteristic interlocking of interests. Technological innovation provides women over 40 years of age with new opportunities to reproduce, while gynaecology, obstetrics, reproductive technology and more recently the prospect of employing cloning to assist reproduction are responding vigorously to an expanding economic market.

REPRODUCTION, RELIGION AND NEW TECHNOLOGIES

In traditional societies, marriage as an economic contract could not be lightly entered into. Warfare and violence meant that eligible bachelors were often in short supply, and hence there was historically a surplus of women. Because more women are now likely to reproduce over a longer period of their life cycle than in previous generations, the spinster as a social role has almost disappeared. The seventeenth-century word 'spinster' typically referred to an occupational category of women who were spinners. By the eighteenth century, it had become a legal category to describe unmarried women, who were often referred to disparagingly as 'old maids'. By the 1820s the term 'spinsterhood' had emerged to provide a collective designation of unmarried and predominantly childless women. The disappearance of the status of spinster tells us a great deal about the changing role of women and the expansion of reproductive rights and opportunities that are characteristic of modern society.

New reproductive technologies have made it possible in principle for more women to achieve successful reproduction, despite the practical limitations of the technology. While delayed marriage, high divorce rates, serial monogamy and the rise of the lone-parent household have raised questions about the continuity and viability of the nuclear family, one important consequence of both medical and social change is that more women today experience pregnancy as a normal event in their life cycle than in previous epochs. In traditional societies, households were not formed through legal marriage until a niche became available in the social structure (Laslett, 1965). There was a Malthusian constraint on resources and scarcity controlled the opportunities for marriage and reproduction. The marriage market is a good deal more flexible in our own times, and delayed marriage does not inevitably mean that women cannot successfully reproduce. While the majority of women still conceive while they are in their twenties, there have been consistent increases in the number of older women who are reproducing: in England and Wales the pregnancy rate among women over 40 years of age has increased by more than 40 per cent in the past decade.

New reproductive technologies are socially important for two reasons. In principle they expand the range of reproductive choices for women, and they separate sex from reproduction. The main constraints on the availability of new reproductive technology, apart from financial hardship, have been created by legislation. The law has sought to limit these technological opportunities for assisted reproduction to married women or women in stable heterosexual relationships, whose age is not thought to prevent them from providing effective and continuous care for their children. These reproductive trends mean that reproduction is now the normal experience of women (with or without marriage), and secondly that reproduction is normal across an increasing age range from teenagers to pensioners. Infertility in the UK is increasingly regarded as socially undesirable and as a medical condition producing severe and distressing psychological consequences. As a result, there are political pressures to recognize assisted reproduction as a medical procedure for infertile couples that should be funded within the National Health Service (NHS). In 1973 a committee chaired by Sir John Peel had recommended that AID (artificial insemination by donor) should be available on the NHS, but it was not until 1990 that an Act of Parliament recognized children conceived by AID as legitimate.

Both medical technology and legal change have expanded the reproductive options that are available to women (and men). Reproduction, in addition to natural pregnancy and adoption, now includes sperm donation, egg donation, surrogacy and a variety of technological interventions. These technological changes have created new social relations that are highly complex and for which the law has few secure solutions. Perhaps the most complex case in recent British legal history was that of Mrs Diane Blood. In 1995 she requested doctors to remove semen without consent from her husband while he was in a coma. Mr Blood did not recover and his semen was frozen. Mrs Blood then requested artificial insemination with the semen after his death, but the Human Fertilization and Embryology Authority (HFEA) refused permission on the grounds that there had to be written permission from both parents if a child is to be born posthumously (Warnock, 2002: 4). She subsequently conceived through the use of her dead husband's semen in Belgium, where these rules do not apply. Two children were subsequently born to Mrs Blood, but the case is still controversial because lawyers are now challenging the Human Fertilization and Embryology Act which takes the common-sense view that a

man who begets a child after his death cannot be regarded as the child's legal father.

The legal situation is complex because English law often falls foul of the European Convention on Human Rights. In many recent cases, where sexual rights have been expanded, English law has been in conflict with European human rights legislation, partly because the Human Rights Act was crafted to preserve the juridical supremacy of the UK Parliament. These tensions have been characteristic of much of the expansion of gay and lesbian rights in contemporary Britain. While social prejudice against gay and lesbian sexual orientations is pervasive, there has been some recognition of gay and lesbian rights. Because there is greater acceptance of gay and lesbian sexuality, gay and lesbian people are achieving some degree of civic recognition. Adoption by gay fathers or surrogacy for gay couples and reproduction for lesbian couples through sperm donation and other means have brought about the normalization of different sexual orientations.

Although gay, lesbian and transsexual communities continue to suffer from social exclusion, they are, through an expansion of sexual citizenship, slowly being incorporated into mainstream social life – on the implicit condition that their sexual preferences assume the characteristics of normal, that is heterosexual, partnerships. Becoming a stable couple helps to normalize otherwise deviant identities. In British legal history several landmark decisions have contributed to this process of recognition. In 1970, the High Court judged that transsexuals could not be legally married; in 1996 the European Court of Justice ruled that transsexuals should have protection from discrimination in the work place; in 1999 the High Court recognized the right of transsexuals to have sex change operations on the NHS; in 2000, a transsexual born with a 'micro penis' won the right in the High Court to be declared a woman. The most recent development in this process of reconciling English law with European human rights legislation occurred in July 2002 when Christine Goodwin, who had since 1984 lived as a woman, won a legal case to be recognized as a woman with a right to marry. Miss Goodwin, who, prior to sexual reassignment surgery had fathered four children in a relationship, had been denied a new National Insurance number, and had experienced persistent harassment (Woolf, 2002). The failure of British common law to recognize changes in gender identity has caused considerable problems for the estimated five thousand transsexuals who have difficulties acquiring mortgages, insurance and welfare benefits under their new gender identities. Medical intervention in such cases brings considerable psychological benefits to transsexuals, and sexual reassignment is an important step in the normalization of their identities. In his study of 55 male-to-female transsexuals, Frank Lewins (1995) found that sexual reassignment was successful in resolving the biographical tensions between gender and sex. While Lewins (1995: 30–1) is well aware that the precise relationship between gender and sex is socially constructed, he also recognized that, passing for a woman required certain bodily techniques relating to walking, sitting and general deportment. The majority of these transsexuals achieved personal satisfaction when they could pass socially rather than biologically as normal, married women.

There have been important legal changes that explicitly or implicitly recognize an expansion of sexual rights to gay and lesbian couples. Recent changes in British law have made it possible for gay couples to function as 'normal' partnerships. The Adoption and Children Bill (2002), for example, which replaces the outdated Adoption Act (1976), allows unmarried and same-sex couples to adopt. The provisions on gay adoption were opposed by the Conservative Opposition but defeated by 301 to 174 votes in the House of Commons. Although a British Social Attitudes Survey found that 84 per cent of the public rejected adoption by homosexual men, Members of Parliament were concerned by the possibility that UK legislation would be yet again out of step with European legal arrangements. Similar legal changes have been taking place elsewhere in Europe, where for example the Swedish government in March 2002 proposed a law to let same-sex couples adopt children, and for lesbians to be artificially inseminated in public hospitals. These legal

changes are perhaps inevitably uneven and inconsistent. For example, the Scottish courts ruled that a gay man, who acted as a sperm donor for a lesbian couple, should be granted full parental rights to give him access to the child, and the ruling has been attacked by the Lesbian Mothers Scotland group because it does not treat lesbian couples as a legal family unit.

What was previously regarded as sexually deviant, namely gay and lesbian sexuality, is now progressively regarded as normal if it can be incorporated within a pattern of more or less permanent partnering, including reproduction and adoption. These changes in sexual rights imply of course that the institution of marriage itself is changing rapidly. A quarter of the children born in England and Wales are born to cohabiting couples, and a recent Social Attitudes Survey found that only a quarter of the population believe that married couples made better parents than unmarried ones. In a context where three in every five marriages are civil marriages, the Church of England is divided over the remarriage of divorcees.

The paradox is that if marriage is beneficial to society as a whole, then there is a rational interest to make it available to everybody on an equal basis. In the UK these arguments about the liberalization of entry into and exit from marriage have not been significantly overshadowed by religious conflict. Religion obviously plays a much smaller part in shaping social policy in the UK than in United States, where Christian fundamentalism has been a direct response to secular humanism. Fundamentalist movements are committed to the restoration of family values, improvement of Christian education and protection of children from the liberal sexual mores of popular culture. Under the Bush administration, the pronatalist religious movement has vigorously re-affirmed the importance of 'family values' in American politics, and has been hostile to homosexuality, divorce on demand, abortion and feminism. This perception of the erosion of American values was at the heart of the Moral Majority that was formed in 1979 under the leadership of Jerry Falwell. However, the original inspiration for this movement came from political groups that were frustrated with the Republican Party, and it included Protestants, but also Roman Catholics, Mormons and Pentecostalists. US domestic and foreign policy had to be based on the Bible, and in order to restore America to its true mission it was necessary to struggle against the 'moral minority' that exercised power over the government. The New Christian Right, as they came to be known, was against abortion, against gay rights and against drug liberalization. Fundamentalists regarded feminism as a 'disease' and equated homosexuality with pederasty. It was 'secular humanism', a catchall phrase including feminism, that had emasculated American men. In this respect, fundamentalism was able to address a range of popular anxieties about male impotence, high divorce rates, female self-assertiveness, the decline of the family and low birth rates.

American fundamentalism responded to this cultural and political crisis in a number of ways. From the late 1980s, there were aggressive, and occasionally violent, campaigns against abortion clinics by so-called moral 'rescuers'. In the educational system, Christian creationists led an attack on evolutionary science and Darwinism in an effort to assert the literal truth of the Book of Genesis. In terms of family life, fundamentalists re-asserted what they claimed to be the biblical view of marriage, namely the importance of male headship. For example, the Southern Baptist Convention meeting in 1988 amended its *Baptist Faith and Message Statement* to declare that a woman should 'submit herself graciously' to the leadership of her husband. The result of the amendment by the largest American Protestant denomination was to jettison the principle of an egalitarian family. This assertion of male leadership was seen to be a necessary step in restoring the family, which is seen to be fundamental to the continuity of Christianity and to the health of the nation. In practice, Christian interpretations of what leadership actually means in day-to-day terms are variable and pragmatic, but the influence of these fundamentalist ideas has been significant, as illustrated by President Clinton's eventual confession of sinfulness to a breakfast meeting of Christian leaders.

Although American fundamentalism has been predominantly a Protestant religious movement of the southern states, there has also been a remarkable convergence of opinion between fundamentalism, the political right, Catholic conservatives and, ironically, components of the women's movement around pronatalism. These diverse movements have in various ways rejected liberal America in favour of the regulation of pornography, anti-abortion legislation, the criminalization of homosexuality and the virtues of faithfulness and loyalty in sexual partnerships. In short, these values confirmed a religious view of sexual and marital relationships that transcended denominational affiliation.

In the UK, there has been opposition from fundamentalists in the Church of England to the liberal endorsement of gay marriage, and the acceptance of gay bishops in the Episcopal Church of the United States has threatened to divide the Anglican communion as a whole. Despite religious opposition, the law has been slowly changing to recognize the demands of lesbian couples to enjoy the same social benefits and entitlements that characterize heterosexual marriages. While heterosexual marriage confers economic and social privileges from which lesbian couples have been traditionally excluded, human rights legislation has forced governments to recognize grudgingly rights of unmarried women and lesbian couples to adopt and reproduce in relationships that are recognized by the law. The recognition that lesbian couples can enjoy a reproductive relationship has contributed to their normalization. Lesbianism has been historically regarded by the law as deviant, but it was also a 'condition' of medical interest (Foucault, 1980). However, by taking on the responsibilities of parenthood, lesbian couples can participate in the normality of parenthood, thereby removing themselves from the medical gaze.

The development of gay marriage, adoption and parenting is a normalization process that is constructed around the social ideal of the couple, and several European countries have recently legislated in favour of adoption by same sex couples. The UK government has been concerned to reduce the time that children wait to be adopted, but in supporting same-sex adoption it is out of step with public opinion where, according to a British Social Attitude poll, 84 per cent of the public oppose adoption by homosexuals. However, representatives of child welfare agencies have pointed out that, with 15 per cent of couples now living together but outside marriage, the government will have to accept unmarried couples if it is to achieve the target of increasing the number of children in care by 40 per cent. In addition, following the case of a young mother who was denied a pension, because she was not married to the soldier who was the father of her child and who was killed in action in Sierra Leone, the House of Lords has debated a bill that would give formal status to 'civil' partnerships. The bill, which has been introduced by Lord Lester, allows couples, including same sex couples, to register their relationship to make legal provision for their joint protection (Perkins, 2002). The underlying legal problem in the British system is that the law commission has failed to find a precise solution that will resolve the legal problems surrounding the property rights of cohabiting couples in the event of their death or separation. The Law Society has argued that cohabitation for three years or the birth of a child should give a right to apply to a court for a share of the partner's capital.

In addition to these legal difficulties, modern medical technology is creating new social possibilities in situations where the law has few precedents on which to base its decisions. A number of legal cases in 2002 tested the implications of medical science and technology for new social relationships, demonstrating that reproductive technology is creating social opportunities that lie outside the framework of the law. The development of so-called 'designer babies' has caused considerable legal and social uncertainty about the role of genetic counselling in the reproductive process. In the United States, the decision of Sharon Duchesneau and Candy McCulough, a lesbian couple who are deaf, to have a deaf baby by deliberate choice has been controversial. In Britain, there have been two cases with the support of the HFEA where parents have conceived a child in order to provide an existing infant with genetic therapy in order to seek a cure for leukaemia and thalassaemia.

While these cases will continue to multiply, their regulation will often be beyond the control of the professions and governments, because the globalization of the medical market will support competition between national teams for medical prestige and influence. Furthermore, the notion of therapeutic cloning is sufficiently elastic to permit continuous experimentation on human reproductive options. In short, scientific competition will have the often-unintended consequence of expanding reproductive rights and further enhance the medicalization of 'natural' reproduction. Indeed there are some medical developments that lend support to the radical feminist argument that the medical control of the womb converts women into reproductive laboratories (Raymond, 1993). In several research laboratories in the United States and Japan, scientists have been developing artificial wombs that could be used to support fetuses that require intensive care when the mother is too ill to sustain a child in her own womb. In any case, scientists as a matter of routine fertilize eggs and keep the embryos alive in incubators prior to implantation in a womb. The basic issue behind these developments is that a variety of medical procedures and reproductive arrangements – surrogacy, IVF, egg donation and cloning – effectively separate reproduction from sexual intercourse. Artificial wombs could be in hypothetical terms an alternative to caesarean section where a woman's chances of natural reproduction are limited, but it would also free men from dependence on women. Gay couples could reproduce through egg donation in their 'own' artificial womb (Rifkin, 2002).

These changes point towards a new medicalization of parenting in which a range of technologies and legal entitlements have expanded reproductive rights making possible a situation of parenting for all. A concatenation of circumstances is producing an alignment of reproductive needs, technological innovation and market opportunity to bring about a medicalization of coupling arrangements. While marriage and the family remain popular social institutions, women will continue to face reproductive choices that are not easily reconciled with professional and work commitments. Delayed reproduction and its dangers provide an ideal environment within which research on reproduction can flourish to find safer alternatives to natural processes. Delayed marriage and delayed reproduction have been the social context for an increase in caesarean delivery but also for a variety of forms of assisted reproduction. In short, the expansion of reproductive rights has occurred in a setting of enhanced technological opportunities. Other legal changes that are connected with human rights legislation have also expanded sexual citizenship (or reproductive citizenship) for lesbian and gay couples. In the future, egg donation and artificial wombs may allow married gay couples to reproduce with increasing regularity and normality, resulting in the reproductive homosexual household.

In the long term, therefore, the law may legalize gay and lesbian marriage in order to protect the children who became involved in such unions. In 2003 the Massachusetts Supreme Court ruled in favour of gay marriage because it was concerned about the denial of children's rights. It argued that it is not rational to penalize children by denying them state benefits merely because the state disapproves of their parents' sexual orientation. It is ironic that public hostility to children being raised in gay partnerships may produce the most secure route to gay marriage in order to protect the children involved. Adoption by gay couples is increasingly popular in the United States, and around 60 per cent of adoption agencies currently accept applications from homosexual couples. However, the adopted children of same-sex households do not enjoy full legal protection if and when their parents separate, and hence there is considerable legal and social pressure to recognize gay marriage. The decision of the Massachusetts Supreme Court is being challenged by neoconservative groups, such as Focus on Family, who believe that strict adherence to heterosexual marriage is the only

real defence of traditional marriage. A lobby for a federal constitutional amendment, formed in the US House of Representatives, has the support of President George W. Bush. There have been similar developments in Canada, where in June 2003 an Ontario court ruling stated that denying marriage to same-sex couples was against the constitution.

THE FAMILY, SOCIAL CAPITAL AND HEALTH

In summary, the traditional family has important economic functions in the production of goods and services through the household, social functions in terms of the reproduction of children, and political functions in establishing legitimate patterns of inheritance. There is considerable concern (religious, moral and legal) about the impact of family change on society as a whole. Given the importance of the family to the organization of society as a whole, public anxieties about social order are often articulated as political anxieties about the stability and continuity of the family. In the seventeenth century political concerns about the authority and legitimacy of the monarchy were focused on the question of authority within the household. In 1680 Sir Robert Filmer, in his *Patriarcha: A Defence of the Natural Powers of the Kings against the Unnatural Liberty of the People*, expressed an anxiety about the future of the patriarchal principle against the emergence of individualistic theories of social contract in a period where the stability of the kingdom was seen to be a reflection of the stability of the family (Schochet, 1975). In the late Victorian period, the psychoanalytic studies which Sigmund Freud undertook of sexual repression within the nuclear family have been interpreted by sociologists and historians as expressions of social instability in the Jewish bourgeoisie of Vienna (Shorter, 1994). In the twentieth century, anxieties about the decline of the nuclear family have disguised more general fears about male/female relationships, heterosexuality and the reproduction of the nation as a necessary component of imperialism. The erosion of the nuclear family has been a persistent feature of twentieth-century social policy, reflected in the debate about the decline of the nuclear family. Talcott Parsons's analysis of the isolation of the nuclear family (Parsons, 1943; Parsons, 1956) has been much criticized, but it is generally recognized that the modern family is small rather than extended, separate from major economic activities and specialized around the provision of intimacy and affection. As a result of legal change, the stability of marriage is compromised by the availability of 'divorce on demand'. While there is no systematic evidence to suggest that the family is disappearing from modern society, there is ample comparative evidence of significant social change, if not crisis in kinship and familial relationships.

Does marriage protect us from mental instability and poor health? In contemporary medical sociology, the family has been both condemned and defended by reference to different experiences of health and illness by men and women in terms of their marital status. While women live longer than men, they have historically higher rates of illness, report lower levels of subjective health, visit doctors more frequently, have higher rates of depression, and consume more drugs than men. For all social classes, women's self-reported health is lower than men. Causes of death tend also to be gender-specific, with men having higher rates of lung cancer, industrial injuries, homicides and car accidents than women. The traditional explanations of these differences have been in terms of the burden of childbearing and domestic duties. Feminist theorists have argued that married life had negative consequences for women because men did not share household duties (Oakley, 1993: 99). Therefore marriage is beneficial for men's health but detrimental to women's health (Clarke, 1983).

Recent research indicates that this historical pattern of gender differentiation is changing. For example, lung cancer has fallen in men, but increased significantly in women. Alcohol consumption has risen for women, with an associated increase in breast cancer. In short, as women have entered the formal labour force, their health status begins to approximate that

of men. Recent research findings have challenged the traditional feminist argument, suggesting that married men and women report better health than any other marital status. For both sexes, divorced and separated people have the poorest health. Single men and women have an intermediate position between people who are married and those who are divorced. Children do not appear to cause a decline in health, but lone and isolated mothers record the worst health and experience high levels of depression (Brown and Harris, 1978). Women in employment report better health than unemployed women, but women in senior positions, who smoke and drink more than their male peers, have increased episodes of illness. These findings (Annandale and Hunt, 2000) point towards one conclusion: the poor health of women historically is a function of their social isolation. Marriage, work and social involvement promote good health outcomes, as social capital theory would predict (Turner, 2003).

THE PROBLEMS OF THE TWENTIETH-CENTURY FAMILY

As we have seen, there is a significant contemporary debate about the future of the family in modern society. However, anxiety about the family has been more or less continuous through the twentieth century. Sociologists have traditionally associated the troubles and difficulties of the family with the impact of industrialization, urbanization and secularization (Davis and Warner, 1937). Whereas social researchers like Charles Booth, B.S. Rowntree and the Webbs had been concerned to study the impact of poverty on the family, later sociologists came to ask more fundamental questions about the very survival of the family. William F. Ogburn (1933) suggested that the family had experienced a profound 'loss of function', because many of the economic needs of individuals were no longer serviced by the family. Parsons in his 'The Kinship System of the Contemporary United States' (Parsons, 1943) and 'The American Family' (Parsons, 1956) agreed with Ogburn's diagnosis, but went on to suggest that the family had been differentiated from the wider social structure to become a more specialized agency as a place of intimacy for child socialization and the nurturing of personality through socialization. The primary function of the nuclear family is the socialization of its members and the transmission of the values of the cultural system. This development was indicated by the urban isolation of the nuclear family, which was increasingly isolated in residential terms. Suburban sprawl has meant that family members work and play outside the structures of an extended kinship system. Because the isolated nuclear family is small, this structure can place enormous emotional burdens on members of the family, especially on the mother.

Parsons's sociology of the family has been extensively criticized. It has been argued that his perspective on the family failed to take family conflict and disharmony seriously, because his theory promoted an idealized vision of middle class family life, which was far removed from the realities of the poverty-stricken families of the urban ghetto or the emotionally burdened middle class family. It failed to take account of important variations in family life in the United States between, for example, different ethnic communities. Against Parsons, many sociologists (Fletcher, 1966) argued that the family was still a crucial institution of modern society, because it is responsible for maintaining the health and well-being of its members. It is also clear from empirical research that the nuclear family is deeply embedded in extensive kinship networks and connections (Bott, 1957). There are important social class variations in family and kinship solidarity. While the traditional picture of working class life in Britain was one of significant geographical stability and extensive kinship interaction (Stacey, 1960; Tunstall, 1962; Wilmott and Young, 1967), it is doubtful that these traditional relationships and community structures have survived urban redevelopment and city modernization (Allan, 1979). There is also some historical evidence to suggest that the extent of the traditional extended family may also have been exaggerated by sociologists (Anderson, 1975). While

kinship relations may be much reduced in modern suburban cultures, the middle class appear to have extensive friendship networks that may to some extent have replaced more conventional kinship ties. These studies suggest that the modern family is a modified extended family in which there are important kinship networks between relatives who do not live with each other, and consequently there is widespread dependence on non-kin relations for support. In the modern inner city, there is empirical evidence that we are witnessing the emergence of isolated geriatric ghettos, where the vulnerable elderly exist in poverty. Urban alienation is particularly prevalent among elderly men who have become isolated from their families and receive relatively little support from welfare services (Klinenberg, 2002).

ROMANTIC LOVE, THE MEDIA AND THE FAMILY

In retrospect the debate about marriage and family life in the twentieth century has revolved around the so-called romantic love complex, in which love is the basic motivation for marriage and intimacy is thought to be the foundation of marital happiness. The conjunction of marriage and love is a thoroughly modern development. Throughout the medieval period in Europe, there was a tension between passionate love and the institution of marriage (Rougemont, 1983). Marriage was essentially a contract between families, which was designed to legitimize sexual intercourse in order to guarantee the continuous ownership and distribution of property through new generations. In the tradition of Courtly Love (Lewis, 1936), passionate relations were driven by an irrational romantic attachment, which was the basis of a counter-institution, namely the romantic tradition of adulterous love. Modern marriages represent a revolutionary transformation of this traditional pattern, because they attempt to base marriage on romantic attachment and to maintain marriage on the basis of reciprocal intimacy. There has been for decades a social emphasis on the importance of courtship and dating behaviour in youth culture (Waller, 1937). Love rather than an economic partnership or a familial alliance becomes the primary justification for marriage, following a romantic courtship (Luhmann, 1986).

This emphasis on romantic love places major emotional burdens on the married couple, because they are committed to fulfilling high expectations of intimacy and sexual gratification. Sincerity, trust and emotional satisfaction are norms of an ideal marriage but they result somewhat paradoxically in widespread marital unhappiness, because it is difficult to achieve these norms of romantic intimacy. High expectations necessarily produce more disappointment in marriage. Sociologists have conventionally claimed that the result is a paradoxical situation of high rates of marriage, high incidence of adultery, high levels of remarriage and extensive intra-familial conflict across generations (Davis, 1940). Romantic disappointment in marriage has become a dominant theme of popular culture, where chat shows, such as the Oprah Winfrey Show, have turned personal failure into 'a glamour of misery' (Illouz, 2003).

This interpretation of the modern marriage as a 'transformation of intimacy' (Giddens, 1992) has been an influential theme of contemporary sociology, where the ideal of a 'pure relationship' of love rather than calculation is seen to be the historical outcome of the rise of the romantic love complex, the quest for a democratic relationship in marriage by the women's movement, the critique of traditional double standards in marriage by feminism, and the emphasis on intimacy which is associated with gay and lesbian politics. Although these features – equality, sexual satisfaction, intimacy and sincerity – are important values in modern marriage, this theory of the modern marriage has its antecedents in the notion of the companionate marriage from an earlier period. In the United States, the companionate relationship was seen to be the emerging pattern of marriage in the 1930s. It was defined as a state of lawful wedlock, which was entered into for the sake of intimate companionship rather than for the procreation of children (Nimkoff, 1934). The companionate relationship was associated with social and geographical

mobility, with a leisure life-style referred to as 'hotel living', and with a transient existence. Indeed these relationships were described as the 'hotel family' to indicate their mobility and impermanence (Hayner, 1927). These companionate unions were assumed to be increasing, with the result that the postwar family was evolving from an institution to companionship (Burgess and Locke, 1953).

Of course, companionate love assumes that adequate contraception is available to prevent companionate childlessness becoming a conventional family, because the companionate relationship will become 'orthodox' in the absence of conscious and successful family limitation. The evolution of intimacy and the emphasis on sexual satisfaction in the twentieth century have followed closely on the evolution of effective contraception, the availability of legal abortion, governmental support of child-care institutions and the economic employment of women in the formal labour market. The separation of economic activities and reproduction within the family is the most significant social change in family life, which is a condition for the emergence of the companionate relationship. Where primogeniture is the principal means of economic accumulation across generations, there will be a tendency to exert close control over women to ensure legitimacy, security and stability of inheritance. In the modern family, the nexus between economic accumulation and legitimate reproduction has been broken by the modernization of the economy, the separation of ownership and control of production, the creation of a mass shares market, and the transformation of laws of inheritance. It is this structural differentiation, which was recognized by Parsons in his analysis of the isolation of the nuclear family, that produces the social conditions under which the romantic love complex can flourish. The survival of the family in the twenty-first century will depend on its place in this romantic love complex as a social arrangement for the satisfaction of sexual needs and emotional companionship rather than as an institution, which exists to produce children and to orchestrate domestic economic activity.

The companionate marriage is also the product of Western individualism, and the emphasis on emotional gratification is an aspect of the legacy of Protestant revivalism. The importance of individual emotional attachment and loyalty in intimate relationships in a secular age can be taken, therefore, as an indication of the continuity of religion in Western societies. From Protestantism, Western societies have acquired an emphasis on the individual and individualism through such religious practices as conversion, a personal relationship to Jesus, private devotion and Bible study. Conversion experiences emphasized the importance of experiencing a loving relationship with Jesus, where emotional intensity was a measure of spiritual intensity. Individualism in modern society has also become increasingly emotional and erotic. Beck and Beck-Gernsheim (1995: 179) argue that love is now our 'secular religion', and claim that as 'religion loses its hold, people seek solace in private sanctuaries', but this interpretation fails to recognize that modern erotic, sentimental and private love is itself part of the social legacy of Protestant pietism. This emotional component of religious experience in eighteenth-century England was associated with the Methodist movement, specifically the evangelical field preaching of John Wesley and the evocative hymns of Charles Wesley. With the routinization of the Methodist fellowship, hymn singing and extemporary prayer preserved a tradition of emotional expressivity. However, it was in German pietism that one finds the broad origins of this emotional trend in Christian spirituality. For example, Friedrich Schleiermacher (1768–1834), who defended religion against the rationalist criticisms of the Enlightenment, argued that religious feelings of dependency are the foundation of religious faith. Schleiermacher's 'anthropology' recognized a common humanity that was articulated through feeling. From this religious tradition, one can derive the modern notion that private and intimate experiences are fundamental to our notion of the self, and that a successful marriage is primarily about establishing satisfactory relations of intimacy (Morrison, 1988). These ideas have been especially potent in the United States in the New Age Movement and

more generally in popular religious approaches to marriage (Heelas, 1996: 99).

In recent years, sociologists have turned to the more contemporary themes of romance and intimacy (Beck and Beck-Gernsheim, 1995; Giddens, 1992; Illouz, 1997; Luhmann, 1986). Romantic love in modern societies is contradictory because it requires or at least celebrates erotic, intense, fleeting and contingent relationships, and at the same time values enduring, permanent and faithful relations of love. These transformations include the secularization of love, the growing prominence of love in film and advertising, the celebration of love in popular culture and its equation with personal happiness, the association of love with consumption and the insertion of 'fun' into the definition of marriage and domesticity. If Courtly Love expressed a feudalization of love in the Middle Ages, the secularization of modern society is expressed in the commercialization and democratization of love.

The love utopia of popular culture was based on the democratization of love by the film industry and by the creation of mass consumption. 'Love for everyone' was combined with 'consumption for all'. However, social reality constantly brought the utopia into question. Marriage guidance experts began to devise a battery of practical solutions to inject fun into marriages, because it was assumed that the companionate marriage was inadequate if it could find space for erotic love and enjoyment. The rise of the 'dating system' also illustrates the new emphasis on youth culture, and the cultural importance of intimacy and the private sphere. The romantic focus on 'going out' and 'dining out', together with the package holiday, are components of a mass market that promotes dating, romantic attachments, courtship, coupling and marriage. For example, romanticized advertisements rarely picture the couple at home with children, but emphasize instead the couple as tourists in a landscape, at a romantic restaurant or in an up-market hotel (Illouz, 1997). The commodification of love has become part of the American Dream.

The paradigm of romantic love, sexual satisfaction and youthfulness is now sufficiently powerful in popular culture to influence older generations who expect either to enjoy love and romantic attachment into old age, or that they can avoid growing old in order to maintain their romantic attachments (Riggs and Turner, 1999). These assumptions underpin popular commentaries on love and the ageing woman in for example Betty Friedan's *The Fountain of Age* (1993). While the elderly are encouraged to sustain romantic love, there has been what we might call an 'infantilization' of romance by which infants and teenyboppers have been drawn into the complex of consumption and romance through popular music. These changes in expressiveness, romance and youthfulness constitute what Talcott Parsons called the expressive revolution, a social change that he regarded as 'a new religious movement of far-reaching importance' (Parsons, 1999: 316). This American religious revolution involved a shift from the cognitive-instrumental values of early capitalism to an affective-expressive culture. Perhaps in support of Parsons's argument one could refer to Madonna, whose popular songs 'Like a Prayer' and 'Open Your Heart' have been interpreted as aspects of popular religion, whose themes are often compatible with liberation theology (Hulsether, 2000: 92).

CONCLUSION: CURRENT TRENDS AND FUTURE DIRECTIONS

Perhaps the most significant causes of change in the Western family system can be attributed to the growth of contraception and the decline of infant mortality in the nineteenth century, the development of no-fault divorce legislation in the post-war period, and the rise of new reproductive technologies in the late twentieth century. Technological changes in reproductive medicine proved to be causally important. In recent years, the globalization of culture and economic relations is producing the diasporic family that is held together by the new information technology. Family life will become increasingly dispersed in global cities through networks of migration and settlement. These global changes may give rise to what we can call the e-family. Global dispersion will also underpin the current trend in many societies towards the fatherless family. With the decline of the traditional family, we have also seen a decline in fatherhood as the normal role of adult men. This development has contributed to a general crisis of masculinity in the modern world. These social changes are closely connected with changes in the economy, especially the rise of female employment and the casualization of employment. With the growth of the lone-parent family, the feminization of poverty will continue in those liberal societies where there is little appetite for increasing taxation and welfare expenditures.

The most significant material change has been the decline of the household as an economic unit in which marriage was a labour contract. Where divorce has become easily available as a result of legal change, the main justification for marriage is now emotional compatibility and companionship. The twentieth century, as a result of the expressive revolution of the 1960s and 1970s, became obsessed with intimacy. Romantic love has been embraced as the dominant theme of popular music and is celebrated throughout popular culture. If information society is producing the e-family, it is also creating opportunities for the cyber romance. The Web is ideally suited to the cultivation of transient, free-floating, ethereal love. The growth of the gay and lesbian couple is further evidence of the expressive revolution, because these relations are often taken to illustrate a 'pure relationship' free from economic or patriarchal components. These changes as a whole represent an important evolution of sexual citizenship in which claims to sexual rights have had the unintended consequence of promoting the diversification of the family form.

While these social changes represent powerful forces that are propelling the family into unchartered waters, there are other processes that may contribute to the preservation of the traditional nuclear family. Although the heterosexual nuclear family has been transformed in the twentieth century, the revival of fundamentalist religion has had an important conservative impact on social policy, especially in the United States. It is likely that fundamental-ism may reverse existing legislation on such controversial matters as divorce, contraception, abortion and gay marriage. Fundamentalism has been able to appeal to the underlying pronatalism ideology that contradicts many trends in secular society, for example towards low fertility rates. While infertility is regarded as an unfortunate, if not tragic, medical condi-tion, voluntary childlessness is deviant. We can anticipate that new reproductive technologies will help more and more women in middle if not old age to reproduce. It is also possible with donation and artificial wombs that gay men can reproduce.

The connection between marriage, family formation and economics has not been entirely broken in modern societies, but the emphasis is on consumption rather than production. In most Western democracies, especially Australia, the UK and the United States, home ownership is an important aspect of both privacy and democracy. Home ownership is an important step towards self-autonomy and independence from the home of origin, but it is, with low interest rates and easy access to mortgages, a sig-nificant aspect of social mobility and affluence. There is a significant nexus (between individu-alism and privacy, consumerism and social status, marriage and independence) that con-tributes to the attraction of family life. Credit cards, bank overdrafts, share ownership, female employment and dual career families have con-tributed to a consumer society in which histor-ically high levels of personal indebtedness are tolerated, if not sponsored, by banks, building societies and credit agencies. The obsessive fas-cination for intimacy, love and sexual satisfac-tion in the modern family provides a magic thread, that Karl Marx would have clearly rec-ognized as a form of religious alienation, that connects couples and capitalism.

REFERENCES

Allan, G.A. (1979) *A Sociology of Friendship and Kinship*. London: George Allen and Unwin.

Anderson, M. (1975) *The Sociology of the Family*. Harmondsworth: Penguin.

Annandale, E. and Hunt, K. (eds) (2000) *Gender Inequalities in Health*. Buckingham: Open University Press.

Barbalet, J. (ed.) (2002) *Emotions and Sociology*. Oxford: Blackwell.

Beck, U. and Beck-Gernsheim, E. (1995) *The Normal Chaos of Love*. Cambridge: Polity Press.

Bell, D. and Binnie, J. (2002) 'Sexual citizenship: marriage, the market and the military', in D. Richardson and S. Seidman (eds), *Handbook of Lesbian and Gay Studies*. London: Sage. pp. 443–58.

Bott, E. (1957) *Family and Social Network: Roles, Norms and External Relationships in Ordinary Urban Families*. London: Tavistock.

Brown, G.W. and Harris, T. (1978) *Social Origins of Depression*. London: Tavistock.

Burgess, E.W. and Locke, H.J. (1953) *The Family: From Institution to Companionship*. New York: American Book Co.

Clarke, J.N. (1983) 'Sexism, feminism and medical-ism: a decade review of literature on gender and illness', *Sociology of Health and Illness*, 5 (1): 62–82.

Davis, K. (1940) 'The sociology of parent–youth conflict', *American Sociological Review*, 5: 523–35.

Davis, K. and Warner, W.L. (1937) 'Structural analysis of kinship', *American Anthropologist*, 39: 291–313.

Dore, R.P. (1958) *City Life in Japan: A Study of a Tokyo Ward*. Berkeley, CA: University of California Press.

Duby, G. (1978) *Medieval Marriages: Two Models from Twelfth-century France*. Baltimore, MD/ London: Johns Hopkins University Press.

Elliott, A. (2001) 'Sexualities, social theory and the crisis of identity', in G. Ritzer and B. Smart (eds), *Handbook of Social Theory*. London: Sage. pp. 428–38.

Fletcher, R. (1966) *The Family and Marriage in Britain*. Penguin: Harmondsworth.

Foucault, M. (1980) *Herculine Barbin, being the recently discovered memoirs of a nineteenth-century French Hermaphrodite*, Brighton: Harvester Press.

Friedan, B. (1993) *The Fountain of Age*. New York: Simon and Schuster.

Giddens, A. (1992) *The Transformation of Intimacy: Sexuality, Love and Eroticism in Modern Societies*. Cambridge: Polity Press.

Goode, W.J. (1959) 'The sociology of the family', in R.K. Merton, L. Broom and L.S. Cottrell (eds), *Sociology Today: Problems and Prospects*, vol. 1. New York/Evanston, IL: Harper and Row. pp. 178–96.

Goode, W.J. (1970) *World Revolution and Family Patterns*. New York: The Free Press.

Greenfield, D.N. (1999) *Virtual Addiction: Help for Netheads, Cyberfreaks and Those that Love Them*. Oakland, CA: New Harbinger Publications.

Hayner, N.S. (1927) 'Hotel homes', *Sociology and Social Research*, 12: 124–31.

Heelas, P. (1996) *The New Age Movement*. Oxford: Blackwell.

Hulsether, M.D. (2000) 'Like a Sermon: popular religion in Madonna videos', in B.D. Forbes and J.H. Mahan (eds), *Religion and Popular Culture in America*. Berkeley/Los Angeles, CA: University of California Press. pp.77–100.

Illouz, E. (1997) *Consuming the Romantic Utopia: Love and the Cultural Contradictions of Capitalism*. Berkeley, CA: University of California Press.

Illouz, E. (2003) *Oprah Winfrey and the Glamour of Misery. An Essay on Popular Culture*. New York: Columbia University Press.

Kiernan, K. (2003) 'Changing European families: trends and issues', in J. Scott, J. Treas and M. Richards (eds), *The Blackwell Companion to the Sociology of Families*. Oxford: Blackwell. pp. 17–33.

Klinenberg, E. (2002) *Heat Wave: A Social Autopsy of Disaster in Chicago*. Chicago/London: University of Chicago Press.

Laslett, P. (1965) *The World We Have Lost*. London: Methuen.

Laslett, P. (ed.) (1972) *Household and Family Life in Past Time*. Cambridge: Cambridge University Press.

Laumann, E.O., Gagnon, J.H., Michael, R.T. and Michaels, S. (1994) *The Social Organization of Sexuality*. Chicago: University of Chicago Press.

Lechner, F. and Boli, J. (eds) (2004) *The Globalization Reader*. Oxford: Blackwell.

Lewins, F. (1995) *Transsexualism in Society: A Sociology of Male-to-Female Transsexuals*. Melbourne: Macmillan.

Lewis, C.S. (1936) *The Allegory of Love: A Study in Medieval Tradition*. Oxford: Oxford University Press.

Luhmann, N. (1986) *Love as Passion: The Codification of Intimacy*. Cambridge: Polity Press.

MacIver, R.M. (1937) *Society: A Textbook of Sociology*. New York: Farrar and Rinehart.

Marshall, H. (1993) *Not Having Children*. Melbourne: Oxford University Press.

Morrison, K.F. (1988) *'I am You': The Hermeneutics of Empathy in Western Literature, Theology and Art*. Princeton, NJ: Princeton University Press.

Newman, D.M. and Grauerholz, L. (eds) (2002) *Sociology of Families*. Thousand Oaks, CA: Pine Forge Press.

Nimkoff, M.F. (1934) *The Family*. Boston, MA: Houghton–Mifflin.

Oakley, A. (1993) *Essays on Women, Medicine and Health*. Edinburgh: Edinburgh University Press.

Ogburn, W.F. (1933) 'The family and its functions', *Recent Trends in the United States*. Report of President's Research Committee on Social Trends. New York and London: McGraw–Hill. pp. 661–707.

Parsons, T. (1943) 'The kinship system of the contemporary United States', *American Anthropologist*, 45: 22–38.

Parsons, T. (1956) 'The American family', in T. Parsons and R.F. Bales (eds), *Family, Socialization and Interaction Process*. London: Routledge and Kegan Paul. pp. 3–33.

Parsons, T. (1999) 'Religion in postindustrial America', in B.S. Turner (ed.), *The Parsons Reader*. Oxford: Blackwell. pp. 300–20.

Perkins, A. (2002) 'Tories soften line on gay partnerships', *Guardian*, 25 July, p. 14.

Raymond, J.G. (1993) *Women as Wombs: Reproductive Technologies and the Battle over Women's Freedom*. New York: HarperCollins.

Rifkin, J. (2002) 'The end of pregnancy?', *Guardian*, 17 January, p. 17.

Riggs, A. and Turner, B.S. (1999) 'The expectation of love in older age: towards a sociology of intimacy', in M. Poole and S. Feldman (eds), *A Certain Age: Women Growing Older*. St Leonards: Allen and Unwin. pp. 193–208.

Rose, A.M. (1968) *Sociology: The Study of Human Relations*. New York: Alfred A. Knopf.

Rougemont, D. de (1983) *Love in the Western World*. Princeton, NJ: Princeton University Press.

Schochet, G.J. (1975) *Patriarchalism in Political Thought*. Oxford: Oxford University Press.

Shorter, E. (1994) *From the Mind into the Body: The Cultural Origins of Psychosomatic Symptoms*. New York: The Free Press.

Smith, J.I. (1999) *Islam in America*. New York: Columbia University Press.

Spickard, P.R. (1989) *Mixed Blood: Intermarriage and Ethnic Identity in Twentieth Century America*. Madison, WI: University of Wisconsin Press.

Stacey, M. (1960) *Tradition and Change*. Oxford: Oxford University Press.

Tunstall, P. (1962) *The Fisherman*. London: MacGibbon and Kee.

Turner, B.S. (1998) 'The origins of the sociology of the family', in B.S. Turner (ed.), *The Early Sociology of the Family*. London: Routledge/Thoemmes Press. pp. 1–18.

Turner, B.S. (2003) 'Social capital, inequality and health: the Durkheimian revival', *Social Theory and Health*, 1 (1): 4–20.

Veevers, J.E. (1980) *Childless by Choice*. Toronto: Butterworth.

Waller, W. (1937) 'Rating and Dating Complex', *American Sociological Review*, 2: 727–34.

Warnock, M. (2002) *Making Babies: Is There a Right to Have Children?* Oxford: The Clarendon Press.

Weber, M. (1978) *Economy and Society: An Outline of Interpretive Sociology*, Berkeley/Los Angeles, CA: University of California Press.

Widmer, E. (2004) 'Couples and their networks', in J. Scott, J. Treas and M. Richards (eds), *The Blackwell Companion to the Sociology of Families.* Oxford: Blackwell. pp. 356–73.

Willmott, P. and Young, M. (1957) *Family and Kinship in East London.* London: Routledge and Kegan Paul.

Willmott, P. and Young, M. (1967) *Family and Class in a London Suburb.* London: Nel Mentor.

Woolf, M. (2002) 'Transsexual born a man wins right to be recognized as a woman', *Independent*, 12 July, p. 2.

8

The Social Institution of Money

GEOFFREY INGHAM

INTRODUCTION

Money is one of the modern world's essential 'social technologies'. Sociology, however, which is claimed to be the distinctive intellectual framework for understanding 'modernity', seems to have ignored money because it is not 'sociological enough' (Collins, 1979). A recent revival of interest in the subject only serves to highlight the longer-term neglect (Dodd, 1994; Zelizer, 1994; Leyshon and Thrift, 1997; Ingham, 1996, 1999, 2000a,b, 2001, 2002; Hart, 2000). Aside from reiterating the obvious importance of 'trust', sociology has not addressed the problem of the *actual social production of money* as an institution. Rather, sociology is concerned with very general descriptions of the consequences of money for 'modern' society (Giddens, 1990), its 'social meanings' (Zelizer, 1994) and, more indirectly, with the Marxist problem of 'finance capital'. This one-sided treatment would not matter if economics provided an adequate explanation of money's existence and functions, but it does not (Ingham, 1996).

Mainstream economics contains what appear to be contradictory conceptions of money. On the one hand, as in common sense, money is a quantifiable commodity that 'circulates' with a 'velocity'. In fact, this notion was already anachronistic at the time of its classical statement in Fisher's 'quantity theory' (1907). By the

early twentieth century, almost all capitalist transactions were carried out by a stroke of the pen in the book clearing of debits and credits in the banking giro, not by the circulation of 'money-stuff'. None the less, a hundred years on, in the era of so-called 'virtual' e-money, the analytical structure of 'quantity theory' continues to inform orthodox economics (Smithin, 2000; Issing, 2001). On the other hand, neoclassical economic 'high' theory asserts that money is relatively unimportant. Money is no more than a 'neutral veil' over transactions in the 'real economy'. Neoclassical economics' most prestigious paradigm (general equilibrium theory) acknowledges that it has no place for money in its mathematical models (Hahn, 1982: 1).

This state of affairs is a result of the division of intellectual labour between economics and sociology that followed the methodological dispute (*Methodenstreit*) in the social sciences at the beginning of the twentieth century (Hodgson, 2001). Money was placed under the jurisdiction of economics; but it is the conception of money held by economic 'theorists' that accounts for the inadequate understanding of money in both disciplines. Sociology should reclaim the analysis of money. Not only is money socially produced, it is actually constituted by structures of social relations (Ingham, 1996, 2000a).

During the *Methodenstreit*, an alternative to the economic commodity-exchange theory of money was advanced by the broad 'Historical School' and influenced contemporary sociological and heterodox economic thinking. Here, money is neither a 'commodity' nor mere 'neutral veil'; rather, it is a 'claim' or a 'promise' of payment – that is, a *social relation*. Banished from mainstream economics and, as a result of economic theory's hegemony, neglected by modern sociology, this analysis almost was lost to mainstream social science. It is claimed that Marxism avoided these errors (Fine and Lapavitsas, 2000), but this analysis has also been weakened by a conception of money as a 'mask' or 'veil' over an underlying 'reality' (Ingham, 2001).

Differences between the two conceptions are evident in the emphases that they give to money's 'functions'. By the late nineteenth century, the question of what money *is* had given way, in economic analysis, to an evasive functionalist definition, which remains the standard textbook approach. Money *is* what money *does*, and it is said to do three things. It is (1) a measure of value (unit, or money of account); (2) a medium of exchange and means of payment; (3) a store of value. From this deceptively simple starting point problems soon become apparent. Do *all* the functions have to be performed? Are they all of equal importance? If not, which is definitive? Mainstream economics has focused on money as a *medium of exchange*; the other functions are assumed to follow from it. The 'historical' alternative stresses the importance of *money of account* as an abstract measure of value, which is stored and transported through time. The issues concern the nature of the relationship between the realm of commodities and the realm of money. Are they one or two realms? Is money any more than an expression of the realm of commodities? Can it have a value outside this realm?

MONEY IN ECONOMICS

Economic orthodoxy: money in the 'real economy'

Modelling itself on the natural sciences, economics sought to establish deductive generalizations based on the axioms of individual rational choice maximization of utility and the associated equilibrium model of the perfectly competitive market (Machlup, 1978). The ideal type of the 'economy' comprises exchange ratios between commodities (*object–object relations*) expressed in money prices, established by individual acts of utility calculation (*individual–object relations*). These *object–object* and *agent–object* relations constitute what is known as the 'real' or 'natural' economy. *Agent–agent* or *social relations* form no part of the model (Weber, 1978: 63–4; Ganssmann, 1988).

The 'real' economy is essentially a model of a simple 'natural' (moneyless) barter economy (for the classic description, see Schumpeter, 1994 [1954]: 277; NB its Aristotelian origins). It describes exchange ratios between commodities, determined by individual calculations of their utilities in bilateral barter exchanges. The key assertion is that barter transforms myriad exchange ratios into a single price for a uniform good. Money is introduced into the model as a commodity that acts as a medium of exchange to facilitate the process – for example, cigarettes in prison. Money is only *a medium of exchange*. As a commodity, the medium of exchange can have an exchange ratio with other commodities. Or as a symbol, it can directly represent 'real' commodities. It is in this sense that money is a 'neutral veil' that has no efficacy other than to overcome the 'inconveniences of barter' which, in the late-nineteenth-century formulation, result from the absence of a 'double coincidence of wants' (see Ingham, 2000a). Money is more efficient than barter, but analytically they are structurally identical.

Menger's (1892) rational choice analysis of the evolution of money remains the basis for all neoclassical explanations of money's existence (Dowd, 2000; Klein and Selgin, 2000). Money is the unintended consequence of individual economic rationality. In order to maximize their barter options, it is argued, traders hold stocks of the most tradable commodities which, consequently, become media of exchange – beans, iron tools, etc. Coinage is explained with the further conjecture that precious metals have additional advantageous properties – such as durability, divisibility, portability etc. Metal is *weighed* and minted into uniform pieces and the commodity becomes money. In short, orthodox economic accounts of money are commodity-exchange theories. Both money's 'historical' origins and its 'logical' conditions of existence are explained as the outcome of a natural process of economic exchange (Ingham, 2000a).

The 'dematerialization' of money broke this explanatory link between individual rationality and system benefits. Paradoxically, for Menger, 'institutions such as money make for the common interest, and yet … conflict with the nearest and immediate interests of contracting individuals'. Why should the 'individual be ready to exchange his goods for little metal disks apparently useless as such, or for documents representing the latter?' (quoted in Jones, 1976: 757). Today, neoclassical economics tries to resolve the problem by showing that holding (non-commodity) money reduces transaction costs for the individual (Dowd, 2000; Klein and Selgin, 2000), but only succeeds in exposing the logical circularity of neoclassical economics' methodological individualism. It can establish only that it is 'advantageous for any given agent to mediate his transactions by money *provided that all other agents do likewise*' (Hahn, 1987: 26). Of course, it is not so much a question of whether it is advantageous to use money if others do, but rather that agents *cannot* use money *unless* others do likewise. To state the sociologically obvious: the advantages of money for the individual presuppose the existence of money as an institution.

There are other problems. First, the 'barter → commodity → money' transition is not supported by the historical record (Ingham, 2000a; Wray, 2000). Second, the model of the natural barter economy with its 'neutral veil' of money is singularly inappropriate for the capitalist monetary system. In the Commodity → Money → Commodity (C–M–C$_1$) sequence of the 'real' economy, money exists only as a medium for the gaining of utility through the exchange of commodities. The financing of production does not take place in the model. In the early twentieth century, attempts were made to explain the fact of bank credit, within the

framework of 'real' analysis. For example, Wicksell's 'natural' rate of interest is a measure of the 'natural' propensities and productivity in the 'real' economy and not, for example, the power of bankers to set a 'money rate'. The 'natural rate of interest' is an extension of the 'neutral veil' concept insofar as money, in the last instance, can only reflect or express the 'real'. In contrast, as we shall see, Weber and Keynes saw that capitalism involves a Money → Commodity → Money sequence (M–C–M$_1$) in which the money side is relatively autonomous. The act of bank lending *creates* money-capital to finance the future production of commodities (on Keynes, see Smithin, 1994: 2). The bank loan – that is, the capitalist's debt – pays wages which are spent as money.

After the mid-twentieth-century's Keynesian interlude, orthodox economic theory was restored in Friedman's 'monetarism', and further problems soon became apparent (Smithin, 1994). In 'monetarism', money is a 'thing' whose supply is quantifiable and controllable. (*Ceteris paribus*, an increase in the supply of money will increase prices.) However, it soon became apparent that it was not clear what should be counted as money – notes, coins, current bank accounts, savings accounts etc. The issue is complex, but the concept of money as a quantifiable and controllable 'stock' produced policy incoherence in the continuous proliferation of measures of money – M$_0$, M$_1$, … M$_{10}$ and so on. Moreover, by the 1990s, monetary aggregates increased as inflation fell, in contradiction of the theory.

However, the fundamental problem in economic orthodoxy, from which all the other difficulties stem, is the misunderstanding and neglect of *money of account*. Medium of exchange is the key function and it is assumed that all the others follow from it. The 'natural' market produces a transactions-cost efficient medium of exchange that becomes the standard of value and numerical money of account. Coins evolved from weighing pieces of precious metal that were cut from bars and, after standardization, counted. However, there are a priori and empirical grounds for reversing the sequence. Money of account is logically anterior and historically prior to the market (Keynes,

1930; Hicks, 1989; Hoover, 1996; Ingham, 1996, 2000a,b; Orléan, 1998; Wray, 2000).

Without further assumptions, it is difficult to envisage how a money of account could emerge from myriad bilateral barter exchange ratios based upon subjective preferences. One hundred goods could yield 4950 exchange rates (Davies, 1994: 15). How could discrete barter exchange ratios of, say, 3 chickens to 1 duck, or 6 ducks to 1 chicken, and so on, produce a single unit of account? The conventional economic answer that a 'duck standard' emerges 'spontaneously' involves a circular argument. A *single* 'duck standard' cannot be the equilibrium price of ducks established by supply and demand because, in the absence of a money of account, ducks would continue to have multiple and variable exchange values. A genuine 'market' which produces a single price for ducks requires a money of account – that is, a stable yardstick for measuring value. As opposed to the *commodity duck*, the *monetary duck* in any duck standard would be an *abstract duck*. If the process of exchange could not have produced the abstract concept of money of account, how did it originate? The question is actually at the very heart of a problem that distinguishes economics from sociology. Can an *inter*-subjective scale of value (money of account) emerge from myriad subjective preferences? Posed in this way, the question of money is at the centre of the general question in Talcott Parsons's sociological critique of economic theory – although it has not been seen in this light. From its starting point of individual subjective preferences, utilitarian theory cannot explain social order (Parsons, 1937).

Economic heterodoxy: money as abstract value and token credit

Heterodox monetary analysis has two sources. On the one hand, it can be traced to analyses of the credit-*money* that appeared in Western Europe in the sixteenth century. The new forms of money were not simply credit in the sense of *deferred payment*; rather, these 'credits' were 'money', in that mere 'promises to pay' (IOUs), issued outside the sovereign mints,

began to circulate as *means of payment*. Only later were they backed by metal in a hybrid bank credit/gold standard. The general use of transferable debt is specific to capitalism. 'Depersonalized' and hence transferable debt is used as means of payment to a third party: A's IOU held by B is used to pay C (Ingham, 1999). After over two thousand years during which coin and money were synonymous, this new money-form posed intellectual puzzles (Sherman, 1997). Some of the answers gave rise to an analysis of money that departed from the Aristotelian theories of commodity money to which all orthodox economic theories may be traced. They led to the idea that *all* money was constituted by *social relations* of credit and debt (Ingham, 2000a: 23).

A second source of heterodox analysis accompanied the construction of the nineteenth-century German state. Money's role in taxation and as the expression of national integrity and power were emphasized (Schumpeter, 1994 [1954]). Knapp's *State Theory of Money* (1973 [1924]) challenged economic explanations of money's properties in terms of the exchange value of its commodity form. By declaring what it will accept for the discharge of tax debt, denominated in its own unit of account, the state creates and establishes the 'validity' of money. Private bank notes become money when they are denominated in the state's money of account and accepted as payment of tax debts owed to the state and reissued in payment to the state's creditors (Knapp, 1973 [1924]: 95, 143, 196). Money consists in a *reciprocal relationship*: states issue 'credits' to pay for their goods and services which, in turn, must be acquired for payment of taxes. New money cannot be created without the creation of a complementary debt (Gardiner, 1993). Money is a social relation, not a thing.

Money is a 'token' that 'bears' units of abstract value. 'State theory' is also known as 'chartalism' (from *charta*, the Latin for token) and sometimes as monetary 'nominalism' (Ellis, 1934). Regardless of its specific form, money is, generically, a credit – that is, it is a claim on goods. 'State theory' was anathema to the early-twentieth-century proponents of the commodity-exchange theory of value – that value can *only* be established in exchange determined by the forces of supply and demand. In objecting that states could not establish the purchasing power of money, the economic theorists misunderstood Knapp. In fact, his argument helps to resolve commodity theory's difficulty in trying to identify the 'moneyness' by its utility or exchange value alone. Economic theory cannot uniquely specify money – that is, distinguish money from other commodities. Following Knapp, money becomes a commodity with an exchange value only *after* it has been constituted as money by a social and political process. States establish the 'validity' of money by the 'proclamation' of the nominal unit of abstract value and the 'acceptation' of the tokens that correspond to it.

Together with early English 'credit theory', 'state theory' influenced Keynes's *A Treatise on Money* (1930). During his 'Babylonian madness' in the 1920s, Keynes studied the German Historical School's work on ancient Near Eastern money. During the third and second millennia BC, their economies were organized with a *money of account*, but payments were made in commodities, labour service, silver by weight etc. (Ingham, 2000a). 'Money' existed for several thousand years before the first use of coinage around 700 BC: 'Money of Account, namely that in which Debts and Prices and General Purchasing Power are expressed is the primary concept of a Theory of Money.' Forms of money such as coins '*can only exist* in relation to a Money of Account' (Keynes, 1930: 3; emphasis added). In other words, the quality of 'moneyness' is conferred by the abstract measure of value that is imposed by the state when it writes the monetary 'dictionary' (Keynes, 1930: 4–5, 11–15).

Keynes also identified 'Acknowledgements of Debt' as forms of money (Keynes, 1930: 6–9). The chapter 'The "Creation" of Bank Money' provides a description of the creation of new deposits of money by the act of lending in a way that is relatively independent of the level of incoming deposits of savings: 'There is no limit to the amount of bank-money that banks can safely create provided that *they move forward in step*' (emphasis in original). Bank chairmen believe that 'outside forces', over which they have no control, determine their decisions. '[Y]et the "outside forces" may be nothing but himself and his fellow chairmen, and certainly not his depositors' (Keynes, 1930: 26–7). The analysis points to the socially constructed reality of the norms of banking practice. Bank money is the result of the act of lending – that is to say, the social relation of debt constitutes money.[1]

Keynes's analysis is continued in the heterodox post-Keynesian theory of 'endogenous' money (Wray, 1990; Smithin, 1994; Rochon, 1999). French and Italian 'monetary circuit' analysis also has Keynesian roots (Parguez and Seccareccia, 2000). The idea that all money is debt is also found in the work of French interdisciplinary social scientists (Aglietta and Orléan, 1998). Other post-Keynesians have returned to Keynes's inspiration in Knapp to build a distinctive 'neo-chartalist school' (Wray, 1998; Bell, 2000, 2001).

MONEY IN SOCIOLOGICAL THEORY

Both economic traditions have influenced sociology, but orthodoxy has had much the greater impact. (Social anthropology has been similarly affected, see Hart, 2000).[2] Weber and Simmel were influenced by the heterodox 'Historical School', but it is precisely these parts of their work that have been seriously neglected.

Money as a symbolic medium

Parsons's early work played a part in confirming the terms of the division of intellectual labour between economics and sociology. They are distinct, but complementary as he was assured of 'the essential soundness, from a sociological view, of the main core tradition in economics' (Parsons, 1991 [1953]). From a sociological standpoint, money is a symbolic generalized medium of communication and interaction (Parsons and Smelser, 1956; Dodd, 1994). It facilitates the integration of the functionally differentiated parts of the social system – in an analogous way to integration through prices in economic theory. But as a 'symbol' money is 'neutral' insofar as it does not affect the underlying constitution of either the 'real' economy or social system. Parsons followed economics' axiom that value is only realizable in exchange and that money is only a symbol of value – that is, money, as symbolic medium, is without value (Ganssmann, 1988: 308). Like its economic parent, this notion does not grasp the obvious fact of money as a store of abstract value that may be appropriated. Furthermore, Parsonian sociology not only failed to take into account that domination derives from the *possession* of money, but also that it derives from control of the actual process of money's *production* by states and banks. Apart from a description of money's integrative functions, all other questions could be left to economics.

This general orientation has persisted in sociology. Habermas, Luhmann and Giddens, for example, have all followed this concept of money as a 'symbolic token' or 'media of interchange [*sic*]' (Giddens, 1990: 22; see Dodd's (1994) secondary analysis of Habermas and Luhmann). Money promotes 'systemic complexity' and the 'time space distanciation' of modernity; but its existence is taken for granted. The importance of 'trust' is repeated, but this has 'as much explanatory value as saying that credit comes from *credere*' (Ganssmann, 1988). Explaining money involves the historical explanation of a specific form of 'social technology' that accounts for abstract value and transports it through time. To be sure, money has the *consequences* that Giddens and others outline; but only if the social relations of its production remain intact. In the absence of this analysis, sociology implies a functionalist explanation of money's existence that parallels the teleological theorems to be found in mainstream economics. Like economics, much modern sociology has lost sight of the obvious. Money is not merely a symbolic token that integrates 'disembedded' social systems (Giddens, 1990); it is also *value* in itself. Control of money's production is a pivotal social institution.

MARX AND MARXIST ANALYSIS

Parsons's dismissal of Marx as a minor classical economist is a gross exaggeration, but it contains a grain of truth. The labour theory of value committed Marx, and his successors, to a version of the commodity theory of money, with all its attendant errors. To this extent, Marx's general theory of money was mistaken. Most importantly, this attachment to the labour theory of value of commodity money prevented Marx from realizing that his theory of capital as a social relation applied also to money. In particular, he did not fully understand capitalist credit money (Cutler et al., 1978: 24–6). Later Marxist and sociological analyses of 'finance capital' have perpetuated the misunderstanding. (on Hilferding's errors, see Henwood, 1997.)

Like Adam Smith, Marx held that '[g]old confronts other commodities as money only because it previously confronted them as a commodity … It acts as a universal measure of value, and only through performing this function does gold … become money' (Marx, 1976: 162, 188). Precious metal can become a measure of value because mining and minting embody labour which can be expressed in 'the quantity of any other commodity in which the same amount of labour-time is congealed' (p. 186). Forms of 'credit' are derivative: bank notes and bills of exchange are money insofar as they directly *represent* both precious metals and/or commodities in exchange.

But Marx's distinctive departure from classical economics is to show that monetary relationships do not merely represent a natural economic reality, but also mask the latter's underlying reality of the social relations of production. These constitute the reality that appears in a monetized alienated form. For Marx there are *two* 'veils'. Behind money lie 'real' economic forces, as they do in somewhat different manner in the orthodox economics. In turn, behind these economic forces lie the 'real' social relations, which also appear as monetary relations. Tearing away these monetary 'masks' or 'veils' will demystify capitalism and its money, which will become 'visible and dazzling to our eyes' (p. 187).

This kind of reasoning is why Marx is considered as a classical sociologist; but it also implies that money can be analytically 'bracketed'. Notwithstanding the two 'veils', Marx's analytical position is similar to classical economics. Emphasis on the social relations of production of commodities and the labour theory of value prevented Marx (and almost all his contemporaries) from recognizing the relative autonomy of the production of abstract value in the form of credit-money, or the more radical position that all money is token credit. Marx dismissed as 'professorial twaddle' Roscher's complaint that economists 'do not bear sufficiently in mind the peculiarities that distinguish money from other commodities' (n. 13, p. 187). In company with all commodity theorists, Marx failed to consider money as abstract value, defined by a money of account and sustained by its own social relations of production.

At times, Marx appeared to have grasped that capitalist credit-money can be created autonomously outside the sphere of the production and circulation of commodities; but, then it plays an essentially *dysfunctional* role. Bank credit could expand beyond 'its necessary proportions' and become 'the most potent means of driving capitalist production beyond its own limits, and this has become one of the most effective vehicles of crises and swindle' (Marx, 1981: 735–9). Marx was conventional in this view that credit instruments – bills of exchange, promissory notes etc. – were, or rather *should* be in a rationally organized system, no more than functional substitutes for hard cash.

The anachronistic and misleading commodity-exchange theory of money is evident in Hilferding's *Finance Capital* (1981 [1910]), which despite the apparent critique, was entirely consistent with orthodox economic theory of the time. He dismissed Knapp's 'state theory' for 'eschewing all economic explanation'. Rather, 'money … originates in the exchange process and requires no other condition' (Hilferding, 1981 [1910]: 36; see also 376). Credit creation is anchored in the 'real' economy of production and, therefore 'the quantity of credit money is limited by the level of production and circulation' (pp. 64–5). Banks aid the capitalist process by garnering the bourgeoisie's 'idle capital' together with the 'idle money of all other classes for use in

production' (p. 90). All this is perfectly true. But, as Schumpeter and Keynes argued, the *differentia specifica* of capitalism lies in banks' 'endogenous' creation of new deposits of credit-money *ex nihilo* – or, more accurately, out of the social relation of debt. This lending is *new* money and not merely the collection of pre-existing 'little pools' into larger reservoirs (Schumpeter, 1994 [1954]: 1113). In failing to see this essentially capitalist process, Hilferding and generations of Marxists and sociologists have actually *underestimated* the power of 'finance capital'!

Like orthodox economics, the Marxist analysis of money has been disabled by the search for the value of money in the commodity (Fine and Lapavitsas, 2000; and see the critique in Ingham, 2001). It has been unable to consider the proposition that *all* money consists in symbolic 'tokens' of abstract value that signify, and are constituted by, social relations of credit-debt. From a sociological standpoint, these social relations must be considered as the 'reality' of money. We may now turn to those aspects of Simmel's and Weber's work into which these and other 'Historical School' arguments were incorporated.

SIMMEL AND WEBER ON MONEY

The Philosophy of Money

Unfortunately, sociology has taken Simmel at his misleading word that *The Philosophy of Money* is not really about money, but rather about how money expresses the essence of modern life (Dodd, 1994: 175). The modern spirit of discontinuous, fragmented, increasingly abstract impersonal relations finds its most perfect expression in money: 'The more the life of society becomes dominated by monetary relationships, the more the relativistic character of existence finds its expression in conscious life' (Simmel, 1978 [1907]: 512). This form of 'sociation' generates individuality, personal freedom and intellectualism (Dodd, 1994; Turner, 1999). However, in addition to the analysis of the effects of money, *The*

Philosophy of Money contains important, but fragmented, accounts of money's origins, its essential qualities and how these are produced. Two aspects of *The Philosophy of Money* have received less attention than they deserve: the analysis of money as *abstract* value, and as a form of *'sociation'* in itself, that is to say, as constituted by social relations.

Simmel rejects all economic theory, including Marxism, which locates money's value in the specific substance or content of the 'money stuff'. Rather, money is the pure form of abstract value. The value of money does not derive from either the costs of its production, or supply and demand, or labour-value. Rather, '[m]oney is the representative of *abstract* value' (p. 120). Money is 'the value of things without the things themselves' (p. 121). Money is the *abstraction* of the 'distilled exchangeability of objects … the *relation* between things, a relation that persists in spite of the changes in the things themselves' (p. 124; emphasis in original). Simmel's critique of commodity theories of money is developed with a dismissal of the implication that measures must have the same quality as the object to be measured – measures of length are long and, therefore, a measure of value must be valuable (p. 131). Some measures of length are long; but as Simmel argued, this is because measure and measured object *share the same quality* of length. 'To establish a proportion between two quantities, not by direct comparison, but in terms of the fact that each of them relates to a third quantity and that these relations are equal or unequal' is one of society's great accomplishments (p. 146). Thus, following the 'nominalists' of the 'Historical School', Simmel asserts the logical primacy of the abstraction of money of account. Money is 'one of those normative ideas that obey the norms that they themselves represent' (p. 122) (see Orléan, 1998: money is *autoréférentielle*; see also Searle, 1995).

Writing at the apogee of the gold standard, Simmel conceded that '[m]oney performs its services best when it is not simply money, that is when it does not merely represent the value of things in pure abstraction' (p. 165). But he does not lose sight of his essential and prescient point: 'It is not technically feasible', Simmel continues, 'to accomplish what is technically correct, namely to transform the money function into a pure token money, and to detach it completely from every substantial value that limits the quantity of money, *even though the actual development of money suggests that this will be the final outcome*' (p. 165; emphasis added). With the breaking of the link between gold and the dollar in 1971, commodity money ceased to exist.

In contrast to orthodox economics, Simmel understands that exchange by money is structurally different from barter. Money is a form of 'sociation' and not a 'thing': 'When barter is replaced by money transactions a third factor is introduced between the two parties … the direct line of contact between them … moves to the relationship which each of them … has with the economic community that accepts the money.' Simmel then endorses the credit theory of money: '[t]his is the core of the truth in the theory that money is only a claim upon society' (p. 177). Indeed, '[m]etallic money, which is usually regarded as the absolute opposite of credit money, contains in fact two presuppositions of credit which are particularly intertwined' (p. 178). First, the metallic substance cannot be normally tested in cash transactions and is, rather, verified by the secondary characteristics stamped on coins by the issuing authority. Second, people must *trust* that the tokens of value will retain their value. This may be based on objective probabilities; but this 'kind of trust is only a weak form of inductive knowledge' (p. 179). There can never be sufficient information for it to be the only basis for holding money. Additionally, money requires an element of 'supra-theoretical belief' or 'social-psychological quasi-religious faith' (p. 179). 'Money is the purest reification of means, a concrete instrument which is absolutely identical with its abstract concept; it is a pure instrument' (p. 211). And the qualities of this pure abstract value reside in 'social organisation and … supra-subjective norms' (p. 210).

Modern sociology's exclusive emphasis on 'trust' tends to trivialize Simmel's analysis. Like Weber, he saw that the development of modern states and non-metallic, 'dematerialized' money were intimately connected. Modern states built themselves, in large part on the basis of credible metallic standards and coinage. Money led to the dissolution of the personalized bonds of feudal relations and the '*enforcement* of money transactions meant an extension of royal power into areas in which private and personal modes of exchange had existed' (p. 185; emphasis added). However, in a dialectical process, the 'value of money is based on a guarantee represented by the central political power, which eventually replaces the significance of the metal' (p. 184). In this historical process, coercion, as always, preceded any 'trust' in the establishment of a currency. Modern sociological analysis tends to forget that monetary sovereignty was established to a large extent by extreme physical coercion – such as branding on the forehead with coins, and execution for counterfeiting.

However, having rejected essentialist theories of intrinsic precious metallic value and the classical labour theory of value, Simmel is left with the very same problem that the Austrian 'subjectivists' had to face – how can myriad individual preferences produce a scale of inter-subjective value. 'Money as abstract value expresses nothing but the relativity of things that constitute value' (p. 121); but *at the same time*, it transcends the relativity of exchangeable values and 'as the stable pole, contrasts with the eternal movements, fluctuations of the objects with all others' (p. 121; emphasis added). But how does it do it?

Simmel answers the question with a historical analysis of money's transformation from substance to pure abstraction (ch. 2, section III: 168–98). It is full of insights gleaned from the Historical School, but is no more than a *description* of the process of becoming the non-material abstraction he correctly identified as money. Moreover, it is confused. He failed to see that, if all money is credit, Hildebrand's barter → commodity → money → credit evolution is a contradiction.

Two fundamental questions remained unanswered in *The Philosophy of Money*. First, what are the origins of the *concept* of money as value? Simmel agrees with the Austrian economists that money expresses exchangeability, but sees that it cannot have been the result of the process of exchange. Rather, it 'can have developed only out of *previously existing values ...*' (p. 119; emphasis added). But which might these have been? Simmel left no more than scattered clues. Second, how is the abstract value of modern dematerialized money established and maintained? Precious metal is a means of maintaining confidence, but in an 'ideal world' money would be no more than 'its essential function', as a symbol of abstract value. Here, Simmel reverts to a thoroughly positivist economic conception of money: '[M]oney would then reach a *neutral* position which would be as little affected by the fluctuations in commodities as is the yardstick by the different lengths that it measures' (p. 191; emphasis added). In other words, Simmel accepts economists' 'ideal world' in which the value of commodities is the result of the interplay of subjective preferences, mediated by the *neutral symbol* of money. But this 'ideal world' is not explained; it does not have a *social structure*. We need to turn to Weber for a sociological formulation in which the value of money expresses the social conflict that lies behind subjective preferences.

Weber on money

The enormous secondary sociological literature on Weber's analysis of capitalism scarcely refers to his analysis of money. The chapters on money and banking in *General Economic History* have been almost completely ignored (Weber, 1981 [1927]). Emphasis on religion has led to a distorted view of his work: for example, the underdevelopment of capitalism in China was not so much the result of a religious ethic as the fact that its money was 'scarcely as developed as Ptolemaic Egypt' (Weber, 1951: 3). This neglect is more puzzling in light of his lavish praise for Knapp's *The State Theory of Money* (1973 [1924]). One would have expected scholars to have followed Weber's lead in exploring the 'permanently fundamental importance' of this 'magnificent work' (Weber, 1978: 184, 169; also 78–9).

Money expands market, or 'indirect', exchange by which it is 'possible to obtain goods which are separated from those offered in exchange for them in space, in time, in respect of the persons involved, and, what is very important, in respect to the quantity in each side of the transaction' (p. 80). The most important element is not the existence of a commodity-money as a medium of exchange, but the possibility of monetary calculation – 'assigning money values to all goods and services' (p. 81). *Money of account* – the 'continuity of the nominal unit of money, even though the monetary material may have changed' – makes this calculation possible. It is as an *abstraction* that 'the individual values the nominal unit of money as a certain proportional part of his income, and not as a chartal piece of metal or note' (p. 168). Following Knapp, Weber refers to the state's definition of money in terms of a unit of account for the legal payment of debts, as its *formal validity* (p. 169).

Weber upheld Knapp's distinction between the 'valuableness' and 'value' (p. 193; see also 78–9). But, in addition to money's 'formal validity' ('valuableness'), there must also exist the 'probability that it will be at some future time acceptable in exchange for specified or unspecified goods in price relationships which are capable of approximate estimate' (p. 169). In this emendation of 'state theory', Weber followed economic orthodoxy, and his critique of Knapp's analysis of inflation is based, to some extent, upon the commodity and quantity theories of money (p. 192, see also 180–4). Weber deplored the kind of disciplinary segregation that eventually came about after the *Methodenstreit*, but he believed that the analysis of the price of goods – including the purchasing power of money – was more properly part of economics (p. 79). None the less, he was unable to resist, mainly in footnotes, making incisive comments on the nature of economic theorizing. *Economy and Society* contains the germs of a sociological recasting of a 'substantive theory of money' (p. 190) which implies a further departure from orthodox economic thought.

Typically, Weber confronts *both* economic orthodoxy and its socialist critics (pp. 78–80, 107–9). Prices, which in conventional theory are the result of the interplay of supply and demand, are seen as the 'product of conflicts of interest (that) result from power constellations' in 'the struggle for economic existence'. Consequently, money is not economic theory's 'neutral veil' draped over exchange ratios of commodities. Rather, money 'is primarily a weapon in this struggle, and prices are expressions of this struggle; they are instruments in this struggle only as estimated quantifications of relative chances in this struggle' (p. 108).

The market may be a power struggle, but Weber offers no comfort to the socialists, who, following Marx, wished to remedy the inequality by issuing vouchers for an agreed 'quantity of socially useful labour'. But, in order to produce rational calculability, money has to be a weapon in the struggle for economic existence between 'the play of interests oriented only to profitability' (p. 183). The exchange of a socially agreed quantity of labour for specific goods would 'follow the rules of barter' (p. 80), and could not produce a measure of abstract value. Weber agreed with the Austrian theoretical economists in the 'socialist calculation' debate that money can never be a 'harmless "voucher"' as its valuation is 'always in very complex ways dependent on its scarcity' (p. 79). Any equilibrium or price stability in an equation of quantities of money and goods, in particular the interest rate, will be the expression of a *predictable balance of power*. Conversely, in this admittedly incomplete formulation, price instability in general is as much the result of the 'economic struggle for existence' as it is the product of an overabundance (inflation) or scarcity (deflation) of money. In short, socialism could not produce rational monetary calculation. Bureaucratic administration could never produce the '"right" volume or the "right" type of money' because state bureaucracies are 'primarily oriented to the creation of purchasing power for certain interest groups' (including the state itself) – which would cause inflation (p. 183).

Simmel and Weber saw clearly the merits of the 'nominalist', 'state' and 'credit' theories of money. These provide a foundation for a more comprehensive sociological theory of money as a social institution.

FUNDAMENTALS OF A SOCIOLOGY OF MONEY

Attention should focus on three questions. What is money? How is money produced? How does money obtain, retain, or lose its value?

What is money?

Economic theory's focus on money as an actual medium of exchange entails a 'category error' in which specific forms of money have been mistaken for the generic quality of 'money-ness'. This has resulted in long-standing confusion over closely related issues – for example, the distinction between money and credit, the so-called 'dematerialization' of money, the advent of virtual 'postmodern' money (Leyshon and Thrift, 1997), and electronic money and the 'end of money'. (For a discussion of these and related issues, see Ingham, 2002.) The unique specification of money is as a *measure of abstract value* and a *means of storing* and *transporting* this abstract value.

Monetary exchange consists in the calculation and exchange and transfer of debits and credits according to a money of account. Money cannot be created without the simultaneous creation of debt. For money to be money, it presupposes the existence of a debt measured in money of account elsewhere in the social system. The holder of money is owed goods.

> [M]oney is only a claim upon society ... The liquidation of every private obligation by money means that the community now assumes this obligation to the creditor ... [M]etallic money is also a promise to pay and ... differs from the cheque with respect to the size of the group which vouches for its being accepted. The common relationship that the owner of money and the seller have to a social group – the claim of the former to a service and the trust of the latter that this claim will be honoured – provides the sociological constellation in which money transactions, as distinct from barter are accomplished. (Simmel, 1978 [1907]: 177, 174–9)

Money is circulating debt, but perhaps the traditional metaphor of a 'circulation' is inappropriate. Rather, vast dense networks of overlapping and interconnected bilateral credit–debit relationships constitute money. This is more obvious in the case of the 'clearing' of debits and credits in a bank giro, where money-stuff does not actually flow from one account to another. But it applies equally to coins and notes, which might be referred to as 'portable debt' (Gardiner, 1993: 224). The essential point is that the debt is either transferable (bank giro) or portable (coin) because it is denominated in money of account. Money is constituted by the *continuation* of relations of credit–debit. In Marc Bloch's counterintuitive observation, money would disappear if all debts were paid (Bloch, 1954).

This conceptualization becomes clearer with consideration of the multiplicity and dissociation of money 'things' in relation to the abstraction of money. The measure (money of account), means of payment for the unilateral discharge of debt and any media of exchange need not be integrated in single form, as in coinage: Cash, plastic cards, cheques, magnetic traces in computer disks, and so on. The point is clearly expressed in a study of money and national identity in early capitalism:

> By the 1830s, then, Britons could at different times and places have understood gold sovereigns, banknotes, or bills of exchange as the privileged local representatives of the pound ... the pound as an abstraction was constituted precisely by its capacity to assume these heterogeneous forms, since its existence as a national currency was determined by the mediations between them. (Rowlinson, 1999: 64–5)

How is money produced?

Different modes of the production of money may be identified. These consist in social relations between issuers, issuer and users, and the technological means available for the storage and transportation of abstract value – from clay tablets, to coins, to pen and paper, to magnetic traces and so on. However, the fundamental question concerns the 'origins' of money of account; that is to say, the abstract 'idea' of money.

Money of account   'Unless the commodities used for exchange bear some relation to a fixed standard, we are dealing with barter [because] … the parties in barter-exchange are comparing their *individual needs*, not *values in the abstract'* (Grierson, 1977: 16–19; emphasis added). For example, the tobacco used as a medium of exchange in seventeenth-century Virginia only became money when its value was fixed at three shillings a pound (Grierson, 1977: 17). The standard of value, determined by weight (the exchange value of money-stuff), is not the important issue. Rather, 'countability' transforms the 'commodity' (*qua* convenient medium of exchange) into 'money'. This might be 'countable-useful' (slaves, cattle, furs) or 'countable-ornamental' (teeth, beads, shells) (Grierson, 1977: 33; see also Hoover, 1996).

As an alternative to the theory that a measure of abstract value could emerge from subjective preferences in barter, Grierson argues that it originated in a very early social institution for the settlement of disputes, later examples of which are known as *wergeld* (Grierson, 1977: 19). *Wergeld* (worthpayment) sanctioned payment of damages and compensation for injury and insult according to a fixed scale of tariffs.

> The conditions under which these laws were put together would appear to satisfy, much better than the market mechanism, the pre-requisites for the establishment of a monetary system. The tariffs for damages were established in public assemblies, and … [s]ince what is laid down consists of evaluations of injuries, not evaluation of commodities, the conceptual difficulty of devising a common measure for appraising unrelated objects is avoided. (Grierson, 1977: 20–1)

This analysis lends itself to a Durkheimian interpretation in which money of account/ measure of value is seen as a 'collective representation' of fundamental elements of societal structure (Ingham, 1996). If religion, or the sacred, originates in the worship of society, money originally expressed society's conception of its own worth. The punitive and compensatory tariffs expressed both the *utilitarian* and *moral* components of society. *Wergeld* symbolically represents society's two faces in prescribing recompense for both *injury* and *insult*. On the one hand, it accounted for the functional worth of the contribution of social roles to societal welfare by assigning a tariff to the loss or impairment of their individual

incumbents; for example, young men of fighting age were worth more than old women and so on. On the other hand, such schemes of functional or utilitarian worth were embedded in norms and values that directly reflected the hierarchical status order of society. Compensation for the loss of a Russian nobleman's moustache, for example, was four times greater than for the loss of a finger (Grierson, 1977: 20). *Wergeld* was the codification of the social values without which the assessment of functional contribution would have remained *anomic* and open to settlement only by constant recourse to socially and economically debilitating blood feuds.

Standards of value   Once the concept of abstract monetary accounting (unit of account) was available to society, the next step was the development of a standard of value based on commodities, as occurred in the ancient Near Eastern empires in the period from 3000 to 1000 BC (Goldsmith, 1987: ch. 2; Polanyi, 1957). The Babylonian *shekel* was originally fixed at 1 *gur* (1.2 hectolitres of barley) and later at a more manageable 8.3 grams of silver. However, these societies were command economies with only very small trade sectors. The overwhelming majority of payments were rents and taxes to religious and secular authorities. There was no coinage and payment was made in commodities, labour services, or silver by weight (*shekel, mina, talent*) (Goldsmith, 1987). The state not only fixed the standard, but also the prices of taxes, rents, and so on. Money had its logical origins in money of account and its historical foundation in the 'chartal' money of early bureaucratic empires. It was not the spontaneous product of the market.

Coinage   Coinage, which integrated all the attributes (unit of account, means of exchange/ payment, store of value) in the form of money-stuff, came 2000 years later in Lydia and Greece around 600 BC (Davies, 1994). Centralized monarchical states and developments in metallurgy made it possible to embody money of account, standard/store of value and means of payment/exchange in a single object. It is probable that the disintegration of the larger bureaucratic empires into smaller states was important in the development of coinage. Small unstable states were dependent on mercenary soldiers whom they paid in lumps of precious metal. As campaigning soldiers spent their lumps, they greatly expanded the scale and scope of market exchange. Coinage reached its apogee in the Roman Empire and '[i]ts "sound money" was accepted over an area larger than any other before or after the nineteenth century' (Goldsmith, 1987: 36). Taxation was the fundamental money relation and 'there is no reason to suppose that [coinage] was ever issued by Rome for any other purpose than to enable the state to make payments … Once issued coinage was demanded back by the state in payment of taxes' (Crawford, 1970: 46).

Four aspects of coinage should be noted in relation to the commodity theory of money. First, the precious metal coins used for payment of taxes were almost invariably too large for daily use. This medium of exchange function was performed by *base metal tokens*. For example, Rome had the gold *aureus* and silver *denarius*, supplemented by the *sestertius* of copper, zinc and tin (Goldsmith, 1987: 36). Second, coins frequently were not struck with a numerical signifier of their relationship to the money of account. (Further, only the silver penny of Charlemagne's abstract money of account of pounds, shillings and pence was ever minted.) Monetary policy, usually from fiscal motives, involved, on the one hand, 'crying up' or 'crying down' the coinage – that is to say, changing its value in relation to the abstract money of account. On the other hand, it was important to ensure that bullion and nominal values of the precious metal did not diverge to the point where the coins went out of circulation to be melted down (Gresham's Law). Third, the 'token' character of coins is apparent in that debasement of the coinage, by reduction of its metallic content, had very little effect on its purchasing power over considerable periods of time (Einaudi, 1953 [1936]; Innes, 1913; Wray, 2000; and see Goldsmith, 1987: 37 for a discussion of Roman debasement). Fourth, as prices had already begun to

rise sharply decades before the discovery of South American silver, it seems improbable that its importation was the cause of seventeenth-century inflation (Fischer, 1996).

Capitalist credit-money　Until late-sixteenth-century Europe, credit networks were restricted to small mercantile sectors and only very rarely developed fully into 'private' money (Boyer Xambeu et al., 1994). The issue of money remained the sovereign's jealously guarded prerogative. In capitalism, however, monetary sovereignty is shared between the state and the private banking system. The history of the hybridization of precious metallic standard coinage and bank credit-money which persisted until the twentieth century cannot be dealt with here. However, emphasis on the importance of the form of capitalist credit-money entails an amendment of the consensus on the centrality of capital–labour (class) relations of production and the role of religion in the rise of capitalism (see Ingham, 1999).

Early modern banking involving 'the development of the law and practice of negotiable paper and of "created" deposits afford the best indication we have for dating the rise of capitalism' (Schumpeter, 1994 [1954]: 78). Money was freed from the physical constraints of territory and geology and could become an autonomous force of production (Schumpeter, 1994 [1954]: 318). But, this development should not be explained in terms of the functional need for a more 'efficient' money in an economy whose dynamic lay elsewhere in 'real' factors such as technology, the division of labour, or capital–labour social relations of production (Ingham, 1999). Modern forms of credit-money were the result of particular geopolitical conditions and social structural changes in the reawakening of Europe after the collapse of the Roman Empire and its coinage system.

With the fall of Rome, the integration of money and account and means of payment in the form of coins disappeared (Davies, 1994). When minting of coins (*moneta reale*) resumed in the myriad political jurisdictions of fragmented medieval Europe, they were integrated by Charlemagne's abstract *moneta immaginaria* (money of account) (Einaudi, 1953 [1936]: 230). The Christian ecumene of the Holy Roman Empire was too weak to impose a centralized minted coinage, but it was able to provide the normative basis for a common money of account. This dissociation of the two elements of money was of critical importance in providing the conditions for the emergence of merchants' private bank money, which was based on the bill of exchange (Bloch, 1954). These bills were denominated in the *moneta immaginaria* and existed in an unstable relationship with myriad coinages. Eventually, the bills of exchange became detached from the commodities in transit that they actually represented and, resting only on the banker's promise to pay, became autonomous means of payment. In this way, after a long struggle, money ceased to be the monopoly prerogative of the sovereign (Boyer-Xambeu et al., 1994).

With regard to 'state theory', it should be noted that the merchants' private bank-credit money only became widely accepted when the states joined the bank giros (Wray, 1990). The fusion of state and bank credit money developed first in the Italian city-states during the fifteenth and sixteenth centuries, then spread to Holland and, most decisively, to England, with the formation of the Bank of England in 1694. The widespread use of debt as a means of payment outside the networks of traders required the state to establish the legal depersonalization and negotiability of debt by which the simple credit of the personal IOU, recorded in unit of account, could become credit money (Carruthers and Babb, 1996; Ingham, 1999). All subsequent developments have been extensions and refinements of this evolutionary leap in monetary practice.

Modern money is constituted and sustained by two fundamental and reciprocal debtor–creditor relations. First, to pay for their goods and services, modern states issue money, which is required, in turn, to pay taxes. Second, the national debt, held by the state's creditors, comprises a base of 'high powered' money, held in the banking system, from which new money can be 'endogenously' created (Wray, 1990; Smithin, 1994; Ingham, 2000b). Other forms of private or 'near' money exist in capitalist networks and local exchange trading schemes (see Ingham, 2002), but they remain subordinate to state money. However, it is argued that the Internet may yet bring about the purely private 'market' money, or even the 'neutral veil' described in economic theory.

Globalization and the 'end of money'
Although it is not yet fully explored sociologically, the question of money and, moreover, the two conceptions of money, lie at the heart of the 'globalization' debate. Communication and information technology, it is contended, is eroding the power of nation-states from two directions – globally from the 'outside' and also locally from the 'inside'. The advance of transnational capitalism and global e-commerce has been paralleled by the revival of local and 'informal' economies. Both developments make use, in part, of new forms of money, based on communication and information technology (CIT). It is widely thought that these could successfully challenge the state's monopoly and control of monetary production.

Two aspects of this debate should be distinguished. First, CIT is literally *transforming* money. After its material forms of metal and paper, money is now widely thought to be becoming 'virtual' as in, for example, the electronic transmission of payments in the banking system, or in 'electronic purses'. Changes in the mode of monetary transmission may have important implications, particularly over the security of the payments system that constitutes the money (OECD, 2002); but confusion over 'dematerialized' money persists. On the one hand, as all money is abstract value it is 'virtual'. On the other, all *forms* of money have a 'materiality'. 'Book money' in sixteenth-century Italian banks was just as 'virtual' when it was transported through time and space by the stroke of the pen and today's e-money leaves magnetic traces.

It is suggested that CIT makes it easier to create authentically alternative new forms of money that might erode or even displace state money. The development of the 'global' and the 'local' both imply the 'denationalization' or 'deterritorialization' of money (Cohen, 2001). A number of developments on both 'levels' are referred to. At the globalized upper level of capitalism, for example, large transnational corporations might issue their own 'scrip' as media of exchange on Internet transactions. In more extreme vein, others argue that Internet barter-credit transactions might even bring about the 'end of money' and the redundancy of central banks (see references in Ingham, 2002). At the other end of the scale, the informal sectors of many modern economies have developed into local exchange trading systems (LETS) with their own local media of exchange. As the very sovereignty of the state is based upon the twin monopolies of money and coercive force, there are many possible consequences of such a leakage of money from its control. 'Denationalized' and 'localized' money could evade monetary regulation and the reach of the tax authorities with obvious consequences for macro-economic management and social welfare programmes. The potential of e-money also plays a part in liberal and social communitarian hopes for the Internet as a force for human emancipation from the state (Hart, 2000).

The extent to which CIT has and could produce alternative or complementary money has been exaggerated. Moreover, e-money has not grown as expected and with the bursting of the 'dotcom' bubble, most have failed. Much of the conjecture and almost all the hyperbole of the early work on e-money was the result of its conceptualization of money *exclusively* in terms of the function of medium of exchange. The debates are strikingly similar in their confusion to those that arose with the acceleration of the transition from metal to paper during the nineteenth century.

Circuits of economic exchange obviously have been able create their own media of exchange that are based, to some extent, on *interpersonal trust and confidence.* But if the base for the confidence has no foundation beyond the economic exchanges themselves, then the media of exchange will remain what anthropologists refer to as 'limited purpose money'. The Internet is seen by some as the means for a limitless extension of such networks (Hart, 2000). However,

the creation of viable monetary space requires social and political relations that exist independently of any networks of exchange transactions. The extension of monetary relations across time and space requires *impersonal trust and legitimacy.* Historically, this has been the work of states. Monetary space is circumscribed by the authoritative money of account that defines the abstract value that constitutes the legal means of payment for the unilateral settlement of debt. Narrowly, economic relations cannot form the basis for monetary space that enables the extension of these relations across time and space. The Internet extends the technical capacity to expand the economic exchanges to an almost infinite extent, but it cannot provide the monetary space that would enable this to happen.

The value of money

Conventionally, the question of the value of money is considered to be exclusively an economic question. With the failure of 'monetarism', however, it is recognized within economics that economic theory has difficulty in explaining this most basic of questions (Issing, 2001). Sociologically, two aspects are important: the social bases of inflation/deflation, and the ideological construction and projection of the value of money.

The social bases of inflation/deflation
The orthodox quantity theory of money remains, in principle, the underlying basis for orthodox economic monetary analysis. The value of money is a function of the ratio between quantities of money and goods: M (money) $\times$ V (velocity of circulation) $=$ P (prices) $\times$ T (number of transactions). The equation is a logical identity, but it has always been assumed that *causation* runs from left to right; but it makes at least equal sense to reverse it. That is to say, for example, in the 'struggle for economic existence', agents attempt to monetize their positions of power by raising their prices, which are met by the 'endogenous' creation of credit money in the banking system. Monetary policy involves

the attempt to restrict this process by central bank interest rate policy. This is, of course, increasingly recognized within economic analysis, but the social and political process involved is not *theorized*. This idea that inflation results from escalating claims has a long pedigree in Keynesian 'cost push' theory (Fischer, 1996: 232–34). The 'labour standard' replaced the 'gold standard', until the neoliberal measures of the late twentieth century (Hicks, 1989). During the hyperinflation of the 1970s, a promising sociology of inflation was developed (Hirsch and Goldthorpe, 1978), but it waned with its subject matter.

Growing deflationary pressures in the early twenty-first century demand a similar sociological response. For example, the 'economic' puzzle of Japan's protracted recession and deflation since 1990 demands a complementary sociological analysis. Space precludes a thorough analysis and I will refer to only one aspect. With deflation, rational Japanese restrain consumption, as economic analysis suggests, in the expectation of continued falling prices. They fall into Keynes's 'liquidity trap'. Only borrowing and spending can cure the 'debt deflation'. However, the recession has also created a level of insecurity that is a direct consequence of the *social structure* of the Japanese economy. In the postwar reconstruction, the provision of social welfare and security – especially lifelong employment – was assigned to the Japanese conglomerate corporations (*keiretsu*) and not so much to the state as in the West. Eventually, the recession eroded the willingness and ability of the *keiretsu* to continue this role. Regardless of the important political dimensions of Japan's impasse, chronic insecurity resists all conventional economic policy measures to inflate the economy. As Keynes argued in the 1930s, security is sought in money as a store of value which perversely exacerbates the economic recession.

Changes in the balance of power between capital and labour obviously affect inflation/deflation, but arguably the pivotal relation is between creditors and debtors. Fundamentally, capitalism is based on the creation of debt to finance production and consumption. The capitalist's role is defined in terms of its debtor

status (Schumpeter, 1934: 101–3). On the other hand, creditors need to safeguard their position by the minimization of risk through default or the erosion of the value of the debt through inflation. The supply and demand of credit-money creation is mediated by the norms of credit-worthiness and morality of indebtedness. Credit is 'rationed' according to socially constructed criteria, and the normative framing of bankruptcy attempts to distinguish between rogues and genuine losers in the competitive process. For example, successful capitalist economies have largely abandoned the moral condemnation of debt and bankruptcy. On the other hand, it is likely that the stigma it continues to carry in Japan is one of the factors that has inhibited the 'writing off' of the mountain of debt that grinds the economy to a deflationary halt. Sociology has scarcely ventured into this field.

Finally, it is clear that the actual social process of credit-money creation and value stabilization is an independent source of inequality. Existing levels are intensified through 'Matthew Effects' (Ingham, 2000b). For example, those that 'hath' are a lower credit risk and gain more favourable interest rates, whilst those at the other end of the scale that 'hath not' are unable to gain access to the banking system and fall prey to 'loan sharks'. Once again the question is one of the construction of a status hierarchy of the quality of 'promises to pay'.

The ideological construction of abstract value Capitalism is characterized by a constant tension between the expansion of value through the creation of debt and the disintegration of the standard of value through inflation. This is a socially constructed non-mechanical relation and institutions are required to keep the two forces in balance. 'The overriding problem is to find some means to maintain the working fiction of a monetary invariant through time, so that debt contracts (the ultimate locus of value creation …) may be written in terms of the unit at different dates' (Mirowski, 1991: 579). The effectiveness of money as the continuity of stable abstract value through time depends on a commitment to a course of action that is based on trust that others will continue to accept our money. But, as I have stressed, this trust needs to be explained. The problem cannot be pursued beyond brief comments on impersonal trust and the ideological construction of money.

Monetary space is a form of impersonal trust (Schapiro, 1987). In the face of radical uncertainty, self-fulfilling long-term trust is rooted in social and political legitimacy whereby potentially untrustworthy 'strangers' are able to participate personally in impersonal complex multilateral economic relationships. However, the market is not in the business of trust building and the history of successful money is the history of successful states (Goodhart, 1998). Conversely, chronically unsuccessful states fail to produce adequate money precisely because they are unable to forge and sustain the two main monetary relations with their citizens on politically acceptable terms – taxation and government debt. The recent histories of Argentina, Russia and Afghanistan provide compelling evidence for this generalization.

Social conventions based on no more than either an equilibrium of competing interests or consensual agreement are fragile (Douglas, 1986). Enduring social institutions require a stronger foundation. 'There needs to be an analogy by which the formal structure of a crucial set of social relations is found in the physical world, or in the supernatural world, or in eternity, anywhere, so long as it is not seen as a socially contrived arrangement' (Douglas, 1986: 48). If successfully enacted, ideological naturalization conceals the social production and malleability of institutions. Until the twentieth century, the ideological naturalization of money was achieved, and its social construction concealed, by the commodity form of money in the gold standard (see Carruthers and Babb, 1996). With the abandonment of gold, however, the fiction of a universal, immutable, natural monetary standard became increasingly difficult to sustain. None the less, the rhetoric of a 'natural' economic process persists in the theory that underpins monetary policy.

The production of a 'working fiction' of stable money now consists of (1) the attempt to control the price of debt through interest rates and (2) the monitoring of the degree to which this monetary policy is deemed to be managed in accord with orthodox economic theory. Expert economists in independent central banks assess whether economic activity might force interest rates and employment above their 'natural' levels (Issing, 2001). Economic theory plays a rhetorical role in the formation of expectations that define the situation and, consequently, influence the future value of money. Central banks establish their 'monetary credentials', according to this rhetoric, and through the buying and selling of currencies the global money markets deliver their verdicts on the credibility of the 'working fictions'. The process has become increasingly formalized through the use of the hierarchies of credibility of sovereign debt produced by credit-rating agencies such as Standard and Poor and Moody's.

Permanent monetary stability in a capitalist economy can only be considered to be a theoretical possibility if orthodox economic theory's assumptions of neutrality and a natural tendency towards long-run economic equilibrium are accepted. But neither is helpful in explaining money as a social institution. All monetary systems, if they are to produce market prices and produce and store abstract value, are necessarily precarious and unstable. In Weber's formulation, the possibility of the rationality of monetary calculation lies in the substantively non-rational foundations of the 'struggle for economic existence' (see also Holton and Turner, 1989).

Money – as constituted by 'real' social relations – is an autonomous and active element in economic life that has double-edged or contradictory effects. In the classic Keynes formulation, it is the means of creating expanded value in the form of commodities; but it is also the means of their destruction (Schumpeter, 1934 [1912]; Minsky, 1986). This attribution of real force and efficacy to money does not entail a metaphysical 'nominalism' or a form of 'money illusion'. This is so only if the economy is taken to comprise nothing of importance other than commodities and their 'real' relations. Rather, money is an expression of human society's capacity for self-transformation. Arguably, this most powerful of 'social technologies' is one over which we have, inevitably, a most insecure grasp. Money is the clearest expression of the *pure* social construction of risk, and as such it deserves a more thorough sociological treatment.

NOTES

1 However, by the *General Theory of Employment, Interest and Money* (1936), Keynes's implicitly sociological analysis had given way to a more economically orthodox treatment in which investment must also be equal to *ex ante* savings. None the less, Keynes's analysis broke with orthodoxy's preoccupation with the 'things' that function as *media of exchange*. Rather, for Keynes, money is a source of stability that lulls our disquiet; it is a pole of stability that renders social life calculable.

2 The question of 'primitive money' became a central issue in the sterile formalist–substantivist debate on the applicability of deductive economic theory to premodern societies. The 'formalists' defined money as a commodity that functioned as a medium for market exchange, and concluded that 'primitive' non-market societies could not, therefore, possess money as such (Hart, 2000). (For references to the same dispute in the historiography of Greece at the turn of the twentieth century during the *Methodenstreit*, see Davies, 1994.)

REFERENCES

Aglietta, M. and Orléan, A. (eds) (1998) *La Monnaie Souveraine*. Paris: Odile Jacob.

Bell, S. (2000) 'Do taxes and bonds finance government spending?', *Journal of Economic Issues*, XXXIV (3): 603–20.

Bell, S. (2001) 'The role of the state and the hierarchy of money', *Cambridge Journal of Economics*, 25: 149–63.

Bloch, M. (1954) *Esquisse d'une histoire monétaire de Europe*. Paris: Armand Colin.

Boyer-Xambeu, M.T., Deleplace, G. and Gillard, L. (1994) *Private Money and Public Currencies: The Sixteenth Century Challenge*. London: M.E. Sharpe.

Carruthers, B. and Babb, S. (1996) 'The color of money and the nature of value: greenbacks and gold in Postbellum America', *American Journal of Sociology*, 101 (6): 1556–91.

Cohen, B. (2001) 'Electronic money: new day or false dawn', *Review of International Political Economy*, 8 (2): 197–225.

Collins, R. (1979) 'Review of M. Mayer, *The Bankers*', *American Journal of Sociology*, 85: 190–4.

Crawford, M. (1970) 'Money and exchange in the Roman world', *Journal of Roman Studies*, 60: 40–8.

Cutler, A., Hindness, B., Hirst, P. and Hussain, A. (1978) *Marx's 'Capital' and Capital Today, Volume 2*. London: Routledge.

Davies, G. (1994) *A History of Money*. Cardiff: University of Wales Press.

Dodd, N. (1994) *The Sociology of Money*. Cambridge: Polity Press.

Douglas, M. (1986) *How Organisations Think*. London: Routledge.

Dowd, K. (2000) 'The invisible hand and the evolution of the monetary system', in J. Smithin (ed.), *What Is Money?* London: Routledge.

Einaudi, L. (1953 [1936]) 'The theory of imaginary money from Charlemagne to the French Revolution', in F.C. Lane and J.C. Riemersma (eds), *Enterprise and Secular Change*. London: Allen and Unwin. pp. 229–61.

Ellis, H. (1934) *German Monetary Theory 1905–1933*. Cambridge, MA: Harvard University Press.

Fine, B. and Lapavitsas, C. (2000) 'Markets and money in social theory: what role for economics?', *Economy and Society*, 29 (3): 357–82.

Fischer, D. (1996) *The Great Wave: Price Revolutions and the Rhythm of History*. Oxford: Oxford University Press.

Ganssmann, H. (1988) 'Money – a symbolically generalized medium of communication?', *Economy and Society*, 17: 285–315.

Gardiner, G. (1993) *Towards True Monetarism*. London: The Dulwich Press.

Giddens, A. (1990) *The Consequences of Modernity*. Cambridge: Polity Press.

Goldsmith, R. (1987) *Pre-Modern Financial Systems*. Cambridge: Cambridge University Press.

Goodhart, C. (1998) 'The two concepts of money: implications for the analysis of optimal currency areas', *European Journal of Political Economy*, 14: 407–32.

Grierson, P. (1977) *The Origins of Money*. London: Athlone Press.

Hahn, F. (1982) *Money and Inflation*. Oxford: Blackwell.

Hahn, F. (1987) 'Foundations of monetary theory', in M. de Cecco and J. Fitoussi (eds), *Monetary Theory and Institutions*. London: Macmillan.

Hart, K. (2000) *The Memory Bank: Money in an Unequal World*, London: Profile Books.

Henwood, D. (1997) *Wall Street*. London: Verso.

Hirsch, F. and Goldthorpe, G. (eds) (1978) *The Political Economy of Inflation*. London: Martin Robertson.

Hicks, J.R. (1989) *A Market Theory of Money.* Oxford: Oxford University Press.

Hilferding, R. (1981 [1910]) *Finance Capital.* London: Routledge and Kegan Paul.

Hodgson, G. (2001) *How Economics Forgot History.* London: Routledge.

Holton, R. and Turner, B. (1989) *Max Weber on Economy and Society.* London: Routledge.

Hoover, K. (1996) 'Some suggestions for complicating the theory of money', in S. Pressman (ed.), *Interactions in Political Economy.* London: Routledge. pp. 204–16.

Ingham, G. (1996) 'Money is a social relation', *Review of Social Economy,* LIV (4): 507–29.

Ingham, G. (1999) 'Capitalism, money and banking: a critique of recent historical sociology', *British Journal of Sociology,* 50 (1): 76–96.

Ingham, G. (2000a) '"Babylonian madness": on the sociological and historical "origins" of money', in J. Smithin (ed.), *What Is Money?* London: Routledge. pp. 16–41.

Ingham, G. (2000b) 'Class inequality and the social production of money', in R. Crompton, F. Devine, M. Savage and J. Scott (eds), *Renewing Class Analysis.* Oxford: Blackwell. pp. 66–84.

Ingham, G. (2001) 'Fundamentals of a theory of money: untangling Fine, Lapavitsas and Zelizer', *Economy and Society,* 30 (3): 304–23.

Ingham, G. (2002) 'New monetary spaces?', in *The Future of Money.* Paris: OECD. pp. 123–45.

Ingham, G. (2004) *The Nature of Money.* Cambridge: Polity.

Innes, A.M. (1913) 'What is money?', *Banking Law Journal,* May: 377–408.

Issing, G. (2001) *Monetary Policy in the Euro Area.* Cambridge: Cambridge University Press.

Jones, R. (1976) 'The origin and development of media of exchange', *Journal of Political Economy,* 84 (4): 757–75.

Keynes, J.M. (1930) *A Treatise on Money.* London: Macmillan.

Keynes, J.M. (1936) *The General Theory of Employment, Interest and Money.* Cambridge: Cambridge University Press.

Klein, P. and Selgin, G. (2000) 'Menger's theory of money: some empirical evidence', in J. Smithin (ed.), *What Is Money?* London: Routledge. pp. 217–34.

Knapp, G.F. (1973 [1924]) *The State Theory of Money.* New York: Augustus M. Kelley.

Leyshon, A. and Thrift, N. (1997) *Money/Space.* London: Routledge.

Machlup, F. (1978) *Methodology of Economics and Other Social Sciences.* New York: Academic Press.

Marx, K. (1976) *Capital: Volume I.* Harmondsworth: Penguin.

Marx, K. (1981) *Capital: Volume III.* Harmondsworth: Penguin.

Menger, K. (1892) 'On the origins of money', *Economic Journal,* 2 (6): 239–55.

Minsky, H. (1986) 'Money and crisis in Schumpeter and Keynes', in H.-J. Wagener and J. Drukker (eds), The *Economic Law of Motion of Modern Society.* Cambridge: Cambridge University Press. pp. 112–22.

Mirowski, P. (1991) 'Post-modernism and the social theory of value', *Journal of Post-Keynesian Economics,* 13: 565–82.

OECD (2002) *The Future of Money.* Paris: OECD.

Orléan, A. (1998) 'La monnaie autoréférentielle: réflexions sur les évolutions monétaires contemporaines', in M. Aglietta and A. Orléan, (eds), *La Monnaie souveraine.* Paris: Odile Jacob. pp. 359–85.

Parguez, A. and Seccareccia, M. (2000) 'The credit theory of money: the monetary circuit approach', in J. Smithin (ed.), *What Is Money?* London: Routledge. pp. 101–23.

Parsons, T. (1934) 'Some reflections on the nature and significance of economics', *Quarterly Journal of Economics,* 46: 511–45.

Parsons, T. (1937) *The Structure of Social Action.* Glencoe, IL: The Free Press.

Parsons, T. (1991 [1953]) 'The Marshall Lectures', *Sociological Inquiry,* 61: 10–59.

Parsons, T. and Smelser, N. (1956) *Economy and Society.* London: Routledge.

Polanyi, K. (1957) *Trade and Markets in the Early Empires.* New York: Free Press.

Rochon, L.-P. (1999) *Credit, Money and Production: An Alternative Post-Keynesian Approach.* Cheltenham: Edward Elgar.

Rowlinson, M. (1999) '"The Scotch hate gold": British identity and paper money', in E. Gilbert and E. Helleiner (eds), *Nation-States and Money.* London: Routledge. pp. 47–67.

Schapiro, S. (1987) 'The social control of impersonal trust', *American Journal of Sociology,* 93 (3): 623–58.

Schumpeter, J. (1994 [1954]) *A History of Economic Analysis.* London: Routledge.

Schumpeter, J. (1934 [1912]) *The Theory of Economic Development.* Cambridge, MA: Harvard University Press.

Searle, J. (1995) *The Construction of Social Reality.* Harmondsworth: Penguin.

Sherman, S. (1997) 'Promises, promises: credit as a contested metaphor in early capitalist discourse', *Modern Philology,* 94: 327–48.

Simmel, G. (1978 [1907]) *The Philosophy of Money.* London: Routledge.

Smithin, J. (2000) (ed.), *What Is Money?* London: Routledge.

Smithin, J. (1994) *Controversies in Monetary Economics.* Aldershot: Edward Elgar.

Turner, B. (1999) *Classical Sociology.* London: Sage.

Weber, M. (1951) *The Religion of China.* New York: Macmillan.

Weber, M. (1978) *Economy and Society.* Berkeley, CA: University of California Press.

Weber, M. (1981 [1927]) *General Economic History.* New Brunswick, NJ: Transaction Books.

Wray, R. (1990) *Money and Credit in Capitalist Economies.* Aldershot: Edward Elgar.

Wray, R. (1998) *Understanding Modern Money.* Cheltenham: Edward Elgar.

Wray, R. (2000) 'Modern money', in J. Smithin (ed.), *What Is Money?* London: Routledge. pp. 42–67.

Zelizer, V. (1994) *The Social Meaning of Money.* New York: Basic Books.

9

The Sociology of Consumption and Lifestyle

DON SLATER

Consumption has a profound but often problematic and unrecognized place in the social sciences over the modern period. Until perhaps the past two decades, it was less an area for substantive research than a barometer of ethical and political positions on the cultural quality and social health of modern society. For the broad tradition of liberalism, core values resided in the figure of the consumer as a self-defining agent who chooses, and whose autonomous and rational choice is exemplified in market behaviour – the sovereign consumer. For the various critical traditions within social analysis, consumer culture – as opposed to consumption *per se* – has tended to stand for the domination of the capitalist commodity form and industrial processes over culture (both in the restricted artistic sense and the broader sense of lived meaningful social life) and for the harnessing of autonomous social subjects to the logic of modern rationality at the level of their needs and wants. Consumer culture has tended to indicate the dominance of commercial culture over the public sphere, a world awash with advertising, brands and commodities.

At the same time that consumption indicated the cultural and social price that was being paid for capitalist modernization, it was regarded as too trivial to investigate in its own

right. There were various reasons for this. In the broadest sense, social analysis has generally displayed a 'productivist' bias: production is generally assumed to be socially, ethically and methodologically primary, as source of value, as providing the underlying structure of distribution of both goods and incomes and as historically prior to modern consumption (as in the idea that an industrial revolution preceded commercial or consumer ones). Hence, consumption is often seen as a derived or secondary phenomenon, with a low explanatory value. Secondly, the academic study of consumption was tainted by the charges of triviality levelled against its object of study. If consumers and consumer culture are debased, trivial and largely feminine, surely the ambitious academic should stick to serious matters? Finally, sociology fell between various disciplinary stools in relation to consumption: economics concerned itself with only the formal rationality of decision-making, regarding the substantive content of consumption decisions to be irrelevant in understanding economic life; the latter was delegated to a range of disciplines, but largely dominated by psychology and by survey approaches that could measure consumer demand for more practical marketing application. It was not clear what a sociological approach to specific consumption practices would be, or could add, at either the theoretical or practical level.

This long tradition of regarding consumption or consumer culture as morally suspect and analytically secondary has been largely reversed over the past two decades, although many of the issues raised by critiques of consumer culture are still very much in researchers' minds. The starting point of most contemporary work however – particularly in consumption studies outside the United States – is that consumption is a central site of social reproduction whose structure is crucial in understanding processes such as identity construction, social agency and key social relationships. Moreover, it is understood as involving creative and oppositional practices, rather than simply acting as a site of subjugation, and this requires a less moralistic and dismissive approach to the everyday life of modern social actors. It seems vital to approach consumption through the understandings and aims of those who carry it out rather than through positions derived from theoretical critiques of capitalist modernity. One can do this not as a liberal economist, for whom the consumer's preferences are by definition always correct and unchallengeable, but rather as a critical social analyst, for whom the consumption of ordinary people is a valid starting point from which to map the networks of power and process in which they are enmeshed.

The shift is partly a move from critiques of consumer culture to the study of consumption. To clarify these terms: 'consumption' is a general, or even universal term in social analysis. All ongoing social life requires material and symbolic resources in order to reproduce social relations, processes and identities. Consumption in this sense is never purely material or simply tied to basic or natural needs. Eating a meal, for example, always involves socially specific structures of consumption: different cultures have different notions of what is edible and inedible (let alone what is desirable or appropriate to specific consumption occasions); how to prepare these goods, and who is to prepare them; and how food consumption in one household distinguishes it from others while identifying it with others within a culture. In a modern household, the difference between family meals with home-cooked food on the one hand, and 'grazing' on prepared foods, individually and at different times, on the other, will not only say a lot about the different lifestyles and identities in these households but will also play a considerable part in reproducing them as different kinds of families.

Consumption, then, is a general category of social analysis, but one that has been quite underdeveloped within sociology (as opposed to anthropology). Instead, sociology has, until recently, been largely concerned with 'consumer culture', or 'consumer society': the specific organization of consumption that increasingly characterized the West over the modern period and which has been to some extent globalized with the spread of Western capitalism. First, in consumer culture goods and services are predominantly accessed as commodities, purchased in markets, rather than produced for immediate consumption within households or local communities. The material and symbolic means of social reproduction therefore largely emerge from, and are thought to be dominated by, industrial processes (for example, mass production) and commercial processes such as marketing and advertising which give commodities (and their purchase through shopping) particular shapes and meanings in relation to the competitive aims of private firms. The central issue immediately becomes power: to what extent are consumers and their social reproduction dominated by the moments of production and market competition. Secondly, 'consumer culture' usually presumes that market-based values and identities have become central to social reproduction. The idea of being a 'consumer' is a specifically modern one in which individual and collective identities are bound up with making choices between marketed goods, and with constructing lifestyles from knowledge of the public commercial meanings and uses of commodities. Not only are modern subjects able to think of themselves primarily as consumers (as opposed to workers or citizens), and to understand consumption as a primary site for their identities, but the language and values of consumption as market choice seem to predominate in other social spheres. For example, after many years of neoliberal political projects, claims to collective provision (such as the welfare state) have become hard to sustain in comparison to market-derived models of consumer sovereignty.

Insofar as sociology emerged historically as the study of the modern society in which it was born it is not surprising that its focus has been on a critical engagement with consumer culture. It is equally obvious, however, that modern consumption is not simply reducible to the modern structures of consumer culture. Developments in the field have largely waited on serious attention to consumption as a core process in its own right. This attention has finally emerged from a number of different strands, which we will approach throughout the rest of this chapter by exploring some of the key themes in contemporary sociology of consumption.

THE CONSUMER AS SOCIAL AGENT

Critical traditions in sociology have largely regarded consumption in terms of the reduction of individuals' agency, or of the authenticity and autonomy of that agency. One can identify two interrelated strands, the Romantic and the critical (Slater, 1997a). Romanticism was concerned from its birth with asserting the ideal, the spiritual and the authentic in human experience against the materialistic, the industrial and manufactured, the rational and – ultimately – the modern. Consumer culture appeared as a commercially manufactured culture, imposed by rationalizing forces over authentic cultures and identities, and promoting an over-investment in the material world. Rousseau states the theme clearly at the start: modern 'society' (by which he means aristocratic and salon society as much as 'the social') imposes external rules and demands on the individual – such as fashion, emulation and etiquette – alienating him [sic] from himself, and pressuring him to find himself not in what he 'is' but merely in what he 'has'. Lifestyle,

enacted through consumption rituals, is a profound form of social tyranny. While Rousseau represents those who sought the countervailing authenticity of the self in the individual, it has been equally common to locate it in the supposedly organic and authentic cultures of the premodern, or in those vestiges of these cultures which have lasted into the modern age as authentic 'values'. Even Marx relays this Romanticism into the critical tradition, constantly assuming a premodern world that was organized transparently in terms of use values rather than exchange values: the premodern may have been impoverished and oppressive but it was not *alienated*, in that people produced directly in relation to their own clear needs and ways of life. F.R. Leavis (Leavis and Thompson, 1933) had the most profound impact on approaches to consumption by arguing along these lines: he envisaged an 'organic' premodern life in which culture is lived and embedded in ways of doing and making, and in which language and experience are consequently true to themselves. In industrial society, true culture retreats to the rarified, but protected, realm of artistic culture, which preserves the values that have disappeared from the life that is actually lived under modern conditions. The latter is dominated by a manufactured culture, commercial meanings, cheap thrills and materialistic impulses that are tied to the imperatives of mass manufacture.

Leavis's Romanticism is not far from much critical social theory. Adorno might argue that all that separates them is a developed theory of capitalism, Leavis's tendency to blame the masses rather than the culture industries and an undialectical notion of culture. Critical theory – from Lukacs through Adorno – builds its account of consumer culture instead on Marx's analysis of the mystifications – fetishism or reification – that arise from the commodity form and the separation of production and consumption through the intervention of market relations. This produces the dominance of exchange value over use value, whereby object relations (both needs and goods and their meanings) are hitched to the logic of profit and competition rather than the autonomous logic of human development. Human needs and ways of life become positively functional to capitalist reproduction: for example, in Adorno, leisure and consumption – particularly cultural consumption – are reconstructed as 'recuperation', as means to ensure that bodies recover enough of their energies to go back to (alienated) work the next day, and that minds are politically docile, identifying their needs and gratifications with what capitalism can profitably produce. Consumer culture as a whole is an engine for sublimating any glimmers of critical consciousness into commodity desires or – as Lowenthal famously put it – mass culture is 'psychoanalysis in reverse', neurotically miring individuals ever more unconsciously in the conditions that oppress them in the first place. In Lukacs's terms, individuals develop a 'contemplative attitude' to social conditions, an idea later developed by the Situationists as the 'society of the Spectacle': we powerlessly and passively watch the world as if we were viewing a film (or advertisement) in which we cannot intervene.

Marcuse (1964, 1973 [1955]) offers probably the most sustained version of this argument in terms of consumer culture: industrial society has reached a level of productivity that would allow us, collectively, to stop working for survival and instead devote our energies to pleasurable self-development. However, the capitalist form of this industrial rationality would, of course, collapse if people did not consume ever more. The maintenance of the system therefore requires intensified 'surplus repression' – the production of the greater number of needs and wants that the system itself needs and wants. This production of unnecessary needs has to be built upon the individual's real instinctual basis (for example, the advertising association of sexual satisfactions with objects like cars and drinks), but by that very process mystifies the individual's relationship to their real needs, which are the main source of their ability to oppose the system which mystifies them.

Both Romanticism and critical theory, then, if by different routes, arrive at the loss of authentic agency in consumer culture. The individual is alienated from themselves to the extent of not knowing what they really need or feel; and without the capacity for critical reflection that comes from acting in relation to the real sources of the self, which both traditions understand in terms of non-alienated social relations. In its cruder forms, the loss of agency is characterized simply in terms of manipulation and persuasion: advertising, marketing and the self-presentation of consumer society as opulent and materially satisfying simply replace real agency with desires more functional to capitalism.

Although this has been the dominant line of thought, there are others. One crucial theme cuts across both liberal and critical traditions: the idea that an expanding commercial and material world expands the scope of human development. This theme is already clear in Enlightenment thought, particularly in David Hume and Adam Smith, for whom the wider social networks that arise from commercial society (best exemplified in the expanded division of labour and in trade), bring people into wider social intercourse, or 'commerce' in its widest sense, exposing them to the fact of social difference, to experience of other ways of life and to being evaluated by other people (Hirschman, 1977). Both drew on traditions of moral psychology in direct opposition to Rousseau's: the scrutiny of 'society' and the experience of alternative lifestyles through a civil life are not alienating but speak to the very foundation of moral action. This is to be found in our empathy, in that our ability to be moral and social depends on our capacity to see ourselves through the eyes of others. (Compare Colin Campbell's (1989) related but different account of the relation between romanticism and consumer culture which stresses the capacity for 'imaginative longing' that unintentionally arises from the romantic sensibility.)

In Marx and Simmel – working through a Hegelian analysis of subject–object relations through processes of objectification (Miller, 1987) – the expanding world of use values (Marx) or objective culture (Simmel) produced by industrial modernity provides for the (potential) development of the human who is 'rich in needs' (Marx) or for the increasing refinement and sophistication of subjective culture (Simmel). The problem for both Marx and Simmel is that the dialectical expansion of human capacities that should naturally arise from this situation is distorted. Marx points his finger at forms of alienation and exploitation which sunder individuals from the products of their labour either subjectively or materially. Simmel (1950) is pessimistic about the capacity of subjectivities to assimilate the profusion of modern things, a problem glimpsed through the prevalent condition of 'neuraesthenia' in modern urban life which individuals defensively counter through a 'blasé attitude'. In both authors there is also the idea that the development of objective culture is attached to the drives of capitalist competition and the mystifications of the market place, rather than to the autonomous needs of self-developing individuals.

Although this theme was developed through material culture studies mainly within anthropology (see below), the re-assertion of agency in sociological treatments of consumption has largely come through another source – cultural studies. There are at least two bases for this re-assertion. First, cultural studies began with a revaluation of popular culture, including consumer culture. Whatever the worries about it, lived culture was to be treated – more 'anthropologically' – as the actual ground on which social identities and relations were formed and lived out, and as a battlefield for social agency rather than a mausoleum for fallen agents. Responding to the many subcultures and political movements from the 1960s onwards which sought to fashion solidarities and lifestyles out of their engagements with the popular (above all in music and drugs), cultural studies particularly focused on the spectacular subcultures of contemporary youth, which turned consumer culture into resources for the expression of social conflict and negotiation. The mod's dandy-esque obsession with Italian design can be read as an idiom for negotiating their mobility from industrial proletariat to white-collar lower middle classness; the punk's safety pins and bin-liner clothes become an active appropriation, inversion and critique of the promises ('*No* future') of consumer capitalism (Hebdige, 1979, 1988).

Unintentionally, cultural studies tended to find agency only in such spectacular inversions; those which could readily be understood as culturally – or even politically – oppositional. Its opinion of the mundane consumption of ordinary people was not far off that of earlier cultural critics: not worth looking at. It was later moves into feminism (McRobbie, 1989, 1991, 1999) and postmodernism (Fiske, 1989) that focused attention on the creativity and negotiation that goes on in all engagements with consumer culture, including those that are excluded from subcultural memberships. The most measured statement of this approach was produced by Willis (1990), for whom all consumption requires symbolic labour and creativity in order actually to place any objects within our lives; agency is a precondition for consumption rather than a property of more critical or political consumers.

Secondly, agency was reasserted within the tradition of semiotics and structuralism, which proposed that all social objects could be treated as signs that derive their meaning from their relationship to other signs within social codes of meanings. This at first produced highly deterministic – structuralist – accounts of advertising, some of which were closely aligned with structuralist Marxism (e.g., Williamson, 1978). Experience of advertisements (or 'interpellation' by them) constructs subjectivities (or 'subject positions') that are ideologically appropriate to capitalist reproduction. The remnants of this position are still evident in Baudrillard's (1981, 1990, 1998 [1970]) work, in which 'the Code' (a kind of social instantiation of semiotic methodology) dominates – and later obliterates or replaces – social life; any involvement with meaningful social material – even attempted opposition – is absorbed by the Code, which gives it its meaning in the first place. The only available form of agency – apart from the possible implosion of the system under its own weight – is a kind of nihilism in which consumers, by passively absorbing everything it throws at them, somehow turn the power of the system against itself.

However, it was in fact semiotics itself that cracked under its own weight, or rather its structuralist variant imploded and transfigured into poststructuralisms for which the central assumption was the indeterminacy of signs and their meanings. Far from being able to solidify into stable Codes, meaning appears as an ongoing process, and one in which specific social subjects are able to realize possibilities for contradiction, opposition or even invention within the order of signs. Just what kind of agency this allows is still a matter of endless argument, with great warnings as to the dangers of falling back into the 'humanism', as it used to be called, of both romantic and critical theory.

A completely different approach to consumption and agency comes out of the later Foucault, developed under the idea of 'governmentality' (Barry et al., 1996; Miller and Rose, 1997; Rose, 1991, 1992, 1999). Whereas liberals, critical theorists and – latterly – postmoderns debate the actual degree of agency involved in contemporary consumption, governmentality approaches have been concerned with the discourses and practices of agency through which we have been led to understand and construct ourselves. The point is not whether consumers are or are not free or sovereign but the extent to which they have been incited to understand themselves through notions of freedom, choice and autonomy or enterprise. This analytical tactic makes considerable sense in relation to the neoliberal context it sought to critique (Rose, 1999). Neoliberalism explicitly waged a cultural and institutional revolution against what it saw as the passive clientelism of the welfare state by conceptualizing and enacting policies that assumed a self-motivating, choosing and 'responsibilized' individual, a version of subjectivity that drew substantially on the model of the consumer. Hence, for example in education and health care – spheres previously to be protected from commercial relations – individuals were to be addressed and acted upon as consumers choosing through quasi-market mechanisms, rather than as political citizens exercising collective rights.

IDENTITY, STATUS AND DISTINCTION

Second only to sociology of consumption's concern with agency has been its obsession

with the substantive content of that agency: identity. The reasons for this are possibly best expressed, and exemplified, by Giddens's (1991, 1992) accounts of post-traditional society, if in far too general terms. One can crudely contrast the confused pluralism of contemporary society with traditional societies which – if not organic – involved stable status orders that ascribed enduring social positions to people; that supported enduring forms of knowledge and authority; and that involved far less experience of other ways of life mediated to localities through travel, mass media or globalized networks. This traditional world is often characterized through the importance of sumptuary law, in which the most detailed of consumption practices were forcefully and juridically regulated in relation to specific ascribed – and largely inescapable – social statuses and identities.

The post-traditional (in Giddens; 'postmodern' in most other accounts) condition involves a breakdown of stable and unitary collective orders: our experience is one of incessant pluralism; of methodical doubting of all knowledge and authorities, and constant competition between them; of increasing mediation of experience to us through new means of communication and globalization. This is associated with a turn to the individual – rather than collective orders – as necessarily the only agency responsible for itself. Giddens sums this up in the formula that 'We have no choice but to choose,' if only because nothing is either ascribed or stable. It is the individual who must both choose and contain all the different choices within what Giddens calls the 'reflexive narrative of the self' or project of the self, a continual effort to establish self-coherence by connecting past, present and future within a consistent narrative of who one is. In the exemplary arena of choice – consumer culture itself – the result appears to be high levels of anxiety over who we are and what our lives, or lifestyles, should look like. How can we possibly know what is right or wrong in our consumption decisions, and even if we could will that decision still be right tomorrow or across all the different people with whom we interact? The picture that emerges from Giddens is of a kind of permanent identity crisis that is both fed and assuaged by the mechanisms of consumer culture. For example, on the one hand, advertising and marketing offer us images of lifestyles that depict standardized representations of what our choices could add up to. This is akin to Leiss, Kline and Jhally's (1986) description of advertising as providing 'maps of modernity'. All very reassuring except that the same lifestyle depictions compete with thousands of others in the marketplace and mediascape; and that they are constantly renovated according to the rhythms of fashion and style change which exacerbate the very condition they were supposed to solve.

A crucial assumption here is that our consumption choices are indeed profoundly consequential for our identities. Figures like Giddens (1991) and Featherstone (1991) argue that we seem to be capable of choice in almost every aspect of life so that whatever we wear, own or do appears to be an expression of our choosing, and thus implicates our ethical and social identity. In a world of accessible cosmetic surgery and inescapable dietary and other bodily regimes, the fact of having a long nose, small breasts or big belly can be read as a deliberate and active decision *not* to mould oneself to other body ideals. To appear overweight or unfashionably dressed can therefore be treated as a direct judgement on one's self, with direct implications for social status and membership (Finkelstein, 1991). While this is evidently a real and significant strand of contemporary social life – and one that is very explicitly voiced in people's discourses (Miller, 1998) and in public media – there is doubt about whether this leads to such pervasive anxiety for everyone (Warde, 1994a, 1994b; Warde and Martens, 2000), or whether all consumer decisions have the same implications for identity (my choice of loft insulation or soap powder may not provoke the same existential doubt as my clothes or the foods I serve at a dinner party as opposed to a quick sandwich at work – Gronow and Warde, 2001; Shove, 2003). Moreover, there is a tendency to persist in a Veblen style of analysis, in which goods appear simply as markers of status distinction, as status symbols that mark out relative

social position, a formulation that ignores the much more complex – and practical – existence that consumed objects lead within our lives.

From Giddens one can move in two apparently opposite directions. On the one hand, Giddens's reference point is the attempt to stabilize the self under conditions of modern choice. Postmodern, and some poststructural, thinkers have largely treated the maintenance or mythology of the stable self as precisely the most oppressive and normalizing aspect of a disciplinary modernity. The potential opened up by contemporary consumer culture is precisely the possibility of play and irony without commitment or an imperative to cohesion. For example, in contrast to Veblen's status-seeking conspicuous consumers, the (post)modern consumer is more like someone attending a fancy dress party, able to don and doff identities at whim, or to play with them tactically (de Certeau, 1984; Fiske, 1989) in a mobile and fluid game with the system of consumption. For example, both Maffesoli (1996) and Bauman (1990) stress the emergence of neotribalism: in contrast to older class and status orders that had a social structural foundation, contemporary consumers are dealing with fluid social groupings, with low commitment, low entry and exit costs, and membership or identification largely based on shared lifestyle expressions. For example, 'consumption communities' might temporarily bind people on the basis of simply flashing your lights as you pass someone driving the same make of car as you.

On the other hand, Bourdieu (1984) does not point us to the dissolution of social structures in the game of consumption but rather to the greater subtlety and strategic character of their operation. Choices are not matters of mere whim or confusion but emanate from structures of taste which are solidified at the level of the person, and indeed the body (habitus), which represent collective social dispositions that can be analysed in terms of class and other social structures, and which are fought over in substantial social conflicts that are consequential for economic and social careers. When Bourdieu argues that 'taste classifies the classifier' he is asserting (like Giddens or Veblen) that our consumption choices are indeed read as personal choices that socially identify us. However, stating this in terms of classifications emphasizes that tastes are structured (if I buy this kind of watch I might well buy, or aspire to this kind of house, holiday, dress, partner, music and so on). These structures emerge from class experiences (for example, the habitus is a set of dispositions that arise from collective experiences of possibilities and constraints), are deeply and largely unconsciously internalized, and are highly determinative of one's possible social memberships and therefore of the social networks that one is capable of operating within. In the most obvious example, the possession of that ingrained cultural capital that allows one to 'naturally' choose the right fork at a formal dinner, banter about good wines, express appropriate opinions about opera or sports cars and so on ensures one a seat at the kind of upper middle class table (literally and figuratively) on which much else depends: knowledge of and access to economic opportunities, social support, 'connections' and so on. Identity here is not a matter of narrative coherence but of appropriate consumption as essential to the social reproduction of real social networks.

At the same time, Bourdieu is equally concerned with the way in which such structures of taste and lifestyle can act as the medium for changes in the entire structure of status and power. Featherstone (1991), for example, develops Bourdieu's account of the rise of the new middle classes whose fortunes are largely bound up with cultural and interpersonal skills, whether they work in advertising, the media or in new universities and schools. They are characterized as upwardly socially mobile, often largely self-taught and hence uncomfortable with the older cultural capital of the existing bourgeoisie. At the same time, their livelihood is bound up with the newer cultural capital of popular and commercial culture. They therefore have every reason to go into battle over the 'hierarchy of hierarchies' – that is, over the relative merits of different competing structures of taste – and to attempt to denigrate the value of traditional consumption and lifestyle, while asserting a more postmodern revaluation of popular culture, and of ironic

and highly reflexive orientations to cultural consumption.

Finally, it is clear that while these arguments about identity address issues of power they do not adequately take into account inequality in its more conventional sense. Bauman (1990), for example, attempted to distinguish between the 'seduced' (those who are *able* to be troubled by the need to pursue identity through consumption) and the 'repressed' (those who by their poverty, and welfare clientage, are excluded from the whole game). While this captures the sense of insult at being left out of the party, it seems again to confuse the study of consumer culture with the study of consumption: the repressed may be left out of the latter but it is unwise – and even more insulting – to treat them as somehow 'without culture', or possessing a culture structured entirely by their exclusion from contemporary consumption games. Bourdieu veers close to the same position in arguing that the working classes are distinguished by a 'taste for necessity', a notion which – improperly used – makes their consumption appear to be driven by pure need and functionality, rather than meaningfully structured like anyone else's.

MATERIALITY AND SIGNIFICATION

All of these arguments depend on a fundamental premise that needs to be examined: the idea that goods are *meaningful*, rather than simply physical items that functionally satisfy specific requirements or needs. This is a long-established position. On the one hand, it derives from semiotics, in which it was argued that social objects (like linguistic ones) could be analysed as signs within systems of signs. Methodologically, this involves bracketing their objective reference or correspondence to an objective order of things and instead focusing on how they are meaningfully related to other objects as signs. Barthes (1986) made the major step in *Mythologies* by analysing objects such as wines, landscapes and wrestling matches not in terms of their physical properties but rather in terms of meaningful oppositions between wines, national landscapes and other sports. His really enduring move was to treat these oppositions and the systems within which they are organized as profoundly ideological. That is to say, for example, that representations of wines can be used to signify and reproduce versions of nationhood (Frenchness, Spanishness, etc.) and indeed to act as central supports for the entire ideology of nationhood and national identity.

On the other hand, an important related route to a similar position derives from anthropology, and particularly from Mary Douglas (Douglas and Isherwood, 1979). Her account also divides consumption goods from their physicality and functionality, arguing that they should be instead (or additionally) understood as means of communication, and the exchange of both objects and knowledge of objects as complex and necessary information systems within any society. The consumption of goods, and the exchange of knowledge (names) of goods, marks out social occasions and categories (you must have turkey at Christmas, you must have white wine with fish). While Douglas's account, unlike Barthes's, locates the meaning of goods in actual social practices and events rather than in sign systems and ideologies, it none the less also separates – methodologically and analytically – the meanings of things from their practical use and properties.

This separation has been problematic in quite various ways. First, and most crudely, there is a long running tendency to assume that goods *should* be functional and useful, rather than meaningful, and that this meaningfulness is largely the product of capitalist mystification. (Douglas would not argue this, but Barthes actually maintains – rather like Bourdieu – that working class consumption is closer to necessity and therefore less bound up with the meaning of things than with getting enough things.) This obviously flies in the face of the need to treat all consumption as culturally organized, hence as bearing meanings that are inseparable from their practical use. This line of thought has been well represented by the tradition of material culture studies within anthropology. Communities objectify all manner of social relations, beliefs and desires

in their categorizations of things, which come to act as idioms not only for the expression of a social order but for its enactment and reproduction. Consequently, the meanings of goods are essentially implicated in the most mundane uses of them, and not merely in their use to mark out social differences or to reproduce ideological structures. As Douglas herself put it, 'The choice between pounding and grinding (coffee) is … a choice between two different views of the human condition …' (Douglas and Isherwood, 1979: 74).

In contrast, sociology has been haunted by a subterranean naturalism that complements its obsession with meanings and sign, continuing to distinguish between goods as material and goods as meaningful, or signifying. This is often complemented by a distinction between basic needs (such as for food, clothing and shelter which must be met by material things) and wants, luxuries or more cultural needs (which are not necessary for physical survival and which relate more to the meanings of things, or to desires of the mind rather than the body). Moreover, this distinction often serves as a critical standard, on the assumption that material needs are both more objective and more fundamental, whereas wants are personal, subjective and dispensable. Hence a common line of critique is that consumer culture is inauthentic and perverse in that it elaborates new needs and wants that are imaginary or inessential (for example, through advertising). This, however, seems to confuse the issue of power over consumption meanings within consumer culture with the ineradicably cultural organization of consumption in all societies (Slater, 1997b). It also obviously leaves the impossible problem of distinguishing approved Culture (which is not a matter of physical needs but defines us as 'civilized') from inauthentic commercial culture.

One direct consequence of the meaning/function distinction has been a methodological focus on 'reading' objects and their public representations in advertising and design (e.g. Goldman and Papson, 1995, 1998; Wernick, 1991). This was clearly an important move, and a necessary departure from treating goods as purely functional and instrumental objects.

However, it has too rarely been pursued into observation of the actual lifeworlds of consumers, into a fully ethnographic understanding of what people do with things. A good example is the study of shopping. Under the emerging impact of postmodernism from the mid-1980s onwards, sociologists challenged the idea of shopping as a functional activity in which consumers accessed satisfiers for known needs, and attempted to do so in an efficient manner (Shields, 1992). Shopping instead constituted an important social form, and one which was increasingly strategic for modern life and economy. Shopping was (increasingly) akin to leisure, providing spaces and activities for hedonism, fantasy, sociality and social identity. It was a playground of semiosis, in which browsing not only the shop windows but also the passing crowds (in the manner of a *flâneur*) had become the central activity, and the shopper was to be understood as a consumer of signs rather than things. The shopping spaces themselves were to be analysed largely through readings (Gottdiener, 1995; Jameson, 1984).

The case was overstated rather than wrong. More sophisticated geographies (Harvey, 1989; Zukin, 1991) were able to place this shopping-as-leisure within social battles over urban space, involving retail and finance capital, urban governance and competing class-based ways of life (in Zukin's terminology, the 'vernacular'). Ethnographies of shopping (Chin, 2001; Miller et al., 1998) indicated how these hedonistic spaces fit into the different class, gender and ethnic lives of their users. Finally, Miller's (1998) ethnographies of shopping indicated that postmodern discourses of hedonism and identity-centred consumption were articulated by many shoppers but bore little relationship to either the meanings or practices evidenced in their actual shopping. This was largely shopping carried out by women and focused on provisioning their families, and was therefore largely concerned with understanding and negotiating the needs of others as a basis for caring for them and sustaining intimate relationships.

There is another crucial sense in which the focus on the meanings of goods has come to dominate consumption studies, and this involves historical arguments about transformations within capitalism. In these arguments, it is claimed that consumer capitalism has in some sense become 'more cultural', or that cultural processes and their institutionalization have become ever more central in the operation of contemporary capitalist society. For example, early Fordist capitalism relayed the economies of scale of mass production organization into a complementary structure of mass consumption based on standardization of goods, large-scale and relatively undifferentiated national and global markets and a mapping of consumers in terms of highly aggregated demographics. This is often captured in Henry Ford's offer that the consumer could have any colour of car as long as it was black. This mode of organization reached its limits in saturated consumer markets and huge capital investments by the 1970s, and encountered new opportunities in more flexible technologies and marketing strategies, particularly over the 1980s. The ideal of post-Fordism is not mass production for mass consumption but rather flexible small batch production of goods that are customized to respond to specific consumer niche markets. These are not defined by demographics but rather by lifestyles and lifestyle imagery with a cultural rather than social structural logic. Hence, the commanding discourses within consumer-oriented firms are increasingly marketing discourses that seek to orient all aspects of corporate activity to building brands, designs and commercial meanings that fit into shifting consumer lifestyles. The brand has become the major contemporary symbol of these developments, particularly in the work of anti-globalization campaigners such as Naomi Klein (2000). Firms like Nike do not directly own factories and production systems but rather organize vast networks of subcontracting and retail distribution which are knit together through their ownership of brand imagery and a logo that constitutes their real commercial value.

As noted above, Baudrillard's later work similarly depicts a world in which semiotic codes have become the 'genetic material' that generates social (hyper)realities. However, the same kind of argument has been given a new lease of life through concepts of information society, network society (Castells, 1996), new economy, 'economies of signs and space' (Lash and Urry, 1994) and 'linguistic capitalism' (Poster, 2001). Each of these terms points to the centrality of a broad range of actual quite heterogeneous cultural capitals that now provide the sources of value and organization within commercial life. While it is clear that these terms reference real aspects of corporations' self-understanding, as well as the emergence of new business organizations such as consultancies (Thrift, 2000), it is unclear either that they capture actual changes in economic process or that they provide a good conceptual basis for understanding changes in the organization or experience of consumption (Slater, 2002 a and b).

Finally, it is important to point to new perspectives emerging from quite a different direction. Science and technology studies, and particularly actor-network theory, have tried to treat the materiality of the object as continuous with its meanings and uses within networks of social action (Barry and Slater, 2002). This has led, for example, to Callon's (1998, 1999, 2002) treatment of consumer goods as inscribed within socio-technical apparatuses that involve the participation of a broad range of heterogeneous social agencies.

CROSS-CULTURAL CONSUMPTION AND GLOBALIZATION

One area of research that exemplifies many of the issues so far discussed concerns the spread of consumer culture, and of specific commodities, across the globe. This is hardly a new theme. Hume and Smith staked many of their hopes for the civilizing and pacifying potentials of market capitalism on the global interdependencies that would arise from trade and the division of labour (Durkheim had similar hopes, contingent on the emergence of a sustainable moral framework for this activity). Marx saw capitalism, on the other hand, as both intrinsically globalizing in its search for new markets for labour, raw materials and consumption, and as corrosive of any of the social orders that it encountered: commodification

was an irresistible force. The last century of consumption studies largely took the latter view, and generally in the form of the Americanization thesis, arguing that the economic, media and military force of American capitalism was able to spread both specific commercial gains and a general consumerist ideology (Sklair, 1991, 1994). Naomi Klein and the general campaign against globalization fit within this kind of approach. Similarly, Ritzer's (1993, 1999, 2001) McDonaldization thesis argues that American capitalism has produced the increasing dominance of a specific form of rationalization, best exemplified in McDonald's, which incorporates consumers globally within an efficient and standardized consumer experience.

Modifications of this position have come from many directions, in particular through an appreciation of the great complexity of cultural flows (Appadurai, 1990, 1995), regional (rather than simply American) commercial power and resistances (Miller, 2001; Wilk, 2001). However, there has also been a more radical, ethnographic challenge to the idea of globalization as commercial domination. Studies of cross-cultural consumption have emphasized the way in which commercial forces are locally mediated, often involving radical reinterpretations or alternative uses of globally marketed goods: actual consumption practices cannot be simply read off of an analysis of producers' intentions and practices (Haugerud et al., 2000; Howes, 1996a). Some of these examples tend to the exotic and the exceptional ('On the third Thursday of every month Tzotzil elders (Mexico) meet to ceremonially drink Pepsi and *Poch* – an alcoholic beverage – and thereby enter into communion with God' (Howes, 1996b) – this gives an important insight into local appropriations of the goods but might not constitute a very telling argument against the undeniably global spread of this drink). Others give an understanding of the important diversity that exists within the apparent picture of uniform global consumer culture: for example, McDonald's may well produce a highly uniform rationality in its business organization but its consumers use it differently in different places (Alfino et al., 1998; Robison and Goodman, 1996). In the process of their local assimilation, goods are 'hybridized' or 'creolized', merging with local meanings to form new ones which are neither local nor simply global. Moreover, sociology's discovery of local mediation of global goods is matched by the corporate world's discovery of 'glocalization', a shift from attempting to achieve universal and uniform global brands to a recognition of the need to understand, manage and capitalize on local differences (Kline, 1995).

The crucial issue may well be understanding the specific uses of cross-cultural consumption rather than simply demonstrating the fact of difference as opposed to homogenization. Wilk (1995), for example, looks at the way in which local cultures may operate dual and complexly interweaved sets of values in their consumption: inhabitants of Belize are clear that their standards of female beauty differ from those inscribed in beauty contests or in children's dolls, yet they are also highly aware of the 'structure of common differences' in which they have to operate – the global structures of value differences through which they must negotiate their relationship to the rest of the world. Similarly, Miller's (1994, 1995) studies of Trinidad emphasize the ways in which Trinidadians use consumer goods and practices in order to consume global capitalism and modernity in their own terms.

CONCLUSION

It is probably not surprising that favoured methodologies in consumption studies have fluctuated with the problematics of the day and the aims in mind. It is notable that not only in contemporary sociology of consumption, but also increasingly in business studies and corporate practice, there is a major shift towards ethnographic approaches or at least towards richer qualitative methods such as in-depth interviews. This is in tune with many of the issues outlined above: ethnography attempts to situate consumer goods within the entire way of life and its cultural and social organization, stressing the active agency of social groups in assimilating objects into their meanings and practices. Ethnography therefore tries not to read actual consumption practices from public representations such as advertising or from corporate organization. Moreover, it stresses social relationships rather than individual preferences or subjectivities. Finally, ethnography is concerned with the specific local character of consumption and with difference rather than with consumer culture as a site of uniformity.

It could be argued that sociology of consumption has only come into its own in the past two decades but that the terms on which it was constructed are now about to change again. The focus on cultural diversity, agency and local practice that gave it space to develop were articulated against older intellectual frameworks that were centrally concerned with power, structure and political economy. It is possible that we are more than ready for a more nuanced return to these older issues and more critical intentions. Postmodern celebrations of the consumer carnival are now well past their sell-by date, while research into 'cultural economy' (du Gay and Pryke, 2002), chains of provision (Fine and Leopold, 1990) and marketing apparatuses (Callon, 2002) are more commonly on the shelf. This would seem to point to a well-established and now central new sub-discipline within sociology.

REFERENCES

Alfino, M., Caputo, J. and Wynyard, R. (eds) (1998) *McDonaldization Revisited: Critical Essays on Consumer Culture.* London: Praeger.

Appadurai, A. (1990) 'Disjuncture and difference in the global cultural economy', *Theory, Culture and Society,* 7: 295–310.

Appadurai, A. (1995) *Modernity at Large: Cultural Dimensions of Globalization.* Minneapolis, MN: University of Minnesota Press.

Barry, A. and Slater, D.R. (2002) 'Introduction: the technological economy', *Economy and Society,* 31 (2): 175–93.

Barry, A., Osborne, T. and Rose, N. (eds) (1996) *Foucault and Political Reason.* London: UCL Press.

Barthes, R. (1986) *Mythologies.* London: Paladin.

Baudrillard, J. (1981) *For a Critique of the Political Economy of the Sign.* St Louis, MO: Telos.

Baudrillard, J. (1990) *Revenge of the Crystal: Selected Writings on the Modern Object and its Destiny*. London: Pluto Press.

Baudrillard, J. (1998 [1970]) *The Consumer Society: Myths and Structures*. London: Sage.

Bauman, Z. (1990) *Thinking Sociologically*. Oxford: Blackwell.

Bourdieu, P. (1984) *Distinction: A Social Critique of the Judgement of Taste*. Cambridge, MA: Harvard University Press.

Callon, M. (1998) 'Introduction: the embeddedness of economic markets in economics', in M. Callon (ed.), *The Laws of the Market*. Oxford: Blackwell/The Sociological Review. pp. 1–57.

Callon, M. (1999) 'Actor-network theory – the market test', in J. Law and J. Hassard (eds), *Actor Network Theory and After*. Oxford: Blackwell. pp. 181–95.

Callon, M. (2002) 'The economy of qualities', *Economy and Society*, 31 (2): 194–217.

Campbell, C. (1989) *The Romantic Ethic and the Spirit of Modern Consumerism*. Oxford: Blackwell.

Castells, M. (1996) *The Rise of Network Society*. Oxford: Blackwell.

Chin, E. M.L.S. (2001) *Purchasing Power: Black Kids and American Consumer Culture*. Minneapolis, MN: University of Minnesota Press.

de Certeau, M. (1984) *The Practice of Everyday Life*. Berkeley, CA: University of California Press.

Douglas, M. and Isherwood, B. (1979) *The World of Goods: Towards an Anthropology of Consumption*. Harmondsworth: Penguin.

du Gay, P. and Pryke, M. (eds) (2002) *Cultural Economy*. London: Sage.

Featherstone, M. (1991) *Consumer Culture and Postmodernism*. London: Sage.

Fine, B. and Leopold, E. (1990) 'Consumerism and the Industrial Revolution', *Social History*, xv: 151–79.

Finkelstein, J. (1991) *The Fashioned Self*. Cambridge: Polity Press.

Fiske, J. (1989) *Reading the Popular*. Boston, MA: Unwin Hyman.

Giddens, A. (1991) *Modernity and Self-Identity: Self and Society in the Late Modern Age*. Cambridge: Polity Press.

Giddens, A. (1992) *The Transformation of Intimacy: Sexuality, Love and Eroticism in Modern Societies*. Cambridge: Polity Press.

Goldman, R. and Papson, S. (1995) *Sign Wars: The Cluttered Landscape of Advertising*. New York: Guilford Press.

Goldman, R. and Papson, S. (1998) *Nike Culture: The Sign of the Swoosh*. London: Sage.

Gottdiener, M. (1995) *Postmodern Semiotics: Material Culture and the Forms of Postmodern Life*. Oxford: Blackwell.

Gronow, J. and Warde, A. (2001) *Ordinary Consumption*. London/New York: Routledge.

Harvey, D. (1989) *The Condition of Postmodernity: An Enquiry into the Origins of Culture*. Oxford: Blackwell.

Haugerud, A., Stone, M.P. and Little, P.D. (eds) (2000) *Commodities and Globalization: Anthropological Perspectives*. Oxford: Rowman and Littlefield.

Hebdige, D. (1979) *Subculture: The Meaning of Style*. London: Methuen.

Hebdige, D. (1988) *Hiding in the Light: On Images and Things*. London: Comedia.

Hirschman, A. (1977) *The Passions and the Interests*. Princeton, NJ: Princeton University Press.

Howes, D. (ed.) (1996a) *Cross-Cultural Consumption: Global Markets, Local Realities*. London: Routledge.

Howes, D. (1996b) 'Introduction: Commodities and Cultural Borders', in D. Howes (ed.), *Cross-Cultural Consumption: Global Markets, Local Realities*. London: Routledge. pp. 1–16.

Jameson, F. (1984) 'Postmodernism, or the cultural logic of late capitalism', *New Left Review*, 146: 53–92.

Klein, N. (2000) *No Logo*. London: HarperCollins.

Kline, S. (1995) 'The play of the market: on the internationalization of children's culture', *Theory, Culture and Society*, 12 (2): 103–29.

Lash, S. and Urry, J. (1994) *Economies of Signs and Space*. London: Sage.

Leavis, F.R. and Thompson, D. (1933) *Culture and Environment: The Training of Critical Awareness*. London: Chatto and Windus.

Leiss, W., Kline, S. and Jhally, S. (1986) *Social Communication in Advertising: Persons, Products and Images of Well-Being*. London: Methuen.

Maffesoli, M. (1996) *The Time of the Tribes*. London: Sage.

Marcuse, H. (1964) *One Dimensional Man*. London: Abacus.

Marcuse, H. (1973 [1955]) *Eros and Civilisation*. London: Abacus.

McRobbie, A. (1989) *Zoot Suits and Secondhand Dresses*. Basingstoke: Macmillan.

McRobbie, A. (1991) *Feminism and Youth Culture: From 'Jackie' to 'Just Seventeen'*. Basingstoke: Macmillan.

McRobbie, A. (1999) *In the Culture Society: Art, Fashion and Popular Music*. London: Routledge.

Miller, D. (1987) *Material Culture and Mass Consumption*. Oxford: Blackwell.

Miller, D. (1994) *Modernity – An Ethnographic Approach: Dualism and Mass Consumption in Trinidad*. Oxford: Berg.

Miller, D. (1995) *Worlds Apart: Modernity through the Prism of the Local*. London: Routledge.

Miller, D. (1998) *A Theory of Shopping*. Cambridge: Polity Press.

Miller, D. (2001) 'The poverty of morality', *Journal of Consumer Culture*, 1 (2): 225–44.

Miller, D., Thrift, N. and Jackson, P. (eds) (1998) *Shopping, Place and Identity*. London: Routledge.

Miller, P. and Rose, N. (1997) 'Mobilizing the consumer, assembling the object of consumption', *Theory, Culture and Society*, 14 (1): 1–36.

Poster, M. (2001) *What's the Matter with the Internet?* Minneapolis, MN: University of Minnesota Press.

Ritzer, G. (1993) *The McDonaldization of Society: An Investigation into the Changing Character of Contemporary Social Life*. London: Pine Forge Press.

Ritzer, G. (1999) *Enchanting a Disenchanted World: Revolutionizing the Means of Consumption*. London: Sage.

Ritzer, G. (2001) *Explorations in the Sociology of Consumption: Fast Food, Credit Cards and Casinos*. London: Thousand Oaks, CA: Sage.

Robison, R. and Goodman, D.S.G. (eds) (1996) *The New Rich in Asia: Mobile Phones, McDonald's and Middle-class Revolution*. London: Routledge.

Rose, N. (1991) *Governing the Soul: The Shaping of the Private Self*. London: Rouledge.

Rose, N. (1992) 'Governing the enterprising self', in P. Heelas and P. Morris (eds), *The Values of the Enterprise Culture: The Moral Debate*. London: Routledge. pp. 141–64.

Rose, N. (1999) *Powers of Freedom: Reframing Political Thought*. Cambridge: Cambridge University Press.

Shields, R. (ed.) (1992) *Lifestyle Shopping: The Subject of Consumption*. London: Routledge.

Shove, E. (2003) *Comfort, Cleanliness and Convenience: The Social Organization of Normality*. Oxford: Berg.

Simmel, G. (1950) 'The metropolis and mental life', in K. Wolff (ed.), *The Sociology of Georg Simmel*. London: Collier–Macmillan. p. 445.

Sklair, L. (1991) *Sociology of the Global System*. New York: Harvester/Wheatsheaf.

Sklair, L. (1994) 'Capitalism and development in global perspective', in L. Sklair (ed.), *Capitalism and Development*. London: Routledge. pp. 165–88.

Slater, D.R. (1997a) *Consumer Culture and Modernity*. Cambridge: Polity Press.

Slater, D.R. (1997b) 'Consumer culture and the politics of need', in M. Nava, A. Blake, I. MacRury and B. Richards (eds), *Buy This Book: Contemporary Issues in Advertising and Consumption*. London: Routledge. pp. 51–63.

Slater, D.R. (2002a) 'From calculation to alienation: disentangling economic abstractions', *Economy and Society*, 31 (2): 234–49.

Slater, D. (2002b) 'Markets, materiality and the "new economy"', in S. Metcalfe and A. Warde (eds), *Market Relations and the Competitive Process*. Manchester: Manchester University Press. pp. 95–113.

Thrift, N. (2000) 'Performing cultures in the new economy', *Annals of the Association of American Geographers*, 90 (4): 674–92.

Warde, A. (1994a) 'Consumers, identity and belonging: reflections on some theses of Zygmunt Bauman', in R. Keat, N. Whiteley and N. Abercrombie (eds), *The Authority of the Consumer*. London: Routledge. pp. 58–74.

Warde, A. (1994b) 'Consumption, identity-formation and uncertainty', *Sociology*, 28 (4): 877–98.

Warde, A. and Martens, L. (2000) *Eating Out: Social Differentiation, Consumption and Pleasure*. Cambridge: Cambridge University Press.

Wernick, A. (1991) *Promotional Culture: Advertising, Ideology and Symbolic Expression*. London: Sage.

Wilk, R. (1995) 'Learning to be local in Belize: global systems of common difference', in D. Miller (ed.), *Worlds Apart: Modernity through the Prism of the Local*. London: Routledge. pp. 110–33.

Wilk, R. (2001) 'Consuming morality', *Journal of Consumer Culture*, 1 (2): 245–60.

Williamson, J. (1978) *Decoding Advertisements: Ideology and Meaning in Advertising*. London: Marion Boyars.

Willis, P. (1990) *Common Culture: Symbolic Work at Play in the Everyday Cultures of the Young*. Milton Keynes: Open University Press.

Zukin, L.A. (1991) *Landscapes of Power: From Detroit to Disney World*. Berkeley, CA: University of California Press.

10

The Sociology of Mediation and Communication

ROGER SILVERSTONE

INTRODUCTION

Sociology has had a consistently paradoxical relationship with what we now call media and communication. While it is quite possible to see its early development, in the writings of Marx, Weber and Durkheim, as having been at least in part concerned with issues of communication and culture – ideology in Marx, collective representation in Durkheim, rationality and legitimation in Weber – it was not until the work of the American pragmatists and symbolic interactionists that communication, centring on interpersonal communication, came to be seen as a, if not the, central dimension of social life (McQuail, 1984).

In this early twentieth-century work communication was, essentially, a social psychological, possibly also a philosophical, term. It was seen to begin and end with a concern for the individual, and with the individual's place in relation to his or her capacity to connect with others. It was theorized and analysed as a crucial component of social life (Dewey, 1958), the formation of self (Mead, 1964 [1932]) and the enabling of community (Park, 1972). Communication 'of all affairs … the most wonderful' (Dewey, 1958: 166), requires assuming the attitude of the other individual as well as calling it out in the other

and in turn assumes and requires reciprocity (Mead, 1964 [1932]: 254). It is the medium through which the social becomes both possible and manifest; natural language is its paradigm.

If communication was something that takes place principally between individuals, then *mass* communication tended to be seen as a distortion of that. It emerged as both product and precondition of mass society – the *bête noire* of modernity (Giner, 1976). This preoccupation explains one of the drivers of media and cultural analysis throughout the twentieth century, fed by the anxieties that such a distortion created in the otherwise idealized symmetrical position of communication between sender and receiver, especially in the supposed symmetries of the face to face. These anxieties cut both ways, of course. There were those who were concerned with the state's, or especially big business's, capacity to appropriate the mass media for their own propagandist or commercial ends. And there were those who were concerned about the crowd and fearful of the new power that the mass media might give to its radical edge (Rosenberg and White, 1957).

This initial, and orienting, perception of society as communicated and indeed communicable, however, rarely left the symbolic (Burke, 1955; Duncan, 1962). It also rarely left both the ideal and the idealized. Little was said in the nineteenth and early twentieth centuries about the role of the media in enabling perceptions of a different world, or about media technology's ineffable relationship with modernity, or indeed about the rise of the modern press as a key component of nation-building and the formation of national identity. The fear of the popular, or a more general nostalgia for disappearing cultures and connectivities, may have prompted much in the way of the social psychology of the crowd, but it did not lead to a developed analysis of what lay behind cultural change, nor of the institutional transformations that were sustaining mediated communications across an increasingly globalizing world. It enquired into neither cause nor consequence of this progressive, or indeed possibly regressive, mediation of everyday life.

This focus on *mediation* therefore, different from, but complementary to, communication has been a relatively recent and, it has been argued, a rather belated phenomenon (Barbero, 1993; Thompson, 1995). Mediation is a fundamentally dialectical notion which requires us to address the processes of communication as both institutionally and technologically driven and embedded. Mediation, as a result, requires us to understand how processes of communication change the social and cultural environments that support them as well as the relationships that participants, both individual and institutional, have to that environment and to each other. At the same time it requires a consideration of the social as in turn a mediator: institutions and technologies as well as the meanings that are delivered by them are mediated in the social processes of reception and consumption.

To a significant degree taking for granted the symbolic infrastructure of the social, the study of mediation has become increasingly and properly focused on the technologies and the texts of mass, broadcast and, increasingly now, interactive communication. In the twentieth century there was a necessary preoccupation with the mass, with influence and persuasion and with more general but none the less still invasive effects of first film, then radio and television. Social researchers in the United States and elsewhere, often prompted once again both by the moral panics that have erupted with every new media shift and a complementary desire to increase political control over this emerging *deus ex machina* (cf. Debray, 2000), developed elaborate methodologies to investigate the increasingly insistent broadcast media and their capacity both to define cultures and to direct individual values, beliefs and actions.

John Durham Peters (1999) has distinguished between dialogue and dissemination as two distinct modes or ideals of communication (notions of communication are rarely less than normative, one way or the other). Whereas the dialogical has provided throughout the twentieth century, and before, the dominantly valued mode, not least in the work of Jürgen Habermas, Peters argues for the respectability and importance of the disseminative, finding in the model of the gospel a perfectly satisfactory alternative to the conversation as a framework for communicating ideas, values and information. This analysis poses two kinds of communication in counterpoint. But it also creates an awareness of communicative difference and it enables a consideration of their relative and uneven dominance historically and sociologically, especially in circumstances of electronic mediation, and as technologies and cultures change.

As we move into the twenty-first century this concern with mediation becomes even more central and more demanding with the interactivity and networking capacities promised by the latest generation of media technology and by their global reach (Castells, 1996). The political and moral significance of the media are pressing hard on the sociological agenda, and concerns raised by media scholars are being echoed (as well as stimulated) by contemporary social theorists.

In this chapter I intend to identify and discuss some of the dominant preoccupations in sociology's engagement with the media and mediation. While the focus is undoubtedly on the first term of the media and communication couplet, the second term will not be far away; and indeed as the possibilities for a re-appropriation of media technologies by the individual become more of a reality, we will need to return to the issue of interpersonal communication, and the constant irritation and challenge of the face to face. In the meantime the argument presumes that mediation is a component of social communication, but an increasingly central one: it also presumes the 'real reality of the mass media as the communications which go on within and through them' (Luhmann, 2000: 3).

The chapter begins with a framing of mediation in terms of power. Mediated communication must be understood as both producer and product of hierarchy, and as such fundamentally implicated in the exercise of, and resistance to, power in modern societies. This makes all mediated communication, in one sense or another, political: seeking to persuade, seeking to define one reality as opposed to another, including and excluding while at the same time informing or entertaining. This starting point leads to a consideration of the two dominant modes of conceptualizing mediation, that of influence and effects on the one hand, and that of ritual and reflexivity on the other. There follow sections on key dimensions of the social role of media: on the nature of news; on the media's capacity to articulate the global and the local in the experience of the everyday; and on the media's role in defining the relationship between public and private spheres and spaces. The final sections of the chapter address technology and media change and questions of morality and ethics.

POWER

It is possible to suggest that what has driven and continues to drive sociological concern with the media is their power: power in a number of different senses, and along a number of different, contrary and contradictory dimensions. The media are believed to be able to set cultural agendas and to destroy them, to influence the political process as well as being influenced by it; to inform as well as to deceive. They are believed to be at the mercy of state and market as well as to be resistible by informed or active audiences, citizens or consumers. Their presumed power has led to preoccupation with ownership and control, with their direct influence on the minds and actions of those who receive their messages as well as with their capacity to paper over the cracks of the contradictions of global capitalism in the drip feed of ideological framing and naturalization.

The media are believed to reflect reality and also to construct it: they can be seen as window, mirror, or even hologram (Baudrillard, 1983). They create anxiety as well as providing constant reassurance. They enable and disable rights of public speech and access to public spheres, both granting and withdrawing legitimacy and legitimation. They provide frameworks both for remembering and forgetting the past, and for representing and misrepresenting the other. The media are seen to be increasingly central as defining the terms in which the global citizen goes about his or her everyday life as well as increasingly central to the political culture within which that everyday life is in turn conducted.

Whereas once media might have been thought of as an appendage to the political process, a handmaiden for governments and parties, as well as an irritant or a watch-dog, the Fourth Estate, there are many who now suggest that the media have to be understood as fundamentally inscribed into the political process itself (Virilio, 1986; Wark, 1994). Politics, like experience, can no longer even be thought outside a media frame. Whereas once the media were believed to be a guarantor of liberty and democracy, it may now be suggested that the very freedoms demanded by, and granted to, the media and which have served modern society so well in the past, are on the verge of being destroyed by those very same media in their florid, cannibalistic, maturity (Lloyd, 2004).

Media power is power exercised at the conjunction of the economic, the political and the symbolic (Thompson, 1995). But it is not exercised in isolation of other sources of that power. There are dangers, of course, of a kind of media-centrism in such arguments, a perception of the media as being the be-all and end-all of the social which cannot, of course, be sustained. Yet it is precisely media's intrusive ubiquity in the political process at global, national and local levels, both as message and as massage (McLuhan and Fiore, 1967), that continually demands sociological investigation.

Models for the analysis of media inevitably reflect the models that are available for the analysis of the exercise of power in society more generally. McQuail (1994), summarizing and simplifying a wide literature, distinguishes between dominance and pluralist models. The former depends on a perception of society as being dominated by a ruling class or elite, within which the media fall under concentrated ownership, producing standardized and routinized, ideologically informed content to a dependent and passive audience with basically conservative consequences for the social order. The latter, pluralism, sees society as comprising competing political, social and cultural interests and groups, with a range of independent media, who are creative, free and responsive in their production of content to audience demand – that audience itself being fragmented, selective and active. The consequences of such mediation are inevitably numerous and without consistency, predictability of effect, or outcome (1994: 70).

This is perhaps more useful descriptively than analytically. Indeed, McQuail himself acknowledges the obvious limitations of such a dichotomy. As Thompson (1990) points out, it makes more sense to think of power in this context as the differential capacity to mobilize meaning. As such the capacity or incapacity of different groups to exert their power can be 'resolved only by studying how … symbolic forms operate in particular social-historic circumstances, how they are used and understood by the subjects who produce and receive them in the socially structured contexts of everyday life' (1990: 67). This formulation is itself, of course, vulnerable to criticism, unless the institutionalization and transmission, that is, the reproduction, of media power is properly considered (Couldry, 2000; Debray, 2000). As Raymond Williams (1974) notes, 'we should look not for the components of a product but for the conditions of a practice'.

The consequences of such an approach mean that one cannot, despite political economy's privileging the concentration of media power through the ownership and control of production and distribution networks (Golding and Murdock, 2000), simply presume linearity in media effects or media influence. Mediation is not all one way, neither at the global nor at the everyday level of communication. Indeed mediation, and Barbero (1993) uses the term in this sense, extends into a concern with how culture is negotiated in the tactics of everyday life.[1]

What are the empirical implications of this? The first is a recognition of the impossibility of reading from one level of the process of mediation to another: ownership does not determine content; content does not determine reception. The second is the need to recognize flux and fluidity in the production and consumption of media texts and also to recognize that mediated meanings are not exhausted at the point of consumption. The third is to recognize that media power exists as a generalized resource of symbolic definition but at the same time one in which all participants, both producers and audiences, albeit always differentially, are involved (Couldry, 2000) and indeed where alternative sites for its exercise emerge (Downing, 2000; Rodriguez, 2001). And the fourth is to insist on the need both for a general social theory in which an understanding of mediation can be located (Luhmann, 2000) as well as a sense of media's historical specificity. Benedict Anderson's (1983) influential account of the press's nineteenth-century role as creating an 'imagined community' for the emerging nation-states in Europe may possibly be of value in analysing the effects of broadcasting (Scannell, 1988), but only in certain societies, and only too in relation to particular technologies and forms of mediation as well as to some but never all minorities or other social groups.[2]

INFLUENCES AND EFFECTS

It is customary to consider the history of media research in the twentieth century as one that has been marked by quite dramatic swings between models of strong and weak effects. The media have been seen as strongly influential at times of media innovation and when societies themselves might be seen to be vulnerable to propaganda or influence (both political and commercial) for specific historical or social reasons. New media – radio, film, television, video and the home computer in turn – have all spurred exaggerated fears about both direct and permanent influence. Moral panics have focused on personal sexual morality or propensity to violence (the Payne Fund studies of the 1930s (Blumer, 1933); the Surgeon-General's research in the 1960s (Comstock et al., 1978); vulnerability to propaganda (Hovland et al., 1965); or threats to social or psychological health (the home computer as socially isolating), or even to physical health (concerns over the carcinogenic mobile phone). Theories of weaker effects have tended to emerge at periods of social and media stability: in the postwar period of social reconstruction (Katz and Lazarsfeld, 1955; Lasswell, 1948) and in the 1970s and 1990s when broadcasting was well established and Western commodity culture achieved its particular hegemony.

This impotence–omnipotence pendulum (Katz, 1980) was explored and driven by empirical work that moved from laboratory to field; from the psychological to the sociological; from quantitative to qualitative research; from stress on the isolated to that on the socially embedded individual; and from the passive to the active receiver of media's increasingly multiple communications. And back again. These shifts created surprising and unholy intellectual alliances, above all bringing together in the strong effects camp empirical social psychologists, psychoanalytically informed cultural analysts and elitist critical theorists, all of whom saw in the media the capacity to direct and deliver a malleable audience, vulnerable either to direct and specific influence or to long-term ideological management, or both.

Those who opposed this view did so on primary sociological grounds. They argued, of course correctly, that communication was a social matter, and that mediation too had to be seen as both socially produced and consumed.

Despite acknowledging the differential power of participants to define, negotiate or resist the meanings available for mediation, they recognized both that the media were only one component in a complex social reality, both enabling and constraining the production of texts and discourses, and that meanings themselves and their salience for different individuals, groups and institutions were the product of a more subtle process of social construction than those stressing effects and influence would normally grant (Morley, 1992).

Katz and Lazarsfeld's (1955) seminal study of personal influence offered an analysis of what they called the 'two-step' flow of mediated communication, in which the social location of the individual was part of a dynamic social environment crucially providing an 'inter-mediation', a breaking of the linearity and directness of media influence. Conceptually speaking, two steps are better than one, but they are still, arguably, too linear and too individual. Indeed this approach, and that described as 'uses and gratifications' in which members of the media audience are seen as selecting and working with media content on the basis of their own psychological predispositions (Blumler and Katz, 1974), has, arguably, failed fully to engage both with the substantively contextualized active audience on the one hand and, paradoxically, with the *longue durée* of media influence and its intended as well as its unintended consequences on the other.

The latter has been to a degree the focus of a more recent attempt to provide an account of media influence, particularly for those heavy mainstream consumers whose world-view might plausibly be dictated by the consistency of both television content and their viewing behaviour over time. A positive correlation of this kind has been reported by George Gerbner and his colleagues over a number of years (Gerbner et al., 1980, 1986; Shanahan and Morgan, 1999), and although it has been pointed out that correlation does not equal causation, that television content is not as consistent as assumed or analysed by Gerbner and his team, that world-views do not necessarily translate into action, that there is difference between denotational and connotational meanings, and that a considerable degree of the variance could be explained by third factors unrelated to media use (Livingstone, 1990), nevertheless this research is perhaps as close as it gets to making some impression on the workings of ideology as the media create it. It is indeed unlikely that a limited diet of (more or less) consistent television or other media consumption cannot but have some impact on the mind-sets of those so consuming it.

More recent research, on television (Kubey and Csikszentmihalyi, 1990) and on the Internet (Kraut et al., 1998), both based predominantly on survey methodologies and quantitative analysis of findings, has provided some evidence that the media have affects on those that use them, though in both these cases the data suggest a kind of soporific and anti-social response.

It makes no sense to dismiss this work out of hand, though questions of meaning, of indeterminacy, non-rationality, self-referentiality and unpredictability as part of the viewing experience, and the process of mediation more generally, as well as the immeasurable presence of long-term and unacknowledged (because entirely taken for granted) ideological formations in the structure of everyday life, make it certain that there is a need for a more dialectical theory of media effects and differently focused empirical work. It is possible to suggest that this need is still the same, even where research focuses on the active audience, reversing the polarities of effects research, and analysing the capacity of both adults (Liebes and Katz, 1990) and children to appropriate mass-produced meanings to their own agendas and to the experienced realities of their own culturally specific everyday lives (Hodge and Tripp, 1986).

To a degree this has come from qualitative audience research much influenced by British and British-influenced cultural studies, which has examined the active role that readers or audiences are supposed to have in their relationship to mass-mediated texts. Here media are seen to be part of a more widely and deeply embedded culture, and as such they become an essential component of the symbolic space that marks the distinctiveness of life in late modern society, a symbolic space that is in turn regarded as the product of the engaged activity of individuals and groups variously positioned in relation to dominant forms of expression and albeit contradictory ideologies.

In work that in various ways deals with audiences as empowered (Fiske, 1987, 1990), specific dimensions of their social status – class, gender, ethnicity – have been brought to bear to extract from the mediation process a sense of sociologically determined discrimination in the work that can, and is being, done in front of the screen and crucially in the discourses of everyday life that in turn mediate the particularities of the viewing experience. Contemporary media audiences are neither cultural dopes nor dupes (Ang, 1986; Buckingham, 1987, 2000; Morley, 1992). Some of this work is still quite linear in its approach to questions of influence; some of it, equally, is entirely unclear about lines of influence or determination, preferring a model of social inertia to compensate for individuals' otherwise creative engagement. But despite such reservations such work offers a much more sensitive, as well as a more radical, approach to mediation as socially produced and politically effective. It begins to challenge the model of communication that is resolutely one of transmission or transportation, and to shift it perceptibly towards one that has been described as that of ritual (Carey, 1989; Rothenbuhler, 1998).

RITUAL AND REFLEXIVITY

James Carey (1989) has noted that two ways of thinking about communication have been present in American social thought, and also within the more operational categorizations of media theory and research. The first, and this has just been discussed, can be described as the transmission model. It presumes directness and intent, command and influence. The second he calls the ritual view of communication, Durkheimian in origin, in which communication is linked to terms such as 'sharing', 'participation', 'association', 'fellowship' and 'the possession of a common faith'. This definition exploits the ancient identity and common roots of the terms 'commonness', 'communion', 'community', and 'communication'. … [It] is directed not toward the extension of messages in space but toward the maintenance of society in time; not the act of imparting information but the representation of shared beliefs. (Carey, 1989: 18)

If influences and affects models tend to focus the mind on media as disturbances of the social order and on the manifest exercise of symbolic power, then ritual models tend to focus the mind on the media's role in creating and sustaining that social order. Once again, even though the dichotomization is both misleading and too clinical, it is vital to acknowledge this double edge and to ensure that both are held in tension, a tension that has to be historically and sociologically investigated in its specific manifestations if it is to be properly understood.

As Moore and Myerhoff (1977: 3) note, 'Social life proceeds somewhere between the imaginary extremes of absolute order, and absolute chaotic conflict and anarchic improvisation. Neither the one nor the other takes over completely'. The media have been seen to be key institutions in this project of time, space and life management. To suggest that they have such a ritual function, particularly in their broadcast mode – that predominant throughout the twentieth century – is to open an agenda that leads directly to core sociological concerns both at the macro and micro social levels. For social rituals are as much a part of the large-scale social structuring of nations and regions as they are of the small-scale interactions that constitute the fabric of everyday life. In both dimensions the media provide a framework for the ordering of time and space, both through the direct address of their programming and messaging, but also through the secondary discourses (Fiske, 1987) that emerge around them: through the conversations and dreams, realities and imaginaries, that individuals in their everyday lives produce as ways of engaging with the other and with the disturbing specificities of life events.

In this sense the media create bulwarks against anxiety (as well as for its management), and

they also provide frameworks for orientation and mobilization within both national and global cultures. Media events – the deaths of great figures, the celebration of sporting occasions, the reporting of global catastrophes (Dayan and Katz, 1992; Zelizer and Allan, 2002) – are key moments, highly ritualized in their reporting and representation that indeed provide those momentary spaces and times when the profane and ordinary world is put to one side and where the power of the albeit dispersed collective is mobilized in a project of mutuality and togetherness. In this context Victor Turner's (1969) notion of 'communitas' would not be out of place.

However, the ritual function of the media extends beyond the exceptional. Studies of national press and broadcasting cultures, for the most part phenomenologically inspired (Scannell, 1996), have quite properly addressed the media's role in creating and sustaining the ordinariness and normality of everyday life. Just as nations were increasingly ritualized through their representation in the media throughout the twentieth century, so too, in soap operas and situation comedies, in game and talk shows, and in the nightly reflections on the disturbances of the world in the news, the mundane world is offered for reflection and reassurance. The media have become part of the grain of everyday life. In both modes traditions are held, and the world remains, to a degree, but to a still significant degree, enchanted.

This re-enchantment has been noted and criticized, most notably by the first generation of scholars in the Frankfurt School and their heirs and protégés (Horkheimer and Adorno, 1972; Lodziak, 1986; Mander, 1978; Postman, 1986). It provides, for better or worse, of course, a link with premodern cultures where the sacred and the power that may or may not be exercisable through the sacred, held more obvious and more untrammelled sway.

Perhaps the particularly modern twist to this continuing presence of the ritualized and ritualizing in culture comes with the acknowledgement that with modernity came reflexivity. Anthony Giddens argues that this reflexivity is different from that which constitutes the reflexive monitoring of action intrinsic to all human activity. It refers to 'the susceptibility of most aspects of social activity, and material relations with nature, to chronic revision in the light of new information or knowledge' (Giddens, 1991: 20). As he notes, such information is not incidental to modern institutions but constitutive of them. Ulrich Beck (1992) by and large shares this view in his analysis of risk society, although neither of them sees the media as being a central component of this ironically still modern, rather than postmodern, project. Giddens's (1991: 23–27) own discussion of the mediation of experience fails to connect the two processes.

Yet it is obviously the case that the mass media, and increasingly the latest interactional media, have become not just the sites where such reflexivity takes place, but actually provide the terms under which it becomes possible at all. Information and narration, news and stories, communication on a global as well as a local scale, and eternally intertwined, are in their mass mediation the key processes at the core of modern societies. The media are crucial institutions for any understanding of the reflexive capabilities and incapabilities of modernity.

One final dimension of this particular sociology of the media addresses the role of the audience in the process of mediation. As such it brings a postmodern flavour to a discussion that has already blurred the distinction between modernity and its precursor. If audiences are no longer to be seen as passive recipients of the messages they receive; if they are to be understood as actively engaged in the complex interactions of everyday life and the cultures and subcultures that constitute it; if they are also no longer to be seen as singular subjects, but as fragmented in their identities as the communities in which they no longer consistently live, then how are they to be perceived?

Recent work (Abercrombie and Longhurst, 1998; Seiter, 1999) provides both through empirical evidence and theory, as well as via a methodological injunction both to do ethnography and/or to think ethnographically, a reformulation of the relationship between technologies, texts and receivers. Such work involves an engagement with the popular, with the dynamics of consumption, and with the creative possibilities that emerge at the interface between media and daily life. Indeed, to a degree, what informs this analysis is the refusal of this distinction, not in some sense to reify a Baudrillardian world of simulacra, but to pose the audience as a verb rather than a noun, and as an activity, a performance, in which the boundaries between audiences and texts or performances are blurred.

Drawing on the analysis of fan culture, and albeit recognizing its extremes, Abercrombie and Longhurst make a plausible case for what they call the diffused audience, a product of a society of media saturation, of both wide-ranging performance and increasing narcissism (Lasch, 1980; Sennett, 1977) as well as one in which the media are themselves constitutive of the social (Abercrombie and Longhurst, 1998: 175ff.). A diffused audience is an eternal audience, and its acts of audiencing are continuous, but it is also an audience which, in its acts of creative consumption, in displays of style and person, constitutes itself as a performer.

The limits of this analysis are obvious enough, just as they are in the effects model, but so are its possibilities. Juxtaposing the two approaches provides the two arms of the dialectic around the question of media power and our capacity to control or resist it, but it does not as yet provide an adequate synthesis. However, framing it in this way also brings to the foreground a range of other dimensions of media and communication which have been the focus of recent and less recent attention. It is to three of these that I now turn.

NEWS, MEMORY AND FORGETTING

News is a significant strand of mass communication. The increasingly rapid demand for, and provision of, information, of commercial, military and broadly social significance, drove the nineteenth-century press (Chalaby, 1999) as well as providing a staple for broadcasting in the twentieth century. Much of the early sociology of the media found itself investigating news from a number of different perspectives. What united them, and still does in many respects, was the concern with accuracy, truth and trustworthiness.

Yet news quickly became not something that reflected a reality so much as something which constructed it. Work in the newsroom on gate-keeping (Gieber, 1964; White, 1950), on the textuality of news through the analysis of its most significant characteristics (Galtung and Ruge, 1969), on the relationship between news and both the structure of its ownership (Bagdikian, 1997) as well as the organization of its production (Schlesinger, 1978; Tuchman, 1978) together still rarely leave this initial framing. As Michael Schudson points out (2000: 194), these approaches rarely depart significantly from an often unstated normative view that the news' primary function is to 'serve society by informing the general population in ways that arm them for vigilant citizenship'. In other words, we still expect the news to act as the Fourth Estate.

More cultural analysis of news addressed its relationship to the wider symbolic spaces, both professional and nationally specific which, once again, imply an ideological tarnish (Glasgow Media Group, 1976; Hall, 1977). Even in those attempts to generalize the 'cultural air we breathe', the implication is that news remains a distinct product of mediated modernity and is powerful in its significance for defining a reality, a newsworthy reality, for the societies that both produce and consume the daily press and the nightly news bulletin. If they were not powerful then why study them?

Schudson's own view is that the effectivity of news is mostly confined to elites, but that in any event what is missing from the sociology of news is a clear sense of its audiences and its publics. This is not entirely fair, for a number of studies have worked in some detail on how audiences decode or work with news content (Lewis, 1991; Liebes, 1997; Philo, 1990) and there is also work which includes news in the wider category of informational media (Buckingham, 2000; Corner, 1995).

Much of this research and writing, however, takes the transmission approach to the communicational infrastructure of news, and self-evidently also, a communicational rather than a mediational approach to news as a dynamic component of social and cultural life. It also presumes, for the most part, a referential model of discourse and reality, such that some measures of distortion, bias, or construction, will always not be too far away.

In a deliberately provocative introduction to a set of illuminating observations on news as a social phenomenon, Niklas Luhmann (2000) challenges news' elision of information, illumination and truth as well as noting the paradox of its regularity (as a New Yorker cartoon once asked: 'How come they call it the news if it's always the same?', now Luhmann is asking: 'How come it's the news if it happens every-day?').[3] Both questions are important both anthropologically and sociologically. Both lead to a concern with the wider significance of news as a cultural category and its relationship to social and media processes.

Such a concern might even lead to a concern with functions. Indeed, functionalist analysis of the media (as discussed by McQuail, 1994: 78–82) focuses on the media's role in general, and news' in particular, as social glue. Integration, cooperation, order, adaptation to change, mobilization, management of tension and continuity of culture and values are each involved in this broadly functionalist approach. Yet it is clear that the significance of each of these elements can be turned on its head once a parallel but differently valued critique of the exercise of power in society as a whole is advocated.

So it is possible to confront news from quite another perspective. As Bird and Dardenne (1988) have noted, we should take the characterization of news as a *story* rather more forcefully. Doing so opens up a range of counter-intuitive ways of thinking about this so-taken-for-granted aspect of mediation in everyday life. Treading the often thin ice of cultural theorizing, a number of commentators have focused on news as myth and narrative and as such have raised perhaps more challenging questions about news' paradoxical role in the massaging and managing of collective anxiety, and as a central component of a mass culture that privileges forgetting over remembering and dissemblance over resemblance.

News, both because of its dailiness and its epistemological claims to be reporting on the world, has become a key to understanding how the media can be seen to be a prop sustaining the individual's sense of ontological security in perhaps an increasingly unsettling world (Giddens, 1990). Its particular, and remarkably globally homogeneous, structures of story-telling, accounts of heroism and disaster, narrative closure, construction of the newsreader as the nightly teller of tales, and its fixed position in the radio and television schedules[4] together define the genre as crucial in this respect. News becomes then a contradictory component of everyday culture. It provides, through the eternal recurrence of its narrative structures, an essential component of a reassuring mythology for contemporary society. But, at the same time in its decontextualized commitments to telling it how it is, often in real-time or in the as-if of real time, it decontextualizes events from the geography and the history which might give them their meaning and which, some have argued, guarantee the news as a tool both for forgetting, and for morally disengaging from, the world (Baudrillard, 1995; Boltanski, 1999; Silverstone, 1999, in press). Research has suggested how little is remembered from a single viewing of a news bulletin (Gunter, 1987), but the kind of forgetting implied by these arguments is in significant degrees more profound. I will return to the moral issues in the last section of this chapter.

COMMUNITY: THE GLOBAL AND THE LOCAL

Marshall McLuhan's prescient but misleading notion of the global village brings together, however, two important dimensions and consequences of mediation (McLuhan and Fiore, 1968). McLuhan's vision was of their convergence: a presumption that the extension of communicative reach would bring with it an intensification of mostly benevolent social relationships. 'Ours is a brand new world of allatonceness,' he wrote. '"Time" has ceased, "space" has vanished. We now live in a global village ... a simultaneous happening ... Electronic circuitry profoundly involves men with one another' (McLuhan and Fiore, 1967: 63). Such media involvement in the reconfiguring of space and time is difficult to gainsay, despite his own particular kind of hyperbole (Meyrowitz, 1985). But it needs to be unpacked and treated with caution, for he presumes, as have so many others, both a technological determinism and an unproblematic account of the social.

The core questions are those involving ideas and realities of community, and the question of how media, particularly the electronic media, have or have not succeeded in enabling different forms of sociality. Indeed many historians of media and communication technologies, painting the broad analytic brush strokes of massive social, economic and political change, have taken their cue, if their not their methodologies, from McLuhan and convincingly argued for profound and indelible changes in society as a result of certain key technological innovations. If writing, and especially writing on paper and papyrus, led to empire (Goody, 1977; Innis, 1972, 1973), and print (and later broadcasting) led to nations (Anderson, 1983; Eisenstein, 1978), then the latest digital media can be seen to be enabling the conditions for another sea change: a global world of intense connectivity and mutuality. At issue is not just the organization of political life, and the central role of media in providing the channels and networks for interpersonal or interorganizational communication, but these networks' capacity to create a symbolic space where identities can be formed and relationships sustained on a global stage (Thussu, 2000; Tomlinson, 1999). These are questions both of scale and of difference. At issue too are the ways in which the media provide a mesh for the interweaving of global and local frames of reference and spheres of activity.

Mediation involves a shift in the location of interaction from the face-to-face, liberating communication from the constraints of the immediate and the local. If nineteenth-century sociologists, albeit with a focus on other dimensions of modernity, bewailed the decline of community, there are those who have argued since that media provide a compensatory framework, albeit in imagined or indeed virtual space, for the loss. There are symbolic and material dimensions to this argument. Benedict Anderson (1983) takes the symbolic route, arguing for individual participation in the shared ritual of reading the morning paper as a crucial component of the imagined community of the emerging capitalist nation-state. Manuel Castells (1996) sees in the network society a new intensity in the free flowing of information which creates a new materiality for action and connection. He is not alone (Giddens, 1990; Held et al., 1999) in realizing that such changes in the global infrastructure will have profound effects on, and arguably in turn be affected by, local activity. The two are fundamentally intertwined, and it is the media that provide the links in which global forces are (or are not) both appropriated and reflected upon at the local level.

The media can then be seen to be doing community[5] in at least three different ways: expression, refraction and compensation (Silverstone, 1999). Anderson's imagined communities are an example of the first, in which media and media practices enable the creation of community as a symbolic space, mostly but not exclusively for the construction of nationhood. Public service broadcasting in Europe, most particularly in the UK, was seen, even by those building the systems (Scannell, 1988; Scannell and Cardiff, 1991), to be key institutions of modernity in this regard. Contemporary struggles for its survival in the context of an increasingly fragmenting national culture and the availability of multiple communication channels are testament, too, of the significance of this aspect of the media as community-building and community-reflecting institutions.

Refraction is a more complex notion. There is a case for arguing, as Anthony Cohen (1985) indeed argues, that community is claimed through moments of symbolic reversal as much as through moments and activities in which values, ideas and beliefs are represented as being unproblematically shared. Symbolic, often ironic, reversal involves people in not only marking a boundary between their community and others, but also reversing or

inverting 'the norms of behaviour and values which "normally" mark their boundaries. In these rituals of reversal, people behave quite differently and collectively in ways which they supposedly abhor or which are usually proscribed' (Cohen, 1985: 58). The media provide multiple opportunities for such displays of reversal, and although these are inevitably contradictory (inflected as they are by judgements of taste and differences of class) they are a core component of, still mostly national, community. From the tabloid and the yellow press to the confessional talk show, the media are constantly involved in the refractory delineation of difference and similarity (Silverstone, 2000).

These refractions may well not survive the globalization of media, for they depend on local connections and associations for their significance. Yet such mediated globalization can be seen to encourage community in other ways. Arjun Appadurai (1996) argues for a characterization of globalization through a sequence of *scapes* which he identifies as distinct dimensions of global cultural flow. The media in the form of the media-scape is one such dimension, and from the point view of critical and alternative sites for community, the ethnoscape is another. The appropriation of media and the capacity to define their own media space both in production and consumption by the increasingly significant number of global diasporic populations has produced a dimension of media culture which is just beginning to be explored (Dayan, 1999; Gillespie, 1995; Naficy, 1993; Silverstone, 2001). The question of how both old and new media enable the creation of alternative and arguably compensatory forms of community expression is one which will become increasingly important in the new century. It will have profound significance for how both cultural politics and political cultures form and reform within and beyond the boundaries of the nation-state.

PUBLIC AND PRIVATE MEDIATION

In a recent review of the complex and increasingly frustrating relationship between democratic and media theory James Curran

(2000) proposes a set of criteria for the reinvention of a democratic media system as follows:

> It should empower people by enabling them to explore where their interest lies; it should foster sectional solidarities and assist the functioning of organisations necessary for the effective representation of collective interests; it should sustain vigilant scrutiny of government and centres of [both economic and political] power; it should provide a source of protection and redress for weak and unorganised interests; and it should create the conditions for real societal agreement or compromise based on an open working through of difference rather than a contrived consensus based on elite dominance. (2000: 148)

This may seem, and arguably is, a utopian rather than a realistic programme for reform, yet it needs to be understood against the relative failures of media theory in this area (see also Garnham, 2000) and especially the increasing irrelevance of both classic liberal theory's hypostatization of a market-driven and hence state-independent media, as well as Jürgen Habermas's both initial and reformulated accounts of the public sphere (1989, 1992). It also needs to be understood, of course, in relation to the actually emergent properties of media systems in the developed world at least, which have been shown increasingly – and paradoxically – to be both subject to manipulative intent by political classes and transnational corporations, and at the same time to be less than obviously potent in delivering changes in opinion and behaviour. In this context too transmission and ritual models of the processes of mediation contest the terrain.

Critics are concerned not just about the media's vulnerability to influence, but their general contribution to political apathy, and their distortion of the relationship between public and private lives and spaces (Eliasoph, 1998; Putnam, 2000; Thompson, 2000).

The media's thorny relationship between the public and the private can be, and has thus been, understood in a number of different ways and different levels. The root concern is as it has just been defined: the role of the media in enabling citizenship and democracy in an increasingly fragmented, and of course in an increasingly global, society. Such concerns encompass questions of the invasion of privacy, rights of free speech and rights of media access, and surveillance. The assumed rights of intrusion into the private lives of public figures – often spuriously defended in the name of the public interest – as well as the dragging or seducing of private citizens into the public limelight – equally often defended on similar grounds – is threatening to destroy both the media's own freedom and its legitimacy. So too, it can be argued, is the blurring of the boundary between real and mediated lives, and between information and entertainment. Apathy and anomie in the social order rise as trust in dominant institutions falls, though some media analysts have found in this situation the emergence of a possibly different kind of civic culture (Dahlgren, 2000).

Given that the public sphere, however we define or criticize it, is essentially a mediated public sphere,[6] the question arises not only as to how to make sense of its functioning but also how to generate normative criteria for its improvement and regulation. In this area perhaps more than any other in media research, the debates shade into questions of ethics, policy and political action.

As Jürgen Habermas (1992) himself notes in reviewing his earlier position on the effects of the mass mediation on the conduct of political life and the quality of democracy, the position is both complex and contradictory. On the one hand, drawing on the example of television's role in the dismantling of communism in the German Democratic Republic, Czechoslovakia and Romania, he points to how these should be 'properly considered not merely as a historical process that happened to be shown on television but one whose very *mode of occurrence* was televisual' (1992: 456). On the other hand, he suggests that the kind of media determinism offered by Joshua Meyrowitz (1985) misses the point of this complexity by ignoring the range of changes in society which accompany the palpable loss of place in modernity: 'There is considerable evidence attesting to the ambivalent nature of the democratic potential of a public sphere whose infrastructure is marked by the growing constraints imposed by electronic mass communication' (1992: 456–7).

The mass media provide an infrastructure for public participation and debate, or at least they have done so in societies where public service systems dedicated to universal access have emerged and where most households have their own television set. They have provided, historically, in their programming, their schedules and their communicative ethos, a cultural framework for collective identification (Scannell, 1996, 2000), even though this seems now threatened in an increasingly digital age of multiple channels and fragmenting tastes. At the same time the mass media have created an intensely mediated political culture, both carnival and cannibal, which is systematically undermining the legitimacy of established political institutions, and in which politics becomes increasingly a matter of representation (images in place of …) rather than representation (action on behalf of …). New technologies, especially the Internet, are being seen by many as having, in their capacity to enable interactivity, the potential to create new forms of political dialogue and participation, though once again opinions vary as to whether this will lead to a strengthening of existing democratic institutions or their replacement by new forms of political action. Early experiments and studies have proved to be still quite inconclusive, and there are significant ongoing debates as to the various merits of direct, deliberative and representative democracy and as to how the new media can be mobilized to enhance them (Hacker and van Dijk, 2000).

TECHNOLOGY AND MEDIA CHANGE

Technology is the defining characteristic of mediation, though by technology is meant more than the machine. Technologies involve networks, skills and knowledge. Technology is *techne* (Heidegger, 1977): an endless matter of unlocking, transforming, storing, distributing, switching about and regulating knowledges and practices.[7] Technology is also magic: enchantment. It is the focus of a global culture's dreams and fears: both perceived threat and anticipated saviour. Media technologies are

both the focus of these dreams and fears as well as instruments of their perpetration. In a digital world media technologies are being redefined and reclassified, as either (or both) information and communication technologies, signalling a shift in content and function, as well as a recognition that changes of quite a fundamental kind are under way in their role at the centre of social life. Such rewiring and rewriting raise the question of what indeed is new about new media.

Pursuing such a question involves a deliberation on different approaches to technological innovation as well as on the theories of the relationship between technology and social change. Raymond Williams's (1974) account of the development of radio as a broadcast medium stresses that it emerged initially as a result of generalized social needs, those of commerce, trade and empire; but that it was subsequently shaped for increasingly dispersing and suburbanizing urban populations. Its first appearance, in the late nineteenth century, was as a two-way communication device replicating, but also advancing, telegraphy and in some senses at least, telephony. Its second incarnation, after the First World War, was configured as a one-to-many device mobilized by the state and capital as an instrument of solidarity and selling. Such a shifting and a settling of the communicative infrastructure of the modern state was decisive in defining a century's national cultures, and told the lie to any crude theory of technological determinism both here and elsewhere in media history.

The radio story has been one of invented needs and significant appropriations, and when it comes to technological innovation in media and communications it still is. Whereas television followed radio's suit, a more or less seamless shift from one broadcast instrument to another, the consequences of its total cultural dominance in the last fifty years of the century could not entirely be predicted, nor was it the case that populations did not have to learn how to use it, or how to incorporate it into their everyday lives (Spigel, 1992). Media technologies are doubly articulated into the social: both as technologies whose symbolic and functional characteristics claim a place in both institutional and individual practice, but also as media, conveying through the whole range of their communication the values, rules and rhetorics of their centrality for the conduct of the quotidian. We learn through the media why the media are important. We learn through the media how to become consumers of media, and indeed of much else besides. In such can be seen to lie society's total dependence on these increasingly intrusive and ubiquitous machines.

As Carolyn Marvin (1988: 8) has noted in her study of a previous moment in the history of media innovation, 'Media are not fixed natural objects; they have no natural edges. They are constructed as complexes of habits, beliefs and procedures embedded in elaborate cultural codes of communication. The history of media is never more or less than the history of their uses, which always lead us away from them to the social practices and conflicts they illuminate.' Such history, and, one might add also such present and future, 'is less the evolution of technical efficiencies in communication than a series of arenas for negotiating issues crucial to the conduct of social life; among them, who is inside and outside, who may speak, who may not, and who has authority and who may be believed' (1988: 4).

Whereas, then, the story of twentieth-century media culture has for the most part been that of broadcasting, and in the particular terms in which I have discussed the idea, a century of mediation, the twenty-first century might involve – it is certainly being claimed to involve – the return of communication. In John Durham Peters's (1999) terms the pendulum might be seen now to be swinging from gospel to conversation. Only this time the conversation is mediated, on a global scale, in text and in image, by the Internet.

Interactivity arguably offers a new hybridity. But at the same time, from the perspective of communication theory, and indeed from a perspective that takes as its starting point the social and social-psychological theories in which the field was grounded, and this chapter begun, there is not so much, arguably, that is new. The supposedly distinct characteristics of new media – digital convergence, many-to-many

communication, interactivity, globalization, virtuality – are perhaps not quite as novel as they are often believed to be. Face-to-face communication is simultaneous and interactive and does not need a mouse. Globalization is prefigured in both cinematic and televisual culture. Those excluded from full participation in media culture are mostly still excluded. And any entry into electronic space has always presupposed and required a physical and a bodily space as both its beginning and end point. Quantity (especially immediacy and speed), certainly, turns into quality in the matter of communication. Yet this would be the case not just for the Internet but for all media networks. Media change is simultaneously therefore both incremental and radical. Evolutions and revolutions will always shade one into the other.

So if the history and sociology of media technology are a history and a sociology of its uses, there is much to do to understand the particular social consequences of the potential inscribed in the latest digital devices and systems. Whereas much recent work has investigated such key sociological concepts as identity and community and has also found in cyberspace new expressions of, and practices in, economic activity, there is still very little that confronts the relationship between off-line and on-line worlds, and which seeks to make sense of the *socio-logics* of media innovation in this, the core activity of the human race (but see Miller and Slater, 2000).

MEDIATION AND THE MORAL SELF

Bewailing the failure of sociology to address a moral agenda in a technologically pockmarked world of wants and obstacles to their immediate gratification, Zygmunt Bauman points to the disappearance of the moral self both in life and in literature (1993: 198). Others, however, are beginning to examine the moral dimensions of mediation (Boltanski, 1999; Silverstone, in press; Stevenson, 1999; Tester, 2001). At issue are the consequences of the media's capacity to bring people together while simultaneously keeping them apart. At issue too is the capacity of those who receive communications from a world otherwise out of reach to find and act on a moral response to what they see and hear.

Distance is at the heart of the matter, and creating what has been called proximity (Bauman, 1993; Levinas, 1969), or proper distance (Silverstone, 2003) has been seen as being a crucial component of what it is to be moral, to have the capacity to act ethically, in a world of intense and eternal mediation. Levinas's notion of proximity preserves the link between, but crucially also the separation of, self and other, a separation which ensures the possibility of both respect and responsibility for the other. The concept of proper distance is intended to sensitize us to the ambiguities in our relationships to the other, ambiguities that are significantly overdetermined both in broadcast and cyber space.

The media have always fulfilled the function of creating some sense of proper distance, or at least they have tried, or claimed to be able, to do so. The reporting of world events, the production of news, the fictional representation of the past, the critical interrogation of the private lives of public figures, the exploration of the ordinariness of everyday life, all involve in one way or another a negotiation between the familiar and the strange, as the media try, forlornly, to resolve the essential ambiguities of contemporary life.

One of their crucial tasks, as has already been suggested, is to create some kind of comfort and pleasure for those on the receiving end of such mediations, some comfort and pleasure in the appearance of the strange as not too strange and the familiar as not too familiar. However, such mediations also tend to produce, in practice, a kind of polarization in the determinations of such distance – that the unfamiliar is either pushed to a point beyond strangeness, beyond reach and beyond humanity on the one hand (the Iraqi leadership during both the Gulf war and the invasion of Iraq); or drawn so close as to be indistinguishable from ourselves on the other (the many representations of the everyday lives of citizens in other countries, as if the latter were in every respect just like us; or in the incorporation of the 'primitive' and the 'exotic' into Western advertising (Silverstone, 1999). Indifference and guilt vie with each other as consequences of such mediation.

As both Baudrillard (1995) and Luhmann (2000) suggest, in a world in which information is seen to replace knowledge, and reporting substitutes for understanding, it becomes impossible for the receivers of communication to think and act in a meaningful and morally sustainable way. The mediated other makes no demands on us, because we have the power to switch it off, and to withdraw. But for us as moral beings this is something we cannot do. We should not be able to switch it off. 'Responsibility is silenced once proximity is eroded; it may eventually be replaced with resentment once the fellow human subject is transformed into an [o]ther' (Bauman, 1989: 184).

It is suggested, of course, that the new media, especially the Internet, shift the nature of the problem precisely in so far as they enable direct one-to-oneness, or many-to-manyness, through e-mails and chat-rooms and various kinds of groupware. The Internet's claim for interactivity is central and essential (Downes and McMillan, 2000). But the notion of interactivity begs a number of questions, above all about its capacity to connect interlocutors in new and significant ways. It also raises the question of the moral status of those who communicate with each other, and of the ethical status of the kind of communications that are generated on-line. But whereas the latter has been much discussed in addressing practices of gender disguise and similar on-line activities (O'Brien, 1999), the former, the pursuit of the moral self, has been much less the focus of attention. It is of course much more difficult.

CONCLUSION: THE SOCIOLOGY OF MEDIATION

The increasing centrality of media for the exercise of power as well as for the conduct of everyday life in modern society, both for system and for life-world, as well as, crucially, their inter-relationship (Rasmussen, 1996), has drawn the study of mediation to the centre of the sociological agenda. The analysis of mediation, as I have suggested, requires us to understand how the processes of mediated communication shape both society and culture, as well as the relationships that participants, both individual and institutional, have to their environment and to each other. At the same time such analysis requires a consideration of how social and cultural activity in turn mediates the mediations, as institutions and technologies as well as the meanings that are delivered by them are appropriated through reception and consumption.

Mediation, in this double sense, is both literal and metaphorical. The boundaries around media technologies may be visible when we look at the machine or gaze at the screen, but they have become entirely blurred in practice, in use and in fantasy, and as they become incorporated into, or unsettle, the rituals of everyday life. As the borders between real and imagined worlds, between self and other, and between the analysis of, and participation in, media culture become increasingly problematic, both the substantive and methodological challenges posed by the presence of media and communication technologies and systems in contemporary society quickly outrun an otherwise containing and comforting agenda. This is not quite the reductive assumption it appears, however. For the media have to be explained as social just as they are required to be a part of the explanation of the social. What seems now, however, absolutely clear, is that they cannot be ignored.

NOTES

1 Jesus-Martin Barbero (1993) uses the notion of mediation to characterize a set of more specific cultural processes crucially involving social movements and their capacity to resist and to negotiate the otherwise singular communications of the mass media: 'communication began to be seen more as a process of mediations than of media, a question of culture and, therefore, not just a matter of cognitions but of re-cognition. The processes of recognition were at the heart of a new methodological approach which enabled us to perceive communication from a quite different perspective, from its "other" side,

namely, reception. This revealed to us the resistances and the varied ways people appropriate media content according to manner of use' (1993: 2). Barbero calls on Raymond Williams to provide his epigraph.

2 My colleague Nick Couldry has pointed out that it is only when we have a concept of mediation that we can start thinking about how mediation works in different ways and different places (cf. Curran and Park, 2000; Downing, 1996). I am indebted to him for a number of helpful comments and bibliographic suggestions, not just this one.

3 'In this strand the mass media disseminate ignorance in the form of facts which must continually be renewed so that no one notices. We are used to daily news, but we should be aware nonetheless of the evolutionary improbability of such an assumption. If it is the idea of surprise, of something new, interesting and newsworthy which we associate with news, then it would seem much more sensible not to report it in the same format every day, but to wait for something to happen and then to publicise it. This happened in the sixteenth century in the form of broadsides, ballads or crime stories spawned in the wake of executions etc.' (Luhmann, 2000: 25).

4 Controversy in the UK in 2000, of some considerable intensity, over Independent Television's shifting of the time of the nightly news bulletin and the BBC's radical response to do likewise is evidence of the centrality of the ritual character of news, and of the horror generated by changes to that ritualization in everyday life.

5 Community is of course an intensely thorny concept in sociology, and the following discussion glosses over a century of discussion and argument. Craig Calhoun (1998), in a paper exploring the links between the sociology of community and the virtual, offers a characterization which provides a useful touchstone: 'Community life can be understood as the life people live in dense, multiplex, relatively autonomous networks of social relationships … Community, thus, is not a place or simply a small-scale population aggregate, but a mode of relating, variable in extent. Though communities may be larger than the immediate personal networks of individuals, they can in principle be understood by an extension of the same life-world terms. …' (1998: 391). *Doing* community is my way of framing community as performative, as a claim rather than an achievement.

6 'It is not that the media "control" politics as such, rather that they have come to create and constitute the space in which politics now chiefly happens for most people in so called "advanced" societies … Whether we like it or not, in order to engage in the political debate we must now do so through the media' (Castells, 1997: 311).

7 '"[T]echnology" refers to the set of practices whose purpose is, through ever more radical interventions into nature (physical, biological and human), systematically to place the future at our disposal. And technology does so, by and large, … through hastening the achievement of a goal located in the future; through control of what occurs in the future; and through maintaining a given state while containing and reducing the period of deviations from it' (Simpson, 1995: 24).

REFERENCES

Abercrombie, Nicholas and Longhurst, Brian (1998) *Audiences*. London: Sage.

Anderson, Benedict (1983) *Imagined Communities: Reflections on the Origin and Spread of Nationalism*. London: Verso.

Ang, Ien (1986) *Watching Dallas: Soap Opera and the Melodramatic Imagination*. London: Routledge.

Appadurai, Arjun (1996) *Modernity at Large*. Minneapolis, MN: University of Minnesota Press.

Bagdikian, Ben H. (1997) *The Media Monopoly*, 5th edn. Boston, MA: Beacon Press.

Barbero, Jesus-Martin (1993) *Communication, Culture and Hegemony: From the Media to Mediations*. London: Sage.

Baudrillard, Jean (1983) *Simulations*. New York: Semiotext(e).

Baudrillard, Jean (1995) *The Gulf War Did Not Take Place*. Sydney: Power Publications.

Bauman, Zygmunt (1989) *Modernity and the Holocaust*. Cambridge: Polity Press.

Bauman, Zygmunt (1993) *Postmodern Ethics*. Cambridge: Polity Press.

Beck, Ulrich (1992) *Risk Society: Towards a New Modernity*. London: Sage.

Bird, S. Elizabeth and Dardenne, Robert W. (1988) 'Myth, chronicle, and story: exploring the narrative qualities of news', in James W. Carey (ed.), *Media, Myths and Narratives*. Newbury Park, CA: Sage. pp. 67–87.

Blumer, Herbert (1933) *Movies and Conduct*. New York: Macmillan.

Blumler, Jay G. and Katz, Elihu (eds) (1974) *The Uses of Mass Communications: Current Perspectives on Gratifications Research*. London: Sage.

Boltanski, Luc (1999) *Distant Suffering: Morality, Media and Politics*. Cambridge: Cambridge University Press.

Buckingham, David (1987) *Public Secrets: Eastenders and its Audience*. London: British Film Institute.

Buckingham, David (1993) *Children Talking Television: The Making of Television Literacy*. London: Falmer Press.

Buckingham, David (2000) *The Making of Citizens*. London: Routledge.

Burke, Kenneth (1955) *A Grammar of Motives*. New York: George Braziller.

Calhoun, Craig (1998) 'Community without propinquity revisited: communications technology and the transformation of the urban public sphere', *Sociological Inquiry*, 68 (3): 373–97.

Carey, James W. (1989) *Communication as Culture: Essays on Media and Society*. London: Unwin Hyman.

Castells, Manuel (1996) *The Rise of the Network Society*. Oxford: Blackwell.

Castells, Manuel (1997) *The Power of Identity*. Oxford: Blackwell.

Chalaby, Jean K. (1999) *The Invention of Journalism*. Basingstoke: Macmillan.

Cohen, Anthony (1985) *The Symbolic Construction of Community*. Chichester and London: Ellis Harwood and Tavistock.

Comstock, George, Chafee, Steven, Katzman, Nathan, McCombs, Maxwell and Roberts, Donald (1978) *Television and Human Behavior*. New York: Columbia University Press.

Corner, John (1995) *Television Form and Public Address*. London: Edward Arnold.

Couldry, Nick (2000) *The Place of Media Power*. London: Routledge.

Curran, James (2000) 'Rethinking media and democracy', in James Curran and Michael Gurevitch (eds), *Mass Media and Society*, 3rd edn. London: Edward Arnold. pp. 120–54.

Curran, James and Park, Myung-Jin (eds) (2000) *De-Westernising Media Studies*. London: Routledge.

Dahlgren, Peter (2000) 'Media, citizenship and civic culture', in James Curran and Michael Gurevitch (eds), *Mass Media and Society*, 3rd edn. London: Edward Arnold. pp. 310–28.

Dayan, Daniel (1999) 'Media and diasporas', in Jostein Gripsrud (ed.), *Television and Common Knowledge*. London: Routledge. pp. 18–33.

Dayan, Daniel and Katz, Elihu (1992) *Media Events: The Live Broadcasting of History*. Cambridge, MA: Harvard University Press.

Debray, Regis (2000) *Transmitting Culture*. New York: Columbia University Press.

Dewey, John (1958) *Experience and Nature*. New York: Dover Publications.

Downes, Edward J. and McMillan, Sally J. (2000) 'Defining interactivity: a qualitative identification of key dimensions', *New Media and Society*, 2 (2): 157–80.

Downing, John (1996) *Internationalising Media Theory*. London: Sage.

Downing, John (2000) *Radical Media: Rebellious Communication and Social Movements*. London: Sage.

Duncan, Hugh Dalziel (1962) *Communication and Social Order*. Oxford: Oxford University Press.

Eisenstein, Elizabeth (1978) *The Printing Press as an Agent of Social Change*, 2 vols. Cambridge: Cambridge University Press.

Eliasoph, Nina (1998) *Avoiding Politics: How Americans Produce Apathy in Everyday Life.* Cambridge: Cambridge University Press.

Fiske, John (1987) *Television Culture.* London: Methuen.

Fiske, John (1990) 'Ethnosemiotics: some personal and theoretical reflections', *Cultural Studies*, 4 (1): 85–99.

Galtung, Johan and Ruge, Mari Holmboe (1969) 'The structure of foreign news', in Jeremy Tunstall (ed.), *Media Sociology.* London: Constable. pp. 259–98.

Garnham, Nicholas (2000) *Emancipation, the Media, and Modernity.* Oxford: Oxford University Press.

Gerbner, George, Gross, Larry, Morgan, Michael and Signorielli, Nancy (1980) 'The "mainstreaming" of America: violence profile No. 11', *Journal of Communication*, 28 (3): 176–207.

Gerbner, George et al. (1986) 'Living with television: the dynamics of the cultivation process', in Jennings Bryant and D. Zillman (eds), *Perspectives on Media Effects.* Hillsdale, NJ: Lawrence Erlbaum. pp. 17–40.

Giddens, Anthony (1990) *The Consequences of Modernity.* Cambridge: Polity Press.

Giddens, Anthony (1991) *Modernity and Self-Identity: Self and Society in the Late Modern Age.* Cambridge: Polity Press.

Gieber, W. (1964) 'Across the desk: a study of 16 *Telegraph* Editors', *Journalism Quarterly*, 33: 423–33.

Gillespie, Marie (1995) *Television, Ethnicity and Cultural Change.* London: Routledge.

Giner, Salvador (1976) *Mass Society.* London: Martin Robertson.

Glasgow Media Group (1976) *Bad News.* London: Routledge & Kegan Paul.

Golding, Peter and Murdock, Graham (2000) 'Culture, communications and political economy', in James Curran and Michael Gurevitch (eds), *Mass Media and Society*, 3rd edn. London: Edward Arnold. pp. 70–92.

Goody, Jack (1977) *The Domestication of the Savage Mind.* Cambridge: Cambridge University Press.

Gunter, Barrie (1987) *Poor Reception: Misunderstanding and Forgetting Broadcast News.* Hillsdale: Lawrence Erlbaum.

Habermas, Jürgen (1989) *The Structural Transformation of the Public Sphere.* Cambridge: Polity Press.

Habermas, Jürgen (1992) 'Further reflections on the public sphere', in Craig Calhoun (ed.), *Habermas and the Public Sphere.* Cambridge, MA: Harvard University Press. pp. 421–61.

Hacker, Kenneth, L. and van Dijk, Jan A.G.M. (eds) (2000) *Digital Democracy.* London: Sage.

Hall, Stuart (1977) 'Culture, the media and the ideological effect', in James Curran et al. (eds), *Mass Communication and Society.* London: Edward Arnold, pp. 315–48.

Heidegger, Martin (1977) *The Question Concerning Technology and Other Essays.* London: Garland.

Held, David, McGrew, Anthony, Goldblatt, David and Perraton, Jonathan (1999) *Global Transformations: Politics, Economics and Culture.* Cambridge: Polity Press.

Hodge, Bob and Tripp, David (1986) *Children and Television.* Cambridge: Polity Press.

Horkheimer, Max and Adorno, Theodor (1972) *The Dialectic of Enlightenment.* New York: Seabury Press.

Hovland, C.L., Lumsdaine, A.A. and Sheffield, F.D. (1965) *Experiments in Mass Communication.* New York: John Wiley.

Innis, Harold A. (1972) *Empire and Communications.* Toronto: University of Toronto Press.

Innis, Harold A. (1973) *The Bias of Communications.* Toronto: University of Toronto Press.

Katz, Elihu (1980) 'On conceptualising media effects', *Studies in Communication*, 1: 119–41.

Katz, Elihu and Lazarsfeld, Paul (1955) *Personal Influence: The Part Played by People in Mass Communication.* New York: The Free Press.

Kraut, Robert, Lundmark, Vicki, Patterson, Michael, Kiesler, Sara, Mukojadhyay, Tritas and Scherlis, William (1998) 'Internet paradox: a social technology that reduces social investment and psychological well-being', *American Psychologist*, 53 (9): 1017–31.

Kubey, Robert and Csikszentmihalyi, Mihalyi (1990) *Television and the Quality of Life: How Viewing Shapes Everyday Experience.* Hillsdale, NJ: Lawrence Erlbaum.

Lasch, Christopher (1980) *The Culture of Narcissism.* London: Sphere.

Lasswell, Harold (1948) 'The structure and function of communication in society', in L. Bryson (ed.), *The Communication of Ideas.* New York: Harper. pp. 32–51.

Levinas, Emmanuel (1969) *Totality and Infinity: An Essay on Exteriority.* Pittsburgh: Dusquene University Press.

Lewis, Justin Wren (1991) *The Ideological Octopus: An Exploration of Television and its Audience.* London: Routledge.

Liebes, Tamar (1997) *Reporting the Israeli–Arab Conflict.* London: Routledge.

Liebes, Tamar and Katz, Elihu (1990) *The Export of Meaning.* Oxford: Oxford University Press.

Livingstone, Sonia (1990) *Making Sense of Television: The Psychology of Audience Interpretation*. Oxford: Pergamon Press.

Lloyd, John (2004) *What the Media are Doing to Our Politics*. London: Constable.

Lodziak, Conrad (1986) *The Power of Television: A Critical Appraisal*. London: Frances Pinter.

Luhmann, Niklas (2000) *The Reality of the Mass Media*. Cambridge: Polity Press.

Mander, Jerry (1978) *Four Arguments for the Elimination of Television*. Brighton: Harvester Press.

Marvin, Carolyn (1988) *When Old Technologies Were New: Thinking About Communications in the Late Nineteenth Century*. Oxford: Oxford University Press.

McQuail, Denis (1984) *Communication*, 2nd edn. London: Longman.

McQuail, Denis (1994) *Mass Communication Theory*, 3rd edn. London: Sage.

McLuhan, Marshall and Fiore, Quentin (1967) *The Medium is the Massage*. New York: Bantam Books.

McLuhan, Marshall and Fiore, Quentin (1968) *War and Peace in the Global Village*. New York: Bantam Books.

Mead, George Herbert (1964 [1932]) *Mind, Self and Society*. Chicago: University of Chicago Press.

Meyrowitz, Joshua (1985) *No Sense of Place: The Impact of Electronic Media on Social Behavior*. New York: Oxford University Press.

Miller, Daniel and Slater, Don (2000) *The Internet: An Ethnographic Approach*. Oxford: Berg.

Moore, Sally Falk and Myerhoff, Barbara (eds) (1977) *Secular Ritual*. Amsterdam: Van Gorcum.

Morley, David (1980) *The 'Nationwide' Audience*. London: British Film Institute.

Morley, David (1992) *Television, Audiences and Cultural Studies*. London: Routledge.

Naficy, Hamid (1993) *The Making of Exile Cultures: Iranian Television in Los Angeles*. Minneapolis: University of Minnesota Press.

O'Brien, Jodi (1999) 'Writing in the Body: Gender (re)production in online interaction', in Marc A. Smith and Peter Kollock (eds), *Communities in Cyberspace*. London: Routledge. pp. 76–104.

Park, Robert Ezra (1972) *The Crowd and the Public*. Chicago: University of Chicago Press.

Peters, John Durham (1999) *Speaking into the Air: A History of the Idea of Communication*. Chicago: University of Chicago Press.

Philo, Greg (1990) *Seeing and Believing: The Influence of Television*. London: Routledge.

Postman, Neil (1986) *Amusing Ourselves to Death: Public Discourse in the Age of Show Business*. London: Heinemann.

Putnam, Robert D. (2000) *Bowling Alone: The Collapse and Revival of American Community*. New York: Simon and Schuster.

Rodriguez, Clemencia (2001) *Fissures in the Mediascape*. New York: Hampton Press.

Rasmussen, Terje (1996) *Communication Technologies and the Mediation of Social Life*. IMK-report No. 16. Oslo: University of Oslo.

Rosenberg, Bernard and White, David Manning (1957) *Mass Culture: The Popular Arts in America*. New York: The Free Press.

Rothenbuhler, Eric W. (1998) *Ritual Communication: From Everyday Conversation to Mediated Ceremony*. London: Sage.

Scannell, Paddy (1988) 'Radio times: the temporal arrangements of broadcasting in the modern world', in Phillip Drummond and Richard Paterson (eds), *Television and its Audience: International Research Perspectives*. London: British Film Institute.

Scannell, Paddy (1996) *Radio, Television and Modern Life*. Oxford: Blackwell.

Scannell, Paddy (2000) 'For-anyone-as-someone structures', *Media, Culture and Society*, 22 (1): 5–24.

Scannell, Paddy and Cardiff, David (1991) *A Social History of British Broadcasting: Vol. 1: 1922–1939: Serving the Nation*. Oxford: Blackwell.

Schlesinger, Philip (1978) *Putting 'Reality' Together: BBC News*. London: Constable.

Schudson, Michael (2000) 'The sociology of news production revisited (again)', in James Curran and Michael Gurevitch (eds), *Mass Media and Society*, 3rd edn. London: Edward Arnold. pp. 175–200.

Seiter, Ellen (1999) *Television and New Media Audiences*. Oxford: Oxford University Press.

Sennett, Rchard (1977) *The Fall of Public Man*. New York: Knopf.

Shanahan, James and Morgan, Michael (1999) *Television and its Viewers: Cultivation Theory and Research*. Cambridge: Cambridge University Press.

Silverstone, Roger (1999) *Why Study the Media?* London: Sage.

Silverstone, Roger (2000) 'Los nuevos medios y la comunidad', *Intersecciones/Communicación*, No. 1 Segunda Epoca, pp. 25–50.

Silverstone, Roger (2001) 'Finding a voice: minorities, media and the global commons', *Emergences: Journal for the Study of Media and Composite Cultures*, 11 (1): 13–28.

Silverstone, Roger (2003) 'Proper distance: towards an ethics for cyberspace', in Gunnar Liestøl, Andrew Morrison, Terje Rasmussen (eds), *Digital Media Revisited: Theoretical and Conceptual Innovations in Digital Domains*. Cambridge, MA: The MIT Press. pp. 468–90.

Silverstone, Roger (in press) *Morality and Media*. Cambridge: Polity Press.

Simpson, Lorenzo C. (1995) *Technology, Time and the Conversations of Modernity*. London: Routledge.

Spigel, Lynn (1992) *Make Room for TV: Television and the Family Ideal in Post-war America*. Chicago: University of Chicago Press.

Stevenson, Nick (1999) *The Transformation of the Media: Globalisation, Morality and Ethics*. London: Longman.

Tester, Keith (ed.) (2001) *Compassion, Morality and the Media*. Buckingham: Open University Press.

Thompson, John B. (1990) *Ideology and Modern Culture: Critical Social Theory in the Era of Mass Communication*. Cambridge: Polity Press.

Thompson, John B. (1995) *The Media and Modernity: A Social Theory of the Media*. Cambridge: Polity Press.

Thompson, John B. (2000) *Scandal*. Cambridge: Polity Press.

Thussu, Daya (2000) *International Communication: Continuity and Change*. London: Edward Arnold.

Tomlinson, John (1999) *Globalization and Culture*. Cambridge: Polity Press.

Tuchman, Gaye (1978) *Making News: A Study in the Construction of Reality*. New York: The Free Press.

Turner, Victor W. (1969) *The Ritual Process*. London: Routledge & Kegan Paul.

Virilio, Paul (1986) *Speed and Politics*. New York: Semiotext(e).

Wark, Mackenzie (1994) *Virtual Geography*. Bloomington, IN: Indiana University Press.

White, David Manning (1950) 'The gatekeeper: a case study in the selection of news', *Journalism Quarterly*, 27: 383–90.

Williams, Raymond (1974) *Television, Technology and Cultural Form*. London: Fontana.

Zelizer, Barbie and Allan, Stuart (2002) *Journalism After September 11*. London: Routledge.

11

An Entirely Different World? Challenges for the Sociology of Race and Ethnicity

PATRICIA HILL COLLINS

For many around the globe, the events of 11 September 2001 ushered in an entirely different world. September 11 may also reveal how the sociology of race and ethnicity has misunderstood the racial/ethnic politics of the post-Second World War era. As Jalali and Lipset flatly assert, 'race and ethnicity provide the most striking example of a general failure among experts to anticipate social developments in varying types of societies' (1998: 317). Much evidence supports their thesis. For example, because it assumed that the importance of ethnicity would decrease in conjunction with modernization, the sociology of race and ethnicity seemed unprepared for the resurgence of racial/ethnic conflict in the 1990s. Conflicts in places as diverse as Yugoslavia, Rwanda, Canada, Sri Lanka and Malaysia challenged the theoretical consensus among Marxist and non-Marxist scholars alike that industrialization, urbanization and education would foster racial and ethnic group integration into emerging democracies (Jalali and Lipset, 1998). American sociology provides an especially glaring example of this myopia. Its preoccupation with racial attitudes held by White Americans apparently blinded it to the rumblings of African American unrest in its own backyard that exploded into sit-ins, marches, protest rallies and a sustained civil rights movement. As James McKee points out, 'the sociologists of race relations had not simply failed to predict a specific event; rather, they had grievously misread a significant historical development. The race relations that appeared in their writings were incongruent with the race relations to be found in the society around them' (McKee, 1993: 2).

Why has a field whose mission remains the study of social relations of race and ethnicity been repeatedly caught off guard by racial and ethnic conflict? More importantly, in what ways can the sociology of race and ethnicity better analyze how race and ethnicity influence such conflicts? Because these are large questions, this two-part chapter can only sketch out some preliminary answers. In the first part, I examine the relationship between the sociology of race and ethnicity, a sub-specialty within sociology that is housed across a confederation of 'national sociologies', and the increasing significance of the interdisciplinary study of race and ethnicity.[1] I suggest that the historical organization of the sociology of race and ethnicity limits its ability, in isolation, to generate paradigms that adequately explain its own subject matter. At the same time, the burgeoning interdisciplinary field of race and ethnic studies does advance alternative analyses, but an overemphasis on the methodological approaches of humanities and interpretive social science limits its progress. Bridging the gap between these two general areas of inquiry might strengthen both.

In the second part of the chapter, I ask what distinctive contributions the *sociology* of race and ethnicity might offer to the broader study of race and ethnicity. I sketch out two possible directions: (1) developing more complex analyses of the concepts of race and ethnicity that might inform interdisciplinary scholarship, in particular, paradigms of intersectionality; and (2) demonstrating the significance of race and ethnicity as socially structured, institutionalized phenomena in national and transnational contexts. The chapter concludes with a brief discussion of how these new directions might revitalize a commitment to analyzing and solving important social problems, in this case, racial and ethnic conflict.

BRIDGING THE GAP: NATIONAL SOCIOLOGIES AND THE INTERDISCIPLINARY STUDY OF RACE AND ETHNICITY

Studying race and ethnicity from a variety of disciplinary vantage points is not new. Prior to the Second World War, biology, medicine, anthropology, sociology, psychology, law and political science all studied race and/or ethnicity simply because these topics constituted unavoidable elements of their fields (Ross, 1991). Because no compelling reason existed for sustained scholarly collaboration across disciplinary boundaries, academic disciplines agreed to respect each other's academic turf. Believing that objectivity, rationality, and the importance of empirical evidence in scientific research would excise from the scientific research process the seeming biases associated with race and ethnicity themselves, Western

science aimed for a science of society. New scientific knowledge would help better society. Western science certainly produced remarkable technological advances. But as philosophers of race and science remind us, academic disciplines generally failed to achieve their value-neutral aspirations and, during their formative periods, were complicit in reproducing slavery, colonialism and similar racial and/or ethnic hierarchies (Stepan, 1982).

This political and intellectual context framed late-nineteenth- and early-twentieth-century sociology. From the outside, it might have appeared that the science of sociology operated as a seamless whole. In actuality, national histories that distinguished the UK, France, the United States, Germany and other Western nation-states from one another fostered 'national sociologies' with accompanying 'national sociologies of race and ethnicity.' As a result, the sub-disciplinary specialty of race and ethnicity within various national sociologies reflected the distinctive characteristics of their nation-states. At the same time, from the perspective of non-Western populations that were often objects of study, these established national sociologies of race and ethnicity functioned as a transnational, hegemonic discourse unified under the banner of sociology as science.

Currently, established national sociologies of race and ethnicity face several formidable tasks. For one, they can no longer turn inward, attending primarily to the issues of their own national interests. Globalization and transnationalism have greatly changed the contours of labor markets, families, cities and other social phenomena as well as the distribution of racial/ethnic populations across borders. Working solely within nation-state borders limits national sociologies' ability to understand these trends as well as the workings of race and ethnicity within their individual national borders. For another, national sociologies can no longer operate as a closed confederation among a small number of nationally based sociological practitioners. European and American sociologies must acknowledge the growth of national sociologies of race and ethnicity in India, South Africa, Brazil, Israel, Cuba and similar independent nation-states where sociology itself as well as the sociology of race and ethnicity play a different role in nation-state development.

On a fundamental level, the sociology of race and ethnicity often fails to understand important social phenomena because its contemporary organization reflects this history. It is important to stress that during its foundational years and for approximately eighty years thereafter, the sociology of race and ethnicity constituted a field where European and American Whites conducted research on or about peoples indigenous to North America, Africa, Asia, the Middle East, the Caribbean and Latin America, largely with little to no input from the affected populations. Clearly, within these exclusionary practices, the themes, paradigms and methodologies defining this sub-field emanated from within the worldview of a remarkably homogeneous community of practitioners. Whiteness as a 'race' was erased, leaving people of color as the 'others' who were intensely 'raced'. Whether the ethnicity of Italians, Irish, Jews and other white ethnics in the United States, or the ethnic cultures carried by Commonwealth immigrants to the United Kingdom, ethnicity became associated with less developed people of all sorts. Lacking race and ethnicity (for example, possessing whiteness) signaled modernity whereas being assigned race and/or claiming ethnicity signified a less modern, underdeveloped status.

As a result of this history, the sociology of race and ethnicity generally failed to account for two critical factors, namely, the saliency of racial/ethnic identities of all sorts, including biological and/or cultural whiteness, and the meaning of racial/ethnic conflicts that are situated in this context. These limitations occurred primarily because sociologists either did not consider these issues as central to society and/or because they had a vested interest in believing that conflict could be managed via rational planning. For example, a belief in assimilation as the guiding paradigm of race relations helps buttress existing racial hierarchies. Within this logic, when isolated and/or backward racial/ethnic groups assimilate and learn the ways of wider society, race and

ethnicity will disappear as important features of social life. Freeing individuals from racial/ethnic groups and from the fetters of stifling group membership would enable them to claim their rightful place in society. Yet the principle of assimilation has also been accompanied by parallel beliefs that some racial groups are biologically and/or culturally incapable of assimilation (African Americans in the United States), and that some ethnic groups refuse to relinquish their culture and thus remain resistant to assimilation (South Asian ethnic groups in the UK and Latino/a groups in the United States). In Latin American countries, the concept of 'whitening' combines biology and culture to produce a distinctive form of assimilation that upholds racial hierarchy. In Brazil, for example, darker-skinned individuals are encouraged to marry well to produce 'lighter' children who will be better positioned to move up within the social class system. Efforts to claim that racism and/or ethnic intimidation will disappear when the dispossessed become more acceptable to the majority, or when they become 'whitened', or when capitalist marketplace relations are unencumbered by state interference (affirmative action), say more about the world-views of researchers themselves than about racism and/or ethnic relations.

National sociologies of race and ethnicity have made important contributions, but globalization and transnationalism have greatly changed their terms of participation in the construction of knowledge. Contemporary scholarship of race and ethnicity is surprisingly eclectic and crosses many fields, including sociology. Describing the greatly changed context that has fragmented contemporary national sociologies, Donald Levine observes, 'the most interesting work now takes place within other kinds of boundaries: in subdisciplinary specialties, transdisciplinary forays, and supradisciplinary syntheses' (Levine, 1995: 292). In preparing this chapter, I sat down to consider which contemporary social locations are generating substantive theoretical and/or empirical work in the study of race and ethnicity. I was surprised to find so little scholarship done by sociologists who have been housed *exclusively* within the sub-disciplinary specialty of the sociology of race and ethnicity. Sociologists are certainly well represented in new interdisciplinary scholarship, yet thinkers who may have been trained in traditional disciplines such as sociology, but whose work reflects transdisciplinary forays, seem to be at the forefront.

In this context, the sociology of race and ethnicity neither dominates cutting-edge work in this field nor can it claim ownership over the field as it did in the past (Tucker, 1994: 103). Instead, transdisciplinary forays by a range of scholars have catalyzed entirely new overlapping and cross-fertilizing interdisciplinary fields, in particular, those of postcolonial studies, cultural studies, African-American/Latino and similar area studies, and critical race studies. Moreover, these interdisciplinary fields are raising important new questions that filter back into and challenge the assumptions framing sub-disciplinary specialties concerned with the study of race and ethnicity within history, literature, sociology, psychology, education and other traditional disciplines. These emerging areas also advance provocative 'supradisciplinary syntheses' that can emerge from the intellectual dynamism that characterizes interdisciplinary scholarship. As Bulmer and Solomos point out, 'the proliferation of new critical perspectives has radically transformed the whole field of race and ethnic studies in ways which make it difficult to see it as a single recognizable field' (Bulmer and Solomos, 1999: 3).

Take, for example, how the arguments in Edward Said's work have traveled far beyond the boundaries of his field of literary criticism to catalyze considerable scholarship in postcolonial studies (Said, 1993). By arguing that imperialism relies heavily on Western perceptions of Asian, Middle Eastern, African and other colonized peoples, and by using the field of oriental studies to examine how Western colonial powers create racial and ethnic discourses about the colonized that serve their own interests, Said spurred interest in analyzing how the ideas and actions of colonial powers fostered racial/ethnic hierarchies. Said's argument that the knowledge produced by the West more accurately reflects its own needs has

been extended in a variety of directions, among them philosopher Anthony Appiah's contention that discourses about Africa also are 'invented' by both blacks and whites (Appiah, 1992). It has also fostered interest in how racial ideas and practices have been crucial to an array of imperial projects, for example, the study of race, gender and sexuality in British imperialism (McClintock, 1995), how race and gender shaped the field of primatology (Haraway, 1989), and the construction of the idea of the 'primitive' that has been so central to understandings of modernity (Torgovnick, 1990).

Closely associated with postcolonial studies, cultural studies scholarship has also stressed the significance of ethnicity and race. In particular, British sociologist Stuart Hall's thesis of 'new ethnicities' in the 1980s clearly rejected primordial notions of ethnicity and opened up fruitful new avenues of investigation (Hall, 1983). Old ethnicities grounded in images of homeland, roots and essentialist definitions of community and identity were challenged by the actions of new immigrant communities in the UK. New ethnicities reflected the convergence of new transnational and trans-racial identifications that accompanied migration and globalization (Cohen, 1999: 5). Hall's ideas generated important new analyses of ethnicity and race that stimulated new frameworks for the study of ethnicity and race in the UK, for example, the attention paid to concepts such as hybridity (Werbner and Modood, 1997) and diaspora (Anthias, 1998; Gilroy, 1987).

The field of cultural studies has traveled far from its British roots, often in unexpected directions. Racial/ethnic women have found the frameworks of cultural studies helpful in theorizing new directions for scholarship and struggle. For example, Nigerian psychologist Amina Mama's essay 'Shedding the masks and tearing the veils: cultural studies for a postcolonial Africa' details how cultural studies provides an exciting and potentially useful space for African social science. Noting that ethnicity and religion have figured greatly in African colonial and post-colonial histories, Mama sees cultural studies as a space for theorizing culture and for incorporating gender in ways that grapple with religion and ethnicity (Mama, 1997).

Postcolonial and cultural studies emphasize ethnicity to a greater degree than race in a context of globalization and transnationalism, and their accompanying effects of migration and the creation of diasporic communities. In contrast, in the United States, African-American studies, Latino/a studies, Native American studies and Asian studies were catalyzed by historically entrenched social practices and public policies of a white settler society grounded in institutionalized racism and the need to develop counter-arguments and responses to it. These area studies reflect responses to the same civil unrest that left the sociologists of race and ethnicity scratching their heads concerning the militancy of African American, Latino, Native American and Asian students. Responding to the demands of students of color, and designed to give voice to the long silenced groups that were much studied but little understood within traditional studies of race and ethnicity, African-American, Latino, Native American and Asian studies units within higher education grew rapidly in the 1970s.

Black, Latino, Native American and Asian studies all have distinctive histories that collectively frame the study of race and ethnicity. For example, African-American studies has drawn upon rich intellectual traditions that engaged the social problem of racism, not solely from the terrain of abstract academic theory, but as a social force with palpable effects on the lived experiences of people of African descent. Historically, the field has gone through periods where it drew more heavily than others on Pan-Africanist or African diasporic frameworks. Because African Americans have such a long and distinctive history in the United States (slavery and Jim Crow segregation), racism has shaped the everyday lives of African Americans via racial segregation of housing, jobs, schooling, health care facilities and public accommodations. These same institutions have also denied African American intellectuals positions as scholars and thus made it possible for mainstream scholars to ignore African

American intellectual production, both within sociology, and in general. In response, African American intellectuals aimed to reinterpret all dimensions of African-American experience, including their own marginalization, through new paradigms. Recognizing that one important feature of domination consists in objectifying, silencing and erasing the humanity of oppressed peoples, African American intellectuals valorized the agency of people of African descent, primarily by placing their ideas, actions and interests in the center of their intellectual work.

Latino studies followed a different path. Histories of colonization, annexation, and imperialism generated different histories for the Mexican-Americans, Puerto Ricans, Cubans, Dominicans, and Central and South American groups that encompass Latinos/as in the United States. Latinos comprise an ethnic group in the eyes of the US Census that includes national-ethnic groups with very different histories. Moreover, as a population, Latinos include multiple 'races' and degrees of racial mixture among Europeans, indigenous peoples, and Africans. Latino studies reflects this mixture. In the past 30 years, Latino studies has moved from earlier models of case studies of Mexicans in the US southwest or depictions of Puerto Rican urban life to more recent work that focuses on Latino responses to processes of globalization and transnationalism. Changing economic relations between the United States and Latin American countries has produced generally favorable results for professionals, and less favorable results for poor, working class and indigenous peoples. The impact of these changes can be measured by migrations to the United States and through rebellions in places such as Chiapas, Haiti and Ecuador (Velez-Ibanez and Sampaio, 2002: 37).[2]

Also originating in the US setting, critical race studies presents a prototype for a new model of interdisciplinary collaboration that builds upon cultural studies, area studies and American social justice traditions. Originating in American legal scholarship, the burgeoning field of critical race studies has grown far beyond its origins among a small group of progressive African

American, Latino, Asian and white legal scholars. The field of critical race studies has several distinguishing features. One concerns how the field's emphasis on both race and ethnicity allows it simultaneously to investigate the continuing significance of the black/white binary understanding of race in America as well as deploy cultural studies ideas concerning new racial/ethnic formations that take ethnicity and mixed-race identities into account. Including the contributions of Latino and Asian scholars brings a much-needed critical eye that challenges the black/white binary where blacks have 'race' and whites have 'ethnicity'.

Another distinguishing feature of critical race theory is its willingness to interrogate the positivism associated with the US legal system, both on its own terms and by bringing new forms of credible evidence into the legal process. On the one hand, the field treats law as a tool for advancing a social justice agenda. The field values positivistic empiricism, primarily because it recognizes the importance that social science scholarship has had in shaping US public policy. Because law remains so fundamental to American government, developing new ways of addressing issues of social inequality through legal means potentially has great impact on actual, not imagined, systems of power. On the other hand, resonating with the valorization of the humanity of people of African descent within African-American studies, critical race studies breaks new ground by believing the stories of those who have been harmed by racial and ethnic oppression and accepting these narratives as equally credible legal evidence. For example, Mari J. Matsuda, Richard Delgado and Kimberlé Crenshaw rely on victims' narratives to interrogate the connections of hate speech to racial and ethnic violence in US society (Matsuda et al., 1993). Narrative traditions drawn from literary studies permeate the field in other ways. For example, Patricia Williams and Derrick Bell both use fiction and personal stories to construct incisive analyses of race, law and American society (Bell, 1987; Williams, 1991).

Despite their disparate histories and emphases, postcolonial studies, cultural studies,

African-American/Latino/a and similar areas studies, and critical race studies seem joined by one crucial tenet. All of these areas are grounded in cognitive models that value comparative and relational thinking. The increase in comparative work illustrates the first element of this approach. For example, several volumes compare race and ethnic relations in Europe, South Africa, Brazil and/or the United States (Hamilton et al., 2001). Sociologist Howard Winant's volume *The World Is a Ghetto: Race and Democracy since World War II* illustrates the significance of comparative frameworks (Winant, 2001). Winant raises questions concerning the meaning of race to modern history before the Second World War, and suggests that race took on different patterns within different nation-states. He then contrasts this to the post-Second World War period of postcolonialism where race and democracy are being reconfigured in a context of globalization. Winant's volume constitutes one of several that aim to shift from international politics to transnational politics – the former embodies a comparative model whereas the latter stresses relational analyses.[3]

Winant's work demonstrates one step in the process of moving through thinking comparatively on a path toward thinking relationally. Rather than comparing how race and ethnic relations in Europe, South Africa, Brazil and/or the United States are similar and different, a relational model examines their connections. The focus is less on the separate entity of the nation-state or confederation of nation-states as it is on the relationships that join them together. For example, rather than comparing how British and American sociologies of race and ethnicity are similar and different (thinking comparatively) or how national sociologies of race and ethnicity resemble and/or differ from interdisciplinary approaches, one might consider how British and American national sociologies influenced one another and how a recursive relationship links national sociologies of race and ethnicity to the transdisciplinary forays of postcolonial studies, cultural studies, African-American/Latino studies and critical race studies. This is the constructionist framework suggested within cultural studies applied in a new way.

This shift of cognitive map toward relational thinking creates conceptual space for new concepts, paradigms and methodologies. Rather than viewing race and ethnicity, for example, as separate entities, these systems are seen as interrelated, intersecting and/or constructing one another. *Intersectionality* is the term often used to describe these relationships and, as such, constitutes a heuristic device, not a framework for empirical research, although this is certainly a possibility. Rather, intersectionality describes the kinds of questions that are fruitful and the type of theoretical analysis that might be used to explain social phenomena (Anthias and Yuval-Davis, 1992). Paradigms of intersectionality reflect this shift to relational thinking associated with new interdisciplinary work. For example, within interdisciplinary contexts, the study of race and ethnicity has been revitalized by examining how race and ethnicity operate with and through gender, class, nation, sexuality and other systems of social inequality. Overall, intersectional paradigms that emerge from the new interdisciplinary work itself may provide a useful framework for bridging the very gap distinguishing national sociologies of race and ethnicity and interdisciplinary work in this same area.

Extracting the study of race and ethnicity from insular academic disciplines has resulted in vibrant scholarship within postcolonial, cultural, African-American and critical race studies. It has also created possibilities for 'supradisciplinary syntheses' across these interdisciplinary fields such as paradigms of intersectionality. One important task confronting the sociology of race and ethnicity lies in defining a sociological niche within these emerging transdisciplinary approaches to the study of race and ethnicity. How might the sociology of race and ethnicity draw upon and contribute to new supradisciplinary syntheses, in particular, by bringing the *tools* of sociology to this intellectual endeavor? Moreover, given the social problems painfully highlighted by the events of September 11, how might the sociology of race and ethnicity find new ways to study social phenomena that influence its

own practice and where its own practice greatly influences what it discovers?

CONCEPTUAL CLARITY: RACE, ETHNICITY AND INTERSECTIONALITY

Within interdisciplinary scholarship on race and ethnicity, the terms 'race' and 'ethnicity' often lack linguistic clarity. In the current interdisciplinary outpouring of scholarship on 'race and ethnicity', it often remains unclear how researchers and policy-makers define the very concepts that they study. Because national sociologies have long made race and ethnicity central within the discipline, sociology can provide rich albeit competing discussions of these concepts that might help clarify the definitions themselves.

Race and ethnicity do seem to be related, but the question of *how* is subject to debate. For one response, race and ethnicity are often treated as substitutes for one another. For example, British sociologist Phil Cohen suggests that when 'race becomes ethnicised and ethnicity racialized ... both terms can be used interchangeably in a way that allows their respective elements of fixity and permeability to be conjugated into more subtle idioms of attributions than either on their own could achieve' (Cohen, 1999: 2). Substituting race and ethnicity for each other generates more robust understandings of race and ethnicity than the offerings of either term standing alone. A similar substitution occurs in the United States where race and ethnicity are often collapsed together in the term 'racial/ ethnic minorities'.

Another approach to untangling the relationships between race and ethnicity assigns essentialist attributes to both. Via a simple mapping process, 'race' refers to biology and 'ethnicity' refers to culture (Marable, 2000). 'Race' and its accompanying 'racism' are created and maintained from the top down by government, science and industry for the purpose of distributing societal rewards to different 'racial' groups. The creation of race relies heavily on the identification and manipulation of physical differences that distinguish bodies from one another. Racism is seen as something that has been primarily defined by state power and legitimated by a scientific racism that proposes biological notions of racial difference. In contrast, 'ethnicity' reflects pre-existing social and/or cultural organization, largely constructed and expressed from the bottom up. Defining ethnicity as 'group identification, by self or others, on the basis of phenotype, language, religion, or national origin' (Mullings, 1997: 160) installs ethnicity as a more comprehensive, albeit primordial category that might encompass the 'phenotype' assigned to race. The saliency of ethnicity can intensify within the context of a top-down racism – the emergence of ethnicity among contemporary African Americans responding to a 'new' racism constitutes an instructive example (Collins, 2004a) – but ethnicity is rarely *created* by government, science or industry for purposes of distributing social benefits. Rather, ethnicity can be benign until it becomes politicized as the basis for competing for territory, jobs, entitlements or other social benefits.

Treating race and ethnicity in either of these ways may obscure more than it reveals. Facile substitutions and the binary thinking that produces oppositional notions of biology and culture both erase significant differences of how these concepts are understood within national contexts, differences that often have been uncritically imported into national sociologies. Distinctive traditions within American and British national sociologies, for example, generate different meanings of race and ethnicity, as well as different perceptions of their conceptual interconnections. 'Race' more adequately reflects the concerns of American sociology whereas 'ethnicity' has closer ties to the interests of British sociology. Migration from Asia, the Caribbean, Africa and Latin America has challenged historical understandings of race and ethnicity in *both* places, albeit in different ways. For example, ethnicity appears to be much more contradictory, malleable and amenable to both the machinations of the nation-state as well as the goals of new 'racial/ethnic' minorities on both sides of the Atlantic.

The seemingly natural alliance of the terms race and ethnicity within sociology may more accurately reflect the power of established national sociologies to label the field in this fashion than actual social conditions. Joining race and ethnicity together seems to be a marriage of convenience that fosters comparative thinking about the two constructs as compared to an in-depth, relational analysis of how race and ethnicity work together and construct one another. Moreover, race and ethnicity could just as easily be co-joined with other similar concepts as with one another. Social class, gender and/or sexuality might also be bundled together with race and/or ethnicity.

American society's long-standing preoccupation with race signals a concern with biology and body politics that is largely absent from analyses of ethnicity. Nigerian sociologist Oyéwumi identifies a focus on the body and on biology as a major feature of Western sociology. Race constitutes a form of assigning social meanings to individual bodies. Because class disappears into race in the American context, marking individual bodies with race in effect marks them with preliminary social class identities (all blacks are poor, all whites are middle class). Such classification facilitates the distribution of political and economic rights while using the alleged naturalness of biology to mask the workings of the American political economy. A large research tradition documents how from its inception, and through waves of immigration, the US nation-state spent considerable time incorporating previously racially unmarked bodies into the American body politic by assigning bodies racial classifications and their accompanying social meanings. To be 'white', bodies had to be racially pure, an idea that created the so-called one-drop rule, where one drop of black 'blood' made one 'black'.

This process of assigning racial meanings to the body bears close resemblance to assigning gender meanings that are thought to accompany biological femaleness and maleness. Dividing bodies into two biological categories, male and female, and assigning social meanings based on putative biological differences constitute the foundation of sexism as a system of power. Gender identities mark male and female bodies in ways that allow observers quickly to categorize individuals by appearance and attribute social meanings to those classifications. These histories of race and gender remain deeply intertwined, as evidenced by the gendered contours of scientific racism (Stepan, 1990); and studies of women's biology that were deeply racialized (Fausto-Sterling, 1995).

Maintaining racial populations that fostered a white purity juxtaposed to a black other required controlling sexuality, a system of power that is closely associated with disciplining the body. The combination of race, gender and sexuality foster two powerful ideas concerning mate selection – choose a mate of the same race and of a different gender. This system of racially homogeneous heterosexism thus regulated sexuality, marriage and the distribution of marital and family assets from one generation to the next so essential to the social class system (Collins, 2004b). This US system of marking bodies with race and gender meanings, and maintaining these categories across time by manipulating sexuality, resembles the process of creating a permanent, intergenerational identity card that grants differential rights of citizenship. Biology (race and gender) or 'phenotype' becomes a national identity card that sorts a racially heterogeneous population in the United States according to ethnic markers of language, religion, or national origin.

In contrast to the American focus on race, the UK and similar societies that view themselves as being historically racially homogeneous may rely more heavily on ethnicity to distinguish seemingly similar bodies from one another. Here too, structural arguments become essential to understanding the new dynamics of the increasing ethnic diversity within European nation-states. Identifying differences of language, religion or national origin seems more closely associated with long-standing histories in both Western and Eastern Europe of using cultural differences to distinguish among ethnic groups. The shift to forms of government that incorporate multiple ethnic groups within one nation-state produces the similar challenge of distributing differential citizenship rights in ways that privilege some and disadvantage others. The disparate treatment targeted toward Jewish, Irish, Roma peoples and other internal minorities seems much less attentive to degrees of biological difference (albeit, as was evidenced within Nazi science, biology certainly was a factor) than to immutable cultural differences. More recently during the postcolonial period, the migration of visibly identifiable ethnic groups from Asia, Africa, the Middle East and the Caribbean into ostensibly all-white European nation-states allowed this nascent internal ethnic animosity to become more racialized. On the surface, ethnicity seems benign. It merely signals cultural differences that need not be accompanied by power differentials and conflict.

In contrast to the historical bundling of race, gender and sexuality in the United States that masks relations of social class and nation-state, the links between ethnicity and social class in the British context are more prominent and, until recently, masked those of race and gender. Because social class has received greater societal and sociological emphasis, analyses of race and ethnicity must grapple with an established discourse on social class. With the arrival of new immigrant populations of color, this process has become increasingly racialized. Structural approaches generally and class analyses in particular reflect the legacy of a scientific racism and Marxist social theory engaged in prolonged dialogue (Stepan, 1982). Its traditions remain structural, from the scientific empiricism of Darwin, statistics and empiricism through its structural opposite, namely (Tucker, 1994) Marxian sociology (race/class) (Miles, 1989). Historically, British sociology did not concern itself unduly with questions of race and ethnicity because its successful colonial rule kept the objects of study far away. Studying colonial subjects within their native habitat by traveling to the colonies buttressed the type of objective social science advanced via scientific racism and Marxist social thought. In contrast, the migration streams into the UK associated with decolonization as well as the creation of second and third generation communities of color within the UK fostered entirely new social relations described under the rubric of new ethnicities.

As this highly abbreviated discussion suggests, race and ethnicity are not as closely linked conceptually as is commonly assumed. Moreover, this cursory review of the conceptual frame of race and ethnicity also raises another set of questions concerning the conceptual links joining race and ethnicity. Extending the logic of race and ethnicity proves impossible – race expands to a system of power called 'racism' with a pantheon of related terms (institutional racism, structural racism, consumer racism, environmental racism, etc.), whereas ethnicity stimulates no such terminology. There seems to be no 'ism' attached to ethnicity – it operates much more as a politically neutral term that does not seem to be accompanied by a system of power. Is this a small point, or does it signal some important differences that accompany each term? Is the absence of an 'ism' for ethnicity itself a sign of the ability of this system of power to erase its own workings? Considering that racism is the major reason why we pay attention to race at all, it seems curious that ethnicity has no parallel.

NATIONAL AND TRANSNATIONAL STRUCTURES OF RACISM

Another contribution that the sociology of race and ethnicity might make to contemporary scholarship on race and ethnicity concerns using sociological paradigms of social structural and institutional analysis to understand better contemporary racial/ethnic phenomena. What joins much of the disparate interdisciplinary work in race and ethnicity is its reliance on interpretive social science, the storytelling of historiography, and narrative traditions of autobiography, personal essays, and fiction. Narrative strategies such as these strive to give voice to peoples who, within Western science, have been typically objectified and studied as racial and/or ethnic 'others'. In part, the techniques such as autobiography and fiction can serve as especially hospitable locations for racial theorizing because they

privilege narrative forms of analysis over the seemingly 'objective' methodologies of Western social science. Narrative traditions allow objects of study to become subjects with agency. When the lines distinguishing law and literature, science and humanities, fiction and non-fiction, and theory and practice become blurred in this fashion, authors who manage to transcend these various boundaries to say something important about race and ethnicity and say it in a new way become important. For example, Toni Morrison's Pulitzer prize-winning novel *Beloved* is a work of fiction, yet it also can be read as a provocative text of racial theory that tells us much about race in the United States specifically, and about oppression and resistance more generally (Morrison, 1987).

The major limitation that permeates these new interdisciplinary approaches to race and ethnicity may lie in their reliance on the humanities that may have been unduly influenced by postmodern analyses of the 1990s. Taken to its extreme, some versions of social constructionism simply erased social structure itself and/or treated social processes as 'texts' to 'read'. This constructionist corrective to the assumed overdetermination of Marxist-influenced structuralism did create much-needed space to examine the growing influence of culture, especially popular culture, in shaping new racial and ethnic formations and power relations. For example, the resurgence of interest in examining the genealogy of race and racial ideologies (Goldberg, 1993), racial and ethnic images in the media, as well as how race provides cultural capital in everyday social interaction (Essed, 1991), all broke new ground in rethinking culture, and by implication, race and/or ethnicity. Despite these contributions, an overemphasis on cultural production, whether the studies of media, film and other elements of popular culture within cultural studies, or the efforts to valorize African-American culture within Afrocentrism, often fostered a historical amnesia that virtually erased the institutional, structural and material relations that underlie cultural production. As a result, 'the concept of culture has become a central theme in a wide range of debates concerning social change within social and human sciences. In what is referred to as the "cultural turn" there has been a shift away from the study of structure as the privileged feature of social relations accompanied by an increased critical interest in language and how it is used to produce meaning in social life' (Brah et al., 1999: 1). Such approaches do focus on social issues, but are more concerned with the construction of knowledge than with actual power relations. Within cultural studies, the absence of attention to social structure and accompanying social problems has led some to see it as a 'disparate morass of social science and humanities practice, with no particular unifying trait' (Feagin and Vera, 2001: 73).

With its emphasis on bureaucracy, nation-states, social policy, migration and urbanization, sociology brings a much-needed structural analysis to this constructionist corrective. For example, Bonilla-Silva's study of the structures of racism provides a comprehensive interpretation of racism that can ground cultural analyses (Bonilla-Silva, 1996). Winant's analysis of the growth of panethnicity and the growth of new racial subjects in the United States, of the increasing importance of class with African-American communities, and of the crisis of white identity brings an important structural analysis to discussions of the 'new' racism in the United States (Winant, 1998). Beyond this important focus on structure, national differences within sociology provide a more robust picture of social structures across diverse societies.

Structural analyses of this type provide a foundation for analyzing the popular culture and media so necessary to the success of contemporary racial formations. For example, in the United States, new racial formations require participation by the media that obscures, for example, racial segregation in the US by presenting media images of integration (Jhally and Lewis, 1992), and that elevates some ethnic groups over others as 'model minorities' (Tuan, 1998). Obscuring the new racism also requires manufacturing new ideologies that defend what ever inequality breaks through and becomes visible. In this context, the workings of a color-blind ideology increase in importance. Racism is deemed to be a thing of the past and new efforts not to see race by blinding oneself to any racial differences actually work to defend racial inequality (Crenshaw, 1997). Elite authoritative discourse becomes intertwined in reproducing these ideas that defend this new racism (Van Dijk, 1993). Finally, one can see its effects in everyday life – as the term 'everyday racism' describes all of the many ways that African Americans in particular encounter differential treatment on a daily basis (Essed, 1991).

One important development in American sociology concerns a return to studying the structural organization of racism as a social problem, often in terms of how race works with and through ethnicity. In the United States, one of the more powerful structural arguments examines how space has dramatically changed over the past thirty years, from a racially segregated space, to a period of desegregation, to current trends of resegregation. Referring to this new resegregation as 'American Apartheid' (Massey and Denton, 1993), this resegregation belies a belief that a new, multicultural democracy is just around the corner. Despite media scrutiny on immigration, in European nation-states, racial/ethnic populations are small and often in close proximity with other populations. In contrast, urban metropolitan areas of the United States contain vast African American and/or Latino neighborhoods. There talk of hybrid identities and eschewing essentialist political programs is dwarfed by the need to address important social issues such as police brutality, the growth of the prison industrial complex, and deteriorating schools, transportation, health care, and other public services. This new look at the structural scaffolding of racism in the United States has also fostered a new look at social class, long obscured under the label of race. For example, in Black Wealth/White Wealth, sociologists Melvin Oliver and Harold Shapiro argue that the traditional emphasis on income in the labor market be supplemented with the equally important emphasis on wealth (Oliver and Shapiro, 1995). Such a shift enables structural analyses of racism that track its reproduction over time. This growing interest in structural analyses has fueled a closer look at major US social institutions, among them, the racial policies of the welfare state (Quadagno, 1994).

Increased attention to structure within frameworks of relational thinking reveals the connections among race and ethnicity in diverse locations. For example, Latin American sociologies reveal distinctive traditions of race and ethnicity where color and class work in more fluid ways. Issues of race and ethnicity remain vitally important for the new nation-states of Africa, Asia, the Caribbean and Latin America, especially in understanding racial and ethnic conflict. In these regions, as is the case for European nation-states and for the United States, issues of race and ethnicity transcend national borders. In this sense, race and ethnicity already function in a global context and do provide a potentially useful conceptual vocabulary for approaching the diverse ethnic dimensions of global racism (International Council on Human Rights Policy, 2000).

SOCIOLOGY FOR AN ENTIRELY DIFFERENT WORLD

Some argue that, as an academic discipline, contemporary sociology has become increasingly disengaged from important social issues, moving away from the activist and radical traditions that are an important part of its history (Feagin and Vera, 2001). As the events of September 11 suggest, the costs of this type of disengagement may be tragically high. The sociology of race and ethnicity has much to offer not just interdisciplinary scholarship but to efforts to foster a more just global society. A sociological emphasis on important social issues must be revitalized.

During sociology's formative decades as a discipline in 1890s to 1910s in the UK, France, Germany, the United States, and other Western nation-states, sociologists actively investigated important social issues that arose in the context of modernity. They were concerned with the particular interests of their societies, and in doing so, modeled an important synergistic and recursive relationship between sociology

and society that seems to be lacking today. Karl Marx, William E.B. Du Bois, Emile Durkheim and Max Weber among others typically pursued questions that reflected important social issues. The effects of the industrial revolution, the growth of new forms of labor organization, the loosening ties of religion and family, the effects of urbanization on migrant populations, all garnered sociological attention. From a contemporary vantage point, the vitality and vigor of the minds devoted to important social problems during sociology's early days, the lack of consensus among sociologists and the richness of debate that arose among the mélange of thinkers publishing in early sociological journals remains striking.

Contemporary sociologists face a similar challenge concerning postmodernity. Race and ethnicity still matter, are relationally linked to one another and to class, nation, gender and sexuality, and are critical elements of postmodernity. Modernity was actively involved in constructing the modern nation-state where race and ethnicity were central to state formation. Postmodernity is characterized by the creation of transnational structures of power that supersede state power. Violence is still with us, but in new forms that result from new technologies developed in a global marketplace and transported from one society to the next under a politics of transnationalism. Race and ethnicity still matter, but differently. As Ahmed suggests, 'ethnic cleansing' may be the metaphor for our times (Ahmed, 1995).

The sociology of race and ethnicity faces the important challenge of better analyzing how race and ethnicity influence contemporary racial/ethnic conflicts. Despite the fact that established national sociologies historically have elevated their distinctive perspectives on race and ethnicity to claim a universality that was more imagined than real, these sociologies remain valuable. It is equally important to recognize that, when it comes to the reality of race and ethnicity in a transnational context, the sociology of race and ethnic studies must come to terms with one crucial question: 'Who is missing from the field and what might they have to say?' Until recently, the sociology of race and ethnicity has been a field that studies social phenomena that influence its own practice and where its own practice greatly influences what it discovers. This is not a criticism – it is an observation that must be taken into account in order to get any reasonable sense of why we have the sociology of race and ethnicity that we currently do, whether or not we like what we have, and what, if any, changes might need to occur to further the field.

This may be the most difficult question facing the sociology of race and ethnicity because, in the aftermath of September 11, it is painfully obvious how much really is missing. Democratization, inclusiveness and the dialogues that they foster create possibilities for a vibrant, transnational sociology of race and ethnicity. Such dialogues might better equip the field to think through new patterns of race and ethnicity linking the local to the global. It might stimulate provocative research questions and pedagogical initiatives that will help us engage and not run away from the different reality that now confronts us. New ways of doing work on race and ethnicity would recognize the vast differences in how race and ethnicity are conceptualized across societies as well as the power relations that legitimate some scholarship and derogate others. In moving toward democratic inclusiveness, perhaps the field would be better equipped to make sense of why some people deliberately crash airplanes into tall buildings, why African American citizens are still killed by officials of their government, why brown-skinned immigrants remain persecuted in Western European nations, and why ethnic and religious conflict persists in Nigeria, India, Pakistan and other important democracies. If this is an entirely differently world, then we may need a fundamentally different new sociology of race and ethnicity to help us live in it.

NOTES

1 One common approach taken in volumes of this sort consists of surveying and offering critical commentary on the sub-field of sociology of race and ethnicity as a self-contained field of study. Despite many excellent surveys of this sort, even a cursory review reveals considerable disagreement on what now constitutes the 'canon' of the sociology of race and ethnicity. For a range of interesting approaches to the field of race and ethnicity, all done by sociologists see Back and Solomos (2000), Bulmer and Solomos (1999), Cohen (1999), and Guibernau and Rex (1997). In part, this growing disagreement concerning the core concepts, paradigms and methodologies of this sociological sub-discipline reflects fragmentation within sociology itself. Moreover, summarizing the sociology of race and ethnicity's 'canon' inadvertently reproduces the very same social relations that the field aims to analyze, even when such summaries are comprehensive and critical.

2 I do not have sufficient space to discuss the related fields of Asian Studies and Native American Studies. For an overview and thoughtful analysis of Asian Studies see Chow (1993).

3 For a useful overview of comparative work see Fredrickson (2001).

REFERENCES

Ahmed, Akbar S. (1995) ' "Ethnic cleansing": a metaphor for our time?', *Ethnic and Racial Studies*, 18 (1): 1–25.

Anthias, Floya (1998) 'Evaluating diaspora: beyond ethnicity', *Sociology*, 32 (3): 557–81.

Anthias, Floya and Yuval-Davis, Nira (1992) *Racialized Boundaries: Race, Nation, Gender, Colour and Class and the Anti-Racist Struggle*. New York: Routledge.

Appiah, Kwame A. (1992) *In My Father's House: Africa in the Philosophy of Culture*. New York: Oxford University Press.

Back, Les and Solomos, John (2000) 'Introduction: theorising race and racism', in Les Back and John Solomos (eds), *Theories of Race and Racism: A Reader*. New York: Routledge. pp. 1–31.

Bell, Derrick (1987) *And We Are Not Saved: The Elusive Quest for Racial Justice*. New York: Basic Books.

Bonilla-Silva, Eduardo (1996) 'Rethinking racism: toward a structural interpretation', *American Sociological Review*, 62 (June): 465–80.

Brah, Avtar, Hickman, Mary J. and Mac an Ghaill, Mairtain (1999) 'Thinking identities: ethnicity, racism and culture', in Avtar Brah, Mary J. Hickman and Mairtain Mac an Ghaill (eds), *Thinking Identities: Ethnicity, Racism and Culture*. New York: St Martin's Press. pp. 1–24.

Bulmer, Martin and Solomos, John (1999) 'Racism', in Martin Bulmer and John Solomos (eds), *Racism*. New York: Oxford University Press. pp. 3–17.

Chow, Rey (1993) *Writing Diaspora: Tactics of Intervention in Contemporary Cultural Studies*. Bloomington, IN: Indiana University Press.

Cohen, Phil (1999) 'Through a glass darkly: intellectuals on race', in Phil Cohen (ed.), *New Ethnicities, Old Racisms?* New York: Zed. pp. 1–17.

Collins, Patricia Hill (2004a) 'Black nationalism and African American ethnicity: Afrocentrism as civil religion', in Stephen May, Judith Squires and Tariq Madood (eds), *Nationalism, Ethnicity, and Minority Rights.* London: Cambridge University Press. pp. 96–117.

Collins, Patricia Hill (2004b) *Black Sexual Politics: African Americans, Gender, and the New Racism.* New York: Routledge.

Crenshaw, Kimberlé W. (1997) 'Color blindness, history, and the law', in Wahneema Lubiano (ed.), *The House That Race Built.* New York: Pantheon. pp. 280–8.

Essed, Philomena. (1991) *Understanding Everyday Racism: An Interdisciplinary Theory.* Newbury Park, CA: Sage.

Fausto-Sterling, Anne (1995) 'Gender, race, and nation: the comparative anatomy of "Hottentot" women in Europe, 1815–1817', in Jennifer Terry and Jacqueline Urla (eds), *Deviant Bodies: Critical Perspectives on Difference in Science and Popular Culture.* Bloomington, IN: Indiana University Press. pp. 19–48.

Feagin, Joe R. and Vera, Hernan (2001) *Liberation Sociology.* Boulder, CO: Westview Press.

Fredrickson, George M. (2001) 'Race and racism in historical perspective: comparing the United States, South Africa, and Brazil', in Charles V. Hamilton, Lynn Huntley, Neville Alexander, Antonio S. A. Guimaraes and James Wilmot (eds), *Beyond Racism: Race and Inequality in Brazil, South Africa, and the United States.* Boulder, CO: Lynne Rienner. pp. 1–26.

Gilroy, Paul (1987) *'There Ain't No Black in the Union Jack': The Cultural Politics of Race and Nation.* Chicago: University of Chicago.

Goldberg, David T. (1993) *Racist Culture: Philosophy and the Politics of Meaning.* Cambridge, MA: Blackwell.

Guibernau, Montserrat and Rex, John (1997) 'Introduction', in Montserrat Guibernau and John Rex (eds), *The Ethnicity Reader: Nationalism, Multiculturalism and Migration.* Cambridge: Polity Press. pp. 1–12.

Hall, Jacqueline D. (1983) 'The mind that burns in each body: women, rape, and racial violence', in Ann Snitow, Christine Stansell and Sharon Thompson (eds), *Powers of Desire: The Politics of Sexuality.* New York: Monthly Review Press. pp. 329–49.

Hamilton, Charles V., Huntley, Lynn, Alexander, Neville, Guimaraes, Antonio S.A. and Wilmot,

James (eds) (2001) *Beyond Racism: Race and Inequality in Brazil, South Africa, and the United States.* Boulder, CO: Lynne Rienner.

Haraway, Donna (1989) *Primate Visions: Gender, Race, and Nature in the World of Modern Science.* New York: Routledge.

International Council on Human Rights Policy (2000) *The Persistence and Mutation of Racism.* Verisoix, Switzerland.

Jalali, Rita and Lipset, Seymour M. (1998) 'Racial and ethnic conflicts: a global perspective', in Michael W. Hughey (ed.), *New Tribalisms: The Resurgence of Race and Ethnicity.* New York: New York University Press. pp. 317–43.

Jhally, Sut and Lewis, Justin (1992) *Enlightened Racism.* Boulder, CO: Westview Press.

Levine, Donald L. (1995) *Visions of the Sociological Tradition.* Chicago: University of Chicago Press.

Mama, Amina (1997) 'Shedding the masks and tearing the veils: cultural studies for a post-colonial Africa', in Ayesha Imam, Amina Mama and Fatou Sow (eds), *Engendering African Social Sciences.* Senegal: Council for the Development of Economic and Social Research in Africa (CODESRIA). pp. 61–80.

Marable, Manning (2000) 'The problematics of ethnic studies', in Manning Marable (ed.), *Dispatches From the Ebony Tower: Intellectuals Confront the African American Experience.* New York: Columbia University Press. pp. 243–64.

Mason, David. (1999) 'The continuing significance of race? Teaching ethnic and racial studies in sociology', in Martin Bulmer and John Solomos (eds), *Ethnic and Racial Studies Today.* New York: Routledge. pp. 13–28.

Massey, Douglas S. and Denton, Nancy A. (1993) *American Apartheid: Segregation and the Making of the Underclass.* Cambridge, MA: Harvard University Press.

Matsuda, Mari J., Lawrence III, Charles, Delgado, Richard and Crenshaw, Kimberlé (1993) *Words That Wound: Critical Race Theory, Assaultive Speech, and the First Amendment.* Boulder, CO: Westview Press.

McClintock, Anne (1995) *Imperial Leather: Race, Gender, and Sexuality in the Colonial Contest.* New York: Routledge.

McKee, James B. (1993) *Sociology and the Race Problem: The Failure of a Perspective.* Urbana, IL: University of Illinois Press.

Miles, Robert (1989) *Racism.* New York: Routledge.

Morrison, Toni (1987) *Beloved.* New York: Alfred A. Knopf.

Mullings, Leith (1997) *On Our Own Terms: Race, Class, and Gender in the Lives of African American Women.* New York: Routledge.

Oliver, Melvin L. and Shapiro, Thomas M. (1995) *Black Wealth/White Wealth: A New Perspective on Racial Inequality.* New York: Routledge.

Quadagno, Jill (1994) *The Color of Welfare: How Racism Undermined the War on Poverty.* New York: Oxford University Press.

Ross, Dorothy (1991) *The Origins of American Social Science.* New York: Cambridge University Press.

Said, Edward W. (1993) *Culture and Imperialism.* New York: Alfred A. Knopf.

Stepan, Nancy (1982) *The Idea of Race in Science: Great Britain, 1800–1960.* Hamden, CT: Archon Books.

Stepan, Nancy (1990) 'Race and gender: the role of analogy in science', in David Goldberg (ed.), *Anatomy of Racism.* Minneapolis, MN: University of Minnesota Press. pp. 38–57.

Torgovnick, Marianna (1990) *Gone Primitive: Savage Intellects, Modern Lives.* Chicago: University of Chicago Press.

Tuan, Mia (1998) *Forever Foreigners or Honorary Whites? The Asian Ethnic Experience Today.* New Brunswick, NJ: Rutgers University Press.

Tucker, William H. (1994) *The Science and Politics of Racial Research.* Urbana, IL: University of Illinois Press.

Van Dijk, Teun A. (1993) *Elite Discourse and Racism.* Newbury Park, CA: Sage.

Velez-Ibanez, Carlos G. and Sampaio, Anna (2002) 'Introduction: processes, new prospects, and approaches', in Carlos G. Velez-Ibanez and Anna Sampaio (eds), *Transnational Latina/o Communities: Politics, Processes, and Cultures.* Lanham, MD: Rowman and Littlefield pp. 1–37.

Werbner, Pnina and Modood, Tariq (eds) (1997) *Debating Cultural Hybridity: Multi-Cultural Identities and the Politics of Anti-Racism.* London: Zed.

Williams, Patricia J. (1991) *The Alchemy of Race and Rights.* Cambridge, MA: Harvard University Press.

Winant, Howard (1998) 'Contesting the meaning of race in the post-civil rights period', in Michael W. Hughey (ed.), *New Tribalisms: The Resurgence of Race and Ethnicity.* New York: New York University Press. pp. 197–211.

Winant, Howard (2001) *The World Is a Ghetto: Race and Democracy Since World War II.* New York: Basic Books.

12

A Sociology of Information

DAVID LYON

INTRODUCTION

Until quite recently, information was something you could learn from looking at the clouds – a red sky in the morning warns of bad weather – or from tales passed on by your mother, or from flipping the pages of an encyclopedia. Only during the twentieth century did information become central to the social, political and economic organization of life and only late in that century did information become inextricably linked with technology. We still learn from the clouds and from our parents, of course, but these sources are often seen as less central to modern life, less adequate than today's more codified forms. In today's globalizing world the newer sense of information as coded, commodified and computer-compatible is in the ascendancy.

At its most mundane, gluts of useless information clog the arteries of the internet, and yet simultaneously, for some, information promises – or threatens – to supplant reality itself. This is a paradoxical development, given that information was once by definition useful, and helped people be in touch with and cope with everyday reality. Reference to the internet also serves as a reminder that today information cannot be conceived separately from communication. The social repercussions of flows of information through networks – the

internet, cell phones and so on – present one of sociology's most stimulating challenges (Castells, 2001; Urry, 2000). But information itself requires sociological analysis if we are to grasp its connection with crucial issues from identity and inequality to matter and meaning.

Information is central to the social transformations that began after the Second World War and are now visible in globalizing high-technology-based societies around the world. So-called information societies started to appear from the 1960s (Lyon, 1988; Mosco, 2004; Webster, 1995), helping to accelerate capitalist development in the global north, and by the 1990s the internet and other new media had also begun to make decisive contributions to the commercialization of information. Cyberspace, as the realm of computer-mediated communications, was no longer just science fiction. Now networking between remote locations is commonplace, and in everyday life people rely on such systems for a variety of activities such as banking, travel arrangements, entertainment, education, access to government services, news, music and movies.

To explore sociologically the significance of these transformations is to ask about their origins, trajectories and effects. The Second World War, mentioned just previously, is not a mere marker of periods. That war, along with the 'Cold War' that succeeded it, actually stimulated and in important ways guided the development of many microelectronic and communications technologies on which we depend today. But it is not only a question of military origins; the issue of meaning also surfaced decisively in the nascent information theory of the 1950s, and its resolution had profound effects. It enabled a shift from seeing information as primarily instructive to seeing it as technical and then as something valuable as a commodity.

None of these developments occurred according to a predetermined pattern, of course. Although many claimed from an early date that they could perceive the future social impacts of, first, microelectronics, and, later, information technologies, most predictions have turned out to be notoriously inaccurate. The course of change has been one of trial and error, serendipitous choices, and factors that had nothing to do with technological superiority (otherwise, some devotees might assert, everyone would prefer Macs to PCs) or appropriateness. The process of change is in fact deeply social, with economic and political factors playing crucial roles. Capitalism, competing nation-states and cultural commitments play a larger part than 'technology' – if by that term is meant devices or machines – in producing societies that stress the value of information.

The mistake made by many commentators is to see 'information', or more likely 'information technology', as having 'social impacts'. As soon as this move is made, the 'information technology' (or IT) appears as an unquestioned 'black box', something that has a mysterious capacity to produce effects. In fact, IT is always embedded in social, economic and political situations and processes. If one focuses only on 'technical' specifications or promotional descriptions of what technologies can 'do', the material conditions and social environments through which they are produced and through which they operate are thereby obscured. In what follows we shall look at some of what Saskia Sassen (2002) calls the 'mediating cultures' that organize relations between technologies and their users and the complex interactions between material and digital worlds. We shall also see that for all the *differences* in social life that are associated with information and IT, there are also many *continuities* that should not be overlooked.

Because of the volatility that is in part a product of the orientation to information, the consequences of shifts in the social importance of information are still hard to discern with any clarity, still less definitiveness. While some significant debates have occurred regarding the realm of computer-mediated communication often referred to as 'cyberspace', the way this has often been analysed can easily distract attention from the analysis of sociological themes such as identity, inequality and power. As part of a broader trend, the changing role of information is implicated in new ways of understanding social relations, the body and global interactions. But it cannot be detached, either, from equally sociological questions of critique, in which meaning appears again as a contested matter.

THE RISE OF INFORMATION

In the middle of the twentieth century, information was what you asked the telephone operator for when you wanted to find a number, or it was discrete bits of handy lore like recipes or fire route instructions (Roszak, 1986: 3–4). But by the end of that century, information was associated with major technological infrastructures, government policies, educational innovations and commercial and industrial management systems. The word information was used as an adjective to qualify basic descriptive categories: information economy, information society, information superhighway (significantly, because speed, acceleration, mobility, technological obsolescence and some other features make the car–computer analogy an interesting one) and even information age. Information was a commodity; it was cool. For some, it was almost a cult.

This major shift can be explained partly in terms of long-term trends which James Beniger dubs the 'control revolution' (Beniger,

1986). He insists that the so-called information society was structurally present from before the Second World War, well before the word information was in common everyday use. From the 1880s the application of steam power and then electricity stimulated the development of communication and control innovations to monitor, calibrate and coordinate everything from steam ships to factories. The railways with their timetables, factories with scientific management and governments and businesses with their bureaucracies were the outcomes. Each put a new, high premium on information. What Beniger says less about is the political economy that gave much of this its dynamic. The means of greater control were harnessed to the ends of capitalist development and information would become increasingly significant within the process.

But while the longer-term trends are significant, on their own they would not have produced the specific items that appeared in the mid-twentieth century. The military activity that so reshaped the world politically also sparked crucial technical quests, that appeared in the form of radar, transistors and computing machines. It is no exaggeration to say that the Pentagon paid for a large part of the basic research behind what came to be called the information revolution. In the geo-politics of the mid-twentieth century, the threat from the then Soviet Union was paramount. Bell Labs's production of the transistor was at first kept secret from the military because it had such obvious strategic value. Radar systems, set up after the Russians showed that they had nuclear capacities in 1949, needed both computer power to analyse signals, and communications capacity to connect distant monitoring centres. When the Russians upped the ante by launching their first sputnik the Americans responded by funding research into aerospace industries miniaturization in what became Silicon Valley, which in turn stimulated the race for power in space. This is where the 'convergence' between computing and telecommunications began (Lyon, 1988: 26–30; see also Winseck, 1998).

At the same time, information theory was also shaped in ways that proved decisive for both culture and commerce. In the 1950s, Norbert Weiner's 'cybernetics' and Claude Shannon's 'mathematical theory of communication' reduced information to coded transmissions and simultaneously opened new ways for information to be a source of added value (Shannon and Weaver, 1949; Weiner, 1950). I say 'reduced' because both historically, and at the time, information connoted more than 'coded transmissions'. In particular, information was (and is today, by some) viewed by many scholars as having a strong relationship with meaning. The shift, which may have appeared arcane and academic to some, was to have concrete and critical significance in the decades to come.

Looked at historically, information seems basic to social life. In oral cultures, stories and ancestral anecdotes ensure that people know about reality, and some of this involves what might be called 'natural' signs to do with, say, weather or hunting. In modern, literate cultures, artificial signs proliferate, and are frequently associated with social order itself. Signs tell us of distant events, places, persons and processes. Information is relational, connecting by reference persons and things. Intelligence is assumed, as are the reality of things and contexts. But whereas information might once have thrown light on reality, or even, through instructions or recipes, contributed to the transformation of reality, once technological devices become the predominant carriers of information, the distinctions blur. In the well-known illustration of digital music recordings, where what is produced in the studio could not be produced live, information displaces reality (Borgmann, 1999).

The debates over information in the 1950s occurred above all in a significant series of Anglo-American meetings called the 'Macey Conferences'. Shannon's theory tried to isolate discrete bits of information for analysis and measurement. The structure of signs was all important; meaning was for him excluded from information theory. This view, though vigorously opposed by the British School, whose key spokesperson was Donald MacKay (MacKay, 1969), became the standard. To oversimplify, where Shannon (and his champion,

Warren Weaver) saw information as engineering, MacKay saw it as semantics. The consequences of uncoupling meaning and information would prove to be profound. The intellectual struggle also concealed a political and economic one; questions of capital and control would surface in coming years as the so-called information society emerged.

The American School facilitated the quantifying and thus the commodifying of information, which, when associated with the rapid rise of computer science, laid the groundwork for the far-reaching cultural and economic assumption that the value of information does not inhere in its meaning. This first move made possible today's assumption that information is primarily a commodity, rather than a gift or something to be shared communally. Today many companies have information as both raw material and product, across a range of information types. The idea of cybernetics on the other hand, where control is achieved through communication and feed-back loops, was popularized through the work of Norbert Weiner, but did not really come into its own until the widespread computerization of administrative and productive spheres from the late 1960s onwards. Not until William Gibson's novel *Neuromancer* (1984) would the 'cyber' prefix appear in 'cyberspace', now in dystopian rather than utopian guise. It marks no lapse into dystopianism to note that the 'cyber' aspect of 'cyberspace' now relates socially to control and regulation, empirically through surveillance in the broadest sense.

THE TRIUMPH OF INFORMATION

The 'triumph' of information in the last quarter of the twentieth century began with what might be called the demobilizing of military technologies after the Second World War and the establishment of the American School's engineering theory, but it did not end there. The capacities of computing technologies to store and process both data and instructions boosted tremendously their role in control systems. More and more productive and administrative processes became information-dependent as the potential for digitization and automation became evident. Many welcomed this as technological progress, as the promise of lives unburdened from the mundane and the tedious was issued by those who perceived in the union of computing and telecommunication the possibilities for nothing less than a new phase of human existence – the information society (Mosco, 2004; Webster, 2004).

In the 1980s, when talk of the information society became widespread for the first time, key issues appeared in three areas: one, the workplace and the occupational structure; two, the nation-state and democratic processes; and three, in global relations between nation-state and corporations (Lyon, 1988; Webster, 1995). It was discussions of the first, and especially occupational structure, that dominated the pervasively important work of Daniel bell on 'postindustrialism' (1974). He argued that older industrial society models were crumbling under the pressure of evidence of new cadres of 'information' and 'knowledge' workers. The distinction, which was moot when Bell made it, has now become even more problematic in an era when 'knowledge-based' enterprises are seemingly very profitable (but see Duff, 2000 for a defence of Bell).

These issues continue to be highly significant, even though in two major respects they underwent further transformation. First, the technologies developed exponentially during the last part of the twentieth century, and became dominated by the rise of the internet and of multi-media. Second, the old categories and distinctions such as workplace or nation-state began to blur as fresh organizational forms started to displace them.

Information had become central to productive and commercial processes, from the programming of numerically controlled machine tools to the quest for customer data and personal profiling to target marketing. Information flows increasingly through bureaucratic organizations in electronic networks known as Local Area Networks (and on a larger scale, in Wide Area Networks) and office e-mail has become a commonplace administrative tool. The various phenomena known as globalization are also in large measure a product of the same processes, now upscaled. Contemporary globalization is unthinkable without the communication and information technologies that facilitate its flows, not only of information, but also of goods, people, capital, entertainment and ideas. Both capitalist production and commerce develop in increasingly international contexts, dispersed over great distances, but connected through nodes of the network.

This shift towards a so-called 'network society' draws attention to changing modes of organization. In policy areas, talk of the 'information society' is still predominant – the European Union's program 'e-Europe: an Information Society for All' is an example – but the work of Manuel Castells has been especially influential in shifting the focus to 'networks', where flows of information are the life-blood. Castells emphasizes the dynamic, open, innovative nature of networks, especially in management. He sees them as helping to reposition capitalism globally, and in a framework of financial flows (1996: 471).

Castells's trilogy is called *The Information Age*, which indicates the central significance he grants to the category of information. He posits an 'informational mode of development' that is not merely accretions on previous modes, but is flexible, pervasive, integrated and reflexive. The competitiveness of firms now depends on their being able to generate and process information electronically, and this helps to restructure economic activity on a real-time worldwide basis, especially through burgeoning global cities such as New York and Tokyo, but also like Hong Kong, Shanghai and Singapore. Socially, the key consequence of Castells's theory of informational capitalism is an emerging polarity between the 'net' and the 'self' that displays itself in a perturbing pull between the places where people live, and the 'spaces of flows' where they connect to nodes in the net. Identity, experienced as increasingly questioned and unstable, appears in new forms (see Stalder, 1998, 2005 for exposition and assessment).

Just because it is such a far-reaching and well-organized theory, Castells's work has attracted not only wide acclaim but also critical debate. The idea of the informational worker continues to raise questions, for example, just as it did when Bell began to discuss such categories. Frank Webster, for one, comments that this category could be seen in terms of a much longer-term trend towards higher educational levels among the employees of the advanced societies. But he does acknowledge that Castells's 'emphasis on the adaptability and malleability of informational labour does give us a clue to one of the most distinctive characteristics of the present epoch' – workers are expected to 'learn how to learn' (Webster, 2000: 77). Such 'flexibility', however, can be unsettling as well as invigorating.

'Informational workers' not only work 'with' information, information may also work on them. A number of years ago Shoshana Zuboff (1988) examined some worksites which, she argued, were becoming increasingly 'informated'. This term indicates the ways in which work may be (re)organized in new informational ways, to carry forward into a fresh context the control that capitalist employers have always tried to exert over their workers. Other studies (such as Head, 2003) suggest that many jobs do not live up to their 'informated' promises. Simon Head shows that many American doctors now find that their 'informated' work is subject to regimentation, time constraints and such-like, which makes their experiences in some ways not dissimilar from those of call centre workers. Debates in this area are manifold – and often inconclusive – but one thing that is clear is that 'information' in this sense is used to increase the efficiency and productivity of production and consumption processes. Some 'informating' of work situations has improved working conditions and collegial relationships, but this is more likely to be a side-effect of the drive to make units more profitable.

The greater 'flexibility' associated with IT-enabled work situations easily spills over into non-work time, thus drawing all other social relationships into this mode. Network socialities – based on the required flexibility of informational workers (Sennett, 1998) – are another, not necessarily positive, outcome of reliance on information technologies. They are 'disembedded' from older localities and ties.

Richard Sennett sees this in terms of a decline of enduring friendships, responsibility and trust, while Zygmunt Bauman adds that life-long projects and lasting commitments seem to have given way to an 'until further notice' approach (Bauman, 1995), and Ulrich Beck argues that it is part of a process of 'individualization' (Beck, 1999). Fast-food, speed-dating and instant-messaging are no doubt the quotidian signs of similar processes. Of course, these may affect informational and media workers first, but these authors argue that such uncertainties are fairly broadly distributed in what Castells calls network societies.

Several ways exist of considering how IT might relate to forms of human sociality. One helpful approach, from Craig Calhoun (1992), involves a consideration of different levels of relationship. If 'primary' relationships are face-to-face, then 'secondary' ones require some kind of mediation, say through a bureaucratic organization like a bank or a driver's licence department. 'Tertiary' relationships, however, may exist with no direct contact at all, whereas 'quaternary' ones may not even involve human beings. People could be communicating with machines – say, an automated call centre system – or machines could be communicating with each other, but still concerning the activities or virtual traces of humans. Information technology facilitates the last two, which are clearly growing in significance in the twenty-first century and create what is called computer-mediated communication, whose 'environment' is 'cyberspace'.

A number of sociological accounts stress the ambiguity of informational cultures as seen in 'network socialities'. For example, Barry Wellman's research on the diffusion of the internet suggests that social capital is built, and relationships fostered, by on-line activities (2001a). However, Wellman acknowledges that what he is discussing is better thought of as 'networked individualism' (2001b). The sorts of security and social control that characterize all-encompassing communities give way, typically, to fragmented and personal communities marked by opportunity and vulnerability. When people are immersed in asocial activities such as surfing and news-reading they turn away from community even more than television-watchers. But when the internet is used for communicating and coordinating with friends, family and organizations, it is an effective medium for building social capital (2001a: 451).

These kinds of sociological debate will continue, especially in relation to Castells's 'information age' and 'network society' theories. Castells himself is in no doubt that these phenomena represent a phase of capitalist development, and he candidly notes that the chances of poorer countries and sectors making any headway out of their relative deprivation hangs to a large extent on information technology developments. Others fear that this is an overly sanguine and overly technological account, and they refer us back to the putatively prior capitalist need to create value with information commodities. Nicholas Garnham, for instance, sees 'information society' ideas (he discusses Castells's work in these terms, rather than Castells's own 'informationalism') as ideological (1998) in the sense that it obscures the underlying reality of capitalist process. Whether or not one accepts Garnham's critique, it is an important reminder that the 'information society' has a life of its own as a rationale for government policy and commercial innovation, which assumes much that has yet to be demonstrated by sociological research.

CODES, CLASSES, CLASSIFICATIONS

The attempts by conventional sociological and Marxist analysts to discount some of Castells's conclusions about informationalism and the network society are often appropriate but inadequate. Such critiques sometimes miss the point that certain significant changes are indeed under way, and that they relate directly to specific ways of construing and organizing information. If one considers some classic sites for sociological analysis – identity, inequality, power – it is clear that each is deeply affected by informationalism, or what Mark Poster calls the 'mode of information' (Golding, 2000; Poster, 1990). Why is information thus implicated in these basic social processes today?

Because many have associated the emergence of so-called cyberspace with a sense of changing realities, it is not surprising that this includes identity. However, this may be seen in at least three distinct ways. One refers to playful identities beloved of postmodernist cyber-theory – where simulation and spectacle predominate – but which is also treated seriously by theorists such as Sherry Turkle. Particularly in her work on 'life on the screen' she considers how we see ourselves differently when we catch sight of our images in the mirror of the machine (Turkle, 1995). A second insists that interactions with networked machines constitute subjects in new ways. Mark Poster, for example, posits the appearance of cyborgs, or 'humachines' (2001: 38), that represents a new bond between human and machine enabled by computers and especially by the internet. We shall return to these below.

The third, represented by Castells, is more conventional. Although he hints at ways in which new social organizations may mirror the networking logic of informational society (1998: 362) he does not explore this as a structuring of identities. Rather, he sees the 'power of identity' as a key feature of network societies, in which the net-self polarity is the basic social axis. This is best expressed as 'collective identities' that 'challenge globalization and cosmopolitanism on behalf of cultural singularity and people's control over their lives and their environment' (Castells, 1998: 2). Whatever one makes of Castells's categories (see Lyon, 2000) the fact remains that this understanding of identity is tied to action-based notions of nation-states, social movements and politics.

Indeed, Castells sees identity-formation as part of a quest for meaning, in which older sources, such as the nation-state, seem less relevant, if not redundant. Castells argues that this leads either to potentially dangerous, regressive and fundamentalist identities, challenged by the network world, or to more progressive, 'project identities' such as those expressed in environmental or feminist movements. A third category of movements works with 'legitimizing identities'. All movements depend at least in part on new information sources for identity construction. But, direct

communication aside, those new information sources are bound to be circumscribed by the availability of symbols. Large corporations still dominate the circulation of ideas in the era of the internet, and there is strong continuity between them and older media companies.

Not only is identity-construction affected by informational flows, inequality takes on new meanings too. Social inequalities and the uneven distribution of life-chances have been a sociological staple for decades. This has often included studies of how certain kinds of inequalities – especially socio-economic differences – are reproduced across generations. Leaving aside the rosy visions of a world of abundance brought about by the 'information revolution', much has been made of the so-called digital divide in network societies, between the information-rich and information-poor. While visionaries such as Nicholas Negroponte argue that the real divide is between generations (Negroponte, 1996: 6), in fact electronic access to information correlates closely on both regional and international scales with material conditions. Castells talks of certain deprived regions in North America or Europe, or massive areas such as sub-Saharan Africa, being 'switched off' from the benefits of the new information technologies.

Another notable aspect of information inequality – or digital divides – is this. Not only is access *to* information articulated with material differences, but material differences may be reinforced *by* information. For instance, a key means of discrimination between different population groups who are more and less valuable to marketers is the information garnered on consumer behaviour. Although market research was carried out for much of the twentieth century, it only became a major industry in its own right with the advent of appropriate computing machinery. Today a systematic process of 'social sorting', using searchable databases, occurs through gathering publicly held data and matching it with data gleaned from other sources such as warranty forms or internet-surfing habits (Gandy, 1993; Lyon, 2001). The effects of this and other related practices tend to reinforce already existing social divisions of socio-economic class, race and ethnicity, and gender.

Such 'social sorting' (see Lyon, 2003b) is achieved by surveillance which, at its most general, has to do with focused attention to personal details for the purposes of influence, management, care or control. Surveillance is increasingly required in order to meet risks and to provide opportunities and this means gathering and processing information relating to people. Insurance companies want to know about several kinds of risks, marketers want consumer data, police seek information about offenders, welfare departments check their claimants to reduce fraud, and so on. In each case, data are generated by abstracting them from people's behaviours and their bodies and used to make judgements about them either as individuals or as members of a certain population. This means that control over personal information has become a critical political issue in all so-called information societies. Some assume that the main problem is invaded privacy; others that the key issue is excluded persons (and the two are connected).

The exponential growth of communication and information services from the later part of the twentieth century permitted such social sorting to take place across a broad terrain, from voter analysis by political parties, to health data collected by insurance companies, to employment records, screening and monitoring, to opinion polling, as well as the consumer behaviour mentioned above. What Karl Marx called 'frozen labour' – technology – is now given further meaning in a world of digital surveillance. As Geoffrey C. Bowker and Susan Leigh Star suggest, software is frozen decisions and policies that are not very visible but are very influential. So, 'values, opinions and rhetoric are frozen into codes, electronic thresholds, and computer applications' (1999: 135). This resonates with Scott Lash's conclusion about the fresh features of technological capitalism, that it operates more by exclusion than by exploitation (2001: 4–5).

Surveillance today has many facets and it represents a rapidly growing phenomenon in every sphere of life. Personal information from transaction records to street video surveillance images to national identification card numbers flow through the electronic networks that comprise the infrastructure of any modern society. The populations of the global north increasingly inhabit surveillance societies in which simply to navigate through everyday life is to confront constantly the protocols of control; sensors, swipes, image capture, message interception and the like (Lyon, 1994, 2001; Norris and Armstrong, 1999). While many construe this – correctly – as raising questions about 'information privacy', such an approach may also deflect attention from the powerful social forces at work. From a personal perspective, loss of control over personal information may be experienced as an intrusion or a violation. Private space, where legitimate activities may be protected from prying eyes or where the agents of the state may not venture without a warrant, is fully understandable and important from the point of view of both social psychology and democratic practice. But beyond these is a question of power.

The etymology of cyberspace reveals that the 'cyber' component comes from 'cybernetics', the science of control through feedback loops which was mentioned above. The use of personal information drawn from the myriad data, visual and audio protocols of daily life serves to create categories that situate population segments according to their value to the corporation, their reliability in the use of government services, or their risk level as seen by law enforcement or insurance companies. Treatments and judgements are based on these, which – within a feedback loop – affect life chances and choices for better or for worse, thus reinforcing already existing social distinctions and divisions. This is how the 'society of control' as described by Gilles Deleuze (1992) actually works. It exploits difference and individuality to achieve control without conformity, directing desire without discipline. For much of the time, this is construed as producing convenience, comfort and security but it can also mean control. This does not make Foucault's work redundant but it does mean that it is unusable on its own.

In terms of power, then, a picture is already appearing of a world – a 'network society' – in which access to the crucial 'switches' means access to power, informational power. This is both economic, as we have seen, and political. Dreams of digital democracy, for instance, have to confront the realities of access to information sources, of the relative ignorance of many voters, and the fact that whatever entry to government services and information is permitted, governments still hold on tightly to the reins of real power. Moreover, events such as the terrorist attacks of 11 September 2001 indicate how quickly governments that one moment are debating the merits of 'e-democracy' and new information privacy laws can move at the next moment to augment their already extensive control of personal information and communications data (Lyon, 2003a). The enhancing of surveillance occurs in the quest for greater security, producing a greater demand for surveillance information. At the same time, the downward spiral of anxiety and fear that is fuelled not only by palpable risks and dangers but also by attempts to address them with more 'security' facilitates the further supply of information. The cybernetic loops are in this way self-augmenting.

However, this does not leave citizens of network societies in some kind of permanent and hopeless information-deprived or information-governed state. Rather, what the new landscapes of power indicate is that the terrains of struggle are altering, with 'switches' and 'codes' becoming the vital determinants of life-chances and life-choices. Information is power in the sense that it has become a critical component of the capacities of individuals and groups to make a difference in today's world. As the legal theorist Lawrence Lessig points out, the 'code' is a kind of 'law of cyberspace' (Lessig, 1999). The unregulated spaces of liberty that once were proclaimed by the cyber-utopians are chimerical, according to Lessig. Rather, cyberspace is by its very constitution subject to law – the codes embedded in hardware and especially in software already regulate cyberspace. All this means is that the arena of politics – of all kinds – is closely connected with coded information, which is also where the fault-lines of power lie.

BODIES OF INFORMATION: MEANING AND MATTER

I suggested earlier that at the start of the twenty-first century information is a commodity with a price tag, it is cool – this is the *Wired* magazine contribution – and it is almost a cult. In fact, Theodore Roszak (1986) was first to note the cult-like treatment of information, though many others have attacked this 'fetish' or this 'myth'. John Seely Brown and Paul Duguid (2000) point out that the 'myth' of information arises when information is isolated from its context, and seen as a kind of prime mover in social affairs. The 'information revolution' has impacts, it is said, beyond the wildest dreams of the early inventors (say, of silicon chips). Brown and Duguid argue that the alternative is to focus on the 'social life of information' which they trace particularly through organizations. I have painted on an even broader canvas here, showing that the social life of information is today implicated in everything from social and self identities, to new forms of discrimination, to patterns of 'glocalization'.

In this section I question once more those naive assumptions about bodies of information, and consider the relation between information and matter, and indeed, the information of bodies. It is not a question of mere quantities of information, such as the frequently heard assertion that each day's *New York Times* contains more information than a person in Shakespeare's day would have acquired in a lifetime. This in any case reflects confusion about different kinds of information; as Sheldon Ungar argues, we can actually become more ignorant in information-saturated societies because information is increasingly specialized and, paradoxically, less publicly accessible (Ungar, 2000). Rather, what matters here is the meaning of matter and the meaning of information.

Discussions among cyberspace devotees in the 1990s frequently involved assertions about existing electronically in a realm beyond matter. Gibson hinted at this in *Neuromancer* with the thought of leaving the 'meat' behind as one was transported into the 'matrix'. But many other writers who made no claims about producing fiction followed this idea to its logical conclusion: cyberspace made possible disembodied human life on a self-chosen plane of conflict-free co-existence. As Margaret Wertheim observes, this could be read as the return of a repressed desire for heaven, supposedly squeezed out of the Western world's physical cosmos by the scientific revolution (Wertheim, 1999). But it is also a highly individualistic idea – surfing as solipsism? – and one that is hard to square with the longer-term Christian insistence on the materiality of the body which alone make sense of the ideas of incarnation and resurrection – not to mention social justice – in that tradition.

In a critique of what I call 'electronic excarnation' (Lyon, 2005), Kevin Robins argues that the 'consensual hallucination' of cyberspace simply turns a blind eye to the world we live in (1996: 85). As with the earlier discussion about information, if cyberspace is considered in a social vacuum, along with its oft-encountered partner, virtual reality, it will be misunderstood. Robins insists, for example, that analysis should let 'reality intrude' into the argument that self-identity is entirely malleable in cyberspace. After all, virtual identities emerge in a world where larger debates over identity are already under way. It is now a sociological truism that the notion of the self and a life history or narrative is giving way to more fragmented and short-term self-understandings. Robins continues: 'This important cultural shift involves a loss of social meaning, and a consequent retreat from moral engagement' (1996: 92).

Robins's viewpoint is not shared by all commentators, by any means. Mark Poster insists that such action-oriented views that assume 'modern' forms of consciousness are less than adequate for understanding information flows and the internet. As he says, 'Information machines put into question humanity as instrumental agent and thereby disqualify the critique of technology [such as Jacques Ellul's] as "dehumanizing"' (2001: 23). Virtual reality technologies so immerse human subjects that they are reconstituted as elements of the object. This goes beyond Marshall McLuhan's notion of technologies as 'extensions of man'

(1964) such that the internet 'forbodes a reconstruction of the basic elements of human culture' (Poster, 2001: 126). In particular, Poster sees this working itself out in new kinds of post-national identity, and in 'dispersed and multiple subjectivities that have a component of cosmopolitanism' (p. 126).

In her work on informatics and the post-human, Katherine Hayles accedes more to McLuhan than Poster does, and she believes that McLuhan was foreseeing some aspects of the posthuman in his 'extensions of man' (1999: 34). This is not the same as Donna Haraway's more political 'cyborg manifesto', which may downplay the body, but only in the cause of 'imagining a world without gender' (Haraway, 1991). The posthuman, for Hayles, is something seamlessly articulated with intelligent machines, a situation made possible by conceiving bodies as information, which in turn could only have happened after Shannon's information theory became dominant. Genetic coding provides the most obvious example of the 'body as information' but Hayles also sees this in relation to information technology proper.

However, unlike some other theorists she does not simply celebrate the disembodied, decentred subject. While acknowledging that, in the networked conditions of the present, considerations of the posthuman cannot be avoided, she argues that claims about disembodiment are merely a powerful illusion. Spurning the meatless existence of Gibson's hero, Case, which leaves the body behind, Hayles opts rather for the extension of 'embodied awareness in highly specific, local, and material ways that would be impossible without electronic prosthesis' (1999: 291). In the end, she avers, 'Information, like humanity, cannot exist apart from the embodiment that brings it into being as a material entity in the world' (1999: 49).

Embodiment is crucial both to information and to humans. Hayles sees the problem in relation to the Macey Conference debates between Shannon and MacKay – in which MacKay held tenaciously to the idea that information is representational, an action rather than a thing. It thus implies context and embodiment, not to mention reflexivity

(Hayles, 1999: 56–7). However much one seeks the universality and quantifiability of information as a thing (Shannon's position), or to explore the interfaces of humans and machines (as Turkle or Poster do), Hayles's stress on embodiment is a helpful constraint, for it reminds us that whatever effects are achieved by hooking ourselves up to electronic networks, what Robins calls 'the world we live in' is still local and immediate, with real social inequalities, messy politics and agonizing moral dilemmas.

CODES AND CRITIQUE

Information may be viewed historically as something that has recently come to prominence, economically and politically, and has achieved hegemonic power in today's globalized and networked world. Information may be viewed sociologically in terms of its contribution to the diffusion of new social practices and to new fault-lines of inequality and identity. And information may be seen culturally as an aspect of fresh mutations of human self-understanding that bifurcate between those that either elevate or erode meaning and matter.

In each context, the coding of information has become increasingly important and, given the fact that the coding is now facilitated by computer systems, the contexts are increasingly interconnected. This is because the technologically advanced societies depend so heavily on information infrastructures, which enable socially constructed and socially consequential flows of ideas and technologies to exert their influence in diverse settings. The codings carried out by computer scientists are not innocent, by any means; they affect the very regulation of commercial and administrative life as they embody the practices and purposes of firms and government departments, not to mention the internet itself.

It helps to step back for a moment and consider the kinds of changes that occurred in the communication of information during the twentieth century. Although some small-scale experiments had been undertaken in other modes of disseminating information before the turn of the twentieth century, print still dominated the literate world in 1900. By the early decades of the century radio was making strides and after the Second World War television became a rapidly expanding supplement to radio, which would soon take away much of the radio audience for entertainment. The internet became a public medium in the 1990s and today the trend is towards integration of numerous media for channelling information. This is highly suggestive when it comes to 'coding' and the power of information.

In the middle of the last century Canadian communication scholar Harold Adams Innis proposed a theory of the 'bias' of communication (Innis, 1962). He suggested that different media have different capacities or tendencies. Some emphasize time and religious organization, and others, space and political organization. These may occur together, as in the Byzantine empire, where political organization was based on parchment and religious, on papyrus. Parchment use in the West biased organization ecclesiastically, whereas the use of paper enabled more political organization – 'binding space' as Innis said. Print helped to increase literacy and was in turn influential in early nationalism and democratic experiments. 'Lighter' methods, on the other hand, like broadcast media, travel easily and thus help further to 'bind space'. They are conducive to imperial and colonial situations (see also Comor, 2001, who discusses how this might apply to the internet).

Another reason, then, why information has moved towards the centre of political life is that it is seen to be an important aspect of power. In recent decades, for example, government information has been recognized for its critical position in determining the outcomes of law and policy. Thus several countries have passed laws – under a 'freedom of information' rubric – to enable ordinary citizens, or the mass media, to obtain access to what might previously have been inaccessible, or, worse, under a veil of secrecy. Equally, major debates occur, often in the realm of commerce, over intellectual property rights and over computer software monopolies. Again, in these spheres, information has been turned into a scarce resource by those who have succeeded in controlling it, but this move is countered by others who insist that 'open source' software enables all to not only have access but to contribute to it themselves.

A sociology that explores the coding of informational systems cannot ignore the fact that such systems also entail new ways of conceiving and producing human subjects and indeed bodies. Questions of how information touches 'reality' are thus central to, and unavoidable in, debates over social structuring and process today, because information is implicated in the broadest – globalization – and most intimate – the body – levels of sociological analysis. If, as I have argued, information is relational, connecting by reference persons and things, then doubt is cast on the capacity of information actually to displace reality. But the involvement of information in social organization does blur old boundaries and raise new questions. Thus in a world of technologically constituted and communicated information, the risk of displacing reality is always present.

The risk may be confronted, however, by an awareness of the ethical dimensions of information – now assuming once more its association with meaning – in relation to power and accountability, embodiment and responsibility. When the classifying of social groups for administration or policing is automated, algorithmic and dependent on information flows, reproducing social inequality has to be conceived as a socio-technical matter. When the use of body-information for identification or screening raises questions about the conventional anatomical definition of the 'body', new notions of bodily or personal integrity must be sought (Ploeg, 2003). In both cases, information as commodity, as control and as concatenations of abstract data are highly significant. But information is more than a commodity, and more than a means of control. Moreover, embodied persons are more than the abstract data that all too often serve as proxy for them. Notions of 'commodity' may be countered with those of 'resource' and 'stewardship'; notions of control with those of 'accountability' and 'responsibility'. The realization that coded information plays such a profound part in social processes today has to be matched by a search for appropriate modes of critique.

REFERENCES

Bauman, Zygmunt (1995) *Life in Fragments*. Oxford: Blackwell.

Beck, Ulrich (1999) *Individualization*. London: Sage.

Bell, Daniel (1974) *The Coming of Post-Industrial Society*. New York: Basic Books.

Beniger, James A. (1986) *The Control Revolution: The Social and Economic Origins of the Information Society*. Cambridge, MA: Harvard University Press.

Borgmann, Albert (1999) *Holding on to Reality*. Chicago: University of Chicago Press.

Bowker, G.C. and Star, S.L. (1999) *Sorting Things Out: Classification and Its Consequences*. Cambridge, MA: MIT Press.

Brown, John Seely and Duguid, Paul (2000) *The Social Life of Information*. Cambridge, MA: Harvard Business School Press.

Calhoun, Craig (1992) 'The infrastructure of modernity: indirect relations, information technology, and social integration', in Hans Haferkamp and Neil J. Smelser (eds), *Social Change and Modernity*. Berkeley, CA: University of California Press. pp. 205–36.

Castells, Manuel (1996) *The Rise of the Network Society*. Oxford/Malden, MA: Blackwell.

Castells, Manuel (1998) *The Power of Identity*. Oxford/Malden, MA: Blackwell.

Castells, Manuel (2001) *The Internet Galaxy*. Oxford/New York: Oxford University Press.

Comor, Edward (2001) 'Harold Innis in the new century: reflections and refractions', *Canadian Journal of Communication*, 26: 1.

Deleuze, Gilles (1992) 'Postscript on the Societies of Control', *October*, 59 (winter): 3–7.

Duff, Alistair (2000) *Information Society Studies*. London: Routledge.

Gandy, Oscar (1993) *The Panoptic Sort: A Political Economy of Personal Information*. Boulder, CO: Westview Press.

Garnham, Nicholas (1998) 'Information society theory as ideology: a critique', *Loisir et Société/ Leisure and Society*, 21 (1): 97–120.

Gibson, William (1984) *Neuromancer*. New York: Ace Books.

Golding, Peter (2000) 'Forthcoming features: information and communications technologies and the sociology of the future', *Sociology*, 34 (1): 165–84.

Haraway, Donna (1991) 'A Cyborg Manifesto: Science, Technology and Socialist-Feminism in the Late Twentieth Century' in *Simians, Cyborgs and Women: The Reinvention of Nature.* New York: Routledge. pp. 149–81.

Hayles, M. Katherine (1999) *How We Became Posthuman: Virtual Bodies in Cybernetics, Literature, and Informatics.* Chicago: University of Chicago Press.

Head, Simon (2003) *The New Ruthless Economy.* New York/Oxford: Oxford University Press.

Innis, Harold Adams (1962) *The Bias of Communication.* Toronto: University of Toronto Press.

Lash, Scott (2001) *Critique of Information.* London: TCS/Sage.

Lessig, Lawrence (1999) *Code and Other Laws of Cyberspace.* New York: Basic Books.

Lyon, David (1988) *The Information Society: Issues and Illusions.* Cambridge: Polity Press; Malden, MA: Blackwell.

Lyon, David (1994) *The Electronic Eye: The Rise of Surveillance Society.* Cambridge: Polity Press; Malden, MA: Blackwell.

Lyon, David (2000) 'The Net, the self, and the future', *Prometheus* 3: 58–68.

Lyon, David (2001) *Surveillance Society: Monitoring Everyday Life.* Buckingham: Open University Press.

Lyon, David (2003a) *Surveillance after September 11.* Cambridge: Polity Press; Malden, MA: Blackwell.

Lyon, David (ed.) (2003b) *Surveillance as Social Sorting: Privacy, Risk, and Digital Discrimination.* London/New York: Routledge.

Lyon, David (2005) 'New media, niche markets, and the body: excarnate and hypercarnate challenges for theory and theology', in John Wallis and James Beckford (eds), *Religion and Social Theory: Contemporary and Classical Debates.* Aldershot: Ashgate.

MacKay, Donald (1969) *Information, Mechanism, and Meaning.* Cambridge, MA: MIT Press.

McLuhan, Marshall (1964) *Understanding Media: Extensions of Man.* New York: McGraw–Hill.

Mosco, Vincent (2004) *The Digital Sublime: Myth, Power, and Cyberspace.* Cambridge, MA: MIT Press.

Negroponte, Nicholas (1996) *Being Digital.* New York: Knopf.

Norris, Clive and Gary Armstrong (1999) *The Maximum Surveillance Society: The Rise of CCTV.* Oxford: Berg.

Ploeg, Irma van der (2003) 'Biometrics and the body as information', in David Lyon (ed.), *Surveillance as Social Sorting.* London/New York: Routledge. pp. 57–73.

Poster, Mark (1990) *The Mode of Information.* Cambridge: Polity Press.

Poster, Mark (2001) *What's the Matter with the Internet?* Minneapolis, MN: University of Minnesota Press.

Robins, Kevin (1996) *Into the Image: Culture and Politics in the Field of Vision.* London/New York: Routledge.

Roszak, Theodore (1986) *The Cult of Information.* New York: Pantheon.

Sassen, Saskia (2002) 'Towards a sociology of information technology', *Current Sociology,* 50 (3): 365–88.

Sennett, Richard (1998) *The Corrosion of Character: The Personal Consequences of Work in the New Capitalism,* New York: W.W. Norton.

Shannon, Claude, and Weaver, Warren (1949) *The Mathematical Theory of Communication.* Urbana, IL: University of Illinois Press.

Stalder, Felix (1998) 'The network paradigm: social formations in the age of information', *The Information Society,* 14 (4): 301–8.

Stalder, Felix (forthcoming, 2005) *Manuel Castells.* Cambridge: Polity.

Turkle, Sherry (1995) *Life on the Screen: Identity in the Age of the Internet.* New York: Simon and Schuster.

Ungar, Sheldon (2000) 'Knowledge, ignorance, and the popular culture', *Public Understanding of Science,* 9: 1–16.

Urry, John (2000) *Sociology Beyond Societies: Mobilities for the Twenty-First Century.* London/New York: Routledge.

Webster, Frank (1995) *Theories of the Information Society.* London/New York: Routledge.

Webster, Frank (2000) 'Information, capitalism, and uncertainty', *Information, Communication, and Society,* 3 (1): 69–90.

Webster, Frank (ed.) (2004) *The Information Society Reader.* London/New York: Routledge.

Weiner, Norbert (1950) *The Human use of Human Beings: Cybernetics and Society.* New York: Doubleday.

Wellman, Barry (2001a) 'Community in the network society', *American Behavioral Scientist,* 45 (3): 476–95.

Wellman, Barry (2001b) 'Physical place and cyber place: the rise of networked individualism', *International Journal of Urban and Regional Research,* 25 (2): 227–52.

Wertheim, Margaret (1999) *The Pearly Gates of Cyberspace.* New York: W.W. Norton.

Winseck, Dwayne (1998) *Reconvergence: A Political Economy of Communications in Canada,* Cresskill, NJ: Hampton Press.

Zuboff, Shoshana (1988) *Work in the Age of the Smart Machine.* New York: Basic Books.

13

Class and Stratification: Current Problems and Revival Prospects

MIKE SAVAGE

INTRODUCTION

Compared to other disciplines, the catholicism of sociology is striking.[1] Sociologists spend relatively little time policing their boundaries and worrying about what 'real' sociology is (see Urry, 1981; Abbott, 2001). Yet, although this openness opens up all sorts of possibilities for the subject as a kind of mobile discipline, it leads to difficulties in defining what the discipline-specific expertise of sociology actually is. What exactly do sociologists know that those in other disciplines do not? What are sociologists particularly good at? This question is not always easy for sociologists to address: its methods are not distinct to it, most of which are better entrenched in other disciplines. Documentary analysis is lionized by historians, ethnography by anthropologists, and survey methods are used throughout the social sciences. Most of its methods for analysing survey data are shared with other disciplines: there is no sociological equivalent to econometrics.[2] Sociological theory blurs into more amorphous forms of social theory. Attempts to develop distinctively sociological theory, evident in the classic writing of Weber, Durkheim, Simmel and Parsons, have given way to hybrid theory, as likely to draw on literary and cultural theory

and elements of philosophy, rather than any particular sociological canon.[3] It is difficult to find any substantive area of sociological inquiry that is not more strongly anchored in the expertise of other disciplines: consider family and kin (anthropology), urban (geography, planning), work and organization (economics, management), politics (political science), economic (economics) and so on.

One exception to this fluidity, I argue in this chapter, is that way that the study of stratification has acted as a unifying force within sociological analysis, as a distinct area where the discipline of sociology claims distinctive pre-eminence.[4] Classical sociological theorists, notably Marx, Weber, Pareto and, to a lesser degree, Simmel and Durkheim, saw social relationships as fundamentally unequal. Many sociological methods were pioneered as ways of understanding social inequality. Community studies, developed in the UK by Booth and Rowntree, and by Hunter in the United States, were preoccupied by the issue of community power, and the geography of social inequality. After the Second World War, the development of sample surveys was linked to studies of class and mobility (in the UK: Glass, 1954; Goldthorpe and Lockwood, 1968/69; Goldthorpe, 1980; and in the United States: Blau and Duncan, 1967).

Methods of survey analysis were initially used to study inequality. Blau and Duncan (1967) used regression and path analysis techniques as a means of understanding the determinants of status attainment in the United States, Goldthorpe (1980) and his associates (Erikson and Goldthorpe, 1992) used log-linear modelling as a means of exploring trends in class mobility. Bourdieu (1984) used correspondence analysis to examine the affinities between class and cultural taste (Bourdieu, 1984). Bott (1956) launched the tradition of social network analysis as a means of understanding class differences in family relationships. And so on.

To be sure, an interest in stratification is not unique to sociology. However, if we adopt Abbott's (1988) insights into the competitive nature of expertise, with different professional groups struggling against others to maintain jurisdiction over a particular kind of work, we can note that in other disciplines, inequality was seen either as derived from, or as caused by, more fundamental axial concerns. Historians were interested in how class relations generated social change (famously Thompson, 1963 and the myriad debate it inspired), political scientists in how inequalities might affect the polity (Barrington Moore, 1966), and economists in how income differentials were related to the valuation of human capital by market processes (Becker, 1964). In these cases, stratification was relevant to the domain interests of the discipline concerned, but did not stake out its central concern. Sociology became distinctive in putting stratification – its nature, ramifications, causes and consequences – at the heart of its intellectual endeavour. Apparently disparate features of middle and late twentieth century sociology begin to appear more unified and coherent when this point is recognized.

However, although stratification played a core role in defining the discipline's central concerns for much of the twentieth century, this now looks increasingly fraught. Even though the study of stratification is technically sophisticated, it is also seen as old-fashioned, parochial and self-referential, unable to come to terms with fundamental features of contemporary social change (e.g. Bauman, 1982; Pahl, 1989;

Lash and Urry, 1994; Pakulski and Walters, 1996; Crompton, 1998). This challenge is serious and far-reaching, and poses serious questions about the value of sociological perspectives. The second and larger part of this chapter examines this challenge and considers responses to it.

This chapter therefore has four parts. The first part briefly shows how the study of stratification came to play a central role in defining sociological concerns during the middle and later twentieth century through its concern with social relationships. The second part shows how this sociology of social relationships has been undercut over the past two decades in the context of deep-rooted theoretical problems in the study of stratification. This section shows how stratification sociology has increasingly been beset by two powerful critical objections: problems in sustaining an explanatory theory of exploitation, and questions about inter-relating stratification with social and cultural change. Sociologists traditionally saw inequality as produced by relationships of exploitation between social groups, but that this relational approach to stratification has been undercut through criticisms of theories of exploitation. The result is that distinctive sociological perspectives have given way to market-based, economic approaches, and that the marginalization of the sociology of stratification poses distinct problems for the vitality of sociology as a discipline.

The third part of the chapter takes particular stock of debates about exploitation. Although there was considerable virtuosity from the 1980s in developing new approaches to the analysis of exploitation, I argue that they all ran into the problem that axes of inequality could proliferate in a way that seemed to provide a warrant for an anarchic sociology. In the fourth part, I therefore consider how we can think freshly about sociological conceptions of stratification. My main argument here is that we can sidestep debates about exploitation through focusing on the processes by which social resources, assets and capacities are accumulated. By switching our attention in these terms we are better able to align the interests of stratification sociology with broader concerns regarding socio-cultural change that are central to the contemporary sociological imagination. I develop my arguments through a critical engagement with the sociological theory of Pierre Bourdieu, which I think has the most potential here.

THE EMERGENCE OF THE STRATIFICATION PARADIGM WITHIN SOCIOLOGY

Wagner (2001) has shown how early attempts to define sociology as the 'science of society', as championed by nineteenth-century positivists and the classical theorists and institutional leaders of sociology, had largely failed by the 1920s. This positivist vision of sociology[5] required the other social sciences to be subordinate to sociology (since the economy, political system, etc. were seen as parts of a wider society). Such was the entrenched power and institutional strength of (particularly) economics and politics as disciplines in both European and American universities that this was never likely to happen.[6] In addition, an animating force in early sociology saw it as part of a social reform movement, linked to Christian progressivism in the United States (Abbott, 1999) and Fabianism and social planning in the UK (Yeo, 1996), that ultimately required a sociology attuned to practical political issues and concerns, not a sociology of evolutionary social laws and relations. Thus, even the structural functionalism of Parsons, which shored up this classic positivist conception of sociology in the most prestigious American universities into the second part of the twentieth century, rested on shallow foundations. From the 1950s, even as the subject expanded dramatically, sociology fractured, with withering critiques from interactionists and ethnomethodologists (e.g. Garfinkel, 1967), and from those with more radical and practical conceptions of the discipline, such as Marxists and feminists.

In the face of this splintering, sociological champions expounded the virtues of their discipline not in terms of its ability to analyse 'society' (however that might be understood), but rather in terms of the peculiar sensibilities they offered to critical inquiry, a project which included their ability to redefine and illuminate issues developed in other disciplines[7] (see for instance C. Wright Mills, 1959; Berger and Luckmann, 1963; Bauman, 1990). Perhaps the single most important attempt to situate sociology's distinctive critical sensibility was in its sensibility towards stratification, which allowed the subject to be re-positioned as a critical discipline attuned to the fundamentally inegalitarian nature of modern social relations (Lockwood, 1964; Rex, 1968).

Thus it was that stratification sociology emerged, largely un-announced, as an alternative means of reconciling a discipline in need of some kind of unifying framework. An example is Nisbet's (1959) influential attempt to redefine the sociological tradition by invoking its five core unit ideas: status, authority, alienation, community and the sacred. Although outwardly concerned to show the conservatism of the discipline, two of these unit ideas – status and authority – were directly concerned with inequality: two more – alienation and community – were related to it, and only the unit idea of the sacred was largely irrelevant to it.[8] This attempt to redefine the sociological project was compatible with the emerging view that sociology was a critical discipline that questioned established and received ways of thinking. A critical perspective involves a deep scrutiny of social beliefs and perceptions that tend to generate views of the social order as holistic communities of shared interests. Whilst the 'sociology as science of society' school shared such views, seeing society as essentially a version of 'community' (see Therborn, 1976), a commitment to a critical perspective allowed sociologists to define their own distinctive perspective compared to other (supposedly less critical) disciplines.

Sociologists were also able to relate their concerns to political action by anchoring their concerns with stratification to political campaigns. In the UK, links between class politics and sociological concerns could be found in debates about citizenship (Marshall, 1950), cultural change (Hoggart, 1956; Williams, 1958), education policy (Marsden and Jackson, 1962; Halsey et al., 1980). Arguments about social change tended to be couched in terms of discussions about the changing (or unchanging) nature of class (see Savage, 2000 for elaboration). In the American context, sociologists examined the implications of sociological approaches for evaluating the idea that American society was relatively classless (e.g. Blau and Duncan, 1967). Sociology became increasingly seen as composed of writers with distinct claims to analysing inequality (see famously Giddens, 1971, who placed Marx and Weber alongside Durkheim as a key sociologist). For Marx, the extraction of surplus product meant that some social groups could live from the labour of subordinate groups, and this process of surplus extraction coloured all aspects of social and cultural life. Weber's emphasis, in part based on his Nietzschean awareness of the omnipresence of conflicting values, was on the generative role of power, as individual actors attempt to impose their goals and values, and in the process how resources of class, status and command allow some actors to pursue their objectives over others. Much subsequent social theorizing follows in the footsteps of these two thinkers.

Stratification provided a key conduit linking disparate sociological sub-disciplines. Over the past 30 years there has been increased recognition of the plurality of axes of stratification. Issues of gender and of race and ethnicity have been increasingly recognized to be significant forces generating inequality. In these cases, the initial entry of these areas as legitimate within sociology was linked to the recognition – contested in some cases – that they defined a further axis of inequality irreducible to others. Thus the study of gender (rather than the 'family') was introduced into sociology as a result of feminist concerns over structural inequality between men and women (e.g. Oakley, 1973). A similar story can be told for race and ethnic inequalities. Stratification provided one way of defining sociology's domain concerns in a situation of chronic identity crisis (for a recent version of this argument see Turner and Rojek's (2001) rejection of a 'decorative sociology' in

favour of one focused on the topics of 'scarcity and solidarity'). Stratification defined a set of central concerns linking theory, method and sub-areas that allowed sociologists to engage in some kind of dialogue with a degree of shared understanding. To some extent, the chronic disputes on these issues – between micro and macro perspectives, between Marxists, Weberians and others, between those championing class, gender and race as the main axis of inequality – allowed this situation to persist. Because these disagreements were recognized as ones characterizing different sociological positions, they helped nurture a shared set of concerns and understandings, and which united sociologists against other disciplines.

THE ECLIPSE OF THE SOCIOLOGY OF STRATIFICATION

Over the past two decades, however, this core role for stratification sociology has been called into question. The sub-discipline of stratification itself became increasingly insulated from sociology as a whole. As I note elsewhere (Savage, 1994), for much of the post-war period there were no textbooks on the sociology of stratification in the UK, in large part because it could not be easily differentiated from the discipline as a whole. However, during the 1990s a rush of textbooks and edited collections diagnosed the state of the sociology of stratification (Saunders, 1990; Edgell, 1992; Breen and Rotman, 1995; Lee and Turner, 1996; Pakulski and Walters, 1996; Scott, 1996; Crompton, 1998; Devine, 1998; Savage, 2000; Roberts, 2001). The verdicts regarding the prognoses for stratification varied between supporters, critics and revisionists, but what was most important was the scope that these discussions had for generating insularity in the sub-discipline.[9]

There were clearly deep-rooted concerns. One was the emergence of a new way of defining sociological expertise, which saw the discipline as a kind of academic avant-garde, especially well placed to diagnose current forms of social change. This drew upon elements of classical sociology, notably the concerns of early sociologists to situate their discipline in the context of industrialization and the transition to modernity (Nisbet, 1959; Kumar, 1978), as well as the process- and context-oriented sociology associated with the French Le Play tradition or the American Chicago School (see Savage and Warde, 1993; Abbott, 1999: ch. 4). In a period of significant social change, it seemed incumbent on sociologists to propound new syntheses explaining why older social forms were giving way to new ones, and what the main dimensions and contours of change were. The revival of this genre could be traced back at least to Bell's (1973) account of post-industrialism, though his subtitle 'A venture in social forecasting' indicates that he saw this as a rather novel enterprise for a sociologist. However, during the 1980s this kind of sociology mushroomed, nurtured by concerns regarding post-modernism, the collapse of state socialism, new forms of flexible production, globalization, and so forth (Lash and Urry, 1987, 1994; Bauman, 1992; Giddens, 1990; Beck, 1992).[10] During the 1980s it seemed almost mandatory for any (British) sociologist worth his or her salt to come up with some new account of epochal social change. The appeal of sociology was here redefined as its ability to quickly interpret current changes, using whatever new and challenging ideas were being developed in the humanities or (more rarely) other social sciences. In the process, sociological theory became almost completely detached from the day-to-day analyses of empirical sociologists, who became more likely to look for alternative kinds of social theory originating in other disciplines: the advocacy of rational choice theory amongst a number of quantitative sociologists being a case in point. Therefore, although during the 1980s and 1990s empirical stratification sociologists in Europe and the US continued to innovate (e.g. Sorensen, 1986; Erikson and Goldthorpe, 1992; Wright, 1997), their research failed to attract much interest outside the specialist research community.

This excitement about the potential of using sociology as a diagnostic of social change took place at exactly the same time that serious intellectual problems were becoming more manifest in stratification sociology's attempts to understand social change. After all, it had been one of the main claims of stratification sociology that it offered a way of understanding change in terms of processes of class formation (see Abrams, 1981; Savage et al., 1992). This problematic, loosely rooted in the work of Marx and Weber, related social change to the demographic, social, cultural and political organization of social groups, and thereby offered a historically specific account of how inequalities could generate the formation of social groups with shared identities, who would then engage in forms of action and affect historical change. Whilst there were more (generally Marxist) or less (generally Weberian) determinist versions of this approach, some common concerns could easily be seen, and they informed the work of historical writers such as Anderson (1974), Barrington Moore (1966) and the stratification sociology of Goldthorpe (1980). However, this approach depended on showing how social actions, identities and class relations were mutually inter-related. In a period of muted overt class conflict and marked weakness of social solidarities based on class, this tradition offered little purchase on the analysis of contemporary social trends (see Bauman, 1982 for an especially thoughtful account here). In addition, insofar as class formation did appear important it could be interpreted as backward-looking (e.g. Calhoun, 1982) and as failing to have a handle on contemporary social change. However subtle the story might be, it looked difficult to talk of class formation, at least in the classical sense, in any part of the globe at the end of the twentieth century[11]. This partly explains why some stratification sociologists changed their focus completely and emphasized the lack of any association between class positions and group identity. Defenders of class analysis, such as Goldthorpe and his associates in the UK, did not claim that class consciousness and identity were marked, but borrowed the tools of rational choice theory to show how class effects could be produced by rational (and not necessarily class-aware) individual actors (Goldthorpe, 2000; and see the discussion in Savage, 2000). Alternatively, Bourdieu's cultural sociology was deployed to show how cultural and symbolic capital led to the 'dis-identification of class' (see, for example, Skeggs, 1997; Charlesworth, 2000).

However, at the same time as class formation appeared weak and relatively unimportant, sociologists and other social theorists became increasingly interested in the issue of 'identity' (Calhoun, 1994; Rutherford, 1994), though now usually seen as independent of class relations. A major claim here was the argument that identity politics could not be related to prior determinations, but that the 'struggle for recognition' (Honneth, 1985) was an autonomous area of social conflict which could not be related in any obvious way to social inequalities. Indeed, some writers such as Nancy Fraser (1995) emphasized the irreconcilability of the politics of distribution and recognition. With these developments, one of the main 'promises' of stratification sociology, its potential for highlighting the relationship between structure and agency, was undercut.

These problems were compounded by a fundamental problem for classical sociological approaches to class. Classical sociological theory had emphasized that social inequalities were fundamentally produced by divisive social relationships. The advantages of some groups could only be understood as related to the disadvantages of others. This relational perspective took different forms, ranging from Marx's labour theory of value, functionalist accounts of the social value of inequality, Weberian views regarding the omnipresence of competition and its differentiation into class, status and party, and so on. These all offered distinctively sociological ways of understanding inequality, which did not reduce inequalities to purely economic processes, but anchored them in social relationships. However, over the past 30 years all have been largely discredited – or at the least have been subject to withering intellectual critiques, leaving sociologists little alternative but to fall back on the kind of market-based explanations of inequality that have been developed within economics. Let us consider this issue further in the next section.

DEFINING INEQUALITY: THE LIMITS OF RELATIONAL APPROACHES

Social inequality exists in all known societies. These inequalities have numerous dimensions. They include economic inequalities pertaining to the uneven distribution of material conditions of life; status or cultural inequalities relating to the cultural approbation of different kinds of practices and people; and political inequalities relating to the rights and privileges different groups command through various claims to citizenship and entitlement. There are numerous axes of inequality, setting genders, classes, ethnicities, generations, residential groups, sexualities and those with different bodily abilities and aptitudes against each other. The problems of the sociology of stratification cannot therefore be attributed to the fact that social inequality is hard to spot. Rather, the difficulties lie in being able to provide a convincing sociological theory specifying how social relations systematically generate inequality. This is evident if we look at three influential sociological accounts of social inequality, all of which commanded support in the mid-twentieth century. First, the functionalist view can be traced back to Durkheim, and was elaborated by Parsons and in particular by Davis and Moore (1945). This related inequality to the need to reward society's most functionally important occupations. It was thus claimed that social inequalities were generally legitimate and based on shared social values and norms. Economic inequalities could be seen as generally socially sanctioned. One problem with this argument is that there is no obvious popular support for income inequalities and public opinion does not on the whole endorse major income inequalities (see Savage, 2000). Insofar as there is acceptance of inequality, this is generally a blanket endorsement of meritocratic values rather than a specific recognition that particular occupations are more socially valued (e.g. Kluegel et al., 1986). A key element of contemporary acceptance of economic inequalities is the widespread (though not universal) belief that markets are acceptable means for distributing incomes. Brint's (1993) demonstration that over the twentieth century affluent American professionals became ever less likely to justify their relatively strong economic rewards on the basis of their social role, and more likely to justify it in terms of their market position, is a case in point. In the light of issues such as this, the functionalist argument has really become a version of economists' arguments about the effectiveness of market mechanisms, and contains little distinctively sociological content.

Secondly, Marxist approaches saw market processes as derived from more fundamental inequalities in the ownership of the means of production. This offered a robust critique of market-based reasoning, but Marxist perspectives have been deeply troubled by their reliance on the labour theory of value. The argument here was that in capitalist society value is expropriated from workers by the owners of the means of production because workers are not paid an amount equivalent to that which they have invested in the commodities they have produced: in this way surplus value is extracted from the workers. The labour theory of value has been subject to intense critique, much of it, perhaps paradoxically, from Marxists. In part, these criticisms have been based around observations of the difficulty of defining the place of professionals, managers and routine white-collar workers within the surplus extraction process, and hence the difficulty of knowing who exactly extracts the surplus value in an era of impersonal corporate capitalism. But these difficulties are related to more fundamental criticisms from Elster (1985), Wright (1985) and Cohen (1989) who use logic drawn from analytical philosophy and economics to show the difficulty of putting the labour theory of value on acceptable 'micro-foundations'. Cohen, for instance, uses game theory to claim that the labour theory of value cannot hold, because the price of commodities varies over time in response to changing demand. Thus, the price of commodities cannot be seen as linked to the value embedded in them. The traditional Marxist defence to this objection has been to note that Marx never saw the price of commodities as the direct result of the labour value embedded in them (the 'transformation problem'), but once this point is granted, it means that the market cannot be seen as strongly conditioned by the inequalities of capitalist production processes. This thereby undermines the main virtue of Marxist approaches. Because market forces become analytically separable from the extraction of surplus value, market-based accounts of economic inequality are admitted through the back door, so to speak.[12] This therefore leads to a similar outcome to that of functionalist theory. Recent Marxists who have attempted to resuscitate class analysis, such as Wright (1985, 1997) have predominantly used economists' concepts of capital, asset and rent. I discuss the implications of their arguments further below.

Weberian approaches to stratification recognized the pertinence of market processes more than other sociological accounts (see Scott, 1996). Deep in Weber's thinking is an awareness of the omnipresence of competition as fundamental to human social relationships. At the same time, Weber subtly recognized the power of status and party to interfere with 'pure' market mechanisms in generating social inequalities. But the significance of Weber's work in stratification theory has perhaps been over-rated: its popularity has traditionally relied on defining it as a sensible alternative to Marxism, and thereby it implicitly depends on maintaining Marxism as a viable current of work (see Savage, 2000). With the decline of Marxism, however, the reliance of Weberian approaches on a market-based account of economic inequalities became more manifest. Weberians tend to take market-based inequalities as given, with attention directed more to the intersection between economic, status and political inequalities in the generation of social groups. Weberian work could thus easily be incorporated into a descriptive listing of various facets of inequality with relatively little analysis of their inter-relationship. There might thus be seen to be an elective affinity between Weberian approaches to stratification and the kind of variable-centred approach to sociological analysis dissected by Abbott (2002).

These problems explain why the contemporary sociology of stratification has become largely descriptive (Sorensen, 2000). Crompton (1998) demonstrates the steady rise to influence of what she terms 'employment aggregate' approaches to stratification since the Second World War. Employment aggregate approaches to class analysis (Crompton, 1998) conflate class with the division of labour (through their use of a class schema) and seek to demonstrate the links between these employment-based classes and a range of dependent outcomes, such as social mobility prospects (Erikson and Goldthorpe, 1992), voting behaviour (Evans, 1999), health outcomes (Bartley, 2004) and so on[13]. Some sociologists (e.g. Grusky and Sorensen, 1998) argue that the logical consequence of this approach is to decompose classes into more specific occupational groups (hence ultimately making the concept of class redundant). Furthermore, even though this body of work is predominantly descriptive, it could still claim to be important by providing an account of why stratification is socially relevant – a kind of rich description of the extent and pervasiveness of social inequalities in contemporary societies. Furthermore, sociologists in this tradition have not established any close correlation between class position and people's sense of class awareness and identity (Evans, 1992; Breen and Rotman, 1995; Goldthorpe, 2000). This means that there is no clear link between class position, class consciousness and class action in the way that traditional sociologists within the class formation tradition expected. Insofar as class is important, its importance seems to rely on mechanisms that do not depend on recognition and agency.

We thus see stratification theory having two major problems: the lack of a clear sociological theory of exploitation, and the lack of a theory of identity and agency. Instead, contemporary stratification makes do with a kind of rich description of social inequalities. The problems here have best been exposed by Sorensen (2000), who argues that much stratification sociology fails to provide an explanatory framework for stratification theory, and relies on the tautological claim that advantages are generated through being in a position of advantage, which fails to address the issue of how such advantages are structurally generated.

Fundamental to the sociological enterprise, he maintains, is the attempt to show how exploitative processes produce the kinds of inequalities that exist. Without this demonstration, it cannot be established that stratification is a core concern of sociology. Sorensen correctly sees the project of an explanatory stratification theory as fundamental to the sociological enterprise. In the next section I consider how these problems might be addressed by drawing on new developments in economic sociology and Bourdieu's reflexive sociology. I begin by considering how Sorensen's own observations highlight some crucial issues for the study of stratification.

ASSETS, EXPLOITATION AND ACCUMULATION

Like Wright (1985, 1997) and Tilly (1998), Sorensen attempts to renew sociological approaches to inequality by critically reworking the concepts of economic theorists to show how structural inequality is an inherent part of market processes. Rather than attempting to develop a sociological theory of inequality that does not rely on market processes, he shows how it is more useful to develop a distinctively sociological account of markets in order to show that markets depend on social processes. This involves taking the fight to the terrain traditionally occupied by economists. Indeed, over the past 20 years a fertile area of economic sociology has developed, especially in the United States, which shows sociologists no longer taking the market as a given but showing instead how it is socially constructed and embedded (White, 1981; Granovetter, 1985; DiMaggio and Powell, 1991; Roy, 1997; Callon (ed.), 1999; Fligstein, 2001; White, 2003). Strikingly, little of this literature directly attempts to demonstrate how social stratification is embedded within markets, since their concerns tend to be more with the construction of markets as institutions or fields (Fligstein, 2001), though there are some gestures in this direction. Roy (1997), for instance, shows how the rise of large American corporations in the early twentieth century cannot be attributed to their greater efficiency but has to be seen as linked to the power resources of dominant elites in American society.

In order to consider more fully how sociologists can excavate a new place for stratification sociology within a market-based account of social inequality, a distinctive sociology of assets and capital[14] is required. The terms capital and assets have increasingly been extended to a wider array of social practices – for instance, to cover human capital, social capital, cultural capital, symbolic capital and so forth. Some writers, such as Fine (2000), are critical of this development, seeing recent debates over social capital as testimony to the hegemony of economics in the social sciences, and as an indication of the marginalization of sociological and political economy approaches. However, Fine's account misplaces the sociological potential of these intellectual exchanges, and is also open to the criticism that the status of political economy approaches without the labour theory of value is anyway problematic. The work of Roemer (1982) and Wright (1985) on the concept of assets, and Sorensen (2000) on rents, can in fact be seen to perform important intellectual work because it allows a way of conceptualizing class that does not rely on the labour theory of value (see, for instance, Roemer, 1982: 47f., and Cohen, 1989). Rather, class is derived from exchange relations (conceived of as exchanges between individuals in a game-theoretical sense), using concepts from neoclassical economic theory to help model such exchanges. Within such a perspective assets are processes that prevent free markets (in labour, property etc.) operating and which lead to structural inequality, and hence markets can be seen as socially constructed devices.

Therefore, it is possible to see a certain radical potential in the deployment of 'asset' theory. For, whilst these concepts work within the terrain of economic theory, their intent is to demonstrate how market processes are necessarily structured by the causal powers of assets that systematically advantage some agents over others. Roemer (1982), for instance, emphasizes that in reality free markets cannot ever operate, and hence that assets, and thereby class

inequality, are integral to exchange relationships. Once this step is taken, then the potential exists to fully disrupt 'market-logic'. This is especially true if the further step is taken of embedding asset theory within Bourdieu's concept of the field (e.g. Fligstein, 2001), in which the market can be seen as an abstract social construction (hence allowing the monetarization of exchange relations) dependent on certain exclusions and institutional foundations. Here we can see the critical potential for the concepts of asset and capital to be related to the way that they offer a distinctive means of conceptualizing stratification through the critical realist emphasis (Archer et al., 1998) on the generative properties of specific entities (i.e. capitals or assets) in particular kinds of contingent circumstances. It is important to recognize the difference between this realist approach and other forms of class analysis. The differences from other forms of class analysis are importantly highlighted by Sorensen (2000), though similar arguments can be found in Wright (1985, and to some extent 1997). However, if assets are to be defined as a generative causal entity, then how exactly do we recognize an asset, given the realist emphasis that it cannot be directly observed? Realists have tended to skirt round this issue, preferring discussions about the general differences between abstract and concrete research rather than a concise account of which assets are of prime social importance. To put this issue another way, stratification theory needs a way to distinguish assets, as generative entities with causal powers, from contingent correlates of social advantage or disadvantage. The confusion of sociologists on the number and range of assets is itself indicative: Wright distinguishes organization, skill and property assets. Bourdieu distinguishes cultural capital, social capital, economic capital and symbolic capital.

The usual way of handling this issue is to see an asset as intrinsically exploitative and relational. This is the approach famously taken by Wright (1985), who identifies three assets, based on property (owners exploit those without property), skill (those with skill exploit those without) and organization (superordinates exploit subordinates). He can thus distinguish between unequal outcomes generated by one or more of these three exploitative assets, and those caused contingently. For instance, health is undoubtedly a correlate of economic well-being. Since it could be claimed that someone's good health does not entail another's bad health (and hence that someone in bad health would not necessarily be better off by changing the health of the person in good health), then it could be claimed that 'health assets' do not exist. This might be true even though there is a clear association between health and life chances. This would make it possible to distinguish the generative powers of relational assets from outcomes. However, it is actually rather difficult to draw such a clear distinction. Health is a relative state. The employment prospects, for instance, of those in bad health would be improved if those in good health were not in the labour market. A similar example is that of left-handedness. It is known that being left-handed is associated with having a higher mortality rate than right-handers, and this association can probably be explained by the difficulties of left-handers in dealing with right-handed 'technologies'. In this case, one would have to see 'handedness' as a form of exploitative asset. The problem is therefore that using this game-theoretical logic, assets can rapidly be multiplied so that they become diffuse and diverse to the extent that any kind of advantage can be redefined in such terms. It is therefore interesting to see that most sociologists tend to fall back on the established sociological canon, with three assets broadly approximating to class, status and party. The problem, however, is that there is no credible justification for this within the parameters of the theoretical framework they use. In addition, this restriction has had the unfortunate effect of leading to 'recycling of old wine in new bottles', in which only the established, sociological orthodoxies of class, status and power (reworked as property, skill/culture and organization) become defined as assets of class inequality.

In more recent years, Roemer (1988) and Wright (1997) have reacted to the can of worms opened up by claiming that only assets linked to the labour process are 'real' assets. This is a means of reasserting the conventional Marxist emphasis on labour (defined as employment) whilst not using the labour theory of value. For Roemer (1988: 5), 'a class is a group of people who all relate to the labour process in the same way'. Sorensen and Wright's advocacy of rent theory points in a similar direction. However, this approach leads back to the descriptive 'employment aggregate approach', whereas the value of the asset approach was supposed to lie in providing an explanatory alternative to this. It also fails to address the crucial issue that the prime focus on the labour process needs to be justified, not posited through a priori logic.

Recent stratification theory has therefore reached something of a dead end. One way out of this impasse is to use the concept of asset in a way similar to that Bourdieu used the concept of capital in connection with that of the field. In realist terms this involves thinking not only about capitals as generative, causal, mechanisms, but also about fields as the environments in which capitals can be effective. Substantively, this leads us to focus on the accumulatory and convertible potential of capitals (or assets) in different kinds of fields. Stratification can thus be seen as involving the cumulative stacking of advantages over time by those who can draw on assets. In Bourdieu's phrasing,

> Capital, which in its objectified or embodied forms, takes time to accumulate and which, as a potential capacity to produce profits and to reproduce itself in identical or expanded form, contains a tendency to persist in its being, is a force inscribed in the objectivity of things so that everything is not equally possible or impossible. (Bourdieu, 1997: 46)

In Marx's terms, in the capital–labour relationship, it is the daily exchange of labour power for wages, and the routine accumulation of capital, that define the nature of this specific relationship as one pertinent to stratification. Rather than focusing on the abstract, cross-sectional, exchange between social parties, we should look at the cumulative potential of assets to reproduce themselves and to accumulate. This allows us to pay greater attention to the way that certain assets can be *accumulated in various kinds of devices and practices*, or can *convert themselves into other sources of advantage*. This approach draws its inspiration from Marx's definition of capital as lying in its ability to accumulate, through the M–C–M$_1$ cycle. The advantage of this approach is that it does not require a labour theory of value (though it is compatible with it).

This emphasis on how inequalities are reproduced, accumulated or challenged does of course address much work carried out within the sociology of stratification, for instance in the field of social mobility, much of which is concerned with the extent to which advantages can be transmitted inter-generationally and preserved over the life course (Erikson and Goldthorpe, 1992). Devine's recent (2004) qualitative study of how middle class professionals in the United States and the UK were supported by their parents, and also use various strategies to support their own children, is a case in point. Here, the focus on transmission over time allows a more fluid approach to stratification which does not demand a relational theory of class to be useful. Bourdieu is theoretically useful for developing this orientation. Drawing on standard sociological arguments, Bourdieu sees those who have capital as exploiting those who do not. Bourdieu's main innovation can be seen in relating his theory of capital to a theory of the field. Fields are also relational. A field is 'a separate social universe having its own laws of functioning independent of those of politics and the economy' (Bourdieu, 1993a: 162). Because a field has 'its own laws of functioning, its specific relations of force, its dominants and its dominated …' (Bourdieu, 1993a: 163), it defines the stakes around which actors relate in particular contexts (see further, Bourdieu, 1993b). This relationality of the field allows sociologists to relax their assumptions about capitals without losing the central argument that stratification in general is a relational process.

Bourdieu's concept of capital runs parallel to Marx's emphasis on capital as accumulated labour and thereby capital as an inherently relational process of exploitation. Thus cultural capital is defined as dependent on intellectual abstraction that is in opposition to the necessities that lie at the heart of working class and peasant life. Cultural capital stands in direct opposition to the immediacy and practicality of popular culture. Bourdieu (1984) establishes this case in part by showing differences in taste and disposition between classes using surveys of French taste in the 1960s. There is now an extensive debate about whether Bourdieu overemphasizes such differences (Lamont, 1992; Longhurst and Savage, 1996; Bennett et al., 1999), which we need not go into here. What does need reiterating is that even when such differences can be seen, this does not demonstrate that they are relational. A further part of Bourdieu's argument is his rather weakly developed historical insight that the emergence of the Kantian aesthetic can be linked as a reaction to popular culture during the nineteenth century. The elaboration of a skhole (Bourdieu, 1999) based on abstraction and logic involves the distancing of culture from the immediacy and necessity of everyday life, and one can therefore see how the emergence of an academic intellectual elite depended on drawing direct contrast with lay, practical knowledge. Here Bourdieu draws on Durkheimian and Weberian themes regarding the differentiation of modern social relations; he focuses on the slow development of various kinds of intellectual fields, as each becomes more autonomous from economic and political relations.

This process by which fields emerge can rather be seen as one akin to primitive capital accumulation, in Marx's terms. For Marx, primitive capital accumulation depends on creating the initial stock of capital necessary to set the capitalist system in operation, which he saw as critically dependent on the enclosure movement in Britain to expropriate wealth which could then be used for investment. The primitive accumulation of cultural capital, in like manner, involves the formation of an intellectual cadre in key areas of social life who champion and advance the scholastic approach. It is possible to link such a process to that of professionalization. Larson (1977) has famously shown, for the British case, how the middle years of the nineteenth century were especially important in allowing professions to define their skills as being based in science and academic learning (rather than the 'craft' knowledge and practices that they had hitherto relied on), and this process involved the direct de-legitimation of lay knowledge. The case in medicine, where doctors used the monopoly provided by the 1858 Act to make the lay knowledge of 'wise women', herbalists, apothecaries and the like illegal, is especially well known, but similar processes whereby the gap between 'craft' skills and 'academic' expertise was established through the denigration of craft skills by abstract reason can be found elsewhere.

Once the initial stock of capital has been created and the field has emerged that provides the institutional and social context in which further capital can be invested and accumulated, exploitation becomes less visible as it no longer has to be exercised through forcible expropriation. It accumulates through the routine workings of the capitalist economy. If this argument were applied to cultural capital, once the academic and educational system that allows cultural capital to be accumulated and transmitted is set in place, it no longer needs to be overtly and directly contrasted with craft knowledge or popular culture. Whilst Bourdieu's concern to make such implicit contrasts between cultural capital and its plebian 'other' visible is laudatory (see especially 1984) at one level, it also misses the point in that it is precisely the fact that cultural capital does not need to overtly denigrate popular culture in its mature operation that is crucial to its social effectiveness and legitimacy. This point allows current debates about cultural fragmentation to be put in a different context. Thus the observation that many members of the cultured middle class are increasingly likely to 'mix and match' their tastes and are happy to employ certain parts of a popular aesthetic (Petersen and Kern, 1996) can be taken as evidence not that cultural capital does not exist, but rather that mature cultural capital is not contaminated by interaction with a popular culture against which it no longer needs to define itself overtly (see also Bryson, 1996; Warde et al., 1999).

Thus, the relationships embedded in 'mature' capital can be seen as existing in a relatively weak sense, in which the routinization of the organization of capital accumulation serves to make exploitation itself invisible. This is, of course, precisely what Marx saw as fundamental to industrial capitalism, which explains why he began his account in *Capital* with a chapter on commodity fetishism. In this respect my argument is an extension of Marx's arguments about capital and labour to other social processes. It becomes a matter of analytical nit-picking as to whether the exploited groups within these arrangements might be better off in different sets of relationships, since this in no way tells us anything about the possibilities for actually changing such relationships. Returning to our counterfactuals, we can admit that there are a plethora of exploitative relationships. Left-handers are indeed exploited by having to live in a world organized around the implicit needs, values and norms of right-handers: indeed such is the routinization of this form of exploitation that it is hardly ever remarked on. However, and this is the point, what makes capital sociologically interesting is not that this is a form of exploitation – for this is so ubiquitous – but that the social consequences of different kinds of capital depend on relating them to fields that allow the accumulation and convertibilty of capital. Although right-handers could be said to exploit, it is not clear that their advantages accumulate over time, or can be directly converted into advantages in other fields. Those with cultural capital, for instance, are able to use their qualifications to help secure better jobs. Those who are right-handed cannot secure better jobs by virtue of their right-handedness. There may simply be relatively few social implications of right-handedness for accumulation and convertibility. There is no field of handedness in which left- and right-handers play games with each other, and hence there is little investment in handedness as a salient social process.

The reason why 'handedness' is not a class asset is related to the way that it cannot readily be abstracted so that it can be accumulated. The abstraction of capital from embodied social interactions is critical to its potential to accumulate: it is for this reason that economic capital, abstracted through money, is easier to accumulate than any other. The more abstract money is, the more it aids exchange and conversion: consider, for instance, the greater ease of conversion of same currency compared to other currencies. Whereas economic capital is entirely disembodied and depends on being stored in abstract systems, other forms of capital can never be disembodied. Social capital cannot be detached from the actual personal ties between people, and even though its potential for accumulation is still considerable through reliance on weak ties and ties through third parties, it is less easy to accumulate than economic capital. Insofar as cultural capital can be accumulated it depends on being objectified through being instantiated in institutional processes and a canon of 'high culture'.

The counter-point is that the convertibility of capitals depends on agents concretely moving between fields. Convertibility depends on 'particularizing' social relationships. The process of accumulating financial money can largely be left to the routine workings of financial markets once a mature economic field is established. To convert economic capital to cultural capital, an agent needs to make a particular contingent transaction that involves stepping outside the routines of that field. It therefore recognizes a place for agency and identity rather different to that in traditional stratification theory. Traditional stratification theory expects social groups to 'form' cultural and social identities on the basis of their group membership, but the accumulation and convertibility of capital does not require identities of this kind. Identities can be seen as a strategy of the disadvantaged within any field to attempt to gain tactical advances by drawing particular attention to themselves in ways that allow them to stake claims that go beyond the rules of the game as defined within that field. For instance, claiming rights to specific treatment in employment relations through membership of a specific disadvantaged social group claims that the 'normal' rules of the game for hiring employees should not apply. Whilst such interventions may improve the situation for such groups within the field, they can be seen to be limited in that by defining relevant groups as needing special treatment they confirm their inability to 'really' play the game.

Thus whereas both Nancy Fraser (1995) and Miriam Fraser (1999) see recognition politics as involving vital political stakes, there are clearly difficulties for some groups to make claims for recognition (see also Skeggs, 1997). Recognition is a limited tactic of the powerless. The powerful do not wish to draw attention to themselves: their ability to engage in conversion strategies depends on them not having identities that fix them to a particular field. A very wealthy man who wants to convert some of his fortune into political influence is advised not to trumpet his extreme wealth, as it will define him as someone seeking undue influence. And so on. Identities are not to be understood as the outcome of a social position, which attach people to a social group membership, but can be better seen as 'tactical' moves in a field seeking a limited adjustment to the rules of that game. This approach allows us to handle the fragmentation, mutability and complexity of contemporary identities in ways that are entirely explicable within the conceptual apparatus of habitus, capital and field.

These observations suggest the value of relating identities to the network sociology of Harrison White (1992), Mark Granovetter (1985), Mische (2002). In White's simple but important observation, identities are based on contingencies, an awareness that one does not fit routine. Identities need not arise from routine processes of capital accumulation, investment and conversion, but instead develop in the interstices of social relations where particular groups think that they cannot compete in a given field as a result of contingent circumstances that affect them and not others. This allows a way of relating stratification theory to issues of identity and subjectivity that do not rely on the problematic baggage of a class formation approach which assumes that identities are linked to an awareness of group membership and identification.

CONCLUSIONS

In this chapter I have explored how the sociology of stratification can be re-positioned so that it is better able to relate to the central concerns of the discipline as a whole. My basic argument is that we should focus less on the relational nature of stratification, and more on processes of accumulation and convertibility. This approach allows us to take the issue of temporality seriously by posing questions such as how are the advantages of particular social groups sustained; under what situations can they be challenged; what kinds of institutional and cultural contexts allow advantages to be routinely accumulated so that they are not seen as contentious, whereas in others they might be called into question. How can advantages in some situations be converted into advantages in others? These are 'middle-range' questions which are open to empirical investigation and which would renew sociology's critical mission.

We can draw much from Bourdieu, but only if this is approached critically. Rather than focusing specifically on Bourdieu's concept of capital, as most stratification theorists have, we are better advised to reflect on the importance of the field (and on the interplay between field and capital) to bring out the radical potential of his perspective. This allows us to avoid being distracted by problems in sustaining a distinctive relational theory of exploitation which has problematized much stratification sociology. We have seen how this led to defensiveness and introspective inquiry, and empirical stratification researchers losing touch with theoretical debates. Amongst theorists it has led to arcane and esoteric debates about the micro-theoretical foundations of exploitation, and it has made it more difficult for stratification theorists to boldly show how their arguments matter. Using Bourdieu's distinction between capital and fields, we can run with the idea that there are multiple sources of exploitation without this leading to anarchy, since attention can be focused on how intersections between capitals and fields allow some kinds of exploitation to be socially and historically more engrained than others. This allows the prospect for more fertile debate between theorists and empirical researchers than has been the case in recent years.

We are also in a position to examine class formation in a more developed way. In recent years stratification theorists have found the lack of association between class position and class identities problematic. Why does inequality matter if people do not appear to identify with their position? Some stratification theorists have dealt with this problem by operating with largely structural accounts of class process, whilst other cultural theorists have dealt with it by emphasizing the social indeterminacy of identities. In this chapter we can see how a 'tactical' account of identity might be developed that has strong overlaps with network approaches. This is perfectly at home with the recognition of the flexible, fragmented and contextual nature of contemporary identities and allows a way of engaging with current debates in this area. Finally, this interest in accumulation and temporality allows the sociology of stratification to connect with current debates about socio-cultural change in ways that can challenge simple accounts of change and have the potential to offer more nuanced insights into persistence and the remaking of privilege.

NOTES

I would particularly like to thank my colleagues Fiona Devine, Bev Skeggs and Alan Warde for instructive debates on these points.

1 This generalization is particularly true of the UK, and applies less strongly to other parts of Europe, and especially to the US where sociology is more institutionalized and 'bounded'. Readers should bear my location in British academia in mind as they read this chapter, though I do draw attention to international variations and hope to indicate that the issues I discuss here are general to sociology across the globe.

2 There are exceptions here. Sociologists have developed distinctive forms of analysis – for instance modes of categorical data analysis using techniques such as log-linear modelling (Goodman, 1978; Hauser, 1978). After its initial nurturing in anthropology, social network analysis has been developed by sociologists (see generally, Scott, 1991) and is not widely practised elsewhere. Even here, it has drawn on ideas from other disciplines, such as anthropology and physics.

3 The trajectory of Anthony Giddens's work is an interesting example. Whilst originally rooted strongly in the sociological canon of Marx, Weber and Durkheim (Giddens, 1971, 1973), he increasingly roved more broadly, with his 1980s work drawing on the philosophy of Heidegger, the geography of Hagerstrand (Giddens, 1984), the

psychology of Winnicott (Giddens, 1991) as well as synthetic historical periodizations (Giddens, 1985). In the 1990s his work lost any clearly sociological components and became a very general social and political commentary (Giddens, 1991).

4 I am here using the term stratification in a broad sense (similar to Crompton, 1998). Stratification in a narrow sense can imply a commitment to a particular way of thinking about inequality, as seeing society as structured layers, which can be deemed compatible with a functionalist sociology. In the increasingly used wider meaning, stratification is concerned with all facets, mechanisms and processes that generate, sustain and describe social inequalities.

5 There are, of course, many versions of positivism (see Halfpenny, 1982). I am here referring to the Saint-Simonian and Durkheimian project defining sociology as the positive science of society, rather than versions of positivism defending particular naturalistic and empiricist epistemologies. The retreat of the positivist project, especially in the United States, where it is seen as the championing of particular kinds of quantitative methods, would be worthy of fuller study.

6 One of the reasons why Parsons's structural functionalism became the strongest twentieth-century defender of the 'sociology as science of society' approach is that it did offer a way of reconciling sociology with economics (with economics being defined as concerned with the means of social action, and sociology with the ends).

7 Thus Urry's (2000) interesting manifesto arguing for new rules of sociological method which are not premised on the assumption that there are 'societies' can really be seen as the most recent in a long line of cognate arguments.

8 It might be further noted here that claiming the 'sacred' as the province of sociology would be contested by anthropologists!

9 This was especially true for UK-based debates about class analysis that could be made to depend on the interpretation of particular kinds of statistical analysis.

10 Thus the kind of 'futurology' that was widely touted in the 1970s, such as that of Toffler (1970), but which was largely disdained as speculative by sociologists, was increasingly domiciled within sociological debate by the 1980s.

11 The main exception possibly being the formation of a global capitalist class (see Scott, 1997; Sklair, 2001), which still remains a remarkably un-researched social formation.

12 Another tendency within recent Marxist theorizing, evident for instance in Postone's (1993) work, is to define exploitation systemically in terms of the general powers of capitalism over all employees, rather than in terms of the extraction of surplus value (see Savage, 2000: ch. 1 for further discussion).

13 Though employment aggregate approaches also take the step of establishing the criterion reliability of their measures of class through testing that the class schema accurately measures what it claims to be based on, i.e. elements of the division of labour.

14 In the following discussions the concepts of capital and asset are treated as similar unless otherwise specified.

BIBLIOGRAPHY

Abbott, A. (1988) *The System of Professions*. Chicago: University of Chicago Press.

Abbott, A. (1999) *Department and Discipline*. Chicago: University of Chicago Press.

Abbott, A. (2001) *Chaos of Disciplines*. Chicago: University of Chicago Press.

Abbott, A. (2002) *Time Matters*. Chicago: University of Chicago Press.

Abrams, P. (1981) *Historical Sociology*. Shepton Mallet: Open Books.

Anderson, P. (1974) *Lineages of the Absolutist State*. London: Verso.

Archer, M., Bhaskar, R., Collier, A., Lawson, T. and Norrie, A. (1998) *Critical Realism: Essential Readings*. London: Routledge.

Bartley, M. (2004) *Health Inequality: An Introduction to Theories, Concepts and Methods*. Cambridge: Polity Press.

Bauman, Z. (1982) *Memories of Class: The Pre-history and After-Life of Class*. London: Routledge.

Bauman, Z. (1987) *Legislators and Interpreters*. Cambridge: Polity Press.

Bauman, Z. (1990) *Thinking Sociologically*. Oxford: Blackwell.

Bauman, Z. (1992) *Intimations of Postmodernity*. London: Routledge.

Beck, U. (1992) *The Risk Society*. London: Sage.

Becker, G. (1964) *Human Capital*. New York: Columbia University Press.

Bell, D. (1973) *The Coming of Post-Industrial Society: A Venture in Social Forecasting*. London: Heinemann.

Bennett, T., Emmison, T. and Frow, J. (1999) *Accounting for Tastes: Australian Everyday Cultures*. Cambridge: Cambridge University Press.

Berger, P. and Luckmann, T. (1963) *An Invitation to Sociology: A Humanist Approach*. New York: Anchor.

Bhaskar, R. (1979) *The Possibility of Naturalism: A Philosophical Critique of the Contemporary Human Sciences*. Brighton: Harvester.

Blau, P. and Duncan, O.D. (1967) *The American Occupational Structure*. New York: Wiley.

Bott, E. (1956) *Family and Social Network*. London: Tavistock.

Bourdieu, P. (1984) *Distinction*. London: Routledge.

Bourdieu, P. (1993a) *The Field of Cultural Production*. Cambridge: Polity Press.

Bourdieu, P. (1993b) 'Some properties of fields', in *Sociology in Question*. London: Sage. pp. 72–7.

Bourdieu, P. (1997) 'The forms of capital', in A.H. Halsey, H. Lauder, P. Brown and A.S. Wells (eds), *Education: Culture, Economy, Society*. Oxford: Oxford University Press. pp. 46–68.

Bourdieu, P. (1999) *Pascalian Meditations.* Cambridge: Polity Press.

Breen, R. and Rotman, D. (1995) *Class and Stratification.* London: Harvester Wheatsheaf.

Brint, S. (1993) *In an Age of Experts.* Berkeley, CA: University of California Press.

Bryson, B. (1996) '"Anything but heavy metal": symbolic exclusion and musical dislikes', *American Sociological Review*, 61: 844–99.

Calhoun, C. (1982) *Class Struggle and the Question of Community.* Oxford: Blackwell.

Calhoun, C. (ed.) (1994) *Social Theory and the Question of Identity.* Oxford: Blackwell.

Callon, M. (ed.) (1999) *The Laws of the Markets.* Oxford: Blackwell.

Charlesworth, S. (2000) *The Phenemonology of Working Class Experience.* Cambridge: Cambridge University Press.

Cohen, G. (1989) *History, Labour and Freedom: Themes from Marx.* Oxford: The Clarendon Press.

Crompton, R. (1998) *Class and Stratification.* 2nd edn. Cambridge: Polity Press.

Crompton, R. et al. (eds) (1993) *Renewing Class Analysis.* Oxford: Blackwell.

Davis, K. and Moore, W.E. (1945) 'Some principles of stratification', reprinted in L. Coser and B. Rosenberg (eds) (1964), *Sociological Theory.* London: Collier Macmillan.

Devine, F. (1992) *Affluent Workers Revisited.* Edinburgh: Edinburgh University Press.

Devine, F. (1998) *Social Class in Britain and America.* Edinburgh: Edinburgh University Press.

Devine, F. (2004) *Class Practices.* Cambridge: Cambridge University Press.

DiMaggio, P.J. and Powell, W.E. (eds) (1991) *The New Institutionalism in Organisational Analysis.* Chicago: University of Chicago Press.

Edgell, S. (1992) *Class.* London: Routledge.

Elster, J. (1985) *Making Sense of Marx.* Cambridge: Cambridge University Press.

Erikson, R. and Goldthorpe, J.H. (1992) *The Constant Flux.* Oxford: The Clarendon Press.

Evans, G. (1992) 'Is Britain a class-divided society?: A re-analysis and extension of Marshall et al.'s study of class consciousness', *Sociology*, 26: 233–58.

Evans, G. (ed.) (1999) *The End of Class Politics.* Oxford: The Clarendon Press.

Fine, B. (2000) *Social Capital versus Social Theory.* London: Routledge.

Fligstein, N. (2001) *The Architecture of Markets: An Economic Sociology of Twenty-First Century Capitalist Societies.* Princeton, NJ: Princeton University Press.

Fraser, M. (1999) 'Classing queer: politics in competition', *Theory, Culture and Society*, 16 (2): 107–31.

Fraser, N. (1995) 'From redistribution to recognition? Dilemmas of justice in "post-socialist" age', *New Left Review*, 212: 68–94.

Garfinkel, H. (1967) *Studies in Ethnomethodology.* Englewood Cliffs, NJ: Prentice–Hall.

Giddens, A. (1971) *Capitalism and Modern Social Theory.* Cambridge: Cambridge University Press.

Giddens, A. (1973) *The Class Structure of Advanced Societies.* London: Hutchinson.

Giddens, A. (1984) *The Constitution of Society.* Cambridge: Polity Press.

Giddens, A. (1985) *The Nation State and Violence.* Cambridge: Polity Press.

Giddens, A. (1990) *The Consequences of Modernity.* Cambridge: Polity Press.

Giddens, A. (1991) *Modernity and Self-identity.* Cambridge: Polity Press.

Glass, D.V. (1954) *Social Mobility in Britain.* London: Routledge.

Goldthorpe, J.H. (in association with C. Llewellyn and C. Payne) (1980) *Social Mobility and Class Structure in Modern Britain.* Oxford: The Clarendon Press.

Goldthorpe, J.H. (2000) *On Sociology.* Oxford: The Clarendon Press.

Goldthorpe, J.H. and Lockwood, D. (1968/69) *The Affluent Worker in the Class Structure.* Cambridge: Cambridge University Press.

Goodman, L. (1978) *Analysing Qualitative/ Categorical Data: Log-Linear Models and Latent Structure Analysis.* Cambridge: Abt Books.

Granovetter, M. (1985) 'Economic action and social structure: the problem of embeddedness', *American Journal of Sociology*, 91: 481–511.

Grusky, D. and Sorensen, J. (1998) 'Can class analysis be salvaged?', *American Journal of Sociology*, 103: 1187–234.

Halfpenny, P. (1982) *Positivism and Sociology.* London: Allen and Unwin.

Halle, D. (1992) *Inside Culture: Class and Art in the American Home.* Chicago: University of Chicago Press.

Halsey, A.H., Heath, A.F. and Ridge, J. (1980) *Origins and Destinations.* Oxford: The Clarendon Press.

Hauser, R. (1978) 'A structural model of the mobility process', *Social Forces,* 56: 919–53.

Hoggart, R. (1956) *The Uses of Literacy.* Harmondsworth: Penguin.

Honneth, A. (1985) *The Struggle for Recognition,* Boston, MA: MIT Press.

Kluegel, Mason D. and Wengener, B. (1986) *Social Justice and Political Change.* New York: Aldine de Gruyter.

Kumar, K. (1978) *Prophecy and Progress.* London: Penguin.

Lamont, M. (1992) *Money, Morals and Manners: The Culture of the French and American Upper Class.* Chicago: University of Chicago Press.

Larson, M.S. (1977) *The Rise of Professionalism.* Berkeley, CA: University of California Press.

Lash, S. and Urry, J. (1987) *The End of Organized Capitalism.* Cambridge: Polity Press.

Lash, S. and Urry, J. (1994) *Economies of Signs and Space.* London: Sage.

Lee, D. and Turner, B. (1996) *Conflicts about Class: Debating Inequality in Late Industrialism.* London: Longman.

Lockwood, D. (1959) *The Blackcoated Worker.* London: Allen and Unwin.

Lockwood, D. (1964) 'System and social: integration', in G.K. Zollschan and W. Hirsh (eds), *Explorations in Social Change.* London: Routledge.

Lockwood, D. (1966) 'Sources of variation in working-class images of society', *Sociological Review,* 14: 249–67. (Reproduced in M. Bulmer (1975) *Working-Class Images of Society.* London: Routledge and Kegan Paul.)

Lockwood, D. (1981) 'The weakest link in the chain: some comments on the Marxist theory of action', reproduced in D. Rose (ed.) (1988), *Social Stratification and Economic Change.* London: Hutchinson.

Longhurst, B. and Savage, M. (1996) 'Social class, consumption and the influence of Bourdieu: some critical issues', in S. Edgell, K. Hetherington and A. Warde (eds), *Consumption Matters* (Sociological Review Monograph). Oxford: Blackwell. pp. 274–301.

Mann, M. (1970) 'The social cohesion of liberal democracy', *American Sociological Review,* 35: 423–31.

Mann, M. (1973) *Consciousness and Action among the Western Working Class.* London: Macmillan.

Marsden, D. and Jackson, B. (1962) *Education and the Working Class.* London: Routledge.

Marshall, G. (1983) 'Some remarks on the study of working-class consciousness', reproduced in D. Rose (ed.) (1988), *Social Stratification and Economic Change.* London: Hutchinson.

Marshall, T.H. (1950) *Citizenship and Social Class, and Other Essays.* Cambridge: Cambridge University Press.

Mills, C.W. (1959) *The Sociological Imagination.* Oxford: Oxford University Press.

Mische, Ann (2002) 'Cross talk in movements: reconceiving the culture–network link', in Mario Diani and Douglas McAdam (eds), *Social Movements and Networks: Relational Approaches to Collective Action.* Oxford: Oxford University Press.

Moore, Barrington (1966) *Social Origins of Dictatorship and Democracy.* Harmondsworth: Penguin.

Nisbet, R.A. (1959) *The Sociological Tradition.* London: Heinemann.

Oakley, A. (1973) *Housewife.* London: Allen Lane.

Pahl, R.E. (1989) 'Is the emperor naked?', *International Journal of Urban and Regional Research,* 13: 711–20.

Pahl, R. (1993) 'Does class analysis with class theory have a future?', *Sociology,* 27: 253–8.

Pakulski, J. and Walters, M. (1996) *The Death of Class.* London: Sage.

Parkin, F. (1972) *Class Inequality and Political Order.* London: Paladin.

Petersen, P. and Kern, R. (1996) 'Changing highbrow taste: from snob to omnivore', *American Sociological Review,* 61: 900–7.

Postone, M. (1993) *Time, Labour and Social Domination: A Reinterpretation of Marx's Critical Theory.* Cambridge: Cambridge University Press.

Rex, J. (1968) *Classic Problems of Sociological Theory.* London: Routledge.

Roberts, K. (2001) *Class in Modern Britain.* Basingstoke: Palgrave.

Roemer, J. (1982) *A General Theory of Exploitation and Class.* Cambridge, MA: Harvard University Press.

Roemer, J. (1988) *Free to Lose.* London: Radius.

Roy, W.G. (1997) *Socialising Capital: The Rise of the Large Industrial Corporation in America.* Princeton, NJ: Princeton University Press.

Rueschemeyer, D., Stephens, E.H. and Stephens, J.R. (1992) *Capitalist Development and Democracy.* Cambridge: Polity Press.

Rutherford, J. (1994) *Identity.* London: Lawrence and Wishart.

Saunders, P. (1989) 'Left write in Sociology', *Network,* 44: 3–4.

Saunders, P. (1990) *Social Class and Stratification.* London: Tavistock.

Savage, M. (1994) 'Class analysis and its futures', *Sociological Review,* 42 (3): 531–48.

Savage, M. (2000) *Class Analysis and Social Transformation.* Buckingham: Open University Press.

Savage, M., Barlow, J., Dickens, P. and Fielding, A.J. (1992) *Property, Bureaucracy and Culture.* London: Routledge.

Savage, M. and Warde, A. (1993) *Urban Sociology, Capitalism and Modernity.* Basingstoke: Macmillan.

Scase, R. (1977) *Social Democracy in a Capitalist Society.* London: Croom Helm.

Scott, J. (1991) *Social Network Analysis.* London: Sage.

Scott, J. (1996) *Stratification and Power.* Cambridge: Polity Press.

Scott, J. (1997) *Corporate Business and Capitalist Elites.* Oxford: Oxford University Press.

Skeggs, B. (1997) *Formations of Class and Gender.* London: Sage.

Sklair, L. (2001) *The Global Capitalist Class.* Oxford: Blackwell.

Sorensen, A.B. (1986) 'Theory and methodology in stratification research', in U. Himmelstrand (ed.), *The Sociology of Structure and Action: From Crisis to Crisis.* London: Sage.

Sorensen, A. (2000) 'Employment relations and class structure', in R. Crompton, F. Devine, M. Savage and J. Scott (eds), *Renewing Class Analysis.* Oxford: Blackwell. pp. 16–42.

Therborn, G. (1976) *Science, Class and Society: On the Formation of Sociology and Historical Materialism.* London: New Left Books.

Thompson, E.P. (1963) *The Formation of the English Working Class.* London: Gollancz.

Tilly, C. (1998) *Durable Inequalities.* Cambridge, MA: Harvard University Press.

Toffler, A. (1970) *Future Shock.* New York: Random House.

Turner, B.S. and Rojek, C. (2001) *Society and Culture.* London: Sage.

Urry, J. (1981) 'Sociology as a parasite subject', mimeo.

Urry, J. (1990) *Sociology Beyond Societies: Mobilities for the Twenty-First Century.* London: Routledge.

Wagner, P. (2001) *A History and Theory of the Social Sciences.* London: Sage.

Warde, A., Martens, L. and Olsen, W. (1999) 'Consumption and the problem of variety: cultural omnivorousness, social distinction, and eating out', *Sociology,* 33 (1): 105–28.

White, H. (1981) 'Where do markets come from?', *American Journal of Sociology,* 87: 517–47.

White, H. (1992) *Identity and Control.* Princeton, NJ: Princeton University Press.

White, H. (2003) *Markets from Networks.* Princeton, NJ: Princeton University Press.

Williams, R. (1958) *The Long Revolution.* Harmondsworth: Penguin.

Wright, E.O. (1985) *Classes.* London: Verso.

Wright, E.O. (1997) *Class Counts: Comparative Studies in Class Analysis.* Cambridge: Cambridge University Press.

Yeo, Eilien (1996) *The Contest for Social Science: Relations and Representations of Gender and Class.* London: Rivers Oram.

14

The Sociology of Culture

WENDY GRISWOLD

Cultural sociology's boom began in the mid-1980s, and by the turn of the century 'culture', which had been becalmed in a socio-logical backwater during the 1960s and 1970s, was everywhere. Research fell into two camps, close theoretically but distant empirically. First was the old 'sociology of culture' school, whereby culture was a dependent variable produced by and registering some social process or forma-tion. Second was 'cultural sociology', whereby culture was an independent variable shaping socially significant outcomes. Crude as it is, such a categorization helps explain why sociologists who claim to be 'doing culture' often seem to be talking about different things. (For brevity's sake, I call both 'cultural sociology' in this chapter.)

The market for cultural sociology has expanded both inside and outside the academy. Universities and scholarly networks over the past 20 years have increased the institutional venues which promote and disseminate cultural sociol-ogy. The American Sociological Association's Culture Section, formed in the mid-1980s, is one of its largest. The International Sociological Society Research Committee 37 claims to cover 'The Arts' but in fact ranges widely in its cultural concerns. In addition to the standard sociology outlets, journals as diverse as *Signs*, *Poetics* and *Administrative Science Quarterly* repeatedly feature cultural sociology, and the proliferation of jobs, books, centers, courses, programs and newsletters address the putative needs of cultural sociologists and their students. The parallel growth in cultural studies as a cross-disciplinary field has had a largely symbiotic institutional relationship with cultural sociology (despite persistent conflict over methods). Outside acad-emia, the emergence of a multi-centered world with new force fields not necessarily coincident with state boundaries – for example, Islam, state-less nations, the Black Atlantic, international labor migration, global cities – has converged with a revolution in electronic media and a late-modern concern about 'values' to produce public interest in culture that goes well beyond the traditional fine arts or anthropological domains.

This increased demand for what cultural sociologists supply has multiplied the resources, intellectual and material, aimed at the study of culture from a sociological standpoint. It has also produced a rough set of theoretical agreements – intellectual conventions – that coalesced in the 1990s. Cultural sociology has matured in both its institutions and its intellec-tual conventions, and most of this chapter will discuss the zones of agreement that have formed. At the conclusion, however, I suggest that there may be something on the horizon that will overwhelm the general consensus.

MUTUAL CONSTITUTION

Early twentieth-century sociology drew a clear line between culture and society, which was sometimes called structure. Both the Marxian and the Durkheimian traditions regarded culture as a misleading translation of social fundamentals. Religious believers are right about the existence of a powerful force which they call God, Durkheim famously argued, but they are wrong about the source of that very real force, for it emanates not from an external being but from society itself. This is not far from Marx's reflection model whereby a cultural superstructure rests on an economic base. Weber, and Talcott Parsons after him, placed more emphasis on culture's guiding capacities regardless of where it came from, while Simmel saw the tragedy of modernity as involving culture's reduced ability to guide anyone, but they all saw a difference between culture and that which it reflected, guided, or obscured. Disciplinary boundaries seemed to reinforce this distinction. As structural-functionalism's star set in the 1960s and 1970s, most sociologists were happy to leave 'culture' to the anthropologists, and sociology graduate students contented themselves with Lévi-Strauss, Turner and Geertz.

By the end of the twentieth century this model of separate spheres had collapsed. (It had never been as widely accepted in European sociology, where scholars like Norbert Elias and Ferdinand Braudel had maintained all along that culture and society were not analytically distinct.) Not only was the direction of influence called into question, but even the distinction between culture and social structure no longer seemed useful. There have been two types of response to this loss of confidence in the previously assumed analytic categories. In the first, sociologists take culture and society to be mutually constitutive; in the second, sociologists limit their research domains and theoretical claims to precisely specified contexts.

In an influential article setting forth the first of these positions, William Sewell (1992) contended that structure was 'composed simultaneously of schemas, which are virtual, and of resources, which are actual'. While his definition

drew from Anthony Giddens, Sewell rejected Giddens's concept of rules as being too formal and replaced it with cultural 'schemas', the informal presuppositions behind more formal rules. Such schemas can operate at various levels, from trivial points of etiquette to deep values and unconscious binary systems. Schemas are virtual because they can be generalized and transposed to different situations. Resources involve power.

> Structures, then, are sets of mutually sustaining schemas and resources that empower and constrain social action and that tend to be reproduced by that social action. But their reproduction is never automatic. Structures are at risk, at least to some extent, in all of the social encounters they shape – because structures are multiple and intersecting, because schemas are transposable, and because resources are polysemic and accumulate unpredictably. (Sewell, 1992)

Sewell abducted the very word structure, long favored by those who viewed culture as the soft stuff resting on the hard stuff, and pressed it into the service of the mutual constitution model. Although the term 'structure' has not undergone the redefinition Sewell advocates, many sociologists have accepted his image of schemas and resources mutually engaged in constructing the social world.

Under earlier theories of culture, there was a separation between culture and structure. Culture was, in this view, that which expressed an underlying reality, be it society, economic relations, or the structure of the human mind. Studies of nationalism, for example, looked for the political and cultural variables ('the nation' as structure) that gave rise to nationalist ideologies ('the nation' as culture). Contemporary cultural analysis refuses to make this type of structure/culture distinction, or its consequent assumption that the former precedes the latter. Nationalism, Craig Calhoun (1997) points out, did not follow 'the nation' but helped bring it into being:

> "Nations are in part made by nationalism. They exist only when their members understand themselves through the discursive framework of national identity, and they are commonly forged in the struggle carried out by some members of the nation-in-the-making to get others to recognize its genuine nation-ness and grant it autonomy or other rights. The crucial thing to grasp here is that nations exist only within the context of nationalism. (p. 99)

In this type of analysis the distinction between structure and culture is meaningless, for each helps constitute the other (cf. Corse, 1997; Spillman, 1997).

Culture has become as much an analytical strategy as a set of objects. In mutual construction views such as Sewell's, everything is implicated in, and penetrated by, everything else. Therefore it follows that everything represents something else; everything is expressive or can be understood as such. Homicide detectives' jargon, teenage girls starving themselves, spontaneous social movements protesting globalization, couples' ways of handling money, a decline in bowling leagues – all can be (and have been) analyzed as both expressions of and participants in social reality (Bordo, 1993; Jackall, 1997; Melucci, 1989; Zelizer, 1994).

Sometimes the reading of such cultural expressions gives rise to some big story. Putnam's (2000) decline of social capital theory or Maffesoli's (1996) vision of emerging urban tribes are such comprehensive accounts. This was the idea Clifford Geertz (1973) held when he made his influential case for culture-as-text. But by and large social science approaches to culture have moved away from the big stories – modernization, functionalism, Marxism, psychoanalysis, the role of the frontier, etc. – toward more partial, localized, contingent stories (Swidler, 1986).

This type of move constitutes the second response to the culture/structure breakdown: one that does not so much emphasize (or even believe in) mutual construction as local construction, here and now, on the ground. Instead of studying 'Protestants' or 'civic religion', for example, many sociologists of religion study how congregations and or spiritual-therapeutic communities put together meaningful action consistent with their beliefs and circumstances (Becker, 1999; Wuthnow, 1996). This move coincides with the less systematic definition of culture that most sociologists now hold. DiMaggio has characterized the two positions as the 'coherence' view, whereby culture is a coherent system, a latent variable underlying multiple social processes, versus the 'fragmentation' view, whereby culture is disorderly, filled with internal contradictions, and different aspects get triggered or cued by different circumstances (DiMaggio, 1997). While the more systemic view is still around, and may indeed be ascendant again (see below), it seems fair to say that the fragmentation view had captured the sociological imagination at the end of the twentieth century.

BUILDING UP AND TEARING DOWN

Since a culture is no longer assumed to have one big story, social science is listening to and for stories being told by a multiplicity of different tellers. Race and gender in particular have joined class as key sources of expressive variation (e.g. Andersen and Collins, 1998). Whether considered at the micro level of the small group to the macro level of the nation-state and beyond, people tell different stories to account for their different experiences, practices and social locations (Fine, 1996; Lamont, 1992; Pattillo-McCoy, 1999). Interestingly, disciplines within the humanities seem more inclined toward a single big story, usually one intertwining race, postcolonialism and sexual hierarchy, while sociology is currently being more theoretically modest.

Sociology being sociology, class continues to be *sine qua non* in cultural analysis. Here the work of the late Pierre Bourdieu has been the dominant influence in the past 25 years. Beginning with his *Outline of a Theory of Practice* (1977), Bourdieu set forth the idea of the habitus as a set of dispositions that generate practices – innovations, adaptations, tastes – that roughly coincide with those of others sharing the same habitus, these typically being members of the same social class. He worked out the consequences of this insight in *Distinction* (1984), where he mapped the tastes of the wealthy and the poor (for example, rich people favor lean meat, poor people enjoy fatty cuts) and the cultured and less cultured (cultured people chose white wine, less cultured prefer hard liquor). The point, beyond the pleasure of drawing taste maps, is that such tastes constitute cultural capital, a way of signaling social background and aspirations to potential employers, friends, and mates. In a number of institutional fields (and Bourdieu uses the term field in the military sense as a bounded arena for social struggles) Bourdieu and his colleagues worked out the multiple layers of social-via-cultural reproduction. For example, his study of the mid-nineteenth-century literary field showed that Flaubert was torn by a 'double refusal', trying to avoid the seductions both of the market and literary bohemia, and that this same structure of distanced engagement organized his fiction, notably *A Sentimental Education* (1869). To this day this classic offers students a sentimental education about the desirable social position for the man or woman of letters.

Motivated by, yet challenging, Bourdieu, scholars have shown how symbolic boundaries take different forms. Michèle Lamont demonstrated how middle class men set boundaries and hierarchies by assessing cultural refinement, moral integrity and economic clout. Comparing French and Americans, metropolitans and provincials, Lamont (1992) showed that people employ more principles of discrimination than Bourdieu's emphasis on tastes would suggest. For the French, whether or not someone was 'refined' in their cultural appreciation really mattered, while the Americans were oblivious of this domain but cared a lot about honesty and being a team player. Lamont later showed (2000) that French and American working class men – black and white, immigrant and native – want the world to be 'in order' and have little tolerance for ambiguity, but the order they look for is organized along different dimensions. Sometimes American blacks and whites think along similar lines as 'working class men', while other times symbolic boundaries mark racial distinctions. Both blacks and whites share a commitment to family and a belief in upward mobility; in this they differ sharply from their French counterparts, who see class boundaries to be more impermeable. On the other hand, American whites feel superior to people who 'want something for nothing' (read, blacks), while African Americans scorn people who 'don't have any compassion for others' (read, whites). Values are important to these people.

American whites favor immigrants over black Americans because they believe the former share their values (hard work) more than the latter do. French whites favor black Frenchmen over immigrants because of shared values as well, the value here being participation in French culture.

Race above all, but also gender, sexual orientation, cohort, religion, ethnicity, neighborhood and even commitment have achieved either new or rediscovered stature as cultural pivots. Outsiders are in (cf. Zolberg and Cherbo, 1997). This is less a case of different Weberian status groups sticking together (although some groups – gays in times of low tolerance, underground youth – look like this) and more a matter of different dimensions of membership being activated by different contexts and triggers. Social movement research has felt the impact of this way of thinking. Alberto Melucci (1989), to cite one influential example, has studied the protean urban youth groups that episodically emerge to protest global capitalism's environmental and social degradation, then seem to evaporate. Melucci argues that the collective identity behind social action is not something that can be categorically assumed, for example union members or women, but the first object of explanation. 'Only if individual actors can recognize their coherence and continuity as actors will they be able to write their own script of social reality and compare expectations and outcomes' (p. 32). This being the case, Melucci asks how collective identity can be woven together, emerging as action or lying latent as potential.

Collective identity is an interactive and shared definition produced by several interacting individuals who are concerned with the orientations of their action as well as the field of opportunities and constraints in which their action takes place. The process of constructing, maintaining, and altering a collective identity provides the basis for actors to shape their expectations and calculate the costs and benefits of their action. Collective identity formation is a delicate process and requires continual investments. As it comes to resemble more institutionalized forms of social action, collective identity may crystallize into organizational forms … In less institutionalized forms of action its character more closely resembles a process which must be continually activated in order for action to be possible. (pp. 34–35; emphasis in original)

The so-called New Social Movements, wherein collective identity is not prefixed, involve submerged networks of mobile actors whose membership is on the one hand limited and occasional, but on the other hand multi-polar and global. Movements operate not as characters or actors, but as signs.

Social movements may be a specific example of how culture works more generally. In a series of influential writings, Swidler (1986, 1995, 2001) has argued that culture should not be thought of as some master blueprint but as a set of piecemeal orientations available to organize action. These possibilities, to which she has given the memorable image of a cultural toolkit, are neither mutually coherent nor invariably mobilized. Indeed, Swidler points out that people commonly espouse a 'value' while their actual practice contradicts that value; the kid who wants to be a doctor but cuts school, or the husband who asserts that love is a matter of give-and-take yet remains committed to his dying wife unable to give anything, are examples.

It has been firmly established, therefore, that a wide variety of human variation must be included in any analysis of, or statements about, 'culture'. Some have interpreted the results of such variation as constituting a cultural mosaic, for example, America as salad bowl not melting pot: but more persuasive is the image of a cultural swirl of mutual influence, with multiple flows, no impermeable boundaries and few fundamentalists (Hannerz, 1992). Within such a swirl, there is not 'a culture', but a dynamic circulation of objects, ideas and practices, much of which is taking place on a global scale. Such global circulation produces entirely new cultural formations (Appadurai, 1990; Bhabha, 1994). Sociologists have paid particular attention to the resultant class formations (e.g. Lash and Urry, 1994; Sassen, 1991). Some surprising new class/cultures have emerged. It used to be assumed, for example, that cosmopolitans were people having means, education and generally high social status. Rhacel Parreñas (2001) shows that maids and nannies may be as worldly as corporate road warriors. Filipina domestic servants in Rome and in Los Angeles share common grievances, are marginal in the same ways,

and communicate via media and e-mail, thus forming a virtual (and sophisticated) community of outsiders.

Sociologists now take for granted that organizations, industries and individuals interacting with one another produce cultural objects and distribute them through various types of channels and markets (Peterson, 1997). This breakthrough first came in the arts, where sociologists began teasing out the economic and organizational underpinnings to artistic achievement, which most people had associated with individual genius ever since the Romantic period. In the 1970s and early 1980s this collective-production-of-culture was the big news (Becker, 1982; Crane, 1987; Moulin, 1987; Peterson, 1976), and by the 1990s it was taken for granted. Then the big news was the message from the new institutionalism in organization studies, which directed attention to institutional structuring principles – something like an organizational habitus, unconscious but determinative of practice – that shape outcomes in ways that sheer efficiency cannot predict. Comparative studies of similar industries in different contexts, such as Dobbin's (1994) study of how railroad development followed different cultural logics in France, Britain and the United States, Saxenian's (1994) comparison of entrepreneurial cultures in New England and Silicon Valley, and Biernacki's (1995) look at the consequences of the UK and Germany having different conceptions of labor as a commodity (embodied in a product *vs.* measured in time) is one type of neoinstitutionalist application. Another is the consideration of world culture (common, near inescapable structuring properties disseminated globally) by John Meyer and his colleagues (Meyer et al., 1997).

Although neoinstitutionalism locates structural homologies, it pays little attention to the source of the structuring principles in the first place. However a complementary school of research asks this prior question: how and when do ideas get institutionalized. Robert Wuthnow's research has shown that distinctly different dynamics come into play in the appearance, the ascendance and the institutionalization of revolutionary ideologies

(1987, 1989). New ideas proliferate when there is a breakdown in the moral order. They compete for resources in good Darwinian fashion, with a few winners and many losers. However, only when they become absorbed into the handful of social institutions that matter – the state, the educational system, the labor market – can they be said to be securely fixed as schemas in Sewell's sense, that is, integral to the structure of society.

THE DEATH AND REBIRTH OF MEANING

The idea that cultural objects have a fixed but buried meaning, which can be unearthed through analysis, has been declared dead – had a stake driven through its heart – but keeps clawing its way back. Just as casual discourse in the new millennium continues to feature talk about 'meaningful relationship' or work that 'means something', so sociologists have by and large persisted with the idea established by Weber that cultural objects and practices are meaning-full, that they both register and influence thought and behavior. The reluctance of many sociologists to move 'beyond meaning', as Robert Wuthnow (1987) once urged, parallels the reluctance of human beings to live in a world of dancing surfaces, a reluctance that the same Robert Wuthnow has closely studied (1996).

So where does sociological thinking about/ research on meaning now stand? We might divide the thinking between two ideal types: the realists (hard-nosed and pessimistic) and the idealists (flexible and optimistic), bearing in mind that some individuals have taken both positions. Realists stick to the guns offered by Sewell et al.: if the social and the cultural are mutually constructive, with culture part of an ongoing interaction, then pursuing meaning in the Weberian sense of reading a cultural text for the underlying structure is chasing an illusion. Meanings exist in bits and pieces (for example, schemas), but the realists doubt if there is some cultural code that pumps out the values and norms by which people guide their lives. Much study of social problems starts from this assumption: social problems are

not issues that resonate with the collective conscience (let alone concerns at the top of some hierarchy of suffering) but issues that have been inserted into the public agenda by savvy operators (Hilgartner and Bosc, 1988). In this type of analysis to talk of meaningfulness would be beside the point. Indeed, some have suggested that not just sociologists but people in general work hard to avoid saying or doing anything meaningful. Eliasoph (1998) shows, for example, how voluntary and social groups maintain themselves by 'avoiding politics', that is, by not talking about anything that might be divisive. Even activists use humor to paper over their conviction that any consideration of how the object of their activism connects to larger issues – any concern with the big picture, larger meanings – will keep them from getting the job done.

The idealists contend that although meanings may not be holistic or fixed, they still orient social action. Requiring more guidance than their genes provide, human beings use culture to answer, perhaps inconsistently, the 'what shall we do and how shall we live' question (Weber). This happens in at least two ways. The first is when a social group agrees that a certain cultural practice or object is meaningful to them and works at communicating through and about that practice. Ingrid Banks (2000) has shown, for example, how African American women construct a detailed social mapping around the meaning of good and bad hair. Eyerman and Jamison (1998) argue that music doesn't just express and entertain social movement participants but constitutes a meaningful rallying point that can actually create the movement itself. Some such meaning clusters may be short-lived, as with Little League baseball teams that last for only a few months, or may last generations, but in either case they can be very intense (Fine, 1987).

The second way meaning orients is when one set of meanings is privileged over others, and resorted to 'when the chips are down'. Religion, the nation and the family are three of the most potent sources of these 'fundamental meanings', what we mean when we clear the ideological decks and say, 'It all comes down to this'. Sometimes these sources combine to form a core idea cluster, for example, the 'Russian idea' depicted by McDaniel (1996), against which people measure political regimes and social institutions. Meanings may be available but ignored, drawn upon under some circumstances but not always; some meaning clusters are more available and robust than others (for example, those sheltered by educational institutions or organized religion). Meaning happens when there is an engagement between the properties of an idea set embodied in an expressive form (cultural object as solution) and a social collectivities' interests (problem); such an engagement is facilitated by shared schemas (Bijker, 1995; Espeland, 1998).

For meaning to have been resuscitated, there needed to be a reconfiguration of subjectivity. Part of the reaction to structural-functionalism was a repudiation of the idea that sociologists with surveys and interviews could get inside of people's minds. All must be behavior, observable, reliable; psychology was out. This argument was widely accepted, but the nature of the subject itself changed. Cultural sociology came to see people not as possessing a smaller or greater part of their culture, but as occupying different positions in a differential distribution of knowledge and cultural resources. Their subjectivities come from their positions, and are characterized by the possession of specific cognitive schemas (DiMaggio, 1997). They participate in different 'social minds' and to different extents (Zerubavel, 1997).

DiMaggio suggests that we think of the connection between culture and mind as a three-way interaction among the differential distribution of information, different schemas, and available sets of symbolic expressions. Say, for example, that Coca-Cola settles a lawsuit on discrimination, and part of the settlement involves emphasis on affirmative action in hiring. This information will be available to most Americans, but not to those who have no access to media, who are inattentive to media messages, who are unable to process such messages (non-English speakers). Those who receive the information will attend to it insofar as it engages pre-existing schemas. A young

African American woman about to graduate from high school has schemas about how one gets jobs and about her possible future trajectories, that will make the information relevant; a young Inuit man may have schemas that make it irrelevant. Meanwhile there are a variety of symbolic clusters – what Coke represents; what working in business represents; what affirmative action represents – that engage and organize the information. This three-way combination may produce action, both in terms of information processing and job-seeking.

Meaning therefore is cognitive, but this does not suggest that it is strictly private or internal. It can be observed in action, without either imputing universal signification or getting inside anyone's head, by examining group practices. The meaning of a piece of technology, to take Bijker's (1995) research as an example, does not reside in the system or artifact itself; technologies acquire their meanings through social interactions. Something 'works' not by solving a pre-existing problem but by achieving a match with a social group in a position to stabilize its meaning. For example the high-wheeled 'Ordinary' bicycle did not work for women, older men and anyone concerned about safety or ease of use, but it worked beautifully for the macho young Edwardians who liked to ride around the parks impressing the girls. We know this not by inferring their psychological make-up but by looking at their buying patterns. These men had money to spend and prestige to lend, so the vehicle lasted despite its unsafe and awkward design. When the safety bike, equipped with air tires came along, it was not adopted because of its superior safety or comfort, though these were undeniable to any engineer or rider. Only when it was shown to be faster, however, did the new technology 'work' in the social sense. Along quite different lines, Ogasawara (1998) has shown that a trivial practice like giving Valentines to co-workers can work, that is, become meaningful, when Japanese 'office ladies' deploy them to critique gender conventions. Powerful cultural objects work by addressing powerful concerns in ways that provide the satisfactions of both engagement and closure (Griswold, 1987, 2000).

If meaning is socially contingent, then across cultural genres there can be no universally rational basis for hierarchies of value. People evaluate specimens of any particular genre, based on criteria such as complexity or the masterful rendition of conventions (or cleverness at defying them), but distinctions *across* genres – for example, jazz is better than hip-hop – cannot be justified. Boundaries between high and popular, mass and restricted, decent and indecent are social configurations, positions in a social field to use Bourdieu's imagery, and not properties of the cultural objects. Drawing on Bourdieu, whom he helped introduce to English-speaking academics, Paul DiMaggio established this point to the satisfaction of most sociologists in the early 1980s, and it has been hammered home in a variety of contexts ever since (DiMaggio, 1982; Levine, 1988; Beisel, 1997). Some theorists push this to an extreme position, offering a postmodern imagery of multiple, parallel, inter-penetrating, coexisting, flowing in-and-out-of-one-another cultures – jazz flows into hip-hop and vice versa – that reinforces the instability of cultural meanings and the indefensibility of cultural hierarchies. As Manuel Castells memorably expressed it, 'Social meaning evaporates from places … People live in places, power rules through flows' (1989: 349).

Except that life is not always lived in a flow. The same sociologists who suggest a non-systematic or fragmented view of culture have also pointed out that under some conditions meanings get locked in. There are two forms of lock-in: crisis and routine institutionalization. During times of personal or collective instability – Wuthnow's 'disturbances in the moral order', Swidler's 'unsettled times' – cultural bits and pieces take on a more coherent form, for example via ideological utterances. Meanings are demanded, and are produced upon demand. At this point institutions may lock in certain meanings and forms, thus giving them an advantage in entering and enduring the ongoing cultural swirl. Formal education, law and legal definitions, state-sanctioned discourse and elections offer clear cases of such lock-ins (Lee, 2000; Swidler, 1995, 2001).

So does art: the themes and conventions of highly esteemed literary or artistic works set audience expectations and become the target at which other artists aim, via emulation or defiance (Becker, 1982). A talented writer in late colonial Nigeria, for example, depicts how 'things fell apart' when the traditional African village encountered colonialism (Achebe, 1958, as discussed in Griswold, 2000). Taken up by British intellectuals and readers, Chinua Achebe's novel *Things Fall Apart* set the standard for African fiction for the next 40 years. The meaning-fullness of the colonial encounter became more deeply institutionalized in the West – in publishing, in courses on African fiction – than it did in Nigeria, however. Nigerians honor Achebe for being a superb writer, and for being known throughout the world, but his themes have not guided younger writers at home; there, fiction concentrates more on contemporary social problems than on the past. *Things Fall Apart* is meaningful both in Nigeria and in the West, but its themes are locked into the West to a greater extent. In the West, African fiction 'means' village life and social change, while in Nigeria it 'means' urban life and social problems. Both meaning statements are valid.

Not just intellectual interest but sheer market performance can achieve a comparable stability; meaning can lock in just by being successful enough to define the field. Richard A. Peterson shows this in his analysis of 'authentic' country music (1997). Having helped define the production-of-culture approach, Peterson assumed that industrial arrangements and markets shape culture, even where the members of the art world take pains to hide their commercial origins. Starting from 1923, with an Atlanta furniture salesman who tried to sell phonographs by producing some fiddle music recordings, and ending in 1953, when Hank Williams, an Alabama boy dressed up like a dandified cow puncher, became the apotheosis of the country singer, 'authentic' country stabilized. Despite multiple disadvantages – for example, the musicians' union refused to admit country musicians because they couldn't read music – performers responded to mass culture's demand for variety through recordings, radio, touring, song publishing, song writing and singing-cowboy films. Country music, in other words, was commercial from the start. Its claim of authenticity relied on convincing an audience that the performers were the genuine article. This was a challenge because what was 'authentic' was constantly changing, as in the 1930s, see-sawing between wholesome barn dance radio programs and the bawdy honky-tonk of the southwestern roadhouses. Likewise it took decades to settle on an 'authentic' costume: early performers dressed like farmers going to church and it wasn't until the postwar era that cowboy outfits, a honky-tonk fantasy established through cowboy movies, took hold. Market success stabilized country by the 1950s, so now a glittery cowboy outfit 'means' country singer and country music itself 'means' a limited set of emotions and situations drawn from rural working class life.

So the current thinking might be summed up as follows: some sociologists avoid meaning because (1) past claims have been too grandiose and have faltered empirically, and (2) there are plenty of ways to investigate culture without making any assumptions about meaning at all. Others feel that if cultural sociologists do not address meaning, they will miss the key to what culture is and how it works. Meaning is not some sacred umbrella over, or fundamental structure under, social behavior, but it is also not just a grab-bag of justifications or a fig leaf for power. People think and act through drawing analogies, and cultural meanings are analogies that are widely shared. Sometimes these are fleeting, but other times they become institutionalized, and stand like Stonehenge, obdurate structures by which people navigate. While sociologists debate over how the navigation system actually works, it seems difficult to theorize it out of existence.

MEASURING CULTURE

Earlier in this discussion I alluded to the methodological skirmishes that sometimes break out between sociology and cultural studies. Such disagreements point to a vexing problem for cultural sociology: that of measurement. Sociology is a discipline rooted in positivist social science, and although some cultural sociologists have taken the interpretive turn on two wheels, others want to slow down. These latter point out that the discipline's advantage over humanistic and anthropological approaches to culture is its capacity to subject theory to rigorous testing. But if that is the case, the 'culture is everywhere' approach fits awkwardly with the sociological self-definition of people who measure and compare.

This is less trouble for those whose work falls into traditional sociology of culture. It is possible to trace the rise and fall of a type of country music, a genre of fiction, or a taste preference, for these lend themselves to strict definition. Measuring a schema or a discursive formation is more problematic, and is very much on the agenda of cultural sociology at the present.

Most of the solutions that have been offered start with some sort of texts, produced through surveys, interviews, or bureaucratic routines. Using both turn-of-the-centry charity files and later a University of California program directory, John Mohr has constructed relational mapping of discourse structures that show ideological continuities and changes (Mohr, 1994; Mohr and Lee, 2000). Kathleen Carley has drawn on student interviews about comedy and science fiction books about robots to explore techniques of 'mental model extraction' that seek paired concepts (Carley, 1994). Robert Wuthnow has redefined survey responses to be not indicators of values, but behaviors through which discursive communities may be inferred (Wuthnow, 1987, 1996). Lamont and Griswold compare texts (interviews and print, respectively) across communities, contending that systematic textual differences indicate reliable cultural differences regardless of just what is being measured (Lamont, 1992, 2000; Griswold, 1987, 2000). Swidler has interviewed people to see what they have to say about love (2001). Uncovering or putting together some sort of text seems necessary for cultural measurement and comparison. Culture is neither in the air nor in the head; it is on the transcript, the survey sheet, the printed word. While a text may not be the best metaphor for culture (as Clifford Geertz once advocated), it remains methodologically indispensable.

Beyond this, many cultural researchers deny that there is anything peculiarly problematic, methodologically speaking, about culture. Given careful and self-aware methodological practice, they say that surveys *do* give some ideas about values, self-aware ethnographies *do* capture what people are thinking about (Putnam, 2000; Patillo-McCoy, 1999). Jepperson and Swidler (1994) reject any complacency in this area, cautioning that knowing minds, even if it were possible through such methods, is not the same thing as understanding culture; the level of analysis is different, they remind us, and sociologists should always resist the temptation to proceed via aggregation. Figuring out the connection among levels of cultural analysis is the challenge.

ON THE HORIZON

By the late 1990s cultural sociology had stabilized around a general set of agreements:

- Culture and society are mutually constitutive (though they can be conceptualized for research as if they were not).
- Everything is expressive, or can be analyzed as such.
- The search for big stories is likely to be less fruitful than the search for more partial cultural accounts.
- Gender, sexuality, race and ethnicity are as important as class in producing cultural stories.
- Cultural forms participate in a global circulation not successfully dominated by any single center.
- Organizations and industries, often structurally homologous in given settings, organize the distribution of cultural objects.
- People hold different positions in a distribution of knowledge and cultural resources. Subjectivity comes, in part, from positions; people in groups of any size or complexity share cognitive schemas.
- Meaning is not fixed but occurs whenever a number of people apply a cultural solution to a problem question relevant to that social group.

- Cultural hierarchies are produced by and reproduce social hierarchies; they are not based on cultural properties.
- Although meanings are contingent, institutions may lock in certain meanings.

In spite of the high level of agreement around these points, change is on the horizon. Two sources of a disturbance in the intellectual order may converge. First, as far back as the 'resistance through rituals' accounts of the Birmingham School and Raymond Williams's opening up of Marxist cultural theory in the 1970s, there was the idea of 'alternative' cultures, cultural bases from which to critique the mainstream (Hall and Jefferson, 1976; Hebdige, 1979; Willis, 1977). Today the mainstream has become a multicultural delta, and nowhere more so than in cultural sociology. The problem is, for an alternative to have any position from which to critique, it has to be alternative *to* something. There has to be a main stream, a dominant position. The highly fragmented views currently in place deny this, and to the extent that they do, we lose critique as well as hegemony.

This may be why there has been such a vigorous reaction to works like Paul Gilroy's *Against Race* (2000). An established theorist of racial oppression, in this book Gilroy accepted the assumptions just listed and drew the consequence that race (schema) and racism (uneven distribution of resources) are mutually constructed, not given. Racial meanings have been established through institutionalization. It follows, Gilroy argued, that dismantling the conceptual schema – race should be dismissed as the fiction it clearly is – can open up new possibilities for reconsidering the bases for the distribution of social goods. Although this indeed seems to be a logical extension of the current synthesis, Gilroy's book raised a chorus of protest that has echoed W.I. Thomas: race matters, if only because people believe that it represents something real. Deconstruct race, and you deconstruct the politics that attends it. Cultural sociology will need to acknowledge and address this shift in the terrain more than it has done.

The second source of change is in contradiction to the first, and it is from something that the agreed-upon theories predicted: a shake-up (unsettled times; disturbance in the moral order) that has promoted ideological coalescence. Ever since the partial, fragmented view of culture took hold, there has been in the shadows its logical alternative: the old-fashioned idea of a more systematic, coherent view. Some efforts to promote this image of a not-altogether-fragmented cultural world – visions of a 'culture wars' dichotomy in the United States, or splitting the world into a post/premodern divide, McWorld *vs.* Jihad – have met with great skepticism (Barber, 1996). Most vehement has been cultural sociology's rejection of Samuel Huntington's (1996) 'clash of civilizations' hypothesis, which posited that the struggle between the West and the rest was less economic than cultural, a contest between world-views (Western and Islamic especially, but also Eastern Orthodox, Latin American, Japanese, Chinese, Hindu and African). Sociologists found Huntington's analysis to be simplistic, jingoistic, and lacking discrimination, and they rejected it for reasons both political (it seems ethnocentric) and theoretical (it assumes a cultural coherence that sociologists don't believe exists).

Nevertheless, 'clash of civilizations' discourse is everywhere outside the academy. Chinese insistence on its non-Western version of capitalism without democracy, Islamicist views of a war between true religion and the heathen, European Union definitions of human rights pitted against much of the world's practices – all such formations sound quite at home with a culture wars idea. Cultural sociology needs to be able to evaluate these claims or risk irrelevance. 'Culture matters!' assert those promoting the idea of global cultural dichotomies and the impact of values (Harrison and Huntington, 2000). Cultural sociology needs to respond to this ordering of the popular imagination. It may also need to be open to the theoretical possibility that values can indeed steer human behavior, an assumption that most people take for granted. This does not mean that cultural sociologists will or should embrace the populist (and often demagogic) view of us against them, West *vs.* the rest, or submit to simplistic theories of *how and when* culture matters. But acknowledging the possibility of some cultural patterns, some systemic tendencies – for example, cultures where tolerance is a value, institutionally embedded, symbolically elaborated, versus cultures where it is not – seems a step that is both appropriate and, at this point, inevitable.

NOTE

For their careful readings and constructive suggestions, I am grateful to Penny Becker, Paul DiMaggio, Gary Fine, Michèle Lamont, Lynette Spillman, Ann Swidler and Vera Zolberg, as well as to Craig Calhoun.

BIBLIOGRAPHY

Achebe, Chinua (1958) *Things Fall Apart.* London: Heinemann.

Andersen, Margaret L. and Collins, Patricia Hill (1998) *Race, Class, Gender.* Belmont, CA: Wadsworth.

Appadurai, Arjun (1990) 'Disjuncture and difference in the global cultural economy', *Public Culture,* 2: 1–24.

Banks, Ingrid (2000) *Hair Matters: Beauty, Power, and Black Women's Consciousness.* New York: New York University Press.

Barber, Benjamin R. (1996) *Jihad vs. McWorld.* New York: Ballantine Books.

Becker, Howard S. (1982) *Art Worlds.* Berkeley, CA: University of California Press.

Becker, Penny (1999) *Congregations in Conflict: Cultural Models of Local Religious Life.* Cambridge: Cambridge University Press.

Beisel, Nicola Kay (1997) *Imperiled Innocents: Anthony Comstock and Family Reproduction in Victorian America.* Princeton, NJ: Princeton University Press.

Bhabha, Homi K. (1994) *The Location of Culture.* London/New York: Routledge.

Biernacki, Richard (1995) *The Fabrication of Labor: Germany and Britain, 1640–1914.* Berkeley, CA: University of California Press.

Bijker, Wiebe E. (1995) *Of Bicycles, Bakelite, and Bulbs: Toward a Theory of Sociotechnical Change.* Cambridge, MA: MIT Press.

Bordo, Susan (1993) *Unbearable Weight: Feminism, Western Culture, and the Body.* Berkeley, CA: University of California Press.

Bourdieu, Pierre (1977) *Outline of a Theory of Practice.* Cambridge: Cambridge University Press.

Bourdieu, Pierre (1984) *Distinction: A Social Critique of the Judgment of Taste* (trans. Richard Nice). Cambridge, MA: Harvard University Press.

Bourdieu, Pierre (1986) *The Rules of Art: Genesis and Structure of the Literary Field* (trans. Susan Emanuel). Stanford, CA: Stanford University Press.

Calhoun, Craig (1997) *Nationalism*. Minneapolis, MN: University of Minnesota Press.

Carley, Kathleen (1994) 'Extracting culture through textual analysis', *Poetics*, 22: 291–312.

Castells, Manuel (1989) *The Informational City: Information Technology, Economic Restructuring, and the Urban-Regional Process*. Oxford/Cambridge, MA: Blackwell.

Corse, Sarah M. (1997) *Nationalism and Literature: The Politics of Culture in Canada and the United States*. Cambridge/New York: Cambridge University Press.

Crane, Diana (1987) *The Transformation of the Avant-Garde: The New York Art World, 1940–1985*. Chicago: University of Chicago Press.

DiMaggio, Paul (1982) 'Cultural entrepreneurship in nineteenth-century boston', *Media, Culture and Society*, 4: 33–50.

DiMaggio, Paul (1997) 'Culture and cognition', *Annual Review of Sociology*, 23: 263–87.

Dobbin, Frank (1994) *Forging Industrial Policy: The United States, Britain, and France in the Railway Age*. New York: Cambridge University Press.

Eliasoph, Nina (1998) *Avoiding Politics: How Americans Produce Apathy in Everyday Life*. Cambridge/New York: Cambridge University Press.

Espeland, Wendy Nelson (1998) *The Struggle for Water: Politics, Rationality, and Identity in the American Southwest*. Chicago: University of Chicago Press.

Eyerman, Ron and Jamison, Andrew (1998) *Music and Social Movements: Mobilizing Traditions in the Twentieth Century*. Cambridge/New York: Cambridge University Press.

Fine, Gary Alan (1987) *With the Boys: Little League Baseball and Preadolescent Culture*. Chicago: University of Chicago Press.

Fine, Gary Alan (1996) *Kitchens: The Culture of Restaurant Work*. Berkeley, CA: University of California Press.

Gallup, George, Jr (1987) *The Gallup Poll: Public Opinion 1986*. Wilmington, DE: Scholarly Resources.

Gallup, George, Jr (1992) *The Gallup Poll: Public Opinion 1991*. Wilmington, DE: Scholarly Resources.

Geertz, Clifford (1973) *The Interpretation of Cultures*. New York: Basic Books.

Gilroy, Paul (2000) *Against Race: Imagining Political Culture Beyond the Color Line*. Cambridge, MA: Belknap Press.

Griswold, Wendy (1987) 'The fabrication of meaning: literary interpretation in the United States, Great Britain, and the West Indies', *American Journal of Sociology*, 92: 1077–1117.

Griswold, Wendy (2000) *Bearing Witness: Readers, Writers, and the Novel in Nigeria*. Princeton, NJ: Princeton University Press.

Hall, Stuart and Jefferson, Tony (eds) (1976) *Resistance Through Rituals: Youth Subcultures in Post-war Britain*. London: Hutchinson.

Hebdige, Dick (1979) *Subculture, The Meaning of Style*. London: Methuen.

Hannerz, Ulf (1992) *Cultural Complexity: Studies in the Social Organization of Meaning*. New York: Columbia University Press.

Harrison, Lawrence E. and Huntington, Samuel P. (eds) (2000) *Culture Matters: How Values Shape Human Progress*. New York: Basic Books.

Hilgartner, Stephen and Bosc, Charles L. (1988) 'The rise and fall of social problems', *American Journal of Sociology*, 94: 53–78.

Huntington, Samuel P. (1996) *The Clash of Civilizations and the Remaking of World Order*. New York: Simon and Schuster.

Jackall, Robert (1997) *Wild Cowboys: Urban Marauders and the Forces of Order*. Cambridge, MA: Harvard University Press.

Jepperson, Ronald L. and Swidler, Ann (1994) 'What properties of culture should we measure?' *Poetics*, 22: 359–71.

Lamont, Michèle (1992) *Money, Morals, and Manners: The Culture of the French and American Upper-Middle Class*. Chicago: University of Chicago Press.

Lamont, Michèle (2000) *The Dignity of Working Men: Morality and the Boundaries of Race, Class, and Immigration*. Cambridge, MA: Harvard University Press.

Lash, Scott and Urry, John (1994) *Economies of Signs and Space*. London: Sage.

Lee, Orville (2000) 'Hate speech and state speech,' paper presented to the Sociology Colloquium, Northwestern University.

Levine, Lawrence W. (1988) *Highbrow Lowbrow: The Emergence of Cultural Hierarchy in America*. Cambridge, MA: Harvard University Press.

Maffesoli, Michel (1996) *The Time of the Tribes: The Decline of Individualism in Mass Society* (trans. by Don Smith). London: Sage. (First published in 1988 in French as *Le Temps des tribus* by Méridiens Klincksieck, Paris.)

McDaniel, Tim (1996) *The Agony of the Russian Idea*. Princeton, NJ: Princeton University Press.

Melucci, Alberto (1989) *Nomads of the Present: Social Movements and Individual Needs in Contemporary*

Society (ed. by John Keane and Paul Mier). London: Century Hutchinson.

Meyer, John W., Boli, John, Thomas, George M. and Ramirez, Francisco O. (1997) 'World society and the nation state', *American Journal of Sociology*, 103: 144–81.

Mohr, John W. (1994) 'Soldiers, mothers, tramps, and others: discourse roles in the 1907 New York City Charity Directory', *Poetics*, 22: 327–57.

Mohr, John W. and Lee, Helene K. (2000) 'From affirmative action to outreach: discourse shifts at the University of California', *Poetics*, 28: 47–71.

Moulin, Raymonde (1987) *The French Art Market: A Sociological View* (trans. by Arthur Goldhammer). New Brunswick, NJ: Rutgers University Press (Abridged translation of *Marché de la peinture en France*, Paris: Éditions de Minuit, 1967).

Ogasawara, Yuko (1998) *Office Ladies and Salaried Men: Power, Gender, and Work in Japanese Companies*. Berkeley, CA: University of California Press.

Parreñas, Rhacel Salazar (2001) *Servants of Globalization: Women, Migration and Domestic Work*. Stanford, CA: Stanford University Press.

Pattillo-McCoy, Mary (1999) *Black Picket Fences: Privilege and Peril among the Black Middle Class*. Chicago: University of Chicago Press.

Peterson, Richard A. (1997) *Creating Country Music: Fabricating Authenticity*. Chicago/London: University of Chicago Press.

Peterson, Richard A. (ed.) (1976) *The Production of Culture*. Beverly Hills, CA: Sage.

Putnam, Robert D. (2000) *Bowling Alone: The Collapse and Revival of American Community*. New York: Simon and Schuster.

Sassen, Saskia (1991) *The Global City: New York, London, Tokyo*. Princeton, NJ: Princeton University Press.

Saxenian, AnnaLee (1994) *Regional Advantage: Culture and Competition in Silicon Valley and Route 128*. Cambridge, MA/London: Harvard University Press.

Sewell, William (1992) 'A theory of structure: duality, agency, and transformation', *American Journal of Sociology*, 98: 1–29.

Spillman, Lyn (1997) *Nation and Commemoration: Creating National Identities in the United States and Australia*. Cambridge/New York: Cambridge University Press.

Swidler, Ann (1986) 'Culture in action', *American Sociological Review,* 51: 273–86.

Swidler, Ann (1995) 'Cultural power and social movements', in *Social Movements and Culture* (ed. Hank Johnston and Bert Klandermans). Minneapolis, MN: University of Minnesota Press.

Swidler, Ann (2001) *Talk of Love: How Culture Matters*. Chicago: University of Chicago Press.

Willis, Paul E. (1977) *Learning to Labour*. Farnborough: Saxon House.

Wuthnow, Robert (1987) *Meaning and Moral Order: Explorations in Cultural Analysis*. Berkeley, CA: University of California Press.

Wuthnow, Robert (1989) *Communities of Discourse: Ideology and Social Structure in the Reformation, the Enlightenment, and European Socialism*. Cambridge, MA: Harvard University Press.

Wuthnow, Robert (1996) *Sharing the Journey: Support Groups and America's New Quest for Community*. New York: The Free Press.

Zerubavel, Eviatar (1997) *Social Mindscapes: An Invitation to Cognitive Sociology*. Cambridge, MA: Harvard University Press.

Zelizer, Viviana (1994) *The Social Meaning of Money*. New York: Basic Books.

Zolberg, Vera L. and Cherbo, Joni Maya (eds) (1997) *Outsider Art: Contesting Boundaries in Contemporary Culture*. Cambridge/New York: Cambridge University Press.

15

The Sociology of Health and Illness

GARY L. ALBRECHT

Heath is a metaphor for well-being. To be healthy means to be of sound mind and body; to be integrated; to be whole. Over time and across societies, influential theorists have emphasized that health consists of balance, of being centered (Antonovsky, 1979). The concept of health can be applied to human parts, as when we say, 'Your mother has a healthy heart' or 'Your father has a healthy psyche' (Ferreira et al., 2001). More generally, health refers to a holistic notion of individual well-being (Goldstein, 2000; Roose et al., 2001). We indicate this by relating that 'Samantha is a "healthy" person' or 'She is in good health'. By extension, the concept of health is attributed to families, communities and nations (Rubinstein et al., 2000). When we say that 'They are a healthy people', we use a metaphor to imply that this group has a balance, coherence, and that they can be trusted.

One's perspective on health is oriented by cultural values (Gilman, 1995). For example, contemporary Western medicine evaluates the health of a body organ or individual through a series of technological laboratory tests used to determine if indicators of structure, such as readings of radiographs, and function, such as kidney filtration rates, fall within a 'normal' range for this individual in these circumstances. If the tests individually and in conjunction suggest that everything is as expected,

the physician concludes that 'You are in good health'. Other societies impute health to the community. If there are reports of an individual being out of sorts, the doctor, medicine man or shaman looks for problematic social relationships and how they might be resolved as, for example, among the Yanomamö of Venezuela and Brazil (Chagnon, 1992). In this instance, health ultimately resides outside the individual and is situated in the social structure and relationships in the community or inside the individual expressed through dreams and hallucinations about spirits and ancestors. Health is reflected in shared values and membership in the community and in a perceived being at peace or at least feeling in control of a conflict. The worst fate for members of a community in any society is to be ostracized; to be excommunicated from the group. When this occurs, people lose their sense of integrity and belonging. Health also resides in the environment. When we speak of a healthy environment, we refer to the atmosphere of human rights, including work, and freedom of expression as well as clean air, adequate water and a sense of security. This is expressed in epidemiological models in terms of the host–environment interaction.

By contrast, illness refers to imbalance. Something is out of sync. This can be understood in terms of judgments about what constitutes the normal and abnormal (Lock, 2000). These judgments are made in terms of biomedical tests, individual perceptions of 'I don't feel well' and the social construction of the abnormal. Like the analysis of health, an examination of illness can take place on the level of the diseased organ, the individual, the community or the nation. While discussions of pathology dominate the medical literature, social scientists point out that illness is culturally constructed and closely associated with the dominant social, political and moral order (Turner, 2000). Their argument is that regardless of the organic basis of disease, the cultural context and interpretation of illness has profound implications for an individual's sense of well-being and perceived attribution of responsibility. When we say, 'He is sick', we employ a rich metaphor which means much more than the person has been judged to have an organic pathology determined by biomedical tests. We mean that the person is out of balance judged from our perspective. But, that is the point. From whose perspective? Based on whose norms and values?

This chapter explores how the sociology of health and illness helps us better to understand people's place and interactions in society and the manner in which social expectations shape our judgments. I begin by looking at key philosophical questions in historical context and in a cross-cultural framework that undergirds debates in the sociology of health and illness. I will then identify and examine some major fault-lines in the sociology of health and illness. Next, I will point to some of the major advances made in the field and indicate what important work is currently being done. Finally, I will consider what questions need to be addressed in the future and why.

PHILOSOPHICAL QUESTIONS UNDERGIRDING THE SOCIOLOGY OF HEALTH AND ILLNESS

The sociology of health and illness developed in a historical context attempting to understand how social and cultural factors influenced the distribution and understanding of disease, responses to illness, the evolution and operation of health care institutions and development of social policies (Aneshensel and Phelan, 1999; Berkman and Kawachi, 2000; Albrecht et al., 2000; Bird et al., 2000). Many of the fundamental questions addressed were earlier raised by philosophers, healers and revolutionaries (Porter, 1999). Without attempting to be exhaustive, some of these issues are:

- What are the bases for theories of health?
- What is the relationship between the body, mind and spirit?
- How do theories of health imply systems of healing?
- Who is the appropriate healer and what does the healing?
- What is the profession of medicine?
- In medicine, what is the relationship between knowledge and power?
- How should the delivery of health care be organized and paid for?
- Does every citizen have a right to health and to life?

Theories of health have been based on imbalances in the body, in the person or in social relationships. The great healing systems of India, China and Europe, for example, are based on the analysis of and interventions in such imbalances. Ayurvedic medicine is based on the Hindu belief that the body contains three elementary substances representative of the three divine universal forces they call spirit, phelem and bile. These forces are comparable to the Greek 'humours' of blood, yellow bile, black bile and phlegm grounded in the four elements of fire, earth, air and water. In traditional Chinese medicine, there is a dualistic cosmic theory of the yang (the male force) and the yin (the female force). The body is made up of five elements: wood, fire, earth, metal and water. In these systems, specific illnesses were attributed to an inordinate amount of one force, element or humour. For instance in the Greek system, colds in the winter were due to phlegm and diarrhoea in the summer to bile. In these three theoretical systems, health depended on preservation of balance between these forces and it was the task of the healer to bring these forces into equilibrium.

In a review of ethnographic data from 139 societies intended to sample the world's cultures, Murdock (1980) argues that an understanding of illness, and by implication of health, across cultures can be based on theories of natural and supernatural causation. According to Murdock (1980: 9), theories of natural causation consist of 'any theory, scientific or popular, which accounts for the impairment of health as a physiological consequence of some experience of the victim in a manner that would appear reasonable to modern medical science'. Natural causation explanatory frameworks include theories of infection, stress, organic deterioration, accidents and overt human aggression. The germ theory of disease, for example, which drives Western scientific medicine would fall under a natural causation model emphasizing infection. There may, however, be some overlap between the subcategories of the natural causation explanatory paradigms.

The theories of the supernatural causation of disease and health rest on assumptions that scientific Western medicine does not recognize as valid. According to Murdock's (1980: 17–27) analysis, there are three general types of theories of supernatural causation: theories of mystical causation, theories of animistic causation and theories of magical causation. Theories of mystical causation are 'any theory which accounts for the impairment of health as the automatic consequence of some act or experience of the victim mediated by some putative impersonal causal relationship rather than by the intervention of a human or supernatural being' (Murdock, 1980: 17). Some examples are the notion of 'fate' among the Romans and the breaking of food or sex taboos among the Thonga. Theories of animistic causation are 'any theory which ascribes the impairment of health to the behavior of some personalized supernatural entity – a soul, ghost, spirit or god' (Murdock, 1980: 19). An example is the concept of soul loss among the Tenino Indians of Oregon State in the United States. Theories of magical causation are 'any theory which ascribes illness to the covert action of an envious, affronted, or malicious being who employs magical means to injure his victims' (Murdock,

1980: 21). An example is the concept of the 'evil eye' invoked in Mediterranean cultures to explain illness and death. Each of these theories deals with the issues of:

- Agency: Who or what is causing the illness or preserving health?
- Social role: What is the role expected of the patient and of the healer?
- Symbols of knowledge, power and healing: What is the knowledge base of the healer? What symbols distinguish the healer from others in the community? and, What does purging by sweating or colonic therapy mean?
- Structure, process and outcome: Where should one seek help when ill? How does the healing take place? and, How should the healers be treated if they succeed or fail in their endeavors? (Ackerknecht, 1971; Porter, 1999).

Murdock (1980: 88–95) found that nearly 80 per cent of his sample had a notion of mystical retribution expressed through a sense of sin; the belief that acts in violation of some taboo or moral injunction would be followed by punishment of the individual or group. Guilt often accompanied this sense of sin. Malinowski (1944, 1948) made a major contribution to our understanding of theories of health and help-seeking by analyzing how individuals seek help for illness or seek to restore balance when things are out of sorts. In his examination of the workings of magic, science and religion, Malinowski concluded that individuals seek help for maladies according to their cultural and societal frames. What they have learned and experienced gives meaning to and a sense of control over their illnesses. Malinowski and others also discovered that people can use multiple frames of reference in understanding disease and seeking help. For instance, among the Wakomba of Kenya, individuals would often seek help from their medicine man if they were 'sick'. But if that did not work, they might visit a health clinic to try Western scientific medicine delivered through a colored pill or injection by a doctor in a white coat. If the intervention of the medicine man and the doctor did not work, they might turn to their indigenous belief system or to the Christ of the missionaries. Often these approaches for help and interventions are commingled, with no one healer knowing that the others are being simultaneously invoked. The problem that then often arises is who is to be credited if the individual is cured and who is to blame for failure? These same issues play out in Western culture when people seek help from scientific medicine, alternative therapies such as herbs, acupuncture and spas, and traditional or 'new age' religions. For all of the emphasis on scientific medicine, there is substantial evidence that people are using syncretic approaches to explaining health and seeking well-being. Thus, while there are continuous collisions between the proponents of explanatory models of health, people who do not feel 'well' explore a wide range of treatment alternatives in searching for health. This reality portends that there will continue to be a struggle over knowledge and power in health care belief and delivery systems. Ultimately, power, control and money are at stake. These will play out differently according to history, culture and resources.

FAULT-LINES IN THE SOCIOLOGY OF HEALTH AND ILLNESS

The sociology of health and illness has reached a stage of maturity built on over 100 years of work. An assessment of the field provides a satisfaction with the many concepts, theories and findings that help us better understand the place of health and illness in society. At the same time, there is an unease with many unresolved contentious issues, the inability of theory to explain much behavior and the gap between knowledge and practice. One way to examine these issues is to concentrate on the fault-lines in the field; to focus on the deep questions that stimulate debate.

Matters of perspective

Sociologists are masters of the dictum 'It all depends'. In the instance of the sociology of health and illness, one's view of the world does depend on one's perspective. While there is clear acknowledgment that we live in global society, intellectuals and political leaders are struggling to make sense of the new world order (Giddens, 2000). In terms of the sociology of health, it is presumptuous that knowledge of health, illness and medicine generated in North America, Europe and Japan is applied with such ease across those societies and around the globe. Knowledge produced on 11 per cent of the world's population by researchers and clinicians is assumed to be applicable with little interpretation to the rest of the world. Even those studies done in the Third World are typically mounted by Western scholars who are in the field for a limited amount of time or by denizens of the Third world who have been educated and work in the industrialized world. Because of the way knowledge is produced and marketed, a major problem of external validity and generalization exists.

A second disconnect in perspective concerns the inequalities in health experienced within and between countries. There is a persistent finding that differences in social class, gender and racial/ethnic groups account for substantial differentials in access to health care, active life expectancy, morbidity and mortality (Andersen, 1995; Crimmins and Saito, 2001; MacIntyre, 1997; Marmot et al., 1995). Such differences are even more exaggerated between the rich and the poor nations. As Amartya Sen (1999) argues, health and development are representative of freedom. After years of observing the practice of medicine and public health efforts among poor communities in the United States and in numerous countries in Latin America, Waitzkin (2001) concludes that inequalities in health are not just a result of social class position and access to resources but are part and parcel of the underlying political economic forces that evaluate people based on their education, ability to work, citizenship and political power. Again, it is the powerful health care institutions, medical professionals, international pharmaceutical companies and governments that produce research findings and decide how scarce resources should be distributed. In few instances are the voices of the poor and disenfranchised heard in this process.

A third difference in perspective among those who study and intervene in the health arena involves the insider–outsider stance of the observer. Much medical and health care research in industrialized countries is sponsored by governments or businesses such as pharmaceutical companies who have considerable vested interests in the outcome of the research or demonstration projects. Within sociology this conflict in perspective has been characterized by the sociology *in* and sociology *of* medicine positions. The sociologists in medicine typically worked in medical settings and had their salaries paid by medical schools and health care providers. The criticism was that these researchers would be compromised by being co-opted by the 'system'. Sociologists of medicine were those scholars housed in behavioral science departments of universities who did not have a financial interest in the institutions of medicine. Therefore, the logic went that they would be more objective observers. Critics countered that these scholars were but part-time visitors who did not work in nor deeply understand the internal working of the health care enterprise. In fact, both perspectives have produced valuable work over the years and today, the distinction, while appropriate, does not fully capture the complex worlds of those doing health care research. It is difficult to be entirely in one camp or the other.

A fourth difference in perspective concerns the question one is asking and the approaches one takes to answering the question. In parochial terms, the debate is often couched in qualitative or quantitative approaches to gathering evidence. American social science approaches to health have typically used quantitative approaches to gather epidemiological, survey, clinical trial and outcomes data to describe structure, process and outcomes. The key questions are:

- What is the health of the population?
- What are the determinants of health?
- How can society intervene to improve the health of the population given limited resources?
- How can evidence shape salutary social policies?

While there has been extraordinary epidemiological and health services research in Europe, much scholarly work in the UK and on the Continent has also sought to understand the meaning of health and medicine. Thus, the influence of Durkheim, Mannheim, Foucault and Habermas has been on understanding what accounts for differences in health outcomes not just from an empirical but from a deeply theoretical perspective. While there is overlap, Sol Levine contrasted the American approach as 'structure seekers' and the European version as 'meaning seekers'. Clearly both perspectives are needed (Bloom, 2000; Chard et al., 1999).

Pragmatism

Pragmatism had a formative influence on the development of medical sociology, particularly in the United States, because it provided a conceptual framework for thinking about issues of health and illness and indicated the types of data and analysis that should be used to construct arguments. Pragmatism signifies a faultline in the study of health and illness because of its epistemological underpinnings, concern with 'scientific method' and focus on applied and policy-oriented investigations. Not everyone was to agree with this predominantly American approach to the study of health and illness because other scholars placed more of a premium on generating over-arching, explanatory theories; valued the generation of knowledge for knowledge's sake; and were more interested in the meanings of facts than in the facts themselves. As a consequence, there are different intellectual approaches to the study of health and illness depending on one's epistemological predilections, notion of what constitutes 'scientific' inquiry, values, ideology, applied versus theoretical orientation, and the historical and cultural context of the investigation.

Pragmatism is a style of philosophy introduced by Charles Sanders Peirce (1839–1914) and William James (1842–1910) which powerfully shaped the work of Dewey (1859–1952) and Mead (1964/1934) in the early twentieth century and the more recent contemporary philosophical work of Quine (1969), Putnam

(1978), Rorty (1991), Haack (1993) and West (1999). Because of its multiple formulations, it is difficult to characterize the work of all pragmatists under one conceptual umbrella. However, in seeking a common understanding of this approach, Susan Haack (1996: 643) asserts that pragmatism 'is best characterized by the method expressed in the pragmatic maxim, according to which the meaning of a concept is determined by the experiential or practical consequences of its application'. The early pragmatists were attracted by the idea of certainty and formulation of scientific laws that had practical applications. Peirce, for example, reacted to the *a priori* methods traditionally favored by metaphysicians by arguing for a scientific method where the inquirer is ready to 'drop the whole cartload of his beliefs, the moment experience is against them' (Peirce, 1931–58, Vol. I: 14, 55). This approach to scientific method is compatible with Popper's principle of falsification whereby theories are proposed and submitted 'to the severest test we can design' (Popper, 1972: 16). The appeal of this version of the scientific method is that it emphasized objective knowledge and universality; truth lay in tested laws and in the 'facts'.

William James espoused a different flavor of pragmatism. He stressed *praxis*, the practical consequences of believing in a particular concept or social program. In considering the intricacies of metaphysical and moral questions, he says, for instance: 'The pragmatic method in such cases is to try to interpret each notion by tracing its respective practical consequences' (James, 1907: 28). He also acknowledged that there might not be conclusive scientific evidence to settle every disagreement. Therefore, he accepted that 'religious beliefs' which in principle cannot be verified or falsified are often used to make strategic decisions because they fit with the believer's life and have practical consequences. He further recognized that 'truth' is socially constructed and can change over time. Both his acknowledgment of 'religious beliefs' and the social construction of truth laid the foundation for explorations of the subjective meanings of experience.

Pragmatism influenced the development of the sociology of health and illness in three ways. First, pragmatism inculcated in sociologists an early interest in gathering 'objective' data through observations, surveys and censuses that would describe social phenomena and help develop predictive models to test arguments. Second, the pragmatists, exemplified by William James, encouraged the anchoring of analysis in practical realities and social policies. James laid the foundations for grounded theory, the study of social problems, observing behavior in the 'real world', formulating social policies and testing their effects on society. Third, the evolution of pragmatist thinking moved away from the strict 'objectivism' and application of the scientific method advocated by Peirce towards an appreciation of the importance of subjective experience, relativistic and culturally different conceptions of behavior, and paradigm shifts in the gathering and interpretation of behavior. In reviewing a broad range of pragmatic positions, it is noteworthy that in spite of their differences, pragmatists coalesced in their emphasis on attending to how knowledge is generated and that it be evaluated in terms of practical utility.

These themes recur in the current work on health and illness that focus on outcomes research and evidence-based medicine. For example, Donabedian (1980, 1981) and subsequent health services researchers (Andersen, 1995) made important distinctions between structure, process and outcome in evaluating the effectiveness of health care interventions, be they on the patient, community or societal levels. Structural measures primarily reflect the organizational and economic structures within which health care is delivered and the personnel who provide the care. Some examples are the practice of managed care in the United States delivered in for-profit and not-for-profit environments by specialized physicians and the National Health Service model in the UK, which is organized and financed by the British government and delivered through widespread use of primary care physicians and nurses. Process measures of health focus on what is done to patients. These would involve the use of treatment protocols detailing what should be done for a particular condition or circumstance, such as when to do a caesarean section in delivering a baby or when to intubate a patient in respiratory distress. Outcome measures focus on the results of health care intervention. Some examples are changes in days of work lost or death due to influenza as a result of preventive vaccinations or reduction in mortality rates due to coronary artery bypass surgery.

Outcomes research is particularly popular among those clinicians and policy-makers who are trying to improve access, maintain quality and control the costs of care (Stevens et al., 2001). Managed competition, health maintenance organizations (HMOs), preferred provider organizations (PPOs) and national health insurance are all organizational strategies to strike an efficient and effective balance between cost, access and quality (Sullivan, 2000). An example is an examination of how the lack of health insurance ultimately influences the overall health of the elderly (Baker et al., 2001). Outcomes research is a research paradigm designed to test whether these forms of organizational interventions achieve their desired objectives (Cone, 2001).

Evidence-based medicine is a related effort to base clinical practice and social policy on evidence accumulated through previous experience and research. A pioneer in this enterprise, David Sackett, defines evidence-based medicine as 'the conscientious, explicit, and judicious use of current best evidence in making decisions about the care of individual patients' (Sackett et al., 1996). By extension, evidence-based medicine is also used to develop and implement policies on the community or population levels. Health technology assessment likewise is an attempt to measure the impact of technological interventions on health outcomes, costs and quality of care. These two approaches use clinical trials and population-based surveys to determine whether particular courses of action, like population-based inoculation efforts for Anthrax and smallpox in light of the threat of biological terror, are sensible strategies.

An enormous body of work in the sociology of health and illness is not so patently pragmatic but is intent on understanding what it means to be sick, to have a chronic illness or disability, to be a woman, to experience fertility and menopause, to be poor, a member of a minority group and in need of health care and social services (Albrecht et al., 2000; Bird et al., 2000). Here the emphasis in the analysis is less on pragmatic outcomes and more on developing an understanding of health and illness, building concepts and forging theory. The fault-line here lies in the type of questions being asked, the methods used to collect data, the political economy of the research process (who is funding the work and for what purpose?) and the intended use of the studies.

Partitioning the person and holism

Based on persistent philosophical questions of epistemology and ontology, there has been an ongoing struggle in the sociology of health to understand the interrelationship of body, mind and spirit. The philosophical origins of this discussion concern the place of the body in analyses of health and illness. The discussion raises two over-arching theoretical sets of issues: deciding on a unit of analysis and positioning the body in the individual in relation to mind and spirit. Turner (1992), Seymour (1998) and Shilling (1993, 2001) review the historical foundations of this intellectual work from the Greeks, through Western philosophy to contemporary sociological theory. The arguments revolve around cultural context, perspective and meaning. Cultures that emphasize the importance of the community deal with individual bodies as being constitutive parts of the larger society. Sociologists generally take this larger, structural view of the body in analyzing how societies define, represent and control bodies. On the other hand, cultures that place strong value on the importance of the individual deal with the body as an essential element belonging to and under the control of the individual. In terms of perspective, the body is conceived of as being both subject and object and by extension as a cultural subject or a cultural object. In this instance, importance is given to the body in terms of valued personal experiences, utility in sport and military terms or in its representation through size, shape and dress. From this viewpoint, the body also has considerable symbolic meaning expressed in judgments about fertility, pleasure or threat to society posed by deviancy. Social psychologists and cultural studies scholars generally explore these issues.

Research in the health arena reflects these larger theoretical issues and perspectives. There is a chasm between those who study physical health and disability and those who focus on mental health and emotions. Those interested in the spiritual dimensions of health and illness including belief in a higher being, ultimate meanings of existence, hope and feelings of detachment and peace are regarded with suspicion by those grounded in the 'science' of the body (Wuthnow, 1998). Furthermore, epidemiologists, demographers and macrolevel sociologists examine the interrelationships between social variables like age, race/ethnicity, sex, gender and social class on health status and outcomes while clinicians and social psychologists concentrate on individual organisms, diseases and health behaviors. As a consequence of choosing one's level of analysis and perspective, these different brands of investigators rarely talk or listen to each other and define health and illness quite differently among themselves.

One is left with the persistent problem of the whole and the parts. What is the object of our study of the body in the context of health and illness and how are these fragmented perspectives ever to be integrated? In fact, these problems are becoming more acute with the growth of the field of human genetics, the increased use of biological interventions in the body and increasing use of replacement parts like mechanical hearts. Reactions to this Balkanization of the body include a burgeoning of interest in holistic health, spiritual healing, a re-examination of the meaning and value of life and mind–body–spirit inter-dynamics (Albrecht and Devlieger, 1999).

Professions, organizations and institutions

Concurrent with the controversies regarding approaches to analyzing personal and community health have been dramatic changes in the way that we conceptualize health care professions, organizations and institutions. The beginning of the twentieth century witnessed the professionalization of medicine when a broad range of health care practitioners such as homeopaths, chiropractors, naturopaths, osteopaths and allopaths employed a curious mix of interventions including blood letting, application of mercury, colonics, manipulation and surgery to cure illnesses. After a period of sorting out which treatments were thought to bear scientific merit, a re-evaluation of medical training occasioned by the Flexner Report and legal and licensing struggles, allopathic medicine in Western nations was legitimated, achieved dominance and was recognized as a profession (Starr, 1982).

In the mid-century the profession of medicine was the standard by which all other professions were judged. According to Goode (1960: 903), a profession (here read medicine) had two core characteristics: 'a prolonged specialized training in a body of abstract knowledge and a collectivity or service orientation.' Five additional characteristics were derived by Goode from these two foundational principles:

- The profession determines its own standards of education and training.
- Professional practice is often legally recognized by some form of licensure.
- Licensing and admission boards are manned by members of the profession.
- Most legislation concerned with the profession is shaped by that profession.
- The practitioner is relatively free of lay evaluation and control.

In a masterful analysis of the profession of medicine, Freidson (1970) showed how medicine was institutionalized, became specialized, generated knowledge based on 'science' and clinical practice, accumulated and exercised power, socially constructed illness and remained among all potential competitors the legitimate profession deemed competent to and worthy of being paid to treat illness. For years, the institutional power of medicine was not seriously contested in Western countries (Abbott, 1988).

Considerable forces arose, however, in the later third of the twentieth century to challenge the status quo of medicine's knowledge, power and form of practice. After the mid-century, medicine increasingly began to be practiced in groups with peer review and accountability (Freidson, 1975). Then, as medicine became even more technological, it began to resemble an industry with business-like concerns such as optimizing the division of labor, selling new products, expanding into new markets, preserving income and maximizing return on investment (Albrecht, 1992; Light, 2000a; Starr, 1982). The traditional profession of medicine was simultaneously challenged by the twin forces of deprofessionalization and corporatization (Weiss and Fitzpatrick, 1997), first in the United States and then in the UK and in other parts of the world. Consumers began to become more assertive in terms of the care they desired and where they sought it. Physicians increasingly began to work for corporations or the state which demanded more accountability and threatened their autonomy. These changes called for a political economic analysis of health care professions and markets.

Light (2000b) typified this change in professional practice, power, climate and setting in terms of a model of countervailing power. In this framework, the knowledge and power of medicine is counterbalanced by other powerful actors in the health care marketplace including the buyers and sellers of services and products, corporations who now employ substantial numbers of doctors, the government who employs physicians and pays for treatment, insurance companies and the more informed consumer. This fault-line in the sociology of health and illness concerns the theories and practice used to explain the definition of health problems, organization of health care delivery, control of knowledge, power over the consumer and marketplace, consumer actions and guardians of the health of the public. Changing times required new perspectives and models (Ardigó, 1995).

Alterations in the practice of health care have had equally dramatic effects on organizations and institutions in the medical arena. In a careful analysis of the changes in health care

environment, institutions and organizational change that have occurred in the past 25 years, Scott et al. (2000: 360) point out that adoption of managed care has produced heated competition and the unleashing of market forces in the health care arena. As a consequence, 'Governance structures have become more fragmented. … The coherence of organizational boundaries has been greatly reduced. … Practitioners and patients alike are confused. … Consensus about institutional logics has been reduced.' Changes in institutional rules and behavior change such as occurred under managed care produce 'disagreements and disputations over the priorities and goals of the sector and lack of agreement on the appropriate means to be employed in reaching them' (p. 359). Light argues that institutional theorists are able to document changes in the profession of medicine, organization and practice of medicine but are not able easily to explain why this has occurred. In response to this challenge, Light elaborated the theory of countervailing powers to assert that the very dominance of the medical profession evoked reactions from governments and consumers and that the very size of and potential profits in the health care business enticed health care corporations, insurance companies and lawyers to enter and attempt to control the business (2000b). Different approaches to understanding the profession of medicine and health care organizations and institutions demonstrate the theoretical struggle to understand changes in health care institutional dynamics over time (Turner, 1995; Williams, 2001).

Health as a value

The last fault-line centers on the symbolic meaning and value of health, for discussions of health and illness are ultimately based on assumptions about human worth. These assumptions and arguments about human worth have particular relevance to research and social policies towards vulnerable populations like women and children, the elderly, the poor, the inadequately insured, disabled people and those with chronic and/or incapacitating illnesses. In practice, vulnerable populations generally share more than one of these characteristics, increasing their vulnerability and risk of poor health status, low quality of life and even death (Ayanian et al., 2000). While scholars agree that their research on health issues has serious implications for social policy, they often skirt direct examinations of the values, morality and ethics undergirding their work or in the application of their results to social policy. Some researchers believe that they should explore specific issues for knowledge's sake alone while others gather data to argue for specific social policies or undertake research to evaluate the interventions suggested by certain social policies. In any event, there are fundamental questions based on values which are subsumed in all research on health – What is health? Is health a human right? Does every person have a right to health care? Who has the responsibility to provide and pay for health care? Are some people more deserving of health care than others? When is it appropriate to not provide health services? Do members of a community have the responsibility to provide care for all members of their community or for other communities? If so, how much care and under what conditions? – and not all researchers, politicians or moral philosophers agree on the answers to these questions (Blendon and Benson, 2001).

Decades of research on the cost/access/quality trade-off problem in health care in Western countries gave rise to behavioral models of access to medical care, market models that regulate the amount, type and quality of care and ethical arguments about health as a human right (Albrecht, 2001; Andersen, 1995). Aday (2000) added depth to the argument by probing the three philosophical paradigms that ground debates on justice and health equity: distributive justice, social justice and deliberative justice. Distributive justice pertains to health care by applying the principle of need to the allocation of health benefits: 'Integral to the framework is the value judgment that the system would be deemed fair or equitable if need-based criteria, rather than resources (such as insurance coverage or income), were the main determinants of whether or not,

and how much, care is sought' (Aday, 2000: 483). Social justice speaks to establishing and supporting a public health infrastructure and population-based health interventions that will prevent disease and protect those most vulnerable in the society. These efforts are usually undertaken and supported by governments and the state. Shortell et al. (1996) argue that such broad-based, national health care systems in European countries account for their better life expectancy and infant mortality rates than the United States, where a much larger proportion of the gross national product is spent on health care. Deliberative justice is grounded in community participation and empowerment of the people affected by health policies in designing health care systems and programs. Such a paradigm enlightens the State of Oregon's approach to allocating scarce health resources and the World Health Organization's Health Cities and Healthy Communities initiatives in organizing health care in developing countries (Ashton, 1991). This deliberative justice approach is concordant with Sen's (1999) assertion that health is an essential component of economic development and of freedom.

Arguments about the inherent social values shaping research and the allocation of scarce health resources are proposed as the critical issues in global health by Koop et al. (2001). They point out that the application of differential values to the organization and delivery of health services dramatically affects such outcomes as demographic destabilization, accelerating disparities in national development, persistent under-attention to the vulnerabilities and capabilities of girls and women, reliable sources of clean water for the world's population and disposal of waste, and attention to public health problems such as obesity and malnutrition. Likewise, Feagin (2001), in re-focusing attention on the implications of sociological research for social justice, implies that serious attention should be given not only to the social problems before us but to the value systems underlying different intervention strategies and likely outcomes of these different strategies. This is an area of keen debate and one in need of more serious thought.

MAJOR CONTRIBUTIONS OF THE SOCIOLOGY OF HEALTH AND ILLNESS

The fault-lines in the sociology of health and illness tell us where lively debates on over-arching issues are occurring but I would also like to draw attention to some major advances in the field and indicate what specific work is being done. On the social psychological level, Mechanic has extended the early work on the sick role to consider illness behavior and what constitutes trust. Parsons (1951) made a major contribution in identifying the components of the sick role in terms of what was expected of the patient. Over the years, others criticized and expanded this model to include expectations of those with chronic illnesses and disabilities. Mechanic (1962) made contributions in considering what it meant to be ill and how one experienced and expressed illness. This work led him to reconsider the doctor–patient relationship and, on a more macro level, what illness meant in society. This stream of research has laid conceptual building blocks and theoretical foundations that make discussions of trust and social justice more sophisticated. As Mechanic (1989) points out, trust is the social glue that makes diagnosis and treatment possible on the individual level and social policy possible on the community and societal levels.

On the organizational level, studies of national health care services, multiple hospital systems, assisted care facilities, hospices, support groups for those with HIV/AIDS and the environment within which these organizations operate have led to important findings about how the organization of health care directly impacts the cost, access and quality of care. This work is now expanding to important sets of cross-national studies that are examining the essentials of effective health care systems, how different organizational models may produce similar results and how the mix of populations served interact with the organizational structures of the delivery system to yield variable results. In other words, the organization of health care needs to be tailored to the needs of the population and local culture and environment. That is why there is persistent interest in comparative health care

system research between Scandinavian countries, other European countries, the UK, United States, Canada, Cuba and Japan.

Inequality in health has also been a dominant theme of the sociology of health and illness which has evolved from a consideration of differences in behavior and material circumstances to a complex consideration of how health behaviors and material and social resources interact to produce differences in health outcomes both on the individual and community levels. Researchers in this area have illustrated the importance of social capital in dealing with health issues. Social capital refers to the social resources and networks available to individuals that help them define and cope with health problems. Consistent findings show that larger amounts of social capital are predictive of less disability, more support and a higher quality of life. Research on social equity has also highlighted the need to do multi-level analysis; to consider individuals in their environments and as members of a community and nation. Each layer of relationships is likely to explain some of the health outcomes and considering individuals in context permits a more fine-grained analysis of health and disease realities.

Health-related quality of life research has directed attention beyond issues of mortality and morbidity to how people are living (Levine, 1987, 1995). This concept is applicable across the lifespan and groups of individuals. Investigations into quality of life have led to important distinctions between objective and subjective indicators of well-being. Albrecht and Devlieger (1999) discovered, for example, that there was a disability paradox raised by the apparent discrepancies between the quality of life of disabled people as perceived by the general public and those living with the disability. About 50 per cent of the people with serious and persistent disabilities in the study reported that they had a good or very good quality of life even though outside observers might deem otherwise. This type of result suggests that clinical and policy decision-makers need multiple sources of data to understand the desires, wants and experiences of vulnerable and disabled people. As a consequence, quality of life is being incorporated into most judgments of treatment outcomes. Much progress is being made in this area.

This work on health-related quality of life has also drawn renewed attention to the concepts of normalcy and deviancy (Phelan et al., 2000). The women's movement and interest in international health have illustrated how white male norms established at one point in history in postindustrial countries do not serve as useful reference points for the behavior of all people. The acknowledgment of incredible diversity in the distribution and experience of illness and disability have turned the discussion away from that of normalcy to that of the appreciation of difference. As a consequence, the meaning and experience of health are being redefined. Most research has been traditionally done on men by men and for men. Yet, recent research clearly demonstrates that women's health experiences and issues are different from those of men, requiring considerable changes in the conceptualization and delivery of health care for women and children. In fact, one of the major factors in improving the health of a nation is to educate women and make health resources available to them, for women are usually the people who care for children, older parents and disabled people.

FUTURE TRENDS

We now turn our gaze to where the field is going. Research on health and illness has become increasingly interdisciplinary in theory and scope and is utilizing prospective, longitudinal designs to address complex questions about the interaction between different sets of variables. This has heated already contested issues because traditional boundaries have been broken and ownership of parts of the person or of the problem have been challenged. These issues question the knowledge base and power of a discipline. As a case in point, consider the boundaries between the social, the cultural, the biological and the medical aspects of health and illness. For years there were debates over the relative power of

nature or nurture in explaining mental illness, heart disease, cancer, strokes and disabilities. Other research investigated the cultural and institutional contexts of health and illness, producing such theories as the stigmatizing effects of labeling people sick or deviant or of attributing the effects of isolation and institutionalization to an illness not to the social consequences of institutionalization. Further research examined illness in different cultural contexts to ascertain whether or not the 'deviant behavior' was symptomatic of an underlying illness or rather a manifestation of cultural differences.

These questions take on a renewed importance in this age of the new genetics, stunning advances in knowledge about the biological bases of illness and a sharper understanding of the interaction between the genetic and organic components of human beings, their group memberships and environments. For instance, there is accumulating evidence for a genetic basis of Parkinson's disease (Scott et al., 2001). Breast cancer is now known to have genetic, lifestyle and environmental determinants (King et al., 2001). The study of twins offers a powerful design to tease out the differential effects of nature versus nurture on behavior. Goldberg and his colleagues (1990), for example, compared over 2000 military men who served in heavy combat roles in Vietnam to their identical twin brothers who saw less intense action. Those twins who experienced the heavy combat were nine times more likely to report medical symptoms such as stress and battle fatigue syndromes, flashbacks, nightmares, inability to sleep and problems controlling their tempers than their brothers.

Udry (1994, 2000) and Udry, Morris and Kovenock (1995) have caused lively debates over the biological and social construction of gender through their biosocial research on gender. In a number of longitudinal cohort studies beginning in the 1960s, Udry (a sociologist-demographer) and Morris (a physician) collected blood samples to measure hormone levels and other biological factors and simultaneously gathered a host of demographic, social and behavioral data. The general thrust of the findings from many studies based on this approach is that *both* biological and social variables explain gendered behavior in these samples and that both sets of variables independently and in interaction explain such behaviors as delinquency, dating behavior, age of marriage and fertility. They conclude from this body of work that both sets of variables ought to be considered in explaining health, disease and many social behaviors, that there are biological limits to the social construction of gender and that there is a need for the development of sophisticated biosocial models of behavior. Feminist scholars attacked this work calling it 'neuroendocrinological determinism' (Miller and Costello, 2001) and conceptually and methodologically deficient (Kennelly et al., 2001; Risman, 2001). Udry responded to these criticisms:

> Sociologists are very diverse in their theoretical orientations. Some of us work within paradigms that are incompatible with paradigms used by other sociologists, even though we suppose we are working in the same domain – in this case, the study of gender. ... Paradigms with different perspectives are not necessarily mutually exclusive. I can live with the critics' paradigm. But can they live with mine? (Udry, 2001: 616)

Similar approaches are being employed in studies of organizational behavior. Arvey and Bouchard (1994) summarize a body of research on genetics, twins and organizational behavior. The general conclusion is that there are numerous studies illustrating that biological and heritable factors do interact with work and organizational variables to explain job attitudes, satisfaction, interests, performance and tenure.

The interplay of biological and social variables is also evident in the examination of the effects of the environment on health and illness. In reviewing this work, Masters (2001: 345) concludes that:

> (a) Developments in genetics and medicine indicate that governmental policies have greatly underrated the dangers posed by radiation and the social transformations that will result from DNA sequencing. (b) Research on brain structures and neurochemistry shows how toxic chemicals undermine normal emotions and behavior. Heavy metal burdens are higher in violent criminals, and exposure to these toxins is significantly correlated with rates of violence (controlling for socioeconomic, ethnic, and demographic factors). (c) An untested chemical used to treat water supplied to 140 million Americans significantly increases both the odds of dangerous lead uptake and behavioral dysfunctions in children and adults. (d) The complexity of gene–environment interactions challenges accepted theories of gender, sociopolitical inequalities, ethnocentrism and history.

This interdisciplinary work threatens traditional academic boundaries and paradigms, intensifies struggles over ownership of a problem, questions existing knowledge and power and raises moral, ethical, and legal issues. Conrad (2000) argues that advances in biology and genetics threaten to intensify the medicalization of human problems accompanied by significant undesirable consequences for people with differences and for social policies. Cunningham-Burley and Boulton (2000) are more sanguine, recognizing that while many problems exist, the new genetics offers untold opportunities for the understanding of health and illness and the practice of health care. Regardless of one's viewpoint, the interdisciplinary approach to health and illness is here to stay and will revolutionize the way that we define, investigate and understand problems. This approach does force scholars to consider the work of researchers in related fields, to develop and test new theory and design studies to tease out the relative contributions of different sets of variables in better understanding health and illness.

At the same time, changes in the shape of institutions and the globalization of health problems are impelling scholars and policymakers alike to focus on the need for supranational institutions that can deal with borderless health-related problems associated with international development, terrorism, HIV/AIDS, the reappearance of infectious diseases and inadequate public health infrastructures. The arguments over income inequalities within and between nations are expressed in terms of peace, equity and justice over the plight of Iraqi children, the AIDS scourge in Africa and Asia, the health of people in the Balkans and the oppression of women and children (Hayward et al., 2000). These issues focus discussion on the meaning of citizenship, health as a human right and health as a moral good. The work of Lane (1991, 2000) and Sen (1992, 1999) is pertinent in this regard. Lane asserts that international markets should be judged not only by economic growth and profits but by their ability to provide well-being to all citizens. In fact, he argues that we are experiencing a loss of happiness in market democracies due to inequalities in the distribution of wealth and health resulting in want and feelings of insecurity. Sen, in a parallel fashion, points out that freedom is ultimately contingent on equity; on development and citizens' feelings of security, and access to basic material goods and health. More discussions of health and illness will be couched in terms of international security, responsibility and access to the infrastructure and resources that permit a human life.

While this analysis of current thinking about health and illness is not inclusive, it does point to many of the salient issues confronting scholars and policy-makers and points to the future work that needs to be done. May such efforts be energized by the maturation of the field and stimulated by the recognition that we are all interconnected citizens of the world. What happens to others will affect us and vice versa.

REFERENCES

Abbott, Andrew (1988) *The System of Professions.* Chicago: University of Chicago Press.

Ackerknecht, Erwin H. (1971) *Medicine and Ethnology.* Baltimore, MD: Johns Hopkins University Press.

Aday, Lu Ann (2000) 'An expanded conceptual framework of equity: implications for assessing health policy', in Gary L. Albrecht, Ray Fitzpatrick and Susan C. Scrimshaw (eds), *The Handbook of Social Studies in Health and Medicine.* London: Sage. pp. 481–92.

Albrecht, Gary L. (1992) *The Disability Business: Rehabilitation in America.* Newbury Park, CA: Sage.

Albrecht, Gary L. (2001) 'Rationing health care to disabled people', *Sociology of Health and Illness,* 23: 654–77.

Albrecht, Gary L. and Devlieger, Patrick J. (1999) 'The disability paradox: high quality of life against all odds', *Social Science and Medicine,* 48: 977–88.

Albrecht, Gary L., Fitzpatrick, Ray and Scrimshaw, Susan C. (eds) (2000) *Handbook of Social Studies in Health and Medicine.* London: Sage.

Andersen, Ronald M. (1995) 'Revisiting the behavioral model and access to medical care: does it matter?', *Journal of Health and Social Behavior,* 36 (1): 1–10.

Aneshensel, Carol S. and Phelan, Jo C. (1999) 'The sociology of mental health: surveying the field', in Carol S. Aneshensel and Jo C. Phelan (eds), *Handbook of the Sociology of Mental Health.* New York: Kluwer Academic/Plenum. pp. 3–18.

Antonovsky, Aaron (1979) *Health, Stress and Coping.* San Francisco: Jossey–Bass.

Ardigó, A. (1995) 'Public attitudes and changes in health care systems: a confrontation and a puzzle', in O. Borre and E. Scarbough (eds), *The Scope of Government.* Oxford: Oxford University Press. pp. 388–406.

Arvey, Richard D. and Bouchard, Thomas J., Jr (1994) 'Genetics, twins, and organizational behavior', *Research in Organizational Behavior,* 16: 47–82.

Ashton, J. (1991) 'The healthy cities project: a challenge for health education', *Health Education Quarterly,* 18: 39–48.

Ayanian, John Z., Weissman, Joel S., Schneider, Eric C., Ginsburg, Jack A. and Zaslavsky, Alan M. (2000) 'Unmet health needs of uninsured adults in the United States', *Journal of the American Medical Association,* 284: 2061–9.

Baker, David W., Sudano, Joseph J., Albert, Jeffrey M., Borawski, Elaine A. and Dor, Avi (2001) 'Lack of health insurance and decline in overall health in late middle age', *New England Journal of Medicine,* 345: 1106–12.

Berkman, Lisa F. and Kawachi, Ichiro (eds) (2000) *Social Epidemiology.* New York: Oxford University Press.

Bird, Chloe E., Conrad, Peter and Fremont, Allen M. (eds) (2000) *Handbook of Medical Sociology,* 5th edn. Upper Saddle River, NJ: Prentice–Hall.

Blendon, Robert J. and Benson, John M. (2001) 'Americans' views on health policy: a fifty-year historical perspective', *Health Affairs,* 20: 33–46.

Bloom, Samuel W. (2000) 'The institutionalization of medical sociology in the United States, 1920–1980', in C. Bird, P. Conrad and A.M. Fremont (eds), *Handbook of Medical Sociology,* 5th edn. Upper Saddle River, NJ: Prentice–Hall. pp. 11–32.

Chagnon, Napoleon A. (1992) *Yanomamö: The Last Days of Eden.* San Diego: Harcourt Brace Jovanovich.

Chard, Jiri, Lilford, Richard and Gardiner, Derek (1999) 'Looking beyond the next patient: sociology and modern health care', *The Lancet,* 353: 486–98.

Cone, John D. (2001) *Evaluating Outcomes: Empirical Tools for Effective Practice.* Washington, DC: American Psychological Association.

Conrad, Peter (2000) 'Medicalization, genetics and human problems', in Chloe E. Bird, Peter Conrad and Allen M. Fremont (eds), *Handbook of Medical Sociology,* 5th edn. Upper Saddle River, NJ: Prentice–Hall. pp. 322–33.

Crimmins, Eileen M. and Saito, Yasuhiko (2001) 'Trends in healthy life expectancy in the United States, 1970–1990: gender, racial, and educational differences', *Social Science and Medicine*, 52: 1629–41.

Cunningham-Burley, Sarah and Boulton, Mary (2000) 'The social context of the New Genetics', in Gary L. Albrecht, Ray Fitzpatrick and Susan C. Scrimshaw (eds), *Handbook of Social Studies in Health and Medicine*. London: Sage. pp. 173–87.

Donabedian, Avedis (1980) *The Definition of Quality and Approaches to Its Measurement*. Ann Arbor, MI: Health Administration Press.

Donabedian, Avedis (1981) *The Criteria and Standards of Quality*. Ann Arbor, MI: Health Administration Press.

Feagin, Joe R. (2001) 'Social justice and sociology: agendas for the twenty-first century', *American Sociological Review*, 66: 1–20.

Ferreira, Flavio L., Daliana, P.B., Bross, A., Mélot, C., and Vincent, J.-L. (2001) 'Serial evaluation of the SOFA score to predict outcome in critically ill patients', *Journal of the American Medical Association*, 286: 1754–8.

Freidson, Eliot (1970) *The Profession of Medicine*. New York: Dodd, Mead and Company.

Freidson, Eliot (1975) *Doctoring Together: A Study of Professional Social Control*. New York: Elsevier.

Giddens, Anthony (2000) *Runaway World*. London: Routledge.

Gilman, Sander (1995) *Health and Illness: Images of Difference*. London: Reaktion Press.

Goffman, Erving (1961) *Asylums: Essays on the Social Situation of Mental Patients and Other Inmates*. Chicago: Aldine.

Goldberg, J., True, W.R., Eisen, S.A. and Henderson, W.G. (1990) 'A twin study of the effects of Vietnam war on posttraumatic stress disorder', *Journal of the American Medical Association*, 263: 1227–32.

Goldstein, M.S. (2000) 'The growing acceptance of complementary and alternative medicine', in Chloe E. Bird, Peter Conrad and Allen M. Fremont (eds), *Handbook of Medical Sociology*, 5th edn. Upper Saddle River, NJ: Prentice–Hall. pp. 284–97.

Goode, William J. (1960) 'Encroachment, charlatanism, and the emerging profession: psychology, medicine and sociology', *American Sociological Review*, 25: 902–14.

Haack, Susan (1993) *Evidence and Inquiry: Towards Reconstruction in Epistemology*. Oxford: Blackwell.

Haack, Susan (1996) 'Pragmatism', in N. Bunnin and E.P. Tsui-James (eds), *The Blackwell Companion to Philosophy*, Oxford: Blackwell. pp. 643–61.

Hayward, Mark D., Crimmins, Eileen M., Miles, Toni P. and Yang, Yu (2000) 'The significance of socioeconomic status in explaining the racial gap in chronic health conditions', *American Sociological Review*, 65: 910–30.

James, William (1907) *Pragmatism*. Cambridge, MA: Harvard University Press.

Kennelly, Ivy, Merz, Sabine M. and Lorber, Judith (2001) 'What is gender?', *American Sociological Review*, 66: 598–605.

King, M.C., Weiland, S. and Hale K. (2001) 'Tamoxifen and breast cancer incidence among women with inherited mutations in BRCA1 and BRAC2: national surgical adjuvant breast and bowel project (NASBP-P1) breast cancer prevention trial', *Journal of the American Medical Association*, 286: 2251–6.

Koop, Everett, Pearson, Clarence E. and Schwartz, M. Roy (eds) (2001) *Critical Issues in Global Health*. San Francisco: Jossey–Bass.

Lane, Robert E. (1991) *The Market Experience*. Cambridge: Cambridge University Press.

Lane, Robert E. (2000) *The Loss of Happiness in Market Democracies*. New Haven, CT: Yale University Press.

Levine, Sol (1987) 'The changing terrains in medical sociology: emergent concern with quality of life', *Journal of Health and Social Behavior*, 28: 1–6.

Levine, Sol (1995) 'Time for creative integration in medical sociology', *Journal of Health and Social Behavior*, Extra Issue: 1–5.

Light, Donald (2000a) 'The sociological character of health-care markets', in Gary L. Albrecht, Ray Fitzpatrick and Susan C. Scrimshaw (eds), *Handbook of Social Studies in Health and Medicine*. London: Sage. pp. 394–408.

Light, Donald (2000b) 'The medical profession and organizational change: from professional dominance to countervailing power', in Chloe E. Bird, Peter Conrad and Allen M. Fremont (eds), *Handbook of Medical Sociology*, 5th edn. Upper Saddle River, NJ: Prentice–Hall. pp. 201–16.

Lock, Margaret (2000) 'Accounting for disease and distress: morals of the normal and abnormal', in Gary L. Albrecht, Ray Fitzpatrick and Susan C. Scrimshaw (eds), *Handbook of Social Studies in Health and Medicine*. London: Sage. pp. 259–76.

MacIntyre, Sally (1997) 'The Black report and beyond: what are the issues?', *Social Science and Medicine*, 44: 723–45.

Malinowski, B. (1944) *A Scientific Theory of Culture*. Chapel Hill, NC: University of North Carolina Press.

Malinowski, B. (1948) *Magic, Science and Religion*. Glencoe, IL: The Free Press.

Marmot, Michael G., Bobak, Martin and Davey Smith, George (1995) 'Explanations for social inequalities in health', in Benjamin C. Amick III, Sol Levine, Alvin R. Tarlov and Diana Chapman Walsh (eds), *Society and Health*. Oxford: Oxford University Press.

Masters, R.D. (2001) 'Biology and politics: linking nature and nurture', *Annual Review of Political Science*, 4: 345–69.

Mead, George Herbert (1964/1934) *Selected Writings: George Herbert Mead* (ed. A.J. Reck). New York: Bobbs–Merrill.

Mechanic, David (1962) 'The concept of illness behavior', *Journal of Chronic Diseases*, 15: 189–94.

Mechanic, David (1989) 'Medical sociology: some tensions among theory, method, and substance', *Journal of Health and Social Behavior*, 30: 147–60.

Miller, Eleanor M. and Yang Costello, Carrie (2001) 'The limits of biological determinism', *American Sociological Review*, 66: 592–8.

Murdock, George P. (1980) *Theories of Illness: A World Survey*. Pittsburgh: University of Pittsburgh Press.

Parsons, Talcott (1951) *The Social System*. Glencoe, IL: The Free Press.

Peirce, C.S. (1931–1958) *Collected Papers* (eds C. Hartshorne, P. Weiss and A. Burks). Cambridge, MA: Harvard University Press.

Phelan, Jo C., Link, Bruce G., Stueve, Ann and Pescosolido, Bernice A. (2000) 'Public perceptions of mental illness in 1950 and 1996: What is mental illness and is it to be feared?', *Journal of Health and Social Behavior*, 41: 188–207.

Popper, Karl R. (1972) *Objective Knowledge: An Evolutionary Approach*. Oxford: The Clarendon Press.

Porter, Roy (1999) *The Greatest Benefit to Mankind: A Medical History of Humanity from Antiquity to the Present*. London: Fontana Press.

Putnam, Hillary (1978) *Meaning and the Moral Sciences*. London: Routledge and Kegan Paul.

Quine, W.V. (1969) *Ontological Relativity and Other Essays*. New York: Columbia University Press.

Risman, Barbara J. (2001) 'Calling the bluff of value-free science', *American Sociological Review*, 66: 605–11.

Roose, S.P., Glassman, A.H. and Seidman, S.N. (2001) 'Relationship between depression and other medical illnesses', *Journal of the American Medical Association*, 286: 1687–90.

Rorty, R. (1979) *Philosophy and the Mirror of Nature*. Princeton, NJ: Princeton University Press.

Rorty, R. (1991) *Objectivity, Relativism and Truth*. Cambridge: Cambridge University Press.

Rubinstein, Robert A., Scrimshaw, Susan C. and Morrisey, Suzanne E. (2000) 'Classification and process in sociomedical understanding: towards a multilevel view of sociomedical methodology', in Gary L. Albrecht, Ray Fitzpatrick and Susan C. Scrimshaw (eds), *Handbook of Social Studies in Health and Medicine*. London: Sage. pp. 36–49.

Sackett, D., Rosenberg, W., Gray, J., Haynes, R. and Richardson, W. (1996) 'Evidence-based medicine: what it is and what it isn't', *British Medical Journal*, 312: 71–2.

Scott, W.K., Nance, M.A., Watts, R.L. and colleagues (2001) 'Complete genomic screen in Parkinson disease: evidence for multiple genes', *Journal of the American Medical Association*, 286: 2239–44.

Scott, W. Richard, Ruef, Martin, Mendel, Peter J. and Caronna, Carol A. (2000) *Institutional Change and Healthcare Organizations: From Professional Dominance to Managed Care*. Chicago: University of Chicago Press.

Sen, Amartya (1992) *Inequality Reexamined*. Cambridge, MA: Harvard University Press.

Sen, Amartya (1999) *Development as Freedom*. New York: Alfred A. Knopf.

Seymour, Wendy (1998) *Remaking the Body: Rehabilitation and Change*. London: Routledge.

Shilling, Chris (1993) *The Body and Social Theory*. London: Sage.

Shilling, Chris (2001) 'The embodied foundations of social theory', in George Ritzer and Barry Smart (eds), *Handbook of Social Theory*. London: Sage. pp. 439–57.

Shortell, Steven M., Giles, R.R., Anderson, D.A., Erickson, K.M. and Mitchell, J.B. (1996) *Remaking Health Care in America: Building Organized Delivery Systems*. San Francisco: Jossey–Bass.

Starr, Paul (1982) *The Social Transformation of American Medicine*. New York: Basic Books.

Stevens, Andrew, Abrams, Keith, Brazier, John Fitzpatrick, Ray and Lilford, Richard (2001) *The Advanced Handbook of Methods in Evidence-Based Healthcare*. London: Sage.

Sullivan, Kip (2000) 'On the "efficiency" of managed care plans', *Health Affairs*, 19: 139–48.

Turner, Bryan S. (1992) *Regulating Bodies: Essays in Medical Sociology*. London: Routledge.

Turner, Bryan S. (1995) *Medical Power and Social Knowledge*. London: Sage.

Turner, Bryan S. (2000) 'The history of the changing concepts of health and illness: Outline of a general model of illness categories', in Gary L. Albrecht, Ray Fitzpatrick and Susan C. Scrimshaw (eds), *Handbook of Social Studies in Health and Medicine*. London: Sage. pp. 11–23.

Udry, J. Richard (1994) 'The nature of gender', *Demography*, 31: 561–73.

Udry, J. Richard (2000) 'Biological limits of gender construction', *American Sociological Review*, 65: 443–57.

Udry, J. Richard (2001) 'Feminist critics uncover determinism, positivism and antiquated theory', *American Sociological Review*, 66: 611–18.

Udry, J. Richard, Morris, Naomi M. and Kovenock, Judith (1995) 'Androgen effects on women's gendered behavior', *Journal of Biosocial Science*, 27: 359–68.

Waitzkin, Howard (2001) *At the Front Lines of Medicine*. Lanham, MD: Rowman and Littlefield.

Weiss, Marjorie and Fitzpatrick, Ray (1997) 'Challenges to medicine: the case of prescribing', *Sociology of Health and Illness*, 19: 297–327.

West, Cornel (1999) *The Cornel West Reader*. New York: Basic Civitas Books.

Williams, Simon J. (2001) 'Sociological imperialism and the profession of medicine revisited: where are we now?', *Sociology of Health and Illness*, 23: 135–58.

Wuthnow, Robert (1998) *After Heaven: Spirituality in America since the 1950s*. Berkeley, CA: University of California Press.

16

The Sociology of Religion

BRYAN TURNER

INTRODUCTION: THE ORIGINS OF THE SOCIOLOGY OF RELIGION

Religion refers to those processes and institutions that render the social world intelligible, and which bind individuals authoritatively into the social order. Religion is therefore a matter of central importance to sociology. To write sociologically is inevitably to work within a particular tradition that has in advance identified certain issues and themes that are salient in the definition of social phenomena. The fact that a classical sociological tradition has already defined the field in advance appears to be particularly important in the case of religion (O'Toole, 2001; Robertson, 1970). In this overview of the sociology of religion, I pay considerable attention to the legacies of Émile Durkheim and Max Weber, who defined the principal issues within the field, with respect to the analysis of the sacred and charisma. Within this tradition, I take the study of institutions to be our primary concern, partly as an analytical strategy to affirm that our topic of inquiry is not with individuals or persons. If we define sociology as the study of institutions, then religious institutions have been a central preoccupation of sociologists. Indeed, the study of religious phenomena, including magic, ritual and myth, was an important feature of the intellectual origins of both anthropology and

sociology. A number of social and cultural changes in the Victorian period created the intellectual context within which the sociological study of religion began to flourish in the late nineteenth century. In particular empirical evidence drawn from reports from Africa and Australia by colonial administrators, missionaries and amateur anthropologists fired speculation about the origins of religion. The theory of animism suggested that 'primitive mentality' was a flawed attempt to understand Nature in the absence of experimental science.

While this interest in primitive religion was overtly located within an emergent social science of comparative civilizations, the covert theme in these Victorian inquiries into primitive society was in fact the growing ambiguity and uncertainty of the role of the Christian church within a social and cultural environment which was itself increasingly secular and where intellectual debate was dominated by the assumptions of natural science and Social Darwinism rather than theology. While these early contributions to sociology and anthropology probed the beliefs and practices of primitive cultures, they were equally, but more obliquely, an investigation of the role and nature of Christianity within a society where the moral and social authority of the church was being steadily undermined. Anthropological fieldwork inevitably raised relativistic problems about the truth of religious beliefs in primitive society and as a consequence they inevitably raised relativistic questions about the rationality and validity of Christian mythology. These tensions between science and religion in Britain were beautifully illustrated in Mrs Humphrey Ward's novel *Robert Elsemere*, in which Elsemere's faith is gradually compromised and finally undermined by his exposure to the relativistic theme of anthropological research, resulting in his transition from Unitarian belief to humanistic scepticism to socialism (MacIntyre, 1969).

The rise of the anthropology and sociology of religion should also be seen against the background of the dominance of natural scientific thought in the second half of the nineteenth century, namely a mode of scientific thinking that was shaped by an evolutionary paradigm. Charles Darwin's theories of evolution and natural selection were translated into a general theory of society in Social Darwinism, within which Christianity was simply an aspect of social evolution. Christianity as a religion had no particular or privileged position in cultural evolution. Social Darwinism, with its emphasis on conflict and struggle as the motors of evolutionary adaptation, provided a general social theory of historical development and social differentiation. Karl Marx integrated political economy and social Darwinism into a powerful theory of history and social formations, in which the stages of the mode of production were linked together into an evolutionary chain from primitive communism, through feudalism, to capitalism and socialism.

While Marx's philosophy of history was a product of this combination of social Darwinism and political economy, his analysis of religion was based upon a critique of Hegel's idealism and Ludwig Feuerbach's sensualism (Turner, 1991). In Marx's theory of ideology, religious beliefs were representations of the particular economic conditions of specific modes of production. Thus, Roman Catholicism was well suited to the political and economic structures of feudalism, whereas the individualistic beliefs of Protestant Christianity were seen to be an expression of the possessive individualism of competitive capitalist economies. Marx,

adopting an evolutionary view of religious beliefs, assumed along with Engels that religion would evaporate once exposed to 'critical criticism' and scientific socialism. The social crisis of Victorian Britain that produced the sociology of religion included the erosion of Christianity, the political threat of working class socialism and the intellectual threat of Social Darwinism and evolutionary thought (Burrow, 1966).

Nineteenth-century theories of economic industrialization provided the foundations of early theories of secularization. It was assumed that the transition from rural to urban society, or from *Gemeinschaft* to *Gesellschaft*, with the growth of industrial capitalism, had destroyed the social and moral basis for the church's authority over society. The social and historical development of Europe was conceptualized chronologically into separate ages of faith and ages of secularity. For writers like Claude Saint-Simon, the 'feudal-theological system' was gradually being replaced by a new social order based upon the industrial classes and positivistic science. In the industrial-scientific system, the government of human beings would be transformed into the administration of things. He predicted the rise of a new religion based on humanism and science that he called the New Christianity. For Auguste Comte, in his positivistic and humanist philosophy, medieval society, which was characterized by the dominance of the Catholic Church and by militarism, would be replaced by a new social system in which scientists and industrialists would occupy the dominant social roles. He anticipated the creation of a religion of humanity which replaced the derelict Christianity of his period (Wernick, 2001). In the sociological writings of Herbert Spencer, the separation of military from industrial society had become a common assumption of dissenting liberals. The collapse of the old military-theological system created a crisis in social organization and individual consciousness; especially for the social establishment and conservative thought.

While the sociology and anthropology of religion was sharply divided into a variety of competing theories, there was a core of assumptions about the nature of religion and science which provided the underlying framework in the late nineteenth century for the analysis of religion (Marrett, 1909; Tylor, 1891). The first assumption was that rationality, defined operationally by the methods of experimental science, was the guiding principle of industrial society. Truth was produced by the evidence made available to human reason by the intervention of experimental science. Positivistic science was the unambiguous benchmark for the evolution of civilization, a benchmark that neatly contrasted the primitive mentality with the modern mind (Levy-Bruhl, 1923, 1985). In primitive religion, individuals were thought to make sense of their natural environment through a system of magical and erroneous beliefs. The emphasis was upon the cognitive apprehension of reality by isolated individuals who were quaintly perceived as 'ancient philosophers'. The second assumption was that human history was characterized by an evolutionary scheme in which societies passed through a series of definite and necessary stages from simple to more complex forms. Within this evolutionary scheme, humanity passed from primitive magic and fetishism through religion to contemporary science. Third, along with the assumptions of the dominant system, individualism was taken to be the primary moral and political characteristic of an advanced civilization.

Although these evolutionary theories were designed to understand primitive cultures, they represented a major intellectual challenge to Christianity. One significant problem for Protestant intellectuals was how to explain the differences between primitive rituals such as a communal meal and Christian practice such as the Eucharist. One solution was to appeal to evolutionary theory itself in order to argue that Protestantism was the most highly evolved religion, and that its rituals and beliefs were essentially abstract propositions that could be justified by rational argument. Christian theology attempts to express religious truths through abstractions that have replaced the concrete metaphors and ideas about actual relationships. This solution was adopted by W. Robertson Smith, whose *Lectures on the Religion of the Semites* (1997 [1889]) were particularly important for Durkheim's sociological

understanding of the functional significance of rituals.

Interpretations of the intellectual origins of the sociology of religion have contrasted the sociological emphasis on collective rituals with psychological theories of individual cognition. In *Theories of Primitive Religion*, E.E. Evans-Pritchard (1965) distinguished early psychological approaches, starting with R. de Brosses's theory of fetishism and theories of the soul in the work of E.B. Tylor, Max Müller and J.G. Frazer from the sociological theories of Émile Durkheim, Robert Hertz, Henri Hubert and Marcel Mauss. Frazer's (1935 [1890]) *The Golden Bough* was characteristic of speculative reflections on the evolutionary and comparative significance of mythology. In a definitive overview of the early tradition, William J. Goode (1951), in his *Religion Among the Primitives*, distinguished between animistic–manist theories which were particularly influential among the English anthropologists, naturalistic theories which were embraced by writers like Müller (1997 [1892]), psychoanalytic theories which were developed by Sigmund Freud in his *Totem and Taboo* (1950), and sociological interpretations of religion in the work of Smith, Durkheim and Mauss.

Although these nineteenth-century theories of religion were influential, they have come under extensive intellectual criticism, which laid the foundation of modern approaches to religion in anthropology and sociology. Theories of animism–manism and naturism shared, as I have indicated, a common set of assumptions – the centrality of the individual, positivism, natural science as an exclusive paradigm of rationality, and evolutionism, which were challenged in Durkheim's *The Elementary Forms of the Religious Life* (1961 [1912]). Durkheim rejected any discussion of the truth or falsity of religious belief as simply misplaced: 'there are no religions which are false. All are true in their own fashion, all answer, though in different ways, to the given conditions of human existence' (Durkheim, 1961: 15). The task of sociology was to discover 'the ever-present causes upon which the most essential forms of religious thought and practice depend' (Durkheim, 1961: 20). The individualistic definitions of religion in animism were too specific, because belief in spiritual beings was not universal to religions. For example, Theravada Buddhism is non-theistic. Durkheim defined religion as a 'unified system of beliefs and practices relative to sacred things, that is to say things set apart and forbidden – beliefs and practices which unite into one single moral community called a Church, all those who adhere to them' (Durkheim, 1961: 62). Cognitive approaches such as Tylor's minimalist definition of religion as belief in spiritual beings, by concentrating on the individual's rational apprehension of the world, failed to draw attention to the emotional and performative character of religious practices, and the obligatory nature of involvement in religious institutions. Durkheim, along with R.R. Marrett, William McDougall and Arnold van Gennep, rejected Frazer's 'intellectualist psychology of religion' in which the primitive community was composed of a collection of discrete minds directed at a rational evaluation of nature (Ackerman, 1987). Unlike the intellectual beliefs of philosophers, belief in the sacred character of the totem was not a voluntary or private option. Durkheim also dismissed Müller's naturism as merely the vision of nature of modern city-dwellers. In traditional societies, nature was more likely to be seen as regular and monotonous, and totemic objects are often far from awe-inspiring. Durkheim's sociological perspective laid the foundation for subsequent approaches to the sacred, especially in the French tradition of the work of Marcel Mauss (2001 [1902]), Robert Hertz, Henri Hubert, Roger Callois and René Girard (1988 [1972]). Durkheim's approach also contributed fundamentally to the social anthropology of Robert H. Lowie (Murphy, 1972) and Mary Douglas (1966, 1970).

DURKHEIM ON CLASSIFICATION, KNOWLEDGE AND RELIGION

Durkheim took the decisive steps towards a genuine sociology of religion in which he interpreted religion as a collective classification of reality. The implications of Durkheim's approach are that religion involves a special type of knowledge that is embedded in collective practices that are reinforced by shared emotions. *The Elementary Forms of the Religious Life* had three distinctive aims. The first was to study a simple religious system, namely Australian totemism, in order to understand the elementary forms of religious life. The second was to study elementary forms of thought such as the distinction between sacred and profane, and finally to establish generalizations about social relations and classification in all human societies.

Primitive Classification Durkheim and Mauss (1963 [1903]) clearly anticipated the more complex and complete presentation of *The Elementary Forms of the Religious Life* (1961[1912]). Both publications attempt sociologically to understand forms of classification, especially forms of religious classification that divide the world into the sacred and the profane. Durkheim's intention was also to give a sociological account of the fundamental forms or structures of consciousness.

The basic argument exhibits the classic features of Durkheim's sociology. We cannot understand forms of consciousness by a study of the consciousness of separate individuals. More specifically, we cannot grasp the nature of thought through a psychological study of the contents of human minds. The social comes before the individual, and thus to understand consciousness (or classification) we need to study its social forms: 'it is enough to examine the very idea of classification to understand that man could not have found its essential elements in himself … Every classification implies a hierarchical order for which neither the tangible world nor our mind gives us the model' (Durkheim and Mauss, 1963: 7–8). It is the social divisions of society that provide the divisions of classification, and so the first logical categories were social. However, the force of these categories depends on their affective force. Thus 'for those who are called primitives, a species of things is not a simple object of knowledge, but corresponds above all to a certain sentimental attitude. All kinds of affective elements combine in the representation … it is this emotional value of notions which plays the preponderant part in the manner in which ideas are connected or separated. It is the dominant characteristic in classification' (Durkheim and Mauss, 1963: 85–6).

We may re-state their argument as claiming that the authority of a classification system receives its force from classificatory systems that are collective, and which are sustained by a shared emotional life. However, this argument raises the obvious question about modern society, namely what happens to the authority of classificatory systems where the force of collective emotions is diminished by the secularization of religious systems? This question was anticipated very directly in their thesis: 'Thus the history of scientific classification is, in the last analysis, the history of the stages by which this element of social affectivity has progressively weakened, leaving more and more room for the reflective thought of individuals' (Durkheim and Mauss, 1963: 88). Thus the collective and emotional character of classificatory practices in modern societies has broken down, and there is more indeterminacy and uncertainty because individuals can become more reflexive and classificatory principles are contested.

Durkheim's sociology of classification was the basis of his sociology of religion, in that religion is a method of apprehending reality in terms of the force of the classificatory principle: sacred/profane. His approach also anticipated a major theme of the secularization thesis, which is concerned with the bases of social order in societies where the traditional force of classificatory schema have collapsed. Although the secularization debate has a decisively historical framework, Durkheim's analysis of classification was typological rather than historical. Durkheim's pragmatist and functionalist account of the social consequences of religious practice neglected the historical dimensions of religious institutions, especially the organizational structures and roles of ecclesiastical organizations. Ernst Troeltsch and Max Weber developed these historical aspects of religion in the German tradition of the sociology of religion. Whereas British and French anthropologists had concentrated on the generic nature of religious and magical symbols and customs, German sociology arose from a specific concern with the historical role of Christianity in Western society, and with the organizational forms of Christian institutions. In *The Protestant Ethic and the Spirit of Capitalism*, Weber (1930 [1904–5]) analysed the relationship between Protestant beliefs and the individualistic and secular culture of emerging capitalism. In *The Social Teaching of the Christian Churches*, Troeltsch (1931 [1912]) developed a contrast between sect and church as a model of organizational development and change in Christianity, a model which used Weber's analysis of charismatic breakthrough (Weber, 1966).

MAX WEBER: SOCIOLOGY AND THE SECULARIZATION DEBATE

Sociology has been specifically concerned to understand the origins and development of modernity, and it has seen religion as a crucial component of the social process of modernization. This interest in religion and modernity had three distinctive components: the impact of religion on economic norms and behaviour; the contribution of religions to the development of political regimes such as democracy; and the consequences of religion for cultural development broadly conceived.

Weber's sociology involved the study of the economic and political ethics of the world religions (Weber, 1966). Weber was concerned to understand whether Christianity, as a cultural precondition for rational economic behaviour, could ultimately survive capitalism and whether the democratic ethos of secular institutions would eventually undermine the hierarchical notions of charismatic authority that underpin ecclesiastical organizations. Weber's sociology was characterized by the theme of the fatefulness of Western institutions, namely how values can be self-destructive (Turner, 1996). For example, religious asceticism was self-defeating in producing the spirit of capitalism, which came eventually to negate

Christian spirituality. Weber also thought the modern power politics that was made possible by the separation of religion and politics in Christianity would corrode the tradition of Christian brotherly love. While historians have disputed the validity of Weber's historical sociology of religions, his sociological questions about religion, politics and economics have proved to be extraordinarily productive and imaginative.

In his introduction to Weber's *The Sociology of Religion*, Talcott Parsons (1966) argued that Weber's sociology of religion was concerned to understand the social leverage that religion has exercised over processes of social change. This social leverage is an effect of the strength and tenacity of the division between the sacred and the profane, or between religious ideals and the world. The confrontation with the world produced a range of different soteriologies or doctrines of salvation. These soteriologies in Weber hinge critically around the dichotomy between asceticism and mysticism. Asceticism was particularly important in the rational response of Protestantism to the control of sexuality and money, but this-worldly soteriologies are not peculiar to Christianity. For example, within the Abrahamic religions, politics and religion have remained in a dialectical tension, and this tension has played a creative role in the development of democratic politics as an urban form of participatory politics. Because the Abrahamic religions shared a universal notion of justice, they have the potential to function as a powerful critique of earthly politics.

The doctrine of the church as a community free from coercion provided a powerful contrast to the state which Weber (1978) famously defined as an institution that has a monopoly of violence within a given territory. The church as a parallel society provided normative criteria by which bad government could, in principle, be evaluated. The church provided a public space within which concepts of justice, equality and community (or brotherhood) evolved as components of a theology of political institutions. However, the association of the church with this world exposed the religious community to corruption and co-optation. For example, the rise of the national church

involved religious functionaries in power-sharing. Thus, the dialectic of sacred and profane can be seen paradoxically as a force that assisted the rise of the modern citizen (Weber, 1958). This dialectic is not peculiar to Western culture; similar arguments can be and have been made about the relationship between Buddhism and society, specifically between the monastic order and the secular state. In Buddhist legend, King Asoka was both conqueror and Buddhist monk.

This interweaving of religion and politics, brotherly love and violence constituted the tragic vision of Weber's sociology. Politics requires authoritative methods for the distribution of resources and must resort to coercive means to establish order. In the last analysis, politics is about the prudent use of force in society to preserve order. For Weber, religious institutions are channels of symbolic (charismatic) violence that coerce behaviour through sacred force, while political institutions require secular force. While political institutions must exert violence, religious communities are based on 'brotherly love' and therefore politics and religion must exist in a state of mutual tension. Paradoxically, they are both required for the creation of social order.

The core feature of this theory is the explication of the historical role of charisma in human societies. Weber employed a theory of charismatic breakthrough to understand the secular dynamic of authority and leadership in social institutions. His main intention was to compare and contrast three types of authority: charismatic, traditional and legal-rational. In *Economy and Society* (Weber, 1978: 241), the term charisma is 'applied to a certain quality of an individual personality by virtue of which he is considered extraordinary and treated as endowed with supernatural, superhuman, or at least specifically exceptional powers or qualities'. Traditional authority involves the acceptance of an implicit rule that expresses a custom, namely an established pattern of belief or practice. Finally, legal-rational authority is typical of bureaucracies in which formal conduct is underpinned by procedural norms. These forms of authority are in turn modes of compliance. Tradition depends on compliance through empathy; legal-rational authority rests on rational argument; and charismatic leadership requires inspiration.

Charismatic authority is confronted by a generic problem of succession with the death of the leader and charismatic authority is consequently unstable. With the death of the charismatic leader, the disciples typically disband, but occasionally alternative solutions for continuity will be developed. In the case of the Christian Church, the charismatic authority of Christ was invested in the church itself (as the body of Christ) and thus in the bishops who, by their control over the 'keys of grace', enjoy a stable vicarious authority. This 'institutionalization of charisma' becomes over time increasingly formal, bureaucratic and impersonal. Weber defined the 'routinization of charisma' in terms of the transformation of the charismatic power of Christ into a set of formal procedures and bureaucratic rules. Charisma is institutionally important in the definition of different religious roles and patterns of organization. For example, Weber distinguished between the prophet who, as a charismatic figure, has a personal call, and the priest who has authority by virtue of his office in the church and his service in a sacred tradition. The prophets, who may emerge from the ranks of the priesthood, are unremunerated, and therefore depend on gifts from followers (Weber, 1952).

The institutions through which people gain access to charismatic gifts have important implications for broader issues of social organization and political power. Where the church was able to claim an exclusive monopoly of the means of grace, then there was a rigid and detailed hierarchy of authority between priests and laity, and the hierarchies of earthly power were a reflection of sacred hierarchies. The democratization of religious membership, which has been characteristic of modern societies, contrasts sharply with the idea that authentic charisma is unequally distributed through human societies or that some people are constitutionally unmusical. The notion that the stratification of religious charisma lies at the foundation of the world religions was central to Weber's sociology of religion. Whereas Troeltsch had developed the idea of church-sect typology, Weber constructed his analysis of religious authority around the idea of virtuoso and mass religiousness. The virtuosi, both ascetic and mystical, are detached from mundane constraints (typically of work and reproduction) and in exchange for their charismatic gifts (prophecy, visions and healing) they receive tributes (money, food and shelter) from the laity. The history of religious institutions is the history of, more or less unsuccessful, attempts to routinize the channels of charisma through the official agencies of the church. The institutionalization of these sacred powers also produced Weber's view of the historical dynamic of church and state, in which the church strove to monopolize symbolic force, and the state to achieve a monopoly of physical violence in a given territory. When these two systems coalesced into Caesaropapism, total power precluded any dynamic social change.

Given the mundane needs and demands of everyday life, only the virtuosi (the monks and priests) can fully embrace the religious commandments and ritual practices that are required to achieve salvation. The laity are in this sense parasitic on the efforts of the elite to seek out salvation on their behalf. It is for this reason that the evangelical revolution of the eighteenth century, which through field preaching took religion to the people, brought about a profound political revolution. It began the modern process of the democratization of religion that overthrew the ancient division between the religious elite and the masses (Sharot, 2001). In his visit to the United States in 1904, Weber was obviously aware of the elective affinity between capitalism and the Baptist sects, but he did not grasp the full spiritual implications of democracy for the American soul. This theme was powerfully developed by Alexis de Tocqueville (1968 [1835–40]) in *Democracy in America*, for whom voluntary associations such as religious denominations were an essential component of democratic participation at the local or community level.

AMERICAN DENOMINATIONS AND
RELIGIOUS PLURALISM

The American War of Independence and the framing of the Constitution specifically precluded the idea of an established church with a special relationship to the state, and as a result denominational pluralism has been a fundamental aspect of social and political life in the United States. With every wave of migration, the settlers built their own churches and created a dynamic mosaic of religious belief and practice. This process was important in the building of national identity, since, while the church and state were separate, religion became an important foundation of social membership and identity. Will Herberg (1955) developed the classic explanation of the relationship between religion, ethnicity and identity, in *Protestant, Catholic, Jew* in terms of a theory of generational loyalties. First generation migrants to America clung to the religion of their homeland out of sheer necessity. The second generation typically rejected the religious commitments of their parents as they became acculturated in secular society, and became Americans. The third generation returned to religion as a form of social membership and identity in a world that was alienated by the new corporate culture and individualism. In short, people could retain their religious identities provided everybody became American. Some critics of American religiosity have, however, argued that the denominational label was bought at the cost of any content. President Eisenhower was alleged to have remarked that every American should have a religion, and he didn't care which one it was. Religion appeared to meld into secular culture as a form of personal comfort. David Riesman (1950) in *The Lonely Crowd* analysed the American personality as the other-directed character that depends on constant approval and affirmation from others. In *The Organization Man*, W.H. Whyte (1956) described the company executives of corporate America, who are mobile, disconnected from their local communities and dedicated to personal achievement within the organization. These organizational commitments encouraged conformity and

alienated these executives from family and community. Religion provided an anchor in this fragile world of urban sprawl, consumerism and mobility.

While generational changes can explain membership of the churches, sociologists of religion regarded this enthusiasm for religious belonging as evidence of secularization, because denominational loyalties appeared to have more to do with social membership than with faith (Wilson, 1966, 1976). Indeed, much of the statistical evidence on religious commitment demonstrated that orthodox belief and knowledge of the Christian faith were declining despite high levels of organizational involvement (Glock and Stark, 1965). Denominational competition often meant that the demands of religion were reduced in order to make membership a comfortable experience. Peter Berger (1969) in *The Social Reality of Religion* and Thomas Luckmann (1967) in *The Invisible Religion* argued that in modern society denominational pluralism had come to resemble a spiritual marketplace in which the laity could pick and choose whatever beliefs and practices satisfied their individual needs. The result was the gradual erosion of orthodox belief and religious discipline. The religious supermarket was perfectly in tune with the cultural climate of the 1960s as an age of experiment and individualism (Edmunds and Turner, 2002). The growth of fundamentalism in the United States has been in part a critical response to the spread of liberal theology in the churches, to feminism in education and secular culture in the media (Armstrong, 2001).

The boundaries of popular religion are constantly redrawn under the impact of large postwar generations, facilitated by an expanding religious marketplace. It is impossible therefore to understand religion in contemporary America without taking into account the impact of the 'baby boomers' (Roof, 1993). The culture wars of the postwar period radically reorganized the map of mainstream religion in North America. Denominational pluralism is a spiritual marketplace that, in the absence of an established church, stimulates organizational innovation and cultural entrepreneurship. The concept of a spiritual supermarket was originally developed by Peter Berger to describe secularization and the crisis of plausibility in a religious context where individuals can shop around to solve their spiritual needs. The market for religious innovations is a response to massive social change in contemporary America in which an expanding consumer culture has produced the self as the principal target of consumption. There was an 'expressive revolution' (Parsons, 1999), in which personal identity was sought and explored through a new subjectivity. In the market place of seekers, five major subcultures have been identified: dogmatists (for example fundamentalists and neo-traditionalists), mainstream believers, born-again Christians (including evangelicals, Pentecostalists and charismatics), metaphysical believers and seekers, and secularists (Roof, 1999). The baby-boomer culture promoted the idea of religion as a personal quest. While Americans may invest less time in voluntary associations and are less certain about traditional Christian values than previous generations, they are significantly involved in spiritual searching that has produced a deeper emphasis on self-understanding and self-reflexivity. As the baby-boomers mature they are moving out of the narcissistic culture of the 1960s into a deeper, more serious quest culture. If traditional religious cultures depended heavily on the continuity of the family as an agency of socialization, the transformation of family life and the entry of women into the formal labour market have radically destabilized religious identities and cultures.

Within this marketplace, the conservative churches continue to have an important appeal (Smith, 2000). The reasons why conservative Christian churches have been more successful than liberal Christianity is somewhat obvious. Conservative Protestants have more children, and discourage contact with people who are childless or divorced (Ammerman, 1987). People in conservative churches retain their membership, because they want their children to be raised through a religious education. We can understand why people stay in conservative churches, but why proportionately do

more liberals join conservative churches? Why are the mainline churches such as the Presbyterians and Methodist denominations in decline, while the more conservative denominations such as the Southern Baptist Convention and the Assemblies of God are flourishing?

Dean Kelley (1977) provided one classic explanation for success in terms of a theory of the costliness of commitment. Kelley's thesis is that the content of a religious message is less important for success than the demands it places on its members. Costliness is measured by control over members' lifestyles, the development of a strong church and the seriousness of religious commitment. Kelley's successful churches require a totalitarian and hierarchical form of authority and homogeneous communities; such successful congregations are unlike liberal religious groups that impose few sanctions on their members. Kelley's thesis has been widely influential, but contemporary research provides only partial support for the strong church thesis (Tamney, 2002). Conservative congregations support a traditional gender division of labour and conventional gender identities; in a society that is deeply divided over gender issues, such reassurance is psychologically attractive. Secondly, in a relativist culture, the certainties of religious teaching on morality are supportive. Finally, traditional religious orientations may serve to articulate political commitments around major issues relating to abortion, gay and lesbian sexuality, education and the family. American society is a spiritual marketplace in which the loyalty of congregations cannot be taken for granted. Religion has to be sold, alongside other cultural products, and the religious market is volatile, with people moving in and out of congregations in search of an appropriate niche.

Behind these developments in the American religious marketplace stands the figure of Alexis de Tocqueville. His view of religion was conservative in that religion in America could exercise moral constraint over the masses, but remain separate from the state, and hence the dangers of revolutionary France could be avoided (Wolin, 2001: 237–8). However,

Tocqueville was also struck by the importance of association for democracy. Religious pluralism, an emphasis on self-realization and voluntary association membership, and local responsibility are manifestations of the democratic revolution, and constitute a democratization of religion. The revolutionary assumption that everybody has religious opinions and that all opinions are equally valid has produced the American religious marketplace, where priestly authority and ecclesiastical hierarchy do not find comfortable locations. In this sense, Methodism with its commitment to the priesthood of all believers, lay participation, emotional subjectivity and congregational autonomy was the harbinger of religious modernization, the logical outcome of which is a society in which everybody has his or her own personal religion.

RELIGION AND POLITICS IN EUROPE

By comparison with the United States, the Christian churches in Europe have since the beginning of the nineteenth century been subject to a profound process of secularization. There is clear evidence of secularization in the sense that membership of and participation in Christian churches have declined (Wilson, 1976). However, religious identity continues to play an important role in national identity and consciousness, for example in Ireland and Poland. In *The Social Teaching of the Christian Churches,* Troeltsch (1931) had argued that the oscillation between church and sect that had shaped much of European history had come to an end with the final collapse of the universal church. While sects continue to flourish, there is incontrovertible evidence of institutional decline of mainstream Christianity (Wilson, 1970). Within this general pattern of decline, there are, however, discernible differences between the predominantly Roman Catholic and Protestant regions and states (Martin, 1978).

Catholicism, prior to political liberalization in the late twentieth century, was central to the expression of nationalism in continental Europe and remained a major counter-weight to communism. Catholicism exercised hegemonic moral leadership over the working class in European politics (Gramsci, 1971). This social and cultural hegemony has been closely associated with religious control over education, and the dominance of the Catholic Church on the European right guaranteed that regional, party and class divisions were often drawn along religious lines. This hegemonic influence continued after the Second World War, when Catholicism played an important cultural and political role in relation to atheist communism. The Polish Solidarity movement and the revival of Russian Orthodoxy demonstrated decisively the capacity of religion to survive communism and to act as a platform of social protest and national renewal. Irish national identity and republicanism have also been thoroughly merged within the Catholic tradition, and as a result the Protestant–Catholic divide in Northern Ireland has remained an obdurate fact of political life. In Spain, General Franco, who came to power in 1936 following his attack on the socialist government, was decidedly Catholic and supported traditional values against godless atheism. The collapse of the Franco regime following his death in 1975 has resulted in the rapid diminution of the public authority of the church in Spanish politics. With the end of the Cold War and the fall of communism, Catholicism has played a diminished role in the articulation of nationalism and national identity. Economic prosperity, growing multiculturalism and migration have brought about a partial divorce between state and church.

In Protestant Europe, the relationship with the state has been more remote, and hence the political influence of the churches has been less significant. While the Catholic Church resisted Protestant infiltration in France, Spain and Italy, the Protestant countries have been religiously more diverse and Protestant churches have enjoyed a privileged rather than monopolistic social position (Robertson, 1970: 125). In the Lutheran traditions of Scandinavia, the churches have been incorporated into the state, and religious functionaries were a component of the official bureaucracy. In Norway, the constitution both proclaims the existence of religious freedom and recognizes the Evangelical Lutheran religion as the official religion of the state. In practice, the separation of church and state is recognized, despite the fact that the cabinet has the right to appoint bishops. In the United Kingdom, the Church of England functions as a national church with the monarch as head, but religious tolerance and pluralism have been accepted principles of British liberalism. The political transition from a confessional state to religious pluralism has been typical of English political gradualism in which discriminatory laws against Catholics and Jews were pragmatically abandoned rather than rejected explicitly by an assertion of religious freedom. While the devolution of powers to regional parliaments in Scotland and Wales has weakened the political significance of the Church of England, Anglicanism remains an important ingredient of the conservative vision of Englishness, but there are important elements of cosmopolitanism among the English establishment that are not defined by religion (Edmunds and Turner, 2001).

The political history of religion in Western Europe was dominated by two issues, namely church–state relations and the cultural divisions between Protestantism and Catholicism. This historic pattern has been slowly broken by migration, the globalization of the European economy and the emergence of multicultural politics. Postwar European economic prosperity has combined with a greying population to produce a multicultural society that has satisfied its labour market needs by encouraging migrant labour. The working-age population of Europe is declining rapidly and by 2030 it is estimated that the ratio of working taxpayers to pensioners in Germany and Italy will drop to below 1:1. In the UK the census report of the office of National Statistics has shown that in 2001 there were more people over 60 years of age than under 16 years of age. Young migrants whose fertility rates are typically higher than the host population have filled the gap between workers and the retired section of the population. Economic dependency on foreign labour has drawn in significant numbers of non-Christian migrants, whose presence is permanently changing the cultural map of Europe. In many European countries the foreign migrant community represents 10 per cent of the host population. The most significant group, both in numbers and influence, is Muslim. There are 10–13 million Muslims in Europe, and in Germany foreigners will make up 30 per cent of the population by 2030.

Ageing populations and labour shortages in the developed world will ensure that immigration and religion remain on the political agenda of European societies. Migrants from Pakistan to Britain, from Turkey to Germany, from the Middle East and North Africa to France, from Indonesia to the Netherlands have produced a diasporic politics that has raised fears about the impact of Islamic fundamentalism on cultural and political institutions. In Germany, Turks and Kurds entered the labour market in the 1960s and 1970s and these 'guest workers' now constitute a more or less permanent second generation, amounting to approximately 2 million people. While many of these migrants are secular, Islamic organizations play an important part in their social and political organization. In France, there is a strong nationalist feeling that North African Muslims cannot assimilate to the secular culture of the French republic. The *hijab* case (*l'affaire des foulards*) in 1989 caused a divisive public debate over the desire of Muslim girls to wear the *hijab* (headscarf) in state schools. The French intellectual left regard secular schools as important for personal liberation from religious ideology, while the right interpret the *hijab* as an attack on French national custom (El Hamel, 2002). In English culture, where there has been a historical tradition of distrust towards Islam, a *fatwa* against Salman Rushdie for his publication of *The Satanic Verses* in 1989 polarized British public opinion, and reinforced the public perception of Muslims as fanatics whose culture is fundamentally incompatible with parliamentary democracy and liberal values. In recent legislation there has been some accommodation to the beliefs and practices of other religions, such as the acceptance of customs relating to the wearing of turbans by Sikhs, animal slaughter and solemnization of marriages.

Latin Christianity had created a common religious and political culture in medieval Europe. The Reformation and the division of

Europe broke this dominant culture into competing states with distinctive national religions. The growth of nationalism in Europe had diverse consequences for the churches, but religious symbols, often combined with epic literature and folk culture, have been indispensable for the creation of nations as 'imagined communities' (Anderson, 1983). Conservative governments, against the threat of secular communism, have often harnessed the political vitality of religious symbols in nation formation. The collapse of communism as a significant atheist alternative to religious belief systems had important implications for Christianity, but Islam has been ideologically constructed to fill the space left by communism.

In addition to the growth of Islam, there has been an important growth in sectarian and cultic religion. European governments have frequently attempted to curb the development of such sects by legislative means; there is considerable public hostility to 'new age' groups, Scientology and Jehovah's Witnesses (Hamilton, 1995; Heelas, 1996). In 1995 the British Home Secretary refused entry to the Reverend Sun Myung Moon, who had planned to enter the UK to hold services for the Unification Church, and in Germany, the federal government has identified 25 'sects' that are seen to be a threat to 'democratic values'. These religious tensions of a multicultural society are now a persistent aspect of European politics, and are an indication of the fact that the traditional Protestant–Catholic division of European politics has been further complicated by social hybridity. Changes in the nature of the study of religion as a European institution are thus reflections of the growth of global religious cultures (Robertson, 1992).

CONTEMPORARY SOCIOLOGY OF RELIGION: GLOBALIZATION AND FUNDAMENTALISM

The sociology of religion had become during the 1960s and 1970s an important component of mainstream sociology in both Europe and the United States. Drawing its intellectual inspiration from Weber and Durkheim, the sociology of religion was primarily concerned with the church-sect typology and the secularization debate. In the UK, Wilson and Martin dominated an empirical research tradition while in the United States Berger, Luckmann and Robertson provided an integration of the legacies of Marx, Weber and Durkheim, and developed the sociology of knowledge around the theme of the social construction of reality. However, during the 1980s and 1990s, the sociology of religion went into steep intellectual decline in Europe, and became marginal to mainstream sociology in the United States.

There has been an important revival of the study of religion in contemporary sociology, but with a different intellectual agenda. Fundamentalism and modernity, globalization and inter-cultural conflict, religion and politics, religious movements and ethnic identity are the key issues for sociological analysis. The debate about the clash of civilizations (Huntington, 1997) has propelled the phenomenon of the sacred, especially the Islamic version of fundamentalism, into sharp political focus. Whereas religion was thought to be on the social margins in the 1980s, it is now regarded as a constitutive feature of modern social movements. In classical sociology, the main issues were the impact of the capitalist economy on organized religion, and the capacity of organized Christianity to contain radical working-class politics. In contemporary sociology, the issues are the place of religion in globalization, the tensions between fundamentalism (in Judaism, Christianity and Islam) and modernity, and the role of religion in providing an ideological conduit for the frustrations and anger of alienated youth. There is a dilemma for Islam and Christianity in that their very success in addressing the secular issues of politics may compromise their capacity to address the traditional issues of spirituality (Luhmann, 1984).

While mainstream Christianity declined in Europe throughout the twentieth century, there has been a significant growth of Pentecostalism and its charismatic penumbra, and approximately one-quarter of a billion people are adherents, or one in twenty-five of the global population. The growth of fundamentalism and charismatic Pentecostalism are both aspects of globalization (Martin, 2002). In Latin America and Africa, Pentecostalism recruits among the 'respectable poor' whose ambition is successfully to enter the modern world, and in West Africa and Southeast Asia, it is most prevalent among the new middle classes, including the Chinese diaspora. Pentecostalism has also expanded among social minorities in Nepal, the Andes and inland China. While in Latin America Pentecostalism functions as a religion of the oppressed, offering them hope, social inclusion and welfare services, in North America and Europe Pentecostalism has spread through charismatic movements within the existing churches and denominations.

Pentecostalism can be interpreted sociologically through a comparison with the history of Methodism, which spread in the eighteenth and nineteenth centuries among the working and lower middle classes. While its inclusive Arminian theology and emotional evangelism proved attractive to the poor and the socially deprived, Methodist discipline, teetotalism and literacy helped the laity ascend the social ladder. In the United States, employers favoured Methodist workers, who were hard-working and reliable (Pope, 1942). Contemporary Pentecostalism has similar characteristics. The 'Pentecostal virtues' include betterment through education, self-discipline and control, social aspiration, responsibility and hard work. These technologies of the self produce socially mobile people, but Pentecostalism also offers psychological liberation. There is an elective affinity between Pentecostalism, the spread of liberal capitalism and 'the expressive revolution' (Parsons, 1999). Pentecostalism, which as an organization is devolved, voluntary and local, works within a religious market that offers spiritual uplift, social success and emotional gratification. Whereas Methodism supplied the work ethic of early capitalism, Pentecostalism is relevant to the work skills and personal attributes of the postindustrial service economy, especially self-monitoring and a refusal to accept social failure.

The sociological study of Pentecostalism is important, because it raises serious questions about the assumption that fundamentalist movements are traditional, or indeed anti-modern. Pentecostalism is highly congruent with the voluntaristic and plural ethos of liberal capitalism, and appears to promote rather than reject the emotional individualism of late modernity. Similar conceptual problems arise with the perception that Islam is a traditional religion. In the popular press, fundamentalism is normally equated with radical Islam, and Islam is understood to be hostile to modernity. Fundamentalism has a number of defining themes. The emphasis on scripture requires a literal belief in the inerrant nature of the fundamental scriptures, and the quest for legitimacy and authority by reference to those scriptures. There is an emphasis on seeing the relevance of traditional scriptures to contemporary issues. In addition, there is a personal quest for purity in an impure world, and an attempt to reject the division between the sacred and the profane. Fundamentalism involves confrontation with the secular world, by violent means if necessary, and a worldview that understands the modern world in terms of an endless struggle between good and evil.

The study of fundamentalism has therefore become a major preoccupation of contemporary sociology of religion (Hassan, 2002). In terms of their core membership and leadership, fundamentalists are recruited from the educated but alienated urban social classes. They are frustrated science teachers, unpaid civil servants, disillusioned doctors and underemployed engineers. In short, fundamentalists are recruited from those social groups that have failed to benefit fully from secular nationalist governments and aborted modernization projects. Their principal recruiting ground has been the new technological universities that were built by nationalist governments as aspects of the project of modernization. These technical students have been at the forefront of the 'Islamization of knowledge' which has attempted to challenge Western systems of science and humanities (Abaza, 2002).

This pattern of recruitment suggests that fundamentalism is not a traditional protest against modernity, but instead these social movements are characterized by their selective approach to modernization and their controlled pattern of acculturation (Antoun, 2001). Selective modernization refers to the process whereby certain technological and organizational innovations of modern society are accepted and others are rejected. The second characterization refers to the process whereby an individual accepts a practice or belief from another culture (the secular world) and integrates it into their value system (the religious world). One illustration of the process of selective modernization is the use of television and radio by fundamentalist Christian groups in the United States. Pat Robertson's Christian Broadcasting Network (CBN) is now the third largest cable network in America, and funds the CBN University, offering courses on media production techniques. James Dobson's radio programme *Focus on the Family*, which offers psychological advice and counselling services, is another example.

Among Islamic radical groups, modern technology is also avidly embraced. In Beirut the militant Hezbollah group has an information network with mobile phones, computers and multiple-version website. Controlled acculturation is a common strategy of Jewish and Muslim fundamentalists that involves physical separation between the religious and secular world. In Israel, Jewish fundamentalists who have to take university courses in academic settings that are secular and liberal have negotiated special arrangements, for example to be taught by men. In Saudi Arabia, fundamentalists have used distance learning techniques to avoid contact with women who are thought to be immodestly dressed. Fundamentalist groups are not therefore wholly opposed to modernity, and have adapted various modern technologies to improve their organizational and communications effectiveness.

Thus, fundamentalists are not traditionalists; on the contrary, they are specifically hostile to traditional religion, which in their view has compromised the fundamental tenets of faith, and by embracing modern technology and organizational forms fundamentalist

movements are, often as an unintended consequence, ushering in radical modernity. This interpretation of fundamentalism is perfectly compatible with the Weber thesis in which the Protestant sects were the reluctant midwives of modernization. Political Islam, with its emphasis on discipline, asceticism, hard work and literacy, and its hostility to traditional Islam in the shape of the Sufi lodges, may also have similar cultural consequences.

Islam has been placed firmly on the agenda of modern sociology of religion by the crisis in international relations and the clash of civilizations. Political Islam is the consequence of the social frustrations resulting from the economic crises of the global neoliberal experiments of the 1970s and 1980s. The demographic revolution produced large cohorts of young Muslims, who, while often well educated to college level, could not find economic opportunities to satisfy the social aspirations that had been inflamed by the rise of nationalist governments in the period of de-colonization. Broadly speaking, we can identify four periods of Islamic political action in response to the social and cultural crises that were associated with foreign domination and civil struggles. These religious movements that have critically attacked contemporary political and military weakness appeal to the early community of the Prophet as a model of social order, and hence they have been labelled 'fundamentalist'. In the nineteenth century, these reformist movements which were hostile to both traditional folk religion and the external Western threat included Wahhabism in Arabia, the Mahdi in the Sudan, the Sanusis in North Africa, and the Islamic reform movements of Egypt. The second wave of activism came in the 1940s with the growth of the Muslim Brotherhood in Egypt, and the third movement began in the aftermath of the Arab defeat in the 1967 war with Israel. It reached a crescendo with the Iranian Revolution in 1978–9 and the Russian incursion into Afghanistan. The contemporary wave of resistance commenced with the Gulf War in 1990, when the presence of American troops on Saudi Arabian soil created the groundwork for the formation of Al-Qaeda networks.

The most influential interpretation of political Islam has been developed by Gilles Kepel (2002) in his *Jihad*. His thesis is simply that the past 25 years have witnessed both the spectacular explosion of Islamism and its failure. In the 1970s, when sociologists assumed that modernization meant secularization, the sudden irruption of political Islam, especially popular protests in Iran that were framed within Shi'ite theology, appeared to challenge dominant paradigms of modernity. These religious movements forced women to wear the *chador* and excluded them from public space. Although leftist intellectuals originally defined religious fundamentalism as religious fascism, Marxists came to realize that Islamism had a popular base and was a powerful force against colonialism. Western conservatives were attracted by Islamic preaching on moral order, obedience to God and hostility to impious materialists, namely communists and socialists.

We can interpret Islamism in sociological terms as the product of generational pressures and class structure. It has been embraced by the youthful generations of the cities that were created by the postwar demographic explosion of the Third World and the resulting mass exodus from the countryside. This generation was poverty-stricken, despite its relatively high literacy and access to secondary education, but Islamism also recruited among the middle classes – the descendants of the merchant families from the bazaars and souks who had been pushed aside by decolonization, and from the doctors, engineers and businessmen, who, while enjoying the salaries made possible by booming oil prices, were excluded from political power. At the local level the ideological carriers of Islamism were the young academics and students, who were recently graduated from technical and science departments and who were inspired by the Muslim ideologues of the 1960s. Islamic themes of justice and equality were mobilized against those regimes that were corrupt, bankrupt and authoritarian, and often supported by the Western governments in the Cold War confrontation with the Soviet empire.

Islamism has failed to fill that gap, and political Islam has been in decline since 1989,

despite the dramatically successful attacks by Al-Qaeda on the United States in 2001. The political opponents of radical Islam have been able to exploit the divided class basis of the movement. For example, the fragile class alliance between the young urban poor, the devout middle classes and alienated intellectuals meant that Islamism was poorly prepared to cope with long-term and systematic opposition from state authorities. Over time governments found ways of dividing these social classes and frustrating the aim of establishing an Islamic state within which the religious law or *Shari'a* would have exclusive jurisdiction. Kepel considers the extreme and violent manifestations of Islamism – the Armed Islamist Group in Algeria, the Taliban in Afghanistan and the Al-Qaeda network – as evidence of its political disintegration and failure. This collapse was detonated by the military invasion of Kuwait in 1990, which was calculated to galvanize the Arab urban poor against the elites of the oil-rich states. The Iraqi attack destroyed the Islamic consensus that the Saudis had established, and the presence of American troops encouraged the growth of dissident Islamic groups in the Saudi kingdom and elsewhere. After the fall of Kabul in 1992, Muslim fighters were dispersed to other conflict regions such as Bosnia, Algeria and Egypt. In Bosnia they failed to insert Islamism successfully into the conflict – a political failure made evident by the Dayton Accords in 1995. In Algeria, extreme violence against civil groups cut off their popular support, and the Berber population remained hostile to Islam. In Egypt, while radical groups had assassinated Sadat, they were unable to sustain broad political support. In Afghanistan, the Taliban lost local and international support through its brutality towards women and opposition groups.

By 1997 there was growing evidence that support for radical Islamism was on the wane. Often with reference to human rights abuse and the need for democratization, the middle class and women's groups who had been targets of religious controls challenged the political dominance of the conservative mullahs and their followers. The election of President Mohammed Khatami in Iran with the support of the middle classes and a generation born after the revolution was achieved against the will of the religious establishment. In Indonesia, a secular president, B.J. Habibie, was elected to replace Suharto, who had fallen from office in 1998, having failed to cope with the financial crises that had undermined the currency. Habibie was ineffectual and indecisive, but he did not directly oppose the process of social and political reform. In Algeria, the new government of Abdelaziz Bouteflika included both secularists and moderate Islamist leaders. In Pakistan, Pervez Musharraf replaced Prime Minister Nawaz Sharif, who had supported the Islamist movement. In Turkey, the Islamist Prime Minister Necmettin Erbakan was forced out of office, thereby breaking the precarious alliance between the middle classes and the radicalized young urban poor. Finally, in the Sudan, the Islamist leader Hassan al-Turabi was forced out of office. For Kepel (2004), the terrorist attacks of 11 September and the Afghan war are further evidence of the political erosion of extremist Islamist movements, because Al-Qaeda has been unable to mobilize a mass movement behind its vision of a global religious war.

In its response to globalization, fundamentalism and the rise of political Islam, the sociology of religion has once more become a major field of study within contemporary sociology. In this chapter, I have concentrated on Christianity and Islam as examples of the fundamentalist challenge, but similar examples could have been taken from Judaism or from Hinduism. Paradoxically, this revival of sociological interest in religious movements has involved an intellectual return to its classical roots in Durkheim and Weber. I have argued that religion was important as an issue in classical sociology, because it posed interesting questions in relation to the growth of rational capitalism, but also because religion was politically important in relation to the rise of a radical working class. In the modern world, religion has become politically important as an active response to the secular implications of globalization. In the United States, Christian fundamentalism has become an important force in the revival of right-wing politics. In Israel,

Jewish fundamentalism has played an important part in re-shaping secular politics, and political Islam has been a major conduit of social and political protest against both corrupt nationalist governments and Western dominance. These intellectual changes in research focus in response to global political developments have had the consequence of revitalizing the sociology of religion as an important component of contemporary sociology.

REFERENCES

Abaza, M. (2002) *Debates on Islam and Knowledge in Malaysia and Egypt. Shifting Worlds.* London: Routledge Curzon.

Ackerman, R. (1987) *J.G. Frazer. His Life and Work.* Cambridge: Cambridge University Press.

Ammerman, N.T. (1987) *Bible Believers. Fundamentalists in the Modern World.* Brunswick, NJ: Rutgers University Press.

Anderson, B. (1983) *Imagined Communities.* London: Verso.

Antoun, R.T. (2001) *Understanding Fundamentalism. Christian, Islamic and Jewish Movements.* Walnut Creek, CA: Altamira Press.

Armstrong, K. (2001) *The Battle for God. Fundamentalism in Judaism, Christianity and Islam.* London: HarperCollins.

Berger, P.L. (1969) *The Social Reality of Religion.* London: Faber and Faber.

Burrow, J.W. (1966) *Evolution and Society: A Study of Victorian Social Theory.* Cambridge: Cambridge University Press.

Douglas, M. (1966) *Purity and Danger: An Analysis of Concepts of Pollution and Taboo.* London: Routledge and Kegan Paul.

Douglas, M. (1970) *Natural Symbols. Explorations in Cosmology.* London: Penguin.

Durkheim, E. (1961) *The Elementary Forms of the Religious Life.* New York: Collier.

Durkheim, E. and Mauss, M. (1963) *Primitive Classification.* London: Cohen and West.

Edmunds, J. and Turner, B.S. (2001) 'The re-invention of a national identity? Women and "cosmopolitan" Englishness', *Ethnicities,* 1 (1): 83–108.

Edmunds, J. and Turner, B.S. (2002) *Generations, Culture and Society.* Buckingham: Open University Press.

El Hamel, C. (2002) 'Muslim diaspora in Western Europe: the Islamic headscarf (*Hijab*) in the media and Muslims' integration in France', *Citizenship Studies*, 6 (3): 293–308.

Evans-Pritchard, E.E. (1965) *Theories of Primitive Religion*. Oxford: The Clarendon Press.

Frazer, J.G. (1935) *The Golden Bough*. New York: Macmillan.

Freud, S. (1950) *Totem and Taboo*. London: Routledge and Kegan Paul.

Girard, R. (1988) *Violence and the Sacred*. London: Athlone Press.

Glock, C.Y. and Stark, R. (1965) *Religion and Society in Tension*. Chicago: Rand McNally.

Goode, W.J. (1951) *Religion Among the Primitives*. New York. The Free Press.

Gramsci, A. (1971) *Selections from the Prison Notebooks*. London: New Left Books.

Hamilton, M.B. (1995) *The Sociology of Religion. Theoretical and Comparative Perspectives*. London: Routledge.

Hassan, R. (2002) *Faithlines. Muslim Conceptions of Islam and Society*. Oxford: Oxford University Press.

Heelas, P. (1996) *The New Age Movement*. Oxford: Blackwell.

Herberg, W. (1955) *Protestant, Catholic, Jew*. New York: Doubleday.

Huntington, S.P. (1997) *The Clash of Civilizations and the Remaking of World Order*. New York: Simon and Schuster.

Kelley, D. (1977) *Why Conservative Churches Are Growing*. New York: Harper and Row.

Kepel, G. (2002) *Jihad. The Trail of Political Islam*. London/New York: I.B. Tauris.

Kepel, G. (2004) *The War for Muslim Minds*. Cambridge, MA: The Belknap Press.

Levy-Bruhl, L. (1923) *Primitive Mentality*. London: Allen and Unwin.

Levy-Bruhl, L. (1985) *Primitive Mythology*. St Lucia: Queensland University Press.

Luckmann, T. (1967) *The Invisible Religion. The Problem of Religion in Modern Society*. New York: Macmillan.

Luhmann, N. (1984) *Religious Dogmatics and the Evolution of Societies*. New York/Toronto: The Edwin Mellen Press.

MacIntyre, A. (1969) 'The debate about God: Victorian relevance and contemporary irrelevance', in A. MacIntyre and P. Ricoeur (eds), *The Religious Significance of Atheism*. New York/London: Columbia University Press. pp. 3–55.

Marrett, R.R. (1909) *The Threshold of Religion*. London: Methuen.

Martin, B. (1978) *A General Theory of Secularization*. Oxford: Blackwell.

Martin, D. (2002) *Pentecostalism: The World Their Parish*. Oxford: Blackwell.

Mauss, M. (2001) *A General Theory of Magic*. London/New York: Routledge.

Müller, M. (1997) *Anthropological Religion*. London: Routledge/Thoemmes.

Murphy, R.F. (1972) *Robert H. Lowie*. London/New York: Columbia University Press.

O'Toole, R. (2001) 'Classics in the sociology of religion: an ambiguous legacy', in R.K. Fenn (ed.), *The Blackwell Companion to Sociology of Religion*. Oxford: Blackwell. pp. 133–60.

Parsons, T. (1966) 'Introduction' to Max Weber *The Sociology of Religion*. London: Methuen. pp. xix–lxvii.

Parsons, T. (1999) 'Religion in postindustrial America' in B.S. Turner (ed.), *The Talcott Parsons Reader*. Oxford: Blackwell. pp. 300–20.

Pope, L. (1942) *Millhands and Preachers*. New Haven, CT: Yale University Press.

Riesman, D. (1950) *The Lonely Crowd. A Study of the Changing American Character*. New Haven, CT: Yale University Press.

Robertson, R. (1970) *The Sociological Interpretation of Religion*. Oxford: Blackwell.

Robertson, R. (1992) *Globalization, Social Theory and Global Culture*. London: Sage.

Roof, W.C. (1993) *A Generation of Seekers: The Spiritual Journeys of the Baby Boom Generation*. San Francisco: Harper.

Roof, W.C. (1999) *Spiritual Marketplace. Baby Boomers and the Remaking of American Religion*. Princeton, NJ/Oxford: Princeton University Press.

Sharot, S. (2001) *A Comparative Sociology of World Religions. Virtuosos, Priests and Popular Religion*. New York/London: New York University Press.

Smith, C. (2000) *Christian America? What Evangelicals Really Want*. Berkeley, CA: University of California Press.

Smith, W. Robertson (1997) *Lectures on the Religion of the Semites*. London: Routledge/Thoemmes.

Tamney, J.B. (2002) *The Resilience of Conservative Religion. The Case of Popular, Conservative Protestant Congregations*. Cambridge: Cambridge University Press.

Tocqueville, A. de (1968) *Democracy in America*. Glasgow: Collins.

Troeltsch, E. (1931) *The Social Teaching of the Christian Churches*. New York: Macmillan.

Turner, B.S. (1991) *Religion and Social Theory*. London: Sage.

Turner, B.S. (1996) *For Weber. Essays on the Sociology of Fate*. London: Routledge.

Tylor, E.B. (1891) *Primitive Culture. Researches into the Development of Mythology, Philosophy, Religion, Language, Art and Customs.* London: John Murray.

Weber, M. (1930) *The Protestant Ethic and the Spirit of Capitalism.* London: George Allen and Unwin.

Weber, M. (1952) *Ancient Judaism.* New York: The Free Press.

Weber, M. (1958) *The City.* New York: The Free Press.

Weber, M. (1966) *The Sociology of Religion.* London: Methuen.

Weber, M. (1978) *Economy and Society. An Outline of Interpretive Sociology.* Berkeley, CA: University of California Press.

Wernick, A. (2001) *Auguste Comte and the Religion of Humanity.* Cambridge: Cambridge University Press.

Whyte, W.F. (1956) *The Organization Man.* New York: Simon and Schuster.

Wilson, B. (1966) *Religion in Secular Society.* London: Watts.

Wilson, B. (1970) *Religious Sects: A Sociological Study.* London: Weidenfeld and Nicolson.

Wilson, B. (1976) *Contemporary Transformations of Religion.* London: Oxford University Press.

Wolin, S.S. (2001) *Tocqueville between Two Worlds. The Making of a Political and Theoretical Life.* Princeton, NJ:/Oxford: Princeton University Press.

17

Leisure and Tourism

CHRIS ROJEK

The sociological study of leisure and tourism is a relatively novel sub-discipline in the field. Over a decade and a half ago, Neil Smelser's (1988) *Handbook of Sociology* could find no place for a chapter on the subject. Early sociological contributions tended to be either based in ethnographic work or social surveys. Typically, they focused only on working class leisure and to conflate this subject with questions of social reform (Rowntree, 1865; Booth, 1902–3; Rowntree, 1901; Lynd and Lynd, 1937). Interestingly, with the exception of Veblen's (1899) brilliant study, the subject of the leisure forms and practices among the rich was neglected.[1]

It is widely agreed that the period between the 1880s and 1920s consolidated the key features of consumer culture as we understand them today (Cross, 1993; Kammen, 1999). In particular, many of the national commodity and leisure markets established during this period remain intact. The emergence of national sports, like soccer in the UK and baseball in the United States, and the development of revolutionary new domestic, electronic leisure forms like the phonograph and radio, which are compatible with the development of high levels of privatized fantasy content, created significant national audiences based around leisure activity. Yet curiously, the institutional sociology of the day remained relatively silent about this transformation. It was not until the 1940s that sociologists began to address the significance of new types of leisure as society-wide socio-technical systems involving manipulation and control. This occurred in the contribution of mass society theory, which emphasized the manipulation and standardization of the masses (Riesman, 1950; Packard, 1957) and the Frankfurt School (Adorno and Horkheimer, 1944). Even then, leisure can hardly be said to have been the *focus* of theory or research.[2]

The first academically significant attempts to institutionalize the study of the meaning of leisure in people's lives and the effects of leisure on community occurred *outside* sociology. In the postwar period, questions of leisure and tourism were initially pursued by departments of Parks, Recreation and Leisure Studies, of which the department at the University of Illinois, Urbana headed by Allen V. Sapora was one of the most influential. The development of Leisure Studies and, later, Tourist Studies in the academy acted as a catalyst for the sociology of leisure and tourism, rather than the other way around.

Why did institutionalized sociology neglect the subjects of leisure and tourism for so long? There were two main reasons. First, the mainstream functionalist bent of Western postwar sociology followed the lead of the classical tradition and identified work as the central life interest. Durkheim (1933: 26) himself proposed that leisure belongs to 'the less serious side of life'. In the nineteenth century and for much of the twentieth century work was regarded as the cornerstone of personality, the foundation of family life, the basis of community and the core of the central value system that under-pinned social order. This emphasis was itself the consequence of many factors. The residue of the doctrine of Christian self-help embodied in the work ethic, which assigned respectability to a paid labourer or recognized the rights for welfare entitlement of a dependant of a paid labourer, was a significant factor. However, the standard connotation between paid labour and respectability was far from being a mere reflection of Christian doctrines of self-help and the work ethic. It also mirrored the fiscal assumptions behind the welfare state which identified continuous paid employment and member-ship of the nuclear family as preconditions for public entitlement. Welfarism carried with it an unparticularized set of moral judgements concerning 'respectable leisure' which assumed the normative status of heterosexual marriage in a nuclear or extended family and the recog-nition of legal parental responsibilities with respect to children. Of course, provision existed for unemployment and ill-health benefit for those who had not fiscally contributed to state resources. However, the a priori of untested enti-tlement was a *career* of fiscal contributions to the state derived from paid labour or legally validated relations of dependency with an indi-vidual occupying this status.

In the 1960s and 1970s many of these assumptions were criticized, particularly by feminists, who pointed to entrenched structural inequalities in the labour market in respect of differences in pay and promotion prospects between the sexes. The gay and lesbian move-ment also questioned the heteronormative bias of welfare state ideology and policies on entitle-ment. Yet welfare ideology bequeathed a curi-ously narrow conception of leisure forms and practice in everyday life founded in heteronor-mativity, paid labour and monoculturalism.

The second main reason for the neglect of leisure and tourism was related to the presump-tions behind the notion of 'the affluent society'.

For example, the influential 'logic of industrial-ization' thesis proposed that the distribution of resources for leisure and tourist activities was fated to expand progressively as science and technology eliminated the human burden of engaging in lifelong paid labour (Kerr et al., 1973). Some commentators predicted the emer-gence of 'the leisure society' in which leisure forms and practices would replace work as the focal point of group identity (Dumazedier, 1967, 1974). Today, this is generally regarded as an optimistic view of social development in the advanced industrial societies. The lily was gilded with the correlative proposition that more afflu-ence and leisure would produce higher levels of social integration and reduce social conflict. Kerr and his associates envisaged the emergence of what they termed the 'new bohemianism' in people's leisure and tourist practices. New levels of creativity and diversity were predicted which would make old models of the 9-to-5 work treadmill redundant. Postindustrial society theory generally supported this perspective (Touraine, 1971; Bell, 1973). It maintained that resources for leisure and tourism would expand as an inevitable consequence of the greater wealth created by science and technology. Similarly, it was assumed that the forms and practices asso-ciated with these activities would contribute to social integration and harmony.

With hindsight, it was an excessively melior-ist, over-rational projection of leisure and tourism that took insufficient allowance of reli-gious divisions, cultural and subcultural differ-ences and the capacity of the welfare state to withstand the challenge of neoliberalism. It failed to recognize that social values of leisure are sources for conflict as well as cohesion. In addition, it was ethnocentric, taking little inter-est in questions of hunger, illiteracy, poverty and morbidity in the Third World. Nor did it raise the question of the sourcing of leisure com-modities in the West from Third World labour. Today, we recognize that Nike, Gap, Champion, Wal-Mart and Reebok make extensive use of low cost labour in the developing countries to assemble their products (Klein, 2001; Smart, 2003: 160). But the leisure society view repro-duced a stage theory of social development, in which it was assumed that the advanced industrial societies presented the developing world with the face of its own future. Above all, traditional mainstream views of leisure and tourism in the 1960s and 1970s depended upon what now reads as a peculiarly deterministic, under-examined view of technology and welfarism that predicted the expansion of free time and affluence as the inevitable consequence of improvements in science and technology, but paid scant attention to globalization, the distribution of power and the politics and dilemmas of personal freedom and choice.

THE EARLY INSTITUTIONAL SOCIOLOGY OF LEISURE

The early sociology of leisure identified three principal functions of leisure: *rest and replenishment* from toil, *reward* for physical and mental exertion and *enhancement* of the bonds between the individual and the community. This was formalized in influential studies by Wilensky (1960) and Parker (1971). They followed the precedent of functionalism in locating leisure values amidst a variety of variables such as class, age, gender, status and work. Of these, overwhelmingly the most important relationship was identified as that between work and leisure. For example, Wilensky (1960) distinguished between 'spillover' and 'compensatory' work–leisure patterns. In spillover patterns a determining role was attributed to work. Thus, sedentary work practice such as clerical filing or secretarial work was theorized as eliciting passive leisure practices such as watching television or reading magazines. In compensatory patterns leisure practice was theorized as making up for the deprivations of work. Work that demanded low levels of intellectual involvement, such as assembly-line production, was postulated to stimulate leisure forms based in high levels of social involvement, such as pub cultures or hobbies requiring planning, coordination and engagement, such as pigeon racing (Friedmann, 1961). Parker (1971) took over many of Wilensky's theoretical assumptions in the development of his 'extension', 'opposition' and neutrality' patterns of work–leisure relations.

What is now conspicuous about this early work is its naïve humanism. The leisure society is depicted as an unequivocal good for mankind. It is held to inevitably enlarge individual freedom, and create the basis for new forms of solidarity. The divisions in access to surplus time, the antagonisms of class, gender, race and status, the thorny question of distributive justice, which later generations of students in leisure studies fastened upon, are absent (Clarke and Critcher, 1985; Deem, 1986; Henderson et al., 1989, 1996). Instead the functionalist sociology of leisure and leisure society theory portrayed leisure forms and practice as enhancing social harmony and integration. Arguably, this climaxed in Cheek and Burch's (1976: 156) proposition that 'leisure activities serve as an expression of social solidarity and norms to reaffirm the larger social order'. Their study tries to apply the Parsonian social systems approach in the sphere of leisure behaviour. Leisure is twinned with the central social problems of social order and growth. Through socialization in primary institutions, the most notable of which are the family, school and community, individuals acquire role models, taste cultures, expressions of commitment and trust relations that equip them for the remainder of the life course. The acquisition of these social assets is theorized in terms of a unifying *central value system*. It is precisely these propositions that have been attacked by the critical sociology of leisure.

CRITICAL VIEWS OF LEISURE BEFORE THE 1970S

Without doubt, the critical sociology of leisure was under-researched and under-theorized in the Western tradition until well into the 1970s. The sub-discipline did possess one *bona fide* classic, in Thorstein Veblen's (1899) extraordinary book *The Theory of the Leisure Class*. This study introduced the concept of *conspicuous consumption* to describe the spectacular expenditure of wealth in leisure practice as a mark of social status. It related this to a complex theory of the power hierarchy in American society.

Veblen submitted that the dominant moneyed leisure class applied leisure forms and practices to symbolize their superior social status. In particular, they organized their leisure activities around conspicuous consumption not only of economic capital, but also cultural capital. Thus, in addition to holding extravagant parties and balls, the leisure class cultivated leisure forms and practices that automatically symbolized voluntary abnegation from paid labour. Among Veblen's examples are the preindustrial pursuits of heraldry, equipage and learning dead languages like Ancient Latin and Ancient Greek. Veblen's theory can be read as an early attempt to explain how leisure practice operates in the semiotics of status distinction and the pursuit of power.

Some alternative critical contributions were made by the various studies associated with the Chicago School in the 1920s and 1930s and the British Mass-Observation studies of the late 1930s and 1940s which sought to use methodological techniques from anthropology and ethnology to document ordinary urban-industrial life in the West. In particular, the work of the Lynds (1937) in the United States and Tom Harrison, Humphrey Jennings and Charles Madge in the UK (Calder and Sheridan, 1985) provided data on habitual leisure practice which revealed the depth and vitality of counter-cultural values in ordinary leisure practice. Interestingly, it was, by and large, free of the moralizing tendency that was so evident in the social survey work of the late nineteenth and early twentieth centuries. Yet while this work attracted a good deal of contemporaneous media attention, the research that it generated tended to be too inchoate and too multi-dimensional to constitute the basis for a coherent critical theory of leisure.

It was left to historians and general commentators on Western civilization like Johan Huizinga (1947) and Louis Mumford (1967, 1970) to inject a degree of vitality into theoretical debates on leisure. Huizinga's model of *homo ludens* argued that leisure is the basis of culture – a proposition developed in the 1950s by the philosopher Josef Pieper (1952). Mumford also emphasized the importance of play in human evolution and criticized the work ethic as an iron principle of advanced industrial civilization. Mumford submitted that more flexible relationships between work and leisure were possible as a result of automation, science and technology. In particular, his work raised questions of a new position on retirement policy and the identification of institutionalized learning with the period of schooling in the life cycle. But these interventions did not crystallize into a critical position in the sociology of leisure and tourism. For one thing, they emerged from outside the discipline of sociology. In addition, they were attached to wider critical accounts of the evolution of Western culture and civilization in which contemporary leisure and tourist forms did not form the focal point of interest.

THE FRANKFURT TRADITION

A sociological counter-balance was provided between the 1930s and 1960s by the Frankfurt School tradition of sociology and philosophy. This neo-Marxist tradition argued that in 'one dimensional society', leisure is subject to manipulation and control (Adorno and Horkheimer, 1944; Marcuse, 1964; Adorno, 1998). Although the question of leisure was examined only *en passant* in this approach, Frankfurt School theorists were antagonistic to the concepts of individual freedom and choice under capitalism. Because leisure is conventionally regarded as the embodiment of these qualities, it was intrinsically held to be a suspect category. For example, Adorno (1998: 173–5) referred dismissively to what he called *pseudo-activity*, that is, free-time activities that lionize the values of freedom, choice and diversity. He maintained that in the context of capitalist consumer culture, these activities provide distraction and the illusion of autonomy. 'People', he wrote (1998: 173), 'prefer to let themselves be distracted by spurious, illusory activities, by institutionalized vicarious satisfactions rather than to face the realization of just how much the possibilities for change are blocked today. The pseudo-activities are fictions and parodies of the productivity society on the one hand incessantly demands and on the other hand confines and in fact does not really desire in individuals at all.' For the Frankfurt School, consumer culture inevitably produces mass conformity in leisure choice and practice. The culture industry, which regulates the various forms of mass entertainment and media information exchange, requires domination over individual choice and practice. So individual choices in leisure practice are ultimately programmatic in that they either follow the dictate of the culture industry or are eventually co-opted by the same means.

This critical analysis of leisure brought with it difficulties of its own. While it contributed to a more politicized reading of leisure and tourism, it provided a position on freedom and choice that many took to be over-reductive. The pronounced importance given to the culture industry amounted to a new essentialism in which leisure choice was attributed ultimately to class-controlled institutions. The Frankfurt School position on leisure provided no solace for activists committed to the progressive change of leisure and tourism. Indeed, Adorno's (1992) response to activism was to call for a sympathetic but ultimately dismissive version of 'resignation'. He regarded the demands of the 1960s counter-culture to be extravagant and unrealistic because the economic, political and cultural preconditions for the transformation of capitalism were not yet extant.

THE SOLIDIFICATION OF CRITICAL PERSPECTIVES

The solidification of the sociology of leisure as a sub-discipline occurred in the mid-1980s. Four positions have emerged as central: the cultural studies approach, feminism, post-work theory and the over-work thesis:

Cultural studies

The expansion of interest in leisure and tourism is partly an expression of 'the cultural turn' in sociology that began in the late 1970s. In the UK the main catalyst was the emergence of cultural studies, notably through the work of Stuart Hall at the Birmingham Centre for Contemporary Cultural Studies. Hall (1970) actually published a paper on leisure as early as 1970; however, its focus was not on the institution or ordering of leisure practice in modern urban-industrial society but on the relationship between leisure and mass communication. This reflected the early importance assigned by Birmingham to the media in the representation of social order. This interest crystallized in what is, arguably, the most significant book published by researchers in the Centre, namely *Policing the Crisis* (Hall et al., 1978). Alongside the role of the media in the regulation of everyday life, Birmingham researchers attributed equivalent influence to the state. Drawing on the work of Gramsci and Althusser, the Centre outlined a position on the state that placed it at the centre of culture and leisure. Any concession that the state granted to the public expansion of culture and leisure through, for example, increased state funding, was theorized as part of a complex 'war of manoeuvre' designed to maintain hegemony.

This was a notably different approach to leisure than anything produced by the early sociology of leisure. Most importantly, it placed power and politics at the heart of analysis. Leisure practice is alluded to in most of the significant publications that emerged from the Centre in the 1970s and 1980s, notably in respect of the use of rituals, media representation in free time and the influence of race in determining access and participation (Hall and Jefferson, 1975; Hall et al., 1980; CCCS, 1982). However, the Birmingham approach to leisure is realized most powerfully in Clarke and Critcher's (1985) influential book on class, culture and leisure. Both had been students in the Birmingham Centre and both collaborated with Hall. Their study harnessed the central theoretical preoccupations of Birmingham and applied them to leisure. The cultural studies position is delineated as a clear alternative to functionalist approaches. Leisure is analysed as both an axis of control and forum of resistance. The study provides a detailed historical account of class and leisure and demonstrates how class and gender shape leisure access and participation. Consumer choice is theorized as conditioned by the logic of capitalist accumulation. While leisure is recognized to offer the means of challenging hegemony, the capacity of capitalism to co-opt forms of resistance is duly noted. The authors argue for the revitalization of socialism by using leisure practice as one means of reconnecting the private to the public.

Although most of the cultural studies work in Birmingham was confined to the British case, many of the central ideas have been successfully transplanted and developed elsewhere. In the United States the work of Larry Grossberg (1997) has expanded the notion of resistance in relation to rock music and other forms of American popular culture. In Australia, often with the inflection of ideas from Foucault and Bourdieu, CCCS ideas have been exploited and developed in the analysis of soap opera, audiences and taste cultures in leisure practice (Ang, 1985, 1996; Bennett et al., 1999).

Feminism

Feminist contributions argue that women's 'free' time and participation in leisure culture is positioned by patriarchy. Studies in the UK by Deem (1986) and Green et al. (1990) and in North America by Henderson et al. (1989, 1996) and Hochschild (1997) maintain that gender is constructed around a sexual, economic and social division of labour in which women are primarily located as domestic labourers, emotional managers and low-paid workers. Gender construction operationalizes an internal and external system of regulation. Internally, the importance of physical appearance in female identity presupposes a lack of equal entitlement to leisure compared with men. The focus upon questions of embodiment in female identity, together with the structural constraints upon females in the labour market, direct women to develop dependency relationships upon men or the welfare state. Externally, women's participation in leisure is generally impeded by a lack of money and time compared with males in the same class formation. Symbolically, women are interpellated in a relation of dependence to male culture, which assigns pronounced importance to female sexuality and restrains women's

access to public leisure space. Feminist arguments therefore destabilize traditional functionalist notions of choice, freedom and spontaneity as universal characteristics of leisure practice.

Recent developments in the feminist position draw on aspects of postcolonialism to question not merely the validity of patriarchy, but *all* forms of identity thinking. Identity thinking is criticized for operating through untenable binary oppositions such as male/ female, mind/ body, culture/nature and work/ leisure. The pervasive character of male hegemony continues to be stressed, but this is explored in relation to hybrid relations involving class, race, nation and collateral dimensions of power (Aitchison et al., 2000; Fullagar, 2002).

Post-work theory

Utilizing many aspects of the Frankfurt School critique of instrumental reason, post-work theory submits that the productive forces of advanced industrial society permit the drastic reduction of work time and the corresponding increase in leisure time. Work is no longer regarded as the central life interest. According to Gorz (1982), most workers relate to paid labour as the means to finance leisure activities rather than the means to forge self worth. Citing the dehumanizing effects of the managerial technoculture, Aronowitz and Di Fazio (1994: 349–58) call for the establishment of an adequate income for all; the regulation of capital to allocate more resources to leisure; and the introduction of fiscal and moral incentives to use leisure time to enlarge social capital. They envisage a grass-roots transformation in the body politic in which organized labour and social movements will play a leading role.

Without meaning to, Aronowitz and Cutler (1998) support Putnam's (2000) proposition that leisure can operate as a significant means of enhancing social capital. Citing Di Fazio's (1985) research on unemployment among longshoremen in Brooklyn, they reject the premise of the work ethic that unemployment produces dysfunctionality in individuals and disintegration in the community. The unemployed longshoremen did not turn to drink or violence. On the contrary, many collaborated more in child-rearing and voluntary unpaid labour in the community.

The post-work position challenges orthodox conceptions of identity formation and community integration which have traditionally emphasized the fundamental importance of paid labour. Echoing the work of Gorz (1982, 1983), this approach maintains that individuals in advanced capitalist society are no longer psychologically bound to work as the source of the central meaning in life. Rather, most people now relate to paid labour as the means to finance leisure activity and travel. On this account, the casualization of labour cannot be understood merely as a structural transformation in the nature of work. In addition, it arises from conscious lifestyle choices made by individuals to diversify and enrich their experience. It is this same desire for diversity and enrichment that will shift society to recognize the post-work mode by eventually instituting a minimum wage and the assignment of prestige to non-work values, especially those directed at enhancing social capital.

The over-work thesis

The diametric opposite of the post-work thesis is Juliet Schor's (1991) book on 'the over-worked American'. Schor argues that while strong ideological attachments remain to leisure as an esteemed life value, the trend is towards simultaneous multiple paid employment. Through a variety of social and economic arrangements, such as combining part-time and full-time labour contracts and participation in the invisible or 'black' economy, workers spend more time in accumulating disposable income. The psychological irony behind the phenomenon of over-work is that workers are motivated to extend participation in paid labour activities in order to increase access to consumer culture. However, the result of working longer is a deficit in time so that workers have less opportunity to enjoy the fruits of their labour.

Contemporary leisure experience must be understood in terms of the 'harried leisure class' or 'time famine' (Linder, 1970; Hochschild, 1997).

This condition is associated with a variety of psycho-somatic anxieties. Schor lists stress, coronary disease, strokes, strain in the management of intimate relations, the production of latch-key children and the deterioration of community solidarity.

Historians of leisure have not been so effusive about the medical, psychological and social effects of over-work, but they confirm the general proposition that modern men and women have exhibited a strong tendency to trade off more leisure for the accumulation of higher economic value through greater participation in relations of paid employment. Hunnicutt (1988) argues that this is evident in the collective bargaining processes of organized labour. Until the 1920s, a prominent goal of organized labour was to increase paid holiday time. Since this period, most unions have down-played this role in favour of right-to-work objectives. The latter have taken the form of extending employment opportunities for the unemployed but also sanctioning the right to overtime work for the employed.

The over-work thesis proposes high levels of integration between individuals and consumer culture and widespread perceptions of time famine as hallmarks of the modern condition. Interestingly, quantitative analysis of time use in the West, suggests that both propositions are faulty (Gershuny, 1978, 2000; Robinson and Godbey, 1999). Research in the United States estimates that since 1965 Americans have gained an extra hour's free time per day. Interestingly, while Americans imagine that they have only 18 hours of free time per week, analysis of time diary data suggests that they actually have more than twice that amount (Robinson and Godbey, 1999). *Pace,* the overwork thesis, these findings imply that the perception of a generalized time famine owes more to the mechanics of how life is *represented.*

Gershuny's (2000) work provides a variant of postindustrial society theory. He argues that as labour becomes more highly skilled and adds higher value through the labour process, it achieves higher rewards. By increasing the hourly rate of reward, skilled workers have leverage to decrease the hours of paid work and boost spending on the leisure sector, thus increasing the numbers employed therein. These hypotheses are extrapolated from time-budget data and may be criticized for paying insufficient attention to the condition of low-skilled workers, the unemployed and women workers. None the less, they provide a counter-point to the over-work thesis by suggesting that skilled workers have been more successful in increasing the rate of economic reward for their labour and decreasing work-time.

A unifying feature of all of these positions is the recognition that leisure choice and practice are political. Sometimes they exaggerate the potential of leisure for building consensus. I think this applies to the contribution of Clarke and Critcher (1985) and Aronowitz and Cutler (1998). Against them, it is necessary to stress that leisure is a source of dissent as well as con-sensus and to insist that the role of leisure in crystallizing conflict and precipitating social change must be acknowledged. However, recog-nizing that leisure is political is a considerable gain over the functionalist positions that domi-nated the sub-discipline until the late 1970s.

THE SOCIOLOGY OF TOURISM

If the sociology of leisure struggled to cohere as a recognized field in the discipline, it took even longer for tourism to become established. Adrian Franklin (2003: 29) has commented on the irony that the massive expansion of tourism in the West during the 1950s and 1960s was met with relative indifference in the disciplines of sociology, geography and business studies that now champion the subject. Dean MacCannell's (1976) path-breaking work on tourist experi-ence provided an exception to the rule. It deployed an interesting mix of methods and arguments from the traditions of social semi-otics and symbolic interactionism to highlight the significance of the boundaries between tourist sights and everyday life in the organiza-tion of tourism. Conversely, it replicated the tra-ditional associations of tourism with escape and the quest for authenticity. This mirrored central themes in the critical sociology of the day having to do with the bureaucracy, standardization and

alienation of urban-industrial life. The division between authentic and inauthentic experience and its connotation with tourist and routine urban-industrial existence was reproduced in the functionalist analysis of Krippendorf (1984) and Cohen's (1988, 1995) social psychology of tourist types. However, it was quickly recog-nized to be unsatisfactory. The casting of tourism as a quest for authenticity glossed over the routine character of much tourist experi-ence; it promoted a false conceptual dichotomy between authentic and inauthentic experience; and it failed to conceptualize the meaning of tourist flow in relation to central questions of modernity.

John Urry's (1990) influential study *The Tourist Gaze* endeavoured to overhaul this state of affairs. Instead of focusing on the character of tourist *experience*, he concentrates upon the *representation* and *sign-world* of tourist sights. His study identifies tourism with the attempt to visually embrace and record different and unusual landscapes, objects and urban milieux. It was obviously influenced by the cultural turn in sociology, especially in respect of the signifi-cance of visual culture, surveillance and hyper-reality in ordering everyday life. However, it is an oddly restrained book, which does not fully engage with the challenges that the debate on modernity and postmodernity present to a sociological and geographical understanding of tourism (Harvey, 1989; Crang, 1999; Franklin, 2003). For example, it tends to present tourism uncritically as a personal and social benefit. The environmental consequences of mass tourism, the development of the sex work sector in tourist destinations and the manipulation of the tourist sign economy are recognized but not adequately investigated. The significance of tourism in providing subjectively meaningful orientation in the lives of tourists tends to be rejected in favour of an emphasis upon the sur-face or superficial aspects of tourist experience. Finally, while the significance assigned to embodiment in tourist experience is welcome, it presents an over-pronounced emphasis upon the visual and under-develops the importance of sensuality in tourist exchange.

Ethnographic and historical studies of the relationship between the beach, heritage sites and nature and tourism have proliferated in the sociology of tourism (MacDonald, 1997; Edensor, 1998; Desmond, 1999; Lencek and Bosker, 1999; O'Reilly, 2000). This work echoes the theme of the Other, sketched out in postcolonialism. It raises the question of hybrid, cosmopolitan and 'transnational' forms of identity which destabilize the dichotomy between tourist and native. It explores how tourist identity is coded and themed and the dilemmas that it poses for 'natives'. These are often directly expressed in the incursion of tourist physical space into native settings. But there are also complex layers of cross-cultural positioning in tourist flows which involve positioning the tourist as the Other. Western tourists have been defined as anything from ambassadors of friendship to symbols of imperialist domination. The questions of how tourist space and how tourists are themselves coded and themed illustrates the importance of examining tourism as a system of representation. This approach lends itself to a variety of discursive methods of analysis which are likely to prove fruitful in further research.

At the level of theory, the most significant work investigates the relationship of tourism to modernity and postmodernity (Gottdiener, 1997; Franklin, 2003). This work draws on globalization theory and multiculturalism to explore travel and difference as the crucial motifs of contemporary urban-industrial identity. Urry (1999) has contributed to this debate with his argument that traditional static concepts of society as a hermetic, sealed identity should be replaced with the concept of flow which highlights movement, porosity and hybridity. At the crux of this work is the proposition that globalization has collapsed modernist divisions of emplacement. It is no longer meaningful to operate with the dichotomy between 'home' and 'abroad'. The work of Ritzer (1992, 1995, 2004a, 2004b) and Gottdiener (1997, 2000) in the sociology of consumption illustrates how new ways of theming urban-industrial space erode the boundaries that separate tourism from everyday life. The emergence of Mediterranean or Caribbean villages in urban-industrial Western shopping malls, the development of heritage sites in deindustrialized landscapes and the proliferation of various forms of multicultural cuisine in Western city centres and suburbs, contribute to the de-differentiation of space. Traditional modernist distinctions between home and abroad, and the attendant anxieties and stereotypes attached to them, which the first and second generation package tour operators of the postwar tourist boom exploited to manage foreign holidays for Westerners, have lost ground. The main challenge facing them has come from new forms of tourism in which consciousness of global interdependence and the division of power between the core and the periphery is pronounced. The extraordinary expansion of the Internet in the past decade has significantly contributed to this process. It has vastly increased the flow of information about other countries, ethnicities, religions and cultures and made virtual forms of travel a habitual feature of life for anyone with access to a computer.

PROSPECTS FOR THE SOCIOLOGY OF LEISURE AND TOURISM

The past 25 years have witnessed the gradual ascent of leisure and tourism as recognized fields in sociology. This has not replaced modules and research groupings organized around the family, education, gender, inequality, health and illness, race, social policy and work on undergraduate courses. But these staples of the core curriculum are now pursued in a context in which the questions of leisure and tourism are widely acknowledged meta-themes in contemporary social life. There are three main reasons for this.

First, demographic changes, especially the ageing of populations in the West, have generated new sociological interest in the place of leisure and tourism in the organization of lifestyle and the composition of society (Gershuny, 1978). Compared with 25 years ago, tourism and leisure are already more prominent features at every stage of the lifestyle. As average life expectancy increases in the West, people are likely not merely to live longer but a significant number will generate enough disposable income to travel more and experience longer periods of retirement for leisure. The place of leisure and tourism in identity and identity politics is likely to grow.

Secondly, the rise of the sociology of consumption has magnified interest in the role of leisure and tourism in configuring identity and practice (Ewen, 1976; Featherstone, 1991; Ritzer, 1992, 2004a). The development of themed shopping environments, which deploy markers of travel as standard design features, has made motifs of leisure and tourism pronounced features of most Western city consumer centres.

Thirdly, the phenomenal expansion of interest in globalization has created new interest in questions of population flow, the physical and symbolic importance of leisure and travel and the relationship between tourism, leisure and multiculturalism. Indeed, Urry (1999) questions the validity of the traditional concept of society in the midst of new global flows of finance, tourists and information. Perhaps this underestimates the continued importance of nation-states and nationalism as foci of solidarity. Certainly, it applies more to conditions in the advanced Western powers than in the developing countries. None the less, globalization has undoubtedly increased popular consciousness of heterodox forms of cultural, political and physical emplacement and embodiment.

Leisure and tourism are particularly rich subjects for sociological inquiry because they continuously pose questions of individual freedom. Parker (1981) defined leisure as possessing the characteristics of freedom, choice, flexibility and spontaneity. This definition expressed a perspective of atomistic individualism, in which the characteristics of leisure are analysed from the standpoint of the individual. Since then, the trend in the sociology of leisure and tourism has been to root analysis in the concept of the *situated* actor. Sociologists differ about what aspects of the situated nature of action are most important. As we have seen in the foregoing discussion, industrialism, class, gender and race have all been presented as key structural influences. Perhaps one way of dealing with the question of situation is to recognize the *embodied, emplaced* character of human action. By treating all humans as already embodied and emplaced, a perspective on the situated nature of action can be developed which is more inclusive than structuralist interpretations. Be that as it may, because leisure and tourism are ideologically constructed as the times and spaces in which individuals possess most freedom and choice, they have enormous sociological potential for revealing how ideology operates to position subjects and how subjects challenge and resist regimes of power. The relationship of leisure and tourism to Western ideology promises to yield some of the most interesting gains in future research.

NOTES

1 Veblen's study is wholly a work of history and theory. His attribution of the functions of 'conspicuous consumption' and the 'pecuniary canons of taste' is based upon no empirical content. This, together with the eccentricities of his academic career, referred to by C. Wright Mills (1957: ix–x) in his 'Preface' to the Third Impression of the book, diminished the impact of Veblen's arguments.

2 Despite their differences, mass society theory the Frankfurt School, presented contemporary, everyday life as subject to an increasing regime of standardization, regimentation and manipulation. These motifs are also evident in Ritzer's (1992, 2004a) thesis of McDonaldization and the globalization of nothing.

REFERENCES

Adorno, T. (1992) *The Culture Industry* (ed. J. Bernstein). London: Routledge.

Adorno, T. (1998) *Critical Models.* New York: Columbia University Press.

Adorno, T. and Horkheimer, M. (1944) *Dialectic of Enlightenment.* London: Verso.

Ang, I. (1985) *Watching Dallas.* London: Methuen.

Ang, I. (1996) *Living Room Wars.* London: Routledge.

Aronowitz, S. and Cutler, J. (ed.) (1998) *Post-Work.* New York: Routledge.

Aronowitz, S. and Di Fazio (1994) *The Jobless Future.* Minneapolis, MN: University of Minnesota Press.

Aitchison, C., MacLeod, N. and Shaw, S. (2000) *Leisure and Tourism Landscapes.* London: Routledge.

Bell, D. (1973) *The Coming of Post-Industrial Society.* Harmondsworth: Penguin.

Bennett, T. et al. (1999) *Accounting for Tastes.* Cambridge: Cambridge University Press.

Booth, C. (1902–3) *Life and Labour of the London Poor.* London: Macmillan.

Calder, A. and Sheridan, D. (eds) (1985) *Speak For Yourself: Mass-Observation Anthology 1937–49.* Oxford: Oxford University Press.

Cheek, N. and Burch, W. (1976) *The Social Organization of Leisure in Human Society.* New York: Harper and Row.

Clarke, J. and Critcher, C. (1985) *The Devil Makes Work.* London: Macmillan.

Cohen, E. (1988) 'Traditions in the qualitative sociology of tourism', *Annals of Tourism Research,* 15: 29–46.

Cohen, E. (1995) 'Contemporary tourism – trends and challenges', in R. Butler and D. Pearce (eds), *Changes in Tourism.* London: Routledge.

CCCS (Centre for Contemporary Cultural Studies) (1982) *The Empire Strikes Back.* London: Hutchinson.

Crang, M. (1999) 'Knowing tourism and practices of vision', in D. Crouch (ed.), *Leisure/Tourism Geographies.* London: Routledge. pp. 238–56.

Cross, G. (1993) *Time and Money.* London: Routledge.

Deem, R. (1986) *All Work and No Play.* Milton Keynes: Open University Press.

Desmond, J. (1999) *Staging Tourism.* Chicago: University of Chicago Press.

Di Fazio, W. (1985) *Longshoremen.* South Hadley: Bergin and Garvey.

Dumazedier, J. (1967) *Towards a Society of Leisure.* London: Collier–Macmillan.

Dumazedier, J. (1974) *The Sociology of Leisure.* Amsterdam: Elsevier.

Durkheim, E. (1933[1902]) *The Division of Labor.* New York: The Free Press.

Edensor, T. (1998) *Tourists at the Taj.* London: Routledge.

Ewen, S. (1976) *The Captains of Consciousness.* New York: McGraw Hill.

Featherstone, M. (1991) *Consumer Culture and Postmodernism.* London: Sage.

Franklin, A. (2003) *Tourism.* London: Sage.

Fullagar, S. (2002) 'Narratives of travel', *Leisure Studies,* 21 (1): 57–74.

Friedmann, G. (1961) *The Anatomy of Work.* London: Heinemann.

Green, E., Hebron, S. and Woodward, D. (1990) *Women's Leisure, What Leisure?* London: Macmillan.

Gershuny, J. (1978) *After Industrial Society?* London: Macmillan.

Gershuny, J. (2000) *Changing Times.* Oxford: Oxford University Press.

Gorz, A. (1982) *Farewell to the Working Class.* London: Pluto.

Gorz, A. (1983) *Paths to Paradise.* London: Pluto.

Gottdiener, M. (1997) *The Theming of America.* Boulder, CO: Westview Press.

Gottdiener, M. (ed.) (2000) *New Forms of Consumption.* Lanham, MD: Rowman and Littlefield.

Grossberg, L. (1997) *Bringing It All Back Home.* Durham, NC: Duke University Press.

Hall, S. (1970) 'Leisure, entertainment and mass communication', *Society and Leisure,* 2: 28–47.

Hall, S. and Jefferson, T. (eds) (1975) *Resistance Through Rituals.* London: Hutchinson.

Hall, S. et al. (1978) *Policing the Crisis.* London: Macmillan.

Hall, S. et al. (1980) *Culture, Media, Language.* London: Hutchinson.

Harvey, D. (1989) *The Condition of Postmodernity.* Oxford: Blackwell.

Henderson, K., Bialcheski, D., Shaw, S. and Freysinger, V. (1989) *A Leisure of One's Own.* State College, PA: Venture Press.

Henderson, K., Bialcheski, D., Shaw, S. and Freysinger, V. (1996) *Both Gains and Gaps.* State College, PA: Venture Press.

Hochschild, A. (1997) *The Time Bind.* New York: Metropolitan Press.

Huizinga, J. (1947) *Homo Ludens.* London: Routledge and Kegan Paul.

Hunnicutt, B. (1988) *Work Without End.* Philadelphia, PA: Temple University Press.

Kammen, M. (1999) *American Culture, American Tastes.* New York: Basic Books.

Kerr, C. et al. (1973) *Industrialism and Industrial Man.* Harmondsworth: Penguin.

Klein, N. (2001) *No Logo.* London: Flamingo.

Krippendorf, J. (1984) *The Holidaymakers.* London: Heinemann.

Lencek, L. and Bosker, G. (1999) *The Beach.* London: Pimlico.

Linder, S. (1970) *The Harried Leisure Class.* New York: W.W. Norton.

Lynd, R. and Lynd, H. (1937) *Middletown in Transition.* New York: Harcourt Brace.

MacCannell, D. (1976) *The Tourist.* New York: Schocken Books.

MacDonald, S. (1997) 'A people's story: heritage, identity and authenticity', in C. Rojek and J. Urry (eds), *Touring Cultures.* London: Routledge. pp. 155–75.

Marcuse, H. (1964) *One Dimensional Man.* London: Abacus.

Mills, C.W. (1957) 'Introduction', in T. Veblen (ed.), *The Theory of the Leisure Class*. London: Allen & Unwin.

Mumford, L. (1967) *The Myth of the Machine*. London: Secker and Warburg.

Mumford, L. (1970) *The Pentagon of Power*. New York: Harcourt Brace Jovanovich.

O'Reilly, K. (2000) *The British on the Costa Del Sol*. London: Routledge.

Packard, V. (1957) *The Hidden Persuaders*. Harmondsworth: Penguin.

Parker, S. (1971) *The Future of Work and Leisure*. London: MacGibbon and Kee.

Parker, S. (1981) 'Choice, flexibility, spontaneity and self-determination', *Social Forces*, 60 (2): 323–31.

Pieper, J. (1952) *Leisure: The Basis of Culture*. New York: Pantheon.

Putnam, D. (2000) *Bowling Alone*. New York: Touchstone.

Riesman, D. (1950) *The Lonely Crowd*. New York: Basic Books.

Ritzer, G. (1992) *The McDonaldization of Society*. Thousand Oaks, CA: Pine Forge Press.

Ritzer, G. (1995) *Expressing America*. Thousand Oaks, CA: Pine Forge Press.

Ritzer, G. (2004a) *The Globalization of Nothing*. Thousand Oaks, CA: Pine Forge Press.

Ritzer, G. (2004b) *Enchanting the Disenchanted World*. Thousand Oaks, CA: Pine Forge Press.

Robinson, J. and Godbey, G. (1999) *Time For Life*. University Park, PA: Penn State Press.

Rowntree, J. (1865) *Pauperism in England and Wales*. London: Macmillan.

Rowntree, S. (1901) *Poverty, a Study of Town Life*. Bristol: Policy Press (centennial edition, 2001).

Schor, J. (1991) *The Over-Worked American*. New York: Basic Books.

Smart, B. (2003) *Economy, Culture and Society*. Milton Keynes: Open University Press.

Smelser, N. (ed.) (1988) *Handbook of Sociology*. Newbury Park, CA: Sage.

Touraine, A. (1971) *The Post-Industrial Society*. New York: Random House.

Veblen, T. (1899) *The Theory of the Leisure Class*. London: Allen and Unwin.

Urry, J. (1990) *The Tourist Gaze*. London: Sage.

Urry, J. (1999) *Sociology Beyond Society*. London: Routledge.

Wilensky, H. (1960) 'Work, careers and social integration', *International Social Science Journal*, 4: 543–60.

18

The Sociology of the Environment and Nature

STEVEN YEARLEY

SOCIOLOGY'S AMBIVALENCE ABOUT NATURE AND THE ENVIRONMENT

In much of Europe at least, sociology was far slower than other social sciences, notably economics, anthropology, politics and geography, to interest itself in the environment and in nature. In part this tardiness was due to the reluctance of sociologists to take the environment at face value (see Newby, 1991). Sociologists had generally adopted a constructivist attitude towards the natural world and were accustomed to treating claims about the 'naturalness' of things as an ideological front. Claims about the 'natural' differences between the sexes or between races had been rejected by the majority of sociologists; more interest was shown in the business of 'deconstructing' these claims. A consequence of this outlook was that more or less any claims about the supposed natural underpinnings of societal arrangements were viewed with scepticism and were seen as less intellectually interesting than critiques of false naturalization. The incorporation of environmental concerns into such sociological analyses appeared to demand a suspension of this deconstructive attitude and was accordingly unattractive.

Admittedly, some sociologists were not subject to these aversions. Neo-Marxist analysts were often quite happy to interpret environmental problems as further evidence of the real, and in that sense natural, damage done by the capitalist system (Schnaiberg, 1980). The standard lists of concerns over alienation and exploitation could be extended to include the exploitation of nature. And, given the apparent reluctance of the industrialized world's working classes to object to capitalist oppression and to engage in the class politics anticipated by mainstream Marxists, the damage done to the environment seemed to offer an attractively concrete case in point for demonstrating the perils of capitalism. Marxists were joined in their ready acceptance of the reality of environmental concerns by some proponents of the more pluralistic traditions of North American sociology. Without a firm and exclusive commitment to specific foundational explanatory factors, these sociologists were more easily able to add environmental considerations to their lists of influential variables (see Buttel and Humphrey, 2002). This strategy gave rise to the so-called New Ecological Paradigm (NEP) in North American sociology which sought to include an environmental dimension in its analyses (Dunlap, 1994, 2002). As Dunlap et al. have recently argued, this called for environmental sociology to recognize its 'core as the

study of societal-environmental interactions'
(2002: 20).

Sociologists who were attracted to neither of
these approaches, neither the neo-Marxist nor
the NEP, have been faced with the challenge
of reconceptualizing sociology's approach to
environmental issues and with having at the
same time to face up to problems with sociological conceptualizations of nature (Benton,
1991). Accordingly, the strategy of this chapter
is to identify the key areas in this sociological
re-writing of environmental themes and in
sociology's approach to nature.

MODERNITY AND CULTURES OF ENVIRONMENTAL CONCERN: OR WHY DO WE CARE ABOUT NATURE AND THE ENVIRONMENT?

In an important sense, the key sociological
question about recent environmental concern
is why it has risen to prominence at all. By the
start of the twenty-first century, environmental
movements – and the movement organizations
which often guided them – had consolidated
their position in Western industrial societies. In
opinion polls, populations frequently pronounced themselves highly concerned about
environmental problems (Office for National
Statistics, 1999: 184). Environmental organizations, both 'traditional' conservation groups
and those of relatively recent descent such as
Greenpeace, had large memberships, typically
on a par with mainstream political organizations and within an order of magnitude of
the membership of trade unions. In the 1990s
the British conservation and bird-enthusiast
group the Royal Society for the Protection of
Birds passed the million-member mark, easily
three times the typical size of the Labour or
Conservative party during that decade. And in
many countries, particularly where the electoral
system facilitated the development of small
parties, Green parties were enjoying moderate
success, even forming the smaller 'half' of the
ruling partnership in Germany after the 1998
elections and again when the government was
re-elected in 2002. The Green political philosophy,

commonly referred to as ecologism, had become
the first successful, progressive mainstream
'ism' to enter politics since socialism's rise over
half a century before (for an exploration see
Dobson, 1995).

On the face of it, the explanation for this
social and political innovation appears straightforward. The increasing frequency and severity
of environmental problems, together with
enhanced expert understanding of complex
ecological topics, forced the issue to the forefront of public life and policy intervention. This
line of reasoning is fundamentally supported
by 'realist' social analysts of all colours (see
Murphy, 1995), including the advocates of the
NEP and neo-Marxists described above (for a
recent example see Dickens, 1992). Though it
appears to have much in its favour, one difficulty
it faces is that many environmental issues – even
if real – are plainly remote from everyday experience so that their reality is not apparent to
ordinary citizens. Certain kinds of air pollution
can be smelled and tasted, but damage to the
ozone layer (some thirty kilometres above
the earth's surface) is not apparent to anyone.
And one cannot easily claim that in those cases
where citizens lack direct experience of environmental realities they accept the testimony of
scientists about the underlying truths. In several
notable cases, such as over nuclear safety, over
the risks from mobile phones and the acceptability of genetically modified organisms (GMOs),
members of the public have shown themselves
reluctant to accept the official proclamations of
the scientific establishment.

The realists' explanatory storyline can be
strengthened somewhat by adding a complementary idea commonly known as the 'post-
materialism thesis'. Suggestions about post-
materialism are usually traced back to the
work of Maslow, a psychologist who advanced
the proposal that humans have a hierarchy of
needs (1954). On this view, it is only when
basic needs for survival are met that human
cultures can concern themselves with longer-
term material and psychological demands.
When these in turn are satisfied, people can
look to various personal development needs,
relating to psychological satisfaction and other
non-material goods. The post-materialist

hypothesis suggests that, in the second half of the twentieth century, populations in the advanced industrial countries were able to attend to less immediate needs and became receptive to messages and values concerning more intangible goods including environmental protection. In a series of empirical studies, mostly conducted using attitude surveys, researchers claim to have detected broad trends towards the espousal of post-material values and an associated rise in environmental concern in wealthier societies. Sensitized to the importance of non-material goods, populations are receptive to claims about environmental protection which chime with their post-material values (see Inglehart, 1990).

This line of reasoning can also be bolstered by considering the socio-economic roots of many environmental problems. In essence, commentators have argued that environmental problems have lately become particularly pervasive for four kinds of reason. First, with the systematic development of industrialism, human societies are able to exert an unprecedented impact on the environment. Though humans have always transformed their environments, often destructively, we are now able to exaggerate that impact. We are able to operate on an unparalleled scale, digging huger mines, fishing more exhaustively and deforesting more thoroughly than ever before. Additionally, two specific aspects of liberal capitalism also tend to promote environmental damage. The first aspect of capitalism is its commitment to growth. The greatest boast of the capitalist system is that it has generated more economic growth than any other system. Even if the free market tends to generate large disparities in wealth within societies, societies as a whole tend to become consistently wealthier in formal economic terms. Apologists for the free market accordingly argue that even the poor are better off under capitalism since, though they may never get close to the wealth of the rich, because of general growth they will tend to experience a rising trend in personal income. Competition between firms also tends to promote growth since companies that fail to grow face being driven to the wall by expanding competitors. Firms cannot content

themselves with mere success but must strive for ever-greater success. The consequence of this is that, on average, mature capitalist economies experience growth every year. Even an economy such as that of the UK which has performed rather modestly since the 1970s has averaged more than a 2 per cent annual growth rate over that period. Given compound interest, this results in the doubling of the economy with nearly every generation, entailing an ever-bigger demand for energy, agricultural products and raw materials. Growth, a seeming imperative of the capitalist system, appears to impel the system towards environmental harmfulness (see Yearley, 1992b: 144–7).

The third consideration (and the second one tied to the functioning of capitalism) relates to the operation of the pricing system. Many environmental problems can be seen as the result of people benefiting from the resources of the natural world without paying for those resources. For example, car drivers contaminate the air with the emissions from their exhaust pipes but do not have to pay for the diminution of air quality or for the consequential impacts on, for example, pedestrians who have to breathe the sullied air. Advocates of the free market argue that market systems succeed so well because the price mechanism sends signals to consumers and producers, and allows them to match their desires with the supply of goods and services. However, since so many environmental goods are left outside this system of prices – the worth of clean air, the value of landscapes and wildlife, the benefits of a dependable climate – the free market cannot but turn out to be injurious to environmental interests. Of late, economists have sought to argue that the way to remedy these problems is not to reject the wisdom of the market but to introduce reforms that assign prices to environmental goods (Pearce et al., 1989). People happily pay for 'pure' bottled waters, so there is evidently an economic value in clean water supplies. However, it is by no means clear that economic values could be attached to all aspects of the environment that people value (Jacobs, 1994). Worse still, many analysts doubt the wisdom of accepting that environmental values can all be measured in financial terms: this would appear to imply that all environmental goods have their price and that, for the right price, it would be reasonable to accept the disappearance of the blue whale or the pervasiveness of foul air in our cities. Environmental economics equates the 'correct' value of the environment with its market value, not with the ecological importance or value of a process, species or habitat (O'Neill, 1993).

Lastly, it is commonly noted that the operation of modern liberal democracies tends to lead governments to adopt relatively short-term policy strategies. With elections every four or five years, governments are encouraged to favour policies that will result in popularity before the date of the next election; they have little incentive to focus on issues that will pay dividends only in subsequent decades. There has therefore been a systematic temptation to favour the short term over the long, to prize house- and road-building over habitat protection and to privilege the use of natural resources to create jobs and material wealth.

It is important, however, to acknowledge one weakness in the line of reasoning outlined in the foregoing paragraphs. It is notable that the majority of the emphasis in the social scientific and economic study of environmental problems has been placed on the production side. It is somehow palpable that environmental despoliation can occur in the course of production, whether from mining and other extractive industries, from the use of solvents in industrial processes or from the energy consumed during manufacture. However production makes no sense without consumption, and interesting arguments have arisen of late among cultural analysts of consumption (Shove and Warde, 2002). To some extent these ideas revolve around a reasonably straightforward investigation of consumption patterns. The point is that environmental and allied concerns can spread back from the consumer to the producer so that, for example, consumer resistance to genetically modified foodstuffs in the late 1990s in Europe and parts of East Asia had a big impact both on farmers' planting decisions – even in the United States, where farmers had to make guesses about the future preferences of European customers for their

exports – and ultimately on the fortunes of GM-seed-producing companies. In this sense, Marxist-style arguments about the treadmill of production need to be complemented by analyses of straightforward consumer pressure. Consumption itself may be susceptible to the logic of ecological reform (see Spaargaren, 1997: 161–201): consumer pressure or concerted lobbying about the containers in which, say, hamburgers are served can lead companies to use less harmful or more readily recyclable materials and so on.

But there is a rather more subtle point, namely that in high-modern cultures consumption appears to have moved even further from simple provisioning (providing the necessities of life) to an apparently autonomous activity in its own right. Going shopping is perhaps the leading leisure activity in Britain, Japan and many parts of North America. Consumers seem to favour confirming (perhaps even 'constructing') their individuality through their purchasing decisions and accordingly the market for 'designer' goods and for apparel bearing the maker's label has swollen dramatically. Ecological concerns have not meshed easily with this process to date since environmentalists' favourite arguments about sufficiency appear to miss the mark altogether. Admittedly, certain brands (most famously perhaps the Body Shop) have sought to build their appeal around their environmentally benign corporate philosophy. But in most cases the connection (if there is any at all) has tended to be a negative one; brands represent values at odds with conservationist philosophies. Brands that have built an image around a value (such as excelling at competitive sports) more or less irrelevant to environmental performance or to observance of human rights among developing-country workers have been targeted for protests on account of their environmental or employment standards. Even where these protests have been effective, they have not got at the heart of what brands and shopping are about but have been largely tangential since they fail to recognize the contemporary social functions of consumption. The shopping experience (Falk and Campbell, 1997), precisely because it is no longer about getting the most goods for the least money, is not readily susceptible to the imposition of direct environmental performance standards.

In these ways, environmental harms appear to be the more-or-less automatic consequence of modern industrial, consumerist, liberal capitalism. The realist view (shared by neo-Marxists and adherents of the NEP) is that environmentalism is the counter-reaction. This reaction is most pronounced where socio-economic circumstances have promoted post-material values.

ENVIRONMENTALISM AND THE SPECIFICITIES OF LATE-MODERN CULTURE

In recent years, other analysts have taken a rather more sceptical view of the post-materialist interpretation of the rise of environmentalism and environmental movements. The idea that the key thing about contemporary environmentalism is the presence of novel values has met with suspicion. In part, this suspicion is generic, directed at any sociological explanations that depend on the autonomous power of values (see Barnes, 1995: 233–34). Critics note that while people may espouse values in attitude surveys, they do not necessarily live according to the precepts which might be thought to derive from those values. In any event, values are typically insufficiently precise to shape how people will act in specific practical situations. These critical points have left space for other sociologists to advance alternative interpretations of the specifics of contemporary environmentalism.

Among the more concrete of these has been the argument made by Berger (1986) that susceptibility to claims about the need for environmental protection is most pronounced in a subset of the middle classes. Berger develops the well-known argument about the rise of a new middle class, which he calls the knowledge class. This class fraction differs from the 'old' middle class in that the raison d'être of characteristic occupations is not to serve the interests of business and capital (as accountants and surveyors typically do) but to use specialist

skills to address the problems created by contemporary social life. Characteristic knowledge class jobs include social work and counselling. This class fraction accordingly has two key interests: an interest in the legitimacy of intervention and regulation and an interest in securing respect for status based on qualification rather than on straightforward commercial competitive success. Berger argues that members of the knowledge class are therefore likely to be predisposed towards such causes as environmental intervention, both because the cause demands regulatory intervention and because the 'reality' of the problem is attested to by scientifically and technically credentialled spokespersons.

This is not to suggest that all environmentalists are members of the knowledge class or that all those who work in knowledge class occupations support environmentalism. Other people may have an interest in the identification and resolution of environmental problems, including people from commercial middle class or from working class backgrounds who happen to develop an interest in, say, bird-life or whose lives expose them or their families to rankly polluting industry. Equally, there are other causes to which members of the knowledge class may be attracted. Problems of human rights, of the plight of refugees, of the exploitation of animals or over the compassionate treatment of farm livestock, along with several others, fit the profile for appealing to the knowledge class. Members of the class have, one might say, an elective affinity with these causes. But to account for the relative success of these competing causes one needs to turn to a different set of factors, factors concerned with the 'marketing' of the different causes.

Accordingly, the explanation offered by Berger is often accompanied by ideas about competition between organizations or individuals that make claims about problems in need of solution (Yearley, 1992a: 47–76). In the context of the environmental movement, these are commonly 'movement organizations' such as Friends of the Earth or the World Wide Fund for Nature (WWF). To some extent these environmental groups are in competition with each other, for members, sponsors and publicity. But they are also part of a bigger competition to have their problem-claims recognized in the media, by officials and by politicians. They need endangered animals and threatened environments to be recognized as social problems ranking alongside or above 'rival' causes such as social discrimination and the plight of homeless young people.

At this point, this interpretation seems to come close to the realist outlook for, if there is really nothing to justify the environmentalists' alarm calls, the success of claims-making organizations is hard to understand. However, repeated case study analyses have indicated that in many cases the actual extent of the problem is hard to gauge. For example, the issue may be very remote, as with the ozone layer, it may be inevitably conjectural, as with the consequences of climate change, or it may be a matter of probabilities, as with the potential hazard from nuclear waste repositories. The compellingness of environmentalists' problem-claims thus appears only partially related to direct evidence about the severity of an issue, and to be significantly related to the groups' success in 'marketing' the problem-claim (see Hannigan, 1995: 38–57; Yearley, 1992a: 74–6). Thus, while it is hard to imagine how environmental organizations could make problem-claims in the absence of any environmental threats at all, their ability to make persuasive claims does not appear to be at all closely tied to the demonstrable nature of particular problems. The character of environmentalism is accordingly shaped in an iterative fashion between the claims-making strategies of campaign organizations and the sensibilities of the receptive audience. To put this another way, environmentalism is socially constructed through this process of iteration.

In the past decade an alternative interpretation has been put forward and has won wide support. On this view, what we have come to recognize as 'ecological concerns' are only concerns about the natural world in a limited sense; they are as much concerns about people's behaviour as about the natural environment. To explain why, we need to place contemporary environmental concerns in a broad historical context. Early modern societies, before the industrial revolution, were characterized by many worries about the external environment. Harvests and food supply depended critically on climate conditions, societies experienced periodic problems of shortages with natural resources, and communications could be completely disrupted by adverse weather. During the nineteenth and early twentieth centuries the common experience was that the external environment was coming more and more under human control. Weather forecasting and climatological understanding improved; enhanced farming techniques seemed to free societies more and more from abject dependence on nature. And even if the degree of control over the environment was still highly limited, there was at least optimism that the control would progressively increase. The present was reasonably bright and the future brighter still.

The key recent development has been the reversal of this optimism. Critically, this reversal has happened not so much because the environment has not submitted to further controls, but because the controls themselves have caused new and unexpected harms. Control over food production seemed to be offered by industrial agrochemicals but these turned out to be potentially harmful to consumers and to the wildlife we had come to value. Mass generation of energy freed us from a kind of dependency on the climate by allowing buildings to be warmed or cooled as much as wished, but the nuclear power which offered to give us bountiful energy turned out to have hazards of its own. Accordingly, the central claim here is that modern environmental concern is not so much a concern about the external environment but anxiety about a humanized nature; as Beck slightly gnomically puts it, 'the ecological movement is not an environmental movement but a social, inward movement which utilizes "nature" as a parameter for certain questions' (Beck, 1995: 55). Societies are freed from dependence on the vagaries of the weather but are now dependent for their security on the good behaviour of the operators of nuclear power stations. The new GM food production techniques currently on offer boast of a future free from anxieties about food scarcity, but leave us dependent for our food safety and environmental well-being on the adequacy of the regulatory system and the scientific testing of GMOs. Where we feared nature, we now worry about the dependability of organizations and regulatory systems.

On this view, therefore, modern environmental concern is an anxiety about the environment only in a special and rather confined sense. More important, this kind of anxiety is not limited to topics commonly thought of as environmental. For example, a parallel story can be told about medical control over nature. Early modern worries about external sources of disease were partly displaced by optimism about new drugs and treatments, before it turned out that modern medical and animal-management practices using rather indiscriminate dosages of antibiotics were leading to 'super-bugs' and treatment-resistant illnesses. Most recently, there has been widespread concern about possible military uses of smallpox. This disease was all but eradicated worldwide, and held only in research facilities in the two leading Cold War powers. In a smallpox-free world vaccination programmes had largely been suspended. Worry about an external threat from a marauding disease is now replaced by concerns about the integrity and dependability of the scientists and technical officials guarding the virus samples. We realize we have delegated control over much of the environment to a few agencies and people; environmental concern is a concern that these agencies may be no safer than 'wild nature' previously was. In extreme cases – as with terrorist access to biological weapons, possibly based on smallpox – harms may be imposed deliberately not adventitiously. On this view, contemporary (late-modern) societies are characterized by continuing concerns over potential self-imposed risks: they are 'risk societies'. Environmentalism is simply one symptom of late-modern risk anxiety (see Giddens, 1994: 202–12).

KNOWING NATURE

Though, as Berger and Beck acknowledge, environmental anxieties are similar to many other current social concerns in terms of the character of the attentive audience and of the kinds of arguments mobilized in public debate, environmental problems tend to be distinctive in one particular dimension. Environmental problems are problems in the natural world and are therefore frequently understood, expressed and debated in scientific terms. The threat of climate change, for example, only makes sense within the context of scientific understandings of atmospheric chemistry, solar radiation and meteorological patterns. Common-sense and everyday experience are not good guides to whether climate change is occurring. In particular, they are not good guides to whether climate change is occurring because of releases of additional greenhouse gases or for some other reason, nor to what the implications of climate change may be a decade or more from now. The politics and culture of environmentalism accordingly have a closer relationship with scientific expertise than most other areas of public life (Yearley, 1992c).

On the face of it, one might suppose that this scientific component of environmental knowledge would tend to assist those making claims about environmental problems since they would have scientific 'facts' on their side. One might also expect that the prevalence of scientific considerations would promote agreement since the scientific results would usher people on opposing sides of any dispute into accord. One can point to instances where the central role of scientific knowledge has had something like these favourable consequences. Thus, without simplifying dramatically, one can argue that members of the university-based scientific community worked out that there was a hypothetical pollution risk from substances (most notoriously CFCs) that might degrade the ozone layer (see Benedick, 1991). The suspected ozone depletion was then detected by scientific equipment deployed in the upper reaches of the atmosphere and, subsequently, government officials organized teams of scientific advisers to work out strategies for agreed international reductions in ozone-depleting substances.

However, the relationship between science and environmental protection has not always been this straightforward (and indeed was not that straightforward in this case either, see Yearley, 1996: 110–15). On the contrary, environmentalists have commonly seen demands for scientific 'proof' used to delay or avoid action on ecological problems. For example, up to the 1990s, environmental organizations and many scientists repeatedly expressed concerns about acidic emissions from power stations, factories and vehicles. They proposed that these gas emissions were responsible for the increasingly acid character of rainwater which appeared to be falling in neighbouring regions, a few hundred kilometres away. This 'acid rain' was said to be causing trees to die in large numbers and to be harming wildlife by making rivers and lakes too acidic. By and large, the attitude of the authorities was to accept that this story was possibly true. But they demanded more scientific evidence before they would take any action to curb acid emissions since it would – they said – be irresponsible to impose costs on the power industry and on consumers without being sure that such action would have demonstrable environmental benefits. Much more recently a similar pattern of argument has surrounded debates over the environmental safety of genetically modified organisms (GMOs), particularly foodcrops genetically engineered for resistance to weedkillers or to exhibit resistance to certain insect pests. In the past, farmers have not needed special environmental authorization to plant new varieties of foodcrops; environmentalists argue that GM crops are different and need to be thoroughly checked for adverse consequences before they can be planted. The authorities argue that tests to date have shown the crops to be harmless and that there should be no further restriction unless undesirable side effects become manifest. In both these cases, the experience of environmental campaigners has been that demands for scientific proof have tended to be used to defend the status quo. Thus, far from the centrality of science ensuring that agreement is reached, science's role can sometimes appear to be that of protecting the existing state of affairs from environmental reform.

In other ways too scientific reasoning may be used to thwart environmentalists' objectives.

During the Reagan years (most of the 1980s) in the USA, industrialists challenged a series of environmental standards and regulations which had been introduced by the Environmental Protection Agency (EPA). They sought judicial review of the EPA's regulations, arguing before the courts that their industries had been unfairly treated. Using rather idealized notions of standards of scientific proof, industry representatives argued, often successfully, that the EPA's rulings had not been based on the most rigorous science (Jasanoff, 1990: 180–207; see also Yearley, 1997). The weakening of environmental regulations which Reagan and his political allies sought was achieved as much through these indirect means as by explicit changes to the EPA and to environmental legislation.

One further dimension in which the practical weakness of science has been manifest can be demonstrated through the case of climate change. Climate change resulting from the enhanced greenhouse effect is thought by very many to be among the most severe international environmental problems. It could result in dramatic alterations in the climate with more intense storms and flooding, in rises in sea-level as the seas expand and as ice melts into the oceans, and in threats to wildlife as habitats are transformed by changing weather patterns. For obvious reasons, much of the running on the diagnosis of this problem and on forecasting its implications has been made by scientific bodies. But even in this urgent and dramatic case, the involvement of scientists has not guaranteed agreement. For one thing, the necessary predictions are technically very difficult. Ordinary weather forecasting runs up against limitations after approximately two weeks; it is accordingly difficult to have great confidence in climate predictions which are made decades into the future. Worse still, these predictions necessarily depend on making assumptions about how the overall weather system will respond to warming; it may be that the relatively settled patterns of air and water flows which underlie current weather forecasts will themselves be altered by global temperature rises. These inherent difficulties with the business of climate prediction are compounded by other factors: for example, as climate models demand enormous computing power, the leading models are concentrated in the developed world. Lacking ownership of – and possibly even access to – these models, policy-makers from countries of the South may treat the models with a certain degree of suspicion (see Yearley, 1996: 102–7). Equally, the models need to be checked against data on climate conditions supplied from around the world, but it is hard to ensure that similar standards of data quality are observed everywhere. Sophisticated models may be fed dubious data. On balance, even though concerns about climate change are fundamentally based on appeals to science, that does not guarantee that policy-makers are knowledgeable or agreed about the extent of the problem.

One final issue needs to be considered in this section. It seems quite reasonable for social scientists to want to have an assessment of the seriousness of environmental problems. Evidently, there is some presumption that environmental difficulties are serious enough to merit all the regulation and social movement activity that surrounds them. And, of course, realist social scientific explanations treat the severity of ecological problems as the key component in their accounts of the rise of environmentalism as a social phenomenon. However, there are considerations of humility which should stop social scientists straying too far in this direction. The extent of many environmental problems, even the most important ones, is not easy to determine, as is evidenced by the succession of contradictory 'state of the world' assessments which have been published (see Lomborg, 2001 for a well-known example). This is both because the biggest problems, such as suspected global climate change, are exceedingly hard to prove conclusively and because the human health effects of environmental pollutants appear to be complex and multicausal. To illustrate these in turn, it is accepted by all commentators that climates are subject to unpredictable variations. Accordingly, there will for many years be reasons to suppose that any apparent climate change is down to natural variations rather than to humanly induced climate shifts. If policy actions are to be taken in a timely way, they will have to be initiated before irrefutable evidence

of alterations in the climate is available; policy-makers therefore inevitably run the risk of taking actions based on erroneous suppositions. Second, it is widely accepted that air pollution can have serious health effects. But with mobile populations, with the fact that over their working life workers are exposed to a great variety of different gases, and with changing patterns of vehicle pollution, it is hard to know in many cases exactly which air-borne chemicals are the causes of particular disorders. Environmentalists themselves, sensing the precariousness of binding themselves to the factual correctness of each and every one of their claims, have often preferred to talk about generalities rather than specifics. So complex and uncertain are these issues acknowledged to be, that attempts to give an assessment of the state of the environment have, at the start of the twenty-first century, come to be as much a right-wing as an environmentalist or left-wing preoccupation.

ASSESSING NATURE: LIMITS TO MODERNIST APPROACHES

If it is difficult to arrive at an agreed and scientifically supported 'objective' characterization of environmental issues, there is one further complication besetting the involvement of scientific forms of reasoning in making environmental decisions. Very often, choices between policy options are defended on the basis of a cost-benefit calculation. Cost-benefit analyses (CBAs) attempt to evaluate policy alternatives by systematically comparing their respective advantages and drawbacks. The assumption is that a policy (for example, the construction of a new road link or a new bridge) is to be looked on with favour if its overall benefits outweigh its costs, particularly if the balance in its favour is larger than the benefit in favour of rival schemes. CBAs have become a central component of modernist approaches to environmental policy-making since they provide a way of comparing alternative policies and since they appear to offer an objective way of aggregating the benefit that people will derive. A new by-pass road will, for example, provide benefits to many travellers and businesses but will increase the nuisance to people and wildlife living along the proposed route; it may also harm some small businesses that are by-passed. A CBA should allow this balance to be assessed systematically.

However, CBA-like activities have come under criticism on numerous occasions, from affected parties and from the environmental lobby. There have been two principal forms of objection. First, it may not be possible to assess the costs and benefits in an agreed way. When officials none the less proceed on the basis of CBAs, the procedure itself and the people who carry it out may come to be viewed as illegitimate. CBAs depend on the same assumptions about the objective nature of technical assessments as were reviewed in the last section above. Projections about the number of road users on a new by-pass, for example, are inevitably conjectural so that the benefits and costs cannot be weighed with confidence. Worse still, there have often been good grounds for public scepticism about the confidence they can place in the technical analysts called in to carry out CBAs. Experts may not have sufficiently detailed local knowledge or they may apply general principles in ways that do not work out in practice. In the extreme case, CBA technicians may favour the interests of the developer over local objectors and let that interest guide their interpretations; for example, the 'costs' of diffuse environmental harms may appear slight when measured against tangible increases in road traffic capacity or shorter projected journey times.

But if the technical difficulties were not daunting enough, the whole utilitarian background to CBAs can itself come under critical scrutiny. CBAs 'work' because they offer to balance advantages against detriments so as to produce a calculation of net societal benefit. But this calculus itself may not be met with acceptance. The basis for the calculation may be rejected because people may not agree about what the relevant social unit of assessment is. Installing a park-and-ride scheme for visitors to a tourist city may bring pollution-reduction benefits to the city centre, but it may only exacerbate pollution problems around the out-of-town parking areas. Constructing a dam may yield advantages (including environmental benefits) for areas that receive the hydroelectric power but produce intense problems for people whose homes or farmlands are flooded behind the dam. In such cases, the outcome of the CBA depends critically on how the boundaries around the exercise are drawn. CBAs thus depend on essentially political decisions about the extent of the community whose interests are to be added up. CBAs commonly take political units for granted thus legitimizing the imposition of environmental harms on minority communities for the sake of the greater good of all. In the United States, where waste sites and polluting industry have recurrently been concentrated in ethnic minority areas, minority rights groups have rejected the idea that, for example, Native Americans' areas can 'rationally' be polluted for the sake of the good of the overall US economy. Supposedly 'technical' forms of assessment such as CBAs have accordingly been opposed by many campaigns, campaigns that have called instead for 'environmental justice' (for an overview see Ringquist, 2000).

On top of this, campaigners have opposed CBAs because of the underlying assumption that all benefits and harms can be weighed on a single scale. They argue that some things may simply not be tradable for others: no amount of reduction in commuting times for example would be 'worth' the equivalent of the elimination of rare bird nesting sites (O'Neill, 1993). Proponents of CBAs argue that their techniques simply systematize the way we naturally think about comparing alternatives. But opponents claim that CBAs impose an alien decision-making strategy; such techniques, it is argued, are attempts to 'colonize the mind' (see Mulkay et al., 1987).

Very similar issues arise in relation to the way that policy analysts talk about risks. As mentioned above, Beck and other sociologists have attempted to characterize contemporary industrial societies as preoccupied with risks. But a more 'modernistic' conception of risk has proved attractive to many policy-making agencies which have used risk calculations as a way of rationalizing approaches to environmental dangers. As an example, environmental campaigners have long protested about the likely hazards of nuclear power. The nuclear industry has preferred to frame the issue in terms of risks. Industry spokespersons point out that many activities entail risks – driving a car, working in a coal mine, living in an earthquake zone as in San Francisco, or using a mobile phone. They claim that the risks of nuclear power need to be set alongside those attaching to other (widely accepted though still risky) social activities. Adherents of this line of reasoning typically suggest that a risk should be understood as the chance of the event happening multiplied by the impact of the event; on such a basis, nuclear power can look rather less risky than many accepted activities, including popular but dangerous sports. Official agencies in many Northern countries are inclined to tackle the majority of environmental problems, from nuclear safety, through 'mad cow disease' to policy towards GMOs, on the basis of the language of calculated risks.

However, using numerous case studies, sociologists have again pointed out limitations to this point of view. For one thing, generalized calculations of risk do not necessarily correspond well to specific cases. Airlines are obliged to work out how quickly aircraft can be evacuated, but empirical tests of evacuation procedures inevitably have to make assumptions about the time of day and weather conditions during evacuation and about how many children, pregnant women or people with disabilities are in an 'average' passenger cohort. The risks for passengers on any particular flight are thus imprecisely related to the standard figures. Moreover, many topics of environmental concern translate imperfectly into the standard calculus of risk. In the case of 'mad cow disease', it is thought that the incubation time of the disorder may run into decades. Accordingly, the risk to which populations may be exposed is as yet fundamentally unclear. The calculative language of risk cannot plausibly be applied if the probability of the problem is not known with much accuracy. Similarly, the likelihood of a nuclear reactor going wrong in the coming years cannot be calculated even on the basis of past experience since the reactors themselves are ageing and, in many cases, they are being managed in unprecedentedly cash-strapped times. Though

we may live in risk societies, officially sanctioned techniques for calculating and distributing risks have time and again run into profound problems of legitimacy. Officials' preference for technocratic analyses of risk has not won people over to the view that policy towards major environmental problems can best be worked out by trading risks against benefits to arrive at a socially optimal outcome (Wynne, 1996).

ENVIRONMENTALISM AND THE SOCIOLOGY OF THE FUTURE

Though seeming to start out as an application of well-tried sociological approaches (the sociological study of particular environmental problems and of popular and often successful pressure groups), environmental sociology has offered to become much more. Several authors have interpreted environmentalism itself as a social construction, while others have used anxieties over environmental risks to re-characterize the central preoccupations of contemporary Western societies. Writers in the latter tradition have proposed that environmental concerns are just one element in a denser fabric of anxieties and concerns over the growing 'humanization of nature', thus tying environmental sociology into an understanding of a culture of pessimism in late modernity.

The sociological study of environmental topics has also helped to open up the topics of the source of value and the nature of rational choice in contemporary culture. Alongside persistent public unease over judgements about the value of life (as revealed, for example, in disputes over human cloning and over the right way to allocate scarce health care resources), it is contemporary disputes over the applicability of economic models and CBAs to environmental 'goods' that have formed the major challenges to the hegemony of market-led and utilitarian approaches to public policy. In particular, the unwillingness of publics to accept official assessments and allocations of risk – together with the growing popularity of environmental justice campaigns – has resulted in repeated, successful challenges to mainstream risk assessments. As yet, it is unclear how (or if) this void can be filled; to date the official preference has been to try to make the assessments more scientific or more accurate, thus failing completely to address issues at the heart of much of the discontent (Jasanoff, 1990: 232–50).

Finally, environmental sociologists have stopped worrying so much about the debate over the 'reality' of environmental problems. Realists and constructivists can readily agree about the intractability of risk evaluations; they can both see that climate change models are inevitably imprecise. And they can both acknowledge that the key issues in the public politics of risk assessments are not usually narrow technical ones over whether the risk calculations are 'correct' or not. Instead, environmental sociologists find that their studies lead them to investigate pivotal issues in the way that contemporary cultural institutions try to fit modernist conceptual tools to the evaluation of culture and nature. In this sense the sociology of the environment is part of the enterprise of seeing beyond present practices and techniques to the sociology of the future.

NOTE

My thanks to Colin Campbell, Claire Haggett, Tee Rogers-Hayden and the editors who kindly commented on earlier drafts of this paper.

REFERENCES

Barnes, Barry (1995) *The Elements of Social Theory*. London: UCL Press.

Beck, Ulrich (1995) *Ecological Politics in an Age of Risk*. Cambridge: Polity Press.

Benedick, Richard E. (1991) *Ozone Diplomacy: New Directions in Safeguarding the Planet*. London: Harvard University Press.

Benton, Ted (1991) 'Biology and social science: why the return of the repressed should be given a (cautious) welcome', *Sociology*, 25 (1): 1–29.

Berger, Peter L. (1986) *The Capitalist Revolution: Fifty Propositions About Prosperity, Equality and Liberty*. New York: Basic Books.

Buttel, Frederick H. and Humphrey, Craig R. (2002) 'Sociological theory and the natural environment', in Riley E. Dunlap and William Michelson (eds), *Handbook of Environmental Sociology*. Westport, CT: Greenwood. pp. 33–69.

Dickens, Peter (1992) *Society and Nature: Towards a Green Social Theory*. Hemel Hempstead: Harvester Wheatsheaf.

Dobson, Andrew (1995) *Green Political Thought*, 2nd edn. London: Routledge.

Dunlap, Riley E. (1994) 'Struggling with human exemptionalism: the rise, decline and revitalization of environmental sociology', *American Sociologist*, 25: 5–30.

Dunlap, Riley E. (2002) 'Paradigms, theories and environmental sociology', in Riley E. Dunlap, Frederick H. Buttel, Peter Dickens and August Gijswijt (eds), *Sociological Theory and the Environment: Classical Foundations, Contemporary Insights*. Lanham, MD: Rowman and Littlefield. pp. 329–50.

Dunlap, Riley E., Michelson, William and Stalker, Glenn (2002) 'Environmental sociology: an introduction', in Riley E. Dunlap and William Michelson (eds), *Handbook of Environmental Sociology*. Westport, CT: Greenwood. pp. 1–32.

Falk, Pasi and Campbell, Colin B. (eds) (1997) *The Shopping Experience*. London: Sage.

Giddens, Anthony (1994) *Beyond Left and Right: The Future of Radical Politics*. Cambridge: Polity Press.

Hannigan, John (1995) *Environmental Sociology: A Social Constructionist Perspective*. London: Routledge.

Inglehart, Ronald (1990) *Culture Shift in Advanced Industrial Society*. Princeton, NJ: Princeton University Press.

Jacobs, Michael (1994) 'The limits to neoclassicism: towards an institutional environmental economics', in Michael Redclift and Ted Benton (eds), *Social Theory and the Global Environment*. London: Routledge. pp. 67–91.

Jasanoff, Sheila (1990) *The Fifth Branch: Science Advisers as Policymakers*. London: Harvard University Press.

Lomborg, Bjørn (2001) *The Skeptical Environmentalist: Measuring the Real State of the World*. Cambridge: Cambridge University Press.

Maslow, Abraham H. (1954) *Motivation and Personality*. New York: Harper and Row.

Mulkay, Michael, Pinch, Trevor and Ashmore, Malcolm (1987) 'Colonizing the mind: dilemmas in the application of social science', *Social Studies of Science*, 17 (2): 231–56.

Murphy, Raymond (1995) 'Sociology as if nature did not matter: an ecological critique', *British Journal of Sociology*, 46 (4): 688–707.

Newby, Howard (1991) 'One world, two cultures: sociology and the environment', *Network* (*Bulletin of the British Sociological Association*), 50: 1–8.

Office for National Statistics (UK) (1999) *Social Trends 29*. London: The Stationery Office.

O'Neill, John (1993) *Ecology, Policy and Politics: Human Well-Being and the Natural World*. London: Routledge.

Pearce, David W., Markandya, Anil and Barbier, Edward B. (1989) *Blueprint for a Green Economy*. London: Earthscan.

Ringquist, Evan J. (2000) 'Environmental justice: normative concerns and empirical evidence', in Norman J. Vig and Michael E. Kraft (eds), *Environmental Policy*. Washington: CQ Press. pp. 232–56.

Schnaiberg, Allan (1980) *The Environment, from Surplus to Scarcity*. New York: Oxford University Press.

Shove, Elizabeth and Warde, Alan (2002) 'Inconspicuous consumption: the sociology of consumption, lifestyles and the environment', in Riley E. Dunlap, Frederick H. Buttel, Peter Dickens and August Gijswijt (eds), *Sociological Theory and the Environment: Classical Foundations,* *Contemporary Insights*. Lanham, MD: Rowman and Littlefield. pp. 230–51.

Spaargaren, Gert (1997) *The Ecological Modernization of Production and Consumption: Essays in Environmental Sociology*. Wageningen: Landbouw Universiteit Wageningen.

Wynne, Brian (1996) 'May the sheep safely graze? A reflexive view of the expert–lay knowledge divide', in Scott Lash et al. (eds), *Risk, Environment and Modernity: Towards a New Ecology*. London: Sage. pp. 44–83.

Yearley, Steven (1992a) *The Green Case: A Sociology of Environmental Issues, Arguments and Politics*. London: Routledge.

Yearley, Steven (1992b) 'Environmental challenges', in Stuart Hall et al. (eds), *Modernity and Its Futures*. Cambridge: Polity Press. pp. 117–67.

Yearley, Steven (1992c) 'Green ambivalence about science: legal-rational authority and the scientific legitimation of a social movement', *British Journal of Sociology*, 43 (4): 511–32.

Yearley, Steven (1996) *Sociology, Environmentalism, Globalization*. London: Sage.

Yearley, Steven (1997) 'Science and the environment', in Michael Redclift and Graham Woodgate (eds), *The International Handbook of Environmental Sociology*. Cheltenham: Edward Elgar. pp. 227–36.

19

Poverty and Life Chances: The Conceptualization and Study of the Poor

DALTON CONLEY

INTRODUCTION: POVERTY AMID PLENTY

This chapter is concerned with the theoretical conceptualization of poverty in rich, developed countries and the estimation of its effects on offspring. The difficulties of conceptualizing poverty amid plenty are perhaps best illustrated by a speech given by a member of the Forbes 400 richest Americans, Thomas Monaghan, who himself rose to great wealth from meager origins. 'To me one of the most exciting things in the world is being poor,' he began his lecture. To explain what he meant, Monaghan cited a study that concluded that a family of four could survive on $68 per year back around 1970 (which would make it $256 today). 'Now you're probably wondering how you can live on $68 a year. The first thing you do is go to the Farm Bureau and buy a hundred-pound bag of powdered milk … While you're at the Farm Bureau you buy yourself a bushel of oats or wheat or corn, and you mash that stuff up … And you grow some vegetables and you get a few vitamin pills to supplement your diet. And I think that's exciting.' He went on to talk about how cheaply he lived in a house trailer, calling it 'the

greatest living I ever did'. He concluded his speech with a rhetorical appeal: 'Oh gosh,' Monaghan said, 'I'd love to talk to all these people who say they can't get by.'[1]

We could debate the actual numbers – that is, exactly how cheaply someone could survive in the contemporary United States or a similarly developed country – and we could question the hypocrisy of a man worth hundreds of millions of dollars castigating the poor for their implied whining, but that would miss the deeper point that Monaghan raises. Namely, what does it mean to be poor in a country when starvation and death from the elements is rare? This question inevitably leads us to the debate over absolute versus relative measures of poverty. As we will see, Monaghan's reasoning is not that far afield from a long tradition of absolute poverty measurement that has based its calculations on the cost of food.

Since the end of the eighteenth century, many individuals and institutions have tried to come up with the magical perfect *absolute* measure of poverty. This led theorists to attempt to quantify the basic necessities needed to live; more to the point, they tried to define poverty in terms of food requirements. Specifically, a household fell into poverty if its income fell below the necessary level to purchase food to physically sustain itself.[2] Attempts to establish such a minimal standard started in England in 1795 when the town of Speenhamland 'instituted a relief program that made up the difference between a worker's wage and the cost of bread sufficient to feed him and his family' (Stone, 1994: 85). In 1901, Rowntree attempted to devise a specific measure in York, England when he documented an income level below which the necessities to maintain one's physical efficiency could not be afforded. His approach was institutionalized in the United Kingdom by the Beveridge Report in 1942.

The most famous American rendition of the food-based measurement of poverty status was that of Mollie Orshansky in her 1963 article 'Children of the Poor'. To estimate the poverty line, she used a strategy not unlike that implicit in Monaghan's speech. She took the US Department of Agriculture's recommendations for the minimum amount of healthy food, estimated the cost for a variety of family types (62 in all) and multiplied this figure by a factor of three.[3] Soon, this became the official poverty line of the United States. As such, it has been the definition of poverty that has most frequently served as the straw man against which researchers have suggested alternatives.

Orshansky has been assailed from all sides for the choices she made in 'drawing the line' in the United States. Early criticism revolved around her choice of three as the multiplier. Rose Friedman, for example, argued in 1965 that three was too high since the poor often spent a greater proportion of their income on food during this time period (the actual figure being closer to 60 per cent, according to Friedman). Friedman's estimation lowered the poverty threshold substantially and halved the number of individuals living in poverty at the time. However, Friedman's argument appears flawed because of its circularity: namely, the poor may have been spending more of their resources on food since they were poor. In other words, since food is the most basic necessity of all, we do not know what other necessities the poor may have been forsaking due to the fact that they

were spending over half their money to keep themselves fed (such as medical care, adequate shelter, and so on). Alternatively, Alan Haber (1966) argued that Orshansky's survey data from the 1950s overestimated the percentage of family income spent on food in the 1960s, suggesting that it had fallen to one-fourth, as illustrated by the 1960–1 Consumer Expenditure Survey. The percentage of family income spent on food has steadily dropped since this period as well. Now housing makes up a much larger proportion of household budgets.[4]

Another conservative line of argument for change is to adjust what we call total family income. Some analysts have argued that total family income is a weak measure of the consumptive power of the poor since many receive in-kind benefits such as food stamps and Medicaid that raise their standard of living but which are not counted as income. Liberals counter that if we include in-kind benefits for the poor, we should include them for everyone. Thus, private health insurance paid for by employers, subsidized student loans, per student expenditures on public education and even the home mortgage interest deduction should be figured into the distribution of resources, making it even more unequal than it is now. (But, of course, that would not affect absolute poverty measures.)

More recent criticisms have sought to change the Orshansky threshold by de-emphasizing its emphasis on food expenditures as the basis of what are considered 'necessities'. Specifically, some researchers argue that the 'market basket' of necessities has expanded since the early 1960s to include such items as indoor plumbing (which many of the rural poor did not enjoy in the 1950s) and telephones. Today is television a necessity? Working heat and air conditioning? How about a computer? With these concerns in mind, many analysts have argued that it is impossible to adjust the poverty threshold over long periods of time using the inflation rate (Consumer Price Index) but that the poverty measure must be reformulated from scratch every so often since what is a 'necessity' changes from period to period, from society to society (Hobjin, 2002).

The US poverty threshold is further criticized because it does not take into account regional variation in the cost of living.[5] Living on 8000 dollars in Mississippi is a lot different than trying to survive on that same income in New York City. Finally, there is the issue of assets and debts. Poverty is measured with respect to income alone. But income only tells part of the financial story for most American families. There is also significant variation in family wealth levels. (Family wealth – also known as assets or net worth – is calculated as total saleable assets minus outstanding debts (at the family/household level); insurance, annuities, received or anticipated social security and other non-fungible assets are not included in this measure.) This variation in net worth – over and above income levels – means that being 'poor' can be a very different economic experience for families with the same income levels. This issue is particularly salient to the study of race, poverty and life chances in America. Currently, the median African American family owns about one-eighth the net worth that the median white family does (Wolff and Leone, 2002). This difference is not explained by income or other demographic characteristics (Oliver and Shapiro, 1995). For example, among families who earned less than 15,000 dollars per year in 1994, the median net worth for white families was 10,000 dollars; the corresponding figure for African American families was zero. More than half the black population in this income bracket has no net worth or is in net debt. Meanwhile, being poor and white typically means living with a 10,000-dollar asset cushion. Income-based measures obscure this difference. There are many potential ways to integrate income and wealth into a poverty measure (such as annuitizing wealth levels and adding them to annual income). However, policy-makers stick to the traditional income-based poverty measure; given that many federal funds are allocated based on the proportion of a state's population that is poor, the Orshansky line has a political inertia that is difficult to alter. Likewise, researchers have only just begun to take into account assets in explaining the impact of poverty on life chances – largely because good measures of family

wealth have not been available until fairly recently (as of 1984).[6]

All this criticism leads to the question of whether an adequate *absolute* measure of poverty is ever possible to arrive at. If we strictly define necessities as those goods without which we cannot survive, then by definition there are no poor among the living. Recognizing this, most scholars define necessities as what is required to live *with dignity*. Of course, if what is necessary to live with dignity in a given society is socially defined, then is not every measure of poverty a relative measure? In other words, if what is a necessity is what most of us have then there will always be people who do not have those things in any market-based economy. In other words, the poor will always be with us – but to greater or lesser degrees depending on how unequally income and wealth are distributed. This is one of the ways that wealth creates poverty – by ratcheting up the social definition of necessity. Theorists who are of the view that all poverty is relational have argued for the implementation of *relative* measures of poverty, most frequently operationalized by considering anyone with less than one-half the median income to be poor (alternatively, researchers use a cut-off of 40 per cent of the median income) (Fuchs, 1967; see also Rainwater, 1974). This sort of measure has become standard in the literature on international comparisons of poverty rate, since it provides an obvious yardstick that is commensurable across nations. However, it really measures income inequality at the bottom half of the distribution.

When using a poverty line set at 40 per cent of the median income of a given country, a comparison of poverty rates among developed nations reveals that the United States is indeed a laggard with respect to the rest of the developed world. Just less than 11 per cent (10.7) of the US population enjoys incomes less than 40 per cent of the median. The next closest country is Australia, with a rate of 7 per cent, Canada at 6.6 per cent and the United Kingdom at 5.7 per cent (Smeeding et al., 2000: Table 2). (If we use the US poverty line and compare countries, we find that Australia and the United Kingdom have higher poverty rates – 17.6 and 15.7 per cent, respectively, as compared to the 13.6 per cent figure for the US in the mid-1990s; Smeeding et al., 2000: Table 1). What is striking is that all of the countries that are the worst when it comes to relative income distributions are of Anglo origin – following cultural lines rather than geographical ones.

Once we dip into the middle of the pack, we find that there is no obvious pattern to which countries outrank others with respect to their poverty rates on either absolute or relative measures. For instance, in absolute rates, what Gøsta Esping-Andersen (1990) calls corporatist welfare state regimes do worse than social-democratic (or universalist) ones. Using the US standard, France has a poverty rate of 9.9 per cent and Germany 7.3 per cent. The Scandinavian countries do better, with Sweden at 6.3 per cent, Finland 4.8 per cent and Norway at 4.3 per cent. But when we switch to the relative rates, Sweden at 4.6 per cent comes out worse than Germany (4.2) or France (3.2). It should be clear that what income is counted, what conversion rate is used (PPP or exchange rate) and a host of other issues cloud international comparisons, making finely graduated rankings almost meaningless. More important are overall patterns, such as the Anglo countries doing the worst of all.[7]

THE EXPERIENCE OF POVERTY: OUTPUT MEASURES

A newer line of argument coming out of British and Irish scholarship focuses on outputs rather than inputs. Traditional measures classify as poor those who do not have the economic ability to meet basic needs within the behavioral (that is to say, budgeting) expectations of the community. Direct measures of poverty identify individuals or families whose *actual* consumption levels do not meet such basic needs.[8] This distinction carries important implications for the way in which the poor are conceptualized and treated. In some senses, the minimum resource conception treats the poor with more respect than the minimum standard of living measure since it merely sets

a resource level that is perceived as adequate and does not make any judgments or assumptions as to how the poor will spend these resources. A standard of living measure distrusts the poor in a certain way since it implies that given a certain amount of resources, the poor may not be efficiently maximizing the acquisition of necessities in the household (*à la* Monaghan). It is also assuming a singular definition of what constitutes a decent standard of living when groups – such as the poor – may differ in what they value.

On the other hand, the minimum standard of living threshold may better measure the reality of life for the poor and is not subject to the vagaries of price and income fluctuations or differential household needs (such as the comparison between an elderly couple and a single mother with a young child illustrates).[9] Some researchers have attempted to resolve this tension between the alternative conceptions of poverty. Stephen Ringen (1988), for example, advocates the use of a combination of income thresholds and a measure of deprivation to measure poverty. The concept is appealing in that people with low incomes but who are not feeling the pinch – on account of generous in kind benefits, asset wealth, etc. – would not be counted as poor. Likewise, those who were 'misers' – that is, those who experienced deprivation despite being able to afford to satisfy their needs – would not be counted among the poor either. Only if a household met the dual criteria of low income and enforced 'lack' of socially defined necessities would Ringen consider them poor.

In this vein, many scholars have worked to develop an adequate measure of deprivation. The first step is to define a basket of necessities. For example, one study surveyed residents of Ireland to come up with a list of socially defined necessities (including, for example, a telephone, two pairs of strong shoes, a color television and a dry dwelling) (Callan et al., 1993). The poor are those who are low-income and who lack a certain number of the 20 necessities.[10] While this move towards a deprivation–income combination would seem to eliminate many of the practical problems with input-only measures of poverty, some theorists want to push further toward a universal set of 'necessities'. These would be constant over time and place and – as such – would facilitate comparisons across very diverse cultures and epochs. The challenge inherent in designing such a poverty measure is no less than defining universal 'goods'.

An early such attempt to operationalize a cross-society, comparable 'universalistic outputs' measure of poverty – moving away from material goods – was the Physical Quality of Life Index (PQLI). Using three basic indicators of the quality of life, in 1979, Morris David Morris (1979) constructed a scale for use in measuring the condition of the world's populations. The components of this scale are: infant mortality, life expectancy at age 12 months and basic literacy. Morris admits that this measure does not capture intangible goods such as freedom or justice; however, Morris suggests that these three are as close as one can arrive to a 'universal' – that is, non-ethnocentric – criterion for well-being. (Human rights, for example, can be defined very differently in one context than another; and freedom is always a matter of negotiation – between yours and mine.) Morris purports that all peoples want their children to live (that is, lower infant mortality) and that all peoples want to live long themselves (that is, life expectancy). Further, he claims, 'even if the desire for literacy *per se* is not widely shared – literacy could serve as a surrogate for (although it does not guarantee) individual capacity for effective social participation' (1979: 3). From these three indicators, he constructs a scale to measure over-time and cross-sectional differences in the quality of life of the world's people.[11] The result is a universal index that allows for comparisons across various societies, sub-populations and cohorts without running into major incomparability issues.[12] The most obvious drawback is the fact that – by definition – individuals or family units do not have a score on the PQLI, only populations do.

Nobel Prize winner Amartya Sen is among those who would go further than Morris. He shares with Morris the desire to push for a measure that is less solely reliant on the distribution of material goods, but Sen seeks to expand the relevant outcomes well beyond those of the PQLI. The leitmotif that organizes the themes of poverty and deprivation for Sen is the question of freedom – that is, freedom to reach our full potential. Deprivation, in Sen's schema, occurs when we are prevented from reaching our full human capabilities. The task at hand for Sen is to define a basket of 'human capabilities' and then investigate what forces enable or limit those (e.g. Sen, 1995, 1999, 2000). The material distribution of resources is a main – but not sole – element of the distribution of freedom to develop our human capabilities. Wealth makes us free – from, say, having to work, having to stay in one place, having to sell our dearest possessions and so on – but there are other dimensions of freedom as well. Freedom, obviously, has a political dimension. Wealth is less valuable if our voice and our actions are constrained by a totalitarian state. Freedom has basic health dimensions as well. If we do not live long, we enjoy our economic assets less. In short, you have to be alive to be free and to develop your human capabilities. You also have to be relatively absent of crippling disease.

For Sen, financial or material limitations are but one way that capabilities can be deprived. That is, market-based distribution mechanisms (economies) represent one allocation avenue among many. Poverty measures that examine only material inputs or outputs may neglect resource inequity based in the political sphere, for example, or to take another case, within the household (particularly with respect to gender inequities) (e.g. Brannen and Wilson, 1987; Glendinning and Millar, 1987; Jenkins, 1991). For instance, he claims that there has never been a massive famine in a democratically run nation, since elected regimes are responsive to the needs of their populations. Politics matters as much as economics. Or rather, they cannot really be separated from each other.

There is a tension in this discussion between wanting to develop a robust measure of poverty that accounts for all sorts of deprivation, on the one hand, and the fear of losing the analytic focus on specifically *economic* sources of deprivation, on the other. If we broaden the concept of poverty too widely, we risk making it conceptually and empirically ineffective by conflating a variety of types of deprivation, oppression and domination. For example, is it really worthwhile to talk about political detainees as part of the poverty problem? We may want to keep these forms of 'capabilities' deprivation separate. At the same time, it is not always easy to parse the analytic distinction. Sen and others have shown us how these worlds act and react on each other. This is a tension that will not be resolved here but should serve as grist for sociologists, economists and political scientists for some time to come.

THE EFFECTS OF POVERTY ON CHILDREN'S LIFE CHANCES

Ultimately, the value of a measure of resources (such as a poverty line) is how well it predicts outcomes we care about. There has been much research assessing the association between income in general – and poverty in particular – and health status, political participation, deviant behavior and so on. One area in particular that has been a fruitful focus of research is with respect to the effects of low income on the outcomes of offspring. An intergenerational lens is particularly appealing to researchers for both political and methodological reasons. Politically, children are almost universally seen as members of the 'deserving' poor in the moral discourse on poverty (and welfare). In other words, while it may be debated whether or not a poor adult has reached this social position through ascription (assignment through birth) or achievement (through their own actions), almost by definition it is the case that children who are poor find themselves in this condition through ascriptive forces beyond their control (that is, into which family they happen to be born). Thus, by focusing on the effects of economic resources on children, the current generation of researchers gets away from the rhetorical trap of 'blaming the victim' that plagued (and ultimately dampened) much research on poverty that took place during the 1960s.

Second, children offer a potential methodological solution to the problems of reverse and spurious causation. Namely, if we examine the relationship between, say, poverty and health among the elderly, we are haunted by the question of whether any observed association results from poverty causing (ill) health status; or health status impacting income; or some third factor – say cognitive ability – affecting both. Children – with no earnings of their own – would seem to offer the ideal 'subjects' for examining the effects of poverty on life outcomes since the poverty in which they may find themselves is largely not due to their own choices, abilities and so on.[13] However, while a focus on children may largely solve the reverse causation issues, by itself such a focus does not adequately address the unobserved heterogeneity issue, also known as spurious effects (more on this later).

The research tradition on poverty and child outcomes is vast and cannot be done justice in the brief space here (see, e.g., Hauser, 1994). That said, this literature is perhaps best summarized in a cumulative, life-course framework over childhood (see Bronfenbrenner, 1979). Starting with birth, much research has shown that low income and its covariates such as low maternal education and minority racial status lead to a greater risk for delivering a low birthweight baby, due to both prematurity and intrauterine growth retardation (Cramer, 1995; Gortmaker, 1979; Starfield et al., 1991; Stockwell et al., 1995). This higher incidence of low birth weight among the poor population partially, but not completely, accounts for the higher infant mortality rates among this group (Cramer, 1995; Gortmaker, 1979; Tresserras et al., 1992). If children survive the first year of life, those from lower SES families face increased risks of childhood mortality, primarily due to increased chance of accidental death (Mare, 1982; Wise et al., 1985).[14] Aside from increased mortality rates, children from poor families suffer from other developmental risks as well (Egbuonu and Starfield, 1982; Wise and Meyers, 1988). For instance, there is an inverse relationship between child blood lead levels and SES (Brody et al., 1994; Klerman and Parker, 1990; Mahaffey et al., 1982; Quah et al., 1982).

Likewise, Sanders Korenman and Jane Miller (1997) showed that poor children are more likely to exhibit low height-for-age (stunting) or low weight-for-height (wasting), two reliable indicators of nutritional status which, in turn, predict other health outcomes.[15] Others have shown an effect of poverty on children's number of bed days and school absences (McGaughey et al., 1991), on acute illnesses (Starfield, 1991) and on chronic conditions such as asthma (Ernst et al., 1995).

In addition to physical health problems, children from poor families tend to enjoy worse mental health and display more behavioral problems than their non-poor counterparts, particularly when poverty is long-term (Campbell, 1995; McLeod and Shanahan, 1993). Poverty may also affect cognitive development. For example, a number of researchers have found that income is correlated with child cognitive indicators such as the Peabody Individual Achievement Tests and the Peabody Picture Vocabulary Test (Chase-Lansdale et al., 1997; Duncan et al., 1994; Korenman et al., 1995).[16] Judith Smith and her colleagues found that between the ages of 3 and 8, relatively small increases in income can lead to substantial changes in intellectual skills. A one-unit increase in the ratio of a family's income to a family's need was associated with a 3–3.7 point increase in measures of verbal and math ability in this study (Smith et al., 1997). At young ages, children in poverty are also much more likely than children who are not in poverty to exhibit behavioral problems in the forms of aggression, tantrums, anxiety and moodiness. At older ages, after entrance into school, children in poverty begin to show further disorders in the forms of learning and attention problems and school disengagement.[17] Of course, however, these income differences were not randomly assigned.

Furthermore, much of this research has been done on US and British populations – where we have already seen relative income inequality to be at its worst in the developed world – so it is not clear whether these effects would persist in societies where income inequality is less pronounced and where more basic services – such as housing and childcare – have been decommodified. One way to ask about the impact of poverty on offspring in a cross-national perspective is to look at intergenerational earnings elasticities. In a meta-analysis Gary Solon (2002) finds that here too the United States does among the worst of all, having the lowest degree of income mobility across generations; to be fair, however, most of the data from European countries have only respondents who are young and/or use only single-year measures of income. For instance, using the German Socio-Economic Panel, Kenneth A. Couch and Thomas A. Dunn (1997) find a father–son elasticity of a multi-year income measure of only 0.11.[18] (Though, using later waves of the same dataset, Johannes Wiegand (1997) puts the German figure at 0.34.) The next lowest estimates of 0.13 come from Sweden – from Swedish income tax records (three-year averages for both fathers and sons) – and from analysis of the Finnish census data (a three-year average for the sons and two-year average for the fathers) (Solon, 2002).[19] The highest estimate of 0.57 comes from the British National Child Development Survey, where the respondents (children) were 33 years of age. (It used a single-year earnings measure for fathers and only a predicted earnings measure for the sons, based on education and social class). The data for the United States, using multiple year income measures for both fathers and sons, is upward of 0.40 (Solon, 2002). In this framework, a low father–son correlation coefficient might suggest that poverty is less damaging in that country; or it might not, since income–health gradients have been found in all countries (though flatter in nations with less income inequality).

Explanations for these various income gradients can roughly be divided into three camps. First, some researchers focus on the *material deprivations* that low SES induces, such as poor nutrition, lack of adequate medical care or unsafe environments (e.g. Callan et al., 1993; Mack and Lansley, 1985; McGregor and Borooah, 1992; Ringen, 1987, 1988). Take the case of food – the most basic necessity of all (along with water). Studies of severe famine in the Netherlands during the Second World War have found that consuming fewer than 1000 calories per day results in dramatic reductions in pregnancy weight gain and infant birth size (Lumey and Van Poppel, 1994; Smith, 1947; Stein et al., 1975). This association between caloric intake and health displays a very clear relationship between access to resources and the biological condition of health and approaches a causal relationship since the famine was an exogenous shock to Dutch society. In a contemporary US context, however, results from nutritional studies yield far weaker results. Studies of diet in the United States have found that, while poverty increases reported difficulty in affording food, quality of diet itself does not affect birthweight (Rogers et al., 1998; Widga and Lewis, 1999). That said, studies examining the effects of improved nutrition obtained through participation in the Supplemental Food Program for Women, Infants and Children (WIC) have revealed somewhat larger effects. WIC benefits have been found to reduce low birthweight rates by up to 25 per cent and very low birthweight rates by up to 44 per cent (Avruch and Cackley, 1995). But, at the same time, because WIC provides social services beyond supplemental food, part of these WIC effects may be the result of factors independent of nutrition. Severe malnutrition is clearly not healthy – as data from the Dutch famine study suggests – but malnutrition also does not appear to be a widespread mechanism connecting economic impoverishment with poor outcomes in the contemporary United States and like societies. However, research in this tradition has gone beyond basic needs such as nutrition to show that low-income households do experience other forms of material deprivation, which may explain part of the effect of income on child cognitive outcomes (Mayer, 1997). For instance, some work has shown that poor children are less likely to have educational toys or books in the household, and such items are positively associated with healthy cognitive development (Duncan et al., 1994; Smith et al., 1997; Zill, 1988; Zill et al., 1991). It is hard to imagine, however, that toys and books explain a very large share of the effect of low income on children.

A second paradigm, often called the *parenting stress hypothesis*, sees low income, variable employment, a lack of cultural resources and a feeling of inferiority from relative social class comparisons as exacerbating household stress levels which, in turn, lead to detrimental parenting practices such as yelling, shouting and hitting, which are not conducive to healthy child development (Conger et al., 1992, 1994; Elder et al., 1995; Hanson et al., 1997; Hashima and Amato, 1994; Lempers et al., 1989; McLeod and Shanahan, 1993; Whitbeck et al., 1991). Further, care for low-income children generally involves fewer positive interactions between the child and the caregiver and less opportunity for play (Howes and Olenick, 1986; Howes and Stewart, 1987; Phillips et al., 1987). Research suggests that parents living in poverty are more likely than parents in better conditions to display punitive behaviors – such as shouting, yelling, slapping – and less likely to display love and warmth through behaviors like cuddling and hugging (Conger et al., 1992, 1994; Elder et al., 1995). A great deal of evidence has connected such parenting practices to low IQ scores and to behavioral disorders (Conger et al., 1994).[20]

What is notable about these two theories of the effects of poverty on children is how individualistic and behavioralist they are. Poverty, it seems, can either cause a family not to have enough material resources, or it can cause the parents stress, which in turn leads to bad parenting practices. Either way, the causal arrow runs from the social condition of deprivation (either absolute in the first case, or relative *and* absolute in the second), through the conditions of the home and the behavior of the parents and only then to the child. Parents are where the buck stops – either by not providing the resources their children need or through bad parenting practices. The bottom line is that poverty works through the family environment, so the family is ultimately responsible for mediating its impact on children. Put another way, poor heroic parents could blunt the deleterious effects by being savvy enough to provide a stimulating educational environment in the home on the cheap, or by not letting financial stress get between their children and themselves. The direct impact of relative income on children – mediated by peer groups, community conditions and society-wide institutions such as the mass media – are not possible to consider within this framework. Of course, it is a lot easier – methodologically speaking – to look for mediating pathways within the household, rather than through wider social contexts (more on this later).

Given this ideological frame, it is not surprising that a third theory asserts that it is not poverty, lack of non-monetary resources or relative inequality that is so detrimental to child development as much as it is the fact that poor parents differ from higher-income parents (Mayer, 1997). Scholars in the *no effect* camp assert that the association between SES and child developmental outcomes is largely spurious. They claim that the same parental characteristics that lead to low income, education and occupational prestige also lead to detrimental developmental outcomes for offspring. These unmeasured characteristics may range from parenting styles to aspirations to genetic endowments. This last paradigm – though generally considered significantly more conservative than the former two – shares most of the same aspects of the 'material deprivation' and 'parenting stress' hypotheses. Namely, it is a causal (or rather non-causal) story about parents. The difference boils down to the fact that the material deprivation and parenting stress models optimistically believe that mediating factors can be measured and therefore manipulated, while the 'no effect' camp is more sanguine on ever explaining the unexplained variance between poor and non-poor families on child outcomes. This difference has, of course, enormous political and policy implications and thus is the focus of the ensuing section.

SLOUCHING TOWARD CAUSATION …

The causal pathways that I outlined above for the material deprivation and parental stress hypotheses could be altered without reducing the feasibility of the paradigms. For instance, rather than a lack of income leading to poor parenting practices and such parental characteristics then leading to a child's low educational attainment, it could alternatively be the case that parental characteristics are leading to low income *as well as to* a child's low educational attainment. Let us say a parent is particularly short-tempered; we could imagine that this tendency would make it hard for this parent to keep a job, while also having negative consequences on his or her child's development. In this case, it is non-economic characteristics that are leading to economic circumstances, not the other way around. We may be dealing here with a case of reverse causation: because certain non-economic characteristics tend to be accompanied by certain economic characteristics, it can be difficult to tell whether income is leading to non-economic characteristics (like temperament and parenting techniques) or whether such non-economic characteristics are leading to income levels. Of course, the order which these different elements follow essentially determines what (income or non-economic characteristics) is in a position to determine children's outcomes.

This potential role of non-economic characteristics in explaining the association between poverty and children's outcomes has been most thoroughly explored by Susan Mayer (1997) in her book *What Money Can't Buy: Family Income and Children's Life Chances.* In this book, Mayer takes several steps to untangle the effects of parental income from parental characteristics. To begin with, she compares the effects of different sources of income on children's outcomes. Parents may get money from several different sources – earnings, government transfers, etc. – and Mayer assumes that each of these different sources of income are associated with parental characteristics to differing degrees. For instance, earnings and welfare payments are likely oppositely associated with education. Focusing on the effects of unearned income on kids' outcomes, Mayer compares the effects of parents' welfare receipts (which are strongly associated with parental characteristics) to other forms of unearned income (which are so diverse as to be only weakly associated with parental characteristics). If income helps children, a dollar from welfare should be as valuable as a dollar from other sources of unearned income. Such a uniform effect does not appear to be the case, however. The effect of other forms of unearned income (that is, not welfare) is smaller than the effect of total income. Thus, it seems that parental characteristics may be significantly bound up in the effects of income.

To further sort out the effects of income and parental characteristics, Mayer takes advantage of the role of temporal ordering in causality. For a factor to cause an outcome, the factor must generally occur temporally prior to that outcome. Any statistical effect of a supposedly causal factor that is found after the outcome has already taken place cannot possibly be playing a causal role in the outcome. Using such logic, Mayer compares the effects of parental income before an event, like a teenager having a baby or dropping out of high school, with the effect of parental income after the event. If the effect of income after the event is sizable, it may be assumed that there are significant underlying factors in this measure. Mayer does, indeed, find that 'post-event income' is a strong predictor of children's outcomes, and argues that income effects on children's outcomes may be acting simply as a proxy for unmeasured parental traits.

Mayer further tests some of the more popular theories about income and parental traits – first, by comparing how rich and poor parents spend their money. Mayer finds that high-income parents tend to spend their excess income on larger homes, cars and eating out more often – all items and practices which likely have little effect on children's outcomes. (However, this is questionable since things like a large house may send subtle messages to children about values and status.) On the other hand, the material items that are widely believed to facilitate child development and improve outcomes, such as books and visits to a museum, Mayer finds are only weakly related to income. So, rich and poor children appear about equally likely to have the amenities that are believed to be important to outcomes. Mayer suggests this is likely because these items cost so little that their distribution depends more on parental tastes than actual income. Next, Mayer considers the effect of income on parents' psychological well-being, testing the hypothesis that poverty leads to bad

parenting via stress. Mayer finds very little support for this hypothesis, though, and documents only a weak relationship between parents' income and how they interact with their children. Thus, it also does not appear that income appreciably influences children's outcomes through its influence on parents' psychological well-being or their parenting practices. Mayer is quick to note, however, that her findings are only meaningful once children's basic material needs are satisfied. In other words, she interprets her results to mean that once a certain income threshold is passed, characteristics of the parents become more important than anything additional money can buy.

Mayer's book has received a great deal of attention and casts serious doubts on much of the prior research documenting the importance of income on children's outcomes. In fact, if explaining poverty without 'blaming the victim' was the rallying cry for researchers in the 1960s and 1970s, accounting for unobserved characteristics of rich and poor folks is the major challenge to researchers in the first decade of the twenty-first century.

It should be noted, however, that even in a work as sophisticated as hers we encounter potential sources of bias. Specifically, some of Mayer's techniques may bias the effects of income in the opposite direction from traditional analysis – that is, toward no effect of income *per se*. For example, when considering the comparison of different sources of parental income, we must wonder what is included in the category of 'parents' other unearned income'. Mayer is talking about the following: inheritance, profit from investments, gifts and other windfalls. These sources of income are associated with very atypical events and, therefore, may be related to other changes – such as death of a relative – which may have negative impacts on children. The one source of income here that would seem the most pure of other relevant changes – investment income – is really moot for the poor since they get almost none of their income from this source. This potential role of wealth also means that if income is non-linear in its effects (as Mayer herself argues when saying that her results are only meaningful when basic needs are satisfied), the income changes that are reflected in the effects of 'parents' other unearned income' are largely among the already well-off, where they should matter less anyway.

Additionally, Mayer's comparison of the effects of income before and after an event, as well as her analyses of parents' spending habits and stress levels, could be interpreted as support for traditional arguments of economic causation. That is, what Mayer calls spurious effects of income could be indirect effects of income. We cannot be certain that parental characteristics independent of income at one point in time are indeed truly separate from prior economic conditions. That is, parents' 'non-economic' characteristics may in fact be related to prior socio-economic conditions that Mayer is unable to measure. If this is, indeed, the case, we may encounter patterns of economic causation that simply span a very long period of time.[21]

Consider, for instance, explanations of differences between rich and poor children that focus on the so-called 'culture of poverty'. Some authors posit that because of relative position at the bottom of the social hierarchy poor parents develop norms that are problematic in terms of larger society.[22] If generations of irregular employment and discrimination result in street skills seeming more valuable than academic skills, parents will be more likely to encourage their children to acquire street skills than to study or stay in school. A simpler account would alternatively state that parents act as role models not in behaviors as much as in delineating the possible and probable in terms of status attainment. That is, parents who experience a lack of upward socio-economic mobility – no matter their values or parenting practices – may send an implicit message that achievement and attainment are impossible. These differences in values and messages are definitely not economic. Yet, they are so closely associated with economic conditions that to consider them apart from income is foolish. Mayer's data do not allow her to consider such possibilities and, thus, the divisions that she draws between economic and non-economic factors may not be entirely definitive.

While Mayer has been assailing 'traditional' poverty research for confusing correlation with causation, much of the research community has been moving right ahead and addressing larger contextual spheres of economic inequality. Earlier I mentioned that much of the research on the impact of poverty on the health, well-being and life chances of children had a parental or household focus with respect to mediating mechanisms. In other words, causation (or lack thereof) was presumed to run through the family unit. Recently, however, some researchers have been arguing that economic inequality at an aggregate level – such as the neighborhood, state or nation – plays an important role in the well-being of children and populations more generally. This line of research has two distinct strands worth mentioning.

First, a substantial literature on 'neighborhood effects' has largely grown out of William Julius Wilson's book *The Truly Disadvantaged*. In this 1987 book, which was partly a response to conservative arguments about the existence of an urban underclass made by pundits such as journalist Ken Auletta in a 1981 *New Yorker* article.[23] Wilson argues that the mobility of jobs and wealthy urban residents to suburban communities has led to a situation in which the urban poor are more socially isolated than they have ever been. Additional researchers have come along to document both the exodus of jobs from urban America and the increased segregation of the urban poor. These facts are generally not contested (e.g. Jargowsky, 1997). Rather, the question that this book and the larger underclass debate pose is whether the greater spatial concentration of the poor has an effect of its own – net of the individual level circumstances in which poor families find themselves. Hence the question of whether 'neighborhood effects' exist.[24] This is a growing literature; however, it is a research tradition that is plagued by the same kind of unobserved heterogeneity that Mayer takes note of at the family level. In some senses, the problem of selection bias may be even worse at the community level thanks to the very trend that Wilson identifies: self-selection out of poor urban neighborhoods. That is, given the substantial amount of residential mobility that occurs in and out of neighborhoods, it is not clear whether the impact of 'per cent poor' in a neighborhood on child (or adult) outcomes such as school performance, delinquency and crime is a result of social contagion and environmental conditions in poor neighborhoods, or simply the social sorting process that takes place when families move (or do not move). In other words, 'per cent poor' and other such community-level measures may merely be acting as proxies for unobserved characteristics of the individual families who live there and not actually picking up some ecological-level trait. Even semi-experimental assessments of programs like Moving to Opportunity (MTO) – in which public housing residents were 'scattered' into neighborhoods of varying socioeconomic circumstances – are plagued by issues of selection bias since it is somewhat voluntary who participates and since there are major issues of contagion between 'treatment' and 'control' groups.

A second potential pitfall for community-level research on poverty relates to aggregation bias when effects of income at the family level are non-linear.[25] Namely, if the effects of income are non-linear at the individual or family level (as they should be), aggregate measures may generate spurious correlations if they are not properly linked back to family units. This latter issue is much more tractable than the former issue of selection bias, as it only requires researchers to shun aggregate correlations for multi-level models. However, current researchers should be aware of this potential hazard to inference.

poverty over time or across place must come up with viable measurements that really get at what we mean by the term 'poverty' in diverse settings. Researchers who wish to investigate claims about the impact of household (or community) poverty on the outcomes of children or adults must grapple with issues of selection bias if they are going to be taken seriously in the scientific and public debates around this important issue. Whether it be through natural experiments, instrumental variables, family and community fixed effects models, or some other innovative statistical approach, researchers who wish to make claims about the effects of poverty must go beyond traditional regression models to have their claims taken seriously in a social and political environment where it is presumed that the poor – and not poverty – are responsible for their own reproduction.

This chapter has not done justice to wide swathes of the sociological research tradition on poverty. I have also not reviewed the illustrious tradition of community, ethnographic studies of the poor, extending all the way back to the Chicago School of the early twentieth century onward through global ethnographies of the twenty-first. This kind of qualitative research does much of the legwork in generating the causal stories to undergird the statistical associations that the quantitative poverty researchers document. These two intellectual traditions must be in constant dialogue – each moving toward the other – in order to solidify the foundation of our knowledge about economic inequality and deprivation in rich countries.

CONCLUSIONS

There is much research to do with respect to poverty in rich countries (and the policies that affect the poor). This chapter has focused on two research strands among many: (1) the conceptualization measurement of poverty and (2) the impact of poverty on the life chances of offspring. There are major challenges to both these research traditions. Researchers who wish to conduct robust research and assessment of

NOTES

1 For the text of the speech see *Harpers* (August 1990), p. 22.

2 Such a conception fits very well with Karl Marx's notion of the physical reproduction of labor.

3 She based this multiplier on results from the Consumer Expenditure Survey of the mid-1950s, which estimated that families spent – on average – 35 per cent of their household budgets on food.

4 Some scholars have called for replacing food with housing as the basis for need calculations since housing

now makes up the largest proportion of household budgets. See Ruggles: (1990) for a discussion.

5 There is, indeed, a fair amount of evidence that suggests that the US federal poverty measure is somewhat crude. Living technically above the poverty line may not necessarily imply that one has access to the resources one needs to live with dignity. Families categorized as near-poor generally have incomes between 100 and 185 per cent of the poverty line, yet, despite their incomes, frequently have trouble making ends meet. Further, because the near-poor are generally ineligible for many government programs, they may be in even more dire straights than the officially poor – again, despite their higher incomes – when trying to provide food, shelter and medical care. For example, in many states Medicaid is available only to those families with incomes below 133 per cent of the poverty line, leaving women and children with low incomes that are just above the 133 per cent cut off without access to health care (Ku et al., 1999; Stevens, 1974).

At the same time, we can also note problems of heterogeneity even among those who fall below the poverty line. Evidence suggests that poverty comes in several varieties, and the single measure that accompanies the question of basic necessities may simply be unable to capture such diversity. To begin with, there is significant variation in the duration of poverty, so that some individuals fall into poverty because of a temporary spell of economic deprivation – often resulting from divorce or unemployment – while others, particularly minorities, may be poor for longer periods of time with little upward mobility over the life course. There is also significant variation in the severity of poverty. In 1999 7 per cent of children lived in extreme poverty – meaning they lived in families with incomes below 50 per cent of the poverty line (in 1999, the extreme poverty line was $6145 for a family of three) (Child Poverty Fact Sheet, 2001).

While the transitory poor and those above the extreme poverty line far outnumber the consistently poor and the extremely poor, this inequality in representation is more than made up for by the implications of duration and severity (Duncan and Rodgers, 1988). Those who are persistently poor and those who are extremely poor are at significantly higher risk for many adverse outcomes, compared to those who are transiently poor, not extremely poor, and non-poor. For instance, children who experience prolonged spells of poverty or severe poverty show larger deficits in cognitive ability and socio-emotional development than children who only experience less severe poverty or poverty for a short period of time. (For a discussion of poverty and children's outcomes see Aber et al., 1997; Duncan and Brooks-Gunn, 1997; Duncan et al., 1998; Smith and Dixon, 1995).

6 Making this difference in wealth levels all the more significant is the fact that Conley (1999) has found that family (parental) wealth is a strong predictor of teenage and young adult outcomes ranging from teenage premarital childbearing to educational attainment to welfare dependency to filial wealth accumulation. In many cases, when parental wealth is taken into account, black–white differences are eliminated or even flip direction. While parental wealth is just beginning to become taken into consideration in intergenerational studies, it has been neglected in the race, socio-economic status (SES) and child outcomes literature.

7 For a discussion of this see Iceland (2003).

8 Adrian Atkinson (1987) makes a similar distinction between measures of a minimum level of resources versus a minimum standard of living.

9 In fact, in the UK Patrick McGregor and Vani Borooah (1992) find that two substantially different sets of people are identified as poor depending on what conception is used.

10 Their list of 20 is based on the work of Joanna Mack and Stewart Lansley (1985), who sought to develop a deprivation scale.

11 His scale is much simpler than earlier versions which were developed by the Organization for Economic Co-operation and Development (OECD), the United Nations and the United Nations Research Institute for Social Development (UNRISD), but which later floundered under the political weight of their own complexity.

12 Even with these relatively straightforward measures, there is a degree of cultural difference in how they are measured. Take infant mortality, for instance. The World Health Organization has defined a live birth as a product of conception that shows signs of life irrespective of its gestational age. However, there is dramatic variation in the clinical practices of classification. Most US states use the WHO definition or something close to it. By contrast, a birth can be recorded up to 48 hours after the time of delivery in France. As a result, many infants who die before registration (when infant mortality rates are highest) may be recorded as a stillbirth. Likewise, in Japan, infants less than 22 weeks of gestation or with congenital abnormalities are reported as stillbirths regardless of the presence of signs of life. These examples are meant to show how difficult it is to come up with even the most basic measures that will be 'universal' across time, place and culture.

13 I say 'largely' since there is a literature in economics which examines the impact of children on their parents' income. For an example with respect to child health see, e.g., Rosenzweig and Wolpin (1988).

14 These increased risks may be compounded by the more limited access to health services on the part of this population (Newacheck and Halfon, 1986; Perrin et al., 1989; St Peter et al., 1992).

15 On the effects of nutritional status see Elo and Preston, 1992; Martorell and Ho, 1984; Miller et al., 1989.

16 For a general summary see Aber et al., 1997; Duncan and Brooks-Gunn, 1997.

17 For a review see Aber et al., 1997.

18 Their corresponding figure for the United States (using the Panel Study of Income Dynamics) is only 0.13. Solon (2002) comments that these low figures are likely to result from the unusually young ages of the samples.

19 The Swedish estimate comes from Osterberg (2000); the Finnish result is from Osterbacka (2001).

20 While the stress paradigm has received a great deal of attention and a fair amount of empirical support – particularly with respect to health status – it has also been criticized for

detracting attention from the primary factor of these models: social position. Bruce Link has argued that 'research on the biological consequences of stress … is seen as an exciting new development [and] … in general, interest has followed the most recent step in the progression toward disease outcomes, while concern with the earlier foci has dissipated' (Link and Phelan, 1995). In other words, as new developments have emerged, researchers have paid more attention to the biological specifics of stress and less attention to the question of why social position is so strongly related to stress in the first place. Offering an alternative to the stress paradigm, Link has proposed the fundamental cause hypothesis. Similar to the stress hypothesis, the fundamental cause hypothesis suggests that relative social positions (e.g. income levels) have inherent qualities that may promote or hinder health and child development. Rather than pointing to inherent levels of stress, however, Link suggests that social positions provide people with resources like knowledge, money, power and prestige that can be used to obtain health resources: 'As new risk factors become apparent, people of higher socioeconomic status are more favorably situated to know about the risks and have the resources that allow them to engage in protective efforts to avoid them' (Link and Phelan, 1995: 86). For example, some authors have suggested that around the 1960s, when evidence of the risks of smoking began to emerge, a new class pattern developed in these behaviors. There is no evidence that, prior to the 1960s, rates of smoking were higher among lower socioeconomic groups. However, during the 1960s individuals of higher socioeconomic status were more likely to quit smoking and current research finds strong socioeconomic gradients in smoking behavior (Ernster, 1988; Norton et al., 1988). In other words, wealthier people learned about the heath risks of smoking more quickly than poorer people and could then mobilize resources to more effectively change their behavior. The same dynamic may hold with respect to parenting. In other words, income may be acting as a proxy for position in a social hierarchy.

21 Other research uses a technique similar to her 'before and after' approach called sibling fixed effects models, which compares family income at various times in siblings' childhoods to determine if and when it matters – net of family characteristics that remain constant (such as genes and the like). One notable study does indeed find an effect of income early in childhood using some of the same data that Mayer uses (the PSID).

22 For discussion of the literature see Mayer, 1997: 50.

23 Wilson was also responding to Charles Murray's 1984 book, *Losing Ground*, which argued that the persistent plight of the poor was partly a result of aid to the poor. In other words, an expanding welfare system, Murray argued, has caused a rise in economic dependency and a concomitant change in the culture of urban poverty.

24 Some important articles in this tradition include Brooks-Gunn et al. (1993); Crane (1991); Garner and Raudenbush (1991); Sampson and Groves (1989).

25 This criticism has been made most vocally at the literature on income inequality and health. For the view that income inequality is related to health status of adults and children see, e.g., A. Deaton (2001); Friscella and Franks (1997); Kennedy et al. (1996, 1998); Lochner (1999); Soobader and LeClere (1999); Wilkinson (1992).

For the view that it is a statistical artifact of aggregation bias see, e.g., Gravelle (1998) and Mellor and Milyo (2001).

REFERENCES

Aber, J., Bennett, N., Conley, D. and Li, J. (1997) 'The effects of poverty on child health and cognitive development', *Annual Review of Public Health*, 18: 463–83.

Atkinson, Adrian B. (1987) 'On the measurement of poverty', *Econometrica*, 55: 749–64.

Avruch, S. and Cackley, A. (1995) 'Savings achieved by giving WIC benefits to women prenatally', *Public Health Reports*, 110 (1): 278–84.

Brannen, J. and Wilson, G. (eds) (1987) *Give and Take in Families*. London: Allen and Unwin.

Brody, D.J., Pirkle, J.L., Kramer, R.A., Flegal, K.M., Matte, T.D. et al. (1994) 'Blood lead levels in the US population', *Journal of the American Medical Association*, 272: 277–83.

Bronfenbrenner, U. (1979) *The Ecology of Human Development*. Ithaca, NY: Cornell University Press.

Brooks-Gunn, J., Duncan, G.J., Klebanov, P.K. and Sealand, N. (1993) 'Do neighborhoods influence child and adolescent development?', *American Journal of Sociology*, 99: 353–95.

Brooks-Gunn, J., Duncan, G.J. and Aber, J.L. (eds) (1997) *Neighborhood Poverty: Context and Consequences for Children, Volume I*. New York: Russell Sage Foundation.

Callan, Tim, Nolan, Brian and Whelan, Christopher T. (1993) 'Resources, deprivation and the measurement of poverty', *Journal of Social Policy*, 22: 141–72.

Campbell, S.B. (1995) 'Behavioral problems in preschool children: a review of recent research', *Journal of Child Psychology and Psychiatry*, 36: 113–49.

Chase-Lansdale, P. Lindsay, Gordon, Rachel A., Brooks-Gunn, Jeanne and Klebanov, Pamela (1997) 'Neighborhood and family influences on the intellectual and behavioral competence of preschool and early school-age children', in Jeanne Brooks-Gunn, Greg Duncan and J. Lawrence Aber (eds), *Neighborhood Poverty: Volume I*. New York: Russell Sage Foundation. pp. 79–118.

Child Poverty Fact Sheet (June 2001) National Center for Children in Poverty. Available at http://cpmcnet.columbia.edu/dept/nccp/ycpf.html.

Conger, R.D., Conger, K.J., Elder, G.H., Lorenz, F.O., Simons, R.L. and Whitbeck, L.B. (1992) 'A family process model of economic hardship and adjustment of early adolescent boys', *Child Development,* 63: 526–41.

Conger, R.D., Ge, X., Elder, G.H., Lorenz, F.O. and Simons, R.L. (1994) 'Economic stress, coercive family process, and developmental problems of adolescents', *Child Development,* 65: 541–61.

Conley, D. (1999) *Being Black, Living in the Red: Race, Wealth and Social Policy in America.* Berkeley/Los Angeles, CA: University of California Press.

Couch, Kenneth, A. and Dunn, Thomas, A. (1997) 'Intergenerational correlations in labor market status: a comparison of the United States and Germany', *Journal of Human Resources,* 32: 210–32.

Cramer, J.C. (1995) 'Racial and ethnic differences in birth weight: the role of income and financial assistance', *Demography,* 32: 231–47.

Crane, J. (1991) 'The epidemic theory of ghettos and neighborhood effects on dropping out and teenage childbearing', *American Journal of Sociology,* 96: 1226–59.

Deaton, A. (2001) 'Health, inequality and economic development', *Research Program in Development Studies Working Paper.* Woodrow Wilson School of Government, Princeton University.

Duncan, G. and Brooks-Gunn, J. (1997) *Consequences of Growing up Poor.* New York: Russell Sage Foundation.

Duncan, G. and Rodgers, W. (1988) 'Has children's poverty become more persistent?', *American Sociological Review,* 56: 361–75.

Duncan, G.J., Brooks-Gunn, J. and Klebanov, P.K. (1994) 'Economic deprivation and early childhood development', *Child Development,* 65: 296–318.

Duncan, G., Brooks-Gunn, J., Yeung, J. and Smith, J. (1998) 'How much does childhood poverty affect the life chances of children?', *American Sociological Review,* 63 (3): 406–23.

Egbuonu, L. and Starfield, B. (1982) 'Child health and social status', *Pediatrics,* 69: 550–7.

Elder, G.H., Van Nguyen, T. and Caspi, A. (1995) 'Linking family hardship to children's lives', *Child Development,* 56: 361–75.

Elo, I.T. and Preston, S.H. (1992) 'Effects of early-life conditions on adult mortality: a review', *Population Index,* 58: 361–75.

Ernst, P.K., Joseph, D.L., Locher, U. and Becklake, M.R. (1995) 'Socioeconomic status and indicators of asthma in children', *American Journal of Respiratory Critical Care Management,* 152: 570–5.

Ernster, V. (1988) 'Trends in smoking, cancer risk, and cigarette promotion', *Cancer,* 62: 1702–12.

Esping-Andersen, G. (1990) *The Three Worlds of Welfare Capitalism.* Princeton, NJ: Princeton University Press.

Friedman, Rose (1965) *Poverty: Definitions and Perspective.* Washington, DC: American Enterprise Institute.

Friscella, K. and Franks, P. (1997) 'Poverty or income inequality as a predictor of mortality: longitudinal cohort study', *British Medical Journal,* 314: 1724–8.

Fuchs, Victor (1967) 'Redefining poverty and redistributing income', *Public Interest,* 8: 88–95.

Garner, Catherine L. and Raudenbush, Stephen W. (1991) 'Neighborhood effects on educational attainment: a multilevel analysis', *Sociology of Education,* 64: 251–62.

Glendinning, C. and Millar, J. (eds) (1987) *Women in Poverty in Britain,* Brighton: Wheatsheaf Books.

Gortmaker, S.L. (1979) 'Poverty and infant mortality in the United States', *American Sociological Review,* 44: 280–97.

Gravelle, H. (1998) 'How much of the relationship between population mortality and unequal distribution of income is a statistical artifact', *British Medical Journal,* 316: 382–5.

Haber, Alan (1966) 'Poverty budgets: how much is enough?', *Poverty and Human Resources Abstracts,* 1.

Hanson, T.L., McLanahan, S. and Thomson, E. (1997) 'Economic resources, parental practices and children's well-being', in Greg J. Duncan and Jeanne Brooks-Gunn (eds), *Consequences of Growing Up Poor.* New York: Russell Sage Foundation. pp. 190–238.

Hashima, P.Y. and Amato, P.R. (1994) 'Poverty, social support and parental behavior', *Child Development,* 65: 394–403.

Hauser, R.M. (1994) 'Measuring socioeconomic status in studies of child development', *Child Development,* 65: 1541–5.

Hobjin, B. (2002) 'On both sides of the quality bias in price indexes'. Federal Reserve Bank of New York Staff Report No. 157.

Howes, C. and Olenick, M. (1986) 'Family and child influences on toddlers' compliance', *Child Development,* 26: 292–303.

Howes, C. and Stewart, P. (1987) 'Child's play with adults, toys, and peers: an examination of family and child care influences', *Developmental Psychology,* 23: 423–30.

Iceland, John (2003) *Poverty in America: A Handbook.* Berkeley, CA: University of California Press.

Jargowsky, Paul (1997) *Poverty and Place: Ghettos, Barrios, and the American City.* New York: Russell Sage Foundation.

Jenkins, Stephen, P. (1991) 'Poverty measurement and the within-household distribution: agenda for action', *Journal of Social Policy*, 20: 457–83.

Kennedy, B., Kawachi, I. and Prothrow-Stith, D. (1996) 'Income distribution and mortality: cross-sectional ecological study of the Robin Hood Index in the United States', *British Medical Journal*, 312: 1004–7.

Kennedy, B., Kawachi, I., Glass, I. and Prothrow-Stith, D. (1998) 'Income distribution, socioeconomic status, and self-rated health: a US multi-level analysis', *British Medical Journal*, 317: 917–21.

Klerman, L.V. and Parker, M.B. (1990) *Alive and Well? A Review of Health Policies and Programs for Poor Young Children*. New York, NY: National Center for Children in Poverty, Columbia University of Public Health.

Korenman, S. and Miller, J.E. (1997) 'Effects of long-term poverty on physical health of children in the National Longitudinal Survey of Youth', in G.J. Duncan and J. Brooks-Gunn (eds), *Consequences of Growing Up Poor*. New York: Russell Sage Foundation. pp. 70–99.

Korenman, S., Miller, J.E. and Sjaastad, J.E. (1995) 'Long-term poverty and child development in the United States: results from the NLSY', *Children Youth Services Review*, 17: 127–55.

Ku, L., Ullman, F. and Almeida, R. (1999) 'What counts? Determining Medicaid and CHIP eligibility for children', Urban Institute Discussion Paper No. 99–05. Washington, DC: The Urban Institute Press.

Lempers, J.D., Clark-Lempers, D. and Simons, R.L. (1989) 'Economic hardship, parenting and distress in adolescence', *Child Development*, 60: 25–39.

Link, B. and Phelan, J. (1995) 'Social conditions as fundamental causes of disease', *Journal of Health and Social Behavior*, Extra Issue: 80–94.

Lochner, K. (1999) 'State inequality and individual mortality risk: a prospective multi-level study'. PhD Dissertation, Harvard University.

Lumey, L. and Van Poppel, F. (1994) 'The Dutch famine of 1944–1945: mortality and morbidity in past and present generations', *Social Historical Medicine*, 7: 229–46.

Mack, Joanna and Lansley, Stewart (1985) *Poor Britain*. London: George Allen and Unwin.

Mahaffey, K.R., Annest, J.L. and Roberts, J. (1982) 'National estimates of blood lead levels: United States, 1976–1980: Association with selected demographic and socio-economic factors', *New England Journal of Medicine*, 307 (1): 573–9.

Mare, R. (1982) 'Socio-economic status and childhood mortality', *American Journal of Public Health*, 72: 539–47.

Martorell, R. and Ho, T.J. (1984) 'Malnutrition, morbidity, and mortality', *Population and Development Review. Child Survival: Strategies for Research*, 10: 49–68.

Mayer, Susan (1997) *What Money Can't Buy: Family Income and Children's Life Chances*. Cambridge, MA: Harvard University Press.

McGaughey P.J., Starfield, B., Alexander, C. and Ensminger, M.E. (1991) 'Social environment and vulnerability of low birth weight children: a social-epidemiological perspective', *Pediatrics*, 88: 943–53.

McGregor, Patrick P.L. and Borooah, Vani K. (1992) 'Is Low Income or Low Expenditure a Better Indicator of Whether or Not a Household is Poor', *Journal of Social Policy*, 21: 53–70.

McLeod, J.D. and Shanahan, M.J. (1993) 'Poverty, parenting and children's mental health', *American Sociological Review*, 58: 351–66.

Mellor, Jennifer M. and Milyo, Jeffrey (2001) 'Reexamining the evidence of an ecological association between income inequality and health', *Journal of Health Politics Policy and Law*, 26: 487–522.

Miller, C.A., Fine, A. and Adams-Taylor, S. (1989) *Monitoring Children's Health: Key Indicators*, 2nd edn. Washington, DC: American Public Health Association.

Monaghan, Thomas (1990) *Harpers*, August p. 22.

Morris, Morris David (1979) *Measuring the Condition of the World's Poor*. New York: Pergamon Press.

Murray, Charles (1984) *Losing Ground: American Social Policy, 1950–1980*. New York: Basic Books.

Newacheck, P.W. and Halfon, N. (1986) 'Access to ambulatory care services for economically disadvantaged children', *Pediatrics*, 78: 813–19.

Norton, T., Kenneth, E., Juliette, K. and Remington, P. (1988) 'Smoking by blacks and whites: socio-economic and demographic differences', *American Journal of Public Health*, 78: 1187–9.

Oliver, Melvin and Shapiro, Thomas (1995) *Black Wealth, White Wealth: A New Perspective on Racial Inequality*. London: Routledge.

Orshansky, Mollie (1963) 'Children of the poor', *Social Security Bulletin*, US Department of Labor.

Osterbacka, Eva (2001) 'Family background and economic status in Finland', *Scandinavian Journal of Economics*, 103: 467–84.

Osterberg, Torun (2000) 'Intergenerational income mobility in Sweden: What do tax-data show', *Review of Income and Wealth*, 46: 421–36.

Perrin, J.M., Homer, C.J. and Berwick, D.M. et al. (1989) 'Variations in rates of hospitalization of children in three urban communities', *New England Journal of Medicine*, 320: 1183–7.

Phillips, D., McCartney, K. and Scarr, S. (1987) 'Child care quality and children's social development', *Developmental Psychology*, 23: 537–43.

Quah, R., Stark, A. and Meigs, J.W. (1982) 'Children's blood levels in New Haven: a population based information demographic profile', *Environmental Health Perspectives*, 5: 128–34.

Rainwater, Lee (1974) *What Money Buys: Inequality and the Social Meanings of Income.* New York: Basic Books.

Ringen, Stephen (1987) *The Possibility of Politics.* Oxford: Oxford University Press.

Ringen, Stephen (1988) 'Direct and indirect measures of poverty', *Journal of Social Policy,* 17: 351–66.

Rogers, I., Emmett, P., Bailer, D. and Golding, J. (1998) 'Financial difficulties, smoking habits, composition of diet and birth weight in a population of pregnant women in the South West of England', *European Journal of Clinical Nutrition,* 52 (4): 251–60.

Rosenzweig, M.R. and Wolpin, K. (1988) 'Heterogeneity, intrafamily distribution, and child health', *Journal of Human Resources*, 23: 437–61.

Ruggles, Patricia (1990) *Drawing the Line: Alternative Poverty Measures and their Implications for Public Policy.* Washington, DC: Urban Institute Press.

Sampson, Robert J. and Byron Groves, W. (1989) 'Community structure and crime: testing social-disorganization theory', *American Journal of Sociology*, 94: 774–802.

Sen, Amartya (1995) *Inequality Reexamined.* Cambridge, MA: Harvard University Press.

Sen, Amartya (1999) *Commodities and Capabilities.* Oxford: Oxford University Press.

Sen, Amartya (2000) *Development as Freedom.* New York: Anchor Books.

Smeeding, Timothy, Rainwater, Lee and Burtless, Gary (2000) 'United States poverty in a cross-national context', Luxembourg Income Study Working Paper, No. 244.

Smith, C. (1947) 'The effects of wartime starvation on pregnancy and its products', *American Journal of Obstetric Gynecology*, 53: 599–608.

Smith, J.R., Brooks-Gunn, J. and Klebanov, P.K. (1997) 'Consequences of living in poverty for young children's cognitive and verbal ability and early school achievement', in G.J. Duncan and J. Brooks-Gunn (eds), *Consequences of Growing Up Poor.* New York: Russell Sage Foundation. pp. 132–89.

Smith, S. and Dixon, R. (1995) 'Literacy concepts of low- and middle-class four-year-olds entering preschool', *Journal of Educational Research*, 88: 243–53.

Solon, Gary (2002) 'Cross-country differences in intergenerational earnings mobility', *Journal of Economic Perspectives*, 16 (3): 59–66.

Soobader, M. and LeClere, F. (1999) 'Aggregation and the measurement of income inequality: effects on morbidity', *Social Science and Medicine*, 48: 733–44.

Starfield, B. (1991) 'Childhood morbidity: comparisons, clusters, and trends', *Pediatrics*, 88: 519–26.

Starfield, B., Shapiro, S., Weiss, J., Liang, K.-Y., Ra, K., Paige, D. and Want, X. (1991) 'Race, family income, and low birth weight', *American Journal of Epidemiology*, 134: 1167–74.

Stein, Z., Susser, M., Saegner, G. and Marolla, F., (1975) *Famine and Human Development: The Dutch Hunger Winter of 1944–1945.* New York: Oxford University Press.

Stevens, R. (1974) *Welfare Medicine in America: A Case Study of Medicaid.* New York: The Free Press.

Stockwell, E.G., Goza, F.W. and Roach, J.L. (1995) 'The relationship between socioeconomic status and infant mortality in a metropolitan aggregate, 1989–1991', *Sociological Forum,* 10: 297–308.

Stone, Deborah A. (1994) 'Making the poor count', *The American Prospect*, 17: 84–8.

St Peter, R.F., Newacheck, P.W. and Halfon, N. (1992) 'Access to care for poor children: separate and unequal?', *Journal of the American Medical Association,* 267: 2760–4.

Tresserras, R., Canela, J., Alvarez, J., Sentis, J. and Salleras, L. (1992) 'Infant mortality, per capita income, and adult illiteracy: an ecological approach', *American Journal of Public Health*, 82: 435–8.

Whitbeck, L.B., Simons, R.L., Conger, R.D., Lorenz, F.O., Huck, S. and Elder, G.H. Jr (1991) 'Family economic hardship, parental support, and adolescent self-esteem', *Social Psychology Quarterly*, 54: 353–63.

Widga, A. and Lewis, N. (1999) 'Defined, in-home prenatal nutrition intervention for low-income women', *Journal of the American Dietetic Association*, 99 (9): 1058–62.

Wiegand, Johannes (1997) 'Intergenerational earnings mobility in Germany', Unpublished paper cited in Solon (2002).

Wilkinson, R. (1992) 'Income distribution and life expectancy', *British Medical Journal*, 304: 165–8.

Wilson, William Julius (1987) *The Truly Disadvantaged: The Underclass and Public Policy.* Chicago: University of Chicago Press.

Wise, P.H., Kotelchuck, M., Wilson, M.L. and Mills, M. (1985) 'Racial and socio-economic disparities in childhood mortality in Boston', *New England Journal of Medicine*, 313: 360–6.

Wise, P.H. and Meyers, A. (1988) 'Poverty and child health', *Pediatrics Clinic of North America*, 35: 1169–86.

Wolff, Edward and Leone, Richard (2002) *Top Heavy: The Increasing Concentration of Wealth in America and What Can Be Done About It*, 2nd edn. New York: The New Press.

Zill, N. (1998) 'Behavior, achievement, and health problems among children in stepfamilies: findings from a national survey of child health', in E.M. Hetherington and J. Arasteh (eds), *Impact of Divorce, Single Parenting and Stepparenting on Children*. Hillsdale, NJ: Lawrence Erlbaum Associates.

Zill, N., Moore, K. Smith, E., Stief, T. and Coiro, M.J. (1991) *The Life Circumstances and Development of Children in Welfare Families: A Profile Based on National Survey Data*. Washington, DC: Child Trends.

20

Globalization: Sociology and Cross-Disciplinarity

ROLAND ROBERTSON AND KATHLEEN E. WHITE

[W]e are going through [a] major intellectual sea change, a shift in perspective. Somehow, the world appears to have changed: people everywhere seem to accept the once preposterous notion that local events can only be understood through a global lens and to view social processes primarily as local manifestations of global patterns. Internationally, human character and social relations appear to be going through a dramatic upheaval – judging by a sudden and overwhelming concern with the way local lives are shaped by global flows, as politicians, business leaders, and academics assume that globalization is a primary dynamic in all our lives. (Seidman, 2000: 339)

INTRODUCTION: CROSS-DISCIPLINARITY

Since the early 1980s the theme of globalization has had an increasingly significant presence in the discipline of sociology. It would not be too much to say that 'the global paradigm' (Robertson, 1990) has transformed (and continues to transform) sociology, as well as numerous other academic disciplines – not to speak of various professions and occupations. At the same time it has become a much-used, double-edged buzzword and/or blameword. The attendant confusion between academic and general use in a number of arenas – political and ideological, business and advertising, and others – has been and remains considerable.

Indeed, the shaping and commodification of the globalization motif has placed long-time academic analysts of it in something of a quandary; insofar as some have had, in effect, to choose between persisting with the tangle of conceptual offshoots of globalization or latching onto other evolving conceptual formulations. Thus, there are those who now prefer the term 'transnational' to global, so as to distance themselves from what they perceive as the morass of 'global babble'. The position taken here is to stay with the use of the term globalization and to continue with the research program mapped by sociologists in the early 1980s, some years before the term became commonplace in business and politics. Nonetheless, extra-sociological or extra-social scientific issues cannot entirely be excluded. To take but one such issue: recent years have witnessed the rapid growth of what are often called anti-globalization movements – usually concentrating on the economic dimension of globalization. These demand sociological analysis – as part of the family of so-called new social movements (cf. George, 2004).

Some readers may think that we are here engaged in a semantic quibble, of which sociologists are so often accused. While there may be a little of this, for the most part the issues involved are very challenging. For a start, let us prioritize those that appear to be the most salient and controversial:

1 The origins and historical length of globalization.
2 The motor, or driving, force of globalization, if any.
3 The relationship between heterogeneity and homogeneity – difference in relation to sameness – as the process(es) of globalization proceed.
4 The much-heralded problem of the relationship between the local and the global and the degrees to which the former is produced by the latter.
5 The question of the fate of the nation-state, within the historical frame of globalization.
6 The difficult problem of the relationship between globality (or globalities) and modernity (or modernities).
7 The fast-growing recognition that so-called globalization is social (interactional and communicative), as well as cultural, political and economic; much irony lying in the fact that many sociological analysts of globalization entirely omit the social as a dimension of globalization.
8 The increasing use of the concept of glocalization as a gloss on or even a substitute for globalization, this proposition being closely related, of course, to the global–local issue.

These themes will appear at various points in what follows.[1]

It should be evident, even at this very early stage, that our discussion crosses – indeed, transcends – academic disciplines. In other words, globalization and its numerous related topics are not by any means a solely sociological issue. By now it encompasses virtually all social and humanistic disciplines (and has also made a number of inroads into the natural and physical sciences). So, when we speak, in a sociological context, of globalization, we must be clear about this. Whereas it would be more than reasonable to suggest that sociology – as an embryonic discipline of the mid-nineteenth century – constituted the truly effective foundation of 'global

studies' and the global paradigm, there can be no neglecting the fact that a large number of disciplines have contributed considerably both to the development of the latter and to the more specific focus on the contested theme of globalization. Study of the latter is, perhaps, the exemplar of current cross-disciplinary 'confusion'.

Many of the matters addressed nowadays under the heading of globalization had been considered for centuries by theologians, philosophers, historians and, later, by social scientists without using that specific term. And in the two hundred years or so prior to 1980, there had been increasing concern with world – or global – history and with 'distant' continents and 'other' civilizations and regions. Thus alterity has become a central feature of the overall globalization process in a phase of postdisciplinarity, transdisciplinarity and anti-disciplinarity. The latter part of the eighteenth and the whole of the nineteenth centuries constituted a period in which such influential writers as Kant, Hegel, Marx, Saint-Simon and Comte, as well as numerous influential historians and historiographers, paid considerable attention to such matters. In their work one finds, to different degrees, acknowledgment of the great changes that had occurred earlier in the century with respect to travel and communication – changes that made it increasingly clear that a new kind of world was emerging, new particularly in the sense of its potential oneness. Kant had set the tone for much of this when he spoke of our living, in a global sense, increasingly side by side.

It should be said, that, while these world-compressing trends continued with increasing rapidity towards the end of the nineteenth century and the early years of the twentieth century, the great sociologists of the so-called classical period (1880–1920), such as Durkheim, Max Weber, Simmel and Toennies, almost entirely neglected such vital specific developments as the establishment of the telegraph, the telephone, the airplane, and World Time, to name but a few of the advancements that fundamentally – at least in the Northern Hemisphere – altered the experience of time and space (Kern, 1983). Instead, their focus was mainly upon social formations, more particularly the temporal transitions away from premodern sociocultural and economic circumstances, although the work of Durkheim and Weber certainly did involve *comparison* of different social forms and civilizations. Weber obviously became increasingly aware of the worldwide reach of modern capitalism and Durkheim showed much interest, particularly towards the end of his life, in the problems of the compatibility of different moral and ethical patterns, in relation to his growing concern with 'international society'. Nonetheless, even though this was almost certainly not their principal intention, classical sociologists, with the aid of other developing human sciences, marked out the focus on 'national societies' as the domain of sociology.

In sum, globalization is a site upon which relationships between disciplines are being restructured. Social science textbooks, which are notoriously well behind the main, innovative trends of their respective disciplines, have only very recently begun to reflect the global turn that has been evident in scholarship for at least twenty years (e.g. Beynon and Dunkerley, 2000; Cohen and Kennedy, 2000; Lechner and Boli, 2000; O'Donnell, 2000; Steger, 2003). It is also worthy of note that in bookshops, especially in the UK and the USA, special sections entirely devoted to works on globalization are becoming quite common.

DIMENSIONS OF GLOBALIZATION

Even though we have highlighted at the outset the multi-disciplinary features of the present study of globalization, ours will be an approach that is centered on – but emphatically, not confined to – the discipline of sociology. Since sociology itself is, like a number of academic disciplines, in a state of great flux, this is much less a statement of *disciplinary* inclination than it may seem to be. Nonetheless we should note the irony of the social dimension being very frequently omitted by sociologists, as well as others, as a major aspect of globalization. For example, while insisting that the first distinctive features of globalization are those of 'stretched social relations', Cochrane and Pain (2000: 15) argue that such relations

involve 'the existence of cultural, economic and political networks of connection across the world'. Or 'as social relations stretch there is an increasing interpenetration of economic and social practices' (Cochrane and Pain, 2000: 16). The second statement somewhat contradicts the first, but our argument here is not to make points against these, and other writers, but to draw attention to a problematic lacuna in much of the sociological study of globalization.

To some considerable degree the absence of explicit focus on 'the social' is being rectified by the sheer ubiquity of the new electronic means of communication. For example, the Internet is giving rise to new modalities of self-identification (Turkle, 1995) and sociation. More specifically, the *virtual social* is an increasingly significant form of social communication. Sociality occurs more and more in cyberspace (e.g., Porter, 1997; Hakken, 1999: 93–173; Jordan, 1999). Knorr Cetina (2001) has argued, in this and other related senses, it would perhaps be more accurate to say that we live in a *postsocial* environment in which 'social principles are thinned out with other cultural elements and relationships replacing them, mediating between them and in some measure [collapsing] in on social relations and structures' (Knorr Cetina, 2001: 520). Whether this helps to explain why the social dimension has been neglected in the discussion of globalization is not entirely clear; but, in spite of the importance of Knorr Cetina's argument, we will here conflate the ideas of social relationship and communication, acknowledging that this may be only a provisional move. We will take up some aspects of this again when we come to discuss the 'microscopic' aspects of globalization. But we would be remiss were we not also to mention the crucial contributions of McLuhan in anticipating new electronic forms of sociality and his conception of a highly contentious global village (McLuhan with Fiore, 1968) – this not being the conventional way of invoking McLuhan.

With these considerations about the social in mind, we stipulate that the four major dimensions of globalization are: the *cultural*, the *social*, the *political* and the *economic*. These are analytic dimensions, subject to further refinement (cf. Scholte, 1993: 100–18; Anderson, 2001). In any case, in the real world which we study, there are never *solely* economic, *solely* political aspects, or whatever. Every phenomenon has elements of all four major dimensions, in spite of the fact that, most clearly in Western philosophy and social science, there has been an ongoing – we believe, futile – debate about the primacy of one dimension over others. The issue of dimensionality is intimately related to that of disciplinarity for there are a number of discourses of globalization (Robertson and Khondker, 1998), some of them corresponding to disciplinary perspectives.

DIRECTIONALITY AND GLOBALIZATION

The analysis of globalization has been plagued by the *Problemstellung* of its directionality. We maintain that globalization has to do with the movement of the world as a whole in the direction of unicity – meaning oneness of the world as a single, sociocultural place. This, in turn, indicates that the singularity of the world increasingly diminishes the significance of territorial boundaries – territoriality having for much of human history been a basic geographic strategy of control (Sacks, 1986; cf. Lewis and Wigen, 1997). Hence the emphasis on borderlessness in much of the literature on globalization (e.g., Jacobson, 1996; Shapiro and Alker, 1996). Nonetheless there are some respects in which borders are becoming more rather than less salient, as is clearly to be seen in the current concern in both ugly and relatively benign ways in more or less worldwide controversies about restrictions on immigration, cultivation of restrictive national identities and the like (Papastergiadis, 1999). There is, admittedly, a fuzziness about the concept of unicity (to be distinguished from its use to refer to a unified *urban* complex) in that there are no criteria for deciding when unicity has been obtained. However, as will also be discussed at a later point, there is available to us a way of talking about globalization as an ongoingly self-limiting process via the concept of glo*c*alization (Robertson and White, 2004).

Various terms have been used to describe the present world circumstance that is being consolidated (or even consummated) by globalization – for example, *world society, world-system, global ecumene, global system, global society, the-world-as-a-single-place* and even more. Some of these entail substantial analytical arguments, while others are in themselves atheoretical. Yet other terms, such as *global arena* and *global field*, have been more calculatedly employed so as to maximize distance from any particular image of the globe or the world. Of at least equal importance are the actual quotidian 'images of the world' to be found in different places and/or among different groups of people (Robertson, 1992: 61–84; Hannerz, 1996; Holton, 1998: 33–41), for such images have great consequences for political movements. To put this more concretely, it makes a lot of difference whether the world as a whole is conceived of as being a *series of nation-states*, as *centered upon inter-national relations* or as a *system of societies*, seen as *a very large collection of individuals*, or as *defined by the human species relative to its environment* (Robertson, 1992: 61–84). These four basic possibilities – which can be combined into a number of images of the world – constitute, in fact, the form globalization has taken over the past five hundred years or so.

THE FORM OF GLOBALIZATION

There are, in principle, a number of different ways in which the world as a whole could have moved in the direction of unicity, which is most certainly *not* to be confused – as, in one way or another, it often is – with the idea of global integration or unification. This is a mistake that a number of individuals frequently make when they insist on the fragmentary aspects of globalization in binary opposition to its integrative aspects. A strong drive towards unicity could have happened under the aegis of a universal church, such as the Roman Catholic Church, as a world empire, or in yet other ways. Indeed, at various points in human history a number of projects for world organization have been advanced and serious steps taken towards implementing these, such as – in addition to our previous examples – international communism after the Russian Revolution of 1917 and the

Japanese project of the world under one Japanese roof, the latter being fully developed in the early 1940s. In very recent times a variety of world-encompassing, primarily religious, movements have arisen, notably in East Asian contexts. On the other hand, notwithstanding a considerable number of imperial projects, as well as religio-ideological ones, none has actually been successful, even though from the world-systems perspective of Wallerstein and the many who have been influenced by him different social formations and nation-states have been hegemonic at various points in history (Wallerstein, 1974, 1980, 1989; Chase-Dunn, 1989; Arrighi, 1994; Arrighi and Silver, 1999). In any case, the contributions to world formation made by projects of world domination or organization cannot be neglected. Currently there are many intellectuals and political leaders and activists who regard the United States as being engaged, particularly since September 11, 2001, in a project of world domination. In this respect the issues of Americanization and anti-Americanism have become central features of global culture (Robertson, 2003). The American policy of 'full spectrum dominance' announced in 2002 by the Bush administration in connection with the war against terrorism has raised this to new heights. The crucial subject of the place and the role of the United States in the contemporary world as a whole cannot entirely be ignored here, particularly because it occupies a complex mixture of centrality and marginality in the global circumstance. This was indirectly acknowledged by George W. Bush in his second inaugural Presidential address on January 20 2005, when he insisted that the future of 'freedom' and 'liberty' in the USA depended upon the achievement of these same ideals around the world.

As the world moves towards a condition of unicity, the temptations and the opportunities for world domination by an empire, ideology, religion or alliance of nation-states becomes that much more likely. Indeed, the events since September 11, 2001 have produced a global circumstance that illustrates very well the kind of catastrophic downside of globalization that a few writers, including the present authors, have been predicting as a possibility for the past twenty years or more. As globalization proceeds, it facilitates the kind of circumstance that has emerged since 9/11, in terms of electronic means of communication, rapid movements of peoples with the subsequent creation of diasporas, reappropriation of histories, 'familiarity' with distant regions of the world and so on.

Let us return more directly to the question of how the world has become increasingly characterized by (1) *extensive connectivity*, or interrelatedness, and (2) *extensive global consciousness*, a consciousness which continues to become more and more reflexive (Robertson, 1983; Tomlinson, 1999; Beck, 2000). These are, indeed, the two most important general features of the overall process of globalization. We can speak of cultural, social, political or economic globalization (or any combination thereof) in a general sense or we can deliberate upon the globalization *of* certain practices, activities, institutional structures and so on; but when we talk of globalization *per se*, we are referring to the two features of the human condition that have been specified concerning connectivity and global consciousness. These, in combination, constitute the move in the direction of global unicity, although the second has been much neglected relative to the first.

The form or, alternatively, the structural pattern that globalization has taken, certainly in recent centuries, consists of the four major components mentioned before: nation-states, inter-national relations, individual selves and humankind. Particularly since the fifteenth and sixteenth centuries, this form has been generalized beyond its home – namely Europe – and came much later to constitute the basis upon which the United Nations organization was established soon after the conclusion of the Second World War (1939–45). In spite of the importance of calculated projects of world formation on the part of specific organizations, movements, empires and so on, globalization is best seen in its most general sense as a relatively unguided process over the long haul. Hence the distinction between globalization as project(s) and globalization as process(es). But it must be emphasized that although this distinction is analytically easy to make, it is very difficult empirically to distinguish between the two at any given point in time. Long-term globalization is surely a mixture of project and process. Moreover as contemporary 'anti-globalization' movements have rapidly flourished in recent years, ideas concerning 'globalization from below' or people taking the control of globalization into their own hands have given a new significance to globalization-as-project.

Much of the literature on globalization has emphasized Western imperialism of one kind or another – as if imperialism were a Western invention (Spivak, 1999: 37) – and the hegemonic position of Western nation-states during the past five hundred years or so. Thus, for some, globalization has been a Western (more specifically, an American) project with the former colonies, and other dominated or threatened areas, being cast as victims of Western globalization. We, however, consider it to be necessary, for a number of reasons, to move away from this stress on victims, in order to make analytic space for the past, present and potential contributions of non-Western societies to globalization in its multidimensional sense – without going to the other, absurd extreme and regarding the world as one of relatively equal nation-states. In sum, a balance should be struck between a paradigm of blame involving simply exploiters and victims, on the one hand, and a paradigm of equality in which there is no room for power and inequality, on the other. In this regard, it is necessary to recognize that what are often called postcolonial studies have become part of the general globalization debate, as have closely related subaltern studies (e.g., Dirlik, 1994, 1996; Hall, 1996; Gandhi, 1998; Spivak, 1999; Sandoval, 2000; Robertson, 2005). The issues of postcoloniality and subalternity cannot, for reasons of space, be elaborated here. But this is certainly not intended to marginalize them, not least because a very emphatic feature of recent anti-globalization/anti-capitalist demonstrations has involved the very poor and exploited.

In the present era many international and transnational movements and international pressure groups have joined in the shaping of the world, although we should not neglect the transnational character of much older movements, of which the anti-slavery movement in the late eighteenth and nineteenth centuries is an excellent example. Nor should the transnational

nature of nationalist movements in the same and later periods be overlooked; this refuting the all-too-common tendency to think that globalization and nationalism are necessarily at odds with each other (compare Meyer, 1980 with, for example, Barber, 1995). In this connection it must be said that a very common mistake in the human sciences is to conflate analytical with empirical modes of inquiry. Specifically, there is a major difference between talking about, for example, world order in an analytical sense and, on the other hand, addressing this issue in empirical terms. There is, in other words, a distinction between the patterns that the analyst can discern at a high level of abstraction and the tangible fragmentation or, indeed, the conflict that he or she perceives.

It should be transparent that we conceive of globalization as a very long-term process, extending back through thousands of years. Many contributors to the discussion of globalization have seen it, on the other hand, as a relatively recent characteristic of the world as a whole. Our commitment to the perspective of globalization as a very long process raises the question as to the difference, if any, between it and the history of the world, or what some now call global history. Unfortunately, space limitations prevent discussion of this here, but it must be said that the interest in the history of the world has grown concomitantly with acceleration in the pace of globalization. Nonetheless, the current interest in globalization – at least in political and economic terms – in large part derives from the fall of the Berlin Wall late in 1989 and the subsequent and widespread belief that the world would, with the very extensive decline in communism, be 'globalized'. The latter meant in its more ideological form the marketization of the entire world, involving the triumph of neoliberal economic ideology with its commitment to free trade, privatization and deregulation.

There can be no easy answer to the question as to the difference between globalization and global history, although there are less than satisfactory ways of doing this. The most clear-cut case is if one maintains that globalization is a relatively recent process – a good example of this being Giddens's influential – but, we think, flawed – *The Consequences of Modernity* (1990), in which the author regards globalization as being facilitated, precipitated, even caused by, the rise of Western modernity (cf. Rosenberg, 2000). In this and other cases where globalization is conceived of as a recent phenomenon then it *is* simple to argue that our present interest in global history has been brought about because globalization has necessarily pushed us in that direction. As the world has moved – almost dramatically – toward unicity, then it is inevitable that we become ever more concerned with the whole rather than its parts. Moreover, since increasing connectivity and reflexive global consciousness involve much *compression* of the world (Harvey, 1989), then different regions and smaller parts of the world – notably, nation-states – are both constrained and enabled to identify themselves by producing their own unique histories and collective memories. Globalization, then, is the major factor in the current concern with the invention of tradition (Robertson, 1992: 146–63), much of it generated by Hobsbawm and Ranger (1983).

Thus, insofar as one regards globalization as a recent process, then one can acknowledge that it opens the way to interest in global history. If, however, one thinks of globalization as a very long historical process, then such acknowledgment is not so simple and the question of the degree to which global history and globalization are identical processes becomes much less avoidable. The skeleton of a solution lies in the following formulation. Whereas global history is, in its broadest scope, concerned with the history of mankind, globalization, on the other hand, dwells upon those aspects of global history that can plausibly be seen as related to the question as to moves towards or away from global unicity. This, of course, includes ostensibly anti-global movements.

OPPOSITION AND RESISTANCE TO 'GLOBALIZATION'

Much of that which has been included under the rubric of anti-globalization movements and activities has involved thinking of globalization not merely as an economic process but, even more narrowly, as a capitalist-economic one (cf. Mittelman, 2000: 163–249). To be sure, the leaders of many of these movements have come to the realization that globalization cannot, in one sense, be overcome for the, by now obvious, reason that the more that demonstrations against and communication about (capitalistic) globalization have proliferated and expanded, the more that globalization in a broader, more comprehensive sense is actually intensified. This applies most clearly to the period which began with the, particularly successful, demonstrations against the World Trade Organization (WTO) in Seattle, USA at the end of 1999. So anti-globalization in a primarily economic sense leads to *more* globalization in its comprehensive, multi-dimensional meaning (cf. Held and McGrew, 2002).

This in large part accounts for the emergence at the end of the 1990s of the theme of *globalization-from-below* (e.g., Falk, 1993). Globalization-from-below indicates a notable acceleration in the growth of global consciousness. More specifically, it represents a shift from the idea of an overarching macro process, a tidal wave overwhelming local specificities and self-identities. In any case, the theme of globalization-from-below is clearly related to ideas about global citizenship, cosmopolitan democracy, global ethics and new, extranational types of governance. These and other motifs are each related to the recently and widely thematized notions of (global) civil society and the (global) public sphere. These became particularly conspicuous topics of study among intellectuals and politicians following the collapse of much of Communism in late 1989. It was widely observed that totalitarian societies lacked a civil realm standing between and relatively detached from governments and individuals or their families, a realm in which debates and communication about human affairs could take place and movements could be mobilized. It is upon the back, so to speak, of the focus on national civil society in formerly Communist societies that much of the interest in (global) civil society has grown.

It will be recalled that, certainly over the past five centuries or so, the form, or structure, of the world as a whole has been centered on four major points of reference (Robertson, 1992):

(1) nation-states; (2) inter-national relations; (3) individual selves; and (4) humankind. Each of these has become more tangible – at first most clearly in Central and Western Europe – over the centuries, in such a way that together they form in the most general sense the world as a whole. Even though there is an ongoing debate as to whether the nation-state is in decline, there can be little doubt as to its still being the major container of human beings. Similarly, relations between and among nation-states remain crucial features of the global-human condition, notwithstanding aggregations of states such as the European Union (EU) or the North American Free Trade Association (NAFTA). Individual selves are clearly of major importance, as is well recognized, for example, in the discussion of and conflict about human rights (Ignatieff, 2001a). Humankind has come to be regarded as a concrete reality rather than a philosophical or theological idea, notably in the past one hundred and fifty years or so, via a variety of global-human tragedies such as slavery; two world wars, the European Holocaust and other more recent projects of ethnic cleansing; the use and spread of nuclear weapons; threats to the human species posed by disease (such as AIDS and SARS); extensive famines and national disasters; civil wars; the proliferation of a number of means of mass destruction; as well as the globe-wide, but fragile, institutionalization of the principle of crimes against humanity.

These four components of the global field (Robertson, 1992, 1994; cf. Robertson and Chirico, 1985) should be regarded for the most part as becoming more and more differentiated from each other over time, although differentiation should not be thought of as separation or fragmentation. Differentiation here refers to a process, or processes, of concretization of the components in relationships of *autonomy-within-reciprocity*. In other words, the components become more distinct but at the same time increasingly (and often problematically) interdependent. In addition, each component changes internally, often traumatically and conflictfully. The nation-state becomes more multicultural and/or polyethnic (e.g., Cornwell and Stoddard, 2001); international relations become more

polycentric and less predictably polarized (e.g., Keohane and Nye, 1989; Rosenau, 1990); selves become less singular, identities less fixed and loyalties more fluid (e.g., Elliott, 2001); and conceptions of humankind become unstable (Ignatieff, 2001b; Yearley, 1996) and less clearly bounded *vis-à-vis* nature and the growth in artificial modifications and extensions of human bodies. Along such lines different phases of globalization (Robertson, 1992; Waters, 1995) during the past five hundred years or so can be delineated. But it should be generally recognized that through the eighteenth and nineteenth centuries the idea of the world as a singular entity grew.[2] For example, by 1740 in the texts of French freemasons the world was being described as a single great republic, in 1784 Immanuel Kant spoke in his *On Perpetual Peace* of a cosmopolitan world (see also, Johnson, 1991; Messner, 2002: 22).

In this perspective globalization is obviously not a distinctively macro process. It is not something that occurs over and beyond our quotidian lives. In other words, globalization is not simply a horizontal, compressing process; it is also a vertical one. It pertains not just to the big phenomena of sociocultural life but also to the small aspects such as the life cycles of increasingly protean individuals. If we are addressing the subject of globalization, we are likewise interested, at least in principle, in everything pertaining to the most salient characteristics of the world as a whole.

Often this consideration has been approached in terms of the global/local distinction. Here similar problems arise, not least because it can well be argued that the local comes into focus the more that we are sensitized to the global (Appadurai, 1995; Dirlik, 1996). But there is in fact much to be said for the argument that the local is globally – or, at least, panlocally – produced. This may appear to some to be counter-intuitive, but there are both empirical and analytical reasons for insisting that there has to be a conception of the context before the text, of the universal before the particular, of the whole before the part, and so on (Robertson, 1992). Thus, the idea of the global is an all-encompassing one that does not entail the exclusion of what may simplistically be called the local, nor the microscopic. These ideas apply particularly to our inclusion of the individual self in the global field. Beck and Beck-Gernsheim (2002) have well demonstrated the significance of relatively recent processes of institutionalized individualization, which was also a major theme in the work of Parsons (Bourricaud, 1981). Parsons put much stress on the increasing complexity of social systems and the requirement that they need more and more constructive inputs from individuals. But this does not mean that such inputs are readily forthcoming, this having much to do with rising crime rates and lack of citizenly involvement. The complexity of the modern – or postmodern – world, with its very problematic emphasis upon the extension of *choice*, has much to do with consumerism, which we will consider briefly elsewhere.

For Beck and Beck-Gernsheim, as well as for Parsons, but for somewhat different reasons, individualism is a *structural feature* of much of the contemporary world. And here it is necessary to bring into consideration the innovative work of Meyer, who has convincingly shown during a long period of highly productive dedication to the analysis of world society, that the modern individual self is remarkably similar all over the world – although with local, particularistic variations. So much so that both of the two main aspects of the contemporary individual are shaped by global culture (Meyer, 1987; cf. Robertson, 2002a). These two aspects are the routinized individual playing standardized roles in contemporary, organized settings, on the one hand, *and* the existential self with her or his personal predilections and desires, on the other. Meyer's major point here is that both – the routinized and the existential – aspects are parts of the *institutionalized* individualism of which we have been speaking.

Another important aspect of the micro/macro and the local/global problem(s) is provided by Knorr Cetina and Bruegger (2001) and is associated with the previously mentioned work of Knorr Cetina on the postsocial. The paramount idea in the present context is the wish of Knorr Cetina and Bruegger to find analytic space within global theory for a *microsociology*

of such. This they do by employment of the concept of *global microstructures*, their empirical exemplification of this concept being the virtual societies of financial markets. The concept of global microstructure is of great relevance in the present context because it draws attention away from the macroscopic, tidal wave view of globalization. But, more important, in the writings of Knorr Cetina new categories of analysis directly relevant to the theme of globalization are suggested (although often in continuity with classical themes of social science). And it is via her work that we can move to a short consideration of the important writings of Manuel Castells (Castells, 1996, 1997, 1998; Castells et al., 1999).

Wittel (2001) sees significant affinities between, *inter alia*, the writings of Castells, Sennett (1978, 1998), Beck (1999), Lash (2002) and Knorr Cetina. As Wittel (2001: 64) puts it: 'Knorr Cetina has one foot in individualization theory, and another in actor-network theory, and provides a framework for connecting both of them.' In the present context we indicate the significance of individualization, de-socialization and network solidarity principally in order to highlight the so-called microscopic aspects of globalization and to demonstrate, to use McLuhan's evocative words, that 'world life' (McLuhan and Powers, 1989) is, when all is said and done, at the heart of the discourse of globalization. Nonetheless, Wittel's proposition is that rather than speaking of de-socialization, as Knorr Cetina does, it is better to speak of 'a shift away from regimes of sociality in closed social systems and towards regimes of sociality in open social systems' (Wittel, 2001: 64–5). So the basic question here is whether network sociality is merely a technological sociality or not. Our own inclination is to argue that there is much continuity between 'pure sociality' (Simmel) and cyberspatial sociality. Indeed, we are prepared to say that to cling to pre-electronic forms of sociality as the real, authentic – even essentialistic – type of sociality is a form of nostalgia. In any case, it should be said in reference to Castells's work that his is normally regarded as a global *macro-sociology* of the information age (Wittel, 2001: 51). Wittel's strategy is attractive – namely, to translate this macro-sociology of a network society into a micro-sociology of the information age. This involves focusing not on 'networks themselves, but on the making of networks'. In other words, 'what kind of sociality is at stake in the information age?' (Wittel, 2001: 52).

ALIGNING THE GLOBAL AND THE LOCAL

In one respect, the use of the term glocalization (Robertson, 1992, 1994, 1995a; Robertson and White, 2004) may be regarded as a way of slicing through the numerous conundra thrown in our paths by the insistence on the significance of the global/local distinction, while in so doing it draws definite attention to *spatiality*. For while globalization *per se* refers to a *temporal* process, glocalization injects a spatial dimension in its emphasis upon the *necessarily* spatial distribution of that which is being globalized (Robertson, 1995a; Robertson and White, 2004). In other words, rather than stating that a big problem arises from the latter, we can obliterate much of it by responding that the concepts of the global and the local can, and should, be synthesized, even that they are complicitous (Stanford Friedman, 1998: 110). A second and more substantial reason for elevating the concept of glocalization within the array of globalization-relevant motifs is that it has a strong bearing on the homogenization thesis. It is in relation to the latter that the concept of glocalization is most usefully elaborated (Robertson, 1995a). This thesis pivots on the claim that the central – for some the defining – aspect of globalization is that the world is being swept by forces making for sameness, for global standardization of culture and institutional structures. Much of this contention adheres to the cultural imperialism argument that a few societies of the West or a single society, the United States, impose(s) culture upon many other societies. This has been encapsulated in the influential McDonaldization thesis (Ritzer, 2000, 2002), which claims that the fast-food preparation methods of McDonald's restaurants, originating in the United States, are dominating the world in a heavily standardized way,

extending well beyond McDonald's restaurants themselves, including the most intimate aspects of our lives. In other words, McDonald's production and promotion methods are taken as a paradigm of Americanization, one which has increasing applicability to a number of Western-based transnational corporations, as well as to smaller enterprises – indeed, to much of everyday life.

While the McDonaldization argument can be subsumed under the thesis of cultural imperialism (although strictly the former is not confined to culture *per se*), there is another aspect of sameness that is of equal importance when discussing the homogenization proposition. This has to do with the fact that we can see around the world much similarity with respect to the various structural features of nation-states. In other words, there is a remarkable degree of *isomorphism* with respect to the structure of modern nation-states, a key feature of the work of Meyer and those influenced by him. Some would try to account for this in terms paralleling the cultural imperialism thesis, others would argue that isomorphisms can be accounted for in terms of the *diffusion*, without imperialist intent, of structural forms – the diffusionist argument also being applicable to culture (cf. Buell, 1994). But a third way of considering this crucial issue, a way that is not by any means entirely at odds with the isomorphism argument, is in terms of the concept of glocalization. For whereas the isomorphism approach depends much on the idea of there being a world culture that provides models for structural and other phenomena, the glocalization tack underlines the more processual aspect of what is approximately the same problem (Meyer et al., 1997).

Although the term glocalization as such is not used in the book edited by Watson (1997) on McDonald's in East Asia, he argues, apparently contra Ritzer, that McDonald's is a vehicle for *localization*. In other words, the cities in East Asia examined by Watson and his contributors each have their own particular variation on the *universality* of McDonald's. Thus although we are not arguing that the issue of the economic strength of transnational corporations is thereby diminished, the argument in Watson's volume is but part of a growing literature on the ways in which the particular enables the universal to work and, indeed, how homogenizing forces actually produce heterogeneous tendencies. In certain respects, the world *is* becoming very similar. But at the same time, this similarity is *sustained by difference.* Products of various kinds gain purchase in specific locales, particular ethnic and gender groups, and so on, through adaptation to these *different* circumstances. Thus we can most usefully speak of *sameness-within-difference.*

It may be said that globalization cannot occur without the global spread of ideas and models being adaptable to particular circumstances – circumstances that should not be regarded in an essentialistic way, for they may be invented, particularly, but not only, for niche marketing, in the broadest sense. Globalization must have some limits – unless one thinks in terms of its leading inexorably to a highly standardized, claustrophobically compressed and entropic world – and so it then behooves us to be aware of these. Our contention is that there *are* built-in brakes on globalization, namely those inherent in the unavoidable necessity of adaptation to – or 'production' of – particular circumstances. Hence the proposition that globalization is self-limiting. Moreover, what is often called local resistance against globalization is a reflexive form of glocalization. We can, in fact, speak of *normative* glocalization. People consciously attempt to localize seemingly homogenizing forces, this being a particularly contemporary form of *reflexive* global consciousness.

In the hands of Meyer, Boli, Thomas and others, isomorphism among social-structural, cultural and individual features of the world occurs as the consequence of models provided by world culture, models which are *enacted* by the many, many collective and individual actors in the global arena.[3] There is in this perspective, however, relatively little attention given to the *selective emulation* or *incorporation* of the features of some nation-states rather than others (Westney, 1987; Robertson, 1995b). In contrast we argue that emulation and rejection have been core features of global change – more specifically of globalization and glocalization – through much of human history, but particularly since the advent of the nation-state.

IMPLICATIONS OF ECONOMIC REDUCTIONISM

During the 1990s globalization became a new way of speaking of capitalism with special reference to the global, or – in the cogent perspective of Hirst and Thompson (1996) – international, economy; and a new international, or supranational, organization, the World Trade Organization (WTO), was created to enforce the rules of globewide capitalism. The blatant signs of increasing international (and intranational) inequality have exacerbated opposition to transnational corporations and to capitalistic globalization. This has been made the more intense by various decisions of the International Monetary Fund (IMF) and the World Bank, centered on the manner in which, often very heavy, constraints were placed on countries needing loans to allow them some chance of overcoming big economic problems. Often nation-states have been required seriously to cut back on their educational and welfare services – in sum, to reduce substantially state expenditure in order to facilitate the repayment of loans granted by the IMF. The whole problem of Third World debt and agitation for the forgiveness thereof has very often been at the center of so-called anti-globalization demonstrations. The latter have included opposition to G8 summits, the annual assemblies of the world's major economic superpowers.

Having said this in a somewhat anti-capitalist vein, there is a not entirely ineffective case to be made *for* economic globalization in this regard. Many of the anti-globalization demonstrations draw upon ill-informed views concerning the operation and principles of the IMF, the WTO and the World Bank – more particularly the long-term effects of relatively capitalistic globalization. In rhetorical terms, if not in practice, many prominent world politicians, including Western ones, have conceded that international inequality is unacceptable. Simply put, we have yet to see whether the ostensible liberalization of markets will bring significant benefits to the deprived and exploited. Nor have we, on the other hand, sufficiently contemplated the protectionist implications of much of the anti-globalization movement. For a relatively rare argument against globalization by a mainstream economist, see Stiglitz (2002) and, for a contrasting view, see Sen (2000).

One of the most addressed aspects of globalization has been that of consumerism (e.g., Featherstone, 1991; Urry, 1995; Sklair, 1995; Howes, 1996; Jameson, 1998; de Mooij, 1998; Ritzer et al., 2001). It is with regard to this topic that we can readily see the ways in which globalization and glocalization have gained so much momentum in the past fifty years or so (Robertson, 1994, 1995a). For one of the seeming ironies of globalization is that capitalism has highlighted the salience of global culture.

So-called micromarketing (Tharpe, 2001) is in fact a central feature of what Sklair (1995, 2001) calls the culture-ideology of consumerism; even though he neglects the vitality, at least in a superficial sense, supplied to worldwide capitalism by the phenomenon of glocalization. Thus, cultural difference – not to speak of culture production – is crucial to modern capitalism. Currently there is much emphasis on stress as a motivation for purchasing goods and services. It has been shown in a number of European countries that purchasing fragrances, cosmetics, desserts, confectioneries and wine is being undertaken by half of the consumers of such as a means of alleviating stress. But, of course, stress is in large part a *product* of advertising strategies and of excessive choice (as 'real' as stress itself may also be). Jameson (1998: 69) has effectively put the issue: 'the reason why so many people feel that this boring and archaic thing is sexy … results from the sweetening of this pill by all kinds of images of consumption as such: commodity, as it were, becoming its own ideology' (Jameson, 1998: 69).

Clearly, in spite of claims to the contrary, people do not simply consume things because they autonomously desire to do so. Most forms of consumption are embedded – like capitalism(s) itself/themselves in culture (more narrowly, ideology) – which is not to deny that those cultures or ideologies are themselves 'simply there'. The fact is that we live at a time when culture and economy are ever-more intertwined (cf. Ray and Sayer, 1999; Thrift, 1999). The economy is culture-producing and commodifying.

We must recognize that the economic reductionist stance has facilitated the opening up of new domains of analysis – notably the study of global civil society, post-national, regional and global shifts in the conception of citizenship, and transnational forms of governance. So in spite of narrowing even more the capitalistic leanings of many current understandings of globalization, the anti-globalization – increasingly called the anti-capitalist (or, not infrequently, the 'anarchist') – movement has helped in prising open even more areas of inquiry that might not otherwise have received as much attention as they have. Of these not the least important is the growing interest in the organization of global and transnational movements (Guidry et al., 2000), even though this concern with capitalistic-economic globalization should not, by any means, be considered as *the* determinant of expanding interest in global civil society, global citizenship, global or transnational government and so on. Rather, the economization of the idea of globalization gave much of such interest an extra push. Moreover, the idea of global civil society was developed relatively independently in media studies (e.g., Volkmer, 1999; Keane, 2003), while environmental, legal and health questions have also led to these expanding foci.

Definite, conceptual use of the idea of globalization began, as we have seen, around 1980; although the work of a number of sociologists, political scientists, media analysts and others prepared the way for this by stepping out of their disciplinary boundaries to study transnational and global phenomena. For the most part, matters beyond societal boundaries were studied only by specialists in the field of international relations (cf. Nettl and Robertson, 1968). One of the stimuli within sociology and political science for moving towards a global perspective was located in the field of modernization studies. With the wave of decolonization which began after the end of the Second World War in 1945 and accelerated considerably in the late 1950s and early 1960s – as well as with the Allied attempts to reconstruct (West) Germany and Japan that had been envisaged before 1945 and then put into operation in the years following the end of the war – there arose a considerable interest in nation-building and the prospects for progress within newly independent nations. But, for the most part, the *comparison* of nations within the Third World category, and with nations that had moved upwards and beyond it was undertaken with little or no regard for the *interaction* of nations.

Eventually, during the late 1960s and early 1970s a few sociologists and political scientists began to see that comparison by the political leaders and intellectuals within nation-states of the conditions of their own nations with other nations was a crucial factor in coming to terms with international inequality and the concept of modernization. To this extent it was necessary also to comprehend how the modern world-system had come into existence at all, including the part played by international, inter-regional and intercivilizational factors (Nettl and Robertson, 1968; Wallerstein, 1974, 1980, 1989; Bergesen, 1980; Nelson, 1981).

Thus by the late 1970s and early 1980s the scene was set for the development of intellectual work concerned with study of the world as a whole. It was in these years that the concept of globalization first began to be used with any frequency or emphasis. Those already within or moving into the field of analyzing the making of the modern world, needless to say, did not do so in a consensual way or with the same motivations. Some of the earlier sociological contributors of significance to the discussion of the world as a whole were concerned above all with peace-making; others were primarily concerned with the demise of world capitalism and the coming of world socialism, most notably the American historical sociologist, Immanuel Wallerstein. Yet others were primarily analytical social scientists with no set political agenda (see also Lagos, 1963; Horowitz, 1966). A particularly crucial, but greatly neglected venture into the analysis of the world as a whole was that of Talcott Parsons (1971), whose approach had some affinity with that of Nettl and Robertson (see also Luhmann, 1997).

Of the perspectives just mentioned – and there were also others – it was that of Wallerstein which most emphasized the causal significance of economic-material factors, relegating other aspects to epiphenomenal status. But its emphasis upon the economic dimension in socialist perspective was so distinctive as to make it immune from being associated with the *capitalistic* advocates of globalization who became increasingly numerous from the late 1980s onward. Thus world-systems analysts could easily, for the most part, take an anti-globalization posture when such became fashionable in the mid-1990s. In fact, without using the exact term globalization they, particularly Wallerstein himself, had been doing that for quite a few years before then (Robertson and Lechner, 1985). Ironically and somewhat perversely, it was largely 9/11 that made the multi-dimensional character of globalization very apparent again – notably with its clear reintroduction of cultural and religious factors into the debate. But quite apart from these post-9/11 circumstances, the focus of the anti-globalization movement and talk of *globalization-from-below*, rather than stressing the local against the global, enhanced existing interest in new forms of citizenship, civil society and the like (e.g., Mander and Goldsmith, 1996). In fact much of the debate about these arose within the context of concern with economic inequality, global justice and lack of control over the activities of transnational corporations. But this is not to say that interest in such grew only within the anti-globalization perspective, but such interest was certainly given an extra push by anti-globalization activity. Indeed, the anti-globalization movement provided a great impetus for the expansion of NGOs in cyberspace, as has the Al-Qaeda movement (Naim, 2002), which Chandra and Talbott (2001: xi) speak of as 'the ultimate NGO'.

GLOBAL CITIZENSHIP, GLOBAL CIVIL SOCIETY AND HUMAN RIGHTS

The idea of global citizenship grew in a general sense through the 1980s and 1990s (Rotblat, 1997) as part of what has been called the global turn. One particular result of this was the expanding focus on environmental issues. This was reflected in the growth of Green political movements in a number of European countries and more diffusely in the increasing attention to environmental themes in what at first, particularly in the United States, was called international education. We should not, however, privilege environmental concerns too much, for the peace movement which grew in Europe in the 1950s and 1960s in response to the nuclear threats posed by the Cold War was also crucial. The nuclear threat and fear of environmental damage were closely linked. More recently this form of pedagogy has just as often been called, more accurately, global education. The intensification of globalization has simultaneously increased educational foci around the globe both on the wider world and, reactively, upon national identity. In fact these two opposing tugs are a major feature of educational debates in a number of countries; although concern with nationalism and national identity is *part-and-parcel* of the general globalization process.

The swelling interest in the late 1980s and the 1990s in the ideal of global citizenship was also part of growing academic concern with citizenship generally, much of it being the result of interventions by feminist theorists (e.g., Duran, 2001) and/or writers specializing in ethnicity and race (cf. Delanty, 2000). But since the main paradigm for studying citizenship had, prior to the 1980s, been developed in terms of *national* citizenship, the advent of the focus on the global circumstance has necessitated rethinking. Much of the latter has been occasioned by the multicultural/polyethnic stance brought about by waves of migration, residence abroad, the flight of refugees and ethnic cleansing (cf. Jacobson, 1996). For long, particularly from the mid-eighteenth century onward, the idea of the nation-state had entailed the homogenization of newcomers (McNeill, 1986), but by the 1960s it was becoming clear that the idea of the national society being a melting pot – a much-used characterization of the United States from the 1920s through the 1960s – was giving way to what had by the 1980s widely come to be labelled the multicultural society. Or, as McNeill (1986) argued, we have been experiencing the return of the polyethnic norm.

But the widely recognized, but not as widely accepted, conception of the multiculturality, or polyethnicity, of the nation-state at the beginning of the twenty-first century has brought with it a concern with problems of social cohesion within and loyalty to nation-states. In fact, 9/11 produced a particular panic in some Western societies as to whether refugees or immigrants were being sufficiently socialized into their new national homes. At this time of writing the fear of immigration and concern with enforcing citizenly commitment on immigrants is growing ever-stronger. There has developed at one and the same time a concern with cohesion, common values and national identities and traditions (Macedo, 1999) and the opposing thematization of cosmopolitanism, the latter being of great importance as a feature of globalization. Cosmopolitanism entails the idea of people – both as individuals and as collectivities – being open to and involved, to varying degrees, in nations other than their own. Indeed, in a highly cosmopolitan world, many people would have multiple nationalities, or, conceivably, none. As Nussbaum points out, the very old ideal of the cosmopolitan referred to a person whose allegiance was to the worldwide community of human beings (Nussbaum, 1996; also Rapoport, 1997; Robbins, 1999: 147–68). In our time, however, there is a plurality of cosmopolitanisms, in large part because cosmopolitanism as a phenomenon actually exists in a variety of, sometimes banal, forms in different parts of the world (Robbins, 1998: 2). Many people are increasingly cosmopolitan by virtue of travel, communication, long-distance friendship, fashion, entertainment, museum attendance, e-mail and so on, but they do not – apparently, for the most part – reflect upon what this means for humanity (as far as we can tell). In any case, the recent increase in various types of tourism – for example, faith, ecological, archaeological, gastronomic, espionage, battle, sex, medical and cosmetic surgical – has been considerable (Urry, 2002).

These are the kinds of consideration which are of particular concern also to those involved in considering the present condition of citizenship (van Steebergen, 1994; Beiner, 1995; Delanty, 2000). The specific notion of *global* citizenship can be looked at from two main viewpoints. It can, on the one hand, be discussed in terms of empirical trends, insofar as one can generalize across the world about such. On the other hand, global citizenship can be thought of normatively, as an ideal to which we should aspire out of necessity and/or as a global virtue. As far as the first of these is concerned, national citizenship has become problematic – quite apart from the apparent alienation of the adult populations of many nation-states from their governmental affairs – because of the fact that large numbers of people now live in nation-states of which they are not *national* members. It has also become problematic because there are so many matters of *governance* that cannot be dealt with entirely by the governments of nation-states (Falk, 1994, 2000a; Held, 1995; Kennedy et al., 2002). Some of these we have touched on before, but in any case problems of governance include, *inter alia*, transnational crime, 'terrorism', environmental issues and refugees.

All in all, particularly in view of the two major general aspects of globalization – increasing connectivity and increasing reflexive global consciousness – the concerns of individuals as to the way in which they are governed tend to lead either in the direction of a minimalist conception of cosmopolitan citizenship or to detachment from citizenship, as conventionally understood, altogether. The latter entails an emphasis upon *universal personhood* (Soysal, 1994) or even *netizenship*, participation in global or transnational affairs on the basis of Internet communication and the establishment and reading of websites. Thus when global citizenship is advocated as a desirable state of affairs, this must take full account of the actually existing *form* – the parameters – of the global circumstance, this having been discussed in a different respect in much of the above. At the same time, the current state of globalization compels us to advocate global citizenship, even though it is not easy to see how such would actually operate in a formal sense. This problem is bound up with the equally important, but certainly not unproblematic, phenomenon of cosmopolitan *governance* (Held, 1995; Archibugi et al., 1998). The normative ideal of global citizenship is sometimes used simply to refer to an attitude, or as a mode of being-in-the-world.

Or it may involve an active participation in and/or contribution to what one perceives as the good of the world – for example, dedicating oneself to teaching about the world as a whole, writing about it, or organizing and taking part in a movement whose purpose is to improve a particular aspect of the world as a whole. Yet in talking in this way one has to be very conscious, at least from the analytic standpoint, of the fact that conceptions of what constitutes the world will vary according to which of the four main components of the global field is (are) emphasized the most; although full awareness of the different components will make it more likely that a person will not *reduce* his or her understanding of the world to one or two components. This means that reading, thinking and teaching about comprehensive, long-term globalization should increasingly become a pivotal feature of citizenship education and learning.

The strongly emerging theme of civil society is a relatively untheorized concept, but refers minimally to the social space that lies between the state and the individuals in their familial networks. Totalitarian and highly authoritarian societies lack such space. The addition of the qualifier 'global' to civil society raises the slightly different question as to an analytic space for debate about the future of world or global society and the conduct of cultural, social, political and economic affairs within it, as well as the relationship between this society and its natural and cosmic environment. To be more specific, global civil society is a domain where values and ideas concerning the affairs within and between nation-states, as well as the global–human situation as a whole, can be debated. A particular problem in this regard is the principle of non-interference in the internal affairs of member nation-states of the UN, a protocol which, strictly speaking, clashes with the idea of a global civil society that sets standards through dialogue and debate, for various internal matters, notably human rights. Likewise, the European Union has steadily increased the demands that it makes on its nation-state members through a range of laws that were previously regarded as entirely matters for internal legislatures. The need for a global civil society has developed in tandem with the speed and scope of globalization. Or to put this another way, the more differentiated the four major components of the global field become, the more there is a sphere of discourse to deal with this differentiation. This means that discussion of global society is located in diagrammatic terms *in the middle region* of our four-fold depiction of the global field.

Such developments have either been interpreted as an expansion of global civil society (e.g., Archibugi et al., 1998; Scholte, 2000; Edwards and Gaventa, 2001) or as the growth of a transnational public sphere (Calhoun, 2002). Although on occasions a distinction is made between the two notions, such is not necessary here. Suffice it to say that a development of this kind has undoubtedly been a prerequisite for the burgeoning of concern with human rights, global citizenship and matters of family resemblance. Of these it is the theme of human rights to which we must now turn, bearing in mind that it is the drive toward unicity which encourages this issue. But it should also be kept in mind that, while, for many, human rights is a matter of strictly ethical concern, being closely tied in fact to the problematic of global ethics (Dower, 1998; Robertson, 2001b), it has likewise become central to international relations, or world politics, in combination with national strategies (or *Realpolitik*).

Sensitivity to human rights has greatly expanded since the late eighteenth century (Lauren, 1998; Falk, 2000b), with the Napoleonic War, plus the two world wars of the twentieth century, occasioning numerous declarations, protocols and laws. The early twentieth century witnessed an acceleration of this, centered on the Standard of Civilization in what some have called international society (Gong, 1984). This standard had its heyday in the first quarter of the twentieth century and became a crucial feature of international law. It was to a considerable extent a consequence of the imposition on East Asian countries of the domestic laws of European nation-states in the areas seized by the latter. During the various catastrophic events of recent decades, human rights have been the object of growing agitation and declaration.

With the extensive amount of migration, the creation of transnational diasporas (Portes,

2000; cf. Gilroy, 1993; Cohen, 1997) and the slow and uneven acceptance around much of the world of the multicultural/polyethnic nation-state, there has arisen a number of problems in connection with the idea of human rights. To put it more concretely, there has been in the United States – until recently, at least, the paradigm case of a multicultural/polyethnic society – the so-called cultural defense. This involves defendants in court cases claiming that what they have been charged with is a generally accepted practice in their country of origin. This defense has been made in such cases as female genital mutilation (or female circumcision), wife beating, animal sacrifice and other practices alien to Western norms and laws.

Much of the tension resulting from clashes over human rights comes from the *relativization* of certain worldviews and practices. In fact, relativization is one of the core aspects of globalization over the long haul (Robertson, 1985, 1992). To put this mythologically, one might well say that when the first two 'tribes' met, then began globalization. For each group the encounter with the Other inevitably had very significant consequences. There was the option for one or both to adhere steadfastly to the original worldview(s); there was the option, at the other extreme, of one or both deciding to co-exist with the Other. Global history generally can be considered in such terms, but with respect to the more specific issue of globalization, it is, we would maintain, *the* central thematic. In other words, the unicity – but not, of course, integration – of the world has been formed through a very lengthy series of constructions and counter-constructions of collective Selves and collective Others. Once relatively well established, these Selves and Others have been involved in encounters with each other, continuously raising problems of relativization. Thus, the historical and geographical dimensions of these constructions are highly relevant to globalization as well as to the issue of relativization – which has a great bearing on the current conflict between Islam and the West.

But we cannot go into details of relativization here. The general point is that increasing connectivity – which may range from complete symmetry to much asymmetry with respect to power – has crystallized over the centuries, as has global consciousness, in the sense that such encounters involve elevating *the problem* of shared consciousness, that problem having become worldwide in its reach. This is, in more technical terms, the problem of value generalization, as well as that of greater inclusion (Parsons, 1977). Throughout world history, encounters between, as well as social constructions of, civilizations have been of profound – and often very long-run – significance (e.g., Beardsell, 2000; Fey and Racine, 2000; Hallam and Street, 2000; Hendry, 2000; Nelson, 1981; Roudometof and Robertson, 1995). They have, of course, been the cause of wars – which must *also* be included in the odyssey of globalization. In fact, the designation of 'the global age' (Albrow, 1996) as the period of the Third World War (frighteningly, for most people) consolidates this thesis.

CONCLUSION: SOCIOLOGY AND DISCIPLINARITY

Bauman (2003: 156) has written that:

> at no other time have the keen search for common humanity and the practice that follows such an assumption been as urgent and imperative as they are now. … In the era of globalization, the cause and the politics of shared humanity face the most fateful of the many fateful steps they have made in their long history.

As has been emphasized at the outset we live now at a time of great disciplinary mutation. The position of sociology in this situation of flux is not at all clear. However it can certainly be said that the theme of globalization has been the major site upon which these changes have been and continue to be wrought. Moreover, it seems very clear to the present authors that not merely has globalization been a field of study which has led to rapid disciplinary mutation, it has also resurrected the old question as to what Comte called the hierarchy of the sciences. We dare to reiterate that sociology was, so to say, in from the outset of the current interest in globalization and related issues. More accurately, the disciplines of sociology, anthropology and religious studies were particularly conspicuous in the rapid development of 'the global paradigm'. To be sure, it is only fair to say that other disciplines, or sub-disciplines, were working along lines similar to those which have been laid down

during the last twenty-five years or so. Nonetheless the question here has to be confronted as to the related matters concerning whether, on the one hand, we are passing through a stage of the reconstruction of the disciplines as we have canonically known them for the last hundred years or, on the other hand, we are participants in the demise of disciplinarity.

In either case it is here postulated that sociology has an increasingly significant role, even if that role may only be fuzzily demarcated. We conclude simply by stating that sociology, in whatever form, is at the fulcrum of the globalization debate. Moreover, this new type of sociology will undoubtedly transcend old issues concerning 'value-neutrality', 'objectivity' or their opposites. We are now, as Bauman suggests, unavoidably participants in struggles about the way in which the world is becoming for-itself, as opposed to being merely in-itself.

NOTES

1 The overall discussion here draws quite a lot from Robertson (1992), Robertson and White (2003) and Robertson and White (2004). It is crucial for the reader to recognize that the present chapter was largely written when the events of 9/11 and their aftermath were particularly salient. Much of relevance has occurred since then, notably the Tsunami earthquake of late December, 2004.

2 There is a great need for serious analysis of *ancient* ideas about the terrestrial world (Robertson and Inglis, 2004; Inglis and Robertson, 2004).

3 The very important issue of culture is not directly discussed much in the present context. It has, however, been crucial in the development of the study of globalization, most notably in the writings of the present authors and in the work of the so-called Stanford school led by Meyer.

BIBLIOGRAPHY

Albrow, Martin (1996) *The Global Age: State and Society Beyond Modernity*. Stanford, CA: Stanford University Press.

Anderson, Walter Truett (2001) *All Connected Now: Life in the First Global Civilization*. Boulder, CO: Westview Press.

Appadurai, Arjun (1995) 'The production of locality', in Richard Pardon (ed.), *Counterworks: Managing the Diversity of Knowledge*. London: Routledge. pp. 204–25.

Archibugi, Daniele, Held, David and Kohler, Martin (eds) (1998) *Re-imagining Political Community: Studies in Cosmopolitan Democracy*. Cambridge: Polity Press.

Arrighi, Giovanni (1994) *The Long Twentieth Century: Money, Power and the Origins of Our Times*. London: Verso.

Arrighi, Giovanni and Silver, Beverly J. (1999) *Chaos and Governance in the Modern World System*. Minneapolis, MN: University of Minnesota Press.

Barber, Benjamin (1995) *Jihad vs. McWorld*. New York: Ballantine Books.

Bauman, Zymunt (2003) *Liquid Love*. Cambridge: Polity Press.

Beardsell, Peter (2000) *Europe and Latin America: Returning the Gaze*. Manchester: Manchester University Press.

Beck, Ulrich (1999) *World Risk Society*. Cambridge: Polity Press.

Beck, Ulrich (2000) *What is Globalization?* Cambridge: Polity Press.

Beck, Ulrich and Beck-Gernsheim, Elizabeth (2002) *Individualization*. London: Sage.

Beiner, Ronald (ed.) (1995) *Theorizing Citizenship*. Albany, NY: State University of New York Press.

Bergesen, Albert (ed.) (1980) *Studies in the Modern World System*. New York: Academic Press.

Beyer, Peter F. (1994) *Religion and Globalization*. London: Sage.

Beynon, John and Dunkerley, David (eds) (2000) *Globalization: The Reader*. London: Athlone Press.

Boli, John and Thomas, George M. (eds) (1999) *Constructing World Culture: International Non-governmental Organizations Since 1875*. Stanford, CA: Stanford University Press.

Bourricaud, François (1981) *The Sociology of Talcott Parsons*. Chicago: University of Chicago Press.

Buell, Frederick (1994) *National Culture and the New Global System*. Baltimore, MD: Johns Hopkins Press.

Calhoun, Craig (2002) 'Imagining solidarity: cosmopolitanism, constitutional patriotism, and the public sphere', *Public Culture*, 14 (1): 147–71.

Castells, Manuel (1996) *The Rise of the Network Society*. Oxford: Blackwell.

Castells, Manuel (1997) *The Power of Identity*. Oxford: Blackwell.

Castells, Manuel (1998) *End of Millennium*. Oxford: Blackwell.

Castells, Manuel, Flecha, Ramon, Freire, Paulo, Giroux, Henry A., Macedo, Donaldo and Willis, Paul (1999) *Critical Education in the New Information Age*. Lanham, MD: Rowman and Littlefield.

Chandra, Nayan and Talbott, Strobe (2001) 'Introduction', in Strobe Talbott and Nayan Chandra (eds) *The Age of Terror: America and the World After September 11*. Oxford: Perseus Books. pp. vii–xix.

Chase-Dunn, Christopher (1989) *Global Formation*. Oxford: Blackwell.

Cochrane, Allan and Kathy Pain (2000) 'A globalizing society', in David Held (ed.), *A Globalizing World? Culture, Economics, Politics*. London: Routledge. pp. 5–45.

Cohen, Robin (1997) *Global Diasporas: An Introduction*. London: UCL Press.

Cohen, Robin and Kennedy, Paul (2000) *Global Sociology*. Basingstoke: Palgrave.

Cornwell, Grant H. and Walsh Stoddard, Eve (eds) (2001) *Global Multiculturalism: Comparative Perspectives on Ethnicity, Race and Nation*. Lanham, MD: Rowman and Littlefield.

Delanty, Gerard (2000) *Citizenship in a Global Age*. Buckingham: Open University Press.

de Mooij, Marieke (1998) *Global Marketing and Advertising: Understanding Cultural Paradoxes*. Thousand Oaks, CA: Sage.

Dirlik, Arif (1994) 'The postcolonial aura: Third World criticism in the age of global capitalism', *Critical Inquiry*, 20: 328–56.

Dirlik, Arif (1996) 'The global in the local', in Rob Wilson and Wimal Dissanayake (eds), *Global/Local: Cultural Production and the Transnational Imaginary*. Durham, NC: Duke University Press. pp. 21–45.

Dower, Nigel (1998) *World Ethics*. Edinburgh: Edinburgh University Press.

Duran, Jane (2001) *Worlds of Knowing: Global Feminist Epistemologies*. London: Routledge.

Edwards, Michael and Gaventa, John (eds) (2001) *Global Citizen Action*. Boulder, CO: Lynne Rienner.

Elliott, Anthony (2001) *Concepts of the Self*. Cambridge: Polity Press.

Falk, Richard (1993) 'Revisiting globalization-from-above through globalization-from-below', *New Political Economy*, 2 (1): 17–24.

Falk, Richard (1994) 'The making of global citizenship', in Bart van Steenbergen (ed.), *The Condition of Citizenship*. London: Sage. pp. 127–40.

Falk, Richard (2000a) 'The quest for humane governance in an era of globalization', in Don Kalb et al. (eds), *The Ends of Globalization: Bringing Society Back In*. Lanham, MD: Rowman and Littlefield. pp. 369–82.

Falk, Richard A. (2000b) *Human Rights Horizons*. New York: Routledge.

Featherstone, Mike (1991) *Consumer Culture and Postmodernism*. London: Sage.

Fey, Ingrid E. and Racine, Karen (eds) (2000) *Strange Pilgrimages: Exile, Travel, and National Identity in*

Latin America, 1800–1990s. Wilmington, DE: Scholarly Press.

Gandhi, Leela (1998) *Postcolonial Theory: A Critical Introduction.* Edinburgh: Edinburgh University Press.

George, Susan (2004) *Another world is possible if …* London: Verso.

Giddens, Anthony (1990) *The Consequences of Modernity.* Stanford, CA: Stanford University Press.

Gilroy, Paul (1993) *The Black Atlantic: Modernity and Double Consciousness.* Cambridge, MA: Harvard University Press.

Giulianotti, Richard (2005) *Sport: A Critical Sociology.* Cambridge: Polity Press.

Giulianotti, Richard and Robertson, Roland (2001) 'Glocalization, transnational corporations and democratic governance: an analysis of the globalization of football', in Peter Loesche, Undine Ruge and Klaus Stolz (eds), *Yearbook of European and North American Studies,* Vol. 5. Goettingen: University of Goettingen Press. pp. 219–51.

Gong, Gerrit W. (1984) *The Standard of Civilization in International Society.* Oxford: Oxford University Press.

Guidry, John A., Kennedy, Michael D. and Zald, Mayer N. (eds) (2000) *Globalizations and Social Movements: Culture, Power and the Transnational Public Sphere.* Ann Arbor, MI: University of Michigan Press.

Hakken, David (1999) *Cyborgs @ Cyberspace: An Ethnographer Looks to the Future.* London: Routledge.

Hall, Stuart (1996) 'When was the post-colonial? Thinking at the limit', in I. Chambers and L. Curtis (eds), *The Post-Colonial Question: Common Skies, Divided Horizons.* London: Routledge. pp. 242–60.

Hallam, Elizabeth and Street, Brian V. (eds) (2000) *Cultural Encounters: Representing Otherness.* London: Routledge.

Hannerz, Ulf (1996) *Transnational Connections.* London: Routledge.

Harvey, David (1989) *The Condition of Postmodernity.* Oxford: Blackwell.

Held, David (1995) *Democracy and Global Order: From the Modern State to Cosmopolitan Governance.* Cambridge: Polity Press.

Held, David, McGrew, Anthony, Goldblatt, David and Perraton, Jonathan (1999) *Global Transformations: Politics, Economics and Culture.* Stanford, CA: Stanford University Press.

Held, David and McGrew, Anthony (2002) *Globalization and Anti-Globalization.* Cambridge: Polity Press.

Hendry, Joy (2000) *The Orient Strikes Back: A Global View of Cultural Display.* Oxford: Berg.

Hertz, Noreena (2001) *The Silent Takeover: Global Capitalism and the Death of Democracy.* London: Heinemann.

Hirst, Paul and Thompson, Grahame (1996) *Globalization in Question.* Cambridge: Polity Press.

Hobsbawm, Eric J. and Ranger, Terence O. (eds) (1983) *The Invention of Tradition.* Cambridge: Cambridge University Press.

Holton, Robert, J. (1998) *Globalization and the Nation-State.* London: Macmillan.

Horowitz, Irving, L. (1966) *The Three Worlds of Development: The Theory and Practice of International Stratification.* New York: Oxford University Press.

Howes, David (1996) *Cross-cultural Consumption: Global Markets, Local Realities.* London: Routledge.

Huntington, Samuel P. (1996) *The Clash of Civilizations and the Remaking of World Order.* New York: Simon and Schuster.

Ignatieff, Michael (2001a) 'The attack on human rights', *Foreign Affairs,* 80 (6): 102–16.

Ignatieff, Michael (2001b) *Human Rights as Politics and Idolatry.* Princeton, NJ: Princeton University Press.

Inglis, David and Robertson, Roland (2004) 'Beyond the gates of the *polis*: Reconfiguring sociology's ancient inheritance', *Journal of Classical Sociology,* 4 (2): 165–89.

Jacobson, David (1996) *Rights Across Borders: Immigration and the Decline of Citizenship.* Baltimore, MD: Johns Hopkins University Press.

Jameson, Frederic (1998) *The Cultural Turn: Selected Writings on the Postmodern, 1983–98.* London: Verso.

Johnson, Paul (1991) *The Birth of the Modern World: World Society, 1815–30.* New York: HarperCollins.

Jordan, Tim (1999) *Cyberpower: The Culture of Politics of Cyberspace and the Internet.* London: Routledge.

Kant, Immanuel (1784) *On Perpetual Peace.* Indianapolis: Hackett.

Keane, John (2003) *Global Civil Society.* Cambridge: Cambridge University Press.

Keohane, R.O. and Nye, J.S. (1989) *Power and Independence,* 2nd edn. Glenview, IL: Scott Foresman.

Kennedy, Paul, Messner, Dirk and Nuscheler, Franz (eds) (2002) *Global Trends and Global Governance.* London: Pluto Press.

Kern, Stephen (1983) *The Culture of Time and Space, 1880–1918.* Cambridge, MA: Harvard University Press.

Klein, Naomi (2000) *No Logo.* London: Flamingo.

Knorr Cetina, Karin (2001) 'Postsocial relations: theorizing sociality in a postsocial environment', in George Ritzer and Barry Smart (eds), *Handbook of Social Theory*. London: Sage. pp. 520–34.

Knorr Cetina, Karin and Bruegger, Urs (2001) 'Global microstructures: the virtual societies of financial markets', *American Journal of Sociology*, 107 (4): 905–50.

Lagos, G. (1963) *International Stratification and Underdeveloped Countries*. Chapel Hill, NC: University of North Carolina Press.

Lash, Scott (2002) *Critique of Information*. London: Sage.

Lauren, Paul Gordon (1998) *The Evolution of International Human Rights: Visions Seen*. Philadelphia, PA: University of Pennsylvania Press.

Lechner, Frank and Boli, John (eds) (2000) *The Globalization Reader*. Oxford: Blackwell.

Lewis, M.W. and Wigen, K.E. (eds) (1997) *The Myth of Continents: A Critique of Metageography*. Berkeley, CA: University of California Press.

Luhmann, Niklas (1997) 'Globalization or world society: how to conceive of modern society?', *International Review of Sociology*, 7 (1): 67–80.

Macedo, Donaldo (1999) 'Our common culture: a poisonous pedagogy', in Manuel Castells et al., *Critical Education in the New Information Age*. Lanham, MD: Rowman and Littlefield. pp. 117–38.

Mander, Jerry and Goldsmith, Edward (eds) (1996) *The Case Against the Gobal Economy and For a Turn Toward the Local*. San Francisco: Sierra Club Books.

McLuhan, Marshall with Fiore, Quentin (1968) *War and Peace in the Global Village*. New York: Oxford University Press.

McLuhan, Marshall and Powers, Bruce R. (1989) *The Global Village: Transformations in World Life and Media in the 21st Century*. Oxford: Oxford University Press.

McNeely, Connie L. (1995) *Constructing the Nation-State: International Organization and Prescriptive Action*. Westport, CT: Greenwood Press.

McNeill, William H. (1986) *Polyethnicity and National Unity in World History*. Toronto: Toronto University Press.

Messner, Dirk (2002) 'World society – structures and trends', in Paul Kennedy, Dirk Messner and Franz Nuscheler (eds), *Global Trends and Global Governance*. London: Pluto Press. pp. 22–64.

Meyer, John W. (1980) 'The world polity and the authority of the nation-state', in Albert Bergesen (ed.), *Studies of the Modern World System*. New York: Academic Press. pp. 109–37.

Meyer, John W. (1987) 'Self and life course: institutionalization and its effects', in George M. Thomas,

John W. Meyer, Francisco O. Ramirez and John Boli (eds), *Institutional Structure: Constituting State, Society, and the Individual*. Cambridge: Cambridge University Press. pp. 309–30.

Meyer, John W., Boli, John, Thomas, George M. and Ramirez, Francisco O. (1997) 'World society and the nation-state', *American Journal of Sociology*, 103 (1): 144–81.

Mittelman, James H. (2000) *The Globalization Syndrome: Transformation and Resistance*. Princeton, NJ: Princeton University Press.

Naim, Moises (2002) 'Al-Qaeda, the NGO', *Foreign Policy*, March/April, pp. 100–99.

Nelson, Benjamin (1981) *On the Roads to Modernity* (ed. Toby H. Huff). Totowa, NJ: Rowman and Littlefield.

Nettl, J.P. and Robertson, Roland (1968) *International Systems and the Modernization of Societies*. New York: Basic Books.

Nussbaum, Martha C. with respondents (1996) 'Patriotism and cosmopolitanism', in *For Love of Country: Debating the Limits of Patriotism*. Boston, MA: Beacon Press. pp. 2–20 and 131–44.

O'Donnell, Mike (2000) *Classical and Contemporary Sociology: Theory and Issues*. London: Hodder and Stoughton.

Papastergiadis, Nikos (1999) *The Turbulence of Migration: Globalization, Deterritorialization and Hybridity*. Cambridge: Polity Press.

Parsons, Talcott (1971) *The System of Modern Societies*. Englewood Cliffs, NJ: Prentice–Hall.

Parsons, Talcott (1977) *The Evolution of Societies* (ed. Jackson Toby). Englewood Cliffs, NJ: Prentice–Hall.

Porter, Roy (ed.) (1997) *Internet Culture*. London: Routledge.

Portes, Alejandro (2000) 'Globalization from below: the rise of transnational communities', in Don Kalb, Marco van der Land, Richard Staring, Bart van Steenbergen and Nico Wilterdink (eds), *The Ends of Globalization: Bringing Society Back In*. Lanham, MD: Rowman and Littlefield. pp. 253–70.

Rapoport, Anatol (1997) 'The dual role of the nation state in the evolution of world citizenship', in Joseph Rotblat (ed.), *World Citizenship: Allegiance to Humanity*. New York: St Martin's Press. pp. 91–125.

Ray, Larry and Sayer, Andrew (1999) 'Introduction', in Larry Ray and Andrew Sayer (eds), *Culture and Economy After the Cultural Turn*. London: Sage. pp. 1–24.

Ritzer, George (2000) *The McDonaldization of Society: New Century Edition*. London: Sage.

Ritzer, George (2002) *McDonaldization: The Reader*. Thousand Oaks, CA: Pine Forge Press.

Ritzer, George, Goodman, Douglas and Wiedenhoft, Wendy (2001) 'Theories of consumption', in George Ritzer and Barry Smart (eds), *Handbook of Social Theory*. London: Sage. pp. 410–27.

Robbins, Bruce (1998) 'Introduction Part I: Actually Existing Cosmopolitanism', in Pheng Cheak and Bruce Robbins (eds), *Cosmopolitics Thinking and Feeling Beyond the Nation*. Minneapolis, MN: University of Minnesota Press. pp. 1–19.

Robbins, Bruce (1999) *Feeling Global: Internationalism in Distress*. New York: New York University Press.

Robertson, Roland (1983) 'Interpreting globality', in *World Realities and International Studies Today*. Glenside, PA: Pennsylvania Council on International Education. pp. 7–20.

Robertson, Roland (1985) 'The relativization of societies: modern religion and globalization', in Thomas Robbins, William C. Shepherd and Jack McBride (eds), *Cults, Culture and the Law*. Chico, CA: Scholars Press. pp. 31–42.

Robertson, Roland (1990) 'The globalization paradigm: thinking globally', in David G. Bromley (ed.), *Religion and the Social Order: New Directions in Theory and Research*. Greenwich, CT: JAI Press. pp. 1–10.

Robertson, Roland (1992) *Globalization: Social Theory and Global Culture*. London: Sage.

Robertson, Roland (1994) 'Globalization or glocalization?', *Journal of International Communication*, 1 (1): 33–52.

Robertson, Roland (1995a) 'Glocalization: time-space and homogeneity-heterogeneity', in Mike Featherstone, Scott Lash and Roland Robertson (eds), *Global Modernities*. London: Sage. pp. 25–44.

Robertson, Roland (1995b) 'Theory, specificity, change: emulation, selective incorporation and modernization', in Bruno Grancelli (ed.), *Social Change and Modernization: Lessons from Eastern Europe*. Berlin: Walter de Gruyter. pp. 213–31.

Robertson, Roland (2001a) 'Globalization theory 2000+: major problematics', in George Ritzer and Barry Smart (eds), *Handbook of Social Theory*. London: Sage. pp. 458–71.

Robertson, Roland (2001b) 'Kung's global ethic: parametric lacunae', *International Journal of Politics, Culture and Society*, 14 (3): 657–65.

Robertson, Roland (2002a) 'Le Dimensioni della cultura globale', in Elisabetta Batini and Rodolfo Ragionieri (eds), *Culture e Conflitti nella Globalizzazione*. Florence: Leo S. Olschki. pp. 17–30.

Robertson, Roland (2002b) 'Globality', in Neil J. Smelser and Paul B. Baltes (eds-in-chief), *International Encyclopedia of the Social and Behavioral Sciences*, Vol. 9. Oxford: Elsevier/Pergamon Press. pp. 6254–8.

Robertson, Roland (2002c) 'Opposition and resistance to globalization', in Richard Grant and John Rennie Short (eds), *Globalization and the Margins*, New York: Palgrave. pp. 25–38.

Robertson, Roland (2003) 'Rethinking Americanization', in Natan Sznaider, Ulrich Beck and Rainer Winter (eds), *Global America? The Cultural Consequences of Americanization*. Liverpool: University of Liverpool Press. pp. 257–64.

Robertson, Roland (2005) 'Global history in a post-colonial age', in Roland Robertson with Kathleen E. White, *Globality and Modernity*. London: Sage.

Robertson, Roland and Chirico, JoAnn (1985) 'Humanity, globalization and worldwide religious resurgence: a theoretical exploration', *Sociological Analysis*, 46 (3): 219–42.

Robertson, Roland and Inglis, David (2004) 'The global animus: In the tracks of world consciousness', *Globalizations*, 1 (1): 38–49.

Robertson, Roland and Lechner, Frank J. (1985) 'Modernization, globalization, and the problem of culture in world-systems theory', *Theory, Culture and Society*, 2 (3): 103–18.

Robertson, Roland and Khondker, Habib H. (1998) 'Discourses of globalization: preliminary considerations', *International Sociology*, 13 (1): 25–40.

Robertson, Roland and White, Kathleen E. (2003) 'Globalization: an overview', in Roland Robertson and Kathleen E. White (eds), *Globalization: Critical Concepts in Sociology*, Vol. 1. London: Routledge. pp. 1–44.

Robertson, Roland and White, Kathleen E. (2004) 'La glocalizzazione rivisitata ed elaborata' in Franciscu Seddu (ed.), *Glocal: sul presente a venire*. Rome: Luca Sossella Editore. pp. 13–41.

Rosenau, James N. (1990) *Turbulence in World Politics: A Theory of Change and Continuity*. Princeton, NJ: Princeton University Press.

Rosenberg, Justin (2000) *The Follies of Globalisation Theory*. London: Verso.

Rotblat, Joseph (ed.) (1997) *World Citizenship: Allegiance to Humanity*. New York: St Martin's Press.

Roudometof, Victor and Robertson, Roland (1995) 'Globalization, world-system theory, and the comparative study of civilization: issues of theoretical logic in world-historical sociology', in Stephen K. Sanderson (ed.), *Civilizations and World Systems: Studying World-Historical Change*. Walnut Creek, CA: Altamira Press. pp. 273–300.

Sacks, Robert D. (1986). *Human Territoriality: Its Theory and History*. Cambridge: Cambridge University Press.

Sandoval, Chela (2000) *Methodology of the Oppressed*. Minneapolis, MN: University of Minnesota Press.

Scholte, Jan Aart (1993) *International Relations of Social Change*. Buckingham: Open University Press.

Scholte, Jan Aart (2000) *Globalization: A Critical Introduction*. Basingstoke: Macmillan.

Seidman, Gay W. (2000) 'Adjusting the lens: what do globalizations, transnationalism, and the anti-Apartheid movement mean for social movement theory?', in John A. Guidry, Michael D. Kennedy and Mayer N. Zald (eds), *Globalizations and Social Movements: Culture, Power, and the Transnational Public Sphere*. Ann Arbor, MI: University of Michigan Press. pp. 339–57.

Sen, Amartya (2000) *Development as Freedom*. New York: Anchor.

Sennett, Richard (1978) *The Fall of Public Man*. New York: Alfred A. Knopf.

Sennett, Richard (1998) *The Corrosion of Character: The Personal Consequences of Work in Late Capitalism*. New York: W.W. Norton and Company.

Shapiro, Michael J. and Alker, Hayward R. (eds), (1996) *Challenging Boundaries: Global Flows, Territorial Identities*. Minneapolis, MN: University of Minnesota Press.

Sklair, Leslie (1995) *Sociology of the Global System*. Baltimore, MD: Prentice–Hall/Johns Hopkins University Press.

Sklair, Leslie (2001) *The Transnational Capitalist Class*. Oxford: Blackwell.

Soysal, Yasmine N. (1994) *Limits of Citizenship*. Chicago: University of Chicago Press.

Spivak, Gayatri Chakravorty (1999) *A Critique of Postcolonial Reason*. Cambridge, MA: Harvard University Press.

Stanford Friedman, Susan (1998) *Mappings: Feminism and the Cultural Geographies of Encounters*. Princeton, NJ: Princeton University Press.

Steger, Manfred B. (2003) *Globalization: A Very Short Introduction*. Oxford: Oxford University Press.

Stiglitz, Joseph E. (2002) *Globalization and Its Discontents*. London: Allen Lane.

Tharpe, Marye C. (2001) *Marketing and Consumer Identity in Multicultural America*. Thousand Oaks, CA: Sage.

Therborn, Goran (1995) 'Routes to/through modernity', in Mike Featherstone, Scott Lash and Roland Robertson (eds), *Global Modernities*. London: Sage. pp. 124–39.

Thrift, Nigel (1999) 'Capitalism's cultural turn', in Larry Ray and Andrew Sayer (eds), *Culture and Economy After the Cultural Turn*. London: Sage. pp. 135–61.

Tomlinson, John (1999) *Globalization and Culture*. Chicago: University of Chicago Press.

Turkle, Sherry (1995) *Life on the Screen*. New York: Weidenfeld & Nicolson.

Urry, John (1995) *Consuming Places*. London: Routledge.

Urry, John (2002) *The Tourist Gaze*, 2nd edn. London: Sage.

van Steebergen, Bart (ed.) (1994) *The Condition of Citizenship*. London: Sage.

Volkmer, Ingrid (1999) *News in the Global Sphere: A Study of CNN and its Impact on Global Communication*. Luton: University of Luton Press.

Wallerstein, Immanuel (1974, 1980, 1989) *The Modern World System*, 3 vols. New York: Cambridge University Press.

Waters, Malcolm (1995) *Globalization*. London: Routledge.

Watson, James L. (ed.) (1997) *Golden Arches East: McDonald's in East Asia*. Stanford, CA: Stanford University Press.

Westney, D.E. (1987) *Imitation and Innovation: The Transfer of Western Organizational Patterns to Meiji Japan*. Cambridge, MA: Harvard University Press.

Wittel, Andreas (2001) 'Toward a network sociality', *Theory, Culture and Society*, 18 (6): 51–76.

Yearley, Steven (1996) *Sociology, Environmentalism, Globalization: Reinventing the Globe*. London: Sage.

21

The Sociology of Gender Relations

SYLVIA WALBY

INTRODUCTION

Sociology has contributed to the transformation of the traditional perception of the relations between men and women from one primarily rooted in biology to one that acknowledges their social constitution, and hence variability and malleability. The fundamental re-thinking of this aspect of life is a process in which sociology has played a significant role alongside popular movements.

There is today a mountain of empirical research in sociology that thoroughly documents the variations in patterns of gender difference and gender inequality across a myriad of social domains, including employment, caring, politics, violence, culture, sexuality, development, globalization and many more. This work is rich, diverse, innovative and comprehensive. A large part of this chapter will be devoted to an account of the themes and contributions of this research.

Yet, despite this very broad development of the analysis of gender relations within sociology, gender is not often regarded as core to traditional sociological theory. This is not to say that there is not theoretical work on gender. There is such work, but this has been largely, though not exclusively, within the realm of cultural theory rather than sociological theory. This has occurred partly because gender was neglected in much of the sociology that has been considered to be classical, and hence not been regarded as core to the central concerns of the traditional sociological canon; partly because the gender field matured at a time when cultural theory was in the ascendance, especially in the UK; and partly because of the interdisciplinary location of much gender analysis which draws on literary and cultural theory as well as social theory.

However, there always has been a strand of gender analysis within comparative and historical research and within sociological theory, although this has been less visible, and it is here that the promise especially lies for the development of the next wave of analysis of the sociology of gender that more decisively connects gender to the core concerns of sociology in general and sociological theory in particular.

What started as a special field of sociology has now developed way beyond any narrowly defined 'woman question' – few, if any, areas of social life are now considered to be entirely ungendered. This increase in scope has, in recent years, been tempered by a greater realization of the importance of other forms of social relations in the construction of specific forms of gender relations, so that gender is less frequently considered in isolation from ethnicity, 'race', class and other social divisions.

The argument of this chapter is that a proper integration of gender into the classical themes of sociology would benefit both sociological theory and the understanding and explanation of gender relations. Recent developments in comparative and historical work on gender are taking this agenda forward.

The chapter is in four parts: first, a summary of the main contributions of sociology to popular understandings of the relations between men and women; second, a critical analysis of the theoretical debates within the sociology of gender; third, a review of the rich and diverse empirical work in the field; fourth, a discussion of promising contemporary developments.

SOCIOLOGICAL CONTRIBUTIONS TO THE UNDERSTANDING OF GENDER IN THE WORLD

Sociology has made several key contributions to the popular everyday understanding of gender relations as well as to social scientific analysis: that gender is socially constituted; that gender is different from biological sex; that there are variations in the patterns of gender relations.

Popular understandings of the differences between women and men have, in previous eras, been rooted in notions of essential unchanging differences. A major contribution of sociology, now widely taken for granted, is that gender is socially constructed. The social constitution of gender is sociology's claim and its taken-for-granted project. The social rather than biological basis of the differences between women and men has been established in contemporary thought through developments in sociology in tandem with waves of feminist activity. One of the instruments taking this forward was the development of a new vocabulary to articulate new conceptualizations of the relations between men and women, not least the devising of the concept of 'gender'. This term, previously restricted to usage in the arcane niceties of grammar, has been reinvented as the cornerstone of a new understanding of the relations between men and women as one that is inherently social. The word has entered the public vocabulary and, slowly, parallel words have been devised in languages other than English.

The analytic separation of sex and gender represents a key sociological intervention, changing language, not only in the academy but also in the policy world, and beyond. Oakley's (1985) work is a key example of this conceptual innovation.

Associated with the notion that gender is social not biological, is the notion that gender is changeable rather than fixed. In different times, places and social locations gender relations take different forms. This was an insight of the early anthropologists, once closely associated with the discipline of sociology, who took as core to their discipline the exploration of different patterns of family and kinship. Mead (1928) is only the most famous of these early pioneers investigating the variations of the constitution of gender relations through the different configurations of social institutions. This understanding of gender as malleable is a key assumption of many feminist movements seeking to change the context within which gender is constituted. Despite the development of evolutionary psychology in notions such as 'the selfish gene', that contest the extent of this variability (Rose and Rose, 2001), the sociological understanding arguably remains dominant. The analysis of the variations in these forms of gender relations is now a key part of the field of gender studies.

GENDER AND THE DISCIPLINE OF SOCIOLOGY

Historical development

The location of gender analysis in sociology has a long and varied history. It is often presumed that there were no leading intellectuals writing on gender relations in and around the discipline of sociology during its foundation in the nineteenth century. However, this absence is exaggerated in at least two ways. First, at the turn of the nineteenth and twentieth centuries a strong and vigorous women's movement generated several leading intellectual figures and writers. One of these was Charlotte Perkins Gilman (1966 [1898]), who wrote of the significance of the confinement of women to the home as the basis of not only their subordination but also of their cultural differences from men, and who published not only books translated into many languages (*Women and Economics* ran to seven editions in seven languages), but also in the *American Journal of Sociology* (Gilman, 1909). But she is rarely recognized as part of the sociological canon. Second, at the same time sociology and anthropology were often considered a single discipline, while core to anthropology was the analysis of family and kinship. This located gender issues at the core of the combined discipline. When the disciplines split, the analysis of family and kinship was left primarily located in anthropology (Coward, 1983). The construction of what constituted the sociological canon in the latter part of the twentieth century left on the margins those writers who had addressed gender issues.

Gender: everywhere or particular institutions?

One of the strategic analytic choices in locating gender within sociology is that of whether gender is considered, first, to be relatively concentrated in a few specific social institutions or, second, to affect all domains and levels of abstraction. The most important example of the first route is where gender is seen as primarily constituted by processes within the family (Parsons and Bales, 1955), though there are further examples, such as sexuality (MacKinnon, 1989). By contrast, in the second route gender is seen as constituted in more or less all social domains (Walby, 1990). The first, more focused, analytic strategy used to be common, but has increasingly given way to the second.

Specialized or mainstream

There is an enduring tension between the development of gender analysis as a specialized sub-field within sociology (considered either in particular institutions or spread across all social domains), or integrated, mainstreamed, into the discipline as a whole. This is both an organizational and an intellectual issue. On the one hand, in order to develop the specificity of the analysis, focused discussions in specialized academic units, conferences and journals seem appropriate. On the other, the relevance of gender to the breadth of sociology may be best realized in integrated departments and academic spaces. In practice, complex combinations of strategies were often used (Platt, 2003).

National differences

There are national differences in the analysis of gender relations. In the second half of the twentieth century, the United States led the analysis of gender in sociology, first in functionalist analysis of the family, then in the development of women's studies. Today, the US has perhaps a more classical approach to the analysis of gender within sociology than some other countries. In the UK, the cultural turn has had a great influence on the analysis of gender relations. However, interest in many of the less developed countries has led to many international debates, with concerns for postcolonial perspectives as well as difference and ethnicity. Perspectives from the South have perhaps also been more concerned with classical issues of social inequality.

Inter-disciplinarity

The development of women's studies and gender studies since the 1980s has been an interdisciplinary development, rather than one that is located simply within sociology. In the early years sociology was central to the development of the interdisciplinary field. However, more recently the interdisciplinary field has been increasingly dominated by cultural and literary disciplines. This is represented in the contents of leading interdisciplinary gender journals, such as *Signs*. The interdisciplinary development of gender studies has had implications for the development of the analysis of gender within sociology.

The presence of literary theories and methodologies has been one of the influences on the epistemological underpinnings of the field that has moved it away from a realist concern with scientific procedures and the cumulation of knowledge to a concern with different perspectives and a move towards, though not always embracing, relativism. This has affected the analysis of gender within sociology, not least because of the operation of many gender specialists within the interdisciplinary field of women's/gender studies as well as their home discipline.

A key achievement of classical sociology was that of the grasping of the macro and micro levels within one overarching theory, and the development of a deep ontology of the social as a consequence. This has been in danger of being lost in a move towards cultural and literary theory and away from sociological theory. However, this is not inevitable and there are contrary developments.

THEORETICAL DEBATES

Gender and class

The relationship between gender and class was one of the early concerns of gender analysis, with many critiques of traditional theorizing of class and capitalism for positioning gender in a residual or marginal location in sociological theory (Crompton and Mann, 1986), resulting in at least some incorporation of gender into contemporary class and stratification analysis (Erikson and Goldthorpe, 1992). The feminist debates addressed the nature of the entwining of gender and class relations, some using a theoretical vocabulary that kept these sets of social relations analytically distinct, such as in dual systems theory (Hartmann, 1976), while others analytically integrated them more fully. These theoretical questions still underlie contemporary analysis of new developments in the economy, from flexibility to globalization and the knowledge economy (McCall, 2001).

Class is not the only form of deeply structured social inequality that cross-cuts gender; rather, there is a multiplicity of these, not the least of which is ethnicity. The recognition of

the significance of these other social divisions was key to the development of a literature on differences and inequalities of many kinds.

Difference and essentialism

The analysis of 'difference' has become one of the central theoretical issues within gender analysis, as it has in some other parts of sociology (Calhoun, 1995). This debate addressed ways in which gender relations were differently constituted in different ethnic groups (Bhopal, 1997), the ways in which different nations and national groupings were gendered (Yuval-Davis, 1997), and how perspectives from the South were to be understood and integrated (Mohanty, 1991). A key underlying theoretical question was that of how the standard for justice should be determined, including the implications of statements either that different social groups had divergent conceptions of justice (Young, 1990), or that all people had fundamentally the same agenda for the achievement of human capabilities (Nussbaum, 2000). A related issue was the nature of the relationship between difference and inequality (Meehan and Sevenhuijsen, 1991; Scott, 1988), the ontological status of difference (Felski, 1997), whether sensitivity to different value systems necessarily leads to social relativism (Fraser, 1997; Walby, 2001b), and the implications of feminism for an analysis of fundamentalism (Afshar, 1998; Moghadam, 1994). The theoretical concern with difference in feminist theory fuelled the turn to postmodern approaches.

Feminist theory struggled to address the critique that it insufficiently addressed social fissures other than that of gender, especially those associated with racialization, ethnicity and postcolonialism (Mohanty, 1991). This issue related to an extensive theoretical debate around 'essentialism'. This concerned the question of whether the process of abstracting the core features of gender relations tended to underestimate the significance of differences among women and to exaggerate the stability and cross-cultural relevance of the categories. Was feminist analysis that took as its main focus the oppression of women by men, necessarily essentialist, reducing complex social processes to simple biological dichotomies (Segal, 1987), or was this critique simply a caricature (Bell and Klein, 1996)? The focus on difference was associated with debates as to whether it was possible to use the categories 'woman', 'patriarchy' and 'gender' without succumbing to essentialism. Should feminism embrace womanhood or de-gendering (Lorber, 2000)? Was the process of stabilization of the categories needed to specify and compare significant differences between women inherently one that rigidified and essentialized these distinctions? Indeed, could there be an adequate analysis of difference that avoided the trap of essentialism (Ferree et al., 2002)? The prioritization of difference, indeed the ontologizing of difference, was sometimes considered to be at the expense of the concept of 'woman' and 'gender', and that such prioritization of difference over gender had gone too far, that the ontologizing of difference was to the detriment of the analysis of gender itself (Felski, 1997).

Some analytic strategy of abstraction, whether called 'essentializing' or not, is always necessary in order to build categories sufficiently stable for practical analysis (Fuss, 1990). The alternative strategy of analytic dispersal of gender in order to avoid essentialism can lead to the absence of a category adequate to include gender in analysis in any meaningful way, since if gender is considered to be a different phenomenon within specific forms of ethnicity, culture or historical periods, it can never be possible to have an analysis of gender *per se*. That is, if gender is analytically dispersed and embedded in other forms of social relations, as argued by Holmwood (2001), then it is hard to have an explanatory analysis of the forms of variations in gender (Sayer, 2000). The way forward is not to disperse gender, but rather to develop concepts and analytic strategies that are sensitive to variations in the form of gender without losing meaning. Even the concept of patriarchy can be developed so as to be sensitive to historical change and ethnic and national difference (Medaglia, 2001; Walby, 1990, 1994). This development has been

associated with the revitalization of realism and interest in classical sociology, and a concern to build an ontology of the social using abstraction at different levels, and in which a robust category of gender is preferred.

METHODOLOGY AND EPISTEMOLOGY

Science itself has been taken as an object of study and been found to be gendered (Rose, 1994). The implications of this for feminist methodology (Reinharz, 1993) and feminist epistemology (Harding, 1986) are profoundly contested (McLennan, 1995).

Harding (1986, 1991) considers that a standpoint epistemology, based on women's experiences, is a route to improved objectivity, and is preferable to what she calls 'feminist empiricism' and postmodernism. She argues that knowledge about gender is best investigated using qualitative methodologies that centre on the voices of women. This epistemological and methodological stance has been widely endorsed in much of women's and gender studies, including that within sociology. In particular, it has been core to the preference for small-scale qualitative studies in this field.

One line of criticism of this stance came from those who queried the existence or validity of a notion of a unified women's standpoint, in light of the significance of difference and diversity, not least that associated with ethnicity. This is associated with a move towards a postmodern understanding of the social. A second critique came from a defence of science for feminism, such as that of Nelson (1990), who argues for a revised feminist empiricism based on Quine. Indeed, since science is neither a mirror of nature nor a mirror of culture, neither absolutist position (science as truth or social relativism) is tenable (Walby, 2001a). Rather, it is necessary to utilize the methods of science, piecing together evidence and theories in socially located networks.

While there have always been those who rejected standpoint epistemology and a preference for reporting on women's voices using qualitative methods, the strictures of 'feminist methodology' have been to the detriment of the development of an analysis of gender relations in sociology, unduly restricting the range of methodology deemed appropriate within a feminist stance, especially in the UK, where in particular it reduced the propensity to use quantitative methodologies (Kelly et al., 1992). However, with the erosion of this epistemological and methodological stance, the range of methodologies used in the sociology of gender has broadened significantly.

EMPIRICAL SCIENCE OF GENDERED SOCIAL INSTITUTIONS

There is a wide, rich and diverse set of empirical studies of gender relations that address most of the empirical fields within sociology. This myriad of empirical studies explores the form and implications of different forms of gender relations in different social institutions and social locations. The following are illustrative of such developments.

Employment

Rather than treating women as a unity, analyses of employment have teased out the complex forms of old and new inequalities consequent on industrial and political restructuring and the transformation of work (Walby, 1997; Crompton, 1997). The debates on new forms of flexibility at work have been gendered, and used to inform a range of empirical studies, ranging from part-time work (O'Reilly and Fagan, 1998) to home-working (Phizacklea and Wolkowitz, 1995). These have addressed the way and extent to which the extension of women's employment has been in forms of employment that are casualized, insecure and low-paid, or whether women can benefit from the new flexibility. Occupational segregation was investigated as a tenacious feature of the gendered labour market, despite changes in its forms (Reskin and Roos, 1990; Hakim, 1992; Scott, 1994). The complex impacts of policies and laws to regulate equal opportunities

(Cockburn, 1991; England, 1992) and work-life balance such as maternity leave (McRae, 1993), especially those associated with the increasing integration of the European Union (Hoskyns, 1996; Rees, 1998; Walby, 1999), were investigated. The complexity of the interrelationship between gender and ethnicity among women workers, where paid work has varying locations in the lives of women from different social locations, was explored (Brah and Shaw, 1992; Phizacklea, 1990). The increasing significance of the European Union has produced interest in the comparative analysis of gendered labour markets in the member states of the European Union and the explanation of the differences found (Rubery et al., 1999). The influence of the cultural turn in gender studies may be seen in the interest in the role of sexuality in the workplace (Adkins, 1994), and the role of culture in restricting women's success in management.

Violence

The significance of male violence in women's lives was demonstrated by many studies overturning traditional assumptions that such violence was the result of psychological or biological forces, whether as a result of a few deranged men or some evolutionary male imperative. The social shaping of patterns of violence and social responses to this violence have brought this field firmly within a sociological frame of inquiry. The relationship between violence and socially structured gendered power relations has been key to this field, though not uncontroversially so.

The methodology used by UK sociologists in this area has been primarily qualitative (Dobash and Dobash, 1980; Hearn, 1998). In the United States, the methodology has been more diverse, including large-scale surveys (Straus and Gelles, 1990), the findings of which were subject to considerable debate (Dobash et al., 1992), leading to methodological revisions as surveys around the world learned from and improved the methodology in earlier ones (Johnson, 1996; Walby and Myhill, 2001). Only later were large-scale surveys conducted in the

UK, which confirmed the finding that violence against women was widespread (Mirrlees-Black, 1999). There has been a steady uncovering and naming of more diverse forms of violence against women. This includes not only rape, sexual assault and domestic violence, but also child sex abuse, sexual harassment, stalking and trafficking in women, which are all part of a continuum of violence against women (Hester et al., 1996; Kelly, 1989). The critical analysis of the response of the criminal justice system and relevant agencies to gendered violence again demonstrated the importance of social context and social response in structuring the impact of the violence (Mooney, 2000; Taylor-Browne, 2000).

Politics

The gendering of sociological debates on welfare and on citizenship has taken as its starting point the critique of the neglect of the care work that is so often performed by women to a greater extent than men. Debates on citizenship often took as their starting point a public conception of the citizen. The feminist critique demonstrated that such a theorization effectively marginalized the contribution of women to society, especially their contributions in the home as mothers (Lister, 1997). The implications of different forms of state support for care work for gender relations has become the new focus in this field (Hobson, 2000; Jenson, 1997; O'Connor et al., 1999; Sainsbury, 1996).

Within the analysis of the state, a key question has been the extent to which women articulated different political interests than men, and the implications of any such divergences for the form and actions of the state. After much scepticism, a gender dimension to political interests was demonstrated in analyses of voting behaviour, in that employed women are more likely to vote left than men and non-employed women, at least in the United States (Huber and Stephens, 2000; Manza and Brooks, 1998). A higher proportion of women elected representatives was also found to make a difference to the extent to which representatives were likely to

support a feminist agenda, at least in the US (Thomas, 1991) and Sweden (Wängnerud, 2000). Political pressure by women was also found to make a difference even when women do not have the franchise (Skocpol, 1992). The combination of different forms of women's representation, in elected representatives, gender machinery in the state such as women's units and civil society or social movements may be the most likely to make a difference (Mazur, 2002; Vargas and Wieringa, 1998).

US Sociology has led these debates on political sociology especially those involving quantitative analysis. Within the UK, the sociological focus has been more frequently on cultural politics than the state, reflecting the cultural turn in British sociology and women's studies (Franklin et al., 1991), tending to leave the analysis of the state to political scientists (Norris and Lovenduski, 1995).

Sexuality

The debates on the place of sexuality within the analysis of gender relations have drawn on a range of sources of theoretical inspiration from Freud to Foucault (Richardson, 2001). Despite the lack in Foucault's own work of much in an explicit and direct way about gender, his conceptualization of sexuality and power became very influential in the 1990s in theories of gender and sexuality, though not uncontroversially so (Ramanzanoglu, 1991). The sociological analysis of gender and sexuality might be considered to have been 'mainstreamed' by Giddens's (1992) work on changes in the patterns of intimacy associated with changing patterns of gender relations.

Substantive research topics have included that of the subordination of women and girls within sexual practices; the use of demeaning sexualized stereotypes to attempt to control women's and girls' conduct, for instance as 'slags' or 'drags' (Lees, 1993); the construction of heterosexuality (Jackson, 1999); the diversity of sexual moralities (Weeks, 1995); and the exploitation of women's sexuality at work (Adkins, 1994). Not all research has seen sexuality unambiguously as a terrain of male power, some seeing it as a site of negotiation, while there has been much attention to powerful female icons such as Madonna.

Culture

Feminist cultural studies has been one of the areas within the sociology of gender and women's studies in the UK that has developed most extensively, with the establishment of several journals, as well as many books, at the point of intersection of women's studies, sociology and cultural and literary theory. The initial interest in the content analysis of images presented by advertising, television and the media, has been replaced by sophisticated textual analysis informed by the discourse analysis of Foucault and the deconstructionism of Derrida (Franklin et al., 1991; McNay, 1992). A key feature of these analyses has been the breaking down of any remaining monolithic notions of femininity, or indeed, masculinity (Connell, 1995; Hearn, 1998; Morgan, 1992), and the exploration of the diversity found, especially that associated with ethnicity (Mirza, 1997). There has been a tendency to celebrate women's agency, including that of non-feminist female icons such as Princess Diana and Madonna.

Feminist cultural analysis had a tremendous influence on the forms of theorizing in women's studies during the 1980s and early 1990s, leading to a shift away from analysis in terms of social structures to those of discourses and of agency. Further, there has been the problematization of the notion of a coherent monolithic subject, for instance, in Butler's (1990) work on 'performativity'. Here gender is merely what exists at the moment of performance, that is, the notion of a stable gender identity is rejected by Butler because it is considered to be overly essentializing. However, Butler's analysis has tended to lead away from the sociological analysis of the social institutions that provide the framing for any such performance.

Today the analysis of culture is largely integrated into analyses of gender, rather than constituting a separate field. The term gender itself has been subject to extensive reconsideration in the light of so much deconstructionist analysis (Hawkesworth, 1997).

Caring and the household

The sociology of the family was traditionally a strong area of sociology, but in the early development of women's studies this field tended to be side-lined in favour of newer substantive fields of inquiry. However, there has been a strong strand of research into caregiving. This includes analysis of kinship and marital obligations for caring between generations (Finch, 1992), and between spouses (Delphy and Leonard, 1992). The significance of this unpaid care work and the burdens that are placed on women in this regard is a continuing theme in this work (Folbre, 1994; Gardiner, 1989; Sevenhuijsen, 1998).

During the 1990s the increased diversity of household forms has been the subject of sociological inquiry, especially that of the increasing proportion of lone mothers (Ford and Millar, 1998; Phoenix, 1991); and gay and lesbian households (Weeks, 1995). The changes in household forms have generated interest in how young people actually manage the transitions between different household forms and stages (Irwin, 1995), especially the diverse transitions by young women to either employment or to motherhood, which vary significantly by ethnicity and by education (Bhopal, 1997).

Within the analysis of caring runs an underlying theoretical question as to why so many women actively choose to care when it reduces their access to many conventional forms of social power. Housewives and their choices are one of the substantive issues that drive the feminist interest in the agency/structure debate.

Nature and science

The relationship between the biological and the social has always been an area of debate in the sociology of gender. Early attempts by radical feminists to incorporate the body into their work on patriarchal domination (Firestone, 1974) were often condemned as essentialist, and as leading inevitably to the reduction of gender to biology and hence to ahistoric and falsely universalistic analysis (Segal, 1987). However, today it is widely accepted in mainstream sociology that it is necessary to have a conception of the body in sociology (Turner, 1984). While the early radical feminist texts might have been unsubtle in their conceptualization, their critics' assertions that their concern with bodies and biology was necessarily essentialist are incorrect.

There have been debates as to whether the new reproductive technologies, especially those that assist fertility, such as IVF, empower women or whether they take away a source of women's power, placing it in the hands of male doctors, who use it for mere medical experimentation. These analyses of the new reproductive technologies have explored the interconnections and tensions between scientific developments and social relations, often considering them as primarily cultural processes (Franklin, 1997). Science and the environment have been analysed as gendered issues, demonstrating how far the range of the field of gender studies can extend.

Contemporary debates are about the two-way traffic between concepts originating in the social and the biological fields of inquiry (Haraway, 1997), rather than assuming that any reference to biology will dominate or in some way inappropriately contaminate a sociological analysis. Biology, in the age of the genome project, which has mapped the shape of the human genes, is no longer seen as a fixed entity, but as a fluid area of discovery. Haraway's work shows how metaphors migrate in both directions between the social and the biological fields, taking some of their meaning from one and transposing it in the other. In so doing, the concepts with which we think gender are changing.

Globalization and development

There has long been a gender analysis in development studies (Moser, 1993), which is now frequently framed by the debates on globalization. The analysis of development as gendered processes includes: the relationship between women around the world, both economically (Mies, 1986) and politically (Berkovitch, 1999; Moghadam, 2000); whether economic development is necessarily or likely to improve or make worse the position of women; women's relationship to national projects, world religions and states (Kandiyoti, 1991); and women's engagement with the rise of fundamentalism (Afshar, 1998). The way that increasingly powerful international bodies, such as the World Bank, the World Trade Organization and the United Nations, affect the gendered strategies available in specific locations, is a newly developing area of gender studies. These bodies both enhance the power of global capital and yet also facilitate global feminist networking (Walby, 2000). These developments add a new twist to the debates on diversity within feminist theory, since no community can be hermetically sealed, all are connected and thus ultimately comparable. In such a new context the local is always already framed by the global, and a retreat to local specificity can never be a full answer.

SOCIAL STRUCTURE AND GENDER

Social structure is a key sociological concept (López and Scott, 2000), important in providing a basis to theoretical claims as to ontological depth. The reconsideration of the issues of agency and structure in mainstream sociology (Giddens, 1992) had a resonance in feminist debates. Macro accounts of women's oppression by men were criticized for giving too much weight to structure and insufficient to women's active agency. While feminists in economics criticized their discipline for an overly individualistic account of human economic action (see *Feminist Economics*), the revisionists in sociology were criticizing their discipline for placing too much importance on structure at the expense of agency.

There are two main problems with traditional forms of analysis of social structure. First, macro-level concepts have been insufficiently gendered, thus making it hard to develop gender-sensitive macro-level analyses. Second, traditional forms of development of concepts of social structure and social system have emphasized dichotomous rather than plural cleavages. One of the issues here is that of the use of institutional rather than relational conceptions of social structure (see Walby, forthcoming, 2006).

These problems are being addressed in new developments in the comparative and historical analysis of gender relations.

CONTEMPORARY DEVELOPMENTS IN COMPARATIVE AND HISTORICAL ANALYSIS

There has been development of comparative analysis of gender relations with a historical dimension in several locations, especially welfare regimes, political movements and employment. The most developed is that associated with the debate initiated by Esping-Andersen (1990, 1999) on the nature of welfare state regimes. The three-fold typology of liberal, social democratic and corporatist forms was criticized for underestimating the significance of gender in these differences. Key to the debate was the differential location of women in relation to the process of commodification which was highlighted as core to a contradiction in his analysis (Orloff, 1993). On the one hand, it appeared that de-commodification, a move from market- to non-market-based forms of support, was interpreted as progressive and associated with social democracy. On the other, the movement of women's labour from the home to the market was also seen as progressive and associated with social democracy. Yet this was a process of commodification, not de-commodification. Gender is a critical intervening variable, necessary to explain the difference. The gender debate went on to make sophisticated distinctions between the implications of different kinds of state support of care work for patterns and inequalities in gender relations, especially that between support paid in cash and support made in kind by the public provision of services (Jenson, 1997; O'Connor et al., 1999; Sainsbury, 1996). A second major programme of work is that concerning the comparative investigation

of the nature and impact of women's politics, investigating in particular three types of representation of women and their interests – elected representatives, gender machinery or women's units in the state, and civil society and social movement – comparing political processes across policy domains and between different countries (Mazur, 2002; Vargas and Wieringa, 1998). A third area of comparative research is that concerning different patterns in gender relations in employment. Among the numerous projects, probably the most significant is that of Rubery et al. (1999), comparing practices within the EU. A fourth approach is to compare gender regimes rather than particular institutions of gender relations (Walby, 1994, forthcoming 2006).

These research programmes both engage with central sociological debates in their own terms as well as gendering them. They are based on theoretical questions, the answering of which is advanced by theoretically driven empirical research. They are cumulative, building on previous findings and theories. They are cross-disciplinary, indeed the welfare debate is on the borders of sociology and social policy, the political movements on the borders with political science, and employment on the borders with economics and management.

CONCLUSIONS

Rather than rejecting the sociological canon, it needs to be deepened. The way to theorize gender is to deepen and develop the classical sociological heritage, not to dismiss or ignore it. While some have claimed that feminism must do this by rejecting old methods, that 'the master's house cannot be re-built using the master's tools', this chapter argues that these are everybody's tools, and can be used to good effect. The key aspects of classical sociological theory that are best retained in theories of gender relations are especially those of depth in ontology, the grasping of macro- and micro-level phenomena within the same overarching theory, and a scientific epistemology and pluralist approach to methodology.

There are many rich, diverse empirical studies of gender relations. The rebuilding of sociological theory of gender, which both enables a better explanation of patterns of gender relations and a better sociological theory of social relations, is just begun.

Standpoint epistemology has led much sociology of gender in the direction of relativism, though this has rarely been adopted unequivocally. Methodologically, this epistemology has led to a dubious prioritization of qualitiative methodologies listening to women's voices, and to the neglect of the potential of quantitative methodologies. Yet, the range of questions in the field suggests that a plurality of methodologies is more appropriate. This requires the rejection of feminist standpoint epistemology and the embrace of a realist approach to knowledge. It requires empirical studies to be oriented more systematically to taking forward large theoretical questions.

The ontology of gender needs to be deepened using classical sociological theory, rather than flattened through a disproportionate focus either on agency or through the use of cultural theory. Only then can we adequately compare the forms of gender regime, not merely micro-level patterns of gender relations. The dispersal of the category of gender implied by the ontologizing of difference and influenced by poststructuralist and deconstructionist approaches needs to be curtailed so that sufficient abstraction is conducted so as to enable categories and concepts to be developed that are firm and stable enough for comparative analysis.

Only if we can explain the world can we know how to change the world. The cumulative nature of scientific knowledge is not the enemy of a critical gender analysis, but its ally.

REFERENCES

Adkins, Lisa (1994) *Gender Families and Work*. Milton Keynes: Open University Press.

Afshar, Haleh (1998) *Islam and Feminisms: An Iranian Case-Study*. Basingstoke: Macmillan.

Bell, Diane and Klein, Renate (eds) (1996) *Radically Speaking: Feminism Reclaimed*. London: Zed.

Berkovitch, Nitza (1999) *From Motherhood to Citizenship: Women's Rights and International Organizations*. Baltimore, MD: Johns Hopkins University Press.

Bhopal, Kalwant (1997) *Gender, 'Race' and Patriarchy: A Study of South Asian Women*. Aldershot: Ashgate.

Brah, Avtar and Shaw, Sobia (1992) *Working Choices: South Asian Young Muslim Women and the Labour Market*. Department of Employment Research Paper No. 91. London: Department of Employment.

Budig, M.J. and England, P. (2001) 'The wage penalty for motherhood', *American Sociological Review*, 66 (2): 204–25.

Butler, Judith (1990) *Gender Trouble*. London: Routledge.

Calhoun, Craig (1995) *Critical Social Theory*. Oxford: Blackwell.

Castells, Manuel (1997) *The Information Age: Economy, Society and Culture. Volume II: The Power of Identity*. Oxford: Blackwell.

Cockburn, Cynthia (1991) *In the Way of Women: Men's Resistance to Sex Equality in Organisations*. London: Macmillan.

Connell, Robert W. (1995) *Masculinities*. Cambridge: Polity Press.

Coward, Ros (1983) *Patriarchal Precedents: Sexuality and Social Relations*. London: Routledge and Kegan Paul.

Crompton, Rosemary (1997) *Women and Work in Modern Britain*. Oxford: Oxford University Press.

Crompton, Rosemary and Mann, Michael (eds) (1986) *Gender and Stratification*. Cambridge: Polity Press.

Delphy, Christine and Leonard, Diana (1992) *Familial Exploitation*. Cambridge: Polity Press.

Dobash, Rebecca Emerson and Dobash, Russell (1980) *Violence Against Wives: The Case Against the Patriarchy*. Shepton Mallet: Open Books.

Dobash, R.P., Dobash, R.E., Wilson, M. and Daly, M. (1992) 'The myth of sexual symmetry in marital violence', *Social Problems*, 39 (1): 71–91.

England, Paula (1992) *Comparable Worth: Theories and Evidence*. New York: Aldine de Gruyter.

Erikson, Robert and Goldthorpe, John H. (1992) *The Constant Flux: A Study of Class Mobility in Industrial Societies*. Oxford: The Clarendon Press.

Esping-Andersen, Gøsta (1990) *The Three Worlds of Welfare Capitalism*. Cambridge: Polity Press.

Esping-Andersen, Gøsta (1999) *Social Foundations of Postindustrial Economies*. Oxford: Oxford University Press.

Felski, Rita (1997) 'The doxa of difference', *Signs*, 23 (1): 1–22.

Ferree, Myra Marx, Gamson, William A., Gerhards, Jürgen and Rucht, Dieter (2002) 'Four models of the public sphere in modern democracies', *Theory and Society*, 31: 289–324.

Finch, Janet (1992) *Family Obligations*. Cambridge: Polity Press.

Firestone, Shulamith (1974) *The Dialectic of Sex: The Case for Feminist Revolution*. New York: Morrow.

Folbre, Nancy (1994) *Who Pays for the Kids? Gender and the Structures of Constraint*. London: Routledge.

Ford, R. and Millar, J. (eds) (1998) *Public Lives and Private Responses – Lone Parenthood amd Future Policy in the UK*. London: Policy Studies Institute.

Franklin, Sarah (1997) *Embodied Progress: A Cultural Account of Assisted Conception*. London: Routledge.

Franklin, Sarah, Lury, Celia and Stacey, Jackie (eds) (1991) *Off-Centre: Feminism and Cultural Studies*. London: HarperCollins.

Fraser, Nancy (1997) *Justice Interruptus: Critical Reflections on the 'Postsocialist Condition'*. London: Routledge.

Fuss, Joanna (1990) *Essentially Speaking: Feminism, Nature and Difference*. London: Routledge.

Gardiner, Jean (1989) *Gender, Care and Economics*. Basingstoke: Macmillan.

Giddens, Anthony (1992) *The Transformation of Intimacy: Sexuality, Love and Eroticism in Modern Societies*. Cambridge: Polity Press.

Gilman, Charlotte Perkins (1966 [1898]) *Women and Economics: The Economic Factor Between Men and Women as a Factor in Social Evolution*. New York: Harper and Row. (Originally published Boston, MA: Small, Maynard and Co.)

Gilman, Charlotte Perkins (1909) 'How home conditions react upon the family', *American Journal of Sociology*, 14 (5): 592–605.

Hakim, Catherine (1992) 'Explaining trends in occupational segregation: the measurement, causes and consequences of the sexual division of labour', *European Sociological Review*, 8 (2): 127–52.

Haraway, Donna (1997) *Modest_Witness@Second_ Millennium. FemaleMan_MeetsOncomouse: Feminism and Technoscience*. New York: Routledge.

Harding, Sandra (1986) *The Science Question in Feminism*. Ithaca, NY: Cornell University Press.

Harding, Sandra (1991) *Whose Science? Whose Knowledge? Thinking from Women's Lives*. Milton Keynes: Open University Press.

Hartmann, Heidi (1976) 'Capitalism, patriarchy and job segregation by sex', *Signs*, 1 (3): 137–69.

Hawkesworth, Mary (1997) 'Confounding gender', *Signs*, 22 (3): 649–85.

Hearn, Jeff (1998) *The Violences of Men: How Men Talk About and How Agencies Respond to Men's Violence to Women*. London: Sage.

Hester, Marianne, Kelly, Liz and Radford, Jill (eds) (1996) *Women, Violence and Male Power*. Buckingham: Open University Press.

Hobson, Barbara (ed.) (2000) *Gender and Citizenship in Transition*. London: Macmillan.

Holmwood, John (2001) 'Gender and critical realism: a critique of Sayer', *Sociology*, 35 (4): 947–65.

Hoskyns, Catherine (1996) *Integrating Gender: Women, Law and Politics in the European Union*. London: Verso.

Huber, Evelyne and Stephens, John D. (2000) 'Partisan governance, women's employment, and the social democratic service state', *American Sociological Review*, 65: 323–42.

Irwin, Sarah (1995) *Rights of Passage – Social Change and the Transition from Youth to Adulthood*. London: UCL Press.

Jackson, Stevi (1999) *Heterosexuality in Question*. London: Sage.

Jenson, Jane (1997) 'Who cares? Gender and welfare regimes', *Social Politics*, 4 (2): 182–7.

Johnson, Holly (1996) *Dangerous Domains*. Toronto: Nelson.

Kandiyoti, Deniz (ed.) (1991) *Women, Islam and the State*. Basingstoke: Macmillan.

Kelly, Liz (1989) *Surviving Sexual Violence*. Cambridge: Polity Press.

Kelly, Liz, Regan, Linda and Burton, Sheila (1992) 'Defending the indefensible? Quantitative methods and feminist research', in Hilary Hinds, Ann Phoenix and Jackie Stacey (eds), *Working Out: New Directions for Women's Studies*. London: Falmer Press.

Lees, Sue (1993) *Sugar and Spice: Sexuality and Adolescent Girls*. London: Penguin.

Lister, Ruth (1997) *Citizenship: Feminist Perspectives*. Basingstoke: Macmillan.

López, José and Scott, John (2000) *Social Structure*. Buckingham: Open University Press.

Lorber, Judith (2000) 'Using gender to undo gender: a feminist degendering movement', *Feminist Theory*, 1 (1): 79–95.

McCall, Leslie (2001) *Gender, Class and Race in the New Economy*. London: Routledge.

MacKinnon, Catherine (1989) *Toward a Feminist Theory of the State*. Cambridge, MA, USA: Harvard University Press.

McLennan, Greg (1995) 'Feminism, epistemology and postmodernism: reflections on current ambivalence', *Sociology*, 29 (2): 391–409.

McNay, Lois (1992) *Foucault and Feminism: Power, Gender and the Self*. Cambridge: Polity Press.

McRae, S. (1993) 'Returning to work after childbirth', *European Sociological Review*, 9 (2): 125–38.

Manza, Jeff and Brooks, Clem (1998) 'The gender gap in US Presidential elections: When? Why? Implications?', *American Journal of Sociology*, 103 (5): 1235–66.

Mazur, Amy (2002) *Theorizing Feminist Policy*. Oxford: Oxford University Press.

Mead, Margaret (1928) *Coming of Age in Samoa: A Study of Adolescence and Sex in Primitive Societies*. Harmondsworth: Penguin.

Medaglia, Azadeh (2001) *Patriarchal Structures and Ethnicity*. Avebury: Ashgate.

Meehan, Elizabeth and Sevenhuijsen, Selma (eds) (1991) *Equality, Politics and Gender*. London: Sage.

Mies, Maria (1986) *Patriarchy and Accumulation on a World Scale*. London: Zed.

Mirrlees-Black, C. (1999) *Domestic Violence: Findings from a new British Crime Survey Self-completion Questionnaire*. Home Office Research Study 191. London: Home Office.

Mirza, Heidi Safia (ed.) (1997) *Black British Feminism: A Reader*. London: Routledge.

Moghadam, Valentine M. (ed.) (1994) *Identity Politics and Women: Cultural Reassertions and Feminisms in International Perspective*. Boulder, CO: Westview Press.

Moghadam, Valentine M. (2000) 'Transnational feminist networks: collective action in an era of globalization', *International Sociology*, 15 (1): 57–85.

Mohanty, Chandra Talpade (1991) 'Under Western eyes: feminist scholarship and colonial discourses', in Chandra Talpade Mohanty, Ann Russo and Lourdes Torres (eds), *Third World Women and the Politics of Feminism*. Bloomington, IN: Indiana University Press.

Mooney, Jayne (2000) *Gender, Violence and the Social Order*. Basingstoke: Macmillan.

Morgan, David H.J. (1992) *Discovering Men*. London: Routledge.

Moser, Caroline, O.N. (1993) *Gender Planning and Development: Theory, Practice and Training*. London: Routledge.

O'Reilly, Jacqueline and Fagan, Colette (eds) (1998) *Part-Time Prospects: An International Comparison of Part-Time Work in Europe, North America and the Pacific Rim*. London: Routledge.

Nelson, Lynn Hankinson (1990) *Who Knows: From Quine to a Feminist Empiricism*. Philadelphia, PA: Temple University Press.

Norris, Pippa and Lovenduski, Joni (1995) *Political Recruitment: Gender, Race and Class in the British Parliament*. Cambridge: Cambridge University Press.

Nussbaum, Martha (2000) *Women and Human Development: The Capabilities Approach*. Cambridge: Cambridge University Press.

Oakley, Ann (1985) *Sex, Gender and Society*. London: Gower.

O'Connor, Julia S., Orloff, Ann Shola and Shaver, Sheila (1999) *States, Markets, Families: Gender, Liberalism and Social Policy in Australia, Canada, Great Britain and the United States*. Cambridge: Cambridge University Press.

Orloff, Ann Shola (1993) 'Gender and the social rights of citizenship: state policies and gender relations in comparative perspective', *American Sociological Review*, 58 (3): 303–28.

Parsons, Talcott, with Bales, Robert F., Olds, James, Zelditch, Morris and Slater, Philip E. (1955) *Family Socialization and Interaction Process*. Glencoe, IL: The Free Press.

Phizacklea, Annie (1990) *Unpacking the Fashion Industry*. London: Routledge.

Phizacklea, Annie and Wolkowitz, Carol (1995) *Homeworking Women: Gender, Racism and Class at Work*. London: Sage.

Phoenix, Ann (1991) *Young Mothers?* Cambridge: Polity Press.

Platt, Jennifer (2003) *The British Sociological Association: A Sociological History*. Durham: Sociology Press.

Ramanzanoglu, Caroline (ed.) (1991) *Up Against Foucault: Explorations of Some Tensions Between Foucault and Feminism*. London: Routledge.

Reinharz, Shulamit (1993) *Feminist Methods in Social Research*. New York: Oxford University Press.

Rees, Teresa (1998) *Mainstreaming Equality in the European Union: Education, Training and Labour Market Policies*. London: Routledge.

Reskin, Barbara and Roos, Patricia (1990) *Job Queues, Gender Queues: Explaining Women's Inroads into Male Occupations*. Philadelphia, PA: Temple University Press.

Richardson, Diane (2001) *Rethinking Sexuality*. London: Sage.

Rose, Hilary (1994) *Love, Power and Knowledge: Towards a Feminist Transformation of the Sciences*. Cambridge: Polity Press.

Rose, Hilary and Rose, Steven (2001) *Alas Poor Darwin: Arguments Against Evolutionary Psychology*. London: Vintage.

Rubery, Jill, Smith, Mark and Fagan, Colette (1999) *Women's Employment in Europe: Trends and Prospects*. London: Routledge.

Sainsbury, Diane (1996) *Gender Equality and Welfare States*. Cambridge: Cambridge University Press.

Sayer, Andrew (2000) 'System, lifeworld and gender: associational versus counterfactual thinking', *Sociology*, 34: 707–25.

Scott, Alison (ed.) (1994) *Gender Segregation and Social Change.* Oxford: Oxford University Press.

Scott, Joan W. (1988) 'Deconstructing equality-versus-difference: or, the uses of poststructuralist theory for feminism', *Feminist Studies*, 14 (1): 33–49.

Segal, Lynne (1987) *Is the Future Female? Troubled Thoughts on Contemporary Feminism.* London: Virago.

Sevenhuijsen, Selma (1998) *Citizenship and the Ethics of Care.* London: Routledge.

Skocpol, Theda (1992) *Protecting Soldiers and Mothers: The Political Origins of Social Policy in the United States.* Cambridge, MA: Belknap Press.

Straus, Murray A. and Gelles, R.J. (eds) (1990) *Physical Violence in American Families.* New Brunswick, NJ: Transaction Books.

Taylor-Browne, Julia (ed.) (2000) *Reducing Domestic Violence: What Works?* London: The Stationery Office.

Thomas, Sue (1991) 'The impact of women on state legislative policies', *Journal of Politics*, 53 (4): 958–76.

Turner, Bryan (1984) *The Body and Society: Explorations in Social Theory.* Oxford: Blackwell.

Vargas, V. and Wieringa, S. (1998) 'The triangles of empowerment: processes and actors in the making of public policy', in G. Lycklama a Nijeholt, V. Vargas and S. Wieringa (eds), *Women's Movements and Public Policy in Europe, Latin America and the Caribbean.* New York: Garland.

Walby, Sylvia (1990) *Theorizing Patriarchy.* Oxford: Blackwell.

Walby, Sylvia (1994) 'Methodological and theoretical issues in the comparative analysis of gender relations in Western Europe', *Environment and Planning A*, 26: 1339–54.

Walby, Sylvia (1997) *Gender Transformations.* London: Routledge.

Walby, Sylvia (1999) 'The new regulatory state: the social powers of the European Union', *British Journal of Sociology*, 50 (1): 118–40.

Walby, Sylvia (2000) 'Gender, globalization and democracy', *Gender and Development*, 8 (1): 20–8.

Walby, Sylvia (2001a) 'Against epistemological chasms: the science question in feminism revisited', *Signs: A Journal of Women in Culture and Society*, 26 (2): 485–509.

Walby, Sylvia (2001b) 'From community to coalition: the politics of recognition as the handmaiden of the politics of redistribution', *Theory, Culture and Society*, 18 (2–3): 113–35.

Walby, Sylvia (forthcoming, 2006) *Complex Social Systems: Theorizations and Comparisons in a Postcolonial Global Era.* London: Sage.

Walby, Sylvia and Myhill, Andrew (2001) 'Comparing the methodology of the new national surveys of violence against women', *British Journal of Criminology*, 41 (3): 502–22.

Wängnerud, Lena (2000) 'Testing the politics of presence: women's representation in the Swedish Riksdag', *Scandinavian Political Studies*, 23 (1): 67–91.

Weeks, Jeffrey (1995) *Invented Moralities: Sexual Values in an Age of Uncertainty.* Cambridge: Polity Press.

Young, Iris (1990) *Justice and the Politics of Difference.* Princeton, NJ: Princeton University Press.

Yuval-Davis, Nira (1997) *Gender and Nation.* London: Sage.

22

Population and Society: Historical Trends and Future Prospects

CHARLES HIRSCHMAN

The statistics of population behavior in the mass are a dry topic treated in isolation, though they possess their own fascination and rational structure. But they measure events, which are central to the life of men and women in all ages. Once attention is turned outward from the events themselves to the social and economic environment in which they occur, the appeal and importance of demography is apparent. The pressures of hard times and the opportunities of happier periods are reflected in historical demography like images in a camera obscura. The picture always needs interpretation and may lack the polychrome fullness of historical reality but it forms a clear and dependable outline to which color may be added as the population characteristics are related to their setting. (Wrigley, 1969: 28)

INTRODUCTION

The population of the world grew by 50 per cent from 1900 to 1950, and then increased by 200 per cent over the next 50 years to reach 6 billion just before the turn of the twenty-first century. Even with fertility declining and a slower rate of population growth in most countries, the United Nations predicts a global population of about 9 billion in 2050 – eventually stabilizing at about 10 billion by the end of the century. Large numbers, such as these, tend to

dull the senses and elicit little response from sociologists or the public at large. Yet, these bare demographic facts reveal the absolutely amazing progress of humankind during the twentieth century.

After a century with two world wars, the Holocaust, a Cold War that legitimated the theory of mutually assured destruction, the failed experiment of communist regimes, and the spread of HIV/AIDS – to name only a few of the twentieth-century horrors, it may seem counter-intuitive to speak of progress in modern times. In general, sociological accounts and theories offer little respite from the general tendency to point to the many failings of the modern world. As a discipline, sociology often focuses on the study of social problems, and there is a thin line between the sociological perspective and social criticism. Yet, a critical awareness of the many shortcomings of the contemporary world must be balanced with an historical awareness that most present-day societies are much less dangerous, stratified and autocratic than the agrarian world (and the early industrial world) of previous generations.

Perhaps the best evidence of improvement in the human condition is the demographic change that has taken place over the past two-and-a-half centuries. For all species, population growth is the best measure of adaptation to local ecological niches. Throughout human history, the size of a local population was considered an index of prosperity (Livi-Bacci, 1997: 1). At the eve of the first industrial revolution around 1750, the world's population was about 770 million, reflecting an average growth rate of only slightly above zero for the entire course of human history. From 1750 to 1950, the growth rate of the world's population 'took off', with an annual average rate of 0.7 per cent and reached a level of 2.5 billion by 1950 (Livi-Bacci, 1997: 31). Then, the world's population literally exploded from 1950 to 2000, with a growth rate of over 1.8 per cent per year, and humanity now numbers more than 6 billion souls.

How did this happen? The most proximate answer is that mortality began to decline in poor countries as well as rich ones with the control of infectious diseases through the diffusion of public heath programs and modern antibiotics. But there is a longer story that includes the expansion of agricultural production and economic growth in many countries, the development of local and long-distance communications and transportation systems, and a world system that included the World Health Organization and international assistance to head off epidemics and famines. Compared to what they should be or could be, social and economic conditions around the world are deplorable, but relative to past times, the twentieth century, and especially the second half of it, looks pretty good.

Population growth is a two-edge sword. In the short term, growth reflects good times, but if maintained for any period of time, increasing numbers put pressure on resources, especially food production. In the world of nature, rapid growth in the numbers of any species soon leads to a population implosion, as the carrying capacity of the local environment is exceeded. *Homo sapiens* has had, on occasion, a few ways out of the Malthusian trap of a population growing faster than its subsistence. The first is migration, and much of human history has taken the form of expansive societies spilling outwards to nearby and distant lands. The second means is technological and organizational change, which has allowed human societies to extract more subsistence and energy from natural resources. A spectacular growth in knowledge, and the

organizational and technological means to apply it, has been the engine that has allowed contemporary populations to far exceed any historical limits on subsistence.

Can this continue? Even with renewable sources of energy and materials, there would be an eventual collision between continued population growth and a finite world. But the collision may be averted because population growth has been slowing in recent decades, not from rising mortality, but because of voluntary controls on fertility. Fertility declines began in several rapidly modernizing countries in the late nineteenth century and spread to most Western countries in the early decades in the twentieth century. Then quite unexpectedly, fertility declines began in several Asian countries in the 1960s and then spread to many developing countries in Latin America and Africa in the last two decades of the century. If current trends continue, the world's population will grow by only 50 per cent from 2000 to 2050 and then gradually level off at about 10 billion. Although public policies may help to speed the process, fertility transitions appear, in ways not fully understood, to be endogenous to the process of socio-economic development and improvements in the human condition.

Although much of the sociological interest in population trends relates to the consequences of current and future population trends (for example, Can the world sustain a population of 10 billion? Do population growth and density affect state formation and political integration? What are the effects of population growth and age composition on savings rates and economic growth?), most demographic research has focused on the somewhat less complicated questions of the determinants of population trends, and in particular on mortality, fertility, migration and urbanization. Demographers, most of whom are sociologists, have accumulated a substantial reservoir of empirical generalizations on all of these topics and have also generated several theoretical interpretations of demographic transformations that have accompanied the creation of the modern world. This chapter is a preliminary overview of some of the major research findings, empirical generalizations and theoretical debates on the relationship between social change and population trends, with a primary focus on the twentieth century, which witnessed the most dramatic demographic changes in human history.

POPULATION GROWTH AND MIGRATION IN HUMAN HISTORY

Modern human beings (*Homo sapiens*) are the most recent branch of the hominids that emerged in Africa around 100,000 years ago (Cavalli-Sforza et al., 1994; Diamond, 1993). The development of language (which was dependent on the human ability to speak) allowed human beings to accumulate and share knowledge and to coordinate group actions in order to collect and hunt for food more effectively than any other large animal. The ability to communicate through language allowed humans to rise to the top of the food chain and created the first population explosion, or 'great leap forward', with early humans spreading to all corners of the globe, beginning around 50,000–60,000 years ago.

McEvedy and Jones (1978: 14) estimate that the average density of hunting and gathering human populations was about 1 person per 10 square kilometers, though it could have been somewhat higher in bountiful environments. Even with modest levels of population growth, most Paleolithic bands could have begun to exceed the carrying capacity of their local environment within a few generations. Migration is probably the first human response to population pressure (Davis, 1974). As families moved to new areas, they had to learn how to adapt to new climatic zones and to survive on different flora and fauna. But human societies have proved extraordinarily adaptable, and within a few tens of thousands of years, human settlements had spread to most of the major regions of the world (Cavalli-Sforza et al., 1994; Davis, 1974; McNeill, 1984). Although archeological evidence is sketchy, human societies reached Asia around 60,000 years ago, the Americas between 15,000 and 30,000 years ago, and finally spread to some of the small Pacific Islands only within the last millennium (Cavalli-Sforza and

Cavalli-Sforza, 1995: 122; Diamond, 1997: 341). This early population explosion, though modest by modern standards, revealed the potential reproductive capacity of human beings and the flexibility of human societies to respond to population pressure by developing varied cultures adapted to local ecosystems.

The most consequential response to population pressure in prehistory was the domestication of plants and animals about 10,000 years ago (Harris, 1977: ch. 3). Although settled agricultural communities created the conditions for an expansion of population growth and the great civilizations of antiquity, the shift from migratory foragers to farmers was probably involuntary, and the last resort when populations had run out of all other options for survival. Even today, hunting and gathering populations generally resist efforts by states and missionaries to settle them in permanent villages and adopt farming. Agricultural populations generally work longer hours and consume less than hunting-and-gathering populations, in addition to enduring the oppression from the ruling class that inevitably arises in societies with agriculture (Harris, 1977; Boserup, 1981).

Population pressures (perhaps accompanied by coercion from elites) led to the independent 'invention' of agriculture in numerous places from around 8500 to 3000 BC, including Southwest Asia (the 'Fertile Crescent'), China, New Guinea and multiple locations in the Americas and Africa (Diamond, 1997: 100). For a few generations, agriculture can provide a safety valve for population growth. For the same unit of land, agricultural production can support a much denser population than hunting and foraging. Agriculture also changes the conditions affecting fertility and mortality dynamics, including the motivation for children.

Fertility levels in hunting and gathering societies were probably lower than in agricultural populations. Most pre-agricultural populations are (were) migratory and mothers had to carry small children for long distances. Since a woman could carry only a single child at a time, the optimal fertility pattern would be one with long inter-birth intervals. Infanticide was a common cultural practice in such populations if one birth followed too soon after another. The availability of edible plants and animals usually set an upper limit on the population that could survive in a local environment. If the population of a band exceeded the carrying capacity of the local environment, the welfare of the community would be endangered until some persons died or left the band. A stable population size was more adaptive for most hunting and gathering populations than a growing population.

The higher level of fertility in agricultural societies was fundamentally a response to the higher incidence of mortality in the large densely settled agrarian populations. This structural necessity (high fertility needed to offset high mortality) was accompanied by a variety of economic and social incentives for high levels of childbearing at the household level (Cavalli-Sforza and Cavalli-Sforza, 1995: 134). Children were a primary source of labor in agricultural communities. On farms, even small children can provide productive hands by watching over farm animals or doing routine chores. An increase in the population of an agricultural community could generally be absorbed through expansion as nearby lands were cleared and brought into production.

The tendency of agrarian populations to spread to new areas, coincident with the displacement of hunting and gathering peoples, reveals the close parallels between demographic and social change. Analyses of the genetic heritage of the contemporary populations of Europe reveals that outward migration of agriculturalists from the Middle East gradually populated most of Europe from about 9000 to 6000 years ago (Cavalli-Sforza and Cavalli-Sforza, 1995: ch. 5). Although there were certainly admixtures from both the indigenous Mesolithic hunter–gatherers and Neolithic farmers, the higher densities of agricultural populations gave them a demographic edge that probably led to military dominance and greater contributions to the gene pool of subsequent generations. This process has been repeated in modern times with the expansion of Europeans to Australia and the Americas, Russians to Siberia, and Chinese to their southern frontiers.

Population data for ancient times are crude estimates based on limited information

and extrapolations (Coale, 1974; Durand, 1977; Livi-Bacci, 1997: 31; United Nations, 1973: ch. 2). From the origins of humankind around 100,000 years ago to the dawn of agriculture (about 10,000 BC), the human population of the world increased to about 6 million. Although this figure may seem tiny, it included tens of thousands of hunting and gathering societies, whose presence had spread to virtually all corners of Europe, Africa, Asia, Australia and the Americas. As more and more populations became dependent on agriculture, human population densities increased in most regions: the world's population grew to approximately 250 million by the year 1 AD. About two-thirds of this population lived in Asia (including the Middle East, China and South Asia), but there were about 30 million in Europe, 25 million in Africa and perhaps 12 million in the Americas. The growth from 6 to 250 million over 10,000 years represents an average rate of less than 0.04 per cent per year.

Just as the world had probably reached its carrying capacity for hunting and gathering populations at about 6 million (or 5–10 million) around 10,000 BC, agricultural populations probably oscillated with years of expansion followed by contractions caused by famine, epidemics and wars. The estimated world population growth rate over the next 1000 years of approximately zero does not mean that agricultural societies maintained a sustainable balance with their environments. Indeed, many early civilizations in the Middle East, Asia and the Americas experienced demographic implosions as precarious irrigation systems or trade networks were destroyed because of invasions, plagues, or breakdowns in social systems.

The population on all continents increased from the year 1000 to 1750 at an average annual rate of about 0.01 per cent – about double the estimated growth rate from 10,000 BC to the year 1 AD. Again, the historical trends are uneven, with decades or even centuries of population decline followed by periods of expansion as ascendant empires developed trade networks and lessened local warfare. Some scholars have speculated that the diffusion of crops from the New World (potato, maize, manioc) contributed to the expanded food production in Asia, Europe and Africa after 1500 (Durand, 1977). European expansion, however, had deadly consequences for the peoples of the New World. The indigenous American peoples, estimated to number over 40 million in 1500, were decimated by European diseases and conquest.

The next major turning point in world demographic history is the industrial revolution, which is usually dated with its origins around 1750. It is more realistic to consider industrialization as a process, which began in eighteenth-century England and spread throughout much of the world over the next two-and-a-half centuries. Indeed, the full weight of the industrial and urban revolutions in Asia, Africa and Latin America is still in the future. The breath-taking changes in scientific knowledge, transportation and communications, economic productivity and the structure and role of governments have few precedents in human history. In turn, these social, economic and political changes have transformed the conditions under which human communities live, with revolutionary consequences for health and well-being. Initially, the impact on human mortality was modest, with perhaps less frequent periods of crisis mortality in the nineteenth and early twentieth centuries than in earlier eras. The major real gains in life expectancy occurred in the twentieth century, especially during the second half of the century.

It is difficult to fully understand the enormity of the demographic consequences of the declines in mortality as the world's population grew from 1 billion shortly after 1800 to 6 billion shortly before 2000. Livi-Bacci (1997: 32–3), drawing upon the work by Bourgeois-Pichat, helps to convey these almost unfathomable magnitudes by interpreting current population numbers as fractions of the human population that has ever lived on Earth. For example, the population alive in the year 2000 represents almost 8 per cent of the estimated 82 billion humans ever born. If we were to weight each birth by longevity, then the estimated person-years lived by those alive in 2000 represent almost one-fifth of the person-years lived since the origins of the species. Whatever the human potential for good or evil, more possibilities are present today than ever before in history.

POPULATION CHANGE IN THE TWENTIETH CENTURY

Although world population size began to slope upward in the eighteenth and nineteenth centuries, the major drama of world population growth is a twentieth-century phenomenon. The basic facts of twentieth-century population growth are presented in Table 22.1, with figures of the estimated population of the major world regions for 1900, 1950 and 2000, and the medium variant projections for 2050. The 1950, 2000 and 2050 figures are from the most recent edition of the United Nations's *World Population Prospects*, and the estimates for 1900 are based on the medium value of the estimated range reported by John Durand (cited in United Nations, 1973: 21).

The three top panels in Table 22.1 show the estimated populations, the percentage distribution by major world regions, and the estimated rates of annual population growth. Trends in population growth over the twentieth century reveal the impact of varied social, economic and political changes across major world regions as well as the diffusion of ideas and institutions designed to reduce mortality and morbidity.

In 1900, Europe and North America were ascendant. Although comprising less than one-third of the world's population, European nations had, through their military might and industrial economies, colonized much of Asia and Africa and organized a world economic system that directed a disproportionate share of the profits of global production (from plantations, mines, trade and transportation) to Europe. Demographically, Europe had experienced a substantial recovery from the Black Death of the fourteenth century, and population growth rates accelerated with the developments in agriculture, industry and governance in the nineteenth century (Durand, 1977).

In 1900, the greatest concentration of the world's population was in Asia, where more

Table 22.1 Estimates of population trends and medium variant projections of population size, fertility and mortality for the world and major world regions, 1900 to 2050

	Population (000)				Percentage distribution				Ave. annual growth rate (%)		
	1900	1950	2000	2050	1900	1950	2000	2050	1900–50	1950–2000	2000–50
World	1608	2519	6057	9322	100	100	100	100	0.9	1.8	0.9
Africa	120	221	794	2000	7	9	13	21	1.2	2.6	1.8
Asia	915	1399	3672	5428	57	56	61	58	0.8	1.9	0.8
Europe	423	548	727	603	26	22	12	6	0.5	0.6	−0.4
Latin Am. and Caribbean	63	167	519	806	4	7	9	9	1.9	2.3	0.9
North America	81	172	314	437	5	7	5	5	1.5	1.2	0.7
Oceania	6	13	31	47	0	1	1	1	1.5	1.7	0.8

	Total fertility rate			Life expectancy at birth (both sexes)		
	Estimated		Projected	Estimated		Projected
	1950–55	1995–2000	2045–50	1950–55	1995–2000	2045–50
World	5.01	2.82	2.15	46.5	65.0	76.0
Africa	6.71	5.27	2.39	37.8	51.4	69.5
Asia	5.88	2.70	2.08	41.3	65.8	77.1
Europe	2.66	1.41	1.81	65.7	73.2	80.8
Latin Am. and Caribbean	5.89	2.69	2.10	51.4	69.3	77.8
North America	3.47	2.00	2.08	68.9	76.7	82.7
Oceania	3.87	2.41	2.06	60.9	73.5	80.6

Source: United Nations, 1953: 11; 2001

than 900 million people lived (double the size of Europe) – almost six in ten of all humanity. The large Asian population reflects the legacy of history; even in antiquity, the populations of China and India numbered in the tens of millions (Durand, 1977). Fertile river valleys, complex irrigation systems, extensive trading systems, and strong states created agrarian civilizations with extensive peasant populations. Over the centuries, these civilizations expanded and contracted with accordion-like waves of demographic growth and decline. Asia had fallen behind the European economic and technological advances in the eighteenth and nineteenth centuries, but Asian populations had, overall, continued to grow during this period (Durand, 1977).

At the margins, with collectively less than one-fifth of the world's population in 1900, were Africa, Latin America and northern America (this UN classification puts Mexico and Central America in Latin America). Although thickly populated in places, Africa did not have the densely settled agrarian empires of Asia nor the several centuries of economic expansion that Europe had experienced. After being virtually depopulated by European diseases and conquest, the Americas had been growing rapidly by migration and natural increase for several centuries, but only comprised less than 10 per cent of the world's population in 1900.

During the twentieth century, there were two dominant demographic trends: unprecedented rates of population growth and a shifting of the balance of the world's population to the poorer regions of Africa, Latin America and Asia. This second trend will accelerate during the twenty-first century. The combined populations of Europe and northern America were 30 per cent of the world's population in 1900, 29 per cent in 1950, 17 per cent in 2000 and will be only 11 per cent in 2050. Over this 150 year period, Asia will roughly hold its own, with almost 60 per cent of the world's population, the African share will triple from 7 to 21 per cent and the Latin American proportion will double to 9 per cent. This redistribution of the world's population is reflected in the differential rates of population growth in the right-most

panel of Table 22.1. For most of the twentieth century, the European population was growing at a rate only half or one-third of that in other world regions. During the second half of the twentieth century, Europe grew at 0.6 per cent per annum while Asia, Africa and Latin America grew at almost 2 per cent per year or even higher. The medium level UN population projections from 2000 to 2050 show that Europe will experience negative growth, most other regions will be below 1 per cent, and African rates will decline to just below 2 per cent per year.

Because of the large initial populations and the very high rates of growth in Asia, Africa and Latin America, the projected levels of absolute numbers are staggering. In 1900, the population of Africa was about one-quarter that of Europe; by 2000, the two regions had about the same demographic weight, and by 2050, Africa will be three times larger than Europe. The projected African population of 2 billion in 2050 will be considerably larger than the world's population in 1900. The population of Asia in 2000 is already twice the world's population a century earlier and even exceeds the world's 1950 population by 50 per cent. Not only will Europe and other 'developed regions' represent a smaller share of the world's population, they are likely to be smaller in absolute terms. The United Nations medium projections, based on rather conservative criteria, predict that Europe will have 100 million fewer persons in 2050 than in 2000. The power of compound interest (or of geometric increase in Malthus's memorable phase) can lead to huge increases in population size in only a few decades. This power is a valuable trait when a society is recovering from a major demographic catastrophe, but it can lead to trouble in a world of fixed resources.

How will the world be different with more persons from the poorer regions and less from the contemporary advanced countries? This is an important topic, but one that has hardly been addressed in sociological research. In general, sociology as a discipline has been primarily focused on the study of the United States and a few other industrial societies (Hirschman, 2003). The fields of international and comparative sociology will become increasingly important, as sociologists begin to address questions about the full range of contemporary and historical societies.

The contemporary period of population growth is unique, not only because of the huge numbers involved, but also because the values of the components of growth have changed. Historically, population growth occurred under conditions of high fertility and moderately high mortality. The mortality declines of the twentieth century have no parallel in human history. In the context of very low mortality, even moderate levels of fertility have given rise to substantial population growth. The bottom panels of Table 22.1 show estimates of mortality and fertility by world regions for the middle (1950–5) and late (1995–2000) twentieth century with projections to the mid-twenty-first century prepared by the United Nations.

The mid-twentieth-century estimate of life expectancy for the world as a whole, about 46 years, is an average of two wildly divergent patterns. In the developed regions of northern America and Europe, life expectancy was 65 years or higher, while average life expectancy was 51 years in Latin America, 41 years in Asia and only 38 years in Africa. The range of mortality in the poorer regions of the world at mid-century, from life expectancies in the high 30s to the low 50s, were comparable to those prevailing in Europe and areas of European settlement around 1900 (United Nations, 1973: 116). The progress in lowering mortality in the developed world during the first half of the twentieth century was a harbinger of comparable progress in the developing world in the second half of the twentieth century. At century's end, average life expectancy in Latin America and Asia had risen to 65 or higher, and was only a few years lower than the life expectancies in Europe and northern America, which stood in the mid-70s. Although significant absolute progress was registered in raising life expectancy in Africa to about 51 years by the late 1990s, a huge gap in mortality remains between Africa and developed countries and even relative to most of Asia and Latin America.

The United Nations mortality projections for the mid-twenty-first century predict convergence with life expectancy of about 80 in Europe and northern America, the high 70s in Latin America and almost 70 in Africa. These optimistic projections assume that present trends will continue, and that there will be no major societal breakdowns or demographic catastrophes. The HIV/AIDS pandemic has had catastrophic effects on mortality in some African countries, but its overall impact on world population growth is fairly modest, perhaps lowering the rate of world population growth from 1.5 to 1.4 around the year 2000 (Caldwell, 2000: 117).

These declines in mortality have been accompanied by parallel trends in fertility over the twentieth century. Table 22.1 shows Total Fertility Rates (TFR), an index of period fertility for a population, constructed to correspond to the average number of births per woman at the completion of childbearing. At mid-century, women in developed countries had two to four children – these rates were actually somewhat higher than those prevailing in the 1930s because of the post-Second World War baby boom. From 1870 to 1930, most Western countries experienced fertility transitions of 50 per cent or more – from five to six children per couple to only two to three. Given that mortality was falling even faster, most Western countries experienced rapid population growth during the first half of the twentieth century.

In contrast to declining fertility in Europe and northern America during the first half of the twentieth century, fertility remained high in Africa, Latin America and Asia. In the mid-1950s, TFRs in Asia and Latin America averaged just below six children per couple and almost seven children per couple in Africa. During the second half of the century, especially after 1970, fertility declined everywhere in the world. In advanced countries, the baby boom of the 1950s gave way to below replacement level fertility (replacement level fertility is defined as two surviving children per woman in the reproductive age range). In Asia and Latin America, fertility declined by more than 50 per cent during the second half of the century, with average fertility of less than three children per couple in the late 1990s.

Only in Africa does aggregate fertility remain high. The UN estimates in Table 22.1

show that African fertility declined from 6.7 to 5.3 births per woman from the 1950s to the 1990s. The United Nations projects an accelerating pace of the African fertility decline in the early decades of the twenty-first century, and a predicted TFR of 2.4 births per woman at mid-century. For the balance of the world, fertility projections hover around the replacement level for the mid-twenty-first century. The one exception is Europe, where current fertility is around 1.4 births per woman, and the projections suggest a recovery to a TFR of 1.8. Since projections typically try to extrapolate recent changes into the future, there is much more uncertainty when it is assumed that a lower asymptote (replacement level fertility) is being approached or a change in direction is likely.

The theories behind these global changes are addressed in the following sections on mortality and fertility transitions.

THE RETREAT OF MORTALITY

Prior to the past 100 years, high 'normal' levels of mortality and periodic episodes of crisis mortality were part of the fabric of every society. Good times without war, famine or epidemics meant that only 2–4 per cent of a population would die in a year. When disaster struck, as it periodically did, up to 10 per cent of a population might perish in a single year. In societies with 'normal' high death rates, parents could expect to lose one or more of their children in infancy, and marriages were typically broken by the death of one spouse before old age was reached.

By the middle of the twentieth century, average death rates in industrial societies were routinely less than 1 per cent per year, and most children could expect to reach maturity experiencing only the occasional death of an elderly relative. Nowadays, it is taken for granted that most parents can expect to live to see all of their children reach adulthood and to anticipate grandparenthood. It was not always so. Only a few generations ago, infectious diseases were an ever-present danger that took the lives of people at all ages and in all social classes. At present, the rare deaths of children and young adults are primarily

due to accidents and violence. Although there are many problems and great tragedies in industrial societies, the retreat of death from the young and middle ages is a social achievement that is all too rarely acknowledged.

The conquest of high death rates was not a smooth trend over the millennia or even during the first century of the industrial era. Rather, progress in lowering mortality is a product of the socio-economic development, and especially of scientific advances, in the twentieth century. For example, the germ theory of disease, which laid the groundwork for modern medicine, only originated with the scientific work of the Pasteurs in the late nineteenth century, and it was some decades before the medical establishment adopted procedures that reduced the spread of infectious diseases. But we are getting ahead of the story. To understand why and how mortality declined in the twentieth century, we need to understand what factors kept mortality high throughout most of human history and the conditions that allowed for modest progress before the twentieth century.

Early theories postulated that the expansion of the food supply (with agriculture and domesticated animals) led to larger populations because of improved nutrition and lower levels of mortality (Childe, 1951[1936]). Agriculture did lead to larger populations and more dense settlements, but not because of improvements in health and lower mortality. Indeed, most research points to the conclusion that hunting and gathering peoples were healthier and had longer lives than settled agricultural populations (Davis, 1974; Livi-Bacci, 1997: 37–47). Oppression and high taxes by ruling elites meant that peasant populations probably had poorer and less varied diets than hunters and gatherers. But the primary reason for higher mortality in settled agricultural populations was the spread of infectious diseases.

Initial encounters between parasitic microorganisms and human populations often lead to epidemic diseases that kill off a high percentage of the exposed population. Over time, epidemic diseases often become endemic as the population develops resistance and the microorganism 'adapts' to become less lethal to its host. Although susceptible to epidemics, most hunting and gathering bands were simply too small in population numbers to sustain endemic diseases. Moreover, frequent movement from place to place provided some protection from the environmental conditions that favored breeding grounds for parasitic microorganisms.

Infectious diseases were much more likely to spread when large numbers of humans (and animals) were living in close proximity. Water sources in densely settled communities in premodern times, especially cities, were generally polluted because pathogens in human waste contaminated rivers, streams and backyard wells. The development of urban sanitary systems and modest improvements in the living conditions of urban workers in the nineteenth century were the essential first steps in lowering the spread of communicable diseases in cities. One of the few exceptions to the demographic sinkholes that characterized premodern cities was Japan. Cities in premodern Japan were much larger (and healthier) than cities in Europe because human waste was systematically collected for its value as fertilizer in Japanese agriculture (Hanley, 1987).

Life expectancies in premodern times ranged from the mid-20s to the mid-30s. Although there were systematic patterns in mortality across time and between societies, there is little evidence of long-term trends before the nineteenth century. William McNeill (1976) has argued that the prevalence of plagues (the most common form of crisis mortality in agrarian societies) was highly correlated with the rise and fall of empires and other epoch-making events in history. Since there was no scientific understanding for the occurrence and spread of disease, effective means of control and superstition were often confounded. Cultures and religious teachings that encouraged care for the sick, frequent bathing and basic sanitation could have had consequential impacts on mortality and population growth.

There appear to have been moderate declines in mortality in Europe in the eighteenth and nineteenth centuries that preceded the impact of any health and medical interventions. Perhaps the one consequential intervention was the vaccination against smallpox developed by Jenner in the late eighteenth century. Although vaccination was slow to spread throughout the world, the deadly scourge of smallpox was dramatically reduced by 1900. The most influential interpretation of the overall decline in the nineteenth century is the improvement in nutrition hypothesis by Thomas McKeown (1976). Based on detailed study of the decline in mortality in England and Wales of specific infectious diseases from the mid-nineteenth to the mid-twentieth century, McKeown shows that most of the declines preceded any effective medical treatment. Indeed, the mortality declines of many infectious diseases occurred before there was any scientific identification of the pathogen and understanding of transmission. McKeown argues that the expansion in agricultural and livestock production, and especially transportation networks, allowed populations to improve their diets and therefore develop greater resistance to disease. Critics have raised questions about McKeown's data on the expansion of food supplies and have suggested other possible reasons for the declines in mortality in the nineteenth century, including the shift to cotton clothing, which allowed for more frequent washing of clothes and related improvements in personal hygiene, including the widespread use of soap (Razzell, 1974).

The magnitude of these early declines in mortality was relatively modest compared to the much more dramatic declines in the twentieth century. For example, the average gains in life expectancy in Western nations in the nineteenth century were about 10 years of life (from the high 30s to the high 40s), while the gains in the twentieth century averaged about 30 years of life (to the high 70s) (Livi-Bacci, 1997: 121). Moreover, the declines in mortality spread beyond the industrial world to Latin America, Asia and Africa in the decades after the Second World War. The gains in life expectancy in the developing world during the second half of the twentieth century rival those registered in the developed world during the first half of the century.

Although some details remain in dispute, the major cause for the worldwide progress in lowering mortality is the scientific knowledge that has advanced medical science, public health programs, and changes in behavior. Samuel

Preston (1976: ch. 4) decomposed changes in life expectancy from the 1930s to 1960s for all countries in the world for which adequate mortality data were available. Less than 20 per cent of the average world-wide progress in life expectancy from the 1930s to the 1960s could be accounted for by increases in income. The balance, more than 80 per cent of the gains in life expectancy, is due to other factors, such as modern medicines and vaccinations that were widespread in the 1960s, but could not have been purchased for any price in the 1930s.

The lack of scientific knowledge to control mortality in past times is best illustrated by the very modest differentials in infant and child mortality by social class in the United States in 1900 (Preston and Haines, 1991: ch. 3). The children of physicians experienced death rates higher than those of farmers (Preston and Haines, 1991: 184–9). The major correlate of child mortality around 1900 was urban residence. Although incomes were generally lower in rural areas, the less dense environments of rural areas provided a modicum of protection from the transmission of communicable airborne and waterborne diseases that were ubiquitous in cities. Within the first few decades of the twentieth century, however, the mortality rates of children in urban middle class families dropped substantially, although the major breakthroughs in curative medicines did not appear until the 1940s and 1950s. Knowledge, derived on the germ theory of disease, allowed advantaged families to practice a number of sanitary measures, such as pasteurizing milk and sterilizing bottles, washing hands before preparing meals and not allowing foods to become contaminated, which dramatically improved the survival chances of their children (Preston and Haines, 1991: 209).

In the 1930s and the 1940s, sulfa drugs and antibiotics were discovered, which were followed by the development of other 'miracle drugs' to combat infectious diseases. For the first time in human history, medical science was able to cure many illnesses quickly and relatively inexpensively. These medical breakthroughs were accompanied by a wide range of preventive inoculations for infants and young children. The impact on health conditions and mortality has been incredible. The death rate in the United States declined by 30 per cent from 1940 to 1954, and almost all of the change is attributable to declines in deaths due to infectious diseases (Crimmins, 1981: 236).

After the conquest of infectious diseases in industrial countries, it was expected that there would be only modest progress in lowering mortality because chronic conditions that primarily affected the elderly (such as heart disease and cancer) were much less susceptible to the tools of modern medicine. Indeed, during the 1950s and 1960s there was a plateau in mortality levels, especially among adults (Crimmins, 1981: 236). During the 1970s and 1980s, however, there were significant gains in life expectancy, including among persons above age 65 (Crimmins et al., 1997). The reasons for this continued progress are not completely understood. New medications have been effective in the treatment of high blood pressure and other conditions that affect the elderly. There have also been important, though not universal, changes in lifestyles, such as reduced smoking and increased exercise. Although some of the earlier gains in life expectancy among the elderly appeared to be primarily to increase the 'years living with a disability', the latest evidence for the 1980s suggests that most of the additional years of added life are without disability (Crimmins et al., 1997).

After the Second World War, modern medicines and public health programs, often sponsored by the World Health Organization and other international organizations, spread around the globe. The impact, in the words of Kingsley Davis (1956), was 'an amazing decline in mortality' in Asia, Latin America and Africa. Based on the summary measures reported in Table 22.1 (United Nations estimates from the mid-1950s to the mid-1990s), life expectancy increased by more than one-third in Latin America and Africa, and by almost 70 per cent in Asia. The interventions responsible for most of these dramatic declines in mortality are immunizations, antibiotics, insecticides, and improved sources of purified water and sewage disposal (Preston, 1980: 300).

In the 1980s, there were claims of a slowdown in mortality progress in the developing world, but the evidence seems to point to continued declines in mortality (Hill and Pebley, 1989).

There remain, however, wide gaps in health and mortality between the developing world and Western industrial countries, although the gap is even wider between many of the rapidly modernizing countries in Asia and the very poor regions of Africa and Latin America. Poverty and malnutrition remain basic obstacles to improving health in many regions in of the world. There are also a number of major new health risks in many countries, including the epidemic spread of HIV/AIDS and the breakdown in the health care infrastructure in the former Soviet Union.

Estimates of those infected with HIV and future projections vary widely. Bongaarts (1996: 22) relies on WHO estimates to report a cumulative total of around 18.5 million adults infected by HIV worldwide from the mid-1970s to 1995. Caldwell (2000: 117) estimates that by the end of 1999, 50 million persons will have died of AIDS or will be infected and will likely die. The incidence and impact of AIDS is particularly severe in sub-Saharan Africa, and especially in East and South Africa. In Zimbabwe, where the HIV prevalence rate exceeds 25 per cent (Caldwell, 2000: 118), adult mortality rose dramatically, with the likelihood of death from age 15 to 60 rising from 0.20 in 1982 to 0.50 in 1997 for females, and from 0.31 to 0.65 for males (Feeney, 2001: 779). For sub-Saharan Africa as a whole, it is estimated that AIDS mortality raised the crude death rate (CDR) by about a point (from 13.8 to 14.8) in 1995 and is projected to have a somewhat larger impact in 2005 (raising the CDR from 11.2 to 12.7) (Bongaarts, 1996: 38).

Although there has not yet been a medical breakthrough to cure or prevent HIV infections, the incidence of HIV/AIDS has been dramatically reduced through behavioral changes (such as using condoms, needle exchanges) in a number of countries. Thailand has been an exemplary model of how government public health efforts and media attention can reduce the spread of HIV/AIDS (Hanenberg et al., 1994). The prevalence of HIV infection continued to rise in sub-Saharan Africa in the last decade of the twentieth century, and there appears to be insufficient political will in many African countries to launch public health campaigns to arrest the spread of HIV/AIDS (Caldwell, 2000).

FERTILITY TRANSITIONS

One of the major turning points in human history, though its significance was only recognized decades later, was the sustained decline in human fertility that began in a number of Western European countries and North America in the late nineteenth century that eventuated in replacement level fertility (about two surviving children per couple) within a span of 50–70 years. Although fertility levels had fluctuated throughout human history as resources waxed and waned, the range of variation was from moderately high to very high levels, say from four to eight children per couple. Motivations for high levels of childbearing were part of the core culture in all human societies. Not only was high fertility an essential requirement for societal survival in the face of high mortality (and periodic waves of crisis mortality), but social institutions and cultural patterns were organized to support and encourage high levels of childbearing within marriages. The sustained decline in fertility that began in the late nineteenth century was not only a demographic revolution, but also the beginnings of a profound redefinition of the family and the adult roles of women and men. Modern societies are still in the process of adapting old (and creating new) institutions and gender roles in the wake of the transition to low fertility.

About a hundred years after the beginnings of fertility declines in Western Europe and North America, a similar process began in the developing countries of Asia, Latin America and Africa. This second wave of fertility transitions began in the late 1960s and early 1970s in a few Asian countries and small island societies. By the 1990s, signs of declining fertility had reached almost every part of the globe, including areas of persistently high fertility in South Asia and sub-Saharan Africa. Although these fertility transitions are still in process, the end is in sight. Replacement level fertility has been achieved in some East and Southeast Asian countries in the 1980s and 1990s, and the United Nations predicts (medium variant) that almost all developing countries will reach replacement level fertility by the middle of the century (United Nations, 2001).

Much of demographic science has been devoted to documenting and measuring the scope, character and pace of fertility transitions. The pace of fertility transitions is affected by the tempo and quantity of children born in reproductive unions: couples typically have two decades (or more) of potential childbearing, and births can be accelerated or postponed within the childbearing career. Translating these life cycle patterns of childbearing into aggregate temporal patterns of fertility creates considerable analytical complexity that has stimulated substantial efforts to formulate mathematical models that capture the significant aspects of fertility transitions. Even more complex and daunting are the efforts to explain historical and contemporary fertility transitions in terms of the social, economic and cultural changes.

The earliest efforts to account for fertility declines in the West by Warren Thompson (1929), Kingsley Davis (1945) and Frank Notestein (1945, 1953) created what is generally labelled as the theory of the demographic transition. Although sometimes glossed as simple theory, which posits that modernization or socioeconomic development leads to declining fertility, the original accounts of the theory specified a variety of causal mechanisms, including the declining role of the family in economic organization, the independence of women from traditional roles, and the shift to rationality spurred by popular education.

Up until the 1970s, the theory of the demographic transition was widely accepted by specialists and was widely presented in introductory textbooks and beyond through stylized graphs and an interpretation of declining fertility in response to the forces of industrialization and urbanization. These processes had occurred in many Western countries during the nineteenth and twentieth centuries and were presumed to be on the horizon of many developing countries. Relative to most other branches of the social sciences, the theory of the demographic transition represented one of the more successful efforts to explain social behavior and social change.

The generality and universal scope of demographic transition theory were, however, sometimes a liability. Almost any indicators that could be linked with urbanization and industrialization were considered interchangeable and equally valid as predictors of the transition from high to low fertility. Although there were many potential hypotheses about specific aspects of social change, such as the changing cost of children in rural and urban environments, these were rarely differentiated from the broader story about industrialization and urbanization. The empirical evaluations of the theory were also quite general, typically with parallel time series on indicators of modernization and declining fertility. Although there were many empirical studies of fertility during the 1950s and 1960s, often with anomalous patterns, there was no challenge to the theory of the demographic transition.

In the 1970s and 1980s, two important developments in demographic research shattered the hegemony of demographic transition theory. The first was surprising findings from the Princeton European Fertility Project, initially noted in an article by Knodel and van de Walle (1979) and later developed in the volume by Coale and Watkins (1986). Although the European Fertility Project was envisaged as an empirical test of demographic transition theory on its home ground, the results showed that the pace of fertility decline across provinces and regions of Europe was only modestly correlated with the socio-economic variables that played such a prominent role in the standard account of demographic transition theory. Instead, the patterns and pace of fertility decline appeared to be associated with regions that shared common languages and culture.

The second challenge to demographic transition theory came from the comparative syntheses of results from the World Fertility Survey (WFS) project (Cleland and Hobcraft, 1985, Cleland and Scott, 1987). The WFS project consisted of a series of cross-sectional studies of individual-level correlates of fertility behaviors and attitudes and contraceptive practice in developing countries around the globe. Although these studies showed that, in general, fertility was correlated in the expected direction with female education, urban residence and other socio-economic variables, the relationships were often modest and many exceptions could be found. Following on these findings and research of Lesthaeghe (1983; Lesthaeghe and Surkyn, 1988), John Cleland and Chris Wilson (1987) wrote a bold essay that directly challenged demographic transition theory and suggested that an alternative model of culture and fertility, labeled ideational theory, would be a more appropriate theoretical framework than demographic transition theory. Ideational theory holds that cultural values have long-term consequences on human fertility and are only slowly (and partially) eroded by socio-economic changes.

Karen Mason (1997) cogently argued that much of the debate on the causes of fertility transitions is largely over variations in the proximate conditions that influence the timing of fertility declines, and that there is considerable agreement over the long-term historical factors, especially mortality decline, that have led to fertility transitions. The portrayal of demographic transition theory as a universal model of modernization and fertility decline is too general and vague (Hirschman, 1994; Kirk, 1996), but there is a considerable body of evidence that socio-economic development has been more influential in shaping historical (Friedlander et al., 1991; Lee et al., 1994) and contemporary (Bongaarts and Watkins, 1996) fertility declines than many critics have acknowledged. There are, of course, considerable variations in the timing of the onset and the pace of fertility declines across populations, and across groups and regions within populations, which are often associated with linguistic and cultural factors. In particular, the diffusion of knowledge of fertility control generally follows cultural boundaries. The influences of socio-economic and ideational factors are complementary, not opposing, elements of an integrated theory of fertility change. Fertility, and population growth more generally, responds to societal pressures that threaten the survival and well-being of human communities (Davis, 1963; Wilson and Airey, 1999). Socio-economic development is surely a major force influencing demographic processes in modern times, but it is not the only source of population pressures that may generate demographic, technological and social change in varied circumstances.

The impact of public intervention, and family planning programs, on fertility trends continues to be debated. The conventional wisdom, initially proposed in the classic study by Freedman and Berelson (1976), is that the combination of effective family planning efforts and a favorable socio-economic setting produce conditions most likely to lead to lowered fertility. Sorting out the independent and joint effects of setting and policy has been remarkably elusive. The initiation of family planning programs tends to be endogenous to the process of development itself, and it is difficult to obtain independent empirical assessments of each. Successful governments tend to have effective public programs, including well-managed family planning programs. Within countries, family planning clinics are not distributed randomly, but are typically placed in areas of high fertility. Thus, the bivariate association between proximity to family planning services and fertility is usually positive. The results of more complex multivariate models are heavily dependent on initial assumptions and the analytical formulations. Several studies show only modest effects of family planning programs (Gertler and Molyneaux, 1994; Molyneaux and Gertler, 2000; Prichett, 1994), but others have reported more positive assessments (Ahlburg and Diamond, 1996; Bongaarts et al., 1990; Tsui, 2001).

The end of fertility transitions was never defined beyond the general expectation that low fertility would approach the replacement level (around two children per couple) within some modest range of fluctuation. This has generally been the case in the United States, when the total fertility rate (births per woman) dropped a little below 2 in the mid-1970s, and then rose slightly to around 2 births per woman in the 1990s. In Europe, however, fertility continued its downward descent, and by the late 1990s fertility was well below the replacement level and showing no sign of changing (Frejka and Ross, 2001.) In some eastern and southern European countries, average fertility appears to be approaching one child per couple. One school of thought holds that this is a temporary phenomenon, driven primarily by poor economic conditions and a temporary rise in the average age of childbearing (Bongaarts, 2001). Fertility expectations data show that most couples still desire to have two children. Other observers believe that the costs of childbearing (social and economic) are so high in modern industrial societies that below replacement fertility is likely to remain indefinitely with the prospect of declining population size in industrial societies (Chesnais, 2001).

MIGRATION

The massive movements of peoples across the globe, including refugees fleeing war and political instability, dispossessed peasants entering the urban proletariat and international migrants seeking their fortune in distant lands, have given rise to the claim of the distinctly modern 'Age of Migration' (Castles and Miller, 1998). Although the scope and volume of contemporary migration are probably unique, human history is replete with major waves of migration to nearby and distant regions (Davis, 1974; McNeill, 1984).

The portrait of immobile communities wedded to the land and local villages over the millennia, only to be disrupted by modern civilizations and global capitalism is, at best, a very partial view. Local communities did persist over long stretches of human history, but the peoples who inhabited them were connected to frontier regions and cities through periodic waves of out-migration in times of population surplus. Moreover, local villages and communities were periodically subjected to conquest that led to displacement, enslavement, or absorption into dominant populations. Patterns of uneven population growth, environmental changes and technological differences between populations inevitably made migration, voluntary and involuntary, a recurrent feature throughout history.

The image of immobile populations and the historical record of periodic large-scale population movements can perhaps be reconciled with the distinction between two types of social settings: normalcy and periods of political turbulence. Most of the moments of significant human migration – especially of large numbers of people moving long distances – occurred during periods of ecological catastrophe, famine, revolution, war, or during political or economic breakdowns. Although moments of turbulence

may appear to be almost continuous in many historical accounts, there were undoubtedly long stretches of normalcy over the long sweep of history. During such periods, the overwhelming majority of most peoples lived out their lives within a very narrow radius from their place of birth. This was especially true in agricultural societies, where investments in land and the seasonality of production tied the bulk of the population to semi-permanent rural communities that spanned generations, with few internally generated sources of social or cultural change.

In every traditional society, there have always been groups that were prone to migration, including merchants, soldiers, and others in the retinue of elites, and those belonging to deviant or persecuted ideologies. And in many traditional societies, there was usually a 'floating population' – persons who did not have claims to land or social position. Depending on the times and conditions, these people served as a class of expendable labor who often joined the military expeditions or who sought refuge by settling the frontier.

The modern era is distinctive because of higher levels of long-distance migration, which occur during periods of normalcy as well as during periods of political turbulence. Beginning during the eighteenth century, and accelerating during the nineteenth and twentieth, a series of technological, economic, social and demographic forces have contributed to much higher levels of migration, both local and long-distance. These movements are not just responses to crisis (though this condition continues in many parts of the globe), but have become part of the routine fabric of modern societies.

One of the most important distinctions between the premodern and modern eras was the widening geographic imbalance between demographic pressures and economic opportunities, and the consequent awareness and ability of persons to respond through migration. The acceleration of population growth, especially in the nineteenth and twentieth centuries, created immense strains in many oversaturated agrarian societies, which were becoming increasingly commercialized. From East Asia to Europe, successive cohorts of peasants faced not only poverty, which was part of the normal order, but also the collapse (or weakening) of traditional feudal or semi-feudal economies and the moral order that tied peasants to the land. The breakdown of traditional patron–client social institutions eliminated the safety nets in rural economies and accelerated out-migration to urban places or to distant lands.

Although most migration responses in modern times are from rural villages to nearby urban areas (or rural frontiers), the spread of long-distance communication and the cheapening of transportation costs meant that major waves of migration could develop on a global scale. During the nineteenth century, a large share of the surplus population that was being shed by rural economies in Europe was absorbed into the rural frontiers of America. In the later decades of the nineteenth and the opening decades of the twentieth centuries, the dynamic economies of the New World continued to be a major destination for redundant peasant labor from Europe and to a lesser extent from Asia. The migration to the New World was monumental, both in its demographic size and the diversity of its origins. For the 75 year period from the mid-nineteenth century to the end of the first quarter of the twentieth century, almost 50 million Europeans migrated to the United States alone (Massey, 1988). Global patterns of labor migration also developed in response to colonial needs for cheap labor in plantations, mining and other extractive industries in Asia and Africa.

Just as long-distance migration across international borders was becoming a characteristic feature of the emerging modern world, the door began to close. Modern states, legitimated by the potent ideology of nationalism, began to issue passports and regulate who entered their countries (Torpey, 2000). During the nineteenth and twentieth centuries, the political map of the world was transformed with the dissolution of empires, the rise and fall of imperialism, and the emergence of many new states. In many cases, state formation was based on a claim of nationalism, which usually implied an ethnic homeland or a sense of belonging to a common people. Although there is no simple one-to-one correlation between nationalism and the tightening up of international boundaries to migration, the logic was similar. Although William McNeill (1984: 17)

observed that the 'barbarian ideal of an ethnically homogeneous nation is incompatible with the normal population dynamics of civilization', nationalist leaders considered open borders to be inimical to the construction of the 'nation-state'.

Another factor that probably helped to turn the tide against an open system of international migration was the increasing rate of population growth. For most of the nineteenth century, migration had been a necessity because of the high mortality in cities and a general shortage of labor to settle the frontier and to work in the factories of the new industrial age. With declining levels of mortality in the early twentieth century, most countries were generally able to meet their labor needs from natural increase. In such circumstances, nationalist and racial ideologies were, perhaps, given a freer hand to legitimate restrictive immigration policies.

The nationalist impulse, which sought to limit and control international migration, waned during the last few decades of the twentieth century. The United States adopted a less restrictive policy of immigration in the 1960s and there have been comparable developments in other countries. In the early 1970s, Australia ended its 'White Australia' policy and allowed significant numbers of Asians to immigrate. In the early 1990s, the countries of the European Economic Community loosened restrictions on inter-state migration. Citizens of any country in the EEC (now the European Union, with 25 member states) can move to any other country and are free to seek employment or attend schooling on equal terms with natives of the member state.

These common patterns in a number of countries and regions are suggestive of underlying shifts in political, economic and demographic forces. The contradictions between tightly regulated international borders and the modern world economy are becoming increasing clear. The first sign was 'labor demand' in industrial countries that could not be met by domestic supply, at least not at the wages offered. Employers found it more desirable to import labor from abroad than to raise wages or to mechanize production. The demand for 'cheaper immigrant labor' is evident in many sectors (agriculture, manufacturing, construction, repair services, restaurants and child care) in most industrial countries, including a growing number of rapidly growing developing countries. The increasingly global international economy seems to create recurrent needs for labor greater than that available from domestic population growth.

The demand for immigrant labor is not restricted to unskilled manual labor. The United States and other industrial countries have encountered a shortage of scientific and engineering workers, particularly in the high-tech sector. This demand has been met, in part, by allowing many talented foreign students in American universities to convert their student visas to immigrant status. There has also been a gradual shift over the past few decades to more open immigration policies for a variety of reasons – refugees, agricultural workers, 'illegal' immigrants with long residences in the country, people in countries that have few kinship ties to American citizens, and workers in high demand by US employers. The prejudices against immigrants and nativist fears have not entirely disappeared, but their open expression has been sharply reduced in many modern industrial societies. These changes in economics, demography, labor demand and ideology contributed to a much freer flow of international labor migration in the late twentieth and early twenty-first centuries.

At the core of most theories of migration is an economic model which posits that people move from places of labor surplus (low wages and high unemployment) to areas of labor scarcity (low unemployment and high wages). Social attractions (and dis-attractions) are added to economic motives as the central elements of the 'push–pull model' presented in Everett Lee's (1966) theory of migration. Lee framed his theory as an update of Ravenstein's statement on the 'laws of migration', which was first presented in 1885. In addition to noting the forces attracting and repelling migrants, Lee and Ravenstein provide a very helpful summary of the many other regularities of the types of migration and the characteristics of migrants in different situations.

The primary limitation of most push–pull (economic) theories of migration is that the reasons for pushes and pulls are exogenous to the theory (Portes and Rumbaut, 1996: ch. 8). Individuals, at least some individuals, do respond to the uneven spatial distribution of opportunities by moving from one location to another, but this begs the question of why there is an imbalance between the availability of workers and the availability of economic opportunities across countries and across regions within countries.

In a very ambitious essay, Wilber Zelinksy (1971) proposed a theory of the mobility transition to parallel the theory of the demographic transition. According to Zelinsky, the pace of mobility increased from premodern to modernizing societies with the increasing differentiation of geographical areas and shift from agriculture to industry. As geographical areas become more similar to one another in fully modern societies, Zelinsky predicts the pace of permanent migration will decline, but that circular migration would increase. Although Zelinsky has captured some important insights, the theory of the mobility transition has not become part of the theoretical corpus of modern demography. Without an underlying biological model (as with mortality and fertility) and with wide inter-societal variation in economic and political conditions (transportation systems, labor demand, government policies, etc.), it has been impossible to formulate an abstract model of expected changes in migration levels and patterns over the course of socio-economic development.

Between the narrow economic approach and Zelinsky's attempt at a grand theoretical synthesis, there are a number of alternative theoretical approaches to the study of historical and contemporary patterns of migration. But with sharp differences in disciplinary approaches and limited data sources on migration, the general tendency is for fragmentation of the field into different research communities that espouse independent theories. However, in a comprehensive review of the research literature, Massey and his colleagues (1998) argue that the major theories in the field of international migration are not mutually exclusive. In contrast to the standard practice of ignoring or denigrating the utility of theoretical perspectives beyond one's own field, they find empirical support for a variety of hypotheses, ranging from neoclassical economics to world systems theory (Massey et al., 1998). This work suggests that the efforts at developing a comprehensive theory of migration must seek to integrate the leading ideas from different fields.

The single most important finding from the empirical literature, which is frequently rediscovered by researchers in different disciplines and areas, is the salience of collective forces on individual decisions to migrate. There are some self-directed persons – pioneers – who weigh the economic and social costs of migration and then set out on their journeys to distant and unknown lands. Much more numerous, however, are the followers, whose decisions to migrate are buoyed by the family and friends who have gone before. Return migrants at the point of origin can provide information and encouragement, and advance financial support for the journey. Even more important are friends and family at the destination site, who can provide temporary housing and sustenance as well as assistance in finding employment. This cumulative character of migration (Massey et al., 1998) leads to chain patterns of migration that link origin and destination communities, often over long distances and time periods.

LOOKING AHEAD IN THE TWENTY-FIRST CENTURY

The major demographic trend of the twentieth century was the rapid expansion of the world's population fueled by unprecedented declines in mortality in both developed and developing countries. At the turn of the twenty-first century, population growth was close to zero in most industrial countries (below zero in most of Europe) as a result of fertility transitions that began more than a century ago. The global fertility transition spread to Asia, Latin America and Africa during the last third of the twentieth century. Although population growth rates remain high in most developing countries, continued declines in fertility and the gradual shift to an older age structure will lead to the cessation of world population growth later in this century.

Although demographic theories do not provide precise predictions of the threshold values of social conditions needed to affect demographic change, there is a general consensus on the factors that have shaped modern demographic history (Mason, 1997; Preston, 1976). The growth of scientific knowledge, and the accompanying changes in production, health care and personal behavior, have led to much lower levels of mortality. And declines in mortality and changes in the role of the family have led to lower incentives for childbearing in modern societies. Wide variations in demographic trajectories in different places and occasional reversals do not negate the overall account.

Even though absolute population attributes can only be predicted within wide bands of uncertainty, there are a number of new demographic realities on the horizon. Demographic momentum and the slower pace of demographic transitions in some poorer regions in the world will contribute to the current trend of an increasing fraction of the world's population living in Africa and Asia. Unless there are significant increases in international migration to Europe and North America, the absolute, as well as the relative, size of the populations in industrial Western countries will shrink. Although current levels of economic welfare around the world are certain to change, the likely imbalance between larger numbers of people living in the poorer regions of the world and fewer persons living in the traditional wealthier regions is likely to contribute to increasing political tensions. Of course, it is not just relative numbers of persons in poor and rich countries that shape political discontent, but also the awareness of differential levels of consumption and economic opportunities in countries at different levels of development.

The long-term consequences of a population of 6 billion, rising to 10 billion, on the world's resources and ecosystem, is largely unknown. The dramatic increase in population numbers during the twentieth century appeared to have only modest effects because scientific applications increased agricultural and industrial production while increasing utilization of the world's supply of fossil fuels. But rising living standards (and consumption) of an increasing fraction of the world's population will add new pressures on the world's supply of natural resources and food production. Perhaps, renewable resources and new energy supplies can be developed to create a sustainable world economy and ecosystem, but this positive scenario assumes rapid technological progress and a world political environment that can balance long and short-term demands as well as the interests of societies at different levels of development. If significant global climate change is produced by human activities, the transition to a sustainable world ecosystem with 10 billion people expecting high levels of consumption will be all the more difficult.

As noted earlier, many of the historical constraints on long-distance migration were eased in the last decades of the twentieth century. Traditional immigration policies are residues of the first half of the twentieth century, when regulated borders were a hallmark of the modern statecraft of nation-building states. Restrictive border policies originated in Europe and then spread around the globe, including the traditional immigrant-receiving societies in the New World and even to former colonial societies in Asia and Africa.

These policies 'worked' because domestic population growth in most countries was sufficient to meet labor demand. Although rapid population growth created immense pressures in many labor surplus countries, there were few places that needed additional labor or allowed open migration. Passport controls were expensive and irksome to many, but they became accepted as normal features of modern states. Over the past few decades of the twentieth century, however, strains in the system of tight immigration policies were beginning to show.

In addition to larger numbers of people, twenty-first-century human societies will also have to adapt to a much older age composition than ever before in human history. Population aging is primarily determined by fertility decline, and secondarily by increases in longevity. The very low levels of fertility and mortality in industrial countries have led to population fractions of about 13–14 per cent above age 65 in the year 2000, rising to almost 29 per cent in Europe and 21 per cent in North America by 2050 (National Research Council, 2001: 32). The changes in Latin America and Asia will be even more rapid,

with the fraction over 65 rising from 5–6 per cent in 2000 to about 18 per cent in 2050. The percentage of elderly in Africa will rise only slightly from 2000 to 2050 because of the much slower pace of fertility decline.

The rising share of the elderly (and declining fraction of children) will have profound effects on the economic, social and cultural fabric of future human societies. One of the defining attributes of modern welfare states is the transfer of income from the working age population to the dependent elderly, thereby relieving individual families of the historic burden of caring for elderly relatives. As the ratio of elderly to the working age population increases, the average cost (tax) per working adult will increase, putting additional pressures on the fiscal system of modern welfare states. It is possible to imagine rosy scenarios including rapid economic growth, a healthier elderly population and delayed retirement that might reduce the welfare state's fiscal burden of supporting an increasing share of dependent older population. However, other factors, including the increasing costs of health care and pharmaceutical drugs, the weakening of familial intergenerational support obligations (Lye et al., 1995), and the increasing political power of a larger elderly population may work in the opposite direction. The impact of population aging may be even more acute in developing countries that have much weaker institutional infrastructures and the health of the elderly population may be much more precarious (Palloni, 2001: 55–61).

The impact of an aging population on many social institutions may be equally significant. In general, older persons tend to be risk-averse and less willing to vote for taxes for education and other governmental programs that benefit children and younger persons. The consumption needs of the elderly will create different economic demands and perhaps the pace of social and cultural change will slow as markets and institutions shift their priorities. Older persons have been accorded high status and deference in traditional family systems in Asia and elsewhere, but these cultural values arose in demographic settings where the elderly have been relatively rare. The obligations of caring for the relatively few elderly were generally shared by a large number of adult children and their families. It remains to be seen whether these family values stay intact in settings with many more older relatives and when the cultural distance between aging parents and their adult children has been stretched by rapid social change.

Family patterns have already begun to change with declining numbers of children and more elderly. If children are not anticipated (or desired), there are fewer incentives for young couples to enter into formal marriages. It is increasingly common for young adults to live together in a common residence, either as an alternative to, or as a prelude to marriage (Bumpass, 1990; Cherlin, 1992). Indeed, age at marriage has increased in the United States, although the average age of cohabitation has not. Declining adult mortality during the twentieth century lengthened the average duration of married life with fewer marriages broken by spousal death at younger ages. On the other hand, marriages have become more unstable with the recent rise in the risk of divorce in many Western countries, especially in the decades after the Second World War. The increase in the divorce rate may be partially affected by demographic factors (longer marital duration, fewer children in marriages), but the long-term secular rise in divorce is probably because modern societies allow individuals greater freedom to act on individual preferences (Preston and McDonald, 1979). Although individual marriages may be more fragile, most divorced persons remarry, suggesting that dissatisfaction with a particular partner does not signify any declining interest in marriage as a social institution. These changes in marriage and family life are likely to continue in the coming decades and probably spread to countries that are in the early stages of industrial development.

As the opening quotation by Anthony Wrigley suggests, the demographic picture always needs interpretation and may lack the polychrome fullness of historical reality, but even in black and white, demographic patterns and social demographic analyses remain a central prism to perceive and to understand social change and human welfare. This is the reason why the sociological imagination must always remain tethered to its demographic anchor.

NOTE

I thank Stewart Tolnay, Bussarawan Teerawichitchainan and Susan Wierzbicki for their thoughtful comments on an earlier draft.

REFERENCES

Ahlburg, Dennis A. and Diamond, Ian (1996) 'Evaluating the impact of family planning programs', in Dennis A. Ahlburg, Allen C. Kelley and Karen Oppenheim Mason (eds), *The Impact of Population Growth on Well Being in Developing Countries*. Berlin: Springer. p. 299–336.

Bongaarts, John (1996) 'Global trends in AIDS mortality', *Population and Development Review*, 22: 21–45.

Bongaarts, John (2001) 'Fertility and reproductive preferences in post-transitional societies', in Rodolfo A. Bulatao and John B. Casterline (eds), *Global Fertility Transition*. Supplement to Vol. 27 of *Population and Development Review*. pp. 260–81.

Bongaarts, John, Parker Mauldin, W. and Phillips, James F. (1990) 'The demographic impact of family planning programs'. *Studies in Family Planning*, 21: 299–310.

Bongaarts, John and Watkins, Susan C. (1996) 'Social interactions and contemporary fertility transitions', *Population and Development Review*, 22: 639–82.

Boserup, Ester (1981) *Population and Technological Change*. Chicago: University of Chicago Press.

Bumpass, Larry (1990) 'What's happening to the family? Interactions between demographic and institutional change', *Demography*, 27: 483–98.

Caldwell, John C. (2000) 'Rethinking the African AIDS epidemic', *Population and Development Review*, 26: 117–35.

Castles, Stephen and Miller, Mark J. (1998) *The Age of Migration: International Population Movements in the Modern World*, 2nd edn. New York: The Guilford Press.

Cavalli-Sforza, L. Luca, Menozzi, Paolo and Piazza, Alberto (1994) *The History of Geography and Human Genes*, abridged edn. Princeton, NJ: Princeton Unviersity Press.

Cavalli-Sforza, Luigi Luca and Cavalli-Sforza, Francesco (1995) *The Great Human Diasporas: The History of Diversity and Evolution*. Cambridge, MA: Perseus Books.

Cherlin, Andrew (1992) *Marriage, Divorce, Remarriage*, revised and enlarged edn. Cambridge, MA: Harvard University Press.

Chesnais, Jean-Claude (2001) 'Comment: A march to population recession', in Rodolfo A. Bulatao and John B. Casterline (eds), *Global Fertility Transition*. Supplement to Vol. 27 of *Population and Development Review*. pp. 255–9.

Childe, V. Gordon (1951[1936]) *Man Makes Himself*. New York: New American Library.

Cleland, John and Hobcraft, John (eds) (1985) *Reproductive Change in Developing Countries: Insights from the World Fertility Survey*. Oxford: Oxford University Press.

Cleland, John and Scott, Christopher (1987) *The World Fertility Survey: An Assessment*. New York: Oxford University Press.

Cleland, John and Wilson, Chris (1987) 'Demand theories of the fertility transition: an iconoclastic view', *Population Studies*, 41: 5–30.

Coale, Ansley J. (1974) 'The History of Human Population', in *The Human Population* (A Scientific American Book). San Francisco: W.H. Freeman. pp. 15–25.

Coale, Ansley J. and Watkins, Susan Cotts (1986) *The Decline of Fertility in Europe*. Princeton, NJ: Princeton University Press.

Crimmins, Eileen M. (1981) 'The changing pattern of American mortality decline, 1940–77, and its implications for the future', *Population and Development Review*, 7: 229–54.

Crimmins, Eileen M., Saito, Yasuhiko and Ingegneri, Dominique (1997) 'Trends in disability-free life expectancy in the United States, 1970–90', *Population and Development Review*, 23: 555–72.

Davis, Kingsley (1945) 'The world demographic transition', *Annals of the American Academy of Political and Social Science*, 237: 1–11.

Davis, Kingsley (1956) 'The amazing decline of mortality in underdeveloped areas', *American Economic Review*, 46: 305–18.

Davis, Kingsley (1963) 'The theory of change and response in modern demographic history', *Population Index*, 29: 345–66.

Davis, Kingsley (1974) 'The Migrations of Human Populations', in *The Human Population* (A Scientific American Book). San Francisco: W.H. Freeman. pp 53–65.

Diamond, Jared (1993) *The Third Chimpanzee*. New York: Harper Perennial Library.

Diamond, Jared (1997) *Guns, Germs, and Steel: The Fates of Human Societies*. New York: W.W. Norton.

Durand, John D. (1977) 'Historical estimates of world population: an evaluation', *Population and Development Review*, 3 (3): 253–96.

Feeney, Griffith (2001) 'The impact of HIV/AIDS on adult mortality in Zimbabwe', *Population and Development Review*, 27: 771–80.

Freedman, Ronald and Berelson, Bernard (1976) 'The record of family planning programs', *Studies in Family Planning*, 7 (1): 1–40.

Frejka, Thomas and Ross, John (2001) 'Paths to sub-replacement fertility: the empirical evidence', in *Global Fertility Transition*, ed. Rodolfo A. Bulatao and John B. Casterline. Supplement to Vol. 27 of *Population and Development Review*. pp. 213–54.

Friedlander, Dov, Schellekens, Jona and Ben-Moshe, Eliahu (1991) 'The transition from high to low marital fertility: cultural or socioeconomic determinants', *Economic Development and Cultural Change*, 39: 331–51.

Gertler, Paul J. and Molyneaux, John W. (1994) 'How economic development and family planning programs combined to reduce Indonesian fertility', *Demography*, 31: 33–63.

Hanenberg, R.S., Rojanapithayakorn, W., Kunasol, P. and Sokal, D. (1994) 'Impact of Thailand's HIV-control programme as indicated by the decline of sexually transmitted diseases', *Lancet*, 344: 243–5.

Hanley, Susan (1987) 'Urban sanitation in preindustrial Japan', *Journal of Interdisciplinary History*, 18: 1–26.

Harris, Marvin (1977) *Cannibals and Kings: The Origins of Culture*. New York: Random House.

Hill, Kenneth and Pebley, Anne R. (1989) 'Child mortality in the developing world', *Population and Development Review*, 15: 657–87.

Hirschman, Charles (1994) 'Why fertility changes', *Annual Review of Sociology*, 20: 203–33.

Hirschman, Charles (2003) 'The development of the social sciences prior to globalization and some thoughts on the future', *Southeast Asian Studies for the Twenty-First Century: Pacific Perspectives*, ed. Anthony Reid. Temple, AZ: Program for Southeast Asian Studies, Arizona State University. pp. 157–78.

Kirk, Dudley (1996) 'Demographic transition theory', *Population Studies*, 50: 361–87.

Knodel, John and van de Walle, Etienne (1979) 'Lessons from the past: policy implications of historical population studies', *Population and Development Review*, 5: 217–46.

Lee, Everett (1966) 'A theory of migration', *Demography*, 3: 47–57.

Lee, Ronald D., Galloway, Patrick R. and Hammel, Eugene A. (1994) 'Fertility decline in Prussia: estimating influences on supply, demand, and degree of control', *Demography*, 31: 347–73.

Lesthaeghe, Ron (1983) 'A century of demographic and cultural change in Western Europe: an exploration of underlying dimensions', *Population and Development Review*, 9: 411–35.

Lesthaeghe, Ron and Surkyn, Johan (1988) 'Cultural dynamics and economic theories of fertility change', *Population and Development Review*, 14: 1–45.

Livi-Bacci, Massimo (1997) *A Concise History of World Population*, 2nd edn. Malden, MA: Blackwell.

Lye, Diane N., Kelpinger, Daniel H., Hyle, Patricia and Nelson, Anjanette (1995) 'Childhood living arrangements and adult children's relations with their parents', *Demography*, 32: 261–80.

Mason, Karen (1997) 'Explaining fertility transitions', *Demography*, 34: 443–54.

Massey, Douglas S. (1988) 'Economic development and international migration in comparative perspective', *Population and Development Review*, 14: 383–413.

Massey, Douglas S., Arnago, Joaquin, Hugo, Graeme, Kouaouci, Ali, Pellegrino, Adela and Taylor, J. Edward (1998) *Worlds in Motion: Understanding International Migration at the End of the Millennium*. Oxford: The Clarendon Press.

McEvedy, Colin and Jones, Richard (1978) *Atlas of World Population History*. New York: Penguin.

McKeown, Thomas (1976) *The Modern Rise of Population*. New York: Academic Press.

McNeill, William H. (1976) *Plagues and Peoples*. Garden City, NY: Anchor.

McNeill, William H. (1984) 'Human migration in historical perspective', *Population and Development Review*, 10: 1–18.

Molyneaux, John and Gertler, Paul (2000) 'The impact of targeted family planning programs in Indonesia', in C.Y. Cyrus Chu and Ronald Lee (eds), *Population and Economic Change in East Asia*. Supplement to vol. 26 of *Population and Development Review*. pp. 61–85.

National Research Council (2001) *Preparing for An Aging World: The Case for Cross National Research*. Washington, DC: National Academy Press.

Notestein, Frank W. (1945) 'Population – the long view', in T.W. Schultz. ed. *Food for the World*, Chicago: University of Chicago Press. pp. 36–57.

Notestein, Frank W. (1953) 'Economic problems of population change', in *Proceedings of the Eighth International Conference of Agricultural Economists*. New York: Oxford University Press. pp. 13–31.

Palloni, Alberto (2001) 'Living arrangements of older persons', *Population Bulletin of the United Nations*, Special Issue No. 42/43: 54–110.

Portes, Alejandro and Rumbaut, Ruben G. (1996) *Immigrant America: A Portrait*, 2nd edn. Berkeley, CA: University of California Press.

Preston, Samuel H. (1976) *Mortality Patterns in National Populations*. New York: Academic Press.

Preston, Samuel H. (1980) 'Causes and consequences of mortality declines in less developed countries during the twentieth century', in Richard, Easterlin (ed.), *Population and Economic Change in Developing Countries*. Chicago: University of Chicago Press. pp. 289–360.

Preston, Samuel H. and Haines, Michael R. (1991) *Fatal Years: Child Mortality in Late Nineteenth Century*. Princeton, NJ: Princeton University Press.

Preston, Samuel H. and McDonald, John (1979) 'The incidence of divorce within cohorts of American marriages contracted since the Civil War', *Demography*, 16: 1–26.

Pritchett, Lant H. (1994) 'Desired fertility and the impact of population policies', *Population and Development Review*, 20: 1–55.

Razzell, P.E. (1974) 'An interpretation of the modern rise of population in Europe: a critique', *Population Studies*, 28: 5–17.

Thompson, Warren (1929) 'Population', *American Journal of Sociology*, 34: 959–75.

Torpey, John (2000) *The Invention of the Passport: Surveillance, Citizenship, and the State*. Cambridge: Cambridge University Press.

Tsui, Amy (2001) 'Population policies, family planning programs, and fertility: the record', in Rodolfo A. Bulatao and John B. Casterline (eds), *Global Fertility Transition*. Supplement to Vol. 27 of *Population and Development Review*. pp. 184–204.

United Nations (1953) *The Determinants and Consequences of Population Trends*. New York: United Nations.

United Nations (1973) *The Determinants and Consequences of Population Trends: New Summary of Findings of Demographic, Economic, and Social Factor*. New York: United Nations.

United Nations (2001) *World Population Prospects: The 2000 Revision. Volume 1: Comprehensive Tables*. New York: United Nations.

Wilson, Chris and Airey, Pauline (1999) 'How can a homeostatic perspective enhance demographic transition theory?', *Population Studies*, 53: 117–28.

Wrigley, E.A. (1969) *Population and History*. New York: McGraw–Hill.

Zelinksy, Wilber (1971) 'The hypothesis of the mobility transition', *Geographical Review*, 61: 219–49.

Part 3

Primary Debates

23

A New Approach for Theoretically Integrating Micro and Macro Analysis

JONATHAN H. TURNER

One of the most contentious issues in sociology is over the question of how to integrate micro and macro levels of analysis. At the empirical level, it is rather easy to make micro–macro connections. For example, traditional survey research almost always does so when it regresses measures of behavior and psychological states (the micro) against background variables like a socio-economic status (SES) index (the macro). Of course, even here the linkage is more illusionary than real since the macro variable is really an aggregation of individual responses to questionnaires rather than a measure of the actual properties of social structure; and the behavioral or psychological measure is merely what people say they do or think (of course, people lie or become delusional all of the time). None the less, the SES index, and perhaps some intervening variables, are often seen to 'cause' the dependent variable, often consisting of another index summing up responses on questionnaires or interviews about behavior and thought. Such 'explanations' are, in reality, time-bound descriptions about what people say about their background, behavior and thinking. Still, sociologists appear to be relatively satisfied with these kinds of empirical efforts linking the macro and the micro.

It is when we turn to explanations by more general and abstract theories about social structure, culture and behavior that problems of how to integrate the micro and macro become evident. At the heart of the issue is how explanations of population-level or societal-level phenomena are to be reconciled with explanations about behavior and interpersonal processes. Once this turn is taken, the problems of linking the macro and micro, or of filling the micro–macro 'gap', become ever-more salient. And, over the past two decades, sociological theorists have become concerned, if not a bit obsessed, with how to close this conceptual gap (e.g., Alexander et al., 1987; Blalock and Wilken, 1979; Eisenstadt and Helle, 1985; Gurvitch, 1964; Hechter, 1983; Kemeny, 1976; Knorr Cetina, 1981; Ritzer, 1985; 1988a,b, 1990, 1991; Smart, 2001; Wiley, 1988). Apparently many sociologists feel uncomfortable with distinct theories designed to explain diverse levels of reality, and we might ask why this is so, especially since far more mature sciences than sociology live with their own micro–macro gaps without undue agonizing. Even physics has not reconciled general relativity with sub-atomic physics, and certainly a field like economics lives comfortably with a clear division between macro and micro economics. But social theorists appear to be dissatisfied with such divisions.

As a result, a good many theories in sociology claim to address the problem of linking the micro–macro divide, but as I will emphasize, these efforts are about as illusionary as the efforts of survey researchers who think that they have measured social structure and culture with aggregated responses to questionnaires. In this chapter, I propose one way of closing the theoretical gap between the micro and the macro (Turner, 2000, 2002), but first, let me briefly review some of the obfuscating issues before turning to the strategies that prominent theorists have employed.

OBFUSCATING ISSUES

One obfuscating issue is the agency versus structure debate which is often viewed, particularly in European social theory circles, as another way of phrasing the micro versus macro question (e.g., Archer, 1982, 1988; Giddens, 1984). Those arguing for the primacy of human agency typically want to see humans as having some degree of free will, whereas those pushing the more structural side will tend to see human action as highly circumscribed by cultural and structural parameters. There is nothing inherently contradictory about these two positions, since human action can be constrained without being determined, while structures can be reconstituted by acts of individuals. But, simply saying this does not explain anything; and when the agency–structure question is conflated with the micro–macro issues, theories are typically rather vague. For example, Anthony Giddens's (1984) view of structure as 'rules and resources' that agents use in practice connotes an interplay between structure and agency but does not really say how this interplay operates, except with rather vague pronouncements about structural 'principles', 'sets', 'properties' and 'contradictions' on the structural side and equally unclear notions of 'unconscious motives and pressures', 'practical consciousness', 'discursive consciousness' and the

like on the micro side. What emerges in Giddens's theory of structuration is a category system but the dynamic relations among categories are not specified. Indeed, they are often connected by lines in diagrams, but the lines have no arrows or signs and, hence, it is difficult to know how the concepts relate to each other. As a result, 'explanation' of an empirical case becomes an exercise in using the categories as a conceptual scheme for interpreting empirical events. The scheme thus becomes an interpretative framework that allows the analyst to talk about micro and macro events, but without really integrating micro or macro dynamics *theoretically*.

Similarly, Pierre Bourdieu's (1984) notion of 'habitus' is equally vague, arguing that individuals' modes of classification, appreciation, judgment, perception and behavior are connected to their place in social structures, particularly the class system, and that individuals' acts reinforce this structure. In Bourdieu's scheme, neither the micro–macro question nor the agency–structure issue is resolved; rather the issue is simply relabelled. 'Habitus' says very little about what aspects of individual cognition, perception, thought, or behavior are influenced by what dimensions of social structure, and vice versa; we are simply told that the connection between structure and agency is mediated by habitus which gives us a name for a process but little else.

Another obfuscating issue is the distinction between the subjective and objective (Berger and Luckmann, 1967; Ritzer, 1988b: 516–18). Presumably, the subjective is what goes on inside of people's heads, while the objective is what we can see outside of people's heads. Those emphasizing the subjective often side with those pushing human free will and agency, and they generally argue for a socially constructed view of the universe, while those arguing for objective reality see the world as structured and as amenable to analysis scientifically. Like most dualisms, this one contains a false assumption – in this case, that the subjective cannot be observed or studied objectively. Rapid advances in imaging technologies that can map the neurology of the brain will soon explode this dichotomy, rendering it as meaningless as similar views that the mind and body are somehow separate or that rationality is distinct from emotions. Of course, individuals think, but why is this process not amenable to objective inquiry? Thus, like many older philosophical distinctions, the dichotomy between the subjective and objective is best abandoned because it will not help us deal with the micro–macro problem. Indeed, adhering to a view of an unobservable and, hence, mysterious subjective realm precludes the possibility that micro processses can be reconciled theoretically with the macro processes that presumably can be studied objectively.

Another popular gloss on the micro–macro question is to assert that the social universe is multi-dimensional, consisting of 'action and order', which simply renames the structure–agency question once again. For example, Jeffrey Alexander (1982) makes such a distinction and, then, breaks down action and order into somewhat different types. Action is rational and nonrational (in my mind, a false dichotomy), while order reveals both integration and conflict. Further distinctions that define each are offered by Alexander but such schemes only define the territory; they do not explain either action or order, nor do they help explain the linkages between the two. Again, we are given a category system without theoretical statements on the linkages among categories.

Further illustrations of obfuscation could be offered, but let me end with this assertion: the micro–macro distinction will not be theoretically resolved by talk about multi-dimensionality or recourse to tired old dichotomies like agency–structure, rational–nonrational, subjective-objective, action–order and so on. Instead, we need to be much more specific on the properties of the social universe that are denoted by the labels of micro and macro. If we cannot do this, then the micro–macro becomes yet another tired dichotomy that we can throw on our philosophical heap of vague verbiage. Aside from these obfuscating approaches, sociologists have employed a number of strategies to close the perceived 'gap' between the micro and macro realms (Turner, 1983; Turner and Boyns, 2002).

STRATEGIES FOR DEALING WITH THE MICRO–MACRO GAP

Micro chauvinism

In this strategy, it is assumed that the micro universe takes precedence in theoretical explanations. There are several versions of such chauvinism. One argues that social structure and other such 'macro' views of the social universe are reifications by sociologists since the only empirically observable processes are individual people engaged in face-to-face interactions (Berger and Luckmann, 1967). Another version of this approach is that since all social structures are ultimately built from micro encounters among people, understanding of larger-scale structures is only possible by examining the micro processes by which they are built up (e.g., Blumer, 1969; Coleman, 1987, 1990; Collins, 1981a,b; Hechter, 1983, 1987). Here the reality of macro structure is not questioned, but the view that it can be understood in terms of its own 'emergent' properties is challenged. All that can really be seen and observed is individual people moving in space and interacting; and so, the macro can only be analyzed from its constituent acts and episodes of interaction.

Macro chauvinism

This strategy makes the opposite claim, in several ways. One is that all micro encounters are embedded in larger-scale social structures, and that the dynamics of face-to-face interaction can only be understood by examining the forces constraining all action and interaction among individuals (e.g., Mayhew, 1980, 1981; Turner, 2002). Another macro chauvinist approach argues that rates of interaction are what are important to know, not the precise mechanisms of interaction; and such rates are determined by the structural parameters that influence individuals' opportunities for interaction (Blau, 1977a,b, 1994). And a third macro approach simply asserts that once social structures exist, they represent emergent properties that are only understandable in their own terms (Parsons, 1951). These emergent properties reveal dynamics of their own that cannot be reduced to, nor explained by, micro processes, and hence, micro analysis is simply irrelevant to the study of macrodynamics (Turner, 1995).

Theories of the 'middle range'

Robert Merton (1968) once made a call for theories of the middle range, whereby the global conceptual schemes of grand theory (particularly that of Talcott Parsons) and the empirical generalization of substantive research were to meet in the middle. Theory would develop more abstract generalizations for substantive areas of inquiry, with general theory awaiting its 'Einstein' only after middle-range theories had accumulated. This strategy tended to produce what I have called 'theories of ____' (fill in the blank with a substantive field, e.g., family, delinquency, ethnic antagonism, gender inequality, etc.); and these theories were, in reality, empirical generalizations made to look theoretical.

Conceptual stepping stones

Probably the most prevalent strategy for bridging the gap between the micro and macro has been the micro-to-macro conceptual progression, whereby the properties of action and interaction are first analyzed, followed by conceptualizations of ever-more macro phenomena. Max Weber's (1968 [1921]) analysis of action, social relationships, associations and legitimated orders represented one early effort; Talcott Parsons's (1951) analysis of action, interaction in status-roles and social systems represented a similar strategy. The assumption is that by adding new concepts as more macro phenomena are conceptualized, the 'emergent' properties of relations among phenomena can be captured and, yet, remain connected to micro-level concepts, but typically, these schemes leave as many gaps as they close. For example, in Parsons's and Weber's movement from conceptualizations of action through interaction to, respectively, social systems or

legitimated orders, the process of interaction is given short shrift; and since this process stands between action and structure, the gap between the micro and macro remains.

Formal sociology

Georg Simmel introduced the idea that rather than address the nature of the units in a social relationship, one should focus on the properties and dynamics of the relationship *per se*. In this way, it makes little difference if the actors are micro (people) or macro (organizations or nation-states), because it is the form of the relationship which is to be the subject of theory. Peter Blau's (1964) early exchange theory, Richard Emerson's (1962) network analysis of exchange and network theory in general (Burt, 1980; Wellman, 1983) all adopt this strategy. While it is often true that there is an isomorphism in the nature of relations among micro and macro units, such is not always the case; the nature of the unit can make a difference in the dynamics involved, and so formal sociology has only limited utility as a strategy for bridging the gap between micro and macro sociology.

Deductive reductionism

In this strategy, high-level axioms about the nature of micro processes (for example, individual behavior or interaction) are placed at the top of a deductive system, with the laws of social structure being deduced from these axioms. George Homans (1961) was, of course, the most famous advocate of this approach, seeing sociological explanations as deducible from a few axioms about human behavior. Peter Blau's (1994) more recent work has elements of this strategy as he seeks to deduce rates of interaction from simple axiomatic assumptions about the nature of social relationships. This solution to the micro–macro problem is elegant, but its execution rarely gives much attention to the properties and dynamics of those more macro structures whose dynamics are 'deduced' (translation: glossed over) in such deductive schemes.

In sum, these strategies for reconciling macro and micro processes fail to resolve the problem. And, if we add the agency–structure approaches of much European theory and the various multi-dimensional approaches typical of Americans to this list of strategies, it is evident that the problem is compounded rather than resolved. Most current strategies, to my mind, simply define the problem, asserting that action is constrained by structure, and structure is reproduced or changed by action. Yet, asserting a reciprocal relation only states the problem again, although we are often given a category system that obscures the failure to link the macro and micro conceptually. And so, if none of the various strategies that have been proposed conceptually link the micro and macro, we can ask: is the problem resolvable? The most advanced science, physics, and every science below physics have all failed to link fully the properties and dynamics of their macro and micro universes; and hence, sociologists should not be too upset if they cannot do so.

One solution to the problem of micro–macro linkage is one that I proposed a long time ago (Turner, 1983): stop worrying about it. Whether one uses micro-level concepts, macro-level concepts, or concepts in between is dependent on the nature of what we are trying to explain. If we assume that social reality exists at levels – that is, there are emergent properties in the social universe – then we choose the theories that best suit the level of phenomena we seek to explain. If we analyze world system dynamics, then symbolic interactionism is not very useful; or if we focus on an episode of emotionally charged interaction, then world system's theory or any macro theory does not have much to offer analysis. This was so obvious to me two decades ago that the whole question of micro and macro linkage seemed to be a red herring for sociology. Why waste our time on it? I still hold this view, but confess that it would be elegant if we could achieve some degree of theoretical integration across levels of reality. But if we are to approach this problem with any hope of success, we have to recast the issues and avoid the mistakes of the approaches I have briefly reviewed thus far.

AN ALTERNATIVE APPROACH TO LINKING THE MICRO AND MACRO

It is often said that distinctions between micro and macro are analytical; that is, they are abstractions that we can use in analysis, but they are not reality itself. I have come to the view that these terms represent more than analytical distinctions; they are *the way reality actually unfolds* (Turner, 2002). I would add a 'meso level' here in drawing this conclusion, and so I am asserting that the social universe operates at micro, meso and macro levels. These levels *are* reality. Thus, my alternative approach asserts that these are not just analytical distinctions, and of course they are this too, but that these distinctions capture one of the most fundamental properties of the social universe: its operation at three basic levels of organization. The micro, meso and macro *are* reality, and hence, we will have three general classes of theories. This begs the question as to whether or not these theories can be integrated, but let me not get ahead of myself on this critical question. If reality unfolds along three levels, then we must develop some way to conceptualize the properties and dynamics of each level.

I propose that we begin to conceptualize social reality as driven by basic and fundamental *forces* operating at three levels: the micro, meso and macro. I use the term 'forces' much as it is employed in physics, as when gravity and electromagnetism are seen to push phenomena in certain ways. The idea of social forces is, of course, an old one; I propose that we revive the notion of social forces as originally intended in early sociology. Thus, theoretical sociology develops principles that explain the operation of forces, and in my view, we need theoretical principles about the forces operating at the micro, meso and macro levels of reality. In Table 23.1 I list the forces that I see as critical to each level. These look very familiar because they have been a part of sociology for a long time; what I argue, then, is that we think of these phenomena in a somewhat different way – that is, as forces driving the operation and organization of the social universe.

These forces first generate, and then operate within, particular kinds of structures. At the

Table 23.1   *Forces of the social universe*

Macro-level forces	
Population	The absolute number, rate of growth, composition, and distribution of people
Production	The gathering of resources from the environment, the conversion of resources into commodities and the creation of services to facilitate gathering and conversion
Distribution	The construction of infrastructures to move resources, information and people in space as well as the use of exchange systems to distribute resources, information and people
Reproduction	The procreation of new members of a population and the transmission of culture to these members
Power	The use of coercion, administrative structures, manipulation of material incentives and symbols to control members of a population as well as the degree of centralization/ concentration of each and the bases of power
Meso-level forces	
Segmentation	The generation of additional corporate units organizing activities of individuals in the pursuit of ends or goals
Differentiation	The creation of new types of corporate units organizing activities of individuals in pursuit of ends or goals and new categoric units distinguishing people and placing them into socially constructed categories
Integration	The maintenance of boundaries, the ordering of relations within corporate and categoric units, and the ordering of relations among corporate and categoric units
Micro-level forces	
Emotions	The arousal of variants and combinations of fear, anger, sadness and happiness
Transactional needs	The activation of needs for confirmation of self, positive exchange payoffs, trust and predictability, facticity or the sense that things are as they appear and group inclusion
Symbols	The production of expectations (normatization) with respect to categories of people present, nature of the situation, forms of communication, frames of what is included and excluded, rituals and feelings
Roles	The presentation of sequences of gestures to mark a predictable course of action (role-making) and the reading of gestures to understand the course of action of others (role-taking)
Status	The placement and evaluation of individuals in positions *vis-à-vis* other positions and creation of expectation states for how individuals in diverse and differentially evaluated positions should behave
Demography	The number of people co-present, their density and their movements, as well as the meanings assigned to number, density and movements of individuals
Ecology	The boundaries, partitions and props of space as well as the associated meaning of boundaries, partitions and props

macro level, the structures generated by the forces are *institutional systems*; at the meso level, these forces form *corporate* and *categoric* units; and at the micro level, the forces sustain *encounters*. Thus, the structural units and the forces driving their formation and operation constitute the social universe; and the goal of sociological theory should be to develop principles on the dynamics of each force as well as on the relationships among forces. It is in this latter concern with the relationships among the structures formed at each level that linkages among the macro, meso and micro occur, but before exploring these linkages, let me briefly review each of the forces listed in Table 23.1.

Macro-level reality

The macro level of reality consists of larger numbers of individuals organized in space over longer durations of time. The macro level of reality ultimately deals with the relationship of a population as a whole with its social and biophysical environments. In traditional functionalism (e.g., Spencer, 1874–96; Durkheim, 1893; Parsons, 1951), these forces are often conceptualized as 'requisites' or 'needs' that must be met if a population is to survive in its environment, but this mode of analysis should be avoided; instead we should conceptualize the organization of a population as driven by forces. There are, I believe, five such forces at the macro level of reality (Turner, 1995).

Population   Population is more than a demographic variable; it is a force that drives all aspects of human social organization. In particular, the size and rate of growth of the population are the most dynamic features of this force, although the composition, movements and distribution of a population are also critical properties of this force. Population sets into motion other forces; and when a population grows, as both Herbert Spencer (1874–96) and Émile Durkheim (1893) recognized, production must expand to sustain its members, distributive infrastructures and exchange become more extensive, reproductive forces become more complex and move outside kinship alone, and power must be consolidated to coordinate and control the larger social mass.

Production   To sustain themselves, people must secure resources and convert them into commodities; and this process is one of the driving forces of human organization, creating the economy as an institutional system. The level of production is related to a number of key elements: technology, physical and human capital, property systems and entrepreneurial mechanisms for coordinating these elements. The higher the values for these elements, the greater the level of production, and vice versa.

Reproduction   Humans must reproduce themselves both biologically and socio-culturally, and this force pushes for the initial formation of key institutional systems such as kinship. And as the complexity of a society increases, reproduction generally drives the formation of additional institutional systems, ranging from education through science and medicine to religion. Thus, socio-cultural reproduction becomes an ever-more powerful force in human societies, generating new kinds of institutional domains.

Distribution   There are two elements to distribution: first, infrastructures for moving people, information and resources about a territory, and second, systems for exchanging resources, information and people. Although they mutually influence each other, these two aspects of distribution need to be analyzed separately because they drive human organization in somewhat different ways. As infrastructures expand and as exchange occurs in markets using liquid media of exchange, the way a population is organized is dramatically transformed; and so as the scale of human organization increases, distribution forces become as important as production forces.

Power   Two aspects of power are critical in understanding this force: first, the level and profile of *consolidation* of power around varying bases, including coercion, administrative control, symbolic manipulation or use of material incentives; and second, the degree of *centralization* of power along any one or all of these varying bases. When populations are very small, this force is not visible, but as a population grows, power becomes a dominant force in determining the way in which the institutional systems coordinating people's activities operate.

What I am asserting here is that, at the macro level of human organization, these five forces – population, production, reproduction, distribution and power – determine the organization of the population as a whole and the cultural systems that are used to sustain this organization. The key structural units generated by these forces are institutional systems – that is, economy, polity, kinship, education, science, religion, law and the like – and the culture of these systems. Macro-level theory is, therefore, about these forces as they generate and sustain institutional systems and culture. At the most general level, we should seek to develop abstract laws about the dynamics of each force (for my best effort, see Turner, 1995).

In terms of linkages among levels of social reality, the institutional complexes and culture generated by these forces are parameters within which the forces operating at the meso and micro levels of social reality operate. Reciprocally, institutional systems at the macro level are composed of the structures generated at the meso level, and the forces driving the formation and operation of these meso-level structures. But we need to do more than assert this fact; we must develop principles that explain the dynamics of this embeddedness. Before suggesting how we can do so, however, let me complete the review of the forces operating at each level of reality. Still, to anticipate my argument: the effects of macro forces on the meso and micro are more constraining than the reverse, and this fact needs to be taken into consideration in developing theoretical principles that link these levels of reality.

Meso-level reality

There are three forces operating at this level – segmentation, differentiation and integration – and the structures generated by these forces are what Amos Hawley (1986) has termed *corporate* and *categoric* units. A corporate unit is a structure and its related culture organized to pursue goals or ends (for example, group, community, bureaucracy), whereas a categoric unit is a social category which makes a difference in terms of how people act and are treated by others (for example, gender, ethnicity, age, social class). Thus, institutional systems are ultimately constructed from corporate and categoric units, but are not reducible to them; the forces driving the macro level are different than the forces of segmentation, differentiation and integration that drive corporate and categoric units.

Segmentation This force causes the formation of structurally and culturally equivalent corporate units. Thus, when more of the same type of nuclear families, bureaucratic structures and villages or towns are created, these are manifestations of segmentation. Segmentation operates mostly among corporate units, because to create a new social category is evidence of differentiation as a force.

Differentiation This notion of differentiation is as old as sociology, and it simply emphasizes that differences are generated in human organization. Differentiation can operate at all levels – as when people play distinctive roles (micro level) or differences in institutions are evident (macro level) – but the origin of differentiation at either the micro or macro level is the meso level of reality. Differentiation at the micro or macro level is a reflection of the forces driving the formation of corporate and/or categoric units. People play different roles, for example, at different points in the division of labor of an organization or on the basis of being a member of a social category, and the differences among institutional systems are in the nature of, and the relations among, distinctive types of organizational units and social categories (for example, family *vs.* factory, father *vs.* worker).

At the most general level, corporate units vary in terms of some key elements (Turner, 2000, 2002):

1 The size of the unit
2 The integrity of its boundaries and internal partitions
3 The formality of its structure
4 The explicitness and extensiveness of its horizontal division of labor
5 The nature of its vertical division of labor
6 The explicitness of the ends or goals it pursues.

Similarly, categoric units vary along a number of dimensions:

1 The degree of homogeneity or heterogeneity of members
2 The clarity and discreteness of the markers distinguishing members of categoric units
3 The inequalities in rank and evaluation of social categories

4   The correlation among memberships in different social categories
5   The correlation of categoric distinctions with the division of labor in corporate units.

A theory differentiation must, therefore, explain the dynamics of, and relations among, these elements.

Integration   When corporate or categoric units are generated, forces are activated to order relations within and between them. For integration within corporate units, these forces revolve around the structural and cultural constraints imposed by the institutional domain (for example, family, economy, religion) in which a corporate unit operates, and the dynamics inhering in the administrative structures used to coordinate and control activities in the division of labor. Integrative dynamics for relations between and among corporate units revolve around such processes as:

1   The level of structural interdependence
2   Structural inclusion (of units inside of each other)
3   Structural overlap
4   Structural segregation of units from each other
5   Structural mobility of members across units
6   Structural domination of one unit by another (Turner, 1996).

Integrative forces for categoric units cohere around:

1   The degree to which the structure and culture of institutional domains define distinctions among social categories and sustain these distinctions through the division of labor of the corporate units making up this domain (for example, the social category of 'father' is defined by the culture of kinship, and sustained by family corporate units).
2   The extent to which distributive processes, particularly exchange dynamics, differentially allocate material and cultural resources so that members of a categoric unit have common shares (for example, social class is defined by the common shares of material and symbolic resources held by its members).

3   The degree to which these differences in shares are defined as legitimate by members of a categoric unit (for example, do women accept traditional definitions of them and the options for employment and income?).
4   The rates and patterns of intra- and inter-category interaction (for example, social class mobility). (For a more detailed discussion of integrative dynamics for corporate and categoric units see Turner, 1996; Turner and Boyns, 2002.)

Just as institutional domains constrain the operation of meso-level forces, so corporate and categoric units circumscribe the operation of micro-dynamic forces. True, in some ultimate sense, corporate and categoric units are constructed from episodes of face-to-face interaction, but like institutional domains which are built from these meso units, the dynamics of corporate and categoric units cannot be explained by their constituent encounters. Segmentation, differentiation and integration are forces of the meso level, and they are very different from those forces driving episodes of face-to-face interaction.

Micro-level reality

The micro level of reality consists of episodes of face-to-face interaction, or what Erving Goffman (1961) termed 'the encounter'. In *focused encounters*, individuals face each other in an ecological huddle and generally have a common focus of attention, while in *unfocused encounters*, people avoid direct face-to-face engagement but none the less monitor each other's actions in public space. As a distinctive level of reality, encounters are driven by basic forces unique to this level: emotions, transactional needs, symbols, roles, status, demography and ecology. These are summarized in Table 23.1, but let me briefly elaborate upon each.

Emotions   All interaction involves the arousal of variants and combinations of at least four primary emotions: fear, anger, happiness and sadness (Turner, 2000). Without emotions individuals cannot think, role-take and role-make effectively, or forge social bonds. Emotional arousal – whether positive or negative – drives all episodes of face-to-face interaction.

Transactional needs   All interaction is motivated or energized by certain fundamental needs (Turner, 1987, 1988, 2000, 2002): the need to confirm self or identity, the need to receive positive exchange payoffs, the need for predictability in the responses of others and the perception that others can be trusted to behave appropriately, the need to perceive that a situation is real and is as it appears, and the need for group inclusion or to feel part of the ongoing interpersonal flow. These needs, I argue, are always activated when humans engage each other in encounters, and their fulfillment drives what people do and how they respond to the actions of others.

Symbols   All interactions are guided by cultural forces, which I label the *process of normatization* (Turner, 2000, 2002) in which people develop mutual expectations for categorization (of others and the situation), frames (what is to be included and excluded from the encounter), forms of communication (appropriate genres of talk and body language), ritual (stereotyped sequences of communication to open, close, structure and repair the flow of gestures in the encounter) and emotions (the type and level of affect to be revealed). The viability of the encounter is, I believe, dependent upon the extent to which it has been successfully normatized along these dimensions.

Roles   In all interactions, individuals use and read each other's gestures in order to present a role to others and to understand the role that others are trying to make for themselves (that is, they mutually role-make [R.H. Turner, 1962] and role-take [Mead, 1934]). I believe that individuals are driven to discover the role of others so that they can make a complementary role (or, if conflict is intended, make a contradictory role). There are several types of roles (Turner, 2002): 'pre-assembled roles', in which the gesturing marking the role is well known to all (for example, being a father), 'combinational roles', where elements from different roles are combined to make a meta-role (for example, a daughter who is a host at a family gathering must combine the roles of daughter and host), 'generalized roles', where gestures mark the style or expressive content of a role (for example, being shy or aggressive), and 'trans-situational roles', which are often associated with categoric memberships and played out in most encounters (for example, the role of being a male).

When individuals successfully role-make and role-take along these dimensions or types of roles, the encounter becomes more viable.

Status   Individuals not only role-take, they also 'position-take' in encounters, looking for signs and signals of the position of others with respect to diffuse status characteristics (for example, male or female), relative evaluation (prestige) of status, place of status in a network or division of labor, and clarity of status relative to other potential status positions (Turner, 2002). When individuals can successfully determine each other's status, the interaction proceeds smoothly, and conversely, when status is unclear or contested, the interaction will be tense.

Demography   The number of people present, their characteristics (as members of social categories), their movements in and out of a situation, and their density all shape the flow of face-to-face interaction. Individuals understand the meanings associated with these facets of interpersonal demography, and these understandings drive how they respond to each other.

Ecology   The organization of space is the final micro-level force, and this force concerns such issues as the amount of space, its boundedness, its partitions, its usable props and other spatial and physical features of the place where the encounter occurs. Like demographic cues, individuals understand the meanings of different configurations of space, and they respond accordingly.

These, then, are the forces driving how individuals behave in, and organize, encounters.

Emotions, need states, norms, roles, status, demography and ecology all exert independent effects on the flow of face-to-face interaction, but it is rare for an encounter *not* to be embedded within corporate and categoric units. Even if individuals are not part of a group, organization or some other structure with a division of labor, they are typically members of social categories – for example, gender, class, ethnicity and age. This embedding of the encounter within corporate and/or categoric units gives us a clue as to how to proceed in linking the meso and micro levels of reality. And in turn, since corporate and categoric units are embedded in institutional domains, my argument suggests the structure of linkages among all three levels of reality. But a typology of structure is insufficient; we need to theorize about *the dynamics* of this embedding process.

THE DYNAMICS OF EMBEDDING

Encounters are embedded in corporate and categoric units, with these meso structures embedded in institutional domains. At any given time, then, embeddedness appears to work from macro down rather than the other way around. The point is buttressed by the simple fact that it takes many iterated encounters to sustain or change either a categoric or corporate unit, to say nothing of an institutional domain. No one encounter within meso structures, nor no one corporate or categoric unit within an institutional domain, is likely to effect much change. But a change in a meso structure, such as reorganization of the division of labor in a corporate unit, can influence many encounters; or if a new technology is introduced into the economy, many meso structures within this domain may be altered. To assert, as micro chauvinists do, that the meso and macro are constructed of chains of micro events may be true in some ultimate metaphysical sense, but this assertion does not get around the problem of aggregation. It takes many aggregated micro events to influence more macro ones, and this fact alone, I believe, makes it unlikely that meso and macro structures are going to be explained by the dynamics

of encounters. In a very small meso structure, such as a group, this might be the case, but the group is, in turn, probably embedded in a larger corporate structure and even more likely to be embedded in categoric units. These more inclusive meso units are not so likely to be explained by micro processes. I will have more to say about how the micro *can* work changes on the meso and macro, but the general point here should be emphasized: reality itself, not perceptions of analysts, reveals a macro-to-micro bias.

If we want to explain reality at all levels, then, we will probably explain much more if we engage in a top-down analysis. That is, how are the forces operating within institutional domains altering those at the meso level; and in turn, how is the embedding of encounters in corporate and categoric units shaping the operation of forces at the micro level? We will explain more by answering these top-down questions than by asking the reverse: that is, how does the encounter explain meso structure, and how do corporate and categoric units explain institutional domains? Thus, in making theoretical linkages among levels of reality, we should begin with a macro-to-micro approach. We do not have to be chauvinists and dismiss the meso or micro; obviously, we could not explain a corporate unit or an encounter solely in terms of macro-level forces. Rather, the macro loads the values for the meso forces, and the meso loads the values for those driving the micro; we still explain each level in terms of its own distinctive forces, but by knowing in which institutional domains corporate and categoric units are embedded and in which meso structures an encounter is embedded, we can construct explanations that link the macro, meso and micro.

Cultural embeddedness

At all levels of social organization, culture is generated and used to regulate actions. The culture of a society – its technologies of information about how to manipulate the environment, its values specifying right and wrong and its texts of lore, history, aesthetics and philosophy – is translated into the culture of

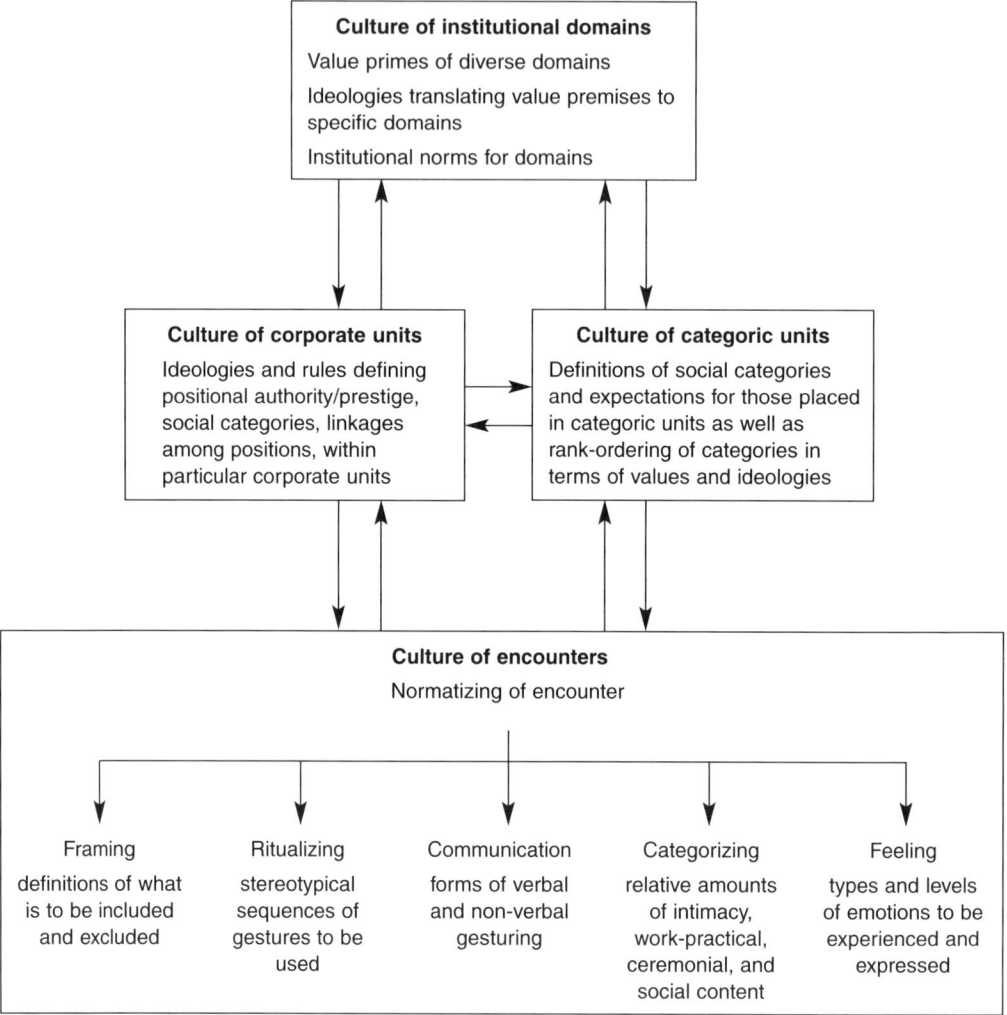

Figure 23.1   *Culture and levels of reality*

institutional domains, and from there into the culture of corporate and categoric units which, in turn, provide the cultural parameters for normatization of episodes of face-to-face interaction in encounters. Figure 23.1 outlines what I see as the critical translations of culture that follow from the embedding. At the most micro level, culture is manifest in the process of normatization, but the contents of these expectations come from the broader societal culture as various elements are adapted to institutional domains and, then, to the corporate and/or

categoric units in which the encounter is embedded. Talcott Parsons was not too far off the mark in his view of a 'cybernetic hierarchy of control', but he did not specify the structural units to which culture is attached, and as a consequence, the connections among levels of reality were left rather vague. New cultural contents can, of course, be added from bottom-up processes, perhaps beginning with chains of iterated encounters but more likely from new kinds of meso structures that, in turn, begin to alter the structure of institutional domains and, perhaps, the broader culture of a society as a whole, or even a world system of societies.

Structural embeddedness

As emphasized, encounters are embedded in the structure and culture of meso-level units that, in turn, are embedded in institutional domains. Thus, corporate and categoric units will reveal structures that reflect the blueprints of culture and the structural arrangements of institutional domains. For example, businesses look very much alike in all capitalist societies because of their embeddedness in an institutional domain driven by similar production and distribution forces as well as similar cultural elements. Encounters in such equivalent corporate structures will be normatized in similar ways because of this embeddedness in similar types of corporate units, although there are always cultural variations across societies and even within societies. For categoric units the process is much the same. For example, the class distinctions of most Western, capitalist societies are very similar because they are embedded in similar institutional domains, and interaction among people of the same or different classes will be very similar because of the encounter's embeddedness in the social categories marking the class system. At times, corporate and categoric unit memberships are interwoven when, for example, a position in a corporate unit – say, student in a university – is also a social category; in such cases, interaction among students or between students and others, such as professors, will be much the same cross-culturally because of the similarities in the division of labor of corporate units and social categories linked to this corporate unit.

Macro-to-meso-to-micro theorizing

It is one thing to assert the power of embedding, but quite another to develop theoretical models and principles explaining the nature of the linkages across levels. There is insufficient space in this chapter to perform this critical task, and indeed, I have not done it for all levels. But I have sought to develop theoretical principles on the dynamics of encounters as embedded processes, seeing the values for each force operating at the level of the encounter as being constrained by embedding in corporate and categoric units and, by extension, in institutional domains (see Turner, 2000, 2002). This effort is not just a programmatic statement, as this chapter must be by necessity, but a preliminary effort to specify the abstract principles explaining relationships among levels of reality. For me, this is the only way to make linkages among micro, meso and macro levels of reality.

I do not want to end here with what may seem like a vague programmatic statement. Let me elaborate and illustrate with one example the kind of theoretical linkages that I have in mind. Any micro-level encounter is embedded in a meso-level structure, driven by the forces of the meso level. The approach that I am advocating does not try to connect the principles explaining the operation of forces at different levels of reality; these are unique to each level and are not, in my view, reducible to each other. What can be reconciled, however, are the effects of meso structures (produced by meso-level forces) on the loadings for each micro-level force, whether emotions, transactional needs, status, roles, symbols, demography or ecology. That is, the embedding of an encounter in corporate and/or categoric units will help explain the loadings of each micro-level force; and when we add to this variations in structure and culture of the corporate and categoric units, we can theoretically link the meso and micro. The same is true for linkages between the macro and meso levels of reality. To illustrate what I am arguing, take the force of 'normatization' as a micro-level force. The values for each element of this force – expectations for categorization of others and situations, for appropriate frames, for forms of communication, for rituals and for expressions of emotions – are determined by embeddedness in corporate and categoric units as much as by the actual flow of interaction. My argument is more complex than the illustration here, but none the less, let me offer two examples of the kinds of propositions that can be developed. First, the more an encounter is embedded in a corporate unit, and the more bounded, formal and hierarchical is the division of labor of this unit, the more clear-cut are expectations for the nature of the situation, for the forms of communication, for frames, for rituals and for the expression of feelings. Second, the more salient are categoric-unit memberships of those in an encounter, and the more discrete (for example, men–women) and differentially evaluated these categories (for example, black–white), the more clear-cut are categorizations of others; and, other things being equal, the more strained are efforts to establish mutual frames, forms of communication; and hence, the more ritualized are interactions and the greater is the potential for the emotional arousal exceeding feeling rules. These two propositions state in more precise ways how the properties of meso units – formality, hierarchy and boundedness for corporate units and discreteness and differential evaluation of categoric units – will load the values for a micro-level force, in this case different aspects of normatization. Thus, we have actual propositions and predictions about how the variable properties of one level will affect the operation of a force at another level. For me, this is a theory that connects the levels rather than being a general metaphor or ad hoc assertion. Obviously, these two propositions do not capture the full complexity of what is involved (see Turner, 2002, for more details), but the connection is at least theoretical. And as I have sought to do (Turner, 2000, 2002), linked theoretical proportions can be systematically generated once we begin to view the variable properties of the structures emerging at one level as imposing constraints on the loadings of forces operating at the next level down. In my illustration, the properties of the structures generated by meso-level forces constrain the values for the forces operating in micro-level encounters. Similar arguments could be made for how the properties of various institutional systems load the values for the forces – segmentation, differentiation, and integration – operating at the meso level. In this way, I believe, we can generate *real theoretical linkages* among the levels of reality.

Micro-to-meso-to-macro theorizing

Before closing, let me theorize about how micro dynamics can effect meso and macro processes – if only to avoid the label of being a macro chauvinist. To argue that society is chains of interaction rituals (Collins, 1981a,b), symbolic interactions (Blumer, 1969), rational choices (Coleman, 1990), unit acts (Parsons, 1937) and the product of other micro processes does not specify *how* the meso and macro are constructed or changed by these micro processes. Most proclamations are highly metaphorical, but we produce more than metaphors. What is required are statements about the mechanisms by which micro processes can affect the meso and macro, as well as the conditions under which these mechanisms are likely to be activated. Again, I cannot go into much detail, but let me outline some of the ways that micro forces can and do alter the structures and cultures in which they are embedded (Turner, 2002; Turner and Boyns, 2002).

Power and status dynamics The power and status of individuals in an encounter influence their capacity to exert effects on the meso structures in which the encounter is embedded. The more power and prestige enjoyed by individuals, the greater their effect on the flow of encounters and, hence, potentially on corporate and categoric units. Moreover, the more membership in categoric units serves as a basis for the creation of corporate units (as in social movement organizations), the greater will be this potential for micro-to-meso influence.

Centrality, density and embeddedness of networks The more an encounter is embedded and central in a network of relations among encounters, and the more dense are such networks among encounters, the greater will be the potential impact of the encounter on meso structures. For as change in a central encounter occurs, its effects flow across networks of ties to other encounters, thereby altering the division of labor in corporate units or the social distinctions of categoric units.

Institutional domains Encounters in some institutional domains will have greater effects than in others. In general, encounters in institutions dealing with the external environment will have a greater impact on meso structures than those revolving around internal system processes such as reproduction (Hawley, 1986). Thus, encounters that alter the meso structures of the economy or polity will be more likely to alter macro structures than those encounters in families, schools, churches and other internal institutional systems.

Iterations A single encounter rarely exerts much influence on meso and macro structures or culture. Rather, it takes repetitions of encounters to increase the potential for change; and the more the conditions outlined above prevail, the more likely are changes in iterated encounters to exert effects on corporate and categoric units and, by extension, institutional domains.

Size The larger is the number of individuals in an encounter, the greater will be its potential effect on the meso structures in which it is embedded. This effect can be direct, as when large numbers of individuals can sustain a focus on change, or it can be indirect, as members of a change-oriented encounter disperse to other encounters.

Visibility Encounters that are visible to others within corporate and categoric units will have more influence on meso structures than those that are not. Communication technologies can greatly enhance visibility (and size of the encounter as well), especially when the encounter uses public rituals to arouse more intense emotions among larger numbers of individuals. When encounters become emotionally charged media events, then they can have far-reaching effects on meso and macro structures.

Emotional energy As noted above, emotions are a powerful force. When encounters arouse intense emotions, these emotions can push individuals to seek change. Moreover, emotions are contagious, and if these emotions are orchestrated by rituals for specific ends, they can reach larger numbers of individuals in other encounters and work to generate change in meso and macro structures.

Deprivations and negative emotions When individuals' transactional needs are not realized, they will experience negative emotions. When such emotions are consistently aroused in encounters or across encounters, they motivate individuals to change the circumstances in which they must operate. More generally, any time expectations are not realized, whether from the failure to meet needs or some other source of dissonance, negative emotions are aroused and lead individuals to seek change. Thus, corporate and categoric units that consistently deprive people and arouse negative emotions will be easier targets for micro-to-meso influence than meso structures in which needs are realized and expectations confirmed.

In sum, then, we can see that there are many paths for micro events to influence meso and macro events. In emphasizing that embeddedness gives corporate and categoric units and their respective cultures more influence on the flow of face-to-face interaction than vice versa, I do not want to imply an extreme macro chauvinism. Still, these paths to micro influence on the meso and macro are relatively rare compared to the influence of macro on meso, and meso on micro; it takes a confluence of these paths for change in corporate and categoric units to occur as the result of micro social processes. The world is not static, of course, and constant pressures are exerted on the meso and macro from the micro level, but if we are to explain a given situation at any level of reality, we first must deal with the unique forces operating at that level as they generate structural and cultural arrangements; and as we do so, we should also turn to the constraints imposed by the embedding of the micro in the meso and the meso in the macro because the values of each force will be determined, in large part, by this embedding. We will get far more explanatory power from theories that are constructed in this way than we will with grand pronouncements that the macro and meso are 'merely' chains of micro events. To make such micro chauvinist arguments true, it is necessary to specify just how and in what ways the micro obviates the emergent properties of the meso and macro levels as well as the forces driving these properties. No micro chauvinist has ever done so. We can list the paths of influence, as I have done above, but this is far different than specifying the conditions under which micro events will structure corporate and categoric units as well as institutional domains.

CONCLUSIONS

Sociologists must, I believe, recognize that the social universe unfolds along micro, meso and macro domains. Humans have created institutional systems to adapt to their environments, both the biophysical and socio-cultural environment of their own creation. These institutional systems are built from units that aggregate and order encounters into corporate units coordinating activities and into categoric units making social distinctions. The most fundamental structural units – institutional systems, corporate and categoric units, and encounters – are the outcome of forces driving their formation, maintenance and change; and these forces are unique to each level of reality. Theories on the forces at one level are not reducible to theories about the forces at another level. This conclusion does not mean, however, that we cannot address the connections between levels, but it does mean that sociologists must stop being metaphorical, vague and chauvinistic about how to develop explanations that take account of what occurs at each level.

My view is that reality itself, rather than the analyst, reveals a bias toward macro-to-micro order. True, in the sociological equivalent of the Big Bang (perhaps the 'little bang') individual people (hunter–gatherers) created institutional systems and meso structures from their encounters, but once these came into existence, they almost always have constrained what transpires at the micro level. I am not being chauvinistic in drawing this conclusion because the forces operating at each level cannot be reduced to each other, or explained in terms of the forces of another level. Rather, I am arguing that the values for forces at one level are loaded by the structures in which this level is embedded – that is, the values for micro forces are very much constrained by the nature of corporate and categoric units, and the values for the meso level are determined, in part, by the structure of the institutional systems in which they are embedded.

From this view of reality, theories about social reality should, first and foremost, be about the operative dynamics of the forces operating at any given level. Without models and abstract principles about how these forces operate, we will never explain the social universe and, for the purposes of this chapter, we will never integrate micro-meso-macro theorizing. With the theoretical principles about the dynamics of each force at each level of reality, we are then in a position to make the linkages to another level of reality. But we cannot do so by trying to integrate the principles about forces; rather, we make the theoretical linkages by seeing how the outcome of these forces – corporate and categoric units at the meso level and institutional systems at the macro level – load the values of the forces operating at the level below them. Such linkages are made by seeing how the specific properties of structures at either the meso or macro levels will influence the forces at the next level down. When theorizing is done in this way, we can develop explicitly theoretical statements about how a property at one level will change the valences for a force at another level.

We would be wise, I believe, to focus on top-down linkages following this strategy, at least for a while. As I tried to illustrate, we can also move bottom-up, but these theoretical principles will be more complex and difficult to construct and test. Indeed, computer simulations may be the only realistic way to test their viability. But, it will be possible to make theoretical statements about the conditions under which the structure of encounters will affect the valences of the forces driving corporate and categoric units (and their cultures) and about the conditions under which the structure of corporate and categoric units will load the valences for institutional systems (and their cultures). But before this kind of analysis is pursued, we need to develop principles moving top-down; we will advance much more rapidly as a science when this latter strategy is emphasized.

REFERENCES

Alexander, J.C. (1982) *Theoretical Logic in Sociology, Volume 1*. Berkeley, CA: University of California Press.

Alexander, J.C., Giesen, B., Münch, R. and Smelser, N. (eds) (1987) *The Micro–Macro Link*. Berkeley, CA: University of California Press.

Archer, Margaret S. (1982) 'Morphogenesis versus structuration: on combining structure and action', *British Journal of Sociology*, 33: 455–83.

Archer, Margaret S. (1988) *Culture and Agency: The Place of Culture in Social Theory*. Cambridge: Cambridge University Press.

Berger, P. and Luckmann, T. (1967) *The Social Construction of Reality*. Garden City, NY: Anchor.

Blalock, H. and Wilken, P. (1979) *Intergroup Processes: A Micro- Macro- Perspective*. New York: The Free Press.

Blau, P.M. (1964) *Exchange and Power in Social Life*. New York: Wiley.

Blau, P.M. (1977a) *Inequality and Heterogeneity: A Primitive Theory of Social Structure*. New York: The Free Press.

Blau, P.M. (1977b) 'A macrosociological theory of social structure', *American Sociological Review*, 83: 265–54.

Blau, P.M. (1994) *Structural Context of Opportunities*. Chicago: University of Chicago Press.

Blumer, H. (1969) *Symbolic Interaction: Perspective and Method*. Englewood Cliffs, NJ: Prentice–Hall.

Bourdieu, P. (1984) *Distinction: A Social Critique of the Judgement of Taste*. Cambridge, MA: Harvard University Press.

Burt, R. (1980) 'Models of network structure', *Annual Review of Sociology*, 6: 79–82.

Coleman, J.S. (1987) 'Microfoundations and macrosocial behavior', in J.C. Alexander, B. Giesen, R. Münch and N. Smelser (eds), *The Micro–Macro Link*. Berkeley/Los Angeles, CA: University of California Press.

Coleman, J.S. (1990) *Foundations of Social Theory*. Cambridge, MA: Belknap Press.

Collins, Randall (1981a) 'Micro-translation as a theory-building strategy', in Karin Knorr Cetina and Aaron Cicourel (eds), *Advances in Social Theory and Methodology*. New York: Methuen.

Collins, Randall (1981b) 'On the microfoundations of macrosociology', *American Journal of Sociology*, 86: 984–1014.

Durkheim, E. (1893) *The Division of Labor in Society*. New York: The Free Press.

Eisenstadt, S.N. and Helle, J.H. (eds) (1985) *Macro-Sociological Theory: Perspectives on Sociological Theory*, 2 vols. London: Sage.

Emerson, R.M. (1962) 'Power-dependence relations', *American Sociological Review*, 17: 31–41.

Giddens, Anthony (1984) *The Constitution of Society: Outline of the Theory of Structuration*. Berkeley/Los Angeles, CA: University of California Press.

Goffman, E. (1961) *Encounters: Two Studies in the Sociology of Interaction*. Indianapolis, IN: Bobbs–Merrill.

Gurvitch, G. (1964) *The Spectrum of Social Time*. Dordrecht: D. Reidel.

Hawley, A. (1986) *Human Ecology: A Theoretical Essay*. Chicago: University of Chicago Press.

Hechter, M. (ed.) (1983) *The Micro Foundation of Macrosociology*. Philadelphia, PA: Temple University Press.

Hechter, M. (1987) *Principles of Group Solidarity*. Berkeley/Los Angeles, CA: University of California Press.

Homans, G.C. (1961) *Social Behavior: Its Elementary Forms*. New York: Harcourt and Brace.

Kemeny, J. (1976) 'Perspectives on the micro–macro distinction', *Sociological Review*, 24: 731–52.

Knorr Cetina, K.D. (1981) 'Introduction: the micro-sociological challenge of macro-sociology: towards a reconstruction of social theory and methodology', in K.D. Knorr Cetina and A. Cicourel (eds), *Advances in Social Theory and Methodology*. New York: Methuen.

Mayhew, Bruce H. (1980) 'Structuralism versus individualism: part 1, shadowboxing in the dark', *Social Forces*, 59: 335–75.

Mayhew, Bruce H. (1981) 'Structuralism versus individualism: part 2, ideological and other obfuscations', *Social Forces*, 59: 627–48.

Mead, G.H. (1934) *Mind, Self and Society*. Chicago: University of Chicago Press.

Merton, Robert (1968) *Social Theory and Social Structure*, enlarged edn. New York: The Free Press.

Parsons, T. (1937) *The Structure of Social Action*. New York: McGraw–Hill.

Parsons, T. (1951) *The Social System*. New York: The Free Press.

Ritzer, G. (1985) 'The rise of micro-sociological theory', *Sociological Theory*, 3: 88–98.

Ritzer, G. (1988a) 'The micro-macro link: problems and prospects', *Contemporary Sociology*, 17: 703–6.

Ritzer, G. (1988b) *Sociological Theory*, 2nd edn. New York: Alfred A. Knopf.

Ritzer, G. (1990) 'Micro-macro linkage in sociological theory', in *Frontiers of Social Theory: The New Synthesis*. New York: Columbia University Press.

Ritzer, G. (1991) *Metatheorizing in Sociology*. Lexington, MA: Lexington Books.

Smart, B. (2001) 'Micro-macro analysis', in G. Ritzer and B. Smart (eds), *Handbook of Sociological Theory*. London: Sage.

Spencer, H. (1874–96) *The Principles of Sociology*, 3 vols. New York: Appleton–Century.

Turner, J.H. (1983) 'Theoretical strategies for linking micro and macro processes', *Western Sociological Review*, 14: 4–15.

Turner, J.H. (1987) 'Toward a sociological theory of motivation', *American Sociological Review*, 52: 15–25.

Turner, J.H. (1988) *A Theory of Social Interaction*. Stanford, CA: Stanford University Press.

Turner, J.H. (1995) *Macrodynamics: Toward a Theory on the Organization of Human Populations*. Brunswick, NJ: Rutgers University Press.

Turner, J.H. (1996) 'A macro-level functional theory of societal disintegration', *International Journal of Sociology*, 16: 5–36.

Turner, J.H. (2000) 'A theory of embedded encounters', *Advances in Group Processes*, 17: 285–322.

Turner, J.H. (2002) *Face-to-Face: A Sociological Theory of Interpersonal Behavior*. Stanford, CA: Stanford University Press.

Turner, J.H. and Boyns, D. (2002) 'The return of grand theory', in J.H. Turner (ed.), *Handbook of Sociological Theory*. New York: Plenum Press.

Turner, R.H. (1962) 'Role-taking: process versus conformity', in A. Rose (ed.), *Human Behavior and Social Processes*. Boston, MA: Houghton Mifflin.

Weber, Max (1968 [1921]) *Economy and Society*, 3 vols. Totowa, NJ: Bedminster Press.

Wellman, Barry (1983) 'Network analysis: some basic principles', in Randall Collins (ed.), *Sociological Theory – 1983*. San Francisco: Jossey–Bass.

Wiley, N. (1988) 'The macro–micro problem in social theory', *Sociological Theory*, 6: 254–61.

24

Global Inequality: Bringing Politics Back In

JAN NEDERVEEN PIETERSE

INTRODUCTION

The data on contemporary human inequality are dramatic and widely known:

> Consider the relative income shares of the richest and poorest 20 per cent of the world's people. Between 1960 and 1991 the share of the richest 20 per cent rose from 70 per cent of global income to 85 per cent – while that of the poorest declined from 2.3 per cent to 1.4 per cent. So, the ratio of the shares of the richest and the poorest increased from 30:1 to 61:1. … by 1991 more than 85 per cent of the world's population received only 15 per cent of its income. (UNDP 1996: 13)

At the beginning of the twenty-first century about a third of the world population – 1.3 billion people – live on incomes of less than one dollar a day. Taking two dollars per day as the poverty line, 2.8 billion out of 6 billion people lived in poverty in the early 1990s (Walton, 1997: 2).

Overall discrepancies in income and wealth are now vast to the point of being grotesque. It is obvious that we inhabit a global theatre of the absurd. The discrepancies in livelihoods across the world are so large that they are without historical precedent and without conceivable justification, economic, moral or otherwise.

Several circumstances with regard to global inequality stand out. While global economic integration has grown over the past decades, global inequality has increased. Global inequality has increased sharply since the 1980s, in a clear rupture with the pattern over previous decades. The growth of extreme poverty coincides with an explosion of wealth over the same time period. Conventional arguments to explain global inequality have been losing their validity over time, rapidly so in light of the recent increase in global inequality.

Economists lead the way in global poverty research; operational research and technical analyses predominate and research and policy focus on global poverty rather than global inequality. While international institutions set the agenda in world development, their institutional maneuvering room is restricted; accordingly, there is an apolitical strand in approaches to global inequality. This may explain why current approaches to reducing global poverty are fundamentally uneven and incoherent.

These are the main concerns and the main line of argument in this chapter. After introducing the theme of global inequality, the chapter turns to measurements of global poverty and next to the question of global inequality. This leads to the question what light does growing global inequality shed on the conventional arguments that explain inequity and inform policy?

The closing section examines contemporary perplexities by taking into account forward-looking perspectives on global inequality.

GLOBAL INEQUALITY

The emergence of global inequality as a theme implies a horizon that is global and adopts human equality as a norm. Equality as a general sensibility has come with liberalism and socialism (Franklin, 1997). As a theme, global inequality goes back by and large to the mid-twentieth century. As a global sensibility it is part of the postwar era shaped by the United Nations and the adoption of the Universal Declaration of Human Rights. UN agencies such as the UN Development Programme, UNICEF and UNESCO have done much work to monitor and report on world-scale inequality. As part of the creation of global order and representing a world-wide momentum that places all nations on a common platform, UN agencies embody and have educated the world to a global sensibility, while being part of the international power structure.

Global inequality evokes what has been termed the 'second great transformation', the transformation from national market capitalism to global capitalism. Themes that ring familiar from the time of the first great transformation – the 'social question', the 'victims of progress', Dickens's 'two cities' – are now amplified on a world scale. Domestic differences endure and now come back as global differences too. Yet, the global setting is quite unlike the national settings in which these questions were first faced.

One hurdle is that while in domestic society the good life can be discussed, the international domain has long been viewed as an anarchic, Hobbesian domain of 'mere survival'. Within societies there is a social contract, but on a world scale? There are cross-border rights, such as the right to development, but is there a cross-border social contract? Solidarity has deep cultural and national roots but so far, according to many, thin transnational roots. The question 'can egalitarianism survive internationalization?'

(Cohen and Rogers, 1997) elicits profoundly different answers. Differences run between perspectives that take the viewpoint of moral obligation or the viewpoint of risk, and between egalitarian and non-egalitarian perspectives on global inequality.[1] With regard to social justice, the spectrum of views ranges from distributive statism to distributive cosmopolitanism, with moral federalism as an in-between position (Hinsch, 2001: 59). These wide disparities match the uneven character of contemporary international relations. Hurrell (2001: 35) signals a 'combination of *density and deformity*' in international society:

> There is now a denser and more integrated network of shared institutions and practices within which social expectations of global justice and injustice have become more securely established. But, at the same time, our major international social institutions continue to constitute a deformed political order, above all because of the extreme disparities of power that exist within both international and world society.

MEASURING GLOBAL POVERTY

> Humans measure what they treasure. (Hazel Henderson, 1996: 115)

When we see the first major overall gap in human inequality emerge in the wake of the industrial revolution the differences are not yet large. They have been widening ever since, though not in a steady fashion. Estimates (UNDP, 1997: 3) of the income gap between the fifth of the world's people living in the richest countries and the fifth in the poorest are as follows:[2]

1820	3 to 1
1870	7 to 1
1913	11 to 1
1960	30 to 1
1990	60 to 1
1997	74 to 1

The earliest measure of world-scale inequality, Gross National Product, is followed by GNP per capita. The Gini coefficient that measures inequality within societies (in which 0 means everyone shares equally and 1 means one individual receives all income and wealth) applies on a global scale as well. The basic human needs conceptualization, prominent in the

1980s, has been virtually abandoned in poverty research (Novak, 1996: 53). While the consensus is that poverty refers to lack of resources, the most common measure remains income poverty. UNDP uses the notion of *human poverty*, measured in terms of education, health, housing and income; the Human Poverty Index is related to the Human Development Index (UNDP, 1997: 17). A further yardstick, *capability poverty*, 'reflects the percentage of people who lack basic, or minimally essential, human capabilities', which gives rise to a capability poverty measure (UNDP, 1996: 27). Initially the unit of analysis was typically the nation, matching the UN frame of the world, and what was taken as global inequality was an aggregation of national statistics. Subsequently, differences *within* societies – rural and urban, gender, regional, ethnic, ecological – have been taken into account; reports now also often recognize the difficulties of adequately measuring poverty.

Major sources of data, such as the World Bank's World Development Reports and the Human Development Reports of the UNDP, set forth global poverty data in language as plain as the newspaper business pages with easily assimilated graphs and diagrams. The reports use occasional striking comparisons. This particular finding has been taken up by many newspapers: 'Today, the net worth of the world's 358 richest people is equal to the combined income of the poorest 45 per cent of the world's population – 2.3 billion people' (UNDP, 1996: 13). Another report notes that the wealth of the world's three richest men is now greater than the combined gross national product of all the least developed countries, which have a total population of 600 million (World Bank, 2000).

Statistics on global poverty are now abundantly available; it would not be difficult to fill this chapter entirely with data, along with laments on difficulties of measurement and hand-wringing policy perspectives. The measures and data are problematic indeed. A handbook of poverty research identifies the following under-researched areas: the power structure and its implications for poverty, the control and manipulation of statistics, and the structural framework of primary research (Samad, 1996: 36). These gaps also apply to global poverty research. The power structure is entirely absent from the leading accounts; the manipulation of statistics makes for an interesting subtext of world poverty research;[3] and macro-economic research tends to be concentrated in the international institutions.

Global inequality as a late-modern notion implies an economic turn; it brings us into a world of economic statistics. With this comes an air of matter-of-factness, which is quite unlike earlier ideas and measures of difference (along the lines of religion, race, civilization, or nation). The terrain of poverty and inequality is dominated by economists and empirical sociologists, and defined and communicated by means of numbers. That with regard to poverty we inhabit a statistical universe is not unusual; numbers lead the way also in studies of development, population and environment. From the way global inequality is conceived it follows that economists do the primary research. The salience of economics is appropriate in that without economic data we could not map or conceive of world-scale poverty; yet it implies that the parameters of debate in economics frame the perceptions of global inequality.[4] Much debate concerns econometrics and technical questions of measurement – which are appropriate measures: purchasing-power parity, by actual exchange rates, according to which US dollar value, weighted by population, whether and how to draw the poverty line, etc.?[5] With regard to poverty research in the United States, Mishra (1996a: 482) observes, 'The near-obsessive concern with the definition and the count of the poor is clearly driven by the ideology and politics of social welfare' and by disputes between conservatives and liberals, and to some extent this holds true for the global situation.

What is missing is a problematization of poverty itself. Economists tend to use culturally flat definitions of poverty, as if monetary income measures hold universal validity. Wolfgang Sachs (1999) distinguishes a wide register of *frugality*, as in subsistence economies; *destitution*, which can arise when subsistence economies are weakened through the interference of growth strategies; and *scarcity*, which arises when the logic of growth and accumulation has taken over and commodity-based need becomes the overriding logic. Of course it is possible to capture this under 'poverty', but is it insightful?

The data on global poverty have become part of a new conventional backdrop. Since the early 1990s and in the wake of the 1995 UN Social Summit in Copenhagen, poverty alleviation has become an international policy focus. Declarations on the part of governments and intergovernmental institutions to eliminate or reduce poverty by half by 2015 were the common fare of *fin-de-millénium* international politics. This policy objective exists side by side with the dominant policy framework of neoliberalism in a highly uncomfortable and uneven policy consensus – *bien étonnés de se trouver ensemble*.

The emphasis in research and policy is on *poverty* rather than on inequality. In most societies, poverty is a politically sensitive theme while inequality is not. Inequality is a relatively safe theme, for after all there are many positions, philosophical and political, in relation to inequality. It may be viewed as necessary, inevitable, or even beneficial in relation to a particular mode of progress. According to a classic liberal view, inequality of outcomes may be acceptable as long as there is equality of opportunity. Poverty, on the other hand, is politically sensitive and challenging for it undermines social cohesion; hence the conceptualization and measurement of poverty are matters of political dispute.[6]

On a world scale, arguably, it is the other way round. Here poverty is a safe theme: the numbers are worrying, but isn't poverty mostly concentrated in distant lands? Has unequal development not been the rule of history, particularly since the industrial revolution? Doesn't contemporary technological change make poverty inevitable? Of course developing countries are lagging behind, particularly in Africa and South and Southeast Asia, but the rising tide of free trade and global economic integration will eventually lift all boats.

Global inequality is a different kind of theme for it measures not just the condition of the world's majority but the gap, and the growing gap, between them and the prospering minority. In that global inequality maps relative deprivation it challenges the legitimacy of world order in a way that mere poverty statistics, accompanied by benevolent policy declarations, do not. According to Robert Wade, 'New evidence suggests that global inequality is worsening rapidly. There are good reasons to worry about that trend, quite apart from what it implies about the extent of world poverty' (2001: 72). Phrased in a different way: 'The non-poor and their role in creating and sustaining poverty are as interesting an object for research on poverty as are the poor' (Øyen, 1996: 11). Economists and the international institutions that employ them habitually ignore differences of power; by prioritizing poverty over inequality, differentials of power, and the responsibilities this entails, are eliminated from the picture.

EXAMINING GLOBAL INEQUALITY

On the assumption that knowledge and power interact, it would stand to reason that the findings on global inequality cannot be neatly separated from the world order that produces global inequality. One way to enter into the core of global inequality is to ask where the data depart from the conventional policy wisdom.

1   A general assumption is that inequality within countries is largest in the poor countries. The figures, however, bear out that the steepest inequality is within the United States and the UK. Considering the comparative degree of income inequality within countries, Bob Sutcliffe observes, 'It is common to read disparaging references in the Western press to the inequality in a country such as India, so it is salutary to note that ... inequality in the UK and in the USA is much greater than in India ... in the richest country of all, the USA, the poorest part of the population are poorer than in almost any other developed country' (Sutcliffe, 2001: 10, 13). 'The per capita income of the poorest 20 per cent in the United States is less than one fourth of the country's average per capita

income – in Japan it is nearly half' (UNDP, 1996: 13). The second steepest social inequality is documented for the UK, where inequality has been increasing since the 1970s (Bornschier, 2002). In both countries inequality has risen in recent decades. In the United States the Gini coefficient began to rise in the 1970s: 'In the period 1977 to 1990, the Gini coefficient for distribution by individuals of disposable household income in the United Kingdom rose by some 10 percentage points, from around 23 per cent to around 33 per cent ... this increase is 2½ times the increase in the United States over that period' (Atkinson, 1999: 3). The trend of growing inequality since the 1980s is being observed throughout Europe as well, also in staunchly egalitarian societies such as Scandinavia and the Netherlands (Atkinson, 1999).

2   The conventional assumption is that the rising tide of neoliberal globalization and free trade lifts all boats. However, those countries and time periods where this policy has been most consistently implemented show the steepest *increase* in inequality: the United States, the UK and New Zealand in the 1980s to 1993.[7]

This effect is being replicated the world over and is confirmed in all reports. An overall growth rate of 5 per cent during the postwar 'golden age' of capitalism (1950–73) was accompanied by decreasing inequality between and within societies. There has been a sharp break in this pattern, except in East and Southeast Asian countries. 'For the majority of the developing and transitional economies, the North–South and East–West income gap in the late 1990s is higher than it was in the 1980s or 1960s.' Since the early 1980s income concentration has risen virtually everywhere: 'this trend towards an increase in inequality is perplexing and marks a clear departure from the move towards greater egalitarianism observed during the 1950s and 1960s' (Cornia, 1999: 1–2).

All reports and analyses document the same pattern: 'Between 1987 and 1993 the number of people with incomes of less than $1 a day increased by almost 100 million to 1.3 billion' (UNDP, 1997: 3). Taking the 1985 US dollar standard, the number of persons who live on less than one dollar per day 'rose from 1.2 billion in 1987 to 1.5 billion today and, if recent trends persist, will reach 1.9 billion by 2015' (World Bank, 1999: 25). Robert Wade concludes that:

> the bulk of the evidence on trends in world income distribution runs against the claim that world income inequality has fallen sharply in the past half-century and still faster in the past quarter-century ... world income distribution has become much more unequal over the past several decades and ... inequality accelerated during the 1980s, whether countries are treated equally or weighted by population. ... world income distribution became markedly more unequal between 1988 and 1993 ... World inequality increased from a Gini coefficient of 62.5 in 1988 to 66.0 in 1993 ... the share of world income going to the poorest 10 per cent of the world's population fell by over a quarter, whereas the share of the richest 10 per cent rose by 8 per cent. (2001: 74)

3   The 'East Asian Miracle' is often presented as a major turnaround in international development. While East and Southeast Asian countries as a whole deviate from the pattern of increasing global inequality, inequality *within* these societies has increased: 'In some economies, including China, Hong Kong, Malaysia and Thailand, there have been significant increases in inequality, especially in the past ten or fifteen years', associated with differences between high- and low-skill groups, between rich and poor regions and rural–urban differences (Walton, 1997: 4; Wade, 2001).

4   To the equation of growing global inequality there are two sides at least. The least developed, poorest countries are lagging more and more behind, and within countries the number of the poor is growing; on the other side of the split screen is the explosive growth of wealth of the hyper-rich.[8] The world's 7 million millionaires include 512 billionaires and 52,000 'ultra-high net worth individuals' (Sutcliffe, 2001: 12). It makes sense to consider extreme poverty and riches within a single picture frame, which is brought out by examining global inequality, and not just global poverty.[9]

5   The nexus between global inequality and domestic inequality is insufficiently examined. Thus, a common view is that 'increased wage dispersion in the OECD countries is due to increased competition from low-wage economies' (Atkinson, 1999: 1), while 'globalization of capital gives business a great deal of

leverage in vetoing national policies' (Mishra, 1996b: 324). Pressures on wages, productivity, labour conditions and trade unions in advanced countries have been rationalized by referring to labour conditions and discipline in low-wage countries, particularly in East and Southeast Asia.

The general observation is that global and domestic inequality tend to move in tandem. Increasing global inequality, accordingly, is, grosso modo, accompanied by growing domestic inequality. There may also be more subtle interconnections. In advanced countries domestic inequality (even growing inequality as in the United States and the UK) may seem acceptable in light of glaring and growing global inequality. Perceptions of poverty in the UK are now more shaped by images of Third World poverty than by the images of the Depression (Street, 1994). Televised images of extreme poverty in Africa and Asia may work not merely as a compassion wake-up call but also as a domestic pacifier. Global inequality, then, overtly as well as covertly tends to sustain power structures and inequality in advanced countries and helps privileged strata to maintain their status.

6   The risks that global inequality poses are discussed with increasing frequency. Economic failure, according to Jeffrey Sachs, raises the risk of state failure as well. 'Failed states', he continues, 'are seedbeds of violence, terrorism, international criminality, mass migration and refugee movements, drug trafficking, and disease', and this 'significantly affects US interests in military, economic, health-related, and environmental areas' (Sachs, 2001: 187, 189). Robert Wade (2001) mentions another angle: 'The result is a lot of unemployed and angry young people, to whom new information technologies have given the means to threaten the stability of the societies they live in and even to threaten social stability in countries of the wealthy zone.' A conventional assumption is that it is possible to contain these risks within the global margins and that a combination of 'aid governmentality', tactical sorties and enhanced border security can control their spillover effects.[10] Yet, environmental degradation does not recognize borders and also

migration, transnational crime and terrorism show otherwise.

7   Finally, conventional wisdom holds that free markets and democracy advance together. But what is the role of democracy and how does it function in the face of growing inequality? One consideration is that 'democracy has made income gaps in regions such as Latin America more visible and looks more and more like an accomplice in a vicious circle of inequality and injustice' (Birdsall, 1998). John Gray observes that in societies that follow neoliberal policies middle classes are falling and working classes are being 'reproletarianized'. 'Meanwhile, the overclass increasingly plants itself behind the high walls of suburban developments, Latin American plantation style, where private funding, not taxation, covers all services. The whole picture of democracy and free markets advancing together, of free-market capitalism sprouting bourgeoisies all over the world, is generally false in today's world' (Gray, 1996: 42). The conventional assumption of the Washington Consensus that civil society acts as a countervailing power and democracy keeps government in check does not apply if official corruption is sustained by transnational forces beyond the reach of the domestic public.

CONVENTIONAL WISDOM FOR BEGINNERS

Global poverty and inequality trail the career of modern development policy as its dark shadow. The career of development policy stretches over some fifty years. During this time standard arguments that have conventionally served to neutralize findings on global inequality have been losing their validity, and the recent increases in global inequality are not much help.

According to a classic argument of Simon Kuznets, income inequality in developing countries would first rise as workers left agriculture for industry and then fall as industrialization took hold, so inequality would follow an inverted U pattern, the so-called Kuznets curve. This has been applied on a world scale as a global Kuznets curve. 'The global economy would be viewed as having weak stratification if there is significant "mobility" of nations between groups of nations changing rank or catching up' (Park and Brat, 1995: 106). In other words, the prediction is that of long-run economic convergence. Subsequent research qualifies this as *conditional convergence*, conditional upon human capital and R&D investments (Park and Brat, 1995: 128; World Bank, 1997). The sharp increase in global inequality from the late 1980s, however, belies this expectation (Atkinson, 1999).

Another conventional argument goes back to classical political economy and early catch-up strategies from Central Europe and the Soviet Union onward: through modernization and industrialization latecomers to development will be able to catch up. Modern development theory adapted these expectations, as in Rostov's take-off stage of industrialization. Dependency theory challenged this assumption: the timing and geopolitical context of catching-up matter and entrenched patterns of dependence and structures of power intervene. With the advent of high technology and the information revolution arguments centred on technological change go through another cycle of high expectations and low outcomes. The scope for 'associated dependent development' through technology transfer by means of foreign direct investment is limited by the assembly and *maquiladora* type of low-wage industrialization and by patenting arrangements through which transnational corporations control technological innovation and dissemination (Smith, 1993). Do the newly industrializing countries break out of this pattern? In spite of their efforts at industrial upgrading East Asian tiger economies such as Korea continue to be characterized by technological dependence on advanced countries and transnational corporations (Smith, 1997). Information technology does not essentially change this equation and the scope for technological leapfrogging is limited; witness the global digital divide (Burkett, 2000).

A stubborn argument throughout the career of development thinking has been that the best anti-poverty strategy is economic growth, with a few variations as to how best to achieve this; in other words, the trickle-down approach. On this ground 'economists who espouse the cause of the poor' are routinely accused of 'becoming unwitting accomplices in the perpetuation of poverty' (Bhagwati, 1998: 45). The real friends of the poor are market forces and market-friendly policies (a 'pull-up approach', according to Bhagwati). First, this ignores the question of the *quality* of growth; a major contribution of human development economics has been to build the case for pro-poor growth as the most *efficient* growth. Second, the trend of widening global inequality in tandem with world economic growth falsifies this expectation at a general level, while ample country experiences discount it as well. Third, more significant still is the trend of widening inequality in advanced countries, again in conjunction with economic growth: if trickle-down does not occur in these robust democracies and middle classes live in 'fear of falling' (Ehrenreich, 1990), then on what grounds is this supposed to deliver in the weaker polities of developing countries, and on a world scale?

Economic growth, industrialization and conditional convergence are clearly far too generalizing arguments to be useful and are on the whole falsified by several decades of accumulated experience. If these conventional views explain convergence, how then to explain the actual experience of divergence? Current discussions signal various causes of growing inequality, some of which were also in effect before the 1980s (faster population growth in developing than in developed countries, and deteriorating unequal terms of trade) and others that are specific to the recent period, in particular technical change and financial liberalization (e.g. Atkinson, 1999: Wade, 2001). Cornia (1999) attributes the increase in income inequality to a rise in earnings inequality and emphasizes as the main explanations skill-based technical progress (reducing demand for unskilled labour), the impact of trade liberalization, IMF policies generating recessions (which adversely affect income distribution), financial deregulation and enlargement of the financial sector (resulting in a shift to non-labour incomes) and the erosion of labour institutions (greater wage flexibility, reduced regulation, erosion of the minimum wage, dilution of trade union power and higher labour mobility). Technical changes aside, most of these trends are the expressions or outcomes of neoliberal policies. The potential and effects of technical change can be channeled by means of industrial policy interventions, as in most newly industrializing countries, but neoclassical policy pressures delimit this option. Liberalization and deregulation, on the whole, bet on the strong, privilege the privileged, help the winners, expose the losers and prompt a 'race to the bottom'. While this is a broad stroke representation, it is plausible to view neoliberal policies as the central dynamic in widening domestic and global inequality since the 1980s.

The perception that global inequality is more threatening a theme than poverty holds widely, yet it may be less pertinent in the case of the United States. The United States has greater tolerance for inequality than any advanced society – materially and socially, as the most unequal among developed societies, and in terms of political culture and development philosophy. In the United States:

> the Reagan administration replaced the war on poverty with a war on the poor. ... Not poverty as such but pauperization, i.e. dysfunctional and deviant behaviour on the part of the poor was now identified as the main problem of the 1980s, and the early 1990s reflected this shift in agenda from a concern with poverty to a concern with the poor. ... From this viewpoint, then, poverty is no longer an issue. The social problems confronting Americans are now those of welfare dependency, out of wedlock births, criminality and other dysfunctional behaviour on the part of the lower strata of the population. (Mishra, 1996a: 403, 404)

The prevailing political discourse blames the victims, defines welfare dependency as the problem and thus views government rollback and welfare cutbacks as the main remedies. Inequality is taken as a matter of course and poverty is targeted as an enemy in that it shows up the cracks in the culture of success. This deeply embedded strain has been reinforced in recent years.[11]

Transposed on a world scale this entails a policy of slashing foreign aid, upheld by Congressional majority, in a nation that ranks already as the world's stingiest foreign assistance donor (the United States at the beginning of the new century transfers a little over 0.1 per cent of its GNP to developing countries while the internationally agreed UN target is 0.7 per cent of GNP). As part of a relentless campaign towards corporate deregulation, conservative think-tanks rail against 'foreign welfare' on the same basis as welfare is blamed in the United States: 'economic assistance impedes economic growth'. International welfare does not work, Congress should eliminate aid, adopt a long-term policy for eliminating development assistance, and instead adopt policies to promote 'economic freedom' (read: deregulation, free trade) in developing countries (Johnson and Schaefer, 1998).[12]

Thus, while international institutions declare reducing world poverty to be a global priority, in the host country of the headquarters of most of these institutions poverty does not rank as a viable political issue. The international institutions are part of an institutional power network whose global impact and dynamics they measure and report on, and as such are subject to ample political pressure. They are intermeshed with and politically and financially dependent on the international political and economic balance of forces. The international institutions based in the United States depend on Congressional budget allocations, US Treasury backing, trustees appointed by the US government and commercial financial infrastructures and credit ratings (the World Bank is also a bank). Subject to multiple pressures, from the Treasury, Wall Street and neoconservative US politics, and from critical NGOs and social forces in the South, the international institutions have little room to maneuver. A way out of the crossfire is to depoliticize the global situation and agenda as much as possible. By this logic, what is at issue is not global inequality but global poverty, the instrument of analysis is economic data processing, and the bottom line remedy is freeing up market forces, now with a human face.

As a consequence, a general trend in policy and discourse is towards hegemonic compromise and papering over significant differences in approach on the part of powerful stakeholders, for instance by using the same terms with different meanings.[13] This trend bemoans outcomes and confines discussion of causes to technical analyses. For international institutions this may translate to intricate balancing acts between signaling concern without rocking the boat. UNDP typically follows a two-track approach, addressing 'aid fatigue' on the one hand (so it is necessary to demonstrate success) and urgency on the other. For instance: 'human development over the past 30 years is a mixed picture of unprecedented human progress and unspeakable human misery – of human advances on several fronts and retreats on several others' (UNDP, 1996: 17).

With regard to poverty research in North America, Mishra distinguishes between social engineering and social structural approaches; the former

> tends to concern itself with research problems closely related to issues of policy and administration. It could also be described as 'operational' research. ... The social engineering approach tends to abstract the problem of poverty from the larger social structure and sees it largely as an administrative problem that can be solved by policy makers by applying 'rational' methods. (1996a: 485)

The social structural approach, in contrast, is not policy oriented; the focus is 'on broader structural issues and their relationship to poverty' (p. 485). These different perspectives, in his view, match differences between economic and sociological approaches.

In relation to global inequality the social engineering approach prevails, as it does in development thinking and policy generally. 'Operational research' is the overriding tendency in development studies, which are dominated by the international institutions that produce and supply the economic data, embedded and enframed in their institutional discourses. The development industry is to a significant degree a subcontracting industry of the international institutions and their intergovernmental infrastructures. The apolitical disposition of the international institutions is passed on to development studies generally in various ways. The international institutions exercise their influence not merely directly (by subcontracting research, funding NGOs, etc.) but through their agenda-setting influence, much like the *haute couture* houses set the tone in another fashion-conscious industry.

Development studies focus on questions of regional, national or local development; when it comes to the global level, 'world development' is hardly on the map beyond the macroeconomic data of the IMF, World Bank, UNDP, OECD and WTO. The research capacity to address world development tends to be concentrated in the international institutions.

The human development approach, currently the most influential synthesis in development thinking, centers on capacitation, enablement, empowerment. This is part of a wider 'capabilities turn' from development economics to business management, and one of the responses to the massive increase in global inequality. Empowerment is now upheld across the world as a magic wand to dispel growing inequalities. Capacities however do little to alter unequal relations of power. The old saying is give a man a fish and he will eat for a day, teach a man how to fish and he will eat always. But nowadays in many places by the time people have learned how to fish they will likely find their shores emptied by large, high-tech fishing vessels from Japan, Europe or North America, under contract with their own governments. Governments North and South hammer on education and training as today's magic charm. But training, in poor neighborhoods, does not solve the problem of employment growth (Wilson, 1996: 30). In business management, empowerment means skill upgrading for lower cadres so that with the downsizing of middle management they will supervise themselves and junior staff. Capabilities, skills and education are resources and forms of power themselves, but there is more to poverty than a deficit of skills.

It may help to place this in historical perspective. Paul Bairoch (1980) notes that around 1750 the share of the Third World, China included, in world industrial production stood at about 73–78 per cent, dropped to 17–19 per cent in 1860, and to a minimum of 5 per cent in 1913. Technological change alone does not explain this precipitous decline, which is not intelligible without political intervention of the kind usually summed up under the heading 'imperialism'.[14] In view of this historical backdrop, to account for contemporary unequal development chiefly in terms of unequal capabilities seems shallow to the point of being unreal; or rather, if capacities matter, so do relations of unequal wealth and power.

The remedies for poverty proposed by international institutions – such as good governance, accountability, 'reinforcing democracy by strengthening civil society', empowerment – are welcome in themselves; yet, in the absence of scrutiny of international power dynamics and macro-economic policies, they exonerate the powers that be and, at the end of the day, abide by the conservative cliché that the poor are to blame for their fate. These approaches now come in standardized packages such as the World Bank's *Participation Sourcebook* (1996) and UNDP's *Overcoming Human Poverty* (2000). These treatments seem to address a parallel universe in which there are no major powers – transnational corporations, banks, Western governments, international trade barriers and institutions – that *produce* poverty and inequality. Detailing micro-economics while ignoring macro-economics, probing micro-politics while skipping macro-politics, they are profoundly apolitical texts. Good governance, democracy, participation? How about good governance, democracy and participation in the IMF and the World Bank? How about transparency and accountability of Wall Street, the US Treasury, the IMF and the World Bank?[15] Is combating poverty in retail while leaving it alone wholesale a persuasive position? If these policy recommendations were accompanied by equivalent inquiries into the role of corporations and governments in the North, by advocating changes in international standards and law, they might be credible; without it they come across as fig leaf exercises in hegemonic compromise.

Thomas Pogge (2001b: 19–21) draws attention to the international borrowing privilege – regardless of how a government has come into power it can put a country into debt; and to the international resource privilege – regardless of how a government has come into power it can confer globally valid ownership rights in a country's resources to foreign companies. He observes that in sub-Saharan Africa a transition to democracy has only been achieved in resource-poor countries (with South Africa as an exception). In view of these international privileges, corporations and governments in the North are accomplices in official corruption; thus, placing the burden of reform solely on poor countries only reinforces the existing imbalance.

To gain deeper insight we must turn to social structural approaches. Attempts to conceptualize global inequality in terms of established frameworks in sociology, however, have been less successful. Global stratification (e.g., Raichur, 1979; Connell, 1984) has gradually faded as a theme; class analysis transposed on a transnational scale presents problems of its own, including data incompatibilities. Concepts such as a 'transnational managerial class' or 'transnational capitalist class' (Cox, 1996; Sklair, 1997) face methodological problems (Embong, 2000) and fall short of an overall global stratification analysis. The contemporary dispersal of capital, the complex interweaving of capital, finance and governance and the intermediary role of international institutions defy the conventional instruments of class analysis.

Several frameworks that sociologists have typically brought to bear on global inequality have gradually been relegated to the margins or overshadowed by other themes. World system theory posited world inequality as a major theme (Wallerstein, 1975). But this approach itself is tied to macro-economic data, particularly the long wave (the Kondratieff cycle), and in the end follows economistic lines of analysis, verging on a capitulation of sociology to evolutionary economics or bookkeeping on a world scale. Analyzing global stratification by core, semi-periphery and periphery countries (Arrighi and Drangel, 1996) does not differ much from the stratified country datasets (such as high-, middle- and low-income developing countries) used by the UN and Bretton Woods institutions. Dependency theory has been sidelined by the development of the newly industrializing countries and emerging markets, particularly in East Asia. It has been overtaken by the wider debate on globalization, which now dominates in sociology as elsewhere. Terrains in which sociology, anthropology and geography make distinctive contributions are migration, changes in labor markets, ecological changes brought about by the dynamics of globalization, and gender, race and class dimensions of global inequality. Several of these concern the downstream consequences of macro-economic policies; they reflect that the main strength of sociological methodology and theory remains the 'society' while transnational sociology is as yet not as well developed. Similarly, the nexus between poverty and migration, poverty and violence and political instability, examined in political science and geography, is relevant enough; yet it fails to penetrate the core issue of global inequality.

Several studies straddling international political economy, sociology, political science and other disciplines probe dimensions that depart fundamentally from the dominant economic approaches to inequality; by combining them, a full and plausible perspective may emerge. Moving from the general to the specific, this includes the following lines and levels of inquiry:

- At a structural level, examine inequality of power between and within states (e.g. Hurrell and Woods, 1995, 1999).
- At a general procedural level, examine how inequalities of power affect decision-making processes (e.g. Beitz, 2001).
- Examine the institutional location and workings of major international institutions (e.g. Chossudovsky, 1998; Wade and Veneroso, 1998).
- Examine policy frameworks and policies (Wade, 2002).
- Examine decision-making processes on a case-study basis (McMichael, 1996).
- And examine policy outcomes.[16]

The upshot of these analyses is to bring politics back in and to zero in on the actual role of unequal power relations as a major factor in growing global inequality. This includes the massive and growing body of work that criticizes the worldwide trends of liberalization, deregulation and privatization, IMF and World Bank policies of structural adjustment, the WTO framework, and the neoliberal policy regime of accumulation that they are part of.

At the core of the problem of global inequality, then, are unequal relations of power. Imperialism, a classic conceptualization of unequal power relations, is a hypothesis that is now often revisited.[17] If the alternative is a liberal pluralism that fails to recognize power differentials, an approach that focuses squarely on unequal power is preferable. The advantage of these analyses is that they highlight power differentials; the disadvantage is that in doing so they recycle old paradigms and underplay the contemporary multiplicity of actors and interests. 'Imperialism' is an analytical and political shortcut. Imperialism was state-centric, centrally orchestrated and territorial, none of which applies to contemporary globalization. A further difference is that the cultural and normative environment has significantly changed: human rights are now widely recognized.

PERPLEXITY AND POLITICS

What kind of world economy grows and yet sees poverty and global inequality rising steeply? The foregoing analysis suggests several observations. The set of policies of neoliberal globalization are to a large extent responsible for rapidly growing global inequality in the past decades. The shift in influence from social democratic to Anglo-American free enterprise capitalism, from stakeholder to shareholder capitalism means a general shift in outlook from social responsibility to private responsibility which is not conducive to an international policy that protects and aids the poor. Most research and policy accounts are of an 'operational' nature. Their outlook is ahistorical and apolitical. In view of over-reliance on neoclassical economics it is atheoretical as well. Their matter-of-factness is a matter of impression management only: under the surface are many conflicts about the measurements and their implications. In that they are morally flat, they deny the fundamental interconnections that exist between the poor and privileged. Growing worldwide cultural interconnections and the growing density of international networks (the 'associational revolution') generate growing pressures for global reform. International power structures and institutions, however, are tied in with neoliberal policy frameworks either because of profound commitments (in the case of the United States and to some extent Britain, home of the nineteenth-century Manchester School) or through hegemonic compromise (European Union, Japan, OECD). What ensues is fundamental policy incoherence between upholding neoliberal policies that widen global inequality, on the one hand, and attempts to reduce global poverty, on the other.

According to Ruggie (1997), what is needed is 'a new embedded liberalism compromise'. Proposals for global reform, such as a 'global third way' (Kapstein, 1998–99), a global new deal, global social policy (Deacon et al., 1998) are increasingly widely discussed (e.g. Nederveen Pieterse, 2000a). Yet the contemporary international conditions of *density and deformity*, referred to above, both account for (density) and delimit (deformity) these contributions.

In 1979 Thomas Rowe distinguished four different approaches to poverty domestically and internationally: *socialization, integration, isolation* and *revolution*. It is interesting to reflect on how they come across now, juxtaposed to current approaches to global inequality.

- *Socialization*: '[The] deprived must acquire the values and behavior that bring rewards to the more privileged in the dominant system. With self-help and aid from the privileged the shortcomings of the deprived must be eliminated' (Rowe, 1979: 224). Here the basic source of the problem is viewed as internal to the deprived. This describes the thrust of mainstream development policy; it may be termed a disciplinary approach in that aid is conditional.
- *Integration*: '[The] deprived must be allowed to participate as equals in the system. Exclusive attitudes and behavior on the part of the privileged and dependent and exploitative relationships between deprived and privileged must be broken' (p. 224). Here the basic source of the problem is viewed as external to the deprived. This describes the critical approaches of dependency theory,

the New International Economic Order, and contemporary global justice.
- *Isolation*: '[The] deprived must reclaim or develop the values and behavior necessary for the good life. … the values and behavior derived from the dominant system are inherently destructive and must be rejected' (p. 224). Here Rowe concentrates on isolation 'from within', on the part of radical social movements of a traditionalist or 'fundamentalist' kind. We may also describe this as voluntary delinking or dissociation from the dominant system, or localism, as in post-development approaches. Isolating the deprived however is also a major policy imposed from without – as politics of containment, that is, the concentration of the poor in ghettoes or, internationally, in the 'global margins'.
- *Revolution*: 'Escape from inequalities requires fundamental change in the dominant system' (p. 224). Revolutionary approaches have been waning after the end of the Soviet and Chinese alternatives. Growing differentiation in the South has further undermined joint collective action. Most armed struggle movements in the South have shifted from the bullet to the ballot (Rocamora, 1992), with the exception of secessionist struggles, armed Islamic groups from Algeria to the Philippines, and armed insurgency in Nepal.

Presently, more than two decades hence, three of these approaches are being implemented side by side by the same and by different actors; a précis, updating and expanding on Rowe's categories and with brief notes on contemporary outcomes, is offered in Table 24.1.

Policies of isolating 'others', or the deprived, go back a long way; 'beyond the pale' is an old expression. In the 1960s Maurice Duverger spoke of the metropolitan world 'slipping into a comfortable and mediocre civilization of consumption, a sort of air-conditioned Late Roman Empire … in which the essential is to hold the barbarian beyond the *lines*' (quoted in Buchanan, 1985: 92). J.M. Albertini, about the same time, saw the industrialized world, both capitalist and socialist, becoming 'islands of

Table 24.1   *Four approaches to global inequality*

Approach	Prescriptions	Policies	Outcomes
Socialization	Deprived must conform to standards set by the privileged	Modernization, human capital, capabilities, empowerment, good governance, civil society	Capacitation does little to alter the overall structure of power and privilege
Integration	Deprived must be treated on equal terms	Foreign aid, foreign direct investment, democracy, participation	Aid is decreasing, FDI is concentrated in the North, international institutions are not democratic
Isolation	Deprived must stay apart, or be kept apart; the effects of poverty must be contained	From without, contain: • migration • conflict • disease	Strong borders, rising visa restrictions, 'humanitarian intervention'
		From within: • delinking, localism • separatism • 'fundamentalism'	Neonationalism remains attractive, yet delinking is a cul-de-sac
Revolution	Achieve break in global system	Armed struggle in favour of delinking or radical change	Waning after end of Soviet and Chinese alternatives; shift from bullet to ballot.

prosperity which can maintain their position only by atomic power' (quoted in Buchanan, 1985: 92). The two zones of prosperity and deprivation are now also identified as zones of peace and of conflict (Nederveen Pieterse, 2004).

Between the zone of peace and the zone of war, there is no peace. The borders are ever turbulent. They are the terrain of enhanced border security, rising visa restrictions, human trafficking. Instability and conflict in the zones of poverty, and dreams of greener shores (e.g. Lundgren, 1988), create refugee streams, asylum seekers and human smuggling. At the same time, declining fortunes and 'fear of falling' amid the depressed middle and working class in the advanced countries fosters the rise of right-wing political forces, as in several European Union countries, and an association between immigration and crime. The human rights of those who cross the border between zones do not rank high on their profile. Australia's policy of detention of refugees, in effect for ten years, is a case in point. Their remote location, deep in the interior in Woomera, confined and kept from inspection,

is telling in itself. On one side of the border, in the global margins, there is discipline – the financial and developmental regimes of the international institutions and conditional aid, or coercive intervention in case of turbulence (as in Rwanda, Somalia, Bosnia etc.). In the ghettoes, *banlieux* and *favelas*, another discipline and surveillance is in operation – the discipline of 'zero tolerance' policing, 'racial profiling' and incarceration. Those who cross the border zone do so at their peril, facing humiliation, disenfranchisement, punishment, and risking death.

Three of the four approaches outlined by Rowe are now simultaneously in effect. In addition, they interact in several ways, so that perhaps they can be viewed as three modalities of the same approach. *Socialization* has increasingly become the imposition of disciplinary regimes, as in IMF stabilization lending, World Bank structural adjustment and WTO stipulations. *Integration* into the world order is taking place as the 'human face' that comes with policies of structural adjustment and, accordingly, on a conditional basis. *Isolation*, or social exclusion, then, comes in only as part of a wider picture: the same areas and people that are being marginalized (cordoned off by low credit ratings, trade barriers, security measures, immigration rules) have first been incorporated into disciplinary regimes of debt repayment, stabilization lending and aid governmentality. Together, these policies could all be viewed as different modalities of a single process of *conditional, asymmetric integration*. Thus, global apartheid and global integration, scenarios that are usually viewed as being wide apart, are being practiced simultaneously, with the note that integration refers to *hierarchical integration*. It goes without saying that these processes of asymmetric inclusion are deeply uneven and internally contradictory. Cultural and political globalization, promoted by transnational enterprises, media and intergovernmental arrangements, militates against isolation policies. Disciplining, democratization and containment are out of step with one another. Thus, global hierarchical integration has turbulence built-in. It is against this dramatic and turbulent backdrop that we may consider the main perspectives that now underlie policies in relation to global inequality: global risk management and global justice.

During the golden age of postwar capitalism, a guiding principle in international policies was mutual interest. In the 1960s and 1970s this was the guiding principle of international cooperation for social democratic, socialist and developing countries: helping developing countries achieve development and equal status is in the interest of advanced countries which stand to benefit from a growing and balanced world economy both economically and in terms of political stability. This inspired proposals for a New International Economic Order, the Brandt Commission and the North–South Commission. This outlook has gradually faded for several reasons. The new international division of labor and investment in low-wage economies changed, with wages rising in newly industrializing countries, the decreasing share of labor in production due to technical change, and concentration of investments in the advanced economies and selected emerging markets; transnational corporations can achieve growth without investing in the least developed countries. The end of the

Cold War and developments in military technology lower the security risk from poor countries. Yet, some risks have increased. Risk assessment and management have moved up accordingly on the agenda of international policy-making.

After spelling out the risks global poverty poses to the strategic interests of the United States, Jeffrey Sachs pleads for 'a strategy of foreign assistance that is commensurate with US strategic interests'. This involves income transfers to poor countries which, however, do not have to be large: 'small amounts of help at crucial moments can tip the balance toward successful outcomes' (2001: 197). In other words, this is a plea for the status quo, now no longer as muddling through, but with the novel dignity of a 'strategic approach'.

Risk management raises many questions. Who defines what risk is? Risk to whom? In this example, risk is defined solely by reference to national interest and so is in effect a realist balance of power approach. This ignores *global risk*. Alongside global inequality, environmental risk, international financial and economic instability, conflict, transnational crime and terrorism, and migration are the most salient global problems. These cannot be properly understood or conceived from a 'national interest' point of view. This underlies current discussions about a new architecture of international finance and the provision of international public goods. Yet, international cooperation towards equity is but one way to manage global risk; unilateral policies are another. In promoting the interests of American corporations world-wide the United States actively promotes globalization, yet the risks this entails and generates it tends to view mainly from the standpoint of its national interest. For security, a missile defence shield; to contain 'rogue states', regional and international policies; to contain local conflicts, humanitarian intervention. In relation to environmental risk, the United States pulls out of the Kyoto agreement.

Amidst contemporary changes considerable mentality changes are under way. The justice claims of developing countries are widely perceived as legitimate. Yet they are being neutralized by international institutions that translate development rights and needs into disciplinary regimes, or are kept from acting on more critical assessments by the existing international balance of forces. Media personnel in the advanced countries have seen their personal fortunes improve and keep a considerable moral investment in the overall system.

Global justice, the normative approach of global ethics and human rights, is an essential strand of contemporary dynamics. It shows that the global rendezvous is not merely a large numbers game but a matter of human engagement and solidarity; the world is becoming more interconnected also emotionally and morally.

Global poverty reduction is morally right: 'The new global economic order we impose aggravates global inequality and reproduces severe poverty on a massive scale. On any plausible understanding of our moral values, the prevention of such poverty is our foremost responsibility' (Pogge, 2001a). It is economically beneficial, as human development economics and growth and equity analyses demonstrate. Global poverty reduction meets the mutual interest of stakeholders. It confers strategic benefits by contributing to political legitimacy and stability and reduces the risk of conflict. Besides, it is doable: 'For the first time in human history it is quite feasible, economically, to wipe out hunger and preventable diseases worldwide without real inconvenience to anyone – all the more so because the high-income countries no longer face any serious military threat' (Pogge, 2001b: 14). Why, then, in the face of moral, economic and strategic considerations – each weighty and together overwhelming – is there no significant action to address global poverty? If we discount the conventional argument according to which economic growth is *the* anti-poverty strategy as falsified generally and a fortiori by recent trends, the sole plausible remaining reason is of a political nature (using 'politics' in a wide sense).

In the twentieth century many more people have died from poverty than from violent conflict. Yet conflict management ranks much higher on the agenda than combating poverty. Why are Western governments 'doing so very little toward the eradication of severe poverty abroad even while they are prepared to spend billions on other humanitarian initiatives, such as the NATO bombing of Yugoslavia?' A cynical answer, according to Pogge, is that 'helping the world's poorest populations emerge from poverty tends to strengthen their states and thus to weaken our own, while bombing Yugoslavia tends to reinforce the existing power hierarchy' (2001a: 3). Addressing global poverty will affect global inequality, which, in turn, will affect domestic inequality and thus reduce the maneuvering room of leading political and economic forces. This suggests that we must consider global inequality as part of the balance of power, and global poverty as part of the price being paid for maintaining global inequality.

Balance of power is not meant here in a realist sense, as inter-state balance of power, but as *rapports de force*, a loose constellation of interwoven political and economic interests that is not unified or homogeneous but yet, so far, has sufficient momentum to deflect alternatives. It need not be assumed that this is a conscious strategy or design, at any rate in its overall outcomes, but is rather the outcome of many diverse acts of self-interest and risk avoidance on the part of privileged actors. Let us assume that many among the privileged abhor poverty – but blame the poor and rely on economic growth as a remedy, and yet, if these beliefs fail they may still desire privilege, or fear losing it, more than they abhor poverty. Then, the charms of power, the trappings of privilege, the cult of celebrity, the logics of neoclassical economics, all concur to maintain the overall balance of power. And so the world's hyper-rich and the poor majority are intertwined in a joint rendezvous, mirrors to one another – but at quite a distance.

The global justice approach has hurdles to spare. If social justice and ethical standards do not apply domestically the likelihood of their prevailing transnationally is even less. Is it not a strange expectation that poverty elimination world-wide could succeed at a time when the middle class and working class in developed countries see their incomes stagnating or falling and are increasingly exposed to risk affecting their job security, social benefits and pensions? If socio-economic inequality is increasing in developed countries, what would be the prospect of its diminishing on a world scale? Yet, this may be one of the most sensitive pressure points in the global situation.

Perhaps revolution does come in, but in quite a different fashion than the old state-centric notions of revolution. A contributor to a discussion on the implications of technological change notes: 'Poverty is a choice the world has made. It is a political choice. The information revolution will be another instrument to implement that choice. Only a governance revolution would represent a real change. And to link the information revolution with democratization is naïve in the extreme, parallel to the current leap of faith linking democratization and open markets' (in Hedley, 1999: 86). John Gray strikes a different note, along the same lines: 'I fear that, given the strength of the project of a global free market, it will take some significant economic upsets and some significant political turmoil for social thought to be sufficiently reworked so that the operation of the world will be more compatible with vital human needs' (Gray, 1996: 45). Only a governance revolution …

Perhaps the points of greatest vulnerability are the following. First, the policies that are now in place are fundamentally incoherent: neoliberal policies widen global inequality while poverty alleviation policies seek to mitigate it. Second, unilateralist politics in the midst of global realities of complex multilateralism invites instability. Third, if we assume that global injustice is being neutralized by clichés and passé economics, this is not the case with domestic injustice. Growing domestic inequality in advanced countries cheek by jowl with stupendous wealth from financial transactions and rising remuneration of CEOs, even as their companies are collapsing, may lead to growing protest. Fourth, the combination of density and deformity in international conditions makes for fundamental instability, witness social movements from Seattle onward.

NOTES

1 As non-egalitarian values that are reasons for concern, Beitz (2001) mentions those associated with poverty and material deprivation, humiliation, the impact of inequality on the capacity for self-control and self-government, and the unfairness of political decision-making procedures with large economic inequalities in the background.

2 'At the global level, the ratio of average income of the richest country in the world to that of the poorest has risen from about 9 to 1 at the end of the nineteenth century to at least 60 to 1 today. That is, the average family in the United States is 60 times richer than the average family in Ethiopia' (Birdsall, 1998). Cf. Sutcliffe, 2001: 83.

3 Pogge argues that in its *World Development Report 2000* the World Bank newly specified the international poverty line by replacing the purchasing power of 1 US dollar in 1985 with the purchasing power of 1.08 US dollars in 1993, without adequately factoring in US inflation between 1985 and 1993: 'This revision thus lowers the international poverty line by 19.6 per cent and thereby conveniently reduces the widely publicized number of global poor without cost to anyone' (Pogge, 2001b: 7 n4).

4 'Up-to-date data are necessary to ensure that the poor and the intensity of poverty are kept visible to the public eye, but it may still be wise to put somewhat less energy into sheer measurement research, and instead turn to issues that yield more in poverty understanding' (Øyen, 1996: 10).

5 On difficulties of measuring poverty and inequality see among others Sutcliffe, 2001; Wade, 2001; Babones, 2002. 'From the United States comes the observation that, for all its usefulness, the poverty line has two major economic weaknesses: (1) it relies too heavily on annual money income, which is extremely difficult to obtain accurately from the households surveyed, and (2) the monetary income itself is an inadequate indicator of command over resources' (Wilson, 1996: 21).

6 'Poverty itself is a highly political issue where power and interest groups have had a significant (some would say overwhelming) influence on patterns of distribution and the existence of poverty' (Wilson, 1996: 24).

7 On the United States, see Mishra, 1996a: 472–3: 'In the United Kingdom … the richest 20 per cent earned seven times as much as the poorest 20 per cent in 1991, compared with only four times as much in 1977. The British gap between males with the highest wage rates and those with the lowest is larger now than at any time since the 1880s, when UK statistics on wages were first gathered systematically' (Frank and Cook, 1995: 5).

8 'Social science and politics have defined poverty as a pathological symptom of society but, illogically, not riches' (Sutcliffe, 2001: 12).

9 Enron fits neatly into this equation: 'The company embodied the get-obscenely-rich-quick culture that grew up around the intersection of digital technology, deregulation and globalization. It rode the zeitgeist of speed, hype, novelty and swagger. Petroleum was hopelessly uncool; derivatives were hot. Companies were advised to unload the baggage of hard assets, like factories or oilfields, which hold you back in the digital long jump, and concentrate on buzz and *brand*' (Bill Keller, 'Enron for dummies', *New York Times*, 26 January 2002).

10 On new politics of containment see Duffield (2001) and Nederveen Pieterse (2004).

11 Karlyn Bowman (2000) refers to the declining interest in economic inequality in the United States: 'Today, Democratic politicians talk about the digital divide, often as a surrogate for the old discussions of income inequality. This new formulation is less likely to irritate allies and funders on Wall Street than criticism of salaries and stock options'.

12 In Senator Jesse Helms terminology foreign aid goes down 'foreign rat-holes' (quoted in Bandow, 1996). On the relationship between US domestic policies and globalization policies see Nederveen Pieterse (2004, Chap. 8 'Hyperpower Exceptionalism').

13 Nederveen Pieterse (2001) discusses hegemonic compromise in development policy.

14 For example, Stavrianos (1981) discusses several episodes of destruction and sabotage of industrial capabilities in the Third World during colonialism and imperialism.

15 On financial practices in the World Bank see, e.g., Adams (1997); on political influences in IMF lending see, e.g., Thacker (1999).

16 This is a wide, multi-level research agenda too large to address here, and since on most of these themes there is extensive literature, indicative references must suffice.

17 For example, Bienefeld (1994), Hardt and Negri (2000) and Petras and Veltmeyer (2001). A rejoinder to globalization equals imperialism is Nederveen Pieterse (2000b).

BIBLIOGRAPHY

Adams, Patricia (1997) 'The World Bank's finances: an international debt crisis', in C. Thomas and P. Wilkin (eds), *Globalization and the South*. London: Macmillan. pp. 163–83.

Arrighi, G. and Drangel, J. (1996) 'The stratification of the world economy: an exploration of the semi-peripheral zone', *Review*, 10: 9–74.

Atkinson, Anthony B. (1999) *Is Rising Inequality Inevitable? A Critique of the Transatlantic Consensus*. Helsinki, UNU WIDER Annual Lectures 3.

Babones, S.J. (2002) 'Population and sample selection effects in measuring internal income inequality', *Journal of World-Systems Research*, 8 (1): 8–29.

Bairoch, Paul (1980) 'Le bilan économique du colonialisme: mythes et réalités', in L. Blussé et al. (eds), *History and Underdevelopment*. Leiden University.

Bandow, Doug (1996) 'Shaping a new foreign aid policy for today's world', *USA Today*, 124 (May): 16–18.

Beitz, C.R. (2001) 'Does global inequality matter?', *Metaphilosophy*, 32 (1): 95–112.

Bhagwati, Jagdish (1998) 'Poverty and reforms: friends or foes?', *Journal of International Affairs*, 52 (1): 33–45.

Bienefeld, M. (1994) 'The New World Order: echoes of a new imperialism', *Third World Quarterly*, 15 (1): 31–48.

Birdsall, Nancy (1998) 'Life is unfair: inequality in the world', *Foreign Policy*, 111 (Summer): 73–94.

Bornschier, V. (2002) 'Changing income inequality in the second half of the 20th century: preliminary findings and propositions for explanations', *Journal of World-Systems Research*, 8 (1): 100–29.

Bowman, Karlyn H. (2000) 'The declining political potency of economic inequality', *Los Angeles Times*, 13 June.

Buchanan, Keith (1985) 'Center and periphery: reflections on the irrelevance of a billion human beings' *Monthly Review*, 37 (July–Aug): 86–97.

Burkett, Ingrid (2000) 'Beyond the 'information rich and poor'; futures understandings of inequality in globalising informational economies', *Futures*, 32 (7): 679–94.

Chossudovsky, M. (1998) 'Global poverty in the late 20th century', *Journal of International Affairs*, 52 (1): 293–311.

Cohen, J. and Rogers, J. (1997) *Can Egalitarianism Survive Internationalization?* Bonn: Max Planck Institute for the Study of Societies Working Paper 97/2.

Connell, R.W. (1984) 'Class formation on a world scale', *Review*, 7 (3): 407–40.

Cornia, G. Andrea (1999) *Liberalization, Globalization and Income Distribution*. Helsinki, UNU Wider Working Paper 157.

Cox, R.W. (1996) 'A perspective on globalization', in J. Mittelman (ed.), *Globalization: Critical Reflections*. Boulder, CO: Lynne Rienner.

Deacon, B., Hulse, M. and Stubbs, P. (1998) *Global Social Policy*. London: Sage.

Duffield, Mark (2001) *Global Governance and the New Wars: The Merging of Development and Security*. London: Zed.

Ehrenreich, Barbara (1990) *Fear of Falling: The Inner Life of the Middle Class*. New York: Harper Perennial.

Embong, Abdul R. (2000) 'Globalization and transnational class relations: some problems of conceptualization', *Third World Quarterly*, 21 (6): 989–1000.

Firebaugh, G. (1999) 'Empirics of world income inequality', *American Journal of Sociology*, 104: 1597–630.

Frank, R.H. and Cook, P.J. (1995) *The Winner-Take-All Society*. New York: The Free Press.

Franklin, Jane (ed.) (1997) *Equality*. London: Institute for Public Policy Research.

Gray, John (1996) 'After social democracy and beyond Anglo-Saxon capitalism', *New Perspectives Quarterly*, 13 (4): 40–6.

Grove, D. John (ed.) (1979) *Global Inequality: Political and Socioeconomic Perspectives*. Boulder, CO: Westview Press.

Hardt, M. and Negri, A. (2000) *Empire*. Cambridge, MA: Harvard University Press.

Hedley, R.A. (1999) 'The information age: apartheid, cultural imperialism, or global village?', *Social Science Computer Review*, 17 (1): 78–87.

Henderson, Hazel (1996) 'Changing paradigms and indicators: implementing equitable, sustainable and participatory development', in M.J. Griesgraber and B.G. Gunter (eds), *Development: New Paradigms and Principles for the 21st Century*. London: Pluto. pp. 103–36.

Hinsch, W. (2001) 'Global distributive justice', *Metaphilosophy*, 32 (1–2): 58–78.

Hurrell, A. (2001) 'Global inequality and international institutions', *Metaphilosophy*, 32 (1–2): 34–57.

Hurrell, A. and Woods, N. (1995) 'Globalisation and inequality', *Millennium*, 24 (3): 447–70.

Hurrell, Andrew and Woods, Ngaire (eds) (1999) *Inequality, Globalization, and World Politics*. Oxford: Oxford University Press.

Johnson, B.T. and Schaefer, B.D. (1998) 'Congress should slash – or kill – foreign welfare', *Human Events*, 54 (22): 24–7.

Jolly, Richard (1997) *Human Development: The World After Copenhagen*. Providence, RI: ACUNS Reports and Papers 1997 No. 2.

Kapstein, E.B. (1998–99) 'A global third way', *World Policy Journal*, 15 (4).

Landes, David (1998) *The Wealth and Poverty of Nations*. New York: W.W. Norton.

Linklater, Andrew (1999) 'The evolving spheres of international justice', *International Affairs*, 75 (3): 473–82.

Lundgren, Nancy (1988) 'When I grow up I want a TransAm: children in Belize talk about themselves and the impact of the world capitalist system', *Dialectical Anthropology*, 13 (3): 269–76.

McMichael, P. (1996) *Development and Social Change: A Global Perspective*. Thousand Oaks, CA: Pine Forge Press.

Miller, M. (2000) 'Poverty as a cause of war', 50th Pugwash Conference on Science and World Affairs, Cambridge, 3–8 August.

Mishra, R. (1996a) 'North America: poverty amidst plenty', in Øyen, E., Miller, S.M. and Samad, S.A. (eds) (1996) *Poverty: A Global Review. Handbook on International Poverty Research*. Oslo: Scandinavian University Press. pp. 453–93.

Mishra, R. (1996b) 'The welfare of nations', in R. Boyer and D. Drache (eds), *States against Markets: The Limits of Globalization*. London: Routledge. pp. 316–33.

Nederveen Pieterse, J. (ed.) (2000a) *Global Futures: Shaping Globalization*. London: Zed.

Nederveen Pieterse, J. (2000b) 'Globalization North and South: representations of uneven development and the interaction of modernities', *Theory Culture and Society*, 17 (1): 129–37.

Nederveen Pieterse, J. (2001) *Development Theory, Deconstructions/Reconstructions*. London: Sage.

Nederveen Pieterse, J. (2004) *Globalization or Empire?* New York: Routledge.

Novak, Mojca (1996) 'Concepts of poverty', in Øyen, E., Miller, S.M. and Samad, S.A. (eds) (1996) *Poverty: A Global Review. Handbook on International Poverty Research*. Oslo: Scandinavian University Press. pp. 47–61.

Øyen, E. (1996) 'Poverty research rethought', in Øyen, E., Miller, S.M. and Samad, S.A. (eds) (1996) *Poverty: A Global Review. Handbook on International Poverty Research*. Oslo: Scandinavian University Press. pp. 3–17.

Øyen, E., Miller, S.M. and Samad, S.A. (eds) (1996) *Poverty: A Global Review. Handbook on International Poverty Research*. Oslo: Scandinavian University Press.

Park, W.G. and Brat, D.A. (1995) 'A global Kuznets curve?', *Kyklos*, 48 (1): 105–31.

Petras, J. and Veltmeyer, H. (2001) *Globalization Unmasked: Imperialism in the 21st Century*. London: Zed.

Pogge, Thomas (2001a) 'Introduction: global justice', *Metaphilosophy*, 32 (1–2): 1–5.

Pogge, Thomas (2001b) 'Priorities of global justice', *Metaphilosophy*, 32 (1–2): 6–24 .

Raichur, S. (1979) 'International inequality and national income distribution', in John Grove (ed.), *Global Inequality: Political and Socioeconomic Perspectives*. Boulder, CO: Westview Press. pp. 77–89.

Rocamora, Joel (1992) 'Third world revolutionary projects and the end of the cold war', in C. Hartman and P. Villanova (eds), *Paradigms Lost: The Post-Cold War Era*. London: Pluto. pp. 75–86.

Rodrik, Dani (1998) 'Globalisation, social conflict and economic growth', *The World Economy*, 21 (4): 143–58.

Rowe, E. Thomas (1979) 'Strategies for change: a classification of proposals for ending inequality', in John Grove (ed.), *Global Inequality: Political and Socioeconomic Perspectives*. Boulder, CO: Westview Press. pp. 221–36.

Ruggie, J.G. (1997) *Globalization and the Embedded Liberalism Compromise: The End of an Era?* Bonn: Max Planck Institute for the Study of Societies Working Paper 97/1.

Ruiz, P.O. and Minguez, R. (2001) 'Global inequality and the need for compassion: issues in moral and political education', *Journal of Moral Education*, 30 (2).

Sachs, J.D. (2001) 'The strategic significance of global inequality', *Washington Quarterly*, 24 (3): 187–98.

Sachs, W. (1999) *Planet Dialectics: Explorations in Environment and Development*. London: Zed.

Samad, Syed Abdus (1996) 'The present situation in poverty research', in Øyen, E., Miller, S.M. and Samad, S.A. (eds) (1996) *Poverty: A Global Review. Handbook on International Poverty Research*. Oslo: Scandinavian University Press. pp. 33–46.

Sklair, L. (1997) 'Social movements for global capitalism', *Review of International Political Economy*, 4 (3): 514–38.

Smith, D.A. (1993) 'Technology and the modern world-system: some reflections', *Science, Technology and Human Values*, 18 (2): 186–96.

Smith, D.A. (1997) 'Technology, commodity chains and global inequality: South Korea in the 1990s', *Review of International Political Economy*, 4 (4): 734–62.

Stavrianos, L.S. (1981) *Global Rift: The Third World Comes of Age*. New York: Morrow.

Street, Brian (1994) 'The international dimension', in U.H. Meinhof and K. Richardson (eds), *Text, Discourse and Context: Representations of Poverty in Britain*. London: Longman. pp. 47–66.

Sutcliffe, Bob (2001) *100 Ways of Seeing an Unequal World*. London: Zed.

Thacker, S.C. (1999) 'The high politics of IMF lending', *World Politics*, 52: 38–75.

UNDP (1996) *Human Development Report*. New York: Oxford University Press.

UNDP (1997) *Human Development Report*. New York: Oxford University Press.

UNDP (2000) *Poverty Report 2000: Overcoming Human Poverty*. New York: UNDP.

Wade, R. (1996) 'Japan, the World Bank and the art of paradigm maintenance: the East Asian Miracle in political perspective', *New Left Review*, 217: 3–36.

Wade, R. (2001) 'Winners and losers', *The Economist*, 359 (28 April–4 May): 72–4.

Wade, R. (2002) 'The United States and the World Bank: the fight over people and ideas', *Review of International Political Economy*, 9 (2): 201–29.

Wade, R. and Veneroso, F. (1998) 'The Asian crisis: the high debt model versus the Wall Street–Treasury–IMF Complex', *New Left Review*, 228: 3–24.

Wallerstein, I. (ed.) (1975) *World Inequality: Origins and Perspectives on the World System*. Montréal: Black Rose Books.

Walton, M. (1997) *Will global Advance Include the World's Poor?* Broadway, England: Aspen Institute, International Peace and Security Program.

Wilson, F. (1996) 'Drawing together some regional perspectives on poverty', in Øyen, E., Miller, S.M. and Samad, S.A. (eds) (1996) *Poverty: A Global Review. Handbook on International Poverty Research*. Oslo: Scandinavian University Press. pp. 18–32.

World Bank (1996) *The World Bank Participation Sourcebook*. Washington, DC: World Bank.

World Bank (1997) *The State in a Changing World: World Development Report 1997*. New York: Oxford University Press.

World Bank (1999) *World Development Report 1999*. Washington, DC: World Bank.

World Bank (2000) *A Better World for All: World Development Report 2000*. Washington, DC: World Bank.

25

Sociology and the Body

NICK CROSSLEY

INTRODUCTION

Although sociological interest in the body is by no means as new as some accounts suggest, the growth of a sociological 'industry' of body studies has been one of the most notable developments in the discipline over the past 20 years. Key texts by Bryan Turner (1984, 1992) and John O'Neill (1985, 1989) constitute founding moments of this new wave of interest, at least in the English-speaking sectors of the sociological field, and date it at the mid-1980s (see also Frank, 1990, 1992; Shilling, 1993). Since that time a massive body of work has accumulated, covering a wide range of issues and sociological perspectives. New objects of interest have emerged and many old ones have been returned to and examined in new ways. The sheer volume and diversity of this work defies any possibility of summarizing it in just one chapter and I do not pretend to attempt that here. Many good overviews are available (Shilling, 1993; Williams and Bendelow, 1998). What I will present here is an overview of five issues which I take to be central to much of the sociological debate surrounding the body:

- The dualisms: mind/body, body/society and biology/culture
- The problem of intellectualism
- The socialization of the body

- The embodiment of society
- Reflexive embodiment.

A multitude of important thinkers and works could be discussed in relation to each of these issues but, again, it would be impossible to do justice to them in the space available. I have been highly selective by force of necessity.

THE DUALISMS

One of the persistent claims of the pioneers of the sociology of the body, as well as those who have argued for a closer relationship between sociology and biology, has been that sociology manifests a Cartesian tendency towards mind/body dualism (Turner, 1984; Shilling, 1993; Williams and Bendelow, 1998; Burkitt, 1999). There are many problems with this claim in my view. For our purposes here, however, suffice it to say that it overlooks the reflections of the discipline's founder. In his essay, 'Individual and Collective Representations', Durkheim clearly marks his distance from the dualist position:

> There is no need to conceive of a soul separated from its body maintaining in some ideal milieu a dreamy and solitary existence. The soul is in the world and its life is involved with the life of things, or we could say that all thoughts are in the brain. (Durkheim, 1974: 28)

In this particular passage the key to Durkheim's post-dualism appears to be the brain, thus suggesting that his position is a variety of vulgar and reductive materialism. Elsewhere, however, he is at pains to distance himself from this position too, stressing that mental life is organized through meanings and representations which are strictly irreducible to the chemical interactions upon which they rest:

It is obvious that the condition of the brain affects all the intellectual phenomena and is the immediate cause of some of them (pure sensation). But, on the other hand … representational life is not inherent in the intrinsic nature of nervous matter, since in part it exists by its own force and has its own particular manner of being. […] the relations of representations are different in nature from those underlying neural elements. It is something quite new which certain characteristics of the cells certainly help to produce but do not suffice to constitute, since it survives them and manifests different properties. (Durkheim, 1974: 23–4)

His position here is relationalist. Human beings are entirely physical beings. We are composed of one substance (matter) not two (mind and matter) as Descartes (1968) suggests. However, an adequate account of human behaviour and experience, as it takes shape in the structured and processual interaction between the human organism, functioning as an integrated whole, and its environment involves emergent properties which, by definition, are irreducible to the basic properties of matter. Norbert Elias makes a similar claim:

complexes of physical events organised as organisms, plants and animals, possess regularities and structural characteristics which cannot be comprehended by merely reducing them to physio-chemical reactions. … organised units at a higher level of integration are relatively autonomous with respect to events on the next lower level of integration. And distinctive forms of thought and methods of research are needed if scientists are to comprehend correctly the forms of organisation of the higher levels of integration. (Elias, 1978: 105)

Amongst the emergent properties considered by Durkheim are consciousness and symbolic meaning. Human behaviour, though entirely embodied, is not the mechanistic effect of physical forces acting upon the organism but rather a *purposive interaction* with a *meaningful situation*, meaning being strictly irreducible to the physical properties of the situation.

In *The Elementary Forms of the Religious Life*, for example, he claims that:

We know what the flag is for the soldier; in itself, it is only a piece of cloth. […] A cancelled postage stamp may be worth a fortune; but surely this value is in no way implied in its natural properties. […] Collective representations very frequently attribute to the things to which they are attached qualities which do not exist under any form or to any degree. Out of the commonest object, they can make a most powerful sacred being.

Yet the powers which are thus conferred, though purely ideal, act as though they were real; they determine the conduct of men with the same degree of necessity as physical forces. (Durkheim, 1915: 260)

This does not preclude the possibility that events best conceived in physical terms can have psychological effects. Eat magic mushrooms and your representations will change. Conversely, as Peter Freund's (1988) important work suggests, effects may pass in the opposite direction. Read a sad novel and its meaning will have a physiological effect. It is important to emphasize, however, that these are not 'interactions' between different 'substances' or 'things' but rather consist of a single event which can be described at different structural levels. For example: sadness does not cause physiological change; rather 'physiological change', on those occasions where it coincides with 'sadness', is a partial and lower level description of 'sadness'.[1] More to the point, most actions, most of the time, can only be explained by reference to the meaningful-representational level, for Durkheim. The same physical 'stimulus' will have a very different effect on our action if, for whatever reason, it assumes a different meaning.

Durkheim's challenge to mind/body dualism is brief. It is little more than an outline. We can flesh out the argument, however, by reference to a very similar argument made by Merleau-Ponty (1962, 1965, 1968). Descartes and those who follow him, Merleau-Ponty observes, conceive of the 'substance' of the body in terms of brute physical matter, such that it is defined entirely in terms of its sense-perceptible properties. The Cartesian body is an object that fills space, can be seen, touched and smelled etc., and which is moved only by the action of other external bodies upon it:

[By 'the body'] I understand all that can be terminated by some figure; that can be contained in some place and fill a space in such a way that any other body is excluded from it; that can be perceived, either by touch, sight, hearing, taste or smell; that can be moved in many ways, not of itself, but by something foreign to it by which it is touched and from which it receives the impulse. […] I am not this assemblage of limbs called the human body; I am not a thin and penetrating air spread through all these members ... (Descartes, 1968: 104–5)

This concept of the body is extremely limited and one-sided. As such it effectively forces Descartes into a dualistic position. It refers exclusively to perceptible properties of the body, for example, failing to account for the nature of the being who perceives them, and it precludes any recognition of the phenomenological sense Descartes has of his own being. Hence his claim, in the above passage, 'I am not this assemblage of limbs called the human body.' If this is what the body is then Descartes is not a body. He must be something else. This 'something else', for Descartes, is a distinct 'substance' which he calls 'mind', a substance which parallels 'body' or 'matter' and yet is radically different from it. To avoid dualism, it follows, we must rethink our concept of the body in such a way as to remove the necessity of invoking something other or extra. This is just what Merleau-Ponty does.

The definition of the body which Descartes arrives at, Merleau-Ponty notes, is derived from the definition of matter which was achieving purchase in the emerging scientific culture of his day. It is Galileo's definition (see also Ryle, 1949; Husserl, 1970). This is methodologically problematic because Descartes's *Meditations* are supposed to be foundational philosophical reflections that will establish a basis for science. They should not, therefore, be reliant upon scientific definitions. More to the point, it is his acceptance of this scientific definition of matter, as noted above, which generates the need for a dualistic schema in the first place. In contrast to this, Merleau-Ponty encourages us to recognize that 'matter' is a scientific typification which abstracts certain aspects of physical being, bracketing out others, for the purposes of its investigations. For these purposes it is perfectly legitimate and adequate but only for these purposes. He suggests that for philosophical and human scientific purposes we look beneath and beyond this typification to a more primordial layer of

physical being, which is both sentient and sensible. He terms this more primordial layer of physical being 'the flesh'. This is a complex aspect of Merleau-Ponty's (1968) later philosophy which I do not have the space to explore here. Suffice it to say, however, that the flesh of the human body is 'reversible'; that is, it is both sentient and sensible, perceiving and perceptible, seeing and seen etc. The body is a sensuous or sentient as well as a sensible being. It is not merely a being which can be seen, touched, smelled, tasted and heard, a slab of meat, but also a being which 'has' sensations of sight, touch etc. Like Durkheim, Merleau-Ponty conceives of this in structural terms. The 'flesh', at least of human and other animate bodies, is a higher level structure of physical being than that abstracted in the concept of 'matter'. Furthermore, like Durkheim, Merleau-Ponty emphasizes both that the sensations of the flesh form meaningful *gestalts*, such that perception amounts to an intentional apprehension of a meaningful world, and that these meanings are socially shared and constructed.

We should add here that Merleau-Ponty's agent responds purposively to the meaningful situations which comprise its 'milieu'. This touches upon a further aspect of his critique of the Cartesian-inspired conception of the body. The Cartesian conception of the body, he argues, implies that human behaviour should be conceived mechanically, as movement caused by the action of external physical forces upon it. At Merleau-Ponty's time of writing this conception was being championed by the psychological behaviourists, and much of his early work, inspired by Goldstein (2000) amongst others, was devoted to a critique of this school. I do not have the space to discuss this critique in detail (see Crossley, 2001a) but its basic outline is important. First, Merleau-Ponty (1962, 1965) assembles a mass of both empirical and philosophical materials to establish that the behaviourist programme is flawed. It is not borne out by experimental and other empirical studies and is theoretically incoherent. Human behaviour cannot be explained in terms of physical stimulus–response reflexes. Secondly, he argues that the same empirical materials which refute behaviourism are most parsimoniously accounted for in terms of an account that emphasizes the role of 'meaning' and 'purpose' in the interchanges between the organism and its milieu. Finally, like Durkheim, Merleau-Ponty argues his case in broadly relational terms. The agency of the body is not the result of an addition of something to the flesh and bones of the organism, for him, but rather of the irreducible structure formed through the interaction of its parts both between themselves and with the immediate environment.

THE EMBODIMENT OF SOCIETY: NATURE AND CULTURE

Durkheim's structuralist critique of mind/body dualism is, for him, little more than a stepping-stone towards an argument for which he is much better known. Just as the parts of the body interact between themselves and with the physical environment, giving rise to a psychological life, he observes, the interaction of individual psychological beings gives rise to a still higher structure, society:

> When we said elsewhere that social facts are, in a sense, independent of individuals and exterior to individual minds, we only affirmed of the social world what we have just established for the psychic world. Society has for its substratum the mass of associated individuals. [...] In such a combination, with the mutual alterations involved, *they become something else*. (Durkheim, 1974: 24–6; emphasis in the original)

In the essay from which this passage is taken Durkheim argues that the representations integral to the mental life of the social agent derive from the higher level structure of collective life. The soldier perceives coloured cloth as a flag and acts and emotes appropriately, to return to earlier quotation, because that is how the cloth is defined in the system of representations of the society to which he belongs. Collective representations are but one aspect of the *sui generis* order that Durkheim conceives of, however, as is widely acknowledged (Durkheim, 1954, 1962).

The various pros and cons of Durkheim's *sui generis* argument are well rehearsed in the literature. I will not revisit them here. What is important, from our point of view, is the implication of his view that the physical, psychological and social 'worlds' are different levels of organization of what Merleau-Ponty (1968) calls the 'flesh'. Without denying the possibility of tensions and mutual adjustments between these successive orders of reality (see below), this conception effects a pre-emptive strike against any inclination we may have to conceive of body and society or nature and culture in dualistic terms:

> ... even if society is a specific reality it is not an empire within an empire; it is part of nature and, indeed, its highest representation. The social realm is a natural realm which differs from the others [e.g. the chemical, biological and psychological realms] only by a greater complexity. (Durkheim, 1915: 31)

> Society is also of nature and yet dominates it. Not only do all the forces of the universe converge in society, but they also form a new synthesis which surpasses in richness, complexity and power of action all that went to form it. In a word, society is nature arrived at a higher point of its development, concentrating all its energies to surpass, as it were, itself. (Durkheim, 1974: 97)

We cannot reduce society to either psychology or biology. Each is a distinct and irreducible structure. For this same reason, we cannot, contra the claims of naïve positivism, study society and social relations in *exactly* the same way as we study other natural structures. The particular nature of social phenomena must be attended to. However, society and culture are structures of the natural world, albeit higher level structures, and we must refuse the temptation to think otherwise. Thus, if human beings are cultural or social beings this is not at the expense of them also being natural or biological beings. This is not to deny that there are uses and meanings of the term 'natural' which necessarily juxtapose it to 'social'. In some cases, for example, it may mean 'innate' as opposed to 'learned'. In the broad ontological sense under discussion here, however, society is a part of nature.

At the level of the individual this implies, as Merleau-Ponty (1962), Elias (1978) and a number of more progressive biologists have argued, that human beings are biologically equipped for a cultural and historical life (Levins and Lewontin, 1985; Lewontin, 2000). That is to say, the process of natural selection has in the case of human beings given rise to a creature characterized by a capacity for intelligent innovation and invention, as well as learning and habituation; a creature who, in interaction with others, plays a considerable role in fashioning the environment (social and material) in which they live, investing it with normative and semiotic structures, and who both incorporates those innovations, in the manner of habits (see below), such that they acquire the force of nature or instinct, and passes them on to offspring equipped to learn and incorporate them also. The human organism is a historical being in the fundamental sense that it is disposed to take over the 'story' from its ancestors and push the 'plot' forward.

This conceptual schema implies no concession to vulgar varieties of materialism or naturalism which seek either to explain social phenomena by reducing them to lower level biochemical orders or to naturalize them by way of pseudo-evolutionary 'just so' stories. To the contrary, it offers a strong critique of reductionism and effectively calls for a much more expansive and progressive view of the natural world. We must not adjust our conception of society or human beings to fit 'naked ape' conceptions of the world. Rather we must expand our conception of nature to fit the evident facts of human social life and history. Nature is a far more complex phenomenon than natural science inclines us to recognize because it contains the constantly changing structures of the social world. Integral to this, however, is the imperative to resist both the tendency to think of society in disembodied terms, in isolation from the embodied practices in which it consists, and the tendency to think of these social practices as outside of or above 'nature'.

As it stands this argument is quite abstract and focused on some of the more fundamental ontological assumptions of social science. We can advance this position by considering the more concrete level at which society is embodied. I mean two things by this. First, as Durkheim himself reminds us, society is generated by way of interactions between (embodied) social agents. It is 'done' by human agents and that 'doing' is necessarily embodied. It is perhaps obvious that our manipulation and transformation of the world presuppose our own physicality but this is no less true of our social interactions, both direct and mediated.

We exist for each other only insofar as we are perceptible to each other, which entails our bodily being, and we communicate meaning only through the embodied media of gesture and language (written, spoken, broadcast etc.). In this sense the social world presupposes what Merleau-Ponty (1968) calls 'the chiasm' or 'intercorporeality'; an 'intertwining' of bodies which see and are seen, touch and are touched, hear and can be heard. The networks comprising the social world are intercorporeal networks. Secondly, the embodiment of structure entails that social structures are incorporated within our bodies, in the form of 'habitus', such that our various interactions, which reproduce society, do so in ways specific to that society and its historical trajectory. In what follows I seek to elucidate this. I begin with Merleau-Ponty's critique of intellectualist conceptions of agency, a critique which itself begins with the Cartesian view of perception.

INTELLECTUALISM, PRACTICAL AGENCY AND HABITUS

For Descartes the meaning of our perceptions is determined by a mental act of judgement or interpretation. What we perceive is not what we see with our eyes, hear with our ears etc., but rather what we judge to be before us with our minds:

> If I chance to look out of a window at men passing in the street, I do not fail to say, on seeing them, that I see men [...] and yet, what do I see from this window, other than hats and cloaks, which can cover ghosts or dummies which move only by means of springs? But I judge them to be really men, and thus I understand, by the sole power of judgement which resides in my mind, what I believed I saw with the eyes. (Descartes, 1968: 110)

Similarly 'action', qua physical movement, is not intrinsically meaningful, intelligent or purposive, but only acquires meaning, intelligence and purpose by virtue of the deliberations, plans and judgements of reflective consciousness. The body, for Descartes, as we saw in the quotation cited earlier in this chapter, 'can be moved in many ways, not of itself, but by something foreign to it by which it is touched and from which it receives the impulse' (Descartes, 1968: 104). The mind, which bestows meaning upon the world by way of acts of judgement, instructs the body how to act in that world. This is problematic on a number of counts.

First, the account of perception is flawed. Insofar as Descartes identifies an active element in perception on behalf of the perceptual agent we might be persuaded to concur. What we perceive is not merely what is 'there' before us, as any number of perceptual illusions and ambiguous images illustrate. We can make sense of the same perceptual materials in very different ways and might fail to see what could be seen because we do not configure our perceptual field appropriately. It is for this reason that we are inclined to reject empiricist accounts of perception which explain it as the caused effect of the objects of perception. Nevertheless, there is a flaw in Descartes's account also. His account of how perception works, which emphasizes the reflective activities of a thinking subject, collapses into infinite regression. It presupposes a prior perception to have occurred and cannot explain this prior perception without presupposing a further perception and so on ad infinitum. In the particular illustration that he gives in the passage quoted above, for example, Descartes claims that his perception of 'men' is, in fact, a judgement. He has judged the hats and coats which he sees before him to be 'men'. This begs the question of how we are to explain his perception of hats and coats. That cannot be explained by reference to an act of judgement unless we presuppose an earlier perception still, which is judged to be hats and coats, and so on. There is no escaping this problem because acts of judgement, interpretation or similar such predicative acts, will always presuppose perceptual materials which are judged or interpreted.

For this reason Merleau-Ponty, in his account, reverses the Cartesian position and argues that we do, indeed, perceive with our eyes and not by way of any abstract predicative mental processes, such as judgement. Like Descartes, Merleau-Ponty believes that perception is an active process in which perceptual meaning is constructed but the activity is that of a sensuous bodily whole which scans the environment, focusing in and out, foregrounding

different elements and pushing others to the background. This is an activity of the eyes but also of the head, neck, feet, indeed of the whole body functioning as an integrated system. Furthermore, he suggests that this process of interrogation and the meaningful *gestalts* it settles upon are the outcome of a process of learning in which habitual schemas of perception are acquired:

> every perceptual habit is still a motor habit and here equally the process of grasping a meaning is performed by the body. [...] The gaze gets more or less from things according to the way in which it questions them, ranges over or dwells on them. To learn to see colours is to acquire a certain style of seeing, a new use of one's own body; it is to enrich and recast the body image. (Merleau-Ponty, 1962: 153)

Reading a written text or listening to a speech provide a very clear illustration of this. It is obvious that the meaning of our perceptions, in these cases, is conventional and based upon the acquisition of particular perceptual schemas. We cannot understand texts written in languages we have not learned. This also illustrates the active element in perception, the element of 'reading', because the same text may be meaningful to one agent (who has acquired the language) but not another (who has not), such that the difference must involve something that they are able to do; that is, read this or that text. And yet texts and speeches generally strike us as immediately meaningful and we are not generally aware of the active processes we are instigating. The activity of reading is conducted, for the most part, at a level of pre-reflective habit. This same point applies to all perception, for Merleau-Ponty. We 'read' social situations as surely as we read written texts, and the role of pre-reflective schemas of perception is just the same.

A very similar argument can be made with respect to 'action'. Ryle (1949), for example, has noted that the Cartesian conception of action, which understands it to be an outcome of deliberation or planning, necessarily collapses back into an infinite regression. If actions must be deliberated upon or planned in order to be meaningful and intelligent, he asks, then where does this leave planning and deliberation? They too are acts and one assumes that they must be intelligent and meaningful in order to bestow meaning and intelligence on that which they deliberate upon or plan. If Descartes is correct, therefore, then plans and deliberations must be planned and deliberated upon too. The problem, of course, is that these prior plans and deliberations too must be planned and deliberated upon and so on ad infinitum.

Merleau-Ponty comes at this same point from a more phenomenological angle. Descartes's argument implies that I enjoy the same relationship to my body as to any 'other' external objects in my world, he notes. But I do not. When I move an object I do something in order to move it and am generally aware of doing so. To move the fridge in my kitchen I must first grab it, position myself appropriately relative to it and so on. I do not 'move' my body in this way, however. It just moves, or rather I, qua corporeal agent, move. I do not have to locate my arm in order to then lift it above my head and I cannot tell you how I lift my hand above my head. I don't know how I do it because, as far as I am concerned, I don't do anything. I simply am my body and its actions are my actions. I enjoy a pre-reflective mastery over both my body and its immediate spatio-temporal milieu. Merleau-Ponty refers to this basic pre-reflective bodily sense and practical mastery as the 'corporeal schema' and he views this corporeal schema as the fundamental basis of our agency (see Crossley, 2001a for an elaboration).

Integral to this notion of the corporeal schema is a concept of embodied 'knowledge' and 'understanding'. The Cartesian conceptualizes knowledge and understanding in reflective and predicative terms. Knowledge is conceived in propositional terms as 'knowledge-that', a reflective awareness and positing that 'x' is the case. Similarly, understanding is conceived as a reflective and conceptual achievement. This definition is flawed on a number of counts (see Ryle, 1949; Merleau-Ponty, 1962; Crossley, 2001a), not least of which is that it ignores a whole range of more practical forms of embodied 'know-how'. Consider, for example, my ability to type. I can type and that means that I 'know' where the various letters are on the keyboard in front of me. But in what way do I know? I do not think about where

the keys are before I type. I just do it. More to the point, I could not say where the keys are if I were asked. I do not know, in a reflective way, where the keys are. My knowledge is an embodied knowledge; knowledge which is indissociable from my ability to do certain things. This is a relatively mundane example but the same might be said of my higher order competencies, such as my ability to 'philosophize' and play the philosophical 'game' or my ability to lecture or make polite conversation. Each entails a form of embodied know-how which consists entirely in my ability to do this or that activity. Kuhn's (1970) work on the philosophy of science provides an interesting example here. There are few more 'cerebral' activities than science. And yet, as Kuhn argues, the doing of science rests upon a range of practical skills, schemas and forms of competence which the budding scientist must both acquire and take for granted. The reflective and discursive aspect of science rests upon and presupposes this pre-reflective and practical work (see also Polanyi, 1966).

The acquisition of these various corporeal skills and 'principles' constitutes a modification and enlargement of the corporeal schema, and Merleau-Ponty generally refers to such modifications in terms of 'habit'. However, he is sure to distance his conception of habit from the narrow and mechanistic version of the concept which rose into prominence in the early twentieth century (Camic, 1986). Habits, for Merleau-Ponty, are flexible, intelligent and multi-track[2] dispositions. They are embodied, practical and pre-reflective ways of understanding the world:

> If habit is neither a form of knowledge nor an involuntary action what then is it? It is knowledge in the hands, which is forthcoming only when bodily effort is made, and cannot be formulated in detachment from that effort. The subject knows where the letters are on the typewriter as we know where one of our limbs is, through knowledge bred of familiarity which does not give us a position in objective space. (Merleau-Ponty, 1962: 144)
>
> …
>
> We said earlier that it is the body which understands in the acquisition of habit. This way of putting it will appear absurd, if understanding is subsuming a sense datum under an idea, and if the body is as an object. But the phenomenon of habit is just what prompts us to revise our notion of 'understand' and our notion of the

body. To understand is to experience the harmony between what we aim at and what is given, between the intention and the performance – and the body is our anchorage in a world. (p. 144)

This practical, embodied understanding and knowledge lies at the root of human being-in-the-world, for Merleau-Ponty. It subtends even our most reflective postures. The reflective subject of the Cartesian schema is not therefore the bottom line on human subjectivity, as Descartes famously takes it to be. Beneath and before our more theoretical modes of dealing with the world we are practical beings. Following Husserl, Merleau-Ponty marks his distance from Descartes on this point by arguing for the primacy of the 'I can' over the 'I think'. Even this formulation fails to capture the radical nature of his argument, however, at least insofar as reference to 'I' invokes an image of a reflexively aware and reflective ego. The 'I' of Merleau-Ponty's 'I can' is an anonymous being which subtends the life of the reflective ego. One is reminded of Zarathustra's message to the 'despisers of the body':

> You say 'I' and you are proud of this word. But greater than this – although you will not believe in it – is your body and its great intelligence, which does not say 'I', but performs 'I'. (Nietzsche, 1969: 62)

None of this is intended to deny that human agents do indeed reflect upon their possibilities for action and entertain conscious thoughts. However, Merleau-Ponty performs a similar 'deconstruction' on the process of reflective thought as upon perception. In the first instance he argues that reflective thought is achieved in and through speech and thus language. This is not a matter of arguing that language 'causes' thought or vice versa. Causation is only possible between two independent beings but thought and speech are not separate, for Merleau-Ponty. They are two sides of the same coin or 'flesh'. Speech (or writing) is the 'body' of reflective thought and thought is the sense or meaning of speech (or writing). More to the point, both speech and thought are practical activities rooted in acquired forms of habitual competence. My ability to speak, forming thoughts in the words of my native language, is a practical activity whose physical mechanisms and linguistic principles I am unable

to explain. I 'understand' language and its rules but in a practical rather than a theoretical or reflective way. It is an activity I perform without thinking about it. And given the linguistic basis of reflective thought, this too must be underscored by practical and embodied activity. I may of course prepare my thoughts and utterances before expressing them but only by means of prior expressions and linguistic uses which I have not prepared in this way. If it were necessary to think about thinking before doing it then my mental life would collapse back into a black hole of infinite regression.

HABIT, HABITUS AND BODY TECHNIQUE: THE SOCIALIZATION OF THE BODY

Through his concept of habit Merleau-Ponty opens the door to a distinctly sociological conception of the body. Human beings do not have fixed instincts, he argues, but our embodied ways of being do nevertheless achieve a degree of stability and regularity in virtue of our habits:

> Although our body does not impose definite instincts upon us, as it does other animals, it does at least give to our life the form of generality, and develops our personal acts into stable dispositional tendencies. In this sense our nature is not long-established custom, since custom presupposes the form of passivity derived from nature. (Merleau-Ponty, 1962: 146)

Here Merleau-Ponty rejoins my earlier claim, in respect of Durkheim, regarding nature/culture dualism. Human beings are 'creatures of habit' but this is not contrary to 'nature'. It is what we are by nature. More importantly, however, Merleau-Ponty recognizes that the habits which shape our subjective lives and actions are often shared. Our individual biographical histories, which give rise to our habits, are interwoven with the lives of others in collective histories, such that our habits are shared too. Hence his reference to custom.

This claim overlaps in important ways with Mauss's (1979) observations on 'body techniques'. Mauss observes that there is variability in the ways in which individuals in different social groups 'use'[3] their bodies. There are, he notes, different ways of, for example, walking, speaking, eating, sleeping and making love, and these different forms of activity tend to follow a social distribution, such that we speak of them as 'social facts' in Durkheim's (1982) sense. These different 'uses' of the body are not mere differences in the mechanics of movement, however. Rather, they are collective techniques for getting a grip upon the world, making sense of it and making out within it. Like Merleau-Ponty's habits they are embodied forms of understanding and knowledge. They give shape to purposive action and, as such, they form an integral part of the 'practical reason' of a particular group. In an effort to capture both this purposive understanding of body techniques and their social facticity, Mauss elects to use the concept of the habitus:

> Please note that I use the Latin word – it should be understood in France – *habitus*. The word translates infinitely better than '*habitude*' (habit or custom), the '*exis*', the 'acquired ability' and 'faculty' of Aristotle (who was a psychologist). It does not designate those metaphysical *habitudes*, that mysterious 'memory', the subject of volumes or short and famous theses. These 'habits' do not vary just with individuals and their imitations; they vary between societies, educations, proprieties and fashions, prestiges. In them we should see the techniques and work of collective and individual practical reason rather than, in the ordinary way, merely the soul and its repetitive faculties. (Mauss, 1979: 101)

'Body techniques' mirror Durkheim's 'collective representations'. They are elements of a collective psychological life. But they entail a pre-representational level of collective life, such as is identified in Merleau-Ponty's critique of intellectualism and his concept of the corporeal schema. Specific social groups share a habitus and specific body techniques. They share a manner of being-in and practically understanding the world.

Within more recent sociology the work of Pierre Bourdieu has done most to explore and develop these notions of habitus and body techniques. He draws upon both Merleau-Ponty and Mauss, extending the concerns of Mauss in particular by reflecting upon both the causes and the consequences of a social distribution of habitus or body techniques. Different social groups can be identified by their body techniques, he argues. In particular he has focused upon differences relating to

class and gender, and he has often returned to the uses of the mouth as his example:

> Language is a body technique, and specifically linguistic, especially phonetic, competence is a dimension of bodily hexis in which one's whole relation to the social world, and one's wholly social informed relation to the world, are expressed. [...] The most frequent articulatory position is an element in an overall way of using the mouth (in talking but also in eating, drinking, laughing etc.) [...] in the case of the lower classes, articulatory style is quite clearly part of a relation to the body that is dominated by the refusal of 'airs and graces' [...] Bourgeois dispositions convey in their physical postures of tension and exertion ... the bodily indices of quite general dispositions towards the world and other people, such as haughtiness and disdain. (Bourdieu, 1992b: 86–7)

The bourgeoisie use their mouths differently to the proletariat in speech. Furthermore, their oral hexis, which Bourdieu deems 'tight-lipped', embodies their broader manner of being-in-the-world. They are, in Bourdieu's view, generally 'up tight'.

The precise reason why specific groups have particular body techniques is never made explicit in Bourdieu's work, but there are hints. At one level his position is purely relational. There is nothing intrinsic to either groups or body techniques which links them, he suggests. Rather, groups-in-formation seize upon arbitrary body techniques in an effort to construct a sense of collective identity and distinguish themselves from other, particularly 'lower' groups. On this point Bourdieu overlaps with Durkheim, who, in his study of the totemic clans of Australia, notes how their members alter the external appearance of their bodies in various ways as a means of marking out group identity and proving group loyalty and belonging:

> They do not put their coat-of-arms merely upon things which they possess, but they put it upon their person; they imprint it upon their flesh; it becomes part of them, [...] it is more frequently upon the body itself that the totemic mark is stamped; for this is a way of representation within the capacity of even the least advanced societies. It has sometimes been asked whether the common rite of knocking out a young man's two front teeth at the age of puberty does not have the object of reproducing the form of totem ... (Durkheim, 1915: 137)
>
> ...
>
> The best way of proving to oneself and to others that one is a member of a certain group is to place a distinctive mark on the body. (p. 265)

By bearing the mark of the group the individual announces its existence and their belonging to it to both 'outsiders' and 'insiders', thus reproducing the sense that the group has of itself. Group members do this, Durkheim argues, because they feel the force of the group pressuring them to do so. The collective generates a demand for its members to identify with it. The body is particularly important here on account of its public and perceptible presence. To wear a sign of group belonging upon the body is instantly and immediately to communicate one's group belonging.

In addition to these processes of group formation and distinction Bourdieu has observed how the habitus of specific groups is shaped by the social and material environment in which the group exists. Circumstances cultivate a shared attitude towards life, which is reflected in body techniques and sedimented in the habitus. Habitus are shaped by the jobs people do, the demands these jobs make, the resources of time, money etc. that are available to groups, the conditions in which they live and so on. Habitus, in this respect, are adaptive phenomena, although again Bourdieu is concerned to emphasize that they sediment and assume a more durable form. Habitus outlive their conditions of production and whatever adaptive functions they may serve therein.

Embodied styles achieve more than the marking of identity in Bourdieu's view, however. They contribute to the reproduction of social hiearchies. His arguments on this matter are complex and cannot be expounded satisfactorily here. It must suffice to make two points. First, embodied dispositions can function as cultural or physical capital, generating advantages for those they dispose in a variety of different situations. Liza Doolittle, in Shaw's *Pygmalion*, is a classic literary illustration of this. To better herself and secure employment in a 'posh' flower shop she must become a lady; that is, acquire the hexis and social competencies of a middle class woman. Secondly the embodiment of class difference by way of hexis has the effect of making social inequalities appear 'natural' – in the sense of 'non-variable'. Acquired competence and style assume the appearance of innate qualities and talents which, in turn, justify inequities in life chances.

In addition to this, challenging the tendency in theories of the social contract, legitimation and ideology to locate the 'agreements' which hold society together at the level of conscious reflection and belief, Bourdieu argues that the domination of the state is secured at the corporeal level. The cognitive structures which support the state 'are not forms of consciousness', he argues, 'but *dispositions of the body*' (1998a: 54; emphasis in the original). He continues:

> The social world is riddled with calls to order that function as such only for those who are predisposed to heeding them as they awaken deeply buried corporeal dispositions, outside the channels of consciousness and communication. (Bourdieu, 1998a: 55)

Furthermore, extending his argument to engage with the notion of 'false consciousness', he adds,

> to speak of ideologies is to locate in the realm of representations – liable to be transformed through this intellectual conversion called 'awakening of consciousness' – what in fact belongs to the order of belief, that is, to the level of most profound corporeal dispositions. Submision to the established order is the product of the agreement between, on the one hand the cognitive structures inscribed in bodies by both collective history (phylogenesis) and individual history (ontogenesis) and, on the other, the objective structures of the world to which these cognitive structures are applied. (p. 55)

What Bourdieu means by this is never clearly spelled out. There are at least three aspects to his basic point, however. At one level, paralleling certain of Durkheim's (1915, 1974) reflections on the forms of solidarity generated through collective effervescence, he appears to be advancing the idea that agents are bound to the social order through collectively held and generated sentiments which become attached to social symbols (flags, anthems etc.). This seems, at least, to elucidate his notion of 'calls to order'. On occasion the state is able to maintain order through an appeal to the patriotic sentiments and identifications of its citizens, reaching behind the domain of rational discourse to the domain of deeply rooted bodily feeling.

Secondly, he is arguing that discursive persuasion is not necessary for effective legitimation most of the time because much of the consent which social agents grant to the state and the *status quo* is granted tacitly at a habitual level. Agents do not decide anew each day to support the *status quo*. Indeed, insofar as events conform to their general expectations they do not question it at all. They participate in society, reproducing it, and they do so with great competence and skill. But their participation is rooted in their habitus; in the dispositions and skills that they have acquired through earlier participation and from the patterns of participation of their parents. They 'play the game' but neither the game nor their participation in it are thematic or reflective issues for them. This is not to say that these assumptions and beliefs have never been discussed or argued over. They may once have been fought over but they are now repressed, pushed out of the narratives of collective memory and existing in the silence of the pre-reflective world of the corporeal schema:

> What appears to us today as self-evident, as beneath consciousness and choice, has quite often been the stake of struggles and instituted only as the result of dogged confrontations between dominant and dominated groups. The major effect of historical evolution is to abolish history by relegating to the past, that is, to the unconscious, the lateral possibles that it eliminated. (pp. 56–7)

Crises and the social movements that sometimes grow out of them might suffice to raise these corporeal dispositions into public consciousness, whereupon they can be debated. But they remain effective to the degree to which they function at the pre-reflective and pre-discursive level of the habitus and the body.

Thirdly, echoing Foucault (1979), Bourdieu notes that and how the dispositions presupposed by the reproduction of political domination are themselves reproduced in the context of a variety of social fields, particularly the educational system. Bodies are disciplined in schools, families, workplaces etc.

What is true of the specific forms of inequality and domination referred to here is, for Bourdieu, true of the social world more generally. Through participation in the games or fields comprising the social world agents acquire, as habitus, the dispositions necessary to continue and reproduce those games. The habitus is thus both shaped by the social world and lends shape to that world. It is a system of durable, transposable dispositions, structured structures predisposed to function as structuring structures, that is, as principles which generate and organize practices and representations that can be objectively adapted to their outcomes without presupposing a conscious aiming at ends or an express mastery of the operations necessary in order to attain them. Objectively 'regulated' and 'regular' without being in any way the product of obedience to rules, they can be collectively orchestrated without being the product of an organizing action of a conductor. (Bourdieu, 1992a: 53)

This claim connects with the concern for 'the body' on two counts, both already noted in this chapter. First, it emphasizes that social worlds are sites of practical and embodied activity. Social worlds consist in practices and practices have to be 'done', not by way of disembodied mental acts but through the practical activities of embodied agents acting in concert. Secondly, the duality of the habitus qua structured and structuring structure, which is central to the reproduction of the social world, rests upon the peculiar configuration of the human organism which enables it to innovate, to 'conserve' innovations in the form of habits and to absorb the innovations of others by a process of learning.

Habitus and asceticism

Bourdieu's concept of the habitus, though entirely corporeal, is much broader than either Mauss's or Merleau-Ponty's concept of habit. Alongside the dispositions and forms of competence recognized by these two writers it includes tastes, sensibilities and broader aspects of lifestyle. All of these elements, Bourdieu maintains, are incorporated within the corporeal schema. In addition, it at least hints at the asceticism imposed upon the body by dint of social membership. The middle class habitus, for example, is deemed more restrained than the working class habitus. This notion of asceticism is important for any sociological discussion of embodiment and requires brief elucidation. We can take our lead from Durkheim.

Societies, to reiterate, are composed of interactions and interdependencies between individual psychological beings, for Durkheim, but these interactions and interdependencies give rise to *sui generis* dynamics and processes. This generates specific demands which act back upon agents. In particular, Durkheim argues, collective life demands that individuals subordinate certain of their specific and particular desires and demands to those of the group. Asceticism is a necessity of social life. There are two reasons for this. First, as writers from Hobbes through Freud and beyond have recognized, the particular desires and impulses of individuals are not necessarily conducive to a just, ordered or harmonious social order. Individual wants often clash and there is a necessity, therefore, that some, at least, are repressed. Secondly, however, and rejoining our earlier point about the relationship of the body to processes of group formation and solidarity, Durkheim argues that the collective psychology of the group generates a demand for all of its members to demonstrate their loyalty to it, putting it above themselves, and that this involves specific tests of loyalty. Rites of passage, for example, specifically those which entail pain, can be understood as ways of training individuals to subordinate themselves to the group and demanding of them that they demonstrate this sacrifice. Similarly with those forms of ritual and taboo which serve no obvious material function. The individual must learn to put the rules and values of society above their own immediate impulses and must demonstrate their willingness to do so. The endurance of pain and discomfort are dramatic ways of doing this.

These observations come from Durkheim's (1915) analysis of totemic clans in Australia and certain of the details of his account are specific to that society. His basic point has a general resonance, however, and has been touched upon by other key figures from the sociological tradition. Weber's (1978) analysis of the protestant work ethic, for example, quite clearly explores the relationship between a specific ascetic regime and the type of society it has given rise to, that is, early industrial capitalism. And coming at the relationship from the other side, Elias (1984) has argued that increased societal differentiation and the concentration of the means of legitimate violence in the centralized state have both led to an increased 'social restraint towards self-restraint'. The more complex societies have become, Elias argues, the more complex, differentiated and sensitive human behaviour must

become, and thus the greater the demand for self-restraint. Not that social agents are necessarily aware of this. Self-restraint is learned and is practised to such a point that it becomes habitual and automatic; a structure of the habitus.

In an interesting argumentative twist, Durkheim (1915) argues that it is this internalized self-control and the reflexivity it imposes upon the agent which gives rise to the belief in (mind/body) dualism. By internalizing the demands of society and applying them to their self the individual experiences a division 'within' their self which they are apt to interpret as a division of body and soul.

REFLEXIVE EMBODIMENT: BODY PROJECTS

This division and reflexivity is not simply a matter of internalized control, however. Within the context of the social interactions comprising society embodied agents become aware of themselves qua 'bodies'. The embodied 'I' becomes aware of itself qua embodied 'me' (Mead, 1967). And this in turn generates a context in which bodies become (reflexive) objects of (self) transformation. In this respect, furthermore, the body is a central element in identity. Agents recognize and become conscious of their selves as 'bodies' and work upon their bodies, both as decorative objects and behavioural systems, in an effort to secure recognition for their identity from others.

Some of this 'body work' is quite mundane and is quickly absorbed within the habitus. We brush our teeth, wash, comb our hair etc. without thinking about doing so. In many respects, however, our bodies remain thematic within the reflexive process of self-hood and are consciously worried over and worked upon. Modern bodies are trimmed down by diet and exercise; built up through the use of weights and exercise; painted and decorated; altered through surgery; pierced, tattooed and even branded. Such activities are often deemed highly personal but like many personal acts their distribution and rates of participation betray a social dynamic. Furthermore, they generally entail 'collective action', at least in the sense that they presuppose organized social worlds or 'fields' for their successful execution and reception.

This point overlaps with much of what I have already said in this chapter, at least with regard to collective identity. There is more to contemporary 'body work' than is captured by the concept of collective identity building, however, at least in the traditional sense of collective identity considered hitherto in this chapter, and not only because 'the cult of the individual' has seemingly achieved dominance over more traditional identity forms – though that is important. In the modern context technological developments and possibilities have shattered traditional ways of thinking about the body and its limits, whilst social changes have undermined the traditions which root both identity and bodily life (Giddens, 1991). Body and identity are now both constituted as objects of choice and, insofar as they meld, objects of the same choice. Furthermore, this is complicated by the advance of medical science which, contrary to earlier expectations, has introduced great uncertainty into bodily life, rendering the body at 'risk' (Giddens, 1991). The authority of tradition has been usurped by authorities who no longer feel capable of offering us certitude and offer us, instead, a balance of probabilities and risks: 'x' reduces the chances of 'y' but increases the chances of 'z'. It is in this context that the modern agent plays out their reflexive relationship to their self; balancing risks and striving to build an embodied self which will be recognized and valued in a post-traditional and uncertain context.

CONCLUSION

In this chapter I have attempted to offer a brief introduction to some of the key arguments and issues surrounding the surge of interest in the body within sociology in the past twenty years. One central theme has been the need to challenge mind/body and nature/culture dualisms, re-rooting both society and the social agent within 'the flesh'. This is not to the detriment of what we might call dualities. It does not preclude the fact that, for example, 'bodies' can be subject to various attempts to (socially) control them and indeed to curb apparently 'natural' tendencies. However, it means that we must seek to understand such dualities from within a non-dualistic framework, and that very often means a reflexive framework. If the demands of civilized society conflict with the demands of unsocialized nature this is not because culture and nature are distinct realms. It reflects rather a torsion with nature (or the flesh) itself, between its higher and lower levels of integration.

Remembering these points forces us to rethink certain of our key concepts. We are required to conceptualize society as a web of interactions between embodied agents but also to reject the vestiges of Cartesianism evident in overly reflective models of the actor. We are required to attend to the pre-reflective and habitual basis of agency. In doing this, moreover, as Bourdieu's work in particular suggests, we can begin to address a further dualism of sociological thought; that of structure and agency. The concept of the habitus captures for us the way in which the body is moulded by the social world but in such a way that it is then disposed to reproduce the social world by way of its (inter)actions.

The body is not merely a pre-reflective and practical agent, however. It is equally an object of a variety of forms of explicit practices of moulding and modification, particularly in the context of late modernity. Through involvement in society embodied agents become aware of themselves qua 'bodies' and are thereby led to act, by way of their bodies, upon their own bodies. In the late modern context this is a process complicated by multiple uncertainties and risks.

NOTES

1 This is a complex point which I do not have the space to explore adequately here. I have argued elsewhere, for example, that specific physiological changes are neither necessary nor sufficient to the meaning of emotional concepts (Crossley, 1998, 2000, 2003). The point here,

however, is that this lack of coincidence derives from the logic of the different levels of description and not from the fact that these levels refer to distinct events. They do not. Clearly 'emotion' and 'physiological change' would have to be separate in order for the one to cause the other.

2 I have borrowed this description, 'multi-track disposition', from Ryle (1949). It refers to a disposition which may manifest in a wide range of actual behavioural responses. My disposition towards speaking the English language, for example, is not a disposition to always say the same thing. Similarly, my competence in statistical modelling will vary according to whatever I am modelling. Finally, my jealousy (an emotional disposition) may result in me behaving in a whole range of different ways, or not behaving in certain ways, according to context.

3 Mauss's use of the term 'use' in this context is potentially problematic, at least insofar as it implies that the body is subject to the manipulations of an already self-conscious and reflexive subject. Body techniques are, for the most part, pre-reflective and the agent is ordinarily unaware of them as such.

BIBLIOGRAPHY

Bourdieu, P. (1977) *Outline of a Theory of Practice.* Cambridge: Cambridge University Press.

Bourdieu, P. (1984) *Distinction.* London: Routledge and Kegan Paul.

Bourdieu, P. (1992a) *The Logic of Practice.* Cambridge: Polity Press.

Bourdieu, P. (1992b) *Language and Symbolic Power.* Cambridge: Polity Press.

Bourdieu, P. (1998a) *Practical Reason.* Cambridge: Polity Press.

Bourdieu, P. (1998b) *On Television and Journalism.* London: Pluto.

Bourdieu, P., Darbel, A. and Schnapper, D. (1990) *The Love of Art.* Cambridge: Polity Press.

Bourdieu, P. and Wacquant, L. (1992) *An Invitation to Reflexive Sociology.* Cambridge: Polity Press.

Burkitt, I. (1999) *Bodies of Thought.* London: Sage.

Camic, C. (1986) 'The matter of habit', *American Journal of Sociology*, 91: 1039–87.

Crossley, N. (1998) 'Emotion and communicative action: Habermas, linguistic philosophy and existentialism', in G. Bendelow and S. Williams (1998) *Emotions in Social Life.* London: Routledge. pp. 16–38.

Crossley, N. (2000) 'Emotion, psychiatry and social order', in S. Williams, J. Gabe and M. Calnan (2000) *Medicine, Health and Society.* London: Routledge. pp. 277–96.

Crossley, N. (2001a) *The Social Body: Habit, Identity and Desire.* London: Sage.

Crossley, N. (2001b) 'The phenomenological habitus and its construction', *Theory and Society*, 30: 81–120.

Crossley, N. (2003) 'Prozac nation and the bio-chemical self', in S. Williams, G. Bendelow and J. Burke (eds), *Debating Biology.* London: Routledge. pp. 245–58.

Descartes, R. (1968) *Meditations.* Harmondsworth: Penguin.

Durkheim, E. (1915) *The Elementary Forms of the Religious Life.* New York: Free Press.

Durkheim, E. (1954) *Suicide.* London: Routledge.

Durkheim, E. (1962) *The Division of Labor.* New York: The Free Press.

Durkheim, E. (1974) *Sociology and Philosophy.* New York: The Free Press.

Durkheim, E. (1982) *The Rules of Sociological Method.* New York: The Free Press.

Elias, N. (1978) *What is Sociology?* New York: Columbia University Press.

Elias, N. (1984) *The Civilising Process.* Oxford: Blackwell.

Foucault, M. (1979) *Discipline and Punish.* Harmondsworth: Penguin.

Frank, A. (1990) 'Bringing bodies back in', *Theory, Culture and Society*, 7 (1): 131–62.

Frank, A. (1992) *At the Will of the Body.* Boston, MA: Houghton Mifflin.

Freund, P. (1988) 'Understanding socialized human nature', *Theory and Society*, 17: 839–64.

Gibson, J. (1979) *The Ecological Approach to Visual Perception.* Boston, MA: Houghton Mifflin.

Giddens, A. (1991) *Modernity and Self-Identity.* Cambridge: Polity Press.

Goldstein, K. (2000) *The Organism.* New York: Zone Books.

Husserl, E. (1970) *The Crisis of the European Sciences and Transcendental Phenomenology.* Evanston: Northwestern University Press.

Kuhn, T. (1970) *The Structure of Scientific Revolutions.* Chicago: University of Chicago Press.

Levins, R. and Lewontin, R. (1985) *The Dialectical Biologist.* Cambridge, MA: Harvard.

Lewontin, R. (2000) *The Triple Helix.* Cambridge, MA: Harvard University Press.

Mauss, M. (1979) *Sociology and Psychology.* London: Routledge and Kegan Paul.

Mead, G. (1967) *Mind, Self and Society.* Chicago: University of Chicago Press.

Merleau-Ponty, M. (1962) *The Phenomenology of Perception.* London: Routledge and Kegan Paul.

Merleau-Ponty, M. (1964) *Signs.* Evanston, IL: Northwestern University Press.

Merleau-Ponty, M. (1965) *The Structure of Behaviour.* London: Methuen.

Merleau-Ponty, M. (1968) *The Visible and the Invisible.* Evanston, IL: Northwestern University Press.

Merleau-Ponty, M. (1969) *Human and Terror.* Boston, MA: Beacon Press.

Nietzsche, F. (1969) *Thus Spoke Zarathustra.* Harmondsworth: Penguin.

O'Neill, J. (1985) *Five Bodies.* New York: Cornell University Press.

O'Neill, J. (1989) *The Communicative Body.* Evanston, IL: Northwestern University Press.

Polanyi, M. (1966) *The Tacit Dimension.* Garden City, NY: Doubleday.

Ryle, G. (1949) *The Concept of Mind.* Harmondsworth: Penguin.

Shilling, C. (1993) *The Body and Social Theory.* London: Sage.

Turner, B. (1984) *Body and Society.* Oxford: Blackwell.

Turner, B. (1992) *Regulating Bodies.* London: Routledge.

Weber, M. (1978) *The Protestant Ethic and the Spirit of Capitalism.* London: George Allen and Unwin.

Williams, S. and Bendelow, G. (1998) *The Lived Body.* London: Routledge.

Young, I. (1980) 'Throwing like a girl', *Human Studies,* 3: 137–56.

26

The City: Its Return as a Lens for Social Theory

SASKIA SASSEN

The city has long been a strategic site for the exploration of many major subjects confronting society and sociology. But it has not always been a heuristic space – a space capable of producing knowledge about some of the major transformations of an epoch. In the first half of the twentieth century, the study of cities was at the heart of sociology. This is evident in the work of Simmel, Weber, Benjamin, Lefebvre and, most prominently, the Chicago School, especially Park and Wirth, both deeply influenced by German sociology. These sociologists confronted massive processes – industrialization, urbanization, alienation, a new cultural formation they called 'urbanity'. Studying the city was not simply studying the urban. It was about studying the major social processes of an era. Since then the study of the city, and with it urban sociology, gradually lost this privileged role as a lens for the discipline and as producer of key analytic categories. There are many reasons for this, most important among which are questions of the particular developments of method and data in sociology generally. Critical was the fact that the city ceased being the fulcrum for epochal transformations and hence a strategic site for research about non-urban processes. Urban sociology became increasingly concerned with what came to be called 'social problems'.

Today, as we enter a new century, the city is once again emerging as a strategic site for understanding some of the major new trends reconfiguring the social order. The city and the metropolitan region emerge as one of the strategic sites where major macro- and micro-social trends materialize and hence can be constituted as an object of study. Among these trends are globalization, the rise of the new information technologies, the intensifying of transnational and translocal dynamics, and the strengthening presence and voice of specific types of socio-cultural diversity. Each one of these trends has its own specific conditionalities, contents and consequences. The urban moment is but one moment in often complex multi-sited trajectories.

Urban sociology can capture some of these features. Other branches of sociology can use the urban moment to construct their object of research even when it is non-urban. Cities are also sites where each of these trends interacts with the others in distinct, often complex manners, in a way they do not in just about any other setting. This resurgence of the city as a site for research on these major contemporary dynamics is also evident in other disciplines. Anthropology, economic geography, cultural studies and literary criticism, all have developed an extensive urban scholarship; most recently, economists are beginning to address the urban and regional economy in their analyses in ways that differ from an older tradition of urban economics, one that had lost much of its vigor and persuasiveness.

All of this raises one of the questions organizing the chapter. Can the sociological study of cities produce scholarship and analytic tools that help us understand the broader social transformations under way today as it once did early in the preceding century? One critical issue here is whether these larger transformations evince sufficiently complex and multivalent urban instantiations as to allow us to construct such instantiations as objects of study. The urban moment of a major process makes the latter susceptible to empirical study in ways that other phases of such a process might not. At the same time, this (partial) urbanization of major dynamics repositions the city as an object of study: what is it we are actually naming today when we use the construct city? This is the second question organizing this chapter.

The chapter examines these questions of research and theorization by focusing particularly on globalization, the rise of the new information technologies, the intensifying of transnational and translocal dynamics, and the strengthening presence and voice of specific types of socio-cultural diversity. All of these are at a cutting edge of actual change that social theory needs to factor in to a far greater extent than it has. By far the best developed conceptually and empirically is socio-cultural diversity. Thus as regards this subject I will confine my treatment here to those issues of socio-cultural diversity that are bound up with the other major trends on which I am focusing. There is a strong emerging new literature on the other three trends, but mostly in disciplines other than sociology and, specifically, urban sociology.

These trends do not encompass the majority of social conditions; on the contrary, most social reality probably corresponds to older continuing and familiar trends. That is why much of sociology's traditions and well-established subfields will remain important and constitute the heart of the discipline. Further, there are good reasons why most of urban sociology has

not quite engaged the characteristics and the consequences of these three trends as they instantiate in the city: current urban datasets are quite inadequate for addressing these major trends at the level of the city. Yet, although these three trends may involve only parts of the urban condition and cannot be confined to the urban, they are strategic in that they mark the urban condition in novel ways and make it, in turn, a key research site for major trends.

CONCEPTUAL ELEMENTS

Among today's dominant forces reconfiguring the social, the economic, the political and the subjective are globalization and advanced forms of telecommunication. These in turn have enabled a proliferation of transnational and translocal networks that cut across the boundaries of cities and states – and hence also across the boundaries of major sociological framings and datasets. The traditional tools of sociology and social theory, let alone urban sociology, can accommodate only some aspects of these trends. The exception is an early generation (e.g., Castells, 1989; Chase-Dunn, 1985; King, 1990; Rodriguez and Feagin, 1986; Gottdiener, 1985; Sassen, 1981; Timberlake, 1985; Zukin, 1991, to cite but a few) of what is today a still small but rapidly growing sociological scholarship that explicitly sought to theorize these new conditions and to specify them empirically. Economic geography (e.g., Knox and Taylor, 1995; Short and Kim, 1999) and cultural studies (e.g., Palumbo-Liu, 1999; Watson and Bridges, 1999) also produced key contributions.

A number of social theorists (e.g., Beck, 2000; Brenner, 1998; Giddens, 1990; Taylor, 1996) have examined the 'embedded statism' that has marked the social sciences generally and become one obstacle to a full theorization of some of these issues. At the heart of embedded statism is the explicit or implicit assumption that the nation-state is the container of social processes. To this I would add two further features: the implied correspondence of national territory with the national, and the associated implication that the national and the non-national are two mutually exclusive conditions.

These various assumptions work well for many of the subjects studied in the social sciences, but they are not helpful in elucidating a growing number of situations when it comes to globalization and to a whole variety of transnational processes now being studied by social scientists. Nor are those assumptions helpful for developing the requisite research techniques. Further, while they describe conditions that have held for a long time – throughout much of the history of the modern state since the First World War and in some cases even earlier – we are now seeing their partial unbundling.[1] For instance, one of the features of the current phase of globalization is that the fact a process happens within the territory of a sovereign state does not necessarily mean it is a national process. Conversely, the national (for example, firms, capital, cultures) may increasingly be located outside national territory, for instance, in a foreign country or in digital spaces. This localization of the global, or of the non-national, in national territories, and the localization of the national outside national territories, undermines a key duality running through many of the methods and conceptual frameworks prevalent in the social sciences – that the national and the non-national are mutually exclusive.

This partial unbundling of the national has significant implications for our analysis and theorization of major social transformations such as globalization and the possibility of focusing on the city to get at some of their critical empirical features; and it has significant implications for the city as an object of study. The city has long been a construct subject to debate, whether in early writings (Lefebvre, 1991/1974; Castells, 1972; Harvey, 1973) or in very recent ones (Brenner, 1998; Paddison, 2001; Drainville, 2004; Lloyd, 2005). Today we are seeing a partial unbundling of national space and of the traditional hierarchies of scale centered on the national, with the city nested somewhere between the local and the region. This unbundling, albeit partial, makes it problematic to conceptualize the city as nested in

such hierarchies. Major cities have historically been nodes where a variety of processes intersect in particularly pronounced concentrations. In the context of globalization, many of these processes are operating at a global scale cutting across historical borders, with the added complexities this brings with it.

Cities emerge as one territorial or scalar moment in a transurban dynamic.[2] This is, however, not the city as a bounded unit, but the city as a complex structure that can articulate a variety of cross-boundary processes and reconstitute them as a partly urban condition (Sassen, 2001). Further, this type of city cannot be located simply in a scalar hierarchy that puts it beneath the national, regional and global. It is one of the spaces of the global, and it engages the global directly, often by-passing the national. Some cities may have had this capacity long before the current era; but today these conditions have been multiplied and amplified to the point that they can be read as contributing to a qualitatively different urban era. Pivoting theorization and research on the city is one way of cutting across embedded statism and capturing the *rescaling* of spatial hierarchies under the way.

Besides the challenge of overcoming embedded statism, there is the challenge of recovering place in the context of globalization, telecommunications and the proliferation of transnational and translocal dynamics. It is perhaps one of the ironies at the start of a new century that some of the old questions of the early Chicago School of Urban Sociology should resurface as promising and strategic to understand certain critical issues today. One might ask if their methods might be of particular use in recovering the category place (Park et al., 1967; Suttles, 1968; see also Duncan, 1959) at a time when dominant forces such as globalization and telecommunications seem to signal that place and the details of the local no longer matter. Robert Park and the Chicago School conceived of 'natural areas' as geographic areas determined by unplanned, subcultural forces. This was an urban sociology that used fieldwork within a framework of human ecology and contributed many rich studies mapping detailed distributions and assuming functional complementarity among the diverse 'natural areas' they identified in Chicago.[3]

Yet the old categories are not enough. Some of the major conditions in cities today, including the urban moment of non-urban dynamics, challenge the mainstream forms of theorization and urban empirical analysis. Fieldwork is a necessary step in capturing many of the new aspects in the urban condition, including those having to do with the major trends focused on in this chapter. But assuming complementarity or functionalism brings us back to the notion of the city as a bounded space rather than one site, albeit a strategic one, where multiple transboundary processes intersect and produce distinct socio-spatial formations. Recovering place can only partly be met through the research techniques of the old Chicago School of Urban Sociology (see, for example, the debate in *City and Community*, 2002; Dear, 2002; Soja, 2000; see also Smith, 1995). I do think we need to go back to some of the depth of engagement with urban areas that the School represented and the effort towards detailed mappings. The type of ethnographies done by Duneier (1999), Klinenberg (2003) and Wright (1997), the scholars in Burawoy et al. (1991), the type of spatial analysis developed by Sampson (2001), are excellent examples, using many of the techniques yet working within a different set of framing assumptions.

But that is only part of the challenge of recovering place. Large cities around the world are the terrain where multiple globalization processes assume concrete, localized forms. These localized forms are, in good part, what globalization is about. Recovering place means recovering the multiplicity of presences in this landscape. The large city of today has emerged as a strategic site for a whole range of new types of operations – political, economic, 'cultural', subjective (Abu-Lughod, 1994; Allen et al., 1999; Anderson, 1990; Bartlett, 2005; Clark and Hoffman-Martinot, 1998; Fincher and Jacob, 1998; Hagedorn, 2004; Krause and Petro, 2003; Lloyd, 2005; Watson and Bridges, 1999; Yuval-Davis, 1999). It is one of the nexi where the formation of new claims materializes and assumes concrete forms. The loss of power at the national level produces the possibility for new forms of power and politics at the subnational level. Further, insofar as the national as container of social process and power is cracked (e.g., Garcia, 2002; Parsa and Keivani, 2002; Sachar, 1990; Taylor, 1995) it opens up possibilities for a geography of politics that links subnational spaces across borders. Cities are foremost in this new geography. One question this engenders is how and whether we are seeing the formation of a new type of transnational politics that localizes in these cities.

Immigration, for instance, is one major process through which a new transnational political economy is being constituted both at the macro level of global labor markets and at the micro level of translocal household survival strategies. It is one largely embedded in major cities insofar as most immigrants, certainly in the developed world, whether in the United States, Japan or Western Europe, are concentrated in major cities (Bhachu, 1985; Boyd, 1989; Castles and Miller, 2003; Georges, 1990; Hondagneu-Sotelo, 1994; Mahler, 1995). It is, according to some scholars (Castles and Miller, 2003; Ehrenreich and Hochschild, 2003; Samers, 2002; Sassen, 1998: Part One; Skeldon, 1997), one of the constitutive processes of globalization today, even though not recognized or represented as such in mainstream accounts of the global economy. The city is one of the key sites for the empirical study of these transnational flows and household strategies.

Global capital and the new immigrant workforce are two major instances of transnationalized actors with features that constitute each as a somewhat unitary actor overriding borders while at the same time in contestation with each other inside cities (Sassen, 1998: ch. 1; Ehrenreich and Hochschild, 2003; see also, e.g., Bonilla et al., 1998; Cordero-Guzman et al., 2001). Researching and theorizing these issues will require approaches that diverge from the more traditional studies of political elites, local party politics, neighborhood associations, immigrant communities, and others, through which the political landscape of cities and metropolitan regions has been conceptualized in sociology.

In the next three sections I focus on some of these issues in greater detail.

THE CITY AS A SITE FOR RESEARCH ABOUT THE GLOBAL INFORMATION ECONOMY

The concept of the city is complex, imprecise and charged with specific historical meanings (e.g., Park et al., 1967; Castells, 1972; Harvey, 1985; Sennett, 1994; Thrift and Amin, 2002). A more abstract category might be centrality, one of the properties constitutive of cities, and, in turn, one they have historically provided and produced. Historically, centrality has largely been embedded in the central city. One of the changes brought about by the new conditions is the reconfiguring of centrality: the central city is today but one form of centrality. Important emerging spaces for the constitution of centrality are the new transnational networks of cities, global city-regions and electronic space (Abrahamson, 2004; Castells, 1996; Graham and Marvin, 1996; Rutherford, 2004; Sassen, 2001; Scott, 2001; Simmonds and Hack, 2000).

A focus on centrality does not necessarily address matters such as the boundaries of cities or what cities actually are. These are partly empirical questions (each city is going to have a different configuration of boundaries and contents) and partly theoretical ones (is a city necessarily a civitas, is any large urban agglomeration a city?). The question is, rather, what are the conditions for the continuity of centrality in advanced economic systems in the face of major new organizational forms and technologies that maximize the possibility for geographic dispersal at the regional, national and global scale, and ensure simultaneous system integration?

A second major issue for thinking about the city as a site for researching non-urban dynamics concerns the narratives we have constructed about the city and its relation to the global economy and to the new technologies. The understandings and the categories that dominate mainstream discussions about the future of advanced economies imply the city has become obsolete for leading economic sectors. We need to subject these notions to critical examination. There are at least two sets of issues that need to be teased out if we are to understand the role, if any, of cities in a global information economy, and hence the capacity of urban research to produce knowledge about that economy. One of these concerns the extent to which these new types of electronic formations, such as electronic financial markets, are indeed disembedded from social contexts. The second set of issues concerns possible instantiations of the global economy and of the new technologies that have not been recognized as such or are contested representations. I have addressed these issues at greater length elsewhere (2003, 2004) and return to them only briefly in the last two sections of this chapter.

Finally, and on a somewhat more theorized level, there are certain properties of power that make cities strategic. Power needs to be historicized to overcome the abstractions of the concept. Power is not simply an attribute or a sort of factor endowment. It is actively produced and reproduced. Many of the studies in urban sociology focused on the local dimensions of power (e.g., Domhoff, 1991; Logan and Molotch, 1987; Nakhaie, 1997; Porter, 1965) have made important contributions in this regard. Beyond this type of approach, one of today's aspects in the production of power structures concerns new forms of economic power and the re-location of certain forms of power from the state to the market, partly due to deregulation and privatization. In the case of cities, this brings with it also questions about the built environment and the architectures of centrality that represent different types of power (Krause and Petro, 2003). Cities have long been places for the spatialization of power. More generally, we might ask whether power has spatial correlates, or a spatial moment? In terms of the economy, this question could be operationalized more concretely: Can the current economic system, with its strong tendencies towards concentration in ownership and control, have a space economy that lacks points of physical concentration? It is hard to think about a discourse on the future of cities that would not include this dimension of power.

To some extent, it is the major cities in the highly developed world which most clearly display the processes discussed here, or best lend themselves to the heuristics deployed. However, increasingly these processes are present in cities in developing countries as well (Cohen et al.,

1996; Knox and Taylor, 1995; Santos et al., 1994; Stren, 1996). Their lesser visibility is often due to the fact they are submerged in the megacity syndrome. Sheer population size and urban sprawl create their own orders of magnitude (e.g., Dogan and Kasarda, 1988; Gugler, 2004); and while they may not much alter the power equation I describe, they do change the weight, and the legibility, of some of these properties (e.g., Cohen et al., 1996; Marcuse and Van Kempen, 2000; Portes et al., 1989; Stren, 1996).

One way of framing the issue of centrality is by focusing on larger dynamics rather than beginning with the city as such. For instance, we could note that the geography of globalization contains both a dynamic of dispersal and of centralization, the latter a condition that has only recently been recognized in macro-level globalization studies. Most of these have focused on dispersal patterns. Yet the massive trends towards the spatial dispersal of economic activities at the metropolitan, national and global levels which we associate with globalization have contributed to a demand for new forms of territorial centralization of top-level management and control operations (Sassen, 2001: Parts One and Two). The fact, for instance, that firms world-wide now have well over half a million affiliates outside their home countries signals that the sheer number of dispersed factories and service outlets that are part of a firm's integrated operation creates massive new needs for central coordination and servicing. In brief, the spatial dispersal of economic activity made possible by globalization and telecommunications contributes to an expansion of central functions *if* this dispersal is to take place under the continuing concentration in control, ownership and profit appropriation that characterizes the current economic system.

It is at this point that the city enters the discourse. Cities regain strategic importance because they are favored sites for the production of these central functions. National and global markets as well as globally integrated organizations require central places where the work of globalization gets done. Finance and advanced corporate services are industries producing the organizational commodities necessary for the implementation and management of global economic systems. Cities are preferred sites for the production of these services, particularly the most innovative, speculative, internationalized service sectors.[4] Further, leading firms in information industries require a vast physical infrastructure containing strategic nodes with hyperconcentration of facilities; we need to distinguish between the capacity for global transmission/communication and the material conditions that make this possible. Finally, even the most advanced information industries have a production process that is at least partly place-bound because of the combination of resources it requires even when the outputs are hypermobile; the tendency in the specialized literature has been to study these advanced information industries in terms of their hypermobile outputs rather than the actual work processes, which include top-level professionals as well as clerical and manual service workers.

When we start by examining the broader dynamics in order to detect their localization patterns, we can begin to observe and conceptualize the formation, at least incipient, of transnational urban systems. The growth of global markets for finance and specialized services, the need for transnational servicing networks due to sharp increases in international investment, the reduced role of the government in the regulation of international economic activity and the corresponding ascendance of other institutional arenas with a strong urban connection – all these point to the existence of a series of transnational networks of cities. These are of many different kinds and types. Business networks are probably the most developed, given the growth of a global economy. But we also see a proliferation of social, cultural, professional and political networks connecting particular sets of cities.

To a large extent the major business centers in the world today draw their importance from these transnational networks. There is no such entity as a single global city – and in this sense there is a sharp contrast with the erstwhile capitals of empires.[5] These networks of major international business centers constitute new geographies of centrality. The most powerful of these new geographies of centrality at the global level binds the major international financial and business centers: New York, London, Tokyo, Paris, Frankfurt, Zurich, Amsterdam, Los Angeles, Sydney, Hong Kong, among others. But this geography now also includes cities such as Bangkok, Seoul, Taipei, Shanghai, Saō Paulo, Mexico City. The intensity of transactions among these cities, particularly through the financial markets, trade in services, and investment, has increased sharply, and so have the orders of magnitude involved. There has been a sharpening inequality in the concentration of strategic resources and activities between each city and others in its country. This has consequences for the role of urban systems in national territorial integration. Although this role has never quite been what its model signals, the last decade has seen a further acceleration in the fragmentation of national territory. National urban systems are being partly unbundled as their major cities become part of a new or strengthened transnational urban system.

But we can no longer think of centers for international business and finance simply in terms of the corporate towers and corporate culture at their center. The international character of major cities lies not only in their telecommunication infrastructure and foreign firms: it lies also in the many different cultural environments in which these workers and others exist. This is one arena where we have seen the growth of an enormously rich scholarship (Feagin and Vera, 1996; King, 1990; Ruggiero and South, 1997; Skillington, 1998; Smith and Guarnizo, 2001; Valle and Torres, 2000; Zukin, 1991). Today's major cities are in part the spaces of postcolonialism and indeed contain conditions for the formation of a postcolonialist discourse. This is likely to become an integral part of the future of such cities.

A NEW TRANSNATIONAL POLITICAL GEOGRAPHY

The incorporation of cities into a new crossborder geography of centrality also signals the emergence of a parallel political geography. Major cities have emerged as a strategic site not only for global capital, but also for the transnationalization of labor and the formation of translocal communities and identities or subjectivities (e.g., Boyd, 1989; Cordero-Guzman et al., 2001; Mahler, 1995; Smith, 1995). In this regard cities are a site for new types of political operations. The centrality of place in a context of global processes makes possible a transnational economic and political opening for the formation of new claims and hence for the constitution of entitlements, notably rights to place. At the limit, this could be an opening for new forms of 'citizenship' (e.g., Dawson, 1999; Holston, 1996; Sassen, 2003; Torres et al., 1999). The emphasis on the transnational and hypermobile character of capital has contributed to a sense of powerlessness among local actors, a sense of the futility of resistance. But an analysis that emphasizes place suggests that the new global grid of strategic sites is a terrain for politics and engagement (Abu-Lughod, 1994; Drainville, 2004; King, 1996; Sandercock, 2003).

This is a space that is both place-centered in that it is embedded in particular and strategic locations, and it is transterritorial because it connects sites that are not geographically proximate yet are intensely connected to each other through various networks. Is there a transnational politics embedded in the centrality of place and in the new geography of strategic places, such as is, for instance, the new worldwide grid of global cities? This is a geography that cuts across national borders and the old North–South divide. But it does so along bounded 'filières', (e.g., Bonilla et al., 1998). It is a set of specific and partial rather than all-encompassing dynamics. It is not only the transmigration of capital that takes place in this global grid, but also that of people, both rich, that is, the new transnational professional workforce, and poor, that is, most migrant workers; and it is a space for the transmigration of cultural forms, the reterritorialization of 'local' subcultures.

If we consider that large cities concentrate both the leading sectors of global capital and a growing share of disadvantaged populations – immigrants, many of the disadvantaged women, people of color generally and, in the megacities of developing countries, masses of shanty dwellers – then we can see that cities have become a strategic terrain for a whole series of conflicts and contradictions (Allen et al., 1999; Body-Gendrot, 1999; Drainville, 2004; Isin, 2000; Massey and Denton, 1993; Sennett, 1990; Soja, 2000; Wilson, 1997). We can then think of cities also as one of the sites for the contradictions of the globalization of capital, even though, heeding Katznelson's (1992) observation, the city cannot be reduced to this dynamic.

One way of thinking about the political implications of this strategic transnational space anchored in cities is in terms of the formation of new claims on that space. The city has indeed emerged as a site for new claims: by global capital which uses the city as an 'organizational commodity', but also by disadvantaged sectors of the urban population, frequently as internationalized a presence in large cities as capital. The 'de-nationalizing' of urban space and the formation of new claims by transnational actors, raise the question Whose city is it?

Foreign firms and international business people have increasingly been entitled to do business in whatever country and city they choose – entitled by new legal regimes, by the new economic culture and through progressive deregulation of national economies. They are among the new city users. The new city users have made an often immense claim on the city and have reconstituted strategic spaces of the city in their image. Their claim to the city is rarely contested, even though the costs and benefits to cities have barely been examined. They have profoundly marked the urban landscape. For Martinotti (1993), they contribute to change the social morphology of the city; the new city of these city users is a fragile one, whose survival and successes are centered on an economy of high productivity, advanced technologies, intensified exchanges. It is a city whose space consists of airports, top-level business districts, top-of-the-range hotels and restaurants, in brief, a sort of urban glamour zone. Urban tourism further adds to this emergence of city users (Fainstein and Judd, 1999).

Perhaps at the other extreme are those who use urban political violence to make their claims on the city, claims that lack the de facto legitimacy enjoyed by the new 'city users'. These are claims made by actors struggling for recognition, entitlement, claiming their rights to the city (Body-Gendrot, 1999; Hagedorn, 2004; Wacquant, 1997). These claims have, of course, a long history; every new epoch brings specific conditions to the manner in which the claims are made. The growing weight of 'delinquency' (for example, smashing cars and shopwindows; robbing and burning stores) in some of these uprisings over the past decade in major cities of the developed world is perhaps an indication of the sharpened socio-economic inequality – the distance, as seen and as lived, between the urban glamour zone and the urban war zone. The extreme visibility of the difference is likely to contribute to further brutalization of the conflict: the indifference and greed of the new elites versus the hopelessness and rage of the poor (Merrifield and Swyngedouw, 1997).

There are two aspects in this formation of new claims that have implications for the transnational politics that are increasingly being played out in major cities. One is the sharp and perhaps sharpening differences in the representation of claims by different sectors, notably international business and the vast population of low income 'others' – immigrants, women, people of color generally. The second aspect is the increasingly transnational element in both types of claims and claimants. It signals a politics of contestation embedded in specific places but transnational in character. One challenge for urban sociology is how to capture such a cross-border dynamic with existing or new categories and, in doing so, how not to lose the city as a site.

CITIES AND POLITICAL SUBJECTIVITY

This chapter started with a consideration of the Chicago School of urban sociology and its possible contribution to some of the challenges current developments pose for urban theory. This concluding section of the chapter goes back to Weber's *The City* in order to examine the production of political subjectivity signaled by the preceding section.

In his effort to specify the ideal-typical features of what constitutes the city, Weber sought out a certain type of city – most prominently the cities of the late Middle Ages rather than the modern industrial cities of his time. Weber sought a kind of city which combined conditions and dynamics that forced its residents and leaders into creative and innovative responses/adaptations. Further, he posited that these changes produced in the context of the city signaled transformations that went beyond the city and could institute often fundamental transformations. In that regard, the city offered the possibility of understanding far-reaching changes that could – under certain conditions – eventually encompass society at large.

There are two aspects of Weber's *The City* that are of particular importance here. Weber helps us understand under what conditions cities can be positive and creative influences on people's lives. For Weber, cities are a set of social structures that encourage individuality and innovation and hence are an instrument of historical change. There is in this intellectual project a deep sense of the historicity of these conditions. Modern urban life did not correspond to this positive and creative power of cities; Weber saw modern cities as dominated by large factories and office bureaucracies. My own reading of the Fordist city corresponds in many ways to Weber's in the sense that the strategic scale under Fordism is the national scale and cities lose significance. It is the large Fordist factory and the mines which emerge as key sites for the political work of the disadvantaged and those without or with only limited power.

Struggles around political, economic, legal and cultural issues centered in the realities of cities can become the catalysts for new trans-urban developments in all these institutional domains – markets, participatory governance, rights for members of the urban community regardless of lineage, judicial recourse, cultures of engagement and deliberation. For Weber, it is particularly the cities of the late Middle Ages that combine the conditions that pushed urban residents, merchants, artisans and leaders to address them and deal with them. These transformations could make for epochal change beyond the city itself: Weber shows us how in many of these cities these struggles led to the creation of the elements of what we could call governance systems and citizenship.

The particular analytic element I want to extricate from this aspect of Weber's understanding and theorization of the city is the historicity of those conditions which make cities strategic sites for the enactment of important transformations in multiple institutional domains. Today a certain type of city – the global city – has emerged as a strategic site for innovations and transformations in multiple institutional domains. Several of the key components of economic globalization and digitization instantiate in this type of city and produce dislocations and destabilizations of existing institutional orders and legal/regulatory/normative frames for handling urban conditions. It is the high level of concentration of these new dynamics in these cities which forces creative responses and innovations. There is, most probably, a threshold effect at work here.

The historicity of this process rests in the fact that under Keynesian policies, particularly the Fordist contract, and the dominance of mass manufacturing as the organizing economic dynamic, cities had lost strategic functions and were not the site for creative institutional innovations. The strategic sites were the large factory at the heart of the larger process of mass manufacturing and mass consumption, and the national government where regulatory frameworks were developed and the Fordist contract instituted. The factory and the government were the strategic sites where the crucial dynamics producing the major institutional innovations of the epoch were located. With globalization and digitization – and all the specific elements they entail – global cities emerge as such strategic sites. While the strategic transformations are sharply concentrated in global cities, many are also enacted (besides being diffused) in cities at lower orders of national urban hierarchies.[6]

A second analytic element I want to extricate from Weber's *The City* is the particular type of embeddedness of the transformations he describes and renders as ideal-typical features.

This is not an embeddedness in what we might think of as deep structures because the latter are precisely the ones that are being dislocated or changed and are creating openings for new fundamental arrangements to emerge. The embeddedness is, rather, in very specific conditions, opportunities, constraints, needs, interactions, contestations, interests. The aspect that matters here is the complexity, detail and social thickness of the particular conditions and the dynamics he identifies as enabling change and innovation. This complexity and thickness also produces ambiguities in the meaning of the changes and innovations. It is not always clear whether they are positive – where we might interpret positive as meaning the creation or strengthening of some element, even if very partial or minor, of participatory democracy in the city – and in what time frame their positiveness would become evident. In those cities of the late Middle Ages he saw as being what the city is about, he finds contradictory and multi-valent innovations. He dissects these innovations to understand what they can produce or launch.

The argument I derive from this particular type of embeddedness of change and innovation is that current conditions in global cities are creating not only new structurations of power but also operational and rhetorical openings for new types of political actors which may have been submerged, invisible or without voice. A key element of the argument here is that the localization of strategic components of globalization in these cities means that the disadvantaged can engage the new forms of globalized corporate power, and secondly that their growing numbers and diversity in these cities under these conditions assumes a distinctive 'presence'. This entails a distinction between powerlessness and invisiblity/impotence. The disadvantaged in global cities can gain 'presence' in their engagement with power but also vis-à-vis each other. This is different from the 1950s–1970s period in the United States, for instance, when white flight and the significant departure of major corporate headquartes left cities hollowed out and the disadvantaged in a condition of abandonment. Today, the localization of the global creates a set of objective conditions

of engagement. Examples are the struggles against gentrification, which encroached on minority and disadvantaged neighborhoods and led to growing numbers of homeless beginning in the 1980s, and the struggles for the rights of the homeless, or demonstrations against police brutalizing minority people. These struggles are different from the ghetto uprisings of the 1960s which were short, intense eruptions confined to the ghettos and causing most of the damage in the neighborhoods of the disadvantaged themselves. In these ghetto uprisings there was no engagement with power.

An important element is Weber's emphasis on certain types of innovation and change: the construction of rules and norms precisely because deeper arrangements on which norms had been conditioned are being destabilized.[7] Herein also lie openings for new political actors to emerge, as well as changes in the role or locus of older norms, political actors and forms of authority. This is a highly dynamic configuration where older forms of authority may struggle and succeed in reimposing themselves.[8]

The conditions that today mark the possibility of cities as strategic sites are basically two, and both capture major transformations that are destabilizing older systems organizing territory and politics, as briefly discussed in the first half of the chapter. One of these is the re-scaling of what are the strategic territories that articulate the new politico-economic system. The other is the partial unbundling or at least weakening of the national as container of social process due to the variety of dynamics encompassed by globalization and digitization.[9] The consequences for cities of these two conditions are many: what matters here is that cities emerge as strategic sites for major economic processes and for new types of political actors. More generally one could posit that insofar as citizenship is embedded and in turn marked by its embeddedness (Turner, 1993), these new conditions may well signal the possibility of new forms of citizenship practices and identities.[10]

What is being engendered today in terms of political practices in the global city is quite different from what it might have been in the medieval city of Weber. In the medieval city we see a set of practices that allowed the burghers to set up systems for owning and protecting property and to implement various immunities against despots of all sorts.[11] Today's political practices, I would argue, have to do with the production of 'presence' by those without power and with a politics that claims rights to the city rather than protection of property.[12] What the two situations share is the notion that through these practices new forms of political subjectivity are being constituted and that the city is a key site for this type of political work. The city is, in turn, partly constituted through these dynamics. Far more so than a peaceful and harmonious suburb, the contested city is where the civic is getting built. After the long historical phase that saw the ascendance of the national state and the scaling of key economic dynamics at the national level, the city is once again today a scale for strategic economic and political dynamics.

NOTES

1 There have been many epochs when territories were subject to multiple, or at least more than one, system of rule. In this regard the current condition we see developing with globalization is probably by far the more common one and the period since the First World War – when we saw the gradual institutional tightening of the national state's exclusive authority over its territory – the historical exception. However, the categories for analysis, research techniques and datasets in the social sciences have largely been developed over the last 70 years. Thus we face the difficult and collective task of developing the theoretical and empirical specifications that allow us to accommodate the fact of multiple relations between territory and institutional encasement, rather than the singular one of national state and sovereign rule.

2 I have theorized this in terms of the network of global cities, where the latter are partly a function of that network. For example, the growth of the financial centers in New York or London is fed by what flows through the worldwide network of financial centers given deregulation of national economies. The cities at the top of this global hierarchy concentrate the capacities to maximize their capture of the proceeds, so to speak.

3 We can see this in early works such as *The Taxi Dance Hall* and *The Gold Coast and the Slum* and later in, e.g., Suttles (1968).

4 For instance, only a small share of Fortune 500 firms, which are mostly large industrial firms, have their headquarters in New York City, but over 40 per cent of firms

who earn over half of their revenues from overseas are located in the city. Furthermore, even large industrial firms tend to have certain specialized headquarter functions in New York. For instance, Detroit-based General Motors has its headquarters for finance and public relations in Manhattan.

5 The data are still inadequate; one of the most promising datasets at this time is that organized by Taylor and his colleagues (GaWC, 1998); see also Meyer (2002) and Smith and Timberlake (2002). But much remains to be done in this field.

6 Furthermore, in my reading, particular institutions of the state also are such strategic sites even as there is an overall shrinking of state authority through deregulation and privatization.

7 Much of Weber's examination focuses on the gradual emergence and structuring of the force-composition of the city in various areas under different conditions and its gradual stabilization into a distinct form. He traces the changing composition of forces from the ancient kingships through the patrician city to the demos of the ancient world, from the episcopal structures and fortresses through the city of notables, to the guild-dominated cities in Europe. He is always trying to lay bare the complex processes accompanying the emergence of urban community, which for Weber is akin to what today we might describe in terms of governance and citizenship.

8 Cf. his examination of how these types of changes and innovations derive from his key concepts, or categories for analysis: social actions, social relations and social institutions – all critical to his theory of the urban community.

9 The impact of globalization on sovereignty has been significant in creating operational and conceptual openings for novel actors and subjects. At the limit this means that the state is no longer the only site for sovereignty and the normativity that comes with it, and further, that the state is no longer the exclusive subject for international law and the only actor in international relations. Other actors, from NGOs and minority populations to supranational organizations, are increasingly emerging as subjects of international law and actors in international relations.

10 This can also be extended to the transnational level. The ascendance of a large variety of non-state actors in the international arena signals the expansion of an international civil society. This is clearly a contested space, particularly when we consider the logic of the capital market – profitability at all costs – against that of the human rights regime. But it does represent a space where other actors can gain visibility as individuals and as collective actors, and come out of the invisibility of aggregate membership in a nation-state exclusively represented by the sovereign.

11 This raises a number of questions. For instance, in Russia, where the walled city did not evolve as a centre of urban immunities and liberties, the meaning of citizen might well diverge from concepts of civil society and cities, and belong to the state rather than the city.

12 I use the term presence to name a particular condition within the overall condition of powerlessness. There is a distinction to be made between powerlessness and being an actor even though lacking power. In the context of a strategic space such as the global city, the types of disadvantaged

people described here are not simply marginal; they acquire presence in a broader political process that escapes the boundaries of the formal polity. This presence signals the possibility of a politics. What this politics will be will depend on the specific projects and practices of various communities. Insofar as the sense of membership of these communities is not subsumed under the national, it may well signal the possibility of a transnational politics centered in concrete localities.

BIBLIOGRAPHY

Abrahamson, Mark (2004) *Global Cities*. New York and Oxford: Oxford University Press.

Abu-Lughod, J.L. (1994) *From Urban Village to 'East Village': The Battle for New York's Lower East Side*. Oxford: Blackwell.

Abu-Lughod, J.L. (1999) *New York, Los Angeles, Chicago: America's Global Cities*. Minneapolis, MN: University of Minnesota Press.

Allen, J., Massey, D. and Pryke, M. (eds) (1999) *Unsettling Cities*. New York: Routledge.

Anderson, E. (1990) *Streetwise*. Chicago: University of Chicago Press.

Bartlett, Anne (2005) 'Political subjectivity in the global city'. PhD Dissertation, Department of Sociology, University of Chicago.

Beck, Ulrich (2000) *The Risk Society and Beyond: Critical Issues for Social Theory*. Thousand Oaks, CA: Sage.

Bhachu, P. (1985) *Twice Immigrants*. London: Tavistock Publications.

Body-Gendrot, S. (1999) *The Social Control of Cities*. Oxford: Blackwell.

Bonilla, F., Melendez, E., Morales, R. and de los Angeles Torres, M. (eds) (1998) *Borderless Borders*. Philadelphia, PA: Temple University Press.

Boyd, M. (1989) 'Family and personal networks in international migration: recent developments and new agendas', *International Migration Review*, 23 (3): 638–70.

Brenner, N. (1998) 'Global cities, glocal states: global city formation and state territorial restructuring in contemporary Europe', *Review of International Political Economy*, 5 (1): 1–37.

Burawoy, M. et al. (1991) *Ethnography Unbound: Power and Resistance in the Modern Metropolis*. Berkeley, CA: University of California Press.

Castells, M. (1972) *La Question urbaine*. Paris: Maspero.

Castells, M. (1989) *The Informational City*. Oxford: Blackwell.

Castells, M. (1996) *The Networked Society*. Oxford: Blackwell.

Castles, Stephen and Miller, Mark J. (2003) *The Age of Migration*, 3rd edn. Basingstoke: Palgrave Macmillian.

Chase-Dunn, Christopher K. (1985) 'The system of world cities, 800 AD–1978', in M. Timberlake (ed.) *Urbanization in the World Economy*. Orlando, FL: Academic Press.

City and Community (2002) 1 (1).

Clark, T. and Hoffman-Martinot, V. (eds) (1998) *The New Public Culture*. Oxford: Westview Press.

Cohen, M., Ruble, B., Tulchin, J. and Garland, A. (eds) (1996) *Preparing for the Urban Future. Global Pressures and Local Forces*. Washington DC: Woodrow Wilson Center Press (distributed by The Johns Hopkins University Press).

Cordero-Guzman, Hector R., Smith, Robert C. and Grosfoguel, Ramon (eds) (2001) *Migration, Transnationalization, and Race in a Changing New York*. Philadelphia, PA: Temple University Press.

Dawson, M. (1999) 'Globalization, the racial divide, and a new citizenship', in R. Torres, L. Miron and J.X. Inda (eds) (1999) *Race, Identity and Citizenship*. Oxford: Blackwell. pp. 373–85.

Dear, Michael (2002) 'Los Angeles and the Chicago School: invitation to a debate', *City and Community*, 1 (1): 5–32.

Dogan, M. and Kasarda, J.D. (eds) (1988) *A World of Giant Cities*. Newbury Park, CA: Sage.

Domhoff, G.W. (1991) *Blacks in White Establishments: A Study of Race and Class in America*. New Haven, CT: Yale University Press.

Drainville, Andre (2004) *Contesting Globalization: Space and Place in the World Economy*. London: Routledge.

Duncan, O. (1959) 'Human ecology and population studies', in P. Hauser and O. Dudley (eds), *The Study of Population*. Chicago: University of Chicago Press. pp. 678–726.

Duneier, M. (1999) *Sidewalk*. New York: Farrar, Straus & Giroux.

Ehrenreich, Barbara and Hochschild, Arlie (eds) (2003) *Global Woman*. New York: Metropolitan Books.

Fainstein, Susan and Judd, Dennis (eds) (1999) *Urban Tourism*. New Haven, CT: Yale University Press.

Feagin, J.P. and Vera, H. (1996) *White Racism*. New York: Routledge.

Fincher, Ruth and Jacob, M. (1998) *Cities of Difference*. New York: Guilford.

Garcia, Linda D. (2002) 'The architecture of global network technologies', in S. Sassen (ed.) *Global Networks: Linked Cities*. New York: Routledge. pp. 39–70.

Georges, E. (1990) *The Making of a Transnational Community: Migration, Development, and Cultural*

Change in the Dominican Republic. New York: Columbia University Press.

Giddens, A. (1990) *The Consequences of Modernity.* Cambridge: Polity Press.

GaWC (Globalization and World Cities Study Group and Network) (1998) http://www.lboro.ac.uk/departments/gy/research/gawc.html

Gottdiener, M. (1985) *The Social Production of Urban Space.* Austin, TX: University of Texas Press.

Graham, S. and Marvin, S. (1996) *Telecommunications and the City: Electronic Spaces, Urban Places.* London: Routledge.

Gugler, Joseph (2004) *World Cities Beyond the West.* Cambridge: Cambridge University Press.

Hagedorn, John (ed.) (2004) *Gangs in the Global City: Exploring Alternatives to Traditional Criminology.* Chicago: University of Illinois Press.

Harvey, David (1973) *Social Justice and the City.* Baltimore, MD: John Hopkins University Press.

Harvey, David (1985) *The Urbanization of Capital: Studies in the History and Theory of Capitalist Urbanization.* Baltimore, MD: John Hopkins University Press.

Harvey, Rachel (In process) 'Global cities of gold'. PhD Dissertation, Department of Sociology, University of Chicago.

Holston, J. (ed.) (1996) 'Cities and Citizenship'. Special Issue of *Public Culture*, 8 (2).

Hondagneu-Sotelo, P. (1994) *Gendered Transitions.* Berkeley, CA: University of California Press.

Isin, Engin F. (ed.) (2000) *Democracy, Citizenship and the Global City.* London/New York: Routledge.

Katznelson, I. (1992) *Marxism and the City.* Oxford: The Clarendon Press.

King, A.D. (1990) *Urbanism, Colonialism, and the World Economy. Culture and Spatial Foundations of the World Urban System.* The International Library of Sociology. London/New York: Routledge.

King, A.D. (ed.) (1996) *Representing the City. Ethnicity, Capital and Culture in the 21st Century.* London: Macmillan.

Klinenberg, Eric (2003) *Heat Wave: A Social Autopsy of Disaster in Chicago (Illinois).* Chicago, IL: University of Chicago Press.

Knox, P. and Taylor, P.J. (eds) (1995) *World Cities in a World-System.* Cambridge: Cambridge University Press.

Krause, Linda and Petro, Patrice (eds) (2003) *Global Cities: Cinema, Architecture, and Urbanism in a Digital Age.* New Brunswick, NJ/London: Rutgers University Press.

Lefebvre, Henri (1991/1974) *The Production of Space.* Oxford: Blackwell.

Lloyd, Richard (2005) *NeoBohemia.* London/New York: Routledge.

Logan, J.R. and Molotch, H. (1987) *Urban Fortunes: The Political Economy of Place.* Berkeley, CA: University of California Press.

Mahler, S. (1995) *American Dreaming: Immigrant Life on the Margins.* Princeton, NJ: Princeton University Press.

Marcuse, Peter and van Kempen, Ronald (2000) *Globalizing Cities: A New Spatial Order.* Oxford: Blackwell.

Martinotti, G. (1993) *Metropolis.* Bologna: Il Mulino.

Massey, D. and Denton, N. (1993) *American Apartheid.* Cambridge, MA: Harvard University Press.

Merrifield, A. and Swyngedouw, E. (eds) (1997) *The Urbanization of Injustice.* New York: New York University Press.

Meyer, D. (2002) 'Hong Kong: global capital exchange', in S. Sassen (ed.), *Global Networks, Linked Cities.* London/New York: Routledge. pp. 249–72.

Nakhaie, M. (1997) 'Vertical mosaic among the elites: the new imagery revisited', *Canadian Review of Sociology and Anthropology*, 34 (1): 1–24.

Paddison, Ronan (ed.) (2001) 'Introduction', *Handbook of Urban Studies.* London: Sage.

Palumbo-Liu, D. (1999) *Asian/American.* Stanford, CA: Stanford University Press.

Park, R.E., Burgess, E.W. and McKenzie R.D. (eds) (1967) *The City.* Chicago: University of Chicago Press.

Parsa, Ali and Keivani, Ramin (2002) 'The Hormuz Corridor: building a cross-border region between Iran and the United Arab Emirates', in S. Sassen (ed.), *Global Networks, Linked Cities.* New York/London: Routledge. pp. 183–208.

Porter, J. (1965) *The Vertical Mosaic.* Toronto: University of Toronto Press.

Portes, A., Castells, M. and Benton, L. (eds) (1989) *The Informal Economy: Studies in Advanced and Less Developed Countries.* Baltimore, MD: Johns Hopkins University Press.

Rodriguez, N.P. and Feagin, J.R. (1986) 'Urban specialization in the world system', *Urban Affairs Quarterly*, 22 (2): 187–220.

Ruggiero, V. and South, N. (1997) 'The late-modern city as bazaar: drug markets, illegal enterprise and the barricades', *British Journal of Sociology*, 48 (1): 54–71.

Rutherford, Jonathan (2004) *A Tale of Two Global Cities: Comparing the Territorialities of Telecommunications Developments in Paris and London.* Aldershot/Burlington, VT: Ashgate.

Sachar, A. (1990) 'The global economy and world cities', in A. Sachar and S. Oberg (eds), *The World Economy and the Spatial Organization of Power.* Aldershot: Avebury.

Samers, Michael (2002) 'Immigration and the global city hypothesis: towards an alternative research agenda', *International Journal of Urban and Regional Research*, 26 (2): 389–402.

Sandercock, Leonie (2003) *Cosmopolis II: Mongrel Cities in the 21st Century*. New York/London: Continuum.

Santos, M., De Souze, M.A. and Silveira, M.L. (eds) (1994) *Territorio Globalizacao e Fragmentacao*. Saõ Paulo: Editorial Hucitec.

Sassen, Saskia (1981) 'Exporting capital and importing labor: Caribbean migration to New York City', *Occasional Papers No. 28*. New York: Center for Latin American and Caribbean Studies, New York University.

Sassen, S. (1998) *Globalization and Its Discontents*. New York: New Press.

Sassen, S. (2001) *The Global City: New York, London and Tokyo*, 2nd edn. Princeton, NJ: Princeton University Press.

Sassen, S. (2003) 'The repositioning of citizenship: emergent subjects and spaces for politics', *Berkeley Journal of Sociology: A Critical Review*, 46: 4–26.

Sassen, S. (2004) 'Local actors in global politics', *Current Sociology*, 52 (4): 657–74.

Scott, A.J. (2001) *Global City-Regions*. Oxford: Oxford University Press.

Sennett, R. (1990) *The Conscience of the Eye*. New York: Alfred A. Knopf.

Sennett, R. (1994) *Flesh and Stone: The Body and the City in Western Civilization*. New York: W.W. Norton.

Short, John Rennie and Kim, Yeong-Hyun (1999) *Globalization and the City*. Essex: Longman.

Simmonds, Roger and Hack, Gary (2000) *Global City Regions. Their Emerging Forms*. London/New York: E&FN Spon/Taylor & Francis.

Skeldon, R. (1997) 'Hong Kong: colonial city to global city to provincial city?', *Cities*, 14 (5): 265–71.

Skillington, T. (1998) 'The city as text: constructing Dublin's identity through discourse on transportation and urban re-development in the press', *British Journal of Sociology*, 49 (3): 456–74.

Sklair, L. (1991) *Sociology of the Global System: Social Changes in Global Perspective*. Baltimore, MD: Johns Hopkins University Press.

Smith, David (1995) 'The new urban sociology meets the old: re-reading some classical human ecology', *Urban Affairs Review*, 30 (3): 432–57.

Smith, D.A. and Timberlake, M. (2002) 'Hierarchies of dominance among world cities: a network approach', in S. Sassen (ed.), *Global Networks, Linked Cities*. London/New York: Routledge. pp. 117–43.

Smith, M. Peter and Guarnizo, Luis (2001) *Transnationalism from Below*. New Brunswick: Transaction Publishers.

Soja, Edward W. (2000) *Postmetropolis: Critical Studies of Cities and Regions*. Oxford: Blackwell.

Stren, R. (1996) 'The studies of cities: popular perceptions, academic disciplines, and emerging agendas', in M. Cohen, B. Ruble, J. Tulchin and A. Garland (eds), *Preparing for the Urban Future. Global Pressures and Local Forces*. Washington, DC: Woodrow Wilson Center Press (distributed by Johns Hopkins University Press). pp. 392–420.

Suttles, G.D. (1968) *The Social Order of the Slum*. Chicago: University of Chicago Press.

Taylor, Peter J. (1995) 'World cities and territorial states: the rise and fall of their mutuality', in P.J. Taylor and P.L. Knox (eds), *World Cities in a World-System*. Cambridge: Cambridge University Press. pp. 48–62.

Taylor, Peter (1996) 'On the nation-state, the global and social science', *Environment and Urban Planning*, A28: 1917–28.

Thrift, Nigel and Amin, Ash (2002) *Cities: Reimagining the Urban*. Cambridge: Polity Press.

Timberlake, M. (ed.) (1985) *Urbanization in the World Economy*. Orlando, FL: Academic Press.

Torres, R., Miron, L. and Inda, J.X. (eds) (1999) *Race, Identity, and Citizenship*. Oxford: Blackwell.

Valle, Victor M. and Torres, Rodolfo D. (2000) *Latino Metropolis*. Minneapolis, MN: University of Minnesota Press.

Wajcman, Judy (2002) 'Information Technologies and the Social Sciences'. Special Issue of *Current Sociology*, 50 (May).

Wacquant, L. (1997) 'Inside the zone', *Theory, Culture, and Society*, 15 (2): 1–36.

Watson, S. and Bridges, G. (eds) (1999) *Spaces of Culture*. London: Sage.

Wilson, W.J. (1997) *When Work Disappears*. New York: Alfred A. Knopf.

Wright, T. (1997) *Out of Place*. Albany, NY: State University of New York Press.

Yuval-Davis, N. (1999) 'Ethnicity, gender relations and multiculturalism', in R. Torres, L. Miron and J.X. Inda (eds), *Race, Identity, and Citizenship*. Oxford: Blackwell. pp. 112–25.

Zukin, S. (1991) *Landscapes of Power*. Berkeley, CA: University of California Press.

27

Sociology of Deviance: the Disciplines of Social Exclusion

HEINZ STEINERT

INTRODUCTION: DEVIANCE AS A FIELD OF SOCIOLOGICAL STUDY

This chapter interprets recent thinking about deviance in Western Europe and the United States in its relation to the social changes in the last 20 years of the twentieth century. The last two decades of a century of counter-Enlightenment marked a distinctive phase of economic and social development. The predominant Fordist mode of production, which mostly meant lifting all obstacles to consumerism, hedonism, individualism and informality, has been supplanted by globalization, neoliberalism and the service- or knowledge-economy. The new formation includes a new praxis of politics with (and concomitant knowledge about) deviance. The sociology of deviance is an adaptive or oppositional part of this.

To begin to understand this phase it is useful to see the sharp contrast to the Fordist formation in the 1960s and 1970s. Then we generally had a public attitude of supporting the needy, of resocialization and of democratic inclusion. If in doubt, it was the social norm that had to be re-examined, not the deviation from it. The predecessor chapter to this, by Andrew Scull (1988), was written under this perspective: it took a relatively consolidated labeling theory and a

politics of benign social control for granted. In contrast to this, we now have a relatively consolidated politics of social exclusion. The deviant, the foreign and the poor are now met with a considerable willingness to get them out and to keep them out. Prison rates since the 1980s have more than tripled in the United States and drawn equal with the former USSR. Everywhere in the West there have been attempts to curb immigration. It is no exaggeration to call this politics of social exclusion a new wave of nationalist, race and class discrimination. In the now dominant populist politics, knowledge about deviance has taken on a new function: to target the 'losers', the 'underclass' and the 'superfluous', as they are now called.

Certainly this general tendency does not go uncontested. And it is itself not unitary, but rather the result of diverse forces supporting and contesting each other, with some unexpected outcomes. To understand the development of knowledge about deviance in some detail, a broad and multi-faceted discourse has to be considered.[1]

Two approaches to such an analysis are used here: placing academic contributions in the wider discursive field (which is mainly determined by relevant social movements) and describing 'defining experiences' in this field, nodal points of confluence in which the interplay of forces becomes visible.

PROBLEMS OF DEFINITION

Deviance is the subject of (mostly introductory) courses in the social sciences. But it is not one of the consolidated sub-fields of sociology. Rather, its subject matter is spread over a number of specializations, from criminology and abnormal psychology to historical ethnographies of rural resistance or Holocaust studies. The textbooks on deviance usually cover a field narrowed in three ways.

First, by a normative assumption, only phenomena that are undesirable – that ought not to occur – are seen as deviant (Black, 1984: 5; similarly Tittle, 1995: 132). Positive deviance (Goode, 1991) is excluded.[2]

Second, there is an under-representation of state-organized crime. The historical examples of slavery and colonialism or the great European witch craze, all powerful examples of state- and church-organized violence and destruction, are quite well researched and theorized but rarely brought into the field of the sociology of deviance. Neither is the research on 'death by government'.[3] Connected to this is the amazing fact that the whole topic of state-organized crime treats the example of genocidal states, including the Nazi state, marginally if at all.

Third, there is a strong tendency to regard as deviant only those categories that are seen as social problems, which mostly constitute a middle ground of tolerated deviance. Youths, fashions and fads, 'nuts, sluts and perverts', the subcultures of more or less bizarre activities and predilections, and the harmless and often transitory deviance of otherwise respectable persons are examples.

The politics of deviance comprises the drawing and patrolling of society's boundaries. In its harsher forms this means varying degrees of social exclusion. At the extreme, the utmost negative valuation defines the category as less than human: barbarians and savages or slaves and serfs. External and internal enemies often get dual ascriptions: despised and ridiculed,

but at the same time exalted to super cruelty, baseness and threatening to all humanity.[4] Regrettably, the examples for this are not only historical.

Institutions of deviance

Deviance, in a sociological understanding, is not a specific behavior or characteristic of a category of persons. Rather, deviance is a social relation: a set of social institutions, in which such behaviors and characteristics are defined, recognized and processed. We can distinguish four such structured, habitual and organized ways of processing deviance. The main institutions are *crime and punishment* (organized in criminal law, the judiciary and corrections) and *weakness and care* (the illness and the infirmity models supported by psychiatry, clinical psychology, social work and welfare). Obviously, these institutions are related to poverty, which, interestingly, is not seen as deviant *per se*. The institutions of *neutralization* are organized in 'safety-valve activities' like sports and tourism or in niches (clubs, carnivals, the artists' subculture and nightlife) set aside so they do not bother the rest of society too much. Most consequentially, there are institutions of *subhumanity and social exclusion*, organized in slavery, colonialism and in some forms of enemy treatment, especially mass murder and genocide.

All these institutions sort actions and human beings into broader or narrower categories. These are primarily derived from the regulatory needs of these institutions, not from persons' inherent characteristics. Immigration offices sort us into nationalities – and then based on the security we can give that we will behave according to regulations. They do not do this because we have passports; rather we carry passports because they want to do this sorting.[5]

There is a necessary individual complement to this. We are not just passive objects of such identification, but take an active part in the creation of categories as well as in the sorting – of others and of ourselves. The period under consideration has produced an enormous literature concerned with identity.[6] Finding, negotiating, projecting, hiding, assuming an identity, but mainly insisting on having our identity recognized, was one of the big topics of these 20 years.[7]

The social science study of deviance is one special endeavor to produce knowledge about these processes of categorizing and institutional subsumption. It is not the only source of such knowledge and not the most powerful player in the field. To describe social knowledge about deviance, and the place of the sociology of deviance in it, this contested terrain has to be mapped.

MAPPING THE DISCURSIVE FIELD

Relative to the 1960s and 1970s, the most obvious changes in the phase under consideration are modifications in the status of a number of forms of deviance brought about by (new) social and political movements. These movements act in a changed arena, as the whole field of politics has moved onto the stage of an advanced culture industry (Steinert, 2003). Strange habits and predilections that we once tried to hide have become marketable commodities on TV talk shows. Experts now peddle their wares in competing culture-industry formats, and politics in general has become more populist. Academic life has changed under the influence of movements and culture-industry involvement.

The discursive field of deviance can be described through the social movements that scandalize or normalize deviance and the academic contributions to these struggles.

Normalizing and scandalizing movements

Most of the movements to be considered here continue a struggle that started much earlier. They do their present work on the backdrop of that history and often with the impression that conditions have become harsher for them. But they also do it in the spirit of success, from which they will not slide back. The distinction I suggest refers to whether they aim at alleviating some entrenched understanding of some

'deviance', or whether they need to produce awareness that something is not as it should be in the first place.

Perhaps the most successful *normalizing movement* has been the gay and lesbian movement, which made the former deviance of homosexuality an accepted variant of the private pursuit of happiness. Legislation decriminalizing homosexuality was enacted in the 1970s in many countries, and since then the normalizing struggle has been a political and social success.[8] Even beyond formal rules, the emotions of horror and shame this 'vice' once elicited have substantially disappeared.

Somewhat less radically, the former deviance of physical and mental handicap has lost much of its stigma. In the Western world, great efforts have been made to integrate such children into schools and grown-ups into the workplace and all into family life. Physical arrangements have slowly been adapted to their special needs (Fleischer and Zames, 2001).

A second group of movements could be called *scandalizing movements*. They have turned formerly taken-for-granted discriminations into visible and unacceptable domination – and have thereby created instances of deviance that formerly did not appear as such.

The feminist movement broke the taken-for-granted male perspective and produced theories of male dominance and/or patriarchy (which is an important difference). It successfully scandalized male violence against women, redefining rape, domestic violence and child abuse. What before was seen as the husband's legal right was turned into deviance and crime.

In other fields, the feminist movement had normalizing as well as scandalizing effects. Prostitution was normalized to a degree in campaigns to make it a service profession like others, renaming prostitutes 'sex-workers', or even 'sex-therapists'. On the other hand, there were other forms of prostitution, especially in the context of neocolonialism, that had to be scandalized as slavery and trade in women. Pornography, too, has been scandalized, becoming the (demeaning) theory to the (violent domination) practice of rape.

Similarly, the anti-racist, postcolonialism and multiculturalism movements, and the prolongation of the civil rights movement, scandalize other formerly taken-for-granted forms of discrimination. They have broken down the dominant white perspective in movements against superiority, against elitism and elite self-images and generally against 'Herrenmenschentum' (claim for super-humanity and master-race status). The deviance resulting from this scandalization is that of the racist, the xenophobe, the authoritarian and the prejudiced person (and occasionally stronger words, like fascist or Nazi).

The ecological movement, too, had to be mostly a scandalizing movement, showing up the dangerous and hidden-costs side of an industrial economy. Again, new forms of deviance were created, in law as ecological crime, and socially as a new form of morality. Connected to this is a form of health consciousness that has produced new norms of diet and lifestyle. Included here we have the most amazing example of the creation of a new form of deviance: the complete turnaround in the norms of smoking tobacco.

Counter-movements

There certainly are counter-movements to all of these. They can be grouped into *reaffirmation-of-order* and *market-populist, neoliberal* movements.

Reaffirmation of order is most obvious in government, with its wars on drugs and crime which have replaced the war on poverty. It is also visible in religious fundamentalists' battles against abortion, homosexuality and divorce. Movements that put a high value on the family usually do this in the expectation that the functioning family is a nucleus of order and authority. This can be directed against feminism, which is then seen as breaking up the family. The more extreme articulations affirm male and white supremacy, and in the even more racialized version, Aryan supremacy. In these cases, a clear order of domination is sought.[9]

The market-populist, neoliberal development is the most vigorous and the most consequential of these past 20 years. It has inaugurated a whole new set of values and rationalities centered on a conception of universal and unrestrained competition, which lets the 'invisible hand' bring about the result most beneficial for all. With shares in the hands (or at least the pension funds) of everyone, and a strict shareholder-value (in contrast to a long-term managerial) orientation, this unfettering of markets is believed to enrich labor as well as capital. Labor is strictly individualized (no collective, unionized or state-guaranteed solutions for them) and redefined as 'labor-power entrepreneurs.'[10] With this goes a belief in some 'knowledge economy' that has replaced the former economy of material production. The traditional working class, and its manual work, is declared to be vanishing fast (together with its necessary masculinity).

The deviance defined by this approach relies on state regulations and transfers (not so much to capital, as these are not usually talked about, but to labor). Poverty is redefined as laziness, a parasitic attitude and a lack of moral fiber. The welfare mother and the junkie are two exemplary figures of the passive type, the mugger and the pusher of the active.

On the less obviously political side of the knowledge economy, consulting and, more specifically, 'psychobabble' have contributed through popular thought and entertainment[11] to create new forms of deviance. The sale of consultant literature and services presupposes a 'problem', a need or, at least, the hope of self-improvement in performance, functioning or looks on the buyer's side.[12]

Academic contributions to the discourse

There are some striking examples of a seeming dependence of practical politics on research results. William Bratton's New York police reform, for example, explicitly claimed adherence to a specific piece of criminological knowledge: the 'broken windows' dynamic. (Signs of neglect in a neighborhood [can] lead into a downward spiral of deterioration, including crime.)

The politics of massive incarceration had a school of juridical thinking, 'just deserts', to support it. Politicians may not have needed this scientific input to get ideas like 'let's try to take all the potential criminals out of circulation by tough sentences', or 'let's not tolerate easily detectable misbehavior, perhaps this way we can deter more serious crime too'. But it certainly was a welcome help to be able to elevate such rules of thumb to the status of theory and cite a professorial authority to confirm common-sense knowledge.

Rather than being useful in such a directly instrumental way, academic work has traditionally performed a synthesizing and reflexive function. Historically this meant the enlightening critique of programs and historical narratives propounded by major religious and political movements. Now, however, instead of, say, five such institutional positions (two churches and three political parties), multiple religious and political movements and numerous TV stations, journals, university departments, think-tanks, publishing houses, free-floating artists and intellectuals all take part in the public competition for having their say. Originality and sensationalism reign. Every position has a counter-position; the serious character of the question is diluted into entertainment. All positions are equally (in)valid.[13]

The academic task has been made more difficult by the multiplication of forces and tendencies. It is endangered by the culture-industry embeddedness. It has, through the same multiplicity, gained in irrelevance as well as possible autonomy.

THE PUBLIC DISCOURSE AND THE SOCIOLOGY OF DEVIANCE

In what follows, four forms of academic contribution will be described. Interspersed are short sketches of exemplary content: the main defining experiences for the sociology of deviance over the past 20 years.

The academic branches of social movements

All of the movements described above have academic representation. But for some, like the feminist or the postcolonial movements, their academic branch is of particular importance, having spawned new specializations, specific studies and research agendas. These have contributed to a redefinition of the sociological enterprise by bringing their specific criticisms to bear upon a discipline dominated by the perspective of 'dead white European males'. This process of widening the perspective of the discipline is far from complete and certainly not uncontested.

The changes concern the very concepts we use. Feminist sociology, for instance, has irreversibly altered the meaning of 'work' in social theory by focusing on household or reproduction work. This has at the same time affected the understanding of family. Gender roles and sexuality have come under inspection and revision in a radical way. Patriarchy as a form of domination, and its function in a capitalist regime, has become a renewed subject of analysis. Processes of exclusion and boundary maintenance, including social definitions of 'sub-humanity' in war, slavery, colonialism and internal servitude, as basic for the capitalist formation, have found attention and interest.

The reaffirmation-of-order and especially the market-populist movements have certainly had their academic representations too. These have reinforced the orthodox explanations of all 'social problems': family breakdown and a general decline of community norms. Women play a special role in this breakdown: the pill and labor force participation set them free. As the predominance of the male breadwinner sags, the result is crime, teenage pregnancy and poverty.[14]

There was a certain convergence in that some former critics took up these topics. 'Taking crime seriously' became a watchword in British critical criminology. In view of conservatives' electoral success in making crime policy a campaign topic, the 'left realist' school shifted its concerns toward victim protection and prevention (Lea and Young, 1984; Young and Matthews, 1992). Among the new victimist agenda groups to be protected (by state punishment) were lower class persons, immigrants, women and children.[15] A relatively broad consensus developed on what has been termed 'populist criminology' (Steinert, 1997b; Cremer-Schäfer and Steinert, 1998). Punitiveness was strengthened. While the movement towards liberation was successful in some fields (homosexuality, handicaps), poverty and criminality, especially in combination with (illegal) immigration, were answered with an exclusionary rhetoric to fit the praxis.

In practically all Western countries the difference between the rich and the poor grew greater. For a time this was conceptualized as 'split society' and 'two-thirds society'. But with gradual resignation to two-digit unemployment figures in Europe, the current concept became 'exclusion'. Just as the eighteenth century had to invent 'class' to conceptualize developing forms of inequality, so do we struggle for a new concept to grasp today's inequalities. 'Exclusion' is one candidate.

Defining experience (I): the New York Zero Tolerance story

The New York Zero Tolerance episode occurred during a period in which, by all available measures, crime was high and on everyone's mind. Politicized by populist politics, this awareness of crime was loaded not only with fear of the 'dangerous classes' again, but with race fears as well.

Politics instigated and instrumentalized fear of crime in a number of electoral campaigns and, significantly, in Ronald Reagan's programs of massive imprisonment and prison privatization, creating a 'prison industry' with its own dynamic in the United States (Christie, 1993; Donziger, 1996, esp. ch. 3; Baer and Chambliss, 1997; Dyer, 2000; Garland, 2001a; Gest, 2001). The contribution of criminologists to such fear-mongering has not been researched systematically. Their use of concepts like 'underclass' or 'persistent offender' (in the German discussion '*Intensiv-Taeter*'), not to mention inventions like 'superpredators' (DiIulio, 1996), would be prime starting points for such analyses.[16] Politics with the fear of crime could, in varying degrees and without the creation of a prison industry, be observed in Europe too.[17]

Bratton's New York police reform, which became famous under the label of 'Zero Tolerance', can be seen as the local contribution – at a rather late point in the process – to the politics of massive punishment and incarceration. In the first place, though, the New York Zero Tolerance experiment was a radical organizational reform. It exchanged high-level personnel and flattened hierarchies, decentralized police work and responsibility for its local effects, and at the same time centralized control by a new computerized system of describing the local crime situation and the famous CompStat sessions at headquarters, in which police activities were programmed and controlled.

This was also one of the best-publicized such reforms ever, but after only two years Bratton was dismissed from his position as police commissioner (by all current accounts, he became too much of a rival for Mayor Rudolph Giuliani). The New York model, often in comparison and in competition with the Chicago community policing one (Skogan and Hartnett, 1997), became a national and international export article.[18]

Bratton attributed his success to a criminological idea: the 'broken windows' model of downward escalation that can be stopped by early intervention, first published by Wilson and Kelling in 1982. It was operationalized by making police intervene actively on minor infractions and on suspicion in the streets. Its campaign against fare-dodgers in the subway, squeegee men and drug couriers, whatever its other effects, certainly changed police work in a radical way. A demoralized organization became active again.

During the same time, crime statistics began to drop quite dramatically, in New York as elsewhere. Obviously, Bratton had to claim this as his success, as did Giuliani. And so did criminologist Kelling (Kelling and Coles, 1996). New York became an export article not only for police reform but also for criminological theory. Practical effect was explicitly made the criterion of valid theory.

More complex interpretations of the drop in crime could be offered: the consolidation of the crack market that ended the warfare over participation, shifts in age composition, an improved employment situation, the simple dislocation of poverty and criminal activities from highly visible inner-city sites to outlying places (if not to the vastly increased prisons), better technical protection of apartments and cars, disarmament efforts, etc. Such lists are, of course, quite unsatisfactory for political as well as scientific debates, even if adequate to describe a multi-faceted reality. They simply make it clear that such 'natural experiments' are not very well suited for theory testing. Good research into the complicated net of effects – not least on the statistics we use – is hard to come by and takes time (see Harcourt, 2001; Taylor, 2001).

The Zero Tolerance experiment has produced high social costs too. Its toughest criticisms arose from the cases of police misconduct encouraged by it, the most scandalous of which were shootings and even torture (Abner Louima). The everyday costs, borne especially by African American and Hispanic communities, still go undocumented.

Defining experience (II): the multiple-personality disorder (MPD) recovered memory incest-and-abuse story

Child abuse, the sexual exploitation of children, is particularly abhorrent, but some aspects of the recent campaign to make the public aware of this problem have been difficult to accept. A lot of the initial evidence came from allegedly therapeutic sessions of 'recovered memory', sometimes with the help of hypnosis. Other evidence came from difficult-to-interpret children's accounts. Some accusations could not be confirmed by additional, independent evidence and did not hold up under rigorous judicial challenge. Accusations were sometimes even put into the context of hard-to-digest phenomena like Satanism. It is not easy to establish whether they are literary fictions and fearful-lusty fantasies or what exactly their reality may be.[19] There were situations that reminded observers of witch-hunts organized by child protection activists. The consequences for those accused, even if not found guilty, were quite real.

The movement to uncover child abuse became organized and international fast. Recovered memory and multiple-personality disorder also became strong movements with their own practitioners and gurus.[20] MPD is a state of person dissociation into at least two, and sometimes a multitude, of roles between which there is no conscious connection. It is understood to be the answer to early experiences of abuse.[21] Recently, at least, the attention these phenomena get seems to have declined. Counter-movements of parents falsely accused of incest have helped to shift the public understanding from 'recovered memory' to 'false memory'.[22]

There has from the beginning been an academic branch to these currents. Efforts were made to produce tenable figures and research information on the phenomena not only of incest and child abuse, but more generally of violence against women. Often this academic branch seems to have been embarrassed by the seeming irrationality of movements, but at the same time there is reluctance to support those who want to deny the relevance of child abuse completely. It is interesting to note that even in an empirically minded setting the point of reference is not 'truth' but political correctness.[23] Recently historical interpretations have gone back to framing the issue in terms of the social meaning of children, taking up where the social history of childhood (Aries, 1962; deMause, 1974) had made an interesting start in the 1960s, but was neglected in the abuse debate (Kincaid, 1998; Heins, 2001).

The academic elaboration of this kind of topic has a tendency to use a broader context of 'violence against women' on the one hand, and of 'masculinity' on the other.[24] The broad information and discussion on rape and wife battering[25] can be joined with the child abuse debate to interpret all these phenomena in the context of a theory of gender relations or of patriarchy. The theoretical formulations also use a conception of patriarchal domination, combined with some class distinctions (Connell, 1987, 1995; Messerschmidt, 1993; Kersten, 1997; Cossins, 2000). In this case, a social-problems-oriented and movement-driven debate has finally produced theoretical interpretations that are seen by many as one of the more interesting innovations in criminology.

Another topic that has been changed enormously by feminist efforts, is hysteria. It has long been noted that the defining illness of the nineteenth century and of psychoanalysis has disappeared in the forms Breuer and Freud studied (Gilman et al., 1993). But increasingly hysteria is being interpreted as a female defense against the many indignities and unrealistic demands of Victorian (and later) gender relations, including relationships with doctors (Showalter, 1985; Bronfen, 1998; Maines, 1999; Bollas, 2000; Mitchell, 2000). These social and historical studies have produced excellent and detailed confirmation and modification of Foucault's (1975) contention that Western sexual and gender relations are a history of the 'production', not the 'repression' of sexuality. There certainly is domination at the basis of this 'illness', which is at the same time one form of negotiating the gender relation.

These lines of theory development converge in, put bluntly, the dismounting of psychoanalysis. The traditional attacks in the name of experimental science, which accused psychoanalysis of being untestable and of unproven effectivity as a therapy, were joined by feminist critique. The much and easily ridiculed idea of 'penis envy' was a bad enough blow, but what really finished Freud for feminists was the assertion that he had, by assuming there were traumatic fantasies of incest, denied the very real sexual abuse of girls rampant at his time – and today (Masson, 1984; Miller, 1984; for a survey of feminist critique see Buhle, 1998).

The lure of general theory

There is a striking proliferation of claims to have produced a general theory for the field in the 20 years surveyed here. The first of these is Donald Black's 'General Theory of Social Control' of 1984 (two edited volumes), later (1993) complemented by his own systematic formulation. Then we have Gottfredson and Hirschi's (1990) 'General Theory of Crime'. Tittle (1995) presents a 'General Theory of Deviance'. Akers (1998) summarizes long years of his work in a 'General Theory of Crime and Deviance'.

There are three ways of deriving a general theory. The *historical critique* surveys the history of relevant thought and identifies a shared and emerging problematic that is identified as 'general'. This classic procedure, as used from Parsons to Habermas, is rarely encountered in criminology. The *subsumption technique* discusses the principal approaches of textbook renown and claims that one of them (in a new modification), or a further concept the author proposes, integrates all the others. The *ordering approach* aspires not so much to structure theories, but the subject matter of a discipline, and offers a general model of factors or (micro and macro) levels and feedback loops between them.[26]

The Gottfredson and Hirschi offer has the highest appeal. Hirschi is on second place in the criminology citation index (Cohn et al., 1998), and there is a growing corpus of empirical work that draws on this theory. By 2000, the number of such reports was big enough to warrant a meta-analysis and the drawing of a balance (Pratt and Cullen, 2000). The point that was taken to be the single most important piece of information in that theory, as shown in what exactly was tested in this corpus of work, was the basic self-control hypothesis: crime is the result of low self-control. The second element is the biographical production and consequent stability of such self-control. According to the theory, it is produced by strict parental control during childhood and is stable afterwards. The third element is the generality of the self-control effect. It applies to all forms of crime and 'analogous behavior' (deviant acts of all kinds below the crime threshold, such as smoking, drinking, involvement in accidents, gambling, loitering).[27] There seems to be a lot of confirmation for the first assumption, whereas for the other two the evidence is not fully consistent. This first assumption, though, has been charged as being a tautology[28] and, further, has a striking similarity to popular and legal assumptions about crime and criminals: they lack self-control. The popular assumption is that self-indulgence problems (in contrast to psychopathology and ability deficit) can and have to be overcome by willpower (Furnham, 1988: 98ff).

One of the conditions of success for a criminological theory is the possibility of deriving feasible[29] research projects from it. The Gottfredson and Hirschi theory meets this condition. We therefore see a little Gottfredson-and-Hirschi-testing industry in the journals. The obvious ideological fit of a reaffirmation that the cause of crime is the criminal's lack of self-control may have advanced its public and political appeal at a time of 'lock-them-up-and-throw-away-the-key' politics. But that alone would not explain the academic success.

Beyond academic competition and claims to fame, the proliferation of general theories must be seen as an answer to the fragmentation of the field. Criminology is widely perceived by its practitioners as having split up into theoretical (or rather, paradigmatic) subcultures none of which can become hegemonic.[30] The general theory attempts seek to reconstitute a common field of the discipline. A strong motivation for ordering is fear that the field is falling apart – or hope for an opportunity to occupy a field that has already fallen apart.

Defining experience (III): the (state-)organized crime story

There was a curious development in European (mainly German-language) criminology in the 1990s. The traditional concept of 'Wirtschaftskriminalität' (economic crime, the German equivalent of white-collar crime) practically disappeared from the discourse and was replaced by 'organized crime' (Pilgram and Kuschej, 1997). The reason is quite obvious in retrospect: the concern over the opening of Eastern Europe and what the demise of communist order and stability there would mean for Western Europe. Also, there was a new danger to be named – the 'Russian Mafia'. Relative to this, the old concerns about EU-subsidies fraud and fraudulent bankruptcies paled. This new form of organized crime became part of the new xenophobia in Western Europe after 1989.

This type of organized crime (OK, as it quickly became known) has slightly contradictory features, combining familial/tribal, military and ultra-capitalist elements in its organization. The fear was that the moderate welfare-capitalist forms of doing business in the secure framework of state guarantees (still current in Western Europe) could not hold up to this predatory competition. In the wider public sphere, OK was, and is, a vehicle to discuss business ethics in a xenophobic context. The seeming absence of an analogous change in US criminology corresponds to the fact that the change to a neoliberal economy was only a small step there. Reagan's unfettering of banking and the stock market with the corresponding new instruments of speculation has not had a very great impact on criminology (although it could and perhaps should have: see Calavita et al., 1997).

The difficulties of 'studying upwards' seem to be even greater in the field of state-organized crime.[31] The topic has been thematic as 'elite deviance' (Simon and Eitzen, 1990) or 'official deviance' (Douglas and Waksler, 1982) before, but the historical dimension had been missing. The literature also makes this into a new specialization of criminology with little relation to other topics – not to mention political science or sociology. Barak (1991) uses the category of 'crimes of omission' which could open the field to general studies of inequality and domination. Hagan (1997) uses the category of 'patriarchal crime' (similar to Messerschmidt, 1986), which, with the exception of gender-specific criminal law (for example, female in contrast to male adultery in some states), also incorporates 'crimes of omission'. He also includes slavery as a political crime. Such possibilities to connect the field to broader studies typically are not followed up.

Thus these interesting approaches fall short of the complex connections Chambliss (1988) could identify inside the political and economic machine of a US city. Similarly, the potential of C. Wright Mills's (1956) concept of 'higher immorality' still needs elaboration. What Bauman (1989) has done for sociology – reminding the discipline of the relevance that studies of the dictatorships and the genocides of the twentieth century have for social theory – still needs to be done for criminology. As long as they, as well as colonialism and slavery, remain outside the field of studies, the basic insight that it is states that organize criminal and other forms of exclusion on a mass scale is hard to come by.

One important development in the field is the emergence of organizations to document business and government misconduct. Amnesty International and other human rights groups and organizations have done more to document torture and political repression than any social science research ever could. Initiatives like 'Corporate Crime Reporter' and 'Multinational Monitor' (Mokhiber and Weissman, 1999), the Center for Public Integrity (Lewis and Allison, 2001) or, for that matter, Transparency International (monitoring corruption), and others, will provide data beyond that of mainstream journalism.

Creating conceptual units – suggesting comparisons

General concepts are among the decisive contributions of academic work. The abstraction under a general concept like deviance of such behaviors as petty theft, wife beating, campaign finance fraud, genocidal politics (past and present) and different ways of seeking sexual pleasure, to name but a few, is alien to the common-sense and political discourse on any of these topics. Its usefulness, if any, lies in making these different phenomena comparable and thereby better understood. By looking for common features between phenomena seen as 'incomparable' by taken-for-granted cultural knowledge, societies, through social science, can learn about general mechanisms regulating both.

One well-known example of this procedure is an article by Charles Tilly (1985), in which war and state-making are compared to the classical protection racket: states, in exchange for a sizable contribution, offer their citizens the protection they would not need without states. This bold comparison opens up questions about different forms of such 'extraction', the reasons why people accept and even defend them, about possible redistributions – and the violence and force states exert on their own citizens. It does a similar service for organized crime, bringing the 'order function' of local regimes of domination into the spotlight.[32]

There is another principle of finding useful comparisons implicit in this example: the principle of genealogy and historical facilitation. It

is much easier to see connections, causations and functions in historical examples than it is in contemporary ones. Once identified in historical material, concepts can be applied to contemporary states.

What we can call 'strong functionalism' is another model that can help us to get beyond taken-for-granted cultural assumptions. It is particularly useful in questions of deviance in that it makes us look for functions – contributions to a regime of domination – in phenomena that are generally regarded as 'dysfunctional'. The most famous recent example is Foucault's (1975) assumption that the prison's failure to re-socialize may be its exact function. It creates, this way, a subculture of outcasts who can be used to render services not available legally but still needed now and then. Their very existence can, on the other hand, be used to justify ever-new reforms and attempts to make the prison 'effective', which keeps it alive.

Prison failure and prison reform, then, are integral parts of this form of punishment. (Petty) criminality, used by quite respectable people, may be the other side of the equation. Illegal immigrants as farm hands during the harvest in California, Spain and elsewhere are a well-studied example. Crimes without victims, in general, become 'normal', or at least useful (if not necessary), parts of society and its economy. This again connects the study of deviance with that of labor markets and social security in an obvious way. The 'informal economy' partly consists of activities which, if provided legally, would be too expensive or morally unbearable. But there is demand for these services, a demand that mostly arises within respectable society. This is certainly true for drug consumption, for many sexual and entertainment services, for unregistered labor and household services. And it is true for what is prosecuted as corruption (see Clinard, 1990; Lee-Chai and Borgh, 2001), industrial espionage and illegal arms trade (see US Congress, 1991; Navias and Willet, 1996; Tirman, 1997), or, recently, the trade in body parts (Andrews and Nelkin, 2001). From an understanding of the prison's 'failure' we are led right into an analysis of market regulations in general (Taylor, 1999; Ruggiero, 2000).

Another old and well-known application of the same 'strong functionalism' found in Foucault's work is the interpretation of prostitution as a necessary complement to bourgeois monogamy (Davis, 1961). In an interesting way, this understanding, provocative at the time, has become obsolete and superseded by two others. One, the Dworkin type, says prostitution (and pornography, pre-marital sex and, finally, all hetero sex) is coercion, rape and a form of slavery; the other takes a sociology-of-the-professions approach (see Scambler and Scambler, 1997; Weitzer, 2000).

According to this second understanding, prostitution is a profession that needs to be treated as one, and given the organizational and infrastructural status and resources given to all registered businesses. 'Sex work' is seen as a possible line of self-employment with a relationship between labor and income that is better than in most factory or office work. It just needs to be kept free of exploitation and violence (see Vance, 1984; Nagle, 1997; Sullivan, 1997; Phoenix, 1999; O'Neill, 2001). Also, the connection with drug dependence, under-age status and immigrant illegality needs to be severed. It is argued that moralistic regulations make life unnecessarily difficult for the women in the trade and prevent the kind of protective regulation they need (Brock, 1998).

The other approach, seeing itself as more radically feminist, cannot conceive of such a taming of sex work by state regulation. Instead, it sees (and documents) the coercive and abusive forms of war prostitution (Barstow, 2000), sex tourism (Ryan and Hall, 2001) and its sex-industry counterpart, de facto slavery (Barry, 1984, 1995), as the norm.[33] In this perspective, even self-chosen prostitution as a source of income cannot really be a deliberate choice and, in even the best case, the activity still implies demeaning and instrumentalizing oneself.

By taking the perspective of the women in the business, a new model – comparing sex work to other types of service in a capitalist economy – made the old functionalist interpretation obsolete. And its one-sided perspective – taking insatiable male sexual wishes for granted – has become visible. The new perspective has opened up new questions and possible interpretations: sex (and even love) could be analyzed as service, its rewards could be systematized beyond the piecework financial relation in prostitution, which then links in with the debate about household work and its remuneration. The second perspective, which concentrates on coercion and violence, also connects prostitution to forms of domination central to the present mode of production, not least including neocolonialist forms of exploitation.

Again, deviance is shown as not necessarily marginal, but is connected right into the center of contemporary institutions. Looking at them from the deviance perspective adds to understanding these institutions properly. New insight does not necessarily need general theory. New interpretations emerge by subsuming phenomena under general concepts, which make them appear in a novel light.

Defining experience (IV): the racism story

The Bell Curve debate in the United States focused on a national sensitivity: racism in relation to African Americans. In Europe, the corresponding category is the less specific 'foreigners'. The discussion is about the justification of social inequality and its consequences. It is about 'keeping them out' in Europe (increasingly in the United States too), and about welfare benefits and their reduction. Herrnstein and Murray (1994) offer a biologistic and a meritocratic argument joined together. In a deeper layer, it is also about history and its relevance for present conditions – a denial of history in favor of some genetic essentialism.[34] This debate is about claims and rights, but it is also and foremost about the reverse: white predominance and superiority.

What is interesting about the Bell Curve debate is the return of scientifically supported elitist biologism *and* the sharp reaction against it. Obviously political, the debate is about welfare policies and affirmative action, as well as the possibility of racist models in social science. Many of the analyses countered Herrnstein and Murray not by a critique of ideology (an exercise in obviousness), but by a critique of statistical methods (in fact, the Devlin et al. (1997) book is explicitly placed in a statistics and methods context) and stringency of argument. One of the insights to be gained from this debate is that racism today hides in (the fallacies of) 'hard' science. Our dominant ideas about measurement of abilities and of causation in social relations are (part of) the background to the overwhelming plausibility of the Bell Curve argument. People are different in their intellectual abilities and these differences matter a lot for their success in life. The critics just do not share the self-satisfied pride some high achievers show by celebrating IQ.

The study of deviance finds one of its most important topics in the study of racism with its claims to superiority and its justification of privilege. Racism is not primarily about the inferiority of the other, but about the superiority of the racist.[35] Racism is about the colonialist's right and duty to rule (the 'white man's burden'), and it is about today's claims for supremacy, not least those put in terms of IQ.

In this formulation, the current bias that racism is some sort of prejudice or stereotyped thinking that can be overcome by proper schooling and mutual acquaintance becomes a little less plausible. The idea of a 'master race' has its historical roots and many centuries of praxis in slave economies and colonialism. Western thinking in terms of subordination and rule has only recently been contested. European colonial rule ended no more than 50 years ago. Only 100 years ago there were still freak shows and 'Negro kraals' in world exhibitions. And slavery is an institution of thousands of years which was formally ended less than 200 years ago and which *de facto* still exists in various forms (see Bales, 1999, 2000). Slave labor remains an economic factor of some importance.[36] Penal servitude is a special form ('one dies, get another') of de-humanization (Mancini, 1996).

The understanding of slavery as compatible even with Enlightenment ideas (see Thomas Jefferson) depends on a variant theory of history that sees some parts of the world, and those who inhabit them, as more advanced,

more civilized than others. The Darwinist idea of a *development* of species from 'primitive' to 'higher' forms gave an excellent justification for the superiority of conquerors, that was actually based on more destructive weaponry[37] and the lack of resistance indigenous populations had to imported germs and illnesses. 'Savage' and 'primitive' are categories of deviance that automatically included domination and exploitation rights – down to the right to eradicate.

In this set of colonialist practices, from conquering to enslaving, the material power of stigma becomes impossible to deny. To see as a 'prejudice' what was actually a right to dehumanize is a rather euphemistic concept. The instrumental understanding of other human beings has a material force. Nowhere has this been more terribly effective than in the Nazi application of racism to an 'internal enemy'. On the basis of nineteenth-century 'racialization' of European (formerly religious) anti-semitism, they were able to install diverse organizations of destruction, from the sterilization, then euthanasia programs via massacres and mass executions to the death factories of the extermination camps. It is this material (and division of labor) organization of a 'sub-human' position – often supported by biological, medical, statistical and engineering sciences – that gives racism its destructive edge.

The noble idea of human rights is only slowly, if at all, gaining an organizational basis that may counter some of this.

Rewriting the disciplinary history

In social science, an interesting and radical way of integrating new developments is the rewriting of the discipline's history under the newly established perspective. Aspects of this history that have been neglected or suppressed (as the accusation often goes) can be reconstructed as what looks, superficially, like a whole new development. This has been done in the sociology of deviance to a remarkable degree. Criminology has recaptured its less-than-noble ancestry in a number of detailed studies (Strasser, 1984; Beirne, 1993; Rafter, 1997; Wetzell, 2000). Similarly, the histories of psychiatry and of social welfare have been re-examined.

One result of this re-examination is the rediscovery of the racist, biologist and exclusionary strand of Western social thought. While once (in the 1970s) sociology was seen as a 'liberal', 'critical', if not 'revolutionary' way of thinking, the deeply conservative lines in its history are now acknowledged. It is by now standard to include the British (and later American) eugenics movement in histories of psychology as well as sociology (see, for example, Fienberg and Resnick, 1997; Dikötter, 1998). Darwinism, the model of 'selective breeding of the fittest', linked with ideas about 'degeneration', 'corruption' and 'parasitic' relationships,[38] has proved important in the development of sociology. If Darwinism and its radicalized applications to human society integrated an understanding of 'master race' and 'subhumanity' into a schema of development, social Darwinism was a 'naturalized' replacement for a philosophy of history. Instead of 'liberation', this vision implied a progress of domination: the 'higher' race has to rule and to defend against possible 'degeneration'.[39]

There is no way to deny this strong and consequential current in Western thinking about state and society. It has today, after the Nazi delegitimization, shed its most reckless rhetoric. But the basic pattern can still be recognized in its present, relatively cautious, reduction of genders and races to heredity.

We can no longer be sure that sociology is *per se* a science of inclusion. With biological and otherwise exclusionary thinking forcefully returning we are made aware that the liberal inclusionary consensus of sociology is just one side of a social process, in which inclusion and exclusion are negotiated, conceptualized and executed in diverse ways. The other side consists of the sciences of social exclusion, the institutions of social exclusion and the social experiences connected to them.

We are in the middle of a change in Western self-interpretation: diversity and inequality are again described by 'natural' categories. New hierarchies are being negotiated. The 'masters of the universe' are willing to push aside any obstacle to the project of a global competitive market. Deviance that is not useful is excluded – not without scientific support.

NOTES

This chapter represents an abstracted and condensed version of a manuscript double its length which was finished in Spring 2002. Thanks to Bill Chambliss, Wolf Heydebrand and particularly Kathy Laster for helpful comments. Thanks to David Greenberg and participants for a discussion in his colloquium. Thanks to Craig Calhoun for encouragement, comment and editorial help.

1 Savelsberg (1994) has, in a comparison of Germany and the United States, developed a set of hypotheses on how political processes and academic knowledge production are interlinked. Garland (2001b) has set out a 'thick description' of these same recent changes in crime policy, comparing the US and the UK. O'Connor (2001) presents an analogous description and analysis for what she aptly calls 'poverty knowledge', an important dimension of knowledge about deviance. The present chapter similarly uses a sociology-of-knowledge framework to structure its descriptive task.

2 The positive side is definitely under-studied: 'saint' and 'genius' categories hardly ever figure as sociological topics.

3 Recent exceptions are Ben-Yehuda (1985) and Oplinger (1990). Rummel (1994) and Coony (1997) show that all through history more deaths have been caused by states than by private initiative. Highly relevant fields of deviance are confined to specialist volumes. Piracy, to pick just one of the more exotic and fascinating examples of the intersection of state-organized (or licensed) crime, war and military organization, all-male gangs, violence and popular fantasies, is seriously under-studied. Piracy is also – via Robinson Crusoe – connected to the early history of the bourgeois individual (Watt, 1957). Turley (1999) shows the connection by comparing Defoe's *Crusoe* with his pirate novels, especially *Captain Singleton*. For a further analysis of crime and the constitution of the bourgeois individual, using the example of Daniel Defoe, see Faller, 1993.

4 Studies of war propaganda show this clearly: see, e.g., Duster (1971), Gay (1993) and Keen (1986).

5 This insight and interest of labeling theory has been followed up through the period surveyed here in a number of impressive studies: for instance Bowker and Star (2000), Lerman (1996) and Zuberi (2001); applied to achievement and psychological tests, see Sacks (1999) and Lemann (1999).

6 Any library search for titles containing 'identity' will come up with several thousand. Except for the traditional female identity, which is widely seen as an instrument of domination, there is little in this literature that analyses how people are 'identified' for a purpose by the powers that be. If this is the focus the concept is 'stereotype' or 'stigma' (see Falk, 2001; Pickering, 2001). 'Identity', in contrast, is mostly seen as something we crave. Only rarely are the two sides brought together.

7 A strong case can be made for seeing the abstraction of a person as 'labor power' as the basis of a general 'instrumental' subsumption of persons. The conception of such 'instrumental reason' is, of course, the core of Critical Theory (see Horkheimer and Adorno, 1947; Horkheimer, 1947).

8 This is certainly not to say that the struggle for the emancipation of homosexuality is over and done. There are, after all, quite a number of states (in the US too) and whole cultures with homosexuality paragraphs still on the book. For histories of the struggle and (on the whole, positive) balances drawn at different points in time see Greenberg (1988), Cruikshank (1992), Plummer (1992), D'Emilio et al. (2000) and Fone (2000).

9 This is the 'old' conservatism in the United States that has a long tradition of racism and was noticed and studied by sociologists back in the 1960s (see Bell, 1963; Hofstadter, 1965). Militias and rural sects can give backing to persons who then blow up a building in Oklahoma City or send anthrax letters to family-planning centers and abortion clinics (see the report by Mead, 2001), but they clearly constitute a fringe. Similarly with neo-Nazis in Europe. Not a fringe are the right-populist parties which organize and instrumentalize xenophobic resentments. They mostly also have (neo-)fascist connections. In power, as in Austria and Italy, they opt for neoliberal politics like (and in coalition with) conservatives.

10 This new US conservatism shares a core of family and anti-government values with the old, but is on the whole a successful ideological restructuring that dates from the 1980s. McGirr's (2001) summary of this difference is the shift 'from a discursive preoccupation with public, political, and international enemies (namely, communism) to enemies within our own communities and families (namely, secular humanists, women's liberationists, and, eventually, homosexuals)' (p. 15). The adherents of the new conservatism are 'a highly educated and thoroughly modern group of men and women' (p. 8), successful and well-heeled, proud of their entrepreneurial effort and therefore convinced of the tough but advantageous rulings of markets. As a generation they are 'the other radicals of the 1960s' (p. 6) (see also Diamond, 1995, 1998). For accounts of the development see Hunter (1991), Hixson (1992), Shibley (1996) and Isserman and Kazin (2000). For a comprehensive account of the diverse sources of this conservative 'market populism' see Frank (2001).

11 This has already been described dating back to at least the early twentieth century: see Jacoby (1975), Rosen (1977), Ehrenreich and English (1979), Herman (1995), Cushman (1995), Pfister and Schnog (1997) and Moskowitz (2001). For description and critique of the present situation see Sykes (1992) and Peele (1995).

12 The techniques are those of classic advertising and have stayed much the same since the propagation of 'sin'. They have just, with the invention of 'B.O.', expectations for the 'whiteness' of sheets and other norms of private hygiene, been taken over by a scientifically oriented, non-denominational industry.

13 German allows the pun of an equivalence between 'gleich gültig' (equally valid) and 'gleichgültig' (indifferent) here. It is easy to see that this is the situation named and theorized as 'postmodernism'. The decision to abandon the search for one 'truth' but rather to allow a multitude of 'realities' limits competition by splitting the field into compartmentalized units between which contact is reduced. It is a strategy of 'peaceful coexistence' in an abundant market.

14 The most elaborate formulation of this orthodoxy, based on international comparison, is Fukuyama (1999). But the same position can already be found in Harris (1981) and a host of publications in between. For the very similar communitarian position see Putnam (2000). In the Fukuyama version a reconstruction of morality is on its way – it will not be imposed by state or other institutions but be developed spontaneously, because people need order and cooperation. Other, especially European, versions are less optimistic.

15 The irony that women and children are the prototypical objects of 'protection' in a patriarchal regime, seemingly did not always register.

16 For a time the 'welfare mother' was the threatening figure held up to illustrate the fear that the welfare state may have gone too far (Katz, 1989; Gans, 1995). In the more economically minded literature this was discussed as the 'welfare trap' or 'poverty trap' (Butler and Kondratas, 1987).

17 This makes it obvious that it cannot be explained by crime figures; it is, rather, a function of a *populist structure* of politics (Steinert, 1999).

18 See the autobiographic descriptions of the adventure by Bratton and Knobler (1998) and Maple (1999).

19 Cuneo (2001) reports ample evidence that exorcism is still practiced in the United States and even with church (or sect, i.e. evangelist) sanction. He also makes it plausible that demon beliefs are picked up from popular fiction, not least from the Hollywood products in this field. The same may be true for 'Satanism' blasphemy and group-sex games, although the horrible crimes like killing babies ascribed to them are a little too reminiscent of the anti-semitic and anti-dissenter myths of old (Cohn, 1961, 1975) and would not likely go unnoticed. One Australian study (Schmuttermaier and Veno, 1999) shows that child protection social workers are more likely to believe there is Satanism the better schooled they are in detecting hidden signs of child abuse.

20 The name of Cary Hammond repeatedly appears in the literature. Cuneo (2001: 207) cites him as 'a Utah-based psychologist … and expert in hypnotherapy and a heavyweight in the recovered memory field …'.

21 See Ofshe and Watters (1994), Nathan and Snedeker (1995) and Pendergrast (1995); see also the relevant chapters in Ben-Yehuda (1985) and Showalter (1998) for interpretations in the wider context of esoteric phenomena in a media society. In Adorno's (1957) study these are interpreted as symptoms of resentment and authoritarianism (intolerance of ambiguity).

22 For an early analysis of 'child abuse' as a moral-entrepreneur issue see Pfohl (1977); more recently, now describing the decline of the movement, Best (1990), Myers (1994) and Beckett (1996).

23 For instance, Flathman (1999), in an article reviewing empirically based knowledge, needs to say it even in the abstract: 'This review aims to draw balanced conclusions about trauma and memory … In order that the debate … not divert attention from the reality of child abuse and its damage, child abuse issues begin and end the review.' In these postmodern times the claim for 'truth' seems to have become the sign of the fanatic and authoritarian,

whereas science presents a 'balanced' view. Scott (2001) takes this one step further by analyzing how victims of 'ritual abuse' suffer from the 'discourse of disbelief'. Even if the ritual-abuse accusations are not 'true', they have therapeutic truth in the 'reconstructed life narratives' of children who mostly had histories of abuse, rape and prostitution.

24 Such widening of the field was also due to counter-accusations like husband battering or violence against parents and older people. Publishers' interest in uncovering the latest variant of sexual abuse is illustrated in titles like 'Female Sexual Abuse of Children: The Ultimate Taboo' (Elliott, 1993). Another widening included professional relations that can be sexually exploited (physicians, psychotherapists, teachers, nurses). Another form of net widening is, of course, the sensibilization for lesser forms of violence like 'emotional incest' (Love and Robinson, 1990). A convincing case can be made that the proper theoretical category has to be a broader concept like 'sexual exploitation' or patriarchal domination. See e.g. Russell (1984) and Walby (1986, 1990).

25 Both of these issues have, especially since the 1970s, been researched broadly. The shelter movement has given a constant influx of experience. The practical changes brought about, both socially as well as legally and in organizations of control, have been marked and remarkable. See among many, Stanko (1985), Scully (1990), Buzawa and Buzawa (1992), Dobash and Dobash (1992, 1998), Newburn and Stanko (1994), Matthews (1994) and Bolen (2001).

26 An analogous attempt in German is Hess and Scheerer (1997). By necessity these compilations are eclectic, trying to integrate a diversity of materials and theoretical approaches into a model that orders them and gives them a place in a grander scheme. Often the result is an ordering framework for a criminology textbook, sometimes so complicated (Figure 7.1 in Tittle, 1995: 173, is a good example) that it is hard to see how this collection of variables of disposition, situation and constraint differs from the multi-factor enumerations that have traditionally dominated textbooks.

27 List given by Paternoster and Brame (1998).

28 Akers (1991) rightly points out that we cannot use crime as the indicator of low self-control and explain it by that same variable. But even the independent measure he demands does not help much if the crimes to be explained are impulsive acts that give immediate gratification. The tautology still lies in the concept, not in its measurement.

29 Feasibility mainly means a size of the project that can still be managed in a PhD dissertation and a plausibility that makes funding easy (in an increasingly competitive market). Nothing is better than an accepted 'theory' that needs testing with an accepted instrument for doing so at hand. This instrument at hand is a questionnaire scale to measure self-control, provided by Grasmick et al. (1993). In fact this scale was the measure in 11 of the 21 tests used in Pratt and Cullen's (2000) re-analysis, a slightly modified version of it several more. Only one of the measures for self-control was behavioral. A more recent survey of the empirical evidence is provided by Greenberg et al. (2002).

30 Ericson and Carriere (1994) see this as a problem, but also a chance.

31 Since Chambliss (in his 1988 presidential speech) urged the American Society of Criminology to have this topic on its agenda, there have been a number of studies and publications. But in the program of the 2001 ASC meeting in Atlanta no more than five of the 400-plus sessions could be counted into this category (unless we include the numerous sessions on police and corrections, against the organizers' objections).

32 This idea of Tilly's caused a little stir of excitement but did not dramatically alter the course of state theory – which is a pity because it could have been connected back to Horkheimer's 'racket' theory of the (fascist) state – and to research into the connections of corruption and organized crime with state functions.

33 The evidence compiled by human rights organizations is overwhelming, so there cannot be any doubt that prostitution often implies some slave-like form of forced labor. There is also no doubt that there is the fantasy of 'white slavery', exploited by the culture industry, with its deeply patriarchal character. To protect women and children against outside predators – other patriarchs' warriors – is one of the patriarch's main duties. So the fantasy certainly tells 'women to beware the city, the immigrant, her sexuality, and ultimately, her freedom' (Grittner, 1990: 9). But that refers to women on the brink of emancipation in the metropolitan parts of the world, not to those in a (neo-)colonial situation.

34 The dispute is well documented in a number of books: Fraser (1995), Jacoby and Glauberman (1995), Fischer et al. (1996), Kincheloe et al. (1996), Devlin et al. (1997).

35 Galton's eugenic ideas were first directed at cultivating and breeding *genius*. The race theories of Gobineau and Chamberlain celebrated the genius of the Germanic and Aryan race – as did Hitler's *Mein Kampf*. Nietzsche was popularly used for his idea of the 'super-man' (*Übermensch*) mainly. See Schmidt (1988) and Becker (1978).

36 For reviews of the 'broader perspectives' see Davis (2000) and Bush (2000).

37 According to Hanson (2001), a ruthlessly massmurderous way of fighting may be the secret of Western military superiority. Certainly the military understanding of '*Menschenmaterial*' ('human material') or 'losses' does nothing to counteract an instrumental treatment of soldiers. Since war is no longer confined to soldiers, this has been generalized to civilians as, e.g., 'collateral damage'.

38 Such ideas were endemic in the European *fin de siècle* and the flip side of its great cultural advances. On Max Nordau, the inventor of 'degeneration', see Schulte (1997); on the nineteenth century legacy that culminated in such ideas, see Gay (2001); on the 'scientific culture' of the *fin de siècle*, see Steinert (1997a, 2001).

39 Elements of this racial understanding can be found in many scientific treatises of the nineteenth and twentieth centuries, from Galton and Pearson in the UK through Ploetz, Schallmayer and Guenther in Germany to Dugdale and McLaughlin in the United States (Haller, 1984; Weingart et al., 1988; Degler, 1991; Reilly, 1991; Tucker, 1994; Kuehl, 1994; Hasian, 1996; Clarke, 1998; Staudinger,

1999; Kappeler, 2000). Even social democrats in Germany and Austria were attracted to the scientific promises of social Darwinism (Byer, 1988; Schwartz, 1995). Perhaps even more of a shock was the discovery that this kind of thinking – and the praxis of sterilizations – had also taken root in the model welfare states of Scandinavia (Broberg and Rolls-Hansen, 1996).

REFERENCES

Adorno, Theodor W. (1957) 'The stars down to earth: the Los Angeles Times astrology column. A study in secondary superstition', *Adorno Gesammelte Schriften*, Band 9.2: 7–120.

Akers, Ronald L. (1991) 'Self-control as a General Theory of Crime', *Journal of Quantitative Criminology*, 7 (2): 201–11.

Akers, Ronald L. (1998) *Social Learning and Social Structure: A General Theory of Crime and Deviance*. Boston, MA: Northeastern University Press.

Andrews, Lori and Nelkin, Dorothy (2001) *Body Bazaar: The Market for Human Tissue in the Biotechnology Age*. New York: Crown.

Aries, Philipe (1962) *Centuries of Childhood: A Social History of Family Life*. New York: Vintage.

Baer, Justin and Chambliss, William J. (1997) Generating fear: the politics of crime reporting, *Crime, Law and Social Change*, 27 (2): 87–107.

Bales, Kevin (1999) *Disposable People: New Slavery in the Global Economy*. Berkeley, CA: University of California Press.

Bales, Kevin (2000) *The New Slavery: A Reference Handbook*. Santa Barbara, CA: ABC–CLIO.

Barak, Gregg (ed.) (1991) *Crimes by the Capitalist State: An Introduction to State Criminality*. Albany, NY: State University of New York Press.

Barry, Kathleen (1984) *Female Sexual Slavery*. New York: New York University Press.

Barry, Kathleen (1995) *The Prostitution of Sexuality*. New York: New York University Press.

Barstow, Anne Llewellin (ed.) (2000) *War's Dirty Secret: Rape, Prostitution and Other Crimes Against Women*. Cleveland, OH: Pilgrim Press.

Bauman, Zygmunt (1989) *Modernity and the Holocaust*. Cambridge: Polity Press.

Becker, George (1978) *The Mad Genius Controversy: A Study in the Sociology of Deviance*. London: Sage.

Beckett, Katherine (1996) 'Culture and the politics of signification: the case of child sexual abuse', *Social Problems*, 43: 57–76.

Beirne, Piers (1993) *Inventing Criminology: Essays on the Rise of Homo Criminalis*. Albany, NY: State University of New York Press.

Bell, Daniel (ed.) (1963) *The Radical Right*. New York: Doubleday.

Ben-Yehuda, Nachman (1985) *Deviance and Moral Boundaries: Witchcraft, the Occult, Science Fiction, Deviant Sciences and Scientists*. Chicago: University of Chicago Press.

Best, Joel (1990) *Threatened Children: Rhetoric and Concern about Child Victims*. Chicago: University of Chicago Press.

Black, Donald (ed.) (1984) *Toward a General Theory of Social Control*, 2 vols. Orlando, FL: Academic Press.

Black, Donald (1993) *The Social Structure of Right and Wrong*. San Diego, CA: Academic Press.

Bolen, Rebecca (2001) *Child Sexual Abuse: Its Scope and Our Failure*. New York: Kluwer.

Bollas, Christopher (2000) *Hysteria*. London: Routledge.

Bowker, Geoffrey C. and Star, Susan Leigh (2000) *Sorting Things Out: Classification and Its Consequences*. Cambridge, MA: MIT Press.

Bratton, William with Knobler, Peter (1998) *Turnaround: How America's Top Cop Reversed the Crime Epidemic*. New York: Random House.

Broberg, Gunnar and Rolls-Hansen, Nils (eds) (1996) *Eugenics and the Welfare State: Sterilization Policy in Denmark, Sweden, Norway, and Finland*. East Lansing, MI: Michigan State University Press.

Brock, Deborah R. (1998) *Making Work, Making Trouble: Prostitution as a Social Problem*. Toronto: University of Toronto Press.

Bronfen, Elisabeth (1998) *The Knotted Subject: Hysteria and its Discontents*. Princeton, NJ: Princeton University Press.

Buhle, Mari Jo (1998) *Feminism and its Discontents: A Century of Struggle with Psychoanalysis*. Cambridge, MA: Harvard University Press.

Bush, Michael L. (2000) *Servitude in Modern Times*. Cambridge: Polity Press.

Butler, Stuart and Kondratas, Anna (1987) *Out of the Poverty Trap: A Conservative Strategy for Welfare Reform*. New York: The Free Press.

Buzawa, Eve S. and Buzawa, Carl G. (eds) (1992) *Domestic Violence: The Changing Criminal Justice Response*. Westport, CT: Greenwood.

Byer, Doris (1988) *Rassenhygiene und Wohlfahrtspflege: Zur Entstehung eines sozialdemokratischen Machtdispositivs in Oesterreich bis 1934*. Frankfurt: Campus.

Calavita, Kitty, Pontell, Henry N. and Tillman, Robert H. (1997) *Big Money Crime: Fraud and Politics in the Savings and Loans Crisis*. Berkeley, CA: University of California Press.

Chambliss, William J. (1988) *On the Take: From Petty Crooks to Presidents*. Bloomington, IN: Indiana University Press.

Christie, Nils (1993) *Crime Control as Industry: Towards GULAGs Western Style?* London: Routledge.

Clarke, Adele E. (1998) *Disciplining Reproduction: Modernity, American Life Sciences, and 'the Problems of Sex'.* Berkeley, CA: University of California Press.

Clinard, Marshall B. (1990) *Corporate Corruption: The Abuse of Power.* New York: Praeger.

Cohn, Ellen G., Farrington, David P. and Wright, Richard A. (1998) *Evaluating Criminology and Criminal Justice.* Westport, CT: Greenwood Press.

Cohn, Norman (1961) *The Pursuit of Millennium.* New York: Harper.

Cohn, Norman (1975) *Europe's Inner Demons: An Inquiry Inspired by the Great Witch Hunt.* New York: Basic Books.

Connell, Robert W. (1987) *Gender and Power: Society, the Person and Sexual Politics.* Cambridge: Polity.

Connell, Robert W. (1995) *Masculinities.* London: Allen and Unwin.

Coony, Mark (1997) 'From warre to tyranny: lethal conflict and the state', in *American Sociological Review*, 62: 316–38.

Cossins, Anne (2000) *Masculinities, Sexualities and Child Sexual Abuse.* The Hague: Kluwer.

Cremer-Schäfer, Helga, and Steinert, Heinz (1998) *Straflust und Repression. Zur Kritik der populistischen Kriminologie.* Münster: Westfälisches Dampfboot.

Cruikshank, Margaret (1992) *The Gay and Lesbian Liberation Movement.* New York: Routledge.

Cuneo, Michael W. (2001) *American Exorcism: Expelling Demons in the Land of Plenty.* New York: Doubleday.

Cushman, Philip (1995) *Constructing the Self, Constructing America.* Boston, MA: Addison–Wesley.

D'Emilio, John, Turner, William B. and Vaid, Urvashi (eds) (2000) *Creating Change: Sexuality, Public Policy, and Civil Rights.* New York: St Martin's Press.

Davis, David Brion (2000) 'Looking at slavery from broader perspectives', *American Historical Review*, 105 (2): 452–66 (plus comments on this article in the same issue).

Davis, Kingsley (1961) 'Prostitution', in Robert K. Merton and Robert Nisbet (eds), *Contemporary Social Problems.* New York: Harcourt. pp. 262–88.

Degler, Carl N. (1991) *In Search of Human Nature: The Decline and Revival of Darwinism in American Social Thought.* Oxford: Oxford University Press.

deMause, Lloyd (ed.) (1974) *The History of Childhood.* New York: Psychohistory Press.

Devlin, Bernie, Fienberg, Stephen E., Resnick, Daniel P. and Roeder, Kathryn (eds) (1997) *Intelligence, Genes, and Success: Scientists Respond to the Bell Curve.* New York: Springer.

Diamond, Sara (1995) *Roads to Dominion: Right-Wing Movements and Political Power in the United States.* New York: Guilford Press.

Diamond, Sara (1998) *Not By Politics Alone: The Enduring Influence of the Christian Right.* New York: Guilford Press.

DiIulio, John (1996) *How to Stop the Coming Crime Wave.* Princeton, NJ: Princeton University Press.

Dikötter, Frank (1998) 'Race culture: recent perspectives on the history of eugenics', *American Historical Review*, 103 (2): 467–78.

Dobash, R. Emerson and Dobash, Russell P. (1992) *Women, Violence and Social Change.* London: Routledge.

Dobash, R. Emerson and Dobash, Russell P. (eds) (1998) *Rethinking Violence against Women.* Thousand Oaks, CA: Sage.

Donziger, Steven R. (ed.) (1996) *The Real War on Crime: The Report of the National Criminal Justice Commission.* New York: Harper.

Douglas, Jack D. and Waksler, Frances C. (1982) *The Sociology of Deviance: An Introduction.* Boston, MA: Little, Brown & Co.

Duster, Troy (1971) 'Conditions for guilt-free massacre', in Nevitt Sanford, Craig Comstock et al. (eds), *Sanctions for Evil.* San Francisco: Jossey–Bass. pp. 25–36.

Dyer, Joel (2000) *The Perpetual Prisoner Machine: How America Profits from Crime.* Boulder, CO: Westview Press.

Ehrenreich, Barbara and English, Deirdre (1979) *For Her Own Good: One Hundred Fifty Years of Experts' Advice to Women.* Garden City, NY: Anchor.

Elliott, Michele (1993) *Female Sexual Abuse of Children: The Ultimate Taboo.* Harlow: Longman.

Ericson, Richard and Carriere, Kevin (1994) 'The fragmentation of criminology', in David Nelken (ed.), *The Futures of Criminology.* London: Sage. pp. 89–109.

Falk, Gerhard (2001) *Stigma: How We Treat Outsiders.* Amherst, NY: Prometheus.

Faller, Lincoln (1993) *Crime and Defoe.* Cambridge: Cambridge University Press.

Fienberg, Stephen E. and Resnick, Daniel P. (1997) 'Reexamining the Bell Curve', in Bernie Devlin, Stephen E. Fienberg, Daniel P. Resnick and Kathryn Roeder (eds), *Intelligence, Genes and Success: Scientists Respond to the Bell Curve.* New York: Springer. pp. 3–18.

Fischer, Claude S., Jankowski, Martin Sanchez, Lucas, Samuel R., Swidler, Ann and Voss, Kim (eds) (1996) *Inequality by Design: Cracking the Bell Curve Myth.* Princeton, NJ: Princeton University Press.

Flathman, Marcus (1999) 'Trauma and delayed memory: A review of the "repressed memories" literature', *Journal of Child Sexual Abuse*, 8 (2): 1–23.

Fleischer, Doris Zames and Zames, Frieda (2001) *The Disability Rights Movement: From Charity to Confrontation*. Philadelphia, PA: Temple University Press.

Fone, Byrne (2000) *Homophobia: A History*. New York: Metropolitan Books.

Foucault, Michel (1975) *Surveiller et Punir: Naissance de la Prison*. Paris : Gallimard.

Frank, Thomas (2001) *One Market Under God: Extreme Capitalism, Market Populism, and the End of Economic Democracy*. New York: Doubleday.

Fraser, Steven (ed.) (1995) *The Bell Curve Wars: Race, Intelligence, and the Future of America*. New York: Basic Books.

Fukuyama, Francis (1999) *The Great Disruption: Human Nature and the Reconstitution of Social Order*. London: Profile Books.

Furnham, Adrian F. (1988) *Lay Theories: Everyday Understanding of Problems in the Social Sciences*. Oxford: Pergamon Press.

Gans, Herbert J. (1995) *The War against the Poor: The Underclass and Antipoverty Policy*. New York: Basic Books.

Garland, David (ed.) (2001a) Special Issue on Mass Imprisonment in the USA. *Punishment and Society*, 3 (1).

Garland, David (2001b) *The Culture of Control: Crime and Social Order in Contemporary Society*. Chicago: University of Chicago Press.

Gay, Peter (1993) *The Cultivation of Hatred*. New York: W.W. Norton.

Gay, Peter (2001) *Schnitzler's Century: The Making of Middle-Class Culture 1815–1914*. New York: W.W. Norton.

Gest, Ted (2001) *Crime and Politics: Big Government's Erratic Campaign for Law and Order*. Oxford: Oxford University Press.

Gilman, Sander, King, Helen, Porter, Roy, Rousseau, George and Showalter, Elaine (1993) *Hysteria Beyond Freud*. Berkeley, CA: University of California Press.

Goode, Erich (1991) 'Positive deviance: A viable concept?', *Deviant Behavior*, 12: 289–309.

Gottfredson, Michael R. and Hirschi, Travis (1990) *A General Theory of Crime*. Stanford, CA: Stanford University Press.

Grasmick, Harold J., Tittle, Charles R., Bursik, Robert J. Jr and Arneklev, Bruce K. (1993) 'Testing the core empirical implications of Gottfredson and Hirschi's General Theory of Crime', *Journal of Research in Crime and Delinquency*, 30: 5–29.

Greenberg, David F. (1988) *The Construction of Homosexuality*. Chicago: University of Chicago Press.

Greenberg, David F., Tamelli, Robin and Kelley, Margaret S. (2002) 'The generality of the self-control theory of crime', in Elin Waring and David Weisburd (eds) *Advances in Criminological Theory, vol. 10: Crime and Social Organization*. New Brunswick, NJ: Transaction Books. pp. 49–94.

Grittner, Frederick K. (1990) *White Slavery: Myth, Ideology, and American Law*. New York: Garland.

Hagan, Frank (1997) *Political Crime: Ideology and Criminality*. Boston, MA: Allyn & Bacon.

Haller, Mark J. (1984) *Eugenics: Hereditarian Attitudes in American Thought*. New Brunswick, NJ: Rutgers University Press.

Hanson, Victor Davis (2001) *Carnage and Culture: Landmark Battles in the Rise of Western Power*. New York: Doubleday.

Harcourt, Bernard E. (2001) *Illusion of Order: The False Promises of Broken Windows Policing*. Cambridge, MA: Harvard University Press.

Harris, Marvin (1981) *America Now: The Anthropology of a Changing Culture*. New York: Simon and Schuster.

Hasian, Marouf Arif, Jr (1996) *The Rhetoric of Eugenics in Anglo-American Thought*. Athens, GA: University of Georgia Press.

Heins, Marjorie (2001) *Not in Front of the Children: 'Indecency', Censorship, and the Innocence of Youth*. New York: Hill & Wang.

Herman, Ellen (1995) *The Romance of American Psychology*. Berkeley, CA: University of California Press.

Herrnstein, Richard J. and Murray, Charles (1994) *The Bell Curve: Intelligence and Class Structure in American Life*. New York: Basic Books.

Hess, Henner and Scheerer, Sebastian (1997) 'Was ist Kriminalität? Skizze einer konstruktivistischen Kriminalitätstheorie', *Kriminologisches Journal*, 29 (2): 83–155.

Hirschi, Travis (1969) *Causes of Delinquency*. Berkeley, CA: University of California Press.

Hixson, William B. (1992) *The Search for the American Right Wing: An Analysis of the Social Science Record, 1955–1987*. Princeton, NJ: Princeton University Press.

Hofstadter, Richard (1965) *The Paranoid Style in American Politics*. New York: Alfred A. Knopf.

Horkheimer, Max (1947) *Eclipse of Reason*. New York: Oxford University Press.

Horkheimer, Max and Adorno, Theodor W. (1947) *Dialektik der Aufklärung. Philosophische Fragmente*. Amsterdam: Querido.

Hunter, James Davison (1991) *Culture Wars: The Struggle to Define America*. New York: Basic Books.

Isserman, Maurice and Kazin, Michael (2000) *America Divided: The Civil War of the 1960s*. New York: Oxford University Press.

Jacoby, Russell (1975) *Social Amnesia*. Boston, MA: Beacon.

Jacoby, Russell and Glauberman, Naomi (eds) (1995) *The Bell Curve Debate: History, Documents, Opinions*. New York: Times Books.

Kappeler, Manfred (2000) *Der schreckliche Traum vom vollkommenen Menschen: Rassenhygiene und Eugenik in der Sozialen Arbeit*. Marburg: Schueren.

Katz, Michael B. (1989) *The Undeserving Poor: From the War on Poverty to the War on Welfare*. New York: Pantheon.

Keen, Sam (1986) *Faces of the Enemy: Reflections of the Hostile Imagination*. San Francisco: Harper and Row.

Kelling, George L. and Coles, Catherine M. (1996) *Fixing Broken Windows: Restoring Order and Reducing Crime in our Communities*. New York: The Free Press.

Kersten, Joachim (1997) *Gut und (Ge)schlecht: Männlichkeit, Kultur und Kriminalität*. Berlin: deGruyter.

Kincaid, James R. (1998) *Erotic Innocence: The Culture of Child Molesting*. Durham, NC: Duke University Press.

Kincheloe, Joe L., Steinberg, Shirley R. and Gresson, Aaron D. III (eds) (1996) *Measured Lies: The Bell Curve Examined*. New York: St Martin's Press.

Kuehl, Stefan (1994) *The Nazi Connection: Eugenics, American Racism, and German National Socialism*. Oxford: Oxford University Press.

Lea, John and Young, Jock (1984) *What Is to Be Done about Law and Order?* Harmondsworth: Penguin.

Lee-Chai, Annette Y. and Borgh, John A. (eds) (2001) *The Use and Abuse of Power: Multiple Perspectives on the Causes of Corruption*. Philadelphia, PA: Psychology Press.

Lemann, Nicholas (1999) *The Big Test: The Secret History of the American Meritocracy*. New York: Farrar, Straus and Giroux.

Lerman, Hannah (1996) *Pigeonholing Women's Misery: A History and Critical Analysis of the Psychodiagnosis of Women in the Twentieth Century*. New York: Basic Books.

Lewis, Charles and Allison, Bill (2001) *The Cheating of America: How Tax Avoidance and Evasion by the Super Rich Are Costing the Country Billions – and What You Can Do About It*. New York: William Morrow.

Love, Patricia with Robinson, Jo (1990) *The Emotional Incest Syndrome: What to Do When a Parent's Love Rules Your Life*. New York: Bantam.

Maines, Rachel P. (1999) *The Technology of Orgasm: 'Hysteria', the Vibrator, and Women's Sexual Satisfaction*. Baltimore, MD: Johns Hopkins University Press.

Mancini, Matthew J. (1996) *One Dies, Get Another: Convict Leasing in the American South, 1866–1928*. Columbia, SC: University of South Carolina Press.

Maple, Jack (1999) *The Crime Fighter: Putting the Bad Guys out of Business*. New York: Doubleday.

Masson, Jeffrey Moussaieff (1984) *The Assault on Truth: Freud's Suppression of the Seduction Theory*. New York: Farrar, Straus, Giroux.

Matthews, Nancy A. (1994) *Confronting Rape: The Feminist Anti-Rape Movement and the State*. London: Routledge.

McGirr, Lisa (2001) *Suburban Warriors: The Origins of the New American Right*. Princeton, NJ: Princeton University Press.

Mead, Rebecca (2001) 'The usual hate mail', *The New Yorker*, 29 October, p. 34.

Messerschmidt, James W. (1986) *Capitalism, Patriarchy, and Crime*. Totowa, NJ: Rowman and Littlefield.

Messerschmidt, James W. (1993) *Masculinities and Crime: Critique and Reconceptualization of Theory*. Lanham, MD: Rowman and Littlefield.

Miller, Alice (1984) *Thou Shalt Not Be Aware: Society's Betrayal of the Child*. New York: Farrar, Straus, Giroux.

Mills, C. Wright (1956) *The Power Elite*. New York: Oxford University Press.

Mitchell, Juliet (2000) *Mad Men and Medusas*. London: Allen Lane.

Mokhiber, Russell and Weissman, Robert (1999) *Corporate Predators: The Hunt for Mega-Profits and the Attack on Democracy*. Monroe, ME: Common Courage Press.

Moskowitz, Eva S. (2001) *In Therapy We Trust: America's Obsession With Self Fulfillment*. Baltimore, MD: Johns Hopkins University Press.

Myers, John (ed.) (1994) *The Backlash: Child Protection under Fire*. Thousand Oaks, CA: Sage.

Nagle, Jill (ed.) (1997) *Whores and Other Feminists*. London: Routledge.

Nathan, Debbie and Snedeker, Michael (1995) *Satan's Silence: Ritual Abuse and the Making of a Modern American Witch Hunt*. New York: Basic Books.

Navias, Martin and Willet, Susan (eds) (1996) *The European Arms Trade*. Commack, NY: Nova Science Publishers.

Newburn, Tim and Stanko, Elizabeth A. (eds) (1994) *Just Boys Doing Business?* London: Routledge.

O'Connor, Alice (2001) *Poverty Knowledge: Social Science, Social Policy, and the Poor in Twentieth-Century U.S. History.* Princeton, NJ: Princeton University Press.

O'Neill, Maggie (2001) *Prostitution and Feminism: Towards a Politics of Feeling.* Cambridge: Polity Press.

Ofshe, Richard and Watters, Ethan (1994) *Making Monsters: False Memories, Psychotherapy, and Sexual Hysteria.* New York: Charles Scribner's Sons.

Oplinger, Jon (1990) *The Politics of Demonology: The European Witchcraze and the Mass Production of Deviance.* London: Associated University Press.

Paternoster, Raymond and Brame, Robert (1998) 'The structural similarity of processes generating criminal and analogous behavior', *Criminology*, 36 (3): 633–69.

Peele, Stanton (1995) *Diseasing of America: How We Allowed Recovery Zealots and the Treatment Industry to Convince Us We Are Out of Control.* New York: Lexington Books.

Pendergrast, Mark (1995) *Victims of Memory: Incest Accusations and Shattered Lives.* Hinesburg: Upper Access.

Pfister, Joel and Schnog, Nancy (eds) (1997) *Inventing the Psychological: Toward a Cultural History of Emotional Life in America.* New Haven, CT: Yale University Press.

Pfohl, Steven (1977) 'The discovery of child abuse', *Social Problems*, 24: 310–23.

Phoenix, Joanna (1999) *Making Sense of Prostitution.* New York: St Michael's Press.

Pickering, Michael (2001) *Stereotyping: The Politics of Representation.* Basingstoke: Palgrave.

Pilgram, Arno and Kuschej, Hermann (1997) *Beobachtungen zum Diskurs über 'Organisierte Kriminalität'.* Vienna: Institut für Rechts- und Kriminalsoziologie.

Plummer, Ken (ed.) (1992) *Modern Homosexualities: Fragments of Lesbian and Gay Experience.* New York: Routledge.

Pratt, Travis C. and Cullen, Francis T. (2000) 'The empirical status of Gottfredson and Hirschi's General Theory of Crime: A meta-analysis', *Criminology*, 38 (3): 931–64.

Putnam, Robert D. (2000) *Bowling Alone: The Collapse and Revival of American Community.* New York: Simon and Schuster.

Rafter, Nicole Hahn (1997) *Creating Born Criminals.* Urbana, IL: University of Illinois Press.

Reilly, Philip R. (1991) *The Surgical Solution: A History of Involuntary Sterilization in the United States.* Baltimore, MD: Johns Hopkins University Press.

Rosen, Richard R. (1977) *Psychobabble: Fast Talk and Quick Cure in the Era of Feeling.* New York: Atheneum.

Ruggiero, Vincenzo (2000) *Crime and Markets: Essays in Anti-Criminology.* Oxford: Oxford University Press.

Rummel, R.J. (1994) *Death by Government.* New Brunswick, NJ: Transaction Books.

Russell, Diana E.H. (1984) *Sexual Exploitation: Rape, Child Sexual Abuse and Workplace Harassment.* Newbury Park, CA: Sage.

Ryan, Chris and Hall, C. Michael (2001) *Sex Tourism: Marginal People and Liminalities.* London: Routledge.

Sacks, Peter (1999) *Standardized Minds: The High Price of America's Testing Culture and What We Can Do to Change It.* Cambridge, MA: Perseus.

Savelsberg, Joachim J. (1994) 'Knowledge, domination, and criminal punishment', *American Journal of Sociology*, 99 (4): 911–43.

Scambler, Graham and Scambler, Annette (eds) (1997) *Rethinking Prostitution: Purchasing Sex in the 1990s.* London: Routledge.

Schmidt, Jochen (1988) *Die Geschichte des Genie-Gedankens in der deutschen Literatur, Philosophie und Politik 1750–1945.* Darmstadt: Wissenschaftliche Buchgesellschaft.

Schmuttermaier, John and Veno, Arthur (1999) 'Counselors' beliefs about ritual abuse: an Australian study', *Journal of Child Sexual Abuse*, 8 (3): 45–63.

Schulte, Christoph (1997) *Psychopathologie des Fin de Siècle: Der Kulturkritiker, Arzt und Zionist Max Nordau.* Frankfurt: Fischer.

Schwartz, Michael (1995) *Sozialistische Eugenik: Eugenische Sozialtechnologien in Debatten und Politik der deutschen Sozialdemokratie, 1890–1933.* Bonn: Dietz.

Scott, Sara (2001) *The Politics and Experience of Ritual Abuse: Beyond Belief.* Buckingham: Open University Press.

Scull, Andrew T. (1988) 'Deviance and social control', in Neil J. Smelser (ed.), *The Handbook of Sociology.* Newbury Park, CA: Sage. pp. 667–93.

Scully, Diana (1990) *Understanding Sexual Violence: A Study of Convicted Rapists.* Boston, MA: Unwin Hyman.

Shibley, Mark A. (1996) *Resurgent Evangelicalism in the United States: Mapping Cultural Change since 1970.* Columbia, SC: University of South Carolina Press.

Showalter, Elaine (1985) *The Female Malady: Women, Madness and English Culture.* New York: Pantheon.

Showalter, Elaine (1998) *Hystories: Hysterical Epidemics and Modern Culture.* New York: Columbia University Press.

Simon, David R. and Eitzen, D. Stanley (1990) *Elite Deviance*. Boston, MA: Allyn and Bacon.

Skogan, Wesley and Hartnett, Susan M. (1997) *Community Policing, Chicago Style*. New York: Oxford University Press.

Stanko, Elizabeth (1985) *Intimate Intrusions: Women's Experience of Male Violence*. London: Routledge.

Staudinger, Roland (1999) *Rassenrecht und Rassenstaat: Die nationalsozialistische Vision eines 'biologischen totalen Staates'*. Hall: Berenkamp.

Steinert, Heinz (1997a) 'Fin de siècle criminology', *Theoretical Criminology*, 1 (1): 111–29.

Steinert, Heinz (1997b) 'Populist criminology and the politics of social exclusion', in Grat van den Heuvel and René van Swaaningen (eds), *Criminaliteit en Sociale Rechtvaardigheid*. Nijmegen: Ars Aequi Libri. pp. 45–52.

Steinert, Heinz (1999) 'Kulturindustrielle Politik mit dem Großen und Ganzen: Populismus, Politik-Darsteller, ihr Publikum und seine Mobilisierung', *Internationale Gesellschaft und Politik*, 4/1999: 402–13.

Steinert, Heinz (2001) 'Kunst und Wissenschaft im Wien der Jahrhundertwende: Gesellschaftliche Grundlagen von Theoriebedarf', in K. Ludwig Pfeiffer, Ralph Kray and Klaus Städtke (eds), *Theorie als kulturelles Ereignis*. Berlin: de Gruyter. pp. 181–204.

Steinert, Heinz (2003) *Culture Industry*. Cambridge: Polity Press.

Steinert, Heinz and Pilgram, Arno (eds) (2003) *Welfare Policy from Below: Struggles Against Social Exclusion in Europe*. Aldershot: Ashgate.

Strasser, Peter (1984) *Verbrechermenschen: Zur kriminalwissenschaftlichen Erzeugung des Bösen*. Frankfurt: Campus.

Sullivan, Barbara Ann (1997) *The Politics of Sex: Prostitution and Pornography in Australia since 1945*. Cambridge: Cambridge University Press.

Sykes, Charles J. (1992) *A Nation of Victims: The Decay of American Character*. New York: St Martin's Press.

Taylor, Ian (1999) *Crime in Context: A Critical Criminology of Market Societies*. Cambridge: Polity Press.

Taylor, Ralph B. (2001) *Breaking Away from Broken Windows: Baltimore Neighborhoods and the Nationwide Fight against Crime, Grime, Fear, and Decline*. Boulder, CO: Westview Press.

Tilly, Charles (1985) 'War making and state making as organized crime', in Peter B. Evans, Dietrich Rueschemeyer and Theda Skocpol (eds), *Bringing the State Back In*. Cambridge: Cambridge University Press. pp. 169–91.

Tirman, John (1997) *The Spoils of War: The Human Cost of America's Arms Trade*. New York: The Free Press.

Tittle, Charles R. (1995) *Control Balance: Toward a General Theory of Deviance*. Boulder, CO: Westview Press.

Tucker, William H. (1994) *The Science and Politics of Racial Research*. Urbana, IL: University of Illinois Press.

Turley, Hans (1999) *Rum, Sodomy, and the Lash: Piracy, Sexuality, and Masculine Identity*. New York: New York University Press.

US Congress (1991) *Global Arms Trade*. Washington: USGPO.

Vance, Carol (1984) *Pleasure and Danger: Exploring Female Sexuality*. Boston, MA: Routledge.

Walby, Sylvia (1986) *Patriarchy at Work: Patriarchal and Capitalist Relations in Employment*. Minneapolis, MN: University of Minnesota Press.

Walby, Sylvia (1990) *Theorizing Patriarchy*. Oxford: Blackwell.

Watt, Ian P. (1957) *The Rise of the Novel: Studies in Defoe, Richardson, and Fielding*. Berkeley, CA: University of California Press.

Weingart, Peter, Kroll, Juergen and Bayertz, Kurt (1988) *Rasse, Blut und Gene: Geschichte der Eugenik und Rassenhygiene in Deutschland*. Frankfurt: Suhrkamp.

Weitzer, Ronald (ed.) (2000) *Sex for Sale: Prostitution, Pornography, and the Sex Industry*. New York: Routledge.

Wetzell, Richard F. (2000) *Inventing the Criminal: A History of German Criminology, 1880–1945*. Chapel Hill, NC: University of North Carolina Press.

Wilson, James Q. and Kelling, George L. (1982) 'The police and neighborhood safety: broken windows', *Atlantic Monthly*, 1982/3: 29–39.

Young, Jock and Matthews, Roger (eds) (1992) *Rethinking Criminology. The Realist Debate*. London: Sage.

Zuberi, Tukufu (2001) *Thicker than Blood: How Racial Statistics Lie*. Minneapolis, MN: University of Minnesota Press.

28

Globalizing Business

STEWART R. CLEGG

INTRODUCTION

Since the time of the earliest civilizations, trade across frontiers and regions has occurred. Economy and society involving exchange of raw materials, animals and crops, semi-finished and finished goods, services, money, ideas and people, has existed since the dawn of civilization (Diamond, 1997). For several hundred years from the sixteenth century onwards, trade between European state systems and their colonial offshoots defined international trade. Such trade involved the world's major trading companies, organized religions and local chiefs and merchants. Often it comprised plunder and looting, dealing in slaves as well as precious and rare commodities. Only later, with the advent of industrialization, did it involve more mundane commodities spreading globally, often replacing indigenous products, propelled by the artillery of cheap prices. Some of the earliest struggles against globalization, as it was experienced in terms of political colonialization, used usurped domestic commodities symbolically in their struggle: Ghandi's domestic cotton spinning wheel, for instance, recalling the village craft displaced by the Lancashire textile industry.

Once national markets were relatively well established, business became organized in what some theorists refer to as 'organized capitalism' (Lash and Urry, 1987). Essentially, this meant national firms with strong identities in their domestic markets would move to capture non-national markets, based on this expertise. Inter-continental markets have been around for nearly 150 years. They are the result of the extensive laying of submarine telegraph cables from the 1860s onwards, making possible virtually instant trade across thousands of miles. Bond markets also became closely interconnected, and large-scale international lending – both portfolio and direct investment – grew rapidly during the latter half of the nineteenth century (Hirst and Thompson, 1996). Foreign direct investment (FDI) grew so rapidly that in 1913 it amounted to over 9 per cent of world output (Bairoch and Kozul-Wright, 1996: 10).

By the early years of the twentieth century significant transnational activity was established, characterized by the transfer of resources, especially capital and to a lesser extent labour, from one national economy to another. The process was uneven: in many countries the patterns of imperial preference in trade meant that semi-peripheral economies in the world system did not compete directly with core countries in manufacturing finished goods but instead concentrated on primary production for the global market that the core countries structured. For instance, much of Central America fell under the sway of the United Fruit Co., which dominated the trade in bananas and other tropical fruit to the US market. Not only was primary production colonized: when finished goods were required the core countries could provide them. In the 1920s the Sydney Harbour Bridge was fabricated bit-by-bit, piece-by-piece, in the North East of England, and shipped halfway around the world to be constructed. Only after the emergence of a national economic industrial capacity during the Second World War, when the old patterns were disrupted, did Australia fully develop industrial capabilities. In the past, typically, where national firms expanded into other markets, this involved the creation of other country production capacities through direct subsidiaries, acquisitions or various types of cooperation (commercial, financial, technological and industrial). This is how the car industry spread globally to countries such as Mexico, Brazil and South Africa. Today, international ventures are commonplace and transnational corporations (firms with a global national presence) have become the major forces driving globalization, opening up global production and markets.

DEFINING GLOBALIZATION

Goran Therborn (2000a: 154) defines globalization as 'tendencies to a worldwide reach, impact, or connectedness of social phenomena or to a world-encompassing awareness among social actors'. He also says that 'the current overriding interest in globalization means two things. First of all, a substitution of *the global* for *the universal*; second, a substitution of *space* for *time*' (Therborn, 2000b: 149, original emphasis).

First, let us consider the triumph of the global over the universal. That the global is being substituted for the universal means that, whereas in the past one might have regarded the most developed nations and their organizations as heralding the universal form of the future, now one is more inclined to think that dominant organizations globally need not necessarily tell us anything about the future: they advise us only about the present and the past, times when they were able to command the

economic heights. But today, the commanding economic heights are easily lost: 20 years ago, among the world's major firms were companies such as Pan Am and TWA – major players in the archetypically global business of airlines. Today, neither exists. Past dominance is no guarantee of future success.

Second, the dominance of space rather than time will be the focus of what follows. Space remains important: the ultimate contradiction of the Internet revolution is that although firms could be located anywhere in cyber space they still seem to cluster together in global cities such as New York, London and Sydney (Castells, 2001). Moreover, on the average, in the OECD economies about 36–40 per cent of what is spent in the economy is spent by the national state, in terms of defence, health, education etc., and these sorts of expenditures tend to be well grounded in national capabilities and concentrated in national space. Space is superseding time because, in a world of trade in symbolic images such as software, currencies and other forms of representation, time is no longer an issue. If you have trading facilities in the right time zones, for instance, you can trade 24 hours a day, moving money, or other 'signs' of commerce, symbolically, across the globe, from London to New York to Tokyo to Sydney to London. There is an increasing separation of the 'real' economy of production and its simulacra in the 'symbol economy' of financial flows and transactions. A new international division of labour compresses and fragments both space and distance in such a way that not only production but also various business-service industries become distributed in unlikely places. Global currencies facilitate trade across the world: Masters of Business become global warriors in the new world order. New divisions restructure geographic space. In principle, anywhere is virtually immediately accessible by information and communication technologies. In practice, most national capitals can be reached within 24 hours' air travel.

Third, globalization does not mean that everyone now lives in a 'borderless world' (Ohmae, 1990) in which nation-states are of diminished significance. Some national governments, notably the United States, play an extraordinarily strong and unilateral role in the global *political* economy, as the war and subsequent occupation in Iraq demonstrate. To the extent that the world is becoming *economically* global, it is a world dominated by US, Japanese and Southeast Asian, West European and allied interests. Technological, economic and cultural integration is developing within and between these three regions and is evident in the patterns of international trade and investment flows. Inter-firm strategic alliances are heavily concentrated among companies from these countries. It is here that scientific power, technological supremacy, economic dominance and cultural hegemony are concentrated (Petrella, 1996: 77).

GLOBAL FLOWS

The characteristics of contemporary globalization include: the internationalization of financial markets and corporate strategies and the diffusion of technology and related R&D and knowledge worldwide, as well as the emergence of global media. These help transform consumption patterns into cultural products through worldwide consumer markets. A global political economy, its social and ecological impact, as well as critical responses to it, is now reported widely (Therborn, 2000b), if largely still with a focus skewed by Western interests. While the focus on globalization has been dominated by discussion of global business interests it is apparent that social identities, just as much as business, are now being organized through a system of global flows.

People only develop a sense of self in relation to others. For most of human history, these others were framed by what was available at the local, often village, level. Today, even the most remote villager can see him- or herself against the mirror that the media projects into their communities. Everything relational flows through space: what it means to be human; what it means to be a member of a society; what it means to be a part of a society within a world system of states – all of these are infinitely expandable once the security of village perimeters is breached. Each of us has to consider ourselves in relation to those others that

flow through and colonize the spaces we are in. Two of these flows are of particular importance. First, the global flows of money, knowledge, people and politics: the material flows of the global world. Second, the invisible flows: trade in the export of cultural consciousness and changing conceptions of the self. It is the latter that always pose the fundamental question of identity: where and how in the world do I fit in – or who and what am I?

At the core of globalization are the investment decisions of states and corporations. When writers refer to globalization as a process they tend to focus mostly on European, North American and Japanese trade, investment and financial flows. Globalization is marked by the integration of deregulating markets and technology and facilitated by telecommunications and ease of transport. International activities enable firms to enter new markets, exploit technological and organizational advantages as well as reduce business costs and risks. These organizations are known as transnationals because they extend beyond national space in their routine activities. Transnational organizations have significant control over both production and consumption in more than one country. They dominate world trade. In principle, they have sufficient geographical flexibility to shift resources and operations between global locations. In practice it may be a bit more difficult. There is a plurality of transnational corporations, which neither dominate national industrial sectors in all markets nor operate without regard for more or less sovereign states. The power of transnationals can easily be overestimated. Only a small number of transnational corporations are truly global and not all transnational corporations are necessarily large in conventional definitions of that term. Global patterns differ markedly according to the national origin of the firms. New supplies and sources of transnational corporations evolve as the world economy evolves, so that now there are emergent markets transnational corporations in newly industrializing countries.[1]

In *Scale and Scope*, Chandler (1990) argues that the global corporation is the final stage in the transformation of industries in search of economies of scale, economies of scope and national differences in the availability and cost of productive resources. Business history suggests that organizations learn in tandem with technological changes (Chandler, 1993). In many industries, economies of scale are such that volumes exceeded the sales levels individual companies could achieve in all but the largest countries, forcing them to become international or perish. The minimum efficient level for capital-intensive plants is 80–90 per cent of capacity in contrast to labour-intensive industries. The costs and profits of capital-intensive industries are determined by plant utilization and throughput, rather than by the simple amount produced.

Less capital-intensive industries are not as affected by scale economies. But opportunities exist for scope economies through worldwide communication and transportation networks. Trading companies handling the products of many companies can achieve greater volume and lower unit cost. With changes in technology and markets came requirements for access to new resources as lower factor costs. Cheap labour may be important but not as much as one might think. It is misleading to assume that the search for cheaper labour in itself is the central driving force of the increasing internationalization of many industries. In most industries there are more important factors than labour costs, including access to markets, technology and other resources. Increasingly industry requires more highly skilled labour and the possession of relevant skills is more immediately important than the price of labour. A focus on globalization that sees it in terms of economies of scale and scope, or the search for cheap labour, or in terms of the business strategies of transnational corporations, is not necessarily wrong. But it is limited.

GLOBAL FLOWS OF CAPITAL, ORGANIZATION, POLITICS AND JOBS

Capital

It is a familiar comment that the economic scale of the largest giant corporations now exceeds the gross domestic product of most countries. International financial flows and foreign currency exchanges now dwarf the value of international trade in goods. Financial services are fundamental to the operation of every aspect of the economic system. Each element of the production chain depends upon necessary levels of finance to keep it in operation (Dicken, 1992: 358). A look at the relative size and value of some well-known countries and companies compared in terms of the value of the GDP reveals some surprises (Table 28.1). The fourth largest entity, Euronext, is the combined single stock market of France, the Netherlands, Belgium and Portugal. While most of the listed entities are US-based not all are. It is also a dynamic list, with a number of new entrants. Of course, there are other ways of assessing the relevant data that might throw up a different set of rankings but the important point is that the rank order demonstrates clearly the significance of the listed entities: there are 28 countries and 72 listed public companies in the top 100.

What is notable is the potential that corporations have to shape policy within nation-states. There are two effects of this: in the host nations it remains the case that politicians have to be mindful of the adage that what is good for national champions is good for the national state. In countries that are competing with one another for foreign direct investment from these global entities, then, in a process more akin to a beauty contest than any economic planning model, less developed nations will sometimes compete against each other in terms of tax incentives, grants and other inducements to attract firms to their country. Within countries regional policies operate similarly to try to bring investment to particular regions. Of course, these corporations are not entirely footloose and fancy-free: often they are deeply embedded within specific locales, perhaps because of a specific infrastructure, suppliers, or university research centres. However, there are a lot more firms than countries in the world. UNCTAD – which hosts the United Nations Centre on Transnational Corporations – estimates that there are 60,000 transnational corporations globally. Because states are spatially fixed they are immobile compared to firms and

Table 28.1   *The world's 100 largest economic entities: national stock markets and publicly listed companies in terms of turnover*

Rank	Economic entities	$US bn	Position in 2002
1	USA	13,778	1
2	JAPAN	2750	2
3	UK	1936	4
4	Euronext (Europe)	1936	4
5	GERMANY	979	5
6	CANADA	855	7
7	HONG KONG	680	9
8	SWITZERLAND	677	6
9	SPAIN	653	10
10	ITALY	584	8
11	AUSTRALIA	566	11
12	CHINA	484	–
13	TAIWAN	356	13
14	General Electric (US)	308	14
15	SWEDEN	298	20
16	Microsoft (US)	294	12
17	SOUTH KOREA	287	17
18	INDIA	274	–
19	Pfizer (US)	264	18
20	Exxon Mobil (US)	264	15
21	SOUTH AFRICA	256	22
22	Citigroup Inc. (US)	247	19
23	Wal-Mart (US)	229	16
24	Intel (US)	204	32
25	BRAZIL	203	29
26	BP (Europe)	181	24
27	FINLAND	171	26
28	AIG (US)	169	23
29	Vodaphone (Europe)	169	28
30	MALAYSIA	165	30
31	Cisco (US)	164	35
32	IBM (US)	160	25
33	Johnson & Johnson	150	21
34	HSBC (Europe)	149	39
35	SINGAPORE	142	41
36	GlaxoSmithKL (Europe)	137	31
37	Berkshire Hathaway (US)	128	37
38	Procter & Gamble (US)	127	34
39	Coca-Cola (US)	122	33
40	Bank of America (US)	118	38
41	MEXICO	118	45
42	Toyota (Japan)	116	45
43	DENMARK	114	50
44	TotalFinalElf (Europe)	112	46
45	Altria (US)	110	42
46	NTTnDoCoMo (Japan)	109	–
47	Royal Dutch (Europe)	107	44
48	Merck (US)	100	27
49	Wells Fargo (US)	99	48
50	Nestlé (Europe)	99	55
51	GREECE	98	61
52	THAILAND	95	–
53	Verizon (US)	94	36
54	Telecomm Italia (Europe)	91	75
55	Chevron Texaco (US)	90	54

Table 28.1 (*Continued*)

Rank	Economic entities	$US bn	Position in 2002
56	PetroChina (China)	89	–
57	NORWAY	88	65
58	Dell Computer (US)	67	62
59	Royal Bank of Scotland (Europe)	85	60
60	UPS (US)	84	56
61	SBC Comm (US)	83	43
62	AstraZeneca (Europe)	82	76
63	CHILE	81	90
64	TimeWarner (US)	81	63
65	PepsiCo (US)	80	43
66	Nokia (Europe)	79	49
67	Eli Lillly (US)	79	52
68	Amgen (US)	79	64
69	Home Depot (US)	79	83
70	IRELAND	77	73
71	Viacom (US)	76	51
72	Nippon T&T (Japan)	76	78
73	Eni (Europe)	75	70
74	Deutsche Telkom (Europe)	74	72
75	J.P. Morgan Chase (US)	74	80
76	Abbott Labs (US)	73	71
77	Telefonica (Europe)	73	82
78	Comcast (US)	72	67
79	Fannie Mae (US)	72	57
80	USB (Europe)	72	74
81	Shell Trading (Europe)	71	66
82	Roche (Europe)	70	68
83	HewlettPackard (US)	69	69
84	Oracle (US)	68	58
85	ISRAEL	68	–
86	3M (US)	66	89
87	France Telcom (Europe)	63	–
88	Morgan Stanley (US)	62	93
89	American Express (US)	62	84
90	Wachovia (US)	60	81
91	China Mobile (Hong Kong)	60	100
92	Barclays (Europe)	59	100
93	Medtronic (US)	58	77
94	Wyeth (US)	57	–
95	BHP-Billiton (Australia)	57	–
96	USBancorp (US)	57	98
97	Samsung Group (South Korea)	56	95
98	Banco Santander (Europe)	55	–
99	Kraft Foods (US)	55	59
100	L'Oreal (Europe)	54	85

Source: Merged data from the International Federation of Stock Markets and the Yahoo! Finance Stockscreener, cross-referenced against the *Financial Times*' FT Global 500, reported in Sheehan (2004)

so their governments have to struggle with the policy implications of globalization: they cannot decamp or disengage. Most of these global corporations are domiciled in relatively few countries: firms from Japan and the United States dominate the list of global 500 firms. There are twice as many US firms (nearly 200) as Japanese (about 100). Germany, the UK and

France each have nearly half as many as Japan, with numbers distributed around forty. After these few countries, most other countries hardly rate, with the exceptions of Switzerland, Italy, South Korea and Canada, who each have about ten such firms, while there are a small handful of firms from the remaining OECD countries as well as one or two from China, Taiwan, Venezuela and some other industrialized economies (Bergesen and Sonnett, 2001).

The impact and contribution of global financial institutions on the processes of globalization are extremely significant. Institutions such as the IMF, according to ex-World Bank economist Stiglitz (2002), have had a deleterious developmental effect by patterning development on a limited number of assumptions and models. Such institutions have a convergent effect in patterning globalization. However, as he makes clear, this patterning should be countered with that encouraged by other related institutions, such as the World Bank, which in recent years have sought to encourage development based on local initiatives and resources, not just those deemed appropriate in terms of hegemonic models. Equally, it is important to note that recent years have witnessed the rise of well organized, anti-globalization campaigns. The upshot of such activity is that protestors target the meetings of the finance ministers of the developed world. Seattle, Prague etc. have been the locations for the disruption of the financial establishment.

The liberalization of the financial system that took place in the 1980s, accelerating through the 1990s, together with digital revolution in information technology (IT), led to the widespread use of new financial instruments, such as junk bonds, leveraged buy-outs and currency speculation, which became *de rigueur* as finance capital took on a hyperreal quality. One consequence of globalization, Harvey (1992: 194) suggests, is that the financial system has achieved an unprecedented degree of autonomy from real production, becoming dominated by an economy of signs representing capital flows rather than an economy of things. What globalizes an economy of signs are the instantaneous representational possibilities afforded by new communications technology (Harvey, 1992). The rapid spread of IT systems links markets globally such that, for instance, differentials in interest rates between states can lead to rapid, almost instant transfers and movement of large volumes of capital, sometimes with speculative effect, as currency traders take a punt on short-term futures markets for the currency in question.

The global integration of financial markets collapses time, creating instantaneous financial transactions in loans, securities and other innovative financial instruments while the deregulation and internationalization of financial markets creates a new competitive spatial environment (Harvey, 1992: 161) in which globally integrated financial markets increase the speed and accuracy of information flows and the rapidity and directness of transactions.

The increasing coordination of the world's financial system emerged to some degree at the expense of the power of nation-states to control capital flows and hence fiscal and monetary policy. At times when confidence in a national currency is tested it is evident that the definition of a weaker nation-state is that it can no longer hold the line. The UK, for instance, is a country with a history of foreign exchange crises. In 1992, it left the European Monetary System following its inability to hold its exchange rate. 'Black Wednesday', as it was called, cost the UK government billions of pounds, much of which went straight into the bank account of George Soros, a celebrated player on global money markets. Instantaneous financial trading means that shocks felt in one market are communicated immediately around the world's markets.

Perhaps the most striking example in recent years of the globally speculative basis of much of the financial system as a global economy of signs occurred during the dot.com boom. In the late 1990s and up until the middle of 2000, one of the most remarkable share booms in history took place. Amazon.com, the on-line book retailer, was worth US $30 billion at the height of the boom, which made it worth far more than many established manufacturing multinationals. In itself this is perhaps unremarkable, until one considers the circumstances of the

Amazon.com story. In 1999 the organization lost US $700 million and in 2000 was losing some $100 million a month. The collapse in the share price in Amazon was mirrored throughout the dot.com sector, as many shares became, quite literally, worthless. The investment public was for a short time mesmerized by the notion that huge sums of money could be made from Internet sites that purported to sell goods and services. What followed was a hyperreal boom in which the mantra of the new economy was accompanied by images of trendy young people becoming millionaires with apparent ease. When the public woke up to the idea that most of these companies had few customers, huge running costs and very little income, the crash ensued. Like every other bubble in history, the dot.com boom was ultimately unsustainable. Perhaps if the dot.commers had been more familiar with economic history or had taken the time to read more novels they might have been less captivated with illusory numbers and might have realized that, just like tulip fever, dot.com fever would burn out (Moggach, 2000).

Organization

Outside of the economy of signs represented in dot.com fever, a major mechanism of global integration occurs through frequent collaborations and strategic alliances. Alliances are essentially an intermediate strategic device, and part of a web that includes many other transactions. Yoshino and Rangan (1995: 17) define alliances as 'cooperation between two or more independent firms involving shared control and continuing contributions by all partners'. They identify the major strategic objectives of alliances as maximizing value, enhancing learning, protecting core competencies and maintaining flexibility. 'The more a company becomes globalized, the more it is likely to lose its own identity within a tangle of companies, alliances and markets,' suggests Petrella (1996: 76). Particularly in industries where there is a dominant worldwide market leader, strategic alliances and networks allow coalitions of smaller partners to compete against the leading companies rather than each other.

Strategic alliances help transfer technology across borders. Access to new markets is facilitated by using the complementary resources of local firms, including distribution channels, and product range extensions. Alliances allow partners to leverage their specific capabilities and save costs of duplication. Strategic alliances are a way of focusing investments, efforts and attention only on those tasks that a company does well. All other activities can be out-sourced either through alliances or subcontracting. Another way of looking at virtual companies, alliances and joint ventures is as the out-sourcing of risk, allowing organizations at arm's length from the parent companies to take risks more freely, something which the parent organization wishes to avoid.

Transnational activity is not easily managed, precisely because it transcends so many spaces: it involves negotiation with different states, interest groups, suppliers, customers etc., which adds to the burden of senior managerial complexity. For instance, different mentalities and business institutions will be located in different countries: UK and US companies are stock-price-oriented, while, in contrast, Japanese, Dutch and Swiss companies are less sensitive to stock prices. Indeed there has been much debate on the role that the City and financial institutions play in Anglo-American organizations. Critics such as Hutton (1996) argue that the primacy of finance creates an atmosphere in which a short-term orientation prevails, as companies aim to satisfy shareholders, who can easily sell their stock. He contends that this stifles innovation and makes for capricious organizations. In contrast, he notes that the means of ownership of German and Japanese companies enable them to plan for the medium and long term. Around half of all cross-border strategic alliances terminate within seven years. Often, where one or other of the partners purchases the alliance then its termination does not necessarily mean failure – but it does suggest a taxing of managerial capabilities.

Globalization is driven by the strategic responses of firms as they exploit market opportunities and adapt to changes in their technological and institutional environment, and attempt to steer these changes to their advantage. The most important competitive force in the global economy is the capacity for innovation, a thesis powerfully illustrated by Porter (1990) in *The Competitive Advantage of Nations*. Porter correlates the advance of knowledge, achievement in innovation and national competitive advantage. In his search for a new paradigm of national competitive advantage Porter starts from the premise that competition is dynamic and evolving, whereas traditional thinking had a static view on cost-efficiency due to factor or scale advantages. But static efficiency is always being overcome by the rate of progress in the change in products, marketing, new production processes, and new markets. Firms gain competitive advantage by changing the constraints within which they and their competitors operate. The crucial issue for firms, and nations, is how they 'improve the quality of the factors, raise the productivity with which they are utilised, and create new ones' (Porter, 1990: 21). The capacity to successfully innovate on a worldwide basis becomes the key competency of leading international companies. It frequently leads to substantive injustices as employees' knowledge in one part of the world is used to deliver cheaper and more efficient manufacturing in another part of the world, and then their jobs are scrapped (Clegg, 1999).

Market imperfections and high transaction costs provide an incentive for firms to internalize firm-specific knowledge and expertise; additionally, another incentive is to protect intellectual property rights within the firm. Intellectual property is information that derives its intrinsic value from creative ideas. It is also information with a commercial value that can be realized through its sale on the market. Intellectual property rights are bestowed on owners of ideas, inventions and creative expression that have the status of property. Like tangible property, they give owners the right to exclude others from access to or use of their property. What protects intellectual property rights are national laws centred on specific legislative spaces and environments. Intellectual property rights are probably most easily understood through the example of

music. (Music is an interesting metaphor to keep in mind because once it flows in an immediate and unmediated way the central issue becomes how it is that corporations are able to retain their central nodal point in its distribution and channel profit from the transactions.) When a CD is sold, some of what is paid is in part for the intellectual property rights embedded in it. Some elements of royalty will flow to the artists and the composers, as well as the record company. When someone downloads from the Web then these rights are not waived and may be breached. Legally, this is theft of these rights from those who have a legal entitlement to see them protected.

Politics

Ohmae (1990), an opponent of the thesis that national, state-based spaces are still significant, insists that the nation-state is now a dysfunctional unit defining no meaningful flows of economic activity – which sounds like a social democrat's nightmare and a neoliberal's dream rather than an accurate picture of most states in the world today. Not that the supporters of neoliberalism in the economic sphere are lonely voices: indeed, in many ways they comprise a new orthodoxy. It is economic rationality as neoliberalism defines it – the triumph of markets over politics. Efficiency has become a universal value. What it means in a global world is that capital should move freely, anywhere. (People, however, are another matter. Border protection is a term more often used in connection with policing people movements rather than the flow of money in or out of a national space.) Firms should be rent-seekers, searching the globe for competitive advantage, according to this scenario of restless corporations. Ordinary people are expected to accommodate to the new global world order, one in which states no longer protect citizens through delivering citizenship rights so much as structure markets in which they can compete efficiently.

A fundamental tension exists between national governments and transnational companies. Transnationals want unrestricted access to resources and markets throughout the world and freedom to integrate manufacturing and other operations across national boundaries, as well as an unimpeded right to try to coordinate and control all aspects of the company on a worldwide basis. Thus, governance of the corporation, especially as a taxable entity, can frequently cut across government of the territories in which it operates, especially as a taxing authority (Bartlett and Ghoshal, 1995). For instance, Hutton (1996) discusses the tax avoidance schemes of numerous multinational firms, a theme also explored in an article by Mathiason (2003). He reveals that Newscorp Investments, Rupert Murdoch's main UK holding group, paid no corporation tax throughout the 1990s. The theme of Murdoch's taxes are addressed by the Australian Broadcasting Corporation, pointing to the way in which much of Newscorp's profits flow through to countries with low-tax regimes, such as the Dutch Antilles, the Cayman Islands and Hong Kong ('Not Shaken, Not Stirred: Murdoch, Multinationals and Tax', *Australian Broadcasting Corporation News*: http://www.abc.au/news/features/tax/page3.htm). Such a strategy has led to huge reductions in the amount of corporation tax paid. There is no suggestion that any of this activity is illegal – quite the contrary – but it does attest to the difficulties that governments face when dealing with multinationals. Some flows are, as we have remarked, easier to police and more front-page newsworthy than others.

Not the least pressure under which transnational corporations operate is the countervailing tendency of states to try to secure national spaces to their advantage. In a world where traditional protectionism increasingly seems not to be an option – other than for the most powerful players such as the EU (agriculture) and the US (steel as well as agriculture) – states have to make a choice between the prospects of free trade with associated costs, or developing the conditions for managed trade. Many countries join trade blocs, such as NAFTA or the EU, whilst building a regulatory environment within which they offer incentives for economic growth through institutional arrangements that protect national economies from international economic disorder (Tyson, 1992).

Governments face demands from business to make their economy more competitive. To do so they often seek to lighten the regulatory frameworks and eliminate unnecessary government expenditures. It is difficult to reconcile extensive social programs for health, education and retirement with these demands. At risk, as governments seem increasingly to have realized, are those many fibres of a civil society, its 'social capital', that enable a market economy to operate efficiently: markets work best when they are socially embedded rather than disembedded. If you, as a consumer rather than as a citizen, must learn to rely on yourself to fund your education, health and retirement, rather than the state, then many vital economic development functions will be abrogated as state managers cede control to transnational corporations less able to exercise strategic control. Moreover, turning citizens into consumers may only be good for business in the short term – while they have effective demand. If they lose it, as in Argentina in the crises that have dogged the economy since its meltdown in 2001, but which were long prefigured, then no one benefits and everyone loses. Transnational corporations represent important external sources of investment, technology and knowledge for national and regional governments. These may further national priorities, including regional development, employment creation, import substitution and export promotion, but they will only do so within explicit policy frames that state managers set. The failure of state managers in this respect might explain, in part, why students increasingly have to pay for their own education when the companies that might hire them in the future are not always making their contributions through the tax system.

Government priorities to develop prosperous national competitive economies demand tax receipts that transnationals, as rational economic actors, will seek to minimize in the interest of their major stakeholders, the shareholders. Governments conceive of capturing global competitiveness within the national economy while transnational organizations think of global competitiveness globally. If, in terms of the global system, it is economically more rational to move call centre jobs to India, then, even when the company is 50 per cent owned by the government on behalf of the taxpayers, it is not surprising that it will do so – whatever the embarrassment to the government may be. A case in point is Telstra, the national telecoms corporation in Australia. The rationalities of government and commerce differ greatly: the transnational company has a bottom line to which it can reduce costs and benefits, while governments have a far more complex and ambiguous set of life-chances to deal with. They have to manage changing definitions of what constitute 'citizenship rights', such as taxpayer-funded provision of big-ticket items like health and education, or else they have to manage to persuade people who once saw themselves primarily as citizens to become consumers in markets that transnational corporations are only too keen to enter.

Governments seek to prevent the use of 'screwdriver plants' to evade trade restrictions, through simple assembly of products essentially manufactured overseas, because, as well as relatively small tax receipts, these plants offer low-skilled employment, with little local value-added, minimal new technology and few multiplier effects. Governments have learned that very often, as soon as the grants and subsidies come to an end, the transnational seeks a new state offering a fresh bounty. The corollary of such experiences is that governments increasingly apply investment regulations that define specific levels of local content, technology transfer and a variety of other conditions, in an effort to make transnational companies increase the extent of their local activities.

Transnationals expect states to cover the costs of basic infrastructure. These include things such as funding of basic and high-risk research; universities and vocational training systems; promotion and funding of the dissemination of scientific and technical information and technology transfer, as well as economic and physical security and a communications infrastructure, such as up-to-date and high-speed international rail links. Additionally, companies often expect states to provide tax incentives for investment in industrial R&D and technological innovations, as well as guarantees that national enterprises from the given country have a stable home base. Privileged access to the domestic market via public contracts (defence, telecommunications, health, transport, education and social services) is also often required. Transnational firms also expect appropriate industrial policies, particularly for those in the high technology strategic sectors (defence, telecommunications and data processing). An important feature of the military-industrial complex is the extent to which large corporations rely upon government contracts. For instance, in 1999 the US government funded defence contracts to the value of $118 billion, of which 26 per cent went to Boeing, Lockheed Martin and Raytheon (http://www.cdi.org/issues/usmi/complex/). Such policies protect designated sectors of the domestic market from international competition, as well as support and assist (through regulatory, commercial, diplomatic and political means) local companies in their efforts to survive in international markets, issues addressed by Charles Perrow (1972) in his seminal study of *The Radical Attack on Business*.

The expectation that states will support business is often represented in terms of capital mobility and its logic. That is, if the local state does not provide the required sweeteners, mobile capitalism will simply exit the scene and set up where the benefits sought can be ensured. The thesis is overstated because in terms of the important criteria of share of assets, ownership, management, employment and the location of R&D, home bases remain important. Very few firms are genuinely transnational in these respects (Weiss, 1997: 10, citing Hu [1992]). With Petrella (1996) and Weiss (1997), one can conclude that states can adapt and innovate around their specific national institutional frameworks.

Government actions often work well for transnationals: for instance, downsizing of the state often produces new commercial opportunities in fields such as defence contracting and telecommunications. Most of the social and economic programs of national governments, even though they have been subject to severe efficiency drives, and a transformation in management, resources and methods of delivery, are still in existence. Even after the great waves of privatization that have swept the world, nation-states remain in charge of essential parts of their sovereignty, such as legislation and the formation of national economic policy. Globalization is itself in part a consequence of adaptations and innovations by firms to state capacities in these areas.

Jobs

There is no doubt that globalization spreads certain universal values and attachments through its world of global consumer products and brands. Rolex, Chivas Regal and Porsche spell success in just about every language. All young global symbolic analysts, whether working on the semiotics of money, films or words, would recognize such symmetry. From Reich's (1991) perspective, these people are the research scientists, new professional engineers, public relations executives, investment bankers, lawyers, real estate developers and creative accountants; management, financial, tax, energy, armaments, agricultural and architectural consultants; management information and organization development specialists; strategic planners, corporate headhunters and systems analysts as well as advertising executives, marketing strategists, art directors, architects, cinematographers, film editors, production designers, publishers, writers and editors, journalists, musicians, television and film producers, and even a few global university professors. Symbolic analysis manipulates symbols to solve, identify and broker problems. It simplifies reality into abstract images by rearranging, juggling, experimenting, communicating and transforming these images, using analytic tools, such as mathematical algorithms, legal arguments, financial analysis, scientific principles, or psychological insights that persuade, amuse, induce, deduce, or somehow or other address conceptual puzzles (Reich, 1991).

To what degree are these symbolic analysts or knowledge workers different from what has gone before? What marks out their professional identity? Management analysts, such as (Mats Alvesson 1993; Alvesson and Karreman, 2001), have argued that what marks such work

as different are its linguistic and symbolic accomplishment in circumstances of high ambiguity and uncertainty. In such circumstances, there is not one correct answer; instead there are a number of competing, plausible alternatives. It places the persuasive abilities of the knowledge worker to the fore, comprising both their image intensity (the suit they wear, the briefcase they carry, the sleekness of their PowerPoint presentation) and the persuasiveness of their rhetoric (the robustness of their argument, their vocabulary, their accent). These workers are global, working for Big 4 firms or their small boutique equivalents; they regularly move between the great commercial capitals of the world, creating genuinely international corporate elites. Such transience, perhaps, fosters networking skills and alters sensibilities around risk, two other important characteristics of the symbolic analysts. In summary, they are the stressed-out but well-remunerated shifters and shapers of money, meanings and markets, doing deals, making business, moving from project to project (Garrick and Clegg, 2001).

The evidence of these jobs suggests that, despite attention to the issues of wages and associated cost of taxes raised by journalists and politicians, transnational companies do not, by and large, invest their main facilities where wages and taxes are the lowest. If they did the theory of comparative costs would work far better than it does. The reasons are self-evident: wages are often a minor cost-factor; greater transaction costs are associated with the presence or absence of densely embedded networks for business in particular locales, such as the world cities of New York, London, Paris and Tokyo, which are likely to remain so. Additionally, domestic linkages institutionally frame businesses in embedded relationships with universities, financial institutions, government institutions and so on. Government–business relations typically have an exclusive rather than open character and can be an important component in building national competitive advantage (Porter, 1990), which then attracts globally skilled knowledge-workers.

The international flow of expert migrant professional and knowledge workers helps create a global labour market in a growing number of occupations, not only those that are glamorous. Supporting the cars, shopping, apartments and travel of these wealthy symbolic analysts is all the dirty work done by those who cook, wash and clean up, who pack and sell convenience foods, who park and service cars, who tend and care for appearance: the face workers, nail workers and hair workers – necessary body maintenance to keep all the wealthy and beautiful people sweet. In global cities such as Hong Kong and Singapore you can see street-level globalization in the form of the mainly Filipina and Sri Lankan female domestic workers who congregate in the public spaces of the Central Business District on their day of rest, Sunday. The rest of the week it is more likely to be thronged with global business people while the maids, chauffers and other domestic servants make global households run smoothly.

Additionally, there is a shadow-labour force of workers in the symbolic sphere – but workers who are tightly scripted, operating in unambiguous and simple environments, unlike their symbolic analyst counterpoints. Outside of the confines of the corporate glitterati and the symbolic analyst elite there is a category of dis-aggregated work quintessentially associated with globalization: that of call centres. Enabled by developments in technology, call centres were ushered into existence in the 1990s, the idea being particularly attractive to corporations as it allowed them to downsize parts of the organization and establish call centres in relatively deprived areas where wage rates were lower and the workforce more pliable. The growth of information technology allows for the increasing codification of knowledge reducing the need for physical contact between producers and consumers, of which call centres are the perfect example – they can be located anywhere. Work is cheapened by routinization of existing tasks; re-engineered tasks can then be moved to places where wages are cheaper. The transaction costs associated are not great: satellites and computers can ensure virtual linkage. The blueprint is clear: rationalize parts of the organization; introduce jobs at just over minium wage in deprived, postindustrial parts of the country; institute a system of surveillance aimed at maximizing efficiency.

By 2002, 3 per cent of the US workforce and 1.3 per cent of the European workforce were making a living from working in call centres, otherwise termed 'factories of the future'. To put a more concrete number on this, in 2002 there were 650,000 call centre workers in 3300 call centres in the UK (ContactBabel, 2002). A good deal was written about the repetitive nature of the work, the exacting management controls and the sheer amount that operatives were expected to do. The last few years have seen call centres go global, as it were. Increasingly, corporations are shifting their operations out of relatively poor areas of developed countries into the developing world. For instance, BT, the telecoms corporation, is cutting back its UK call centres, in favour of opening up operations in Delhi and Bangalore. Once call centres are established, they are estimated to be considerably cheaper to run in India than in the UK. For instance, in 2003, a British call centre worker would typically earn £13,000–14,000 a year: in India a worker doing a similar job will make £1200. The move to India is continuing apace, to the extent that a report in the *Guardian* (Tran, 2003) suggests that by 2008 there will be around 100,000 call centre jobs created by British companies alone. The Philippines, the Czech Republic and South Africa are also among the nations attempting to make inroads into the call centre industry, to a sufficient extent that they form an important pillar of each nation's economic policy.

In terms of globalization, there are also 'grunge jobs' (Jones, 2003: 256). Jones sees grunge jobs as essentially bifurcated: first there are the semiskilled workers who work in the lower reaches of the supply chains established by the global giants, which Castells (2000) estimated at about 35 per cent of the jobs in the US economy. It is a contingent, easily dismissible and re-employable mass of people who can be used and laid off to absorb transaction costs and cushion demand for the core transnational companies globally. When these transnational companies react to signs of economic distress then it is these subcontract workers in the supply chain who bear the pain first, buffering the core company employees. These workers are low skill, add little value and are easily disposable, but at least they may have social insurance and do work in the formal economy.

The second element in the composition of the grunge economy comprises an underclass of workers who are often illegal immigrants working sporadically in extreme conditions outside of the formally regulated labour market: think of sweatshops in the garment industry, for instance. As Jones (2003) reports, there is research from Deloitte and Touche (1998) that suggests that informal sector activity ranges from 40 per cent in the Greek economy, through to 8–10 per cent of the UK economy. States often encourage the informal sector as an arena from which 'street level' and taxable entrepreneurs might develop in enterprises other than the marketing of drugs, prostitutes and the proceeds of crime (Deloitte & Touche, 1998; Sassen, 1998).

Of course, transnationals also create jobs when they employ people indirectly through global supply chains. Transnational corporations often get a bad press for their subcontracting practices in the Third World. For instance, writers such as Naomi Klein (2001) are extremely critical of the role that transnationals play in the developing world. Her argument is that transnationals behave irresponsibly by employing subcontractors who pay low wages, have poor working conditions and potentially abusive environments. She singles out the famous companies whose brands are known the world over. In a campaign by Oxfam – a nongovernmental organization – Nike have been taken to task over these issues. One thing that such campaigning activity has delivered is assurance from Nike that such concerns have been addressed, which for many is a contestable point. On balance it is fair to say that they may be positive agents of change. It is clear that transnationals have the potential to create stable, long-term jobs with decent pay and conditions. Those that do not will be subject to campaigns throughout the Western World. Thus, potentially they deliver better jobs and better wages in many economies: additionally, they set standards that local industry has to aspire to in both labour and industry practice. If there really were 'no logos' it would be much harder to police these standards as there would

be no brand differentiae offering opportunities for discrimination between the choice of one T-shirt or another. One would expect that in such a situation price signals would be even more sovereign and would exercise still stronger downward pressure on local wages and conditions in the Third World. Fair logos rather than no logos might be a better policy. Subcontract manufacturing jobs also create higher export earnings domestically, which potentially enhance the tax base of national governments. Potentially, because often these companies are quite sophisticated in moving tax losses around their global operations and using transfer pricing of internally traded goods to minimize liabilities where they will attract the highest regimes of tax.

The employees in the sweatshops of the Third World are in some respects fortunate: it all depends on the point of comparison. They have jobs: they are not hustling on the street, selling gum to standing motorists, shoe-shines to seated customers in restaurants on the street, or their bodies to whosoever wants to buy their services. In the cities of the Third World and in the ghettoes of the First World, many people on the mean streets of the barrios and *favelas*, desperate and poor, are in this underclass position. For them any organizational employment would be a step up the ladder of opportunity. It seems perverse, in these circumstances, for Western liberals to oppose the opportunities that they actually get on the basis of standards never applied to life lived on the streets.

GLOBAL IDENTITIES

People go where they think jobs will be, especially those without many opportunities where they are. In the United States, with its porous land borders, wealthy middle class people in major cities live off the backs of such migrant, often illegal, labour. Victor Villaseñor's (1992) book *Rain of Gold* tells a moving story. He writes of a Mexican-American friend who swam the Rio Grande five times, before he became a hybrid, and of another who lived and raised a family in New York City for 17 years.

When he first came, he told him, it was difficult to adapt because there were no shops selling the ingredients of Mexican cooking, no chillies, *tomatillos*, or *masa de harina*. Now those items can be bought five minutes from his New York home. Even in cities such as Melbourne or Manchester, far from Mexico, it is possible to buy these things. The globalization of languages, food and cuisines, together with the spread of places of worship, is a good index of globalization because wherever people move they take their everyday material cultures with them, and their language, religion, and food are the most evident manifestations of such culture.

As culture travels it becomes interpenetrated with traces of the places it visits and the peoples it encounters and undergoes metamorphosis. More complex notions of personal identity emerge as a result of globalization, attendant upon revolutions in gender, sexual, ethnic and racial mores leaving their traces on hitherto more restricted societies. The interpenetration of culture and economy produces new micromarkets. These markets are for branded goods and services premised on the differentiation of cultural identities based on the possession of positional goods: things whose value is wholly culturally defined by who has them and who does not. The drivers for this differentiation occurred first within sophisticated societies, whose market niches were increasingly distributed by global corporations, and were then spread through the global reach of mass media of communication. Watch the advertisements between CNN news stories to get the picture. If the proposition that globalizing strategies form a singular rationality were true, the homogenization of taste and consumption would inevitably lead to standardization of products, manufacturing, marketing and trade. Such a saturation of markets, with a few common products gaining enormous profit, is manifested in McDonaldization. You might think that with so much homogenizing pressure the world and its peoples are becoming more one-dimensional, less complex and differentiated, and more alike. However, standardization has its limits, and there are important cultural, political and economic forces for local differentiation

that have emerged powerfully in recent years to question the logic of globalization.

The differentiation of identity opens up new opportunities for market differentiation. Not all questions of identity can be resolved through markets, however. Old questions of identity re-emerge in the global era, partially as a consequence of the breakup of state socialist hegemony, principally in the former USSR and the Balkans, but also through the assertion of religious identities founded in Islam, Orthodox Christianity and, sometimes, as in East Timor, Catholicism. These issues frame the global world of consciousness within which Western diplomats, politicians, generals and international managers operate, and which they must navigate.

Most major social theorists of the past, such as Karl Marx (1976) and Talcott Parsons (1966), agreed on one thing: that the future would be much more homogeneous than its past and that the trajectory of future development would be towards convergence rather than divergence. We are now living in the futures that they foresaw but do we live in a moment of global convergence? On the contrary, suggest a number of influential analyses. What might once have been thought imminently extinguishable is now as often celebrated as hastened to its doom – although the celebrants and the hasty rarely share the same interests.

Partly inspired by a broader debate about culture, a number of writers have suggested that the strengths of indigenously embedded ways of doing things need re-evaluation (Yeung, 2000). The interest in indigenous peoples is not just restricted to liberals interested in different philosophies of the world. Some pharmaceutical transnationals, seeking to develop new drugs to deliver more growth, higher earnings and profits, are taking a keen interest in indigenous peoples. Their interest is in patenting their DNAs, in case they should contain genetic secrets that can help treat contemporary Western diseases. In some respects such reappraisal often attaches itself to postmodern themes where there is the implicit idea that stages may be jumped and that societies can move from premodernity to postmodernity

(Clegg, 1990). Convergence may neither be necessary nor desirable. Individual identities, it is realized, differ greatly across national societies as well as within them. Culture is increasingly seen as critical and convergence is seen as less likely and less productive than divergence.

The spread of the mass media, especially television, means that in principle almost everyone can be instantaneously exposed to the same images. However, the world is becoming less a 'global village' and more a 'global market', in which privileged commodities for sale are often based on hybridization, created from the intermingling of peoples and items from different cultures. Once more, music is a good example, with the huge growth in the 'World Music' market from the 1990s, when, encouraged by the example of Jamaican Reggae superstar Bob Marley, Third World musicians became global stars in the new niche market. But to do so they had to move through the circuits of power of the global recording companies, such as BMG, Sony and so on. Maybe now, in the days of MP3 and i-Pod, this will no longer be the case? Music flows digitally and seamlessly in the global economy.

It could be argued that inter-subjective experience has become global today through exposure to international media reporting. However, what such reporting means may be highly variable. While there may be no one who cannot recall the images of the planes ripping into the World Trade Center the images mean very different things for different political actors in different parts of the world. The consequences of global exposure are profound: states wage war pre-emptively against concepts, such as 'Terror', attached to socio-religious movements in a world where states are no longer the only organizations controlling use of the means of violence. In the nineteenth century, as a sign of global power, Europeans could shell the coastline of the African jungle in a vain assertion of their technological superiority (read Joseph Conrad's [1970] *Heart of Darkness*). Today, America and its allies can bomb anywhere on the planet as a sign of their global reach while adversaries in 'The War on Terror' can cause carnage through lower tech but no less fearsome weapons. Ceaseless detail

is broadcast about the latest 'victories' and 'advances' in this war from Al-Jazeera and CNN – although the detail of what is a victory or a defeat may vary with what one watches and where one watches it. The emergence of global communication gives rise to a global consciousness that is hotly contested. The freedoms offered by a market-based culture can be seen as residing anywhere on a continuum from seductively glamorous to threateningly dangerous – depending on the presuppositions that one starts with. Not all religions, ideologies or belief systems want the liberation that a consumer society offers their members.

Globalization exacerbates tensions between local senses of self, of who you are, and who you could be. And these are not free-floating signifiers of equal weight in dreamtime stories that imagine futures now rather than pasts lost but are stories that lodge in different forms of consciousness. Some are encoded in the lore of the elders, the wisdom of the tribe, while others present themselves through the news on the airwaves, the sights and sounds that come down the tube, the transmissions through the satellites, optical cables and microwaves. The local is now truly global.

Some global significations route more global imagination than others. CNN is not the only global media entity. The Murdoch News Corporation satellite now spreads its Fox footprint over almost all of Europe, North America and the Asian region. Certainly, there is considerable fixity to the messages that the media transmits but, recalling the error with which McLuhan (1964) started the whole globalization debate, there is also considerable diversity in the way in which they are interpreted, instantiated and used. That forms of production and distribution are fixed in a technological form does not mean closure in forms of cultural consumption. Murdoch discovered this when he found that his analysis that the digital age meant the end of dictatorship was a message received extremely coolly in Beijing. His subsequent ditching of the BBC from his satellite broadband, for unfriendly reporting, helped appease sensibilities somewhat, as have critical remarks about the Dalai Lama and the decision not to print Chris

Patten's (1998) book based on his experiences as the last Hong Kong Governor, as well as the diplomatic efforts of Chinese-born Wendy Deng, who is also Mrs Rupert Murdoch.

Globalization in the cultural sphere has meant the global proliferation of norms of individualized values, originally of Western origin, in terms of a discourse of 'rights' (Markoff, 1996). In some views, such as those of the Bush administration, these rights should increasingly shape identities. Such discourse is not unproblematic: it meets considerable opposition from religious, political, ethnic, sexual and other rationalities tied to the specificities of local practices, but it does provide a framework and set of terms through which resistance to these might be organized. One theorist who has realized this is Barber (1996), who has popularized the idea that the world is set on a collision between McWorld and Jihad, where convergence in the form of primarily US business interests meets stubborn and deep-seated sources of local resistance, embedded in religious world-views. From this perspective, the trajectory of convergence produces a globalization of culture, technologies and markets against which local forms of retribalization, through Jihad, will react.

Perhaps the clearest expression of the emergence of a discourse of global rights occurs in relation to the status of women. Moghadam (1999: 368), for instance, suggests that:

> [T]he singular achievement of globalization is the proliferation of women's movements at the local level, the emergence of transnational feminist networks working at the global level, and the adoption of international conventions such as the *Convention on the Elimination of All Forms of Discrimination Against Women* and the *Beijing Declaration and Platform for Action of the Fourth Conference on Women.*

Such doctrines are clear expressions of a global discourse of rights applying to just over a half of humankind. However, at the same time as these rights documents are issued globally, other aspects of globalization have contradictory effects. In many ways, suggests Moghadam (1999: 376), working class and poor urban women have been the 'shock absorbers' of neoliberal economic policies. Structural adjustment policies that increase prices, eliminate subsidies, diminish social services and increase fees for essentials hitherto provided by the state, place women at greater risk of ill-health and poverty. By contrast, however, to the extent that transnationals enter into employment in these regions then they represent unparalleled opportunities for employment outside of either the informal sector of dubious work and conditions or outside domestic service, opportunities that are often accompanied by education programs, as governments seek to equip their human capital with the upgradeable skills that will attract further investment.

Purser, Park and Montuori (1995) suggest that if one focuses only on the economic dimension, considered in relation only to those selves whose profits are served by corporate power, anthropocentrism will result. The global constituents of the environment, including other selves, humankind and the natural environment will suffer, particularly where there is a high degree of separation of simulacra from the real economy. Real economies root themselves in places; simulacra are free-floating signifiers that invest in signs that translate only randomly into decisions that affect the lives and deaths of people in real economies remote from the centres of financial flows.

The subjects who are adversely impacted by the experience of globalization are not only human. Some subjects cannot articulate discursively the momentous changes occurring in their constitution. One can think of whales, seals, or 'mad' cows whose rights to be ruminants have been violated by organized agri-industry and have had to be reasserted by government policies, and other species that have been the subject of organized campaigns to represent or save them in some way. Animal rights are now well established (Singer, 1976).

The ecosystem as a whole is now often ascribed rights and interests, in the name of sustainability. Other entities incapable of interest representation, such as fetuses, those who are on life-support systems, and so on, are also ascribed rights. All of these are represented as global subjects with assigned rights and interests that some organizations violate, others ignore and a few choose to represent (Meyer, 2000: 239). It matters not whether a cow is British or French in an economy where meat, sperm, livestock and meat-derived products, such as gelatine and cosmetic additives, trade globally. Greenpeace, as an organization for expressing a standardized moral consciousness that can mobilize activists anywhere, can represent Canadian seals as easily as those that are Russian and, through global media, can act its way into the global consciousness. Local species can become global icons.

GLOBAL WINNERS AND LOSERS

News Corp and some other global media companies such as CNN are undoubted winners from globalization – but there are also losers. Some of these losers are the organizational behemoths created in response to the opportunities for global action that the digital world presents, companies that simply overreached their corporate governance and integrative capabilities. A case in point, staying in the media space, would be the TimeWarner/AOL merger, which created an overvalued corporate entity with a difficult blend of organizational cultures. Indeed, ungovernable entities that are too complex culturally, organizationally and financially could be seen as one aspect of the collateral damage that globalization has inflicted on the ranks of business. But these are neither the primary nor the most desperate casualties.

The primary casualties of globalization appear to be low-skilled grunge workers in traditional manufacturing countries who either lose their jobs to overseas, or experience a painful slide in their wage rates as employers strive to reduce costs. Particularly vulnerable are the relatively unskilled and under-educated, especially in labour market systems that do not develop very active and interventionist labour market policies. Wood (1994) reckons that trade with developing countries is the prime suspect for the increase in inequality *within* industrial countries. He estimates that it has reduced the demand for low-skilled workers in rich economies by more than a fifth. Against this, however, you must balance the fact that most jobs are still in spatially discrete and non-tradeable sectors. A wharfie in Australia cannot easily relocate to become a longshoreman in the United States. And even for the 16 per cent of US workers who make their living in manufacturing, the overlap of production with low wage countries is relatively small. Their main competitors in most sectors are workers in other high wage countries, as is true of most OECD states.

It should also be noted that global capital markets provide poor countries with better access to capital and thus to transferable technology. For instance, Sri Lanka is a poor country – but it has some of the most technologically sophisticated jersey textile plants in the world, such as JerseyLanka, staffed by technology and management graduates from Sri Lankan universities, trained by British, Australian, and South African expatriates, producing knitted jersey destined for manufacture by contractors fulfilling orders for Marks & Spencer. None the less, the main beneficiaries of globalization are undoubtedly the employees of the transnational companies and those symbolic analyst professionals who service these companies: lawyers, researchers, consultants, IT experts and so on. Meyer (2000: 240–1) is unequivocal that those who organize scientific and professional activity on a global scale are the real winners. Professional associations represent such people; international knowledge-businesses, universities and research laboratories employ such people, as do international governmental associations and agencies. These are the people at home in airport lounges, with frequent flyer programmes, and portable computers as global talismans of their universality. The winners also include not just those whom he identifies as being able to make universalistic claims about rights, science or any other form of expert knowledge, as well as the digital content providers, but also include those who are experts in various global sports, representing sponsors such as Nike, Adidas and other transnational sports companies whose brands are ubiquitous, as well as the global entertainers, the J-Los and Kylies. Global brands and those who sustain then are unequivocal winners from globalization.

With the emergence of global brands, international out-sourcing and supply chains, there is a natural tendency for the market leader to get further ahead, causing a monopolistic concentration of business (Arthur, 1996). Real dangers attach to winning when the losers are excluded and abandoned to their situation. The winners can come together and increasingly integrate with one another. Where such processes occur within societies serious consequences may result in terms of increased poverty, unemployment, alienation and crime. But the consequences are of a higher order of magnitude when the processes of exclusion and alienation involve countries and whole regions of the world. The share of world trade in manufactured goods of the 102 poorest countries of the world is falling as the share of the developed world increases. There is a de-linking of the less from the more developed world, particularly in Africa. The core of an increasingly globally integrated world economy excludes those countries from the margins. For instance, the World Bank Poverty Report (2001: see http://www.worldbank.org/poverty/wdrpoverty/index.htm) highlights that 'Of the world's 6 billion people, 2.8 billion live on less than $2 a day and 1.2 billion on less than $1 a day. Eight out of every 100 infants do not live to see their fifth birthday. Nine of every 100 boys and 14 of every 100 girls who reach school age do not attend school.' One can only speculate on the political consequences of such a new global division: they are unlikely to be integrative for the world system as a whole (Petrella, 1996: 80–1).

Attitudes toward the overwhelming political and economic forces for globalization range from enthusiastic integration to determined isolation, and from a belief that the free market will resolve all resulting tensions, to a commitment for comprehensive political regulation. 'New Right' politicians are against globalization: it brings people they don't want to their nation; it threatens them with ideas they don't like, and while it sells them lots of cheap goods that they can afford it does so at the cost of vulnerable jobs in previously protected parts of the domestic economy – the heartland of their political support. They see globalization

as fragmenting national identities. Those under threat demand to be protected from its adverse effects. Ethnically distinct identities (those who do not share what extremists constitute as national identity, usually because of skin-colour or religion, or both) are denounced and marginalized as denying the majority of 'ordinary people' their rights to economic surplus, relief, jobs, housing, or whatever.

The New Right sometimes meets the Old Left in the shadows cast by politics. One also finds S11 anarchists, agreeing, in Sklair's (1999: 158) words that 'globalization is often seen in terms of impersonal forces wreaking havoc on the lives of ordinary and defenceless people and communities'. As he goes on to say, it 'is not coincidental that interest in globalization over the last two decades has been accompanied by an upsurge in what has come to be known as New Social Movements (NSM) research (Spybey, 1996; Sklair, 1999).' NSM theorists argue for the importance of identity politics (of gender, sexuality, ethnicity, age, community and belief systems) in the global era. S11 are a perfect example of this – and their strategies are based on global tactics. They do not seek to build effective conventional political alliances and positions but use the tools of globalization, such as the Internet, to create activist happenings as spectacular media events whenever the leading global players meet internationally. But if you are against a concept such as globalization, which seeks to capture a broad array of social detail, which bits of it are you most against? And what is the alternative to globalization: is it protectionism? Of course, there is an argument that sometimes protectionism, especially where it preserves unique intellectual/cultural property, such as national cinema or television, is necessary if the juggernaut of cheap mass-produced and McDonaldized products is not to eliminate cultural differences (Ritzer, 1993, 2004).

And in the world at large, the effects of globalization can be seen through studying the GNPs of the world of nations in the postwar eras. Those that have been phenomenally successful in lifting themselves up those tables, have, by and large, engaged, and been engaged with, the world globally. The states that have not been engaged or have remained disengaged have remained poor and real losers from globalization.

LOCAL SPECIALIZATION IN A GLOBAL WORLD

Some writers, following Robertson (1992), such as Clarke and Clegg (1998) and Helvacioglu (2000), have referred to the phenomenon of the interpenetration of the global in the local and vice versa, as 'glocalization'. It is a paradoxical consequence of increasing globalization that there is a concentration of clusters of world-class expertise in specialist industries in different local economies around the world. The significant local dimension of the globalization phenomenon consists of regional economies built upon interlinked networks of relations among firms, universities and other institutions in their local environment (see de Vet, 1993; Storper and Scott, 1993; OECD, 1996). Early specialization is reinforced by the growth of similar firms and institutions to create highly competitive industrial and service clusters.

The OECD (1996: 52) explains the rationale for the local concentration of specialist industry in terms of the advantages of being in the same location as similar firms, specialized suppliers and contractors, as well as knowledgeable customers. Additionally, these locations tend to provide a good technological infrastructure, and specialist research institutions, as well as a highly skilled labour force, where specialization within firms enables extensive outsourcing (vertical disintegration) and encourages similar new firms to be set up in the location (horizontal disintegration). For instance, Lash and Urry (1994) discuss the importance of local concentration in the making of movies, while a number of UK authors have described the networks and clusters associated with 'Motorsport Valley' – a small area north of London which accounts for most of the automotive innovation associated with Formula 1 Motor Racing (Tallman et al., 2004).

Local geographic concentrations of three broad groups of industrial and service activities have been noted. First are highly competitive traditional, labour-intensive industries, which are highly concentrated, including textiles and clothing in Italy. Second, are high-technology industries that often cluster around new activities, such as biotechnology in San Francisco, semi-conductors in Silicon Valley, scientific instruments in Cambridge (UK) and musical instruments in Hamamatsu (Japan). Third, services, notably financial and business services, such as advertising, films, fashion design and R&D activities, concentrate in a few big global cities such as Los Angeles, Tokyo, London, Paris, Sydney and Shanghai. Globalization increases the competitiveness of these local economies by attracting international firms with their own specific advantages, and enhancing established sourcing and supply relations. Local firms individually may respond to heightened competition through improving their innovative performance. Innovation may be extended through developing greater interactions between firms, suppliers, users, production support facilities, and educational and other institutions in local innovation systems. Local firms, particularly if they are highly specialized, will cooperate with international firms seeking complementary resources in the specialized assets of small firms. It is not only in areas of straightforward global business, such as manufacturing, that locality can become a source of competitive advantage: it can also be built from marginalized and powerless local cultures. Think of hip-hop, now the dominant popular music trend globally. It emerged from the ghetto culture of alienated black youth in the big cities of the United States.

Global projects often work against the interests of local people. For instance, indigenous people from the Mexican state of Oaxaca are pitted against transnational agri-business, struggling not only over sustainable agriculture but also for their way of life. The irony is that the struggle is over a crop that is indigenous to the region of Oaxaca, over which the giant US transnational Monsanto now claims intellectual property rights. On the morning of 15 October 2003, 16 paramilitaries attacked a meeting in the village of Santa Maria de Yaviche (Oaxaca, Mexico), which was being held by CIPO-RFM (Consejo Indígena Popular de Oaxaca – Ricardo Flores Magon). One participant was killed by paramilitaries and eight others were seriously wounded. None of the participants of the meeting was armed. CIPO-RFM had been the target of earlier paramilitary attacks and had suffered from other kinds of persecution. The CIPO-RFM has been active in the campaign against globalization, because of their traditional role as maize farmers. The people of Oaxaca call themselves 'people of maize' and were the originators of corn as a crop. A spokesman for CIPO-RFM explains: 'Our ancient varieties are being destroyed by GM corn coming in from the US, cheaper than we can produce.' Last year, university researchers discovered that between 20 and 60 per cent of traditional maize varieties of crops in CIPO-RFM's community were contaminated with modified genes from imported Monsanto gene-patented corn. These indigenous peoples are struggling for respect for their rights, battling against imprisonments, kidnappings, torture and attacks allegedly supported by officials in the state government. (See http://www.newint.org/features/cancun/index2.htm for more details.)

Although many injustices have occurred to indigenous peoples globally, the situation may be changing with the latest developments in globalization, as the indigenous becomes re-evaluated for its otherness, an otherness that is seen to be in some ways more authentically in tune with nature. As the example of the resistance of the people of Oaxaca might suggest, a terrible irony may attach to these views: either you stay primitive, poor and pure or become involved in the global economy and be exploited. Indigenes can either conform to role in some kind of protected 'natural' theme park, or, with the patina of existential exoticism that the development of 'creole' cultures offers, show positive new sources of hybridity. However, there is a third way that the contributions of the researchers associated with the Odyssey Group at http://www.geocities.com/the_odyssey_group/index.html suggest. New forms of communication based on the Internet

offer opportunities for local and indigenous communities to meet the global market and benefit from it on their own terms. As Diawara (2000) stresses (in a discussion of Western agencies and their work in the Malian Sahara), there is a need for researchers and managers to try to work with, and integrate, local knowledge and culture with expert knowledge – not to oppose them as mutually impermeable spheres, a point also made by Flyvbjerg (2001) in his conclusions.

CONCLUSION

If the aim of international competition is to win, only a few can be winners. A real danger is that the losers are excluded and abandoned to their situation. The winners come together and increasingly integrate with one another. Where such processes occur within societies, serious consequences may result in terms of increased poverty, unemployment, alienation and crime. But the consequences are of a higher order of magnitude when the processes of exclusion and alienation involve countries and whole regions of the world. The share of world trade in manufactured goods of the 102 poorest countries of the world is falling as the share of the three regions of the Triad increases. There is a 'de-linking' of the less from the more developed world, particularly in Africa. The Triad seem to be composing the core of an increasingly globally integrated world economy from which the countries outside the Triad blocs are largely excluded.

Attitudes toward the overwhelming political and economic forces for globalization range from enthusiastic optimism, as one frequently finds in influential editorials in *The Economist*, expressing a belief that the free market will resolve all resulting tensions, to determined isolationism. Isolationists, epitomized by the anti-EU parties in countries such as the UK, yearn for lost days of national self-sufficiency. A motley collection of actors, including the anti-globalization political parties, such as the Australian One Nation Party or Le Pen's followers in France, found themselves in part agreement on the spatial and moral effects of globalization in fragmenting political identities. Such parties denounce those with ethnically or religiously distinct identities as denying 'ordinary people' (those defined by some, usually xenophobic, conception of 'national' identity) their rights – to the surplus, relief, jobs, housing or whatever.

S11 anarchists are equally as opposed to globalization – albeit for different reasons. They do not seek to build effective conventional political alliances and positions but use the tools of globalization, such as the Internet, to create activist 'happenings' as spectacular media events whenever the leading global players meet internationally. These are the liberal international organizations such as the IMF, World Bank, World Trade Organization and OECD, bodies that stress the inevitability of further globalization and the significance of the role of international agencies in fostering understanding and agreement.

George Soros (1998), who, more than anyone, is an unequivocal winner from globalization, fears that regulation of globalization will not emerge in sufficient time, despite the fact that some political bodies, such as the European Community, appreciate new responsibilities, such as respecting international social and environmental regulations and the integrity of different cultures. Others, of course, amongst them the most powerful, do not. Without the recognition of a common interest taking precedence over particular interests, our present system will break down, he suggests. That at the present, in a global system premised on business and national interests, there are no organized capacities that would seem able to produce such an outcome may be the ultimate challenge of globalization.

NOTE

1 Against the rhetoric of liberalization which can overstress the rationality of transnationals, we must counter the reality of them as, by definition, somewhat disembedded in their international operations and realize that this disembeddedness can sometimes cost them dearly. They get things wrong, precisely because they do not really know the contexts in which they operate in a deep and embedded way. When Mitsubishi managers in the United States

managed in their customary ways they did not expect to be landed with a lawsuit for sexual harassment of female employees and for breaches of the equal employment opportunity laws – but they were. Transnational companies are huge and complex organizations to manage, less gazelles than dinosaurs, and open to many sources of pressure, tension and contradiction in their global operations.

REFERENCES

Alvesson, M. (1993) 'Organizations as rhetoric: knowledge intensive firms and the struggle with ambiguity', *Journal of Management Studies*, 30 (6): 997–1015.

Alvesson, M. and Karreman, D. (2001) 'Odd couple: making sense of the curious concept of knowledge management', *Journal of Management Studies*, 38 (7): 995–1018.

Arthur, B. (1996) 'Increasing Returns and the Two Worlds of Business', *Harvard Business Review*, July.

Bairoch, P. and Kozul-Wright, R. (1996) 'Globalization myths: some historical reflections on integration, industrialization and growth in the world economy', UNCTAD Discussion Paper 113.

Barber, B. (1996) *Jihad vs. McWorld*. New York: Ballantine.

Bartlett, C. and Ghoshal, S. (1995) 'Changing the role of top management: beyond systems to people', *Harvard Business Review*, 73 (3): 132–42.

Bergesen, A.J. and Sonnett, J. (2001) 'The Global 500: mapping the world economy at century's end', *American Behavioral Scientist*, 44 (10): 1602–15.

Castells, M. (2000) *The Information Age: Economy, Society and Culture, Volume 1: The Rise of Network Society*, 2nd edn. Oxford: Blackwell.

Castells, M. (2001) *The Internet Galaxy: Reflections on the Internet, Business and Society*. Oxford: Oxford University Press.

Chandler, A.D., Jr (1990) *Scale and Scope*. Cambridge, MA: Harvard University Press.

Chandler, A.D., Jr (1993) 'Learning and technological change: the perspective from business history', in R. Thomson (ed.), *Learning and Technological Change*. New York: St Martins Press. pp. 24–39.

Clarke, T. and Clegg, S.R. (1998) *Changing Paradigms: The Transformation of Management for the 21st Century*. London: Collins.

Clegg, S.R. (1990) *Modern Organizations: Organization Studies in the Postmodern World*. London: Sage.

Clegg, S.R. (1999) 'Globalizing the intelligent organization: learning organizations, smart workers (not so) clever countries and the sociological imagination', *Management Learning*, 30 (3): 259–80.

Conrad, J. (1970) *Heart of Darkness and Other Stories*, with an introduction by Bruce Harkness and suggestions for reading and discussion by Gladys Veidemanis. Boston, MA: Houghton Mifflin.

ContactBabel (2002) *UK Contact Centre Report*. Retrieved from www.contactbabel.com/uk2002report.html.

De Vet, J. (1993) 'Globalization and local and regional competitiveness', *STI Review*, No. 13. OECD: Paris.

Deloitte & Touche (1998) *Informal Economic Activities in the EU*. Brussels: European Commission.

Diamond, J.M. (1997) *Guns, Germs, and Steel: The Fates of Human Societies*. New York: W.W. Norton.

Diawara, M. (2000) 'Globalization, development politics and local knowledge', *International Sociology*, 15 (2): 361–72.

Dicken, P. (1992) *Global Shift: The Internationalization of Economic Activity*. London: Macmillan.

Flyvbjerg, B. (2001) *Making Social Science Matter: Why Social Inquiry Fails and How It Can Succeed Again*. Cambridge: Cambridge University Press.

Garrick, J. and Clegg, S.R. (2001) 'Stressed-out knowledge workers in performative times: a postmodern take on project-based learning', *Management Learning*, 32 (1): 119–34.

Harvey, D. (1992) *The Condition of Postmodernity*. Oxford: Blackwell.

Helvacioglu, B. (2000) 'Globalization in the neighbourhood: from the nation-state to Bilkent Centre', *International Sociology*, 15 (2): 326–42.

Hirst, P. and Thompson, G. (1996) *Globalization in Question: The International Economy and the Possibilities of Governance*, Cambridge: Polity Press.

Hu, Y.-S. (1992) 'Global or stateless corporations are national firms with international operations', *California Management Review*, Winter: 107–26.

Hutton, W. (1996) *The State We're In*. London: Vintage.

Jones, M. (2003) 'Globalization and the organization(s) of exclusion in advanced capitalism', in R. Westwood and S.R. Clegg (eds), *Debating Organizations: Point-Counterpoint in Organization Studies*. Oxford: Blackwell. pp. 252–70.

Klein, N. (2001) *No Space, No Choice, No Jobs, No Logo: Taking Aim at the Brand Bullies*. New York: Picador.

Lash, S. and Urry, J. (1987) *The End of Organized Capitalism*. Cambridge: Polity Press.

Lash, S. and Urry, J. (1994) *Economies of Signs and Space*. London: Sage.

Markoff, J. (1996) *Waves of Democracy: Social Movements and Political Change*. Thousand Oaks, CA: Pine Forge Press.

Marx, K. (1976) *Capital*. London: NLB/Penguin.

Mathiason, N. (2003) 'Corporate tax avoidance is costing us all billions', *Observer*, 29 June.

McLuhan, M. (1964) *Understanding Media: The Extensions of Man*. New York: McGraw–Hill.

Meyer, J.W. (2000) 'Globalization: sources and effects on national states and societies', *International Sociology*, 15 (2): 233–48.

Moggach, D. (2000) *Tulip Fever*. New York: Random House.

Moghadam, V.M. (1999) 'Gender and globalization: female labour and women's mobilization', *Journal of World-Systems Research*, V (2): 367–88.

OECD (1996) *Globalization of Industry – Overview and Sector Reports*. Paris: Organization for Economic Co-operation and Development.

Ohmae, K. (1990) *The Borderless World*. London: Collins.

Parsons, T. (1966) *Societies: Evolutionary and Comparative Perspectives*. Englewood Cliffs, NJ: Prentice–Hall.

Patten, C. (1998) *East and West: The Last Governor of Hong Kong on Power, Freedom and the Future*. London: Macmillan.

Perrow, C. (1972) *The Radical Attack on Business*. New York: Harcourt Brace.

Petrella, R. (1996) 'Globalization and internationalization: the dynamics of the emerging world order', in R. Boyer and D. Drache (eds), (1996) *States Against Markets: The Limits of Globalization*. London: Routledge.

Porter, M. (1990) *The Competitive Advantage of Nations*. Basingstoke: Macmillan.

Purser, R.E., Park, C. and Montuori, A. (1995) 'Limits to anthropocentrism: towards an ecocentric organization paradigm?', *Academy of Management Review*, 20 (4): 1053–89.

Reich, R.B. (1991) *The Work of Nations*. New York: Vintage Books.

Ritzer, G. (1993) *The McDonaldization of Society*. Newbury Park, CA: Pine Forge Press.

Ritzer, G. (2004) *The Globalization of Nothing*. Thousand Oaks, CA: Pine Forge Press.

Robertson, R. (1992) *Globalization: Social Theory and Social Culture*. London: Sage.

Sassen, S. (1998) *Globalization and Its Discontents*. New York: New Press.

Sheehan, P. (2004) 'A rising force in capital and culture', *Sydney Morning Herald*, Weekend Edition, 3–4 January, p. 21.

Singer, P. (1976) *Animal Liberation: A New Ethics for Our Treatment of Animals*. London: Cape.

Sklair, L. (1999) 'Competing conceptions of globalization', *Journal of World-Systems Research*, V (2): 143–62.

Soros, G. (1998) *The Crisis of Global Capitalism: Open Society Endangered.* London: Little, Brown and Company.

Spybey, T. (1996) *Globalization and World Society.* Cambridge: Polity Press.

Stiglitz, J. (2002) *Globalization and Its Discontents.* Victoria, BC: Allen Lane/Penguin.

Storper, M. and Scott, A.J. (1993) *The Wealth of Regions: Market Forces and Policy Imperatives in Local and Global Context.* Los Angeles: Lewis Centre for Regional Policy Studies, UCLA, Working Paper No. 7.

Tallman, S., Jenkins, M., Henry, N. and Pinch, S. (2004) 'Knowledge clusters and competitive advantage', *Academy of Management Review*, 29 (2): 258–71.

Therborn, G. (2000a) 'Globalizations: dimensions, historical waves, regional effects, normative governance', *International Sociology*, 15 (2): 151–79.

Therborn, G. (2000b) 'Introduction: from the universal to the global', *International Sociology*, 15 (2): 149–50.

Tran, M. (2003) 'BT confirms plans for Indian call centres', *Guardian*, 7 March.

Tyson, L. (1992) *Who's Bashing Whom? Trade Conflict in High Technology Industries.* Washington, DC: Institute for International Economics.

Villaseñor, V. (1992) *Rain of Gold.* New York: Delta.

Weiss, L. (1997) 'Globalization and the myth of the powerless state', *New Left Review*, 225: 3–27.

Wood, A. (1994) *North–South Trade, Employment and Inequality.* Oxford: The Clarendon Press.

World Bank (2001) *Poverty Report.* Retrieved from www.worldbank.org/poverty/wdrpoverty/index.htm.

Yeung, H.W.-C. (2000) 'Economic globalization, crisis and the emergence of Chinese business communities in Southeast Asia', *International Sociology*, 15 (2): 266–87.

Yoshino, M.Y. and Rangan, U.S. (1995) *Strategic Alliances: An Entrepreneurial Approach to Globalization*, Boston, MA: Harvard Business School Press.

29

Sex and Power: Capillaries, Capabilities and Capacities

ELSPETH PROBYN

INTRODUCTION

Sex and power: what could be more compelling, and immediate? A once radical, now seemingly mandatory term within sociology and feminism, does the pairing of sex and power need rethinking? In theory, as in practice, the conjoining of sex and power reveals the intricacy of how subjectivities are ordered and identities regulated. By linking sex with power it becomes possible to foreground routes of power that continually cross the macro, the micro, the structural and the subjective, differentially articulating the social, the cultural and the economic.

While the question of sex and power is of crucial importance to sociology, in this chapter I argue that the dominant ways in which it is framed threaten to render it impotent. This is not to say that there have not been innovative ways of addressing the question of sex and power. Increasingly, however, the debate is divided by an insistence on the one side that we privilege a materialist analysis, and on the other that the question is best analysed in terms of discourse and representation. One camp follows a Marxist or a post-Marxist line that calls for – although it does not often deliver – a political economy of sex. The other

camp, which includes some feminisms and much of queer theory, argues that an analysis of the discursive realm of representations provides the most acute understanding of the workings of sex and power.

Dennis Altman's book *Global Sex* (2001) exemplifies and reproduces this division. Altman is a well-known and respected writer on homosexuality and he has been deeply involved in HIV research, especially in terms of the Southeast Pacific region. Given his expertise in matters of sexuality and his commitment to HIV/AIDS research one would think that he is ideally suited to guide us through 'global sex'. Unfortunately, in the stead of a 'thick description', we merely get polemic.

The positions against which Altman argues are variously named as postmodern feminism, cultural studies, queer, or ludic theory. Altman's dismissal of discourse and representation, and the absence in his book of a sustained argument for terms that might replace them, is deeply worrisome for the field of studies on sexuality. It is, as I have suggested, all too common. The deep antipathies that divide the field produce a bifurcated situation, with sociology on the side of the structural and economic, ignoring or repudiating analyses of how hegemony is constituted and maintained symbolically.

As such, *Global Sex* is a clear example of Michèle Barrett's critique of sociology. She argues that traditionally sociology 'overemphasised the determining effects of social structure, at the expense of an understanding of human agency and identity': that 'it viewed inequality in terms of social class' (2000: 15). This is, of course, a broad critique that could be debated. More interesting is her contention that sociology has a problem with 'the imaginative, the sensual, the emotional, the other, for that which we cannot control' (2000: 14). Her list of the areas in which 'sociology is conspicuously inadequate' is of interest: 'Physicality, humanity, imagination, the other, fear, the limits of control; all are missing in their own terms, in their own dynamic' (2000: 19).

The terms Barrett raises are precisely the issues that permeate sex. They are mercurial and hard to study or theorize within a sociological frame. The great challenge is to understand how they connect – are shaped and produced by, or collude – with forms of power. While the division of debate, and the divisive debates that Barrett alludes to are not restricted to the question of sex and power, the limitations of dominant paradigms can be clearly seen in regards to this crucial aspect of life. I will, however, argue that the study of sex and power may also inspire new ways of combining various strands of sociological analysis and thus demonstrate the potential that sociology has always had for incorporating and extending ways of thinking about societies and their structures.

From the slogans of the 1990s such as 'Girl power', the manifold manifestations of alternative or 'resistant' sexualities, to the oppressive regulation of sexuality under various fundamentalist regimes, power appears in many guises, and reveals differing forms of sexuality. The sheer variety of sexual expression is matched by the difficulty of conceptualizing sex and power as objects of study, and the links between them. In evident ways, the term sex is slippery. At one level it can refer to reproduction and ways in which women are confined by the economic implications of reproduction. Sex is therefore always entwined with questions of gender. On another level, sex can mean sexual practices, and often then leads to examinations of how sexual identities both regulate and are regulated by individuals and groups.

CAPILLARIES

> When I think of the mechanics of power I think of its capillary form of existence, of the extent to which power seeps into the very grain of individuals, reaches right into their bodies, permeates their gestures, their posture, what they say, how they learn to live and work with other people. (Foucault, 1977a: 28)

In terms of power, definitions and conceptualizations proliferate. There is, however, an established distinction in terms of conceptualizing power as repressive or conversely as productive. In simple terms, this can be understood as 'power over' versus 'power to'. Repressive power translates more often than not into juridical power which, as Judith Butler states, can be thought of as 'power acting on, subordinating pregiven subjects' (1997: 84). In contrast, productive power concerns the capacity of power to form subjects. Opposing views of the human subject are central to these different definitions: in the one, the subject exists prior to the application of power; in the other, power always already intervenes to produce subjects. The distinction between repressive or juridical and productive is indebted to Foucault, although it obscures many of his finer points regarding the operation of power. However, broadly put, repressive power can be defined as where 'all the modes of domination, submission, and subjugation are ultimately reduced to an effect of obedience' (Foucault, cited in Mason, 2001: 123).

In her book *Spectacles of Violence*, Gail Mason argues that this definition of power of 'power over' is compatible with certain feminist definitions of patriarchal power. In this model, 'power is defined as a form of domination that subjugates women by blocking them from doing certain things or thinking in certain ways; women are controlled through demands for social conformity and obedience' (Mason, 2001: 123). In comparison to repressive power, 'Productive power is defined as a relation between forces that, in passing through discourse and material events, is constitutive of particular social positions and the sense of self that is acquired in the negotiations of these positions' (p. 123).

These are, of course, general descriptions, and as Mason argues, for Foucault and those inspired by his work, the distinction between the two hypotheses is more heuristic than 'real'. However, they have powerfully demarcated areas of research and thinking about power and sex. They have also generated intense disagreement and hostility between camps. The major source of contention lies in what power is seen to do, how it is exercised, and where power is to be located. In terms of the Foucauldian line, a theorization of power is intimately associated with conceptualizations of subjectivity and the formation of the human subject. In Butler's summation, 'subjection is, literally, the *making* of a subject, the principle of regulation according to which a subject is formulated or produced. Such subjection is a kind of power that not only unilaterally *acts on* a given individual as a form of domination, but also *activates* or forms the subject' (1997: 84).

If it is the case that power forms the subject, or in other words that there is no subject that pre-exists power and is able to single-handedly wield power, we need to inquire after the vehicle that carries power. Put in other terms, how are we to study power if it cannot be located as originating in people's hands? For Foucault the answer, in much of his work, was that power is carried by discourse. This in turn leads us directly back to sex, as this quotation from *The History of Sexuality (Vol. 1)*, illustrates:

> What is at issue is the overall 'discursive fact', the way in which sex is 'put into discourse'. … my main concern will be to locate the forms of power, the channels it takes, and the discourses it permeates in order to reach the most tenuous and individual modes of behaviour, the paths that give it access to the rare and scarcely perceivable forms of desire, how it penetrates and controls everyday pleasure – all this entailing effects that may be those of refusal, blockage, and invalidation, but also incitement and intensification: in short, the 'polymorphous techniques of power'. (1980b: 11)

This quotation encapsulates many of the ideas that are continuously interwoven in Foucault's analysis of power. It highlights the nebulous yet tenacious nature of its movement, the way in which power continually penetrates us: its polymorphousness. It is also precisely this type of language which so infuriates his critics. To many 'polymorphous' sounds like merely amorphous and fuzzy. However, at its most basic, discourse designates the way that heterogeneous groups of statements serve to construct regimes of true and false. As Stuart Hall defines it, 'a discourse is a group of statements which provide a language for talking about a particular kind of knowledge about a topic. When statements about a topic are made within a particular discourse, the discourse makes it possible to construct a topic in a certain way. It also limits the other ways in which the topic can be constructed' (1992: 291). While the implications of this definition are large, in terms of everyday life it is usually quite clear when you have stumbled into the land of the false. At an experiential level, you may simply feel wrong: your sexuality, or body, or comportment are at odds with the dominant regime of the true. In this vein, Paul Bové (1995) argues that while Foucault produced a new sense of discourse, it described a familiar phenomenon. At one level, discourse describes and locates the 'self-evident' and the commonsensical that is in operation in all societies. It both names and can be used to analyse what produces, legitimates and supports the 'self-evident'.

In other words, this notion of discourse asks: How does discourse function? Where is it to be found? How does it get produced and regulated? What are its social effects? How does it exist? In more elaborated terms, discourse aims to 'describe the surface linkages between power, knowledge, institutions, intellectuals, the control of populations, and the modern state as these intersect in the functions of systems of thought' (Bove, 1995: 54–5). Clearly from this description, and also following the earlier discussion of the role of power in the formation of subjects, no one person owns a discourse, although they/we reproduce it. In this sense, the function of discourse is anonymous (Bove, 1995: 56).

Butler argues much the same point about the anonymity of power, and relation of discourse to the formation of the subject. In her words, 'The subject is neither a ground nor a product, but the permanent possibility of a certain presignifying process, one that gets detoured and stalled through other mechanisms of power, but which is power's own possibility of being reworked' (1991: 13).

However, just because discourse does not emanate from one body does not mean that certain discourses do not serve certain interests over others. As Foucault argues, 'Posing for discourse the question of power means basically to ask whom does discourse serve? It isn't so much a matter of analysing discourse into its unsaid, its implicit meaning, because discourses are transparent, they need no interpretation, no one to assign them a meaning' (1980a: 133). In other words, discourse analysis looks not to meanings *per se* but to how they function, asking with what other discourses they function, what are their effects? Against certain misreadings ('power is everywhere', 'everything is discourse'), the study of discourse lends itself to a precise and systematic mode of analysis. The problem with many understandings of discourse and power, be they positive or negative, is that they seek to locate these terms in some confined space (for example, in the state, in men's hands, etc.). But the point is to look to their movement, and in terms of power to examine its effects.

In terms of discourse, it is evident that one can and must examine the constitutive elements, the statements that make up a discourse at a given time. In a general manner, we can say that the analysis of discourse is always tied to genealogy: discourse analysis is directed at the conditions of possibility for statements. It asks what had to be in place in order that 'x' or 'y' can be stated? As an intricate system of classification, discourse names, brings into being, and places experience and knowledge. As anyone who has felt their power knows, words matter. As the title of one of Foucault's earlier works puts it, there is an 'order of things' directly related to words, statements – in short, discourse. In fact the title of that book in the original French is 'words and things' (*les mots et les choses*). The common dismissal of discourse as ephemeral is therefore misplaced, if at times understandable. As Foucault aptly writes in *The Order of Things* (1973), humans vainly try to escape the 'heavy materiality of discourse'.

In his inaugural lecture to the Collège de France, 'The order of discourse' (1971), Foucault presented a more elaborated presentation of the systematic workings of discourse. Bové (1995: 58–63) sums up the precise protocol for the analysis of discourse:

- It traces the ways in which discourse constitutes 'objects' and classes of objects.
- Discourse constitutes these objects as subjects of statements which are judged true or false according to the logic of the empowered discourse.
- Discourse is material in its effects – discourse and practices are interrelated.
- 'The analysis of discourse [lies] in its conditions of possibility, its conditions of formation, in the series of its modifications, and in the game of its dependencies and its correlations. Discourse thus appears in a describable relation to the ensemble of other practices'.
- The positivity of discourse is defined as 'practices tied to certain conditions, tied to certain rules, and susceptible to certain transformations caught within a system of correlations with other practices'.

Foucault put these principles of analysis to work in his *The History of Sexuality*. The first volume, 'The Will to Knowledge', is perhaps the more cited in terms of sex. In it he examined the workings of the nineteenth-century discourse on sexuality. As is well known, he argued against the prevailing view that the Victorians were prudes who dared not speak of sex. Famously his rebuttal of 'the repressive hypothesis' raised the ways in which from the late eighteenth century on, Europeans never ceased talking about sex. More to the point, he analysed the emergence of scientific discourses all predicated on the desire to name various elements of sexuality which served to incite talk about sexuality. New fields of study – notably, psychoanalysis, psychology and sexology – invented ever-more nuanced classifications in terms of sexuality.

At the heart of Foucault's argument about sexuality is a conception of power linked to the regulation of truth statements. Power in this definition is dynamic: it doesn't shut down, it actively opens new areas to scrutiny. 'We must cease at once and for all to describe the effects of power in negative terms: it excludes, it represses, it censors, it abstracts, it masks, it conceals. In fact power produces; it produces reality; it produces domains of objects and rituals of truth' (1977b: 194). This mode of exercising power is, for Foucault, a distinctly modern move, exemplified in the relation between power, knowledge and truth. These terms are grouped around sexuality: they make sense of sexuality in particular ways, and sex for us moderns becomes a privileged way of knowing the truth about – of making sense of – ourselves. This is a very different configuration, a distinct and particular mode of operation spawned from a nexus of discourses that emerge at a particular time in a particular place.

The particularity of the analysis is emphasized because Foucault was not arguing about the innateness of the sexualized operations of power, nor did he license an extrapolation of his analysis beyond the European context. Nor, in fact, was he, as many feminists have pointed out, terribly interested in women's sexuality *per se*. In the later volumes of *The History of Sexuality* he turned to an examination of the antecedents of the European sensibility in regards to sex. In *The Use of Pleasure* (1986), and *The Care of the Self* (1988), Foucault examines various texts, manuals and practices undertaken by the Ancient Greeks as 'practices of the self'. These were the routine ways through which citizens of the *polis* produced themselves as such. They included close attention to what they ate, their dreams and their conduct within the community. Sexual practices were mentioned but in and of themselves were not terribly important. Ethical comportment was a central preoccupation and was measured in terms of how a citizen practised the regimen, or the articulation of these techniques of the self.

Foucault posits a rupture in how sexuality was used and thought. If, for the Greeks, sex was one practice amongst several, all coordinated in the service of 'taking care of the self', this is radically at odds with the use of sex that emerges co-extensively with European modernity. Summed up in the Judaeo-Christian injunction to 'know thyself', sex becomes that imperative

which spawns an ever-increasingly intricate measuring of the self. It is the impetus to self-knowledge, and because of its fragility as a knowable object, it spurs us ever on in the quest to be in the true. As the following quotation captures, sex for us is not easy, mired as it is in:

> a process that spreads it over the surface of things and bodies, arouses it, draws it out and bids it speak, implants it in reality and enjoins it to tell the truth: an entire glittering sexual array, reflected in a myriad of discourses, the obstination of powers, and the interplay of knowledge and pleasure. (1980b: 77)

This description of sex's relation to truth, power, knowledge and reality amply demonstrates Foucault's conception of power: 'Power operates not through repression but through the proliferation of discourse and statements' (1980b: 133).

In this manner, and as several commentators have argued, power is conceived of as 'a making possible ... action upon action' (Bové, 1995: 57). But this operation is framed and in turn made possible by the 'materiality of discourse'. As Bové clearly points out, 'discourse makes possible disciplines and institutions which in turn sustain and distribute these discourses' (p. 57). Immediately, power's object, operationalized through discourse, is to control bodies and actions in the most insidious ways – from inside, as it were. As Butler puts it, sexuality for us is our very principle of intelligibility to ourselves and to others: 'the category of sexuality here functions as a principle of production and regulation at once ... here sex is a category, but not merely a representation; it is a principle of production, intelligibility, and regulation which enforces a violence and rationalises it after the fact' (1991: 19). In forceful terms, Butler describes the work of sexuality in ways that emphasize 'the heavy materiality of discourse'.

Those, such as Altman, who would see Foucauldian analyses of sex as 'convoluted theories of desire which evade questions of social and economic power and inequality' (Altman, 2001: 159), would do well to listen more carefully to how discourse works as an analytic entry into power's operations. Power and sex in Foucault's terms can hardly be said to be outside of the workings of the social or the economic. Certainly Foucault operates at a different level, one that sees inequality as more complex than a binary, on/off phenomenon, or that would posit power as causally effecting oppression. Against such reductions, Foucault compels us to conceive of our relationship to power in more challenging, and ultimately more realistic ways: to consider 'that the horizon in which we act is there as a constitutive possibility of our very capacity to act, not merely or exclusively as an exterior field or theatre of operations' (cited in Butler, 1991: 10).

One may justifiably point out that Foucault was overwhelmingly interested in Western systems of discourse, and as Edward Said has stated 'his Eurocentrism was almost total' (in Barrett, 1991: 152). However, the conclusion we must draw from Foucault's analyses of the question of sex and power is that very different bodies will be produced under different discursive regimes, themselves absolutely embedded in local, historical conditions. Following from this, Butler argues that 'the recasting of the matter of bodies as the effect of a dynamic of power, such that the matter of bodies will be indissociable from the regulatory norms that govern their materialization and the signification of those material effects' (1993: 2). In other words, studying the operations of sex and power must of necessity connect the body to the 'geographically and historically specific "norms" within which we each locate, evaluate and understand our bodies' (Bell and Valentine, 1997: 26). In turn we must see these norms as not just impinging on bodies, but as that which produces, as Butler (1993) puts it, the very matter of bodies – that which constitutes the materiality of sex.

CAPABILITIES

Having outlined some of the key terms within a Foucauldian approach to the question of sex and power, I now want to turn to the question that is raised by him about our capacity to act. This is a very practical question, whilst of course it operates philosophically in complex ways. Rather than rest within the universe that Foucault constructs, I will take the question of capacity and attempt to rearticulate it within a very different theory about power, human agency and the ways in which capabilities are extended or curtailed by power. Although I am wary of crossing very different epistemological projects – and as we will see, Foucault and Nussbaum are in many ways incompatible – none the less the practical turn that Nussbaum's philosophy wants to take may be complemented by Foucault's more corporeal conception of power.

Nussbaum, a prolific writer, has recently declared herself to be at war with much of contemporary feminism, at least that which is influenced by Butler. Nussbaum's stinging attack on Butler, published in the *New Republic*, made no bones about the problematic nature of poststructuralist feminism. Butler's project is said to be without hope, to mock the ideals of human dignity, and in a highly quotable sentence she warns that, 'Hungry women are not fed by this, battered women are not sheltered by it, raped women do not find justice in it, gays and lesbians do not achieve legal protection through it' (1999: 45).

In her book *Women and Human Development: The Capabilities Approach* (2000) Nussbaum is more temperate about what differentiates her project from much contemporary social and feminist theory. Nussbaum's proposal for a new way of intervening in the question of human development is firmly grounded in, and expounds, a number of universal postulates. As such, she is immediately at odds with theories of difference, and various forms of social constructionism. It must be stated that her understanding of social constructionism is dated, and as is often the case with arguments outside of sociology, she imputes a purity to the paradigm that most sociologists would not recognize. In other words, few would argue that human experience is purely socially constructed, and would question what indeed that could precisely mean.

Notwithstanding this caveat, Nussbaum's framing is of interest: she firmly posits that 'it is possible to describe a framework … that is strongly universalist, committed to cross-cultural norms of justice, equality, and rights, and at the same time sensitive to local particularity, and to the many ways in which circumstances shape not only options but also beliefs and preferences' (2000: 7). Universalism is, of course, antithetical to much theory that has developed on the back of a critique of liberalism, and Nussbaum is an unapologetic liberalist. Yet her notion of universals is tied to a conception of human capabilities that is not a replica of the familiar figure of liberalism's universal man. In her argument, 'a particular type of universalism, framed in terms of general human powers and their development, offers us in fact the best framework within which to locate our thoughts about difference' (2000: 7).

Her project of 'applied philosophy' draws from the work of John Rawls and Amartya Sen; in other words, it brings together normative philosophy and development economics. If this is already quite a stretch, for sociologists Nussbaum's use of empirical material may be problematic. While she clearly states that her argument is not to be read as sustained empirical research, she nonetheless relies on interviews and 'narrative examples' of Indian women for the rhetorical impact of her argument. As such, the spectre of 'real' women, those whom she earlier claimed were harmed by Butlerian feminist accounts of sex, are crucial to the development of her argument. We already know that sex for Nussbaum will not be the stuff of discourse or queer performativity. Sex here is the reality that impedes women from exercising fully their human capabilities. As such it is thoroughly embued with power, understood as that which prevents, represses and oppresses in clearly defined ways.

I will return to whether and how Nussbaum's project can speak to the Foucauldian understanding of sex and power. But first I want to examine her list of the universals that constitute 'central human functional capabilities'. She lists ten such capabilities. While the absence of sexuality is striking, we may be able to articulate sex as imbricated within, if not central to, her list. The capabilities she lists are:

- Life
- Bodily health
- Bodily integrity

- Senses, imagination and thought
- Emotions
- Practical reason
- Affiliation
- Other species
- Play
- Control over one's environment (2000: 78–80).

Sifting through her description of these categories, we find sex in a number of places. Most obviously in a footnote about 'affiliation', Nussbaum notes that she had not originally placed nondiscrimination on the basis of sexual orientation on her list as she found that it would be premature based on her experience of Indian society. Interestingly enough, it was the Indian reaction to the film *Fire* that has caused Nussbaum to rethink her position and she would now 'add this item to a cross-cultural list that is expected to command overlapping consensus' (p. 80, fn). The 1996 film, by the Indian-Canadian director Deepa Mehta, is a lush bodice-ripper portraying an affair between two middle-class sisters-in-law. It caused a violent scandal in India, and prompted a full-scale debate throughout Indian society including at the level of the Indian government.

Sexuality also figures in the category of 'bodily integrity', which includes security against sexualized forms of violence and 'having opportunities for sexual satisfaction and for choice in matters of reproduction' (p. 78). She supports this with reference to the 1994 International Conference on Population and Development which includes the statement that 'Reproductive health therefore implies that people are able to have a satisfying and safe sex life and that they have the capability to reproduce and the freedom to decide if, when, and how often to do so' (p. 78).

In explicit terms, these are the only instances where Nussbaum relates sexuality to the full expression of 'truly human functioning'. However, one can also use Nussbaum's list to draw out the ways in which power limits connections between sex and other capabilities. For instance, her insistence on the emotions, imagination and play lend themselves to an understanding of sexuality that would be broader than reproduction or sexual orientation. Under the category of 'senses, imagination and thought', she concludes that 'being able to have pleasurable experiences, and to avoid non-necessary pain' could easily be opened to include a call for much wider sexual education that might ameliorate the context whereby children, in both the developing and developed worlds, might gain access to knowledge about different forms of sexual activity. Equally the category of 'emotions' includes 'not having one's emotional development blighted by overwhelming fear and anxiety, or by traumatic events of abuse or neglect' which would support queer and feminist arguments about the violence caused by the obligatory performance of hetero-normativity. This would include Butler but more acutely Eve K. Sedgwick's telling accounts of the effects of normative heterosexuality on children. As Sedgwick puts it in her essay 'How to bring your kids up gay', 'the scope of institutions whose programmatic undertaking is to prevent the development of gay people is unimaginatively large' (1993: 161). Indeed, while Nussbuam and Sedgwick would make strange bed partners, there is a case for suggesting that Sedgwick's *Tendencies* be read alongside Nussbaum. Sedgwick's detailed description of the ways in which normative sexuality orders 'impacted' social spaces, and the way sexual identity comes to rule everything from how you look, with whom you do what, where and how, and the ways that sexual identity forms 'the main locus of emotional bonds' (1993: 7), functions to ground Nussbaum's more abstract argument.

If Sedgwick makes us *feel* the burden of power always exercised through the ways in which normative sexuality curtails human thought and capacity, how does power operate in Nussbaum's argument? Strangely enough, for a book that wishes to intervene in the field of development, there is little overt discussion of power. Certainly we are to understand that poverty and the unequal distribution of resources at both the level of geo-politics and of gender are ever-present limits within which Nussbaum presents her model. And while evidently she has spent some time in India, the choice of India as reference point is far from innocent. As I have mentioned, sociologically

her use of putative empirical material is dubious. She makes constant recourse to seemingly the same four Indian women to add 'narrative colour'. However, her list could have been developed in any situation, and indeed it is precisely her argument that these constitute universal human capabilities. There is therefore no epistemological or methodological rationale for why India is privileged. One has to conclude that it is a rhetorical device aimed at securing her argument as 'real' and not merely representational. As such it is presumably more persuasive to place her argument within a context where the question of power and its effects on people is rendered immediate for a Western audience's 'knowingness' about power differentials in the large sub-continent.

It is a winning ploy in that it operates to place elements that are familiar to Western readers within a 'strange' context. Many of her categories of capabilities could feature in Western women's magazines. By using India as the reference point where we 'know' people are starving, Nussbaum avoids the familiar Marxist conundrum whereby what are now considered 'life-style issues' (the ability to fulfil one's imagination, to affiliate and form friendships with whom we please, to chose sexual partners etc.) do not have to wait until 'after the revolution'. In this way, Nussbaum avoids having to prioritize material needs, as she reworks her list as based in materiality.

It should be clear that I find Nussbaum's proposals provocative, and agree with her on their necessity. I may be much more moved by the generosity of arguments such as Sedgwick's, which argue much the same as Nussbaum but in an open and engaging manner. This is not just a quibble about style; there is a distinct lack of intellectual generosity in Nussbaum's work that is at odds with the purported goal.

Notwithstanding these objections, Nussbaum's text can be read as an invitation to think the question of sexuality more expansively than is often the case in studies focused on 'sex and power'. Sexuality here could be envisioned as both the vehicle for, and an objective of, a reworked notion of human capability. The understanding of power that underlies her model is also consistent with a Foucauldian notion of power even while it is apparently at odds ontologically with his philosophical position. It is clear that in Nussbaum's list power operates as 'an action on actions', as a way of foreclosing human capabilities. Nussbaum presents her argument as 'practical' against the supposed impracticality of work influenced by Foucault. But in fact her argument has no greater or less practical value than Foucault's injunctions that we 'think differently', and that we not accept things as they are. As with Foucault, there is no 'why' in Nussbaum's argument. In other words, they both look not to the cause and origin of power but rather to how it spreads across bodies and societies constantly forming a limit of human capabilities.

CAPACITIES

I now want to turn from Nussbaum's argument to consider another way of viewing sexuality and power. Here I will draw on Deleuze's conception of the body's untold capacities which he takes from Spinoza and which reverberates with his commentary on Foucault's oeuvre. Again, there is considerable difference and tension between Nussbaum's preferred paradigm (reworked liberalism) and Deleuze's philosophy. The coincidence between the key words 'capabilities' and 'capacity' is not to be taken as a reassurance that there is any compatibility between them. Yet I want to follow my intuition that there is a productive tension between these projects that are so differently based in 'the intuitive idea of truly human functioning' (Nussbaum, 2000: 78fn).

For those with only a passing acquaintance with Deleuze, and especially Deleuze and Guattari's co-written work, it may seem filled with arcane jargon. Terms like BwO (Bodies without Organs), molar and molecular, de- and re-territorialization may be daunting and even annoying. However they are merely different ways of trying to describe facets of social, human and nonhuman interactions. Given how radically varied these are, it is perhaps not surprising that Deleuze and Guattari enlist a wide assortment of terms in order to 'figure' human behaviour.

Against Nussbaum's list of ten human capabilities, the Deleuzian notion of the body is quite different. Taking from Spinoza, Deleuze asserts its unknown capacities: 'We still do not know what a body can do.' Notwithstanding this claim, Deleuze follows through on Foucault's 'idea that apparatuses of power have an immediate and direct relation with the body' (1994: 64). We will see shortly how sociology could take up this relation and deepen it. But to frame this simply, crucial to Deleuze's argument is a depiction that insists on the intimate interrelation of society, the social, the psychic, the economic, human and nonhuman bodies. As Elizabeth Grosz argues, 'a Deleuzian model insists on the flattening out of relations between the social and the psychical so that there is neither a relation of causation (one- or two-way) nor hierarchies, levels, grounds, or foundations. The social is not privileged over the psychical ... nor is the psychical privileged at the expense of the social' (1994: 180). To recall Barrett's critique, this is to rethink those aspects that sociology has been slow to analyse: the imaginative, the sensual. More important, it gives us an inkling of how one could go about analysing them.

In Deleuze's framing, a body is both kinetic and dynamic. The body as such is made of infinite 'particles'. The body is a moving assemblage that finds itself enmeshed with other assemblages. This is a complex and yet obvious way of seeing interaction. It depends on an understanding of bodies as multiple and as always engaged with other bodies and entities. Gatens describes how for Deleuze (and following Spinoza) 'the human body is understood as a complex individual, made up of a number of other bodies ... in constant interchange with its environment ... the body as a nexus of variable interconnections, a multiplicity within a web of other multiplicities' (1996a: 7). These connections are called assemblages. Deleuze and Guattari describe the way 'an arrangement ... exists only in connection with other arrangements'. They continue: 'We shall wonder with what it functions, in connection with what it transmits intensities or doesn't, into what multiplicities it introduces and metamorphoses its own' (1987: 3–4).

This language is obviously quite different from traditional sociological description. And it is not description, sociological or otherwise. It is rather a way of figuring interaction, framed in such a way as to open rather than close possibilities. While it lends itself to wild metaphorization, and bad poetry (but then, so can Durkheim), it can also be put to use within sociology to rethink and question what we think we know of human sociability. The emphasis on the milieu, for instance, compels us to place the human body as always interacting and being interacted with on multiple levels. One interesting example of this is Deleuze's re-reading of Freud's 'Little Hans' case. Freud's interpretation was framed and overdetermined by his interest in the Oedipal complex, with little concern for the other systems in which the boy was placed. Countering Freud, Deleuze writes, it is 'as if the "vision" of the street, frequent at the time – a horse falls, is beaten, struggles – wasn't capable of directly affecting the libido, and has to recall his parents having sex' (1993: 84). Against this detachment of the psychic and its forces from the social, Grosz argues that Deleuze directs us to how 'individuals, subjects, microintensities, blend with, connect to, neighbourhood, local, regional, social, cultural, aesthetic, and economic relations directly' (1994: 180).

As such, the body is an assemblage of bodies traversed and formed by various systems. It is important to note that this is not to posit the body as without history; in fact it compels acknowledgement of the different histories of the body: individual, collective and the ways in which the body functions to connect the economic, social and psychological. As Gatens reminds us, 'what a body can do is, at least in part, a function of its history and of those assemblages in which it has been constructed' (1996a: 10). In these terms, this framing can 'take account of the variety of ways in which individual bodies and their capacities are affected by their participation in larger assemblages of family, work and sociopolitical life' (1996a: 8).

In this way, the body is a result of how it has been framed and understood, and it has histories of how it has been affected by social forces. In Gatens's argument, this is why it is so crucial to conduct genealogical analyses of the body's framing. In particular, she analyses the ways in which sociological descriptions of sex and gender have come to form bodies. She traces how Robert Stoller's work in the 1960s on the distinction between biological sex and social gender became the foundation for feminist assertions that bodies are not biologically determined but are socially produced and curtailed by gender. To foreshorten her argument (and see Gatens, 1996b, for a full account of the relation of sex to gender), her genealogical account of the circulation of these concepts finds them deployed within the politics of sexual equality. The assertion of the 'essential sameness of all persons' now figures in any number of legal, educational and governmental assumptions. Laws on equal employment, rape and other dictates of sexual equality have come then to powerfully inform, limit and at times extend what bodies can do in particular circumstances.

The conception of power that circulates through this notion of equality is one that asserts that equality is 'freedom from power'. As Gatens puts it, 'liberation, or freedom, somewhat ironically, was conceived in forms of an equality that would be guaranteed by juridical power' (1996a: 4). Equally ironic is the way in which certain feminist dictates about human nature, such as Andrea Dworkin and Catherine MacKinnon's claims about brute masculine power, have become part and parcel of legal systems. While their particular intervention concerned pornography and its putative relation to male violence against women, this sexualized framing of the body has entered into the everyday: sexual harassment issues and concerns affect behaviour in work places, worries about sexuality enter into how we teach, and more generally what we have come to know of and about sex affects how we conduct ourselves in relationship to others and to ourselves. In this way, power – not at an abstract level, but in concrete ways – is thoroughly sexualized. In Gatens's terms this is to acknowledge how 'each of these designations link a body in a multiplicity of ways to complex networks or assemblages which distribute power differentially according to such designations'. In clear ways, these 'interlocking assemblages of law, medicine, enunciation, sexuality, and so on, determine what this body can do, say, think' (1996a: 10).

In this way, power carried by institutional discourses serves to block, redirect, constrain. The body's 'unknown capacities' are curtailed in much the same way as bodies are deprived of attaining their full human capabilities. Sex in this model is not the only way in which power operates, but it is an important one. It also demonstrates how sex embued with juridical power and paradoxically sustained by a conception of a freedom from power, returns to limit what bodies can do.

MICROPRACTICES

To recap briefly, focusing on Foucault's argument I have sketched the relationship of power to sexuality, detailing the ways in which power operates through discourse. In turn I considered Nussbaum's model of human capabilities and the ways in which power materially intervenes to curtail 'truly human functioning'. I then attempted to complement such a view with Deleuze's notion of the body's unknown capacities, which as we have seen are constantly made knowable and contained within historical and actual assemblages. I acknowledge these leaps transcend at times very different philosophies. I also realize that as yet they may be at most suggestive for another sociological take on sex and power, and at worst just more jargon. In this concluding section, I will therefore try to respond to the question of how these ideas might actually play out in more sociologically attuned analyses.

One of the 'methodologies' that Deleuze raises in regard to his notion of the body's capacity to affect and be affected is that of ethology. Simply put, ethology defines bodies, animals or humans by the affects they are capable of (Deleuze, 1992: 627). Strictly speaking, ethology began as an offshoot of zoology and evolution. One can see the connection between the study of plant and animal evolution and the definition that Deleuze takes from Spinoza: 'ethology studies the compositions of relations

or capacities between different things' (1992: 628). Both require that minute attention be paid to the possibility of change at a micro level. Akin to ethnographic description, although without the metaphysical assumptions that often implicitly guide anthropological description, ethology focuses on breaking down processes of interaction into seemingly insignificant elements. It looks at bi- and multi-lateral movements. Suspending the temptation to name behaviour as sexual, gendered, or indeed as properly economic or cultural or psychological, it focuses on the ways in which particles or entities co-exist and function together. The assemblages that are formed are then somewhat arbitrarily categorized as sexual, or as cultural or economic, and so forth.

It is evidently an experimental way of going about describing behaviour yet its principles can be applied to any number of human assemblages. For instance, in one project I experimented with using ethological principles to describe the field of food media (Probyn, 2003a, 2003b). This entails a noncausal mapping of several systems or assemblages: the circulation of ideas about taste in terms of media production and its economies; close detailing of professions; the ways in which different orders of bodies – professional, ordinary, etc. – incorporate or not ideas about eating; the connections that are forged between what might be called the level of the cultural and the symbolic, and those that are more properly concerned with production, economics and distribution.

Turning from this study, which does not focus on sex and power although it discovers interesting manifestations of it, I want briefly to describe a project that brings many of the theoretical principles described above to bear within a sociological study of sex.

Kath Albury's *Yes Means Yes* (2002) is interesting and exciting for several reasons. Albury is part of a younger generation of scholars who have been greatly informed by feminism, feminist sociology and queer theory, yet who have to work with and against several of their tenets. In particular, as Albury writes, 'feminism has taught me that I have the right to say "no" to unwanted sex. It has also taught me that I can say "yes" to sex' (2002: vii). Given the heavy hand of the feminist notion of 'compulsory heterosexuality', saying yes to heterosex is some ways harder – at a theoretical level, of course – than saying yes to queer sex or saying no to unwanted sex. Albury's project concerns, as the subtitle puts it, 'getting explicit about heterosex'. Her project is unusual in that it does not seek to simply 'queer' heterosexuality, and Albury is quite adamant that such is not the case even when discussing some of the decidedly queer practices of her interviewees. Perhaps more to the point, is that she does not seem to subscribe to a model of resistance. Power here is not that straightforward.

Albury's project is also refreshing in that it acknowledges and works with and within the rich history of feminist writing on sex, and without whingeing. As we know, much of this material has been 'as confusing and contradictory as its subject matter' (2002: 27). And some has also been clearly homophobic as well as deeply distrustful of any sexual pleasure that women might have with men. For instance, she cites Sheila Jeffries, an obvious target perhaps but none the less a very vocal anti-sex feminist, for whom a feminist and socialist 'discussion of "sexual pleasure" is as incongruous as a discussion of "interior decorating" in a feature on homelessness' (p. 26). There is also, of course, a rich line of feminist analysis which is 'prosex'. In the main, however, pro-sex feminists have tended to celebrate lesbian and queer sex; their discussions tend to operate quite outside of a paradigm of heteronormativity. Akin to Gatens's call for a genealogical acknowledgement of how concepts have come to form limits on material practice, Albury's work begins to demonstrate the intricacies of power in contemporary sexual practice.

At an empirical level, Albury's project draws on interviews with women who have experimented with a range of 'unusual' sex practices – from amputee fetishism, different kinds of porn, to anal sex. As a part-time 'sexpert', known as 'Nurse Nancy' in websites and sex advice columns, Albury is well placed to draw out evidence of the fact that so-called straight girls are saying 'yes' to kinds of sex that their often feminist mothers would call 'degrading'. At a

theoretical level (Albury, 2005), she draws on and reworks many of the paradigms that I discussed above. Her critique of some of the larger statements about sex and power, including Anthony Giddens's wide-eyed assumption that gay and lesbian relationships are somehow free of power, is supported by a theory of micropolitics. Drawing on William Connolly's work, and influenced by Foucault, 'micropolitics works at the level of detail, desire, feeling, perception and sensibility' (Connolly, 1999: 149).

This theoretical descriptive statement in turn accords with Deleuze's 'methodological' enlisting of ethology. What Connolly calls the necessity of '*the selective desanctification of elements in … [one's] identity*' (1999: 146; cited in Albury, 2005; emphasis in original) echoes the imperative in ethological analysis to break down 'molar' or sedified entities into their constitutive elements. To recall Deleuze's notion of the body as composed of infinite particles, bodies are assemblages that are ordered and re-ordered by social, political and economic forces. Ethology then analyses the ways in which elements within the assemblage affect and are affected by other elements. This type of analysis precisely looks to detail, desire and feeling and the ways they inflect micro relations within the assemblage. Or, as Connolly puts it, 'as one part of [an individual's] subjectivity … begins to work on other parts' (1999: 146). Some of these parts might be ordered by sex, whereas others may be composed in relation to other levels of practice. In this, it recalls Foucault's discussion of the regimen of the Ancient Greeks where precisely it was the reflection on the relation of different practices to each other, the technologies of the self at work, that constituted the ethics of the self.

These somewhat abstract principles are put to work by Albury in her research on heterosexual practices. From the results, it becomes evident that increasingly 'many western men and women are experiencing forms of heterosexuality that are not clearly bounded by external moral frameworks' (2002: 171). As she notes, many heterosexuals 'negotiate complex relationships on the basis of personal, ethical decisions grounded in their individual beliefs and circumstances' (p. 172).

CONCLUSION

To return to the question of sex and power, it would be ludicrous to say on the basis of the theoretical arguments and the empirical results presented here that sex is now free from power. Nor is it sufficient to celebrate power within sex, although the eroticization of power in consensual practices such as s/m or b/d is important. But it is not a question of being either for or against power in sex, or sex in power. As I hope is clear, the situation is more complex. Sex and power are fundamental to human capabilities, and their seemingly endless combinations along with the pleasures and fears they articulate may be uniquely human. It is also the microanalysis of how they affect and are affected by different forces that attests to Deleuze's dictum about the unknown capacities of bodies.

The arguments I have presented here are compelling; they are also somewhat abstract and probably annoying to many sociologists for whom a reworking of Foucauldian principles may be the last thing on their agenda – especially if they would not read Foucault in the first place. I have little hope that the framework I have presented here will overcome the division between 'materialist' versus 'discursive' analysis, the post-Marxists versus the postmodernists. However, if we are to attend to the challenge that Barrett articulates, as well as that of dwindling numbers of students wanting to study sociology, we will need to listen to alternatives. I am not suggesting that the philosophical analyses of Nussbaum or Deleuze or whomsoever be incorporated wholesale *as* sociology. As I mentioned, Nussbaum, for instance, is weak when she ventures into the realm of the sociological. And while intriguing, ethology is yet to be fully tested as a methodology within sociological analysis, and in some sense it echoes other methodologies such as grounded analysis or 'thick description'. However, if we are to reinvigorate the sociological study of sex and power, and make it equal to and as exciting as its empirical realities, then we are going to have to reconnect sex and power with human sensuality, imagination, physicality – in short, to the awesome questions of human capabilities and capacities.

REFERENCES

Albury, Kath (2002) *Yes Means Yes: Getting Explicit about Heterosex.* Sydney: Allen and Unwin.

Albury, Kath (2005) 'Impure relationships: ethical heterosex in popular culture'. Unpublished thesis, University of New South Wales.

Altman, Dennis (2001) *Global Sex.* Chicago: The University of Chicago Press.

Barrett, Michèle (2000) 'Sociology and the metaphorical tiger', in P. Gilroy, L. Grossberg and A. McRobbie (eds), *Without Guarantees: In Honour of Stuart Hall.* London: Verso. pp. 14–20.

Barrett, Michèle (1991) *The Politics of Truth: From Marx to Foucault.* Cambridge: Polity Press.

Bell, David and Valentine, Gill (1997) *Consuming Geographies: We are Where We Eat.* London/ New York: Routledge.

Bové, Paul A. (1995) 'Discourse', in Lentricchia, F. and McLaughlin, T. (eds), *Critical Terms for Literary Study.* Chicago: University of Chicago Press. pp. 50–65.

Butler, Judith (1991) 'Contingent foundations: feminism and the question of "postmodernism"', in Judith Butler and Joan Scott (eds), *Feminists Theorize the Political.* New York/London: Routledge. pp. 3–21.

Butler, Judith (1993) *Bodies that Matter.* New York/ London: Routledge.

Butler, Judith (1997) *The Psychic Life of Power.* Stanford, CA: Stanford University Press.

Connolly, William (1999) *Why I am a Secularist.* Minneapolis, MN: University of Minnesota Press.

Deleuze, Gilles (1992) 'Ethology: Spinoza and us', in J. Crary and S. Kwinter (eds) *Incorporations.* New York: Zone Books. pp. 625–33.

Deleuze, Gilles (1993) *Critique et clinique.* Paris: Minuit: *Essays Critical and Clinical* (trans. Daniel Smith and Michael Greco, 1997). Minneapolis: University of Minnesota Press.

Deleuze, Gilles (1994) 'Désir et plaisir', *Le magazine littéraire*, 325 (October), pp. 59–65.

Deleuze, Gilles and Guattari, Felix (1987) *A Thousand Plateaus: Capitalism and Schizophrenia* (trans. Brian Massumi). Minneapolis: University of Minnesota Press.

Foucault, Michel (1971) *L'Ordre du discours.* Paris: Gallimard.

Foucault, Michel (1973) *The Order of Things: An Archeology of the Human Sciences.* New York: Vintage.

Foucault, Michel (1977a) *Language, Counter-Memory, Practice* (ed. D. Bouchard, trans. D. Bouchard and S. Simon). Ithaca, NY: Cornell University Press.

Foucault, Michel (1977b) *Discipline and Punish. The Birth of the Clinic.* Harmondsworth: Penguin.

Foucault, Michel (1980a) *Power/Knowledge: Selected Interviews and Other Writings* (ed. C. Gordon). New York: Pantheon Books.

Foucault, Michel (1980b) *The History of Sexuality, Vol. 1* (trans. Robert Hurley). New York: Vintage.

Foucault, Michel (1986) *The Use of Pleasure. The History of Sexuality, Vol. 2* (trans. Robert Hurley). New York: Vintage.

Foucault, Michel (1988) *The Care of the Self. The History of Sexuality Vol. 3* (trans. Robert Hurley). New York: Vintage.

Gatens, Moira (1996a) 'Sex, gender, sexuality: can ethologists practice genealogy?', *Southern Journal of Philosophy*, xxxv: 1–19.

Gatens, Moira (1996b) *Imaginary Bodies: Ethics, Power and Corporeality.* London/New York: Routledge.

Grosz, Elizabeth (1994) *Volatile Bodies. Toward a Corporeal Feminism.* Bloomington, IN: Indiana University Press.

Hall, Stuart (1992) 'The West and the rest: discourse and power', in S. Hall and B. Gieben (eds), *Formations of Modernity.* Cambridge: Polity Press. pp. 245–320.

Mason, Gail (2001) *Spectacles of Violence.* London/New York: Routledge.

Nussbaum, Martha C. (2000) *Women and Human Development: The Capabilities Approach.* Cambridge: Cambridge University Press.

Nussbaum, Martha C. (1999) 'The professor of parody', *New Republic,* 220 (8): 37–45.

Probyn, Elspeth (2003a) 'Eating for a living: a rhizo-ethology of bodies', in H. Thomas and J. Ahmed (eds), *Cultural Bodies: Ethnography and Theory.* Boston, MA: Blackwell. pp. 215–40.

Probyn, Elspeth (2003b) 'Eating into ethics: food journalism and passion', in C. Lumby and E. Probyn (eds), *Remote Control: New Media, New Ethics.* Melbourne: Cambridge University Press. pp. 107–23.

Sedgwick, Eve K. (1993) *Tendencies.* Durham, NC: Duke University Press.

30

The Sociology of the University and Higher Education: The Consequences of Globalization

GERARD DELANTY

The university can be seen as the paradigmatic institution of the public sphere and of modernity more generally, for some of the major transformations in modernity have been reflected in the changing nature of the university. It was central to the emergence of modernity in Europe and America and in the twentieth century it was space that nurtured democracy and citizenship in countries emerging from colonialism. Taking a broader view of knowledge as entailing more than science but also cultural knowledge, the university can be seen as the space where the project of modernity unfolded through cognitive struggles, in particular between science and culture. From the Enlightenment onwards the university was pivotal in the genesis of national consciousness as well as in a wider commitment to cosmopolitanism, first in Europe and later in the rest of the world. Some of the most important cognitive battles took place in the university, such as the conflict over tradition and modernity, secularization and, in the second half of the twentieth century, democracy and human rights. The university is, then, more than an institution of knowledge production but has also nurtured the dominant and emergent

cultural models of society. In the terms of Castoriadis, it might be said that the university is the 'imaginary institution of society', that is, one of the major sites in society where the radical imagination flourishes (Castoriadis, 1987). However, a sociological history of the university has yet to be written. The current tendency is to see it in terms of a model of decline, perhaps because of the wider disenchantment with modernity and the promises of the Enlightenment – promises that were very much connected with the idea of the university.

With the Enlightenment, the overriding belief was that the university is based on the unity of knowledge. This was the view that knowledge is based on a fundamental underlying idea, allowing us to speak of the 'idea of the university'. Knowledge was held to be autonomous, self-legislating and an end in itself; it was located not in society but in the institution of the university, and higher education was merely the dissemination of this idea in a knowledge-bereft society. Briefly, three cognitive shifts occurred in the twentieth century. The first, and discernible from the late nineteenth century, was in the emergence of disciplinary, specialized knowledge, dominated by the experimental natural sciences within the context of national, militarized economies. This led into the age of 'organized', or high modernity, when knowledge entered the economies of the Cold War era and when the university became a central institution of the national state. The second is the democratization of the university in the 1970s when new cultural models in society entered the university (for example, feminism and the New Social Movements) in the age of mass education. This development, marking the extension of social citizenship to higher education, eventually led to a gradual erosion of disciplinarity and undermined the older institution of academic authority based on received wisdom. The third is the shift towards the 'postmodern university' we are currently witnessing and which began in the 1980s when the university embraced the market and began to participate in the global order. In this shift – from the public cultures of modernity to the neoliberal and 'post' cultures of globalization – the erosion of disciplinarity and the autonomy of science become more pronounced and, it is often argued, the very notion of academic autonomy enters a crisis along with the declining authority of national institutions. In this view, the trajectory of the university in modernity is one of the loss of autonomy and the gradual descent from the ivory tower to social, economic and increasingly technological concerns. But, as I shall argue, rather than speak of a model of historical decline, we should see the university as the site in which the social and cultural contradictions of modernity get expressed in battles about the nature and function of knowledge.

In this chapter my aim is to look at how the debate on the university has been refracted through the main sociological theories of higher education. Hopefully this will relativize some of the dire diagnoses of the current situation of higher education. The sociology of the university has been a neglected aspect of the history of sociology. Yet, most of the major sociologists and social theorists from those in the classical tradition such as Weber, Durkheim and Veblen and mid-century sociologists such as Parsons, Bell, Riesman and Shils, to the radical generation – Touraine, Gouldner, Habermas and Bourdieu – wrote extensively on it. In doing so they were not all necessarily working within the sociology of education but, from the broader perspective of social theory and the sociology of knowledge, saw higher education and more generally the institution of the university as central to a wider understanding of modernity. Too much of the debate on the university has been dominated by speculative work on the *idea* of the university. More recently some of this genre has become popular with the thesis of the postmodern university, beginning with Lyotard and reiterated by Bill Readings in an influential philosophical application of Lyotard's ideas. The postmodern theory of the university has been reflected in widespread concerns about the embracing of market values by the university under the condition of globalization. I shall try to demonstrate in this chapter that the sociological works offer an important appraisal of the university as an institution that marks major transformations within modernity. These works put into theoretical and historical perspective a wider view of the university as a resilient institution that both reflects and transforms the society of which it is a part. Thus rather than speak of the demise of the university as a result of the postmodern scenarios of the fragmentation of knowledge, the retreat of the state, the embracing of market values, or the impact of globalization, a sociological approach suggests a more differentiated view of the university. The chapter will show that the discourse of citizenship has been central to the conception of the university in modernity and much of this is still relevant to the current situation.

First I outline the major classical conceptions of the university in social theory; in the following section I discuss the idea of the university in radical social theory; next I turn to contemporary debates on the university and, finally, I offer an appraisal of the current situation of the university in light of these debates.

SOCIAL THEORY AND THE UNIVERSITY IN MODERNITY

Since the Enlightenment the university has been a central theme in many debates on the nature of modernity. From Kant and von Humboldt to Newman and Jaspers much of this revolved around the question of academic freedom and the institutional underpinning of the unity of knowledge that was central to the Enlightenment project. If the Enlightenment promised progress through knowledge, the university was the institution in society that provided the space in which to make possible that goal. With Max Weber the philosophical discourse of the university and the Enlightenment ideal of knowledge and science as an end is put on trial. Weber departed from the Enlightenment-influenced idea in one major respect: he did not think that knowledge had a self-evidently emancipatory function and he strenuously opposed the use of science for politics. The university suffered the same fate as knowledge under the conditions of advanced modernity and the total disenchantment of the world he believed accompanied modern rationalism, the result of which was the irreconcilable conflict between the realms of science, politics, ethics and art.

In his famous lecture in 1918, 'Science as a Vocation' ('*Wissenschaft als Beruf*'), he discussed the role of the university professor in the disenchanted age of modern rationalization (Weber, 1948: 131). Weber noted how the rationalization of the university in Germany is a form of Americanization. 'This development, I am convinced, will engulf those disciplines in which the craftsman personally owns the tools, essentially the library, as is still the case to a large extent in my own field. This development corresponds entirely to what happened to the artisan of the past and is now fully under way.' Weber lamented, but accepted with resignation, the inevitability of the disappearance of the Enlightenment university and the rise of the modern instrumental university. Less critically and in line with his value-neutral conception of science, he noted the separation of science and politics, for the conduct of science under the conditions of modernity allows no room for politics. Science is the product of a rationalized world devoid of personality while politics still offers some scope for personality and the recovery of charisma, is his message. His lecture ends on a note of resignation to meet the 'demands of the day' and the 'intellectual sacrifice' that science as a profession requires. He was unambivalent in his commitment to 'ethical neutrality' for he believed that cultural values could not be judged. Knowledge might gain some power over them if it confined itself to neutral analysis. But even then it will be limited; as he put it in an essay on universities in 1908: 'The freedom of science exists in Germany within the limits of ecclesiastical and political acceptability. Outside these limits there is none' (Weber, 1973: 17; see also Shils, 1973). This was the basis of a view that won widespread support in later decades and is best represented by the German sociologist Helmut Schelsky's term 'solitude and freedom' (Schelsky, 1963). In *Einsamkeit und Freiheit*, a work never translated into English, Schelsky demonstrated, in what to some was unrealistic, the idea of an overarching and transcendent point of unity, which is to be found, he argued, in the 'solitude and freedom' of science and scholarship. However, there was a tension in the view of the relation between higher education and society in some of these early sociological theories.

The Enlightenment model of the university believed the unity of knowledge rested on the unity of teaching and research. Much of the early sociology of the university recognized the breakup of this unified model of knowledge. For instance, Thorstein Veblen in his influential *The Higher Learning in America* (1962), first published in 1918, wrote about the decline of the liberal model of the university which becomes instead a place of research to which teaching is subordinated. This transition was marked by the creation of the PhD, as an attempt to usurp the German liberal humanist tradition of knowledge as an end by institutionalizing a research culture. Recognizing that the twentieth century university would be different from that which preceded it, Veblen nevertheless held onto the Enlightenment humanistic understanding of knowledge as an end in itself. These theories were among the first intimations of the entry of the university into sociological consciousness.

In the 1960s and 1970s, when sociology as a discipline consolidated, several notable sociologists and social theorists wrote about the university and from diverse perspectives. In the United States Daniel Bell saw the university as occupying a central role in the postindustrial society, as did Alain Touraine in France, although from the perspective of radical politics; Riesman charted the course of the university in the age of radical politics; Parsons and Platt wrote a major work on the university as the central institution in professional society; for Gouldner the university was strung between the intelligentsia and radical politics; in Germany Habermas saw the university as a mean of cognitive critique and societal learning; and Bourdieu wrote about the university as an organ of cultural capital which might be the site of new social struggles.

Daniel Bell (1966) was one of the first to recognize the importance of the university for sociology, proposing the thesis that the university is a central part of the postindustrial society and in it a potentially emancipatory 'knowledge class' is to be found. For Bell, this class, essentially the intelligentsia, is composed of the scientific, the technological, the administrative and the cultural. The cultural includes intellectuals in the narrow sense of the term, political and public intellectuals as opposed to experts. Since the postindustrial society depends to a great extent on the production of knowledge, the university will occupy a more important role than before. It would be inevitable that as the university becomes implicated in material production, it would also take on a political role. In his famous work *The Coming of the Postindustrial Society*, Bell defended the relevance of the traditional and the modern functions of the university. The function of the university, he argues

is to relate to each other the modes of conscious inquiry: historical consciousness, which is the encounter with a tradition that can be tested against the present; methodological consciousness, which makes explicit the conceptual grounds of inquiry and its philosophical presuppositions; and individual self-consciousness which makes one aware of the sources of one's prejudgements, and allows one to re-create one's values through the disciplined study of the society. (Bell, 1974: 423)

In this respect Bell identified an important feature of the university: it is one of the few locations in society where many modes of

knowledge are concentrated. Whatever unity is possible in face of such specialization and differentiation consists precisely of this concentration of functions. For Edward Shils this role was inseparable from citizenship. He believed the university had made a major contribution to social and civic citizenship by providing society with some of its essential requirements, in particular a professional class.

For Parsons and Platt (1973) in *The American University*, a major attempt to apply Parsonian structural functionalism and the sociology of knowledge to higher education, the university is the key institution of the 'fiduciary' subsystem, which might be understood as the 'system of trust', and lies in the 'zone of interpenetration' between the cultural system and society. It is interesting to note that Parsons and Platt in this major work on the university do not see a conflict between these two functions. Influenced by functional theory and a liberal political ideology which predisposed them toward a largely harmonious view of society, they saw a complementarity in these functions and believed that the university did not have to compromise its role as the 'trustee of cognitive culture'.

The unity of the university for Parsons is not the unity of a legitimating idea but the functional unity of its structures with respect to the societal community. The two principal features of the American university are: '(1) that it, and with it the institutionalized cognitive complex, has become a differentiated part of a complex society and (2) that it has become upgraded in prestige and influence within the society to the point that some commentators describe it as the central institution in the society' (Parsons and Platt, 1973: 103). The key concept for Parsons and Platt is 'interpenetration', the process by which one subsystem affects another: the university is forced to occupy a zone between culture and society, and therefore must cut across these systems. But the imperatives of differentiation do not preclude the possibility of an overall integration. This complementarity between differentiation and the possibility of integration is the central and unifying theme in Parsons's entire sociology of modernity (Parsons, 1974). It was his firm conviction that there is an overall unity of function in the core components of modern society. In the Parsonian framework this unity of purpose is reflected in the university's interpenetration into the domains of culture and society. Indeed, the very term cognitive rationality embodies both a cultural (cognitive) and a social (rationality) dimension, as Parsons and Platt point out (1973: 38). What is important in the Parsonian framework is that the university is still connected to the non-cognitive structures of the cultural system, while being autonomous from the moral community at large. The complexity of the interrelationships that characterize the university prevents it from being the moral arbiter of society: the modern university cannot function as, they say, the 'Prince's conscience', as in the early modern university (Parsons and Platt, 1973: 47–50).

The university's main functions are: 1 research, 2 professional training, 3 general education and 4 cultural development. Of particular importance is the growing significance of professional training, which they see as a response to the demands of the economic system, which creates the need for a public system of accreditation. These functions are related to the different institutions within the university, research is concentrated in the graduate schools, professional training in the professional schools and teaching in the colleges. Cultural development is not underpinned by a specific domain within the university but is located within society, where professors can gain influence in the public domain either as intellectuals or as professionals. While Parsons and Platt argue that the primary core value of the university is cognitive rationality, they recognize that the university is increasingly becoming a certifier of professional competence within the occupational order. In Parsons's words: 'the university became the primary trustee of that phase of the cultural heritage of modern societies that was important for the grounding of professional competence' (Parsons, 1979: 91). In their framework, intellectuals, who have access to the mass media, are also important in their contribution to the 'general definition of the situation', with respect to the human condition as a whole and the status of

the social sciences. The university, they argue, makes a major contribution to public knowledge which is central to modern society. The public, unlike professional knowledge producers, is concerned less with the problem of explanation than with the problem of meaning (Parsons and Platt, 1973: 279–82).

The American University was a product of disciplinary organized knowledge with politics kept outside. Academic freedom was also a freedom *from* politics. As Parsons (1979: 108) himself admitted, academic freedom 'is closely related to the rights of privacy enjoyed, for example, by the family and (subject to very broad restrictions) the rights of parents to have the main voice in the bringing up of their children'. The role of the university was not to criticize or transform culture and morality but to pass on relatively intact a received tradition to future generations. Clearly this was an inherently conservative function. As Durkheim observed in his history of educational thought: 'the evolution of education always lags very substantially behind the general evolution of society as a whole'. He noted how, for instance, 'a great scientific movement was to be born in the sixteenth century and to be developed throughout the seventeenth and eighteenth centuries without making the slightest impact on the University before the beginning of the nineteenth' (Durkheim, 1977: 1964).

RADICAL SOCIAL THEORY AND THE UNIVERSITY

Until the 1970s, the university occupied a central location in society, but in late modernity the university came gradually to incorporate voices from the margins of society. Cultural revolution in the Western world from the 1960s onwards shattered the cultural framework which carried liberal education (Lipset, 1967). In this period the university becomes less a transmitter of culture than its transformer. In Germany, where de-nazification was a project led by the universities, this was particularly pronounced. What is striking about the revolutionary decades was the emergence of a cultural clash between bourgeois culture and mass culture. New cultural voices emerge: the women's movement, black and ethnic cultures, nationalist liberation movements, Marxism and the postmodern avant-garde which sought to re-link art and politics. As a result of the Vietnam War and the civil rights movement, the American university became a major political site, a factor enhanced by the academicization of Marxism. In the 1960s and 1970s the counter-cultural impulse stemmed largely from the students, a contrast to the other great period of academic revolution – the 1790s and the opening decade of the nineteenth century – when it stemmed from the professors. This is expressed, for example, in a famous incident at Warwick University in 1970 and became the subject of the book edited by E.P. Thompson, *Warwick University Ltd*, when students, protesting about the lack of accountability in the university, occupied the administration and gained access to controversial information relating to what E.P. Thompson later called the 'industrial– intellectual oligarchy' (Thompson, 1970). In a book entitled *Culture in the Plural*, published in 1974, Michel de Certeau discussed the embracing of democratic popular cultures by the university: 'The relation of culture to society has been transformed: culture is no longer reserved for a given milieu; it no longer belongs to certain professional specialities (teachers or liberal professions); nor is it any longer a stable entity defined by universally received codes' (de Certeau, 1997: 41). He believed the introduction of popular culture into the university was leading to the birth of the student worker and the wider abolition of the social divisions of labour. Though this socialism of the intellect and of labour was not to last, the politicization of the university was irreversible.

An important German debate on the university began in the late 1960s with a contribution by Habermas. Habermas's (1969, 1971a, b) intervention concerned the question of democratization and cultural renewal. Rejecting attempts to define the university in terms of the culture of humanism, on the one side, and on the other, as a purely instrumental

institution for providing technical knowledge, he defended the critical heritage of the university. Like many intellectuals on the left, he was aware that the older humanistic model of the university – the subject of Fritz Ringer's famous study (Ringer, 1969) – failed to offer resistance to fascism and consequently needed to recover its moral standing in society. Habermas emphasized the role of the university as an interpreter of a society's self-understanding and not just passing on its heritage in an unmediated manner: 'it belongs to the tasks of the university to transmit, interpret, and develop the cultural tradition of the society' (Habermas, 1971a: 2). The old German university helped to establish the nation-state, but the task of the reformed university is to prepare the way for democratization. However, Habermas believed the reform of the German university was compatible with the *Bildungs* ideal of the older model in so far as this could be transformed into a more critical kind of self-reflection. For Habermas the university was also in danger of becoming dominated by the instrumental rationality of technology and capitalism. The alternative was democratization and the ending of the dualism of academic hierarchy and the administration of departments. In a later essay (Habermas, 1987), he argued that the critical role of the university has remained unrealized but to bring to realization today will require the creation of a 'communication community'. For Habermas, like Parsons, the university is a 'bundle institution', that is it is rooted in the life-world through the bundling of functions, such as research, general education, cultural self-understanding, the formation of public opinion and the training of specialists: 'As long as this complex has not been completely torn apart, the idea of the university cannot be completely dead' (Habermas, 1987). But unlike Parsons, Habermas argued the unity of the university is not to be found in culture or in science but 'in the last analysis it is the communicative forms of scientific and scholarly argumentation that hold university learning processes in their various functions together' (Habermas, 1987). While the older humanistic conception of the university emphasized the professorate as the guardians of culture, Habermas pointed out that it is the students who are now defending the university (Habermas, 1971b). Habermas's theory of the university thus places a central role in his wider social theory of modernity, seeing it as the site of critical and communicative reason. In his work on the public sphere, for instance, modernity is seen as the unfolding of communicative spaces and while many of these spaces have been feudalized or colonized by instrumental reason, the university has remained an important site of critique (Habermas, 1989, 1996). As is also evident in his other work from that period, *Knowledge and Human Interests* (Habermas, 1978), knowledge is a differentiated structure and is linked to society by its inseparable connection with cognitively specific human interests. But what links all the sciences together is not scientific rationality as such but the embeddedness of science in communication, for despite extensive differentiation and specialization the mode of knowledge production within universities has not become totally detached from the cognitive horizon of the life world and to that extent it contains within it a connection with communication. Such a communicative understanding of the university allows us to speak of the 'idea' of the university with a major qualification: the 'idea' of the university does not necessarily derive from the university itself. As Habermas intimated, a 'new life can be breathed into the idea of the university only outside its walls' (Habermas, 1987).

This was also the position that Alain Touraine took. In *The May Movement*, Touraine (1971b) applied his sociology of action to the university. As the paradigmatic institution in the postindustrial society, he believed the university might be the focus of the new kinds of social movements, the first signs of which were the events of May 1968 in Paris. In the postindustrial society, knowledge is the key to the new struggles, he argued in *Post-Industrial Society* (1971a). The implication of this is that the university must decide whether it is to be allied to politics or to capital. Touraine believed the mode of knowledge produced by the university could be used to renew the

cultural models and to lead to the creation of new social practices, a social theory that was elaborated in more abstract terms in *The Self-Production of Society* (1977). He saw a new role for the university emerging as a reflection on society for the 'progress of knowledge is inseparable from the critical self-reflection of society on itself, on its intellectual operations as well as on its social and political organization' (Touraine, 1971a: 332). The university thus exists between politics and knowledge: just as there is no pure or autonomous knowledge neither is there pure politics. 'The university was and is, simultaneously, an instrument to reinforce the dominant scientific creation and a relatively independent center of criticism and cultural change' (Touraine, 1971a: 334). Seeing knowledge and politics as mediated in the cultural model of society, he criticized both the conservatism of the university and the offensive politics of the students. In his subsequent writings, he grew more distanced from the idea of a postindustrial social movement emerging within the university.

A theme that becomes visible in the sociological writing on the university in this period is that the university is a site of cultural contestation. It is a relatively autonomous zone in society where major cultural conflicts are fought out over what might be broadly called 'cultural capital'. This is evident in the work of Riesman, Gouldner and Bourdieu. In *The Academic Revolution* David Riesman and Christopher Jencks (1968) emphasized the rise of the academic profession which reached pre-eminence with the emergence of the student movement. In work published in 1980, *On Higher Education: The Academic Enterprise in an Era of Rising Student Consumerism*, Riesman explored the implications of this confrontation (Riesman, 1998). As a result of the emergence of student revolt there was an inevitable decline in the power of the academic profession in an era of what he called 'student consumerism'. In one of his most famous books, *The Future of Intellectuals and the Rise of the New Class*, Alvin Gouldner explored some of the contradictions of the university in postindustrial society (Gouldner, 1979). Arguing that intellectuals and the intelligentsia together formed a 'new class', a kind of 'cultural bourgeoisie', which is essentially contradictory since it is composed of two overlapping elements, the professions and the radical intellectuals. While both share a social existence in the production of knowledge, the former is embedded in the system of power and the latter is in opposition to it. The New Class differs from the older elites in that it has control over education. The school is the major alienation from the old class, he argues, but the decisive break is in higher education: 'Colleges and universities are the finishing schools of the New Class' resistance to the old class' (Gouldner, 1979: 44). In his view, education is more than just the 'ideological state appara-tuses', as Althusser claimed (Althusser, 1971). Instead, he argued the university is a contra-dictory place in which the New Class may seek alliances with business or with apolitical culture or with political subversion. The univer-sity is, like the New Class itself, internally differentiated:

> To understand modern universities and colleges we need an openness to contradiction. For universities both *reproduce and* subvert the larger society. We must dis-tinguish between the functions universities publicly *promise* to perform – the social goods they are chartered to produce – and certain of their actual consequences which, while commonly unintended, are not real: the production of dissent, deviance, and the cultivation of an authority-subverting culture of critical discourse. (Gouldner, 1979: 45)

Gouldner's thesis is that the New Class, which is much more contradictory than the old class, does not control cultural capital such as knowledge. He believes there is enough empir-ical evidence to suggest that, in particular, in higher education power is loosened not tightened. Higher education thus becomes a major 'cosmopolitanizing influence' in mod-ern society. In it there is a shift from causal to reflexive speech and a discourse emerges in which claims and utterances may not be justi-fied by reference to a speaker's social status. As a result, all authority referring claims are potentially problematic (Gouldner, 1979: 3). As he put it elsewhere: 'The university's central problem is its failure as a community in which rational discourse about social worlds is possi-ble. This was partly because rational discourse

as such ceased to be its dominant value and was superseded by a quest for knowledge products and information products that could be sold for funding, prestige and power – rewards bestowed by the state and the larger society that is bent upon subverting rational discourse about itself' (Gouldner, 1979: 79). In sum, he argued universities foster a 'culture of critical discourse', cosmopolitanism and reflexivity.

We can conclude this discussion of the university in modern sociology by referring to the work of Bourdieu. In his extensive writings on education and the university, in books such as *Homo Academicus* (1988) and *The State Nobility* (1996), Bourdieu presents a view of the university as the paradigmatic site of cultural capital. Although Bourdieu's main studies on higher education are based on research conducted in the late 1960s and 1970s and are very specific to the French context, they provide a striking account of some general trends in the transformation of higher educa-tion. Sharing with Foucault the view that knowledge is power, Bourdieu maintains that knowledge is not primarily emancipatory but is socially located in contexts of power which are in essence classificatory, or cognitive, systems in which the different forms of capital circulate. His concern is to reveal these contexts of power in order that knowledge might be reflexively reconstituted. Bourdieu's sociology of knowl-edge claims that cognitive structures shape, limit and influence the production and circula-tion of knowledge in society. Consequently some of the most important battles over cul-tural capital are fought out in the university. Education thus is a field in which the wider conflicts and sources of inequality in society are manifest. The idea of inequality – in economic capital – the pursuit of distinction – in cultural capital – is very pronounced in education. The expansion of education has not led to greater social equality, according to Bourdieu and Passeron in *Reproduction in Education, Society and Culture* (1977) and *The Inheritors* (1979). Participation in French higher education is pre-dominantly middle and upper-middle class. Lying at the root of this position is a view of education as a form of cultural capital which can lead to economic capital but it is also something that is inherently a source of power in its own right. It is Bourdieu's theory that this kind of power is becoming more significant today as cultural fields become more and more autonomous of the state and of particular social groups such as classes. Education thus becomes a cultural field in which society selects individuals for positions of power and allocates status and prestige. Schools and universities are primarily institutions of selection. It is this functional selectivity that connects the university to society. Since education is then primarily a form of social differentiation it is inherently stratified. Much of Bourdieu's analysis of education centres on the internal structure of power within the university. Power in society is refracted through the prism of the university which produces different kinds of power but which are linked to the reproduction of power in society.

Bourdieu mentions in particular the struggle between three kinds of cultural capital that is fought out in the university. These are academic power, scientific power and intellectual power. Academic power refers to the power of control over the administration of academic resources and the means of career influence. It is the power to preside over credentials and allocate status and as such it is a socially codified power. Scientific power is essentially the power that comes from research reputations based on scholarly publications. It is a matter of prestige deriving directly from knowledge as opposed to the status attached to honorific positions. Intellectual power (or 'intellectual renown') comes from the ability to influence public opinion. It can derive from academic power but it is more likely to stem from scientific power. In France this is represented by membership of the *Académie Française*, writing reviews in the influential weeklies, or in publishing a book with a publisher read by the educated middle classes (Bourdieu, 1988: 78–9). The university thus can be examined as a site of struggle between these three fields of power and where different kinds of cultural capital collide.

There is no doubt that Bourdieu's studies on education and the university stress the autonomy that these institutions have won for themselves in their ability to create 'orders of classification'. There is relatively little in his analysis on the empancipatory struggles that other theorists have emphasized. Thus where Riesman saw a decline in 'faculty dominance', Bourdieu sees only the ascendancy of the professorate and its consolidation as a 'state nobility'. Clearly in the current age of the 'postmodern university' this view of the academic profession is no longer tenable. Although it is allied to particular kinds of power in the wider society, the struggles within the educational field are not significantly shaped by the extra-institutional context. Unlike the work of Riesman in the United States or Touraine in France or Habermas in Germany, Bourdieu ignored the wider social context, preferring to see the crisis as deriving from problems within French higher education. This is particularly vivid in *Homo Academicus* which offers a structural taxonomy of the May 1968 crisis. However, what remains of enduring importance in Bourdieu's work on the university is his account of cultural capital, which serves as a medium of exchange between the various kinds of power. In the context of the debate around the postmodern university this sense of the relative autonomy of the field of cultural capital is important.

THE UNIVERSITY IN CONTEMPORARY SOCIAL THEORY AND SOCIOLOGY

Despite their differences, the classical social theories of modernity, from Weber through Parsons, all took for granted certain assumptions about modernity, such as the relative autonomy of knowledge and the view that technology was contained by science. Such assumptions led them to a view of the university as an autonomous site in modern society. These assumptions were also present in modern social theory, such as in the theories of the university of Habermas and Bourdieu, and other figures in the radical tradition. In recent social theory – which is much more sceptical about the project of modernity – a corresponding uncertainty about the role of the university has become very pronounced amidst a broader recognition of the transformation of scientific knowledge.

There are five main positions on the university in contemporary social theory, which for present purposes will include a broader spectrum of thought than sociology: the liberal critique, the postmodern thesis, the reflexivity thesis, the globalization thesis and the McDonaldization thesis.

The liberal critique   In essence, this is a conservative cultural critique and, although not sociological, is highly influential even within social science. It is primarily concerned with the university as a medium of cultural reproduction. The liberal idea of the university can be associated with the quite different positions of Allan Bloom (1987) and Russell Jacoby (1987). Bloom represents an old-fashioned conservative view of higher education as the preservation of tradition. He thus bemoans the attack on the traditional curriculum in the name of diversity. Jacoby, who represents a more radical liberal position, also attacks the arrival of cultural politics but not because of the greater value of the traditional canon: he regrets the decline of the public intellectual, who has disappeared from the university that has become the retreat of the specialist. Despite the different positions within this broad stance that derives from the neohumanist tradition, the tendency is to see the university in crisis because of the decline of the autonomy of culture, be it the culture of critique or, in its more conservative version, the traditional culture of the canon.

The postmodern thesis   If Bourdieu stressed too much the autonomy of the university as a 'state nobility', more recent theories that were to surface since Lyotard's theory of the university in *The Postmodern Condition* exaggerate the demise of the university as a result of 'material capital' invading the space of 'cultural capital' (Lyotard, 1984). In the postmodern informational society, he argued, the university suffers the same fate as the meta-narratives of modernity. Since there are no longer autonomous spaces, the university does not occupy a privileged site. Lyotard's view of the university is thus a striking contrast to Bourdieu's emphasis on the 'state nobility'. Against Bourdieu's image of a resilient institution of modernity, Lyotard is more sceptical of the institutions of modernity such as the university's ability to offer possibilities for radical politics. He saw the university as based on the principle of unity by which the different kinds of knowledge are part of a universal principle of unity. Universities for Lyotard are based on bounded discourses – such as the department, the faculty, the curriculum – and modern forms of legitimation, such as the lecture and professorial authority. Therefore he did not see the university as central to politics, arguing instead that the postmodern condition is based on a different kind of politics, one of plurality and one that is located far from the jurisdiction of the state. One implication of this is the postmodern thesis of the impossibility of the curriculum. Rejecting the neohumanist ideal of the integration of teaching and research – which in different ways was accepted by Parsons and Habermas in the writings on the university – Lyotard sees teaching as counter-revolutionary while research can be emancipatory so long as it breaks from any criterion of legitimation. Unlike teaching, which he sees as under the control of the state, research can be subversive of all attempts to impose meta-narratives. In postmodern conceptions of the university, such as that of Bill Readings (1996), it is argued that the knowledge has lost its emancipatory role and the very notion of universality, or even that the very idea of a curriculum is now impossible, given the fragmentation of knowledge, as in, for instance, the separation of teaching and research.

The reflexivity thesis   This set of positions is quite separate from the postmodern thesis. It is best associated with the claim that there is a new mode of knowledge based on a more reflexive relationship between user and producer (Gibbons et al., 1984). As a Mode 2 paradigm around applied knowledge emerges, the university – which is caught up in the more hierarchical and disciplinary-based Mode 1 knowledge production – becomes, it is claimed, increasingly irrelevant to the post-Fordist economy in which technoscience is becoming more important. While offering a less dramatic theory of the decline of the university, an assumption of the obsolescence of the institutions of modernity is built into the argument. In more recent work by three of these authors, this prognosis is somewhat qualified (see Nowotny et al., 2001). In general, the point that lies behind this stance is that technical training, the provision of technical expertise and generally technoscience rather than basic science is what is important today and universities are less equipped to deal with it, given that they are located in the nexus of basic knowledge characteristic of the humanities and experimental sciences.

The globalization thesis This body of writing on the university draws attention to the instrumentalization of the university as it embraces market values and information technology, especially in the area of the on-line provision of higher education. Although the proponents of this thesis do not use the language of postmodernism, they share the view that the university, as a modern institution and servant of the nation-state, is embracing consumerism and, as it does so it loses its moral purpose in the global age. While e-programmes are one dimension of the impact of globalization, another is in the area of technoscience. According to various authors, the university is far from irrelevant to capitalism, as the previous thesis would claim, but is in fact fully integrated into it and, as a new managerialism takes over the university, there is a resulting loss of academic freedom (Curie and Newson, 1998; Etzkowitz and Leydesdorff, 1997; Slaughter and Leslie, 1993). This thesis suggests that the university has become a major player in the global market and in information-based capitalism. Slaughter and Leslie (1993) argue in a major study, *Academic Capitalism*, that the changes that took place in higher education in the 1980s and 1990s were as great as the changes that took place in the last quarter of the nineteenth century when the industrial revolution created the wealth that provided the base for

higher education. But in the 1980s and 1990s national systems of higher education are being restructured in order to secure a greater share of global markets. The shift to 'academic capitalism' occurred because universities' search for extra funding coincided with the corporate quest for new products requiring a high input of scientific knowledge. So, rather than universities becoming irrelevant, they are becoming more and more central to capitalism in the provision of technoscience and the university has in fact strengthened its position by participating in the global expansion of capitalism. What in fact exists is a 'triple helix' of links between government, university and industry, to use the term of Etzkowitz and Leydesdorff (1997).

These developments have led to a great deal of speculation about the emergence of global-mega universities, corporate universities, even virtual universities (Miyoshi, 1998; Robins and Webster, 2002; Scott, 1998; Smith and Webster, 1997). Building on industry–university links established since the 1980s, it has frequently been noted, universities are also moving closer to digital degrees. The growth of vocational training, distance learning and the move to make course curricula the property of the university are examples of how universities are reducing labour costs while expanding enrolment. According to Bill Readings in a brilliant study, *The University in Ruins*, the university was created to legitimate and serve the nation-state in a historical mission to provide the nation-state with a cultural project (Readings, 1996). This project, which derived from the Enlightenment, is no longer relevant today since, he argues, the nation-state no longer exists. The university and the state are both modern creations and the fate of the former is inextricably linked to the latter, for globalization has put an end to the university of modernity as it has to the nation-state: 'The University no longer has to safeguard and propagate national culture, because the nation-state is no longer the major site at which capital reproduces itself' (Readings, 1996: 13). In place of defining a cultural project, the 'posthistorical' university is a 'ruined' institution, merely reproducing the corporate ideology of 'excellence' which commodifies all forms of knowledge. These accounts of the postmodern university thus portray it as nothing less than an enclave of global capitalism.

The McDonaldization thesis The notion of the 'McUniversity' indicates the emergence of growing rationalization in the university along the lines of McDonaldization as in the Weberian theory of rationalization. In one version of the argument, new bureaucratic forms of university administration are taking shape diminishing the autonomy of academics and transforming the university into a Fordist organization for the mass production of higher education (Parker and Jary, 1995). Although not amounting to the end of the university, as the postmodern thesis suggests, the idea of McUniversity indicates the arrival of a massified university in which education, professional organization and research are standardized by neoliberal thinking. The McUniversity entails greater managerial power, structural centralization, increased student intake, the casualization of labour and the elimination of inefficiency.

What are we to make of these announcements of crisis and even of the decline of the university? It is possible to agree with many of these theories, especially the latter, which avoids some of the extreme statements associated with the postmodern university. The following section will attempt an appraisal of these ideas.

THE USES OF THE UNIVERSITY: THE UNIVERSITY IN THE KNOWLEDGE SOCIETY

To what extent is the postmodern university a reality? Has the vision of the university in what might broadly be called modern social theory been rendered obsolete by developments that can be described as postmodernization: the penetration of market values into the university, the encroachment of globalization, the possibility of the virtual mega university, the fragmentation of knowledge? Does the McUniversity offer some possibilities for the university to be

a relevant institution? There is clearly much to suggest that the idea of the university in the older sociological theories of Weber, Parsons, Habermas and Bourdieu has been undermined by recent developments and the liberal critique is at best a nostalgic plea for a lost modernity. Whether the assumptions of the older approaches are no longer valid is a different matter and must be soberly addressed.

First, there is a clear need for a historical contextualization of the university. The recent debates on the demise of the university tend to be based on a historically inaccurate view of earlier models of the university. While the augmented instrumentalization of the university by market values is an undeniable and probably irreversible development, it is by no means specific to the contemporary university. Universities have always been deeply involved in industry since the late nineteenth century. German universities since the middle of the nineteenth century were heavily involved in the technological innovations and American universities since the Land Grant Act became deeply embedded in the nascent industrial society.

Second, the globalization thesis exaggerates certain trends, especially relating to the impact of information and communication technologies. Assumptions of technological determinism underlie these notions of the mega-online university replacing all other kinds of higher education. There is no doubt that the delivery of higher education is moving to more and more mixed methods, which will include on-line delivery, and self-governance has been eroded by managerialism. However, current evidence is that the virtual university may be suffering the same fate as the wider virtual economy. The belief that on-line provision will solve the fiscal problem of widening participation is increasingly being doubted, as interactive learning is in fact expensive. A distinction also needs to be drawn between the commercial and educational uses of the new global means of communication. Clearly in the lower end of the market for academic produce, on-line delivery will not decline, and it may also be effective for certain kinds of training, but for most kinds of educational instruction, including much of vocational training, it will not be viable as the exclusive means of instruction. Moreover, it is a fundamental misunderstanding of the social impact of information and communication technologies to assume that they are revolutionary. Current sociological research reveals that in fact these technologies allow people to do what they have always done but in more diverse ways. In sum, technology has a differential impact on social relations.

Third, any sociologically informed account of the transformation of higher education today must recognize the diversity of universities. Much of the current debate tends to assume that American developments in academic capitalism are universally applicable. To an extent this can be generalized to the wider Anglo-American world, but it is highly questionable that it applies to, for instance, the European universities. Moreover, the great diversity within American higher education cannot be ignored. The European context is very different, simply because in most European countries the university is a public institution. Where the United States has been a market-dominated society, the European experience has on the whole given a stronger role to the state. Although this is less the case in the UK, the state tradition, as is reflected in Bourdieu's studies, is a striking feature of the European university tradition. The different state traditions in Europe have given the European university an extraordinary variety of institutional forms. While the economic exploitation of knowledge is becoming more and more globalized, science is still nationally organized and yet is globally interconnected. Nearly all the important organizations of science – *Centre National de Recherche Scientifique* in France, the *Max-Planck-Gesellschaft* in Germany – are nationally funded. The persistence of national foundations for knowledge does not hinder the remarkable growth of global collaboration but makes it possible. In this respect an important consideration is the so-called 'Bologna Process' in Europe within which there is the expectation of a 'Europeanization' of higher education by 2010 along with a growing consciousness of the emergence of a European 'knowledge society'.

In sum, my argument is that the spectre of the postmodern university tends to exaggerate the instrumentalization of the university by global forces and that there is not only a good deal of continuity with the older model of the university, but that much of the so-called instrumentalization is to be contextualized in a more differentiated analysis of the knowledge society where there are opportunities as well as dangers for the university.

I would like to explore three further dimensions to the role of the university in the knowledge society, a term that indicates a social condition in which knowledge is the key to social reproduction and to citizenship. The term knowledge society should be used in a broad sense to include not merely the application of science and technology in the economy nor as another term for the 'information society'. As has been recognized by the sociology of knowledge since Alfred Schutz, knowledge includes science and information but also encompasses cognitive complexes that are embedded in culture and in everyday life as well as self-knowledge and reflexive forms of knowledge. Knowledge is increasingly inseparable from citizenship and from democracy.

First, the postmodern thesis that the turn from the state to the market fundamentally alters the historical purpose of the university can be challenged on the grounds that it exaggerates current developments in the area of the market. What the postmodern position neglects is that the university is still a major vehicle of cultural citizenship, especially in countries where civil society is weak, for example in China, as Calhoun has demonstrated, or in Iran and in numerous other examples (Calhoun, 1994). In Eastern Europe today universities have a major role to play in reshaping societies (see Dahrendorf, 2002). Universities throughout the world have been tremendously important in cultivating democratic values and in the extension of cultural citizenship, for example in bringing about a critical and reflexive awareness of issues relating to minorities, multiculturalism, human rights, feminism, cultural heritage. While in the past much of the critical capacity of the university was subordinated to defining the cognitive structures of the nation-state, today the cultural mission of the university has extended into the broader domain of cosmopolitanism in the cultivation of postnational kinds of citizenship.

The capacity of the university to define cognitive structures for society is one of the major themes in the sociology of the university discussed earlier. There is much in this that is still relevant to the current situation.

Second, in many countries higher education is central to social citizenship. In the UK for instance the question of widening participation in higher education is one of the main aims of government policy in the area of social citizenship. In the view of many critics, this has the disadvantage of a trade-off between the social question of widening participation and the cultural question of an overriding commitment to science. The defenders of liberal education make much of this, seeing only a loss in the cultural dimension. For good or for bad, higher education is being forced more and more to be an agent of social change. There is no sign of this abating and in fact the separation of mass education from research-based activities has for long been a feature of the American university. It is not implausible to suggest, following Parsons, that the university responds to integrative demands by undergoing differentiation. In this way it can achieve a degree of social integration while pursuing cultural goals. One of the best examples of the role of the university in extending social and cultural citizenship is the Open Society Foundation, funded by George Soros. Aside from being an interesting example of how globalization is not undermining higher education but supporting it, the Open Society testifies to the critical role higher education is playing in reconstituting civil society in post-communist societies (see Dahrendorf, 2002).

Third, technological citizenship has become a new form of citizenship, going beyond social citizenship and, indeed also, cultural citizenship, and pertains to challenges to society that the new technologies are creating. In the context of the knowledge society the question of technological citizenship is especially important for the university to define a new identity for itself. Technology, especially technoscience, is shaping the world according to the dictates of global market forces and is one of the major societal discourses today in which rights and democracy are framed. As science is no longer exclusively based in the university, it is not far-fetched to propose that universities have an important role to play in linking technology to citizenship and bringing about a democratization of science and technology (Fuller, 1999). Universities are heavily implicated in the new technoscience, as a result of partnerships with business. But in a situation in which universities do not entirely control the production of science and technology, their significance rather lies in their ability to produce democratic discourse.

There are undoubtedly tensions between these dimensions of citizenship. For instance, widening participation – the dimension of social citizenship – can undermine the cultural role of the university, but it can also enhance it. Perhaps it can be suggested that the term 'university' today means the interconnection of different societal discourses: cultural, social and technological. Where these are fragmented in the wider society, they are connected in the university. The university no longer has a monopoly over knowledge in the broad sense of education and nor does it exclusively define science. Yet, it is a vital institution in the public sphere, contributing to civil society and citizenship by connecting societal discourses. The public sphere today is part of the knowledge society in which knowledge is not only more widely available but is also more and more contested as increasing numbers of social actors are drawn into it. It is possible to see universities in the knowledge societies of the twenty-first century having the role of public spheres, that is discursive sites in society where social interests engage with the specialized worlds of science and where national and global forces meet.

NOTE

This chapter is based on my book *Challenging Knowledge: The University in the Knowledge Society* (Buckingham: Open University Press, 2001).

BIBLIOGRAPHY

Althusser, L. (1971) 'Ideology and the ideological state apparatus', in *Lenin and Philosophy and Other Essays*. London: New Left Books.

Bell, D. (1966) *Reforming of General Education: The Columbia College Experience and its National Setting.* New York: Columbia University Press.

Bell, D. (1974) *The Coming of the PostIndustrial Society.* London: Heinemann.

Bloom, A. (1987) *The Closing of the American Mind.* New York: Simon and Schuster.

Bourdieu, P. (1988) *Homo Academicus.* Cambridge: Polity Press.

Bourdieu, P. (1996). *The State Nobility.* Cambridge: Polity Press.

Bourdieu, P. and Passeron, J.-C. (1977) *Reproduction in Education, Society and Culture.* London: Sage.

Bourdieu, P. and Passeron, J.-C. (1979) *The Inheritors: French Students and Their Relation to Culture.* Chicago: University of Chicago Press.

Bourdieu, P., Passeron, J.-P. and de Saint Martin, M. (1992) *Academic Discourse: Linguistic Misunderstanding and Professorial Power.* Cambridge: Polity Press.

Calhoun, C. (1994) *Neither Gods nor Emperors: Students and the Struggle for Democracy in China.* Berkeley, CA: University of California Press.

Castoriadis, C. (1987) *The Imaginary Institution of Society.* Cambridge: Polity Press.

Curie, J. and Newson, J. (eds) (1998) *Universities and Globalization: Critical Perspectives.* London: Sage.

Dahrendorf, R. (2002) *Universities after Communism.* Hamburg: Körber-Stiftung.

de Certeau, M. (1997) *Culture in the Plural.* Minneapolis, MN: University of Minnesota Press.

Delanty, G. (1997) *Social Science: Beyond Realism and Constructivism.* Buckingham: Open University Press

Delanty, G. (1999) *Social Theory in a Changing World: Conceptions of Modernity.* Cambridge: Polity Press.

Delanty, G. (2000a) *Modernity and Postmodernity: Knowledge, Power and the Self.* London: Sage.

Delanty, G. (2000b) *Citizenship in a Global Age: Culture, Politics, Society.* Buckingham: Open University Press.

Delanty, G. (2001) *Challenging Knowledge: The University in the Knowledge Society.* Buckingham: Open University Press.

Durkheim, E. (1957) *Professional Ethics and Civic Morals.* London: Routledge and Kegan Paul.

Durkheim, E. (1977) *The Evolution of Educational Thought.* London: Routledge and Kegan Paul.

Etzkowitz, H. and Leydesdorff, L. (eds) (1997) *Universities in the Global Economy: A Triple Helix of University Industry Government Relations.* London: Cassell Academic.

Fuller, S. (1999) *The Governance of Science.* Buckingham: Open University Press.

Gibbons, M., Limoges, C., Nowotny, H., Schwartzman, S., Scott, P. and Trow, M. (1984) *The New Production of Knowledge.* London: Sage.

Gouldner, A. (1979) *The Future of Intellectuals and the Rise of the New Class.* London: Macmillan.

Habermas, J. (1969) *Protestbewegung und Hochschulenreform.* Frankfurt: Suhrkamp.

Habermas, J. (1971a) 'The university in a democracy: democratization of the university', in *Toward a Rational Society.* London: Heinemann.

Habermas, J. (1971b) 'Student protest in the Federal Republic of Germany', in *Toward a Rational Society.* London: Heinemann.

Habermas, J. (1978) *Knowledge and Human Interests,* 2nd edn. London: Heinemann.

Habermas, J. (1987) 'The idea of the university – learning processes', *New German Critique,* 41: 3–22.

Habermas, J. (1989) *The Structural Transformation of the Public Sphere.* Cambridge: Polity Press.

Habermas, J. (1996) *Between Facts and Norms: Contribution to a Discourse Theory of Democracy and Law.* Cambridge: Polity Press.

Jacoby, R. (1987) *The Last Intellectuals: American Culture in the Age of Academe.* New York: Basic Books.

Lazersfeld, P. and Wagner, T. (1958) *The Academic Mind: Social Scientists in a Time of Crisis.* Glencoe, IL: The Free Press.

Lipset, S.M. (ed.) (1967) *Student Politics.* New York: Basic Books.

Lyotard, J.-F. (1984) *The Postmodern Condition: A Report on Knowledge.* Manchester: Manchester University Press.

Miyoshi, M. (1998) '"Globalization", culture, and the university', in *The Cultures of Globalization* (ed. F. Jameson and M. Miyoshi). Durham, NC: Duke University Press.

Nowotny, H., Scott, P. and Gibbons, M. (2001) *Re-thinking Science: Knowledge and the Public in an Age of Uncertainty.* Cambridge: Polity Press.

Parker, M. and Jary, D. (1995) 'The McUniversity: organization, management and academic subjectivity', *Organization,* 2 (2): 319–38.

Parsons, T. (1974) 'The university "bundle": a study of the balance between differentiation and integration', in N. Smelser and G. Almond (eds), *Public Higher Education in California: Growth, Structural Change, and Conflict.* Berkeley, CA: University of California Press.

Parsons, T. (1979) *Action Theory and the Human Condition.* New York: The Free Press.

Parsons, T. and Platt, G. (1973) *The American University.* Cambridge, MA: Harvard University Press.

Readings, B. (1996) *The University in Ruins.* Cambridge, MA: Harvard University Press.

Riesman, D. (1998) *On Higher Education: The Academic Enterprise in an Era of Rising Student Consumerism.* New Brunswick, NJ: Transaction Publishers.

Riesman, D. and Jencks, C. (1968) *The Academic Revolution* New York: Doubleday.

Ringer, F. (1969) *The Decline of the German Mandarins: The German Academic Community, 1890–1933.* Cambridge, MA: Harvard University Press.

Robins, K. and Webster, F. (eds) (2002) *The Virtual University? Information, Markets and Managements.* Oxford: Oxford University Press.

Schelsky, H. (1963) *Einsamkeit und Freiheit: Idee und Gestalt der deutschen Universität und ihrer Reformen.* Hamburg: Rowohlt.

Scott, P. (ed.) (1998) *The Globalization of Higher Education.* Buckingham: Open University Press.

Shils, E. (1972) 'The intellectuals and the powers: some perspectives for comparative analysis', in *The Intellectuals and the Powers and Other Essays.* Chicago: University of Chicago Press.

Shils, E. (1973) *Max Weber on Universities: The Power of the State and the Dignity of the Academic Calling in Imperial Germany.* Chicago: University of Chicago Press.

Shils, E. (1997) *The Calling of Higher Education: The Academic Ethic and Other Essays on Higher Education.* Chicago: University of Chicago Press.

Slaughter, S. and Leslie, L. (1993) *Academic Capitalism: Politics, Policies, and the Entrepreneurial University.* Baltimore, MD: Johns Hopkins University Press.

Smith, A. and Webster, F. (eds) (1997) *The Postmodern University?* Buckingham: Open University Press.

Thompson, E.P. (1970) *Warwick University Ltd.* Harmondsworth: Penguin.

Touraine, A. (1971a) *Post-Industrial Society.* New York: Random House.

Touraine, A. (1971b) *The May Movement: Revolt and Reform.* New York: Random House.

Touraine, A. (1977) *The Self-Production of Society.* Chicago: University of Chicago Press.

Veblen, T. (1962) *The Higher Learning in America.* New Haven, CT: Yale University Press.

Weber, M. (1948) 'Science as a vocation', in H.H. Gerth and C. Wright Mills (eds), *From Max Weber.* London: Routledge and Kegan Paul.

Weber, M. (1973[1908]) 'The alleged "academic freedom" of the German universities' (trans. Edward Shils). *Minerva*, 11.

31

Science, Technology and their Implications

KARIN KNORR CETINA

There is a widespread consensus today that contemporary Western societies are in one sense or another ruled by scientific knowledge and expertise. Science and technology were a driving force in the transition from traditional to modern societies and they are central in explaining the great socio-economic transformations early in the industrial revolution and the later progress of industrialization. Today, at the beginning of the twenty-first century, many believe another new epoch is in the making, and science and technology are again deeply implicated in the changes under way. Most of the concepts that have been suggested to refer to the new system, including labels such as 'postindustrial society' (Bell, 1973; Hage and Powers, 1992), 'postcapitalist' society (Drucker, 1993), 'technological society' (see, for example, Berger et al., 1974), 'information society' (see, for example, Beniger, 1986; Castells, 1996), 'risk society' (Beck, 1992) and 'knowledge society' (Stehr, 1994), embody this view. One major line of reasoning holds that the new order is postindustrialist by virtue of moving from a system based on heavy industry where capital and labor are the engines of economic growth to one where knowledge is the main productive force. One recent source of this awareness is Daniel Bell (1973), for whom knowledge in the form of

scientific theory has become an axial principle that accounts for changes in the division of labor, the development of specialized occupations, the emergence of new enterprises and sustained growth. A second line of reasoning centers more on postmodernity as an era of skepticism toward any absolute foundations of knowledge, as one in which a plurality of heterogeneous claims to knowledge has emerged instead and information technologies have become a dominant social force in shaping social life (Lyotard, 1984). This argument has been pushed furthest by Castells (2001: 3), who sees the 'network' as the message of the information technology revolution which, in his view, drives contemporary social transformations. Other assessments have highlighted further aspects of this knowledge and information transformation. For example, Habermas's argument about the 'technicization' of the life-world attempts to understand the spread of abstract systems to everyday life (1981). Giddens (1990), arguing that we live in a world of increased reflexivity mediated by expert systems, extends the impact of knowledge to the self, pointing out that today's individuals engage with the wider environment and with themselves through information produced by specialists which they routinely interpret and act on in everyday life.

Most accounts see knowledge and technology from a social impact perspective: knowledge and technology are the independent variables that have a profound effect on the character of social and economic life. In these accounts, knowledge is sometimes formulated to fit long-standing beliefs about science (an example is Bell's attempt to explicate knowledge in terms of theory, 1973: 44), but it is in effect the last thing to be explained, having no reality independent of analyst's models.

A BRIEF HISTORY OF SCIENCE AND TECHNOLOGY STUDIES

The specialty that attempts to break open such notions as science and technology, or scientific knowledge and information, is the sociology of science and technology. The sociology of science dates back to the late 1930s, when Robert K. Merton (1970 [1938]) displaced the then-existing Marxist perspectives (see, for example, Bernal, 1939; Hessen, 1931) with a genuinely sociological approach to knowledge. In what came to be called the 'institutional approach to science', some of the important questions concerned the social organization of science and the 'institutional imperatives', or norms and values, that sustained the scientific attitude from within (the norms were universalism, disinterestedness, organized skepticism and 'communism' – the collective ownership of scientific results). The generation which followed turned its back on the functionalist mode of reasoning which is evident in these concerns and which Merton, like Parsons, had adopted. It collectively moved away from the focus on social-structural and institutional processes characterizing scientific groups and organizations, arguing that science cannot be understood if the cognitive content of science and technology, and the processes of knowledge and technology creation, are not included in the analysis. This attitude was encouraged by the work of Kuhn (1970 [1962]) and Feyerabend (1975), who espoused a philosophy and historiography of science in which they traced the interdependence of cognitive and social factors in the history of physics and other disciplines. The outcome of this collective change of mind was that the sociology of science and technology turned into a sociology of knowledge, also called 'the new sociology of science' and 'science and technology studies'. Unlike Mannheim (1936) and Scheler (1924), who had proposed a sociology of knowledge in the 1930s but excluded from it the natural sciences, the new generation insisted that the natural sciences must be at the center of attention of social studies of science. Mannheim and Scheler's central thesis was that human thought was socially conditioned, as was knowledge in economics, and more generally in the human sciences; but they assumed, as did most scholars after them, that the natural sciences were exempted from such influence. The common assumption explicitly endorsed by the earlier institutional school had been that sociologists had nothing to say on the practice and content of science; the content of science was, at best, the concern of philosophers of science, who investigated the structure of scientific theories and the logic of discovery and justification. In contrast, what unfolded with the new sociology of scientific knowledge were research programs that took it upon themselves to demonstrate the relevance of empirical sociological analysis in the hardest possible cases, those of the natural sciences and mathematics. The resulting studies showed that the technical core of science could be studied empirically with social science methods to great advantage. Doing science and technology was a form of constructive action in collective contexts; though the processes observed were intricate and complex, they were open to examination to no lesser degree than those in other areas of social life.[1] This new sociology of science was later expanded into a new sociology of technology (Pinch and Bijker, 1984) and both proved tremendously successful, conceptually as well as empirically, yielding a number of new programs and results discussed in the next section.

The seemingly deliberate effort to extend the perspective of the sociology of knowledge to the natural sciences, the very domain which had acquired a monopoly on defining what counts as knowledge from the Enlightenment onward – while at the same time establishing itself as being in some sense 'outside society' when it came to its own internal processes – was the result of the convergence of several independent endeavors originating in the early and mid-1970s (Barnes, 1977; Bloor, 1976; Collins, 1975, 1985; Knorr Cetina, 1977, 1981; Latour and Woolgar, 1979; Lynch, 1985; MacKenzie, 1981; Traweek, 1988; Zenzen and Restivo, 1982). These efforts became enhanced and related to one another by simultaneous early formulations of the 'sociology of knowledge turn' in science studies. The most notable early formulations of the goals and musts of the new research program included Bloor's 'symmetry thesis', Collins's methodological relativism (1985) and Knorr Cetina's and Latour and Woolgar's assessment that scientific activities had to be seen as constructive rather than descriptive and that they are bound to particular sites, scientific laboratories. The symmetry thesis was part of four principles Bloor set out in his 1976 book and which circumscribed the strong program in science studies: the program was to be causal, that is, it should attempt to determine the factors that account for the convictions and knowledge-beliefs of scientists; it should be neutral in regard to true and false knowledge, successful and unsuccessful beliefs, 'rational' and 'irrational' outcomes – meaning both sides of these dichotomies should be explained, not just one; it was to be symmetric, meaning one should be able to make reference to the same causes as explanations of true and false knowledge; and it should be reflexive, meaning the patterns of explanation should be applicable to social studies of science and the results it comes up with. The main thrust of these principles, and notably of the second and the third, has been the symmetric treatment of true and false knowledge in empirical research. These principles declared normal, proper, successful, rational natural science research whose results counted as true or potentially true to be subject to the same scrutiny and explanatory variables as false, irrational, shaky, or politically mandated scientific results – the kind of pseudo-science that had been subjected to social explanations before. Bloor's principles formulated as legitimate and long overdue what he

himself and others in science studies had set out to do: make inquiries into the nature of normal science and 'good', established knowledge processes. The new sociology of science and technology is characterized by a methodological relativism that follows from these ideas. In essence it holds that we must bracket any presumption of the rationality of science and our deeply entrenched beliefs in scientific authority. Only then will it be possible to study scientific practices and beliefs on a par with other beliefs and practices (Rouse, 1996: 5–7). Methodological relativism needs to be distinguished from judgmental relativism that takes all knowledge claims to be equally valid – which is not what the new sociology of science proposed.[2] The constructionist program in the new sociology of science and technology extends the tenets of the symmetry thesis and of methodological relativism by adding an empirical strategy of making sense of science that pays attention to the (humanly) made character of knowledge: 'As we come to recognize the conventional and artifactual status of our forms of knowing, we put ourselves in a position to realize that it is ourselves and not reality that is responsible for what we know' (Shapin and Schaffer, 1985: 344). We shall consider this in more detail, in connection with a host of research results and perspectives that have since emerged in the area under examination.

SELECTED RESULTS OF THE NEW SOCIOLOGY OF SCIENCE AND TECHNOLOGY

Constructionism[3] and laboratory studies

The source of the phrase 'laboratory studies' is a number of early on-site observation studies of knowledge processes in natural scientific laboratories (Knorr Cetina, 1977, 1981; Latour and Woolgar, 1979; Lynch, 1985; Traweek, 1988). For the first time in the history of science studies, these authors made a full-scale attempt to study the process of knowledge production in its natural setting, the laboratory.

Perhaps coincidentally, the first studies were all done in California, a context that proved conducive to the intrusions into the 'cathedrals of knowledge' these authors attempted. The most radical outcome of the two earliest studies was an assessment which has itself developed into a dominating approach in recent science studies: the assessment that science was constructive rather than merely descriptive of the 'nature' it addressed. There are weaker and stronger readings of 'constructionism' in science studies. One of the strongest is that the world as described by science ought to be seen as a consequence rather than a cause of scientific representations.

This claim becomes less radical if one understands it as the outgrowth of an ontological pragmatism characteristic of science and technology studies. Accordingly, one needs to distinguish between the pre-existence of a material world that is granted by every constructionist, and the concrete phenomena of experience that science comes up with and that have specific characteristics. These are thought to begin to exist as entities that can be reliably picked out and encountered only *after* science has articulated and defined them. This is perhaps most evident when the phenomena at stake are remote and invisible – examples are the top quark or the Higgs mechanism, TRF (a hormone releasing factor) and cell mechanisms and viruses. All these were not part of our life before they were named, described and otherwise designated by science. What exists reliably beyond such phenomena are everyday entities, which are always culturally defined and shaped; the classifications and characteristics associated with these entities vary between cultures, and they frequently conflict with the classifications and qualities produced by science. We have no access to any reality independent of such universes of meaning and practice. Hence not only must we see reality (as concretely defined in terms of encounterable entities with specific characteristics) as an outgrowth of everyday cultural or scientific practice, but we can also observe the construction of these objects in terms of changing cultural definitions and articulations, or, in the case of science, in terms of the activities and accomplishments observable in scientific labs. Note

that this interpretation does not imply the sort of judgmental relativism that has been politically suspect to many because it leaves us with no tools to evaluate certain accounts as better than others. The advantage of 'good' scientific accounts, in terms of this notion, is pragmatic and rests with their difference from everyday accounts – good scientific accounts are backed by research programs and instrumental practices that contrast with everyday instrumental practices and backings. Instead of working with realist assumptions about the relationship between representations and nature, which it considers intractable, this sort of epistemic constructionism is based on a logic of differences between universes of knowing which it believes are the only tractable elements available to us. It should also be noted that truth itself is a historical notion, as is 'evidence', 'objectivity', 'experiment' and all other terms used in epistemology. Historical studies conducted in the spirit of the sociology of knowledge have demonstrated the cultural and temporal embeddedness and frequent transformations of these notions, thus making us acutely aware of the fragility and path dependence of their current status and epistemic authority (see, for example, Daston, 1991; Shapin, 1994; Shapin and Schaffer, 1985).

Laboratory studies have been the breeding ground for the notion that science is constructive, and they have sustained the ontological pragmatism just spelled out – among other things by pointing out the artificiality of laboratories and the preconstructed and artificial character of the 'nature' within them. In addition, the laboratory itself has come to be seen as a theoretical notion rather than simply a place where science gets done: the lab, in this view, is a knowledge tool that rests on the reconfiguration of the knower and the known and their relationship. For example, in laboratories scientists no longer confront nature-in-the-raw (like weather conditions, seasonal and temporal constraints on plant growth, the problems of observation in field-astronomy), but a nature miniaturized and remodeled in other ways such that it can be processed in a rationalized and accelerated manner. In the laboratory, nature is subject to 'social overhauls' that prepare it for inquiry. According to this perspective, it is the conventions embodied in laboratories and in the sequential succession of laboratory set-ups – rather than methodological principles of experimentation – that account for some of the successes of science. Laboratory studies have also shown the ambiguities, the 'slack' and the missing elements in research outcomes. Research outcomes are rarely clear, definitive and complete; laboratory studies have traced the negotiations and techniques of persuasion adopted to eliminate slack. Here construction takes on the concrete sense of social negotiation; it points to the interpretative leaps and the creation of 'surplus' meanings that compensate for gaps and ambiguities in scientific data. The constructionist approach is clearly less controversial in the case of technology, to which it has also been applied (see, for example, Pinch and Bijker, 1984; Bijker et al., 1989). Since technologies are artifacts, claiming that they are constructed causes no outrage, though the adoption of a constructionist methodology and a sociology of knowledge perspective by some authors (see, for example, Bijker, 1995; Law, 2002; MacKenzie, 1990) has helped to move technology studies away from a mere history of inventions and to bring into focus the cultural, political, social and other factors and the multiple associations through which technologies are built from within.

The categories introduced by the constructionist research program have been critically examined under the heading of reflexivity (see, for example, Woolgar, 1988; Ashmore, 1989). Taking seriously the reflexivity which Bloor's strong program demanded, and indeed extending its range, Woolgar and Ashmore argued that constructionism is incoherent if it does not interrogate its own constructions of representations of science and technology. In other words, constructionism should not be understood as a program that attempts to improve representations of science, since its own categories and distinctions are equally constructed. Constructionists' texts must be open to reflexive criticism of their own cultural practices and should express this awareness and evince attention to the constructedness of their own texts in their writings.

Studies of experiments

In a post-Kuhnian move away from the hegemony of theory in science, not only sociologists but also social historians of science have given scientific practice more weight in the study of science and technology. In addition to the laboratory, experiments have become a focus of study. This work has produced a number of interesting results, some of which fundamentally challenge traditional beliefs about experiments while others highlight the role experiments play in particular natural sciences. Natural scientific experiments are commonly seen as the most important venue for settling knowledge claims and lending credibility to scientific results. But, as Collins's and Pinch's work has shown (see, for example, Collins, 1985), this assumption is problematic. As described by Collins and Pinch (1998: 11, 25, 98), whether or not scientific results can be replicated and what counts as a valid replication depends on agreements about what the important variables in an experiment are. Such agreements are normally taken for granted but are made explicit during controversies. As a controversy develops, more variables that potentially affect an experiment come to the fore. From the critics' point of view, these can be used as excuses by the proponents of a particular experimental outcome when results cannot be replicated. For the proponents, they are reasons for why the unpracticed may have difficulty with the replication. Whether the experiment is flawed and the sought-after signal is really there or whether the signal is not there and the experiment is valid can only be decided if one knows the correct outcome, which in original research one does not, since finding out the correct outcome is the very point at issue. What the authors call 'the experimenter's regress' is the circle implied by a situation where one has to build a good experimental apparatus to detect a signal, but cannot decide whether one has built a good apparatus until one has tried it and obtained the correct result, which one cannot determine until one has built the apparatus – and so on. Reaching experimental closure, then, in the natural sciences, is not a mere matter of setting up decisive experiments and of experimental replication. Some scientific results become discredited not because there is any published disproof that rests on decisive evidence, but because the field tires of them, a principal investigator dies or loses credit, or because more interesting problems come along. For the sociology of science, this means a large opening for studies that unearth the real venues of consensus formation and result stabilization in science and technology.

A second project centers around experimental systems, a term Rheinberger (1997: 27–30) proposed for a series of experiments connected to one another, and forming the 'smallest integral working units of research'. Rheinberger defines experimental systems as vehicles for materializing experimental questions that center around particular research objects; the notion is also used by scientists themselves to characterize the scope of their activities. Its usefulness lies in its pointing away from the notion of single experiments as the ultimate arbiter of truth. Single experiments can prove little and carry little conviction in scientific controversies. Yet as Rheinberger argues, even the argument about the experimenter's regress embraces, in its very rejection of their decisiveness, the focus on single experiments. Rheinberger uses the notion of an experimental system to examine the history of molecular biology, which he finds to be neither the outgrowth of a unifying theory focused on the notion of information, nor that of the work of a few research groups led by prominent scientists, but of a number of scattered, differently embedded and only loosely connected heterogeneous experimental systems that sought to characterize living beings down to the level of biologically relevant macromolecules. Without explicitly using the term, Galison also examined an experimental system: a series of instrumental technologies defining a sequence of high energy physics experiments which, in this field, take many years and involve large international collaborations of scientists. Galison's work (1997) situates itself more broadly with respect to philosophical understandings of science and with respect to cultural debates over modernity. Like others, he attempts to set the theoretically inclined philosophy of science right by demanding equal rights for theory, experiment and the material technologies of instrumentation. As a result of his studies of high energy physics' experimental technologies in the last decades, he proposes a model of intercalation that splits apart these components of scientific paradigms, arguing that they may develop and change at their own pace relatively independently of other components. Thus the Kuhnian model, according to which science changes via the wholesale replacement of scientific paradigms during scientific revolutions, is not substantiated. Different components of experimental work follow their own logic and dynamics. In high energy physics, they are in the care of specialized and often fragmented epistemic communities (Brown and Duguid, 1991; Saxenian, 1996) that pursue these developments within their own distinctive frames of reference and meaning.

Actor-network theory

The laboratory study perspective has been combined with a network approach to yield what has come to be called 'actor-network theory', an influential approach for analyzing the power struggles embedded in and, according to this view, defining science and technology (Callon, 1986; Callon and Latour, 1981; Latour, 1987, 1988, 1993; Law, 2002; Law and Hassard, 1999). Scientists, engineers and others build heterogeneous networks consisting of non-human objects (like microbes, scallops, or machines), colleagues, financial resources, publications, organizations/corporations and other elements to make their findings successful and unassailable. The emphasis here is on heterogeneity; the defining characteristic of this particular network theory is that it is not limited to human agents, but explicitly recognizes non-human entities as nodes in the network and as actors in any technoscientific game: in fact, non-human agency is a key term in this theory. A second key element is that the network is seen as a stabilizing arrangement. For example, technologies become more widely implemented and more successful as the networks expand; actor-network theory is the approach that has devoted most attention to technology, perhaps because both original proponents, Latour and Callon, work at a technological university (the Ecole des Mines in Paris). But the argument has been extended to science, where it claims, more importantly and more controversially than in the case of technology, that scientific knowledge claims also become more factual as the networks grow. Latour and Callon propose what might be called a network theory of truth, a view according to which the outcome of scientific and technical conflicts is largely determined by an ability to get others to 'align themselves' with a knowledge claim. Fuller alignment is equivalent to more 'stabilized' (more held to be true) knowledge claims that are difficult to call into question; deconstructing them requires significant resources that match those of the existing network. There is no provision in the theory for a master-mind or master-actor orchestrating the alignment (but see Latour's study of Louis Pasteur, 1988). Instead, the non-human actors in a network are as important as the human ones, 'co-constructing' outcomes and their stabilization as well as network expansion. Despite the label 'actor-network theory', which suggests an emphasis on individual agency, the approach tends toward seeing agency as distributed in a network.

If one wanted to read this approach as a causal theory there would be several problems. On the one hand, there is no indication of the conditions under which network construction and expansion are successful. Actor-network theorists appear to consider success a contingent outcome that can only be empirically determined on a case-by-case basis. Second, anything can build a network link; for example one's holding a cup of tea establishes a link between a human actor and an object. Here the approach tends toward tautology and ignores the question of network boundaries: if anything is a link, nearly everything is already interrelated by virtue of anything going on in the world at all, and the theory can neither grasp new links nor explain success in establishing them. Furthermore, equating network expansion with stabilization and success must appear problematic; as we know from political theory, military expansions, colonialism and the like, networks can also become too large to be manageable and effective. Finally, the approach defines science as politics and bases truth on power, that is, on the alliances forged in heterogeneous networks. Yet at the same time, the edge is taken off this audacious hypothesis when objects are brought back into the picture as agents that resist alignment and that co-define network outcomes and scientific representations. In other words, since non-human actors ('nature') determine at least part of the events, realist assumptions creep back in, and, given the lack of a social theory of network construction and expansion, carry some weight in explaining fact-stabilization. Perhaps against the will of the authors, the approach appears to work best when human actors are foregrounded, when the analysts describe how powerful scientists such as Pasteur or Diesel built and shifted allegiances, recruited resources, rhetorically persuaded other parties of their success, and got things to work ('forged alliances') in the laboratory.

The cultural turn in science and technology studies

The turn to the laboratory as the place of science had brought into view a whole universe of cultural activities implicated in research. The shift to analyzing science and technology as process rather than product proved tantamount to seeing science as culture defined in terms of particular sets of practices (Pickering, 1992). Kuhn's views about the role of paradigms as holistic sets of methodological preferences, theoretical beliefs and sample cases that ground normal science had already suggested what Collins (1985) later called an enculturation model – the socialization of scientists into shared and implicit background knowledge that provides the basis for routine work. Since its beginning, the new sociology of science and technology has made references to the cultural make-up of what it was about. None the less, what took precedence in the early period was registering the social processes of formation from which science had been exempted for so long. Perhaps this explains why more focused works on the 'cultural' aspects of science and technology only came later. They look, for example, at the influence the cultural environment exerts on disciplinary, 'culture-free' science and on transnational science. And they have begun to analyze differences in epistemic practices between sciences, leading to the term 'epistemic cultures'.

Consider first the question of whether scientific disciplines ought to be understood as transnational, culture-free traditions or whether these traditions are reworked and transformed as they are implemented in different cultures (Hess, 1995: 39–53, 49). According to Hess, only a small number of studies have addressed this issue, but these studies provide evidence of such transformations in the social and natural sciences. One of the first studies of this kind was Sherry Turkle's comparison of psychoanalysis in France and in the United States (1992). Turkle described how Freudian psychoanalysis became reoriented in the US 'to a message of hope in a culture of pragmatic self-improvement' and accepted by large populations, whereas in France existing research traditions in dynamic psychology led to a rejection of psychoanalysis as a general cure outside small circles of intellectuals, artists and writers. This picture holds until after 1968, when psychoanalysis gained the prominence in French culture that it had long occupied in American culture, although it was also rewritten by authors such as Lacan. While Turkle's study can be interpreted as referring mainly to questions of national reception and to the human sciences, Sharon Traweek's continuing comparisons of American and Japanese professional and organizational cultures in high energy physics have a broader focus (1988). Traweek showed how the funding systems and, as a consequence, detector designs varied across these settings. In the US, the detector design allowed for continuous detector rebuilding and surprise data, while the Japanese design emphasized reliability and precision at the expense of new data (see also Hess, 1995: 50). Similarly, Haraway's study of primatology in Japan, India and the United States (1989) shows how different national beliefs play themselves out in different formulations of primatological methods.

As Hess sums up, the Japanese 'tend to view nature as something to be cultivated by hand', and hence tended to feed primates, whereas Western beliefs in a sharp division between nature and culture led to a rejection of provisioning of animals that are located in natural surroundings seen as wild. Then again, the cultural meaning of monkeys in India as belonging to a sacred supernature and as interacting with humans may have prompted Indian primatologists to investigate the interaction of monkeys and humans, whereas Western scientists focused on studying primates in their original (natural, wild) state (Hess, 1995: 50–1). A particular genre of studies best exemplified by Joan Fujimura's work on transnational genomics (see, for example, 2000) focuses on both transnational science and cultural variations in the implementation of a particular project (see also Fujimura, 1996).

Most accounts of science and technology implicitly or explicitly assume the 'unity of science', a notion associated with positivism and the Vienna Circle of philosophy of more than fifty years ago. Science connoted an attitude of tolerant skepticism and a particular method that promised the accumulation of findings and technical capability in the service of humanity (Rouse, 1996: 51). Postpositivist philosophy (see, for example, Feyerabend, 1975; Hacking, 1983; Kuhn, 1970 [1962]) turned against positivism's formalism and challenged the notions of linear progress and the assumption of a specific rationality of science. But it continued to talk about *science* as if it was somehow unified and all part of one bloc; questions of the epistemic heterogeneity of the natural sciences were simply not addressed, nor were they, until recently, raised by the new sociology of science and technology. For example, the debates raging over realist, skepticist, feminist and other interpretations of science all tend to assume that science is a unitary enterprise to which these interpretations can be applied across the board. This picture has now changed (see, for example, Galison and Stump, 1996), and the second cultural approach to be mentioned can be associated with the change. It brings into view cultural differences within science in regard to the understanding of measurement, the meaning of 'empirical', the configuration of the objects investigated and of what counts as real, the emphasis placed on errors and failures of knowledge, the role and construction of laboratories, and the organizational practices implemented. This work sees different machineries of knowing at work in different scientific fields – composed of different empirical systems, different logics of instrumentation and different systems of epistemic authority and organization. The machineries add up to different 'epistemic cultures'. The first full-scale study of two epistemic cultures compares high energy physics and molecular biology (Knorr Cetina, 1999). Among other things, the study illustrates how high energy physics cultivates a kind of negative knowledge, which is not non-knowledge, but knowledge of the limits of knowing, of the mistakes we make in trying to know, of the things that interfere with our knowing, of what we are not interested in but still have to confront in empirical research. In a sense, high energy physics has forged a coalition with the evil that bars knowledge, by turning these barriers into a principle of knowing. The liminal things high energy physics focuses on are neither the objects of positive knowledge nor effects in the formless region of the unknowable, but something in between: examples are 'limits', systematic errors, efficiencies, acceptances and so on, whose investigation and presentation consume a large part of experimental time. Other aspects of high energy physics experiments include their reflexive turn toward self-understanding, toward replacing the 'care of objects' with the 'care of the self' (Knorr Cetina, 1999: 55ff., 63 ff.). High energy physics experiments may seem remote from particular social interests, but they are not. Apart from the knowledge strategies they exemplify, they illustrate what it might mean to organize global cooperations in a knowledge society outside the realm of large corporations, and to make them work. At the beginning of the twenty-first century, high energy physics experiments are conducted by large global collaborations of up to 2000 physicists and up to 200 physics institutes that work together for approximately 20–30 years, or the better part of the lifetime of a scientist. These collaborations

now involve the largest, longest-lasting and presumably best-integrated epistemic groups. As these groups struggle through the stages of the birth and lifetime of a new experiment, they create and illustrate for us many organizational innovations that are relevant to other areas within (the genome project, for example) and outside science. Another field which may seem equally remote but which has been studied is mathematics, the distinct practices of which differ not only from physics but seem unique among all sciences (Heintz, 2000; Merz, 1999).

Finally, a number of authors have turned to studying scientific texts or to studying scientific theories and research results as narratives and discourse structures (see, for example, Bazerman, 1999). This enables them to follow the metaphors and images that scientists use in their theories and descriptions, and import, or translate from, other cultural orders (Martin (1991) and Haraway (1989) can be interpreted in this way). The cultural turn is exemplified here in the choice of data and approach (scientific texts are analyzed as narratives) as well as in the attempt to trace the flow of cultural symbols (metaphors) through different social domains (science on the one hand and other socio-cultural domains on the other).

Standpoint theory approaches and feminist science studies

The field has not only experienced a cultural turn, but attracted strong feminist scholars who have developed their own viewpoints. One of the first perspectives that developed was a feminist standpoint theory that was continuous with the field's earliest formulations of a sociology of knowledge and was also loosely based on Lukács' theories of class consciousness and reification (1971). What the feminist version of a standpoint theory added, then and now, to the earlier formulations, is a critical edge derived from exploring Western science as a realm of endeavor dominated by white males from privileged backgrounds. Standpoint theory made plausible that science is marked by and perhaps locked into the perspectives of the categories of people who produce it – white males, who are also the oppressors in the sex/ gender structure of Western societies. Feminists argued for the privileged perspective of women in recognizing gender bias. Women, the oppressed, feel the constraints of the structures which dominate them, and hence are more likely to identify these constraining forces; while those who are not oppressed (white males) do not notice such constraints and are blind to their own perspectival biases (Hartsock, 1983; Sismondo, 1996). Later feminist authors have upheld perspectivalism, but have backed away from interpretations of standpoint theory that suggest that there can be a single true story about reality. In her book *The Science Question in Feminism* (1986) Harding acknowledges that there are many forms of oppression, and hence there must be many privileged perspectives.

Haraway (1988) goes a step further in attempting to find some ground for political action while acknowledging the radical contingency of all knowledge claims. She also rejects the possibility of an all-encompassing, objective standpoint, but advocates 'partial perspectives' as a positive tool in producing knowledge: the resulting 'knowledges' are limited and historically contingent, but they are 'about' something. In other words, Haraway advocates a sort of perspectival realism as a remedy for relativism and objectivism, a realism which allows for not just one but many true stories. In a recent book, Harding (1998) also takes a step beyond her earlier works by attempting to work out an anti-essentialist reading of standpoint epistemology. She launches further complaints about the claims to absolute cognitive superiority made by modern technoscience, and discusses the possibility of multicultural knowledges that do not devalue non-Western types of 'science'. Going even further in the direction of approaches that are not in themselves feminist, Longino (2002) points the way for a compromise between constructionist ideas, more traditional philosophical concepts and feminist thinking on science.

It should be noted that feminists have produced a wide range of results revealing gender bias in the content of scientific conceptions and theories, going far beyond the questions of the representation of women in particular positions, access to resources and so on (Fox Keller, 1985; Haraway, 1989; Martin, 1991). For example, Martin has shown how masculine vocabularies and conceptions of heroic conquest are inscribed into biologists' descriptions of sperm and egg activity, and how new views reiterate such trends while ostentatiously undermining an earlier conceptual sexism. While earlier biological conceptions construed the egg as passive and powerless, the newer active egg models transform the passive egg into its opposite, a dangerous female that 'captures and tethers' the helpless male sperm – drawing upon cultural models of the female as a witch or a whore (Hess, 1995: 30; Martin, 1991). A different but important line of research focuses on reproductive technologies and on the development of reproductive science (Clarke, 1998). This work shows, for example, how amniocentesis opens up different choices, opportunities and dilemmas for different groups, while the construction of the technology also shifts dramatically between groups (Rapp, 1990).

PERSPECTIVES

The new sociology of science and technology is a young field: it started off with a bang in the 1970s when it was reworked and revamped as a sociology of scientific knowledge. At that point, the field had a point of intense focus: the question of the social conditioning of knowledge in the natural sciences and mathematics. Since then, the field has expanded in the various directions just discussed, and more. It is now diverse, but it still retains a particular orientation that distinguishes it from other specialties that address knowledge, notably knowledge management, the sociology of information and transformation theories that point toward a knowledge society. The sociology of science and technology retains its orientation towards studying knowledge not just externally, but internally; not just from the outside with respect to its social structural, occupational and other implications, but from the inside, by including in the studies conducted a level of content of knowledge, of knowledge practices and epistemic relations. The vigorous growth and vitality of science and technology studies in the last decades may have something to do with this insistence on getting inside the domains of expertise examined. Accordingly, when students of science and technology and others who took over a 'science studies approach' (identified with the research programs listed) have addressed larger social questions, they have done so in distinctive ways. They have applied science studies concepts and findings to legal battles, pursuing issues of the constructed, networked and translated nature of evidence and techniques in this context; they have also extended the approach to financial markets and economics, to politics, to management and to general questions of classification. They have transferred concepts like that of the laboratory to non-laboratory settings, and they have given their own assessments of what postmodernity might mean. Here are some examples.

One of the strongest consequences of recent studies of science and technology is that it has raised the awareness for the role of non-human objects (animals, other natural objects and technologies) in society, students of science and technology attributing a more active role to such objects than sociologists in general. For example, the actor-network approach treats them as 'actors' according to a semiotic and grammatical (rather than Weberian or phenomenological) definition of action. Presumably, any object can fill the subject's role in a linguistic sentence structure. Analogously, non-human actors (technologies, viruses, scallops etc.) can have agency (for example, have power, provoke effects, create resistance) in scientific and technological settings (for examples of such treatments of non-human actors see Callon, 1986; Latour, 1993; Latour and Johnson, 1988; Pickering, 1995). The discussion resonates strongly with certain traditions of sociological and philosophical research, for example with claims in ecology for the need to reintroduce nature into the social contract (Beck, 1992; Merchant, 1983; Serres, 1990). It also overlaps with a line of work that has grown out of science and technology studies and problem-solving and

has come to be known as 'work place studies', that is, investigations of the usage of (electronic information) technology by workers at their place of work (Suchman, 1987). A further point of contact is given in studies of 'virtual society', electronically connected communities and their relationship to technologies (Pels et al., 2002). But as a rule, sociologists have defined the social world as the domain of human interaction, human institutions, human rationality, human life. As Luckmann pointed out in 1970, we take it for granted that social reality is the world of human affairs, exclusively. Yet why should we take this for granted? As Luckmann also argued, the boundary we assume between the human, social and the non-human, non-social is not an essential structure of the life-world. Latour (1993) has even proposed that what we are taking to be modernity is characterized by a systematic refusal to recognize and incorporate in our thinking the hybrid forms of organization that are neither purely subject nor object. It is the hidden working of these hybrid forms behind our back that makes it possible for us to continue to conceive of ourselves as pure subjects and of society as purely human. Knorr Cetina (1997) has maintained that if the social is not limited to the human, we can begin to develop an analysis of the ways in which major classes of individuals (for example, scientists) have tied themselves to object worlds which situate and stabilize selves, define individual identity just as much as communities and families used to do, and which promote forms of sociality (forms of binding self and other) that supplement the human forms of sociality studied by social scientists. Objects may also be the risk winners of the relationship risks which many authors find inherent in contemporary human relations. The strongest claim is that what lies ahead is a 'postsocial' environment where objects displace human beings as relationship partners and embedding contexts, or increasingly mediate human relationships, making the latter dependent on the former. The 'question of objects' poses a challenge to sociology comparable to that which globalization does. To develop an understanding of global society we need new concepts that point away from conceptions of nation-state societies with which sociological thinking has been bound up in the past. To learn to understand the role of objects in contemporary society we need new theoretical frameworks and conceptual tools, and we must let go of the exclusively human concept of social reality that Luckmann attacked.

There are other, less controversial extensions of science and technology studies to the larger social context. For example, laboratory studies have developed into a laboratory studies perspective that takes its lead from family resemblances between laboratories and other physical and virtual spaces. In this case the notion of a laboratory, and the concepts emerging from laboratory studies, are transferred to areas that are not literally laboratories but can be seen as spaces of knowledge. As a perspective, the laboratory studies approach simply brings *into view* matters with which students of laboratories have concerned themselves in other areas. For example, processes of reality construction are ongoing occurrences in a variety of settings. This is the sense in which the industrial factory itself begins to resemble a laboratory as a site for invention and intervention in which new realities are created (Miller and O'Leary, 1994). We can illustrate this use of the laboratory approach by an example from transsexual research and one pertaining to the factory. In the first case the new sex of a person who desires to have a different sex from the one he or she is born with is seen as a 'fact' that is being constructed in a laboratory that is constituted by the different locations and stages of the treatment that transsexuals undergo (Hirschauer, 1991). The laboratory approach sheds light on the multiple arenas that make up the lab, on the constructive and transformative work involved, and on the heterogeneity of the frameworks of knowledge applied to transsexuality. In the second case, that of the factory, Japan is brought to Illinois, as it were, in the attempt to reconfigure the American factory in the image of global factory modernization, by redesigning shop floors, recalculating new spatial orderings of production, and molding the worker according to the ideal of a 'new economic citizenship' for plant personnel.

Here the factory itself becomes a laboratory for acting upon its own assemblage of locales and internal relations and for refashioning the person who participates in the assemblage (Miller and O'Leary, 1994).

A third research focus where the science and technology studies approach is extended to the wider society concerns the relationship between science and law. Lynch has studied the Iran Contra Hearings and Lynch, Jasanoff and others have examined the OJ Simpson trial in relation to DNA fingerprinting and the failure of science to convince the jury in the trial (see the works collected in Lynch and Jasanoff, 1998). For example, Lynch (1998: 853, 855) reviewed arguments about DNA profiling between the prosecution and the 'dream team' of defense lawyers in the OJ Simpson trial, arguing that the defense lawyers' motions were based on rebuttals to the prosecution's 'realist' claims about the inherent workings of natural and technological processes that paralleled those of constructionists' rebuttals to realist claims about science in general. The motions provided an impressive inventory of uncertainties and contingencies, relating them to political, financial, ideological and career interests of those who collected and analyzed the evidence. The rebuttals rested on exposing sources of uncertainty and contingencies that remained unexamined by official inquiries and hidden from the defense. Jasanoff's work supplements these findings by conceptualizing trials as arenas in which visual authority has to be created and defended. Jasanoff (1998: 713) argues that it is part of the judge's role to construct whose vision will be authorized in trials as expert, and in what circumstances lay vision can take precedence over expert sight.

As these examples show, the sociology of science and technology of today brings its approach to a variety of societal questions where science, technology and technical expertise, or what is sometimes perceived to lie at the center of these domains, the non-human and objectual, are key elements. It also at times brings its approach to bear on questions that do not focus on these elements, but are of fundamental theoretical concern, for example the question of organization (Vaughan, 1996), or that of classification and its consequences (see, for example, Bowker and Star, 1999). Over the past few decades, the field has transformed itself slowly from the pure sociology of science Merton had in mind to the discipline of science and technology studies, which seems at times on the verge of transforming itself further into what is purely an approach (or perhaps a confederation of approaches) applicable to many of the dazzling facets of contemporary life. Since science, technology and knowledge are always 'just around the corner' in contemporary societies, and questions pertaining to research, analysis and information appear to be implicated in most social institutions in the environment in which we live, the field is not likely to lose its footing in the process.

NOTES

1 Scientists have occasionally reacted to these endeavors as if they were invasions of their epistemic territory and authority. But science is not different from (say) government, large corporations or other bodies when it comes to the need for it to remain open to empirical, method-based examination (Gieryn, 1999: 25–35). While scientists themselves have often sought to tell their story and give their trade a definitive shape (Gieryn, 1999: 26), these accounts cannot replace systematic inquiries into particular scientific and technological practices and contexts.

2 Scientific knowledge claims may have legitimate claims to superior evidential substantiation over non-scientific theories within particular historical contexts, but they will none the less have been established relative to historical standards and beliefs.

3 The term constructionism rather than constructivism is used here to differentiate the epistemic constructionism of science and technology studies from social constructivism in sociology (Berger and Luckmann, 1966). For differences between the two approaches and internal differences between the different varieties of epistemic constructionism see Sismondo (1996).

REFERENCES

Ashmore, Malcolm (1989) *The Reflexive Thesis*. Chicago: University of Chicago Press.

Barnes, Barry (1977) *Interests and the Growth of Knowledge*. London: Routledge and Kegan Paul.

Bazerman, Charles (1999) *The Language of Edison's Light*. Cambridge, MA: MIT Press.

Beck, Ulrich (1992) *Risk Society. Towards a New Modernity*. London: Sage.

Bell, Daniel (1973) *The Coming of Post-Industrial Society: A Venture in Social Forecasting*. New York: Basic Books.

Beniger, James R. (1986) *The Control Revolution*. Cambridge, MA: Harvard University Press.

Berger, Peter L., Berger, Brigitte and Kellner, Hansfried (1974) *The Homeless Mind: Modernization and Consciousness*. New York: Vintage Books.

Berger, Peter L. and Luckmann, Thomas (1966) *The Social Construction of Reality: A Treatise in the Sociology of Knowledge*. Garden City, NY: Doubleday.

Bernal, John D. (1939) *The Social Function of Science*. New York: Macmillan.

Bijker, Wiebe E. (1995) *Of Bicycles, Bakelites and Bulbs. Toward a Theory of Sociotechnical Change*. Cambridge, MA: MIT Press.

Bijker, Wiebe E., Hughes, Thomas P. and Pinch, Trevor J. (eds) (1989) *The Social Construction of Technological Systems: New Directions in the Sociology and History of Technology*. Cambridge, MA: MIT Press.

Bloor, David (1976) *Knowledge and Social Imagery*. London: Routledge and Kegan Paul.

Bowker, Geoffrey C. and Star, Susan Leigh (1999) *Sorting Things Out: Classification and Its Consequences*. Cambridge, MA: MIT Press.

Brown, John S. and Duguid, Paul (1991) 'Organizational learning and communities-of-practice: toward a unified view of working, learning and innovation', *Organization Science*, 2 (1): 40–57.

Callon, Michel (1986) 'Some elements of a sociology of translation: domestication of the scallops and the fishermen of St Brieuc Bay', in John Law (ed.), *Power, Action and Belief: A New Sociology of Knowledge?* London: Routledge and Kegan Paul. pp. 196–233.

Callon, Michel and Latour, Bruno (1981) 'Unscrewing the big Leviathan: how actors macro-structure reality and how sociologists help them to do so', in Karin Knorr Cetina and Aaron V. Cicourel (eds), *Advances in Social Theory and Methodology*. London: Routledge and Kegan Paul. pp. 277–303.

Castells, Manuel (1996) *The Rise of the Network Society*. New York: Harper and Row.

Castells, Manuel (2001) *The Internet Galaxy: Reflections on the Internet, Business, and Society*. Oxford: Oxford University Press.

Clarke, Adele (1998) *Disciplining Reproduction: Modernity, American Life Sciences, and the 'Problems of Sex'*. Berkeley, CA: University of California Press.

Collins, Harry M. (1975) 'The seven sexes: a study in the sociology of a phenomenon, or the replication of experiments in physics', *Sociology*, 9: 205–24.

Collins, Harry M. (1985) *Changing Order: Replication and Induction in Scientific Practice.* London: Sage.

Collins, Harry, M. and Pinch, Trevor (1998) *The Golem. What You Should Know about Science*, 2nd edn. Cambridge: Cambridge University Press.

Daston, Lorraine (1991) 'Marvelous facts and miraculous evidence in early modern Europe', in James Chandler, Arnold I. Davidson and Harry Harootunian (eds), *Questions of Evidence. Proof, Practice, and Persuasion across Disciplines.* Chicago: University of Chicago Press. pp. 243–74.

Drucker, Peter F. (1993) *Post-Capitalist Society.* New York: HarperCollins.

Feyerabend, Paul K. (1975) *Against Method.* London: New Left Books.

Fox Keller, Evelyn (1985) *Reflexions on Gender and Science.* New Haven, CT: Yale University Press.

Fujimura, Joan H. (1996) *Crafting Science: A Sociohistory of the Quest for the Genetics of Cancer.* Cambridge, MA: Harvard University Press.

Fujimura, Joan H. (2000) 'Transnational genomics. Transgressing the boundary between the "modern/West" and the "premodern/East"', in Roddey Reid and Sharon Traweek (eds), *Doing Science + Culture.* New York/London: Routledge. pp. 71–92.

Galison, Peter L. (1997) *Image and Logic: A Material Culture of Microphysics.* Chicago: University of Chicago Press.

Galison, Peter L. and Stump, David J. (eds) (1996) *The Disunity of Science: Boundaries, Contexts, and Power.* Stanford, CA: Stanford University Press.

Giddens, Anthony (1990) *The Consequences of Modernity.* Stanford, CA: Stanford University Press.

Gieryn, Thomas F. (1999) *Cultural Boundaries of Science: Credibility on the Line.* Chicago: University of Chicago Press.

Habermas, Jürgen (1981) *Theorie des kommunikativen Handels.* Frankfurt/Main: Suhrkamp.

Hacking, Ian (1983) *Representing and Intervening.* Cambridge: Cambridge University Press.

Hage, Jerald and Powers, Charles H. (1992) *Post-Industrial Lives: Roles and Relationships in the 21st Century.* Newbury Park, CA: Sage.

Haraway, Donna J. (1988) 'Situated knowledge', *Feminist Studies*, 14: 575–609.

Haraway, Donna J. (1989) *Primate Visions: Gender, Race and Nature in the World of Modern Science.* New York/London: Routledge.

Harding, Sandra (1986) *The Science Question in Feminism.* Ithaca, NY: Cornell University Press.

Harding, Sandra (1998) *Is Science Multicultural?* Bloomington, IN: Indiana University Press.

Hartsock, Nancy C.M. (1983) 'The feminist standpoint: developing the ground for a specifically feminist historical materialism', in Sandra Harding

and Merrill B. Hintikka (eds), *Discovering Reality: Feminist Perspectives on Epistemology, Metaphysics, Methodology and Philosophy of Science.* Dordrecht: Reidel. pp. 283–310.

Heintz, Bettina (2000) *Die Innenwelt der Mathematik: zur Kultur und Praxis einer beweisenden Disziplin.* Vienna/New York: Springer.

Hess, David (1995) *Science and Technology in a Multicultural World. The Cultural Politics of Facts and Artifacts.* New York: Columbia University Press.

Hessen, B. (1931) 'The social and economic roots of Newton's "Principia"', in Nikolai I. Bukharin et al., *Science at the Cross Roads.* London: Kniga. pp. 147–212.

Hirschauer, Stefan (1991) 'The manufacture of bodies in surgery', *Social Studies of Science*, 2 (2): 279–319.

Jasanoff, Sheila (1998) 'The eye of everyman: witnessing DNA in the Simpson trial', in Michael Lynch and Sheila Jasanoff (eds), *Special Issue on Contested Identities: Science, Law and Forensic Practice. Social Studies of Science*, 28 (5–6): 713–40.

Knorr Cetina, Karin (1977) 'Producing and reproducing knowledge: descriptive or constructive? Toward a model of research production', *Social Science Information*, 16: 669–96.

Knorr Cetina, Karin (1981) *The Manufacture of Knowledge: An Essay on the Constructivist and Contextual Nature of Science.* Oxford: Pergamon Press.

Knorr Cetina, Karin (1997) 'Sociality with objects. social relations in postsocial knowledge societies', *Theory, Culture and Society*, 14 (4): 1–30.

Knorr Cetina, Karin (1999) *Epistemic Cultures. How the Sciences Make Knowledge.* Cambridge, MA: Harvard University Press.

Kuhn, Thomas S. (1970 [1962]) *The Structure of Scientific Revolutions*, 2nd edn. Chicago: University of Chicago Press.

Latour, Bruno (1987) *Science in Action.* Milton Keynes: Open University Press.

Latour, Bruno (1988) *The Pasteurization of France.* Cambridge, MA: Harvard University Press.

Latour, Bruno (1993) *We Have Never Been Modern.* Cambridge, MA: Harvard University Press.

Latour, Bruno and Johnson, Jim (1988) 'Mixing humans with non-humans: sociology of a door-opener', in Susan Leigh Star (ed.), *Special Issue on Sociology of Science. Social Problems*, 35: 298–310.

Latour, Bruno and Woolgar, Steve (1979) *Laboratory Life: The Social Construction of Scientific Facts.* Beverly Hills, CA: Sage.

Law, John (2002) *Aircraft Stories: Decentering the Object in Technoscience.* Durham, NC: Duke University Press.

Law, John and Hassard, John (1999) *Actor Network Theory and After.* Oxford: Blackwell.

Longino, Helen E. (2002) *The Fate of Knowledge.* Princeton, NJ: Princeton University Press.

Luckmann, Thomas (1970) 'On the boundaries of the social world', in Maurice Natanson (ed.), *Phenomenology and Social Reality. Essays in Memory of Alfred Schutz.* The Hague: Nijhoff. pp. 73–100.

Lukács, Georg L. (1971) *History and Class Consciousness: Studies in Marxist Dialectics* (trans. Rodney Livingston). London: Merlin Press.

Lynch, Michael (1985) *Art and Artifact in Laboratory Science: A Study of Shop Work and Shop Talk in a Research Laboratory.* London: Routledge and Kegan Paul.

Lynch, Michael (1998) 'The discursive production of uncertainty: the OJ Simpson "dream team" and the sociology of knowledge machine', in Michael Lynch and Sheila Jasanoff (eds), *Special Issue on Contested Identities: Science, Law and Forensic Practice. Social Studies of Science*, 28 (5–6): 829–68.

Lynch, Michael and Jasanoff, Sheila (eds) (1998) *Special Issue on Contested Identities: Science, Law and Forensic Practice. Social Studies of Science*, 28 (5–6).

Lyotard, Jean-François (1984) *The Postmodern Condition.* Manchester: Manchester University Press.

MacKenzie, Donald (1981) *Statistics in Britain, 1865–1930.* Edinburgh: Edinburgh University Press.

MacKenzie, Donald (1990) *Inventing Accuracy: A Historical Sociology of Nuclear Missile Guidance.* Cambridge, MA: MIT Press.

Mannheim, Karl (1936) *Ideology and Utopia: An Introduction to the Sociology of Knowledge.* New York: Harcourt, Brace.

Martin, Emily (1991) 'The egg and the sperm: how science has constructed a romance based on stereotypical male–female roles', *Signs: Journal of Women in Culture and Society*, 16 (3): 485–501.

Merchant, Carolyn (1983) *The Death of Nature.* New York: Harper and Row.

Merton, Robert K. (1970 [1938]) *Science, Technology and Society in Seventeenth-Century-England*, 2nd edn. New York: Harper and Row.

Merz, Martina (1999) 'Multiplex and unfolding: computer simulation in particle physics', *Science in Context*, 12 (2): 293–316.

Miller, Peter and O'Leary, Ted (1994) 'The factory as laboratory', *Science in Context*, 7 (3): 469–96.

Pels, Dick, Hetherington, Kevin and Vandenberghe, Frédéric (eds) (2002) *Special Issue on Sociality and Materiality. Theory, Culture and Society*, 19 (5–6).

Pickering, Andrew (ed.) (1992) *Science as Practice and Culture.* Chicago: University of Chicago Press.

Pickering, Andrew (1995) *The Mangle of Practice.* Chicago: University of Chicago Press.

Pinch, Trevor J. and Bijker, Wiebe E. (1984) 'The social construction of facts and artefacts: or how the sociology of science and the sociology of technology might benefit each other', *Social Studies of Science*, 14: 339–441.

Rapp, Rayna (1990) 'Constructing amniocentesis: maternal and medical discourses', in Faye Ginsburg and Anna Lowenhaupt Tsing (eds), *Uncertain Terms: Negotiating Gender in American Culture.* Boston, MA: Beacon Press.

Rheinberger, Hans-Jörg (1997) *Toward a History of Epistemic Things: Synthesizing Proteins in the Test Tube.* Stanford, CA: Stanford University Press.

Rouse, Joseph (1996) *Engaging Science: How to Understand Its Practices Philosophically.* Ithaca, NY: Cornell University Press.

Saxenian, AnnaLee (1996) *Regional Advantage: Culture and Competition in Silicon Valley and Route 128.* Cambridge, MA: Harvard University Press.

Scheler, Max (1924) *Versuche zu einer Soziologie des Wissens.* Munich: Duncker and Humblot.

Serres, Michel (1990) *Le Contrat naturel.* Paris: Bourin.

Shapin, Steven (1994) *A Social History of Truth.* Chicago: University of Chicago Press.

Shapin, Steven and Schaffer, Simon (1985) *Leviathan and the Air-Pump: Hobbes, Boyle and the Experimental Life.* Princeton, NJ: Princeton University Press.

Sismondo, Sergio (1996) *Science without Myth: On Constructions, Reality and Social Knowledge.* Albany, NY: State University of New York Press.

Stehr, Nico (1994) *Arbeit, Eigentum und Wissen. Zur Theorie von Wissensgesellschaften.* Frankfurt/Main: Suhrkamp.

Suchman, Lucy (1987) *Plans and Situated Actions: The Problem of Human–Machine Communication.* Cambridge: Cambridge University Press.

Traweek, Sharon (1988) *Beamtimes and Lifetimes: The World of High Energy Physics.* Cambridge, MA: Harvard University Press.

Turkle, Sherry (1992) *Psychoanalytic Politics*, 2nd edn. New York: Guilford.

Vaughan, Diane (1996) *The Challenger Launch Decision: Risky Technology, Culture, and Deviance at NASA.* Chicago: University of Chicago Press.

Woolgar, Steve (ed.) (1988) *Knowledge and Reflexivity.* London: Sage.

Zenzen, Michael J. and Restivo, Sal (1982) 'The mysterious morphology of immiscible liquids: a study of scientific practice', *Social Science Information*, 21 (3): 447–73.

32

Citizenship, Ethnicity and Nation-States

SINIŠA MALEŠEVIĆ AND JOHN A. HALL

INTRODUCTION

For most of human history, class, gender and social status were the central pillars of exclusion, polarization and conflict. Today, however, it is the question of legitimate membership in a particular state that determines an individual's social standing. As every African or East European knows very well when approaching the European Union, passports determine social position. The speedy, control-free, blue line for European citizens (and unofficially for Americans, Canadians, Australians and members of other stable and 'respectable' polities) stands in stark contrast to the slow green line facing those who arrive from the rest of the world. At such moments a wealthy businessman from Morocco or Ukraine realizes how much worse is his social standing compared to that of a dole-dependent single teenage mother from Ireland or a New Age traveler from Belgium. The possession of a particular passport symbolizes the power of the modern state and its legal and material embodiment in citizenship. However, this profoundly contemporary legalistic underpinning of citizenship, important though it is, does not reveal the internal complexity of states. It frames nation-states as inherently stable and culture-free legislative entities. In order to understand the novelty of contemporary citizenship we will have to engage both historically and geographically with the question of internal cultural diversity.

A central presupposition of this chapter is that the relations between citizenship and ethnicity can only be understood once we realize – as is beginning to happen in contemporary sociology – that the nation-state is not some sort of static entity. We begin of course with abstract discussion of the three terms in the title. But attention then turns to three particular social realms in order to introduce historical and comparative evidence that will allow light to be cast on the theoretical issues raised. Something must be said about European history since its historical record did most to create the conceptual equipment at work in social science. Attention then turns to the United States, the most powerful nation-state in the history of the world, in large part to suggest that this social formation is not as far removed from European experience as its self-image might suggest. This discussion of the core of liberal capitalist society serves as a necessary backdrop to an all-too-brief consideration of the condition of the vast majority of humankind. There can be no more urgent need than that of determining whether the

South is doomed to follow in the footsteps of the North. If there are reasons to fear, let it be said at once that there are rational reasons to hope. A final preliminary point must be made. A particular approach is taken here, namely, one that privileges political explanations on the ground that cultural forms are more consequence than cause of general social development; justifications for this view are offered throughout the chapter.

CITIZENSHIP

Historically, citizenship grew out of popular demand for civil, political and social rights. The classic account of T.H. Marshall (1963) saw this development in evolutionary terms – from acquiring the rights to free speech, worship, property ownership and justice (civil rights) in the eighteenth century via the securing of the right to vote and stand for office (political rights) in the nineteenth century to finally obtaining protection for disadvantaged groups via development of the welfare state (social rights) in the twentieth century.

Michael Mann critically extended this analysis by emphasizing historical particularities and contingency in the development of citizenship in Europe and America. While Marshall's analysis had some empirical backing in the UK it could not properly explain development of citizenship elsewhere. The extension of citizenship rights, in Mann's view, was historically determined by the interests of political, economic and military rulers who were in control of the particular state apparatus. Hence the political elites in the United States and the UK were constrained by the early development of economic liberalism and expansion of the civil rights (in the American case also due to the popular participation in revolution) which led to the development of the constitutional model of citizenship with the institutionalization of repression 'only for those who went outside the rules of the game' (Mann, 1988: 192). In absolutist states such as Germany, Austria, Japan and Russia due to the dominance of agricultural production and the limited size of the working classes, the rulers (church, nobility and monarchs) were in a position to deny universal citizenship rights to all the other strata in society and were eventually forced only to concede limited civil (but not political) rights to the bourgeoisie. According to Mann, other European states moved from contested to merged models of citizenship through deep social and political conflicts between monarchists and clerics on the one hand and secular liberals and socialist revolutionaries on the other (as in Spain, Italy and France), or this struggle went through negotiated social change with the eventual victory of an alliance between small farmers, working classes and bourgeoisie (as in Scandinavia).

Bryan Turner (1994) has expanded this analysis even further, arguing that both Marshall and Mann have neglected the impact of social movements, different religious traditions and the possibility of creating a citizenship from below. In his view various forms of citizenship have developed in a dialectical and parallel interplay between the elite pursuit of control of the state and decisive actions of civil society groups. He builds his theory of citizenship around the dichotomies of private *vs.* public and active *vs.* passive, arguing that specific historical circumstances have determined the form and content of particular citizenship frames. Thus, American and French citizenship developed through revolutionary experience by popular pressure from below leading to an active understanding of citizenship; in contrast, the passive citizenship of England and Germany has its roots in the relatively peaceful way in which it was given from above (whether through the negotiation of competing elites as in England, or by a paternalist authoritarian state employing an instrument of modernization as in Germany). The historical routes taken by these states as well as the contents of particular religious traditions had a decisive impact on general attitudes to public and private spheres. Hence state-suspicious, privately oriented Protestantism had a direct impact on American citizenship, being at once active, individualist and apprehensive towards the state. In contrast, French Catholicism *and* secular Enlightenment-shaped collectivism privileged the public over the private sphere, and led to a collectivist and statist but very active model of citizenship. English Protestantism with no revolutionary tradition but with very developed civil society led to passive and private citizenship, whereas limited political rights coupled with Protestant ethics and authoritarian paternalism led to even more passive and private citizenship in Germany.

Feminists have also contributed to understanding of citizenship (Butler, 1993; Walby, 1994). Their emphasis is on describing the modern forms of citizenship in terms of the institutionalization of gender-biased norms. For one thing, the timetable by which women were accorded rights differed from that of men, thereby putting Marshall's model in question. For another, feminists argue that social and political rights gained through the development and expansion of the welfare state in the West were historically linked to a male-centered life cycle and its corresponding norms that privilege continuous, uninterrupted full-time employment and with profound disregard for the feminine life cycle (with pregnancy, maternity, menopause and menstrual periods). The criticism has been particularly leveled against the strong classical liberal distinction between the public and private spheres where public was traditionally identified with active, productive and socially recognized work (male), while private was relegated to passive, unappreciated and unpaid domestic work (female).

Although all of these approaches have contributed significantly to understanding of citizenship they all share one pronounced weakness. The leading approaches on citizenship have focused primarily on class, gender, religious background and social status in attempting to explain individual differences between societies and have largely neglected the central question of the relationship between citizenship and cultural difference. There are many questions that need to be addressed here. Are universalist premises of citizenship incompatible with cultural particularities of ethnic and national group claims? Is multiculturalism a viable alternative to the melting pot ideology? What is the relationship between modernity and cultural homogeneity? It is questions such as these that make it essential to discuss the

nature of ethnicity and nationalism – and then to provide a sketch for an historical and comparative sociology of the advanced and the developing worlds.

ETHNICITY

Although the term 'ethnicity' has its roots in the Greek *ethnos/ethnikos*, which was commonly used to describe pagans, that is non-Hellenic and later non-Jewish (Gentile), second class peoples, its academic and popular use is fairly modern. The term was coined by David Riesman in 1953 and it gained wider use only in the 1960s and 1970s (Glazer and Moynihan, 1975). However, from its inception 'ethnicity' has remained a 'hot potato' of sociology. Four distinct issues can usefully be highlighted.

First, although the term was coined to make sense of a specific form of cultural difference it generally acquired a rather different set of meanings. While Anglo-American tradition adopted ethnicity mostly as a substitute for minority groups within a larger society of the nation-state,[1] the European tradition regularly opted to use ethnicity as a synonym for nationhood defined historically by descent or territory.[2] At the same time both traditions shared a joint aim to replace until then a very popular, but with the Nazi experiment heavily compromised, concept of 'race'. Nevertheless, popular discourses in both Europe and America have 'racialized' the concept of ethnicity, that is 'race' was largely preserved (in its quasi-biological sense) and has only now been used interchangeably with 'ethnicity'.

Secondly, the collapse of the colonial world in the 1950s and 1960s brought even more confusion on questions of race, culture and ethnicity. The homelands of former European colonizers have quickly become populated with the new postcolonial immigrants who were visibly different. Following now American popular and legislative discourse, these groups have also become defined as 'ethnic' thus simultaneously preserving old definitions of historical ethnicity by descent or territory (for example, Welsh, Flemish, Walloons and Basques) with the new definitions of ethnicity as an immigrant minority (for example, Pakistani, West Indian, Sri Lankan).

Thirdly, the fall of communism and the breakup of the Soviet-style federations along 'ethnic' lines and the emergence of 'ethnic cleansing' policies in the Balkans and Caucasus have further complicated these definitional issues. With wars on former Yugoslav soil, the term 'ethnic', through the extensive and influential mass media coverage of 'ethnic wars', has degenerated into a synonym for tribal, primitive, barbaric and backward.

Fourthly, the ever-increasing influx of asylum seekers, refugees and economic migrants to Western Europe, America and Australia who do not necessarily express visible or significant physical, cultural or religious difference to their hosts, and their legal limbo status (for example, waiting for the decision on asylum) have relegated the term 'ethnic' to a quasi-legislative domain where 'ethnic', just as in the days of ancient Greece and Judea, refers again to non-citizens who inhabit 'our land', that is, to second class peoples.

To clarify all these misuses and misunderstandings one has to explain who exactly is an 'ethnic' and what ethnicity stands for in contemporary sociology. First, ethnicity as used in contemporary sociology is a broad enough concept to accommodate distinct forms of social action defined in collective-cultural terms. Unlike 'race', which is an epitome of a folk concept, often constructed in an ad hoc manner by social actors who are themselves trying to make sense of their everyday reality, the concept of ethnicity allows for sociological generalization without affecting particular instances of it. Although there is a clear genetic and physical variation between human beings such as skin colour, hair type, lip size and so on, as biologists emphasize, there are no unambiguous criteria for classifying people along the lines of these characteristics. Any such classification would artificially create groups where in-group variation would be greater than its presumed out-group variation. In other words 'race' is a social construct where phenotypic attributes are popularly used to denote in-groups from out-groups. Since there is no sound biological or sociological foundation for its use in

an analytical sense one should treat it as no more than a special case of ethnicity. Hence, when the term 'race' is used in a popular discourse it cannot refer to a 'sub-species of *Homo sapiens*' (van den Berghe, 1978: 406) but is applied only as a social attribute.[3]

Secondly, since it was commonly acknowledged that the classics of sociological thought had little or nothing to say about ethnicity,[4] sociologists had to turn to anthropology and in particular to the seminal work of Frederik Barth (1969) in order to explain the power of cultural difference, both historically and geographically. Before Barth, cultural difference was traditionally explained from the inside out – social groups possess different cultural characteristics which make them unique and distinct (common language, lifestyle, descent, religion, physical markers, history, eating habits, etc.). Culture was perceived as something relatively or firmly stable, persistent and definite. Cultural difference was understood in terms of the group's property (for example, Frenchmen have possession of a culture distinct from that of Englishmen). Barth's work provided nothing short of a Copernican revolution in the study of ethnicity. Barth put traditional understanding of cultural difference on its head, that is he defined and explained ethnicity from the outside in: it is not the 'possession' of cultural characteristics that makes social groups distinct but it is the social interaction with other groups that makes that difference possible, visible and socially meaningful. In Barth's own (1969: 15) words: 'the critical focus of investigation from this point of view becomes the ethnic boundary that defines the group, not the cultural stuff that it encloses'. The difference is created, developed and maintained only in interaction with others (for example, the Frenchness is created and becomes culturally and politically meaningful only through the encounter with Englishness, Germanness, Danishness etc.) Hence, the focus in the study of ethnic difference has shifted from the study of its contents (for example, the structure of the language, the form of the particular costumes, the nature of eating habits etc.) to the study of cultural boundaries and social interaction. Ethnic boundaries are explained first and foremost as a product of social action.

Thirdly, Barth's research set a foundation for understanding of ethnicity in universalist rather than in particularist terms. Since culture and social groups emerge only in interaction with others, then ethnicity cannot be confined to minority groups only. As Jenkins (1997: 11) rightly argues, we cannot study minority ethnic groups without studying at the same time the majority ethnicity. The dominant structural-functionalist and modernist paradigm of post-Second World War sociology has traditionally viewed ethnicity as a parochial drawback from the past that will largely disappear with intensive industrialization, urbanization, universal national education systems and modernization (Parsons, 1975). Ethnic difference was understood in rather narrow particularist terms. But if ethnicity is understood more generally in terms of social interaction, culture and boundary maintenance, then there is no culturally and politically aware social group able to create a credible narrative of common descent, without ethnicity. In other words, as long as there is social action and cultural markers to draw upon (for example, religion, language, descent etc.), there will be ethnicity. And this is indeed where sociology comes into play.

Although Barth has provided a groundwork for the elementary understanding of ethnicity his approach fell short of accounting for political and structural repercussions in the organization and institutionalization of cultural difference. Why, when and how do individuals and groups maintain the ethnic boundaries? In trying to explain these questions post-Barthian sociology has drifted in different directions. Rational choice theory focused on individual motives and choices (Banton, 1983: Hechter, 1992). Viewing individuals as utility maximizers who struggle over limited resources, rational choice sociologists believe that ethnicity is no more than an advantage that can be used for individual gain. Speaking the same language, sharing the religious tradition, myths of common descent or any other form of cultural similarity help actors unite, making the price of collective action less 'expensive'. Michael Hechter (1992) argues that ethnic groups

maintain their inter-group solidarity in two principal ways: by providing benefits to their members and/or by restricting and sanctioning their individual choices to prevent 'free riding'. Hence collective action on an ethnic group basis is most likely when individuals can benefit from it or when they fear sanctions from alternative behavior. Although successful in emphasizing the dynamic and manipulative quality of ethnicity, this approach has been criticized, among other things, for neglecting the structural conditions under which individual choices are made (Malešević, 2002b).

Working within the similar economistic tradition, neo-Marxist approaches emphasize what rational choice theory neglects – the structural determination of ethnic group behavior: the state's role in reproducing and institutionalizing ethnically divisive conditions, the function of racist ideology in preventing working class unity or the relationship between economic inequality and ethnic identity (Miles, 1984). While traditionally Marxists have analyzed ethnicity as an ideological mask that only hides class antagonisms focusing almost exclusively on the capitalist modes of production, contemporary neo-Marxism is much more sensitive to autonomy of the cultural sphere. Recognizing limits of class analysis, contemporary Marxism (Solomos and Back, 1995) attempts to widen its analysis of ethnicity by directing its attention to the new social movements and identities other than class (Anthias, 1992). However, these are still, just as in rational choice theory, couched in antagonistic, economist terms where ethnicity remains a second order reality, a tool of exchange and coercion.

Symbolic interactionist perspectives are overtly critical of such a view. Blumer and Duster (1980), Lal (1995) and other interactionists argue that social action is often more symbolic than economic and that ethnicity can most adequately be studied and explained by focusing on the individual and collective subjective perceptions of reality. In this perspective ethnicity is analyzed as a social process through which individuals and groups acquire, maintain, transform or change their 'definitions of situation'. In Lal's words (1995: 432) the perceptions of ethnic ties are 'influenced by the situation in which we find ourselves, the presence of real or imaginary significant others, and "altercasting" as well as positive or negative value we assume a particular identity will confer in a particular context'. Ethnic groups operate through the 'collective definition of situation' on the basis of which they participate in the ongoing processes of interpretation and reinterpretation of their experiences (Blumer and Duster, 1980: 222). As often stressed by interactionists, objective unequal distribution of economic rewards or political power between the ethnic groups does not necessarily result in group conflict. It is rather the nature of their mutual symbolic interpretations and collective perceptions that determines inter- and intra-group relations.

The view that human beings are predominantly symbolic, cultural creatures who create their own worlds of meanings has been put under scrutiny by sociobiologists. Sociobiology starts from a simple and apparent fact that humans are made of flesh and blood, that they need to eat, drink, sleep and copulate, which are features shared with the rest of the animal kingdom. Culture is regarded as important but is seen as being subordinate to nature since it has developed from nature and is dependent on changes in nature. According to sociobiologists, just as animals, humans are genetically programmed to reproduce their genes. When direct reproduction is not possible one will reproduce indirectly – through kin selection. P. van den Berghe (1981) has persistently argued that ethnicity is no more than an extension of kin selection. Ethnic groups are defined by common descent and are seen as being ascriptive, hereditary and generally endogamous. Since ethnic nepotism has biological origins, it is argued that 'those societies that institutionalized norms of nepotism and ethnocentrism had a strong selective advantage over those that did not' (van den Berghe, 1978: 405). Sociobiology is the only sociological tradition that explicitly takes a primordialist stance in the explanation of ethnic relations.[5] Its view that ethnic groups are biologically determined for in-group favoritism has been subject to the critique of most other research

traditions, but power elite theory has provided the most sustained criticism of primordialist positions.

Power elite approaches argue that what is crucial for understanding of ethnic relations is focus on human beings as political rather than biological animals. Brass (1994), Cohen (1981) and others speak of ethnicity in instrumentalist terms. Nevertheless, this instrumentality is not of an economic (as in rational choice theory) but rather of a political nature and it focuses more on the role of individuals and groups in positions of power than on the randomly picked utilitarian agents. Power elite theories are developed around the two spheres of human activity – power (politics) and symbolism (culture). Their argument is that cultural markers are for most of the time arbitrary and what matters in ethnic relations is how, when and by whom can these symbols be manipulated to mobilize social groups. Symbols are considered to be powerful mechanisms of elite control because of their ambiguity and emotional intensity. In this perspective conflicts based on ethnicity are explained as something that 'arise out of specific types of interactions between the leaderships of centralizing states and elites from non-dominant ethnic groups especially, but not exclusively, in the peripheries of those states' (Brass, 1994: 111). Although clearly able to accommodate some propositions of symbolic interactionism (symbolism), rational choice theory (instrumentality of cultural markers) and neo-Marxism (unequal position of social groups), this position has been criticized for treating 'masses' in a passive, conformist and submissive way and for neglecting the study of motives and values behind the ethnic mobilization.

The approach that is most sensitive to the criticisms raised above is a Weberian approach to ethnicity (Collins, 1999; Jackson, 1982/3; Stone, 1995). In fact, contrary to the commonly held view, Weber has provided a fairly developed and articulated theory of ethnicity. Moreover, Weber provided a definition and analysis which allowed for a non-essentialist view of ethnicity long before Barth's path-breaking study. If one reads Weber properly, it is possible to see that Weber did not conceive ethnicity in terms of a 'group property' but rather in terms of social action. Following his ideal-type methodology Weber perceived all social groups as quasi-groups, emphasizing their amorphous and dynamic potential. In the same way ethnicity is understood as a potential social attribute not as an actual group characteristic. Weber defined ethnicity in terms of two key factors – (a) a belief of social actors in common descent based on cultural differences and (b) a political action through which this belief becomes socially meaningful (1968: 385–98). What is crucial here is his view that 'it is primarily the political community, no matter how artificially organized, that inspires the belief in common ethnicity' (Weber, 1968: 389). Hence, this position anticipates Barth's emphasis on boundaries and even goes a step further, accounting for a group mobilization and linking it to some propositions raised by power-elite theories. Furthermore, by introducing the concept of 'monopolistic closure' Weber's theory of ethnicity has room for economic instrumentality broader than rational choice type of analysis. Weber argued that ethnicity can often be explained by looking at how individuals tend to close relationships by using 'any cultural trait' to 'ensure economic opportunities' for their group. This monopolistic social closure of groups ties well into the symbolic interactionist emphasis on symbolism since the Weberian approach stresses the link between ethnicity and status. Ethnicity often becomes a mechanism for the monopolization of status honor since the sense of an ethnic group's honor is rooted in a belief of the group's superiority. As Weber has shown, quite often low economic group standing is coupled with high ethnic group status and vice versa (for example, white manual workers *vs.* 'blacks' in the United States, Fijians *vs.* Indians in Fiji, Serbs *vs.* Albanians in Kosovo). These intergroup relations can also undergo swift transformation with the advent of charismatic personalities who are often able to draw on the power of emotional and value-rational social action to initiate dramatic social change. The link between charismatic authority and value rationality is key for understanding the power of popular appeal that ethnic nationalism can

quickly generate (Malešević, 2002a). In this way Weberian tradition is able to explain individual and group motives behind the ethnic mobilization. The greatest advantage of Weberian tradition over its competitors comes from a simple but crucial idea that although a universal sociological theory of ethnicity is possible, there is a multiplicity of 'ethnic situations'. Ethnicity can overlap with status, class, legal or political rights or with caste. As Rex (1986: 14) points out, ethnic groups 'may be arranged in a hierarchy of honor, they may have different legal rights and they may have different property rights'. Weberian tradition is the most systematic and synthetic approach that anticipates the original Barthian argument which explains ethnicity through the social (inter)action.

NATIONALISM

The distinction which has had the longest intellectual career within the theory of nationalism is that between civic and ethnic nations. This was first introduced by Hans Kohn (1967) and it has recently been given new life by Rogers Brubaker (1992) in an impressive comparative study of French and German citizenship laws. The distinction contrasts French and American nationalism with, above all, those of Eastern Europe. In the former one can become a citizen easily, by accepting local laws and customs – with citizenship being given as of right to anyone born on the territory of the state. In the latter, citizenship rights are reserved to those of a similar ethnic background. Although the situation has just changed, a clear example of this latter situation was Germany's acceptance of ethnic Germans from Eastern Europe and Russia who could not speak the language – and its near refusal to give citizenship to Turkish workers, even though they could speak German and had quite often lived the whole of their lives within that country. It is not surprising that civic has come to be associated with good, and ethnic with nasty – a view particularly clearly articulated by Eric Hobsbawm (1990).

There has been conceptual advance beyond this stark binary opposition. To begin with, we should *not* accept everything that is implied in the formula ethnic/bad, civic/good. There is nothing necessarily terrible about loyalty to one's ethnic group, whereas civic nationalism is not necessarily nice: its injunction can be 'join us or else'. Of course, ethnic nationalism is indeed repulsive when it is underwritten by relativist philosophies that insist that one should literally think with one's blood. Further, civic nationalism becomes more liberal when it moves towards the pole of civility, best defined in terms of the acceptance of diverse positions or cultures. Whether this move is so to speak sociologically real can be measured by asking two questions. First, is the identity to which one is asked to accede relatively thin, that is, does it have at its core political loyalty rather than a collective memory of an ethnic group? Second, are rates of intermarriage high? All this is obvious. Less so, perhaps, is a tension that lies at the heart of multiculturalism. In the interests of clarity, matters can be put bluntly. Multiculturalism properly understood *is* civil nationalism, the recognition of diversity. But that diversity is – needs to be, should be – limited by a consensus on shared values. Difference is acceptable only so long as group identities are voluntary, that is, insofar as identities can be changed according to individual desire. What is at issue is neatly encapsulated when we turn to the notion of caging.[6] If multiculturalism means that groups have rights over individuals – if, for example, the leaders of a group have the power to decide to whom young girls should be married – then it becomes repulsive. Such multiculturalism might seem liberal in tolerating difference, but it is in fact the illiberalism of misguided liberalism, diminishing life chances by allowing social caging. This view is, of course, relativist, and it is related to ethnic nationalism in presuming that one must think with one's group. Importantly, the link to ethnic nationalism may be very close indeed. If there are no universal standards, and ethnic groups are held to be in permanent competition, then it is possible, perhaps likely, that one group will seek to dominate another.

If these are ideal typical positions, a powerful stream of modern social theory in effect suggests that some have greater viability than others. A series of thinkers, interestingly all liberal, have insisted that homogeneity, whether ethnic or civic, is a 'must' if a society is to function effectively. John Stuart Mill made this claim when speaking about the workings of democracy, insisting that the nationalities question had to be solved in order for democracy to be viable (Mill, 1975). The great contemporary theorist of democracy Robert Dahl has reiterated this idea (Dahl, 1977). The notion behind all this is straightforward. Human beings cannot take too much conflict, cannot put themselves on the line at all times and in every way. For disagreement to be productive in the way admired by liberalism, it must be contained – that is, it must take place within a frame of common belonging. Very much the same insight underlies David Miller's view that national homogeneity is a precondition for generous welfare regimes (Miller, 1995). This is correct: the generosity of Scandinavian countries rests on the willingness to give generously to people exactly like oneself. But the great theorist of the need for social homogeneity was of course Ernest Gellner. As it happens, the explanation he offered for this ever more insistently – that of the necessity of homogeneity so that industrial society can function properly – is rather question-begging.[7] But even the most cursory consideration of his life suggests that he captured something about the character of nationalism. Born into Kafka's Czech-German-Jewish world and forced into exile in 1939, he returned in 1945 to find the Jews murdered and the Germans being expelled. A second period of exile ended when he returned when communism fell – to witness on that occasion the secession of the rich majority from the Slovaks. Visceral experience underlay his image of political space moving from the world of Kokoschka to that of Mondrian – that is, from a world in which peoples were intermingled to one in which national homogeneity was established (Gellner, 1983: 139–40).

The claim of those variously stressing the need for homogeneity amounts to saying that we are very unlikely to have civil nationalism, that is, that multinational entities are an impossibility. This is to say that constitutional schemes – federal, confederal and consociational – from which civil nationalism hopes so much are very unlikely to work. That has certainly been a key part of the experience of Europeans, as we shall see, for this has been the dark continent of modernity, with homogeneity being achieved through repulsive means – through population transfers, ethnic cleansing and genocide much more than by voluntary assimilation (Mazower, 1998). The key analytic question within the theory of nationalism – a question with immediate consequences for ethnicity and citizenship – is whether civil nationalism is a realistic social possibility. As noted, this leads to a further question, that of whether the rest of the world follows the European example. If so, the future of world politics looks set to bring us catastrophe, given the complex ethnic intermingling of many states, particularly some of those in the developing world.

As it happens, there is a counter-argument to the pessimistic view associated with Gellner's predominantly socio-economic causation. Advances in sociology suggest that the character of social movements results overwhelmingly from the nature of the state with which they interact. This political sociology may well apply, as noted, to working class behavior. Liberal states that allowed workers to struggle at the industrial level avoided creating politically conscious movements; in contrast, authoritarian and autocratic regimes so excluded workers as to give them no option but to take on the state. This general notion – that the barricades are so terrifying that reform is habitually more attractive than revolution – has very large applications. The case against Gellner is that the politics explain nationalism as much or more than socio-economic factors. More particularly, the secessionist nationalism privileged by his definition of nationalism results more from a reaction to the authoritarianism of empires than from the social inequality faced by a culturally distinct group. Liberalism before nationalism may allow for containment, that is, respect for historical liberties might allow multinational frames to exist.

It is important to stress here that it is liberalism which is at the core of the position that stands as an alternative to Gellner's sociology – for we should not uncritically romanticize democracy. Tocqueville long ago pointed out that majorities could in theory be tyrannical. Whether he was correct or not about the United States, there can be no doubt that in numerous instances – for example, Protestant hegemony in Northern Ireland from 1922 to 1969 – democracy has been exercised freely and fairly, and at the expense of minorities. More generally, democratic participation is not always a good in and of itself, despite the recent vogue for civil society and civic virtue. This suggests an equally important corollary. Bluntly, democracy matters less than liberalism. Liberal regimes may achieve very great stability by diffusing various conflicts through society rather than concentrating them at the political center. Pure democratic participation will destabilize unless it is channeled through social institutions which tend to contain, manage and regulate conflict. The Balkan Wars of the past decade have demonstrated that democratization does not necessarily bring peace and prosperity. However, the collapse of communism did not lead to violence in every instance, suggesting that attention be given to two variables (Snyder, 2000). First, political leaders who imagine that a new world can only bring their downfall may well be tempted to play the nationalist card in order to stay in power (for example, Milošević vs. Klaus). Secondly, democracy may well lead to violence if it lacks the institutional framework that allows it to control its passions, that force it to reflect. Snyder stresses in this context that democratization clearly leads to violence when news comes from a single authority. And all this is to say that in our own time a multinational state, even with the benefits of the purported lessons of the past, utterly failed to successfully transform itself.

The paradox at work can be underscored. The presence of institutions of conflict regulation can shape and channel, even perhaps tame newly emergent popular pressures. In contrast, authoritarian regimes are likely to create social movements armed with total ideologies. The contrast is between societies in which liberalism came before democracy and those in which democracy came before liberalism. Our position as a whole is that of Tocqueville (1955), the central tenets of whose masterpiece are that liberalism and authoritarianism are self-perpetuating. We need not be quite so pessimistic, for some authoritarian regimes have become liberal democracies, but we should be aware how difficult is that transformation – and that the advent of democracy does not necessarily entail sweetness and light.

STATE AND NATION IN EUROPE

Although it is important to note that nationalism was associated with horror in European history, cognitive advance depends upon explaining why this was so. After all, in the middle of the nineteenth century Europe was at the pinnacle of its power, confident that it represented progress. The European balance of power depended on the interactions of Austro-Hungary, Wilhelmine Germany, Imperial Russia, Great Britain and France. The fate of the Ottomans was very much part of the mental world of these great powers; the position of the United States came slowly to assume great significance, especially for Great Britain. If all this suggested ebbs and flows of power and influence, no hint was present that this was the scene for a new, great Peloponnesian War – a conflict so visceral that it knocked Europe off the perch that it held briefly as the leader of the world. What were the essential contours of this conflict? Further, does understanding these variables allow us to suggest that the link between nationalism and nastiness was contingent rather than absolutely necessary?

The rivalry between these states was such that the most immediate structural element at work was that of the need to industrialize. An obvious consequence that troubled ruling elites was the emergence of working classes. In fact, a whole series of sectoral divisions amongst workers meant that no unitary class existed inside a particular state, let alone between them – at least when workers were left to themselves. Extreme repression of radicals combined with liberal treatment of the rest famously created

in the United States a world in which workers began to consider themselves as middle class. Something of the same pattern had put paid to the Chartists in England, but the presence of some, albeit very limited, state interference – that of the Taff Vale court decision which for a short period prevented union organization – ensured that class loyalty was created, that is, socialism was avoided but a Labour Party was created. In contrast, regime exclusion did create socialist class unity. Anti-socialist laws in Wilhelmine Germany created a movement with political and industrial wings, formally wedded to revolutionary ideas but in fact made reformist by the speedy abolition of the laws in question. In Imperial Russia autocracy differed from authoritarianism in being at times even more suspicious of capitalism (McDaniel, 1988). The fundamental factor at work was regime policy. Militancy varied precisely in relation to state actions: reformists came to the fore as the result of the political opening of 1905, whilst revolutionaries triumphed inside the movement once concessions were abandoned. The end result of these policies was the creation of the only genuinely revolutionary working class in human history. In a nutshell, the historical record does indeed support the political sociology of class that was outlined at the start.

To consider industrialization only in terms of its impact on class would be a mistake. Every state sought an exactly similar set of industries in order to maintain its geopolitical independence, and this in turn led to economic tensions. The importance and character of imitative industrialization is captured in the marvelous demonstration by Gautam Sen (1984) that every industrializing state in the nineteenth century sought to have the same basic portfolio of heavy industries – so as to ensure its capacity for geopolitical independence, that is, its ability to produce its own weapons. Differently put, states interfered with markets. In this context, the elements of historical sociology that concern us here revolve around three factors that explain the nature of Europe's twentieth-century disaster. Each factor can be seen as an extension of the beliefs of Max Weber, namely his visceral nationalism, his commitment as a Fleet Professor to an imperial policy, and his insistence that the empire's conduct of German foreign affairs was disastrous. And it should be said clearly that these factors were at work in all the countries involved.

First, developmental states characteristically felt weak when they ruled over a mass of different ethnic and national groupings. For one thing, Britain seemed to gain strength from its homogeneity – although this perception faded once Home Rule politics made it clear that Britain was in its way as composite a state as were other empires. But the determination to copy the ethnic homogeneity of leading European powers had a further element to it, namely that of seeking to strengthen the legitimacy of the state by playing the national card against socialism. Accordingly, nationalism comes to the fore at the end of the nineteenth century as much from above as from below. Perhaps curiously, nationalism had not been enormously successful in the years before 1914. Geopolitical interference stood behind the cleansing of perhaps 5 million Muslims from the new Balkan nation-states (Mazower, 2000). This suggested of course that the stakes of any general conflict, should it occur, might well be very great indeed (Kaiser, 1990: pt 4). But as long as the balance of power remained in operation, nationalism had great difficulty in breaking the established mould of state borders. A clear contrast can be drawn between the logic of the situations facing different empires (Lieven, 2000). Austro-Hungary quite simply had no chance to become a modern nation-state: the dominant ethnicity was simply too small to serve as a *Staatsvolk*. What evolved in consequence was a situation, in Count Taaffe's words, of 'bearable dissatisfaction' (Lieven, 2000: 191). If the Magyars were content, the Slavic nations within the Austrian half were not terribly treated – for all that they hoped that the monarchy would move towards greater constitutionalism. Demands were contained, however, by a clear awareness of geopolitical realities. As early as 1848 the Slavs had realized that to become small but unprotected nations was to risk annihilation should Germany or Russia be drawn into a power vacuum.

The second factor can usefully be introduced by saying, again, that nationalism is an essentially labile force, able to connect with and deeply influenced by the social forces of any particular historical moment. The reference to Max Weber as Fleet Professor brings to attention the crucial fact that nationalism was, in this period, linked to imperialism. There is a sense in which Weber himself should have known better. As Adam Smith had stressed long ago, colonies could be more of a millstone than an advantage. But it is very often the case that what matters socially about economics is less the facts in and of themselves than what people believe to be the facts. In this case, imperial dreams had a very considerable rationale. When Lord Roseberry admitted that the British empire did not pay at the time, he went on immediately to say that it might none the less be absolutely necessary in the longer run.

It is the third factor, the nature of foreign policy-making inside imperial courts, to which attention must be given for an explanation for the breakdown of order that then allowed nationalism and imperialism to cause disaster. A preliminary, scene-setting point is simply that the late nineteenth-century European great powers *were* engines of grandeur, whose leaders habitually wore military uniform. The difficulty that such rulers faced, however, was that making foreign policy was becoming ever more difficult. Jack Snyder has usefully suggested that foreign policy-making tends to be rational when states are unitary (Snyder, 1991; cf. Mann, 1993: ch. 21). Examples of such rational states include the rule of traditional monarchs, the collective domination of a revolutionary party so much in control of a late, late developing society as to have no fear of popular pressure, and the checks and balances on foreign adventures provided by liberal systems. In contrast, late developing societies – which combine authoritarianism with genuine pressures from a newly mobilized population – tend to lack the state capacity necessary to calculate by means of realist principles.

The First World War was not a Clausewitzian affair, in that statesmen lost control of policy-making. Industry applied to war in part explains this, but still more important was the fact that a war of peoples needed justifications other than the merely dynastic or territorial. The chaos that resulted exhausted the European fabric. It was this factor which made the peace treaty disastrous. The lack of genuine geopolitical agreement encouraged the politics of economic autarchy. The failure to solve the security dilemma cemented the link between nationalism and imperialism. This was the world of Hitler and Stalin, of the horrors of ethnic cleansing, population transfer, mass murder, and of total war between the two great revolutions of modernity.

The First World War had ended badly despite the making of formal treaties. In contrast, the Second World War ended well without formal agreements. What mattered most of all was consideration given to power politics, that is, the creation of a secure frame within which economic and social forces could then prosper. Spheres of influence were established between two great superpowers which very rapidly came to understand each other extremely well, not least because the presence of nuclear weapons forced them to be rational. Nationalism was ignored, stability created. There were two elements at work in the reconstitution of Europe (Maier, 1981; Ruggie, 1982). Europeans themselves made a very major contribution. Fascism was thoroughly discredited, beaten in its own chosen arena of military valor. More particularly, French bureaucrats, aware of the devastation caused by three wars with Germany within a single lifetime, effectively changed France's geopolitical calculation. If Germany could not be beaten militarily, it could perhaps be contained through love. The origin of what is now the European Union came from a decision by the two leading powers to give up their geopolitical autonomy, by establishing genuine interdependence in coal and steel – that is, in giving up the capacity to make their own weapons. This move was made possible by the second factor, the presence of American forces. Europeans of course did a great deal to pull Americans in – with Lord Ismay famously arguing that foreign policy should seek to keep the Americans in, the Russians out and the Germans divided.

As Milward (1992) explains, European states had sought, between 1870 and 1945, to be complete power containers, unitary and in possession of markets and secure sources of supply. The fact that this led to complete disaster produced humility – which is not to say for a moment that state power somehow lost its salience. Rather, states discovered that doing less proved to give them more, that interdependence within a larger security frame allowed for prosperity and the spread of citizenship rights. Differently put, breaking the link between nationalism and imperialism enhanced rather than undermined state capacity. However, liberalism in Europe, from the Atlantic to Ukraine, and including most of southeastern Europe, is made easier because very great national homogeneity has been established, in largest part thanks to the actions of Hitler and Stalin.

The fundamental change in geopolitical realities after the collapse of the Soviet bloc certainly played a part in key developments within the European Union, most notably that of binding Germany within Europe by avoiding any German economic hegemony through the Bundesbank. Still, continuities are more important than new developments. For one thing, this liberal democratic league has the capacity, not least given that one cannot be a member without respecting minority rights, to consolidate liberal democracies in Central Europe just as it did in Southern Europe a generation ago. For another, statist calculations remain at play: the Franco-German condominium survives, whilst French determination to balance Germany has led it virtually to rejoin the NATO command structure. Perhaps most important of all, there is no sign of fundamental change to the rules of the geopolitical game. The mere sign of worry, let alone any threat of withdrawal, on the part of the United States has seen Europeans own up to the fact that they wish the American presence to continue, despite its varied imperfections.

Fascism had been defeated in the hottest of wars. In contrast, the Cold War ended with a whimper. The period since 1989 has made crystal clear that the Soviet developmental model was deeply flawed. For one thing, whatever the benefits of initial heavy industrialization and social modernization, there is now no doubt that the absence of market mechanisms doomed Soviet style economies to waste and inefficiency. Socialism as a power system had sought to establish its own channels of control, thereby in effect continuing Tsarism's distrust of independent civil society. When power was absolute, command-administrative methods had great force. Once softer political rule came to the fore, it became obvious that force was linked to rigidity. If the lack of flexibility caused problems, the inability to decompress – that is, the inability of socialism to emulate some authoritarian capitalism regimes in liberalizing from above – resulted from another facet of an atomized society, bereft of social institutions. Liberalization processes depend upon the striking of bargains, often in some round-table negotiations. Gorbachev's difficulty was that there were no leaders of independent organizations, able to control their members, with whom he could negotiate (Bova, 1991). In these circumstances, controlled decompression was impossible. Democratization took the place of liberalization. For another, the national question can be seen to have occupied the new political space, and in such a way as to put the final nail in a social world presumed until very recently to be powerful and permanent. The reconstitution of the empire by 1921 and its expansion in 1939 and in the years from 1944 presented problems with which the Tsars would have been all too familiar. Several systems of rule were again contained within a single political umbrella, with the greatest difficulties again coming from the inclusion of advanced Western nations whose consciousness was so advanced as to make assimilation impossible. The situation was in fact worse than it had been for the Tsars: the Baltic states and Poland had tasted independence, the Czechs knew that socialism was taking away their industrial lead, whilst a united Ukraine, freed from fear of Poland and Germany, concentrated all its ire on Russia. But if the empire became an expensive burden, it is important to remember that the nationalities did less to cause the breakdown of the Soviet bloc than to make sure that reconstitution would be impossible. A political opening increases noise. Nerve is required to put up

with new pressures, so that discontents take a normal form – from revolution to reform. The worst move in such circumstances is – what Gorbachev did – to step backwards, to make the newly vocal fear and thereby to confirm them in their suspicion of the continuity of an old regime. The interventions in Georgia and Lithuania were accordingly utterly disastrous. Yeltsin was given the cards by means of which he was able to destroy the Soviet Union. Rarely has a great power fallen so far, so fast.

THE AMERICAN MELTING POT

The discussion of nationalism in the abstract suggested that civic nationalism was not necessarily as liberal as its defenders imagined. This insight certainly helps us to understand the Leviathan of the contemporary world. Bluntly, the national experience of the United States is not as different from that of Europe as it would like to believe. Civic nationalism in America has encouraged a melting pot, homogenizing the many into a single unit. Differently put, the United States is not a social world favoring diversity. An initial consideration to that effect lies in the simple fact that white Anglo-Saxon settlers more or less exterminated the native population, thereby establishing their own hegemony. Further, the creation of the new state placed a very strong emphasis on uniformity. For one thing, a Constitution was formed, a singular set of ideals created, which thereafter was held to be sacred. For another, the United States was created by means of powerful acts, usually directed from below, of political cleansing. A significant section of the elite – in absolute numerical terms larger than those guillotined during the French Revolution, and from a smaller population at that – that had supported the Crown was forced to leave (Palmer, 1959: 188–202).

Perhaps the most striking general interpretation of American history and society, namely that proposed by Seymour Martin Lipset (1996), is that which insists on the power of these initial ideas, of continuity through continuing consensus. That is not quite right. If some alternatives were ruled out at the time of foundation, others were eliminated as the result of historical events. The two most important examples deserve at least minimal attention. First, we ought to remember that the United States remained unitary only as the result of a very brutal civil war. The Constitution had of course recognized the different interests of the slave-owning southern states, but the difference between North and South grew in the early years of the republic. War destroyed that diversity, with Lincoln trying at the end of the conflict to create unity by means of such new institutions as Thanksgiving. Of course, the South did not lose its cultural autonomy simply as the result of defeat in war, maintaining a key hold on federal politics well into the 1930s. None the less, over time the South has lost its uniqueness, especially in recent years as the result of political change and of population and industrial transfers from North to South. Since no one wants a second civil war of visceral intensity, there is no possibility of the United States becoming a multinational society. The second alternative vision was that of socialism, in one form or another. Revisionist history makes it equally clear that there was a genuine socialist stream of ideas and institutions in American history, represented most spectacularly in the militant unionism of the International Workers of the World. Further proof of the strength of working class activism can be found in the bitterness of labor disputes – whose end result was a very large number of deaths, second only to those at the hands of the late Tsarist empire (Mann, 1993). This is all to say that American ideals of individualism and enterprise were not so powerful or so widely shared as to rule out a challenge. Their ascendancy came about for two fundamental reasons. On the one hand, the fact that citizenship had been granted early on meant that worker dissatisfaction tended to be limited, to be directed against industrialists rather than against the state – thereby limiting its overall power. On the other hand, and crucially for this argument, socialism was literally destroyed – as is made apparent by that very large number of working class deaths. The recipe for social stability, which worked in the United

States, is often the combination of political opening with absolute intolerance towards extremists.

It would be a mistake to leave matters at this point. For the rosier and milder face of the coin of American homogeneity can be seen at work in American ethnic relations. With the clear exception of African Americans, for the majority of Americans, ethnic identity is now, as Mary Waters (1990) makes clear, a choice rather than a destiny imposed from outside. Rates of intermarriage are extremely high, not least for the first generation of Cuban Americans in Florida, more than 50 per cent of whom marry outside their own group.[8] Ethnic identity has little real content. It is permissible to graduate from kindergarten wearing a sari as long as one does not believe in caste – that is, as long as one is American. There are severe limits to difference, but similarity is now often achieved by much more civil means. The powers of homogenization in the United States, deriving as much from Hollywood and consumerism, of course, as from the factors examined here, remain intact. The melting pot still works, but it does so in a far more benign manner.

SPLENDOURS AND MISERIES OF THE SOUTH

It only takes a moment to think of issues in the South affecting the transformation of states. It may be that socialist China can manage to transform itself, both because it placed *perestroika* before *glasnost* and because it has very largely become a nation-state. More generally, however, the North has washed its hands of the South, much of which could drop off the face of the globe without the purportedly global economy even noticing (Hall, 2000). However, despite all the talk about globalization diminishing the significance of ethnic and national attachments, it seems that the opposite process is taking place. First, one of the consequences of more globalized economies is further expansion in migration from the South to the North. Nevertheless, the new cohorts of migrants differ significantly from their counterparts in the postcolonial era: in an environment of instability and insecurity within a globalizing world, assimilation and full citizenship in a host nation-state is often replaced with alternative forms of political loyalties such as dual citizenships, denizenships or living on the legal margins of the asylum system (non-documented immigrants, runaway deportees). Intensified by the development of modern means of transport and communication (Internet, mobile phones etc.) on one hand and economic stagnation in their home countries on the other, the new immigrants often opt for retention of strong ties with their countries of origin. These political, cultural and financial links are often fostered by the governments in the South, who view their transnational emigrants as key source of 'remittances, investment capital and votes' (Itzigsohn, 1999). Secondly, the changing nature of the globalizing economy coupled with the persistence of strong ethnic and national ties with the South creates a situation where new immigrants are less likely to develop a stronger sense of cultural and political membership in the country of immigration. Rather, they are more prone to transnationalism, identifying with ethnic group attachments that cross borders of a particular nation-state (Kearney, 1995). However, one should not overstate this largely economic-centered argument since the technical capacity of the states in the North to control their borders and the movement of people has also dramatically increased. In other words, politics matters as much as economics, if not more. One wonders whether politics can in the longer run be so subject to a new form of international apartheid as is economics. The spread of weapons of mass destruction, especially to states possessed of the fiscal advantages given by the possession of fossil fuel, first presented a crucial problem in the form of Saddam Hussein. It is hard to imagine that his will have been the last challenge, despite America's much vaunted military revolution.

It is beyond our powers to do more than note the salience of these issues. But the perspective that has been argued does suggest the usefulness of considering the situation of multinational regimes in the South. Given that development seeks in its very essence to copy the advanced, it behooves us to ask whether the South's twenty-first century will be as dark as that through which Europe has just passed. If there are obvious reasons to fear, there are – remarkably – reasons for optimism. It should be said immediately that the hope in question is not mere wishful thinking, not the placing of hope above analysis.

Some regimes in the developing world have managed multinationalism far better than did Europe. A general background condition was an initial realization in some quarters that imagination was needed so as to avoid disaster. It was precisely because African borders were absurd that it was, Julius Nyerere argued, essential to maintain them. Equally importantly, few states have an ethnic group of sufficient size that it is able to even imagine complete domination of the territory – there being, for example, perhaps 120 different ethnicities in Tanzania. Politics are therefore pushed towards multinationalism for structural reasons. These circumstances have bred a remarkable substantive achievement, that of the language repertoires of some African states and, above all, of India. David Laitin's analysis of the Indian situation suggests that a fully capable Indian citizen needs a language repertoire of '3 plus or minus 1' languages (Laitin, 1992). Two languages are needed to begin with because India has two official languages, English as well as Hindi – for Nehru's desire to produce a unitary and monoglot society was stymied by the desire of civil servants to maintain their cultural capital, that is, the ability to function in English. A third language is that of one's provincial state. But one only needs two languages when one's provincial state is Hindi-speaking. In contrast, one needs four languages when one is in a minority in a non-Hindi-speaking provincial state. India is the most important exception to Gellner's generalization that homogeneity is a functional prerequisite of modernity. This is a remarkable institutional success story, the creation of an Austro-Hungary that seems to work. And this sort of linguistic arrangement has been complemented in many parts of the developing world by a varied collection of agreements, habitually consociational and regional, which have allowed ethnic groups to survive within a single shell. The complex case of Malaya is a prime case in point (Horowitz, 1986).

Language is of course only one of the markers that can be used as the basis on which to homogenize peoples into a single nation, and one can always fear – though not, to this point, excessively – that religion could again serve as the basis for terrible ethnic cleansing in India. It is worth remembering in this context that the full impact of ethnic superstratification is felt during the process of modernization – which is by no means complete in most of the world's polities. If hope has some descriptive base, the fact that there have been many failures of multinational federations – from Yugoslavia and the Soviet Union, to the Caribbean, sub-Saharan Africa and British Central Africa – should make us realize how very hard it is to make such arrangements work. Still more obvious are the genocidal horrors of Kampuchea and Rwanda – in which other peoples behave as did we Europeans in the very recent past. It is hard to imagine that such actions, now visible on our television screens, will not have any effect on the condition of those who inhabit the more comfortable zones of the world.

CONCLUSION

Our intent in this chapter has been to sound a cautionary note. When a society develops institutions to regulate conflict early on, then it is likely that emergent popular forces will be absorbed within a liberal mould flexible enough to tame and contain them. In contrast, democratization occurring before the advent of liberalism is likely to lead to social disruption, sometimes of the most repulsive sort. Establishing liberal institutions in the midst of fundamental social and political change is very difficult indeed. The world remains a very dangerous place – one in which nationalism may continue to cause disaster. For the characteristic political form of modernity remains that of the nation-state, whose character does indeed revolve around a good

deal of homogeneity. When one remembers the amount of violence involved in creating such entities, one must fear for the future of the world. But this is an area in which a measure of hope is permissible, given the inventiveness of non-Europeans. Differently put, we can hope that they will not copy us. And it would be a terrible mistake to imagine that nationalism is now a problem for others, rather than for our own advanced countries. Brendan O'Leary (2000) has recently pointed out that federalism works best when it has at its core a demographically dominant *Staatsvolk* – the idea being that a ruling people, secure in its position, will be perfectly prepared to allow federal concessions. In the absence of such demographic dominance, federalism only works when consociational measures are added, so as to join different communities. Given that Europe, like Austro-Hungary, simply does not have enough Germans, the European Union would be well advised to retain all the consociational deals that reassure small states – as well as to find ways to give representation to such stateless nations as Catalonia and Scotland. Getting institutional design right even in an economically advanced and politically liberal Europe chastened by memories of its horrible past is going to be very difficult indeed.

NOTES

1 For example R.A. Schermerhorn (1970) defines an ethnic group as 'a *collectivity within a larger society* having real or putative common ancestry, memories of a shared historical past, and a cultural focus on one or more symbolic elements defined as the epitome of their peoplehood.' (our italics).

2 Some good examples of misunderstandings in distinguishing between concepts of 'nation', 'ethnicity' and 'state' in literature are given by Connor (1978).

3 As Collins (1999: 74) rightly argues, 'a sociological distinction between ethnicity and race is analytically pernicious because it obscures the social processes that determine the extent to which divisions are made along the continuum of somatotypical gradations. Race is a folk concept, a popular mythology that elevates particular ethnic distinctions into a sharp break. As sociologists, our analytical challenge is to show what causes placements along the continuum.'

4 See Guibernau's (1996) analysis of Marx, Durkheim and Weber's treatment of ethnicity and nationalism.

5 Some structural functionalist interpretations of ethnicity (Geertz, 1963; Shils, 1957) are also regularly described as 'primordialist', although as Ozkirimli (2000: 213) rightly points out, unlike sociobiology they do not provide primordialist explanations but focus on the ways in which ethnicity is popularly perceived. In other words, they indicate how social actors themselves share the primordialist vision of ethnic reality.

6 The notion of caging is of course that of Michael Mann (1993).

7 For a series of critical reviews on this point see most of the essays in J.A. Hall (ed.) (1998).

8 We rely here on the research of Elizabeth Arias of the State University of New York at Stony Brook.

REFERENCES

Anthias, F. (1992) 'Connecting "race" and ethnic phenomena', *Sociology*, 26: 421–38.

Banton, M. (1983) *Racial and Ethnic Competition*. Brookfield: Gregg Revivals.

Barth, F. (ed.) (1969) *Ethnic Groups and Boundaries: The Social Organization of Culture Difference*. London: George Allen and Unwin.

Blumer, H. and Duster, T. (1980) 'Theories of race and social action', in *Sociological Theories: Race and Colonialism*. Paris: UNESCO.

Brass, P. (1994) 'Elite competition and the origins of ethnic nationalism', in J.G. Beramendi, R. Maiz and Z.M. Nunez (eds), *Nationalism in Europe: Past and Present*. Santiago de Compostela: University of Santiago de Compostela.

Bova, R. (1991) 'Political dynamics of the post-communist transition', *World Politics*, 44: 113–38.

Brubaker, R. (1992) *Citizenship and Nationhood in France and Germany*. Cambridge, MA: Harvard University Press.

Butler, J. (1993) *Bodies that Matter: On the Discursive Limits of Sex*. Routledge: London.

Cohen, A. (1981) *The Politics of Elite Culture: Explorations in the Dramaturgy of Power in a Modern African Society*. Berkeley, CA: University of California Press.

Collins, R. (1999) *Macro-History: Essays in Sociology of the Long Run*. Stanford, CA: Stanford University Press.

Connor, W. (1978) 'A nation is a nation, is a state, is an ethnic group is a …', *Ethnic and Racial Studies*, 1 (4): 377–400.

Dahl, R. (1977) *Polyarchy*. New Haven, CT: Yale University Press.

Geertz, C. (1963) 'The integrative revolution: primordial sentiments and civil politics', in C. Geertz (ed.), *Old Societies and New State*. New York: The Free Press. pp. 105–19.

Gellner, E. (1964) *Thought and Change*. London: Weidenfeld & Nicolson.

Gellner, E. (1983) *Nations and Nationalism*. Oxford: Blackwell.

Glazer, N. and Moynihan, D.P. (eds) (1975) *Ethnicity: Theory and Experience*. Cambridge, MA: Harvard University Press.

Guibernau, M. (1996) *Nationalisms*. Cambridge: Polity Press.

Hall, J.A. (ed.) (1998) *The State of the Nation: Ernest Gellner and the Theory of Nationalism*. Cambridge: Cambridge University Press.

Hall, J.A. (2000) 'Globalization and nationalism', *Thesis Eleven*, 63: 63–79.

Hall, J.A. and Lindholm, C. (1999) *Is America Breaking Apart?* Princeton, NJ: Princeton University Press.

Hechter, M. (1992) 'Rational choice theory and the study of race and ethnic relations', in J. Rex and D. Mason (eds), *Theories of Race and Ethnic Relations*. Cambridge: Cambridge University Press.

Hobsbawm, E. (1990) *Nations and Nationalism since 1780*. Cambridge: Cambridge University Press.

Horowitz, D.L. (1986) 'Incentives and behaviour in the ethnic politics of Sri Lanka and Malaysia', *Third World Quarterly*, 10: 18–35.

Itzigsohn, J. (1999) 'Immigration and the boundaries of citizenship: the institutions of immigrants' political transnationalism', *International Migration Review*, 34: 1126–54.

Jackson, M. (1982/3) 'An analysis of Max Weber's theory of ethnicity', *Humboldt Journal of Social Relations*, 1 (10): 4–18.

Jenkins, R. (1997) *Rethinking Ethnicity*. London: Sage.

Kaiser, D. (1990) *Politics and War*. Cambridge, MA: Harvard University Press.

Kearney, M. (1995) 'The local and the global: the anthropology of globalization and transnationalism', *Annual Review of Anthropology*, 24: 547–65.

Kohn, H. (1967) *The Idea of Nationalism*. New York: Macmillan.

Laitin, D.D. (1992) *Language Repertoires and State Construction in Africa*. Cambridge: Cambridge University Press.

Lal, B. (1995) 'Symbolic interaction theories', *American Behavioral Scientist*, 3 (38): 421–41.

Lieven, D. (2000) *Empire*. London: John Murray.

Lipset, S.M. (1996) *American Exceptionalism*. New York: W.W. Norton.

Maier, C. (1981) 'The two postwar eras and the conditions for stability in twentieth century

Western Europe', *American Historical Review*, 86: 327–52.

Malešević, S. (2002a) *Ideology, Legitimacy and the New State*. London: Frank Cass.

Malešević, S. (2002b) 'Rational choice theory and the sociology of ethnic relations: a critique', *Ethnic and Racial Studies*, 2 (25): 193–212.

Mann, M. (1988) *States, War and Capitalism: Studies in Political Sociology*. Oxford: Blackwell.

Mann, M. (1993) *Sources of Social Power. Volume Two: The Rise of Classes and Nation-States, 1760–1914*. Cambridge: Cambridge University Press.

Mann, M. (1999) 'The dark side of democracy', *New Left Review*, 235: 18–45.

Marshall, T.H. (1963) *Citizenship and Social Class*. London: Pluto.

Mazower, M. (1998) *Dark Continent*. London: Allen Lane.

Mazower, M. (2000) *The Balkans*. London: Weidenfeld & Nicolson.

McDaniel, T. (1988) *Capitalism, Autocracy and Revolution in Russia*. Berkeley, CA: University of California Press.

Miles, R. (1984) 'Marxism versus the "sociology of race relations"?', *Ethnic and Racial Studies*, 7 (2): 217–37.

Mill, J.S. (1975) 'Considerations on Representative Government', in *Three Essays*. Oxford: Oxford University Press.

Miller, D. (1995) *On Nationality*. Oxford: Oxford University Press.

Milward, A. (1992) *The European Rescue of the Nation-State*. Berkeley, CA: University of California Press.

O'Leary, B. (2000) 'An iron law of nationalism and federation?', Fifth Ernest Gellner Memorial Lecture, London School of Economics.

Ozkirimli, U. (2000) *Theories of Nationalism*. London: Macmillan.

Palmer, R. (1959) *The Age of Democratic Revolution*. Princeton, NJ: Princeton University Press.

Parsons, T. (1975) 'Some theoretical considerations on the nature and trends of change of ethnicity', in N. Glazer and D.P. Moynihan (eds), *Ethnicity: Theory and Experience*. Cambridge, MA: Harvard University Press. pp. 53–83.

Rex, J. (1986) *Race and Ethnicity*. London: Open University Press.

Ruggie, J. (1982) 'International regimes, transactions and change', *International Organization*, 36: 379–415.

Schermerhorn, R.A. (1970) *Comparative Ethnic Relations: A Framework for Theory*. New York: Random House.

Sen, G. (1984) *The Military Origins of Industrialization and International Trade Rivalry*. London: Pinter.

Shils, E. (1957) 'Primordial, personal, sacred and civil ties', in *British Journal of Sociology*, 8: 130–45.

Smith, M. (1992) *Power, Norms and Inflation*. New York: Aldine de Gruyter.

Snyder, J. (1991) *Myths of Empire*. Ithaca, NY: Cornell University Press.

Snyder, J. (2000) *From Voting to Violence*. New York: W.W. Norton.

Solomos, J. and Back, L. (1995) 'Marxism, racism, and ethnicity', *American Behavioral Scientist*, 3 (38): 407–20.

Stone, J. (1995) 'Race, ethnicity and the Weberian legacy', *American Behavioral Scientist*, 3 (38): 391–406.

Tocqueville, A. de. (1955) *The Old Regime and the French Revolution*. Garden City, NY: Anchor Books.

Turner, B. (1994) 'Outline of a theory of citizenship', in B. Turner and P. Hamilton (eds), *Citizenship*. London: Routledge.

Walby, S. (1994) 'Is citizenship gendered?', *Sociology*, 2 (28): 379–95.

van den Berghe, P.L. (1978) 'Race and ethnicity. A sociobiological perspective', *Ethnic and Racial Studies*, 1 (4): 401–11.

van den Berghe, P.L. (1981) *Ethnic Phenomenon*. New York: Elsevier Press.

Waters, M. (1990) *Ethnic Options*. Berkeley, CA: University of California Press.

Weber, M. (1968) *Economy and Society*. New York: Bedminster Press.

Index